# RUSSIA IN FLAMES

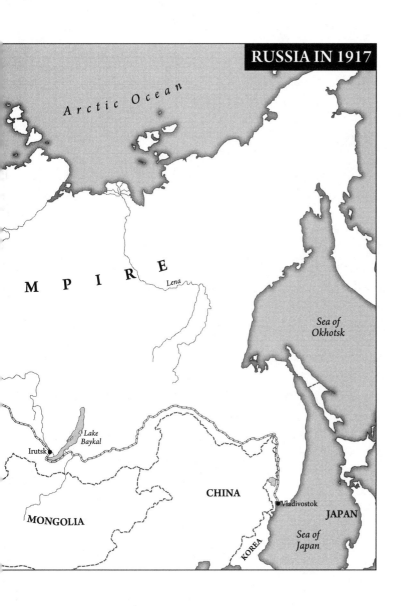

**RUSSIA IN 1917**

*Arctic Ocean*

M P I R E

*Lena*

*Sea of Okhotsk*

Lake Baykal

Irutsk

MONGOLIA

CHINA

Vladivostok

KOREA

JAPAN

*Sea of Japan*

# RUSSIA
## IN
# FLAMES

## WAR, REVOLUTION, CIVIL WAR
## 1914–1921

## LAURA ENGELSTEIN

OXFORD
UNIVERSITY PRESS

## OXFORD
### UNIVERSITY PRESS

Oxford University Press is a department of the University of Oxford.
It furthers the University's objective of excellence in research, scholarship,
and education by publishing worldwide. Oxford is a registered trade mark of
Oxford University Press in the UK and certain other countries.

Published in the United States of America by Oxford University Press
198 Madison Avenue, New York, NY 10016, United States of America.

Library of Congress Cataloging-in-Publication Data
Names: Engelstein, Laura, author.
Title: Russia in flames : war, revolution, civil war, 1914–1921 / Laura Engelstein.
Description: New York, NY : Oxford University Press, 2018. | Includes
    bibliographical references.
Identifiers: LCCN 2017000595 | ISBN 9780199794218 (hardback)
Subjects: LCSH: Soviet Union—History—Revolution, 1917–1921. |
    Soviet Union—History—Revolution, 1917–1921—Causes. | World War,
    1914–1918—Russia. | Russia—History—1904–1914. | Civil war—Soviet
    Union—History. | Soviet Union—Social conditions—1917–1945 |
BISAC: HISTORY / Europe / Russia & the Former Soviet Union. |
    HISTORY / Modern / 20th Century.
Classification: LCC DK265.E476 2018 | DDC 947.084/1—dc23 LC record available
    at https://lccn.loc.gov/2017000595

9 8 7 6 5 4 3 2

Printed by Edwards Brothers Malloy, United States of America

For Michael

О, если б знали, дети, вы,
Холод и мрак грядущих дней!

O, you children, if only you knew,
What hunger and darkness are waiting for you!

 – Alexander Blok, *Voice from the Chorus* (*Golos iz khora*) (1910–1914)

Ешь ананасы, рябчиков жуй,
День твой последний приходит, буржуй.

Gorge on pineapple! Chomp on grouse!
Your days are numbered, bourgeois louse!

 –Vladimir Mayakovsky (1917), in *Vladimir Il'ich Lenin* (1925)[1]

Население, это классовый враг.

The population is the class enemy.

 – Andrei Platonov, *Hurdy-Gurdy* (*Sharmanka*) (c. 1930)

# Contents

# List of Maps

# Author's Note

All translations are my own, unless otherwise indicated. When transliterating Russian from the Cyrillic alphabet, I have used a modified Library of Congress system. In the text, the names of well-known figures are Anglicized—Kerensky, Trotsky (but Kerenskii, Trotskii in the notes); Petr Tchaikovsky, the composer, but Nikolai Chaikovskii, the revolutionary.

Place names offer complications of their own. Some were multiple at the time (Lithuanian Vilnius, Russian Vilna, Polish Wilno; German Lemberg, Polish Lwów, Russian Lvov, Ukrainian Lviv), some changed when borders changed, some were rechristened for political reasons (St. Petersburg, Petrograd). When the differences are part of the story, they will be indicated, but the choice of one over the other should not be taken as endorsement of any current national claim. English equivalents will be used when possible: thus Warsaw, Moscow, Kiev.

As for the issue of dates, the Bolsheviks marked the political rupture by switching to a new calendar. On February 1, 1918, by the Julian calendar used in Russia, the Bolsheviks adopted the Gregorian calendar used in the West, which in the twentieth century was thirteen days ahead. Thus, February 1, 1918 Old Style became February 14, 1918 New Style, although the Russian Orthodox Church and some opponents of the Bolsheviks in the Civil War rejected the change. Up to January 31, 1918, I use Old Style (Julian calendar) dates for domestic events, indicating New Style (Gregorian calendar) for dates of international significance, or when double perspective is needed. Dates in the notes are those used in the various sources cited.

# Introduction

In 1913 the Romanov dynasty celebrated three centuries of rule. In August 1914, Russia went to war against Germany and Austria-Hungary. Less than three years later, in February 1917 by the old Julian calendar, the last of the Romanovs fell from power. Incapable of prosecuting the war, the monarchy had succeeded only in forfeiting the loyalty of its subjects. In February, Imperial Russian society, from top to bottom, rose up against the autocratic regime. Tsar Nicholas II was forced to abdicate, and the leaders of respectable society installed themselves in the seat of power. The workers and soldiers who had brought the monarchy to bay followed the lead of moderate socialists in establishing a political arena of their own. Aware of their tenuous claim to rule, the revolutionaries of the first hour were still saddled with the burden of the war and faced with the popular unrest, now in organized form, which had enabled their own break with the past. In October 1917, as the crisis deepened, Vladimir Lenin's Bolshevik Party staged a coup d'état that dislodged the "bourgeois" officeholders, stole the moderates' thunder, and inaugurated four years of civil conflict, ending in early 1921 with the consolidation of history's first socialist government.

It took more than ten days to shake the world. The monarchy was ousted by the representatives of privileged society, backed by the fury of soldiers, peasants, and workers, whose long-term grievances had been pushed to the edge by the war. The men who assumed the reins of government were constitutional conservatives, aiming to control, not intensify, disorder, but in toppling the sovereign power they had taken a revolutionary step. From the beginning, the revolution held out the possibility of a democratic outcome, a potential dramatized by the remarkable turnout for elections to the Empire-wide Constituent Assembly, even after the Bolsheviks had taken command. The potential for civil war was also implicit in the revolution from the beginning. As the crisis deepened, a group of officers attempted unsuccessfully to seize control and prevent the Left from gaining ground, but it was the October coup that tipped the balance into armed warfare.

The military and social establishment, which had supported the February Revolution in the hopes of prosecuting the war more successfully, rallied its forces against the usurpers, whom they viewed not only as political extremists but as pawns of enemy German power.

The Civil War unleashed by the coup was deep and extensive, embracing every corner of the Empire, from the ethnic borderlands to the peasant heartland, at every rung of the social hierarchy. It was a story of crisis and collapse, but also of surprising resilience. The chaos on the streets and behind the front revealed enduring allegiances and habits of collective action; the institutions of civil society, rudimentary though they were, provided a platform for political mobilization. At the pinnacle of power, the elites battled each other for control. But at the level of the state, the basis of power— political authority, a functioning bureaucratic apparatus, and "monopoly of the legitimate use of physical force," as Max Weber put it—had itself been shaken.[2] Power was not simply there to be seized; it had to be reconstructed. All parties to the Civil War fought with savage intensity. In the end, the Bolsheviks proved the most adept at controlling and deploying violence, at shaping new instruments with which to impose social discipline and compel consent. The Civil War was thus in part a war waged by the monarchy's emerging successor, having repurposed its vestigial institutions, against the remnants of the old society and the old regime, in order to build a radically new social order. Even when it emerged victorious, the Soviet state continued to wage war against the society it had brought into being, as though the process of transformation and subjugation was never complete.

The Civil War was extraordinarily brutal, on all sides. Unfolding over a vast territory, the conflict consisted of many interlocking wars and caused immense material and human damage. Demographers have estimated total losses, military and civilian, between 1918 and 1922, out of a population of about 170 million, at over 15.5 million, or about 9 percent. The total included 2.5 million victims of violence on and off the battlefields, two million victims of terror from all sides, six million who succumbed to starvation and disease, and the five million victims of famine in 1921.[3] None of the contenders were able to control the conduct of the improvised forces they deployed; none shied away from forms of violence, such as hostage-taking, reprisals against civilians, summary executions, rape and torture, and the targeting of ethnic communities, considered at the time as violations of moral, if not also legal, norms. The Bolsheviks, in the end, were most effective in institutionalizing the violence they needed to win—and with which, in its organized form, they proceeded to build a new social order.

At its core, however, the revolution was not a military but a political struggle, in all its interlocking dimensions, and that struggle is the focus of this book. It is a political contest in which the ideal of democracy—of broad participation in the workings of power—achieved enormous resonance, at all levels of society. And was ultimately betrayed. It was a contest in which warfare became a political medium and a substitute for politics. Here was the Bolshevik key to success.

The story of war, revolution, and civil war is very much also an imperial story. In 1914 the Russian Empire extended west to east from the Finnish Gulf to the Pacific Ocean, north to south from the White Sea to the Black Sea. Almost three-quarters of the population lived west of the Ural Mountains, in what was called "European Russia." To the east lay the vast expanse of Siberia. The western border included Finland, the Baltic littoral, a large portion of the former Polish-Lithuanian Commonwealth, and most of what is today Ukraine. The southern periphery included the mountainous Caucasus region and the steppes and deserts of Central Asia, reaching to the Chinese border.

Only 15 percent of the overall population lived in cities. But Russia was rapidly changing. In 1913 the capital, St. Petersburg (renamed Petrograd in August 1914), had 2.5 million inhabitants, Moscow two million. Manufacture, science, and many of the attributes of urban civilization were producing a bourgeoisie, an industrial working class, a professional elite, civic associations, and a market for books, newspapers, and culture—both high and low. Europe took notice. In 1906 impresario Sergei Diaghilev mounted an exhibit of Russian modernist painting in Paris, which was all the rage. In 1913 his Ballets Russes staged Igor Stravinsky's *The Rite of Spring*, creating a sensation with its shocking theme and discordant rhythms—a foretaste of the primitivist modernism that was to characterize the revolutionary years.

There is no doubt that Imperial Russia was evolving. Had it not been for the trauma of the Great War, which also destroyed the Hohenzollern, Hapsburg, and Ottoman Empires, Russia might conceivably have developed toward some form of capitalist society, with a truly representative and empowered political system. Indeed, the monarchy itself actively promoted economic advance. Yet that same regime, which considered itself autocratic down to the very end, clung to its monopoly on power. It was only the Revolution of 1905, roiling the Empire from stem to stern, that extracted the concession of an elected parliament, the State Duma, from the unwilling sovereign, who continued to regard it with disdain and allowed his ministers to limit its operation and diminish its mandate. The contradiction between the persistent traditionalism of the monarchy and the growing pressure for an expanded civic arena and a meaningful political role for the establishment elites, for a share in power—developments which had accompanied the emergence of civil society in the West—led to ever-growing tensions and seemed to justify the posture of the radical political extremes.

   The Great War provided an opportunity for society, in a swell of patriotic fervor, to assert its claim to a role in the management of public affairs. Despite its distrust of independent social forces, however patriotic they might be, the regime was obliged to solicit their cooperation. While increasingly seen as unable to meet the challenge of a war that demanded the engagement of civilian as well as military forces, the monarchy stubbornly refused to broaden access to political life. The chronic friction between the state and its loyal but frustrated public intensified with each passing month. This was, moreover, a war that placed a heavy burden on the mass of the laboring population—peasants in uniform, peasants pressed for grain, industrial workers struggling to feed their families. Above all, it was a war in which the government itself was at cross-purposes, the Army High Command pursuing policies that disrupted the domestic economy and aggravated social tensions, its own propaganda fueling internal conflicts. In short, it must be said, the old regime contributed largely to its own demise.

   In undermining its own authority, the monarchy opened the door to defiance of authority across the board—mutiny, industrial strikes, the burning and pillaging of rural estates. When the revolution erupted in February 1917, however, it was more than a revolt of the masses against the power of their superiors and the demands of the war. The men who took matters into their own hands and turned against the monarchy were the notables of the State Duma, backed by critical figures in the military High Command. Duma deputies representing the propertied and privileged classes then created what they called a Provisional Government. Meanwhile, Duma deputies from the moderate socialist parties formed a leadership organ for the popular movement that had flooded the streets of Petrograd and forced the Duma's hand. They used the model pioneered in the 1905 Revolution to establish the Petrograd Soviet.

   Both the Provisional Government and the Petrograd Soviet defined themselves as place-holders, uneasy in exercising the power they had actively claimed. Yet the ideals and symbols of socialism had broad popular appeal across party lines, and the desire for political representation transcended class divides. It was only toward the end of 1917 that the Bolshevik Party emerged as the sole organized force ready to assert its own right to power in no uncertain terms. The Bolshevik claim was at first very weak, indeed derisory, as some of the leading Bolsheviks themselves understood. Their first move, on Lenin's urgent insistence, was to take Russia out of the war. The war had been the monarchy's undoing and the Provisional Government's Achilles heel. Peace had been a crucial demand of the rebellious soldiers, reacting not only to the strains of prolonged combat, but also to the shortages and hardship on the home front. The promise of peace became a defining feature of the Bolshevik appeal. Yet even a majority of Bolsheviks resisted Lenin's demand to lay down arms, which he viewed as the only means of maintaining their fragile claim to rule. They preferred to pin their hopes for the salvation of the Russian gamble on the outbreak of world revolution.

The October takeover was itself enough to provoke an armed response to the Bolshevik challenge. In the end, however, it was the outrage and enormity of the separate peace concluded with the Central Powers at Brest-Litovsk in March 1918, over the objections not only of Lenin's comrades but of their Left SR allies, that solidified the Bolsheviks' bold assertion of power. It was the opposition to the peace that energized resistance to the Bolshevik move even on the Left, thus compelling the comrades to circle the wagons and deepening their antagonism to competing forces in the political field. Always having an enemy, insisting on the incompatibility of positions, the need for sharp distinctions and clear divides—these had been Vladimir Lenin's political calling cards from the moment of the party's inception. Through relentless propaganda, the organization of language and ideas as well as institutions, the party continually simplified and clarified: who we are, who we are against, "who [bests] whom"—*kto kogo*, in Lenin's brutal shorthand.[4] Now the party was the state, acting upon society, to conquer its resistance and reconstruct it from inside out, erecting a new state structure and a new form of power.

In time and with great effort, the Bolsheviks succeeded, in the course of the Civil War, first of all in reconstituting the army, not only as a fighting force, but as the core of a new social formation, the mechanism for restructuring society itself. Bolshevik victory was an act of war. It was accomplished not only with guns and military discipline but by the onslaught of words and images, visual and verbal. Graphic artists who had filled the satirical journals with their barbs in 1905, playing hide and seek with the censor, now took their aim at new targets. Poets wrote lyrics and ditties, modernist iconoclasts built stage sets, designed spectacles and posters. A new culture with a new vocabulary and a new moral tone was disseminated widely. The newspaper, the slogan, the red banner, the bloodthirsty song.

The Bolshevik idiom was part of a more pervasive socialist culture, which had begun, under the impact of 1905, to expand beyond the radical fringe. The red flag, the "Marseillaise," the idea of the proletariat as a positive moral force became symbols of liberation, of opposition to the autocratic old regime. On a popular level, such attitudes had coexisted with veneration of the monarch and with the aura of traditional symbols, not least those of religion, well into the war, but revolutionary iconography created a shared sense of moral purpose. The socialist repertoire crossed ideological divides, embracing Marxist Social Democrats (SDs)—Bolsheviks and Mensheviks, populist Socialist Revolutionaries (SRs), bomb-throwing anarchist-terrorists, and numerous splinters in between.

Though united by common values and aspirations, the socialist camp was deeply divided on matters of tactics and the use of violence. The grassroots-oriented Mensheviks and moderate SRs endorsed the soviets but opposed the October coup. The more radical Left SRs, by contrast, helped legitimate the regime of the People's Commissars by their participation. After Brest-Litovsk, the SRs helped solidify Bolshevik rule in reverse—by withdrawing their support. Outraged by the treaty and by Bolshevik treatment of the peasantry, the SRs turned against their temporary allies, giving the Bolsheviks an excuse, if one were needed, to intensify their attack on challenges from the Left, eliminating competing claims to authority or allegiance. The Bolsheviks were clarifiers and monopolists. They created a distinctive brand. The original capaciousness of the socialist vision and symbolism, as a language of contestation, at the same time served them as a means of extending and certifying their own rule.

––––––––––

The Bolshevik Revolution inspired generations of idealists, in Russia and the West, with the vision of a just society. From the start, it also inspired fierce opposition, across the political spectrum, as an inherently flawed project. Many of its early champions became disillusioned only later, when Stalin seemed to have betrayed the revolution's original democratic hopes. Nikita Khrushchev's repudiation of Stalin's crimes in his Secret Speech of 1956 left the Leninist ideal untarnished. Once the Soviet Union had crumbled, and with it the official ideology of Great October, and once the archives had opened their files, the question of the revolution's original character acquired a new life. In fact, there were no halcyon days of the Bolshevik Revolution. There was no primal moment of democratic purity that was later betrayed, though the hopes pinned on October were certainly disappointed. The Bolsheviks were ruthless and uncompromising from Day One. Leading Bolsheviks disagreed and argued with each other over tactics. Key decisions met with resistance—notably, the timing of the October coup and the acceptance of Brest-Litovsk—but discipline held. Lenin remained the center of authority, even when challenged. The SRs split, the Mensheviks split, the Bolsheviks, though sometimes divided, did not split. They created organizations, they operated simultaneously on many levels, to mobilize and direct, to punish and penalize.

Alexander Kerensky, the outstanding figure of the early days of the Provisional Government, was a charismatic speaker, the focus of admiration and adoration in the wake of the tsar's ignominious decline. But he had no effective instrument of rule and no clear, always decisive direction. The reasons for the failure of the constitutional experiment of early 1917 nevertheless cannot be reduced to the issue of Kerensky's fall from grace. There is no two-word answer to the question of why the proponents of popular democracy failed and the Bolsheviks managed to impose their vision, especially since success was not instant, but the product of a prolonged and vicious struggle. Ideology was important, but the socialists had a broad, not exclusive, appeal. Mensheviks and SRs posed a real threat to Bolshevik ambitions. The key to Bolshevik victory was their superior ability to mobilize violence, not only as a destructive force but as a tool in the hands of key state institutions—the army and the Cheka, the secret police established within weeks of the October takeover as a bureaucratic organization. The Bolsheviks were relentless state-builders, in the service of a radical social vision, but the state came first.

Bolshevik methods, as well as their goals, generated opposition in many quarters. Inheriting the mantle of empire, the commissars resisted the efforts of outlying regions to free themselves from central rule. Inheriting the need to feed an army and supply the cities, they confronted the same rage and resentment the peasants had earlier directed against the policies of the old regime. They encountered the same defiance of discipline the soldiers had directed against officers with epaulettes. In the heartland, the Russian elites mobilized against them. Career officers in Siberia and the south formed armies and courted a popular following with ideologies of their own, notably anti-Semitism. Political moderates, for their part, were often confronted with difficult, if not impossible, choices between different forms of demagogy and sometimes indistinguishable forms of brutality. Nobody's hands were clean.

In the end, the Bolsheviks prevailed. They succeeded not only because they were determined and ingenious when it came to organization, propaganda, and political maneuvers, or because they were unsentimental in viewing revolution as a form of war. Although their policies generated massive popular resistance, their message resonated deeply among the dispossessed of the old regime. It was a message that summoned—before eviscerating—the longed-for democratic ideal, an ideal embodied in the soviets as well as the Provisional Government; in the Constituent Assembly, for which millions voted while the country was still at war; in the many grassroots committees and provincial City Dumas. There was a propulsive dynamic between the leaders of the Bolshevik Party, especially once they managed to hang onto the instruments of state, and what they called the broad masses. They attracted not only workers, in whose name they spoke, but ambitious young peasant men, out to survive and to change their lives by joining the Red Army. They appealed to Jewish youth and Jewish intellectuals, freed from the anti-Semitism of the old regime, because the Bolsheviks took them on board. Intellectuals—artists, writers, technicians, dramatists, poets, scientists— welcomed the promise of modernity, of a rational society, of a newly imagined future, which they saw themselves as helping to create. The matter of the party's social constituency is not straightforward, however. It is not always clear that barely schooled adherents distinguished this particular version of the socialist appeal from the other varieties of the Left, all signifying a principled antagonism to the old society and its constraints. The Bolshevik temper may, however, have better suited the ferocity of the moment, though the SRs were unscrupulous, too. The followers may have offered their allegiance because the Bolsheviks came to stand not only for resistance to power but for power itself. And many, of course, did not accept them and rebelled, from early on in the party's ascendancy.

How the Bolsheviks managed in the end both to create a new kind of rule and to sustain it is part of the drama that transfigured the lands of the old Empire and transformed the political landscape of the twentieth century. Within the old borders, they were bested only in those peripheral, though important, regions that made their escape and established independent entities of their own. The nationalist leaders of what emerged as Poland, Estonia, Latvia, Lithuania, and Finland also managed to harness popular support for the project of state-building, although not without considerable outside help. Attempts to do the same thing in the Ukrainian provinces, by contrast, were not successful. The drama of the Civil War thus raises a number of key questions—what makes states work and what makes them fail, how authority can be lost and then re-established, how legitimacy is squandered and regained, and what makes a democratic form of government a feasible option.

In the summer of 1917, in the aftermath of a failed popular revolt against the Provisional Government, for which the Bolsheviks were held responsible, Lenin left Petrograd and took refuge in nearby Finland. There he wrote a pamphlet called *State and Revolution*. It projected a future in which the state apparatus would no longer be necessary, since class differences would have disappeared and with them the need for a powerful minority to control and exploit the oppressed. In a state that was no longer an instrument of power— thus, no longer in fact a state—administration would be all that remained, applying technical expertise to the practical matter of running a just and equitable society. This stateless vision of social as well as political justice, which Lenin derived from Marx, is what inspired many intellectuals, as well as ordinary people, at the time and long after. This was the shining destination, but the state was not destined simply to "wither away," in the words of Friedrich Engels, which Lenin insisted had often been misunderstood. The state must first be used to destroy the old order and eliminate the class oppressors rallying in its defense. For this purpose it would have to become more, not less, powerful. During this transitional stage, the proletariat would exercise a ruthless political dictatorship.

*State and Revolution* has been interpreted variously as an expression of Bolshevik utopianism and as an example of Bolshevik authoritarianism.[5] In neither case, however, is Lenin's vision democratic. Lenin does not imagine democracy as a political system. He allows for no political process, no institutional basis for the expression and resolution of conflict, no mechanism for the exercise of power based in society. Lenin's vision as portrayed in *State and Revolution* returns to the pre-1917 model of a central authority presiding over a social organism that lacks the attributes of civil society, in the political sense. It lacks autonomous associations, freedom of expression, and the mechanisms for managing the disparate interests inherent in any complex community. The Soviet Union did not revive the old regime, but it updated some of its essential features. It was undemocratic and unfree and even more brutally repressive. Almost all the political figures mentioned in this account, except those who had died natural deaths, fallen in battle, or emigrated, were murdered in the 1930s purges. The war against itself that Russia inaugurated in 1918 lasted a long time.

This book tells the story of the Russian Revolution, from its roots in World War I to the conclusion of the Civil War in February 1921, as a political drama shaped by immense social forces beyond anyone's control, buffeted by conflicts embedded in the international state system, bearing the imprint not only of the experience of the war but of the legacy of the outmoded autocracy. It is a story that takes divergent paths, as the Empire fragments and political movements come and go. It is hard to do justice to any one of its components, but in outlining its broad contours, some general patterns emerge. The actors in the drama are collective (peasantry, soldiery, workers, cultural communities) and individual, at all levels. No leader acts alone, but some have a decisive impact on events. In this case, the role of Lenin and Trotsky is hard to underestimate. Nothing was inevitable about the outcome of these years of bloodshed and strife. Many decisions mattered. The presence of key players—a Lenin or a Trotsky—is nevertheless not enough to explain the collapse of one civilization and the birth of another. The revolution and civil wars that enveloped the Romanov domains were part of the grand sweep of the World War, but also a product of cultural and institutional patterns rooted in the Imperial Russian past. Their legacy persists in today's Russia, even after the Soviet Union's demise in 1991.

The Russian Revolution hovered over the twentieth century, a beacon to many on the left, a tragedy—or an opportunity—to many who lived through it and later experienced its results, demonic to many on the political right. In 1979 British historian E. H. Carr predicted that historians would continue to consider October 1917 "a turning-point in history," but would disagree on whether it constituted a "landmark in the emancipation of mankind from past oppression,...or a crime and a disaster."[6] In the Soviet Union, of course, the Great October Revolution was celebrated as the regime's foundational moment. In 1996 the holiday was renamed; in today's Russia the date is no longer even marked. President Vladimir Putin has condemned the Treaty of Brest-Litovsk for having "betrayed the national interest."

As a consequence of war, revolution, and civil war, he declares, Russia was "destroyed from within."[7]

Despite such grand pronouncements, scholars in post-Soviet Russia have been intent on getting beyond the political uses of the revolution and beyond the kind of alternatives E. H. Carr proposed. In the past twenty-five years, they have mined the newly opened archives for previously inaccessible documents, which they have published in meticulously annotated volumes for the use of the international scholarly community. This book owes an enormous debt to the work they have done and to the moral passion with which they have attempted to dismantle clichés and think differently. Take, for example, a collection of hitherto unavailable material on the attempt of Central Asian political leaders after October 1917 to establish the basis for self-government against the threat of Soviet domination. Published in 1992 in Almaty, then the capital of the newly constituted Republic of Kazakhstan, when hopes for democracy in the region were running high, the volume begins with a warning "against the mindless rejection of unfamiliar positions, different convictions, other ways of looking at reality."[8]

Insofar as the drama of 1917—and its consequences—have receded into the past, especially for citizens of the West, we need to be reminded of its importance, how unprecedented and monumental the events really were, while avoiding the old antinomies, in which Lenin is either a Hero or a Devil, in which the so-called masses are either paragons of high-minded dedication to a selfless cause or mere perpetrators of mindless violence. October 1917 was indeed a coup, which took advantage of and then deepened a genuine social revolution. It also suffocated the eloquent desire for democratic self-representation displayed by all segments of Imperial Russian society, in their different ways, throughout the revolutionary year and deep into the Civil War.

A hundred years is a long enough distance from which to question the terms in which to consider these world-shaking events. This book tells a story in which all the categories are inevitably laden with moral and political judgments—Proletariat, Counterrevolution, Red Terror—and in which such judgments cannot be avoided, but a story that must be told with some degree of detachment from the ideological positions that animated the revolution in the first place. We live at a time in which the democracy that the trans-Atlantic world has come to take for granted since the end of World War II and the defeat of fascism may be seriously endangered. The great historical moment between 1917 and 1921 in which the cost of democracy's failure became all too apparent deserves our renewed attention.

# RUSSIA IN FLAMES

Boris Kustodiev, "Moscow I: Attack," *Zhupel* [*Bugbear*], no. 2 (1905). Beinecke Rare Book and Manuscript Library, Yale University.

# PART

# I

# Last Years of the Old Empire, 1904–1914

The Russian Empire began the twentieth century—in 1905—with a revolution. Long in the making, it was a surprise nonetheless. Anyone who has read Turgenev (*Fathers and Sons*), Dostoevsky (*The Possessed*, also known as *The Demons*), or Joseph Conrad (*Under Western Eyes*) will know that the dream (or nightmare) of revolution haunted nineteenth-century Russia. The specter of Communism evoked by Marx was most at home on Europe's eastern margins. Yet the revolutionary movement did not create the revolution. The Revolution of 1905 was a product of the dilemma facing Russia's old regime, an autocratic state which had survived into the modern era. To maintain its standing as a Great Power, the Empire had to embrace the very changes that threatened the basis of its rule. It needed industry, technology, and literacy, but without their political consequences—parliaments, public opinion, civil society, and the dread proletariat. To survive as an imperial regime, the autocracy must cease to be autocratic. The results of this tension were explosive.

The upheaval that began in January 1905 lasted for a good two years. The turmoil, once subdued, was followed by a decade of continuing political confrontation between the forces behind the revolution and the regime they had not managed to unseat. This confrontation centered in the State Duma, the elected parliament wrested from the unwilling tsar, who resented the incursion on absolute power but saw no other way to survive. The concessions unwillingly granted were immediately undermined by imperial decree, even before the opening of the Duma's first session. Once the last vestiges of unrest were under control, the electoral laws were changed, also by decree, to restrict the Duma franchise. In the seven years until the outbreak of war in 1914, society continued its battle with the regime, now by means of the Duma, however limited its mandate, and in the court of public opinion, however restricted its scope. It was thus an already mobilized society that encountered the challenge of the Great War, which at first rallied the public in support of the patriotic effort, but soon had the effect of undermining the monarchy altogether.

The political roots of 1905 date to the 1860s. In 1861, as the United States was embarking on the Civil War that ended slavery, Alexander II liberated the Russian serfs by imperial decree. Defeat in 1856 in the Crimean War had shown that Russia could not compete as a Great Power in the modern world with unfree labor and an undereducated elite. Emancipation was followed by the Great Reforms, which created representative organs of local administration (the zemstvos), reshaped the courts, and updated the terms and conditions of military service. Basic education expanded, the universities grew, and the professions developed, yet the emergence of civil society—the sphere of public discussion and association—remained crippled by the monarchy's distrust of its own subjects, even its own elites.

The thinking few were therefore unhappy. They chafed at the limitations on their own freedoms, but were troubled even more by the lot of the vast impoverished peasantry—"the people" (*narod*), constituting 85 percent of the population. Idealistic Russian youth traveled to the villages; they traveled to Europe to get an education. Women studied medicine abroad. Men and women gathered in reading groups to discuss socialist tracts and champion the equality of the sexes. The Populists (*Narodniki*) dedicated to peasant revolution were unsuccessful, however. In 1881 a handful of Populist zealots, disappointed by their own failure and by the inadequate results of the Great Reforms, assassinated the Tsar-Liberator. His arch-conservative son Alexander III reigned for the next thirteen years, followed by his own son, the equally traditionalist Nicholas II. The radicals' bold, yet self-defeating, act increased the regime's sense of embattlement. It magnified the perpetrators' importance in the eyes of contemporaries and in the retrospective genealogy of Bolshevik victory in 1917. Only one of the assassins was Jewish, but the deed unleashed a wave of anti-Jewish pogroms, with ominous portents for the future.

The repressive policies of the last two tsars continued to alienate the privileged classes, attaching the fringe ever more firmly to the goal of revolution, but revolution itself was a product of the modernizing forces the regime both needed and feared. Officials were frightened not only by home-grown firebrands but by the example of Europe, where the development of industrial society had generated a proletariat, the ideology of socialism, and most recently the Paris Commune of 1871. It was not clear at the time that capitalism might in the long term be a recipe for stability rather than upheaval. Nevertheless, the path forward was unavoidable. In the wake of the Great Reforms, the development of railroads and the expansion of cities, commerce, industry, and science had, by the 1890s, created an arena in which the attributes of Western civilization were clearly visible: railways, trams, telephones, automobiles, cinema, advertising, high fashion, department stores, factories, factory workers, newspapers, physicians, physicists, art nouveau. Chemist Dmitrii Mendeleev developed the periodic table; Ivan Pavlov won the Nobel Prize in physiology in 1904.

The figure most closely associated with state promotion of economic development was Count Sergei Witte. A product of the Empire, he was born in the Georgian capital of Tiflis (Tbilisi), where his father held an official position. The family, of Baltic German origin but Orthodox faith, had entered Russian state service in the sixteenth century. Witte's second wife was Jewish. He began his own career in the Ministry of Finance department of railroads and eventually served as minister of finance from 1892 to 1903, peak years of industrial progress, which his policies encouraged.[1]

Reform and modernization, contrary to expectation, seemed at first to increase the stability of public life. The zemstvos created in 1864 hired agronomists, statisticians, physicians, and schoolteachers to work in the villages; they nurtured a culture of civic responsibility among local gentry and offered a chance for the classes to mingle. Russian public life had greater depth and durability than ever before. Yet the elites in the provinces and the capitals were still denied a legitimate outlet for political action or expression. Nicholas II, when he ascended the throne in 1894, rejected what he dismissed as their "senseless dreams" of a constitutional order.

The educated establishment longed to contribute to a functioning society. The heirs of the Populists wanted to destroy it. By the 1890s, in line with the new social landscape, Marxism had challenged the dream of a peasant revolution. The villages had remained quiescent, and revolutionary terror—the assassination of the Tsar-Liberator—had failed to topple the regime. The generation that turned to Marx put their wager on the emerging proletariat—the urban factory workers—and took heart from the inroads of capitalism evident even in Russia. Marx himself postulated capitalism as the precondition for the proletarian revolution. The Russian acolytes felt the future was upon them and conceived of Russia as part of a worldwide chain of historical development.

The most authoritative figure in the emerging radical generation was Vladimir Ilich Lenin. Born Ulianov in 1870 in the Volga River town of Simbirsk (since 1924 Ulianovsk), five hundred miles east of Moscow, he was the younger brother of a Populist radical executed in 1887 for his role in a failed plot to assassinate Alexander III. The first defectors from Populism, led by Georgii Plekhanov, fourteen years Lenin's senior, had founded the Union of Struggle for the Emancipation of the Working Class in 1883. By 1895 it had become the Union of Russian Social Democrats, for which the twenty-five-year-old Lenin drafted the program.[2] In Minsk in 1898, its organizers renamed it the Russian Social Democratic Labor Party (*Rossiiskaia sotsial-demokraticheskaia rabochaia partiia*). Pinning their hopes on Russia's radical potential, the Social Democrats believed the old anger of the peasant masses and the new anger of the factory slaves would combine to dislodge the "feudal" monarchy and its budding capitalist class from power simultaneously. "Combined and uneven development," Lenin's later co-conspirator Leon Trotsky called it. Born Lev Davidovich Bronshtein in 1879 on a farm near the city of Elizavetgrad (later Zinovievsk, then Kirovo, today Kropyvnytskyi, Ukraine) in Kherson Province, north of the Black Sea, Trotsky was not yet twenty in 1898, when he was arrested for revolutionary activity. After a year in prison and another two and a half in Siberian exile (where, in the company of other exiles, he read and wrote and kept abreast of political developments), he fled to Europe, where he joined Lenin and the other comrades, busy plotting revolution.

In 1903 the Social Democrats gathered in Brussels for their second party congress, soon shifting to London to escape the Russian police. It was then, in the course of a contentious vote, that the group split into two factions. Winning by a hair, Lenin's followers adopted the name "Bolshevik"—meaning "those of the majority"; the losers were known as "Mensheviks"—"those of the minority." Iulii Martov, born Iulii Osipovich Tsederbaum in 1873 and raised in Odessa, became the leader of the Menshevik faction.[3] The two sides differed on the fundamental issue of what constituted a revolutionary party and what kind of social movement it should hope to form. Lenin had articulated his vision in a 1902 pamphlet called *What Is to Be Done?*, in which he called for a vanguard of professional revolutionaries to guide the proletariat in the acquisition of Marxian revolutionary consciousness. The Mensheviks rejected the model of a tightly controlled nucleus of party leaders in favor of a more broadly based grassroots party. They were skeptical, as well, of the possibility of launching a proletarian revolution in a country where capitalist society had not yet fully evolved. Bourgeois revolution should come first on the agenda.[4]

The Social Democrats were not alone in plotting revolution in these years. In 1902, the remnants of the old Populist movement had reconstituted themselves as the Socialist Revolutionary Party, which preserved the ideal of a peasant-based communitarian revolution.[5] Like their nineteenth-century predecessors, they believed that Russian peasant culture was intrinsically collectivist and that the evils of capitalism could be avoided if capitalism were bypassed altogether. They also retained the tradition of political terror. In April 1902, for example, the SRs assassinated Minister of the Interior Dmitrii Sipiagin and in summer 1904 his successor, Viacheslav Pleve.[6] Viktor Chernov, born in Saratov Province in 1873, thus of the same generation as the founding Social Democrats, was the party's leading figure and theoretician.[7]

Nor were revolutionaries the only ones forming organizations. In 1902 a group of zemstvo leaders, committed to moderate social reform and Western-style constitutionalism, joined with Petr Struve, one of the original Social Democrats, in founding a journal called *Liberation* (*Osvobozhdenie*). It was to be the masthead of what became known as the "social movement" (*obshchestvennoe dvizhenie*), understood as the mobilization of "society," rather than the laboring masses, either peasant or proletarian. Born in 1870, a son of the governor of Perm Province, Struve was originally drawn to Marxism, mostly for its analysis of the importance of capitalism in historical development. After various troubles with the authorities, obligatory for any activist at the time, he began moving toward the political center and departed for Europe. *Liberation*, published in Stuttgart and smuggled back into Russia, became the rallying point for liberal mobilization in 1905.[8]

Thus, even before the revolution, Russia was equipped with a panoply of political associations dedicated to various degrees of radical change. All were illegal. The Revolution itself, when it came, was not, however, a product of socialist agitation. It began not among the laboring masses, who had their own grievances and goals, but at the top of the social pyramid—from the halls of academe to the provincial zemstvos, the physicians and school teachers, the feminists, the high school and university students and their lawyer fathers. All welcomed the occasion to challenge the regime and present their demands for inclusion in the political life of the Empire, to realize their bid for civil rights and lawfulness. Many of them sympathized with the desire of the radical Left for greater social equality and justice.

———————

The educated establishment's long-standing discontents were exacerbated by the consequences of the war with Japan that began in February 1904. One Japanese victory followed another, and the Empire's state-of-the-art battleships sank to the bottom of the Yellow Sea, the government's prestige sinking along with them. In the autumn of 1904, the same zemstvo circles which had collaborated in creating *Liberation* began, with the acquiescence of Pleve's less draconian successor, to organize congresses of zemstvo delegates. By the end of the year, they had produced a list of demands for political reform.[9]

The aspirations of civil society gave the revolution its political shape and provided the initial momentum, but the anger of the popular classes gave it power. In 1903 the police had introduced a program of officially sponsored labor unions, meant to steal the thunder from radical agitators. They were all too successful. In St. Petersburg the Orthodox priest Father Georgii Gapon created the Assembly of Russian Factory and Mill Workers (*Sobranie russkikh fabrichno-zavodskikh rabochikh*), which grew to considerable proportions. The Assembly had strong support, in particular, at the massive Putilov machine-building works, employing 13,000 workers.[10] At the beginning of January 1905, the Putilov hands struck to protest the firing of four Assembly members, and most of the city's factories soon joined them. In the tradition of humble petitioners, Gapon decided to present the tsar with a list of the workers' demands. The language of socialism was absent, the posture was deferential, but the demands were nonetheless defiant: the eight-hour day and the right to unionize, but also the democratic franchise, civil liberties, and equality before the law.

On Sunday, January 9, 1905, Gapon led a procession numbering tens of thousands of workers and their families, who headed for the Winter Palace, singing hymns as they went. At the Narva Gates, with its great triumphal arch marking Russia's entry into Paris in 1814, they were stopped by a mass of soldiers, who opened fire on the crowd. Gapon made his escape, but other confrontations occurred that day at different points in the city, including in Palace Square outside the Winter Palace. In the end, a hundred fifty marchers were killed and at least three hundred wounded.[11]

"Bloody Sunday," as it was instantly dubbed, elicited an outpouring of public indignation and precipitated an avalanche of labor unrest and popular protest across the Empire. Strikes spread through the cities, peasants torched manor houses, soldiers and sailors mutinied. On the one hand, the lower orders ran amok; on the other hand, organization was everywhere. The Revolution was a festival of mobilization, broader than any of the clandestine plotters could instigate or control. The process of politicization affected associations across the board and engendered new ones. Craftsmen founded unions, professionals created a Union of Unions (*Soiuz soiuzov*), factory workers elected councils, and umbrella councils linked factories and neighborhoods to each other. The Russian word for council is "Soviet" (*sovet*). When activists in St. Petersburg decided in October to establish a command center for the dawning proletarian revolution, they called it the Soviet of Worker Deputies (*Sovet rabochikh deputatov*).

Before that point was reached, however, attempts were made to resolve the growing crisis. In the effort to defuse the widespread labor unrest, in February Nicholas summoned worker delegates to an advisory commission, chaired by the undistinguished bureaucrat Nikolai Shidlovskii, but when the delegates became too demanding, it was dissolved. The workers learned two lessons from the Shidlovskii Commission: the power of self-representation and the futility of playing by the rules. In June the Zemstvo Constitutionalists, as they were now called, delegated the eminent religious thinker and professor of philosophy Prince Sergei Trubetskoi, from one of the empire's oldest aristocratic families, to visit the tsar and make the case for a modicum of reform.[12] Nicholas offered vague promises, but only minor concessions were made.

Meanwhile, the extremes of right and left contributed to the continuing turbulence. In February, Grand Duke Sergei Aleksandrovich, the tsar's uncle and the commander of the Moscow military district, was assassinated by the SR Ivan Kaliaev in retribution for the January massacre. Kaliaev was not Jewish, but anti-Semites blamed the Jews. Pogroms were numerous throughout the revolution, often the work of gangs known as Black Hundreds (*Chernye sotni*). A wave of pogroms had followed the assassination of Alexander II, and the pattern of blaming—and attacking—Jews at moments of social and political vulnerability became well established.

Mob violence and common crime abounded, but ordinary people also displayed a capacity for purposeful collective action. Radical agitators provided slogans—the eight-hour day or the democratic franchise—but strikers focused mainly on achieving decent conditions, shorter hours, and better pay. In the context of revolution, all action acquired political meaning, and any form of mobilization, by definition illegal, was a challenge to authority. At the height of the spring strike wave, Minister of Finance Vladimir Kokovtsov, in the spirit of the police-sponsored program which had produced Father Gapon, proposed that labor unions be legalized, satisfying the workers' desire for self-representation and diffusing their anger. His suggestion was rebuffed, but officials closer to the action realized that organization could be useful, and intransigence was a provocation. When in May massive strikes broke out in Ivanovo-Voznesensk, a textile manufacturing center northeast of Moscow, the local factory inspectors suggested the strikers elect delegates to represent them. The council of worker deputies that emerged was in effect the first "soviet." Yet confrontation remained the norm. Before long, Cossacks were summoned to disperse an unauthorized mass meeting, leaving several of the strikers dead and provoking a burst of uncontrolled anger—stones thrown, shops looted, policemen attacked. Eventually, the strike in Ivanovo-Voznesensk petered out, with little to show for it.

Lenin had always been aware of the potential for spontaneous mass action (*stikhiinost'*) to go awry and of the need to exert ideological control (*soznatel'nost'*). A chapter of *What Is to Be Done?* was devoted to attacking the hope for self-generated revolution. The strikes and grassroots organs of leadership produced in 1905 endowed the factory districts of the urban centers with a sense of power, but Lenin always focused on the ultimate goal of revolution, which was to replace one political system with another. The experience of 1905 developed habits of self-organization that would be repeated, myths of heroism and sacrifice that would be remembered, but the goal was still out of reach. The outcome confirmed Lenin's suspicion of "spontaneous" mass movements. Yet spontaneous mobilization was the first revolution's gift to the revolution that followed a decade later. The experience of 1905 demonstrates that leaders are not enough and that violence itself is rarely devoid of form and purpose, however uncontrolled it may seem, and sometimes may be.

The summer of 1905 was characterized by the continuing proliferation of organizations, failed attempts at compromise, and in August the conclusion of peace with Japan, resulting in the Treaty of Portsmouth. The Russian delegation headed by Count Witte, now chair of the Council of Ministers, a largely honorific position, included Konstantin Nabokov, the novelist's diplomat uncle. The Battle of Tsushima in May had destroyed two-thirds of the Russian fleet and undermined any lingering public support for the war. It seemed time for concessions. In July liberal activists convened a gathering of representatives from City Dumas (city councils) and zemstvos—in effect, the spokesmen of civil society. The more cautious were still reluctant to make serious demands, but the majority formulated a program that called for a constitutional monarchy, with a legislative assembly elected on the basis of the so-called four-tailed suffrage: direct, equal, secret, and universal (though excluding women). Trying to check the momentum, in early August the government offered the model of a parliament with a limited mandate and a restricted franchise. Too little, too late.

The summer was a period of growing ferment. University students had been on strike since the beginning of the year. At the end of August, the universities were granted "autonomy," and the halls and classrooms filled with crowds of students, workers, activists, and ordinary citizens. The authorities seemed to think the continuous meetings in this rare arena for free speech would let off steam, but in fact the pressure only built up. The turning point came in September, when printers in Moscow went on strike, soon attracting other trades in which Social Democratic organizers had been active. A Council of the Five Professions combined printers, carpenters, ribbon-makers, tobacco-factory workers, and railroad workers.[13] These were not standard-issue proletarians, with nothing to lose but their chains—indeed, even in large factories skilled workers took the lead—but the model of worker-representation was catching.

The impact of labor action was powerful not only because it was increasingly well-organized but also because it was part of the mobilization of society across the board. In their self-designation as "proletarians," workers were joining the civic community, a community that itself was taking form as authority at the top weakened. At the beginning of October, the funeral for Prince Sergei Trubetskoi, who in June had approached the tsar with a plea for reform and had now suddenly died at the age of forty-three, drew a crowd of thousands, many sporting red flags. The next day, the Central Committee of the All-Russian Railroad Union (*Vserossiiskii ispolnitel'nyi komitet zheleznodorozhnogo profsoiuza*, shortened as *Vikzhel*), established in April, announced the start of a railway strike, which by the next week had halted all traffic in Moscow, affecting the entire system. The railroad union was a particularly potent political instrument, uniting as it did ticket-office clerks with skilled workers in repair shops and manual laborers serving the tracks, and extending its influence to the farthest reaches of the Empire. A mass meeting at St. Petersburg University approved the call for a general strike, and the movement spread like wildfire. Every possible profession—waiters, pharmacists, bank clerks, theater ushers, actors, ballet dancers, students, telegraph operators—and of course the industrial labor force—declared solidarity, in every city and town. Trams stopped, lights went out. Industrialists collected money to support their employees.

The Bolsheviks were not influential enough in the factories to have played a part in instigating the movement. If any party had an influence among the railroad workers, it was the SRs, who tended to appeal to white-collar employees. Once the strike was under way, the most important role was played by a group of St. Petersburg Mensheviks, who suggested that the factories elect representatives to a citywide Council (Soviet) of Worker Deputies. When the delegates convened in mid-October, they chose an Executive Committee, with a left-liberal lawyer as chair. Similar councils were formed in many cities. The Soviet had now acquired the political meaning it would transmit to 1917, as the tribune of the people—or "the Democracy," as it came to be called. The Bolsheviks stood aside. Lenin appeared in St. Petersburg only in November and was skeptical of the Menshevik idea.

The Russian intelligentsia, whether respectable or confrontational, and the Russian proletariat, whether industrial or artisanal, were not the only players in the drama of 1905. If strikes peaked in January and February, and again from October to December, unrest in the countryside spiked in May, June, and July, diminished during the harvest, then picked up again starting in October. Peasants lashed out at the landowners, taking grain, destroying property and financial records, and felling trees, but rarely harming the owners.[14] They were expressing long-standing grievances, as well as protesting the impact of the military draft and the food shortages caused by a shortfall harvest. When it came to expressing political demands—that is, addressing themselves to "power"—they, like the workers, needed helpers. In this case, zemstvo activists urged them to submit petitions, now welcomed by the authorities as a way to restore calm. Petitioning the higher-ups was a peasant tradition; what was new was the peasants' response to the chance to organize. In July and August, over a hundred delegates arrived in Moscow Province to form what was called the All-Russian Peasants' Union (*Vserossiiskii krest'ianskii soiuz*), guided in its deliberations by activists from the socialist parties. Whether the delegates knew what was meant by a constituent assembly is an open question. At the same time, as unrest continued, soldiers and police set fire to the guilty villages and punished suspected troublemakers with flogging, another imperial tradition.[15]

Peasants were important, moreover, not only in their communes and in the fields, but in uniform. The damage to the tsar's image in the wake of Bloody Sunday and the continuing defeats in the Far East opened the door to defiance. To the discomfort of their commanders, troops were used to suppress domestic disturbances; in the general turmoil it was unclear how long the soldiers would continue to follow orders. Protests might be infectious. Strikes on the railroads slowed the return of units from the Far East after peace was concluded.[16]

The navy was more volatile still, since crews included a high proportion of skilled technical hands recruited from the cities and therefore a potential source of political infection. Already in 1904 there had been signs of unrest. Most dramatic of all—and later dramatized in Sergei Eisenstein's 1925 anniversary film *Battleship Potemkin*—was the mutiny on the Black Sea Fleet battleship of that name in June 1905. Having gained control of the ship, the mutineers arrived at Odessa, where confrontations between strikers and Cossacks had been at fever pitch since the start of the month. Order was soon restored with the liberal application of gunfire. A crowd of civilians was mowed down as they descended the broad steps leading to the harbor. The slaughter provided the subject of one of the great scenes of modern cinema, as eyeglasses shattered and a baby carriage bumped its way down the stairs. The victims were an "innocent," indeed "bourgeois," public.

There was no group in Imperial Russia that did not manifest some form of protest in the course of 1905. Even Orthodox seminarians expressed solidarity with the revolutionary movement. It is not surprising, then, that regions of the ethnic periphery should have been affected as well. Nicholas II's foreign minister, Count Vladimir Lamsdorf, himself of Baltic German descent, made the point in 1906: "it was precisely the various allogenes— the Armenians, Georgians, Letts, Esthonians, Finns, Poles, etc.—who rose one after another against the imperial government for the purpose of obtaining, if not complete political autonomy, at least equal rights with the native population of the Empire."[17]

The large portion of the former Polish-Lithuanian Commonwealth incorporated into the Russian Empire at the end of the eighteenth century as a result of partitions with Prussia and Austria, known as the Kingdom of Poland, or Congress Poland, from 1815 to 1864, had long chafed at its subjection. In 1830 and again in 1863, Poles launched major rebellions. Repression after 1863 had deepened Polish resentment. Anger erupted instantly in 1905. Warsaw and Łódź responded to Bloody Sunday with massive strikes; troops answered with gunfire; martial law was declared.[18] In the Caucasus, Georgia experienced extensive peasant uprisings. In the Baltics, Reval (now Estonia's capital Tallinn) was peaceful, but the industrial city of Riga (today the capital of Latvia) was overrun by strikes, which were met with armed repression. Latvian peasants directed their anger against the German landowners, who formed their own militias but depended on imperial troops to finally restore order.[19]

---

The October General Strike forced the monarchy to its knees. At the urging of Witte and Grand Duke Nikolai Nikolaevich, the tsar's first cousin once removed, on October 17 Nicholas issued the Manifesto that created the State Duma and promised the granting of civil liberties. The Duma would have the power to confirm all laws, thus implicitly limiting the monarch's power, but the principle of absolute rule was never formally abjured, leading to obvious tensions. Witte was named to head the new cabinet. His first appointment, of the reactionary Petr Durnovo as minister of the interior, alienated the liberal figures whom he also invited to join. Durnovo's reputation alone, they felt, would nullify the promise of the new government.[20] Contradictions were thus built into the October settlement from the start, but it was nevertheless an enormous achievement, opening the door to legitimate political participation and public debate.

The new rules of the game allowed for the establishment of political parties, not formally legalized but accepted. The Union of Liberation, born of the journal *Liberation*, gave birth to the Constitutional Democratic Party (*Konstitutsionno-demokraticheskaia partiia*, also known as the Party of the People's Freedom [*Partiia narodnoi svobody*]), for short, KDs or Kadets. A party of professionals, with little resonance outside the urban elites and the zemstvo leadership, it counted among its leaders the historian Pavel Miliukov and Vladimir Nabokov, the novelist's father. (The future author of *Lolita* was now six years old.) A lawyer by training, from a distinguished and wealthy aristocratic family, whose own father had served as minister of justice under Alexander II and III, Nabokov père was a noted defender of Jewish rights and an outspoken opponent of the death penalty. His mother, as the novelist recalled, could not understand why her son, though he "appreciated all the pleasures of great wealth, could jeopardize its enjoyment by becoming a Liberal, thus helping to bring on a revolution that would, in the long run, as she correctly foresaw, leave him a pauper."[21]

The Kadets stood for the rule of law, civil rights, civic equality, and protection of private property. On the key issue of increasing peasant access to land, they accepted the necessity for redistribution, but only with compensation to the present owners. Some even viewed constitutional monarchy as the best model for Russia. The Kadet position, eminently moderate by European standards, expressed the desire of respectable society for an accountable system of power. The intransigence of the absolutist regime had pushed them, however, into alliance with the radical Left, whose tactics—strikes, uprisings, even terror—they accepted during the revolution as a lever with which to advance their own moderate cause. Not all of them endorsed this alliance. The "demarcation line" between constitutional and revolutionary politics, observed Vasilii Maklakov, divided the entire country and ran through the heart of the party as well. A pragmatist on the party's conservative right wing, Maklakov shared the constitutional persuasion.[22]

To the right of the Kadets, but still within the liberal orbit, stood the Union of 17 October (*Soiuz 17 oktiabria*), or the Octobrists, representing the interests of big business. If the Kadets represented the middle class of culture and education, this was the real bourgeoisie, though many of its members earned their living as professionals, not unlike the Kadets. The party's founder was Aleksandr Guchkov, from a wealthy Moscow merchant clan.[23] Where the Kadets saw the October Manifesto as the first step toward further reforms, the Octobrists considered it an adequate basis for reformed monarchical rule. While endorsing civil rights and the legalization of trade unions, the businessmen did not share the Kadets' ambivalent sympathy for the mass movement. They nevertheless shared the broad consensus among the educated public demanding access to political power and greater accountability at the top.[24]

By contrast, ardent defenders of the autocracy, opposed to any kind of change, faced a dilemma. The sovereign had enacted reform by decree. To found a monarchist party was an oxymoron, yet the old principles needed a new defense. Despite their opposition to the Duma, some monarchists used it as a forum from which to attack the principle of parliamentary representation and impede its operations, a form of participatory sabotage. The extreme Right also focused on the Jews, identified as the moving force of the revolution, a view shared in high places. The anti-Semitic Union of the Russian People (*Soiuz russkogo naroda*) received the tsar's tacit endorsement. Nicholas agreed with Foreign Minister Lamsdorf, who remarked in January 1906 that the Jews "figured as a specially active and aggressive element of the revolution, whether as individuals, or as leaders of the movement, or in the shape of entire organizations."[25]

The Manifesto broke the back of the revolution—factories resumed work, parties held conventions. Euphoric crowds filled the streets in a sea of red flags. However, violence did not abate during the so-called Days of Freedom, but only intensified. In issuing the Manifesto, the tsar had confirmed his authority as the ultimate lawgiver, but the decree had—in theory—limited his power. The fact of conceding to pressure signaled weakness, not strength. In search of culprits, Black Hundred gangs sponsored by the Union of the Russian People assaulted pedestrians with a "Jewish appearance," indeed anyone wearing eyeglasses. Across the Empire overall, almost seven hundred pogroms were recorded, almost nine hundred Jews were killed, many thousands were injured, and a vast amount of property was destroyed. The details were reported in the Russian press and damaged Russia's reputation abroad. The single most shocking incident occurred in June 1906 in the heavily Jewish city of Białystok in eastern Poland, in which eighty-eight inhabitants were killed and seven hundred injured.[26] Perpetrated in defense of authority, the pogroms were a symptom of the damage that authority had incurred and the desperation of the monarchy's defenders. Pogroms, of course, damaged authority even further, and though he shared Lamsdorf's diagnosis of the problem, Nicholas did not endorse the riots.

The pogroms were not the only form of disorder that followed the October Manifesto. Peasants interpreted the decree as authorization to take possession of land they felt by rights was theirs. Rural unrest peaked in November 1905 (and surged again between May and August 1906, this time often more deadly).[27] Soldiers and sailors also kept the revolutionary spirit alive. Most dramatically, over three thousand sailors on the Kronstadt naval base in the Gulf of Finland across from St. Petersburg rioted for two days at the end of October, demanding civil rights and better conditions and plundering the town. Loyal troops brought them to order, leaving about two dozen dead. The crews of two Black Sea Fleet warships stationed in the Crimean port of Sevastopol seized their vessels, presented demands, and persuaded the sympathetic Lieutenant Petr Shmidt to assume command. The government punished the malefactors and moved to institute reforms and expedite the demobilization of forces in the East.

Confrontations escalated at the end of 1905, encouraged not only from the reactionary Right but from the radical Left as well. The Soviets continued to function, operating as shadow municipal administrations. The St. Petersburg Soviet created its own militia and encouraged the workers to continue pressing their demands, including the eight-hour day. Bolsheviks and Mensheviks both believed that the fight was not yet over. Trotsky elaborated a theory of "permanent revolution," designed to justify the premature (according to the Marxist timetable) advance to the proletarian phase. The reaction was not long in coming. The industrialists joined forces and imposed a coordinated lockout that left thousands of workers on the street. The regime meanwhile court-martialed the Kronstadt rebels and declared martial law in Poland. The Soviet riposted by calling another general strike, but the summons fell flat. The eight-hour-day campaign and a post and telegraph strike also failed.

Instead of backing down, the socialist leadership resolved on a final confrontation. It was a folie à deux. When the Soviet's chairman was arrested, it renewed its call for a general strike. This time, the entire Executive Committee and two hundred delegates were arrested. Trotsky, then twenty-six, was among those tried in September 1906. In February 1905, he had made his way under cover from Europe to the relative safety of Finland. Appearing in St. Petersburg in mid-October, he joined the Soviet leadership, but how much of a role he played is unclear. During the fifteen months of his sentence, he studied and wrote, as he had during his first confinement—the classic luxury of revolutionaries in tsarist prisons.[28]

After the St. Petersburg arrests, the action shifted to Moscow. The uprising that began in early December, complete with barricades and factory militias, demonstrated both the possibility and the futility of challenging the forces of order head-on. Workers in the factory district of Presnia acquired arms and ammunition; cobblestones and furniture were piled into heaps blocking the streets. A massive strike shut off electricity and transportation. Institutions closed their doors; residents panicked. By the middle of the month, the Semenovskii Regiment had arrived from Petersburg and the Presnia district was subjected to heavy artillery bombardment. When it was over, at least a thousand civilians had lost their lives and hundreds had been arrested, many of whom were executed without trial. The extremism of the socialist parties which had pushed for insurrection was answered by the ferocity of repression.

The public had been frightened by the continued radicalism of the St. Petersburg Soviet and by the aggressive tactics adopted in Moscow. Some liberals moved to the right, but in general the ruthless reprisals forfeited public sympathy for the post-Manifesto regime. As the new year dawned, Witte abandoned his earlier moderation for a concerted campaign of pacification. Punitive expeditions, under military command, went through the countryside executing alleged rebels without trial and burning villages to the ground. Repression was particularly brutal in the Baltic provinces, where Prime Minister Durnovo gave General Vladimir Sukhomlinov carte blanche to apply maximum force. Emergency laws went into effect in two-thirds of the Empire. The crackdown was successful, because the troops obeyed orders. Into 1906, soldiers mutinied sporadically, interpreting the Duma, as they had the October Manifesto, as a sign that supreme power had weakened, yet in the end the balance did not tip.

While the government waged war on its own population, the extreme Left also went on a rampage. Over the course of 1906, SR assassins succeeded in killing hundreds of officials—and numerous bystanders in the process.[29] The Bolsheviks, for their part, financed their own activities by robbing banks at gunpoint. Minister of the Interior Durnovo, meanwhile, purged the ranks of civil servants and professionals suspected of radical sympathies. The censorship, which had relaxed its hold during the upheaval, was now reinforced. Weathering periodic confiscations, satirical journals kept directing their barbs at the "new" regime while canonizing the holy moments of the Revolution, Bloody Sunday and the Moscow Uprising. Potent symbols were born.

---

After the grand finale of 1905, the aftermath was anticlimactic. The Duma franchise was neither universal nor equal. The proportions favored landowners over peasants and workers, in that order. Peasants nevertheless constituted the vast majority of the population, and it was hoped their traditional submissiveness would now return. The Bolsheviks and the Union of the Russian People, at the two extremes, agreed in their antagonism to the Duma. The Bolsheviks declared a boycott, but some monarchists took part in the campaign. The Kadets came away victorious with 40 percent of the seats, while a quarter went to independents and another quarter to a string of left-wing parties. The Octobrists and other moderates emerged with a mere 3 percent of the seats, the radical right with none. Over half the deputies represented the peasantry, over a third the nobility, and about a fifth the urban professions.[30]

Before the deputies could convene in late April, however, Witte, in a preemptive move, secured a large loan from France and other European powers, cushioning his government against the deficit created by the war and avoiding financial dependence on the Duma.[31] The government also managed to retract or undermine some of the central promises of the October Manifesto. In February, the tsar endowed the ceremonial State Council, half of its members appointed by himself, with powers equal to those of the Duma. The Kadets denounced the move as a coup d'état. Then, four days before the Duma was scheduled to open, the Fundamental Laws of the Empire were published. A constitution in all but (objectionable) name, these laws could be changed only by the emperor. The promised civil rights—due process, private property, various liberties—were limited by law. The scope of the Duma was also restricted. Laws could be passed by decree during its recess (in theory subject to later approval), and the tsar was entitled to dissolve it. Miliukov called the Fundamental Laws "a conspiracy against the people."[32]

Another change also altered the landscape, again before the Duma had even convened. Five days before it opened, Witte stepped down and was replaced by Ivan Goremykin. Ten years Witte's senior, Goremykin had been minister of the interior in the late 1890s. He was now appointed over the objections of his colleagues, who considered him inadequate to the job, describing him as rigid, retrograde, and lazy.[33] In another move in the confrontational two-step between ruler and subjects, the Third Kadet Party Congress adopted a series of reform objectives for the coming session that were clearly unrealistic. These included land reform and an official investigation into government repression of the revolution.

The day the Duma opened, soldiers and police were posted throughout the city, anticipating disturbances, but reluctant though he was, Nicholas had decided to demonstrate his imperial pleasure. The deputies were invited to the Winter Palace, where the tsar pronounced a speech. Uniformed bureaucrats and courtiers in formal dress stood to one side, the deputies, from every corner of the Empire and in every possible attire, stood to the other. The speech was lackluster, and so was the deputies' response. After the reception, they proceeded to the Tauride Palace, built in the late eighteenth century under the reign of Catherine the Great for her lover Prince Potemkin, now refurbished to accommodate the new assembly. The deputies were greeted warmly as they passed through the streets.

The establishment of the Duma was supposed to have quieted the revolution, but it met against the background of persistent turmoil. Peasants were not cut off from events in the capital; newspapers reporting on Duma debates reached villages already troubled by the consequences of a poor harvest and the return of demobilized soldiers. The deputies received thousands of petitions from the countryside, transcribed by school teachers, doctors, or clerks, but expressing genuine concerns. Despite the Bolsheviks' disdain for the elections, workers also showed an interest in the Duma. Lenin decided it was worth participating after all, if only to make trouble.[34]

The most difficult problem tackled by the First Duma was the question of land reform, but the most impassioned debate concerned the Białystok pogrom.[35] Speakers focused on the discovery that a secret printing press within the Ministry of the Interior had been issuing pamphlets denouncing the Jews. The most arresting moment in the debate was the speech delivered by Prince Sergei Urusov, lately governor of Bessarabia Province, where he had arrived in the wake of the 1903 Kishinev pogrom, shocking at the time for its ferocity.[36] Urusov denounced the involvement of local officials in the riots and made a plea for the strict enforcement of existing laws against ethnic hatred and mob violence. His words, published in domestic and foreign papers, caused a sensation.[37]

After repeated provocations and mutual insults, barely ten weeks after the Duma opened the government decided it had to go. As troops massed in the capital, almost a third of the deputies retreated to the Finnish town of Vyborg (Viipuri), sheltered from the police, where they formulated what came to be known as the Vyborg Manifesto, titled "To the People from the People's Representatives." It called on the population to withhold taxes and defy military conscription. It was a foolhardy and inconsistent gesture. The Kadets were once again playing with revolutionary fire, only this time there was no spark, and they soon realized their mistake. The signers were eventually brought to court, and 166 were sentenced to three months in prison. All forfeited the right to stand for re-election.

At the end of July, Petr Stolypin, Goremykin's minister of the interior, moved up to take his place. After Witte, Stolypin was the most significant figure in the late years of the Empire.[38] From an old noble family, he had previously served as governor in the provinces of Grodno and Saratov. If Witte had managed to settle the revolutionary earthquake with the October Manifesto, Stolypin had to face the aftershocks. He pursued a complicated strategy of sustaining the Duma while curtailing its powers and working around it. Beginning at the end of 1906, he also instituted a far-reaching program of rural reform, designed to establish a solid landowning class in the countryside with an investment in stability, thereby also depriving the Duma of the initiative. Above all, he applied the strong arm of the state in repressing popular unrest and punishing challenges from the Left. A difficult and self-contradictory program.

Despite the waning of the Soviet's charisma at the end of 1905, the disaster of the Moscow Uprising, and the failure of the Vyborg Manifesto to elicit any kind of response, challenges to authority continued. In his first days in office Stolypin confronted mutiny among the sailors in Kronstadt and the Helsingfors (now Helsinki) fortress of Sveaborg, as well as in Reval. In the cities, by contrast, mass action seemed on the decline. The St. Petersburg Soviet issued and then rescinded the call for a general strike, and its leaders were arrested. An echoing strike in Moscow quickly died down. The second half of 1906 was characterized, however, by a surge in terrorism from both Left and Right. In July assassins paid by the Union of the Russian People murdered a Kadet Duma deputy whom they believed to be Jewish. Mikhail Gertsenshtein had in fact converted to Orthodoxy, but he had spoken out against the pogroms. His funeral drew a crowd of thousands. The perpetrators were tried and convicted, but pardoned by the tsar, who sympathized with their mission. Stolypin thought it wiser, however, to relax the restrictions facing the Jews, which had been increasing since 1881, but the modest proposal he submitted for approval in October 1906 was rejected by Nicholas, at the urging of his "inner voice."[39] In March 1907 another Kadet deputy from the First Duma, one of the signatories of the Vyborg group and a member of the League for Jewish Rights, was gunned down on a Moscow street. Twenty thousand people attended his funeral. The assassin, hired by the Union of the Russian People, escaped abroad.

The SRs, for their part, were also responsible for dramatic gestures. On a Saturday in mid-August, 1906, Stolypin was receiving petitioners at his summer house on one of the islands in the Neva River when three men appeared wearing officers' uniforms and carrying suitcases. In a scenario all too familiar in our own day, the cases exploded, killing them and twenty-seven other people and injuring seventy, including two of Stolypin's children. He himself was barely hurt, his prestige enhanced by his composure.[40] The deed was the work of an SR offshoot calling itself the Union of SR-Maximalists (*Soiuz eserov-maksimalistov*).[41] This and a persistent rain of terror from the Left led the government to institute field courts-martial with the power to impose and execute summary sentences. Until allowed to lapse a year later, the courts applied the death penalty in over a thousand cases and sentences of hard labor in over three hundred. In a seeming echo-chamber of lawlessness, Right and Left pursued their common goal of impeding the emergence of a stable political system.

---

Despite the disqualification of the Vyborg signatories, the Second Duma, which opened in February 1907 after a hiatus of seven months, proved even more contentious than the first. The Right elected its first deputies, the number of socialist seats rose, while the center contracted. The Kadets, however, had become more cautious. Stolypin offered formally to legalize the party, on condition it publicly repudiate left-wing terror. Miliukov entertained the proposition, but the party refused, for fear of seeming to endorse Stolypin's courts-martial. The Octobrist Party had split on that very issue. Over all, the chamber was deeply divided; half its members opposed the Duma's very existence.

In early March, Stolypin appeared before the assembly, in a conciliatory spirit, to outline his program, including pending legislation on land reform. In reply, the Menshevik deputy from Georgia, Iraklii Tsereteli, half the minister's age, delivered a strident condemnation of his government. Tsereteli was denounced from the floor by Vladimir Purishkevich, who soon became known for inflammatory speeches and vulgar anti-Semitic tirades.[42] Stolypin maintained his dignity and refused to be provoked. Throughout April and May, the Kadets persisted in offering plans for agrarian reform more radical than anything the government was likely to accept. Outside the Duma, the government closed newspapers and widened the scope of arrests. Each side reinforced its image of the other.

As the tensions persisted, the police raided the apartments of the SD and SR deputies, charging the Social Democrats with sedition. The Kadets condemned the group's expulsion. Maklakov, at the very right of his party and the least prone to political sentimentalism, explained to Stolypin that accepting the arrest of fellow deputies would sap the party's moral foundation. Stolypin had little room for maneuver. On Sunday, June 3, 1907, at the tsar's insistence, notices were posted at the Tauride Palace, closing the Duma. Its president learned the news from a foreign journalist. Over the next few days, six hundred people were arrested, including the SD deputies in question.[43] In violation of the Fundamental Laws, the Duma franchise was adjusted by decree, to reduce the representation of workers, peasants, and ethnic minorities, eliminating almost the entire geographic periphery. No protests ensued, but arrests continued, more newspapers were shuttered, and recently legalized trade unions were now repressed. Measures against continuing acts of terror and criminality intensified.

The dissolution of the Second Duma and the alteration of the electoral laws were denounced as a coup d'état. Stolypin was an authoritarian pragmatist. He had not hesitated to defy the recent (half-hearted) commitment to legality, but he still viewed the Duma as a useful instrument. He counted on the Third Duma, which opened in November, with its staunchly middle-of-the-road center, to provide a workable base from which to enlist "society" in the project of stabilizing the country through a combination of repression and reform. The public forces which had confronted the regime in 1905 could not simply be ignored. The Octobrists indeed now emerged in the Duma as the single largest party, which, together with other moderate groups, constituted a large majority. The Kadets and far Right balanced each other at the edges, while the Left had been severely reduced. Landowners held 40 percent of the seats.[44] Some key figures survived the reshuffle. Purishkevich reappeared on the right, Miliukov and Maklakov among the Kadets, and Guchkov for the Octobrists.

Over the course of four years, however, Stolypin forfeited the advantage he had gained. His continual violations of the Fundamental Laws, combined with the tsar's own blatant disregard for legality, alienated the Octobrist center, and the party became a less reliable partner. Even Stolypin's sponsorship of Guchkov in 1910 as Duma president did not guarantee support. Nor did the extreme Right mitigate its hostility to the Duma, despite the government funds supplied to the Union of the Russian People and to various reactionary newspapers. The dissemination of propaganda and targeted financial backing of the press were part of Stolypin's overall attempt to shape public opinion. Anti-Semitism was, of course, as much a force for disruption as the calls for class warfare coming from the Left. Altogether, the courtship of reactionary forces did little to strengthen Stolypin's hand. Russia's diminished prestige in the international arena—its loss to Japan in 1905 and its failure to block the annexation of Bosnia by Austria in 1908—undermined Stolypin's position in conservative eyes. In belated reaction to the self-assertion of subject minorities in 1905 and in a gesture extended to frustrated Russian patriots, Stolypin took extra steps to curtail Finland's traditional rights and attempted to limit Polish influence in the Western provinces. Along with official sponsorship of anti-Semitic extremism, the nationalist turn would have unfortunate consequences in the near future.[45]

Stolypin himself did not live to see the end of the Third Duma. On September 1, 1911, Nicholas was in Kiev for the unveiling of a monument to the emancipation of the serfs fifty years before. Stolypin was in the party that attended a performance of Nikolai Rimsky-Korsakov's opera *The Tale of Tsar Saltan* in the municipal theater. During intermission, a young man walked into the minister's loge and shot him in the chest. As Stolypin collapsed into his seat, he cried, rather operatically: "I am happy to die for the tsar!" At which point, Nicholas himself appeared in the box.[46] Four days later, Stolypin died of his wound. The assassin was twenty-four-year-old Dmitrii Bogrov, from a wealthy Jewish Kiev family. Though he considered himself an anarchist, in 1907 he had become an informant for the secret police, reporting on the activities of the local SRs and SR-Maximalists, apparently for the money. When his comrades began to suspect a double-cross, they insisted he prove himself by performing a spectacular act of terror. The tsar's visit provided the opportunity. Bogrov chose Stolypin, not Nicholas, as his target. Having convinced the police that the minister needed protection, Bogrov was given a pass to the theater on the night of the performance. After the shooting, he was taken away, court-martialed, and a week later hanged.[47] Though Stolypin had said he was happy to die for the tsar, by 1911 he no longer had the emperor's whole-hearted backing. His assassination spared him a final disappointment.

In over five years in office, Stolypin had confronted three major challenges: to establish a working relationship with "society," as represented in the Duma; to implement reforms that would change the face of the countryside and reduce the likelihood of peasant unrest; and to manage or counteract the influence of radical ideology, on both Left and Right. He failed on all counts. The Third Duma remained troublesome, the reforms did not have time to produce results, and his support for the organized Right had serious short- and long-term consequences. Nor did the threat of industrial turmoil disappear. Rather, the economic recovery that began in 1910 led to an upsurge in labor activism. A flashpoint came in spring 1912 at the Siberian gold mines on the Lena River owned by a British-Russian joint stock company. When striking workers assembled to protest the arrest of their leadership, they were met by troops who opened fire, leaving over two hundred dead and an equal number wounded. The Lena Goldfields Massacre, as it came to be known—an echo of Bloody Sunday—triggered a rash of strikes in St. Petersburg and Moscow, and the level of worker unrest rose to the highest point since the Revolution.[48] The Bolsheviks now turned their attention to the surviving labor unions, where they began successfully to compete with the Mensheviks for influence, establishing footholds in key industries. In the Fourth Duma, they won a majority of seats held by labor.[49] Another portent for the future.

Duma deputy Alexander Kerensky, elected from the socialist Laborite Party (*Trudoviki*), loosely associated with the SRs, headed an investigation of the Lena events, which was reported in the press. Eleven years younger than

Lenin, Kerensky was also born in Simbirsk, where his father was a school inspector. The two families were acquainted. After 1905, Kerensky made a name for himself in St. Petersburg as a defense lawyer in political trials. He became known in the Fourth Duma for his eloquent speech-making and emerged in February 1917 as the leading figure of the first months of the revolution.[50]

---

The Fourth Duma sat from November 1912 to summer 1913, returning from recess for a second sitting between October 1913 and June 1914, then for a special one-day convocation on July 26, 1914 (August 8, NS), to vote war credits.[51] This assembly was characterized by even greater polarization and party fragmentation than the Third, where the Octobrists had been the mainstay. Now, their numbers diminished, the Kadets held their own, while the Right and the Left grew. Overall, the number of distinct "groups" and "fractions" had increased. Among the Kadets, Maklakov and others on the right criticized Miliukov's leadership as unrealistic, while those on the left urged greater contact with the socialists and the workers' movement. Alliances emerged between progressive industrialists and the professional classes, united around several basic demands (opposition to the so-called June 3rd System, reform of the State Council, the defense of civil liberties, and the demand for a cabinet responsible to the Duma), but no effective opposition emerged.[52]

Not only was the Duma internally divided, but it faced a less united government under Stolypin's successor, Vladimir Kokovtsov, former minister of finance, now serving concurrently in that post. Stolypin's attempt to establish a working relationship with the Duma majority, with the Octobrist Party as key, was often foiled by his own actions. Kokovtsov had no such base, because the parties had begun to fragment and also because he did not have the same goal. Nicholas approved of the new prime minister's seeming disregard for "politicking."[53] His position was weakened, moreover, by obstruction from within his own cabinet. The most hostile and underhanded of its members was Nikolai Maklakov, the Kadet Vasilii Maklakov's younger brother, appointed minister of the interior in February 1913 over Kokovtsov's objections. For the rest of the year, Maklakov did everything in his power to undermine Kokovtsov's authority, urging Nicholas to reduce the Duma to advisory status, diminish the ministers' collective responsibility, and reimpose preliminary censorship on the press. In short, Maklakov made his best attempt to undo the October Manifesto and restore autocratic power. Kokovtsov survived only to the end of January 1914, when he was replaced by the same Goremykin who had followed Witte, in both cases representing a reversion to short-sighted bureaucratic servility. The emperor described the move with satisfaction as a coup d'état.[54]

The entire right wing of the Duma, whatever its internal nuances, was united on the question of the Jews. Nicholas and Count Lamsdorf were not alone in blaming the revolution, the continuing socialist agitation, and the campaign of terrorist assassinations on this familiar scapegoat. Leading ministers such as Witte, Stolypin, and Kokovtsov understood the dangers involved in encouraging the mob to strike out, even in defense of the tsar and the Christian God. They understood that foreign opinion, aroused by news of the pogroms, could damage Russia's reputation, and that cultivating the goodwill of international Jewish finance was a matter of national interest. Yet they were ambivalent and inconsistent on the question of removing existing limitations on Jewish residence, education, and public service. There were good reasons to think, for example, that confining the vast majority of the Empire's 3.5 million Jews to the fifteen southwestern provinces, known as the Pale of Settlement, and another 1.7 million to the Polish provinces contributed to Jewish poverty and encouraged Jewish radicalism.[55] In early 1911, Stolypin seemed to give his approval to a bill introduced in May 1910 proposing the abolition of the Pale.[56] A vote in February 1911 referred the bill to committee, where it subsequently died, but not before eliciting a lively debate on the Duma floor, in which Vasilii Maklakov delivered an impassioned speech in favor not only of abolishing the Pale but of equal rights for Jews.[57]

Meanwhile, in Kiev in March 1911, a Russian boy was found murdered. The local Black Hundreds declared the killing to have the markings of an ancient Jewish ritual in which Christian victims were drained of their blood for use in matzos. At their urging, the Kiev police arrested an employee of a local brick factory by the name of Mendel Beilis, a casually observant Jew who had until then enjoyed good relations with his neighbors. What began as a local case expanded into an international scandal by the intervention of Minister of Justice Ivan Shcheglovitov, who gave the case a top-level imprimatur. After two years in prison, Beilis appeared in a Kiev courtroom, where his trial lasted from late September to the end of October 1913. A jury of peasants heard government-backed witnesses and the testimony of experts asserting the nefarious character of the Jewish faith. They also heard speeches for the defense by a team of lawyers, Gentile and Jewish, mobilized by the Russian Jewish community, including Vasilii Maklakov, who denounced the case as a sham and a disgrace to the Russian judicial system.[58] The trial made front-page news in the Russian press and resonated around the world. The case became a rallying point for the enlightened Russian public, as the Dreyfus affair had been in France. The peasant jury in the end found Beilis not guilty of the crime, but conceded that ritual murder was indeed a credible accusation.[59]

The Beilis case was not the last scandal to blight the final years of Nicholas's reign. The defenders of monarchy who refused to adapt to the demands of modern governance contributed to the autocracy's undoing. But the monarchy depended not only on effective government. It depended also on the special, sacred aura attached to the sovereign's person. Even before the end of the Third Duma, this glow had begun to dim. By 1911 public uneasiness with the tsar's diminishing stature had begun to fixate on the figure of Grigorii Rasputin. A Siberian peasant who had assumed the role of a wandering holy man, Rasputin came to St. Petersburg, where at the end of 1905 he caught the attention of the imperial couple and soon became a regular presence at court. His repute as a miracle-worker or faith-healer and his place in the empress's affections were assured in 1912 when he seemed to cure her son, the tsarevich, of a bout of hemophilic bleeding. Drawing around himself a circle of adoring women, he gained a reputation for sexual promiscuity as well as mystical gifts. He seemed both compelling and repulsive.[60]

The earliest objections to the uncouth figure, with his black cloak and piercing eyes, came not from the public but from top officials. Stolypin and Kokovtsov both tried to get rid of him. In early 1912 Mikhail Rodzianko, the Octobrist leader who had succeeded Guchkov as president of the Duma in March 1911, warned Nicholas that Rasputin belonged to an illegal religious sect, the so-called Self-Flagellators (Khlysty). There is no evidence that Rasputin was in fact anything but a magnificent egotist with powers of seduction, both spiritual and sexual. The charge of sectarianism was designed to discredit him, but it reflected the sinister threat he seemed to embody. For Nicholas, he was a messenger from the divine; for the anxious public, a devil.[61] "Rasputin," Rodzianko warned, "is a weapon in the hands of the enemies of Russia, who use him to undermine the Church and the Monarchy. No revolutionary propaganda could achieve as much as the presence of Rasputin."[62] A year later, with Rasputin still in place, Rodzianko proclaimed before the Duma: "You all know what a terrible drama Russia is living through....At the centre of that drama is a mysterious tragi-comic figure, like a shade of the underworld, or a survivor of the darkness of past centuries, a strange figure in the light of the twentieth century."[63]

Clinging to Rasputin in their isolation from society and even from the government, the imperial couple distanced themselves further not only from the public but from their loyal servitors as well. Ceremonies marking the centenary of Romanov rule that kicked off in February 1913 did nothing to restore the court's luster. As historian Richard Wortman remarks, "Rather than provide an occasion for consensus, the celebration became a focus of contention between diverse understandings of nation—liberal, statist, monarchical, and clerical."[64] Again asserting his divinely inspired mandate, the tsar rode from the Winter Palace to the Cathedral of Our Lady of Kazan on Nevskii Avenue. Police and troops were on the alert for revolutionary demonstrations or a terrorist attack. Anti-Semitic monarchist organizations, including the Union of the Russian People, were prominent in the procession, signaling the tsar's approval. As Wortman notes, "the religious processions had taken on the aspect of a political demonstration in behalf of the tsar." The elected representatives of the people—the unwanted intermediaries between the tsar and his folk, as Nicholas saw them—were demonstratively pushed to the side. The tsar's manifesto omitted mention of the Duma. Rodzianko was slighted at the official banquet. In May the imperial couple toured central Russia, ending their ceremonial journey in Moscow. Visits to holy sites and audiences with humble peasants provided the message of enduring tradition and closeness to the people's heart, but incidents of discord with spokesmen of educated society marked the tsar's distance from forces trying to lead Russia into the future.[65] Spectacle was not enough to reconstitute dynastic authority in the modern world.

It was a sign of how far the monarch's credit had sunk that the well-to-do middle classes now despaired of the political compromise they had earlier embraced. In November 1913, Guchkov expressed regret that the Octobrist Party's attempt "to achieve a rapprochement with the government, the attempt at a peaceful, painless transition from the old order to the new, has failed."[66] It was the Octobrists' duty, he now said, to defend "the state system" against the government itself. Opposition could no longer be relegated to the radical Left, allowing the ministers to claim they were fending off a revolutionary cataclysm. "In actual fact," said Guchkov, the government was "resisting the fulfilment of the most moderate and elementary demands of society." The Octobrists must use every legal means to "defend the govern-ment's authority against the very holders of office."[67] In December 1913, Rodzianko complained to Nicholas that the country was in danger, not from the masses but at the top: "Each minister has his own opinion. For the most part, the cabinet is divided into two parties. The State Council forms a third, the Duma a fourth, and of your own opinion the country remains ignorant. This cannot go on, your Majesty, this is not government, it is anarchy."[68] In short, the governing system established by the October Manifesto, which attempted to reconcile the principle of autocracy with parliamentary power and a unified cabinet, was in dire straits well before the onset of war in August 1914.[69]

Страхъ!..

ИЗД. НОВ. КРИВ. ЗЕРКАЛО.

"Fear!" Postcard, Slavonic Library, National Library of Finland.

# PART II

## The Great War: Imperial Self-Destruction

# I

# The Great War Begins

The fighting in Europe lasted from August 1, 1914 to November 11, 1918—just over four years. For Russia, it lasted only until December 15, 1917 (December 2, OS)—just over three. By then the autocracy had collapsed and the regime that replaced it had fallen. The February and October Revolutions of 1917 drew their explosive potential not only from the grueling experience of battle and home-front privation, but also from the not-so-distant experience of the 1905 Revolution.[1]

What follows is not a history of Russia's war, but a rumination on three themes that bear on the question of what form of politics and what kind of state emerged from the Revolutions of 1917. The first theme concerns the disarray at the highest reaches of power in the monarchy's last years, the fact that authority was already compromised in 1914. The second addresses the patterns of violence that emerged during the fighting and persisted into the Civil War. Extreme brutality, at the front and behind the lines, sometimes enjoyed the sanction of authority, sometimes reflected authority's collapse. The third theme involves the stigmatizing of designated groups—different at different times and in different places, but united by exclusion from the common fold. Together, the weakness of authority, the suspension of moral restraint, and the deepening of social divisions prepared the ground for the ruthless struggle to reassert control and rechannel the volatile forces released by the war—the struggle that lasted four years, from 1917 to 1921, longer than the war itself.

———

Russia did not enter the war from a position of strength. Some historians have argued that it was precisely the Empire's internal weakness that prompted German leaders in summer 1914 to provoke the conflict.[2] Russia enjoyed the advantage over Germany in manpower and natural resources, but these were not yet fully exploited. Both sources of vulnerability—domestic instability and the still unrealized industrial and military potential—were recognized by Russian statesmen at the time. Certain conservative figures, in particular, doubted Russia's capacity to survive more than a few months of war. They feared Germany was too powerful for Russia to handle.[3]

The diplomatic horizon was unquiet, as well. Russia's humiliation in the Bosnian crisis of 1908 was still fresh, and the treaty concluding the Second Balkan War was barely a year old. The educated public was well aware of trouble still brewing in the Balkans and greeted the crisis of July 1914 with apprehension.[4] High-ranking officials were divided on whether Russia's best interests lay in maintaining good relations with Germany or countering German influence by an alliance with France. The Russian Foreign Office heard reports that antagonism to Russia was increasing in Berlin. In the winter of 1913–1914, Germany sent a military mission to the Ottoman Empire under General Otto Liman von Sanders. Achieving control of the Turkish Straits, linking the Black and Aegean Seas, was a long-standing goal of Russian foreign policy. Russian diplomats interpreted the mission as Germany's attempt to establish its own influence there.[5]

This was the context in which Petr Durnovo, arch-conservative minister of the interior in the aftermath of the October Manifesto, warned Nicholas against weakening the German alliance. The opinions he expressed in a memo to the tsar in February 1914 have often been cited as a bellwether of the disaster that ensued.[6] Durnovo belonged to a group of far-right conservatives in the State Council who favored the alliance with Germany as a matter of political principle. They were staunch supporters of unlimited monarchy and regarded the Duma with open distaste, as an institution created under duress and better to have been avoided. Russia and Germany, in Durnovo's words, represented "the conservative principle in the civilized world, as opposed to the democratic principle, incarnated in England and, to an infinitely lesser degree, in France." It was unfortunate that Nicholas had abandoned Russia's "traditional friendly relations, based upon ties of blood, with the Court of Berlin" and drawn closer to England. A European war, Durnovo predicted, would involve "Russia, France, and England, on the one side, with Germany, Austria, and Turkey, on the other." Russia, he feared, was not ready for this confrontation. Nicholas did not share his pessimistic view, but it reflected widespread anxiety about Russia's ability to withstand the domestic consequences of another war.[7]

Liberals in the Duma supported an alliance with England and France for the opposite reasons, as the progressive Western model to which Russia should aspire. Durnovo blamed them for the outbreak of revolution in 1905, when their democratic illusions, he believed, had played into the hands of unscrupulous firebrands. Should Russia be defeated in another war, these same liberals would again open the door to massive social upheaval. Inspired by socialist slogans, peasants would demand the division of land and property, and the defeated army, depleted of its best men, would "find itself too demoralized to serve as a bulwark of law and order." The elites, having forfeited their authority, would be "powerless to stem the popular tide, aroused by themselves, and Russia will be flung into hopeless anarchy, the issue of which cannot be foreseen."

Not all conservatives shared Durnovo's preference for the German alliance; not all were uniformly hostile to the Duma. The lack of coherence among figures at court and high-ranking officials was a symptom of the regime's increasing weakness. Those who distrusted the Duma failed to understand the need to win its support, and thus the endorsement of respectable society, in the face of the very threats Durnovo so presciently detailed in February 1914. His colleague in the State Council, Baron Roman Rozen, a Baltic German of Orthodox faith, also feared the destructive consequences of war with Germany, but he saw the domestic challenge differently. The "real danger of revolution," he noted in January 1914, "is created not by the Utopian demands of extreme radicalism but by the failure to give timely satisfaction to the moderate desires and expectations of educated society, the higher social classes of any nation, which in their great majority have always been loyal."[8]

---

By summer 1914, however, public opinion, as well as many in the officer corps and key figures at court, had turned against Germany. Foreign Minister Sergei Sazonov stressed Russia's interest in maintaining Ottoman control of the Turkish Straits, as crucial to Russian shipping and to keeping Germany from establishing its influence there. Nor could Russia stand by when Austria reacted to nationalist challenges in the Balkans. German support for Austrian interests was sure to follow.[9] Nicholas opted for the alliance with England and France.

Russia soon found itself in exactly the position Durnovo had outlined, with the consequences he and Baron Rozen had foreseen. The political incongruity of Russia's alliance with France was all too apparent. French president Raymond Poincaré visited St. Petersburg in late July, as the prewar crisis was coming to a head. The French ambassador Maurice Paléologue described the pomp and ceremony of the imperial court, as reflected in the precious gems glistening on the well-tended bosoms of the ladies in attendance. Russia, in his view, was an opulent and barbaric vestige of an historic moment the West had already surpassed, but its primitive might was needed to restore the balance of power against the German menace. Poincaré, together with Paléologue and the French prime minister, René Viviani, were escorted to the Peter-Paul Fortress, bastion of tsarist oppression, by "terrifying" red-coated Cossacks, as "the 'Marseillaise' answered to the Russian Imperial Hymn"—"God Save the Tsar."[10] It might seem to a connoisseur of irony, Paléologue observed, as though Poincaré and Viviani, those "avowed revolutionaries," were being led to their prison cells. "Never had the moral contradiction, the tacit ambiguity, at the heart of the Franco-Russian alliance struck me so forcibly."[11]

This was not the only paradox generated by geopolitical concerns. Insofar as liberals in the Duma were anti-German and pro-British, they also defended Russian ambitions in the Balkans and in the Straits, where German and Russian interests collided. This posture would get them into trouble in 1917, when they continued to endorse the monarchy's expansionist vision. The prosperous bourgeoisie, represented in the Octobrist Party, had long supported Russian imperial designs in the Balkans. The Octobrists had advocated a more aggressive Russian stance in the various crises since 1908.[12] By the summer of 1914, the Russian public was primed for confrontation with Germany in this very arena.

The fatal events followed in quick succession. On June 28 Archduke Franz Ferdinand of Austria was assassinated in Sarajevo. A month later, on July 23, Austria-Hungary presented Serbia with an ultimatum. On July 25 (July 12, OS), Nicholas ordered that preparatory steps be taken to support the anticipated mobilization. On July 28, Austria-Hungary declared war on Serbia; Nicholas gave orders to mobilize the four military districts from which an attack on Austria would originate. On July 29 (July 16, OS), Sazonov concluded that full mobilization must go forward.[13] Nicholas at first agreed, but changed his mind that evening upon receipt of a telegram from his cousin, Kaiser Wilhelm II.[14] The following morning, General Nikolai Ianushkevich, the army chief of staff, and Minister of War Vladimir Sukhomlinov, with the endorsement of Mikhail Rodzianko, president of the

State Duma, urged the tsar to take the necessary steps, but he waited until later that day, after meeting with Sazonov, before finally issuing the order to proceed with general mobilization. The announcement came on July 31 (July 18, OS).[15] On August 1, 1914 (July 19, OS), Germany declared war on France and Russia. By the following day, German troops had crossed into Russian Poland. A day later, August 3, they invaded neutral Belgium. Britain declared war on Germany on August 4. On August 6 (July 24, OS) Austria-Hungary declared war on Russia. The Great War had begun.[16]

The participants embarked on this conflict with foreboding; even the German ambassador to St. Petersburg, Count Friedrich Pourtalès, acted with obvious reluctance. After meeting with Sazonov on July 30 (July 17, OS), Paléologue noted, the ambassador looked haggard and seemed unsteady on his feet.[17] The diplomats felt powerless to brake the descent into war. "Individual initiative has disappeared," Paléologue had bemoaned three days earlier. No act of will, no diplomatic move, could stop "the automatic mechanism set in motion." He reports the Austrian ambassador Count Friedrich von Szapary muttering: "La machine roule."[18] After Pourtalès presented the Kaiser's declaration of war to Sazonov, the ambassador burst into tears.[19]

It was perhaps self-serving of Paléologue to present his diplomatic confrères as helpless in the face of events; by the end of July they no doubt felt that war could not be avoided. Nonetheless, decisions were being made. Nicholas had hesitated, but his ministers and the patriotic enthusiasts in the Duma had urged him on. Faced with the German and Austrian challenge, the Empire had no choice, they felt, but to defend its position as a great power or cease to be one. Military reforms implemented in response to the Balkan crises of 1908 and 1912 had strengthened the army. Continuing industrial growth and the extension of the railroad network provided grounds for cautious optimism. In July 1914, Russian ministers imagined the war would be short. It remained unclear, however, how the populace would respond to another military call-up a decade after the Russo-Japanese War and whether the educated classes, represented in the Duma and in public organizations, would rally to the cause.

As Rodzianko had warned Nicholas at the end of 1913, the tsar might want to consider himself all-powerful, but the government was in fact dangerously divided. In August 1914, the regime's inner tensions were all too obvious, pitting the army against the cabinet and the cabinet against itself. On the side of reaction were Goremykin, chair of the Council of Ministers, now seventy-four, and the obstructionist minister of internal affairs, Nikolai Maklakov. Throughout the first half of 1914 and into 1915, Maklakov continued to urge that the Duma be reduced from a legislative to a consultative body, a campaign he had launched in 1913, equally in vain. On the relatively moderate side were the ministers who recognized the need to work with respectable public opinion. Sazonov had been minister of foreign affairs since 1910, and his replacement in July 1916 by Boris Shtiurmer, at the time doubling as prime minister, was correctly perceived by the public as the triumph of reaction. Aleksandr Krivoshein, minister of agriculture since 1908, played a key role in the wartime cabinet as a voice of reason. He lasted in office until October 1915.[20]

Minister of War Sukhomlinov is hard to classify. His career illustrates some of the tensions within the autocratic system that threatened its own survival. A veteran of the Russo-Turkish War of 1877–1878, Sukhomlinov was promoted to general in 1898. He spent the turbulent years from 1899 to 1907 in Kiev, a hotbed of radical anti-Semitism (an outlook he shared), where he served first as chief of staff of the military district, becoming its commander in 1904. In 1906 he was charged with pacification of the Baltic provinces. In 1908 he was promoted to head the General Staff in St. Petersburg. After 1905 the General Staff had been separated from the Ministry of War, to which it was once again subordinated in 1909, the year Sukhomlinov became minister of war, combining the two functions.[21]

Sukhomlinov was ambitious and venal. In the clientelist manner of the tsarist bureaucracy he promoted men loyal to himself, who were not always the best qualified. Yet, in the wake of the Balkan crisis of 1908, he instituted a number of military reforms which emphasized the role of technology, reconfigured the size and number of military units, and challenged the traditional use of cavalry and the defensive reliance on fortresses. Disliked by the Duma, he nevertheless gained its support for increased military spending.[22] The revision of strategic planning and projects for more extensive military reform intensified after 1912, but not enough had been accomplished by 1914. Russia was still deficient in automatic weaponry and underequipped with vehicles and airplanes, railroads were still inadequate, and plans had not been made for a long war.[23] The command still relied heavily on bayonets and fortresses. The reforms, moreover, were resisted by the upper-class officer corps and in particular by the elite Guards officers, first among them Grand Duke Nikolai Nikolaevich, who resented

Sukhomlinov's desire to control finances and appointments and his challenge to traditional tactics and hierarchies.[24]

Since the autocracy was by definition a system of personalities and personal politics, the fact that Sukhomlinov's career had won him enemies was nothing remarkable in itself. Such personal conflicts, however, amplified the administrative tensions between the Ministry of War and the military chain of command (at General Headquarters, or Stavka, seated in the Belarussian city of Mogilev).[25] These tensions were accentuated by the "Regulations on the Field Administration of the Army in Wartime" (*Polozhenie o polevom upravlenii voisk v voennoe vremia*), issued on July 16, 1914 (OS). The Regulations granted the commander in chief unfettered power in the "theater of military activity," defined as occupied territory and areas behind the front, creating a virtual second government free from civilian interference.[26] The fracturing of authority was evident also in the appointment of Grand Duke Nikolai Nikolaevich to this position, a choice considered by some to detract from the tsar's own status. As one general remarked: "You can't tear the feathers from the monarch's crown and distribute them to right and left. Supreme Commander, Supreme Evacuation, Supreme Council—all supreme, only the monarch is nothing."[27]

In short, the tsarist regime approached August 1914 with a seriously disunited cabinet and military command. It encountered a war that straddled modernity and tradition, relying on automobiles, railroads, and airplanes (of which Russia had a miserable few hundred), telephones and bugles, machine guns and sabers, horses and carts. It was a war that affected society from top to bottom and demanded its full engagement, under a regime used to seeing civic initiative as a threat rather than a resource. The public mood was therefore of great importance. In the days before Austria's ultimatum to Serbia, widespread strikes had seized St. Petersburg's largest factories. The authorities blamed them on German agents.[28] By the time the order for general mobilization was announced, however, enthusiasm could be detected even in the working-class districts. Cheering crowds gathered in front of the Winter Palace and the Cathedral of Our Lady of Kazan. Educated society rallied to the flag. Duma president Rodzianko declared the conflicts plaguing Russian society since 1905 to be now forgotten.[29] Socialists, by contrast, predicted a social cataclysm—like Durnovo, but for opposite reasons. In the short term, nevertheless, they urged their followers to accept the draft, on the grounds that war would prove the regime's undoing. They, too, like Durnovo, were prescient.

Mobilizing the monarch's symbolic resources, Nicholas announced the declaration of war on July 20 (August 2, NS) at a ceremony in the Winter Palace that displayed the court in all its opulent glory. A massive crowd gathered on the embankment alongside the palace, Ambassador Paléologue reported, while officers and courtiers in fancy dress assembled inside. A mass was held around an icon of the Virgin Mary of Kazan, chants were sung, and the chaplain read aloud the tsar's manifesto to his people. Slowly, clearly, echoing the words pronounced by Alexander I in 1812, Nicholas then declared: "Officers of my guard here present, I salute in you my entire army and I bless you. I solemnly swear that I will not conclude peace so long as a single enemy remains on the soil of the fatherland." The crowd in the room and the crowd outside broke into "frenetic cheers."[30] Meanwhile, people streamed past the French Embassy, chanting "Vive la France!" French observers assumed they had been recruited by the police.[31]

More spontaneous, perhaps, but also more ominous, was the attack on the German Embassy on St. Isaac's Square. Two days after the tsar's announcement, a mob of several thousand destroyed the entire edifice, as police stood idly by.[32] The building, purchased in 1873, soon after German unification, struck Ambassador Paléologue as a provocation. A redesigned façade of Finnish granite in neoclassical style was unveiled in January 1913 in time for the Romanov Centenary. Its fourteen columns and the two bronze horses mounted on the roof seemed to the Frenchman ponderously Teutonic, "powerfully symbolic" of Germany's intention to dominate Russia.[33] Similar outbursts occurred in provincial cities at the start of the war.[34] Targeting symbolic objects, the people's wrath acquired symbolic status of its own. The neo-Orthodox religious philosopher Vasilii Rozanov, a stringer for the vehemently anti-German *Novoe vremia* (*Modern Times*), celebrated the impulse behind the attack.[35] "Illusions are as sacred as facts," he remarked. "The dear people of Petersburg spent a splendid night of illusions—and God bless them."[36] The liberal press, by contrast, likened the rampage on St. Isaac's Square to the German's own "Teutonic vandalism."[37]

St. Petersburg's liberal mayor, Count Ivan Tolstoi, denounced the riot as "hooliganism," a poisonous byproduct of officially sponsored patriotic demonstrations. Tolstoi was a black sheep: a man of enlightened views, who rejected what he described as the routine prejudices of his milieu. He was outspoken in defense of the Jews and condemned the government's "criminal nationalistic policies of the last twenty-five years."[38] Yet even he was affected by the melodramatic tone of stories focused on German barbarity. A favorite theme concerned the fate of Russians caught by the outbreak of war on German soil—ladies unceremoniously stripped to their underwear, patients taking the waters in German spas dumped unceremoniously in railway stations—the "bestial" conduct, as Tolstoi put it, of the "savage Teutonic barbarians."[39] When, in return, Russian authorities began summarily expelling long-time German residents from the capital, the mayor nevertheless bravely came to their defense.[40]

Tolstoi's own use of patriotic formulas shows how hard they were to resist. Such clichés included not only the image of the Teutonic barbarian, the beast lurking beneath the thin membrane of German culture, but also the obsession with German influence in Russian domestic affairs—violence (*nasilie*), in the one case; domination (*zasil'e*), in the other. Not only did Russia depend on German investment and trade, but for generations the Baltic German nobility had played a central role in Russian official and military life. Among the commanders in this war were Generals Pavel von Rennenkampf, Aleksei Evert, Pavel Pleve, and Baron Anton Zal'ts. Beginning in 1916, the prime minister and minister of the interior was Boris Shtiurmer. In November 1915, the Chief Procurator of the Holy Synod, Vladimir Karlovich Sabler, legally changed his name to Desiatovskii; in August 1915, Rennenkampf converted from Lutheranism to Orthodoxy.[41] Such figures made easy targets. A certain General Aleksandr Preis, for example, received an anonymous letter in May 1915, denouncing him as a spy.[42] Many imperial administrators in Russian Poland had German names, opening them to suspicion and resentment among the Poles.[43] As if practicing a belated exorcism, Nicholas thought in December 1916 of replacing the ubiquitous German terms for positions at court with Slavic equivalents.[44] On August 18 (OS), St. Petersburg was renamed Petrograd, to Slavicize the Germanic form.

---

If crowds thronged the streets and squares of Petrograd and other cities, seemingly moved by patriotic emotion, the villages had no cause for joy. At the beginning of August 1914, approximately 1.4 million men were already in uniform. By the end of the year, another five million had been called up.[45] Men over the age of twenty-one, as recorded in the parish registers, were liable to be drafted. In the villages, account was taken of the number of working men in a household; in the cities, munitions factory workers and policemen were exempt.[46] In 1915 an additional five million were drafted, in 1916 a further three million, in 1917 730,000 more. By the time the war ended in 1917, 15,378,000 men had been conscripted, almost 40 percent of males between fifteen and forty-nine.[47] The proportion of working-age men affected was higher in the villages than in the cities, and higher close to the front than in the interior.[48] Peasants made up 85 percent of the overall population and an even higher proportion of soldiers in the army.[49] Soldiers served together with men drawn from their own areas, but the units were stationed far from home. As a form of preemptive counterinsurgency, Polish conscripts were not stationed in Poland.[50]

Just as critical to the peasant economy as the loss of laboring men was the procurement of horses and draft animals. Peasants were ordered to bring their horses for veterinary inspection, while the more delicate mounts of the neighboring gentry were spared.[51] The military equine census of 1912 recorded over seventeen million horses; during the war, the army requisitioned over 1.5 million, or 10 percent overall, but over one-quarter of agricultural workhorses. The peasants also lost many of their carts,[52] and privately owned automobiles were requisitioned.[53] "The war may be popular in the cities," a letter-writer from Smolensk Province observed, "but the villages are horrified.... When they called up the horses, the cheating was indescribable. I didn't care, because my horses were 'reserved,' but it was unpleasant to watch."[54]

The departure of men from the countryside was a serious blow to the welfare of families and villages. Most complied, but some evaded the summons.[55] The farewell drinking spree was a traditional peasant response to the draft. In 1904, drunkenness had disturbed the orderly call-up for the war against Japan. This time, the declaration of general mobilization was accompanied by prohibition on the sale of alcoholic beverages outside first-class restaurants and clubs, another sign that sacrifice was not to be spread evenly. The ban was extended at the end of August to last the duration of the war.[56] Prohibition did not prevent recruits in many cases from breaking into liquor depots and indulging in drink-crazed mayhem.[57]

Not all the disturbances were fueled by drink. The call-up provoked rioting across Russia. In the cities, police patrolmen were attacked; in the villages, peasants set fire to estates and large farms. Food shops everywhere were looted. A riot in the Urals town of Barnaul caused extensive damage to shops and dwellings, leaving a hundred dead by the time the police restored order.[58] The disorders that accompanied the draft did not necessarily reflect a principled opposition to the war, however. Conscription had not been announced in advance or explained in terms that made sense to the peasants, who in August were busy with the harvest. The provinces were undermanned with police, the cities were overwhelmed with the influx of peasant recruits.[59] Nevertheless, with few exceptions, factory workers expressed patriotic views.[60] Despite the numerous outbursts, people in the capitals had the impression that mobilization had gone smoothly.[61]

Once the war began, violence became a matter of organization, not rage or dismay. Casualty figures rose steeply. Manpower shortages were felt as early as the end of 1914. In 1915 Russia suffered a staggering three million casualties, dead, wounded, or captured, and the draft age was lowered from twenty-one to nineteen. Casualties into 1917 have been estimated at over six million.[62] Exact numbers are impossible to ascertain, but overall three million inhabitants of the Russian Empire are thought to have lost their lives between 1914 and 1917 as a result of the war. The total includes almost two million soldiers who were killed in battle, succumbed to wounds, or died in captivity. A third of the one million civilian deaths resulted from military operations, the rest from hunger and disease.[63] When it came to battlefield deaths, however, no class was exempt. The prewar professional officer corps was decimated in the early months, opening the door to promotions from below and shifting the military's class profile.[64] In round figures, the active officer corps in August 1914 consisted of about 40,000 men. The same number were mobilized right away, and another 220,000 were trained during the war. Of the total 300,000 who fought between 1914 and 1917, 24,000 were permanently lost—killed, incapacitated, or unaccounted for—leaving about 276,000 at the end of 1917 (including 38,000 prisoners of war and severely wounded).[65] Peasants became noncommissioned officers; the proportion of noblemen dwindled. Even before the war, the lower ranks of the officer corps had offered a path to social advancement. Now the process accelerated, at the cost of training and competence. In 1905 noncommissioned and educated reserve officers had helped politicize the ranks. This happened again as the war progressed.[66] Since Jews could not be officers, they were often the best-educated men among the troops, and thus played a disproportionate role in 1917.[67] The loss of well-trained officers with an ethos of service had dire consequences for the army's ability to sustain morale and accomplish its military mission. The greatest burden of sacrifice fell, however, on the peasant masses, and no doubt the absence of good leadership contributed to the tremendously high casualty count.

———

Conscripts may have submitted to the draft with fatalism or repressed resentment, but in an age of media-driven propaganda, submission was not enough. The urban public, even the factory masses, responded to the tsar's appeal, but sentiment in the villages was harder to interpret. Educated people doubted whether peasants understood the purpose of the war or were capable of patriotic feeling. Officers viewed the ordinary man in uniform as simple and childish, guided by rituals and symbols—the mystical formula "For Faith, Tsar, and Fatherland," rather than ideas or political principles.[68] But uneducated people, no less than their social superiors, also needed reasons to fight; they maintained their own catalogue of meanings inherited from the past. Fedor Stepun was a writer and philosopher of mixed Orthodox and German parentage, trained in the reserves, who served at the front as a junior officer. He recorded his impressions at the time and later recalled the attitudes of the men under his command. The troops were not indifferent to the meaning of the war, he observed; they were curious to know how it started and whether the Germans were "baptized or un-Christian, like the Turks." The men were astounded to learn that the enemy was in fact Christian and not an infidel, like the Turks and Japanese in earlier wars. Their conception of the war as a crusade was supported, Stepun supposed, "on the one hand, by sermons about the pious Emperor and the 'Christ-loving host'; and on the other, by soldiers' songs tied to memories of the Turkish campaigns." Siberian peasants did not have an educated person's perspective on "Russia as an empire or the geopolitical laws governing its existence." They did not see beyond the concerns of planting and harvests. Nevertheless, Stepun reported, "despite their civic unpreparedness for war, the brigade fought gallantly."[69]

The Germans soon emerged in wartime propaganda as no less bestial and uncivilized than the Turk, despite the veneer of Western culture.[70] Anxiety about the formidable German colossus was magnified by the fact that the enemy was an invader. Russia had not faced an invader since 1812, when Napoleon had set his sights on Moscow. Russia, now as then, had a long western border, running from the Baltic to the Black Sea. Its most vulnerable extremity, surrounded on three sides by Prussia and Austria-Hungary, was the Polish territory west of the Vistula River. Anticipating the outbreak of hostilities, the authorities ordered the evacuation of personnel, official records, and even local garrisons from the entire region, which was left to fend for itself.[71] Indeed, on July 20 (August 2, NS) German troops crossed the unguarded border and seized the towns of Kalisz, Częstochowa, and Będzin.[72]

Major-General Sir Alfred Knox, the British military attaché, considered these "trans-frontier raids" to be of "little importance."[73] The impact of the German incursion was not military, however, but psychological. In the course of the next two weeks, German troops reduced the center of Kalisz, a major textile center and one of the oldest Polish cities, to ash and rubble, slaughtered many of its inhabitants, and caused others to flee in panic and terror. People were torn from their homes and gunned down in the streets, rabbis and priests taken hostage, corpses left on the pavement to rot, and physicians threatened at gunpoint; the hospital was damaged in artillery fire, and entire city blocks were set aflame. Indeed, the invading Germans treated Kalisz much the way they treated the Belgian city of Louvain two weeks later, causing a worldwide outcry. Stories of the devastation in Kalisz, relayed to Russian journalists by traumatized refugees, set the tone for propaganda fixated on enemy brutality and the uncivilized conduct of war. For Russians, Kalisz became, like Belgium in the West, a symbol of German savagery.[74]

The atrocity theme remained a persistent feature of wartime propaganda, but was especially intense in the first months. A group of German intellectuals publicly defended the war as a campaign against Russian barbarism. Among them were several former and future Nobel Prize winners, including the physicist Max Planck and the playwright Gerhart Hauptmann.[75] In Russia, writers and artists suppressed whatever ambivalence they might have felt toward the imperial regime or toward war in general. They accepted the view that Russia had entered the conflict only in response to German provocation. The description and condemnation of so-called atrocities encouraged intelligentsia patriotism. Accounts of "the Belgian horrors" and the sack of Kalisz also acquainted the reading public—and the populace that absorbed rumors and secondhand news—with vivid descriptions of extreme violence and images of the enemy as unredeemed beasts.[76] In the case of Kalisz, the oft-repeated narrative encouraged Russians to identify the Polish people with the Russian cause, eclipsing the usual suspicion of the Poles under Russian rule as disloyal.

Symbols and rituals were important, and not only for the uneducated. Although the tsar bore full responsibility for the declaration of war, it was obvious that society could not be ignored in such a serious crisis.[77] Nicholas therefore called a special, one-day session of the Fourth Duma for July 26 (OS). The deputies first gathered in the Winter Palace, where they heard their sovereign insist that war had been thrust upon them. He called on them also to shoulder the imperial mission. "We defend not only our honor and dignity on Russian land," he said. "We fight also for the Slavs, our brothers in blood and faith." From the Winter Palace the deputies proceeded along the Neva embankment to the Duma's chamber in the Tauride Palace. Asserting their unity of spirit, the political parties pledged to suspend their mutual antagonism and temper their hostility to the regime; the subject nationalities pledged their loyalty; the mistreated minorities adjourned their resentments.[78] In creating a sense of common cause ("we are all Russians"), an early pamphlet declared, "the German threat has done us a great service—the final service the Germans will perform for Russia."[79]

Faced with the strident nationalism of recently united Germany, the Russian Empire in fact struggled to find a mobilizing idiom in reply. Nationalism was associated with the urges of Poles and Finns to achieve independence—a threat, not a resource. On behalf of society, the Duma deputies endorsed the imperial mission. They hailed Russia's duty to defend not only "the Slavic peoples united with us in faith and blood" but also "the honor, dignity, and integrity of Russia and her position among the great powers."[80] Duma president Rodzianko affirmed the people's faith in their ruler and in God's Providence. Ethnic and cultural minorities might not be expected to display the same patriotic zeal, a vulnerability of which the enemy was well aware. It was necessary therefore to assert "the integrity and unity of the state," Rodzianko insisted. The various peoples on Russian soil would unite, he promised, in one "fraternal family" to defend their "common fatherland." The deputies intoned the Imperial Hymn, "God Save the Tsar"—"Mighty, Sovereign, and Orthodox."[81] Sincere as their patriotism may have been, the tone struck by ministers and deputies in these opening moments of the war was nevertheless defensive. In particular, they rejected the German charge that Russia's early mobilization had been an implicit declaration of war, to which the Central Powers had merely been responding. Foreign Minister Sazonov described the Austrian bombardment of Belgrade in July as a "pogrom" of the peaceful inhabitants. He cited the heroism of the Belgian people and denounced German aggression as a violation of the international laws of war.[82]

As an empire, however, Russia faced dangers from within. In the spirit of national unity, Rodzianko accepted the suspension of the Duma at least into the coming year. His acquiescence, on patriotic grounds, angered a number of party leaders but suited the purposes of Goremykin and Minister of the Interior Maklakov. The Fourth Duma was no threat, of course, to the established order. The moderates welcomed the opportunity for cooperation and the chance to demonstrate support for the war. The relatively more oppositional Kadet Party, in support of the struggle against German domination in Europe, agreed to defer its political goals. Its leader, Pavel Miliukov, vowed that the liberals would fulfill their duty as "citizens of the empire." Whatever their attitude toward the government, their obligation was to suspend domestic conflicts and support the men at the front.[83]

Even the socialists capitulated, as they had across Europe, but without renouncing their critical stance. Alexander Kerensky rose to declare that socialists had no enemies among the workers of other nations, driven into fratricidal conflict by the "ruling classes" of Europe. If all countries were to be guided by the democratic principles of liberty, equality, and fraternity, there would be no war. Kerensky nevertheless pledged "the Democracy" to support the war, but complained that the government, even at this dark moment, continued to exacerbate the country's internal divisions. It mistreated the "non-Russian peoples" and did nothing to relieve the burden of the laboring poor. Peasants and workers must nevertheless rise to the defense of their country. Fight the war to make the revolution![84] Vladimir Lenin, in exile, made no secret of opposing the war, but the handful of Bolshevik Duma deputies kept silent. When they gathered illegally in November, they were arrested, further reducing the size of the Duma Left. If Minister of the Interior Maklakov hoped the arrest would arouse public protest, which could be used as an excuse to suppress the Duma once and for all, he was disappointed. None of the liberals publicly objected. Miliukov, for one, damned the Bolsheviks as traitors. Special legislation nevertheless deprived the Duma of some of its former powers, and Maklakov did all he could to thwart civic initiatives in support of the war. The minister's distrust of public life was particularly incongruous and self-defeating at a moment when the public overwhelmingly favored cooperation.[85]

The troubled minorities in the Duma added their voices to the chorus. The representative of the German-descended population of the Baltic region asserted their loyalty to "throne and fatherland." The Latvian and Estonian deputies declared that "neither nationality, nor language, nor religion prevent us Lithuanians and Estonians from being ardent patriots of Russia, ready to defend our fatherland, shoulder to shoulder with the great Russian people against the arrogant foe."[86] The ghost of nationalism nevertheless hovered over the sentiments expressed by a deputy from one of the Polish provinces, recalling the tragic position of the Polish people, deprived of independence and the expression of their own will. Divided among the warring powers, Poles were tragically pitted against each other. The deputy nevertheless expressed the hope that the united Slavic peoples, under Russia's lead, would repel the advances of mighty Prussia, as Poland and Lithuania had done at the Battle of Grunwald in 1410. To shouts of "bravo" from all sides, he predicted that the fratricidal bloodshed would result finally in the unification of the Polish people.[87] The Jews also harbored resentments. Naftali Fridman, deputy from the Lithuanian province of Kovno, though himself an ardent Zionist, reminded the assembly that the Jews considered themselves "citizens and loyal sons of the fatherland," despite discrimination against them. Russia was their homeland and they would shoulder arms together with everyone else.[88] The deputy from Kazan Province, representing its Muslim population, echoed the general support for the war and expressed loyalty to Russia.[89] Each protestation of loyalty, of course, testified to the danger of betrayal and fragmentation.

While representatives of society across the board made a show of solidarity, the military itself displayed an alarming degree of incoherence. A war plan existed, but differences soon emerged. Minister of War Sukhomlinov insisted Russia concentrate its forces against Germany in the northwest; Foreign Minister Sazonov wanted to direct them first against Austria in the southwest. Sazonov, however, gave in to pressure from France, which urged Russia to distract the Germans from their campaign in the west.[90] When Grand Duke Nikolai Nikolaevich assumed his post as commander in chief, he ordered two Russian armies to cross the border into East Prussia. Though not yet at full strength, the Russian First Army, under General von Rennenkampf, headed west in the direction of Königsberg; the Second Army, led by General Aleksandr Samsonov, was to move west and then north from the Polish provinces. The two forces were to be coordinated by General Iakov Zhilinskii, commander of the Northwest Front. The plan was to encircle the German Eighth Army, under General Maximilian von

Prittwitz, which was positioned between them. On August 17 (August 4, OS), Rennenkampf led his cavalry into East Prussia.

From the very start, most of the problems that would later reach catastrophic proportions were already apparent. These included poor leadership, failures of communication, inadequate transportation, and severe shortages of supplies, guns, and ammunition. They also involved the long-standing divisions within the High Command between reformers associated with Sukhomlinov and the traditionalist followers of the Grand Duke. The traditionalists continued to emphasize the defense of fortresses and the use of cavalry commanded largely by aristocratic officers; the reformers believed infantry and artillery were the key to modern warfare and considered fortresses a strategic and financial waste.[91] When war broke out, conservative commanders gained the advantage over forward-looking administrators, but the tensions persisted. Rennenkampf, for example, was a traditionalist, Samsonov a reformist. Rennenkampf was not on speaking terms with his own chief of staff, who represented the opposite camp. Sukhomlinov hated him with a passion.[92]

The first challenges, however, were not personal but practical—how to mobilize sufficient manpower and resources in time to begin the westward march; how to supply the men with boots, rations, guns, and ammunition, when Russian factories were not geared to war production. They were not geared even to the production of footwear. Men marched with rags on their feet. In early December 1914, General Ianushkevich at Stavka wrote to Sukhomlinov, describing himself as "hysterical": "My hair stands on end at the thought that lack of bullets and rifles will lead to Wilhelm's triumph.... Many of the men have no boots, their feet are frozen, without winter coats they fall sick. As a result, when officers are killed, the men surrender in masses."[93]

The situation with communications was also dramatic. Samsonov had only twenty-five telephones and a few telegraph transmitters with which to reach his own troops and contact the First Army. The Russians, moreover, sent their wireless messages uncoded, which meant the Germans learned their plans in advance.[94] Transportation also put the Russians at a disadvantage, for reasons having to do with politics as much as geography. Russia was of course vastly more extended than Germany and less well served by railroads. The Polish salient was particularly ill-endowed. Intended to impede the progress of invading forces, the limitation now made it harder for Russians to mobilize in the opposite direction. Railroads were in general

overtaxed by the many functions they had to fulfill—carrying troops to and
from the front, the wounded to hospitals, refugees out of the war zone,
supplies, and especially fodder for the horses. Horses were a key element in
the Russian case, and not only on the battlefield. Undersupplied with motor
vehicles and obliged to transport material from the railhead to the front, the
Russians relied largely on horse- and ox-drawn carts.[95] In East Prussia, by
contrast, the Germans were on home turf, well prepared and well supplied,
operating on a compact terrain, where they could rely on support from the
local population.

The first battle in the Eastern theater occurred at Gumbinnen (now
Gusev, in the Kaliningrad district of Russia), directly east of the German
fortress at Königsberg. The Germans had first achieved a minor victory
over the Russians at Stallupönen (today Nesterov), then retreated to
Gumbinnen, where they hoped to dispatch the rest of the First Army
before the arrival of the Second Army from the south. There, on August 20
(NS), Generals August von Mackensen and Hermann von François launched
a devastating barrage that decimated Rennenkampf's forces. The Russians
nevertheless managed to mount a counterattack, achieving their first victory. Rennenkampf then failed to take advantage of this favorable moment,
turning instead to attack the fortress at Königsberg, which the Germans
had abandoned.

The timid Prittwitz was now replaced by the more forceful Paul von
Hindenburg and Erich Ludendorff. With full access to Russian communications, the generals learned that Rennenkampf had stopped for supplies.
Leaving sufficient troops to fool the enemy into thinking it was still in position, the German Eighth Army turned south to meet Samsonov. The First
Army might have attacked the Germans from the rear but failed to do so.
Zhilinskii, who had only the vaguest idea where his own forces were positioned, ordered Samsonov to "intercept the enemy as he retreats before the
advancing army of General Rennenkampf." The enemy was not retreating;
Rennenkampf was not advancing. Samsonov therefore encountered an army
larger than he could have expected, freed by Rennenkampf's negligence to
bring its full force to bear against him.[96]

After six days' march in the August heat, the Second Army finally arrived,
short of supplies and ammunition, at the town of Allenstein (now Olsztyn
in Poland), not far from Tannenberg, where the Germans had been defeated
by the Poles and Lithuanians in 1410. This was the same Battle of Grunwald
invoked by the Polish Duma deputy two weeks before. The fighting, in

what the Germans later dubbed the Battle of Tannenberg to avenge their five-hundred-year-old humiliation, began on August 23 (NS) with what seemed a German retreat. Samsonov concluded that the enemy lacked confidence.[97] Alas, by the next day, the Germans had intercepted all his telegrams. In full possession of his plans, they launched an attack. Rennenkampf, less well informed about his own troop movements than the Germans, had no idea what Samsonov was up to and failed to advance. Indeed, Zhilinskii, also in the dark, ordered Rennenkampf to keep his sights trained on Königsberg. By August 29, when Zhilinskii finally realized that the Second Army was under assault, it was too late. By then, after five days of battle, Samsonov's forces had suffered fifty thousand casualties, including seven thousand dead; hundreds of guns and thousands of horses were captured. Attempting to escape in the dark of night, Samsonov, who suffered from asthma and a weak heart, fell behind his companions and took his own life. His body was found and buried by German soldiers.[98]

The First Army, positioned near the Masurian Lakes, had still made no move. Three days before Samsonov's suicide, however, it was attacked by the combined forces of the German Eighth Army. Unlike Samsonov, who at least had done his best, in the absence of intelligence and backup, to defend the honor of his command, Rennenkampf fled with unseemly haste as far back as Kovno (Lithuanian Kaunas), safe behind the Russian border. Even his defenders had to admit he had lost his nerve.[99] His detractors called him General "Rennen vom Kampf"—"running from battle." In a single month, his First Army had suffered 80,000 casualties, losing 150 guns and half its motorized vehicles. Together the First and Second Armies lost 250,000 men. Zhilinskii was immediately relieved of his command; Rennenkampf hung on a bit longer.[100]

The war against Germany thus began with defeats for the Russian side and the humiliating end of Rennenkampf's career. The myth of Tannenberg, which played a sinister role in later German history, only enhanced the German threat.[101] The armies on the Southwest Front seemed to be in better hands under General Nikolai Ivanov and his chief of staff, General Mikhail Alekseev. Ivanov was limited in his talents as a commander, but admired for his dedication. He had advanced from lowly beginnings, fought with the artillery in the Russo-Japanese War, and enjoyed the confidence of his men. He was now sent, along with the armies under Generals Nikolai Ruzskii, Pavel Pleve, and Aleksei Brusilov, to engage the weaker Austrian opponent.[102]

Things did not begin well here, either. The Russians were defeated first at Kraśnik the day the Battle of Tannenberg began and again at Komarów three days later. But then they pushed the Austrians back at Gniła Lipa and went on to capture Lemberg (Polish Lwów, Russian Lvov, today Ukrainian Lviv). By the first week in September, the Russians were in position to smash the Austrian armies, which got wind of their plans and beat a hasty retreat southward to the Carpathian Mountains. The fortress of Przemyśl, west of Lemberg on the San River, headquarters of the Austro-Hungarian chief of staff, was now surrounded. The Russian siege of Przemyśl began in late September, was lifted briefly in October, resumed in November, and lasted into March 1915, when the Austrians finally surrendered, leaving 110,000 men in Russian captivity.

The Germans responded to Austria's loss of Lemberg by moving troops from East Prussia to a position west of the Polish salient, on a level with Warsaw, which they believed was vulnerable to attack. By the end of September, the new German Ninth Army, under Hindenburg and Ludendorff, was extended in a north-south line from Posen (today Polish Poznań) to Cracow. The Germans began their advance toward Warsaw, aiming for the gap between the Russian Second Army in Warsaw and the Russian Ninth Army on the San, points joined by the north-south Vistula River, parallel to the western Polish border. Unaware of the German position, the Russians had decided to move their troops into this gap. Thus, from mid-September to early October, the antagonists faced each other from opposite sides of the river. The Germans were vastly outnumbered by the Russians, whose guns were not, however, powerful enough to prevail. The confrontation that ensued was known as the Battle of the Vistula River, or the First Battle of Warsaw. By mid-October, as German forces under General Mackensen were approaching Warsaw, further south along the Vistula the Russian Fourth and Ninth Armies were engaging the Austrian First Army. The Germans then decided to retreat, and by the end of the month they were back where they had started. The First Battle of Warsaw was a much-needed Russian victory.

Building on their success, the Russians directed their efforts toward Silesia, the German territory directly west of Kalisz and including the city of Breslau (today Polish Wrocław). Having learned of the Russians' plans, Hindenburg, now in command of the Eastern Front, decided to intercept them. On November 11, Mackensen, capturing over ten thousand men, forced the First Army to retreat from its position south of the Vistula. The

Second Army meanwhile tried to escape encirclement by retreating in the direction of Łódź. The Fifth Army arrived in time to knock out Mackensen's right flank as temperatures dropped with the sudden onset of winter. When Rennenkampf, still commanding the First Army, attacked from the east, the Germans pulled back. By November 22, however, they had surrounded Łódź from three sides. Although the Germans did not manage to complete the circle, the Russians were too weak to hold the city, a textile manufacturing center crowded with thousands of wounded, including Poles fighting on both sides. Among the German commanders was General Karl Litzmann, in whose honor the town was later rechristened by the Nazis as Litzmannstadt, site of the notorious Łódź Jewish ghetto in World War II. Despite the shortage of rifles and ammunition, the Russians had anticipated victory. By the end of November, however, Łódź had fallen into German hands. At this point, Rennenkampf was relieved of his command.

In the end, the Russians had prevented the Germans from taking Warsaw, while the Germans had blocked the Russian move into Silesia. The Russian public might well have been confused by the results of the first months of fighting. Humiliated in East Prussia by the powerful German forces, the Russian armies made a better showing—and under better leadership—against the weaker Austrians. The unexpected loss of Łódź was a blow to patriotic self-esteem. By the end of 1914, Russian forces, on the combined East Prussian, Polish, and Galician fronts, had incurred a million casualties, killed and wounded.[103] Officers were singled out, so losses among the officer corps were extremely high. Already in short supply, weapons were squandered on the battlefield and in retreat. Ill-trained soldiers dropped them as they fled. The Allies were shocked in December to learn the extent to which the Russians lacked guns and ammunition.[104] The military censor assiduously followed the "mood" of the enlisted men by scrutinizing their letters, but not everyone could write.[105] A more direct indication of disaffection was the rate of desertion, which rose with each military setback and continued to grow as the war progressed.[106] By the end of the year, the educated public, at least, already felt a sense of foreboding. The military historian General Nikolai Golovin, in the field during the first months, recalled that "gloomy rumors were finding their way from the army into the country, and tales of disorganization, together with forecasts of an approaching catastrophe, reached even places the most remote."[107]

In fact, in terms of territory the results were something of a draw. On the one hand, the Germans controlled the Polish salient, as far east as Łódź, fifty miles from Warsaw; they had also seized the Latvian port of Libau (after 1918, Liepāja), north of Königsberg on the Baltic coast. On the other hand, Russia occupied both Galicia, including the city of Lemberg, and East Prussia, where they had returned in October. Russia's gains were nevertheless overshadowed in domestic public opinion by the overall impression of disorganization and heavy losses. The distinguished Russian specialist in international law, Baron Mikhail von Taube, later recalled the shock of the early defeats in East Prussia, which "could alas not be erased by the brilliant offensive of our troops in Galicia.... The fact is the defeats on the German front barely a month into the war showed clearly that the Russian army was in no shape to defeat the Germans."[108] Taube had been among the conservatives Cassandras who had predicted disaster to begin with. They seemed ever more prescient as time went on.

# 2

# Germans, Jews, Armenians

If the opening months of fighting had alarmed the newspaper-reading public, 1915 failed to provide relief. A second battle with the Germans at the Masurian Lakes, part of Hindenburg's plan to push the Russians back beyond the Vistula, again resulted in a Russian defeat. The Russian army was encircled in the wintry Augustów Forest (today at the intersection of Poland, Belarus, and Lithuania) and surrendered in late February, at the cost of thirty thousand prisoners.[1] Farther south, however, the Germans had been less successful. Here Przemyśl was still under siege, and they had failed, as noted in the previous chapter, at the Battle of the Vistula (First Battle of Warsaw) in October. They had captured the textile city of Łódź in November, but the Russian forces were not seriously damaged.

In April 1915, after the peak of winter had passed, the Germans decided to strike at the southernmost point on the Eastern Front, the area around Gorlice-Tarnów, southeast of Cracow at the upper end of the Carpathian Mountains. General Mackensen led the combined German and Austrian armies, which attacked with heavy bombardments on May 2 (NS). General Golovin called it "the Mackensen steam roller," a gigantic beast dragging its tail of heavy artillery behind it, battering the defenseless Russians, who lacked the equipment and ammunition to respond.[2] The Russian Third Army under the Bulgarian General Radko Radko-Dmitriev was vastly outnumbered and outgunned. On May 7, Stavka unwisely ordered a counterattack, which ended in a massacre. When Radko-Dmitriev was allowed to retreat three days later, he reached the San River with only 40,000 of an original 200,000 men. Over 140,000 prisoners had been taken; divisions were reduced to mere handfuls of traumatized survivors. Radko-Dmitriev lost his command.[3]

Meanwhile, the Central Powers swept away everything the Russians had previously gained. In June they liberated Przemyśl and retook Lemberg. After turning north toward the Vistula, the Germans forced the Russians, who still lacked guns and ammunition, to abandon the fortress at Ivangorod (Dęblin). In July, Assistant Minister of War General Mikhail Beliaev pleaded with the French ambassador for help. He reminded Paléologue that in some infantry regiments one man in three had no rifle. "The poor fellows wait patiently, under the hail of shrapnel, for their comrades to fall, so they can collect their weapons." If not for the resignation and fortitude of "our peasants," panic would have ensued. France, alas, could not supply her ally with weapons, Paléologue responded.[4] They would have to rely on themselves. In the course of August, the Germans seized Warsaw and took Brest-Litovsk on the Bug River. In September, Hindenburg took Vilna (Polish Wilno; today Vilnius, capital of Lithuania).[5] By then, the Russians had not only been forced to abandon Austrian Galicia, but had lost their Polish territory as well. They were now three hundred miles east of the position they had held in August 1914.[6]

———

Military setbacks fostered an atmosphere of suspicion and xenophobia, which was deepened by official policies and propaganda. Distrust of foreigners affected all the warring nations. In Russia, the fixation on domestic treachery helped undermine the social solidarity needed not only to sustain the war but to maintain the integrity of empire. Foreign subjects were the first target. Almost immediately, the Ministry of the Interior had ordered the round-up of German and Austrian males, who were transported by rail in freight cars to hastily organized camps. The category "civilian enemy aliens," originally encompassing draft-age men, was soon extended, with less justification, to include women and children.[7] Petrograd mayor Ivan Tolstoi complained in October that he was now obliged to supervise the dispossession of foreign subjects who might have spent their entire lives in Russia— wives, husbands, governesses and maids, most who had forgotten they were not Russian. He blamed the right-wing newspapers for inflaming public opinion, but the government was even more to blame. Tolstoi found himself "driven to despair by the idiocy of our domestic policies. They do us no good, but only dishonor us in the eyes of the entire civilized world. The pointless expulsions of German women and children, the pointless cruelties to Jews, the pointlessly chosen moment to impose compulsory use of the Russian language in Finland—all this merely shows the phenomenal stupidity of Maklakov et C[ie]."[8] Ottoman subjects were also unceremoniously rounded up when the Ottomans entered the war in October 1914.[9]

The campaign against Germans affected not only resident foreigners but imperial subjects of German origin.[10] These included the two million colonists whose ancestors had settled in Russia in the eighteenth century. Highly literate, productive farmers, mainly Lutheran, but including some pacifist Mennonites, who refused to serve under any flag. At least a million inhabited the border regions, extending from the Baltic lands through Poland and Volhynia (north of Austrian Galicia in what is now western Ukraine). Beginning in September 1914, continuing at a rapid rate through 1915, and more slowly into 1916, hundreds of thousands of men, women, and children, including the widows and mothers of fallen soldiers, were loaded into railway cars or driven onto the roads, forced to sell or abandon their possessions and farmsteads. City dwellers of German origin were later removed as well. Some were transported under arrest along with common criminals; the majority shared the same fate as other refugees from the western provinces. The end result of clearing a major grain-producing region of its best cultivators was to reduce the Empire's (and army's) supply of grain.[11]

The campaign against domestic Germans, with all its harmful consequences, was promoted by the Army High Command. Grand Duke Nikolai Nikolaevich's chief of staff, General Nikolai Ianushkevich, was animated by a fiercely paranoid hatred. "We must expel this German filth, and no kid gloves," he insisted. "On the contrary—drive them out, like animals." Following the Regulations on Field Administration of the Army in Wartime, Ianushkevich ordered the removal of "suspicious" or "undesirable" persons from areas under his control. The orders were implemented with unalloyed enthusiasm by the commanders of the various armies, even those, like Generals Faddei Sievers and Aleksei Evert, who were themselves of German extraction. When General Brusilov, in October 1915, organized the expulsion of twenty thousand German colonists of both sexes and all ages from the area around Rovno (Polish Równe, Ukrainian Rivne) in Volhynia, he employed the by-then classic excuse—that his victims were "without doubt damaging the telegraph and telephone lines."[12]

When officials described domestic Jews and Germans as exploiters of the Russian people, they stoked popular resentments and encouraged the kind of hot-headed violence that eventually turned against the regime itself.[13] In the case of the Germans, for example, urban mobs felt licensed to loot and pillage property owned by Germans or bearing German-sounding names. Ianushkevich, however, saw no such problem; he insisted on ridding the entire territory of Russian Poland of its German-speaking population. By

April 1915, General Pavel Engalychev, Governor-General of Warsaw, could report success. Many of the local Germans had been placed under arrest and removed together with common criminals en route to Siberia. Thousands of domestic Germans were still being expelled from Volhynia, however, as late as October 1915.[14]

Jews in the western regions were targeted for deportation beginning in September 1914 and continuing into the new year. Animosity against them only grew after the defeats of early 1915, when they were blamed for the military failures.[15] By summer 1915, at least half a million Jews had been uprooted from the provinces of the Pale and pushed eastward into the Russian interior.[16] The methods by which Russian forces emptied the territories of their Jewish inhabitants were unapologetic. Not content with taking hostages from among the educated, they evicted entire families, who set out on foot, without food or clothing. As Ianushkevich put it: "War is waged with fire and the sword; let them suffer."[17] Many did not survive the journey. Authorities in the cities accused the new arrivals of creating havoc and spreading disease.[18] When the German and Austrian armies broke through the Russian front at Gorlice in early May 1915, reaching as far as Jelgava (Mitau), south of Riga, millions of Jews, together with the local Germans, followed the Russian armies in retreat.[19] Many succumbed to smallpox and typhus.[20] Having escaped the onslaught of rape, pillage, and murder committed by the Russian troops passing through their villages, the dispossessed were often set upon by the local inhabitants, who pelted them with stones and accused them of stealing.[21]

These policies aroused public indignation and inspired the mobilization of social forces to cope with the crisis, which was too profound for the government alone to handle. Civilian groups throughout the Empire provided charitable relief. Jewish organizations, for example, sent agents into the field, delivering money and reporting back on what they found. Despite the wartime censorship, details of the tragedy circulated widely.[22] The harm visited upon the Jews of Russia, who only wished to serve their homeland, was eloquently denounced in the July 20, 1915 (OS) sitting of the Duma by Naftali Fridman, the same Kadet deputy who had pledged the loyalty of the Jewish population in August 1914. He now stressed the proven willingness of Jewish men to fight in the Imperial Army at the same time as their families were being dispossessed and chased from their homes under the stigma of treason. Eager to sacrifice for the patriotic cause, Jews were still deprived of their rights and treated with contempt. He deplored the fact that Jewish blood "is being spilled not only by the enemy, not only in the war, but also on the excuse of the war and also without any excuse."[23]

Such brutal methods had harmful consequences not only for their direct victims but also for the Russian population, a consideration the military authorities ignored. Take, for example, the fate of Ottoman prisoners of war transported to Samara, on the Volga River, after the Russian victory at Sarıkamış in Eastern Anatolia in January 1915. They arrived in sealed railway cars, which were left unattended on the sidings for days at a time. A member of a distinguished Samara family wrote to a relative in Petrograd later that month, describing their condition. Covered with lice, many succumbed to dysentery and typhus. Often the cars filled up with corpses. Despite efforts at disinfection, the writer noted, "the sidings, already filthy, are still filled with endless chains of railway cars crammed with infected Turks." Typhus was striking the best doctors and nurses. Abandoning their posts, they left the prisoners "untended or tended by the soldier-medics who are compelled to do so. It is now already winter, and frost is the best disinfectant. But what will happen with the thaw? We may see the kind of epidemic that will claim more victims than the war itself."[24]

Murderous callousness was therefore not reserved for the Jews, but the Jews had pride of place in the official demonology. As Paléologue noted at the end of March 1915, the expulsion of Jews from the frontier zones that began in the first month of the war continued after the new year at an even faster pace and remained "just as abrupt, hurried, and brutal." "Hundreds of thousands of unfortunates wandered over the snow, pushed like cattle by squads of Cossacks, abandoned in distress in train stations, dumped in the open air on the outskirts of cities, dying of hunger, of fatigue, of cold." This, he commented, although over 200,000 Jewish soldiers were serving in the Russian Army "and fighting very well!"[25]

In early July 1915, the ambassador noted that anti-Semitism was gaining ground. "If the Russian armies are beaten, it's naturally the fault of the Jews." He cited a right-wing newspaper that called on the Russian people to *"identify their enemy—the Jew!...From generation to generation, this people, cursed by God, has been hated and despised by everyone. The blood of the sons of Holy Russia, whom they betray every day, cries out for vengeance!"*[26] In early August, at the height of the retreat, he noted the same hasty, brutal methods, leaving the Jews no time to gather their belongings, herding them onto trains and out onto the open roads. As soon as they were gone, he reported, "the Orthodox populace rushes to pillage the ghetto," while the Jews themselves were "reduced to terrible destitution."[27] By the end of 1915, Russian forces had uprooted as many as a million Jews, in the course of which tens of thousands had perished.[28]

---

The same techniques were applied in the areas occupied by Russian forces, beginning with the first invasion of East Prussia. Though the Russians did not remain long enough to carry out their plans, they entered East Prussia intent on inspiring terror and taking preemptive measures against opposition that had not yet occurred.[29] In autumn 1914, more than ten thousand inhabitants of the region were uprooted from their homes. The original idea was to force them westward in the wake of their own retreating armies, but the continued fighting got in the way. The refugees therefore were directed eastward toward the Russian interior. Local authorities on the receiving end objected that no provision had been made for the welfare of the displaced masses; they complained of the added burden.[30] The expulsions were supposed to prevent the local inhabitants from passing information to the enemy or, in the case of adult males, being drafted into military service on the other side. Neither at home nor across the border were the campaigns based on evidence of the treason or espionage they were alleged to prevent. They expressed rather a general atmosphere of paranoia, enhanced by feelings of inadequacy in the face of the formidable German war machine, and sustained by the xenophobic ideology of the radical right, whose influence was felt in the highest places. When Jews in Poland, either sincerely or for effect, made a point of demonstrating their support for the Russian cause, their patriotism surprised Russian observers, who expected to see their prejudices confirmed. When the tide turned, they nevertheless feared, these same Jews might suddenly favor the Germans.[31]

The campaigns against civilians in the areas close to the front, on both sides of the border, reflected the inability to distinguish front from rear or to police the legitimate use of force. They were a symptom of Russia's military weakness, as the more perceptive members of the public, such as Baron von Taube, observed.[32] Each time Rennenkampf's armies entered East Prussia, they found that most of the population had fled, taking as much as possible with them. The few inhabitants that remained were viewed with suspicion. General Vasilii Gurko, then a cavalry commander in the First Army, observed teenage boys on bicycles, whom he imagined were reporting on his movements, and claimed to have discovered soldiers disguised as peasants, even as women, with the same purpose in mind. He noticed the smoke rising from fires set by villagers at the forefront of advancing Russian troops to alert their own forces. The fires indeed betrayed the Russian movements, but they also allowed Gurko to discover where his own troops were headed. In the first days of the invasion, the First Army had few telephones or telegraph with which to connect with its own men. In their blindness and anxiety, the soldiers viewed the local inhabitants as spies. Some no doubt were. Spies or no spies, the Germans were, of course, infinitely better equipped, better prepared, and better able to maneuver on their own territory than the disoriented intruders.[33]

Fear was felt on both sides. Gurko depicts the inhabitants of East Prussia as devious and cocky, but also terrorized by the specter of the so-called Asiatic hordes, a staple of German propaganda.[34] "Our Cossacks in particular were the cause of many a wild rumour of alleged atrocities on the people, rumours, I need hardly say, which…created panic in the German towns."[35] In East Prussia the rumors of Cossack brutality were not unfounded. The area was occupied by Russian forces twice: in August 1914, and again from October 1914 to February 1915. When they returned in October, Gurko recalled, the border areas were deserted. Villages had been looted by both sides and left in ruins. The Russians were convinced, once again, that the few people they encountered were there to collect information.

Such mistrust had consequences. Grand Duke Nikolai Nikolaevich issued an order to the First Army on August 23, 1914 (September 5, NS), justifying retaliation against civilian attack. When civilians opened fire on invading Russian troops, he instructed, the soldiers were to seize any property of military value, then burn the place to the ground, having first allowed women and children to depart.[36] In the heat of the moment, of course, troops were never this careful. There was always an excuse. Locals "signaling" to their own forces was one common charge; sniping from windows or attics was another.[37] The Germans, for example, explained the destruction of Kalisz as a response to concealed sharpshooters. The scale of the so-called reprisals, moreover, was always out of proportion to the alleged cause. In the case of East Prussia, the Russian forces engaged in the widespread rape of women and girls, mistreatment of prisoners of war, and the wanton destruction of property, all of which the German Foreign Office formally denounced as violations of the Geneva and Hague conventions on the laws of war.[38]

Suspicions and abuses of an even more dramatic kind occurred during the Russian occupation of Austrian Galicia and Bukovina from August 1914 to June 1915.[39] Nationalists in the Duma and the press viewed the territory as an original part of the Russian lands (*Chervonnaia Rus'*) and urged its annexation.[40] Almost half the population were Greek Catholic (Slavic) Ruthenian peasants, another two-fifths Catholic Poles, and around 10 percent Jews.[41] When they arrived, the Russians expected the Ruthenians to embrace them. The Jews they distrusted on both sides of the border. In Galicia it was assumed they were loyal to the Hapsburg cause and aware that Jews were worse off in Russia.[42] The notion of the Jews as a transnational fifth column was not an entirely Russian invention. Among assimilated German Jews, who looked down on the Eastern Jews (*Ostjuden*) in Galicia and the Pale as mired in medieval tradition, some viewed them as a resource the Kaiserreich should exploit to promote its own expansionist ambitions.[43]

The Russian army had various reasons to distrust the non-Slavic population across the border, but its reactions were conditioned not only by the murky reality of warfare on foreign soil. They were shaped also by official policies toward the Jews at home and by the anti-Semitic attitudes that prevailed even in educated circles and completely dominated at court. When war began in 1914, right-wing newspapers distributed at the front depicted Jews in uniform and those among the local population as traitors.[44] Jews were accused of shirking the draft in large numbers and also of being physically unfit to serve.[45] After 1905, Polish nationalists raised the banner of anti-Semitism, something they now shared with the anti-Polish Russian right, which was of course pro-Empire.[46] Militant anti-Semites in Russia thought of themselves as bolstering legitimate authority, though in fact the mobilization of angry mobs had the opposite effect. During the war, they no doubt intended to consolidate patriotic feeling by providing a common focus of anger. Instead, their efforts deepened internal fragmentation and threatened the integrity of empire, which depended by definition on the cohabitation of disparate groups.

The key sponsors of this self-defeating policy ignored its risks. General Ianushkevich and the administrators of occupied Galicia were not casual anti-Semites. They were committed to anti-Semitism as a political ideology and a guide to official policy. Ianushkevich's outlook reflected the same "crazed anti-Semitism," in the words of Petrograd mayor Ivan Tolstoi, that permeated imperial government circles.[47] A higher official, for example, had confessed to Tolstoi that he "couldn't lay eyes on a Yid without his hands itching to bash him in the kisser."[48] Tolstoi was publically rebuked when in November 1914 he and his children visited Petrograd's Choral Synagogue, where they occupied an honorary place next to the Gintsburg family, which had financed its construction. The service was attended by wounded Jewish soldiers. The rabbi made a patriotic speech, urging Jewish men to uphold the honor of Israel in defending their Russian homeland, as the Maccabees had upheld Jewish honor in their time.[49]

Hostility to the Jews was not confined to Russia. Anti-Semitism emerged as a powerful current across Europe in the last decades of the nineteenth century. In an ironic footnote to the martyrology of poor violated Belgium, the poet Émile Verhaeren, celebrated in Russia as the bard of his suffering people, blamed the militarism of German culture on the nefarious influence of the German Jews.[50] Sir George Buchanan, the British ambassador in Petrograd, reported to the Foreign Office, mistaking prejudice for fact, "There cannot be the slightest doubt that a very large number of Jews have been in German pay and have acted as spies during the campaigns in Poland. Nearly every Russian officer who returns from the front has stories to tell on the subject."[51] Such officers of course needed no evidence to confirm their firmly held convictions. The circulation of such stories created a general mood of distrust and animosity heightened by the anxiety of war.

Some public figures, such as the well-known writer Leonid Andreev, rejected these assumptions. Ubiquitous as prejudice may have been, Andreev remarked with regret, only in Russia was anti-Semitism associated with physical brutality in peacetime.[52] In wartime, the ideological campaign against the Jews encouraged precisely the kind of violence understood by military and civilian leaders as a violation of international standards. Although the Geneva and Hague conventions did not clearly define what actions constituted war crimes, their provisions were widely interpreted as prohibiting the abuse of civilian populations, the mistreatment of prisoners of war, attacks on medical personnel, and the use of certain types of weapons.[53]

In Kalisz, the Germans had chosen their victims seemingly at random among the town's German, Polish, and Jewish citizens. Rabbis, pastors, and Orthodox priests were among the hostages. The destruction of the city was the result of organized arson and sustained artillery barrage—in short, an act of war. Its justification, however, as an act of self-defense or reprisal echoed a familiar feature of the typical Russian anti-Jewish pogrom. The rioters in Kishinev, Tomsk, Orsha, or Białystok who attacked apparently innocent Jewish families, raping, murdering, and plundering as their fervor grew, routinely described themselves as victims of Jewish aggression. As purveyors of alcohol and rapacious merchants, Jews were said to prey upon the Christian population. They were thought to murder Christian youths for ritual purposes (as in the Beilis case). They were accused of hurling rocks or shooting guns at their innocent neighbors, thus inviting the response they justly deserved. In short, perpetrators of the pogroms thought of themselves as the injured parties.

In Galicia, the Russian military was primed to encounter treachery by reports on the region circulated to the officer corps well before the war, assessing the political attitudes of the local population. The reports stressed, in particular, the insidious behavior to be expected from the Jews.[54] Arriving in autumn 1914, the Russians accused the Austrians of atrocities against the Ruthenian peasants, in which they were allegedly assisted by the Jewish population.[55] Atrocity charges were more or less routine in this early phase of the war, directed by Germany and Russia against each other, often with obvious justification, and just as routinely refuted. Addressing the Duma in January 1915, Sazonov denied the "libelous rumors maliciously spread by Germany," accusing Russian troops of assaulting the Jewish population. If damage had been done, he insisted, "that is one of the unfortunate effects of the war, from which all inhabitants of the front regions suffer." He blamed "most of the devastation in our areas of Poland" on the Austrian and German forces.[56] By the middle of the year, Sazonov was obliged to change his tune. As in Kalisz, in Galicia the violence began with a spree of looting, murder, and rape, this time when the Cossack troops rampaged out of control.[57] Also as in Kalisz, the military command followed the initial outbursts with an organized assault on the civilian population, now focused on the Jews.

Before the war, neither the tsar nor his ministers, hostile to Jews as most of them were, directly instigated or endorsed the outbursts of mob violence. They realized the direction of such anger, once aroused, was not always easy to control. Trials followed most of the peacetime pogroms. Perpetrators were subject to criminal prosecution, although the verdicts were rarely proportional to the crime. During the first occupation of Galicia, by contrast, the Army High Command, which exercised absolute authority in the region, did everything to promote the attitudes that encouraged abuses. The military's campaign again the Jews of Galicia was fully sanctioned at the highest levels by Minister of War Sukhomlinov, as well as Generals Nikolai Ivanov and Evert, Grand Duke Nikolai Nikolaevich, and Nicholas himself.[58] In early February 1915, Ianushkevich issued an order to the occupying forces: "beginning with Bukovina, expel the Jews in the direction of the retreating enemy forces and take hostages from the wealthiest and most prominent

Jews."[59] In March, the tsar declared: "The nationalities hostile to us will answer for the violence and harm they have inflicted on the Slavic and Romanian population of Bukovina."[60] Ianushkevich saw the occupation of Galicia as a chance to punish the Jews while the military still enjoyed unfettered power in the region and before the ministers or the Duma had a chance to interfere.[61]

The animus against the Jews was but one example of the omnibus xenophobia promoted by the authorities and spread by the press, as in other warring countries. In autumn 1914, as part of the attempt to rid East Prussia of civilians likely to betray or impede Russian operations, Jews, along with local Germans, were driven eastward. The same rationale applied in the Caucasian theater, where the target groups were Roma and Crimean Tatars, accused of favoring the Ottoman forces that occupied the region at the end of the year. Thousands were stripped of their property and shipped unceremoniously into the Russian interior, where they were confined to special settlements lacking the basic means of survival.[62] The occupation of Galicia provided the chance to settle other scores, as well. Leaders of the Ukrainian Uniate church, including the metropolitan Andrei Sheptits'kyi, were deported to Siberia, along with prominent Ukrainian figures.[63]

The Jews, however, aroused a special animosity. While the Russian army uprooted the German population in East Prussia and expelled German settlers from the western provinces where they had lived for generations, the Jews both in occupied Galicia and in the Pale experienced a level of aggression in a category of its own. Ianushkevich, like every good pogromist, thought of himself as taking revenge for an injury already—or about to be—inflicted. In this case, he had in mind the harm allegedly done to the Orthodox peasants of Galicia, or the treason and espionage allegedly perpetrated in the border provinces close behind the lines. In Galicia, Ianushkevich's revenge took the form, not only of mass deportations and hostage-taking, but also of seemingly spontaneous pogroms. In the early days of the Russian occupation, troops destroyed the Jewish quarter of Brody in reprisal for the shooting of an officer in front of a Jewish-owned hotel. The soldiers burned the synagogue and killed nine Jews, including the hotel owner's daughter. The writer S. A. An-sky (Rappoport), dispatched by a Jewish relief organization in Petrograd to report on the situation in Galicia and distribute funds, noted that the Cossacks "came up with the lie that would be adopted as the standard pretext for all the pogroms and violence against Jews: a girl standing at her window had fired at the Russian army."[64] A similar rampage, also in response to a purported shot, occurred in Lemberg in late September.[65]

Faced with the chaos they were creating, commanders attempted to reconcile political (or ideological) imperatives with practical results: whether
to expel entire populations—whole families, young and old—from the
front zones, leading to congestion in the interior, or to limit deportations to
hostages. Some supporters of the policy nevertheless objected to the obvious incongruity of sending people stigmatized as dangerous or unwanted
deeper into Russia. Minister of the Interior Maklakov deplored the influx
of Germans. General Alekseev complained in March 1915 with regard to
the eastward expulsion of Galician Jews: "This is unacceptable—we already
have too many of them."[66]

---

Another porous border caused trouble for Russia in the early months of the
war. The Ottoman Empire had at first debated whether to join the Central
Powers or the Entente, but on August 15, 1914 it signed a treaty with
Germany, lured in part by the prospect of acquiring the Russian Caucasus
and recovering the area of Eastern Anatolia, including the fortress of Kars
and the city of Ardahan in the northeastern corner of Erzurum Province,
lost to Russia in 1878 at the Congress of Berlin.[67] At the end of September,
the Ottomans closed the Straits, underscoring the importance for Russia of
establishing control over that critical gateway. On November 10, responding
to German pressure and hostile moves by Britain, Ottoman warships entered
the Black Sea and began shelling Russian port cities. Two days later, Russia
declared war on the Ottoman Empire.[68]

Eastern Anatolia contained a large Armenian population that extended
across the Russian border into the Caucasus. In the 1890s, Ottoman Armenians had begun agitating for national autonomy. Throughout the decade,
Armenian militias had engaged in violent clashes with organized Muslim
bands, sponsored or joined by government forces. Massacres perpetrated or
encouraged by the regime, continuing after the Young Turks came to power
in 1908, resulted in tens of thousands of Armenian deaths.[69] When war
began in 1914, Russian propaganda appealed to the Ottoman Armenians, as
fellow Christians, to support the Russian cause.[70] In September, Nicholas
uttered some vague words endorsing the goal of Armenian autonomy.[71] The
Ottomans, not unjustly, suspected Armenians on the Russian side of promoting rebellion in Turkey, while they themselves encouraged Armenian
nationalists to foment rebellion in Russia, advice that was refused.[72] Rather,

like the Jews, who also straddled a vulnerable border, Armenians on both sides affirmed their loyalty to their respective empires. Armenian leaders in Turkey, fearing reprisals, objected when nationalists based in the Caucasus formed volunteer detachments, which attracted some defectors from the Ottoman army, to fight for independence.[73]

In the end, four Armenian battalions were authorized to fight with the Russian Army.[74] At the same time, the Ottomans sponsored irregular formations among Muslims in the Russian Caucasus.[75] This was a game both sides played.[76] When Russian forces crossed into Anatolia in November 1914, heading in the direction of the Ottoman city of Van, not far from the Persian border, they were accompanied by these Armenian units. In late December, Ottoman forces took Ardahan, just south of Georgia, and proceeded up the Black Sea coast toward Batumi, murdering Christian inhabitants as they went. After the Turks retreated, Cossack troops retaliated with massacres of their own. In early January 1915, when the Russians retook Ardahan, they pillaged and burned the Muslim quarter, slaughtering anyone who had not fled.[77] When the Russians withdrew from northern Persia in mid-December, Ottoman forces organized massacres in the area east of Van, as a way to punish and discourage revolt and collaboration. At least twenty thousand Armenians were slaughtered.[78]

The spiral of pogrom-style violence was a result both of official policy (propaganda and explicit orders) and of the disintegration of discipline among armies on both sides. As on other fronts, commanders expected troops to live off the local population, but the more desperate the need for supplies, the less control the officers exercised over their men. Often, however, the initiative came from the top, following the logic of reprisals. In December 1914, for example, Ottoman troops entered Ajaria, the westernmost region of Georgia, where they massacred the local Armenian inhabitants. When the Russians returned there in January 1915, General Vladimir Liakhov ordered his men to massacre every Muslim they encountered.[79] Armenian militias joined in the action, which the Ottomans claimed resulted in the deaths of at least thirty thousand civilians.[80]

The first major confrontation between Russian and Ottoman armies, lasting from the end of December 1914 to mid-January, 1915, occurred in the town of Sarıkamış, between Russian Kars and Ottoman Erzurum. Fought in rugged mountains under brutal winter conditions, the battle ended with a decisive Russian victory, achieved partly with the help of Armenian volunteers. The Russians had the advantage of a railroad running from Tiflis through Kars; there was no Turkish railroad in Eastern Anatolia. Russia was not strong enough, however, to penetrate deeper into Anatolia.[81] Minister of War Enver Pasha had insisted on the ill-considered engagement, but the Ottoman public blamed the defeat on Armenian treachery. It was at this point, in March 1915, that the government began systematically deporting Armenians en masse from areas near the front lines. Armenian soldiers were demobilized, disarmed, and drafted into labor battalions. Villages were raided and pillaged, inhabitants were murdered in the thousands. The perpetrators included bands of Ottoman army deserters, but also soldiers of the regular Ottoman army. The authorities reacted with draconian reprisals to any disturbance in which Armenians demonstrated the least resistance.[82]

The crisis came to a head in the area west of Lake Van, where Armenian self-defense squads had clashed with Muslim armed bands. In mid-March, a newly installed governor, backed by Circassian and Kurdish troops, requisitioned four thousand Armenian men for labor battalions, threatening to deport or murder their families if they did not appear. When only five hundred complied, punitive squads were sent into the villages, where they began slaughtering the inhabitants, with orders to wipe out the adult male population.[83] The Armenians dug trenches and took shelter inside the city walls of Van, where, from mid-April to mid-May, they withstood the Ottoman siege. Meanwhile, the regime denounced the Armenians as traitors and rebels and began the systematic arrest of Armenian leaders and the mass deportation of Armenians from Erzurum and the surrounding area.[84] When Russian armies returned to the area in May, they discovered fifty-five thousand corpses, amounting to half the former Armenian population of the Van region.[85] The Russians then installed an ethnic Armenian as governor, who ordered the surviving Armenians to loot and torch the dwellings of Muslim villagers to prevent their return. Cossacks and Armenian volunteers, duly authorized, combed the Kurdish villages, murdering survivors.[86]

Both the Russians and the Ottomans thus harnessed ethnic animosities for their own political purposes, encouraging reprisals unrelated to military objectives, but it was at this point that the Ottoman response escalated. At the end of May, Minister of the Interior Talat Pasha denounced the Armenian population as a threat in time of war and issued orders to remove them.[87] This was the onset of the genocide. "From May through November 1915," the historian Ronald G. Suny writes, "almost all Armenians in eastern Anatolia were forcibly driven from their homes, the men usually taken off and killed outside the town, the women and children marched in groups toward the southeast."[88] By the conclusion of the war, 90 percent of Armenians in the Ottoman Empire had been killed or deported or had fled; between 600,000 and one million perished.[89] The slaughter was not a response to a concerted rebellion against Ottoman authority, as the Turkish authorities claimed. It was the continuation of a policy of deportation and massacre of civilian populations, initiated well before the war and intensified after 1914 by the demonization of the Armenians as an ethnic fifth column.[90] These events were well known at the time, and the parallel with the Imperial Army's treatment of the Jews in Russia and Galicia, though relatively less murderous, was noted by observers.[91]

# 3

# Tearing Themselves Apart

Under pressure from the relentless German advance on the Western Front, in early August 1915 General Alekseev ordered Russian forces to begin pulling back. Although the Imperial Army did not collapse, it relinquished an area of more than a hundred thousand square miles, comprising the Polish, Lithuanian, and Belarussian provinces and part of Volhynia, and suffered enormous casualties. The Great Retreat, as it was called, was, in the words of one historian, "a military and political disaster of enormous scale." For each month of the Great Retreat, twice as many men were killed or wounded, and over twice as many taken prisoner, as in any preceding month. Over the course of 1915, two million soldiers were killed or wounded and another 1.3 million captured. Soldiers were deserting in great numbers as well.[1]

The departing troops left devastation in their wake. As the local Poles complained, "They obliterate villages and cities, burn the harvests, destroy everything the inhabitants possess by forcing them to leave their homes and massacring those who refuse to follow. The regions of Chełm, Warsaw, and Łomża are nothing more at this point than heaps of ruins and ashes."[2] Two fortresses surrendered (Novogeorgievsk/Modlin, just north of Warsaw, and Kovno, between Königsberg and Wilno), while further east three were simply left behind (Ivangorod/Dęblin, Brest-Litovsk, and Grodno/Hrodna).[3] The strategy of the fortress-oriented traditionalists had proved a disaster. Patriotic Poles no doubt savored the irony. In 1840 the town of Dęblin had been renamed Ivangorod in honor of the Ukrainian-born Field Marshal Ivan Paskevich, who had suppressed the Polish uprising of 1830–1831. In the same spirit, the town of Modlin had been rechristened Novogeorgievsk in 1834, when the fortress was expanded as a defense against future Polish rebellions.[4]

Military misfortune, however, accounted for only part of the devastation in material and moral terms that the retreat inflicted. The policies of expropriation and deportation implemented by the High Command in autumn 1914 and continued into the new year were applied even more vigorously in spring 1915, after the German offensive—"the Mackensen steam roller"—began. In August, Minister of Agriculture Krivoshein despaired:"No country has ever been saved by tearing itself apart!"[5] Indeed, the destructive policies, driven by maniacal xenophobia, pursued by the all-powerful Russian military command in the occupied territories and behind the front not only harmed their victims but exacerbated the stresses of wartime in the interior. Many Russians accepted the picture of Jews and Germans as spies and saboteurs and welcomed the campaign against them, but the military defeats and growing social crisis of 1915, exacerbated by these very methods, created a sense of panic and foreboding not only among critics of the regime but among its most loyal servants.

There were two centers of potential leadership outside the military establishment during the war, the Council of Ministers and the Duma. Both were impeded by internal dissension and by the tsar's determination to limit their powers. The war offered the perfect occasion for the reassertion of full autocratic rule. It also demonstrated in dramatic terms that autocracy made successful conduct of the war impossible. The tsar's distrust of the Duma, not only as a legislative body (restricted as it was) but also as an expression of public opinion, was reflected in his reluctance to let it meet at all. The Duma had gathered for a ceremonial session on July 26, 1914 (OS), a week into the war, when delegates had pledged their support. In 1915, it met for only two days in late January, then again from mid-July to early September. The Council of Ministers, by contrast, met continuously. Not only were its deliberations characterized by sharp disagreements, but only five of its thirteen members kept their posts to the end of 1915. In short, the Empire's civilian leadership lacked both authority with respect to the military command and internal coherence.

Conflicts over the management of refugees dramatized this disarray. The governors of the provinces where the military planned to settle the thousands of Galician Jews driven from their homes in March were not forewarned. They had not been consulted and dreaded the prospect of coping with the influx of homeless and needy. Frightened of the inevitable turmoil that would result, the Council of Ministers insisted then, and later in April with regard to the Baltic region, that the army restrict itself to deporting hostages, and leave the rest of the population behind.[6] The refugee crisis, however, only worsened. In mid-May 1915, as Russian troops were withdrawing behind the Vistula, the ministers again expressed their alarm. The 300,000 Jews then being expelled from the Baltic region were clogging the railroads already overloaded with wounded soldiers, fuel, and ammunition. "Now, on top of everything," the ministers complained, "the Yids." Minister of the Interior Maklakov confessed: "I'm no lover of the Jews, but I can't approve. Internal danger—pogroms and nourishing the revolution. International danger. Better—hostages." Minister of Finance Petr Bark, a wealthy aristocrat of Orthodox faith—who in 1935 became an English baronet, who is buried in Nice, and whose papers are housed at Columbia University— worried that mistreatment of the Jews would prejudice Jewish banks and make it harder for Russia to borrow money.[7] In January, Sazonov had denied that the Jews of Galicia were being mistreated. Now he declared it was "*nonsens*" to think you could simply drive them forward: "they'll take to the roads—then what?" Krivoshein was the only one to suggest the policy was not only self-defeating but wrong. He denounced the whole operation as "medieval" and immoral.[8]

Opposition to the policy was not necessarily a sign of political enlightenment. Maklakov objected to the fact that Stavka, in acting beyond the war zone, was infringing on the prerogatives of the Ministry of the Interior. He worried, moreover, not only about the disruptions resulting from the influx of refugees into the interior but also about the effects of militant xenophobia on domestic life. The army, for example, had ordered the arrest of Jules Goujon, owner of the enormous Goujon metal works in Moscow, essential to military production, accusing the French national, a longtime resident and prominent public figure, of German sympathies. The Ministry of the Interior secured Goujon's release, but his enterprises had been pillaged.[9]

In fact, the overheated tone of patriotic propaganda resonated strongly in the very places and among the very groups that had responded to revolutionary agitation in 1905. In late May, 1915, workers throughout Moscow went on a three-day rampage against German-owned shops and factories. Participants included almost ten thousand workers from the center as well as the industrial districts. The mob broke into shops and even private apartments, stealing what they didn't smash, setting fires, and denouncing "German domination," the xenophobic catchword. One group murdered a factory manager who tried to stop them. These were not class-conscious proletarians. Some sang the imperial anthem ("God Save the Tsar"). Their motives were not universally condemned. Moscow governor Aleksandr Adrianov praised them as patriotic. The distinguished Moscow linguist Aleksei Sobolevskii acknowledged in a private letter that the violence against Germans and Jews was "excessive," but he found it "easy to understand the workers' indignation and why they took matters into their own hands," since they experienced the control of "the internal German" directly.[10]

The mayhem stopped only on the morning of May 29, when police and soldiers finally intervened. Ten persons had been killed and over thirty wounded. The anti-German mood in Moscow factories persisted into June. The largest, most advanced enterprises were not exempt. Workers at the giant Prokhorov textile mill were convinced the Germans had poisoned the drinking water, causing an outbreak of intestinal disorder; as late as August 1915, workers at the famously radical Putilov machine-building plant in Petrograd demanded that Russian subjects of German origin be fired.[11]

The ministers were indignant that the Moscow authorities, in particular Adrianov and Prince Feliks Iusupov, the city's military governor, had abetted the violence. A prominent society figure of eccentric tastes and fabulous wealth married to the emperor's niece, Iusupov in fact had ordered German and Austrian subjects be confined to what were called "concentration camps." (*kontsentratsionnye lageria*). The police were demanding that Germans be expelled from the factories. When the riots started, Adrianov had done nothing to stop them.[12] Adrianov had gone too far; he was dismissed. Iusupov kept his position.[13] The frenzy of xenophobia was politically dangerous, as the ministers perceived. Rumors of treason spread throughout Moscow. Nicholas, Alexandra, and their controversial spiritual adviser, Grigorii Rasputin—the entire court were said to be German agents.[14] Certain details, excluded from the press, fed the gossip mills. The crowd had supposedly demanded that the empress be imprisoned in a convent, that Nicholas abdicate in favor of Grand Duke Nikolai Nikolaevich, and that Rasputin be hanged.[15] Since the court was not above suspicion, its defenders also fell under a cloud.

Over the course of the war, Rasputin had come, in particular, to symbolize the imperial couple's moral decline. Intimacy with a figure of seemingly sinister powers marked the erosion of sacred charisma on which the tsar's authority relied. The attacks on Rasputin, which had begun well before the war, now added to the atmosphere of menace and suspicion, as though forces beyond human control were moving the empire toward disaster. The real problems were not supernatural, however, but political. In the Council of Ministers, the intransigent Maklakov, the Chief Procurator of the Holy Synod Vladimir Sabler (who became Desiatovskii in November), and Minister of Justice Shcheglovitov, notorious for his role in the Beilis affair, opposed the Duma as an infringement on the tsar's prerogatives and urged him not to convoke it.[16] The more realistic ministers favored cooperation with society, as represented in the Duma. They welcomed the alliance with France and England and called for dismissal of Maklakov, Sabler, Shcheglovitov, and Minister of War Sukhomlinov, whose reputation had been compromised in March by the arrest and execution of one of his subordinates on charges of treason. By the end of July, all four pillars of reaction were gone.[17] Only the aged and implacable Goremykin, protected by Empress Alexandra, survived the house-cleaning, in the key position of prime minister. Foreign Minister Sazonov and the ambassadors of France and England considered the shake-up in the Council of Ministers a reaffirmation of the tsar's determination to fight the war to a victorious conclusion.[18]

The new ministers were not sanguine, however. On the ever-painful subject of the refugee crisis, Prince Nikolai Shcherbatov, the new minister of the interior, complained that "an enormous resettlement of peoples has begun." Galician Jews ("the most dangerous"), German colonists, Poles, Lithuanians, and Latvians ("Cossacks using whips against old people and children") were being driven into the heartland. "Masses clog the roads. Total pandemonium (roads, canons, cholera)....(drought, wagons collapsing, livestock dropping in their tracks)."[19] General Ianushkevich's obsession with the Jews was a disaster. "We cannot fight the war against Germany," Krivoshein sardonically observed, "and at the time same wage war against the Jews. We must separate these two wars."[20] Later in August, by the time the Germans had taken Warsaw, the violence, destruction of property, and general confusion in the western regions had only intensified. The refugees were swarming the cities behind the front like "hungry locusts." Panic was spreading. The ministers needed to establish their authority. "Historians will not believe," said Krivoshein, "that we fought blindly and brought the country to the edge of ruin."[21]

The army's treatment of the Jews was not only of concern to the ministers and the Russian public, but was widely covered in the foreign press. Jewish organizations urged the British Foreign Office to intervene. Hesitant to pressure its Russian ally, Britain was confirmed in its reluctance by reports from its representatives in Russia, Ambassador Buchanan, General Alfred

Knox, and Sir Bernard Pares, who endorsed the Army's view of the Jews as subversive. Anti-Semitism was not confined to Russia. Some Jewish bankers made clear, however, that aid was contingent on support for Jewish rights, an issue raised by Minister of Finance Bark.[22] At home, leaders of the Russian Jewish community urged Prince Shcherbatov to intervene.[23]

The so-called Jewish question had political as well as practical implications. The ministers worried that the consequences of persecution were impeding the war effort and perhaps interfering with Russia's ability to acquire loans. The Kadets debated the issue of Jewish rights at their fifth congress in June 1915, considering it a matter of principle and also a question of Russia's moral standing. The pragmatic Vasilii Maklakov, the dismissed interior minister's elder brother, cautioned, however, that too aggressive a stance in favor of Jewish rights would fail to influence the army and only discredit the party as a tool of the Jews.[24] Miliukov, for his part, noted that the Pale, ironically enough, had been abolished de facto by the very policies based on distrust of the Jews, quipping that "the Pale of Settlement has gone to the devil already" (*Cherta osedlosti ponevole uletela k chortu*).[25] In August, the majority of deputies in the Duma, excluding only the extremes of Right and Left, formed what they called the Progressive Bloc (*Progressivnyi blok*), which endorsed Jewish rights, though on a gradual basis. The need to address this question was recognized even on the Right. Pavel Krupenskii, a deputy from the Nationalist Center representing Bessarabia, declared: "I am a congenital anti-Semite, but I have come to the conclusion that it is now necessary for the good of the homeland to make concession to the Jews. We need the support of the Allies. One cannot deny that the Jews are a great international power and that our hostile policy toward them weakens our credit abroad."[26]

---

The ministers had more on their minds than the Jewish question. A week after his appointment as deputy minister of war in June, General Aleksei Polivanov complained of the deficit of career officers and the drastic shortage of weapons. "We have no guns," he declared. "Misfortune, calamity, I'll be blunt—it's a tragedy."[27] He was frustrated that Nicholas spoke only with Grand Duke Nikolai Nikolaevich and General Ianushkevich, instead of hearing what the commanders in the field had to say. The tsar agreed in principle, on Polivanov's urging, to convene a military council near the front, but seemed in no great hurry.[28] A month later, exactly a year into the war, the Germans had gained control of one-third of European Russia. Polivanov warned his colleagues: "The fatherland is in danger. The troops are definitely exhausted. The Germans are pressing from all sides." Nicholas needed better military counsel, but also "the voice of the Council of Ministers, for we are approaching tragedy, both from within and without."[29] Two weeks later still, he complained: "Demoralization, surrender and desertion are assuming huge proportions. General Headquarters [Stavka] seems to be completely at a loss, and its orders are assuming a hysterical character." The ministers criticized the policy of evacuating the entire western region: "To lay waste a score of provinces and drive their inhabitants into the interior is equivalent to dooming Russia to frightful calamity."[30]

While the ministers were deliberating among themselves, the Duma deputies were gathering in Petrograd, awaiting the new session set to finally open on July 19. In anticipation, the worker districts and even the Petrograd garrisons were in a state of agitation. The deputies, too, felt a sense of emergency, blaming the government (meaning the tsar and the ministers) for the military disaster and demanding a greater role for themselves and for society at large in supporting the war. They denounced the German influence at court, charged Sukhomlinov (no longer minister of war) with mismanagement and corruption, and deplored Rasputin's continuing role.[31]

Events moved quickly. Military defeats and domestic scandals intertwined. On July 23 (August 5, NS), the day after the Germans entered Warsaw, the Duma voted for Sukhomlinov to be brought to trial. In April 1916, he was sentenced to a term in the Peter-Paul Fortress.[32] A socialist deputy was interrupted by the president when he denounced the "tsarist tyranny that has brought Russia to the abyss." More restrained, but in the same spirit, the cautious Vasilii Maklakov demanded (in English) that the regime put "the right men in the right places."[33] On August 17 (NS), the Kovno fortress, defended half-heartedly by hastily trained and inadequately armed soldiers, fell into German hands. General Vladimir Grigor'ev ingloriously abandoned his command and was tried and sentenced to hard labor.[34] Nicholas later refused to commute his sentence, but the tsar was himself under the gun. The deputies blamed him and "the German party" for this latest humiliation.[35] Three days after the loss of Kovno, Novogeorgievsk, the last Russian fort in Poland, also surrendered.

It was at this critical juncture in mid-August 1915 that the Duma formulated an appeal in support of the war. The appeal, which it hoped to present directly to the tsar, deplored the mismanagement of the army, the chaos in the rear, and the refugee crisis. It feared that foot soldiers, resentful at being sent to the slaughter unprepared and unarmed, were losing confidence in their commanders and that the people at large were appalled at the destruction and chaos created by their own leaders. The Duma therefore urged that "society" be allowed to participate fully in supporting the war behind the front and that the tsar assert his sovereign authority to heal the fatal division between Stavka and the civilian government.[36]

Unbeknownst to the Duma, however, Nicholas had already taken the momentous step of transferring Grand Duke Nikolai Nikolaevich to the Caucasian Front and assuming his role as commander in chief. Described by those around him as insecure and indecisive, the tsar made two executive decisions in 1915. In replacing the arch-reactionary ministers with more sensible figures in July, he showed a spark of good sense and a bit of backbone. It was not what Alexandra wanted. When he substituted himself for the popular Grand Duke, he succumbed to her pressure.[37] General Polivanov, a rational man, considered this decision a triumph for the "dark forces" behind the throne.[38] Twelve years the tsar's senior and a good two feet taller, the Grand Duke was handsome and dignified—the symbol of imperial virility. His image appeared on magazine covers and postcards, often astride a white charger, recalling St. George's iconic steed. His popularity in all classes was undiminished by the misfortunes of the war. The tsar, by contrast, was by now perceived as a weak, domesticated figure, under the thumb of his German-born wife and her insidious spiritual consort.[39] With the tsar's absence from the capital, Alexandra's role as conduit between the cabinet and the monarch was considerably enhanced.[40]

Nicholas's defenders in high society claimed he wished to sacrifice himself for the salvation of the Empire. The tsar explained to Nikolai Nikolaevich, as he packed him off to the Caucasus, that in time of crisis the sovereign must put himself on the front lines.[41] The foreign ambassadors preferred to think Nicholas was underscoring Russia's commitment to the war by his personal involvement, but Sazonov was appalled.[42] At the start of the war, the ministers had rejected the idea of Nicholas leading the army; now they had not been consulted. Aleksandr Samarin, chief procurator of the Holy Synod, deplored the "measure directed against the only figure tied to hopes for victory."[43] He feared it was "the beginning of the end."[44] Duma president Rodzianko urged the ministers to lodge a protest. When Goremykin told him to mind his own business, Rodzianko declared, "There is no government in Russia."[45] The ministers in fact would have liked to protest, but Goremykin insisted the tsar's word was beyond question.

The crisis of August 1915 shows how deeply in trouble the regime already was after a single year of fighting. Russia did not lack for intelligent men on the highest rungs of power. They, like Nikolai Nikolaevich and Ianushkevich, served at the tsar's pleasure. But the same system that installed them at the top prevented them from exercising power. Rodzianko was right—there was no government in Russia. At this point, the ministers still tried desperately to save the monarchy, to which they were all deeply devoted, from its own fatal flaws. These included the tsar's ability to shield himself from any kind of pressure. Yet he had yielded under pressure in October 1905. On the evening of August 20 (OS), despite Goremykin, the ministers met with Nicholas in Tsarskoe Selo and urged him to reconsider. He refused.[46]

At the next day's meeting of the Council of Ministers, Sazonov allowed himself to describe the tsar's dismissal of the Grand Duke as "treacherous." It was their duty at least to "open the tsar's eyes—to warn him of the danger." Goremykin was unmoved. Did they dare send the sovereign an ultimatum? Were they in cahoots with "the Left" to undermine the throne? The prime minister boasted of his "archaic" sense of duty. The tsar was anointed by God, the incarnation of Russia, the expression of God's will. Samarin begged to differ. Yes, they opposed the dismissal of Nikolai Nikolaevich. So did all sensible people.[47] Two days earlier, the Moscow City Duma had reaffirmed its support for the war and for the commander in chief, urging cooperation between society and government.[48] This was not "the Left"—it was the country. The time had come to reach out. The ministers needed to work with society, not against it, Polivanov insisted. Minister of Education Count Pavel Ignat'ev ominously warned: "There is no more army, only an armed people."[49]

The conflict between Prime Minister Goremykin and the cabinet showed that the servants of autocracy were pulling away from the person of the tsar. This cleft would prove fatal to Romanov fortunes, but not quite yet. The ministers insisted Goremykin report to Nicholas with their views. "I love the tsar," said Samarin, "but I also love Russia. If the tsar is harming Russia, I cannot go along." Nicholas did not need slavish obedience but honest opinions. They could no longer serve with Goremykin at their head. Goremykin considered it dishonorable to resign. He agreed reluctantly to convey their message, but was sure the tsar would not reply. "The tsar's word is not Scripture," warned Sazonov. "His popularity and authority have been shaken." If his word remained sacrosanct, then they might as well drown themselves.[50]

That evening, August 21, eight of the ministers met in Sazonov's apartment at the Ministry of Foreign Affairs and signed a letter imploring the tsar to reinstate Nikolai Nikolaevich and declaring the impossibility of continuing in their posts with Goremykin as chair. Polivanov and Minister of the Navy Ivan Grigorovich supported their position, but could not as military officers offer their resignations in time of war.[51] The result: Shcherbatov and Samarin were out by the end of September; Krivoshein lasted to the end of October. Goremykin remained as prime minister until January 1916.[52]

---

The change at the top of the army command was not what the Duma deputies had in mind when they pleaded for a unified center of power to coordinate civil and military authority during the war. The reopening of the Duma on July 19, 1915, nevertheless presented a chance for cooperation between "society" and the Council of Ministers. Although the deputies had abstained from demands and criticisms, Maklakov had restricted their sessions to a single day in July 1914 and another three days in January 1915. He had tightened censorship of the press, put the Bolshevik deputies on trial (saved from possible death sentences by the intervention of Grand Duke Nikolai Nikolaevich), and had his own brother and Petr Struve, another moderate liberal, sentenced to two months in prison for their comments on the Beilis case.[53] Now Maklakov was on the sidelines and the ministers were faced with crises of war production, military provisioning, and civil organization that only the industrialists, professionals, and leaders of public opinion represented in the Duma could help them solve. They were obliged now to appeal for public assistance.[54]

In January 1915, the State Council had formed an Economic Commission, involving the participation of leading industrialists. In another example of its self-defeating hostility to "social forces," the government abolished the Commission two months later, at the beginning of April.[55] The military defeats of May prompted the leaders of industry to take a more assertive approach. Until then, the moderate parties had acquiesced in the suspension of the Duma. Now, reflecting the changed mood in propertied circles, the moderates gave up the show of unconditional patriotism. The Congress of Trade and Industry (*S"ezd predstavitelei promyshlennosti i torgovli*) meeting in

Petrograd created a Central War Industries Committee (*Voenno-promyshlennyi komitet*), uniting over seventy local organizations. Chaired by Aleksandr Guchkov, founder of the Octobrist Party, in cooperation with another leading Moscow industrialist, Pavel Riabushinskii, the Committee began pressing for the return of the Duma.[56] By June all the parties of the middle ground had adopted this position and called, in addition, either for a "Ministry Responsible to the Duma," or, less emphatically, a "Ministry of Public Confidence."[57] With the four pillars of reaction—Maklakov, Sukhomlinov, Sabler, and Shcheglovitov—out of the way, the respectable public figures had men they thought they could work with.

From the first days of the war, voluntary organizations had shouldered a number of important tasks seemingly beyond the capacity of the military or civilian authorities. The most important of these independent associations were the Union of Towns and the Union of Zemstvos (*Soiuz gorodov* and *Zemskii soiuz*), formed in 1914 to aid in the care of sick and wounded soldiers. By the end of that year, they were administering 1,700 hospitals and contributing to refugee relief. In June 1915, the two organizations joined to form the Union of Zemstvos and Towns (*ZemGor*), which processed government orders for military procurements, including boots, clothing, and even munitions.[58] Meanwhile, Duma president Rodzianko, himself a wealthy landowner and entrepreneur, together with a group of leading industrialists, had persuaded Grand Duke Nikolai Nikolaevich to create a special council for the coordination of arms supply, with the participation of manufacturers and Duma deputies, to be chaired by the minister of war, answerable directly to the monarch. Once the relatively enlightened Polivanov had replaced the incompetent and corrupt Sukhomlinov, the War Industries Committee was allowed to join the special council.

The question of provisioning was crucial and the situation was dire. The complaints first heard in autumn 1914 about the shortage of ammunition and weapons had only grown more urgent. In August 1915, after he had decided to leave for the front, the tsar approved the creation of four special councils— transport, fuel, food supply, and most important, state defense.[59] Chaired by Polivanov, the latter included government officials, as well as representatives of the War Industries Committee and the ZemGor. Nicholas himself attended the ceremonial opening of the councils in the White Hall of the Winter Palace, to signal his continuing involvement in the management of government behind the front. It was at this point that the ministers presented their plea for the removal of Goremykin, which of course proved entirely in vain.[60]

Polivanov tried to coordinate the activities of the special councils, but to little effect. They worked at cross purposes. The new minister of the interior, Aleksei Khvostov, appointed in September 1915, actively impeded his efforts. Despite these frustrations, the defense council's regional divisions, with the participation of military officers and local voluntary organizations, continued to assist domestic industry in satisfying the military's demands.[61] The entire episode of the special councils illustrated the bureaucracy's need to enlist the cooperation of social forces. It illustrated the extent to which the emergency had impelled the regime, including even the obdurate Nicholas, to relinquish some of its habitual reluctance. It also illustrated the extent to which bureaucratic structures and decades of distrust and intransigence could still prevent the government from utilizing the resources at hand.

The other source of potential support resided, of course, in the Duma. Even at this anxious juncture, the ministers considered the body expendable. Its days were rumored to be numbered. It was now, in August, that a group of deputies met privately at Rodzianko's house to draw up a list of ten key points and form the Progressive Bloc. The initiative obtained the support of sympathetic figures in the State Council, which had cooperated in forming the joint Economic Commission at the start of the year. The Moscow City Duma endorsed the demand for a government of public confidence; other municipalities echoed the call.[62] In reaction to this move, the deputies of the extreme Right formed a "Black Bloc" (*Chernyi blok*), which agitated for dismissal of the Duma—in other words, for their own redundancy. The leader of the Right fraction, the same Aleksei Khvostov appointed minister of the interior in September, launched a tirade, impugning in a single breath the German colonists, unnamed "rapacious capitalists and bankers," and the incompetent bureaucrats who had failed to prevent the mob from ravaging Moscow. It was this expression of pseudo-populist xenophobia that earned Khvostov his cabinet portfolio. The reactionary Council of the United Nobility (*Sovet ob"edinennogo dvorianstva*) warned Goremykin that the Progressive Bloc was taking advantage of the wartime emergency to implement the political objectives of the revolutionary Left.[63]

The Progressive Bloc at first attempted to keep its deliberations secret, but its demands were soon published in the Moscow and Petrograd press.[64] The Council of Ministers, meeting the day the program leaked, debated whether even to consider the proposals. Goremykin advised against it, but Sazonov warned this was a dangerous path. If the Progressive Bloc collapsed, the Duma would move even further "to the left." The ministers were

conflicted: they feared allowing the deputies to continue making speeches—
thus arousing the country; they feared dismissing them, thus also arousing
the country. The Putilov workers were already on a slowdown strike. The
cabinet could ill afford to alienate the war-production workers. Minister of
Trade Prince Vsevolod Shakhovskoi preferred first to appease the Duma,
then send it packing. The deputies needed to be "managed."

Goremykin predictably denounced the Progressive Bloc's entire program,
which Sazonov thought mostly uncontroversial. In fact, the program was not
at all radical or even confrontational. It was designed to alleviate the causes
of conflict and fragmentation and thereby strengthen the basis for fighting
the war. The demands included amnesty for political prisoners, religious
toleration, autonomy for Poland, legal equality for the Jews—introduced
gradually, rights for Finland, freedom of the press in the Ukrainian region,
and the legalization of trade unions.[65] Predictably, Goremykin failed to
understand that a fixation on mythical dangers prevented the emperor from
seeing where the real dangers lay. Nicholas would never lift a finger for the
Jews, he declared.[66]

The other ministers realized, however, that they could no longer afford
merely to ignore or, worse, alienate the public organizations or the war-
production workers. The euphemism of a "cabinet of public confidence"
targeted Goremykin. He was the obstacle that stood between the government and the public, between the ministers and the tsar. Krivoshein, no
democrat, thought the country could dispense with the Duma, but the
ministers needed the power to act and Goremykin would not let them. "We
are not conspirators," Sazonov expostulated. "We are just as loyal as Your
Excellency." Goremykin retreated. He would tell Nicholas first to dismiss
the Duma, then request someone else be appointed in his place.[67]

Delegated to urge Nicholas to compromise with the Progressive Bloc,
Goremykin arrived at Stavka with the suggestion instead that Nicholas close
the Duma down. Nicholas readily agreed. The ministers felt betrayed. Their
resignations were not accepted, although they would be out of office soon
enough. The Duma deputies meanwhile fulminated in private. In any normal country, they would have been able to play a constructive role; here they
were considered revolutionaries.[68] Indeed, this is precisely what some of the
ministers thought.[69] In public, the deputies meekly accepted their fate.[70]

With the announcement of the prorogation on September 3, as the ministers had feared, some Putilov workers emerged in the street singing the
"Marseillaise" and were joined by some at other plants. By the next day, as

many as seventy thousand Petrograd workers had gone on strike. Polivanov feared a general strike was brewing.[71] The ZemGor, meeting in Moscow, demanded the return of the Duma and a ministry of public confidence, but when the tsar refused to receive their delegation, they too folded their tents.[72] The moderates, like the ministers, feared the potential for unrest in the factory districts. Respectable society, which supported the war, had no interest in fomenting disorder or destabilizing the regime. The protests soon subsided, but the specter of revolution haunted everyone's mind.

The lame-duck ministers were nervous. The mood in Moscow was restless. The worker delegates to the War Industries Committee were raising political issues, but arresting them might provoke a strike. Students were reading Marxist pamphlets smuggled from abroad.[73] In 1905 the combination of workers and students had been explosive. As in 1905, the forces of order were showing signs of strain. Policemen and gendarmes were quitting the service; ensigns in Moscow were defying orders.[74] But the ministers were no less worried by the threat to domestic stability posed by the regime itself. The civilian government was powerful enough to impede the activities of civil society, helping obstruct the operation of the Duma or limiting the role of independent associations. The ministers were not powerful enough, however, to alter the way their own government ruled. They were stuck in the contradictions of their own dedication to the monarchy as it actually existed.

Questions of administration and domestic stability were closely related. In September 1915, the ministers were already worrying about possible food shortages in Petrograd and Moscow. Supply was hampered in part because the railroads were clogged with refugees, who continued to pour into the cities, straining resources and administrative ingenuity.[75] In particular, the ministers deplored their own inability to curb the army's crazed obsession with hidden or not-so-hidden enemies. General Ruzskii had dismissed all Baltic officials, including a certain Baron Nikolai Medem, Orthodox by religion, son of the governor of Warsaw, and Goremykin's son-in-law to boot, because of his Germanic background. "It's a madhouse," said Krivoshein. Ruzskii was demanding the evacuation of all males from the province of Livonia (now divided between Latvia and Estonia), threatening Petrograd with a new wave of destitute homeless. General Ivanov, commander of the Southwest Front, was continuing to clean out Poltava and Chernigov provinces. The military were expelling refugees working in Kiev sugar factories. "Complete madness, bedlam," Krivoshein complained.

The chaos on the railroads was appalling: weapons sat for weeks unloaded; some wagons traveled empty, while others were bursting with crowds of displaced people headed nowhere. The lands formerly tilled by the uprooted German colonists were not being sown. The ministers feared the spread of hunger and hunger riots. They blamed the military authorities. The invasion of the southwest region by the general in charge of requisitions did more damage, Polivanov objected, than the enemy. It was the "tragedy of divided power," Krivoshein observed. "Sheer bedlam. The Germans will not conquer us. The quartermaster-generals will destroy everything. Their powers are unlimited, their abilities limited. Words cannot express the horror."[76]

And yet, for all their awareness of the damage the regime's own structures and policies caused, the ministers shared the tsar's deep distrust of independent forces. They feared the Union of Towns was forming a self-defense attachment, that the Union of Zemstvos was forming its own army, that the press was undermining public confidence. On this subject, Krivoshein revealed his deep psychological ties to the same milieu that produced the crazed generals Ruzskii and Ianushkevich. In October 1914, the ministers had criticized the staunchly conservative (and anti-Semitic) newspaper *Novoe vremia*, widely read in educated circles, for its anti-German invective. A year later, Krivoshein complained that *Novoe vremia* had fallen "into the hands of the Yids, a change deeply to be regretted." It was a crime to let the paper be controlled by "suspicious" people, he said.[77] Nicholas was in the habit of finding his own subjects "suspicious," and not just the Jews. The fear was self-fulfilling. Revolutionaries assassinated officials, and respectable liberals agitated for laws that would have curtailed his powers. During the war, the Empire needed the support of its subjects more than ever, and the fear of disloyalty grew with the greater need.

1. "The Emperor and the Grand Duke Nicholas at G.H.Q., 1915," in Sir John Hanbury-Williams, *The Emperor Nicholas II as I Knew Him* (London: Arthur L. Humphreys, 1922). Joseph Regenstein Library, University of Chicago.

**2.** K. K. Bulla, "The Horse Draft." Postcard, Slavonic Library, National Library of Finland.

**3.** "The Second Patriotic War, 1914–1915–1916: Refugees from Galicia." Postcard, Slavonic Library, National Library of Finland.

**4.** "Encounter of Kuban and Ural Cossacks After the Battle." Postcard, Slavonic Library, National Library of Finland.

**5.** Vladimir Mayakovsky, "*Deutschland über alles*–The Germans cry, And from the battlefield they fly." Postcard, Slavonic Library, National Library of Finland.

**6.** Mukhomor, "Hand Over the Tribute!" Postcard, Slavonic Library, National Library of Finland.

**7.** A. F. Postnov, "Down With the Pale of Settlement!" *The Pale no longer restrains us / We're now free on Russian lands / To sell our garlic and sausage / Even where the Kremlin stands.* Postcard, Slavonic Library, National Library of Finland.

**8.** Leonid Pasternak, book cover: *Shchit: Literaturnyi sbornik*, ed. Leonid Andreev, Maxim Gorky, and Fedor Sologub, 3rd ed. rev. (Moscow: Mamontov, 1916) [*The Shield: A Literary Collection*. Russian Society for the Study of Jewish Life]. Joseph Regenstein Library, University of Chicago.

# 4

# Conflict and Collapse

The fear of disloyalty attached itself in particular to the inhabitants of border zones, sometimes linked to communities across the border, who often resented their incorporation into the Empire and its policies of cultural repression. For the Central Powers, Russian-held Poland, the Baltic littoral, Volhynia, Bessarabia, and the Caucasus were all gateways to the heartland. Their populations all had historic ties to enemy powers. In the case of trans-border peoples with national ambitions, Russia's fears were not entirely unfounded. German and Austrian propaganda targeted ethnic minorities with reason to resent imperial Russian rule. In Austria, Ukrainian nationalists formed a Union for the Liberation of the Ukraine (*Soiuz vyzvolennia Ukraïny*) and Józef Piłsudski formed Polish Legions for action across the Russian border. Prisoners held in Austrian captivity divided themselves into separate contingents—Ukrainians, Finns, Poles, Georgians, Jews. On its side, the Russian army encouraged similar groupings among Austrian prisoners, hoping to turn the Czech, Slovak, and Polish soldiers against their Hapsburg rulers. Allowing Armenian nationalists to form volunteer units attached to the Russian army, but destined to foment rebellion on the Ottoman side, was part of this pattern.[1]

The three divisions of pre-partition Poland—East Prussia, Austrian Galicia, and the Russian-held provinces (from 1815 to 1864 known as Congress Poland or the Polish Kingdom—*Tsarstvo Pol'skoe, Królestwo Polskie*)—were at the center of the nationality question. In East Prussia, restrictions on Polish cultural life created resentments on which Russian propaganda could play.[2] In the Russian-held provinces, the imperial regime had inflamed national feeling by decades of political and cultural persecution. The war thus posed a challenge. "The Polish people would gladly support the Russian cause," wrote the Polonophile Slavic linguist Aleksandr Pogodin in the liberal press, "if their national feelings were only respected. Their imperial patriotism has been poisoned by harmful and thoughtless official policies. Will the authorities understand the problem in time to correct it?"[3]

In the first week of the war, the monarchy indeed tried to repair the damage. On August 1, 1914 (August 14, NS) an appeal issued in the name of Grand Duke Nikolai Nikolaevich and addressed directly to the Polish people was disseminated widely. Composed by ministers Sukhomlinov and Sazonov, together with General Ianushkevich, the appeal promised to grant the reunited Polish nation some degree of self-government, "under the Russian scepter," once the Empire had emerged victorious from the war.[4] The Germans responded with an appeal of their own, urging the Polish-speaking population to reject Russian rule.[5]

Russia did not promise to relinquish control over Polish destiny, but the gesture was good publicity for the Russian cause. The *New York Times* believed the appeal would attract the attention of Poles fighting under Prussian and Austrian colors: "Russian Poles Rejoice: Hold It Is Now the Interest of Poles Everywhere to Side with Russia." The appeal's "moral effect," the paper noted, "is calculated to be very great."[6] As for the impact on Russian-Polish relations, Russians themselves were not so sure: "What kind of Pole from Cracow, or even Poznań, wants to find himself under the Russian scepter?" a skeptic from Kiev quipped.[7] Another Russian reported from Vilna: "Not even the Poles are excited about the appeal. Why promise united Poland under Russian rule? Why not full independence?"[8] Independence is what they wanted.[9] The Poles mistrusted the Grand Duke's appeal, and with good reason.[10] Princess Elizaveta Shakhovskaia, wife of the governor of Estland Province (later Estonia), writing to the agronomist Vladimir Evreinov in Petrograd, wondered whether the gesture was serious or "just a brilliant improvisation, like a bit of fireworks?"[11]

Partly to quiet such doubts, another appeal was issued, on August 5, also in the Grand Duke's name. This one addressed the "Russian people" (*Russkii narod*), urging them to live with their neighbors in peace and harmony. "We all have a place in the bosom of Mother Russia," the Grand Duke reminded them. "Do not offend peaceful people, whatever their national identity might be. Do not base your good fortune on the persecution of foreigners, as the Swabians have done. Turn your swords against the enemy and your hearts toward God, with a prayer for Russia and the Russian Tsar."[12] Against the background of the devastation soon to be perpetrated by the Army High Command, the appeal of course rang hollow.

The Polish situation was delicate indeed. Around 600,000 Poles were fighting in the Russian Imperial Army.[13] General Eugeniusz de Henning-Michaelis, stationed with a Polish regiment in Kielce, greeted the Grand Duke's declaration with satisfaction, as the resolution of Poland's "greatest misfortune"—the partitions. Living under three flags, the Poles had gradually lost their moral unity and were "now compelled to fight a fratricidal war." When he realized, however, that "the entire expanse of the Polish Kingdom west of the Vistula, including Warsaw, was excluded from the purview of the Russian army," he was dismayed. Understanding the strategic logic of the decision, he nevertheless feared "the political and psychological impact on the Polish population. Having just promised the Poles the chance to gain national unity and freedom, the Russians delivered a large part of the country into German hands without so much as a struggle."[14]

Piłsudski's supporters were less diplomatic. When the area around the industrial powerhouse of Łódź was occupied by the Austrians in late 1915, it became the headquarters of the Polish Legions, which issued their own appeals. "You cannot be a loyal tsarist subject and a good Pole," warned one of their pamphlets. "You cannot serve both God and the Devil." The Russians, now in a tight corner, were trying "to disarm Polish vigilance with their lies," the text continued. "After the war, once they have won, they will put us in even heavier chains. No tsarist promise or manifesto is worth two cents." The Russians had shown their true colors in Galicia. "Thousands of Polish peasant huts were torched, hundreds of Polish noble estates were completely destroyed, property thoroughly ransacked. Schools, Catholic churches demolished." The Germans had not been kind to Poland, but at least they had been clear. "Better an honest and open enemy than a false and two-faced friend."[15]

Though hailed by progressive Russians as a step in the right direction, since it conceded the possibility of Polish self-rule, the August 1914 Appeal was in fact no more than window dressing. Antonii Ottovich von Essen, the imperial governor-general of Warsaw, with his ostentatiously German names, derided the proclamation as an obvious misunderstanding. Before he had a chance to eat his words, his comment had surfaced in enemy propaganda and had a chilling effect on the Poles.[16] Those among them who hoped for Polish-Russian cooperation were disappointed.

The dilemma faced by such conciliators can be illustrated by the case of Aleksander Lednicki. A leading figure in the Kadet Party, as deputy to the First Duma he had signed the Vyborg Manifesto in June 1906. Now in Moscow, after August 1914 he devoted his energies to the care of Polish wounded from all three armies.[17] The Grand Duke's August promises, he complained, had been undermined by imperial officials in Poland who forbade open discussion of the options implied in the prospect of self-government, while allowing aggressive nationalists to circulate their views. If the Appeal had been respected, it would have taken the wind out of the nationalist sails. Instead, Russian policy seemed intent on pitting one segment of Polish society against another. Lednicki identified a sinister convergence between Polish nationalist and imperial Russian propaganda, which in both cases exacerbated ethnic tensions to the detriment of the common cause. Both, Lednicki complained, used the Jews as a scapegoat. "Polish anti-Semites pointed out that the Russian authorities treated the Jewish population with suspicion, while the Russian authorities cited Polish anti-Semites to the effect that one should treat Jews with suspicion." Damage to the common cause was also inflicted by officials and officers in Poland and Galicia whose conduct, Lednicki complained, was tantamount to treason; extortion, plunder, and dissipation blackened Russia's name.[18]

The Empire was by definition a composite of different peoples—that was its charm, its grandeur, its distinctive character. Its governing and privileged classes were drawn from all corners—the Baltic periphery, the Polish provinces, the Caucasus. Together they constituted a hybrid imperial culture, but the dominant language was Russian and the privileged religion, the sanctifier of autocratic power, was embodied in the Russian Orthodox Church. Lednicki was a Pole loyal to the imperial cause. But these loyalties were unstable, particularly under the pressure of war and the impact of xenophobic propaganda. Reassembled in late January 1915, for three humiliating days after six months of suspension, the Duma deputies had reiterated their support for the *union sacrée*, which they had announced in July 1914, but their affirmations had a sharp double edge. Duma President Mikhail Rodzianko once more invoked the ideal of Slavic brotherhood "in blood and faith."[19] He hailed not only Serbia but Bulgaria, whose independent existence had been sponsored by Russia in 1878, at the end of the Russo-Turkish War. Eight months later, in October 1915, Bulgaria was to join the Central Powers, showing its ingratitude and betraying its supposed Slavic allegiance, but this moral failure still lay ahead.[20] In 1914 Rodzianko had also invoked the "fraternal unity of all the peoples of the Russian land." Yes, intoned Goremykin, Poland and Russia were now brothers. This time, unlike in 1878, Russia would reach Constantinople (today Istanbul). Sazonov denounced German schemes to cause trouble along the borders—in Romania, Bulgaria, and Turkey, and in Galicia with the "so-called Ukrainian movement."[21]

The deputies from the contentious regions struck decidedly ambiguous notes. The August Appeal, whatever its motives, had introduced an insidious idea that was immediately reflected in public discourse. The Duma deputy from Kielce Province (where General Henning-Michaelis had found himself abandoned in the early days of the war) hailed the Allied powers for supporting "the liberation of individual nations." The deputy from the Armenian capital of Erevan applauded Russia's struggle to free "the Armenians from their age-old subjection to the Turkish Yoke." Naftali Fridman from Kovno reasserted the loyalty of the Empire's Jewish subjects. In a transparent rhetorical maneuver, he refrained from enumerating "the insults that have been and are still directed against us." In a similar vein, the deputy from Ufa, in the southern Urals, pledged the loyalty of the Muslim population, despite constant affronts to their religious and "national" feelings.[22]

Thus, in January 1915 the Duma deputies insisted on their imperial loyalty, but they did so in national terms. Indeed, the policies implemented in the western provinces encouraged the stigmatized groups to think of themselves as distinctively "national," in a formal or political sense. Each persecuted community had formed its own charitable organizations. The left and center political parties also had to reconcile support of the war, which entailed a defense of imperial Russian interests, with the democratic principles they hoped the war would promote. The liberal Kadets, who hoped to see Russia emerge with a Western-style constitution, endorsed the Empire's expansionist goals—Russia's historic mission to acquire the "Russian" Carpathians, the Turkish Straits, and Tsargrad (Constantinople), expelling Germany from the Bosporus.[23] Kadet leader Pavel Miliukov considered the August 1914 Appeal a sign of Russia's moral superiority.[24] Further to the left, Alexander Kerensky said he favored peace only if all democratic Europe was behind it and endorsed the struggle of "our citizens of other nationalities" for the "full realization of their national ideals." He took a skeptical view of the August Appeal, which, he charged (to boos from the Right), had not been issued in good faith but in a moment of weakness. Kerensky was nevertheless no fan of Polish independence. Like other progressive intellectuals at the time and like everyone who wished for Russian victory, which depended on the survival of the Empire in one piece, he insisted the Poles could achieve their freedom only by remaining in the Russian fold.[25]

A discordant note was struck by Nikolai Chkheidze, a Menshevik from Tiflis, Georgia, who denounced the army's treatment of the Jews, the brutal policies applied in Galicia, and the continuing demonization of domestic minorities.[26] To whistles from the Right and Center, he protested the arrest of the five Bolshevik deputies the previous November and hailed the recent socialist conference in Copenhagen, which had resolved to work for an early end to the war. Shouts from the center interrupted: "Enough! How much are the Germans paying you?"[27]

Xenophobic stereotypes and images circulated from mouth to mouth, in private correspondence, in the press, and in the flood of pamphlets, albums, posters, and postcards produced during the war. Artists and writers rose to the occasion. Germans were routinely depicted as brutes and barbarians, Austrians as degenerate and effete, Jews as profiteers, spies, and traitors. Among supporters of the patriotic cause, some rejected the aggressively xenophobic thrust of official policy and the right-wing press. They favored a cosmopolitan nationalism befitting an empire of many ethno-national parts.[28] But they were a minority voice.

Russian Jewish leaders, of course, did what they could to combat anti-Semitism and its harmful effects. They had mobilized in relation to the Beilis case, and they organized a charitable response to the wartime refugee crisis. In 1915 a group of activist Jewish lawyers, associated with the prominent Kadet Maksim Vinaver, urged the well-known writer Maxim Gorky to launch a campaign of public education. The modernist authors Leonid Andreev and Fedor Sologub joined with Gorky to sponsor public lectures, questionnaires, and the publication of a volume of essays and fiction, titled *The Shield* (*Shchit*), to which Petrograd mayor Ivan Tolstoi gave his blessing. The trio solicited contributions from a range of Gentile figures of varying political views, but united in the belief that political anti-Semitism was dangerous and morally objectionable.[29] The roster of distinguished figures was no doubt preaching to the choir, but the effort testified to the moral vision of a moderate section of educated society, searching for a middle ground between the radical extremes of social revolution and the frenzy of the anti-Semitic Right. The challenge for this patriotic, yet critically minded, middle was to keep its balance as the country headed ever more recklessly toward social and political collapse.

———————

In Europe, 1916 was consumed by the Battle of Verdun, which lasted from February to mid-December, ten months of attacks, counterattacks, and artillery barrages, inflicting enormous losses on both sides and bringing little advantage to either. Despite some progress in the field, the Russian army began the year with heavy casualties as well. In Galicia, Paléologue noted, "At a single location, in Czartorysk, 11,500 men, blinded by a snowstorm, were mowed down, to the last one, in a few minutes, by the German artillery." "Alas," he observed, "public opinion has become more sensitive to losses than to success."[30]

In March the Allies asked Russia to keep the Germans occupied by launching a campaign in the East. Stavka therefore opened an offensive at Lake Naroch, in Belarussia. Despite their superiority in numbers and massive ammunition supplies, the Russians failed to secure a decisive victory. They began with a prolonged artillery assault that missed most of its targets. Russian soldiers crossing between trenches in massed groups were easily picked off. The infantry bogged down in the early spring mud. Russian casualties far outnumbered the German losses. The assault on Riga, led by General Aleksei Kuropatkin later in the month, also ended in failure, with similarly high casualties. The Russians soon forfeited whatever ground they had gained at the start. Failing to provide the relief the Allies had hoped for, they succeeded only in eroding their own, already shaky, self-confidence.[31]

On the Southwest Front, by contrast, where General Aleksei Brusilov assumed command in March, the mood seemed to be lifting. Responding this time to a plea for relief from the Italians, four Russian armies opened a campaign against the Austrians in Volhynia and eastern Galicia. Beginning in early June and lasting into September, Brusilov's offensive provided Russia's one outstanding achievement of the war. The Germans were too busy at Verdun to support their weaker partner. The Russians took more than 400,000 prisoners, including 9,000 officers, and gained a considerable swath of land. By engaging and knocking out the Austrian armies, the offensive pulled the Italian chestnuts out of the fire. It also relieved pressure on the French and on the Allies in Salonica. Finally, the Austrian defeat brought Romania into the war on the side of the Entente in August 1916.[32]

The Romanian campaign was not, however, a blessing for Russia. Considerable Russian forces were now tied down in the south. The Central Powers, for their part, managed, in the space of a few weeks, using Hungarian railways, to transfer reserves in sufficient numbers to match the Romanian army. The mobilization of reserves in this case was key to the Germans' ability to dominate the contest. Romanian intervention, ending in defeat, provided the Central Powers with the additional resources to continue fighting into 1918.[33] By November 1916, they had gained control of Dobruja, south of Bessarabia along the Black Sea coast. The Russians were unable to transport the required forces in time to save Bucharest from enemy hands. The city fell to General Mackensen in early December 1916.[34]

Alas, as in the fall of 1914, the public paid more attention to the failures (at Lake Naroch and Riga in the north, the losses incurred by General Aleksei Evert in the west, and finally Romania) than to the triumphs in Galicia and the Caucasus. Rodzianko expressed a widespread sentiment when he denounced the ineptitude of the Army High Command, which he believed had destroyed the confidence of its own officer corps. The result was the "absence of initiative and paralysis of bravery and gallantry" at the front.[35]

Indeed, a combination of military and administrative incompetence had produced one of the most dramatic crises of 1916, arousing precisely the kind of hostility on the part of subject peoples the government had been at pains to suppress and providing ammunition for the regime's harshest critics. An ill-advised and poorly implemented decree, announced abruptly in July, which imposed a labor draft on the Muslim population of Central Asia, exempt from military service, gave rise to a massive rebellion throughout the region. General Kuropatkin was sent to repress the insurgency, which was not finally halted until October, at a staggering cost to the native population.[36] A group of Muslim Duma deputies, joined by Alexander Kerensky (who had spent his gymnasium years in Tashkent, where his father was a school inspector), traveled to the region to investigate. At a closed sitting of the Duma in December, Kerensky delivered an impassioned denunciation of official policy, which he blamed for the outbreak of the revolt, and of the brutality of the official response—"Such a government is unaccceptable!" he thundered.[37] The end of this government was in sight.

Kerensky's denunciation, which was not publicized at the time, provided a rhetorical finale to a year in which domestic morale had progressively eroded. Brusilov's summer campaign of 1916, though victorious, had resulted in dramatic casualties.[38] In August, Aleksandr Guchkov, head of the War Industries Committee, wrote to Chief of Staff Alekseev, describing the ominous mood. Prime Minister Boris Shtiurmer had replaced Goremykin in January, then concurrently followed Sazonov at Foreign Affairs in July. With his Germanic name, he was widely suspected of treasonous intentions. His government, Guchkov reported, had lost the confidence of the educated public, which feared not only for the outcome of the war but for the future of the country. Citing "the excited state of the people, especially of the workers," Guchkov warned that "a deluge is approaching—and a pitiful, wretched and flabby government is preparing to face that deluge by taking measures good enough only against a shower. It puts on rubbers and opens an umbrella!"[39]

———————

Guchkov's invocation of proletarian revolution was not merely rhetorical. In the aftermath of 1905, workers for a time had been content with the newfound right to organize, but the 1912 Lena massacre had signaled a return of labor militancy that was still being felt in the first half of 1914. The outbreak of war had sent the workers back to their benches, and the radical parties did not encourage strikes during the war. Nevertheless, the number of strikes and strikers continued to climb. On average, the monthly rate in 1915 was four times that of the final months of 1914, when the factory districts were unusually quiet; the monthly rate in 1916 was almost twice that of 1915.[40] The mounting discontent reflected the increasing shortage of essential commodities—kerosene, soap, wood, coal, salt, sugar, butter, milk, and bread, and the sharp rise in prices. The pinch began to be felt in early 1915; by the end of the year, lines in front of the shops had lengthened, and in 1916 shortages increased more sharply, while prices continued to rise. Along with the strikes, bread riots became more common. Women took out their anger on the shopkeepers, whom they accused of price gouging and profiteering.[41]

The protests were not at first attached to a political agenda. Most workers were not in the mood for trouble. When the five Bolshevik deputies came up for trial in February 1915, the party's call for protests elicited no response.[42] Patriotic appeals seem to have had greater effect. Workers rallied to mark the Russian success at Przemyśl in March 1915; they participated in the anti-German riots of May 1915; they showed their enthusiasm again when Romania entered the war in August 1916. Nor did they always see the different perspectives as contradictory. In 1915 it was still possible for workers with a radical background, such as those at the Putilov machine-building plant, to support the war, the Duma, and the extension of civil liberties and the franchise, while calling for the expulsion of Russian citizens of German or Austrian extraction.[43]

Two incidents in summer 1915 had signaled that the mood was shifting. In Ivanovo-Voznesensk, the textile town to the northeast of Moscow with a history of labor militancy dating back to 1905, a strike began in August in response to the arrest of shop-floor delegates. The local Bolsheviks organized protests, demanding their release and brandishing the slogans "Down with the War!" and "Down with the Autocracy!" When the strikers assembled in front of the prison, the soldier-guards opened fire, killing thirty and wounding twice as many. A similar confrontation in July had occurred in Kostroma, farther to the northeast of Moscow, and had also resulted in the shooting of demonstrating workers. A wave of protest strikes in Petrograd followed on both occasions.[44]

The authorities were aware of the risks involved in alienating the key war industry labor force—not only the industrialist Guchkov, but also the cabinet ministers worried about the effects of growing economic hardship.[45] They feared that dismissal of the Duma on September 3 might arouse protest in Petrograd munitions plants. Indeed, while the police continued to arrest the leading Putilov workers, tens of thousands of strikers in the capitals announced their support for the Duma, even if unsure exactly what it was. Some threw rocks at the police, who responded with gunfire.[46] The Bolsheviks attempted to transform these protests into a larger political movement. Echoing the events of October 1905, a decade earlier, they called for a general strike. The response was disappointing, but calls to commemorate Bloody Sunday at the start of 1916 evoked a response in Petrograd and Moscow.[47] Throughout the fall of 1915 and into the early winter of 1916, the ministers noted signs of discontent at Putilov and among the worker delegates to the War Industries Committees.[48] Protests continued throughout 1916, culminating in an incident in October, when strikes sweeping through Petrograd factories included calls to end the war.[49] Workers hurled stones and fired revolver shots. A regiment was summoned to reinforce the police, but instead turned their guns against them, before being herded back to their barracks. The execution of 150 of the mutinous soldiers ten days later provoked another raft of strikes.[50]

The impact of worker unrest was magnified by the concentration of large industrial enterprises in and near Petrograd, in particular those involved in war production. The Putilov works and other machine-building plants were politically the most active and played a key role in the events of 1917. But workers constituted only a small fraction of the overall population. The peasants, who vastly outnumbered them, suffered doubly from the war—in uniform and in the fields. By 1915 the impact of the draft was making itself felt in the shortage of able male hands and work horses; fields were left unsown. In some ways, however, the villages benefited. Soldiers' wives received allowances, prohibition—and the absence of men—reduced the amount spent on drinking. They were flush with cash, but goods were scarce and expensive. In the northern and industrial provinces, the peasants themselves depended on purchasing bread and suffered from the spike in prices, pushed upward partly as a result of the drop in the yield of grain.[51]

No one had expected a grain shortage during the war, but by the end of 1916 a shortage had emerged. In 1915 peasant women had already begun staging riots, confronting merchants, grabbing sacks of flour, trashing shops in the market place. Such incidents, often involving women—workers' wives or themselves workers, peasant women or soldiers' wives—became more frequent in 1916.[52] In the villages, protesters took out their anger on a range of targets—landowners, peasants who had managed to establish independent farms before the war, the more prosperous German colonists, the authorities in general, merchants, and people perceived as "speculators." Despite the ban on alcohol, moonshine flourished. With older men away, patriarchal authority suffered and the youth that remained ran wild. Early in the war, the ordinary front soldier ate better than he had at home; by 1916 his rations had dwindled, and he felt himself doubly deprived.[53]

The authorities developed various schemes to manage the situation, contemplating a grain levy in 1916, at one point contemplating an economic command center. Civic leaders in the Duma and in the voluntary sector felt a growing panic as the government seemed to be spinning out of control. Desperate to compensate for the economic and administrative chaos that was impeding the war effort and threatening to breed popular unrest, they managed to achieve new levels of coordination, forming independent structures that sought not to challenge but to buttress the regime. They realized that in time of emergency a strong state was needed.

Nicholas and his ministers clung to their prerogatives, but the state they represented was weak and increasingly unable to discharge its primary functions. The tsar seemed to have squandered all the manly virtues—a prey to the wiles of his imperious German wife and the occult sway of the house wizard, Rasputin. Even sensible people spoke of the "dark forces" behind the throne. Affection was important to this ancien régime. When the people stopped loving the tsar, his days were numbered.[54] High society hinted of possible plots to get rid of him.[55] After all, two of the most successful reigns in Romanov history had followed in the wake of palace coups: that of Catherine the Great after the murder of her husband, Peter III, in 1762, and that of her grandson, Alexander I, after the murder of his father, Paul, in 1801.[56] This time, alas, there was no obvious successor.

With Nicholas installed at Stavka, out in Mogilev, Rasputin's influence grew. Following his advice, Alexandra convinced the tsar to replace the more independent and capable ministers with figures known for their "insignificance and servility," as Paléologue noted with regard to the appointment of Shtiurmer as prime minister in January 1916.[57] The rightward shift in the cabinet made the Duma deputies pine for the days of the stubborn but honorable Goremykin.[58] In March General Polivanov was replaced as minister of war by the lackluster General Dmitrii Shuvaev. Polivanov's willingness to work with the despised Duma had angered Alexandra. "Once again," commented Paléologue, "out of weakness, the emperor has sacrificed one of his best servants."[59]

Too little, too late: Nicholas had appeared, for the first time, at the Tauride Palace, to greet the opening of the Duma on February 9, 1916, realizing that some gesture toward the disgruntled public would stand him in good stead. His appearance was greeted by Sazonov and Polivanov as the start of "a new era." It infuriated the delegates on the Right (the Duma's in-house auto-opposition) and the empress. By July Foreign Minister Sazonov and Minister of War Polivanov were gone.[60] In departing, Sazonov was reported to have said: "It's the Emperor who rules, but it's the Empress who governs…under the influence of Rasputin. Alas! God help us!"[61]

Rasputin had also exercised his influence to gain control of the Holy Synod. Krivoshein, who had been ousted from office in October 1915, feared for the future. "The Holy Synod has never before sunk so low!" Paléologue heard him complain. The people were losing their faith, and the Orthodox Church was forfeiting their respect. A moment of danger would come, Krivoshein warned, when the monarchy would turn to the Church for support—to "find nothing was left of it. I, too, am beginning to believe that Rasputin is the Antichrist."[62] Paléologue revealed a streak of anti-Semitic paranoia, no doubt picking up gossip from those around him, when he decided the "miracle-working peasant," to whom Krivoshein attributed Satanic powers, was being manipulated by "a gang of Jewish financiers and degenerate speculators, Rubinshtein, Manus, etc." The empress did his bidding, "not suspecting she was working for Manus and Rubinshtein, who themselves are working for Germany."[63] Ignatii Manus and Dmitrii Rubinshtein were wealthy and influential St. Petersburg bankers who were formally charged with treason in spring and summer

1916. Until then, Rubinshtein had in fact been close to Rasputin. He also held stock in the anti-Semitic *Novoe vremia*, which is perhaps why Krivoshein had complained of the newspaper falling into the hands of "suspicious" people.[64]

Contradictions abounded. Appearances were damaging, bits of information became the kernel of rumors, conspiracy theories flourished. Paléologue was convinced that the "camarilla" around Alexandra was preparing to conclude a separate peace with Germany, extricating Russia from the alliance with democratic England and France.[65] A person at court told him that Rasputin and Shtiurmer were the pawns of a powerful "anonymous syndicate" composed of Baltic German nobles and ultra-reactionaries in high places, eager to take Russia out of the war and prevent revolution.[66] The ministers were accused of manufacturing shortages and inviting worker unrest as an excuse to crush the socialist parties and present themselves in a heroic light. Antiwar pamphlets circulating in the factories, people speculated, must be the work of the Germans or of the tsarist secret police, the Department for the Maintenance of Public Safety and Order (*Otdelenie po okhraneniiu obshchestvennoi bezopasnosti i poriadka*, or Okhrana for short), part of the Ministry of the Interior.[67]

When the Duma reopened on November 1, 1916, the mood was tense. Petrograd workers were striking. The loyalty of the Petrograd garrisons was unclear.[68] The recently appointed deputy minister of the interior, Aleksandr Protopopov, formerly deputy president of the Duma, was now said to be rallying monarchist mobs to stir up the Orthodox peasantry against liberals, intellectuals, and Jews, after which the ministers would move to dispense with the Duma altogether.[69] On the eve of the session, Nicholas heard from Shtiurmer that rumors of treason in high places would be echoed from the podium.[70] On the day itself, the ministers appeared only briefly before leaving the hall. Now both out of office, Krivoshein and Polivanov wrung their hands. "Without the active and friendly cooperation of the Duma," admitted Polivanov, "we cannot succeed in winning the war. It is therefore insane to claim to govern without the Duma. As for governing in opposition to it, I can't believe anyone dreams of this, because it would be the ultimate madness."[71]

The climax came when Pavel Miliukov rose from the floor to deliver the speech Shtiurmer had warned was coming.[72] "Poisonous suspicions," the Kadet leader noted, were circulating among the public with regard to the current government, the same rumors of treason and conspiracy

Paléologue had noted in his journal in the preceding weeks. The ministers willing to work with society had been removed from office. Those that remained, Shtiurmer at their head, were suspected of trying deliberately to arouse domestic discord, as an excuse to dismiss the Duma and conclude a separate peace with Germany. All this in the name of preventing social revolution, which they accused the whole of moderate society—the municipal and zemstvo unions, the War Industries Committees, the liberal organizations—of wanting to provoke by prolonging the war. The idée fixe of revolution, Miliukov declared, was what justified the current ministers' opposition to the war, to the Duma, to the Allies. They were incompetent as well as corrupt. Thanks to them, Russian troops had not reached the Romanian Front in time to achieve victory.

Most incendiary of all was Miliukov's charge that the disloyal ministers, together with Rasputin, formed a "court party" centered around the empress, a claim he cited in German from a German newspaper.[73] "What does it matter, in terms of the practical results," asked Miliukov, in what became his most notorious line, "whether in the present case we are dealing with stupidity or with treason?" In response to the Duma's efforts to organize support for the war, "the government insists that organization means revolution—is this stupidity or treason?" At each point in the speech he repeated the refrain "stupidity or treason?" and each time the deputies echoed "Treason!" Finally, from the Right benches someone called, "And your speech—is it stupidity or treason?" To which Miliukov replied, "My speech is a service to my country." In the end, the ambiguity fell away: "No, gentlemen," he concluded, "there has been too much stupidity.... It would be hard to blame this all on stupidity."[74]

Duma president Rodzianko removed the most egregious phrases from the official minutes and only reluctantly sent the cabinet the full text. The censor obliged the press to insert blank pages where the Duma minutes would usually have been, causing a sensation and whetting the public's appetite for more. Typewriters in government offices worked overtime and unofficial copies began to make the rounds, selling for high prices, discussed over and over again in private gatherings, the effect of Miliukov's words becoming all the more powerful for having been (unsuccessfully) repressed.[75] Prime Minister Shtiurmer, outraged by the speech, recommended the dissolution of the Duma and Miliukov's arrest, but only Protopopov, the minister of the interior, assented. Instead, to the deputies' surprise, Minister of War Shuvaev and Minister of the Navy Grigorovich appeared in the Duma pledging to work together in support of the war. Nine days after Miliukov's performance, Shtiurmer was dismissed. Protopopov remained in office, however, until February 1917, protected by Alexandra.[76]

Paléologue had one last look at the aging minister after his disgrace. As the ambassador drove along the Moika Canal, he noticed Shtiurmer "walking with difficulty against the wind and snow, his back bent, his eyes fixed on the ground, an expression of gloom and devastation on his face....As he stepped off the sidewalk to cross the embankment, he almost fell!"[77] A ghost from Andrei Bely's recent symbolist novel *Petersburg*—a dream evocation of the revolution of 1905, when the authority of old men had crumbled and strange new forces were in play.[78]

The list of figures in the treasonous "court party" invoked by Miliukov included Rasputin. A diabolic figure, even to those for whom demons were metaphoric, Rasputin, so close to the heart of power, provided an explanation for the feeling of helplessness increasingly taking hold, even in rational circles. Peasants were not alone in regarding the monarchy and the monarch as sacred; for those who still did, it made sense to think an evil power had him in thrall.[79] The fixation on Rasputin resonated broadly, moreover, with the cultural moment. At the turn of the twentieth century, intellectuals and artists, in Europe as well as in Russia, flirted with the powers of the unseen, with symbolic meanings and mystical connections, with theosophy and spiritual renewal. Russian thinkers spoke of the Antichrist with no hint of irony. Anti-Semitism was itself a form of occult thinking, imagining a conspiracy of powerful Jews pulling the strings of international diplomacy, funding the world powers, draining the vitality of innocent Christians, exercising supernatural control. Later, in exile in France, the best-selling writer known as Teffi evoked a dinner party she had attended with the philosopher Vasilii Rozanov for the purpose of seeing Rasputin close-up. The mystically inclined Rozanov kept pressing her to elicit some secret clue to the holy man's personality, but she herself was unimpressed. "The hysteria around the name of Rasputin was making me feel a kind of moral nausea," she recalled. Rozanov urged her to extract some kind of revelation, but Teffi remained cool, observing the adoration of the other ladies, but resisting Rasputin's attempt to draw her in. She did remember his parting words, however, or imagined with hindsight what they might have been—"If they kill Rasputin, it will be the end of Russia."[80]

Rasputin's very existence—his alleged sexual prowess, his alleged powers of persuasion and manipulation—thus reflected the "spirit of the times," as

the best-selling novelist Anastasiia Verbitskaia titled one of her sexually ris-
qué novels. The spirit of the times embraced sex, love, occult forces—things
deliciously threatening, unsettling, inexplicable. Now the spirit of the times
included war and the disarray of earthly powers, the dissipation of the
Empire's historic charisma—the empress's "neurotic hallucinations," the
tsar's pale and nervous countenance. Rumors depicted Alexandra as a whore,
a she-devil, the incarnation of evil.[81] Official images of the imperial ladies
dressed as nurses, the tsar's visits to the front—nothing restored their prestige. The very respectable Union of Zemstvos and Towns, in the last days of
1916, did not speak in metaphors when, in Paléologue's words, it declared
that the government "had become the tool of occult forces...and was leading Russia to ruin."[82]

Fear and hatred of Rasputin, despair for the outcome of the war and the
future of the Empire, united the political extremes. In late November, three
weeks after Miliukov's talk of "stupidity or treason," Vladimir Purishkevich
rose in the Duma and made a surprising statement of his own. The ardent
monarchist of strident anti-Semitic views, a long-time member of the Union
of the Russian People, who had founded his own Union of the Archangel
Michael in the same spirit, now denounced the incompetence and disunity
of the current government, which is to say, the new crop of ministers. He
accused them of impeding the war, of destroying the feeling of patriotism at
all levels of society. He also charged them with playing into the enemy's
hands. He attacked Protopopov by name, but he confessed, "Such people,
after all, are merely small fry.... The real trouble comes from those occult
powers and those influences which shove this or that individual into position."[83] This time he did not mean the Jews.

Again, words traveled. People quoted Purishkevich's plea for an end to
Rasputin: "All it takes is a reference from a Rasputin to elevate the most
abject creatures to the highest positions....Arise, gentlemen ministers! If you
are true patriots, go to Stavka, throw yourselves at the feet of the tsar, have
the courage to tell him that the domestic crisis cannot continue, that the
people's wrath is brewing, that revolution is looming, and that an ignorant
*muzhik* must no longer govern Russia!" The Council of State applauded the
tirade.[84] Purishkevich had called for political courage, not murder, but Prince
Feliks Iusupov invited Purishkevich to take action. Iusupov, who had been
military governor of Moscow during the riots of May 1915, now invited
Grand Duke Dmitrii Pavlovich, the tsar's first cousin (and said to have been
the prince's erstwhile lover), to join them. This was indeed the very last of

the Empire's palace coups, directed this time not at the sovereign himself but at a symbolic substitute.

The details were both scandalous and banal. The murder took place in the early morning of December 17, 1916, in the basement of the opulent Iusupov Palace on the Moika Canal.[85] The prince had made friendly overtures toward Rasputin in the weeks before the planned date, as a basis for inviting him to the palace for an evening party. The men gathered in the basement, where Rasputin was offered food laced with poison. When he rose to leave, seemingly unaffected, first Iusupov and then Purishkevich shot him point-blank. His body was transported in a waiting car and dumped under the ice of the frozen river, in hopes the current would carry it away. Police patrolmen had heard the gunfire, and the perpetrators admitted what they had done. News got out, and the press reported that Rasputin had died while attending a party. When the body was discovered two days later, an autopsy confirmed it had been shot three times. Purishkevich was left unpunished, Iusupov sent off to his family estates, and Grand Duke Dmitrii dispatched to serve in Persia. The investigation lasted until the fall of the monarchy, when Kerensky, the new minister of justice, called it off.[86]

The affair had the unreal quality not only of cheap melodrama but also of modernist decadence. Paléologue described Iusupov as a dilettante, "taken with perverse fantasies, literary images of vice and death," who in murdering Rasputin was following "a script by his favorite author, Oscar Wilde." At the Imperial Mariinskii Theater that evening, the ambassador reported, Elena Smirnova was dancing in Marius Petipa's *Sleeping Beauty* and everyone was discussing the news.[87] Purishkevich's version of the events was published in Paris in 1923, three years after his death from typhus in south Russia. In an introduction, Vasilii Maklakov described the memoir, falsely billed as a diary, as "wordy and incoherent," confused and mendacious, a reflection of the "social pathology" behind the murder and of "the confusion in the minds and conscience of people disoriented by what was happening in Russia" at the time. Nevertheless, Maklakov mused, "even conscious untruth can be characteristic and help one understand an era and its moods."[88]

1) Милюковъ П. Н. Министръ иностран. дѣлъ 2) Керенскій А. Ф. Министръ юстиціи 3) Терещенко М. В. Министръ Финансовъ 4) Некрасовъ Н. В. Министръ Путей Сообщенія 5) Коноваловъ А. И. Министръ торговли и промышленности 6) Шингаревъ А. И. Министръ земледѣлія 7) Годневъ И. В. Государственный контроль 8) Мануйловъ А. А. Министръ народн. просвѣщенія 9) Львовъ В. Н. Оберъ-прокуроръ Св. Синода. и 10) Набоковъ В. Д. Управляющій дѣлами Временнаго Правительства,

Provisional Government Ministers. M. K. Sokolovskii and I. N. Bozherianov, *Pervoe Pravitel'stvo svobodnoi Rossii i vystavka voiny* (Petrograd: Obshchestvo popecheniia o bespriiutnykh detiakh, 1917) [*The First Government of Free Russia and the Exhibition on the War* (Petrograd: Society for the Care of Homeless Children, 1917)]. Nicholas Murray Butler Library, Columbia University.

# PART III

## 1917: Contest for Control

# I

# Five Days That Shook
# the World

Like the 1905 Revolution, the revolution that began in February 1917 (March, by the European calendar) had a long fuse but a short, explosive trigger. As in 1905, the political concerns of the privileged elites were given impetus by a sudden surge of popular anger, though ideology was now much more important. In 1905 the socialist parties were just getting their feet wet; by 1917 they had broadened their influence in the factories and the army, exploiting the wartime economic crisis. The symbols and ideas of socialist revolution had had time, over the preceding decade, to penetrate the idiom of everyday life. Yet, as in 1905, the revolutionaries did not start the revolution. They had no direct role in the monarchy's fall.

The supreme authority was already in question, as we have seen, on the eve of 1914. Respectable citizens, such as Aleksandr Bublikov, an engineer and bureaucrat who was to play a small but crucial role in Russia's unfolding drama, expressed a common opinion when he wrote, a year into the revolution, that the monarchy "had not understood that to govern the country against its people was impossible." This was a government that "fought against everyone, feared everyone and everything, oppressed everyone and suffocated all that was young and fresh."[1] By summer 1915, it seemed to many that the challenge of the war, and more specifically, the unwise policies of the Army High Command, had begun to undermine the basis of empire. Looking back a decade later on what he called "the Russian catastrophe," Baron Boris Nol'de, an authority on international law attached to the Ministry of Foreign Affairs, blamed that year's Great Retreat for "destroying Russian military power" and, worse, for "producing the first great crack in the Russian mechanism of state."[2] Vasilii Maklakov believed Nicholas's departure for Stavka in Mogilev had set the disaster in motion.[3]

If respectable society faced a regime that restricted its room for maneuver, while seeming to have lost its own grip on power, it also feared the danger of popular anger, ready to explode as deference to authority eroded. Pavel Miliukov warned his Kadet colleagues, also in summer 1915, that "any carelessly thrown match may kindle a terrible fire. And God save us from seeing this fire. This would be not a revolution but a terrible Russian *riot*, senseless and pitiless. It would be an orgy of the mob."[4] In contrasting revolution, by which he had in mind a civilized challenge to the existing order, with the gathering storm of unbridled rage, Miliukov was citing the famous line from Alexander Pushkin's account of the eighteenth-century peasant revolt led by the Cossack Emelian Pugachev. But even that fearsome rebellion, in which manor houses were torched and their inhabitants slaughtered, had had a logic and coherence, perhaps not evident to its victims, but meaningful to those who comprised what Miliukov called the mob. The logic of 1917 involved purposeful as well as "senseless" violence and also new principles of order. The Miliukovs were challenged to define these principles and enforce them, to reconstitute authority on new grounds.

The combination of a general economic crisis, which the government was powerless to stem, and the legacy of collective militancy set the stage for worker radicalism in 1917. The readiness of workers to take to the streets in the capital cities, where the educated elites and the organs of state power were concentrated, struck at the nerve center of political authority. In confronting the forces of order, Petrograd workers were guided by traditions derived from the experience of 1905, which included the habit of self-organization and a set of symbols and rituals that continued to resonate in society at large. The red flag and the "Marseillaise" stood for vague notions of liberation and resistance to authority. In January 1917, workers struck to commemorate Bloody Sunday, as they had in 1916. They demonstrated in mid-February to welcome the reopening of the Duma. The gesture of support for the Duma had been organized by the Menshevik-oriented workers belonging to the Petrograd Central War Industries Committee, itself a legally constituted body. Their arrest prompted further protests. A strike for higher wages at the massive Putilov works provoked a lockout. Rumors circulated in the capital of an impending general strike that would likely escalate into a challenge to the entire political system.[5]

February 23 (March 8, NS), the day after Putilov shut down, was International Women's Day, a holiday invented by European Social Democrats in 1910 and then largely neglected. During the war, some Russian Social Democrats, including Leon Trotsky, had formed what they called the Interdistrict Group (*Mezhraiontsy*), hoping to unite the two competing factions. Together with some Bolshevik comrades, the group had decided to spread the word about Women's Day in Petrograd factories as part of their ongoing agitation. They were not intending to launch a revolt, but factory women had been striking and staging bread riots throughout the war, as we have seen, and did not need much inducement on this occasion.[6] The issue was food. Flour, sugar, bread were in short supply; the lines were long and often futile. As Paléologue observed, "Petrograd is short of bread and fuel; the people are suffering."[7] The same was true in the provinces.[8] The women in the large textile mills of the Vyborg district, across the Neva from the Winter Palace, now took the matter into their own hands. Thus, on February 23, they made the rounds of nearby metal plants, shouting "Bread!" and urging the men to join them. By noon, fifty thousand workers had left their benches, though most soon drifted back. A determined nucleus of about two thousand made the rounds of the large munitions plants, forcing the workers either to come out or go home. By the end of the day, most Vyborg factories had been affected. Some workers in the Petrograd district, behind the Peter-Paul Fortress, also struck.[9]

More serious than the strikes themselves were the protesters' attempts to reach the center of the city. Unable to get past the armed guards stationed on the Liteinyi Bridge, connecting the Vyborg side to the center, many simply walked across the frozen river. A group headed toward the Cathedral of Our Lady of Kazan on the upper end of Nevskii Avenue, another toward Znamenskaia Square at its lower end. Police prevented most of the demonstrators from reaching their goals. The square, dominated by an ungainly statue of Alexander III on horseback erected in 1909, was named after the church honoring Christ's entrance into Jerusalem.[10]

The chief of police of the Petrograd district in 1917 later remembered how "the dense crowds moved slowly and peacefully along the sidewalks, conversing animatedly and laughing. Around two o'clock you began to hear low-pitched, mournful chanting: Bread, Bread."[11] The tension soon exploded. Toward three o'clock, a large group, composed mostly of women and young people, was queuing for bread at the Filippov bakery on Nevskii. When told the day's supply was exhausted, they went on a rampage, tearing the place apart. Other shops were also looted when a band of young men made the rounds later in the evening. Policemen who tried to interfere were assaulted.[12]

In the Duma, which had resumed its session only a week before, the liberals blamed the government for letting the supply situation get out of hand. In the Vyborg district, Bolshevik activists, who had discouraged the demonstrations to begin with, now decided to call for a general strike.[13] Friday, February 24, the day after the Vyborg events, began with mass meetings in many of the largest factories, at which speakers from the various socialist parties, as well as the more articulate workers from the shop floor, called for an end to the war, an end to the autocracy, and of course bread. They urged their fellows to take their tools, pick up some rocks, and use them to smash whatever shops they passed along the way. The destination: Kazan Cathedral on Nevskii. A large crowd of perhaps forty thousand, drawn from the most important arms and metal-working plants in the Vyborg district, again headed for the Liteinyi Bridge, which was heavily guarded by a regiment of Cossacks. When ordered to charge, the regiment approached the crowd, but kept their sabers and whips in place.[14] When police blocked the bridge, the demonstrators walked across the frozen river, as others had the day before, until halted by troops and policemen on the opposite bank. Workers from the Petrograd district, now joined by students of various ages, approached the Troitskii Bridge, leading to the Admiralty at the head of Nevskii, across from the Winter Palace. Several were shot by policemen blocking their way. Crowds still on the other side of the river broke into food shops, clearing the shelves, taking the cash, and destroying the counters. Police who tried to stop them were pelted with bottles and rocks.[15] This was the same inchoate rage that had fueled the anti-German Moscow riots in 1915 and the periodic attacks on Jewish shopkeepers.

By the end of the morning, the massive crowd, many thousand strong, flooding into the center across the ice-bound river, had filled Nevskii and the other wide avenues. Rallies were held at both ends, in front of the Kazan Cathedral and on Znamenskaia Square. Nikolai Sukhanov, a Left Menshevik close to the Bolsheviks and later a chronicler of the revolution, described a mood of "extreme excitement" such as he had experienced during the Revolution of 1905: "The central districts looked like a continuous mass meeting." On Znamenskaia Square, "from the plinth of the statue of Alexander III, speakers of the Left parties spoke uninterruptedly and without any interference. The basic slogan was, as before, 'Down with the War', which together with the autocracy was interpreted as the source of all misfortunes and especially of the breakdown in supplies."[16] Bystanders and onlookers expressed their sympathy. When a detachment of trainees from the Volynskii Regiment arrived on the square, the crowd urged them not to fire, and their officers held them back. Shops and cafes closed early for the evening. By then the strike had affected almost 160,000 workers throughout the city.[17]

The strike movement and the demonstrations had developed a momentum of their own. Meanwhile, the socialist parties—Bolsheviks, Mensheviks, SRs, the Interdistrict Group—debated how to respond to unfolding events. The Duma deputies, for their part, continued to criticize the government's handling of the food crisis and its general incompetence. Alexander Kerensky demanded the creation of democratic institutions—as a way of controlling the passions unleashed on the streets. That evening, in an attempt to satisfy the Duma's demand for civic participation, the ministers transferred responsibility for food distribution in Petrograd to the City Duma. General Sergei Khabalov, commander of the Petrograd Military District, continued, however, to blame consumers for hoarding and refused to take steps to increase the supply of bread. Despite the rise in attacks on patrolmen during the second day of unrest, Khabalov failed to grasp the seriousness of the situation. Resorting to their usual strategies, the general and his staff focused on the arrest of radical agitators and summoned extra regiments from out of town.[18]

By Saturday, February 25, the strikers from the industrial districts had been joined by shop clerks, waiters, cooks, cabdrivers, and city employees. Students rushed from class to join the crowds. The profile recalled the broad solidarity of 1905. Streetcars were no longer running. Shops were closed. Newspapers had stopped appearing. The marchers were not silent. The air filled with strains of the "Marseillaise," the international hymn of revolution, mingled with the menacing refrains of the "Varshavianka." Created by anti-Russian Polish patriots after the uprising of 1863, provided with Russian words in 1897, and taken up by the Russian Left in 1905, the "Warsaw Anthem" struck a ruthless note: "Into bloody battle, holy and just, march, march, ye, working folk! Thrones drenched in the blood of the people will we redden with our enemies' blood!"[19]

In all this tumult, the ordinary police were nowhere to be seen. Any patrolmen slow to vanish were savaged by the crowds. Mounted police, who carried whips (the notorious *nagaika*) and used them, were now ruthlessly assaulted.[20] On one occasion, as the chief of police led his men through a crowd, he was knocked off his horse. The angry mob snatched his gun and shot him dead. In another incident, when a Guards officer at a striking metal factory on Vasilievskii Island, the district behind the university and the Stock Exchange, shot and killed a worker who had addressed him in rude language, his own men turned against him. Strikers used hand grenades and bombs, taken from arms factories and arsenals, to pick off individual gendarmes and policemen. Their aggression was encouraged by the hesitation of Cossacks and soldiers, torn between sympathy and obedience, who sometimes wavered or failed to intervene. When, in one incident, a mounted policeman struck a demonstrator with his saber, a Cossack attacked the policeman with his sword.[21]

That same Saturday evening at Stavka in Mogilev, Nicholas finally woke to the realization that a crisis was brewing. He telegraphed General Khabalov and ordered him to use force.[22] Khabalov threatened to punish strikers who did not return to work by sending them to the front; he warned that troops were ordered to direct gunfire at anyone gathered in the street. His proclamations were ignored.[23] The decision to use soldiers to fire at the crowds had the effect not of calming the unrest, but of forcing the troops to resolve their conflicted feelings. The strikes and demonstrations might have run their course. These orders drew the military into the maelstrom.[24]

By the next morning, Sunday, February 26, the authorities seemed to have recovered their nerve. Patrols blocked the bridges, isolating some districts. Soldiers were posted at factories, railroad stations, and intersections. An American, writing from Petrograd, described the scene on Nevskii: "You could not imagine a more brilliant and martial sight than the Cossack cavalrymen glittering in the sunlight."[25] The city was in fact well defended. Regiments were stationed strategically. Three were positioned north of the river—in the Vyborg and Petrograd districts and on Vasilevskii Island. Others clustered around key points in the center: the Pavlovskii Regiment between the Winter Palace and the nearby parade ground, the Field of Mars; the Lithuanians, Preobrazhenskii, Volynskii, and the Sixth Engineers (Sappers) between Liteinyi and the Tauride Palace, above Znamenskaia Square; the Semenovskii, Petrograd, and Izmailovskii below the Fontanka Canal; Cossacks on the Obvodnyi Canal. Altogether, the Petrograd garrison contained 180,000 soldiers; another 152,000 were stationed on the city outskirts.[26] The units were intended, when needed, to protect the regime against its own population. In 1905, for example, the Semenovskii had been dispatched to Moscow to suppress the December uprising. Nicholas counted on them now once again.

Khabalov followed the tsar's orders. Though the bridges were raised, people continued to cross on the ice. By early afternoon, the Nevskii had once again filled with crowds from the factory districts. They were startled, this time, when soldiers from the Semenovskii Regiment aimed directly into the crowd, killing several people. Elsewhere, on the Moika Canal and again on Znamenskaia Square, trainees from the Pavlovskii Regiment left dozens of dead and wounded, but the crowds kept reforming. Znamenskaia Square was the scene of confusion, as people pleaded with similar trainees from the Volynskii Regiment not to shoot. Encouraged by a sympathetic twenty-five-year-old sergeant, Timofei Kirpichnikov, the young men hesitated, but the commanding officer, a Major Lashkevich, gave the order to shoot and a lieutenant discharged his gun directly into the throng. The ensuing gunfire left a trail of civilian victims.[27] Khabalov's method seemed to have worked. Sukhanov remembered how the "corpses of innocent passers-by" on Nevskii Avenue had been cleared away, but rumors of what had happened "flew swiftly about the city. The inhabitants were terrorized, and in the central parts of the city the movement in the streets was quelled."[28]

The day's outcome was still uncertain, however. Patrols were occasionally disarmed by the crowds. "Single policemen had long since completely vanished," Sukhanov recalled. "Into every crowd and group an enormous number of soldiers' grey greatcoats had been 'organically assimilated.'" Grenadiers assembled on the Troitskii Bridge stood listening to revolutionary speeches and talking with the crowd, their officers helpless to intervene. The men "were obviously unsuitable material for any active operations," Sukhanov had observed. "For this detachment to take aim and open fire on the people it had been conversing with was unthinkable, and no one in the crowd believed for a moment that it was possible."[29]

The conflict between obedience and sympathy expressed itself vividly in the reaction of the Pavlovskii Regiment. A group of workers approached the barracks on the Field of Mars and reported the bloody events on Nevskii, where the Pavlovskii trainees had mowed down the crowd. The Fourth Company, led by a noncommissioned officer, decided to take action. Equipped with rifles from the company arsenal, they proceeded along the Ekaterininskii Canal (today the Griboedov Canal) in the direction of Nevskii. Along the way, they encountered a crowd of people gathered on the embankment just at the moment when police on the opposite side had opened fire, trying to disperse them. The soldiers returned fire, and the police retired. Having crossed the threshold of mutiny, the company returned to their barracks, but were disarmed and arrested. Sukhanov notes that "this historic incident…marked an abrupt break in the course of events."[30] The minister of war, General Mikhail Beliaev, appointed at the start of the year, proposed executing them all, but Khabalov realized the miscreants were too numerous to punish in this fashion. Instead, he had a handful of supposed ringleaders arrested. The two generals, seeming not to realize what the mutiny portended, concealed the incident from Nicholas at Stavka.[31]

Early that same Sunday morning, February 26, Minister of Agriculture Aleksandr Rittikh and Minister of Foreign Affairs Nikolai Pokrovskii, both in office only since November, met with representatives of the Duma, who continued to press for what they called a responsible government—which is to say, replacement of the current ministers. The cabinet responded by deciding to prorogue the Duma.[32] Meanwhile, though it was Sunday, delegates filled the halls of the Tauride Palace. Duma president Rodzianko appeared in the afternoon and reported on the meeting with the ministers, who had not yet informed him of their decision. Urged by the delegates to protest the shooting of demonstrators, Rodzianko telegraphed the tsar at Stavka, warning him that the situation was serious, that anarchy loomed. Popular unrest in Petrograd "had assumed explosive and threatening proportions." The bread shortage had spread panic. "The government authorities are completely paralyzed and powerless to restore order." The tsar must "save Russia" from "destruction and shame."[33] Having heard from generals Beliaev and Khabalov that Petrograd was under control, Nicholas ignored the warning. "That fat Rodzianko wrote me all kinds of nonsense," the tsar was heard to remark, "to which I will not even reply."[34] Back in the Tauride Palace, at 11 p.m. a group of deputies approached Rodzianko requesting a special Duma session. Rodzianko announced a meeting of the Duma's Council of Elders (*Sovet stareishin*) for noon the following day, to be followed by a "private meeting" two hours later.[35] That same evening, the night of February 26 to 27, Rodzianko received an imperial decree immediately dissolving the Duma. Not having heard from Nicholas, Rodzianko sent a second telegram. The dismissal of the Duma, he declared, had removed "the last bastion of order." "Civil war has broken out and is in full swing." If the movement reaches the army, he prophesied darkly, "the Germans will win and Russia will crumble, and the dynasty with it."[36]

That Monday, February 27, indeed, the old regime effectively crumbled. Nicholas, the supreme commander, was still on the throne but powerless to govern. The transition from popular discontent—the demonstrations and

strikes of thousands of factory workers—to the collapse of the state apparatus hinged on the psychology of the troops quartered in Petrograd. The
chain of events began with the Volynskii Regiment, stationed between the
Tauride Palace and Liteinyi Avenue, which linked the restless Vyborg district to the center. The training detachment that had fired on the crowd the
day before now felt remorse. They were willing therefore to listen to
Kirpichnikov when he again urged them to disobey orders to shoot. Excited
and nervous, the men warned their commanding officer, Major Lashkevich,
to make himself scarce, then shot him in the back as he turned to leave.
They had reached the point of no return.[37]

The spread of mutiny was not a peaceful process. It involved not only the
murder of figures of authority—whether commanding officers or policemen on patrol—but also mutual intimidation. The men who put themselves
beyond the pale had an interest in forcing others to join them. The Volynskii
mutineers proceeded therefore to the nearby barracks of the Preobrazhenskii
and Lithuanian Regiments and the Sixth Engineers. After a scuffle, they
seized the Preobrazhenskii arsenal, freed the prisoners in the stockade, and
murdered an officer. The Lithuanians emerged in a clamor of trumpets, rifle
shots, and shouting. The Preobrazhenskii barracks were surrounded by arsenals, arms factories, and the General Staff Academy, all of which now fell
into the soldiers' hands.[38] An officer was warned by his subordinate: "Your
honor, stay away, they'll kill you! The battalion commander has been murdered, a lieutenant...has been murdered, and several officers are lying near
the gate. The rest have fled."[39] Officers were also murdered at the Engineers'
barracks, after which the men streamed through the gates on the heels of
their marching band. By noon, four regiments had joined the rebellion.[40]

Meanwhile, workers on the Vyborg side, with no news of what was happening across the river, ransacked nearby armories, amassing weapons and
ammunition. They attacked police stations—the police had disappeared—
and the Finland Railway Station, where they overcame the guards and
plundered the weapons depot. As some workers tried to cross the Liteinyi
Bridge, they were targeted by trainees from the Moscow Regiment quartered in the district. The armed marchers fired back, killing the commander
and some of the men. Meanwhile, rebel soldiers crossing the bridge from the
center took some casualties but managed to pacify the Moscow ranks. The
crowd of workers and defiant troops then proceeded north to the Vyborg
side, red ribbons fluttering from bayonets. Following the lead of a Bolshevik
worker and a couple of SRs, a group turned toward the embankment, where

they liberated the inmates of the notorious Kresty penitentiary, to the amazement of the political prisoners and the joy of the actual criminals.[41]

Crime, as well as violence, now spiked. When regiments or detachments resisted, the armed multitudes stormed their barracks and forced them out. Surging throngs of armed workers and young men burned down police headquarters and mercilessly pummeled the odd patrolman unwise enough to have remained on the street. Later the crowd headed toward the Tauride Palace. On the way, they attacked the House of Detention on Shpalernaia Street, freeing more prisoners; they set fire to the Circuit Court, burning all its records (to the dismay of historians ever since); and they plundered the arsenal of the Main Artillery Administration, capturing thousands of rifles, revolvers, and pistols. Careening along Liteinyi Avenue in armored cars draped in red, they shot aimlessly into the air. Everyone in the street, it seemed, had some kind of weapon. Young boys fired exuberantly, endangering civilians foolish enough to venture out.[42]

That afternoon, Sukhanov was making his way on foot from the Petrograd district to the Tauride Palace. The scene was exciting, but menacing—the mixture of exaltation and unfocused aggression that characterized these three intoxicating days. "We met cars and lorries, in which soldiers, workers, students, and young women, some wearing arm-bands, were sitting or standing. God knows where all these came from, where they were rushing to, or with what purpose! But all these passengers were extremely excited, shouting and waving their arms, scarcely aware of what they were doing. Rifles were at the ready, and panicky shooting would have started on the least excuse."[43] Or, in the more eloquent words of the writer Viktor Shklovskii, another left-leaning intellectual, at the time attached to a reserve armored division: "Throughout the city rushed the muses and furies of the February revolution—trucks and automobiles piled high and spilling over with soldiers, not knowing where they were going. . . . They rushed around, circling and buzzing like bees. . . . The city resounded with crashes. . . . I was happy with these crowds. It was like Easter—a joyous, naïve, disorderly carnival paradise. . . . There were plenty of weapons. They went from hand to hand."[44]

By the end of the day, still February 27, almost all the troops garrisoned in the city had heeded the call—170,000 soldiers had mutinied. Once on the street, they went wild, resisting any kind of discipline or leadership. Their officers often retreated for fear of their lives or from a sense of futility. Unable to respond to the emergency, General Khabalov had no viable plan and visibly lost his nerve.[45] The police chief instructed his remaining officers to change clothes and go home. When caught in civilian disguise, they were sometimes executed on the spot. A few climbed onto the rooftops and shot down at the crowds, but the story of machine guns raining fire onto the streets is a legend.[46] A small number of soldiers at this point could still be counted on to obey, but their commanders issued senseless orders.[47]

General Khabalov was not the only one to lose his nerve and his grasp of reality. General Beliaev, the minister of war, had learned of the growing rebellion early that morning. The cabinet met on and off during the day at the private apartment of Prime Minister Prince Nikolai Golitsyn, just ending his second month in office. Not until afternoon did the ministers declare a state of martial law in the city, a useless gesture given the total disarray among police and gendarmes. Power in theory passed to the military command, but it had already lost its ability to maintain any kind of order.[48]

While events in Petrograd were spinning out of control, the group of Duma deputies constituting the Council of Elders met as agreed at noon in the Tauride Palace, where Rodzianko informed them of the decree dissolving the Duma. They proceeded nevertheless to endorse the call for an emergency session that afternoon.[49] They had taken the first steps in the direction of revolution.[50] At one o'clock, an hour after the Elders had assembled, a disciplined regiment led by its officers appeared at the Duma. By 2 p.m., when the general session began, the Tauride was entirely under the guard of revolutionary soldiers. Kerensky and the Menshevik deputy Nikolai Chkheidze gave speeches; the crowd and the soldiers entered the halls.[51] In this tense and fateful moment, the Elders debated what to do next. They were unsure whether the Duma could claim to represent the revolution or whether that was what they wanted it to do. They were unsure the people massed outside would accept them. They were unsure what form a new power might take.

For, indeed, power was the subject of discussion—how to replace the regime dissolving all around them. What was finally resolved at 5 p.m. was the formation of the "Provisional Committee of the Members of the State Duma for the Restoration of Order in the Capital and the Establishment of Relations with Public Organizations and Institutions" (*Vremennyi komitet Gosudarstvennoi dumy*). Even before the new year, in fact, some deputies had been plotting to engineer the tsar's removal, and Rodzianko did not hesitate, when the time came, to endorse the Duma Committee's assumption of authority.[52] The Duma Committee consisted of twelve deputies, including the Octobrist Rodzianko, the Kadet Miliukov, and socialists Kerensky and Chkheidze. It also included Duma deputy Colonel Boris Engel'gardt, who assumed command of the insurgent Petrograd garrison.[53] Engel'gardt played a key role in convincing the officers to support the Duma. By 11 that evening, Kerensky had taken the step of organizing a staff, which, with Rodzianko's endorsement, became the core of a Military Commission, which was decisive in consolidating military support and securing key buildings.[54] Notices were posted throughout the city announcing the Provisional Committee's formation, and telegrams were dispatched to the military command announcing the dissolution of the cabinet and pledging the Duma's full support for the continuation of the war.[55] As Vasilii Maklakov later put it, "From this moment the insurrection had a flag (the Duma) and an army (the Petrograd garrison). The flag inspired the country with confidence. The Duma put its past, its official position, the popularity it had acquired over the years at the service of the insurrection."[56]

The Provisional Duma Committee announced its formation around 5:30 in the evening. At 7 p.m., in the Mariinskii Palace, on St. Isaac's Square, the imperial cabinet met for the last time. The desperate ministers telegraphed Nicholas imploring him to dismiss Protopopov, the despised minister of the interior, negotiate with the Duma, and appoint a military dictator.[57] Without waiting for an answer, Golitsyn himself asked Protopopov to resign. Soon the rest of the cabinet also tendered their resignations, not long after Golitsyn had approved the decree dismissing the Duma, whose support might in fact have helped them stay the course.[58]

That evening, at Stavka in Mogilev, when Nicholas finally learned the true dimensions of the crisis in Petrograd, he demonstrated his characteristic inflexibility. Upon receiving the cabinet's resignation, he refused it. His brother, Grand Duke Mikhail Aleksandrovich, urged him to accede to Rodzianko's persistent demands for the appointment of ministers congenial to the Duma, in essence a constitutional monarchy, but he rejected the advice. Instead, he dispatched General Nikolai Ivanov to the capital with a contingent of supposedly reliable troops from the Northern Front and gave the general emergency powers as dictator of the Petrograd Military District.[59]

Grand Duke Mikhail had decided on the advice he offered Nicholas after meeting with Rodzianko and other Duma deputies in the Mariinskii Palace earlier that evening. They had appealed to him to endorse the transfer of power to the Duma, enabling it "to form a government with sufficient authority to calm the country." The Grand Duke said he lacked the power to do so, but he accompanied the Duma delegation into the cabinet meeting, where he urged Golitsyn to take that very action. Golitsyn informed him that the ministers had already resigned. Mikhail then declined the delegates' proposal that he himself replace Nicholas on the throne. All were anxious to conjure up a source of authority, at a moment when the supreme authority had ceased to function. When the delegates returned to the Duma at 10 p.m., they discovered that the Mariinskii Palace had been surrounded by rebel troops, trapping the ministers inside. While continuing to discuss the need for the Duma to "take executive power into its own hands," the deputies heard that the Preobrazhenskii Regiment had declared its support for the Duma. At 2 in the morning, now Tuesday, February 28, the Duma Committee declared itself the new government and ordered the arrest of the ministers.[60]

An hour earlier, Stavka had received a telegram from Khabalov revealing the true state of affairs. It was too late for any measures to be taken, and in any case the armed forces were no longer under anyone's control. The remaining handful of loyal soldiers was first directed to the Winter Palace, but the commandant there objected to their filthy appearance. Ordered back to the Admiralty, most slipped into their barracks, insulted and now unafraid. Not with a bang, but a whimper. Khabalov, Beliaev, and the cabinet ministers meekly awaited their fate. Apparently, a minister or two cowered under the table when the electricity failed. Meanwhile, the nighttime streets pulsated with red flags and the refrain of revolutionary songs.[61] The red cock had always been the symbol of arson and rebellion—the peasant's favorite weapon. Now the red of burning buildings mirrored the ribbons and banners bedecking the crowds, even in the darkness.

Along with the telegrams to the army, the Provisional Committee issued a proclamation informing the population of its decision to assume power, an act it described as an attempt to get control of the crisis. "Under the difficult conditions of internal collapse, caused by the policies of the old government, the Provisional Duma Committee has found itself obliged to take in hand the restoration of state and public order."[62] This statement has often been interpreted as an expression of reluctance. As Maklakov later put it, "against its will," the Duma, "had *submitted* to the movement, which erupted without it and in the end turned against it."[63] In fact, the Duma deputies were eager to assume control and establish their own authority, even if its nature was yet undefined. Authority was needed. Along with its proclamations, the Committee got to work, appointing commissars (its term) to man the various ministries.[64]

That morning, Duma deputy Aleksandr Bublikov recalled, "the street in front of the Tauride Palace was crammed with trucks overflowing with soldiers. It was impossible to get through the crowd. The Duma was the center of everything." Bublikov had prepared a telegram to be sent to railroad stations across the empire. Equipped with a couple of trucks, Bublikov had led "an eccentric army of soldiers from various units, without a single officer," to "launch an attack on the state power of Russia." An official at the Ministry of Transportation extended his hand and said, "Thank God! Finally! We were already expecting you yesterday."[65] Bublikov's message carried the news of the transfer of power to the farthest corners of the land. The old regime had been superseded.

Ministers, police chiefs, and officers had been lynched or had slunk away in fear and nervous prostration. Some ministers were hauled off by the crowd and taken to the Tauride Palace, where the notorious Ivan Shcheglovitov and Boris Shtiurmer were placed in confinement. To save his skin, Protopopov surrendered. The Duma Committee, under Kerensky's direction and with Rodzianko's approval, had started immediately to impose order, establishing a guard around the Tauride Palace, taking over key buildings and public functions, and trying to exert some control over the rash of arrests. The Committee sanctioned some of the arrests, reviewed and countermanded others, in effect, as historian Tsuyoshi Hasegawa puts it, acting "as a virtual revolutionary power."[66] Kerensky personally prevented the crowd from lynching Protopopov on the spot.[67] Shtiurmer died in the Peter-Paul Fortress at the end of the summer. Protopopov, Nikolai Maklakov, and Shcheglovitov were executed by the Bolsheviks in autumn 1918.[68]

The Duma thus acted in defiance of the lawful government, in the context of uncontrolled attacks on authority of all kinds. In the February turmoil, it was not unusual for commanding officers who tried to restrain their men to be murdered. The sailors on the Battleship *Aurora* killed their commander. The sailors at the Kronstadt naval base stabbed to death the base commander, among other officers killed or imprisoned. Altogether eighty officers in the Baltic Fleet may have been lynched in these early days. Rear Admiral Adrian Nepenin was shot in the back.[69] The Hotel Astoria had been requisitioned to house Allied officers and Russian officers on leave with their families. When a mob demanded that the Russian officers surrender, a general fired down at the street from an upper window. Releasing the foreigners and the families, the besiegers then trained their own machine guns on the hotel doors and stormed the lobby. Among the officers shot dead was the trigger-happy general. Other officers were arrested. The lobby was drenched in blood. The rebels broke into the wine cellar. Relatives escaping the siege took refuge in the nearby townhouse of the Nabokov family.[70]

The Tauride Palace stood at the center of the storm, a bulwark of the revolution, representing the diverse—and incompatible—interests united against the old regime. As the soldiers erupted triumphantly from their barracks into the streets flooded with young people, careening automobiles, and fluctuating eddies of Petrograders drawn by the spectacle, but also no doubt trying desperately to go about their daily lives on the perilous sidewalks, the agitated flood pooled around the Tauride Palace. As the right-wing deputy Vasilii Shul'gin put it, "the people hailed the Duma as a *symbol of the revolution*, but not from respect for the Duma itself."[71] The Duma was not merely a stronghold of the class enemy, but also an achievement of the previous revolution and a thorn in the autocrat's side. Indeed, at this moment of general turmoil and expectation, everyone with any experience of public life—respectable or subversive—was gathering inside the Tauride Palace. The right wing housed the Duma deputies and now the Duma Committee. This wing represented the so-called bourgeoisie, dressed in proper attire, uneasily borne aloft by the waves of the unwashed, pushed well beyond their political comfort zone. They owed their current opportunity to the popular groundswell, which now, at once, challenged their claim to power.

The Palace's left wing, by contrast, sheltered, according to Sukhanov, "the entire Socialist and radical intelligentsia of Petersburg."[72] They too were presented suddenly with the chance to realize their dreams, but felt threatened, no less than the Duma deputies, by the danger of complete social breakdown. As Sukhanov put it, "the armed, hungry, shelterless, terrorized, and ignorant masses of soldiery now represented no less a danger to the cause of the revolution than the organized forces of Tsarism."[73] The men in the left wing also wore jackets and ties. Unprepared for the scale of the disturbances, they had been gathering for the last four days in private apartments, telephoning back and forth to find out what was going on. They had not immediately grasped the fact that revolution was finally occurring.[74]

The idea of forming some sort of coordinating center for the spreading strikes had been circulating in the factories since the first demonstrations on February 23. The model was the Soviet of 1905. A group of Mensheviks, together with representatives from worker cooperatives and the Workers' Group of the War Industries Committee, attempted to create such a center, but were immediately arrested.[75] The imperial secret police, the Okhrana, was still on the job, even as the higher structures were crumbling. At 7 p.m. on Monday, February 27, after the Duma had announced the formation of the Provisional Committee, and while the ministers were holding their final meeting in the Mariinskii Palace, a group of Menshevik Duma deputies met in Room 13 (the budget office) of the Tauride Palace and created the Provisional Executive Committee of what was to be the Petrograd Soviet.[76] Among them were Chkheidze and Kerensky, simultaneously also members of the Duma Committee, and Sukhanov, the later memoirist. The Bolsheviks played no part in the proceedings.[77] There were no workers at this initial meeting. The two wings of the Tauride Palace and the two newborn institutions, the Duma Committee and the Soviet Executive Committee, represented the two strands of the revolution—reformist and radical, establishment and popular. Yet both were emanations of the Duma—in both cases Duma deputies took the lead in replacing the old power.[78]

The Soviet founders represented the moderate side of the socialist movement. The Bolsheviks were in exile or busy in the factories of the Vyborg district. The Mensheviks, who had pioneered the Soviet in 1905 and now revived it, constituted the "legal democracy"—organizers who had cooperated with liberal groups during the war, though representing worker interests.[79] The Executive Committee's first communication was an appeal, circulated by the newspaper of the Petrograd Journalists' Committee, the only newspaper then in print, inviting the workers to hold elections. Activists went from factory to factory spreading the call.

By 9 p.m., that same Monday, the delegates from the factories had assembled in the Tauride Palace. The hastily called elections had produced a majority favoring the Menshevik and SR parties; Bolshevik sympathizers did less well.[80] The proceedings were constantly interrupted by excited soldiers, eager to report the adherence of new units to the cause. This first meeting lasted for eight hours, until 5 a.m. on Tuesday morning. Leaders were elected, all of them socialist intellectuals, including Kerensky. Chkheidze was elected chair. Trotsky did not come on board until September, in time—as we shall see—to engineer the Soviet's self-destruction.[81] Kerensky's role, as a non-party socialist able convincingly to address the angry crowds, was key in these early days. In bridging the Soviet and the Duma Committee, he represented the attempt to build a united front of all the forces backing the Revolution, despite their obvious differences.[82]

Even the architects of the Soviet were divided on their goals. Some thought they were establishing the basis of a revolutionary government, an institution prepared to take power into its own hands. Others believed the Soviet must support the so-called bourgeoisie in its efforts to restore a semblance of order and therefore protect the revolution from possible assault by the remaining forces of the old regime. No one knew how much energy or loyalty was lurking in the country at large. Nicholas was, after all, still in place. From the perspective of the Tauride Palace, it seemed that only the respectable classes would be able to convince the officers to return to their posts, only the Duma delegates could rally the progressive elements of privileged society to the revolution's side, in the name of political reform and wartime patriotism.

As for the soldier masses, hungry, tired, and confused, as Sukhanov recalled the picture, "they huddled together in clusters, meandering around the hall like sheep without a shepherd, and filling up the Palace." The smell must have been overwhelming—"a reek of soldiers' boots and greatcoats."[83] As Nabokov recalled, "Soldiers, soldiers, and more soldiers, with tired, dull faces, seldom gay or smiling faces; everywhere were signs of an improvised camp, rubbish, straw; the air was thick like some kind of a dense fog, there was a smell of soldiers' boots, cloth, sweat."[84] The philosopher and then junior officer, Fedor Stepun, also recalled, in the same vein, "The heavy smell of sweat and cheap tobacco. Slippery under foot, dirty, floor covered with expectorated sunflower seeds and cigarette butts."[85]

Whether or not the Soviet aspired to be a government, the urgent tasks at hand were those of a government in the most immediate practical sense. A committee was charged with the task of finding food to feed the hungry soldier masses, to prevent them from indulging in riots and drunken mayhem. Representatives of the Soviet joined the Duma Committee's Military Commission, but the Soviet also created one of its own.[86] It contacted officers known to have socialist sympathies. Most who responded were noncoms. The men who staffed the Soviet committees were professionals—physicians, statisticians, in one case a colonel professing loyalty to the SR Party, currently employed in the library of the Military Academy of the General Staff.[87]

The Soviet, no less than the Duma, had an interest in halting the descent into chaos. The self-appointed people's spokesmen were not at the moment interested in deepening the crisis or inflaming social conflict. As the SR librarian-colonel put it, there were "crowds of unarmed soldiers roaming about the city, juveniles engaged in arson, and automobiles driven madly about the streets....We had neither artillery, nor machine guns; neither commanding officers, nor communications."[88] One solution was to form worker militias, an idea promoted by Menshevik leaders as a way to stabilize the situation.[89] The militias, like the Soviet, addressed the challenge of corralling the masses, which could only be done by involving them in the process.

On Tuesday morning, after a long night, the Soviet issued an appeal to the people of Petrograd and all Russia. "The old regime has reduced the country to ruin and the people to starvation," it declared. The battle was not yet won, however. The Soviet's goal was "to fight for the complete removal of the old government and the convening of a Constituent Assembly, elected by secret ballot, on a universal, equal, and direct franchise." The form of this "democratic" future government was as yet undetermined.[90] Soon over two thousand of these soldiers and workers crammed into the hall, constituting the Soviet as the locus of "the people's power." They milled about listening to speeches. Real business was conducted by the Executive Committee. Its tasks for the moment were anything but utopian and idealistic. They had more to do with reining in the unbridled impulses of the masses in whose name they spoke and bringing the mechanisms of daily life back into operation. Petrograd, even in revolution, was not Petrograd without telephones, street lights, and streetcars.

Symbolism was itself a potent force. The Soviet represented the power of democracy against the educated elite and against all manifestations of the social hierarchy. If an intellectual in coat and tie was able to hold his listeners' attention in the stuffy hall or on the public square, it was because he spoke from the left side of the Tauride Palace, supposedly on the people's behalf. When Sukhanov entered the Duma chamber on February 28, he watched as soldiers used their bayonets to rip to shreds the larger-than-life portrait of Nicholas II by Il'ia Repin that hung over the speaker's rostrum.[91] Before 1917 it had been a criminal offense to deface or insult any image of the emperor or the imperial family. This was political blasphemy, a popular black mass. It was also an ominous sign of the common people's attitude toward high culture. Repin was a shining light of the artistic elite, though also closely tied to privileged society, an alliance of culture and class power. Repin's career illustrated some of the paradoxes of late imperial society. In 1896 he painted the tsar; in 1903 he produced, on commission, an anniversary portrait of the State Council. In 1905 he celebrated the October Manifesto with a joyous canvas.

Less damaging to the cultural heritage, agitated crowds dragged the Romanov double-headed eagle from façades of buildings and the wrought-iron gates of the Winter Palace. Officers' epaulettes were unceremoniously ripped from their shoulders.[92] An orgy of iconoclasm accompanied the physical assault on men in uniforms. People would recall the anti-German Moscow riots of May 1915 and of course the sporadic anti-Jewish pogroms that usually punctuated moments of intensified social conflict. Now the mobs of exhilarated soldiers and striking workers, along with a smattering of common criminals newly released from jail, directed their aggression against social privilege, pillaging the urban residences of the wealthy and of course helping themselves to the contents of their wine cellars. Drunkenness only stoked the fires of class resentment.[93]

The primary challenge—and most pressing need—for both the Duma Committee and the Soviet Executive Committee was to get the genie back in the bottle. People in the streets were looking for a new authority—they gravitated toward the Tauride Palace and waited for instructions, but would not automatically obey. Though often inspired by men in the noncommissioned ranks, the soldiers directed their anger against their commanding officers, against the very principle of subordination and obedience. The Soviet Military Commission aimed to get the men back to their barracks, willing to follow orders—but from whom? Many career officers sought refuge in the Tauride Palace to escape the wrath of their own men. In the small hours of that momentous Tuesday morning, leaders on both sides acknowledged their common interest in restoring discipline among the runaway troops. The Soviet Executive Committee agreed to allow the Duma Committee to take charge of the Military Commission, hoping to entice the majority of career officers back to their posts. Indeed, many officers pledged their loyalty to the Duma, not only for purposes of self-protection but as a counterweight to more radical extremes.[94]

Cooperation was essential. The Duma moderates could not ignore the charisma of Soviet authority, while the Soviet needed the respectability provided by the Duma Committee. The alchemy of military authority depended on appealing to both sides: the mutinous ranks and their terrified and resentful commanders. The Revolution, which encompassed both the liberal dream of a self-governing political system and the radical dream of a people's state, needed to control the destructive force which had upended the old institutions and presented them with their chance at power. The first order of business for leaders at all levels in these first days, paradoxical as it may sound, concerned the reestablishment of public order. Order could only be established, however, under a new symbolic regime.

Rodzianko and Miliukov desperately tried to convince the soldiers to recognize the authority of the Duma Committee. Using the phrase for the first time, Miliukov insisted there could be no "dual power." Rodzianko finally issued a formal order to soldiers and officers, demanding the units return to barracks and submit to the authority of their commanders and the Duma Committee.[95] The Soviet Executive Committee appealed to the soldiers to obey the joint commission. Attractive as it may have been to career officers, the Duma Committee was not, however, in touch with the sentiments of their men. Fearing they would have their weapons confiscated or be punished for insubordination or even crimes, the soldiers had no interest in resuming their old roles; they demanded Rodzianko's arrest. The mass of Soviet deputies at that day's general meeting also denounced Rodzianko's order. Soviet leaders, committed to sustaining the joint Military Commission, tried to reassure them.[96]

That evening, the Duma Committee consolidated its authority further, incorporating the Military Commission into the reconstituted Ministry of War, now headed by Guchkov, the wealthy Octobrist entrepreneur and former Duma president. This move was calculated to inspire confidence in the officers, but had the opposite effect on the anxious and resentful soldiers—Guchkov became the target of an attempted assassination.[97] Rumors continued to circulate that officers intended to deprive the soldiers of their weapons. The rampaging troops were, after all, mutineers and sometimes also murderers. The process of self-organization among the ranks involved ridding themselves of officers they didn't like and electing new ones. Unpopular commanders continued to be shot or beaten to death. Agitators associated with the Left SRs and the Interdistrict Group were urging soldiers to defy their officers, heightening the already explosive mood.[98]

The two wings of the revolution thus spent Tuesday, February 28, trying, in their respective ways, to consolidate the revolution, to shore it up and prevent it from running wild. The threat of reversal was very real. Early that morning Nicholas had left Stavka to join Alexandra and the children in the imperial residence at Tsarskoe Selo, fourteen miles south of Petrograd. The direct rail line straight north from Mogilev, through Vitebsk and Dno, was reserved for General Ivanov's forces, so the tsar's train and that of his suite were diverted to a longer, more eastern route. There was no sign of disorder or disloyalty along the way, only the usual winter landscape, but bad news kept coming. At 5 p.m. Nicholas learned that the Duma deputies had formed some kind of committee; at 9 p.m. the railway stations received Bublikov's telegram confirming the fact.[99]

In Petrograd, meanwhile, the Duma Committee learned that Ivanov and his troops were on their way to the capital. The Committee feared that a

military assault might succeed in crushing the rebellion and with it the possibility of political change—and at the cost of terrible bloodshed. The
General Staff officers who had committed themselves to supporting the
Duma Military Committee informed Ivanov that the Petrograd garrison
had recognized the Committee's authority. Armed intervention would only
strengthen the hand of the radical Soviet, they warned, at the expense of the
moderate forces. In any case, the soldiers' movement could not be stopped
by bullets alone. As if to demonstrate their point, by the end of the day,
Tsarskoe Selo itself had been overtaken. The imperial palace remained
under armed guard, Alexandra and the children safe inside, but the town
echoed with the sounds of revolutionary songs and of shops being smashed
as waves of defiant soldiers filled the streets, pillaging as they went.[100]

The dynasty's future had not been resolved; the tsar was still a potential
menace. Rodzianko had obtained the support of three Grand Dukes in
drafting a manifesto establishing a constitutional monarchy with a responsible ministry. He continued to resist the pressure coming from the Duma
Committee, which was pressing for the tsar's abdication. Nicholas in fact
had been unable to proceed to Tsarskoe Selo, even by the alternate route,
after learning that the stations ahead were in the hands of insurgent soldiers.
These towns were not yet, in fact, in danger, but the Duma Committee was
happy to create that impression, hoping to delay the tsar's progress toward
Tsarskoe Selo and allow the deputies to solve the problem of what to do
about him.[101]

When the monarch eventually arrived at Pskov, headquarters of the
Northern Front, still 150 miles from his destination, it was 8 p.m. on
Wednesday, March 1. There was no ceremony to greet him.[102] By then representatives of the Duma Committee had arrived in Tsarskoe Selo and managed to calm the agitated throngs. By this time, also, General Mikhail
Alekseev at Stavka, with the tsar's endorsement, had cancelled Ivanov's military operation. Stavka welcomed the Duma Committee's assurance that it
had the situation in hand. Its decision to accept the Committee's mandate
was reinforced the next day, when it learned of rebellions in Moscow and
Kronstadt, as well as mutiny in the Baltic Fleet. Admiral Adrian Nepenin
had managed to reassure his men by recognizing the Duma Committee.[103]
Two days later, Nepenin reported that the Baltic Fleet "as a fighting unit no
longer exists." The day after that, the admiral was murdered.[104]

If a final argument were needed, garrisons along the railway lines connecting Petrograd with the front had begun to mutiny as well. A notably

vicious incident occurred on March 1 in the town of Luga, between Pskov and Tsarskoe Selo. The soldiers there arrested most of their officers, but singled out those with German names, including the commander, whom they bayoneted to death. The pattern of licensed brutality learned during the war—and encouraged by patriotic propaganda—thus easily adapted itself to the expression of new animosities. The Luga rebels also managed to attract the sympathy of some of Ivanov's men. These troops never reached the capital, but they took the experience of politically motivated insubordination back to the front when they returned.[105]

Indeed, it was not unusual for units sent to suppress mutiny to become insubordinate themselves. In self-defense, though possibly also from conviction, the remaining Luga officers formed a military commission loyal to the Duma Committee, convincing the troops that they had gone over to the revolution. General Nikolai Ruzskii, commander of the Northern Front, who had the added incentive of disliking General Ivanov, took the initiative in withholding support for the punitive expedition, whose mandate was in any case soon annulled. After Luga, Ivanov was replaced as commander of the Petrograd Military District by General Lavr Kornilov. By then, the political situation in the capital had altered.[106]

———————

On that same Wednesday, March 1, with the fate of the monarchy still hanging in the air, a turning point was reached in the relationship between the political leaders and the mass of mutinous soldiers on whose support the future of the revolution hung. As the Soviet opened its third plenary session in the Tauride Palace, the proceedings were interrupted when a group of soldiers insisted on answers to their pressing concerns: whom to obey—the Military Commission, now under the Duma Committee's authority, or the Petrograd Soviet? In particular, whether to comply with Rodzianko's order to return to barracks and submit to authority, and, more generally, how to define relations between officers and men under the new conditions? These were leaders drawn from the ranks, affiliated with the SR and Menshevik parties.[107] Finally, a resolution emerged. "The opinion of the Military Commission shall be recognized as long as it does not deviate from the opinion of the Soviet."[108] It was at this point that soldier deputies were added to the Soviet, which was renamed to acknowledge the military character of the revolt, becoming the Soviet of Worker and Soldier

Deputies.[109] It thus departed from the original concept of its socialist founders, who saw the Soviet as the headquarters of the Proletarian Revolution.

The soldiers agreed to surrender their weapons, not to the officers but to the regimental committees being formed by the lower ranks throughout the Petrograd garrison.[110] This "committee spirit" was key to both the workers' and the soldiers' movements. And these were indeed movements, even if they lacked a coherent ideology or formal leadership. It was the soldiers who had dealt the body blow to the old regime, which almost everyone was happy to be rid of. Yet the monarchy was still in place, and the question of the military's loyalty was therefore unresolved, despite the mutiny in the capital. Right now the enlisted men wanted a new kind of army. The Duma Committee may have hoped to reconstitute the old one, but the Soviet, for its part, had no choice but to accede to the pressure for change. Indeed, the Soviet leaders thought of themselves as helping shape a new kind of democratic army. Such an army would consolidate the common soldiers' support for the democratic cause, which in this case depended on cooperation with the politically cautious moderates in the Duma Committee. A complex situation, and one not immediately appealing to peasants in uniform, who feared they might be shot for resisting orders, old or new.

Obeying the Soviet's injunction to present themselves to the Military Commission, a group of soldiers requested that the Commission issue a proclamation depriving commanders of the right to control the distribution and possession of weapons. When Rodzianko and Guchkov refused to endorse their demands, the group, composed once again not of rank-and-file men, but of politically savvy soldiers or former workers now in uniform, returned to the Soviet. There they clustered around a table, while the lawyer Nikolai Sokolov, secretary of the Soviet Executive Committee, took dictation.[111]

This proclamation, based on the demands rejected by the Military Commission, was then endorsed by the Soviet general meeting. It was known as Order No. 1. When it was read out loud from the podium, a participant remembered, "The soldiers and the workers listened to the order in triumphant silence. To understand the revolutionary significance of this order, it was enough to see the faces of the soldiers. Thunderous voices of approval then spread throughout the stuffy, packed room of the Soviet."[112] The text of Order No. 1 was distributed in leaflets the next day, when it was also published in the Soviet newspaper, *Izvestiia* (*The News*). It stipulated that all military units were to elect committees of enlisted men, as well as delegates to the Soviet. In their political activity, the units were to follow the directives of their own committees and the Soviet; orders emanating from the Military Committee of the State Duma were to be respected only if they did not conflict with those of the Soviet. The soldier committees were to exercise control over the distribution of weapons, which were under no circumstances to be surrendered to officers. Soldiers were to observe military discipline when on duty but otherwise enjoy the same rights as civilians. Finally, officers were not to be addressed with traditional terms of deference and were to use the polite form of address toward their men.[113]

While the Soviet plenum was proceeding, the Soviet Executive Committee was meeting with the Duma Committee to define their mutual relations, unaware of the drama leading to Order No. 1.[114] The Duma Committee needed the Soviet's endorsement. The Soviet leaders were willing to negotiate with the representatives of propertied and privileged society, because they believed the time was not yet ripe for the next, socialist, stage of revolution and because they shared the Committee's interest in protecting the revolution against defenders of the old order. They disagreed among themselves, however, on how to define this relationship. The Bolsheviks, the Interdistrict Group, and the SR-Maximalists opposed cooperation altogether, urging the Soviet immediately to declare itself the "provisional revolutionary government," though what that might mean at this stage was unclear. The more cautious wanted to enter into a coalition with the Duma Committee. The majority agreed to support the formation of a provisional government based on the Duma Committee, without Soviet participation but with Soviet support.[115] This support would depend on a series of conditions, which largely overlapped with the wartime platform of the Progressive Bloc. The politically repressive nature of the autocracy guaranteed that the basic demands of establishment society would coincide with those articulated by the intelligentsia on behalf of the angry masses.

The Soviet Executive Committee had an urgent need for the Duma deputies to assume the responsibilities of government, but it could not offer unconditional support without alienating its own followers. At their joint meeting, the Soviet leaders presented a list of terms: amnesty for political and religious prisoners, the guarantee of civil liberties and various forms of popular self-government (militias instead of police, elected local administration, soldier committees and elected officers), and allowing the Petrograd garrison to keep its weapons and remain in the city. It further demanded an end to discrimination based on religion or nationality—always a key element in the liberals' own program. In a somewhat contradictory fashion, the Soviet demanded energetic steps toward the convocation of a Constituent Assembly elected on a democratic franchise, but also the immediate institution of a democratic republic.[116]

In the course of this testy meeting, Vasilii Shul'gin challenged the representatives of the Soviet, one of whom was Sukhanov: "If you feel you have the power, if you intend to govern Russia, if you agree to bear this terrible responsibility, then send us packing, arrest the Provisional Committee, arrest the State Duma, create a government and govern yourselves. But if you lack the nerve and desire to do this, then don't tie the hands of people who have the courage after all to shoulder the burden of governing Russia at such a time."[117] Negotiations continued.

Concessions were made. The Duma Committee objected to the election of officers, a point the Soviet soon conceded, though insisting on the issue of soldiers' rights. The Duma Committee also objected to the demand for a democratic republic, maintaining (as the Soviet did, too) that the final form of the new system should be determined by the anticipated Constituent Assembly. If the Soviet leaders were afraid to challenge the Duma and strike out on their own, the Duma deputies were afraid of abandoning the elements of state authority still remaining. Miliukov insisted on supporting Grand Duke Mikhail as regent, a proposition even Sukhanov did not reject under the circumstances. Both parties agreed to defer the question of the eventual form of government. Guchkov agreed not to mention the commitment to pursue the war to a victorious conclusion; the Soviet agreed to endorse the Duma's role as a provisional government.[118]

This agreement was the origin of the uneasy cohabitation known as Dual Power. But the spokesmen for the soldiers' and workers' revolt did not control their base. This tension was to complicate and eventually destroy the fragile balance. While the moderates on both sides were sealing their agreement on March 1, the soldier leaders down the hall were dictating Order No. 1. The next day, when the Soviet formalized the terms of its support for the Provisional Government, the proclamation stressed the conditional nature of Soviet cooperation—the famous "insofar as" (*postol'ko-poskol'ko*) stipulation.[119]

The Soviet later published an order modifying the conditions for the election of officers, but affirming the other provisions of Order No. 1.[120] It had no choice in the matter. General Alekseev later blamed this document for destroying the Imperial Army. In fact, whatever its long-term consequences,

the Order did succeed at first in reassuring and quieting the Petrograd garrison.[121] Its most important consequence, however, was to undermine the
authority of the Duma Committee.[122] At the same time, it also put pressure
on Soviet leaders, insisting they assume an authority they were reluctant to
accept, since they were committed to their alliance with that same committee. The Soviet and the Duma Committee, together with the City Duma,
also cooperated in establishing worker and citizen militias in the neighborhoods. These were intended to maintain order in the absence of the tsarist
police, which had vanished. In the factory districts, the militias were often
in the hands of workers. In all cases, they were armed. Ordinary people thus
responded to the collapse of existing institutions by creating new ones, but
the question of central authority, or government, was still unresolved.[123]

Before any further steps could be taken, however, the question of the
dynasty had to be settled. The Duma deputies had by now, Thursday, March 2,
accepted the need for Nicholas to step down in favor of his son, Aleksei, with
Grand Duke Mikhail as regent.[124] But legitimacy was still an issue. Who had
the right to decide anything? When Miliukov addressed the crowded
Catherine Hall in the Tauride Palace early that morning, he called for the
soldiers to submit to the authority of commanders who had accepted the
new principles of fair treatment embodied in the revolution. To challenges
from the audience, Miliukov replied, "I am asked: 'Who elected you?' Nobody
elected us, since if we had sat down to wait for an election by the people, we
could not have wrested the power from the hands of the enemy. While we
were arguing whom to elect, our enemy would have had time to organize
and to defeat both you and us. We were elected by the Russian Revolution."
Such arguments, coming from a liberal constitutionalist, were surprising.
Nor did they accord with what followed. When Miliukov announced that
Nicholas was expected to abdicate in favor of Grand Duke Mikhail as regent,
the audience was alarmed. The dynasty must go! Miliukov insisted a monarch was still needed until a new type of government could be democratically formed.[125] That evening, a group of officers frightened of the explosive
anger among the enlisted men, pleaded with Miliukov to renounce the government's support for the dynasty. Side-stepping the issue, Miliukov claimed
the troubling statements reflected merely his own personal views.[126]

In the end, it wasn't the crowd that dethroned Nicholas but the monarch
himself. At 9 p.m. that same day, Guchkov, the wealthy industrialist, and the
right-wing Duma deputy from Kiev, Vasilii Shul'gin, arrived in Pskov, delegated by the Duma Committee to urge the tsar to abdicate in favor of his

son, with Mikhail as regent.[127] The emissaries were unaware, however, that Rodzianko, acting on his own behalf, had already convinced General Ruzskii to pressure Nicholas into abdicating and that Nicholas had already accepted his fate the night before. Indeed, by this time all the front commanders, as well as Grand Duke Nikolai Nikolaevich, had agreed that Nicholas must abdicate to stop the army from further collapse.[128]

Since then, however, Nicholas had revised his decision: he would abdicate also on behalf of Aleksei, since he did not wish to be separated from his son. The emperor did not have the legal right to violate the laws of succession, but it was obvious he would have his way. Guchkov and Shul'gin, the two loyal monarchists representing the Duma Committee, which was not itself buttressed by any law, arrogated to themselves the right to "accept" the emperor's decision. Nicholas agreed to amend the announcement to include a pledge that the future holder of the imperial throne would adhere to whatever constitution emerged from the revolution that had placed him there. That same Thursday night, Nicholas left Pskov to return to Mogilev. News of the abdication reached Empress Alexandra in Tsarskoe Selo the next morning.[129] Before renouncing the throne, the tsar officially endorsed the formation of a new government, to be led by Prince Georgii L'vov, head of the Union of Zemstvos, who was also the Duma Committee's choice.[130] The Provisional Government thus found itself seeking approval both from the regime it had replaced and from the Soviet that threatened to succeed it—in other words, from both the ancien régime and the Revolution.

The next day, Friday, March 3, despite the protests, Miliukov visited Grand Duke Mikhail in his apartment on Millionnaia Street, next to the Winter Palace, and urged him to assume the throne. "If you decline, Your Highness, there will be ruin. Because Russia will lose its axis. The monarch is the axis, the sole axis of the country. Around what will the Russian masses rally? If you refuse there will be anarchy, chaos, bloodshed." Kerensky, who was also present, took the opposite line. "You will not save Russia by accepting the throne," he warned the Grand Duke. The anger of soldiers and workers was focused on the dynasty. "I appeal to Your Highness as a Russian to a Russian. I implore you in the name of Russia to make this sacrifice. If it is a sacrifice. Because I haven't the right to conceal the perils to which you will be personally exposed, should you decide to accept the throne. I cannot vouch for the life of Your Highness."[131]

Not surprisingly after this performance, Grand Duke Mikhail declined to put his life on the line. His statement included a plea to "all citizens of the

Russian State to pay allegiance to the Provisional Government, which has come into being at the initiative of the State Duma and which is endowed with full power, until such time as the Constituent Assembly, to be convened in as short a period as possible on the basis of a universal, direct, equal, and secret vote, by its decision on the form of government, expresses the will of the people."[132]

Despite the best efforts of the moderates and the Army High Command to preserve the edifice without the person, the dynasty had ended. The Soviet insisted that Nicholas be arrested; the Provisional Government was forced to concur, though it refused to send him to the Peter-Paul Fortress. There were no legal grounds for the emperor's detention, but no one, even at court, came to his defense.[133] The charisma of rule, diminished by the war, had by now vanished. The Kadet leader Vladimir Nabokov called Nicholas "an insignificant, hypocritical weakling." By now, he observed, "to be for the tsar meant to be against Russia."[134] The imperial family spent the summer under guard in Tsarskoe Selo, allegedly for their own protection, before being removed to the Siberian town of Tobolsk. Grand Duke Nikolai Nikolaevich, once the symbol of Russian military prowess, restored as commander in chief by Nicholas before he stepped down, was placed under house arrest in the Crimea.[135]

The Romanov dynasty had folded—in the course of one short week, less time than the ten days in the following October that soon "shook the world." The world was already shaken. People on all rungs of society greeted the February uprising and dynastic dissolution as the birth of a new era. Nabokov was not alone in thinking "that something great and sacred had occurred, that the people had cast off their chains, that despotism had collapsed." Together with Baron Nol'de, Nabokov had drafted Grand Duke Mikhail's statement relinquishing the throne.[136] Nabokov focused on the legal niceties, believing, like his fellow Kadets, that even in revolution legality must remain the supreme guiding principle. Having devoted his entire career to the cause of civil liberties and constitutional rule, Nabokov assumed an administrative role in the Provisional Government. It did not provide the expected satisfaction. Looking back on the period between March and October, he later recalled, "these six months were one continuous process of dying."[137]

# 2

# The War Continues

After a year and a half in which his sovereignty continuously eroded, the tsar had abandoned his post without much demur. His successors faced the monumental task of reconstituting authority at the center of government in the face of the crisis that was still in full swing. On the day Grand Duke Mikhail renounced the throne, the Duma Committee announced its formal reconstitution as the Provisional Government. Headed by Prince Georgii L'vov, the cabinet included the major personalities of the Progressive Bloc. Five of the principal figures were Kadets, including Pavel Miliukov as minister for foreign affairs. The Soviet Executive Committee had barred its members from joining them, but Alexander Kerensky eagerly assumed the post of minister of justice, after a dramatic performance before the full Soviet body, in which the crowd loudly acclaimed his choice.[1] Kerensky's theatrical style served him in good stead during the first months of the revolution, when the public and the populace yearned for the charismatic authority they had lost.[2] And everything in those first euphoric and frightening months seemed like a theatrical performance. Was this really happening? Was it real? Emotions were heightened.

March 3 was a key moment in the evolution of revolutionary power. Members of the Duma Committee had disagreed on how to make the transition. Duma president Mikhail Rodzianko wanted to retain the Duma as the new government's legislative arm, preserving a link with the former regime. Indeed, Rodzianko was seen by many people as the obvious new head of state. Surprisingly, given his last-ditch attempt to bring Mikhail to the throne, Miliukov believed, by contrast, that the Duma was tainted by association with the monarchy and that a break was needed. He did not want the new government to defer to the authority of the vestigial body. Kerensky, with one foot in the Soviet, endorsed Miliukov's position, thinking it would increase the government's dependence on the Soviet.[3]

Rejecting Rodzianko's model, the Provisional Government announced it was assuming the full power formerly exercised by the tsar. Unofficial Duma sessions continued into July; the Duma itself was formally dissolved in October. In practical terms, the break indeed meant deferring to the Soviet leadership, expecting the handful of activists to guarantee the new regime's popular support. As Order No. 1 demonstrated, this was an unrealistic hope, yet the basic principles of the new government reflected the need for a popular mandate, however insecure it actually was.[4] The program, as announced on March 3, reiterated the conditions imposed by the Soviet Executive Committee, though omitting any mention of a democratic republic. It affirmed the commitment to soldiers' rights, as outlined in Order No. 1, except for the election of officers.[5] It avoided the issues of war and the distribution of land, on which the Soviet and the Provisional Government disagreed.[6]

That same day, the now superseded Duma Committee published a statement signed by Rodzianko, addressed to the "Citizens of Russia," which announced the end of the "period of transition." The new government would do its best to maintain "order based on freedom" and save the country from military defeat and domestic collapse. "Citizens, excited by events in the capital, must first of all return to a peaceful life of work," Rodzianko exhorted. "The troops must similarly return to normal life."[7] The decisive break with the past had been taken, but the old regime had not yet been entirely swept away and the confusion was far from over.

---

Treated by the emperor with distrust and disdain since its creation, the Duma became a symbol of the people's government, despite its lopsided franchise, but when it seized the reins, it had only the experience of opposition to draw on. The Provisional Government inherited the shell, but lacked the attributes of power and authority. It had no ceremonial, ritual, or symbolic tradition—no costumes, medals, palaces, or charismatic center. The Tauride Palace, for all its imperial pedigree, was a modest structure. The symbols of revolution, dating from 1905, belonged to the socialist repertoire—the red flags and the "Marseillaise," often amended to suit the local idiom with the addition of "war on the vampire-tsar." These emblems were of course problematic for representatives of the liberal revolution, even for the moderate socialists, yet they provided a common language that could not be avoided or refused.[8]

It was Alexander Kerensky who in the early days supplied both symbolism and charisma. A man of unity and compromise bridging the two uneasily allied institutions, he managed at the same time to represent the non-party face of socialism as a generic ideal, while his oratory impressed the angry, distrustful crowds.[9] His volatile personality and theatrical bent suited the moment of constantly changing stage sets and continuously revised scripts, of fluid boundaries and shifting combinations, but he was vulnerable to the fluctuating mood of his fans, no less temperamental than he was. He was the matinee idol of the February Revolution. Offended by his vulgarity and disturbed by his success, liberals took their distance. Thus, Vladimir Nabokov later declared: "The idolization of Kerensky was a sign of some psychosis in Russian public opinion. This may be too mildly stated." He "had neither the merits nor the intellectual or moral qualities that would justify such hysterical and ecstatic attitudes."[10] At the time, however, Kerensky was recognized by a range of figures as the epitome of the Revolution, the central personality, the oracle and emblem of the combined forces of change.[11]

The Provisional Government suffered, of course, from its social profile—the bastion of the privileged upper crust (so-called census society, from the voting categories). The men laboring in the armaments factories and running the railways were loyal, insofar as they were loyal at all, not to the cabinet of industrialists, princes, and professors but to the shared symbols of the Revolution and, more particularly, to the ideologues of the workers' movement, the socialists at the head of the people's assembly, the Petrograd Soviet. The Soviet was itself unable to impose its will—if its intelligentsia leaders could indeed decide in which direction it should be heading. Neither the ministers nor the Soviet disposed of reliable means of enforcement; the tsarist police had vanished, the worker militias were difficult to control, and the soldiers, with the bit between their teeth, were uncertain in their loyalties.

Unauthorized as it was, the Provisional Government was formally recognized by the United States on March 22, and by England, France, and Italy two days later. The Entente was happy to be rid of an awkward ally. French ambassador Maurice Paléologue noted the shabby condition of the Mariinskii Palace, recently occupied by the State Council and now the seat of the Provisional Government, which had moved there on March 20, and the absence of ceremony, when he arrived to make the official presentation. Foreign Minister Miliukov assured the ambassadors of the new government's commitment to pursuing the war.[12] The position of the revolution's socialist leaders was less clear. Kerensky assured his French comrades that workers everywhere would oppose imperialism and strive for peace.[13] The question of foreign policy would indeed prove fatal to the Provisional Government, in more ways than one.

Meanwhile, the new rulers were forced to govern. Although the self-appointed cabinet hesitated to exercise powers it did not legally possess, it nevertheless enacted a series of important measures.[14] During its first month of existence, it removed all governors and vice-governors, replacing them with the chairmen of the local zemstvo boards. Not all the dismissed men were politically hostile or incompetent; not all the zemstvo chairmen were politically sympathetic or independent of the old regime. This was a largely symbolic gesture designed to satisfy the more radical impulses to the cabinet's left.[15] The same problem of personnel, political loyalty, and professional expertise was, of course, to plague the Bolsheviks when they faced an even more radical break with the past. In both instances, the practical demands of governance struggled with ideological and symbolic imperatives. The Bolsheviks were better than the liberals at making ideology an instrument of rule; destruction was also a fundamental aspect of their political project. Though hostile to the old regime, many liberals were more closely tied to the old social hierarchy.

Among its first measures, the Provisional Government restored the right to self-government enjoyed by the Russian-ruled Grand Duchy of Finland until being revoked in 1899. Taking Grand Duke Nikolai Nikolaevich's empty promise of August 1914 a step further, it granted independence to a future united Poland; since the Russian part of Poland was currently under foreign occupation, the decree had, however, little force.[16] In terms of domestic policy, the death penalty was abolished and courts-martial were limited to the area of the front, reducing the extensive authority formerly exercised by the Army High Command. All citizens, regardless of religion or nationality, became equal before the law. The Orthodox Church thereby lost its privileged position as the religion of state; Jews were no longer subject to discriminatory legislation. During the summer, the universal male suffrage established for elections to the Constituent Assembly was extended to include women. (Russian-ruled Finland had granted women the vote in local elections in 1907.)

On the pressing issues of land and food, the Provisional Government displayed greater caution. On the one hand, it created a state monopoly on grain, for purposes of requisitioning and price control. On the other hand, it warned the peasants who were helping themselves to the acreage they had long coveted not to take action until official measures were put in place. A land commission was established to gather information. The land question was to acquire urgency as winter gave way to spring and summer. For men committed to the principle of private property, it was difficult to resolve. The Petrograd Soviet meanwhile instituted the eight-hour day in the factories and endorsed the egalitarian relations between officers and men articulated in Order No. 1.[17]

Beyond Petrograd, the revolution occurred at different speeds and with varied levels of violence and conflict.[18] Dual Power did not occur everywhere. In many provincial centers, society was less polarized, and the professional and propertied classes were active in organizations, such as the City Dumas and zemstvos, that represented the public interest. Of course, these were highly unrepresentative bodies. In Moscow, for example, less than 1 percent of the city population was eligible to vote for the Duma, and only a third of them actually bothered to do so.[19] The Dumas naturally supported the Provisional Government, but they collaborated with the local soviets and trade unions. A broad public sphere to some extent transcended class divides. Improvised bodies emerged to deal with the economic crisis. Moderate socialists retained their popularity in some places well after October.[20] Cooperation or collaboration was the positive aspect of the provincial scene. Disorder, competing authority, or the collapse of authority was the negative result.[21] The major impulse after February was to wrest power from the center and vest responsibility for government and management in local society.[22]

Take, for example, the situation in the Urals. While Petrograd was in turmoil, uncertainty reigned. Just before the Provisional Government announced its existence, a local newspaper reported, "Rumors abound. The editorial offices are under siege. The telephone rings off the hook. Everyone asks: 'What's going on? A new cabinet? A Provisional Government? Is it true?' Orenburg today feels like a desert island. Rumors fly. Something, somewhere has happened, something very important, exactly what all thinking Russia has long yearned for and which will lead us to victory over the enemy. But is it true? Perhaps a canard, mere gossip, a provocation? The phone is silent, like a mysterious sphinx. They say telegrams have arrived, but are not delivered. Anything is possible."[23]

Anxiety was followed by euphoria—red flags, the "Marseillaise," Orthodox priests blessing the new "Russian state," soldiers and local notables marching side by side in the streets. The same "festival of freedom," with the ubiquitous slogans, "Long live free Russia! Victory behind the front means victory at the front! Liberty, equality, fraternity! Long live the democratic republic! Down with the dynasty!"[24] In the Urals, the old regime gave way not so much to Dual Power as to dispersed power, or, as historian Igor Narskii puts it, to no power at all. In place of the former provincial officials, numerous organizations sprang up, combining socialists and liberals, public activists with revolutionary agitators. Along with the zemstvos, local citizens formed "committees of public safety" and soviets.[25] The police were disbanded, prisoners freed, crime and pillaging spiked. Wine depots were a favorite target, although drunkenness was not yet the massive problem it would later become.[26] In short, the same two countervailing impulses were at work everywhere at all levels of the social hierarchy: the revelry of disorder and violence, breaking every former inhibition and bond, and the impulse to organize and gain control over the breakdown.

The revolution began in the factory districts and garrisons of the capital. In both cases, the excited mass of people were led to rebellion by the better-schooled and more politically aware among them—the skilled metal workers of the armaments plants, on the one hand, and the noncommissioned officers, on the other. Workers and soldiers intermingled on the staging ground of power—proceeding across the river from the Peter-Paul Fortress to the Winter Palace, and gravitating to the Duma in the Tauride Palace. The hardships of everyday life occasioned by the war, in proximity to the seat of government, politicized popular discontent behind the front.

Events in the capital also affected the soldiers fighting the war. Despite official efforts to block news of the rebellion from reaching the front, soldiers were constantly moving back and forth and the enemy was quick to spread the information. Behind the scenes, General Alekseev lent his support to the tsar's abdication in an attempt to keep the lid on at the front. In the days of uncertainty, officers feared the impact of rumors. Commanders were eager for an official announcement. Bublikov's telegram about the Provisional Government had arrived the day it was sent; a formal announcement of the dynasty's fate arrived only five days later, after Grand Duke Mikhail had made his final decision. When officers still hesitated to believe the news, Alekseev informed them: "The legal Provisional Government, in view of the manifesto of Grand Duke Mikhail Aleksandrovich, must be recognized by the field army, as only then will we avoid a civil war."[27]

The soldiers' reaction reflected the long months of rumors about the tsar and tsarina's German connections. Officers in general, though credited with patriotism, were suspected of monarchist sympathies; those with foreign names were suspected of being German agents, hence traitors. The men were particularly sensitive to symbolism. The old imperial hymn was a provocation, as were epaulettes and the tsar's personal symbol on the uniform;

regimental flags were suspect. Some officers wore red ribbons as camouflage. Almost all the front headquarters were affected. Order No. 1 reached the front the day after the abdication, followed by Order No. 2, confirming the elections of officers, which had of course already taken place. Stavka had not been consulted, so both orders were an affront to its authority. Alekseev begged Aleksandr Guchkov to intervene. The Provisional Government therefore issued Orders No. 114 and 115, affirming most of the provisions of Order No. 1 (polite address, end to useless formalities, the right to political activity), but asserting the primacy of its own authority.[28]

In fact, the worst violence did not occur at the front but along the railway lines and in urban garrisons. At the front, unpopular officers were arrested and replaced, but rarely murdered. There were problems with the new oath, which affirmed the soldiers' loyalty, no longer to the tsar, but now to "the Russian State and its present head, the Provisional Government." The word for state (*gosudarstvo*) was close to that for sovereign (*gosudar'*), leading some enlisted men to wonder what in fact had changed. Now required to sign the oath, some worried they were signing away their new freedom. One officer commented on the soldiers' perspective: "In their eyes, what has occurred is not a political but a social revolution, which in their opinion they have won and we have lost."[29]

This conflict was to deepen, but until the middle of April the situation at the front was relatively stable. The effect of Order No. 1 was to encourage the formation of soldier committees. These were created not by the common infantry man of peasant stock but by his cultural superiors: junior officers, clerks in the technical services, physicians of Jewish background, noncoms with a modicum of education. These leaders supported the Provisional Government's position on the war; even the Soviet in these early weeks took a so-called defensist stand, which it now interpreted as the army's duty to continue the fight in defense of the country's newfound freedom.

At first, General Alekseev objected that the committees and soldier soviets were bypassing Stavka's authority. He was reminded by Guchkov that the Provisional Government itself could not survive without the endorsement of the Petrograd Soviet, "which enjoys all the essential elements of real power, since the troops, the railroads, and post and telegraph are all in its hands. One can say flatly that the Provisional Government exists only so long as it is permitted by the Soviet. In particular, the War Ministry is able to issue only those directives that are not in essential conflict with positions taken by the Soviet."[30] Alekseev abandoned his attempt to prohibit the formation of committees, welcoming them instead, as a potential way of influencing the ranks. Most officers supported the Provisional Government and also the committees, which had their own reasons for wanting to have orders obeyed. They hoped to bridge the social chasm that now impeded their job, as it had once been its very foundation.

---

The soldiers had been encouraged in their patriotic duty by wartime propaganda, official and unofficial, directed at the Teutonic menace. Anti-German propaganda provided a language in which to express deeper unhappiness with the autocracy; the dynasty itself had been tainted by the xenophobic brush. The loss of Nicholas did not therefore invalidate the purposes of the war. For the first weeks after the monarchy collapsed, soldier committees accepted the Provisional Government as an improvement over the morally compromised old regime. By the end of March, however, they had begun to grasp the appeal of the Soviet position: continued support for the war, but on the basis of a different, more "democratic" vision, in which "peace" rather than "victory" occupied the central place. Despite the disruptive impact of Order No. 1 and the element of self-regulation introduced by the soldier committees, the change of government had not affected the fundamental experience of the front: ordinary soldiers were still dying in what seemed like a losing cause. The Soviet stance provided a step away from full endorsement of the war, without completely crossing the line.

  · The question of the war, as a matter of foreign policy, acquired a class coloration, however, that dramatized the differences between the Provisional Government and the Soviet. The international context shaped the terms in which these differences were expressed. In September 1915, a gathering of socialists in Zimmerwald, Switzerland, had called on the "Proletarians of Europe" to press for an end to the war and "peace without annexations or indemnities." In February 1916, Lenin had used the phrase "peace without annexations."[31] In an address to the United States Senate on January 22, 1917, that circulated throughout Europe, President Woodrow Wilson called for "peace without victory" and asserted that "every people should be left free to determine its own polity, its own way of development."[32] The day after becoming foreign minister, Miliukov affirmed the government's commitment to the Allied cause and to the goals articulated by the now defunct tsarist regime.[33] Ten days later, on March 14, the Petrograd Soviet stressed the resolve of democratic Russia to oppose the German invaders, "guns in our hands." The country "will not retreat before the bayonets of conquerors, and will not permit itself to be crushed by foreign military force." Pointedly, however, the Soviet rejected "the policy of conquest" pursued by Russia's "ruling classes" and called "the peoples of Europe to common, decisive action in favor of peace."[34]

On April 4, 1917 (March 22, OS), the United States entered the war. The next day, Miliukov, now on the defensive, published an interview in which he invoked the principle of self-determination to justify Russia's goal of "liberating the small nationalities" of the Hapsburg and Ottoman empires. Categorizing these ambitions not as "annexations" but as solutions to the nationality question, he nevertheless defended Russia's claim to ownership of the Turkish Straits. "The possession of the Straits is the protection of 'the doors to our home,'" he asserted, "and it is understandable that this protection should belong to us."[35] Miliukov was forced, however, under continuing pressure from the Soviet, to draft an official statement of his government's war aims that reflected the Soviet position. The statement, issued on March 27, asserted that "the aim of free Russia is not domination over other nations, or seizure of their national possessions, or forcible occupation of foreign territories, but the establishment of a stable peace on the basis of the self-determination of peoples." Higher principles demanded the Poles be released from their "shackles," he conceded, but "the Russian people will not permit their fatherland to emerge from this great struggle humiliated and sapped in its vital forces."[36]

The Soviet and the Provisional Government both continued to support the war, but the differences were important. Soviet leaders reaffirmed their earlier statement, urging "the peoples of the world" to work toward peace,[37] reasserting the contrast between "war to victory" and "war without annexations or indemnities."[38] The Provisional Government had been sending emissaries to the front to explain its position. The front committees, in turn, sent mixed delegations of officers and men to visit Petrograd. The delegates met with members of the government in the Mariinskii Palace. The change since February was dramatic. In the days of the State Council, Nabokov recalled, the Palace had been attended by "stately footmen mov[ing] silently about in embroidered liveries and white hose." It was now "invaded by crowds of disheveled and carelessly dressed people in jackets and blouses of the most proletarian kind. The grand and solemn ceremonial of days past was replaced by a vociferous bustle."[39] The soldier delegates also visited the Soviet in the Tauride Palace. They expressed strong support for the war,

going so far as to complain that Order No. 1 had undermined military discipline, and chastised the Petrograd workers still on strike for interfering with war
production. But they also came in contact with the mutinous garrisons and got
an earful of socialist jargon.[40] They returned to their units with greater sympathy
for the Soviet camp and growing suspicion of the "bourgeois" ministers.

The front committees had not abandoned their professional commitment
to the war. The slogan "Down with the War" was not yet popular in the capital. Back in the trenches, however, the defensist position—fight for the new
Russia—was no longer enough. The troops continued to refuse orders. They
continued to arrest unpopular officers. Taking the Soviet at its word and
expecting it to work for peace, they began refusing to fight. Socialist agitators
more radical than the Soviet encouraged a pacifist mood, a tendency the
Germans welcomed. The rate of desertion rose, and whole regiments refused
routine tasks such as repairing trenches. In mid-April, General Alekseev
reported to Guchkov: "The situation in the army grows worse every day."[41]
The commanders still relied on the committees to instill discipline in the
men, but the committees themselves had begun to lose credit.

───────────

The war was the central challenge. Responding to concerns expressed in the
British and French press, Miliukov once again stressed Russia's commitment
to the Allied cause. He also insisted on the validity of the original treaties,
which promised that Russia would secure its "vital interests," which is to say,
the acquisition of Constantinople and the Straits.[42] On April 18, he repeated
Russia's continuing commitment to "observe the obligations taken with
respect to our Allies."[43] While using the new language of democratic Russia
and endorsing the ultimate goal of peace, he made clear that "both the obligations and the rights that bind us to our Allies should be and shall be strictly
observed."[44] The April 18 note, which appeared in the newspapers, provoked
angry protests by workers and soldiers, who had by now absorbed the Soviet
position on war "without annexations or indemnities." Two days later, thousands of soldiers of the Finland Regiment surrounded the Mariinskii Palace,
demanding that Miliukov resign. Banners sported slogans associated at this
point with Bolshevik propaganda: "Down with the Provisional Government!"
"Down with the War!" "All Power to the Soviets!" Workers from the Vyborg,
Petrograd, and Vasilevskii Island districts were joined by an assortment of
urban types, milling about on Nevskii Avenue.[45]

The Soviet leaders had no interest, however, in destroying the Provisional Government. Blaming the demonstrations on Bolshevik agitation, they managed to calm the excited troops and reassure the Vyborg crowds. Similar demonstrations occurred in Moscow as well.[46] On April 21, when the streets of Petrograd filled once again, shots were fired on Nevskii, leaving dead and wounded on the pavement. Unwilling to assume power in their own name, Soviet leaders issued an order forbidding further demonstrations, except when organized by them.[47] General Kornilov, commander of the Petrograd Military District, had contemplated using troops to suppress the disturbances. The Soviet Executive Committee not only insisted he retract his orders, but announced publicly that all military orders must receive explicit Soviet endorsement. The indignant Kornilov resigned his command.[48]

Nabokov later wondered why his fellow liberals had not been quicker to realize the need to exit the war. This would, of course, have meant abandoning the Allies and negotiating with the German occupiers. Even Kerensky did not go that far. The Provisional Government was convinced that a democratic Russia would inspire the common soldier with renewed enthusiasm for the fight. If the Germans had wanted to disable their opponent by fostering revolution, they would learn to their chagrin that democratic Russia had gained in resolve. "I do not know," Nabokov commented in retrospect, "whether anyone really believed such twaddle, but I repeat, it was not only developed in the pages of newspapers, but also repeatedly and persistently formally declared."[49] In his view, the war had been "incompatible with those problems which the revolution raised inside the country and with the conditions under which the problems had to be resolved."[50]

At this point, not even the Bolsheviks had drawn what seemed later to be the obvious conclusions. In mid-March, the Bolshevik newspaper *Pravda* (*Truth*) attacked "secret diplomacy," but supported Russia's participation in the war. On April 3, however, Vladimir Lenin arrived at the Finland Station. Returning to the capital after a decade of European exile, he provided the force of personality and leadership hitherto lacking on the Left. Trotsky arrived in Petrograd a month later. He too had spent ten years in exile abroad, most recently in New York City, where he had been living in the Bronx. Lenin had traveled on a special "sealed" train authorized by the German authorities.[51] As Vasilii Maklakov later remarked, "the Germans did not conceal the fact that they had injected Lenin into Russia as one might inject a poisonous germ."[52] A German diplomat in Moscow in 1918 reflected ruefully that the pro-Entente policy of the Provisional Government had prompted the Germans to "employ Beelzebub, the Devil's boss, to drive out the Devil."[53] Lenin may ultimately have served the Germans' purposes, but he was never their tool. Nor did his arrival cause the Provisional Government to crumble. In April his extreme views were premature, even in his own party. His confounding speeches, philosopher Fedor Stepun observed, "were not speeches but sails to catch the crazed winds of the revolution."[54]

Lenin's arrival, though not immediately decisive, was nevertheless a political turning point and a moment of high drama. Local Bolshevik organizers, with a flair for the ritual occasion, had mobilized a swarm of soldiers, sailors, and workers to meet the train at the Finland Station, situated on the Vyborg side across the river from the Tauride Palace.[55] The scene that later became an icon of Socialist Realism anticipated in real life the later Stalinist aesthetic. As Nikolai Sukhanov remembered that evening, "The throng in front of the Finland Station blocked the whole square, making movement almost impossible and scarcely letting the trams through. The innumerable red flags were dominated by a magnificent banner embroidered in gold: 'The Central Committee of the R.S.-D.W.P. (Bolsheviks)'. Troops with marching bands were drawn up under the red flags near the side entrance, in the former imperial waiting-rooms. There was a throbbing of many motor cars. In two or three places the awe-inspiring outlines of armored cars thrust up from the crowd."[56] Inside, "Banners hung across the platform at every step; triumphal arches had been set up, adorned with red and gold; one's eyes were dazzled by every possible welcoming inscription and revolutionary slogan, while at the end of the platform, where the carriage was expected to stop, there was a band, and a group of representatives of the central Bolshevik organizations stood holding flowers." When the train finally arrived, "A thunderous *Marseillaise* boomed forth on the platform, and shouts of welcome rang out."[57]

Also in attendance at this spectacle were representatives of the Soviet Executive Committee. The Menshevik Nikolai Chkheidze said a few words inviting the Bolshevik leader to work together with the other socialist parties.[58] Lenin, an inveterate monopolist of authority, was, of course, not interested in cooperation. Turning to the crowd, he announced that the time for socialism had come, if perhaps ahead of schedule. "The worldwide Socialist revolution has already dawned…Germany is seething…Any day now the whole of European capitalism may crash. The Russian revolution accomplished by you has prepared the way and opened a new epoch. Long live the worldwide Socialist revolution!"[59] This was a new and daring "voice from outside."

"Suddenly," Sukhanov recalled, "before the eyes of all of us, completely swallowed up by the routine drudgery of the revolution, there was presented a bright, blinding, exotic beacon, obliterating everything we 'lived by.'"[60]

All the way from the station, across the Sampsonievskii Bridge to the mansion of the prima ballerina Matilda Kshesinskaia (Matylda Krzesińska) on the Petrograd side, which had become Bolshevik headquarters, Lenin stopped at every intersection to give a speech. Hurling invective at the "cap-italist pirates" responsible for the war, Lenin made his listeners' "heads spin" with his daring rhetoric. Popular sentiment had not yet completely broken with the war; the socialist intelligentsia was still committed to working with the Provisional Government. Lenin's ideas were a shock, but shock tactics were his trademark. He was not a dramatic speaker, but an authoritative one. In Sukhanov's words, he was "an orator of enormous impact and power, breaking down complicated systems into the simplest and most generally accessible elements, and hammering, hammering, hammering them into the heads of his audience until he took them captive."[61]

In the small hours of the next morning, Lenin brought his relentless style to bear on the Bolshevik activists assembled in Kshesinskaia's mansion. There he articulated what became known as his April Theses. To the shock of his comrades, he denounced the Provisional Government as well as the defensist position on the war espoused by the moderate Soviet leaders, who believed the defeat of Germany was necessary to the revolution. His language was, as usual, contemptuous and aggressive, but even stripped of jargon, his arguments had a compelling ring. Even under Russia's new government, he insisted, the war "remains a predatory imperialistic war" and therefore "not the least concessions to 'revolutionary defensivism' are permissible." The advocates of this position have been "deceived by the bourgeoisie," and must be enlightened: "without the overthrow of capital it is impossible to end the War with a truly democratic and not an annexationist peace."[62] Whether or not the liberals were "agents of capital" or the SRs "petty-bourgeois oppor-tunists," as their Marxist confrères disdainfully charged, none were in fact able to extricate themselves from their commitment to the war, annexationist or otherwise. And the war was crucial to their own survival.

---

On the question of the revolution's ultimate purposes, Lenin envisaged the future socialist state not as a parliamentary democracy but as a republic of soviets, resting on the power of the armed people, which would nationalize the land and institute social equality.[63] Lenin's vision of the soviets as the principal organs of power did not, of course, refer to the currently existing bodies, whose leaders and policies he disparaged. The April Theses were only the first move in a strategy to divest those leaders of their symbolic authority. At a meeting convened the day after Lenin's arrival in an attempt to unify the various Social Democratic parties, Lenin struck a dissonant note. He was, as Sukhanov put it, "the living incarnation of schism."[64] Even his own lieutenants were at first uncomfortable with his extreme position, but by the end of the month the April Theses had been adopted as party policy.[65] As the newspaperman and historian William Henry Chamberlin observed, "Into the formless and inchoate mass which Russian society represented in the first weeks of the Revolution Lenin's sharp, bitter words cut like a knife, revealing and inspiring class antagonism and class hatred. The revolutionary honeymoon when any orator could elicit the applause of almost any crowd was coming to an end. The epoch of clearcut class struggle was approaching."[66] Whether class struggle was ever clear-cut during the revolution is another matter, but it was Lenin's intention to make it seem so. This was not the work of one or two weeks, however. Animosity existed at the grass roots— resentment of hierarchy and authority, and anger at the unequal sacrifices demanded by the war in terms of hunger, suffering, and death. But for the Bolsheviks to turn class warfare into an instrument of political power took the rest of the spring and summer. The conditions for their success were prepared largely by the decisions of their political rivals, though the Bolsheviks made the best of the chances they got.

The immediate impact of Lenin's arrival, however, was to damage his own party. The general press branded him a German agent. The Baltic sailors who had welcomed his return now denounced him; hostile crowds gathered around Kshesinskaia's mansion, others marched through the streets demanding his arrest. In honorable, but naive, comradely fashion, the Menshevik-edited Soviet newspaper, *Izvestiia*, defended his honor, but a demonstration of wounded soldiers proceeding laboriously toward the Tauride Palace proclaimed their dedication to victory, their hatred of the Germans, and their anger at the traitor Lenin.[67] It was easy, as Sukhanov did, to blame the slurs on "provocateurs" and the "capitalist bourgeoisie," but the willingness to blame Germans, both actual and fictive, for all sorts of ills was by now a deeply ingrained habit.

The Bolsheviks in early April proved that they were capable of orchestrating a dramatic welcome at the Finland Station, but they were in no position to implement Lenin's seemingly unrealistic ideas, even if they had been willing to embrace them. Tainted by accusations of treason, they remained on the margins of political life. It turned out, however, that the margins were a good place to be. Those at the center of authority, tenuous as it was, were in the process of exhausting their political credit. Both partners to Dual Power were vulnerable to pressure from below, and in this case the balance tipped in the Soviet direction. The Soviet emerged from the crisis with its authority enhanced, but its leaders were themselves not ready to abandon the war. Nor were they ready to dispense with their bourgeois partners. Instead, they abandoned their earlier objection to closer cooperation. Kerensky, already in the cabinet, pressured fellow socialists to join him. The Provisional Government welcomed the support, and a conference of the Petrograd garrison endorsed the idea. The Mensheviks hesitated, however, for fear that association with the government and failure to satisfy the expectations of the popular base would strengthen "the maximalist sentiments of the masses," in the words of Irakli Tsereteli, head of the Soviet Presidium and its most influential figure.[68] It was only on May 1, when Guchkov stepped down as minister of war, that the Soviet Executive Committee voted to join the cabinet, creating the First Coalition.[69] The following day, Miliukov tendered his resignation, not only on the issue of the April 18 note but to protest the coalition.[70]

The new cabinet, still headed by Prince L'vov, included six socialists (mostly Mensheviks and SRs) and ten "capitalist" ministers.[71] Guchkov was replaced as minister of war by Kerensky, moving from the ministry of justice; the discredited Miliukov was replaced as foreign minister by the politically independent sugar magnate Mikhail Tereshchenko, moving from finance.[72] Despite his anxieties, Tsereteli entered the cabinet as minister of post and telegraph, along with one other Menshevik, Matvei Skobelev, as minister of labor.[73] The coalition was dominated, on the left, by the SR Party (in the key positions of war, justice, and agriculture). Kadets held transport, finance, and education.[74]

From the perspective of doctrinaire Marxists, the arrangement signaled the consolidation of "bourgeois" interests, in all their rainbow hues: from major industrialists and professors to peasant-soldiers, actual peasants, shopkeepers, and low-ranking bureaucrats. The government now also reflected the interests, as Sukhanov put it, of "the great mass of the indigent intelligentsia and all the unthinking ordinary people and odds and ends who had been stirred and shaken up by recent events."[75] The "petty-bourgeois democracy," as he called it, having renounced its independence, had doomed itself to the capitalist fate.

———————

Kerensky, now as minister of war, was responsible for managing the biggest challenge to any successor of the autocratic regime. The Provisional Government had fallen on the question of war aims. The coalition therefore hurried to define its position. Affirming the basic premises of the Provisional Government's earlier declaration, it rejected a separate peace and pledged to pursue the war against the Central Powers while working for a general peace without territorial gains or postwar indemnities, on the Wilsonian model.[76] "The strengthening of the foundations of the democratic army, and the organization and strengthening of its fighting force for offensive as well as defensive operations, will be the chief task of the Provisional Government."[77] The Menshevik Conference that convened in Petrograd in May endorsed the coalition, a position reflecting the moderate wing of the party. When Pavel Aksel'rod and Iulii Martov, the party's intellectual stars, returned from European exile (like Lenin, also on a "sealed train," though with less fanfare), they were dismayed to find their internationalist position superseded.[78]

It was one thing to announce support for the war; it was another thing to fight it. In mid-April the French and British had launched a major offensive, which failed in its objective and resulted in massive casualties, provoking widespread mutiny in the French army. When pressed by the French to provide support with an offensive in the East, Alekseev had objected in March that the Russian army was in no shape to fight. The front commanders journeyed to Petrograd in a spirit of protest but arrived in time to find socialists in the cabinet and therefore committed to pursuit of the war, if only, as the Soviet kept insisting, for the purpose of "the earliest possible attainment of a universal peace."[79] Now Alekseev changed his mind and with the backing of Generals Aleksei Brusilov and Vasilii Gurko, who wished to retain the confidence of the Allies, pressed for an offensive.[80] The plan was to bring three Russian armies, from the Northern, Western, Southwest, and Romanian Fronts, to bear on the German and Austro-Hungarian forces in Galicia.[81] The hope was to force the Germans to their knees before the Imperial Army could deteriorate further, thus preventing its defeat and blocking the

possibility of German penetration into Russia and perhaps also the restoration of the old regime.[82]

Kerensky's role in promoting the offensive was decisive. His amphibious
position, between the "democratic" Soviet and the "bourgeois" government
(no longer entirely "bourgeois"), which so irritated his colleagues on the left
and inspired the liberals' disdain, allowed him to withstand pressure from the
Soviet without losing his revolutionary credentials.[83] On May 11, he issued
the Declaration of Soldiers' Rights, a document drafted earlier by the Soviet,
which had been resisted by Guchkov. The final version reiterated the basic
principles of Order No. 1, but reinforced the authority of officers. It confirmed the responsibility of the army committees to manage practical affairs,
but reserved for commanders the right to discipline officers and enforce obedience in the field.[84] The Soviet supported the Declaration, against objections
from the Bolshevik Left, as an expression of popular sentiment and a "firm
basis for the democratization of the Army."[85]

Reinforcing the message, Kerensky dispatched commissars to the front to
instruct the troops in their duty as soldiers of the democracy. He himself was
dubbed "the persuader-in-chief."[86] The principles of mutual respect, cooperation by consent, equality of civil status—keys to the soldier deputies'
understanding of what the revolution could do for them—were of course
fatal to the military as an institution, as the Bolsheviks were to discover when
they found themselves at the helm. The fact that soldiers needed to be persuaded was itself a problem. Summoning troops to the offensive, Kerensky
exhorted: "In the name of the salvation of free Russia, you will go where
your commanders and your Government send you. On your bayonet-points
you will be bearing peace, truth, and justice. You will go forward in serried
ranks, kept firm by the discipline of your duty and your supreme love for the
revolution and your country."[87]

Kerensky was the personal messenger of war—and here his personality
counted. Now, in May, he embarked on a three-week tour of the front,
where he was greeted enthusiastically by the front committees, themselves
intent on asserting their authority. The ranks, by contrast, were holding their
own meetings, ignoring the committees and deaf to Kerensky's appeal.[88]
Congresses were being held all over the front—the ubiquitous mechanism of
revolution: self-organization, endless debate, a sense of solidarity—but also
frustration with the endless talk and absence of authority. The congresses in
turn elected delegates to the forthcoming All-Russian Congress of Soviets,
scheduled to open in Petrograd in early June.[89]

At this point, late May, the odd Bolshevik agitator was disregarded. General Brusilov, the new commander in chief, accompanied Kerensky on his rounds. At each stop, the General asked: "Can I promise the war minister that you will do your duty to the end, and if I order you to attack, you will attack?"[90] Under the circumstances the question was not rhetorical. No commander in chief should have to ask it. Yet Kerensky's performance succeeded. The committees, composed of literate men with political affiliations who had backed the Soviet call for peace in April, now threw their weight behind the new, revolutionary offensive.[91] These men had no trouble with the eclectic slogan: "For Holy Russia, for the Army, for its chief, Citizen-Teacher Kerensky—Hurrah!"[92]

The month of June was characterized by strenuous efforts on the part of social leaders, at different levels and with different political ambitions, to get a handle on the spiraling violence. As Sukhanov recalled, "Lynch-law, the destruction of houses and shops, jeering at and attacks on officers, provincial authorities, or private persons, unauthorized arrests, seizures, and beatings-up—were recorded every day by tens and hundreds."[93] The troops were central to the problem. In the cities, the garrisons lost the last shred of discipline. Front soldiers deserted in ever greater numbers, heading back home to take part in the dismemberment of landed estates, indulging along the way in "drunkenness, rowdiness, and disorder."[94] The men over forty, who had been drafted to replenish the ranks, now marched in protest on Nevskii Avenue, with signs that complained, "no one is working the land," "our families are starving." They appeared at the Mariinskii Palace demanding to be demobilized.[95] This contingent was clearly better organized—more disciplined—than the men who merely hopped the overcrowded trains back to their home villages. "All over the country," recalled Sukhanov, "disorders, anarchy, seizures, violence, and 'republics' still continued; people took the law into their own hands, soldiers mutinied, and regiments disbanded."[96]

The effort to establish authority over the escalating disorder—Pushkin's "pitiless Russian riot" against which Miliukov had warned—came from two quarters, the vestigial sites of Dual Power. On the one hand, from Kerensky on behalf of the coalition government and the Army High Command in the form of the offensive. Paradoxical as it may seem, the call to patriotism and revolutionary self-defense was calculated to inspire the common soldier to submission, if not valor. The purpose was to save the revolution by a victory that would end the war. On the other hand, the first Empire-wide Soviet Congress opened on June 3 and lasted most of the month. The overwhelming majority of the more than 750 delegates favored the moderate position of the SRs and Right Mensheviks, which is to say the supporters of coalition. The soldier-delegates at the Congress were not men from the trenches but "mobilized intellectuals," in Sukhanov's words, junior officers, the committeemen whose role at the front was to stem the chaos. Lenin spoke for a mere fifteen minutes, a lackluster performance, intended not to persuade but to shock. If no other force was willing to shoulder the responsibility of power, he warned, the Bolsheviks were ready to step into the breach.[97] The Congress itself was far from militant; its basic orientation, after all, coincided with that of the government. Its main accomplishment was to replace the Petrograd Executive Committee with an All-Russian Central Executive Committee. This nucleus included both Lenin and Kerensky, neither of whom ever appeared.[98] The two prima donnas of power.

For all their bravado, however, and for all Lenin's take-no-prisoners approach to the podium, the Bolsheviks were better at cultivating dissatisfaction than giving it shape. The crowds still had the bit between their teeth, as demonstrated by the greatest challenge to the Soviet Congress in the first week of June. Behind the tumult, however, was a growing organizational network. The Bolsheviks were building their base, not only among the amenable Petrograd garrisons but among the workers whose interests they claimed to represent. By mid-April, some of the key Petrograd factories had already adopted Bolshevik slogans. In late May, the workers' section of the Petrograd Soviet endorsed the call (still premature) for "All Power to the Soviets."[99] A week after the Soviet Congress opened, Bolshevik leaders decided to organize a peaceful demonstration, under the banners "Down with the Ten Capitalist Ministers," "All Power to the All-Russian Soviet of Worker, Soldier, and Peasant Deputies," "Time to End the War," "Neither Separate Peace nor Secret Treaties," and "Bread, Peace, Freedom."[100] Hearing the plans for the next day, the Soviet Congress sent delegates to the factories urging workers not to heed the call. That evening the Bolsheviks retracted their appeal, but the Soviet leaders were livid. Tsereteli accused the Bolsheviks of conspiring against the revolution: "The weapon of criticism is being replaced by criticism with weapons," he thundered, referring to the armed soldiers who were sure to have joined the workers in the streets.[101] There was talk of prohibiting all demonstrations without Soviet approval and of "disarming the Bolsheviks," which meant the factory militias and the better organized, more political Red Guards, which had begun forming in April.[102]

In fact, Bolshevik intentions were confused. The thrust of the demonstration was directed against the ministers in the Mariinskii Palace, but if the party was in fact planning a coup, it was unclear who would take power. Not the Soviet in whose name their banners spoke, because the Soviet was collaborating with the coalition government and did not want power on its own behalf. As Sukhanov commented in retrospect: "Lenin's group was not directly aiming at the seizure of power, but *it was ready to seize it in favourable circumstances, which it was taking steps to create.*"[103] When the Bolsheviks had debated what to do, on the night before June 10, opinions were divided. Lenin himself urged caution. His caution carried the day.[104]

Turning the tables, the Soviet Congress summoned a demonstration for June 18, in support of its own position. That Sunday, crowds flooded the Field of Mars, the parade ground not far from the Winter Palace. The weather was warm and sunny. To the dismay of the Soviet leaders, however, the Bolsheviks had the last laugh. Most of the banners held aloft were those prepared for the aborted event of the week before: "All Power to the Soviets!"—"Down with the Ten Capitalist Ministers!" Adding insult to injury, there was "an enormous, heavy, gold-embroidered banner" inscribed with the initials of the Bolshevik Party.[105] "It was a stinging flick of the whip in the face of the Soviet majority and the bourgeoisie," Sukhanov remembered.[106]

The mood in Petrograd was unstable. The day after Bolshevik banners had shone on the Field of Mars, Nevskii filled with crowds, this time welcoming the announcement of the long-awaited Galician offensive.[107] In March, soldiers at the front had reinterpreted the war as a defense of the Revolution, which they equated with the policies and class profile of the Soviet. The front committees continued to promote revolutionary defensism, but as time passed, as disgruntled troops from the urban garrisons appeared at the front as replacements and as front soldiers visited the capital and got an earful of antiwar rhetoric, attitudes in the trenches began to shift.

The Bolshevik Party in Petrograd had meanwhile retreated from its extreme antiwar slogans. The retraction of June 10 reflected its doubts about the readiness of the popular following to reach the obvious conclusions—or the party's readiness to face the logical consequences of its bold words. At the front, however, self-motivated Bolshevik agitators pursued a consistently antiwar line and inspired countless acts of disobedience and resistance. Organizational chaos and social collapse fed on each other. The railway lines were a tinderbox—tight spaces crammed with soldiers being transferred from one place to another, replacement troops en route to the front, over-forty recruits on their way back home, soldiers deserting and deserters returning. Stations became theaters-in-the-round of political agitation, as soapbox orators harangued the ever-shifting crowds. Boozy soldiers ran amok. Some divisions operated their own liquor stills.[108]

If the ordinary recruits followed their blind instincts, whether of self-preservation (going home) or self-destruction (drunken riots), political trouble emanated not from the disgruntled cannon fodder but from those with greater resources and less to fear: men with skills—telephone opera-tors, drivers, sappers, artillerists, mostly employed behind the lines, where discipline and surveillance were laxer.[109] The Bolsheviks at this juncture did not formally oppose the offensive, but their agents in the field undermined the army's capacity to make the offensive work.

The story of the Galician offensive illustrates the nature of the social dis-integration that not only impeded the war effort but created the political crisis that emboldened the Bolsheviks to accept their own dare, as the one force willing to take the risk of power. Preparations for the offensive began in late May, June in the European calendar. The signs were already ominous. Entire companies, even regiments, refused to move to the front; a divisional commander was severely beaten, some officers were murdered. Divisions on the Romanian Front and in the Carpathians established their own "trench republics."[110]

Having backed the offensive, General Alekseev now warned Kerensky, "The troops are no longer a threat to the enemy, but to their own father-land. Admonitions and appeals no longer have an effect on the masses. What is needed is authority, force, compulsion, the fear of punishment."[111] Having called for a return to strict enforcement of the military code and restoration of full disciplinary powers, the general nevertheless issued plans for the offensive to go forward. The next day, he was relieved of his command— dismissed "like a house servant," he grumbled—and replaced by General Brusilov.[112] Alekseev and Brusilov both came from military families. Neither was plebeian, but Kerensky wanted to make the top brass seem more "dem-ocratic" by making his own appointment. He took the occasion to assert his civilian authority. Authority needed assertion.

Kerensky continued to make the rounds, exhorting the men to do their duty, taking his high-drama roadshow to the trenches. Sometimes he was applauded, sometimes humiliated. Intellectuals such as writers Viktor

Shklovskii and Fedor Stepun joined the ranks of the "persuaders." They encountered physical threats and charges of "*burzhui!*"—Russian shorthand for "bourgeois." "How much are they paying you?" The crowds in great-coats were ominous. They were more impressed with a string of obscenities than arguments or appeals to revolutionary principles. Obscenities too crude for any polite setting bridged the gulf between men of education and culture and peasants in uniform with rotting feet.[113] They were a shared breach of decorum—a form of solidarity and an implied threat of violence. Symbolic politics, yet again.

Known as the June Offensive (also as the Summer or Kerensky Offensive), the campaign centered on the border towns of Vilna and Dvinsk (Dünaburg, today Daugavpils) in the north and Tarnopol (today, Ternopil) in the south. Operations were launched on June 18 (July 1, NS), with a two-day artillery assault. Kerensky now pitched catchwords that would later be turned against him: "Soldiers! The Fatherland is in danger. Freedom is threatened, the Revolution stands before the abyss!"[114] Some soldiers, falling back on habits of compliance, still believed that a quick victory was the best path to peace. But the summons activated the new habit of questioning rather than obeying.

The men were by now used to being "persuaded," to hearing endless exhortations and admonitions. Audiences were not passive. The lawyer and Soviet leader, Nikolai Sokolov, who had taken the dictation that resulted in Order No. 1, now traveled to the front to communicate Soviet support for the offensive. He was not welcome. Accused of being an officer in disguise, he was beaten bloody by the men he was trying to inspire. Actual officers were frequently assaulted; meetings continued in permanent session, like a low-grade fever.[115] After two days of unsuccessful fighting, commanders described the men as "in the highest degree demoralized. The consistent flouting of battle orders, unauthorized departures from positions, and refusals to replace other units on the line have become an everyday occurrence. The work of committees of all denominations yields no results."[116]

Distrust was rampant. When officers went over the top and did not return, usually because they had been slaughtered, the men suspected them of desertion.[117] The soldiers themselves often did desert, sometimes in the heat of battle. The Russian capture at the end of June, under General Kornilov's command, of Kalush and Galich in southern Galicia proved the army could still function on occasion, but in the aftermath of success, the troops did what they had done on earlier sorties into the region. They assaulted the local inhabitants, particularly the Jews; raped the women, destroyed property, looted, and got drunk on whatever alcohol they could get their hands on.[118]

The aftermath of defeat produced a similar response. When powerful German forces moved in from the west to rescue their weaker Austrian partners, they seized Tarnopol on July 24 (NS) without encountering resistance. On their way out, the Russians torched the railroad station and the bridges crossing the Siret River, a tributary of the Dniester. The evacuation was disorganized, and again the local population bore the brunt of the soldiers' aggression.[119] "Most units are in a state of ever-growing disintegration," the committee on the Southwest Front reported. "There is already no question of authority and subordination. Persuasion and argument have lost their force. They are answered with threats, sometimes with shooting. Some units leave their positions at will, not awaiting the approach of the enemy. There were cases when an order to move quickly for support was debated for hours at meetings, so that the support was delayed for days.... The situation demands extreme measures."[120]

Stavka had an interest in portraying the fleeing troops as Bolshevik-crazed cowards, or perhaps as the pawns of paid German agents, or as the victims of German agents disguised as Bolsheviks. Many soldiers did, of course, run away, but operations were hindered by the same problems of planning and coordination that had plagued the military throughout the war. The enlisted men, for their part, suspected their officers had betrayed them, aiming to discredit the revolution by making the "democratic" army look bad.[121]

---

While the offensive was falling apart, so was the coalition government. As events in the heart of Russia were taking their course, on March 4, political leaders in the nine mostly Ukrainian-speaking provinces had formed a national assembly, the Central Rada (*Tsentral'na Rada*—Ukrainian for "council"). On June 10, the Rada issued its "First Universal" (a Cossack term for decree, here used in modern political life for the first time), declaring the nation of Ukraine, with its capital in Kiev, to be an autonomous part of the Russian state.[122] The Provisional Government pleaded with the Ukrainians not to break away, declaring that only the Constituent Assembly could decide the fate of the Empire in its entirety, but the ministers soon agreed to acknowledge the Rada at least on a temporary basis.[123] Any concession to Ukrainian aspirations that weakened the bonds of empire was unacceptable, however, to the four Kadet ministers. On July 2, they tendered their resignations, bringing an end to the two-month experiment in political collaboration.[124]

The month of July in the Russian calendar witnessed not only military failure and political crisis, but also a repetition of the June Days, when the streets had pulsated with agitated crowds, bearing Bolshevik slogans that challenged not only the "bourgeois" government but also the moderate socialist leaders of the Soviet. In June these slogans had been too radical even for the Bolsheviks who had launched them. Now, once again, the Bolshevik spirit was alive, but the Bolshevik leaders were still not yet in command. To this point, the program—or the brand—was a symbol of opposition— opposition to whatever forces were sending more men to the front and failing to appease the growing distress at economic hardship. Lenin's goal was to harness the energy of opposition to the party's positive goals, which for him were front-and-center political: the question of power.

The so-called July Days illustrated the delicate mechanism of inspiring but also controlling the popular temper.[125] In the early afternoon of Monday, July 3, the Soviet Presidium was meeting in the Tauride Palace. Sukhanov stepped into the corridor, where he heard a phone booth ring. The speaker identified himself as a worker; he wished to consult with a member of the Executive Committee. His factory committee had heard that workers else- where were launching a demonstration. What were the Soviet's instructions? What should they do?[126] Note: the worker used the telephone, and he both- ered to ask for guidance. Sukhanov told him the Soviet opposed such demonstrations; these must be provocateurs. In fact, the First Machine Gun Regiment was already soliciting support from other units for an armed dem- onstration. The Soviet pondered how to stop them.[127]

As the Soviet pondered, the movement grew. Factories throughout the city went on strike. Trains stopped running. Workers from the Vyborg dis- trict joined the soldiers, some of whom began shooting at random. Cars and trucks rushed about, crammed with soldiers and ordinary people brandish- ing rifles. The soldiers seemed to lack a purpose, Sukhanov observed. They had "nothing but a 'mood.'" Speakers at the Tauride Palace appealed for calm, but the crowd accused the Executive Committee of having "surren- dered to the landlords and the bourgeoisie" and demanded its members be arrested.[128] Bolshevik slogans had a psychological impact that challenged even the party that launched them.

The remaining ministers met in Prince L'vov's apartment to consider the crisis, but they were irrelevant by now.[129] The focus was the Tauride Palace. There Trotsky urged the Soviet to take power in its own name. His listeners seemed to welcome the idea, but the slogan was just that. Soviet leaders rejected the demand as premature and also futile. In the absence of any call to action, the crowd began to dwindle.[130] All through the night, Soviet leaders, together with three hundred assembled delegates, stayed in the hall and continued to argue. The buffet was still serving sandwiches.[131] Early the next morning, the meeting dispatched representatives to the factories to try to calm the mood.[132] Neither the Soviet nor the Bolshevik Party, making mischief with its provocative slogans, was ready to meet the challenge from the street.

That day, July 4, shops were closed and trams were not running. The Tauride Palace was surrounded by chaotic throngs. The Central Executive Committee was still sitting, enveloped by a continuous hubbub. The Bolsheviks, who on one level had called for a "peaceful" march, on another level heightened the tensions. Local party activists had mobilized twenty thousand sailors from the Kronstadt naval base. They had arrived early that morning on warships that docked at the Nicholas Embankment, on Vasilevskii Island. From there a swarm of soldiers, sailors, and workers, accompanied by marching bands, had first headed for Kshesinskaia's mansion on the Petrograd side. Speaking from the balcony, Lenin urged them not to proceed, but at the same time, to cries of "hurrah," denounced the Provisional Government and the Soviet.[133] Nor were these demonstrators peaceful. As they moved from Bolshevik headquarters to the Tauride Palace, gunfire would begin "with a chance shot; panic would follow; rifles began to go off at random. There were dead and wounded everywhere."[134] A report by the Soviet Executive Committee described the behavior of the Kronstadt sailors, who "carry out searches on the pretext that they have been fired on. If anyone is found he is pulled out on the street and lynched."[135] Sukhanov had similar recollections: "Small, isolated pogroms began. Because of shots from houses, or with them as a pretext, mass-searches were conducted by soldiers and sailors. The searches were a pretext for looting. Many shops suffered, mainly wine and food shops and tobacconists. Various groups began to arrest people on the streets at random. Around 4 o'clock, according to rumour, the number of people wounded or killed already amounted to hundreds. Dead horses lay here and there."[136] Troops were sent to stop the mayhem, but panicked at the first shot. In the confusion, it was hard to tell one side from the other.[137]

Meanwhile, in the eye of the growing storm, meetings continued uninterrupted in the halls of the Tauride Palace.[138] Workers demanded that the
Soviet take power and oust "the ten capitalist ministers." "We trust the
Soviet," they said, "but not those whom the Soviet trusts."[139] The most
politicized groups posed the greatest threat. Not only the Kronstadt sailors,
but also the thousands of men from the Putilov works, who were moving
toward the center. Troops accompanied by artillery and machine guns filled
Nevskii and Liteinyi Avenues, until a cloudburst drove them away. It was by
then around 5 in the afternoon, when the twenty thousand Kronstadters
started to pour through the doors and hallways of the Tauride Palace, like
a river breaching its banks. Sukhanov remembered "an endless multitude
packing the entire space as far as the eye could reach. Armed men were
climbing through the open windows. A mass of placards and banners with
the Bolshevik slogans (of June 9th) rose above the crowd."[140]

Martov was among the few Soviet leaders who thought they should
indeed "take power," but the rest refused to give in to pressure.[141] The
Kronstadters, in a hostile mood, demanded to speak to the socialist ministers. When Viktor Chernov, the SR minister of agriculture, appeared before
them, as Sukhanov recalled, the men raised "a frantic din. The crowd, brandishing its weapons, began to surge forward....Chernov was declared under
arrest as a hostage." Trotsky, undaunted, appealed to the revolutionary sentiments of the "Red Kronstadters" to no avail; they considered his defense of
Chernov a mark of treason.[142] Chernov managed to slip away, but it was
clear that anger was easier to arouse than channel—a lesson at the core of
Lenin's political strategy from the very start.

Chkheidze, chair of the Petrograd Soviet, also faced down an angry mob,
this time of Putilov workers, who attempted to lay hands on Tsereteli, the
Menshevik minister of post and telegraph.[143] Chkheidze kept his cool,
accusing them of betraying the revolution, telling them to go away and
mind their own business. The workers backed off. Sukhanov did not then,
or in retrospect, condemn the workers' lynch-mob psychology or question
their distrust of the Soviet leadership. He recalled the image of a "*sans-culotte*
on the platform of the White Hall, shaking his rifle in self-oblivion in the
faces of the hostile 'leaders of the democracy,' trying in torment to express
the will, the longings, and the fury of the authentic proletarian lower depths,
who scented treachery but were powerless to fight against it. This was one
of the finest scenes of the revolution. And with Chkheidze's gesture one of
the most dramatic."[144] At the end of the afternoon, with the Soviet still in

session, a mass of troops as yet unaffected by the Bolshevik spirit finally appeared, to posture in the Soviet's defense.[145] Both the mobs in the street and the loyal regiments considered the Soviet their own. This sense of possession would serve the Bolsheviks well in due course.

By that July 4 evening, the Kronstadters were headed back to base. Next day, the Bolshevik newspaper *Pravda* called for an end to demonstrations. The Bolsheviks tried also to stop the Putilov workers from launching another strike.[146] Late the preceding evening, the Ministry of Justice had published documents purporting to demonstrate that Lenin was a German agent. This charge, though unsubstantiated, had apparently contributed to the soldiers' willingness to come to the Soviet's defense.[147] Despite the party's retreat, it was clear that Bolshevik agitation had inspired the turmoil. The government finally applied some muscle. The *Pravda* office was closed, the staff arrested. When a mob trashed the print shop, the defenders of Bolshevik honor derided the attackers as "Black Hundred elements," though they were perhaps no different from the "*sans-culottes*" who had tried to lynch Tsereteli. Prince L'vov and Tsereteli, who had earned Lenin's contempt, tried to stop publication of the charges against him, but without success. The slanderous cat was out of the bag.[148]

By then, the tumult had largely subsided, though rumors of continuing strikes persisted. In the Soviet Executive Committee, the Left Mensheviks criticized the use of troops to suppress the disorders; they deplored the attacks on Bolshevik activists, now being arrested and sometimes roughed up by the same sort of people who had until then been manhandling police officers, army officers, and shop foremen. The Bolsheviks themselves protested the accusations of treason. At the same time they helped calm the temper of the remaining Kronstadt sailors, who had taken possession of the Peter-Paul Fortress and were only with difficulty persuaded to leave.[149]

On July 6, a mere three days after the start of the disorders, Kerensky returned from his tour of the front and ordered the arrest of Bolshevik leaders, Trotsky among them, and the dismemberment of the rebellious regiments. Lenin crossed the border into Finland, where he remained in hiding until October.[150] The slogan "All Power to the Soviets" was tabled.[151] It had done its work fomenting agitation and disturbing the confidence of the institution it claimed to support, but as a guide to political action it was useless. All sorts of people were at this point ready to believe that Lenin was a German agent. While Martov, on the Menshevik left, continued to defend the Bolsheviks' rightful place in the socialist spectrum, Tsereteli justified the arrests, and Kerensky resolved to destroy the party.[152]

Lenin, in hiding, was confirmed in his belief that one had to adjust one's tactics; Mensheviks were confirmed in their attachment to principle. On Friday, July 7, the Mensheviks voted against continued collaboration with the Provisional Government. That same day, Prime Minister L'vov resigned, on the grounds that the socialists were "sacrificing national and moral values to the masses in the name of demagogy."[153] The SR Party pronounced his political obituary: "Prince L'vov was one of those accidental guests of the revolution....Revolutionaries will come and go, but the revolution, the process of the revolution, will endure until the questions proposed, not by individual parties but by the entire course of Russian history, are solved."[154] Kerensky replaced L'vov as prime minister and set out to rebuild the cabinet.[155] Although the Soviet itself had declined the chance to go it alone (if that chance had ever had any possibility of succeeding), the cabinet, when finally consolidated on July 24, now included a majority of socialist ministers.[156] Known as the Second Coalition, it would have to maneuver between unappeased radicalism on the left and growing impatience on the right. The "process of the revolution" might seem to have a logic and energy of its own, but it depended on the actions of leaders and of the social forces around them.

# 3

# From Putsch to Coup

The months of April, June, and July had each produced an episode in which popular discontent outstripped the capacity of any political leadership to contain or direct it. The factories and the barracks had been stirred up, but the formulas kept changing. In April the issue was foreign policy, a proxy for the visceral question of the war and how long it was going to continue. In June antiwar catchwords combined with a Bolshevik-style challenge to competitors on the left, under the banner "All Power to the Soviets." In neither case did the intellectuals or activists who coined the slogans have the authority or power to channel the response they evoked or the amorphous underlying emotions.

The July Days went a step farther. The contingent of Kronstadt sailors displayed the potential to act in effect as a private revolutionary army. The escalated threat produced an escalated reaction. The government finally cracked down on the Bolshevik Party, correctly held responsible for stimulating the aggressive mood, and turned for support to the Army High Command. As minister of war and head of state, Kerensky was in the position of tacking between "the democracy" and the military chiefs. Among the top commanders, General Kornilov seemed to occupy the same middle ground. He was not soft. In April, he had resigned his position as commander of the Petrograd Military District when the Soviet prevented him from ordering the troops to suppress the unrest. As commander in the field, he demanded restrictions on the front committees' role, but he nevertheless defended their existence, which other commanders angrily opposed.

Now Kerensky seemed to enter into an alliance with Kornilov. Stavka had blamed the Tarnopol defeat in July on the massive desertions and panic among the ranks. It made sense to imagine that Germans and Bolsheviks were in league, for their respective reasons, to undermine the fighting capacity of the Russian army. Within the army committees, the same moderate-left intellectuals as the leaders of the Soviet, along with literate low-ranking officers, supported the command in the push for reinforced discipline.[1] Mayhem, lynchings, and drunken riots were the alternative, not to mention ignominious military defeat. The soldiers, for their part, blamed the retreat on the treachery of their commanders.[2]

While the offensive was already under way, Kerensky had appointed Kornilov commander of the Southwest Front. Kornilov was a Siberian Cossack who had fought in Central Asia and the Far East. He surrounded himself with a bodyguard of Teke Turkmen cavalrymen. The Caucasian Native Mounted Division (*Kavkazskaia tuzemnaia konnaia diviziia*), commonly known as the Savage Division (*Dikaia diviziia*), composed of volunteers from the North Caucasus (in particular Chechnia) and Transcaucasia, had fought as a unit in the Imperial Army, showing particular skill and ferocity in Galicia. It now owed allegiance to Kornilov, who knew the region and spoke a number of its languages.[3] He was not a monarchist, but he distrusted the Soviet as unpatriotic, reviled the Bolsheviks, and wished to restore the army to its professional purpose. Politically unsophisticated, he was described by General Anton Denikin, one of his early supporters and future leader of the anti-Bolshevik White forces, as "a banner. For some of counterrevolution, for others of the salvation of the Motherland."[4]

On the Southwest Front, Kornilov had the support of the front commissar, the erstwhile SR terrorist Boris Savinkov, now Kerensky's deputy minister of war. The same age as Trotsky and Kerensky, Savinkov was born in Kharkov of Russian parents but raised in Warsaw, where his father was serving as a justice of the peace. Attracted to the SRs as a young man, Savinkov had helped organize the assassination of Minister of the Interior Viacheslav Pleve in 1904, that of Grand Duke Sergei in 1905, and the failed attempt on Prime Minister Petr Stolypin's life in 1906. He spent the years between the revolution and the outbreak of war in Europe, where he devoted himself to writing novels on political themes and turned his back on terror.[5] Now an ardent patriot and proponent of the war, he returned to Russia via Finland in April 1917, shortly after Lenin's arrival. His articles for the SR newspaper *Delo naroda* (*The People's Cause*), denouncing the Soviet as defeatist, came to Kerensky's attention. Both outliers in the SR Party, they had met briefly in 1905. The new commissar arrived in Galicia in a fancy uniform and impressed everyone with his fluent command of Polish.[6]

The patriotic Savinkov welcomed Kornilov's attempts to reinforce discipline in the field. The general declared he would treat desertion as treason and ordered his officers to shoot any soldier who tried to walk away. In an obviously futile gesture, he prohibited committees from discussing rather than obeying their officers' commands. He also banned the Bolshevik front newspapers. In July, he demanded the reinstatement of the death penalty at the front, which the cabinet approved, along with the restoration of field courts. Soldiers interpreted this change as a return to the hated old order. The law was rarely applied, but attempts were made to remove the worst agitators from the ranks.[7] Kornilov's moves were endorsed by the front committees and commissars and by Soviet leaders, who did not consider the reinforcement of superior authority an attempt to defeat the Revolution but an effort to keep the army from falling apart. Kornilov, however, also had the support of the Officers' Union, an organization formed in May by Stavka staff officers, who clearly had different expectations.[8] On July 18, Kerensky promoted Kornilov to commander in chief, replacing General Brusilov.[9] The front committees, which had earlier welcomed Kornilov's attempts to impose obedience among the ranks, denounced the appointment as an attempt to halt, if not reverse, the revolution.[10] Deputy Minister of War Savinkov guided Kornilov in the delicate maneuver of seeming to support the "democratic" forces while bringing their institutions (in this case, the committees) under control.[11]

Despite Kornilov's efforts, the June Offensive, which concluded on July 31 (August 13, NS), ended with huge losses among both officers and troops.[12] Two weeks later, in the attempt to reinforce the government's position and rally a broad spectrum of public support, Kerensky convened the so-called State Conference (*Gosudarstvennoe soveshchanie*) in Moscow.[13] On August 12, 2,500 representatives of Russian society gathered in the Bolshoi Theater, symbol and site of imperial high culture, for three days of deliberation. Here were intellectuals, Duma and Soviet deputies, Kadets and moderate socialists, conservatives, zemstvo men, military officers, cabinet ministers, and delegates from the army front committees. Only the Bolsheviks stayed away. Trotsky was in prison, and Lenin was keeping a low profile in Finland. The atmosphere was tense with rumors of an impending coup from the right; posters everywhere hailed Kornilov as the new commander in chief. The Moscow Soviet, for its part, had formed a self-defense committee. Moscow Bolsheviks, ignoring Soviet protests, organized a widespread strike. Trams stopped running, restaurants closed, the nighttime streets were dark.[14]

On the second day of the Conference, General Kornilov, the subject of much speculation, arrived by train, surrounded by his picturesque Turkmen guard.[15] Addressing the assembled company the following day, he warned, "the enemy is knocking at the gates of Riga, and if the shakiness of our troops does not allow us to hold the coastline of the Gulf of Riga, the road to Petrograd will be open." In what later, in retrospect, seemed to be a threat, he added, "It may take the fall of Riga to bring about the restoration of order in the rear."[16] His relatively mild remarks were followed by an outpouring of vitriol against the existing bifurcated regime. The speeches by generals Alekseev and Aleksei Kaledin were particularly dire. "All Soviets and committees must be abolished," stormed Kaledin to applause from the right. "Discipline in the army must be…strengthened by the most resolute measures…The leaders of the army must be given full powers."[17]

The Moscow Conference seems to have convinced Kornilov that he was the man of the hour. Immediately preceding the Conference, the commander had presented a list of demands for the restoration of discipline at the front, which Kerensky had rejected. A week later, once the delegates had dispersed, Kerensky himself drafted a set of regulations in that same spirit. A group of hard-line generals, with Kornilov's support, decided it was necessary to intervene to prevent the Left from organizing mass protests against the new measures. On August 20, they began positioning the most reliable units for transportation to Petrograd.[18] When the Germans entered Riga the next day, Kornilov blamed the disaster on the indiscipline of the troops, which he charged with fleeing the scene in great numbers. By contrast, the Menshevik commissar on the Northern Front, Vladimir Voitinskii, in a telegram addressed to the Petrograd Soviet, defended the soldiers' honor. Widely reprinted in the front newspapers, Voitinskii's message created the impression that Kornilov's dark picture was self-serving—an excuse to justify harsh measures and even a dictatorship.[19]

The relationship between Kerensky and Kornilov at this point is a matter of dispute. On August 23, Savinkov went to Mogilev to meet with Kornilov at Stavka, where he seemed to endorse the plan to seize Petrograd. They agreed that Kornilov would notify Kerensky of the approach of troops, in particular the Third Corps, under General Aleksandr Krymov, as a signal for Kerensky to declare martial law in the capital. Savinkov and Kornilov also negotiated issues concerning the disposition and command of the volatile Petrograd garrison. In the end, both sides seemed to feel they had established the basis for cooperation, a united front of the relatively "democratic" military command with the moderate elements in the Provisional Government against the Soviet, the front committees, and the increasingly menacing Bolshevik threat.[20]

On August 24, with Savinkov en route back to Petrograd, Kornilov and his collaborators made plans for the military occupation of the city. The next day, Kornilov telegraphed Savinkov, as agreed, anticipating the arrival of his forces by August 27 and requesting the declaration of martial law in Petrograd on the 29th. At this point, however, Kerensky discovered that Kornilov in fact intended to install himself as head of an authoritarian government that would dispense with the prime minister altogether. Kerensky then convinced the cabinet to give him full powers to oppose Kornilov's machinations. When this final meeting of the ministers of the Second Coalition concluded early in the morning of August 27, Kerensky ordered Kornilov to step down in favor of his chief of staff, General Aleksandr Lukomskii. The astounded Lukomskii, who along with Kornilov had been convinced of Kerensky's support for their enterprise, refused his unexpected promotion, on the grounds that Kornilov alone could save the army and "save Russia." Most other generals shared this view. The troops dispatched from the front to execute Kornilov's plan were meanwhile drawing closer to their destination. Obliged now to publicize the break with Kornilov, only a week after the general's elevation to commander in chief, Kerensky hurried to prepare the defense of Petrograd. Revealing that Kornilov had intended to "establish a regime opposed to the conquests of the revolution," he announced the commander's dismissal, which Kornilov had not accepted, and the imposition of martial law—now in order to foil, not support, the plan.[21] A few leading Kadets urged Kerensky to step aside in favor of Kornilov, but the Soviet leaders bolstered the prime minister's resolve.[22]

Faced with the challenge from the right, the Soviet marshaled its organizational networks in support of Kerensky and the Provisional Government. Establishing a Committee for the Struggle Against Counterrevolution, which included Mensheviks, SRs, and even the chronically hostile Bolsheviks, the Soviet instructed local soviets, as well as postal, telegraph, and railroad workers, to disregard orders emanating from Stavka and prepare for armed self-defense. Despite their aversion to the moderate socialist leadership, the Petrograd Bolsheviks agreed to cooperate. Lenin denounced his conciliatory comrades as "fools" and "scoundrels," but in August the moderates carried the day.[23] The Bolshevik Military Organization—formed in March as an alternative to the Soviet military organization, the militias, and Red Guard, and as a means of gaining traction among Petrograd soldiers—now insisted that only a government in "the hands of the revolutionary workers and poorest peasantry" would guarantee the full development of the revolution and provide genuine protection against "Kornilov, the Kadets, or the Germans." It nevertheless threw its weight behind the joint effort.[24]

In fact, the grassroots campaign conducted by the Soviet, with energetic Bolshevik participation, was a model of ideological and organizational mobilization. Emergency bulletins were communicated via telegraph, leaflets were printed and distributed, Bolshevik agitators made the rounds of the Petrograd garrison, committees sprang up everywhere. The Committee for the Struggle Against Counterrevolution used a radio transmitter at Tsarskoe Selo to broadcast its messages.[25] The Petrograd City Duma, in which the Bolsheviks were now a considerable presence, sent deputies to nearby Luga to dissuade Kornilov's troops from proceeding with their mission. The Central Soviet of Factory-Shop Committees coordinated action in the factories. The SR-controlled transportation union and the Menshevik-controlled printers' union did their part. The Executive Committee of the All-Russian Railroad Union (Vikzhel) dispatched telegrams throughout the network, instructing railway personnel to block the progress of Kornilov's troops and track their movements.[26]

Workers lined up to join the armed detachments called Red Guards, first formed in April, supplied by the Bolshevik Military Organization with guns and ammunition from the armaments factories and arsenals. The worker militias had been discredited after the July Days, but they were now legitimized and soon embraced as many as 25,000 armed men.[27] Finally, on August 29, three thousand Kronstadt sailors landed on Vasilevskii Island, ready to guard the train stations, the bridges, and the Winter Palace. Kornilov himself remained in Mogilev, but the next day his Savage Division reached a station not far from Tsarskoe Selo, stopped from further progress by impassable tracks. It was met by a unit of Muslim mountaineers, sent to appeal to their co-religionists on the Provisional Government's behalf, which persuaded them not to continue. A few pro-Kornilov officers were murdered by their men, but in the end Kornilov's scheme to save the revolution from itself collapsed without armed confrontation.[28]

The result was to weaken the potential for military opposition and strengthen the forces on the left. The Bolsheviks and Left Mensheviks who had rallied on the Provisional Government's behalf had tempered their cooperation with demands for the immediate declaration of a democratic republic, even in advance of the Constituent Assembly. They demanded the release of the Bolsheviks arrested after July, and they called for the convocation of an exclusively democratic state conference. The biggest winners were the Bolsheviks, who had clearly demonstrated the depth of their influence among the politically most responsive layer of workers and soldiers.

The consequences for the army command were catastrophic. On the Southwest Front, General Denikin was arrested by his own men, Savinkov was dismissed from his post as deputy minister of war, and Kornilov and Lukomskii, together with three other generals, were imprisoned in the town of Bykhov near Mogilev. General Krymov met with Kerensky in the Winter Palace on August 31, still eager to justify his role in what he described as an attempt to constrain the anarchy imperiling the revolution and, of course, the war. He still apparently believed he would have a sympathetic ear, despite all Kerensky's recent pronouncements. Knowing of Kornilov's plan to install military rule, Kerensky accused Krymov of treason. Foiled and no doubt furious, the general retired to a friend's apartment and shot himself in the head.[29]

Kerensky's clumsy attempt to harness Kornilov's ambitions on the government's behalf, against the growing appeal of the Left, thus backfired completely. The push for strongman rule attracted few supporters, while inspiring widespread resistance. This resistance was not formless, but rooted in the organizational structures shaped over the preceding months by the leaders in the socialist camp, both moderate and radical. The reaction gave the Bolshevik Party, at this point still under the post-July cloud, an ideological and organizational shot in the arm. As Lenin had hoped since April, when the notion seemed delusional, the structures built by intellectuals in the name of the dispossessed would provide his own launching pad.

The Bolsheviks could afford at this point to remain on the sidelines, but they were far from inactive. Up and down the front and in all the major Petrograd factories and key cities, grassroots agitators tirelessly hawked the Bolshevik brand. Indeed, the front army was the site of intensive media warfare. Not only did Bolshevik newspapers flood the ranks, but the committees published their own newspapers, which relayed news of events in the capital. The ordinary (literate or semiliterate) soldiers, certainly the noncoms, were fully aware of political developments. By August the troops may have been angry and undisciplined—many indulged in drunken violence, and some murdered their superior officers—but they were not uninformed. Politics saturated the atmosphere everywhere.

The dynamics of the Kornilov plot reveal the process by which the right-wing alternative to the political stalemate of the coalition lost credit, while the credit of the left-wing alternative rose. Symbols were powerful. Kornilov represented the army high command, which is to say, the "gilt-shouldered" officer class, the hierarchy of the old regime, and now also the cabinet ministers who continued to promote the war. The Bolsheviks competed with their rivals for the mantle of "the Democracy," which in its current incarnation the party derided, but whose institutions—the committees and soviets—never lost their popular allure. The challenge was to appropriate the potential authority these institutions seemed to possess but were reluctant to exercise.

The Bolsheviks' power was not entirely symbolic. The mobilization against Kornilov in the cities strengthened the networks of communication and grassroots organization. The same kinds of networks operated also at the front, where committees foiled the officers' attempts to control the flow of information to their men, while transmitting messages from the control centers of "democratic" resistance in the cities. The officers were by and large discredited by the plot. As one front commissar remembered, "The authority of the commanders was destroyed once and for all. The soldier ranks, seeing how a general, the commander in chief, had gone against the Revolution, felt themselves surrounded by treason on all sides and saw in every man who wore epaulettes a traitor. And whoever tried to persuade them otherwise also seemed a traitor."[30] The committees, by contrast, received a needed boost. Many officers were arrested and a few (brutally) murdered, while the committeemen recovered their standing in the eyes of the enlisted men.

Kerensky's reputation suffered from the fiasco, in which he seemed to have conspired, at least at the start. His political instincts, such as they were, failed him in its aftermath as well. At first he insisted the orders issued by Kornilov before the plot were still valid, and then appointed to succeed him the conservative General Alekseev, who had shared many of Kornilov's views, and whom Kerensky had replaced unceremoniously with Brusilov in the spring. Attempting now to circumscribe the newly enhanced power of the front committees and commissars who had rallied to his side, Kerensky issued an order on September 1, limiting their political activity, prohibiting the arrest of officers, and attempting to regain control over the communications network that had facilitated the anti-Kornilov defense.[31] Kornilov was temporarily out of action, but his cause survived. As Voitinskii noted: "Every soldier knew that the conflict between Kerensky and Kornilov had been preceded by negotiations between them, that the subject of these talks had been the death penalty, further restraints on soldiers' organizations, and the return of authority to the officers, in short, to put clamps on the soldier and return him to the control of the 'old regime.'"[32]

At the front, the approach of winter, combined with the "treason" of the highest in command and the activation of committee and soldier networks in response, undermined any remaining willingness of the ranks to obey orders and return to the fight. The ordinary peasant in uniform refused to build winter bunkers, he sold whatever warm clothing he still possessed, he plundered supply trains, resisted orders, requested leave or simply took off, fraternized with the enemy, attended endless meetings and listened to the recitation of endless resolutions. Both commanders and commissars were concerned with the mood and took constant soundings. A report filed on the Southwest Front for the week of September 7–14 noted that the Kornilov affair had deepened the "profound, often blind feeling of mistrust of officers." The soldiers now refused to perform even the "essential military duties, such as repairing the trenchworks and training exercises." Officers had been arrested, threatened, and beaten up. If the men didn't sell their winter clothing, they panicked when there wasn't enough. "The shortage of warm uniforms, boots, and forage continues to excite the soldiers, adversely affecting their mood and evoking a positive horror over the winter campaign."[33] Winter in these parts could begin in mid-October, early November, or at the first freeze.[34]

The soldiers' protests were not merely passive—refusing assignments, avoiding routine duties, making themselves scarce. They more and more frequently went on the rampage, joining peasants in ransacking landed estates, torching food stores, slaughtering livestock, breaking into wine cellars and indulging in alcohol-fueled mayhem. Sometimes the violence was directed against "their own." In Gomel in late September, a mob of nine thousand soldiers demanded an immediate end to the war and responded to threats of discipline by assaulting the assistant commissar and bashing his skull in with a rock.[35]

Meanwhile, there was the dun of constant meetings, repetition of the same slogans—"Peace! Down with the *burzhui!*" The front committees were busy—as they had been from the start—trying to contain the formless violence. Now they were also busy preparing for elections to the long-awaited Constituent Assembly. The Central Soviet Executive Committee announced plans for a second All-Russian Soviet Congress to convene in Petrograd on October 20, to which delegates also had to be elected. In short, the committees, which had emerged from the Kornilov challenge stronger and more authoritative than before, were now burdened by formal duties and the demands of the political process. They explained voting procedures and printed information on the political parties, as though the country were indeed entering a new era of constitutionally mandated modern political life.

In the crush of competing demands, the committees were losing touch, once again, with the temper of the men they were serving. Bolshevik slogans sounded ever more appealing as the summer drew to a close. Troop replacements arrived from the cities poorly trained, undisciplined, and primed with the Bolshevik message. The front committees were weakening "with each passing day," one reported, being challenged, changing their composition, and in general losing the authority they had once possessed. "On the question of the war either the masses have broken with the committees or the committees have adopted the position of the masses."[36]

With Kornilov foiled, the Left now presented the greatest challenge to the survival of a middle-of-the-road political regime. On the one hand, therefore, Kerensky tilted leftward. On September 1, he declared Russia to be a republic (on what authority was unclear). Kornilov was under arrest, Savinkov out of the cabinet. On September 4, Trotsky, in prison since July, was released, along with Vladimir Antonov-Ovseenko, both soon to emerge as key revolutionary leaders.[37] On the other hand, Kerensky played to the Right. He cracked down on the anti-Kornilov committees and continued to rely on the liberals for support, still attempting to sustain the basis of a socialist-liberal coalition. Kadet complicity in the Kornilov affair had, however, pushed the moderate Soviet leaders on whom the success of coalition depended further to the left, and they now opposed Kadet participation. Kerensky therefore formed a five-man Directorate (with the French Revolution in mind), from which the Kadets were excluded.[38]

The socialist parties continued nevertheless to debate the question of collaboration. In the All-Russian Soviet Executive Committee meeting of August 31 to September 2, the point of departure was cautious. The Right Menshevik Irakli Tsereteli, once the preeminent Soviet leader, continued to defend the need for cooperation with "bourgeois" forces (in particular, the Kadets). Lev Kamenev, the most conciliatory of Lenin's inner circle, insisted on the creation of an all-socialist government, working with a full spectrum of "democratic" institutions—the zemstvos, trade unions, and City Dumas, though not what he called the organized "bourgeoisie." This government would initiate a program of deep social reform even before the opening of the Constituent Assembly.[39] Most important among these reforms—the core of the Bolshevik program—were the immediate transfer of land to the peasants, workers' control over production, and the immediate declaration of universal peace. Kamenev's resolution was voted up at a rump session, but superseded by a final vote, which endorsed the position of the mainstream Mensheviks and SRs, who continued to support Kerensky's coalition regime. Only Martov, among the Mensheviks, favored a purely socialist government.[40]

While the former partners to Dual Power and the coalitions were searching for a viable alternative to the failed compromises between "the democracy" and the establishment, the Bolsheviks were also looking for the best way to take advantage of the institutional and political hiatus. Toward the end of summer and into the early fall, they moved from the periphery to the center. In this conjuncture, the tensions between the different aspects of Bolshevism as a political formation, not just a party, proved an advantage. In this phase of its existence, when the situation was fluid, party activists operated at different levels, with a range of tactics not always dependent on decisions at the top. Agitators at the grass roots were able to improvise their own strategies and build a popular following, partly through direct contacts in the factories and the military, partly through the constant flow of newspapers and sloganeering. Though flexible in practice, the party nevertheless struck a consistent note. Their tactics shifted, their slogans ("power to the soviets") came and went, but the Bolsheviks saturated the airwaves with a persistent rhetoric, a terminology, a recognizable signature or brand that created certain expectations.

While commissars and speechifiers stumped the trenches and the factories, the leading figures were busy calculating the best strategy for knocking out the political center. Their ability to do so depended to some extent on the success of their agents in the field. While activists were mobilizing the workers and soldiers to participate in elections—to local and central soviets, to conferences, and ultimately to the Constituent Assembly—Lenin was contemplating the military overthrow of the government in Petrograd, eventually to abolish the elected institutions on whose backs they had climbed to the top. The Bolsheviks were simultaneously using and subverting the democratic process.

Up to the very last minute, the party's brain trust debated how to benefit from their position at the margins of the existing political structures but at the center of the continuing revolutionary process. Lenin had no rival in terms of intellectual authority and force of character. Yet, he could not simply impose his will. He had to argue for his views, and some comrades argued back, notably Lev Kamenev and Grigorii Zinov'ev, both in their thirties, more than a decade younger than the boss.[41] Lenin was insistent, but he altered his assessment of the practical possibilities at every moment along the road to power as circumstances around him changed. He tested and discarded slogans and tactics. He was ideological and flexible at the same time. He was neither tolerant nor democratic, considering those who disagreed with him idiots and fools. The mechanisms of democracy nevertheless stood him in good stead as a springboard to power. The revolutionary months had created a network of communication and political action that embraced millions of men at the front and hundreds of thousands of men and women in the cities; events since February had accustomed the broad public and the far-flung populace to respond to the actions and discourse of political leaders; above all, the war, in its bloody embrace, had focused the attention of the entire Empire. Telephones, newspapers, telegraph, railroads, the post—these bound the classes and regions together and enabled politics to operate in a modern, mass-mobilization mode. The Bolsheviks used them all.

Kerensky, all along, stood for the necessity of keeping the propertied classes and the military command on the side of the revolution. He stood for collaboration and compromise, and when those tactics failed, his star fell. But even the Bolsheviks, right down to the final countdown in October, contemplated compromise—in their case, not with the so-called bourgeoisie but with the other socialist parties. The Soviet, as an institution and a symbol of "people's power," never lost its appeal, no matter who was in charge. Lenin built his entire strategy on this recognition. In April he introduced the "all power" slogan; in June and July the slogan had gotten out of hand and the party retreated. During the crisis of authority in August and September, the Mensheviks and SRs at the helm of the Petrograd and All-Russian Soviets wavered on whether to continue to collaborate with "bourgeois" forces or opt for a purely socialist regime: that is, power—finally—to the soviets. Lenin, still in hiding in Finland, followed events in the mainstream and socialist press, churning out articles on how to maneuver in the shifting political sands. In the first days of September, he advocated cooperation with the Mensheviks and SRs in the name of Soviet power. When they tilted toward Kerensky, he pulled back; when they tilted away, he reconsidered. If, he argued, the moderate socialists were willing to assume the burden of power, then the revolution could proceed on a peaceful

course. "If not," he warned, "then the revolution is lost, and only a victorious uprising of the proletariat can save it."[42]

The Sixth Bolshevik Party Congress at the end of July had rejected any
notion of cooperation with the moderate socialist parties, and the All-
Russian Bolshevik Executive Committee continued to uphold this view. In
the wake of the July Days, the Congress had resolved that "the peaceful
development and painless transfer of power to the soviets was impossible, for
power has already been transferred into the hands of the counterrevolutionary bourgeoisie."[43] The Petrograd Bolsheviks, meanwhile, continued to
concentrate on grassroots mobilization, competing for influence in the
Petrograd Soviet. They also focused on the elections to the so-called All-
Russian Democratic Conference (*Vserossiiskoe demokraticheskoe soveshchanie*),
conceived by the Soviet in the wake of the Kornilov adventure.[44] The
Conference opened in Petrograd on September 14. Its 1,582 delegates represented soviets, City Dumas, cooperatives, and trade unions—the broadly
defined "democratic" spectrum that Kamenev had championed at the All-
Russian Soviet Executive Committee two weeks earlier.[45] The Bolsheviks
had campaigned energetically, but they lost heavily to the other socialist
parties. The SRs won 34 percent of the delegates, the Mensheviks 11 percent,
the Bolsheviks only 9 percent; fully a quarter declared themselves unaffili-
ated.[46] Kamenev and Trotsky addressed the gathering in the spirit of Lenin's
recent articles, favoring an all-socialist solution to the political logjam.[47]

At this juncture, two fights were in progress—one inside the Democratic
Conference on the choice between a bourgeois-socialist or an all-socialist
coalition, and one inside the Bolshevik Party on whether to continue to
work through the "democratic" institutions or confront them from outside.
At the very moment that Bolshevik spokesmen were promoting the all-
socialist option in the Mariinskii Palace, Lenin was writing furiously from
his Finnish outpost. In two letters to the party leaders, he denounced the
Democratic Conference as "petty bourgeois" (the ultimate political put-
down). The party's competitors on the left were in disarray, he reminded
them, the Bolsheviks had obtained their first majorities in the Moscow and
Petrograd soviets, and the Germans were headed toward Petrograd. Now, he
suddenly insisted, was the moment to act. An end to compromise—armed
insurrection was the order of the day. "We could not have retained power
politically on July 3–4, because *before the Kornilov revolt*, the army and the
provinces could and would have marched against Petrograd. Now the picture is entirely different." The Bolsheviks in the Democratic Conference

should demand "the removal of the present government in its entirety ... and ...the immediate transfer of all power to *revolutionary democrats, headed by the revolutionary proletariat.*"[48]

So shocked was the Bolshevik Central Committee, meeting on September 15, by their leader's sudden change of heart that they resolved to keep his letters secret. They continued to pursue their conciliatory line at the Democratic Conference. There the key question of coalition was still unresolved. Most delegates favored some kind of collaboration with the so-called bourgeoisie, but many were resolutely hostile to the Kadet Party, which they still viewed as complicit in the Kornilov affair. On September 19, the Conference delegates finally rejected the possibility of coalition with the Kadets, but only after agonized debate.

With many issues still unresolved, the Conference had decided to create yet another interim body. The series of gatherings, distinguished in various ways one from the other, with closely echoing names hard for historians and readers to keep apart, reflected the unstable political moment. As the American journalist John Reed put it, "there were always three or four conventions going on in Petrograd."[49] The so-called Interim Soviet of the Russian Republic, also known as the Preparliament (*Sovet rossiiskoi respubliki,* or *Predparlament*), scheduled to open on October 7, would consist of a group of delegates from the Democratic Conference, plus representatives of other "democratic" organizations—the soviets, zemstvos, and cooperatives, but also of the propertied classes.[50] The return to the cross-class model of the Moscow State Conference represented a victory for Kerensky's position.[51]

Before the Preparliament could assemble, however, the political forces had realigned. On September 9 the Soviet Executive Committee had decided to allow the Presidium, until now dominated by Mensheviks and SRs, to reflect the strength of the respective parties. By the end of the month, the Bolsheviks, whose influence within the Soviet had been growing, held four of the seven seats. Not only did Trotsky and Kamenev thus join the Presidium, but Trotsky replaced the Menshevik Nikolai Chkheidze as chair, resuming the position he had first held briefly in 1905, thus activating the symbolic link with the earlier revolution and with the origins of the Soviet idea. At the same time, on September 25, against the background of continuing disagreement on the limits and conditions of inter-party cooperation, Kerensky formed a new cabinet, including four of the reviled Kadets. This was to be the final coalition.

The Bolsheviks, meanwhile, were busy defining their relationship to the two vestigial instruments of Dual Power: first, the Preparliament, which, despite all the confusion, still signified an attempt to encompass the broad social spectrum, and, second, the Second All-Russian Congress of Soviets scheduled to begin on October 20, which embraced the full socialist camp.[52] (The first such congress had met for most of June, coinciding with the abortive June Days and the failed June Offensive.) Ignoring Lenin's inconvenient letters from Finland, moderates such as Kamenev, Aleksei Rykov, and Viktor Nogin worried about the dangers of trying to go it alone, still unsure the soldiers and workers would support their bid for power. They viewed the Soviet Congress as the basis for a broad socialist government (a coalition of the Left) to take charge until the advent of the Constituent Assembly. Trotsky, too, viewed the Congress as a launching pad, but with the goal, as he saw it, of an exclusively Bolshevik government.[53] Trotsky wanted the party to boycott the Preparliament, but he was outvoted. In short, as late as the last week in September the leading Bolsheviks (Lenin aside) were committed to working through the institutions: to get out the vote—for the Preparliament, for the Soviet Congress, for the Constituent Assembly.

Lenin had denounced his comrades for agreeing to participate in the Democratic Conference, the progenitor of the Preparliament, and for resisting his call for insurrection. He was particularly annoyed by the idea, propounded by both Kamenev and Trotsky, of using the Soviet Congress as a launching pad. On September 29, he resigned in a huff from the party's Central Committee. The resignation was of course ignored. " 'To wait' for the Congress of Soviets is idiocy," he thundered, "for the congress *will give nothing* and can give nothing.... We have thousands of armed workers and soldiers in Petrograd who could at once seize the Winter Palace, the General Staff building, the telephone exchange and the large printing presses." More emphatic still: "It is my profound conviction that if we 'wait' for the Congress of Soviets and let the present moment pass, we will *ruin* the revolution."[54] And again, as was his style: "To await the Congress of Soviets is a childish play at formality, a shameful play at formality, treachery to the Revolution."[55]

Lenin pursued his campaign in the party's leadership organs. The All-Russian Central Committee had confiscated Lenin's September letters. The Petrograd Committee was itself divided on what to do, but angered by the deception. On October 5, the Petrograd and All-Russian Committees met separately; the former voted to start preparations for an armed insurrection, while the latter, annoyed at not being consulted, voted to boycott the Preparliament. One way or the other, the party, with its inner vacillations, was preparing to make its move. On October 7, Lenin returned to Petrograd to be closer to the action, living clandestinely in an apartment on the outskirts. He was still, officially, a wanted man.

The Preparliament opened that same day, October 7, in the Mariinskii Palace. The occasion was attended by five hundred delegates, the ambassadors of the Allied powers, and a host of journalists—a media moment, a theatrical opening. The Bolsheviks arrived late, fresh from their caucuses in Smolny. After the ceremonial introductions, Trotsky rose to speak. A dramatic and ruthless orator, Trotsky threw down the glove. The Germans were threatening Petrograd, Kerensky was preparing to flee. "The revolution and the people are in danger!" he thundered. "We turn to the people! All power to the soviets! All land to the people! Long live an immediate, just, democratic peace!" And still covering his tracks, he added, "Long live the Constituent Assembly!"[56] After July, Kerensky had denounced the Bolsheviks as German agents; now Trotsky called Kerensky a traitor to the Revolution. And with this rhetorical salvo, the Bolshevik delegates demonstratively left the hall.

The sensation was followed by relief. The troublemakers gone, the delegates in the Preparliament returned to chewing on the same old bones—the army must be restored to fighting shape; the Allies must be induced to negotiate a peace. The Allies, bolstered by the U.S. entry into the war in April, were unreceptive to peace proposals from the Russian side. Miliukov scolded the socialists, Trotsky and Lenin included, who in 1915 had joined an international gathering in the Swiss town of Zimmerwald to condemn the war. This was now an old story, but his words demonstrated how distant he was from political reality.[57] Lenin, the ideologue, had his nose to the wind; Miliukov, the liberal, was a broken record. The real challenge was out there in the streets, where Bolshevik agitators were riding a storm of popular indignation. Kerensky, they said, was preparing to deliver the capital into German hands, evacuating the government to Moscow, transferring the revolutionary garrison out of Petrograd.[58] It was no secret to the public at large that the Bolsheviks were contemplating an insurrection. Bolshevik newspapers published their internal debates on the question of when and how; mass meetings were in permanent session throughout the city.

The meeting of the Bolshevik Central Committee on October 10 is a legendary moment in the story of 1917. It is cited by historians to demonstrate two conflicting points: first, that Lenin was key to Bolshevik success—which no one disputes; second, that the party was not a simple instrument of Lenin's will but a forum for "democratic" discussion. The second point is not self-evident. That evening, three days after Trotsky's melodramatic farewell to the Preparliament, twelve of the twenty-one leading Bolsheviks convened in the apartment of the sympathetic Menshevik Nikolai Sukhanov, whose Bolshevik wife told him to stay away. Among those present were Joseph Stalin, Zinov'ev, Kamenev, Trotsky, the Polish Social Democrat Feliks Dzerzhinskii (Dzierżyński), and the Bolshevik feminist Alexandra Kollontai, all to play leading roles in consolidating Bolshevik power after October.

In his first appearance since returning from Finland, Lenin insisted armed insurrection must be the party's first order of business. Zinov'ev and Kamenev persisted in doubting the reliability of popular support. In fighting Kornilov, the Bolsheviks had successfully allied with the other parties on the left. Now, the two argued, they should use the Constituent Assembly, which had strong symbolic appeal, as their base of operations. The majority, not surprisingly given Lenin's stature, supported his view that insurrection could not wait, but the meeting left questions of technique and timing unresolved.[59]

If disagreement on the tactical issues of how to end up in power qualifies as democracy, then it is fair to say that Lenin did not exercise absolute authority. His views did not automatically command assent within his own inner circle. Nor were his own positions absolute. In these final weeks, he was constantly adjusting his assessment of the situation. In relation to the organized procedures of democratic political life, however, the Bolsheviks were unequivocal. The soviets, the congresses, the committees, the conferences— all were valuable for what they represented (a symbol of the people's voice), not for their own sake. Once these institutions had served to legitimate the party's aspirations, they could be dispensed with, or refashioned as instruments of rule. In that sense, there was nothing democratic about the Bolshevik Party. It needed a popular following in order to achieve its goals; it knew how to generate and respond to popular sentiment. The comrades believed they were serving the best interests of the people, not merely interests of their own. They thought of themselves as democratic in a more profound way than the kind of "democracy" associated with formal institutions. The political arena existed only within the party itself; those outside, even in the socialist camp, were idiots, traitors, and fools.

The moderate socialists had clung to the alliance with the military and civic elites as a hedge against the outbreak of civil war, which they feared would doom the revolution. Lenin saw the situation the other way around. Civil war was the path to triumph. The revolution was in fact from the start a civil war—men versus officers, peasants versus landowners, workers versus factory owners, poor versus rich, drunk versus sober. The political classes

(intelligentsia and professional elite) knew this perfectly well and did everything they could to contain it. The Bolsheviks, by contrast, did everything
they could to make it worse—waving the red flag, they mobilized this very
anger and conflict. It was a dangerous tactic, but it worked. They succeeded
ultimately in managing the definition of who was against whom, turning
conflict from a threat or a danger into a political device. Whether it worked
in terms of the revolution's goals as understood by the majority of its
supporters, in all walks of life, is another question.

# 4

# Bolshevik October

The path from the Bolshevik Central Committee meeting of October 10 to the "fall" of the Winter Palace, and with it the last of the coalition regimes, a mere two weeks later, was full of twists and turns, plans, revisions, and accidents. The Bolsheviks were flexible, but also decisive and duplicitous. They had a wide organizational network to draw upon. The fact that many in the party resisted Lenin's demand that the uprising precede the Soviet Congress actually worked to the party's advantage (and Lenin's) in the end. The division made for a two-pronged approach. On the one hand, Bolshevik newspapers and activists stressed preparation for the upcoming Congress. At the front, agitators used the process of preparing for elections to the Constituent Assembly to disseminate Bolshevik slogans, "which soon became a part of the soldiers' vocabulary and mode of thought," as historian Allan K. Wildman puts it.[1] On the other hand, preparations for insurrection continued.

The Congress of Soviets of the Northern Region met, for example, in Petrograd on October 11–13, to prepare for the bigger congress two weeks later. Dominated by Bolsheviks and Left SRs, chaired by the Bolshevik Nikolai Krylenko, it included the very red Baltic Fleet sailors from the Kronstadt fortress as well as hotheaded Bolsheviks from Russian Finland. Yet the Northern Region adopted the position on which Lev Kamenev and Grigorii Zinov'ev continued to campaign, that it was too risky to act in advance of the All-Russian Congress of Soviets, envisioned as the basis for a future all-socialist, but not exclusively Bolshevik, government, to be finalized by the forthcoming Constituent Assembly. In short, "the democracy" in general, including the majority of Bolshevik leaders, retained even this late in the game a use for politics as a participatory process that conferred legitimacy on power.

The socialist parties competed among themselves, but they also contributed to a joint effort. In building their base, the Bolsheviks benefited from the elections to the Constituent Assembly, which "proceeded like clockwork thanks to the careful organizational work of their political opponents."[2] This tedious activity allowed the parties to establish a real following among the literate upper reaches of the popular classes. It educated these classes in the political process: slates, by-elections, platforms, slogans. The atmosphere was volatile, but the activity was routine. By endorsing the Second Congress, the Bolsheviks put their rivals in a quandary. Still reluctant to promote the idea of Soviet power, the moderates allowed the Bolsheviks to capture the idea, by now deeply embedded in popular consciousness, and hijack their creation.[3]

At the same time, Bolshevik activists continued with the practical tasks of preparing for insurrection in the name of the symbol over which its creators had lost control. Their visits to factories and barracks were no secret. The establishment press and even the Soviet leadership denounced them. Kerensky contemplated using armed force to stop them, but his minister of war reminded him that they had no armed forces to count on. Some Bolsheviks, for their part, worried that the popular mood was unstable. They worried about the reality of armed confrontation, given the paucity of weapons and ammunition on their side. The Red Guards of August had since fallen into disarray. But Lenin, addressing a secret meeting of the Central Committee during the night of October 16 to 17, was emphatic: "We cannot govern ourselves according to the mood of the masses since it fluctuates and is difficult to appraise.... The masses have given the Bolsheviks their trust and demand from them not words but deeds."[4]

Lenin then used the same scare tactics that Kerensky had used earlier in the year. He invoked the perennial bullying point—"the revolution in danger." "The bourgeoisie is intent on surrendering Petrograd as a means of crushing the revolution, and the only way of avoiding this is by taking the defense of the capital into our own hands." This, he insisted, must take the form of an armed insurrection. "Power must be seized immediately, at once. Every day lost could be fatal. History will not forgive us if we do not take power now!"[5]

The majority of Central Committee members endorsed Lenin's demand, but the dissenters were vocal. The most insistent was Kamenev, who published his reservations in Maxim Gorky's non-ideological leftist paper, *Novaia zhizn'* (*The New Life*), on October 18, for anyone with an interest in intra-party Bolshevik squabbles to read. Born Aleksei Peshkov, Gorky was a famous writer who styled himself a man of the people while regarding the people with unsentimental candor. During the war, he had allied with other progressive public figures in combatting official and popular anti-Semitism, which he saw as a moral scourge. Close to Lenin and the Bolsheviks, he maintained his intellectual independence.[6] Now, he offered a platform to Lenin's critics. Lenin's political intuition had led him, however, in exactly the right direction. Kerensky played into his hands.[7] The Germans had taken Riga on August 21 (September 3, NS) and were rumored to be moving toward Petrograd. Citing the threat to the capital, on October 5 Kerensky ordered the transfer of most of the Petrograd garrison to the Northern Front. Indeed, by mid-October German forces, in what they dubbed Operation Albion, had captured three islands in the Gulf of Riga.[8]

The threat to the capital and Kerensky's response were the target of Trotsky's irony at the Preparliament. Kerensky's order was indeed unpopular in various quarters. The commanders at the Northern Front viewed the possible arrival of the rebellious garrison as a threat to discipline. The soldiers themselves refused to budge. Invoking the example of Kornilov, whose rallying cry had been "Petrograd in Danger," the Bolsheviks claimed Kerensky was using the excuse to deprive the Revolution of its protagonists. They countered with the cry: "The All-Russian Congress in Danger!"[9]

The Soviet reacted to Kerensky's new moves as it had to the Kornilov events. As on that occasion, it portrayed its cause as the defense of the Revolution and rallied a popular following. In August it had created a special defense committee to protect the Provisional Government from Kornilov; now, the Provisional Government itself was the threat. On October 9, the Soviet established a Military Revolutionary Committee (*Voenno-revoliutsionnyi komitet*) in support of Soviet authority against the Provisional Government. The next day, the Bolsheviks formed their own military command center, but Lenin insisted they work through the Soviet Military Committee, which was headed by three Bolsheviks and two Left SRs. The Bolsheviks thus used the cover of the Soviet committee to shield their ultimate goal. This goal, as Lenin kept insisting, to the continuing demurrals of some of his lieutenants, was the seizure of power—ostensibly on behalf of the Soviet—before the opening of the Second Congress of Soviets, now rescheduled for October 25.[10]

The Petrograd garrison soldiers, at the heart of this crisis, had selected delegates to a citywide conference, which opened on October 18. The threat of being sent to the front caused them to embrace the summons issued by the Soviet Military Committee to defend the revolution. They did not endorse the call for armed insurrection, however, but urged the upcoming Soviet Congress to "take power in its hands and provide peace, land, and bread for the people."[11] Meanwhile, Bolshevik activists inundated the barracks and factories with a flood of impassioned oratory. Trotsky was particularly effective. "All round me," Sukhanov recalled, "was a mood bordering on ecstasy. It seemed as though the crowd, spontaneously and of its own accord, would break into some religious hymn."[12] The ideas Trotsky presented were well known. "The whole point lay in the mood."[13] Historians often wonder what people were really thinking at great historical moments. People at the time wondered, too. Sukhanov recalled observing "the raised hands and burning eyes of men, women, youths, soldiers, peasants.... Were they in spiritual transports? Did they see, through the raised curtain, a corner of the 'righteous land' of their longing? Or were they penetrated by a consciousness of the *political occasion*...? Ask no questions! Accept it as it was."[14]

The process of "taking power" was in fact already under way. The Bolsheviks may have disagreed among themselves on questions of timing and strategy, but their objective was transparent. Yet no one tried to stop them. Commanders on the Northern Front contemplated sending troops to Petrograd, but nothing came of their plans. Kerensky contemplated arresting the Soviet Military Committee, but General Georgii Polkovnikov, head of the Petrograd Military District, thought he could still persuade the Military Committee to back down. Undaunted, the Committee continued its low-key takeover of military authority, replacing government commissars with its own men, often Bolsheviks, who contravened official government orders. Polkovnikov, who had forfeited the loyalty of his troops, was in fact helpless to prevent them.[15]

Indeed, on October 23 the Soviet Military Revolutionary Committee gained control of the Peter-Paul Fortress and the Kronwerk Arsenal, strategic and symbolic sites. Still uncertain how the garrison and factories would respond to a preemptive strike, Bolshevik leaders continued to frame their moves as a defense of the Soviet Congress and the anticipated Constituent Assembly. Their socialist rivals saw through the masquerade, but took no action.[16] Kerensky, ensconced in the Winter Palace, shuttered the presses of the major Bolshevik newspapers (and a few reactionary rags, for the illusion of balance). This blow at freedom of the press, as the Bolsheviks sanctimoniously dubbed it, occurred in the early morning of October 24.[17] Kerensky's one feeble move thus allowed the Bolsheviks to depict themselves even more vigorously as champions of "the Revolution." "The Petrograd Soviet is in direct danger," they warned their followers: "counterrevolutionary conspirators have attempted to bring cadets and shock battalions from the suburbs to Petrograd during the night.... You are hereby directed to bring your regiment to battle readiness.... Any procrastination or interference in executing this order will be considered a betrayal of the revolution."[18]

Unable to rally the troops, Kerensky repaired to the Mariinskii Palace, where he addressed the Preparliament, which was still in session. There he accused the Bolsheviks of playing into the hands of the German enemy, charging them with "treason and betrayal of the Russian state."[19] For the rest of that fateful day and evening, the Preparliament debated the question of how to respond to the Bolshevik threat. Its failure to achieve a consensus revealed the deep splits within the country's political leadership. This body, which constituted the only alternative to Bolshevik power, was unable to fashion a plausible counter-strategy. On the liberal end of the spectrum, the Kadets urged Kerensky to use force; farther to the right, the Cossack delegates also demanded action. Both the radical and moderate left, by contrast, rejected a military response as unfeasible and also pointless. The only way to counteract the Bolsheviks' appeal was to adopt their platform. The government must embark immediately on the process of suing for peace; it must tackle the land question in the peasants' favor and promote the continuing democratization of the army. They attacked the Provisional Government for opening the door, by its timidity, to the Bolshevik challenge. The Menshevik Internationalists, the left wing of the party, and some delegates identifying as Left SRs demanded the Soviet Congress create an all-socialist government to replace Kerensky's regime.[20]

While this discussion was going on, that regime was systematically being undermined by small acts of subversion. The success of these moves reflected the strength of the organizational structures that the Bolsheviks, under cover of Soviet legitimacy, had already put in place. On the afternoon of October 24, the General Staff gave orders to raise the bridges, blocking access to the center. By the end of the day, however, only two of the bridges over the Neva had been drawn; the others were in the hands of street crowds and garrison soldiers. By then, also, the Military Revolutionary Committee had taken command of the central telegraph office and the wire service. In contrast to June and July, there were no mass demonstrations. Indeed, the center was unusually quiet. Many shops and restaurants closed, as did banks and offices, but pedestrians went about their business, seemingly unaware of what was afoot. In the evening, theatrical performances went on as usual.[21]

While these strategic operations were progressing, Lenin was following events from the safety of a private apartment in the city. The order for his arrest had been reactivated, and the Central Committee ordered him to stay out of sight. From his sheltered perch he pelted the comrades with furious directives. Annoyed with their caution, he demanded immediate action. Trotsky had presented the party's preparations as a defense of the Soviet against the Provisional Government's alleged treachery. Lenin was impatient with this pretense. He insisted the insurrection preempt the Soviet Congress. "It would be a disaster, or a sheer formality," he thundered, "to await the wavering vote of October 25. The people have the right and are in duty bound to decide such questions not by a vote, but by force…The government is tottering. It must be *given the deathblow* at all costs. To delay action is fatal."[22]

In Lenin's view, existing authority must not be allowed to fall by the weight of its own ineptitude; it must be toppled not by some parliamentary process, but by force of arms. Leaving his hiding place, sporting a wig, Lenin made his way through the Vyborg district in an empty streetcar, continuing on foot along Shpalernaia Street, arriving at party headquarters in Smolny around midnight; it was still October 24.[23] By the next morning, the Military Revolutionary Committee had stopped pretending. A company of engineers took control of the Nikolaevskii Railway Station, a commissar cut off power to government buildings, soldiers seized the central post office. The captain of the battleship *Aurora*, later a Soviet museum, was forced to position his ship near the Nikolaevskii Bridge, downstream from the Winter Palace. Sailors occupied the State Bank, and soldiers cut telephone lines to military headquarters and the Winter Palace, where the ministers had been meeting all night. Lenin in Smolny was impatient to have the whole ministerial crew arrested, but it took another twenty-four hours to make the final move.[24]

These twenty-four hours, from early morning on October 25 to the following dawn, contained more elements of comedy than tragedy, though they were tragic in the classical sense. The noblest characters in the drama—the Mensheviks of highest principles—were brought down by these very principles and by circumstances beyond their control. The most ruthless characters in the drama, also true to type, took advantage of those same circumstances. Lenin achieved his goal, because his goal was different and was tied up with his method. This method was characterized by the use of violence as a political tool. The various leaders thrown up by the monarchy's collapse presided over the collapse not only of the monarchical regime, but of the state itself. Lenin was determined to re-establish state power and to do so by using violence on behalf of a new political authority. Under the circumstances, this authority needed the endorsement of the popular forces that had emerged, in chaotic and violent fashion, in the factories, barracks, and villages. Any party that wished to rule had to capture the allegiance, in particular, of the disintegrating armed forces. From Lenin's perspective, however, popular revolution had to be an act of conquest; it did not have to be an act of mass participation. The Bolsheviks were hypocritical only in the minor sense that for as long as possible they claimed to be acting on behalf of "the Soviet," or the collective Left. They were entirely sincere, however, in their claim to express the will of the masses, since they did not in principle accept a parliamentary or "bourgeois" concept of how that will was to be expressed.

What this new state turned out to be was not entirely predetermined by the nature of the acts that began its existence. The civil war unleashed by the coup, the continuing debates within the leadership, the need to secure popular allegiance, the challenge of economic collapse—all helped shape the new order. The character of the Bolshevik takeover between October and December 1917 nevertheless left its stamp. Many of the features associated with Soviet power were already in evidence from the start, when Lenin's role was crucial. Giving the Bolsheviks credit for what they claimed to stand for, Vasilii Maklakov later observed, "Power for them was supposed to be a means of promoting their ideas, of achieving the victory of 'socialism,' and in this they miserably failed. *Their* victory delivered the most devastating blow to socialism possible."[25]

The final act in the Bolshevik seizure of power was primarily—and appropriately—a military operation. At 10 a.m. on October 25 (November 7, NS), while the Bolsheviks were still shaping their plan of action, Lenin composed a statement in the name of the Soviet Military Revolutionary Committee, announcing the fall of the Provisional Government. The message was sent an hour later to all points on the telegraph network: "The Provisional Government has been overthrown. State power has passed into the hands of the organ of the Petrograd Soviet of Workers' and Soldiers' Deputies, the Military Revolutionary Committee, which stands at the head of the Petrograd proletariat and garrison. The cause for which the people have struggled—the immediate proposal of a democratic peace, the elimination of landlord estates, workers' control over production, the creation of a soviet government—the triumph of this cause has been assured."[26]

The government targeted for extinction was in fact dismantled piece by piece. When Kerensky attempted to leave for Pskov at 11 a.m. to rally troops in self-defense, he was unable to use the trains, which were controlled by the Military Revolutionary Committee. In an ironic detail, often later invoked, he was obliged finally to depart the Winter Palace in a car borrowed from the U.S. Embassy. The erstwhile star of the February Revolution, therefore, exited Palace Square through the General Staff arch, American flag flying. Meanwhile, the deputies to the Preparliament, meeting in the Mariinskii Palace, were quick to disperse when soldiers and sailors surrounded the building. At 2 p.m. the ships which had departed Kronstadt in the morning arrived in the city and discharged their men.[27]

Half an hour later, Trotsky opened an emergency session of the Petrograd Soviet in Smolny. The day before, he had denied that the Bolsheviks were plotting an armed insurrection. Now he announced, "On behalf of the Military Revolutionary Committee, I declare that the Provisional Government no longer exists!"[28] Lenin then boasted of the start of a new era in Russian history, the creation of a "proletarian socialist state."[29] Someone in the hall objected that the Bolsheviks were preempting the decisions of the Soviet Congress slated to open later in the day. Trotsky was disdainful. "The will of the Second Congress of Soviets has already been predetermined by the fact of the workers' and soldiers' uprising. Now we have only to develop this triumph."[30] By this time in the afternoon, sailors were in possession of the Admiralty, having arrested the naval command. Soldiers and Red Guards surrounded the Winter Palace and Palace Square.[31]

Inside the Winter Palace, the ministers contemplated the unfolding crisis. Around 7 in the evening, a messenger delivered an ultimatum from the Military Revolutionary Committee demanding that they surrender. The messenger explained that the Peter-Paul Fortress and the *Aurora*, both now in the Committee's hands, were pointing their guns at the Winter Palace. The ministers decided to wait things out, insisting they were duty bound to remain in place until the opening of the Constituent Assembly. The Petrograd City Duma meanwhile formed a Committee of Public Safety. It sent a delegation to the Winter Palace in support of the ministers, which was prevented by the Military Revolutionary Committee from reaching its goal. The protest was, in any case, merely symbolic.[32] Also largely symbolic, though more intimidating, were the blanks fired at 9:30 p.m. from the battleship *Aurora*, as instructed by the Committee, making a loud noise. At 11, shots shattered a window above the chamber in which the ministers were waiting. The few remaining soldiers continued to drift away. When the Soviet Congress finally opened its session in Smolny at 10:40 p.m., on October 25, after an eight-hour delay, the Menshevik Fedor Dan reported that the government, including the socialist ministers, were "under fire at the Winter Palace."[33]

Who constituted this long-awaited gathering of the people? How did they respond to the crisis unfolding around them? Since the First Soviet Congress in June, the proportion of Bolshevik delegates had tripled, giving them about half the total of over six hundred. They did not therefore constitute a majority in their own right, but together with the Left SRs, with 15 percent, they occupied a dominant position. Mensheviks and other SRs accounted for a quarter of the places. Bolsheviks dominated the Presidium, with fourteen of the seats, including Trotsky and Zinov'ev; the Left SRs had another seven; the Mensheviks declined to accept the rest.[34]

Like all the revolutionary institutions of 1917, which were simultaneously iconoclastic and bureaucratic (engaging in raucous debate and assailing established authority, while issuing official passes and identity papers, typing and printing public announcements, and keeping minutes), the Congress surveyed the delegates' political positions. Three-quarters said they favored an all-Soviet government, which is to say, power exercised jointly by the various socialist parties. About 10 percent favored "power to the democracy," which meant some form of authority spread among the variety of participatory institutions spawned by the collapse of the old regime. A mere handful supported a continuing version of Kerensky's coalition government, either with or without the participation of the Kadet Party. No one admitted to wanting an exclusively Bolshevik or SR solution. The majority positions were not incompatible with the Bolshevik line, however. After all, Trotsky still represented the Military Revolutionary Committee, a Soviet organ, as a champion of Soviet authority. The consensus nevertheless confirmed the danger that Lenin wished to avoid—that "Soviet power" in this "democratic" form would merely impede the ultimate Bolshevik objective.

Indeed, when the Congress session opened, the majority of delegates called for the immediate formation of an all-socialist coalition government as a response to the current crisis, what Sukhanov called "a united democratic front." Moderate socialists denounced the military assault on the Provisional Government as "a criminal political venture."[35] Iulii Martov, speaking on behalf of the Menshevik Internationalists, warned that the Bolshevik coup, which he described as "a purely military plot," would unleash the fury of a civil war and result in the triumph of the counterrevolution. He urged fellow Mensheviks and moderate Bolsheviks to make it possible for the Provisional Government to transfer its authority to an all-democratic government by means of negotiation with a broad spectrum of democratic groups and organs.[36] When the moderates threatened to walk out of the meeting, they were taunted by the majority with the by now habitual terms of abuse: "Kornilovites!" "Lackeys of the bourgeoisie!"[37]

It was at this point that Trotsky offered his famous justification for the Bolshevik coup, which he also denied was one. His words echoed Lenin's hard-nosed political realism, as well as his high-handed disdain for political opponents and for anyone, in general, who preferred compromise to confrontation. Continuing to invoke the Soviet Congress as an expression of popular sovereignty, Trotsky ignored the fact that its majority, despite the overall dominance of Bolsheviks and Left SRs, had not endorsed the military takeover in progress outside its doors nor the idea of an exclusively Bolshevik government.

> A rising of the masses of the people requires no justification. What has happened is an insurrection, and not a conspiracy.... The masses of the people followed our banner and our insurrection was victorious. And now we are told: Renounce your victory, make concessions, compromise.... With whom ought we to compromise? With those wretched groups who have left us or who are making this proposal? ...No, here no compromise is possible. To those who have left and to those who tell us to do this we must say: You are miserable bankrupts, your role is played out; go where you ought to go; into the dustbin of history![38]

When Martov rose to leave, Trotsky condemned the Menshevik departure as "a weak and treacherous attempt to break up the legally constituted all-Russian representative assembly of the worker and soldier masses at precisely the moment when their avant-garde, with arms in hand, is defending the congress and the revolution from the onslaught of the counterrevolution."[39]

Trotsky thus provided a classic example of Bolshevik double-talk. Their socialist brothers were now anti-democratic counterrevolutionaries, while the Bolshevik vanguard posed as the champion of the duly elected Congress, whose opinion, of course, had not yet been expressed but which could be counted on to endorse the decisions of their self-appointed Bolshevik leaders. "The departure of the compromisers does not weaken the soviets," Trotsky declared. "Inasmuch as it purges the worker and peasant revolution of counterrevolutionary influences, it strengthens them." The tasks of the Second All-Russian Congress of Soviets "have been predetermined by the will of the laboring people and their insurrection of October 24 and 25. Down with the compromisers! Down with the servants of the bourgeoisie! Long live the triumphant uprising of soldiers, workers, and peasants!"[40]

In retrospect, Sukhanov, who was close to Martov and sympathetic to the moderate Bolsheviks, viewed the walk-out as a tragic mistake. "We completely untied the Bolsheviks' hands, making them masters of the entire situation and yielding to them the whole arena of the revolution. A struggle at the Congress for a united democratic front *might* have had some success.... By quitting the Congress,...we gave the Bolsheviks with our own hands a monopoly of the Soviet, of the masses, and of the revolution. By our own irrational decision, we ensured the victory of Lenin's whole 'line'!"[41] Some even in Lenin's inner circle still had doubts about the wisdom of his impatient move; some may genuinely have felt that socialist victory demanded cooperation among the socialist parties, each of which commanded the loyalty of sections of the popular classes—Mensheviks strong in some working-class quarters, and SRs among the peasants, soldiers, and white-collar ranks. Such a collaboration might have mitigated the hostility of establishment society, perhaps even engaged their cooperation, as a similar configuration had in 1905 and in February 1917. But the mood in the street and in the trenches, if not in the meeting hall, was more violent and agitated than before.

In the small hours of the next morning, October 26, the ministers heard shouting and stamping in the hallway outside their room in the Winter Palace, punctuated by a few random gunshots. The Bolshevik Vladimir Antonov-Ovseenko from the Military Revolutionary Committee entered at the head of an agitated crowd and announced their arrest. He prevented his entourage, disappointed to find the chief culprit—Kerensky—missing, from murdering their captives, whom they instead escorted across the Troitskii Bridge to the Peter-Paul Fortress. The ministers were threatened again with lynching by crowds along the way, before finding refuge in the cells of the notorious tsarist prison.

Back in Smolny, Anatolii Lunacharskii read the manifesto prepared by Lenin in anticipation of this moment. It was the beginning of a new era.

> The Soviet government will at once propose a democratic peace to all nations and an immediate armistice on all fronts. It will safeguard the transfer without compensation of all land—landlord, imperial, and monastery—to the peasant committees; it will defend the soldiers' rights, introducing a complete democratization of the army; it will establish workers' control over industry; it will insure the convocation of the Constituent Assembly on the date set; it will supply the cities with bread and the villages with staples; and it will secure to all nationalities inhabiting Russia the right of self-determination.[42]

At 5 a.m., the Second Congress of Soviets voted to endorse the manifesto, declaring that with the arrest of the ministers power had now passed from the Provisional Government to the soviets, and in particular to the Second Congress, which is to say, to themselves.[43]

Although he had objected to the timing of the coup, Lev Kamenev now introduced a series of decrees (ending the death penalty at the front, releasing political prisoners, ordering Kerensky's arrest), which were then endorsed by the Congress assembly. Lenin himself presented the Decree on Peace (*Dekret o mire*) "without annexations or indemnities" and the Decree on Land (*Dekret o zemle*), the Left SR platform of land seizure without compensation.[44] Everyone on the Left, broadly construed, wanted this by now; the Bolsheviks were agile enough to put their stamp on the least common denominator, thus appropriating the consensus.

Ex post facto, the Bolsheviks then invited the Congress to endorse the form of government the party had already created and which had originated the decrees. This new government consisted of the Council of People's Commissars (*Sovet narodnykh komissarov*, or Sovnarkom), nominally accountable to the Central Soviet Executive Committee (*Tsentral'nyi ispolnitel'nyi komitet*) elected by the Congress before which the Bolshevik leaders now stood. The commissars at this point were all Bolshevik (Lenin at the head, Trotsky at foreign affairs), since the Left SRs had declined to join them.[45] The Bolsheviks were themselves divided on the wisdom of trying to challenge "the democracy" head-on at this early stage, a confrontation they feared might arouse popular resistance. The moderates (Kamenev and Zinov'ev, most prominently) shared the view also held by the party's Left SR allies that the Sovnarkom should be answerable to the Central Executive Committee, which was not exclusively Bolshevik, although the Bolsheviks now had the largest share. Trotsky, by contrast, categorically rejected the idea of collaboration, calling the Mensheviks and Right SRs who had exited the Congress "traitors to the revolution."[46]

The moderate Bolsheviks differed from Lenin and Trotsky not on the ultimate goal—an exclusively Bolshevik government—but on the best way to achieve it. They feared that direct confrontation with their rivals on the left would unleash a civil war. They continued to insist that the Sovnarkom should derive its authority from the Constituent Assembly. Indeed, even Lenin confirmed the dates of the Constituent Assembly elections and its convocation (November 12–14 and 28, respectively). What gave him the authority to do so was entirely unclear. His endorsement was itself an act of subversion.

Lenin and Trotsky had thus succeeded in simplifying the political land-scape. You were either for us or against us. Everyone from the Kadets on the right to the mainstream Mensheviks and Right SRs in the middle denounced the Bolsheviks as usurpers; the Bolsheviks denounced their accusers as ene-mies of the revolution. Their opponents did indeed reject the Bolshevik claim to represent the will of the people. The invective spewed by Bolshevik orators was not mere name-calling, although name-calling had a powerful rhetorical effect. Whoever waved the Soviet banner had the advantage. Despite their claims to speak on behalf of the masses, however, the Bolsheviks fundamentally changed the character of "the Democracy," as the nonpartisan voice of the people at large. As a social force embodied in a range of ad hoc institutions, this democracy had undercut the old structures—destroyed dis-cipline in the army, opened the floodgates to endless discussion and debate, challenged the authority of ministers and bureaucrats. The Democracy had been unable, however, to create the architecture needed to run the successor to the autocratic state and transform the excitement of liberty into a new kind of discipline and power.

The idea of "the Democracy" had not yet, however, lost its hold. On the final day of the Congress, October 27, a representative of the Executive Committee of the All-Russian Railway Union (Vikzhel), which had not been invited to the gathering, rose to challenge its legitimacy and that of the Sovnarkom itself. The Railway Union was, in miniature, an inter-socialist gov-ernment of its own, its leadership including the range of socialist parties, its membership ranging from office clerks to mechanics to manual workers. It had played a key role in 1905 and in stopping Kornilov's progress toward Petrograd in August. Now, the Vikzhel emissary, in excited and menacing tones, denounced the seizure of power by a single party, insisted the revolutionary government must represent the full spectrum of socialist democracy, and threatened to use the Union's power over the vast railway network to reduce Petrograd to star-vation if the Bolshevik usurpers did not back down. His speech created a sensation, but the Bolsheviks immediately launched a propaganda campaign designed to separate the union rank-and-file from its own leaders.[47]

---

Meanwhile, there was mopping up to do. The ministers were behind bars. Kerensky had fled the Winter Palace, heading for Pskov. There he tried to rally the troops, as had General Ivanov on behalf of Nicholas in February and Kornilov on behalf of strong authority in August. Once again, the tactic failed. Bolshevik activists had already gained the support of soldier committees on the Northern and Western Fronts, those nearest to the capital.[48] The morning after the coup, General Petr Krasnov, one of Kornilov's accomplices, occupied Gatchina, twenty-five miles southwest of Petrograd, with a force of seven hundred Cossacks.[49] Back in Petrograd, on October 26, the Mensheviks and SRs on the City Duma, with the support of other democratic organizations, had formed the All-Russian Committee for the Salvation of the Homeland and the Revolution (*Komitet spaseniia rodiny i revoliutsii*), in opposition to the Sovnarkom and Soviet Central Executive Committee—to which the Sovnarkom was technically beholden but which in fact was under Bolshevik control. Like the Bolsheviks, the Committee for Salvation also thought of themselves as defending the revolution. Like the Bolsheviks, they described themselves as representing Soviet power, which, in their case, they viewed as the framework for grassroots participatory democracy and interparty socialist cooperation.[50]

The anti-Bolshevik mobilization elicited broad support. Anticipating General Krasnov's arrival, the Committee planned to attack the Bolshevik strongholds, but the plans were revealed while the troops were still miles away, waiting for reinforcements, and it was forced to take action ahead of time. On October 29, military school cadets took over the central telephone exchange, the Hotel Astoria, the State Bank, and even Smolny. The Military Revolutionary Committee declared martial law, and most garrisons ignored the summons. By the end of the day, the revolt had been snuffed out, leaving two hundred killed or wounded.[51] The Red Guards had been encouraged in their ferocity by Lieutenant-Colonel Mikhail Murav'ev, a rogue Left SR member of the Military Revolutionary Committee who went on to a short and brutal career.[52]

Despite the success in blocking their moderate opponents, Bolshevik victory was far from assured. General Krasnov was still on his way, and the situation in Moscow was highly unstable. There the Soviet also formed a Military Revolutionary Committee, while the City Duma formed a Committee of Public Safety (*Komitet obshchestvennoi bezopasnosti*). Moscow was less polarized than Petrograd, however. Both sides thought of themselves as defending Soviet power, which they expected the Constituent Assembly to endorse. Eager to avoid armed conflict, for two days the parties engaged in negotiations. Fighting began in Red Square only on October 27, when the Committee of Public Safety soon found itself in possession of the Kremlin. The chairman of the Moscow Soviet was Viktor Nogin, a man of the same

age as Trotsky, but one who had actually worked in a factory before beginning a youthful revolutionary career. The cautious Nogin was a conciliator,
as we have seen, who in fact did not think the Bolsheviks ought to have
struck out on their own. His attempt to reach a compromise with the other
socialists failed, however, on the demand that they accept the decrees issued
by the Soviet Congress after the coup.[53]

The Military Revolutionary Committee rallied thousands of Red Guards,
which, as in Petrograd, had formed on the basis of the factory militias, but now
answered to the Soviet. They were young, rowdy, and hard to control, and by
now armed. The fighting did not abate until November 3, not long after the
Military Revolutionary Committee had acquired artillery, which it directed at
the center of the city, from positions on the surrounding hills. Despite the fireworks, the Moscow Bolsheviks remained uneasy with the coup. Nogin and
others in the Moscow Party Committee shared the Menshevik conviction that
Soviet power must involve a broad democratic front. As far as the Moscow
working class was concerned, some embraced the coup, but few were willing
to fight for it. Many were passive, and some followed the Mensheviks in actively
rejecting Bolshevik claims to power.[54]

Back in Petrograd, while the revolt instigated by the Committee of
Salvation was under way and the outcome in Moscow was undecided, on
October 29 Vikzhel threatened to halt the railroads and launch a general
strike if the socialist parties did not agree to negotiate a peaceful settlement
of the crisis. Vikzhel's demand for an all-socialist government was welcomed
by the same parties and grassroots groups that had objected to the Bolshevik
maneuver all along: some Left SRs, Menshevik Internationalists, the Petrograd
Trade Union Council, the Central Soviet of Factory-Shop Committees, the
district soviets.[55] The question raised by Vikzhel's attempt to bring the socialist parties together is whether, even after the coup, there was a chance to
replace the Sovnarkom with a collaborative, purely socialist government.
After all, the multi-party soviets represented the essence of what the populace thought of as "the Democracy." "All Power to the Soviets!" was the slogan
Lenin used to cover the attack on Kerensky's government, knowing it resonated with the populace, whose active or tacit endorsement was key. In
Moscow, the Bolsheviks themselves took this slogan seriously.

Vikzhel faced a dilemma. It rejected the Sovnarkom as illegitimate, but
could not endorse the Committee for the Salvation of the Homeland and the
Revolution, which continued to support Kerensky's government.[56] Yet the
middle ground was not a neutral position. Vikzhel's refusal to transport troops

hindered Kerensky more than Lenin, since the pro-Bolshevik soldiers were already in place.[57] The Mensheviks, for their part, objected strenuously to the inclusion of Bolsheviks in the proposed all-socialist coalition, saying the party had "disgraced itself by its bloody escapades, its unprecedented violence and cruelty," with the result that it was now "hated by the vast majority of the country."[58] But when Vikzhel leaders criticized the Bolsheviks too sharply, their own rank and file objected.[59] The Vikzhel-sponsored negotiations that began on the evening of October 29 involved twenty-six representatives of eight parties and nine organizations, including a few moderate Bolsheviks, such as Zinov'ev and Kamenev, perpetual advocates of compromise within the party. The Mensheviks agreed to participate, causing the defection of part of their own Central Committee. Indeed, the Mensheviks accused Vikzhel, by its apparent neutrality, of working to the Bolsheviks' advantage. They and the Popular Socialists (*Trudovaia narodno-sotsialisticheskaia partiia*), an anti-terrorist offshoot of the SR Party, refused to contemplate a role in any government that included Lenin or Trotsky.[60] In the midst of these squabbles, a delegation of Putilov workers entered the hall and declared, "We will not tolerate the continuation of civil war." Damning both the Bolsheviks and the SRs, they shouted, "To hell with Lenin and Chernov! Hang them both!... We say to you: stop being destructive. Or else we'll deal with you ourselves!"[61]

As most accounts suggest, the mood in Vyborg and other factory districts was militant, if ideologically neutral, while the activists remained stubbornly ideological. Indeed, the leaders were split between those who wanted to compromise with the Bolsheviks—which meant refusing to oppose them—and those for whom civil war was the only acceptable course. Once its initiative collapsed, Vikzhel declared its support for the Sovnarkom, after all. Zinov'ev and Kamenev were censured by the Bolshevik Central Committee, while the Left SRs agreed to join the Sovnarkom, where they remained until March 1918, when the government reverted to its original single-party profile.[62] The external threat was also soon mastered. On October 30, Krasnov's troops were overwhelmed at Tsarskoe Selo in a battle against the more numerous combination of armed workers, soldiers from the Petrograd garrison, and sailors from the Baltic fleet. Krasnov surrendered, and Kerensky once again fled.[63]

———————

In terms of the kind of power that could turn a self-appointed body (whether the Provisional Government or the Sovnarkom) into an actual government, or endow a diffusely elected body (the Petrograd and All-Russian Soviets) with real political authority, the devotion of the armed forces was key. When the army deserted him, Nicholas fell; when it deserted the Provisional Government, that government dissolved. The Bolsheviks had managed, through arduous agitation in the Petrograd garrison and at the front, to secure at least the neutrality of the troops and in some key cases their adherence to what the Bolshevik Party seemed to stand for.

The political events of 1917 unfolded against a background of increasing social disintegration, mounting hunger, and popular outbursts, in which the same troops that often decided the outcome of political contests made it difficult for any kind of leadership to exercise control. Crime and violence, in which alcohol was the incendiary ingredient, had intensified over the course of the year. Soldiers rampaged through the cities, raiding liquor depots, pillaging train stations, attacking merchants. The continuing food crisis produced a feeling of desperation among ordinary working people, who often joined in. A Moscow official identified a common pattern to the disorders, which began "with the trashing of liquor depots, after which the completely drunken crowd moves on to the looting of stores, shops, and houses."[64] The historian Igor Narskii characterizes the rash of drink-fueled riots that followed the change in power in October as a "veritable bacchanalia," a "drunken revolution."[65] Similar marauding affected the countryside as well.[66]

The collapse of social discipline provided the Bolsheviks with an opening, but it was a threat as well. Achieving political authority was obviously a matter of the utmost urgency. It was not enough to declare victory; victory had to be imposed. In the preparation for the final assault, the Bolsheviks always combined two different modes of operation. While Lenin pressed for immediate action and Trotsky led the charge, the many low-level party activists spread the word. They instilled, by constant repetition, the basic party slogans, reminding their listeners, as the Provisional Government and the Soviet sank into passivity, that there was always an alternative waiting in the wings. At the dawn of November on the old calendar, with the Bolsheviks now supposedly in command, the political struggle only intensified. The period has been described as "an incipient civil war," fought not with weapons but with slogans, newspapers, speeches, and elections, in the cities and also at the front in numerous soldier gatherings.[67]

At first, the Bolsheviks were stymied by the anticlimax in Petrograd and by the negotiations forced on the socialist left by the leaders of the Railroad Union, desperate to revive the model of an all-socialist government. The ministers had been deposed, but the second-ranking Provisional Government functionaries continued to meet in a private apartment until the end of November, sequestering state funds to support the strike of civil servants, which lasted for another two months.[68] Finally, as the desultory Vikzhel negotiations collapsed, Lenin returned to the offensive, taking the first dramatic step toward consolidating Bolshevik influence in the army. The party needed not only to finish the conquest of rank-and-file loyalty but also to neutralize the power of the top command. Most urgently, the Bolsheviks needed to take the country out of the war. More accurately, they needed to gain political control over the process already under way—the army's increasing incapacity to fight, the officers' incapacity or unwillingness to lead, the country's vulnerability to continuing German aggression.

The Decree on Peace presented by Lenin at the Second Congress of Soviets invited the Central Powers and the Allies jointly to accept an immediate armistice, to be accompanied by negotiations for a "democratic peace."[69] Receiving no reply from the Allies, on November 8/21 the Sovnarkom ordered Commander in Chief General Nikolai Dukhonin at headquarters in Mogilev to contact the Germans "with the proposal of an immediate cessation of hostilities for the purpose of starting peace negotiations."[70] Dukhonin, who had replaced General Alekseev after Kornilov's attempted August coup, did not recognize Bolshevik authority and delayed his response.[71] Though an imperial holdover, the general was not a monarchist. He appealed to the troops in the name of the democratic revolution. The Allies, he told them, might contemplate a general peace if Russia had a legitimate government with which they could cooperate. The Bolsheviks and the Germans were enemies of the true revolution. "Give the true Russian democracy time to form a government," he pleaded, "and this government, together with the Allies, will immediately give you a lasting peace. Rapprochement with the Germans means new war in the near future. The Germans will not endure a free democratic Russian people on their borders."[72]

On November 9, when the general outright refused to obey, he was replaced as commander in chief by Nikolai Krylenko, a mere ensign.[73] A radiogram was then dispatched to all points in the armed forces, announcing Dukhonin's replacement and issuing a command, widely reprinted in army newspapers and instantly available to the Germans, as it was intended to be.

1. "Burning the Emblems of Royalty. In one instance the crowd seized an American eagle, which shared the fate of its Russian brothers." Stinton Jones, *Russia in Revolution: Being the Experiences of an Englishman in Petrograd during the Upheaval* (London: H. Jenkins, 1917). Joseph Regenstein Library, University of Chicago.

2. "Guns behind barricade commanding the Litainai Prospect and Bridgehead." Stinton Jones, *Russia in Revolution: Being the Experiences of an Englishman in Petrograd during the Upheaval* (London: H. Jenkins, 1917). Joseph Regenstein Library, University of Chicago.

**3.** A. I. Savel'ev, "Bread Lines," Used as title-page illustration, *Iskry: Illiustrirovannyi khudozhestvenno-literaturnyi i iumoristicheskii ezhenedel'nyi zhurnal s karikaturami,* no. 39 (Moscow: Sytin, October 8, 1917). [*Sparks: Illustrated Artistic-Literary and Humorous Weekly Magazine with Caricatures*]. Getty Images.

**4.** K. K. Bulla, "Demonstration of soldiers' wives on Nevskii Avenue, Petrograd, April, 9, 1917." Banners read: "Feed the Children" and "Better Rations for Soldiers' Families Defending Freedom and the People's Peace." Slavic and East European Collections, The New York Public Library.

**5.** Provisional Executive Committee of the State Duma, 1917. Library of Congress.

**6.** "Meeting of the Executive Committee of Worker and Soldier Deputies." Library of Congress.

**7.** Funeral ceremony for victims of the revolution, March 23, 1917. Banners read: "Long Live the Democratic Republic!" Library of Congress.

**8.** Vladimir Il'ich Lenin. Library of Congress.

"Let the regiments at the front immediately elect representatives to open formal truce negotiations with the enemy. The Soviet of People's Commissars gives you this authority." The men were enjoined, however, to protect their officers from "lynchings unworthy of revolutionary armies.... You will maintain the strictest revolutionary and military discipline."[74] When it came to laying down arms, the men did not need to be asked twice. Both the Germans and the Bolsheviks, for different reasons, were anxious to control the process of spontaneous fraternization, but the directive was intended to win the loyalty of men in uniform to the new regime. The injunction to maintain "revolutionary discipline" was, by contrast, much harder to enforce. The Bolsheviks' desire to instill discipline was, moreover, highly ambivalent. In characteristic fashion, they insisted on obedience to the new authorities, while cultivating antagonism (and aggression) with respect to the old.

Having satisfied the deepest desires of the men at the front and allowed them to take direct credit for the peace, Krylenko made the rounds, warning the soldiers to reject "the lies and the false appeals of General Dukhonin's gang." Relieving the key commanders of the Northern Front of their posts, he declared Dukhonin to be "an enemy of the people, for his stubborn refusal to obey the order of dismissal and for his criminal acts which gave a new impetus to civil war. All those who support Dukhonin are to be arrested regardless of their social position, party affiliations, and past record."[75] The Fifth Army Committee in Dvinsk, following the clue, vowed "to wipe out all counterrevolutionary nests that stand in the way of peace and to attack at once the group at Mogilev, including Dukhonin…and other traitors to the revolution."[76]

Dukhonin had no means of defense. The commanders at Dvinsk and Pskov informed him that their men wanted peace and would no longer obey them. They were "helpless to prevent the collapse of the front," they reported.[77] On November 19, the Mogilev soviet formed a pro-Bolshevik Military Revolutionary Committee, which arrested General Dukhonin and his remaining staff.[78] General Kornilov, imprisoned in Bykhov near Mogilev since August, had urged Dukhonin to assemble an anti-Bolshevik contingent. The general refused, but did permit Kornilov and the other commanders in Bykhov, including General Anton Denikin, to escape. The group managed to make their way individually by various means to Novocherkassk, upstream from Rostov at the base of the Don River, where they joined General Alekseev, who had preceded them.[79] This gathering became the kernel of the White movement.

Dukhonin remained at his post to face the danger. When Krylenko arrived by train the next day, he invited the general into his railway car. A crowd of angry soldiers and sailors swarmed the carriage, egged on by one of their own commanders who tossed them the general's epaulettes, the hated sign of military authority. The instigator was the same Lieutenant-Colonel Murav'ev who three weeks before had stopped the revolt of the Committee for the Salvation of the Homeland.[80] The mob then dragged Dukhonin from Krylenko's carriage, beat him senseless and shot him point blank, then stripped and defaced the corpse.[81] Krylenko claimed he had attempted to stop the attack but was overpowered by the "masses," whose "hatred...had boiled over." In a message to the troops, he denounced "the lynching," as a "stain" on "the banner of the revolution."[82] A correspondent at the scene reported, however, that Krylenko had not made a great effort to protect the victim. "Passions were excited to such a pitch that any intervention on his part might mean death to him also. He only clutched at his head and sat for a long time with his face buried in his hands."[83] Krylenko himself had done his best to bring those passions to the boiling point. This incident illustrates the dangers inherent in what was left of the Imperial Army: angry and undisciplined soldiers; commanders hostile to the new regime but unable to rally their forces; new commanders equally unable to impose their authority, but willing to provoke if they could not command.

The Civil War that ensued tested but also hardened the Bolsheviks' hold on power. It gave them time to consolidate and redefine the meaning of Soviet rule. The double-headed eagle and gold-braid epaulettes had to be replaced by something new. A new flag, a new emblem, a new anthem, a new calendar, new orthography, and a new language of state—all emerged fitfully in the course of the Civil War. Even the name of the new regime was unstable for the first few years. The day the Bolsheviks seized the Winter Palace, the Second All-Russian Congress of Soviets of Worker and Soldier Deputies announced the establishment of the Russian Soviet Republic (*Rossiiskaia Sovetskaia Respublika*), adding the middle term to the title adopted by the Provisional Government.[84] Various decrees in early 1918, however, used other labels, sometimes more than one: Russian Federal Republic, Soviet Republic of Russia, Soviet Worker and Peasant Republic, Russian Federal Soviet Republic. The Constitution proclaimed on July 19, 1918, settled on Russian Socialist Federal Soviet Republic, later reshuffled as Russian Soviet Federal Socialist Republic (*Rossiiskaia Sovetskaia Federativnaia Sotsialisticheskaia Respublika*—RSFSR). The RSFSR was the principal republic in what became the Union of Soviet Socialist Republics in 1922. Until then, the country was referred to informally as Soviet Russia, the Republic of Soviets, or the Country of Soviets. Its enemies rejected all these combinations. The Whites used the derogatory "Sovdepia," snidely compressing "Soviet of Deputies." Even the slur acknowledged the core institution and symbol of Bolshevik rule.

# 5

# Death of the Constituent Assembly

The Bolsheviks embraced the use of force not only to establish themselves in power, but also to define the kind of power they intended to wield. But the party, under Lenin's astute leadership, was also good at brand-building, image-making, political theater, and parliamentary maneuvers. They were better than their rivals at leveraging institutions for their own use. Both the Soviet (and its congress) and the Constituent Assembly remained potent symbols of the revolution's democratic appeal for a wide spectrum of Russian society. The Bolsheviks needed to appropriate and neutralize them both.

Opposition to the coup from the socialist Left clarified the Bolshevik position in the political field, but though Lenin and Trotsky had called the shots, the party was not monolithic. At this point, it was broad enough still to include divergent views on the path to victory. Moderates recoiled at the specter of an emerging civil war. Anatolii Lunacharskii, the commissar of education, believed compromise was needed to avoid the use of terror; Trotsky accused him of "petty bourgeois psychology" for considering terror something to avoid.[1] At the Central Committee meeting on November 1, 1917, David Riazanov, chairman of the trade union council, warned against alienating their Left SR allies and creating the impression of having "tricked the masses, having promised them a Soviet government."[2] Another comrade voiced similar doubts: "We must understand that having taken power we will be forced to lower wages, to increase unemployment, to institute terror. We do not have the right to reject these methods, but there is no need to rush into them."[3] The cautious Moscow Bolshevik Viktor Nogin worried that failure to compromise would result in "a purely Bolshevik government maintained by political terror," resulting in "the estrangement of the proletarian mass organizations from those who direct our political affairs, to the establishment of an unaccountable regime, and to the destruction of the revolution and the country."[4] He was no doubt thinking of the armed conflict still raging in Moscow.

On November 4, Nogin, Grigorii Zinov'ev, and Aleksei Rykov resigned from the Central Committee in protest.[5] The Central Committee's rejection of a socialist coalition, they said, contradicted the wishes of "the overwhelming majority of workers and soldiers, eager for the quickest possible end to the blood-letting among the different parties of the democracy." Three weeks later, however, Nogin confessed "his mistakes."[6] He died in 1924, early enough to be buried in the Kremlin wall; Varvarskaia Square in central Moscow was renamed in his honor. Emerging from the Nogin Square metro station in later years, Muscovites would no longer recall that its namesake had once briefly resisted the force of Lenin's will.

Arguments on behalf of socialist cooperation and inhospitable to the use of terror carried no weight with Lenin or Trotsky, yet the party was not yet ready to dispense with the symbolic legitimacy provided by the Soviet Executive Committee. Instead, it counterbalanced the recent addition of peasant delegates favoring the Left SRs by recruiting additional soldiers and sailors. Lenin thus maneuvered under cover of the popular institutions, alienating moderates outside the party, intimidating moderates inside the party, and stacking institutions (the Soviet Executive Committee) to achieve political control. A skillful political operator, Lenin aimed ultimately to abolish politics altogether by abolishing disagreement. Differences were not matters for discussion but grounds for opposition. In 1903, to begin with, the Mensheviks ceased to be comrades who argued, but a separate party. As party leader, Lenin concentrated decision-making in the hands of subordinates he could manipulate or control, even when they showed signs of resistance. The price of resistance was exclusion; dissenters were reluctant to be expelled from the fold, as Nogin's example shows. Already, the Petrograd Soviet had ceased to be a political organ. Its vast plenum continued to gather throughout November, in endless meetings at which no decisions could be made—theater, not politics. Decisions were made in the refashioned Executive Committee and Presidium, composed only of Bolsheviks and Left SRs, both chaired by the moderate Zinov'ev, now also toeing the line. By the end of the year, the Bolsheviks had established their dominance in the district soviets as well.[7]

The focus of attention next turned to the elections for the Constituent Assembly, the last symbol of democracy, aside from the various soviets (by now under Bolshevik domination) remaining from the February Revolution. The Bolsheviks approached the election campaigns with their usual combination of grassroots energy and no-holds-barred intimidation. On the one hand, they worked to get out the vote, wanting to ensure a popular mandate; on the other hand, they threatened to dissolve the Constituent Assembly if the results did not come out in their favor.

The symbol proved to be a true experiment in democracy. About fifty million people, not quite a third of the total population, voted in the elections to the Constituent Assembly. Clearly, the broad populace had some idea of what it meant to make their voices heard. About 15 percent of voters were urban, matching the overall demographic profile, which means that the peasantry took the election more seriously than might have been expected. Over seven hundred deputies were elected, two-thirds SRs (mostly Right SRs), a quarter Bolsheviks, the rest other socialists and the national parties (Ukrainian, Muslim, Armenian, Zionist). The Mensheviks and Kadets earned very few seats. The Bolsheviks alone did not have a majority; they could not yet ignore the SRs. Only in the cities did the Bolsheviks outdo them (34 and 16 percent, respectively), better in Petrograd with 45 percent to the SR 16 percent. Cities also provided the Kadets and Mensheviks with their strongest support (19 and 6.4 percent). Among rural voters, 44 percent chose SRs, 18.6 percent Bolsheviks, a negligible number Mensheviks and Kadets. Confirming the cultural profile, Kadet and Menshevik deputies had the highest level of education; at least a third of SR and Bolshevik deputies had little schooling at all.

The results confirmed the contrast between the Bolshevik appeal among the urban lower classes and the SRs' roots in the countryside. Although the Mensheviks also had working-class followers, they appear here, like the Kadets, as a party of educated people. In terms of ethnic composition, the deputies came from thirty different groups, of which the largest were the Russians (half), Ukrainians (18.7 percent), and Jews (11 percent). According to party affiliation, half the Bolshevik deputies were Russian, 18 percent Jewish, 9 percent Ukrainian; of the SRs two-thirds were Russian, 10 percent Jewish, 9 percent Ukrainian. Put the other way around, two-thirds of Russian deputies were SRs, a quarter Bolshevik, 5 percent Kadet; two-thirds of Ukrainian deputies belonged to Ukrainian socialist parties, another quarter to the SRs, 12 percent to the Bolsheviks. Deputies of Jewish background were evenly divided—about 40 percent each for Bolsheviks and SRs. The body as a whole represented a new generation. Of the 400 or so members of the Fourth Duma, a third were under forty years old, another third over fifty. By contrast, three-quarters of the Constituent Assembly deputies were under forty, a mere 9 percent over fifty.[8]

The overall figures provide a sense of the vast range of representation in the first Empire-wide body elected on a universal suffrage. The deputies themselves included leading figures from all the major parties. Many top Bolsheviks had been elected, including Trotsky, Lenin, and Stalin. The Kadets Pavel Miliukov, Vladimir Nabokov, Maksim Vinaver, and Vasilii Maklakov were elected but did not come. Also on the list were the Zionist former Duma deputy Naftali Fridman, the Georgian Mensheviks Iraklii Tsereteli and Akakii Chkhenkeli, and the Ukrainians Symon Petliura and Volodymyr Vynnychenko, who had already assumed leadership of an embryonic national government. The deputies included only ten women, including the wives of Bolshevik deputies Krylenko (Elena Rozmirovich) and Piatakov (Evgeniia Bosh), and the SR Chernov (Anastasiia Sletova-Chernova). The others had independent reputations as political notables in their own right. Among them, sixty-five-year-old Vera Figner, Mariia Spiridonova, and the legendary Ekaterina Breshko-Breshkovskaia, now seventy-three, were SRs, Varvara Iakovleva and feminist Aleksandra Kollontai Bolsheviks.[9] In short, among the hundreds elected were the cream of the post-imperial political elite.

The Bolshevik attitude toward the Constituent Assembly was purely instrumental, however. The Sovnarkom briefly contemplated the recall of deputies who did not recognize Soviet power, but time was short—and, of course, the action would have been an outright provocation. Instead, the Sovnarkom focused on obstructing any possible action taken in support of the newly elected body, scheduled to open on November 28, two weeks away.[10] Two days after the elections concluded, the Sovnarkom, again on its own authority, ordered the dismissal of the Petrograd City Duma, the remaining center of civil opposition to Bolshevik (coded Soviet) rule. When the municipal deputies continued to meet, some, including Nabokov, were briefly arrested. On November 23, they announced the formation of a Union for the Defense of the Constituent Assembly (*Soiuz zashchity Uchreditel'nogo sobraniia*), subsuming the earlier All-Russian Committee for the Salvation of the Homeland and the Revolution. Composed of Kadets and the socialist parties that rejected the Sovnarkom's claim to represent Soviet power and exercise the functions of a state, the

Union decided to organize a peaceful demonstration for November 28 in defense of the Constituent Assembly, which the Bolsheviks in principle also endorsed.[11]

Within the Bolshevik leadership, the question, once again, was one of tactics. No one in the party defended the Constituent Assembly on principle as the embodiment of true democracy. Their debates focused, rather, on how to get rid of it. They insisted that the question of legitimacy had been decided by the acclamation of the Soviet Executive Committee, which had endorsed the Sovnarkom as the expression of Soviet power. The very idea of legitimate succession was awkward, and not only because of Bolshevik contempt for the formality of the law—and indeed, what law could be invoked? The imperial regime itself had flouted its own laws. The monarch had been deposed by the illegal actions of his military command and parliament. The Constituent Assembly was to accomplish the task of legitimizing the revolution. Now its time had come. Even some Bolsheviks admitted, explaining their reluctance simply to sweep it away, that "constitutional illusions were still very much alive among the masses."[12] These were presumably the same masses whose support the Bolsheviks invoked in justifying their assault on competing centers of popular allegiance.

Certainly, the large procession that made its way along Nevskii and Liteinyi Avenues on November 28 in response to the City Duma's appeal could not be said to represent the people at large, though it marched in support of the democratically elected Constituent Assembly. The crowd of well over ten thousand Petrograders consisted largely of the professional middle classes and leaders of the moderate and liberal parties. But the socialist members of the Soviet Executive Committee and the delegates to the SR Party Congress who marched with them indeed had a claim to a popular mandate. Blocked at gunpoint from entering the Tauride Palace, where the Constituent Assembly was supposed to assemble, a few of the marchers climbed over the fence and held a small meeting, addressed by the SR leader, Viktor Chernov, and other SR and Kadet spokesmen. Late in the afternoon, the handful of Constituent Assembly delegates who had reached Petrograd held a rump meeting that elected Chernov as chair.[13]

In the absence of the majority of elected delegates, this assembly was largely symbolic, but the few vowed to keep meeting until the full complement was ready. When the deputies returned the next day to continue their deliberations, they were expelled from the building and barred from coming back.[14] Some of them, including the Kadet Andrei Shingarev, a physician by training and former minister in the Second Coalition, were arrested.[15] Shingarev, an outspoken former Duma deputy, had provided a continual flow of anti-Bolshevik invective. He spearheaded the group of Kadets who made efforts to resist the Bolshevik move first to delay, then dissolve the Constituent Assembly. The Sovnarkom branded all of them "enemies of the people." Lenin declared them outside the law, invoking the French Jacobin example.[16] The Left SRs, wishing to avoid the impression that their Bolshevik allies were conspiring against the Constituent Assembly, though in fact they obviously were, urged the Sovnarkom to retract the order for the liberals' arrest. The Soviet Executive Committee (not surprisingly) gave the Sovnarkom full powers to act. As Trotsky put it, "There is nothing immoral in the proletariat finishing off a class that is collapsing...You," he addressed the Left SRs, "wax indignant at the naked terror which we are applying against our class enemies. But let me assure you that in one month's time at the most, it will assume more frightful forms....Not the [Peter-Paul] fortress but the guillotine awaits our enemies."[17]

The Bolsheviks needed the Soviet Executive Committee and the Constituent Assembly, just as they needed the Left SRs as partners in the Sovnarkom, only until they felt they could shed the democratic mantle. The most effective slogans leading up to and following the October coup were peace and land. The Bolsheviks shared these catchwords with the SRs, both Right and Left; Lenin therefore needed to make his party indispensable— or unavoidable. The Bolsheviks had first to free themselves from SR interference and then to eliminate them altogether from the political scene, as their last credible rivals. The final move would mean the end of arguments or concessions, unleashing an all-out war against any alternative political force or symbol. The Bolsheviks denounced their opponents as tools of the bourgeoisie, a term of abuse that had long since lost its sociological referent, but which justified the battle as class warfare. It was a political fight to end all politics.

The Left SRs were not passive partners. The Mensheviks had withdrawn from the political arena in protest; the Left SRs continued to protest, condemning the closure of the Petrograd City Duma and the retaliation against defenders of the Constituent Assembly, but at the same time continuing to negotiate. They demanded equal weight in the Sovnarkom, but after prolonged negotiation accepted a quarter of the positions and a third of the seats in the Soviet Executive Committee.[18] Unable as yet to emancipate themselves from their allies, the Bolsheviks took steps to strengthen their hand. On December 7, 1917, they replaced the Military Revolutionary Committee, still nominally answerable to the Soviet Executive Committee, with an independent organ, although its directorship also included Left SRs.[19] This was the All-Russian Extraordinary Commission to Combat Counterrevolution and Sabotage (*Vserossiiskaia chrezvychainaia komissiia po bor'be s kontrrevoliutsiei i sabotazhem*), known as the Cheka (from the initials of "*chrezvychainaia komissiia*").[20] It was headed by the Polish Social Democrat Feliks Dzerzhinskii. Now just over forty, more or less Trotsky's age, he came from a modest gentry family in the Vilna region. Like others of his generation, he became involved in underground political activity in his teens, spending much of his youth in tsarist prisons, from which he was liberated only in March 1917. Cheka headquarters were located in the old Okhrana building in Petrograd, no doubt affording him a particular satisfaction. Like other Polish Social Democrats, Dzerzhinskii found both anti-Semitism and Polish nationalism unacceptable and had close ties to the Jewish socialist movement in Poland.[21]

The Cheka was the ancestor of the later Soviet security organs, known in the West by their Russian acronyms. In 1922 it was replaced by the State Political Administration (*Gosudarstvennoe politicheskoe upravlenie*—GPU), subordinate to the People's Commissariat of Internal Affairs (*Narodnyi komissariat vnutrennikh del*—NKVD). In 1923 the GPU became independent as the OGPU, which in 1934 returned to the NKVD, infamous for the Stalinist purges of the 1930s. In 1941 responsibility for state security was transferred to the NKGB (*Narodnyi komissariat gosudarstvennoi bezopasnosti*), which after further reshuffling in 1954 became the KGB, the organization Vladimir Putin joined in 1975.

Bringing the Left SRs into the government was intended to neutralize their objections and undercut their value as an alternative on the Left. But Lenin's key strategy was always to sharpen the line between friend and foe. Now the enemy included, on the one hand, socialists who had accepted the overturn of the Provisional Government but conceived of the revolution in non-Bolshevik terms. On the other hand, the enemy included a range of groups aiming to turn back the clock—to February, at the least. Among them were the public servants still refusing to perform their functions for the new masters. The Bolsheviks had real enemies, who were indeed conspiring against them. In the absence of any mechanism for political conflict, however, every difference became a casus belli. If war is politics by other means, for Lenin politics was a form of war.

Formal legal principles, derided as bourgeois, were meaningless. When the Left SR Isaak Shteinberg became commissar of justice, he quaintly insisted on freeing prisoners who had not yet committed any crimes. Arrests, however, continued: moderate socialists, Constituent Assembly delegates, including Chernov and Tsereteli. Shteinberg managed to get the pair released. With startling naiveté and tactical ineptitude, amounting either to self-delusion or disingenuousness, he kept insisting the Cheka observe legal norms. His Bolshevik colleagues on the Sovnarkom reminded him that the Cheka was the law.[22]

In a general sense, Red Terror involved a process of incorporating dispersed violence into the formal structures of the state. As Dzerzhinskii put it in 1922, "Assuming that the age-old hatred of the revolutionary proletariat for its slave-masters will necessarily take the form of a whole series of unsystematic bloody episodes, during which the aroused elements of the people's anger will sweep away not only enemies but also friends, not only hostile and harmful elements, but strong and useful ones, I have attempted to introduce the systematization of the penal apparatus of revolutionary power. The Cheka has never been anything other than the rational direction of the punishing arm of the revolutionary proletariat."[23]

If Dzerzhinskii addressed the punitive dimension of the Terror, Trotsky considered its role in the conduct of war. This was not a war in which the contenders expected to conclude a peace and define the terms of future coexistence. "The enemy," Trotsky insisted, "must be neutralized; during war this means—destroyed."[24] As Dzerzhinskii put it, "Justice is not what's needed now. Now it's a fight—face to face, a fight to the death." He therefore demanded "an organization of revolutionary vengeance on the agents of the counterrevolution."[25] For the Bolsheviks, government was itself a form of war—war against the remnants of the old social order, conceived as a perpetually resurgent internal threat. Therefore the terror of wartime became a principle of rule.

---

The continually postponed Constituent Assembly remained an obstacle on the road to assuring the authority of the new, self-declared state. As in the lead-up to the October coup, Lenin faced resistance from the moderates in his own party, who continued to urge the Bolsheviks to work through, not against, the elected bodies representing a popular mandate. Lenin, however, disparaged the Constituent Assembly and demanded it subordinate itself to what he called the more genuinely democratic authority of the soviets. In short, he wanted the Constituent Assembly to lend its authority to the false claims with which the Bolsheviks had masked their preemptive strike in October. He wanted it to expend its last vestige of credit in discrediting itself.

As part of his bid to concentrate authority in his own hands, with respect to other parties, as well as to his own, on December 11 Lenin engineered the expulsion of his moderate critics, including Lev Kamenev, from the Bolshevik faction in the Soviet Executive Committee.[26] Competition from outside had not yet been extinguished, however. The Left SRs in the Sovnarkom pushed to set January 5 as the date for the opening of the Constituent Assembly, after a long month's delay. Anticipating trouble, the Bolshevik-dominated Soviet Executive Committee scheduled soviet and peasant congresses to meet a few days later, presumably as a correction to whatever would have occurred.

Meanwhile, on January 3, 1918, the Soviet Executive Committee endorsed a manifesto defining the character of the new regime. Lenin intended to present this document at the opening of the Constituent Assembly, which in principle alone had the authority to approve it. Modeled on the "Declaration of the Rights of Man and Citizen" issued by the National Constituent Assembly in Paris in 1789, the "Declaration of the Rights of the Toiling and Exploited People" (*Deklaratsiia prav trudiashchegosia i ekspluatirue-mogo naroda*) defined the new state as a "Republic of Soviets of Worker, Soldier, and Peasant Deputies" (*Respublika Sovetov rabochikh, soldatskikh i krest'ianskikh deputatov*), in which the soviets exercised the supreme govern-ing authority. Speaking in the name of the Constituent Assembly, the man-ifesto outlined a program of social, as well as political, transformation. The republic was to be a "federation of National Soviet Republics." It would abolish the private ownership of property in all its forms, which would become henceforth the property of the nation, for the use and benefit of the formerly oppressed classes. "Universal labor duty" would contribute to the eradication of "the parasitic classes." These classes, in the meantime, would be prevented by the "armed toilers" formed into "a Socialist Red Army" from rallying their forces against the revolution.[27]

On the key question of war and peace, the Declaration repudiated the imperial regime's treaties and war aims (as well as its debts to foreign governments and investors), announcing its support for a democratic peace, granting Finnish independence, and promising autonomy for the Armenians—though not for the Poles. Autonomy for the Armenians was less high-minded than it sounded. It was part of the elaborate diplomatic maneuvers among Bolshevik peacemakers, the Central Powers, and the Ottoman Empire, in which the fate of ethnic minorities was used on all sides as a bargaining chip.

The crux of the Declaration, however, was the question of sovereignty. Here, Lenin was ingenious. He called upon the Constituent Assembly to use its (in his mind, illegitimate) prestige to undermine its own waning authority. "Elected on the basis of party lists compiled before the October revolution, when the people could not yet mobilize their massive numbers to rebel against their exploiters, when they did not yet realize the full power of the opposition exercised by their exploiters in defense of their class privileges, and when they had not yet begun the practical task of creating a socialist society, the Constituent Assembly would find it entirely wrong, even from the procedural point of view, to oppose itself to Soviet power." Therefore, the Declaration instructed the Constituent Assembly to affirm that it was stepping aside: "Power must belong entirely and exclusively to the toiling masses and their authorized government—the Soviets of Worker, Soldier, and Peasant Deputies."

This Declaration was, of course, a far cry from the one on which it was modeled. The Declaration of 1789, on behalf not of the toiling masses but of individual men (though still excluding women), as human beings and as citizens, guaranteed the rights of "liberty, property, security, and resistance to oppression." It declared that sovereignty resided in the "Nation." It defined liberty as "the power to do anything that does not harm another," limited only by the right of others to enjoy the same rights, limits which "can only be determined by the law." The French Declaration went on to define what was meant by the law and its protections. Lenin's Declaration, by contrast, said nothing about the law and in fact nothing about rights, either in the moral or legal sense, either for individuals or collectivities. The moral calculus was implicit, nevertheless. The toilers, as a social category, had a right higher than any law or procedure to unseat the privileged classes and rule on their own behalf. What form this rule was to take was a matter for their leaders to determine.[28]

The inconvenience, from the Bolshevik point of view, of democratic procedure was evident in the majority held by SRs, mostly of the Right faction, among the delegates that finally converged on Petrograd. Before they could assemble, however, an event occurred which played into Bolshevik hands. On January 1, 1918, Lenin was the object of a failed assassination attempt. The perpetrators were disgruntled army officers, wishing to protect the Constituent Assembly from Bolshevik schemes. Three weeks later they were arrested. Already concerned that the Union for the Defense of the Constituent Assembly, formed by the Petrograd City Duma in November, had called for a demonstration in support of the opening session, the Bolsheviks immediately accused the SRs of plotting to overthrow Soviet power. Declaring martial law in the city, security forces cordoned off the area around the Tauride Palace and Smolny. Soldiers were planted at various key locations, aircraft flew low over the rooftops, and barricades were raised, as if anticipating an armed assault. The commissar for military affairs arrogated supreme authority to himself—a reprise of the tactics employed on the eve of the October coup, when the Bolshevik-controlled Military Revolutionary Committee had preempted the official Petrograd Military District. Once again, Lenin's party had escalated the level of violence, actual or threatened, after magnifying the danger of opposition.[29] All this before the Constituent Assembly had even opened.

Proceedings were scheduled to begin at one in the afternoon of Saturday, January 5. The marchers assembled by the Union for the Defense of the Constituent Assembly arrived from various parts of the city, planning to converge at the Field of Mars, move toward the Tauride Palace without entering, then turn back toward Nevskii. The Soviet Executive Committee denounced the demonstration as an attack on Soviet power, and thus an attack on the revolution. It warned that participants would be dispersed by gunfire.[30] The Constituent Assembly was still viewed by the general population, not just the few who responded to the call of the Union for the Defense of the Constituent Assembly, as a symbol of the revolution's democratic gains. It constituted a reproach or alternative to the Bolshevik claim to embody the true democratic spirit. The Sovnarkom could not tolerate such competition, nor could it afford to accept the rules of parliamentary debate and democratic elections. It must assert itself as a new style of power. Lenin's signature strategy was to inflate the danger posed by the enemy, however defined, as justification for a demonstratively violent response. Hence the Bolsheviks assumed, sincerely or disingenuously, that the demonstrators would carry arms, and instructed the Red Guards accordingly.

The crowd that assembled on the Field of Mars was not a referendum on popular opinion. Like the multitude summoned by the City Duma at the end of November, it represented the middle range of Petrograd citizens, those "mere inhabitants," whom even the anarchist fellow-traveler Victor Serge derided as inherently counterrevolutionary because they understood the Bolsheviks as fatal to their way of life.[31] Their banners read: "All Power to the Constituent Assembly!" "Down with Political Terror!" "Long Live the Brotherhood of Peoples!" They were unarmed. The first group was stopped by Red Guards in mid-morning, but the marchers ignored the warning to turn back, continuing onward, to the strains of the "Marseillaise," which signaled their dedication to the revolution as they understood it, until the Guards began firing in their direction.[32]

By contrast, a repeat incident later in the day on Liteinyi Avenue resulted in the death of at least twenty-one civilians. Altogether at least ten thousand people, possibly many more, though including few workers, had joined the procession. Despite the marchers' unthreatening demeanor, the Red Guards reacted with frenzy. They shot from roofs and windows, from behind barricades, as though mimicking the imagined behavior of the mythic sharpshooters and demonic civilians featured in every pogrom or atrocity tale. Moscow residents learned of the shooting in Petrograd from the one newspaper still providing information: Gorky's *Novaia zhizn'*.[33] The Mensheviks called the shooting of worker comrades a crime. They called the Bolsheviks and Left SRs traitors to the revolution. They appealed to the Red Guards—"knowing not what they had done"—to join with brother workers in support of the revolution's democratic principles and against Bolshevik terror.[34] By evening, however, the Bolsheviks had shut all the opposition newspapers and threatened with dismissal any workers who heeded the Menshevik call.[35]

The Tauride Palace was itself under heavy armed guard. There were guns, bombs, grenades, and artillery in abundance. The SR Mark Vishniak recalled that "the quantity of armed men, the weapons themselves and their clanking, created the impression of an encampment getting ready either to defend itself or to attack." The arriving delegates were carefully screened.[36] Lenin, at the head of the Bolshevik delegation, waited for the streets to be under control before allowing the proceedings to commence. About half the total deputies elected were present, more than half of those SRs, a quarter Bolsheviks.[37] None of the handful of elected Kadets made an appearance. The session finally opened late in the afternoon with an unseemly brawl. An elderly SR attempted to introduce the session, speaking on behalf of the majority party, but he was rudely pushed aside by the thirty-three-year-old Bolshevik Iakov Sverdlov. Speaking on behalf of the Soviet Executive

Committee, of which he was chair, Sverdlov urged the assembly to acknowledge the authority of the Sovnarkom and endorse the Declaration, which he then began to read, attempting to circumvent parliamentary procedure with a rhetorical fait accompli.[38] The Bolshevik delegates burst out with a loud rendition of the "Internationale" in support of the impending world revolution. The assembly nevertheless elected as chairman the SR leader, Viktor Chernov, thus endorsing his earlier election by the rump assembly on November 28 and signaling continuity with the Provisional Government, since Chernov had served as minister of agriculture in the first coalition.[39]

In the speech-making that followed, Chernov and Tsereteli, the widely respected Menshevik leader, defended the Constituent Assembly as the sole body empowered to confer legitimacy on the revolutionary government. They not only rejected the Bolsheviks' claim to speak "for the people" but pointed to the destructive consequences of their rivals' grab for power. In the chaos they themselves had caused, Tsereteli observed, the Bolsheviks had then suppressed all critical views and blamed the "bourgeoisie" for sabotaging the revolution. Responding to objections from the Left, he riposted: "Let's suppose Kerensky was worse than you are, but that doesn't prove you are better than the Constituent Assembly. At the present time you are fighting neither Kerensky nor Tsereteli but the expressed will of the entire population."[40] When Chernov and Tsereteli continued to press for a joint socialist government, the thirty-year-old Bolshevik Nikolai Bukharin accused them of impeding the march of history. On a first vote, the assembly declined to endorse the Soviet Executive Committee Declaration.[41]

At one in the morning, now January 6, after a short break, the assembly reconvened—typical of the heated, prolonged, and exhausting mass meetings that punctuated the revolution. Lenin, out of sight in the galleries, observing the floor, decided the Bolsheviks should stage a walk-out. The Sovnarkom would then put an end to the entire proceedings, actualizing the threat of violence hovering over the event from the start. A final Bolshevik speaker denounced the assembly as "counterrevolutionary," for rejecting the fruits of "the great October revolution" (later the official Soviet tag). He accused the Right SRs, elected on lists drawn up before October, of promoting "bourgeois" interests. The elections themselves, of course, had occurred after the coup, with the full participation of Bolshevik grassroots activists. At odds with their more militant comrades, the Right SRs yelled back, "Nonsense!" "Lies!" On behalf of his faction, the Left SR commissar of justice, Isaak Shteinberg, once more urged the assembly to approve the

Soviet Executive Committee's Declaration instituting Soviet power, thus simultaneously using and abdicating its own (contested) authority.[42] The assembly proceeded, instead, to endorse resolutions on land and peace presented by Chernov on behalf of the Right SRs, which were virtually identical to the positions included in the Soviet Declaration, while undercutting the Sovnarkom. The assembly also voted to adopt the name of the "Russian Democratic Federative Republic." In fact, Chernov behaved as though the coup had never happened and the Sovnarkom did not exist, proposing what Shteinberg later called "unreal, ghostlike laws," while the same decrees were already being issued by an authority he refused to acknowledge.[43] Moscow residents learned of these resolutions through Menshevik leaflets.[44]

In essence, the entire twenty-six hours of argument involved a struggle for precedence among socialist parties that shared a common vision of the social revolution they wished to accomplish but differed dramatically on the methods they were willing to tolerate. None of the parties to the conflict were either "bourgeois" or "counterrevolutionary." Precisely because they shared so much, it was imperative for Lenin to brand and monopolize the common ground.

The final presentation and votes were interrupted rudely, in the wee hours of the morning, by the intrusion of a pro-Bolshevik anarchist sailor from Kronstadt, who conveyed instructions to have the delegates clear the hall. "The guard is tired," he said. Chernov replied that the delegates were tired, too, but would stay to complete their business. By 6 a.m. the Left SRs and Bolsheviks had already taken their leave, and the remaining delegates emptied the building.[45] They emerged into the darkness; the sun would not, of course, rise in this northern city until well into the morning. Now all Lenin had to do was stage-manage the destruction of the revolution's last elected organ.

That same day, January 6, both the Sovnarkom and the Soviet Executive Committee formally approved the permanent dissolution of the Constituent Assembly, which, in the absence of the Bolshevik and Left SR delegates, Lenin branded a tool of the counterrevolution.[46] These bodies had, of course, no authority to issue such decrees, but they established their authority by acting as if they had. In his address to the Soviet Executive Committee, Lenin offered a paean to the virtues of direct, grassroots democracy, as represented in the soviets. It was an appeal any socialist could welcome. As a corollary, he reiterated his long-nurtured contempt for the formal process of democracy. In December 1917, Lenin had expressed his opinion of "the people's will," as conventionally understood. "If in a burst of enthusiasm the people has elected a very good parliament...then we ought to make it a long parliament, and if the elections have not proved a success, then we should seek to disperse parliament not after two years but, if possible, after two weeks."[47] He gave his own definition of democracy. "The people wanted the Constituent Assembly to be convened. But they quickly realized what it amounted to. And now, once more, we are fulfilling the will of the people, which has declared: All power to the Soviets! And we shall crush the saboteurs."[48]

A few non-Bolsheviks on the Soviet Executive Committee accused Lenin of dictatorial methods and of violating the will of the Second Soviet Congress. A few Bolshevik sympathizers and even some Bolshevik moderates were uneasy with the move, but on January 7 the resolution to dissolve the Constituent Assembly was, not surprisingly, adopted. The Left SR Shteinberg, still commissar of justice, supported the dissolution. Lenin was unabashed. As Trotsky remembered him saying, "The dissolution of the Constituent Assembly by the Soviet Government means a complete and frank liquidation of the idea of democracy by the idea of a dictatorship. It will serve as a good lesson."[49] Three days later, the Third All-Russian Congress of Soviets assembled in Petrograd and retroactively approved all the decrees previously issued by the Sovnarkom and Soviet Executive Committee, thus putting its seal of approval on Soviet power, which in fact meant Bolshevik control.[50]

The danger in declaring the Kadet Party outside the law, and in general vilifying the Constituent Assembly as an arm of the counterrevolution, was vividly illustrated on the night of January 6 to 7. The Kadets Andrei Shingarev and Fedor Kokoshkin, both former ministers in Kerensky's final government, had been arrested on November 28, along with other Kadet delegates to the Constituent Assembly.[51] Weeks in the cold, damp cells of the Peter-Paul Fortress had affected their health, and they were transferred, at Shteinberg's urging, to the Mariinskii hospital on Liteinyi. Soon after their arrival, a group of Baltic Fleet sailors entered their room, strangled Shingarev, and then, for good measure, shot them both as they lay in their beds. The Soviet Executive Committee blamed the murders on the influence of the reactionary Black Hundreds, but people on the street were heard to mutter that the bourgeois agents had got what they deserved.[52] The culprits were not punished.

The two victims were models of democratically minded political moderation. As an acquaintance remarked, "Their whole lives had been spent in disinterested public service. They were Liberals, who had worked incessantly to help the down-trodden and oppressed, and it would have been hard to find two men in public life more free from personal ambition or self-seeking."[53] By this point, however, "moderate positions no longer satisfied anyone."[54] The Bolsheviks' use of physical brutality did not damage their cause. The general public, in the words of a witness, deplored the Constituent Assembly's "cowardly, 'undignified behavior' and Chernov's submissiveness. They cursed the Assembly more than the Bolsheviks who had dispersed it....Indeed, many influential people had lost all interest in political figures and demanded a general, moreover...a Cossack."[55]

---

Some historians have argued that the experience of the Civil War following the October coup and the dissolution of the Constituent Assembly distorted the original character of the Bolshevik Party. The new regime, it has been said, resorted to terror in order to survive the onslaught of armed enemy forces. This view does an injustice to Lenin. The Cheka was established six weeks after the coup, to combat "counterrevolution, speculation, sabotage, and abuse of office." This was before the counterrevolution had taken organized form. The Cheka had the power to conduct searches and arrests, as well as on-the-spot "trials" and on-the-spot executions without trial.[56] Its targets included not only people taking advantage of the economic collapse to turn a profit, but honest traders and political opponents of any stripe.

The actions of the Cheka were mildly restrained at first by the addition of Left SRs to the Cheka leadership on January 7, 1918, but the collaborators' willingness to come on board undercut any moral objections they might still have thought of raising.[57] Lenin, for his part, was unambivalent. In December 1917, he had expounded the Marxist view "that to the transition period from the bourgeois to the socialist society there corresponds a special state (that is, a special system of organized violence against a certain class), namely the dictatorship of the proletariat."[58]

The atmosphere in which political opponents were dubbed "enemies of the people" and summarily arrested—in which officials of the regime were instructed to treat so-called speculators by shooting them on the spot, and the same for "counterrevolutionaries, spies, thugs, saboteurs, and other parasites"—was an atmosphere that encouraged mob violence. Commissar of

Justice Shteinberg commented in retrospect that outlawing the Kadet Party "was, after all, almost an invitation to terror issued by the most authoritative institution in the country. Once the idea of impunity toward supposed counterrevolutionaries penetrated the minds of irresponsible individuals, one could expect lynching incidents to spread among the population."[59]

Lenin was not interested in the fine points of individual guilt or innocence. "It is senseless," Shteinberg remembers him saying, "even to discuss the question of legality. The Kadets, brandishing the slogans of democracy, actually instigated the real civil war. Very well then: investigate these our charges against them and see if you can disprove that the Kadet Party constitutes the general staff of the civil war which is already drenching the country in blood."[60] It was, of course, true, as Lenin claimed, that the Kadets had made contact with the armed enemies of October. A number of party leaders had filtered down to the Don valley to join the officers assembling there.[61] "The Kadets scream 'all power to the Constituent Assembly,'" Lenin said, "but in fact this means 'all power to Kaledin.'"[62] General Aleksei Kaledin had been among the commanders who had supported Kornilov's bid for power in August.

Open opposition was both a threat and an opportunity. Trotsky was even more emphatic. "There is not the slightest doubt," Shteinberg remembered him saying, "that the party of the Kadets is organizing the counterrevolution.... They complain—and sentimental socialists join them in the complaint—at being thrown into jail! Let them instead be grateful. In past revolutions their kind was dealt with differently. They would have been taken to the Palace Square and there made . . . a head shorter!"[63] Shteinberg, whose own moral credentials as a Bolshevik collaborator were none too pure, recalled asking Lenin, "Why do we bother with a Commissariat of Justice? Let's call it frankly the Commissariat for Social Extermination and be done with it!" To which Lenin supposedly replied: "Well put . . . that's exactly what it should be . . . but we can't say that."[64]

———

The October coup provoked real opposition. Kerensky attempted briefly to mobilize an armed rebuttal. The air was electric with violence, threats of violence, and fear. No one was in control. On January 1, 1918, Lenin had been targeted for assassination. After the Constituent Assembly was dispersed, the Kadet Central Committee met secretly in Moscow to debate the party's options. Though committed to parliamentary principles, the Kadets nevertheless hated Chernov and deplored the Constituent Assembly's SR majority. As the election returns had shown, however, they themselves lacked popular appeal. In August 1917, the most conservative Kadets had supported Kornilov's plan for a military dictatorship to suppress the Bolshevik threat; some now believed "a temporary military dictatorship" was needed to cope with the post-October social breakdown and endemic violence and to unseat the usurpers. Once the Bolsheviks had been defeated, new elections would be called. A more representative Constituent Assembly would then define the future government. Others rejected the military option and insisted, rather, on the importance of building a social base. So great were the divisions within the party that the Central Committee conceded to individual members the license to make whatever choices they saw fit.[65] Like the SRs, the Kadets had lost whatever ideological coherence they once had mustered. This was a confusion the relentless Bolsheviks could only applaud. The difficulty of uniting the diverse forces that opposed the Bolshevik regime—for a variety of different reasons, with a variety of incompatible goals, all lacking the necessary resources—was key to the fortunes of the fragmented movement, in which some considered themselves to be defending the revolution and others to be undoing it. Meanwhile, the Bolsheviks used their appropriated status as heads of state to take Russia out of the war and concentrate on defeating their domestic enemies.

# 6

# Politics from Below

The political revolution—February to October—unfolded in Petrograd, the seat of power, sending shock waves throughout the Empire. Both its nodal points can be described as coups. The replacement of Nicholas by a rump committee of the Duma was not a legal move, but a challenge to legitimate sovereignty. The Constituent Assembly was expected to mend the breach with the authority vested in the democratic franchise. Meanwhile, the government was considered provisional. The Bolsheviks, by contrast, had no concern for legality. They considered violence a necessary instrument in the fight for power. In fact, both the respectable figures that dealt the final blow to the monarchy in February and the radical Bolsheviks who drove them out owed their opportunity to the disruptive force of popular discontent. Their success or failure in political terms depended on harnessing the support of the broad population, or at least on deflecting its rage.

Unapologetic about the use of force, the Bolsheviks nevertheless considered October a revolutionary moment, indeed the Great Proletarian Revolution. They claimed, in dislodging not only the Provisional Government but also the Constituent Assembly, to be replacing what they derided as pseudo-constitutionalism with true people's power. They claimed to have a direct mandate from the formerly oppressed classes to challenge the institutions and structures of class society. To call the Bolshevik seizure of power—not only the assault on the Provisional Government but also the destruction of the Constituent Assembly—a coup is to challenge these claims. To call it a coup is to ask whether Lenin and his deputies indeed acted on behalf of the oppressed classes, with their active endorsement and support, or whether they merely took advantage of the massive social breakdown that had undermined existing structures of power, clearing the way for them to assert their own.

But though the Bolshevik bid for power was clearly a coup, it was also an expression of a profound social revolution, in which the populace actively asserted its interests against those of the privileged few. As the Constituent Assembly elections demonstrated, much of the population felt itself empowered by the end of autocratic rule and drawn into a novel political process. At the same time, it was the social revolution of 1917 that enabled the Bolsheviks to seize the reins, destroying the chance for a democratic settlement and crushing the expectations that prospect aroused. The populace was, however, not the passive victim—or tool—of Bolshevik manipulation. The people were angry, aggressive, and out of control. They were also capable of self-organization and self-leadership.

The Russian Empire entered the war divided by region, class, and uneven economic and cultural capital. It experienced not one but many simultaneous revolutions. The rivals for power who succeeded the old regime were obliged not only to outmaneuver each other but to reach beyond the privileged upper crust. They had also to withstand the onslaught directed against them—the men in uniform tired of the war, the villages suffering its impact, and the urban poor pinched by the wartime economy. The politics of the revolution cannot be understood without relation to the vast popular swells that generated their own energy and on which the elites maintained only a fragile hold. The contenders for power did not hover over a void of anarchy and violence, though there was anarchy and violence to spare. The Revolution and Civil War were fueled by vast social movements, in all corners of the empire and at all points on the social scale. The unlettered classes engaged in collective action in pursuit of goals and following a logic of their own, though these actions were largely local, uncoordinated, and unstable. They did not, however, act in a vacuum, and they often derived their symbols and strategies from the culture at large, and from the socialist idiom in particular. Their own culture also provided resources for responding to the crisis around them—a crisis they helped create.

The first question to address in approaching the popular role in the revolution is one of vocabulary. The terms *proletariat* and *peasantry* are generalizations covering vast discrepancies in psychology, social status, economic resources, and cultural traditions. The term *proletariat* is, moreover, often used in a highly ideological way, implying a level of political awareness and an automatic receptivity to the socialist appeal not always evident in fact. Peasants, for their part, varied in their relation to the land, in their connection to industry and the cities, in their local habits, and in their regional distinctions. References to the generic "masses" abound in the polemical literature of the time and in the scholarship that has followed. A less invidious cousin of the "mob," the "crowd," or the "street," it is imprecise and patronizing, yet often unavoidable. Inhabitants of late imperial society themselves distinguished between "society" (*obshchestvo* or *obshchestvennost'*), meaning the educated classes or civil society, and "the people" (*narod*), referring broadly to the laboring folk. The term "social movement" (*obshchestvennoe dvizhenie*) was often used in a capacious manner to designate the mobilization of society at large. Not only were civil society and popular society separated by cultural and economic status, but each was divided within itself. Ethnic distinctions and occupational differences mattered. And yet, as in any society, the components were bound together in relations of dependence and competition. Under the pressure of crisis, however, all potential sources of conflict were inflamed.

---

In 1917 the cities held the key to political power. They contained the institutions of government, the educated classes (civil society), the urban working class, the universities, the presses, the railway depots and transportation hubs, the shops. But the cities depended on the countryside to supply them with food—and taken all together, their populations were vastly outnumbered by the peasants who worked the land and brought the grain and produce to market. As a cultural formation, peasant society had long been an object of scrutiny by thinkers, writers, and socially concerned professionals. The Russian peasant symbolized Russia—its hope and its despair, a moral beacon, a sign of backwardness. Nineteenth-century Russian literature contemplates this puzzle from all sides, from Ivan Turgenev's *Hunter's Sketches* to Tolstoy's many explorations of what he imagined to be the soul of the common folk. Between 1917 and 1921, the villages, expressing long-standing resentments, rose against the local gentry and attacked their more fortunate neighbors. Peasants lashed out at real and symbolic oppressors (landowners, policemen, army officers, and Jews). Some, however, were capable of joining organizations—the unions and soviets organized by political activists. About forty million voted in the Constituent Assembly elections, an astounding fact.

Peasant uprisings had constituted some of the most brutal episodes in Russian history. As the Russian Populists had long recognized, the communal way of life promoted coherent action. Tightly bound to a whole, the normally servile peasants might summon the will to confront outside authority. Traditional villages were regulated by institutions that imposed internal norms and penalized infractions. They mediated between the community and the agents of the state that impinged upon them. This was no egalitarian paradise. Patriarchal to the core, older men ruled their sons, husbands their wives. Elders constituted the village assemblies that governed land use, collected taxes, adjudicated disputes, and punished minor crimes. The tsarist state created institutions of its own that monitored the transactions at a local level: the *volost'* (district) assemblies and *volost'* courts, the zemstvos. Internecine violence was another instrument of peasant self-regulation, notably in the form of wife-beating and *samosud* (lynch law), in which physical brutality imposed discipline and moral norms.

In short, peasants encountered and helped produce the revolution not as an inchoate mass, but in regulated communities. These, of course, had been to some extent destabilized by the rapid modernization of the twenty-five years preceding 1914—men and women together and separately traveling to the cities for paid work; young men returning from the army, from war; the level of literacy rising, though slowly. The Great War affected the villages most directly in terms of the draft—of men, horses, and livestock—and in the form of grain requisitions. Veterans returned, officially or on their own; refugees flooded the hinterland. Transportation was dislocated, markets disrupted.

The peasants were thus linked to the larger society in various ways: to the grain market, through the interface of millers and middlemen; to the estate owner, whose fields they rented and tilled and whose woods and pastures they used; to employers of agricultural labor; to primary schools, either state- or church-run; to the local zemstvos, which employed a range of professionals—schoolteachers, agronomists, physicians, and statisticians; by the flow of seasonal labor to rural factories and to the cities; and by military service. Nor was the peasantry monolithic. The character of landholding, the structure of villages and communities, social distinctions and power relations within them, the kind of agriculture practiced, local traditions, the impact of economic change—all differed from region to region. Some areas produced grain, some needed to import it.

The central, so-called black-earth zone had experienced the brunt of serfdom and the complex process of emancipation after 1861. The commune here was a collective enterprise, in which inequality of wealth among households was mitigated by the periodic redistribution of land. Along the periphery of European Russia, by contrast, the commune was weaker and traditional forms of association and agriculture were losing their hold. In the Baltic, serfdom had been eliminated in 1817 without allotments of land. Peasants there typically worked for wages on large commercial farms geared to European export.

In the Ukrainian provinces, large-scale cultivation also predominated. Peasants often rented their land to sugar-beet producers, which also employed them. Serfdom had not extended to Siberia or the southwest Volga steppe, which were dominated by large-scale, capitalist enterprises growing wheat, tobacco, and cotton for the internal market and for export. A class of prosperous peasants emerged (the so-called *kulaks*—a term already current before 1917), involved in commercial cultivation, while the less successful were no longer able to rent enough land to sustain themselves. The regions that experienced the most intense peasant revolts in 1905 were those caught between traditional ways and newer forms of agricultural production. The memory of those conflicts remained alive in the younger generation, and the process of change that provoked them had only intensified in the decade since.[1]

Overall, the percentage of arable land owned by peasants as personal or communal property had grown over the last quarter century, while the percentage owned by nobles and state officials had dropped. Collectively, the peasantry nevertheless still owned less land overall.[2] In addition to the communes, which controlled social and economic life, the peasants also participated in agricultural associations and cooperatives. In short, peasant society had its own internal structure, within the communes and in relation to production and the market. The peasants were set in their ways, subject to the weather and the agricultural cycle, but they were also attuned to the economic environment and sensitive to alterations in the operation of outside authority. Despite the regional variations, two issues affected peasants everywhere, though in locally specific ways: food—producing and marketing grain on the one hand, and having enough to eat on the other—and land. Both were key elements in the unfolding of revolution in the villages. They were key issues for any group trying to gain and hold onto power on a macro scale.

―――――――――

Remote as the peasants were from the cities where power changed hands, the fall of the old regime affected the countryside directly. First and foremost, the peasants began expelling the landowners and asserting their right to the land. Fearless, they removed the now powerless policemen and officials from their posts. Like everyone else, the villagers began gathering and talking. The older generation no longer monopolized village assemblies; younger men, returning soldiers, even women now spoke up. The new mobilization grew out of the enduring structures of communal life, even with the changing of generations, but peasants were also exposed to the wider world. Socialist activists organized meetings in provincial cities that drew hundreds of delegates from the villages: for example, in Samara in March 1917, and in Saratov in April. Meetings proliferated at all levels. The rural intelligentsia played a key role, but peasants set the agenda.[3]

The fundamental ambivalence of the Provisional Government on questions of basic legislation and state authority shaped its policies on provisioning and land. In late March the new ministers established a state monopoly on grain, demanding that peasants relinquish grain above a fixed amount, compensated at a fixed price. Procurement Committees (*prodovol'stvennye komitety*) were sent to the villages. In April, the government created Land Committees (*zemel'nye komitety*) under the Ministry of Agriculture, which were to gather the data necessary for future reforms, to be implemented by the Constituent Assembly.[4] The peasants, however, did not welcome government food agents, nor did they cooperate with the zemstvos run by local gentry and professionals. When new zemstvo elections were held, the peasants increased their own representation.

In short, after March 1917 traditional village assemblies became the basis for peasant self-mobilization, challenging estate owners over the use of woodlands, pasture, and fields. In the Volga region, the peasants formed Committees of People's Power (*Komitety narodnoi vlasti*) which endorsed the seizure of uncultivated land. The Provisional Government, defending the principle of private property and deferring the land question to the Constituent Assembly, tried to stop the wave of confiscations, but did not have the power to do so. Even the SR activists, for example in Samara and Saratov, who helped articulate peasant goals were unable to set limits to peasant actions.[5]

These actions were orchestrated by the communes. In spring 1917, the communes elected committees to deal with the landowners. Many at first observed what they considered formal procedure—deciding what land to leave for the estate owner's use, justifying the felling of trees, the use of pasture. During the summer, hundreds of estates were besieged by entire villages acting in concert. The peasants would convene at the manor house in their carts, armed with pitchforks, axes, and sometimes guns in the hands of returned soldiers. They would empty the residence and farm buildings of useable equipment, smash the large machines or leave them behind, lead away the livestock, then put the structures to the torch. Many of the owners and stewards would have fled; murders were rare in the early months. The communes acted together, richer and poorer as one, resolving as a collective how to divide the spoils in land. The intensity of the assaults varied with the agricul-tural cycle, the locality, and the influx of soldiers from the front, radicaliz-ing the mood. The communes also took aim at the land of peasants who had established their separate farms after the reforms instituted by Prime Minister Stolypin before the Great War with the aim of creating a prosperous independent farmer class with an investment in order.[6]

Thus, in spring and summer of 1917 all forms of central authority failed. The monarchy had collapsed, and the Provisional Government was unable to prevent the peasants from destroying the class regime in the countryside. The assault on the estate system was not, however, a wild rampage, but the prod-uct of existing and still functioning social institutions: the commune and the local assemblies. The SRs tried to ride the wave, but they did not direct it. The October coup did not constitute a break in this progression, as Soviet historians later claimed. The peasants understood the revolution to have started when they seized the estates, independent of political events in the capital, though the progressive disintegration of central authority enhanced their sense of impunity.[7]

Once again, the Bolshevik takeover involved relabeling as much as creation. The district zemstvos and *volost'* committees—a level above the communes—now became *volost'* soviets. The Decree on Land presented to the Second All-Russian Congress of Soviets on October 26, 1917, endorsed what the peasants were already doing. The Land Committee (*Zemel'nyi komitet*) became the Land Department (*Zemel'nyi otdel*). The same stationery was used, because paper was scarce; the zemstvo agronomists and other tech-nical personnel were still needed, because most peasants could not read or write. By summer 1918, the country was being run by these local "commune-republics," issuing what they thought of as their own laws, restructuring the countryside at the ground level. The Bolsheviks did not control the peasant assault on authority and privilege, but it served their purposes in the early months. The day of reckoning would come later.[8]

The war had put enormous pressure on the economy. In late 1916, the British journalist R. Scotland Liddell reported: "Russia—this great Russia that could feed the world!—was short of food; and very short of other commodities too. . . . There was a scarcity of everything in Russia—food and clothes and boots and petrol and paraffin. What things there were very dear."[9] Prices skyrocketed. Shopkeepers made a killing. Some people had the money to spend, but most people lacked the basics.[10] Bread riots, as noted, became common in the cities that autumn. The crowds, often predominantly of women, frequently vented their anger in trashing the shops. The secret police reported in October, "The food question has become the single and most terrible impulse among the broadest reaches of the huge imperial population, impelling these masses gradually to join the growing movement of dissatisfaction and bitterness."[11]

The February Revolution indeed began as a Petrograd bread riot, when working-class women found the shops running short. The cities hungered because the villages could not or would not market enough to feed both the army and the urban population. Peasant economic behavior was not ideological; it responded to the market in grain and the availability of manufactured goods to purchase with their gains. But economic responses had political consequences. It was the war and hence the government that created the pressure for grain. The collapse of the old regime allowed the peasants to seize the land they coveted, but it did not free them from the demands created by wartime economic and manpower mobilization. The February government inherited both the procurement problem and the administrative habits of the old regime. The key issues for the monarchy and then for the Provisional Government were the relationship between the government and the private sector, between the authorities at all levels and the peasantry. The Bolsheviks would confront the same issues down the line.

The food-supply problem had proved more than the monarchy could handle during the war. A grain shortage was not anticipated at the start. The harvests in 1914 and 1915 were good; grain exports had been suspended. The free market was not enough, however, to feed the army, and the government limited the use of rail transport for non-military purposes, disrupting the normal distribution routes. Shortages emerged in the cities and in the provinces.[12] During the war, both the Ministry of Agriculture and the army were involved in procurement. The Ministry worked through the zemstvos and cooperatives, which dealt directly with the peasants. The government also sent purchasing agents to the villages, but these outsiders often resorted to the services of private grain traders, with better knowledge of storage and transportation needs. In the effort both to extract grain and to retain some kind of regional balance, the government employed both embargoes and requisitioning, but despite the official role middlemen often determined the actual prices. When prices rose, the middlemen or traders were denounced as "speculators." The bogeyman speculator turned out to have a long life. The ministries did a poor job, however, of managing the conflict between civilian and military needs (by 1916 half the marketed grain went to the army), between regulated and market prices, between grain collection and transport. Numerous different organizations were involved, both official and civic, which led to administrative confusion.[13]

In February 1916, the balance tipped in the direction of official regulation of prices Empire-wide. The enhanced role of the state in shaping economic relations was typical of all the wartime powers. In Russia the trend had paradoxical results. The regime that had consistently distrusted the private sector, both civic and economic, now made use of the services of economic experts to extend its own reach. In extremis, it needed the civic sector to help it function more effectively as a state—a lesson the monarchy ought to have learned much sooner. Among the experts was the economist Vladimir Groman. Exiled as a young rebel to Viatka Province in Siberia, he was employed by the local zemstvo as a statistician. Upon release, then back again in Siberia, he continued to work for the zemstvos; in 1905 he was active in the liberal Union of Unions, composed of skilled professionals. During the war, Groman joined a group of economists in forming a committee on prices, which in 1915 published an extensive report on the problem of price inflation. He was selected to represent the Union of Towns on the special government food commission established in August 1915.[14] By conviction a Menshevik, Groman envisioned a planned, state-centered economy, which was compatible with the needs of the imperial regime at war.[15] Iakov Bukshpan, a liberal economist also attached to the special food commission, wrote in 1916: "The war has moved the state into center stage in social life....Industrial mobilization, regulated prices and requisitions, syndicates and monopolies, all of this has created a new current in the national economy and points to unheard-of possibilities for economic creativity."[16]

The problem, once regulation was agreed upon, was how to adjust prices in a way that induced the peasants to sell, while keeping the cost of bread low enough to suit the urban consumers. Traders held onto grain when the price structure did not seem favorable. The Ministry of the Interior understood that creating a food crisis in the cities might lead to popular unrest.[17] It disagreed with the Ministry of Agriculture on how to solve the problem. As it always had, the Ministry of the Interior substituted coercion for civic initiative. It preferred to work through administrative agents. Distrusting social organizations, even the patriotic zemstvos, the police organized raids on railroad depots and stations, looking for unloaded grain and denouncing the culprits. The Ministry of the Interior blamed the high prices and shortages on "speculators"—Germans, Jews, or simply the "dark forces," not excluding the Union of Towns. The Ministry of Agriculture, by contrast, preferred to enlist the civilian sector, hence the recruitment of economists and the Union of Towns.[18] The experts, though nongovernmental, were hardly subversive. They favored centralized authority, a government monopoly on grain, and regulation of prices for manufactured goods as well as grain in order to manage the relationship between town and country. Various plans were put forward by the Ministry of War, the special commission, and the Ministry of Agriculture, which itself courted but also feared public initiative.[19] In short, in trying to be a strong state, the old bureaucracy stumbled over its own inner divisions.

The crisis peaked in November 1916, under the last of the imperial ministers of agriculture, the Livonian nobleman Aleksandr Rittikh. In response to General Brusilov's reports of deficits on the Southwest Front, the government increased its grain purchases and resorted to more energetic requisitioning of surpluses. Rather than use force, Rittikh put pressure on the zemstvos and set quotas. The goal was to supply both the troops and the defense workers. Duma deputies complained that the cities were still short; they objected to the policy of requisition quotas (the *razverstka*), criticized the method of setting prices, and regretted that the government did not trust public organizations, which would do a better job. Even the zemstvos were outsiders to the peasant village, which was itself not enlisted in the task of culling grain. The peasants experienced the official demands as "a simple seizure of grain by an unpopular state authority," as historian Lars Lih puts it.[20]

In mid-February 1917, on the very eve of the imperial collapse, the Duma debated the food question. The Kadet deputy Andrei Shingarev (murdered by enraged sailors a year later) insisted that both peasants and the rural intelligentsia be included in the organizations for procuring grain. Rittikh, by contrast, reproached the zemstvos for focusing on their narrow local needs and stressed the importance of central authority. Frustrated with what he perceived as civic obstructionism, Rittikh instructed commissioners, governors, and zemstvos to extract their quotas by the end of the month or take the grain by force. He admitted to the Duma, however, that he did not have the power to compel delivery.[21]

The Provisional Government followed the same pattern, but with wider public and even peasant involvement. It created a grain monopoly. Peasants could keep what they needed for themselves, but the rest must be delivered to the state at a fixed price. Locally elected food-supply committees and the existing commissioners were to enforce the system. The monopoly did not function, but the government did manage to control transport and hence the movement of grain. The peasants resented the inclusion of educated people in the local committees. They also refused to comply with directives from Petrograd, physically attacking committee members and hiding the grain they refused to deliver at the fixed prices. Complicating the situation was the continuing role of private millers and traders. Because of the industrial breakdown and the diversion of production to military needs, consumer goods were not available for peasants to purchase with whatever cash they acquired or had put away. Grain deliveries were interrupted by fuel shortages. In short, the Provisional Government was no more successful than the monarchy in supplying the army and the cities and satisfying the peasants.[22]

The principal social actors in both February and October were the peasants and the soldiers (peasants as soldiers), but February, as noted, began in Petrograd with a protest led by lower-class urban women, in the wake of strikes in the big Petrograd metalworking plants. These were the same core workers, the most literate and skilled, who in 1905 had responded to the St. Petersburg Soviet, had joined the trade unions permitted to function after 1906, and led the resurgent strike movement in 1912. By 1914 this minority had access to a range of organizations—sick funds, cooperatives, and clubs, as well as labor unions, which together encouraged a common culture and sense of solidarity.[23] These mobilized workers appropriated the language, symbols, and aspirations of their intelligentsia mentors. Socialist-led trade-unionism addressed the desire to ameliorate work conditions and obtain better treatment, to gain some sense of mastery over their own lives. There is less certainty about the meaning for the broad factory masses of the whole arsenal of socialist terminology and the political goals it expressed. Nevertheless, amid the turmoil of unruly returning soldiers and the self-propelled peasant rebellion in the countryside, the factory workers of Petrograd in particular, and of the cities in general, displayed an internal coherence derived from years of contact with socialist organizers and a closer connection to the society around them. Strategically positioned in urban centers, where the struggle for power among contending elites occurred, workers played a role in shaping the outcome of their contest.

The Bolsheviks boasted of having led a proletarian revolution in October, claiming to have mobilized the collective action of workers on the party's behalf, because it was they who expressed the proletariat's true interests. This was, of course, the view required of Soviet-era historians, and some Western scholars have agreed that "the months between March and October were in large part a workers' revolution."[24] Whether or not the Bolsheviks in particular, as opposed to the Mensheviks or SRs, represented worker interests in 1917, it is certainly the case that the industrial labor force across the Empire had by then developed the means to influence the political outcome. They had developed habits of self-organization, electing leaders, holding meetings, endorsing platforms, mobilizing for strikes. During the Great War, some workers had joined the War Industries Committees. Sharing in the general feeling of patriotic purpose, workers at first were relatively quiet. They also shared the xenophobia encouraged by official propaganda. Moscow workers, as we have seen, participated in anti-German riots in June 1915. This too was a form of collective action. Any impulse to strike for material benefits was inhibited by the threat of being drafted. Yet the tradition of radicalism was preserved among the skilled workers in the great armaments plants, who were exempt from military service. The number of strikes increased in 1916, as the conditions of everyday life worsened.[25]

As far as the radical parties were concerned, labor mobilization cut two ways. It had the potential to disrupt production and breed conflict, challenging established authority, yet it allowed the workers to act as a relatively disciplined mass—as a force for order amid the collapse of discipline at all levels. Proponents of revolution needed, on the one hand, to increase the kind of "disorder" needed to topple the old regime and push the revolution forward, while, on the other, channeling the chaos in a useful direction—order in disorder. Worker organizations could and did serve the interests of various competing parties, but they could also stand in the way of any one party's control. Once in the saddle, the Bolsheviks reined them in by means of what was by then their signature tactic—penetrate, mobilize, dominate, liquidate.

The massive strikes in Petrograd's giant metalworking plants at the start of 1917 reverberated throughout the highly concentrated and politically saturated laboring districts of the city. The fall of the monarchy then precipitated a revolution of authority inside the factories—an example of the tight link between embedded social hierarchies and deference to power at the top. Workers in the same highly activated Petrograd plants formed shop-floor committees based on the experience of 1905, led by former delegates to the War Industries Committees. Pledging devotion to the war effort, the committees nevertheless pressured for shorter hours and better conditions. In Petrograd, the employers were themselves organized; they recognized the committees as a positive force and made a number of concessions.[26]

The Bolsheviks did not create the committees, but they drew them together into the Central Soviet of Factory-Shop Committees (*Tsentral'nyi sovet fabrichno-zavodskikh komitetov*), which met first in June 1917. By this time, shortages of food, fuel, and raw material had made themselves felt. Worker cooperatives distributed food; shop committees sent emissaries to the countryside in search of provisions. The committees also tried to counteract the drop in shop-floor productivity and to maintain discipline in the face of hardship, combatting absenteeism and alcoholism.[27] Throughout the year, workers endorsed political resolutions, voted for delegates to the soviets, and contributed precious kopeks in support of various political causes, as well as for relief of soldiers, orphans, and prisoners of war. In short, not all but many workers engaged in continuous political activity of one kind or another throughout 1917, on behalf of the revolution as they understood it.[28]

In addition to the committees, trade unions also flourished in 1917. Their number and membership exploded after February, under the leadership of all three socialist parties. The Second All-Russian Conference of Trade Unions, meeting in July, included over nine hundred unions; Bolshevik delegates constituted the largest single bloc. The skilled workers set the pace here as in the committees, where Bolshevik representation was even more pronounced.[29] Thus, the upper crust of the Petrograd labor force, which was itself relatively sophisticated, generated a factory-based leadership that connected with intelligentsia organizers from the political parties.[30]

The idea of "workers' control," meaning the organized collective oversight of plant management, was the principle behind the committees. It stood for grassroots democracy, the same desire to set the agenda and reject old-regime hierarchies also manifesting itself in soldier committees at the front. In both cases, former subordinates assumed the role of keeping order, while rejecting the need to obey orders themselves.[31] Although in this sense conservative, they offered avenues for revolutionary propaganda. Already primed by the experience of self-activation, the committees could adopt, under pressure of circumstance, more obviously political and disruptive goals.

During 1917 the Bolshevik relationship to the committees was not straightforward. On the one hand, party activists took a leading role in their proliferation and dominated the Central Soviet of Factory-Shop Committees. The committees provided a useful platform from which to pressure the Provisional Government and its socialist allies. On the heels of October, the Statute on Workers' Control (*Polozhenie o rabochem kontrole*), issued by the Central Soviet Executive Committee on November 14, 1917, endorsed this principle.[32] On the other hand, the same pressures from the shop floor—for higher wages, for a greater role in the management of production—now impeded the Bolsheviks' own plans for governing the industrial sector. Lenin recognized that workers were not equipped to run factories. The decree creating the Supreme Council of the National Economy (*Vysshii sovet narodnogo khoziaistva*—VSNKh), a central, party-run organ, appeared two weeks later. Grounds for conflict emerged from the start.[33]

The same tension between grassroots mobilization and political control appeared in relation to the other form of worker activism that emerged after the fall of the monarchy and the collapse of public order: the factory-based armed detachments in Petrograd and other cities. Variously known as militias, *druzhina*s (militia-type brigades), and eventually Red Guards, they were initiated by worker leaders associated with the various socialist parties. The need to find substitutes for failed institutions was not confined to workers, however. City Dumas also created militias after February. The maintenance of order in the face of surging unrest and the disintegration of the imperial police was a general concern.

The worker defense squads formed at the factory level cherished their independence from top party leaders, who in any case took a long time to realize their potential. By the end of August 1917, however, the Bolsheviks had finally established control. In October the Petrograd Red Guards, as we have seen, played a major role in capturing key points in the city, alongside the not always reliable troops. In Moscow they also supported the coup.[34] On January 5, 1918, the Red Guards in Petrograd shot at workers demonstrating against the dispersal of the Constituent Assembly. Six weeks later, the Petrograd Red Guards, whose loyalty the Bolsheviks had come to doubt, were disbanded.[35] The Red Guards were abolished definitively in June, 1918, at the Fifth All-Russian Congress of Soviets, as part of the general move toward suppressing self-activated formations of all kinds and consolidating top-down control.[36] However beholden they were to party leadership, the Red Guards nevertheless maintained something of their original spirit, interpreting the revolution as a challenge to authority and to social elites no matter what their professed intentions.

Post-Soviet historians in Russia have challenged the myth of Proletarian October head on. Sergei Iarov baldly declares, "In the mass, with the exception of individual brigades of worker-activists and the Red Guards, the Petrograd proletariat did not participate in the October armed uprising."[37] The Red Guards in the major cities were indeed composed overwhelmingly of workers, but the vast majority of workers, even in Petrograd and Moscow, took no active part in the October events. The passive majority did, however, vote in great numbers for the Bolshevik slate in the Constituent Assembly elections.[38] At the same time, the politically most sophisticated workers continued to defend the principle of socialist democracy against the single-party rule inaugurated in October.[39] Insofar as the Bolsheviks acted in the name of Soviet power, the more articulate workers could be said to have backed them, but it is clear that the overwhelming sentiment, both in the factories and among socialist leaders, even Bolsheviks, favored an all-socialist, not exclusively Bolshevik, outcome in October. So if October was proletarian, it was an endorsement of the Bolsheviks only in a deceptive sense, and more important, the workers themselves were not the key to the establishment of a new form of power after 1917, as the course of the Civil War was to show.

In the maelstrom of February, it seemed to many in the professional and propertied classes, eager for stability and suspicious of radical ideologues and "the mob," that the soldiers in the streets were guided by nothing but inchoate anger, a desire to tear the old regime apart—its institutions, symbols, authority. Such observers were convinced the slogans and catchwords supplied by the political parties were brandished in the streets without being truly understood.[40] Even some scholars who viewed October as a true "socialist" revolution have observed that socialist ideas were adopted by the rank-and-file workers "not as they appeared in books," as Pavel Volobuev puts it, "but processed in relation to their own interests, filling the socialist slogans with their own content, wrapping their own demands in a socialist cover."[41]

The question of the workers' understanding of political concepts, of their collective goals, and their relationship to educated leaders (their "class consciousness" or "revolutionary class consciousness," in the Marxist lexicon) bedeviled their potential sponsors and has preoccupied historians ever since. The Soviet academic establishment claimed the Bolsheviks had secured a genuine popular following among a class that conformed to Marxist type.

Lenin had contended, however, from the early days of the movement that most actual workers—not to mention the peasants—were not yet capable of recognizing their own supposedly objective interests. The party could rely only on a small trusted group, the so-called worker vanguard, imbued with the proper ideology. In September 1917, he identified the soviets as the vehicle for that group, guided by the vanguard party, which would "elevate, train, educate, and lead the entire mass of people which had remained up to now completely outside political life and history."[42]

Historians in the West, along with their post-Soviet colleagues, have challenged the erstwhile Soviet orthodoxy. Those most hostile to the Communist enterprise find the workers, no less than the peasants, propelled by emotions—fear, resentment, anger—or by immediate material needs, not by ideas. The least sophisticated are prone to purposeless violence, not organized political life; the minority form organizations, but only for practical ends.[43] Other scholars, hoping to salvage the socialist project from its Soviet distortions, look for signs that the workers were motivated by a coherent worldview, if not precisely its Bolshevik rendition. They find that broad socialist slogans functioned as markers of social identity: we are workers, not peasants, and decisively not "bourgeois."[44]

It was a mixed picture. It is clear that words and symbols, songs, slogans, material objects—flags and ribbons, certain styles of dress—had meaning beyond the range of the educated classes. It is also clear that workers and peasants had their own interests and their own manner of interpreting the language and message of their aspiring leaders. They absorbed the socialist idiom; they responded to anti-Semitic clichés; they may not have risen in defense of the Constituent Assembly, but they voted in great numbers. During 1917 socialist rhetoric was actively propagated by all party presses. Thousands of pamphlets delivered the basic message of exploitation and oppression. Socialist symbols came to stand for the revolution itself. Red flags appeared after February, the hammer and sickle already in spring 1917. "Antibourgeois" language spread beyond working-class or even radical circles. A leading Kadet commented on "the fashion for socialism."[45] In the process, socialist terminology escaped its original meanings. "Bourgeois" became an all-purpose term of abuse. It replaced "scoundrel" or worse; it meant selfish, self-serving; it was tossed back and forth in polemics even among socialists themselves.[46]

To a great extent this pervasive language functioned in a purely symbolic register—like the red flag for the revolution. Intellectuals at the time observed that the terms had little to do with their theoretical meanings.[47] A French linguist noted that many labels and turns of phrase became oft-repeated clichés, thus unavoidable, permeating the soundscape; but also that slogans and verbal formulas, crafted by activists who had spent long decades abroad, were often remote from spoken Russian and were indeed hard for the average person to understand. One of the goals and achievements of the Soviet regime was to make a certain lexicon ubiquitous and instinctive.[48] Words themselves became symbols.

In the process of establishing control, the Bolsheviks put their educational apparatus into full gear. Factory meetings were carefully orchestrated for the propagation and endorsement of official formulas and vocabulary. The participants regarded such occasions, which they were compelled to attend, as choreographed spectacles, in which roles were strictly assigned. They quickly learned, under fear of arrest, what was expected of them. Votes were unanimous, because voting was a ritual. The ritual incantation of ideology masked the absence of political understanding.[49] But ideas and slogans cannot simply be imposed, even if they are imperfectly understood. The basic socialist scheme made sense, after all. Workers in the cities were daily confronted with the reality of class difference in the neighborhoods and in the streets; by the authority of management on the shop floor and of policemen on the street corners. In February, factory foremen and police patrols were the first targets of violence. The basic distinction was between them and us, up there and down here. By the beginning of autumn 1917, banners and slogans emanating from the factories reflected a simplified perspective—a contest between "the Democracy" and "the bourgeoisie." "The Democracy" was not in this case a political concept, the liberal notions of rights and institutions, but a social category: the laboring masses, the downtrodden in general, as against the privileged, the propertied—the "bourgeois." The "bourgeois" were the ones with fur collars.[50] It became dangerous to wear a suit and tie.[51] The "dictatorship of the Democracy," a common formulation, was not a contradiction but an expression of what the soviets stood for—class rule, not in the liberal or even Marxist sense.[52] Yet the idea of democracy, even in this form, never lost the core meaning of self-governance and broad participation in political life.

This widespread lexicon, this symbolic repertoire, has been called socialist culture. It was a theory or world view reduced to its primitive components: Lenin's pithy "*kto kogo*"—"who [bests] whom."[53] The philosopher Nikolai Berdiaev commented in 1917: "The social problem has become for us the problem of finding those 'scoundrels' and 'villains,' those 'bourgies,' who are the source of all evil. Extreme moralism has produced morally repugnant results."[54] And epithets were fungible. The reviled bourgeois could easily become the distrusted Jew, class hatred could easily metamorphose into anti-Semitism.

"Ideological metaphors," the historian Boris Kolonitskii notes, "took on a life of their own."[55] It did not matter that the actual bourgeoisie was complex (magnates as well as petty tradesmen), that many caught under the umbrella were not bourgeois in any sense of the word (naval officers, landowners). The term "proletariat," similarly, covered a multitude. Workers did not constitute a single, homogeneous social class, any more than the peasants were uniform across the vast imperial expanse in social customs, agricultural practices, relationship to the labor and grain markets, connection to the cities, or levels of literacy. In the case of workers, the categories under the purview of government factory inspectors varied by craft, type of production, location, degree of urbanization (persistent ties to the village), and so on. Caught in a situation of extreme crisis, workers sometimes responded to leadership (whether their own, or from outside), but the majority often succumbed to collective urges, taking matters into their own hands.

Both Mensheviks and Bolsheviks worried about the tendency of workers to go on the rampage (*goloe buntarstvo*), driven by hunger and anger to resist even their own more sensible or strategic leaders. The parties denounced the "elemental" anarchy that threatened the success of the revolution itself. In mid-1918, a prominent Menshevik commented on the challenge of leading the masses in a politically useful direction. Still in evidence, he complained, were "all the consequences of the age-old lack of culture and the savagery of our working class. Stripped of the fancy dress of revolutionary phraseology, it now appears…as it is in reality, in real life."[56] And the fancy dress itself was a knocked-down model—designed for mass consumption, easy to deploy for unsubtle, or as Berdiaev put it, "morally repugnant" ends. And yet, amid the crime, drunken rampaging, lynch mobs, and general mayhem, a considerable number of peasants and workers, in both cases from the more urbanized, more literate minority, actively engaged in the political process inaugurated by the revolution. They were not simply the dupes of crazed ideologues. As the Civil War will show, ordinary people reacted fiercely when those same ideologues directly harmed their interests and threatened their lives.

Leon Trotsky at Brest–Litovsk, 1918. Getty Images.

# PART IV

Sovereign Claims

# I

# The Peace That Wasn't

The Civil War was to decide the question of power. The Bolsheviks draped themselves in the mantle of statehood. They seized the capital cities and key institutions of imperial rule: the bureaucracy, the army, and the organs of economic regulation associated with the war. But power for its own sake was not the Bolshevik goal. Or rather, the desire to exercise power was tied to the vision of a new social order that would support a new kind of regime. Destruction and reconstruction were the two faces of the Bolshevik agenda. On the one hand, they continued the process of undermining the patterns of authority governing the old society—the class hierarchy, the organs of village self-government, the influence exercised by elites with knowledge and expertise. On the other hand, they needed to implant structures of their own, to create or recreate the organs of a functioning state. Some policies tore at the social fabric; others attempted to re-knit the social web. Some escalated the violence; others aimed to get it under control.

The challenge of the war had defeated both the monarchy and its successor. The war had undermined not only the economy but also the army. Profiting from the resulting instability, the Bolsheviks nevertheless had to eliminate its major cause. Peace was therefore the first item on the Bolshevik agenda. There was no move more calculated to mark the break with the preceding regimes and highlight the Bolshevik role as troublemakers and renegades than the decision to desert the so-called bourgeois democracies and sue for peace with the Central Powers. Germany, for its part, had a vested interest in weakening the Russian state, whatever its political coloration, and in pushing back its western boundaries. The decision to send Lenin back to Petrograd had paid off. In the long term, German and Russian interests were inherently at odds. Their immediate interests, by contrast, coincided. The Central Powers wanted to shut down the Eastern Front and concentrate their forces in the west. The Bolsheviks needed to deliver on the promise of peace. The question was how and on what terms to end the fighting.

By the time the Bolsheviks were in a position to take action, the possibility of ending the war had been on the international agenda for over a year. On September 4, 1914, the Allies had pledged not to pursue a separate peace.[1] An honorable resolution to the conflict therefore must involve a collective effort. In December 1916, Woodrow Wilson had issued the first call to end the war by mutual agreement, challenging all parties to justify the war's enormous costs and losses.[2] The president again claimed the moral high ground on January 22, 1917, in his speech to the U.S. Senate, calling for "peace without victory." The impartial rhetoric did not, however, cure the Germans of the belief that America was too deeply embroiled in the Allied cause, to which it was providing crucial economic backing, to act as a neutral party. The German decision at the end of January to resume unrestricted submarine warfare finally drove the United States into the war.[3] On April 4, 1917 (March 22, OS), the United States voted to send troops to Europe. By then the Romanov dynasty had fallen.

The position occupied by Wilson in January 1917, as leader of a neutral nation, did not survive America's entry into the war on the Allied side. On May 22, Wilson said peace would have to follow German defeat on the battlefield.[4] His original ideas, as adopted by the spokesmen of newly democratic Russia, continued to resonate, however, among European centrists and on the left. As late as July 1917, moderate voices in the Reichstag were urging an end to the war on some kind of "honorable" terms. German Secretary of State for Foreign Affairs Richard von Kühlmann in August envisioned a peace without territorial gains.[5] In autumn, however, when General Erich Ludendorff assumed the Supreme Command, the military gained the upper hand in shaping German diplomatic and imperial ambitions.[6] The Allies, for their part, denounced the Bolshevik move to negotiate on their own with the Central Powers.

It was clear that the new government did not intend to play by the rules of conventional diplomacy, for which the Bolsheviks showed nothing but open contempt. Yet they could not avoid the diplomatic game. In order to extricate themselves from a war that had defeated the two preceding regimes, they could not just walk away—though this was a maneuver they briefly attempted. The process by which Lenin and Trotsky, the principal actors on the Soviet side, managed to rally domestic support for a peace agreement demonstrates the complexity of political life in the wake of October. In asserting their claim to rule, the Bolsheviks had rejected any form of joint or collaborative government, but they could not exercise power at this early stage without the cooperation of socialist rivals.

What is surprising about this interlude—October 1917 to March 1918— is the vigor of political infighting between the Bolsheviks and the other socialist parties, particularly their Left SR partners, but also within the party itself. The grand organs of state power had ceased to function—the incapacitated army was, of course, key—but post-October was not an institutional vacuum. Lenin had to maneuver on the domestic stage in order to operate as a head of state in the international arena. In short, some kind of political process and the organizational framework in which it took place survived the coup and the destruction of the Constituent Assembly. Only the outcome of the domestic squabbling and of the treaty itself enabled Lenin finally to eliminate serious contenders outside the party and challenges from within the Bolshevik ranks.

What is also surprising during the period between the promise of peace in November 1917 and the conclusion of peace four months later is how difficult it still remained to get Russia out of the war. If the Provisional Government or the moderate socialist Soviet leaders had realized in 1917 that they needed to stop fighting in order to preserve the revolution's democratic gains, they might have stolen the Bolsheviks' peace-platform thunder. They might have placated the angry soldier masses. But they feared the wrath of the patriotic Army High Command, which had agreed to the tsar's abdication as necessary for victory in the war, and they shrank from betraying the democratic Allies whose recognition and support they needed. The Bolsheviks were committed to the promise of peace, yet they too at first concealed the radical nature of their isolated gesture. On October 26, 1917, the Second All-Russian Congress of Soviets had issued the Decree on Peace, inviting all belligerent parties, in the interests of the working peoples of the world, to begin immediately to negotiate a "just and democratic peace," "without annexations...and without indemnities."[7] Delivered in person by Lenin, the decree asserted the principle of self-determination for subject nations. This principle was to play a key role, on both sides, in the negotiations with the Central Powers.

By pretending this was a call for international mobilization rather than an admission of defeat, the proclamation covered for the fact that Russia was exhausted and had de facto already stopped fighting. It mimicked Wilson's appeal to the civilized world, understanding this concept differently. "Wars cannot be ended by a refusal [to fight]; they cannot be ended by one side alone. We are proposing an armistice for three months—though we are not rejecting a shorter period—so that this will give the suffering army at least a breathing spell and will make possible the calling of popular meetings in all civilized countries to discuss the conditions [of peace]."[8]

The Decree on Peace introduced the Bolsheviks to the international diplomatic arena, simultaneously borrowing its language and rejecting its rules. As George F. Kennan has pointed out, the decree adopted the terms introduced by Wilson, circulating in European political circles and popular on the international socialist Left, of "peace without victory." Yet talk of a no-fault resolution to the war had gone nowhere since Wilson's first speech. Even he had retracted his plea for the reciprocal renunciation of war aims. Bolshevik use of the language was thus an empty gesture—particularly futile coming from a government with no authority or fighting power, which was losing the war. Yet, it was also a move pregnant with new meaning—it announced a new concept of international politics. The appeal was not submitted to the Allied governments; it was addressed over their heads to the peoples of Europe, imitating the posture of the Zimmerwald socialists in 1915, in the expectation, so stubbornly nursed across the Russian revolutionary spectrum, that the Western nations were ripe for revolution. It was, in fact, as Kennan remarks, a call to revolution.[9] Not surprisingly, the Allies did not respond.[10]

At this point, the Constituent Assembly was still in the offing, and the Decree on Peace left to it the final authority to decide on the conditions of peace from the Russian side. The Bolsheviks were still feeling their way. In another attempt at improvisation, two weeks later, on November 7, as we have seen, they instructed General Dukhonin, who had just replaced Kerensky as commander in chief, to approach the German command with the offer of an armistice. The following day, the Sovnarkom addressed a note to the Allied missions, announcing the existence of the new government. "By implication," Kennan comments, it was "a claim to recognition and an invitation to the establishment of normal diplomatic intercourse."[11]

The day after that, before the Allies had time to respond, which in the end they did not, Dukhonin declared his refusal to act on behalf of the usurper regime. The General was relieved of his command, as we have seen, and troops in the field were instructed to initiate an armistice on their own.[12] At the same time, Trotsky, as commissar of foreign affairs, began, as promised in the peace decree, to publish the texts of the secret treaties concluded by the tsarist regime. "The government of workers and peasants abolishes secret diplomacy with its intrigues, ciphers, and lies," he declared. "We have nothing to hide."[13] No great secrets were in fact revealed, but, as in the case of Wikileaks, the violation of trust angered the parties concerned. The Allied mission chiefs still in Petrograd registered a protest with Dukhonin, who had not yet left his post, warning of "the gravest consequences," but these were mere words.[14] By contrast, the Bolsheviks took action. Trotsky was incensed by the recognition of Dukhonin's continuing authority constituted by the Allied protests.[15] Ensign Nikolai Krylenko, the new Soviet commander in chief, left for Mogilev to enforce the Sovnarkom orders, with the consequences we have seen.

The soldiers had murdered Dukhonin as part of their own protest against a war they were no longer willing to keep fighting. With this in mind, on November 13/26, Krylenko approached the Germans with an armistice offer. When the next day they agreed to a meeting on November 19 (December 2, NS), the Soviet commander in chief telegraphed the army to order an immediate ceasefire.[16] Two days before the proposed date, Trotsky appealed to the Allies to join in negotiating an end to the war, but they did not respond. "We want a general peace," the Bolsheviks riposted, "but if the bourgeoisie of the Allied countries force us to conclude a separate peace, the responsibility will be theirs."[17]

The Allies continued to ignore them.[18] On November 18 (December 1, NS), a Soviet delegation, headed by the former Menshevik and seasoned revolutionary Adolf Ioffe, left for German headquarters in the town of Brest-Litovsk, directly east of Warsaw in occupied Poland, today in Belarus. With no viable army at their disposal, the Soviets had only the chimera of international revolution to strengthen their resolve: "If the German proletariat realises that we are ready to consider all offers of peace," the Decree on Peace had declared, "revolution will break out in Germany, but to agree to examine all conditions of peace does not mean to accept them."[19] It was not clear, however, what leverage the Russians were going to have.

On November 20 (December 3, NS), the two sides concluded a two-week ceasefire.[20] Two days later, when the Allies had still not responded, discussions were suspended. Ioffe then left for Petrograd, seeking authorization to negotiate a separate peace. The Soviets used the pause to circulate propaganda that appealed to German troops to launch their own revolution. The Bolsheviks also announced plans to cancel their debt obligations to the

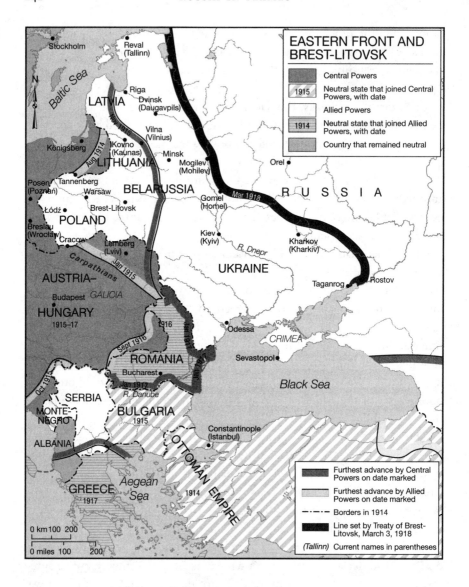

EASTERN FRONT AND
BREST-LITOVSK

| | |
|---|---|
| | Central Powers |
| 1915 | Neutral state that joined Central Powers, with date |
| | Allied Powers |
| 1914 | Neutral state that joined Allied Powers, with date |
| | Country that remained neutral |

| | |
|---|---|
| | Furthest advance by Central Powers on date marked |
| | Furthest advance by Allied Powers on date marked |
| —·—·— | Borders in 1914 |
| | Line set by Treaty of Brest-Litovsk, March 3, 1918 |
| (Tallinn) | Current names in parentheses |

Allies, so far sparing the Central Powers. A few days after that, as we recall, Lenin decided to postpone the Constituent Assembly, which was supposedly to approve the terms of peace.[21]

On November 29 (December 12, NS), the delegations returned to Brest-Litovsk.[22] Three days later, they signed a formal armistice, set to expire January 1/14, 1918.[23] Trotsky explained to the "Toiling, Oppressed, and Exhausted Peoples of Europe" that his government had not deserted the cause of world revolution. The capitalist countries were not "capable of a democratic peace," which must await the triumph of international socialism; meanwhile it was necessary to stop the slaughter and promote the overthrow of capitalism.[24] A face-saving formulation, but also sincere.

On December 9/22, 1917, peace negotiations began. Altogether, four hundred people crammed into the war-ravaged citadel of Brest-Litovsk.[25] At the heart of the Quadruple Alliance (Germany, Austria-Hungary, Turkey, and Bulgaria), the Central Powers were represented by German Secretary of State Kühlmann, accompanied by General Max Hoffmann, chief of staff on the Eastern Front,[26] and Austrian Foreign Minister Count Ottokar von Czernin. Joffe again headed the Soviet delegation. Two contrasting casts of characters; two social systems; two political games. On the one side, professional diplomats and senior commanders; on the other, a ragtag assortment of "common people" (a worker, a peasant, a woman), symbolizing the new democratic order, led by upstart outsiders. The delegation also included two SRs, a Lithuanian, a Ukrainian, and a Pole.[27] Generations separated the two sides, as well. The German and Austrian principals were in their forties; Ioffe was thirty-five, Trotsky just approaching forty, the others younger still.

It is easy to imagine what their opposite numbers thought of the Soviet delegates at the time. As Kaiser Wilhelm put it: "The Russian people have been turned over to the vengeance of Jews, who are connected with all the Jews in the world."[28] In 1938, twenty years after the peace, the British historian John Wheeler-Bennett described Ioffe as "a typical revolutionary intellectual, not unpolished in manner and with a soft pleasant voice. Long hair and beard framed his Semitic face, and pince-nez perched upon his Semitic nose. A similar type, though less obviously Hebraic, was Leo Kamenev, Trotsky's brother-in-law."[29] Ioffe was not, however, a run-of-the-mill revolutionary. Born in the Crimea to a wealthy Jewish family, he joined the Social Democrats while still in his teens. In his twenties, he studied medicine and law in Berlin and Zurich, acquiring the facility in German that would stand him in good stead at Brest-Litovsk. After returning for the Revolution of 1905, he spent four years in Vienna with Trotsky. In 1917 he belonged to the Interdistrict Group, which joined the Bolsheviks in June.[30]

The gulf between the two sides at the bargaining table was bridged by the mutual need for resolution on the Eastern Front and by a common vocabulary. Citing the Decree on Peace, Ioffe repeated the demand for a treaty to be concluded by all the belligerent nations, respecting the principle of national self-determination.[31] Echoing the Reichstag resolution of July

1917, Kühlmann denied the Germans were interested in territorial acquisition.[32] Czernin said the same thing in different terms. The Central Powers
agreed to withdraw their troops from occupied territory only if the Entente
did the same and on condition that Poland, Lithuania, and Latvia be recognized as independent.[33]

On the first point, Allied reciprocity, it was clear the Allies were not coming to the table. Trotsky had invited them repeatedly, but they had not
replied.[34] Fearful that a Russian-German alliance might emerge, British
Ambassador to Russia George Buchanan urged the Entente to release the
Russians from the September 1914 commitment to joint peace-making.
Gathered in Paris on November 30, the Allies had refused, however, to contemplate active relations with the new Russian regime. The French, in particular, would not consider peace at this point in the war, given Germany's
dominant position. Kerensky's final ambassador to France, Vasilii Maklakov,
not surprisingly warned against dealing with the regime that had made him
redundant. The Allies might "proceed to a revision of war aims together
with Russia," he said, once there was "a government aware of its duties
to the country and defending the interests of the country and not of the
enemy."[35] Such honorable intransigence helped isolate Soviet Russia from
its Western allies, leaving it vulnerable to the German military's expansionist
ambitions and exacerbating the conflicts about to erupt in the Civil War.
Maklakov thus did his bit to narrow Soviet diplomatic choices. He had
reason to want the regime to fall.

On the second point, the matter of national self-determination, formal
independence for Russia's borderlands opened the door to German penetration. The Kaiser had recognized Polish independence already in
November, 1916, establishing a compliant occupation regime; German
troops had been in control of the Baltic provinces since the fall of 1917.
The Central Powers were not about to relinquish their conquests; self-
determination was a convenient disguise. As historian Winfried Baumgart
puts it, "The German government intended the appeal to the right to self-
determination as a tactical means of finally detaching these lands from Russia
and binding them to Germany."[36]

Germany's motives were not, however, immediately apparent. On
Christmas Day in the West, Kühlmann and Czernin endorsed the terms of
the Decree on Peace, knowing the enabling condition—Allied participation—
was unlikely to be met.[37] Trotsky, in Petrograd, told the Soviet Central
Executive Committee that "our diplomacy has met with great success."[38]

Talks were then once again adjourned, for another ten days, to permit the Allies to respond.[39] As the recess began, Trotsky issued yet another appeal, "To the Peoples and Governments of the Allied Countries," inviting them to join the proceedings, since the Russians believed the Central Powers had agreed to withdraw from occupied land within Russian borders.[40] The appeal was also a threat. "If the Allied governments, in the blind stubbornness characteristic of declining and perishing classes, again refuse to participate in the negotiations, then the working class will be faced with the iron necessity of wresting power from the hands of those who either cannot or will not give peace to the peoples of the world."[41]

The German High Command, however, rejected the implication that Russia might be allowed to return to pre-1914 borders. The Soviets contended that the regions in question must be allowed to decide their own futures, as a result of democratic procedures, but meanwhile all occupying forces must be withdrawn. General Hoffmann explained to Ioffe that the Germans considered the Baltic states and Poland already to have opted for independence. The Germans were not therefore obliged, under the principle of national self-determination promulgated by the Soviets themselves, to withdraw their troops from areas no longer considered parts of Russia.[42] Ioffe threatened to walk away, but this made no impression. "There was no question of negotiations being broken off," Hoffmann recalled; "the only chance the Bolsheviks had of remaining in power was by signing a peace. They were obliged to accept the conditions of the Central Powers, however hard they might be."[43] Hoffmann's clarification had revealed, as Kamenev put it, that "The Germans have transformed the principle of self-determination from a formula for national liberation into a disguise for annexation."[44]

---

Both economics and geopolitics were at stake. German leaders did not conceal their pressing need during the war to access the resources provided by the Baltic provinces, Poland, and the Ukrainian steppe: grain, industry, and fuel. From the very beginning of the Great War, the Central Powers had lent their support to nascent liberation movements in Russia's western periphery, while also bankrolling the Bolsheviks in the Russian core. The goal was to weaken postwar Russia as a great power while guaranteeing access to economic resources and opportunities in the east.[45] In the words of German Chancellor Theobald von Bethmann Hollweg, "Should the military developments and events in Russia itself make it possible *to thrust the Muscovite*

*Empire back eastward, detaching its western portions,* then our liberation from
this nightmare in the east would certainly be a worthwhile goal, worth the
great sacrifices and extraordinary exertions of this war."[46] The only disagreements among German leaders and between the German and Austrian partners concerned how best to achieve this objective. The terms of the treaty at
Brest-Litovsk evolved over the course of the negotiations, partly in response
to the Soviet role. The civilian and military negotiators on the German side
did not always see eye to eye, a sign that German political opinion was
divided; in the end, the military's aggressive position prevailed.[47]

The new calendar year by European reckoning began with yet another
recess at Brest-Litovsk. During the break, on January 5 (NS), Kühlmann and
Czernin formally repudiated the Christmas agreement, on the grounds that
the Allies had never responded.[48] The talks were complicated further two
days later by the appearance of delegates claiming to represent the Central
Rada formed in June 1917, now the governing council of the self-declared
Ukrainian National Republic (*Ukraïns'ka Narodna Respublika*), announced
on November 7/20, 1917, in Kiev. The Ukrainians arrived in Brest-Litovsk
to begin separate negotiations for a bilateral peace with the Central Powers.[49]
Declaring that "the government of the Soviet of People's Commissars does
not extend over the whole of Russia and is not recognized by the Ukrainian
National Republic," the Ukrainian delegates asserted their right to take
independent action in the international arena until such time as a federation
enjoying the consent of the governed should emerge on the territory of the
former Russian Empire.[50] It was time for hardball on both sides.

Now, however, that the Central Powers had revealed their naked
annexationist motives, it remained for the Allies to position themselves as
standard-bearers of political idealism. On January 8, 1918, the day before
the recess at Brest-Litovsk came to a close, Wilson delivered his Fourteen
Points address to the joint session of the U.S. Congress.[51] Wilson's message reiterated the ideas with which he had been associated since
December 1916, but which had since been promoted most energetically
by the new Soviet regime in earnest of its democratic, liberationist intentions. Instead, however, of unmasking those intentions, Wilson focused
on recapturing the idiom.

The president's motives in delivering the Fourteen Points were ambivalent. On the one hand, he wished to reclaim his original slogans from
their use by revolutionaries intent on upending the world order and
destroying international capitalism; on the other hand, he wished to draw

the Russians away from an alliance with Germany and prevent them from leaving the war.[52] By asserting America's dedication to democratic principles, the statement was intended to counter Soviet accusations that Allied refusal to come to Brest-Litovsk abetted German annexationist ambitions. The statement would also appeal to Central European socialists, themselves critical of these aims.[53]

Like Lenin, Wilson denounced secret treaties and promoted the political rights of minority nations. Though he avoided the catchword "self-determination," he defended the autonomy of the component peoples of the Austro-Hungarian Empire, recognized the independence of Poland as a nation, and asserted the right of colonized peoples to have a voice in shaping their futures. The United States, of course, had by now entered the war on the side of the Entente, with which Russia had not yet officially broken. And, despite the October coup, this was the Russia, still anticipating the convocation of the Constituent Assembly, with a potentially democratic future.

In his opening remarks, Wilson championed the Soviet position at Brest-Litovsk, which he compared to the German's acquisitive ambitions. "The Russian representatives were sincere and in earnest. They cannot entertain such proposals of conquest and domination."[54] He described "the Russian people" as victims of German aggression. "They are prostrate and all but helpless, it would seem, before the grim power of Germany, which has hitherto known no relenting and no pity. Their power, apparently, is shattered. And yet their soul is not subservient. They will not yield either in principle or in action. Their conception of what is right, of what it is humane and honorable for them to accept, has been stated with a frankness, a largeness of view, a generosity of spirit, and a universal human sympathy which must challenge the admiration of every friend of mankind." The President pledged American assistance in helping Russia fulfill her dreams of "liberty and ordered peace."[55] Occupied Russian territory must be evacuated and Russia be assured of "the independent determination of her own political development and national policy and... of a sincere welcome into the society of free nations under institutions of her own choosing." He urged her "sister nations" to put aside their selfish interests and give her all their sincere support (Article 6).[56]

Wilson did not go so far as to offer diplomatic recognition. His rhetoric, moreover, treated the Soviet regime with the condescension usually reserved for colonial subjects or minor ethnic enclaves struggling against imperial domination. Soviet Russia, however, thought of itself as the successor to a grand empire, with condescension of its own to dispense. The promise of independence to Poland (Article 13:"An independent Polish state should be erected which should include the territories inhabited by indisputable Polish populations, which should be assured a free and secure access to the sea, and whose political and economic independence and territorial integrity should be guaranteed by international covenant") had as little appeal to the Bolsheviks as to their patriotic opponents.[57] It was, moreover, inconsistent. "The evacuation of all Russian territory" was incompatible with insistence on the independence of Poland, which as part of the former Russian Empire ought therefore to be restored to Russian sovereignty.[58]

The text of the Fourteen Points was delivered three days after the address in Russian translation to Lenin personally by Edgar Sisson, an employee of the U.S. propaganda office in Petrograd, who later asserted that the Germans were paying Lenin to take Russia out of the war.[59] Neither Lenin nor Trotsky had the slightest regard for the president's professed good intentions, viewing him as nothing more than another imperialist bourgeois hypocrite.[60] Yet Wilson was not entirely wrong to think the question of a separate peace remained undecided. At this point, the idea was not popular in Russia. It was Lenin who was swimming against the tide. Most of his followers, with the exception of a few right-hand men, resisted his insistence on concluding the peace as swiftly as possible. The spirit of revolutionary defensism was still alive.

A separate peace was certainly to the advantage of the Central Powers, but Lenin was unsentimental in his choice of methods. He accepted German money; first undermined, then overthrew the pro-war Provisional Government; and finally managed to take Russia out of the war. All of this promoted German interests. In the long run, however, Lenin embodied Germany's worst nightmare—a leader capable of resurrecting the Russian state as a powerful obstacle to German geopolitical ambitions. In terms of Brest-Litovsk, the more the Bolsheviks dithered, against Lenin's advice, the more the Central Powers were able to demand.[61]

The mastermind of the actual negotiations was not Lenin, however, but Trotsky. At Brest-Litovsk talks had resumed on January 9, 1918, the day after Wilson's address. Trotsky now headed the Soviet delegation, imposing a new discipline on his fellows. The Russians dined by themselves, refused to ride in German cars, and allowed Trotsky to take the lead in public deliberations. They faced not only the representatives of the Quadruple Alliance, but also the Ukrainian delegates and a spokesman for the Polish Regency Council (*Regentschaftskönigreich Polen—Królestwo Regencyjne*), a body established, with German backing, on occupied Polish soil, all of whom expected to benefit from the principal parties' commitment to self-determination.[62] The Bolsheviks were not the only ones claiming to represent a new government on the international stage.

The Germans were pressured by Austria, desperate for food, to conclude an agreement that would guarantee access to Ukrainian grain. The Central Powers thought Trotsky was in an even more desperate position and planned to use the Ukrainian card against him. It was at this point that Kühlmann uttered his later much-quoted remark, "Ils n'ont que le choix à quelle sauce ils se feront manger," to Czernin's disconsolate sigh, "Tout comme chez nous."[63]

Trotsky, however, was not disconsolate but high-handed. Clinging to the language of enlightened diplomacy consistent with the ideals of international socialism, when Hoffmann objected to the Soviet propaganda campaign among German troops Trotsky invoked freedom of the press. He denounced the German version of self-determination as a screen for class and military domination, insisting yet again on the Soviet desire for "a democratic and a just peace."[64] The Soviets remained at Brest-Litovsk, he asserted, to achieve a resolution "without violence to the Poles, Lithuanians, Letts, Esthonians, Armenians, and other nationalities to whom the Russian Revolution, on its part, assures the full right to free development without reservation, restriction, or *arrière pensée*."[65]

It was now January 10 (NS). By this time, Lenin had decided the Soviets had no choice but to accept the draconian conditions presented by the Central Powers and to conclude a separate peace. To many of his comrades in the party, particularly the group by now known as Left Communists, as well as moderate Mensheviks and firebrand Left SRs—in short, the socialist brotherhood across the board—the idea of concession seemed a betrayal of revolutionary principles. The Left Communists insisted that German soldiers were too tired to fight, while Russian soldiers would rally to defend the fatherland. The Petrograd Bolsheviks argued vociferously for a "revolutionary war," a *levée en masse* in defense of the revolution. Lenin, by contrast, acknowledged that the long-expected revolution in Europe was not forthcoming; the Russians would have to go it alone.[66]

Trotsky's strategy at Brest-Litovsk, meanwhile, was to use the common vocabulary to unmask Germany's true intentions, sending a message to the

European public, in particular the European proletariat, from whom the Bolsheviks still hoped to elicit a revolutionary response. Thus, on January 12, Kamenev conceded that Soviet Russia could not lay claim to the old imperial borders: "The new frontiers of the fraternal union of peoples of the Russian Republic and the peoples which desire to remain outside its borders must be defined by a free resolution of the peoples concerned." Russia would not compel them to adopt any "particular form of government." Free self-determination could only occur, however, in the absence of military occupation.[67]

General Hoffmann was provoked. The Russians, he objected, were taking the attitude of victors, whereas in fact they were the ones under occupation. Championing the principle of self-determination, they applied it only to the territories Germany now controlled, while their own government was "based purely on violence, ruthlessly suppressing all who think differently." The German Supreme Command therefore rejected "any attempt to interfere in the affairs of the occupied provinces."[68] In short, the Germans were staying put, although they, too, asserted the right of peoples to determine their own form of government and their national allegiances.[69]

Hoffmann was insolent, but his partner was in a less favorable position. The Soviets were therefore encouraged to stick to their guns. A few days later, workers across Austria went on strike to protest food shortages. On January 17, Emperor Karl warned Czernin that if a treaty did not soon emerge, the result would be revolution.[70] But Austrian desperation was outweighed by German confidence. Hoffmann showed Trotsky a map of German territorial demands. The proposed Soviet border would exclude most of Poland and a good piece of the Baltic provinces. Not only would Russia lose almost 100,000 square miles, Trotsky observed, but the occupied territories would remain under German and Austrian occupation for an indefinite time, unable to control their own destinies. Requesting a ten-day adjournment, Trotsky left for Petrograd.[71]

A day later, the Bolsheviks abolished the Constituent Assembly by force of arms. The British Labor Party and the German Social Democrats condemned the move not only in its own terms but as a sign that the Bolsheviks were clearing away the remaining opposition to a separate peace, reiterating the charge that they were working on Germany's behalf.[72] To counter the impression that Soviet Russia was abetting Germany's expansionist ambitions, Trotsky conceived the ingenious idea of refusing to play the game at all. Since Russia had no military force at its disposal, it would refuse to fight but also refuse to sign a peace dictated by German military superiority. "We declare we end the war but do not sign a peace," he wrote to Lenin. "If they attack us, our position will be no worse than now, when they have the opportunity to proclaim and declare us agents of England and of Wilson after his speech, and to commence an attack."[73] If Germans indeed resumed the attack, it would demonstrate that Russia was signing only under compulsion, not as Germany's agents but as its victims.[74]

While this was going on, delegates were gathering in Petrograd for the Third All-Russian Congress of Soviets of Worker and Soldier Deputies, set for the last week in January, which was to replace the Constituent Assembly as the voice of popular opinion. Lenin outlined the position he would present to the various party gatherings. "Under the circumstances it would be very bad policy to risk the fate of the Socialist Revolution on the chance that a revolution might break out in Germany by a certain date." The interests of the Socialist Revolution, which is to say, Russia's best interests, must take precedence over the principle of national self-determination.[75] They would not go to the mat on the issue of German annexations.

Unequivocal as Lenin always was, his position met with fierce opposition. At a meeting of party leaders on January 8/21, his views received fifteen votes, against thirty-two for the position promoted by the Left Communists, who insisted on the alternative of a revolutionary war, and sixteen for Trotsky's middle ground of agreeing to peace but refusing to sign an agreement. The following day, however, the Bolshevik Central Committee endorsed both Lenin's insistence that negotiations be resumed and Trotsky's theatrical tactic, intended to buy time for the ever-anticipated European revolution to emerge.[76] Despite the heated rhetoric, Trotsky kept seeking an alternative, attempting through informal contacts in Petrograd to elicit the Allies' support—to no avail.[77] Addressing the Soviet Congress, he blamed the Allies for hoping that German aggression would succeed in destroying the revolution. "The peace terms which Germany offers us are also the terms of America, France, and England."[78] For a brief moment, it seemed as though the Left Communists were right. Strikes broke out in Berlin two days later. They were, however, quickly suppressed.[79]

Bolshevik Party leaders thus differed on whether the Central Powers still had the stomach to fight, whether revolution abroad was imminent or unlikely, and whether the Russian peasant-soldiers would rise to the country's defense. By the time Trotsky returned to Brest-Litovsk on January 30 (NS), the various deliberative organs—the Bolshevik Central Committee, the Left SR committee, the Soviet Congress—had endorsed his compromise tactics. Russia would refuse to sign but also refuse to fight—"no peace, no war"—and begin demobilization. The hope was to drag out the negotiations long enough either for the resumption of German aggression to be answered by a spontaneous "revolutionary war" or for the awaited explosion of revolution in Europe. It was at this point, in late January, that the Sovnarkom established the Worker-Peasant Red Army (*Raboche-krest'ianskaia Krasnaia armiia*), as a way to counteract the demobilization of the old Imperial Army.[80]

When talks resumed, attention was focused on the Ukrainian question. Three weeks earlier, on January 7 (NS), as we have seen, representatives of the Ukrainian National Republic, based in Kiev, had claimed the right to negotiate a peace on their own behalf. About ten days earlier, however, the Bolsheviks had proclaimed the establishment of a rival government, the Ukrainian Worker-Peasant Republic (*Raboche-Krest'ianskoe Pravitel'stvo Ukrainy*), based in Kharkov (Ukrainian Kharkiv). Soviet troops were at the moment nearing Kiev, threatening to topple the Rada.[81] Accompanied by delegates from Kharkov, Trotsky now insisted that only they could speak for Ukraine and then only as part of the Russian delegation.[82]

Caught between the two ruthless powers, the delegates of the Ukrainian National Republic invoked the principle that both sides espoused and both shamelessly exploited. Among these delegates was the twenty-seven-year-old Mykola Liubyns'kyi, described by Wheeler-Bennett as "a strange, wild figure in his ill-fitting Victorian frock-coat."[83] A linguist by training, Liubyns'kyi served as the fledgling government's foreign minister until late April 1918, when it was removed in a German-backed coup. With the double anger of an indignant SR and a Ukrainian patriot, Liubyns'kyi denounced the Soviets for betraying the basic ideals of the revolution. "The Government of the Bolsheviks," he declared, "which has broken up the Constituent Assembly, and which rests on the bayonets of hired Red Guards, will never elect to apply in Russia the very just principle of self-determination, because they know only too well that not only the Republic of the Ukraine, but also the Don, the Caucasus, Siberia, and other regions do not regard them as their government, and that even the Russian people themselves will ultimately deny their right."[84] At the end of these passionate remarks, the Central Powers announced their recognition of the Ukrainian National Republic "as an independent, free and sovereign State, which is able to enter into international agreements independently."[85]

On February 6 (NS), after yet another break, during which the Germans returned to Berlin, the sides reassembled. Trotsky was unfazed. He continued to insist the delegates from the Ukrainian National Republic represented no one but themselves. On February 7, the Red Army took Kiev, ousting the Rada. Kühlmann and Czernin nevertheless hoped the threat of a separate treaty would pressure Trotsky into accepting their terms. Ludendorff was adamant that Germany emerge from the proceedings with control over the Ukrainian lands.[86] Finally, the treaty between the Quadruple Alliance and the Ukrainian National Republic was signed on February 9, 1918. It recognized Ukraine as an independent nation, set its boundaries, and stipulated the evacuation of occupying forces after ratification. It renounced "indemnities," but provided for an economic agreement that established German and Austrian claims on Ukrainian grain and other resources.[87] At the signing, the Ukrainians wore tails, starched white dress shirts, and black ties. The occasion was recorded on film.[88]

The treaty with the self-proclaimed Ukrainian government constituted the first formal step in the dismemberment of the old Russian Empire. Back in Berlin, German resolve only hardened. Wilhelm had learned that the Russians were urging German soldiers to mutiny, murder their officers, assassinate the kaiser, and make their own peace with Russia. Baltic German landowners were petitioning for support. Berlin pressured Kühlmann to pursue a tougher line and demand a swift response.[89] Kühlmann accused the Bolsheviks of promoting mutiny and regicide; Trotsky denied the charges, at the same time rejecting the validity of the treaty with Ukraine, which he insisted was still a part of Russia. By now he had the green light from Lenin to launch his coup de théâtre. Not only did Russia repudiate the treaty with the Ukrainian National Republic, he said, but it would sign no treaty itself. "No peace, no war." Russia would demobilize and stop fighting, but would not sign. "We cannot enter the signature of the Russian Revolution under conditions which carry oppression, sorrow, and suffering to millions of human beings." Hoffmann was astounded. Trotsky left the room, the delegation with him. That night, the Russians departed for Petrograd, feeling especially clever for having flouted all the rules.[90]

Trotsky's maneuver achieved two aims. Domestically, it provided a compromise position that softened the opposition to Lenin's demand for capitulation; internationally, it extended the interval in which the European proletariat might finally rise against their own masters. Trotsky himself, of course, hoped for the second outcome and only gradually swung entirely to

Lenin's side, although he avoided putting his signature on the final, humiliating document. He was also angry. Bruce Lockhart, the British journalist, diplomat, and informal agent of the British War Office then in Petrograd, interviewed him during this time. "He has a wonderfully quick mind and a rich, deep voice. With his broad chest, his huge forehead, surmounted by great masses of black, waving hair, his strong, fierce eyes, and his heavy protruding lips, he is the very incarnation of the revolutionary of the bourgeois caricatures. He is neat about his dress. He wore a clean soft collar and his nails were carefully manicured....He is full of belligerent fury against the Germans for the humiliation to which they have exposed him at Brest. He strikes me as a man who would willingly die fighting for Russia provided there was a big enough audience to see him do it."[91]

Meanwhile, the Germans debated how to react to Trotsky's novel procedure. Their decision presents one of the tantalizing "what if" moments in this agonized tale. Czernin and Kühlmann, the civilian negotiators, argued for keeping the territory their troops already occupied and accepting the end of hostilities. General Hoffmann, following Ludendorff, insisted on the resumption of war and the expansion of conquest. Had the general's position not prevailed, the Soviet regime would have been less beleaguered, and its prestige would have been enhanced. It is unclear whether a less humiliating outcome would have softened the opposition to Bolshevik rule coming from their rivals on the left and their sworn enemies to the right and center. In any case, taking the hard line, the Germans threatened to pursue their eastward advance if negotiations did not resume by February 17, a week after Trotsky's provocative gesture.[92] The game was not over yet.

# 2

# Treason and Terror

When the Soviet delegation from Brest-Litovsk reached Petrograd, they reported to Lenin and the Sovnarkom, but also to the Soviet Executive Committee in special session and to its combined Bolshevik/Left SR factions. These were the remaining organs of the revolution not yet exclusively in Bolshevik hands. The revolution was to some extent still a talking shop. While Left Communists and Left SRs comforted themselves with the assumption that German workers would refuse to fight proletarian Russia, the German High Command was preparing to restart the offensive. News of their plans reached Lenin and Trotsky on February 16, 1918 (on the Gregorian calendar, which Russia had now adopted), but they did not make them known until two days later, when the attack had begun and the facts could no longer be concealed.[1] At the beginning, General Hoffmann wondered what to expect. The Central Powers had no choice, he reflected on February 17, otherwise "these brutes will wipe up the Ukrainians, the Finns and the Balts, and then quietly get together a new revolutionary army and turn the whole of Europe into a pigsty....I am very curious to see whether the Russians will defend themselves at all, or whether they will clear out without a fight....The whole of Russia is not more than a vast heap of maggots—a squalid, swarming mess."[2] Indeed, there was not much to stop the invaders. Five days later, Hoffmann remarked, "It is the most comical war I have ever known—it is almost entirely carried on by rail and motorcar. We put a handful of infantrymen with machine guns and one gun on to a train and push them off to the next station; they take it, make prisoners of the Bolsheviks, pick up a few more troops and go on. This proceeding has, at any rate, the charm of novelty."[3]

Lenin employed all his skill as a party infighter to get his comrades to face the facts. On February 17, the Bolshevik Central Committee rejected, by a vote of five to six, his motion to accept the German terms, preferring to defer the decision until after the offensive actually began. The next day, Lenin's appeal was again rejected by a single vote, with Trotsky among its opponents. By then, however, the Germans had reached Dvinsk and were moving towards Ukraine.[4] Lenin observed that since they had demobilized the remains of the army, they could not resist the invaders even if they wanted to. "We cannot joke with war," he admonished. They must immediately accept whatever terms were offered, even if it meant the loss of the western borderlands. "To delay is to betray the revolution."[5] It was only during the night of February 18–19 that his motion carried by a single vote, Trotsky having changed his position. Among the holdouts were Adolf Ioffe and Feliks Dzerzhinskii.[6]

Thus, on February 19, 1918, two months after negotiations had begun, Lenin and Trotsky wired Berlin.[7] They objected to the resumption of the offensive, but conceded that "under the circumstances" the Soviet government was forced to accept the proffered terms.[8] Moving through the Baltic cities, the Germans were getting closer and closer to the capital. The local soviets organized hasty defense squads, which melted away as the invaders approached.[9] Some residents cowered, others awaited the enemy's arrival with excitement. The barely formed Red Army brigades were incapable of fighting. Soldiers clogged the railroads as they fled back east. The Sovnarkom discussed possible ways to mobilize the population in defense of the capital and created an emergency command center, consisting of Lenin, Trotsky, Stalin, and two Left SRs, but there was no force to command.[10]

On February 21, the Germans took the Estonian town of Rezhitsa (Rēzekne), on the way to Pskov, headquarters of the Northern Front, 180 miles south of Petrograd on a direct railway line. Declaring "The Socialist Fatherland in Danger," Sovnarkom placed Petrograd under a state of siege and began organizing its defense. The idea was to combine the model of mass mobilization with class warfare. "All able-bodied persons of the bourgeoisie, both men and women, should be included in the battalions—to dig trenches under the supervision of military specialists—and should work under the eyes of the Red Guard. In case of refusal or opposition, shoot them down." As in patriotic wartime propaganda, the foreign enemy and domestic traitor were linked, but there was less inhibition now about how to respond to the dual threat. "Enemy agents, speculators, burglars, thieves, hooligans, counterrevolutionary agitators, and German spies should be shot on the spot."[11]

In fact, the armistice had not stopped the war. The Allied embassies prepared to leave the city. Trotsky and Georgii Chicherin, his second in the foreign office, approached American and British citizens still in the capital to explore the possibility of Allied help.[12] The feelers went nowhere. Trotsky's clever maneuver had failed. On February 22, Chicherin replaced him as commissar of foreign affairs and chief negotiator at Brest-Litovsk; on March 13, Trotsky replaced Nikolai Krylenko as commissar of war.[13] Chicherin was well suited to the role of high-level diplomat, having served in the Imperial Foreign Office. He came from a wealthy and cultivated aristocratic family, spoke many languages, and had published a study of Mozart's music. Despite his privilege, he became involved in radical politics, ran into trouble with the tsarist police, and spent the war years in London, where he was imprisoned for antiwar agitation, then exchanged for various British subjects still in Russia. Upon his return in early 1918, he joined the Bolsheviks.[14]

The Sovnarkom received the German response only on February 23. The Germans were in no hurry. They had used the interval to move beyond the armistice line and occupy the rest of what soon became Estonia. They gave Russia forty-eight hours to reply, but only one day remained by the time their message arrived and discussions got started.[15] The ultimatum would expire at 7 in the morning on February 24. The Germans also demanded that talks resume in Brest-Litovsk by March 1 and the treaty be signed by March 3. Russia would then have two weeks in which to ratify the agreement. In all that time, the Germans would keep advancing. Lenin said, "It is a question of signing the terms now or of signing the death sentence of the Soviet Government three weeks later."[16]

Into the night and morning, as February 23 became February 24, the Bolsheviks and their Left SR allies debated. Again, Lenin had to browbeat his comrades into compliance. He could not muster a true majority even in the Bolshevik Central Committee: six, including Stalin, supported him; four Left Communists, including Nikolai Bukharin, were opposed; and four abstained—including Trotsky, Dzerzhinskii, and Ioffe! Only procedural sleight of hand allowed Lenin finally to prevail in the Soviet Executive Committee. Ignoring the dire reports on conditions in the army and navy, the Left SRs and Left Communists stuck to their ideological guns. And not just the firebrands. The Menshevik Iulii Martov, still in the Soviet leadership, continued to insist an armed force could yet be mobilized and that, in any case, it was more honorable to go down fighting than preemptively to give in.[17] Lenin's fellow Bolsheviks called him a traitor, a German spy. He was no better than the Mensheviks whom he had always reviled for "compromising with imperialism."[18] Lenin was unmoved. "Let us beware of becoming the slaves of our own phrases," he warned them. "Give me an army of 100,000 men, an army which will not tremble before the enemy, and I will not sign this peace....You must sign this shameful peace in order to save the world Revolution, in order to hold fast to its most important, and at present, its only foothold—the Soviet Republic."[19] It was one thing, however, to force the votes to precarious, hairline majorities. It was another to control the rest of the opposition. A Left SR recalled that people "no longer had any choice but to fight against the peace, and above all against the conscious or unconscious traitors to Russia, the Bolsheviks."[20]

By now, German troops had advanced through the Baltic region and were sweeping south, on a line from Gomel to Rostov, gaining control of a swath of territory extending from the Gulf of Finland to the Sea of Azov and the Black Sea, including the Crimea. In this advantageous position, their terms were harsher than before. They demanded Russia recognize the independence of the Baltic states of Estonia, Latvia, and Lithuania, as well as of Finland, Ukraine, and Georgia, and withdraw any forces still on the ground; they insisted on across-the-board demobilization and disarmament, the payment of indemnities, and the cessation of propaganda in areas under Central Power control.[21]

In the early morning of February 24, as the deadline was fast approaching, after hours of acrimonious debate, Lenin finally secured a slim majority in the Soviet Executive Committee and telegrammed Berlin to accept the terms.[22] But the danger was not yet past. That day, when the Germans entered Pskov, the Red Guards quickly degenerated into a mob that trashed the market. In the course of the pogrom, as the rampage was described, they murdered the chairman of the Pskov soviet. By the night of February 24–25, the Germans had taken the city. Sirens in Petrograd signaled their arrival, but the Petrograd garrison still refused to leave their barracks.[23] The Left SRs appealed to factory workers and created ad hoc fighting squads, but few volunteered. Petrograders were told to expect air raids and gas attacks.[24] Left to defend Pskov were various units of Red Guards, Red Army volunteers, and Latvian Riflemen. The Latvian regiments had been formed as part of the Imperial Army in summer 1915 for the defense of Riga. In 1918, as the Germans advanced, many of them retreated into Russia, providing the Bolsheviks with a disciplined armed force.[25] In Pskov, the Latvians were not enough, however. On February 26, the Sovnarkom decided to move the government to

Moscow, but tried to keep their preparations as quiet as possible, to avoid the impression of taking flight.[26]

The final session at Brest-Litovsk opened on February 28 with the arrival of the Russian delegation, once again led by Ioffe, with Chicherin in a secondary role. No more grandstanding. Time to swallow the bitter pill. But again, for the last time, they were theatrical about their impotence. Refusing to discuss or even read the text, they wired Petrograd saying they were signing and leaving at once.[27] A second wire asked for a train and bodyguards for the return journey. The second wire arrived first, giving the impression the Germans were on their way to the capital. The first wire soon followed, calming the commissars' rattled nerves. Lenin was convinced, nevertheless, that nothing would stop the Germans from continuing their march.[28] To save face, to issue one final propaganda blast, the Russians signed under protest, denouncing the "so-called 'peace by agreement'" as "in fact an imperialistic and annexationist peace." This was "peace dictated at the point of the gun."[29]

By the terms of the Brest-Litovsk Treaty, Soviet Russia lost 34 percent of its population, 32 percent of its agricultural land, 54 percent of its industrial plants, and 89 percent of its coal mines. Germany gained control of territory stretching from the Arctic Sea to the Black Sea, inhabited by 55 million people, rich in wheat, oil, and other valuable resources.[30] Nor did the humiliating surrender end the military threat. During the week between the capitulation on Sunday, February 24, and the signing on Sunday, March 3, the Germans of course kept moving. Petrograd was not out of danger. For all Trotsky's bravado and the magical thinking that generated the Left's stubborn belligerence, the leadership panicked.

Faced with an armed enemy outside the gates and vigorous opposition to its policies from within, the fledgling state returned to the pattern pioneered by the weakened tsarist regime. It used the threat of military attack as an excuse to launch a war against real and imagined domestic enemies. The Cheka, as noted, had been established in December 1917, well before the Germans resumed their advance, but the new conjuncture enhanced its role. The tensions generated at Brest-Litovsk, the German invasion, the rising nationalism on the western periphery among the Poles and the Baltic peoples, as well as the growing opposition to Bolshevik policies, even on the left—all this justified the lumping together of dissident Mensheviks, humanitarian organizations, and opponents of a separate peace under the sign of counterrevolution. And, indeed, the treaty so outraged the non-Bolshevik Left as to push them, despite their differences, into a common camp.[31]

The merging of genuine and fantasized opponents perfectly suited Lenin's style of polarization politics. It also satisfied his inclination to use targeted violence as a political tool. Cheka agents and Red Army men were authorized to "shoot on the spot." Given the undisciplined, ragtag character of the newly christened, still largely notional Red Army, the decrees gave carte blanche to indiscriminate violence.[32] The question of whether to launch a militant crusade had mutated suddenly from a theoretical debate over a possible *levée en masse* (the so-called revolutionary war) to the practical urgency of self-defense. But workers and soldiers refused to be mobilized even in defense of the revolution. Indeed, workers now voted in their soviets in support of the peace. The Left Communist position—*révolution à outrance*—seemed less plausible than ever. Indeed, the German advance had been enabled by the party's reluctance to accept Lenin's initial case for a quick peace.

Once the treaty was signed, the process of ratification began. Again, Lenin had to struggle to get his way. At the Seventh Bolshevik Party Congress in Petrograd, March 6–8, 1918, Lenin blamed the Left SR opposition and Trotsky's stalling maneuver for the delay that resulted in the final escalation of terms.[33] After a long debate, a substantial majority voted to ratify the peace. "In view of the fact that we have no army, that our troops at the front are in a most demoralized condition, and that we must make use of every possible breathing-space to retard imperialistic attacks on the Soviet Socialist Republic, the Congress resolves to accept the most onerous and humiliating peace treaty which the Soviet Government signed with Germany."[34] Trotsky was among the four who abstained from the vote.[35]

The minority clung nevertheless to the Left Communist view that the peace would serve only to demoralize the Russian proletariat and hamper the spread of international revolution. "Under the circumstances," they insisted, "the only proper course to pursue is to wage revolutionary war on imperialism." The radicals argued that partisan warfare, involving workers and peasants, would develop into civil war between the masses and the capitalist classes, which is to say, it would continue the process of deepening the revolution. A "proletarian army" would retard the dissolution of the revolutionary working class, by uniting the workers "as soldiers of the proletarian revolution....In the very course of fighting a strong Socialist army will be developed."[36] Building such an army became Trotsky's mandate as commissar of war. In that sense, the unrealistic expectations of the minority with respect to the external threat anticipated the domestic conflict just then emerging.

The Bolsheviks ended their congress on March 8, 1918, having ratified the treaty and adopted a new name: the Russian Communist Party. They soon had a new capital, as well. On March 12, a week after the signing of the peace, with ratification still in progress, the entire government apparatus— printing office, gold reserves, families, furniture, members of the Sovnarkom, the Soviet Executive Committee, the Bolshevik and Left SR Central Committees, the Cheka (hurriedly executing some political prisoners as they departed, over Shteinberg's objections)—clambered onto trains heading for Moscow. The trains were guarded by the Latvian Riflemen, the only unit with residual discipline and revolutionary spunk.[37] While Lenin settled into the Kremlin, the new symbol of Soviet power, Trotsky remained in Petrograd to organize the Red Army.[38]

Moscow had been the capital of old Russia, before Peter the Great opened his "window onto Europe" in 1703. Soviet Russia had not yet turned in upon itself, but it was covering its flanks. Lenin had entered Petrograd in April 1917 with extravagant fanfare; he now scurried away. Though conceived as a security measure in a moment of alarm, the move nevertheless also represented a symbolic break with the autocracy. The move to Moscow allowed the regime to identify with the deep past, while also shifting the seat of power. If it sheltered the commissars from the German threat, the change did not protect them from the menace of social collapse. Moscow in 1918 was a city of violent contrasts—a luxurious and feverish night life, on the one side; deserted buildings, crime, and desperation, on the other.[39] As in Petrograd, even party officials were attacked on the streets, not because of their politics but for the sake of their fur coats. Daring to walk on foot, a number of important figures were left to make their way coatless in the winter cold, considering themselves lucky to be alive.[40]

Unsure of a majority for ratification of Brest-Litovsk at the Fourth All-Russian Congress of Soviets, scheduled for March 12, Trotsky still hoped to persuade the Allies, through informal contacts in Petrograd, that Russia might be forced to confront the Central Powers after all and therefore needed assistance.[41] President Wilson addressed a message to the Soviet Congress expressing "sincere sympathy...for the Russian people at this moment when the German power has been thrust in to interrupt and turn back the whole struggle for freedom and substitute the wishes of Germany for the purposes of the people of Russia." Alas, the United States was in no position to offer material aid.[42]

The opening of the Fourth Congress was postponed from March 12 to 14, but the Allies still did not respond. By March 15, 1,200 delegates had assembled.[43] Lenin arrived at 11 p.m. and spoke for over an hour: "We have no army....We need peace to gain a breathing-space to give the masses a chance to create new forms of life." Echoing the opposition catchwords, he said the era of imperialist wars had ended. They were now "entering a new period of revolutionary wars on an international scale. We must prepare for the struggle."[44] Speaking for the Left SRs, Boris Kamkov charged that the peace made Russia "a tool of German-Austrian imperialism."[45] Martov, the veteran Menshevik, "congratulated" Lenin: "From now on he is under the protection not only of the Red Guard but also of Kaiser Wilhelm."[46] The treaty was nevertheless ratified by a large majority, though 150 delegates refused to vote. The Left SRs repudiated the treaty as "a betrayal...of the Socialist Revolution."[47] They resigned from the Sovnarkom. *Pravda* accused them of organizing "an insurrection of the leaders of the intelligentsia against the masses."[48]

It took the shock of the separate peace, coming on the heels of the January 6 coup de main, to bring the opposition together. The challenge was to oppose the Bolsheviks "from the left"—or even the center—without abandoning one's principles. It was therefore in mid-March, after Lenin and Trotsky had made their own pact with the devil, that a number of moderate SRs, Popular Socialists, Left SRs, and Kadets, abandoning party constraints, convened in Moscow to coordinate action and set an agenda.[49] In April they dubbed themselves the Union for the Regeneration of Russia (*Soiuz vozrozhdeniia Rossii*), which defined its task as "the resurrection of Russian state authority, the reunion with Russia of the regions forcefully cut off from her, and the defense of these regions from foreign enemies. The task of reunifying and defending Russia should be accomplished, in the Union's opinion, in close agreement with Russia's Allies, while they together carry on the struggle against Germany and the powers allied with her, who have seized parts of Russia's territory. The Union will strive to achieve the task of resurrecting the now corrupted Russian state in accordance with the will of the people, expressed by means of universal and equal elections.... [W]hen the territory of Russia is liberated from its enemies, it will convoke a Constituent Assembly, which will establish the forms of Russia's government."[50]

Indeed, the Treaty of Brest-Litovsk marked a turning point in the high politics of the revolution, which strengthened the Bolsheviks' hand. The Left SRs, which is to say, the radical wing of the SR Party, closest in temperament to the Bolsheviks and willing to join in repudiating the soviet model of broad socialist power, were doubly complicit in their rivals' success. By entering the government (the Sovnarkom and Cheka), they lent it credibility, enabling Lenin to annex SR slogans and constituency. Now, by rebelling against him, they helped consolidate the Bolshevik ranks. Following the contentious ratification, the ensuing Left SR violence against the regime justified the escalation of the Red Terror and motivated the dissident Left Communists to circle the wagons and toe the party line. The convergence of external threat and domestic turmoil created compelling grounds for the application of extreme measures, as they were euphemistically but transparently called.

Lenin had argued that Brest-Litovsk would provide a "breathing space" for the consolidation of power, but even after March 3 the Germans kept coming. Complying with the terms of the treaty, between mid-March and early April the Baltic Fleet withdrew from Finnish territory. Two hundred ships were transferred, assisted by icebreakers, across the frozen Gulf of Finland, under Finnish shelling, to the Kronstadt fortress, but the Germans remained in control of Helsingfors (Helsinki) and the Gulf, the gateway to Petrograd.[51] Despite pressure from the Kronstadt soviet and the Petrograd comrades, the Moscow party leadership also refused to respond when the Germans demanded the surrender of Fort Ino, on the Karelian Isthmus, north of Petrograd. By mid-May, Petrograd was abuzz with rumors of an impending German attack; the Bolsheviks were accused of promoting German interests. Captain Aleksei Shchastnyi, the officer who had organized the heroic rescue of the Baltic Fleet, protested the surrender of Fort Ino. On the evening of June 21–22, 1918, Krylenko, now heading the Soviet Executive Committee Revolutionary Tribunal, had Shchastnyi arrested, tried, and shot.[52]

On June 20, 1918, the day before the captain's execution, V. Volodarskii, an uncompromising Left Communist hostile to the Brest-Litovsk treaty who had nevertheless fallen into line, was assassinated by an even more uncompromising SR.[53] Shchastnyi's execution as an enemy of the revolution had angered Baltic Fleet sailors who opposed the policy of continuing concessions. Their protests were joined by workers at two major Petrograd factories—the Obukhov and Putilov works. Demobilization of the army and lessening demand, together with the fuel shortage, had reduced the level of production at both plants, leading to a rise in unemployment. The dwindling food supply intensified discontent. These were radical workers, ardent in support of the revolution. Angry rallies, in which workers mingled with sailors from nearby ships, invoked the authority of the Constituent Assembly and challenged the Bolshevik monopoly on power.[54] The Petrograd Cheka used Volodarskii's assassination as an excuse to arrest protesting workers. The workers were torn, however, by competing emotions. They cherished Volodarskii as an opponent of Brest-Litovsk, bucking the party line, but he was nevertheless a Bolshevik official targeted by an anti-Bolshevik SR. Shchastnyi, by contrast, had been executed by those same Bolsheviks for sharing Volodarskii's reservations about Brest-Litovsk. Volodarskii's funeral on June 22, which was staged as a massive endorsement of Soviet (that is, Bolshevik) power, resolved the tensions. Remaining doubters among the Baltic sailors were arrested. The troubled factory district was put under martial law; various SRs were also rounded up.[55]

As they had throughout 1917, the Bolsheviks continued to operate in more than one register. On one level, they engaged in what remained of participatory politics—this time campaigning in June 1918 for the upcoming elections to the Petrograd Soviet, while of course doing their best to stifle political rivals. Bolshevik activists in the factories made sure their candidates came out ahead. On another level, Bolshevik officials used the power of office to close opposition newspapers and suppress the activities of independent worker groups. The Left SRs rejected the elections as corrupt but were constrained by their basic support for the Soviet regime. There was less and less room for maneuver, however. Remaining Menshevik and independent SR organizers were denounced as enemies of the people and arrested.[56] The protests centered in the big Petrograd factories ended by cementing support for the Bolshevik state position. Party loyalty overshadowed hostility to the Brest-Litovsk compromise; the threat of counterrevolutionary terror (Volodarskii's assassination) narrowed the political options.

Unrest among the party's popular base, the iconic proletariat, was a worrisome sign, but the angry workers were driven as much by the misery of everyday life as by ideological fervor. The coming of spring was a mixed blessing in Petrograd. Snow still covered the remains of dead animals, and refuse littered the streets; the number of recorded typhus cases had escalated in early March; unemployment exploded (by April almost half the city's labor force was out of work); German occupation of the Ukrainian breadbasket and interference with the railways intensified the existing food shortage; the prisons were filled to bursting, but crime was on the rise. Gangs of criminals disguised as Cheka agents committed theft and murder, untrained Red Army recruits and Red Guards indulged in free-for-alls. Firearms were everywhere, and young men were out of control. This was a level of social disintegration that even the Cheka was unable to contain.[57] The militant workers did not question the revolution; they framed their arguments in terms of loyalty to a cause everyone shared. The Bolsheviks seemed to have abandoned world revolution; the SRs seemed to threaten its survival with their continuing provocations. The feeling that life and death hung in the balance was only heightened in July, when Petrograd experienced a surge of cholera cases and cholera deaths.[58] A consequence of the crisis in living conditions, the outbreak of disease added an apocalyptic element to the political tension.

The major political consequence of Brest-Litovsk was to take the SRs out of the running. From January to April 1918, SR activists had circulated in the countryside, promoting soviet authority on the local level and initiating the process of land reform. The SR Party had published a newspaper oriented toward the peasants. Its activities, while potentially challenging the Bolshevik monopoly on power, in the short run broadened the new regime's base of support.[59] The peace treaty had undermined this collaboration. The Left SRs had resigned from the Sovnarkom at the Fourth Congress of Soviets, although they remained in the Cheka and continued to participate in local soviets. They became increasingly critical of the brutal methods used to undermine the structures of traditional peasant life (more on this below). Hoping to jump-start hostilities on their own initiative, they began sending activists to the Ukraine to harass the occupying German forces.[60]

The anxieties aroused by the faltering negotiations prompted Lenin to expand the internal war on the enemies of the revolution, enlarging the core lexicon of imperial wartime propaganda. The Cheka declared there was "no alternative to annihilating mercilessly on the scene of their crime all counter-revolutionaries, spies, speculators, thugs, hooligans, saboteurs and other parasites."[61] These moves were designed not only to oppose or preempt actual threats, but also to harness the retributive violence enacted spontaneously on behalf of the regime. In January and February 1918, radicalized sailors in the Baltic and Black Sea fleets had murdered their officers by the hundreds.[62] It was easy enough to spot an officer (though divining his politics was harder), but the distinction between friend and foe was not always clear. The Soviet declared the entire Baltic aristocracy, including women and children, "outside the law" and subject to deportation, a move reminiscent of the Imperial Army's campaign against the Jews in the western provinces early in the war.[63]

The Left SRs saw themselves not as "enemies of the people" but as champions of peasant needs and as a restraining influence on Bolshevik violence; hence Justice Commissar Shteinberg's objections to high-handed Cheka methods and Left SR resistance to Bolshevik methods in implementing land reform. Yet the SRs' continuing opposition to ending the war put them at odds with the peasantry's fundamental interests. The breaking point for the Left SRs was not, however, the persecution of their comrades or the targeting of populations innocent of any specific crime but the conclusion of the separate peace, which they interpreted as an abandonment of the cause of world revolution. Ratification of the treaty had not, moreover, removed the threat of war. In Finland and Ukraine, the Germans were throwing their weight behind enemies of the revolution. In March and April, Allied forces had appeared in the north and Far East. In May and June, armed conflicts had broken out in Siberia, where anti-Bolshevik centers had been established, as we shall see.[64]

It was in this atmosphere of menace coming from all sides that on the evening of July 4, 1918, over a thousand delegates assembled in Moscow's Bolshoi Theater, for the opening of the Fifth All-Russian Congress of Soviets. The Bolsheviks had maneuvered to assure themselves a two-thirds majority at the Congress, partly by expelling the remaining Mensheviks and SRs from the Soviet Executive Committee and from local soviets. Most of the other delegates were SRs.[65] On stage sat the members of the Central Executive Committee, described by British agent Bruce Lockhart as "a motley gathering of about one hundred and fifty intellectuals with a strong predominance of Jews."[66] Presiding were Trotsky, Krylenko, Dzerzhinskii, and the Latvian Chekist Iakov Peters (Jēkabs Peterss)—indeed, an ethnic array. "Admission is by ticket only," Lockhart noted, "and every entrance, every corridor, is guarded by groups of Lettish [Latvian] soldiers, armed to the teeth with rifle, pistol, and hand-grenade."[67] In the boxes and galleries, assembled for the opening evening session, sat the various unofficial representatives of the Allied powers still in the capital, and above them the ambassadors of the Quadruple Alliance, including the German ambassador, Count Wilhelm von Mirbach, as though poised for an amusing dramatic performance. They got more than they had bargained for. Voices from the floor shouted, "Down with Mirbach!" "Down with Brest!" Turning toward the ambassador, the Left SRs shouted, "Away with the German butchers! Away with the hangman's noose from Brest-Litovsk!"[68]

During the heated debate that followed, Trotsky denounced as a provocation and treason to the revolution any attacks on the German occupiers in Ukraine, while Kamkov for the Left SRs denounced the treaty as a "ruse," serving only the interests of German capital, and praised the resistance to the German occupiers as a sign of "healthy revolutionary psychology."[69] When Lenin finally appeared, on the evening of July 5, he calmed the tumult, but could not quiet the passions. Kamkov declared: "The dictatorship of the proletariat has developed into a dictatorship of Mirbach.... [W]e are become, not an independent Power, but the lackeys of the German Imperialists, who have the audacity to show their faces even in this theatre."[70] In the end, the Bolsheviks pushed through a decree authorizing summary executions for anyone protesting the German presence on Russian soil.[71]

Excluded from the central organs of power, the Left SRs now resorted to more direct methods. On July 6, both the Soviet Executive Committee and the foreign ambassadors were absent from the theater. In midafternoon, while the session was in progress, two Left SR officials of the Cheka, Iakov Bliumkin and Nikolai Andreev, appeared at the German legation, presented false papers allegedly signed by Dzerzhinskii, and asked to see the ambassador. Once inside his office, they pulled revolvers, shot him point-blank, tossed a bomb, and escaped in a waiting car, which took them to Cheka headquarters, where the SR Central Committee was then meeting. At 5 p.m. Dzerzhinskii showed up to arrest the two culprits, but was himself outnumbered and arrested. The well-known SR Mariia Spiridonova, one of the few women elected to the Constituent Assembly, announced the news to the assembled Congress. The SR Central Committee sent telegrams explaining their deed, which criticized the treaty and denounced the Germans but stopped short of demanding the overthrow of the Sovnarkom.[72]

At Cheka headquarters, Dzerzhinskii was soon freed by the loyal Latvian Rifles. The Left SR delegates to the Congress, unaware of what their colleagues had been up to, were nevertheless all arrested, along with hundreds of SR party members, some of whom were shot.[73] The plot concocted by a handful of Left SR leaders in Moscow thus led to the decimation of the party and its definitive exclusion from political life.[74] Instead of antagonizing the Germans, as the perpetrators had intended, the assassination only strengthened the German resolve to keep the Bolsheviks in place. Interested above all in stability, they withdrew whatever support they had earlier provided to the regime's opponents in the guise of hedging their bets.[75]

---

The SRs indeed seemed to pose a serious threat to the Bolshevik hold on power. On the day of Mirbach's murder, July 6, an armed uprising began in the Volga city of Iaroslavl, 150 miles northeast of Moscow. It was initiated by an organization called the Union for the Defense of the Homeland and Freedom (*Soiuz zashchity rodiny i svobody*), which had been organized by the noted SR terrorist Boris Savinkov, the erstwhile confederate of General Kornilov, in the wake of October. Its goal was to organize opposition to Bolshevik rule in the Russian heartland. The Union obtained funds from General Alekseev and attracted the support of various Mensheviks, SRs, and even some monarchists willing to subscribe to a program of loyalty to the Allies, the unification of Russia, and deference to the authority of the Constituent Assembly. By May 1918, the Union included 5,500 officers. In June the Cheka arrested many of its members, but many escaped and headed for Iaroslavl.[76]

The civic organizations of Iaroslavl had openly opposed the October coup. When Savinkov's Union launched its assault on the local Soviet institutions, it enjoyed wide support among the city's educated classes and even among the broader population. The two thousand participants included a few hundred workers, but most workers continued to view the anti-Bolshevik officers with suspicion, and the local Mensheviks stood aside.[77] The goals of the uprising were those of the February Revolution—not a reversion to the old regime, but a defense of the liberal ideal of a democratic order, with an admixture of populist social reform. The leaders called for the establishment of an elected government, guaranteeing "political and civic freedom and in a strictly legal fashion insuring property in land to the laboring peasants." This government would introduce "a strictly legal order and all violations of person and private property...will be harshly punished."[78]

Iaroslavl was not only an important rail junction but also a center of Red Army concentration. The rebels began by arresting the Communists, imprisoning some eighty of them on a barge, allegedly for their own protection; a number were simply murdered—in violation of orders to try them first.

Red Army troops, reinforced from Moscow, were meanwhile poised on the
nearby heights, from which they began systematic shelling of the city. The
fighting lasted for two weeks. Heavy artillery destroyed entire neighborhoods, churches, and monuments; buildings were burned to the ground.
The Red commander requested and received chemical weapons and
flame-throwers in order "to liquidate the whole business," if need be, but
the weather seems to have prevented their use.[79]

By July 21, the struggle was over. The anti-Bolshevik officers had from
the beginning declared themselves to be at war with Germany, refusing to
acknowledge Brest-Litovsk. German prisoners of war had been confined to
a theater in the center of town throughout the fighting. Rather than capitulate to the Red Army, whose legitimacy they did not accept, the Russian
officers insisted on surrendering to the German officer in charge, who
accepted their gesture, but when threatened by the Red commander handed
them over to the Cheka, with predictable consequences.[80] On the evening
of July 22, upon orders from Moscow, 350 captured insurgents were executed, others later in the year.[81] Savinkov later reflected that the revolt
"cannot be called successful, but it was not useless." It had proved that "not
all Russians were ready to submit to Bolshevik terror. Honor was saved.
Glory to those who fell in battle."[82]

---

The SR turn to terror and armed opposition allowed the Bolsheviks to shed
the fig leaf of coalition. The platform for discussion and potential disagreement had narrowed. According to the new constitution, enacted by the
Fifth All-Russian Congress of Soviets on July 10, 1918, supreme power was
lodged in the All-Russian Congress of Soviets, but over a year then elapsed
before the Sixth Soviet Congress convened in November 1919. The Soviet
Executive Committee, purged of competing parties, met more frequently,
but the exclusively Bolshevik Sovnarkom, in constant session, emerged with
full authority in its hands.[83]

But only eight months after overthrowing the Provisional Government,
whose own authority was anything but secure, the authority vested in the
Sovnarkom was yet to be established. The Red Terror, conceived on the
model of the French Revolution, as a war against the domestic enemies of
the revolution, was the Bolsheviks' method of enforcing their claim to rule.
The revolution had actual enemies, to be sure—monarchist generals, agents

of hostile foreign powers, stubborn defenders of the revolution's original constitutional goals, leaders of breakaway nationalist movements, terrorist-assassins of party leaders and state officials. In that sense, the threat was real and the Red Terror a reaction to imminent danger—and to brutality on the other side. Lenin's Bolsheviks, however, interpreted opposition broadly. They viewed any disagreement or competition for the loyalty of the people as acts of treason, pushing former comrades or troublesome collaborators into the enemy camp.

Overall, the Red Terror was as much a preemptive strike as a reaction. Responding to overt aggression or explicit challenges, the Terror also targeted entire categories of the population that, by virtue of their place in the old order, were unlikely to welcome the new regime. Some of these labels, though clumsy guides to political sympathies, could be identified in formal terms (the aristocracy, the clergy), others were fluid or ambiguous (the "kulaks," the "bourgeoisie"). The Red Terror, in short, was not a purely defensive maneuver but a fundamental aspect of Bolshevik power—state-administered violence as a substitute for the political process and an alternative to the rule of law. Explicitly anti-legal, it incorporated the types of violence stigmatized by the international conventions, to which imperial Russian experts had made a significant contribution, as violations of universally accepted principles—the taking of hostages, summary executions, cruel and unusual treatment of prisoners, and implicitly, the targeting of civilian populations. Before the revolution, however, capital punishment had been associated with the repressive nature of the tsarist regime. Liberals as well as socialists campaigned against it. Some of that aversion even carried over into the new regime, which preferred to employ the euphemism "the supreme penalty" (*vysshaia mera nakazaniia*) to describe it. Most of the executions, whether summary or following a hearing before a revolutionary tribunal, were carried out by firing squad. Lenin, however, was not squeamish. He insisted that enemies of the revolution fully deserved the death penalty. Martov protested, but Lenin rejoined: "There has not been a single revolution, or era of civil war, without executions."[84]

The Red Terror was in principle—and fundamentally—arbitrary. Its categories were boilerplate and their application unpredictable. Its individual victims had not necessarily done anything wrong and did not always fit their generic descriptions. The Terror was not merely the most vivid expression of a new style of rule, however; it was also a response to panic. Brest-Litovsk did not, in fact, eliminate the German threat. German forces were ensconced in the Baltic states and on Ukrainian territory. Nor did the treaty eliminate pressure from Russia's former allies. Dispatched to Russia while negotiations were still in play, their agents remained behind to make mischief. Once it became clear the Bolsheviks were not about to re-engage the Central Powers, distracting their attention from the Western Front, the British, in particular, looked for partners among the regime's committed opponents.

The story of the Red Terror here intertwines with the story of foreign intervention, the mobilization of anti-Bolshevik revolts, and the full flowering of the Civil War. A small contingent of British marines had landed in the northern port of Murmansk in early March, tasked with protecting Allied military stores. Additional troops were sent to Russia in June, but played no role in the unfolding conflict between the nascent Red Army and the various forces arrayed against it. The Cheka was not imagining things, however. British intelligence services were indeed at work in Petrograd, recruiting disaffected Russian officers, providing funds to anti-Bolshevik groups, actively trying to unseat the regime that seemed to be favoring German interests.[85] Until the end of May, the Bolsheviks had nevertheless continued to flirt with the possibility of attracting Allied support against the German threat. Meanwhile, London debated whether to intervene on behalf of the Bolsheviks, against them, or not at all.[86] On August 2, additional British troops landed in Arkhangelsk. The German Navy still hovered in the Gulf of Finland. The Baltic Fleet was alerted, the Petrograd Cheka began rounding up officers and anyone suspected of Allied sympathies. Proponents of all-out Terror now gained the upper hand even in the Petrograd branch of the party, which had until then shown a certain restraint. Trotsky and Iakov Sverdlov, president of the Central Executive Committee, visiting from Moscow, urged the Second Northern Regional Congress of Soviets, meeting in Smolny on August 1–2, to endorse "mass terror" against "the counterrevolutionary bourgeoisie."[87] On August 19, the Petrograd Cheka adopted the policy of summary executions that was already the hallmark of the central Cheka under Dzerzhinskii's direction.[88]

The Terror unleashed a vicious cycle of violence that only amplified the dangers it was supposed to deflect. Agitated speech-making and inflamed headlines had generated a radicalized mood. Local soviets called for the "annihilation of all leaders of the counterrevolution to a man."[89] In this spirit, on August 21 Moisei Uritskii, the heretofore relatively moderate head of the Petrograd Cheka, ordered the execution of a group of twenty-one

detainees. Among them were common criminals, Petrograd Cheka operatives of supposedly dubious character, and political prisoners. The latter
included a young man whose execution inspired a friend to take revenge.
On August 30, Leonid Kannegiser, a twenty-two-year-old former cadet
from the Mikhailovskii Artillery Academy, assassinated Uritskii in the office
of the Commissariat of Internal Affairs (NKVD), shooting him in the head
with a Colt pistol. The young man fled, first on bicycle, then on foot, but
was soon arrested. In October he was executed.[90]

Uritskii's biography was almost identical to that of Volodarskii, assassinated two months earlier, though he was a generation older and somewhat
less precocious. Born to a Jewish family in 1873 in a town near Kiev, Uritskii
joined the Social Democratic Party at its inception in 1898, sided with the
Mensheviks after 1903, was arrested and exiled after 1905, spent the war in
New York City (together with Trotsky), returned after February 1917, joined
the Bolsheviks before October, and, as a member of the Petrograd Military
Revolutionary Committee, helped engineer the coup. In 1918, like Volodarskii,
he sided with the Left Communists on the issue of Brest-Litovsk, but his
loyalty to the regime was undimmed.[91] As head of the Petrograd Cheka, he
tried to steer a moderate course, but he remained at the helm when the
mood shifted.

Uritskii's assassin also came from a Jewish family, but his grandfather had
been ennobled and his father was a prominent engineer. Himself trained as
an engineer, Kannegiser found his vocation as a poet, but after February
1917 he entered the military academy. While Uritskii was organizing the
overthrow of the Provisional Government in October, Kannegiser, along
with other cadets, was defending the Winter Palace, but he made his peace
with the outcome. Close to the SRs, he turned against the Bolsheviks only
after Brest-Litovsk.[92] Kannegiser's interrogators insisted he must have acted
from a commitment to either Zionist or SR ideology, but it appears that his
motives were entirely personal.[93] His SR sympathies had not involved him
in party work, let alone a counterrevolutionary conspiracy. The incident
recalled the famous 1878 case of Vera Zasulich, who had avenged an abused
comrade by shooting a tsarist official. Astonishingly, she had been exoner-
ated at her trial and managed to flee. This time there was no trial and no
escape. The sixty-nine-year-old Zasulich was herself now living in Petrograd,
where she expressed her disapproval of the Bolshevik regime. "At the present moment," she declared, "socialism has no more ferocious enemies than
the gentlemen from Smolny."[94]

The day of Uritskii's murder, August 30, Lenin was in Moscow, visiting the factories. At the conclusion of one of his speeches, he was approached by a young woman who pulled a gun and tried to kill him. Unlike Uritskii, Lenin survived the attempt on his life, though he was seriously wounded. The earlier attempt, on January 1, had done no harm. Now the party trembled for a few days, until the leader emerged from danger. The would-be assassin was Fanny Kaplan, the same age as Volodarskii and from the same background. Born in 1890 in the Pale of Settlement to a traditional Jewish family, in 1906, at the age of sixteen, as the 1905 Revolution was in its dying days, she fell under the influence of anarchist firebrands, whom she assisted in preparing explosives destined for the assassination of Kiev Governor-General, Vladimir Sukhomlinov. The material exploded prematurely, damaging her vision, alerting the police, and leading to her arrest. This was the same General Sukhomlinov who was forced to step down as minister of war in 1915 and arrested in 1916, charged with responsibility for the army's disastrous lack of munitions and supplies. He was tried on the same charge again in September 1917 by representatives of the Provisional Government. Amnestied and released from prison after October on grounds of advanced age, he spent his last years in German emigration.

Kaplan, for her part, spent the war years in prison, where she encountered the charismatic Mariia Spiridonova, who recruited her to the SR Party. Freed after the February Revolution, Kaplan objected to the dissolution of the Constituent Assembly. When interrogated, she explained, "I fired at Lenin because I consider him a traitor to the revolution and his continuing existence has undermined the faith in socialism. What his undermining of faith in socialism consists of I will not say."[95] She denied any connection with a plot or political party. She was executed four days later, on September 3, 1918.

The two terrorist acts of August 30, 1918 are often blamed for the onset of the Red Terror, but the key elements were already in place when the "Red Revolutionary Terror!" was officially announced on September 5, 1918.[96] The authorities needed no proof—and had none—that either of these overheated young persons was tied to an SR conspiracy or connected to British or French agents, but the Cheka cast its nets wide, trawling for suspects and ordering the execution of hostages already in custody. On the nights of August 30–31 and August 31–September 1, while Lenin lay in critical condition, as many as five hundred hostages were executed in Petrograd alone. The Kronstadt Cheka shot half the one thousand hostages in its custody.

The newspaper headlines were virulent—"Blood for Blood!" They kept up a steady refrain linking the internal enemy to the armed foreign powers poised at the borders and boring from within.[97]

From the beginning, the Cheka operated as a bureaucratic institution, its directors holding regular meetings, keeping minutes and records of arrests (in three copies). Agents were expected to wear leather jackets and carry flashlights.[98] Its archives classified cases according to social origin, nature of the crime (White Guard organizations, armed action, anti-Soviet agitation), and punishment (execution, concentration camp, fine, confiscation of property, exile—from Moscow, from Russia).[99] The Cheka published lists of people shot, selected from all walks of life, sometimes at random—ministers, army officers, lawyers, students, priests, civil servants—all described as "bourgeois."[100] The lists were a warning. Though Lenin had not been killed, the Cheka cautioned, "The criminal attempt on the life of our ideological leader, comrade Lenin, prompts us to abandon sentimentality."[101] Red Terror was defined as "an inoculation" against future and continuing threats.[102] "For each of our Communists we will obliterate hundreds, for each attack on our leaders thousands and tens of thousands of these parasites."[103]

There was also a comic-opera dimension to the assassination scare, which involved actual British agents still in Petrograd, who were in fact trying to organize an anti-Bolshevik conspiracy, with the help of a couple of agents provocateurs. A Cheka raid on the British Embassy in Petrograd resulted in the death of one of the agents and many arrests; British and French consular staff were arrested in Moscow as well. All were exchanged for Maksim Litvinov, the Soviet representative in Britain, who had been interned in retaliation. A storm in an ideological teacup. The British plots were real, if nugatory; the charges that foreign powers were behind the attacks on Volodarskii, Uritskii, and Lenin were invented.[104]

The mix of truth and fabrication provided cover for an orgy of reprisals perpetrated by the Petrograd Cheka, which arrested hundreds of citizens of the newly independent Baltic states (still occupied by the Germans, who protested on their behalf!), and many artists, performers, and skilled professionals, as exemplars of "the counterrevolutionary bourgeoisie."[105] The Petrograd Cheka persisted in taking and shooting hostages, reporting over six thousand arrests since early in the year and up to eight hundred executions. Local Cheka branches had begun imitating their example. Conditions in the prisons were appalling enough to shock comrades visiting from Moscow.[106]

The rhetoric was vulgar and belligerent; the application was ruthless and blunt. Hostage-taking was used liberally. The Grand Prince of anarchism, Petr Kropotkin, now seventy-six years old, complained that the policy was a reversion to "the Middle Ages and the era of religious wars."[107] SRs, anarchists, and Kadets already in prison were shot.[108] "If the bourgeois reptile raises its head, the heads of hostages will fall."[109] The bloodthirsty language was disseminated "in meetings, in newspapers, on posters, in resolutions."[110] The Terror was more than a reaction to any specific act. It was a way of thinking, a method of rule designed to paralyze resistance and opposition. Whether in relation to the wives and children of officers who fought for the Whites or the families of peasant "bandits," the logic was the same.[111]

---

The emergence of the Red Terror must, of course, be understood not only in the context of internecine political wrangling but also against the background of armed threats to the existence of the new regime. These came not only from foreign powers but from remnants of the Russian imperial military command and from the embryonic nations taking advantage of the imperial collapse and the post-October crisis to escape the old borders altogether. Yet the organizational basis for the Terror was established before these threats had actualized, in expectation that the revolution would necessarily provoke a response.

Lenin justified Brest-Litovsk as a breathing space, but it magnified domestic opposition. By the time the Germans were defeated on the Western Front, the Russian Civil War was in full swing. It is interesting to imagine what might have happened had Lenin not insisted on signing the treaty at Brest-Litovsk, had the Bolsheviks instead accepted the idea of a popular mobilization, the *levée en masse* or revolutionary war promoted from the socialist left, thus inviting the Germans to keep coming, the way Alexander I had allowed Napoleon to keep coming in 1812. The German Army might well have been unable, so late in the war, to maintain control of extended Russian territory; the Bolsheviks would not have been able to dispense so easily with the original, populist soviet model. Instead of provoking the virulent opposition of the Left SRs and using the occasion to smash them, the Bolsheviks could have retained them as collaborators. They would have needed to forfeit the slogan of peace, but they could have blamed its failure on the Allies' unwillingness to accept the offer extended by the Decree on

Peace. Lenin was truly alone in pushing for surrender; even his own party didn't want it. Given his political profile, it is possible to understand his drastic maneuver as intended for the sole purpose of pitting the Bolsheviks against everyone else, a kind of all-or-nothing wager on the authoritarian, single-power outcome. It is surprising nevertheless that Lenin got his way in the face of so much opposition. It thus seems more unexpected than inevitable that his model of the bully-party and the bully-state should have prevailed.

# 3

# Finland's Civil War

Not surprisingly, events in the imperial capitals were immediately reflected in the near periphery. The northwest borderlands were Russia's interface with Europe. Having felt the brunt of fighting on the Eastern Front during the war, they profited from the collapse of central authority and the presence of enemy troops to break away.[1] By the end of 1918, five new countries had declared their independence here: Finland, Estonia, Lithuania, Latvia, and Poland.

The area that later constituted Finland had been acquired in 1809 as a result of war with Sweden. Consolidated in 1812 as the Grand Duchy of Finland, it retained its governing institutions (a Senate and a Diet), an army, courts and laws, currency, and tariffs.[2] In the 1890s, a shift in policy toward the region resulted in these privileges being gradually curtailed. The army was dissolved, Russian was introduced as the official administrative language, and the governor-general acquired absolute power.[3] As the Empire began to behave more like a nation-state than an empire, attempting to suppress regional and cultural differences in favor of centralized control and uniform administration (on paper, at least), it stimulated a powerful sense of national pride among local leaders and their constituencies. In the case of Finland, the loss of the Duchy's original rights deepened the sense of shared identity between Swedish and Finnish speakers.

Regional nationalism was, of course, no simpler than the nationalism of a Russia that was only partly Russian. A remnant of the days of Swedish rule, the Finnish elite was largely Swedish-speaking. Finnish society was also divided along class lines, the division becoming ever sharper as Finland began to industrialize and its population expanded from 1.7 million in 1870 to 3.2 million in 1917. The country remained primarily agricultural, but as cities grew, so did the working class. The workers here too became targets of revolutionary agitation. Finland developed a strong German Social

Democratic or Menshevik-style trade-union-oriented labor movement. By 1905, the Finns therefore displayed the full panoply of grievances affecting other regions: local resentment against the imperial center, desire for a greater role in political life, and the basis for class conflict.[4]

The 1905 Revolution itself demonstrated the ease with which endemic social tensions could escalate into civil war. Forced to make constitutional concessions after 1905, the tsar restored Finland's traditional rights, pleasing the moderate, establishment parties. On the left, however, Finnish socialists were faced with the militancy of their own popular base. The same Baltic sailors who were to fuel Bolshevik radicalism in 1917 attempted mutiny in 1906, without the backing of party leaders. Indeed, in Finland the 1905 Revolution turned in against itself, as newly formed Red Guards battled middle-class Home Guards. Even the Social Democrats participated in elections to the Finnish parliament, but in 1908, Russifying policies went back into effect, and the parliament lost the rights it had recently regained. The Finnish political classes became increasingly anti-Russian, while the workers became increasingly radical in their resentment of class privilege.[5]

The outbreak of war in 1914 presented the leaders of Finnish society with a dilemma. Grand Duke Nikolai Nikolaevich's proclamation to the Poles in August 1914 led them to await a similar promise of postwar autonomy, but none was forthcoming. Instead, the Finnish parliament was suspended, delegates were imprisoned or exiled. As the Empire weakened, some Finns therefore made overtures to the Germans, who could be expected to hasten that progress by endorsing Finnish independence. The idea of German backing attracted support not only among the Swedish-speaking elite but also among socialist leaders, who expected the German Social Democrats to embrace their cause. Germany made no firm promises, but did allow Finnish volunteers to form a Jäger Battalion in the Prussian army. The Battalion's role was unclear and was still under discussion when the monarchy collapsed and the situation changed completely.[6]

Though Finland was technically at war, along with the rest of Russia, the Finns were not subject to conscription.[7] Though shielded from the full impact of combat and occupation, Finland instantly felt the shock of revolution. On February 28, 1917, the General Staff ordered troops stationed in Finland to march on Petrograd and crush the revolt. Rear Admiral Adrian Nepenin, commander of the Baltic Fleet, at first declared a state of siege, but once the Duma Committee emerged, he accepted the new authority. By March 3, the sailors of the Baltic Fleet stationed at the Sveaborg Fortress in

THE BALTICS

—·— Border of Russian Empire, 1914
······· Boundaries between provinces of Russian Empire
——— Borders of states that became independent by 1921

(Tallinn) Current names in parentheses

▨ Became part of Lithuania by 1921

Helsinki harbor had mutinied, murdering thirty-eight officers, including Nepenin, who refused to relinquish his post without orders from the new government. He was shot in the back.[8] Dual power with a vengeance.

Soviets emerged in Finland, as everywhere else, and adopted the posture of conditional support for the Provisional Government. In Finland the situation was complicated by the division between the relatively moderate local Social Democrats and the more extreme soviet leaders representing the Russian soldiers and sailors stationed in Helsinki and Vyborg, eighty miles northwest of Petrograd.[9] Not only were the troops foreign, but they were out of control. "The first days of the revolution in Helsingfors," the social psychologist Henning Söderhjelm recalled, "took the shape of a huge riot of the soldiers and the mob. Detachments of naval and land forces dashed about in the motor cars of their commanders, all with rifle or revolver in hand, with the finger on the trigger, firing volleys of shot into the air for joy, or shooting straight before them in order to increase the din and noise caused by the furious speed. They were hunting for the officers who had concealed themselves. The latter were killed wherever they were found, in their houses, in the street, or on staircases. . . . The city was entirely in the power of the Russian soldiers."[10] The forces of order had become forces of disruption.

The national question and the class question converged on the issue of lower-class militancy and aggression. Russian troops were not the only threat to the propertied classes. Everyday life had been a potential battlefield, Söderhjelm observed. "It was felt in the streets and in tram-cars—everywhere where people of different classes came together—that Finland had got a ruler, that the working-men with the assistance of the Russian soldiers had come to feel that their 'class' was the one that ruled the country."[11]

The Provisional Government, for its part, was eager to prevent the kind of social conflict in Finland that would open the door to German penetration. It therefore restored the former duchy to its original rights under the monarchy. It authorized the return of the parliament, entrusted with drawing up a new constitution. Despite their political differences, socialists and constitutionalists agreed to work together. Assuming it had the full sovereign power to do so, the Provisional Government issued a manifesto on March 7, which defined the interim status of Finland within the Russian state. It acted despite the fact that in relationship to Russia as a whole the new ministers claimed only temporary authority pending final resolution by the anticipated Constituent Assembly.[12]

Pleased as they were with this turn of events, Finnish leaders overlooked the manifesto's basic contradiction. By reversing the monarchy's discriminatory policies, the Provisional Government restored Finland to political life, while still asserting the authority of the capital. Acting as the successor to Nicholas as Grand Duke of Finland, it at the same time granted Finland "internal independence."[13] By accepting these terms, the Finns claimed the right to self-rule while also acknowledging their constitutional link to Russia. The principle of national self-determination, invoked instead by some Swedish-speaking deputies, would have resolved this tension. The Provisional Government, for its part, was content with the latent contradiction, as it had no interest in promoting the breakup of the state now in its hands.[14]

Faced with the Provisional Government's adherence to the idea of constitutional succession (what or who was to replace Tsar Nicholas as Grand Duke of Finland), socialist and bourgeois deputies to the Finnish parliament joined to pass a bill, asserting that body's executive competence. Leaving military and diplomatic affairs to Petrograd, Finland would exercise domestic self-rule. The proclamation, endorsed by the Finnish soviets, was issued during the July Days, when the Petrograd government seemed about to topple. Unaware of what exactly was happening in the capital, the Finnish Bolsheviks learned belatedly that the government had not in fact fallen. Following the party line, they retroactively denounced the attempt at insurrection as untimely.[15]

In response to the bill, the Provisional Government, its energy now restored, sent troops into Finland. None of the bill's sponsors wished to provoke an armed confrontation, however, not even the socialists.[16] With the backing of those who hoped new elections would reduce the socialist majority, Kerensky dissolved the parliament, on the grounds that Finland had no right to challenge the current government's authority or to preempt the decisions of the future Empire-wide Constituent Assembly. The destiny of the Finnish nation, he declared, "can only be decided on the basis of agreement with the Russian nation." The Petrograd Soviet endorsed the dissolution of the parliament, accusing the Finns of putting the Revolution itself in jeopardy.[17]

Of more immediate concern than the Constituent Assembly, however, was the threat of armed violence, both on the part of the same rebellious soldiers and sailors who were making the revolution in Petrograd and in the event of German invasion and Russian retreat.[18] The Northern Corps of the Imperial Army, composed of Russian soldiers under the command of General Vladimir Oranovskii, was stationed in Vyborg. In response to Kornilov's move on Petrograd, the Vyborg soldiers and sailors had formed a Military Revolutionary Committee. When General Oranovskii naturally refused to submit to its authority, the committee had him and a number of his officers arrested. Confined to a guardhouse, the captives were soon assailed by a crowd of angry soldiers, who mocked and beat them, then threw them into a canal and gunned them down as they tried to climb out. The Helsinki Soviet justified the murders as an expression of righteous anger. Lenin commented: "The Vyborg soldiers have demonstrated the full power of their hatred for the Kornilovite generals."[19]

The Russian forces still on Finnish soil remained under the authority of the government in Petrograd, but when in mid-October Kerensky tried to activate the Vyborg garrison, he was informed by the new commander that the troops would not obey.[20] The Bolsheviks' influence in Finland, as demonstrated in the case of General Oranovskii's murder, was concentrated in the armed forces. By late September 1917, they dominated not only the Northern Army but also the so-called Regional Committee of Finland (*Oblastnoi komitet Finliandii*), representing Soviet Russian interests and Russian military personnel still in Finland. The Regional Committee competed with the Finnish Soviet, created on the Russian model but representing the ethnically Finnish working class. The essential conflict between the Finnish Social Democrats, close in spirit to the Russian Mensheviks, and the Russian-centered Bolsheviks is the key to the Finnish story: two models of socialism face to face and complicated by the ethnic (national) factor.

By early October, the Bolsheviks had also gained control of Tsentrobalt, the committee representing the sailors of the Baltic Fleet. Lenin counted on the radicalized troops and sailors across the nearby Finnish border as backup for the anticipated takeover in the capital. The Finnish Social Democrats had other concerns. At the end of September, as a result of new elections, they lost their parliamentary majority. They did not therefore hurry toward armed confrontation, although they did establish an official Red Guard. The Bolsheviks were unwilling, however, to provide them with arms, since the Finns could not promise that their men would fight on the Russian side, even in the case of a German invasion.[21] The Finnish comrades were not only obstinately moderate but also patriotic.

In the aftermath of the parliamentary elections, the Provisional Government decided the safest way to ensure stability in Finland, as a bulwark against German aggression, was to grant self-government in advance of the Constituent Assembly. This was also a way of winning the support of the Finnish bourgeois parties, which opposed the more radical socialist program. The Provisional Government thus issued a decree on October 24, renouncing its "sovereign prerogatives over Finland, with the provision that foreign affairs be retained, as at present, by the supreme authority of Russia, and that Finland shall not alter the military legislation, or the laws concerning Russian nationals and institutions in Finland, without the consent of the Russian Government."[22] The Provisional Government, which did not have the legal right to do so, thereby devolved the authority formerly exercised by the Grand Duke onto the governing bodies of Finland. The formulation angered the socialists, who contended that parliament already exercised the authority the Provisional Government did not have the right to bestow. Delegates from Petrograd arrived in Helsinki with the government's response on October 25, just as the Bolsheviks were unseating its ministers in the capital. The decree was therefore moot.[23]

---

The Finnish Social Democrats had been unaware of the Bolshevik plans to seize power, but Bolshevik activists in Finland played a key role in Lenin and Trotsky's scheme, by mobilizing the sailors and garrison in support of the takeover. The Finnish socialists would have preferred to avoid direct confrontation with the bourgeois parties. They were not sure the Bolshevik victory would last; they were not ready for actual class warfare. Their hand was forced, however, by the Bolshevik activists in Helsinki, who threatened to provoke the Finnish workers to revolt, over the heads of their own Social Democratic leaders; indeed, the Bolsheviks had already established a presence in the Finnish Red Guard.[24]

Marxists of all shades on both sides of the border shared the conviction that socialism in Russia could survive only in the context of a pan-European workers' revolution. Lenin believed that Russia should nevertheless set the pace. The Finnish socialists, like the Russian Mensheviks, felt the time was not ripe. They pressed for the current parliament to accept the socialist program and then resign, allowing a peaceful transition, which would not alienate the Finnish bourgeoisie, whose historical moment had not yet passed. The socialist leaders spoke of legality and the need to avoid armed confrontation. Finnish delegates visited Lenin in Petrograd, where he urged them to follow the Bolshevik example, but they left with the impression that the survival of Bolshevik power was not a sure thing, which of course it wasn't.[25]

The Finnish socialists thus dickered in exactly the manner that most annoyed Lenin, for whom actions shaped reality, not the other way around. Finally, on November 1 / 14, a general strike was declared, which was intended as a show of strength but not as a bid for power. In the big cities, the Finnish Red Guard, buying or borrowing weapons from the Russians, who were unwilling to give them away, easily gained control. Their members were untrained and inept, but met little resistance. The Russian-led Tsentrobalt did not offer to help them. The strike was successful, but the socialist leaders did not seize the reins. The most important result of the strike was to enhance the power and confidence of the Red Guards.[26]

Finally, ten days later, parliament convened, with a mix of socialist and bourgeois deputies. The Social Democratic congress meeting at the same time continued to debate whether the moment was yet right for the proletarian revolution in Finland. The Helsinki Red Guard sent a delegation which demanded the seizure of power, but the party refused to be pushed.[27] The socialists had avoided confrontation, and little blood had been shed. Altogether thirty-four people had been killed in the confrontations between the bourgeois Home Guard and the Red Guard, most by the latter. While the socialists debated, on November 13/26, the bourgeois parties in parliament appointed their own government, headed by Pehr Evind Svinhufvud. The goal was statehood, not social transformation.[28] In November 1917, Svinhufvud was almost fifty-six years old. A lawyer and judge from a Swedish-speaking middle-class family of aristocratic origin, he was dismissed from the Finnish court of appeals in 1902 for resisting the policy of Russification. From 1907 to 1912, he was the speaker of the Finnish parliament, but his renewed resistance to Russian policies landed him in Siberia, from which he returned only after the February Revolution.[29]

Like the Provisional Government, the Finnish parliamentary leaders were obsessed with legality and procedure, which they saw as the key to legitimacy and hence to authority and power. Russia still had legal sovereignty over Finland, but Svinhufvud's government did not want to negotiate with the new Bolshevik rulers. The upstarts were not sure to last, but before departing the scene they might intervene on behalf of their socialist comrades. The Finnish government therefore invoked the authority of the anticipated all-Russian Constituent Assembly. The socialists, by contrast, despite their earlier reluctance to claim power in their own name, preferred to recognize the Bolshevik regime and accept the offer of immediate independence extended by the commissar of nationalities, Joseph Stalin.[30]

The contrast between the positions of the two Finnish camps resulted in a war of manifestos. On November 21 (December 4, NS), the bourgeois government presented a constitution that declared Finland an "independent republic," with "parliament as the holder of the sovereign power." The socialists echoed the key phrase but insisted that "an effort must be made to realise this independence by negotiating an agreement with Russia."[31]

A vote was taken, and the bourgeois version prevailed. December 6, 1917, became Finnish Independence Day, but the final outcome was yet to be determined and was not exclusively in Finnish hands.[32]

As part of their bid to free themselves from Russian domination (regardless of the ideological color of its regime), in November the Finns had sent a delegation to Berlin, requesting German intervention. General Ludendorff rejected the idea. Instead, he presented the Finns with conditions that took into account the recently expressed Soviet interest in opening separate peace negotiations. Once the Germans and Russians had concluded an armistice, Finland was to "claim the right to self-determination," insist that Russian troops withdraw, and explicitly request German support, in exchange for which Ludendorff promised to include the issue of Finnish independence in the peace negotiations. The terms of the armistice with Russia in December, however, did not mention Finland.[33]

It was difficult for the Finns to find a sponsor. The Entente would not support Finnish independence because the anti-Bolshevik groups they did support insisted on maintaining the old borders. Nevertheless, the Finns could not afford to be openly pro-German.[34] The Bolsheviks, by contrast, officially proclaimed their readiness to recognize a free Finland. What they meant by this was clear from the fact that they were also encouraging the Finnish proletariat to "take power into their hands." Such independence was to involve a special, federative relationship with Russia.[35] "We are now conquering Finland," Lenin declared, denying this was a form of imperialist aggression. Once the Finnish workers had conquered power at home, they would naturally ally with their socialist brethren, accomplishing the triumph of the international proletarian revolution. Whether cynical or sincere, such a vision was entirely consonant with the Marxist world view on both sides of the border.[36] Russian troops of course remained in Finland, to guard against possible German advance. The Soviets did, however, begin partial demobilization. Many soldiers simply deserted; whole divisions self-demobilized. Lenin was ready in any case to forfeit Finland and the Baltic states for the sake of peace with Germany; the Finns did not believe this and continued to badger the Allied and Scandinavian powers for recognition.[37]

Russia still called the shots. The day parliament announced its sovereignty, the Sovnarkom declared the Regional Committee to be "the highest organ of Russian state power in Finland."[38] Despite Russia's military and economic leverage, the parliament nevertheless persisted in ignoring the new regime.

The Finnish socialists, on their side, presented the December 6 declaration of independence directly to Lenin and Stalin, but Svinhufvud communicated only with the vestigial representatives of the overthrown Provisional Government, on the grounds that the Constituent Assembly was still to come.[39] Finally, on December 12/25, the Finnish Social Democratic Party appealed to the Sovnarkom to recognize Finland's independence, hoping to take the wind out of the bourgeois nationalist sails.[40] The parliamentary Finns, for their part, could not be sure if the Constituent Assembly would meet at all or whether it might not deliver a government less hospitable to Finnish desires. The respectable politicians arrived in Petrograd, where they were subject to a series of petty humiliations until the Sovnarkom on December 18/31, proclaimed its readiness to support "the separation of Finland from Russia."[41] Lenin apparently believed the concession was a relatively painless way of gaining propaganda points on the issue of national self-determination.

A few days later, though still regretting the reluctance of the Finnish socialists to take power into their own hands, the Congress of Soviets Executive Committee gave its approval; only the SRs demurred, still invoking the authority of the impending Constituent Assembly. Lenin, though reluctantly, met with Svinhufvud as two heads of state. Finnish independence was recognized in short order by Sweden, Denmark, Norway, France, and Germany. Britain and the United States held out, hoping still to get Russian forces back into action against the Central Powers.[42] On December 26, 1917 (January 8, 1918, NS), Svinhufvud told parliament that "the Russian people has generously fulfilled its promise to realize the right of self-determination of small nations." Finland declared itself neutral.[43]

Secession from the former Empire did not, however, separate Finland from Russian politics or from social conflicts that ignored the border. As in Russia, the Left was fragmented. The Finnish Social Democrats, despite Lenin's urging, refused to launch their own revolution, but they were not in control of the forces they themselves had set in motion. The Red Guards had flexed their muscles during the general strike. In Helsinki the Red Guards and the Bolsheviks were particularly aggressive, engineering attacks on government personnel and property, defying not only Svinhufvud's government but the Social Democratic leadership as well. Independent of the Regional Committee or the Bolsheviks, the Red Guards also managed to gain control of the city of Turku, where they set about pilfering government property, intimidating public servants, and looting and trashing shops. On the Red side, to sum up, there were therefore at least five centers of power or potential influence in Finland: the Finnish Social Democratic Party; the Red Guards established by that party but escaping its control; the Finnish Bolshevik Party organization in Helsinki, the Russian-dominated Regional Committee; and the Bolshevik Party in Petrograd.[44]

The Svinhufvud government and its supporters dismissed the Red Guards as bandits or criminals, encouraged in their rampages by the Russian troops. As one parliamentary deputy remarked, "It is certainly not a question of a struggle between different social classes, as long as our socialist gentlemen do not wish to line up with criminals, but it is a question only of a struggle between society... and criminal gangs."[45] The Russian garrisons sometimes supplied the Red Guards with weapons, but the Petrograd Bolsheviks were reluctant to equip the Guards, which they did not themselves control. The Red Guards were not in fact composed of Russians, as some conservatives alleged, or of criminals, but mostly of native Finnish workers. It was the overheated Helsinki Red Guards that on January 8, 1918, the day Svinhufvud praised Russian generosity, took over the mansion of the former governor general. Rejecting the authority of the bourgeois government, they renamed the building Smolny, after Bolshevik headquarters in Petrograd. The Social Democrats accused them of "terrorism... against the party," but did not try to stop them.[46]

The Red Guards were, moreover, only one side of the increasingly marked split in Finnish society. The next day, the Svinhufvud government's Military Commission decided to purchase arms and uniforms from the Germans and retrieve the Finnish Jäger Battalion, which had been fighting in the Prussian army. The parliament then voted by a narrow margin to authorize the creation of a security force to oppose the Red Guards. One socialist deputy protested that the "bourgeois government has created a class-war army which is directed against the Finnish working people."[47] The Social Democrats had been reluctant to launch this war, but were unable to keep their followers in check. Now they faced the consequences. The government security force was intended initially to replace the police, which had dissolved, and the militia, which was unable to perform its functions. It consisted of the existing Home Guards, bolstered by the returning Jägers, who provided training and leadership. Financed by Finnish businessmen, the Home Guards bought weapons on the Russian black market or purchased them in Petrograd and smuggled them back home. Later they bought arms from the Germans.[48]

All this activity was ill-coordinated and amateurish. A skilled commander was needed. On January 2/15, 1918, after some hesitation, the Military Commission appointed General Baron Carl Gustaf Emil Mannerheim to lead the new force. In some respects, he seemed an unlikely candidate. Raised in an upper-class Swedish-speaking family, Mannerheim spoke Finnish poorly. Excluded by his background from a role in domestic politics, he made a career in the tsarist army, was fluent in Russian, and had spent many years outside Finland. Though not a democrat, as an officer in what had been an Allied army he favored the Entente over the Central Powers. After the Bolshevik takeover, he resigned his commission and returned to Helsinki. The Finns at this point knew little about him, but he proved an inspired choice.[49] His evolution from imperial servant to national icon personified the tectonic shift in the region's political life.

Mannerheim set up his military staff in Vaasa, two hundred miles north of Turku on the Gulf of Bothnia.[50] From this point on, Finland backed into revolution and civil war, with the Germans and Soviet Russians in supporting roles. Other than Mannerheim, no charismatic figure emerged to lead the political charge on either side. The conflict escalated not as a result of foreign interference but as a byproduct of Bolshevik agitation among the Russian armed forces and in the Finnish factories. As the two sides—Finnish Reds versus Finnish Whites—tried to gain control over the exercise of armed force, the Germans tipped the balance.

Although the Russians, first as the Provisional Government and then as the Sovnarkom, had endorsed Finnish independence, Russian forces remained in place. As long as the peace talks at Brest-Litovsk were still in progress, the Germans were obliged to stay out. As Adolf Ioffe put it, "in practice the separation from Russia is not yet completed." In theory, therefore, the Regional Committee continued to represent Russian authority in Finland. By this point, however, the Russian garrison was in the process of dissolution and could not be used as a fighting force.[51]

Conflict escalated, as a result not of policy decisions but of the confrontation between volunteer armed groups, not yet constituting armies. On January 19 in Vyborg, site of the main Russian garrison, Russian soldiers together with local Red Guards took control of a factory that had been used to store Home Guard weapons. Skirmishes between Red Guards and Home Guards occurred in a number of other places as well. The Reds had held Vyborg only for three days, however, when the Home Guards chased them out.[52] By now Lenin had decided to help arm the Red Guards. Fearing the

Home Guards might seize the expected shipment from Petrograd, the Helsinki Red Guard leadership called for a general strike throughout southern Finland, a decision the Social Democrats did not endorse, but could not avert.[53]

Russian leaders in Finland were no more in control than the Finnish comrades. When Svinhufvud went to talk with the Tsentrobalt sailors on January 11/24, they briefly detained him. The move was condemned by Ivar Smigla, the Latvian-Russian head of Tsentrobalt and of the Regional Committee. He had no control over his own men, however, and no hand in the decision of the Finnish Red Guards the next day to arrest Svinhufvud's government and take power into their own hands. Smigla promised to send arms but pledged otherwise to stand aside. Having so far tried to avoid open conflict, Svinhufvud warned that any attack on the Home Guards, renamed the White Guards, would constitute an attack on the legal government—which, of course, is exactly what the Finnish Reds intended. Mannerheim, for his part, decided it was time to disarm the Russian garrison, the remnant of the Imperial Army that the Bolsheviks by now had thoroughly secured, which he correctly judged too weak to resist.[54]

On January 13/26, fearing the impending Red Guard attack, the ministers hurriedly abandoned Helsinki. The next day, the Red Guards declared their intention of creating a "Social Democratic revolutionary government" to replace them.[55] The Regional Committee prepared to support the Red Guards, who were dragging their own reluctant Social Democratic leaders after them, but Trotsky assured Svinhufvud that "the violent intervention of Russian military units in Finland's internal affairs is not allowed."[56] The Regional Committee ordered the garrison not to get involved; for its part, the government ordered the White Guards to hold back. While leaders on all sides—Svinhufvud, the Finnish Social Democrats, the Bolshevik Smigla—were retreating, the Red Guards managed easily to seize the government buildings in Helsinki. By January 15/28, they were in control of the capital. The following day, Mannerheim, on his side, had captured Vaasa and disarmed the Russian garrison there.[57] Red versus White—not Finn versus Russian, but Finn versus Finn—were in position.

Before the ministers closed shop in Helsinki (some going into hiding, a few making it up north), the parliament issued a final statement, urging the population to give their allegiance to General Mannerheim. "Part of the Finnish people," it declared, "relying on foreign forces and foreign bayonets, has risen in revolt against Finland's parliament and Finland's government."[58] By early February (NS), Mannerheim had secured northeast Finland and part of Karelia, the easternmost part of the country, extending north from Petrograd (and today part of Russia), for the White—that is, anti-socialist (anti-Bolshevik, all the more so) Finnish nationalist—cause.[59] The Finnish nation had acquired its general.

In Helsinki, meanwhile, the newly established government, having ousted the parliament, declared itself the Finnish People's Deputation and adopted a vague program of gradual social transformation—not at all Leninist in spirit. Because there was no military opposition, the ragtag Red Guards on which it relied easily took control of the key cities of Vyborg, Tampere, and Turku. The Sovnarkom sent them some weapons, and some Red Guards came over from Petrograd to fight on their side. When, however, the Regional Committee ordered the garrison troops to fight on behalf of their Finnish comrades, they refused to obey.[60] The most the Sovnarkom could deliver was rhetorical endorsement. On January 17/30, it recognized the People's Deputation as the "new socialist government of Finland." Trotsky in Brest-Litovsk said, "We greet the working class of Finland which has seized power from the hands of the bourgeoisie." Belittling the fact that the comrades had not only ousted the so-called bourgeoisie but broken away from the Russian motherland, Lenin predicted that "more and more diverse confederations of free nations will group themselves around revolutionary Russia." In principle, at least, the Russian Bolsheviks saw their Finnish counterparts as taking the first steps toward pan-European revolution.[61] On March 1, 1918, Soviet Russia signed a peace treaty with allegedly socialist and independent Finland that emphasized Russia's continuing relationship of dominance.[62]

The Finnish comrades were not, however, Bolshevik-style Social Democrats. The Finnish party leaders tried to bring the People's Deputation under control, to impose some restraint on the Red Guards, which had not reformed their headstrong ways. They warned that "revolution is not the same thing as criminal violence."[63] Essentially in the Menshevik mold, these Social Democrats defined their goal as a democratic parliamentary republic, with a mixed capitalist-socialist economy.[64] This late in the game, with Petrograd in Bolshevik hands, they behaved as though it were still March 1917, while the Red Guards behaved as though it was January 1918, which indeed it was.

The die was cast. On both sides of the Finnish civil divide, the challenge was to create a more or less reliable fighting force motivated by political goals. The Whites represented what remained of the former parliamentary government, recognized by certain Western powers, and initially by the Sovnarkom as well. They defined their cause not in ideological terms but as the defense of law and order against "criminals and traitors," whether Russians or Finnish Reds. "The struggle which is now in progress in Finland is not a class war," they declared, "but is a collision between, on the one side a legal social order...and on the other side plain terrorist activity."[65] Mannerheim denounced "the mutilated bodies of murdered citizens and the ruins of burned villages," demanding "revenge on the country's traitors."[66] The aim was to liberate the south from the "terrorist regime" that was "murdering, plundering, imprisoning and torturing the peaceful and law-abiding inhabitants."[67] Some lurid details were embroidered, as in all atrocity propaganda, but the essentials were correct—for both sides. Here was the same logic as the Bolshevik Terror—again, coming from both sides.

The Red Guards were volunteers; they supplied themselves by what they called requisitioning, sometimes offering compensation but often resorting to outright plunder. They were egalitarian and bucked all authority. There were few officers to lead them in any case.[68] Before the onset of the German offensive on February 18, 1918, the Sovnarkom continued to promise support, but when it came to accepting the German peace conditions, Lenin said, "Let them take revolutionary Finland. The revolution will not be lost if we give up Finland."[69] Pro-Bolshevik Russian officers did fight for the Reds, mostly in Karelia, but the Finns resented them, while the ordinary Russian soldiers hurried to board the trains leaving for Russia. They were harassed and robbed by the Finnish Red Guards, trying to stop them from taking provisions and equipment along with them.[70] By contrast, the People's Deputation was relatively staid. It inherited the old government institutions and the civil servants, who only briefly struck in protest.[71] Without an armed force or police, it was unable to curtail the looting, intimidation, and bloody settling of scores perpetrated by the Finnish Red Guard, which between January and March 1918 committed some 1,650 murders. Most victims could reasonably be identified as supporters of the White cause; some were prisoners or hostages. Unlike the Red Terror in Russia, which had almost immediately acquired an organized form, these reprisals were spontaneous. The Deputation opposed them.[72] The tactics, though brutal, were largely ineffective. The government ministers survived in hiding in Helsinki, Svinhufvud was smuggled out to the north, Mannerheim managed by subterfuge to dismantle the Russian artillery on the Sveaborg Fortress in Helsinki harbor, White propaganda circulated unobstructed. The

Sovnarkom insisted the telegraph service remain in Russian control; the staff feigned allegiance and reported back to the Whites.[73]

The White forces countenanced political terror of their own. They shot prisoners taken in combat; they shot and otherwise executed civilians thought to belong to or support the Red Guards. While condemning such excesses, Mannerheim did little to stop them and encouraged the attitudes that justified them. He told a German journalist, "The revolutionaries have made themselves guilty of high treason and insurrection and the punishment for that is death." Saboteurs and spies behind the lines, he ordered, should be "shot on the spot."[74] The Finnish Red Terror was not institutionalized; the Deputation had no political police. The Finnish White Terror combined spontaneous social warfare with official policy. Better organized and led, the Whites emerged victorious, and as a consequence the toll they eventually exacted was higher.

Not unlike Lenin, Mannerheim had no objection to the use of force, but he wanted to be in control. Like the Red Guards, the White Guards were volunteers; they too resisted discipline and hierarchy, and there were too few of them to build a real army. Conscription was therefore introduced, with the fiction of reactivating the 1878 imperial law, suspended since 1900, a gesture at legality that only underscored its reverse. Not everyone drafted, moreover, could be trusted, since a large share of the population had voted socialist. Finding commanders also raised issues of allegiance. Since there were few native Finns with professional military training, Mannerheim drew on colleagues from the Russian Imperial Army, on officers from Sweden, and finally on the Germans, dispersing the handful of well-trained Jägers throughout the army to drill the recruits.[75] The Finnish foot soldiers, however, disliked the Russian officers Mannerheim recruited, because they were Russian. They disliked Mannerheim himself and other officers, like Ernst Berthold Löfström (Ernest Levstrem), who also had Swedish names. The language of command in the Finnish White army was Swedish![76] Since Swedish was used by the Finnish upper classes, there was a social dimension to the soldiers' resentment.

The Reds were ensconced in the south, in possession of the capital, Helsinki, enjoying Soviet Russian support. Fearing they would not be able to dislodge them, Svinhufvud's deposed government urged the Germans, still negotiating at Brest-Litovsk, to insist on Russian withdrawal and provide the Whites with direct military backing.[77] Mannerheim, for his part, did not believe the Germans would win the war and insisted that Finland must liberate itself from Russian domination and the Red threat by its own native efforts. He nevertheless realized that he needed the Jägers and, in the short run, German help. The Finnish appeal was indeed self-abasing. On February 14, 1918, the government requested the dispatch of German troops to Finland. This would be "the most effective way of saving the country: may we therefore be permitted to propose this form of intervention."[78] The Germans of course had their own reasons for including in the March 3, 1918, Brest-Litovsk treaty the complete withdrawal of Russian troops, warships, and Red Guards from Finland. A treaty then signed on March 7, 1918, between Germany and the independent nation of Finland named the price. Germany would have privileged access to Finnish resources, control over foreign trade and foreign relations, and the right to maintain a military presence. Finland, as Mannerheim had feared, emerged a German client.[79]

Mannerheim remained first in command of Finnish forces, but the German general Count Rüdiger von der Goltz called the shots.[80] The Germans declared: "we come as friends to help you, so that order, justice and liberty will again rule in your country.... We do not come as conquerors." Svinhufvud affirmed that the Germans intended "to fight together with us against the plague from the east and to destroy the Red terror."[81] On April 3, 1918 von der Goltz's nine-thousand-man Baltic Division landed in Hanko, a port eighty miles west of Helsinki. On April 6, the Deputation decided to relocate to Vyborg; some of its members even wanted to capitulate.[82] That same day, Mannerheim's army had captured Tampere, a hundred miles north of Helsinki, without German help. It was a moral as well as military victory. Over two thousand Red fighters were killed, another eleven thousand captured.[83]

Both the fighting and the retribution were bloody. Mannerheim ordered that prisoners were not to be "shot out of hand," as was the expectation and largely the practice, but brought before tribunals. During the battle, however, his forces showed no restraint, lobbing hand grenades into windows at the slightest movement, on the excuse that snipers might be lurking. At the end, those captured were massed in warehouses at the train station, then taken out to be shot, despite the General's order. Special care was taken to execute all the Russians. A witness described the scene near the station as a "slaughter," which left "a heap of bleeding bodies lying on the ground." The massacres, in which Russians were summarily executed, tarnished Mannerheim's reputation at the time, but did him no lasting harm.[84] By contrast, when von der Goltz entered Helsinki on April 14, he encountered no organized defense but only sporadic Red Guard action. The hidden ministers emerged to form a government, and the bourgeois Finns rejoiced. In its ease and symbolic significance, von der Goltz's success overshadowed Mannerheim's achievement and emphasized the importance of the Germans' role.[85]

By April 1918, Mannerheim had fashioned a working army and prepared to take Vyborg. The Deputation appointed a military dictator to organize its defense. It ordered those Red Guards no longer needed in the west to retreat eastward and leave their families behind. The Guards indeed began moving east from Turku, but took their families with them, clogging the railroads, plundering and murdering hundreds of civilians as they went. The Deputation met for the last time in Vyborg on April 21, 1918. It decided that the core leaders should take refuge in Russia, to prepare for a return engagement.[86] The Red Guards in Vyborg nevertheless did put up a fight, against both the White Army and von der Goltz's Baltic Division. The Finnish General Löfström declared: "Red leaders and Russian soldiers who fight are outside the law and can be treated accordingly."[87] The Baltic Division had taken as many as twenty thousand prisoners. On May 1, Mannerheim held a victory parade. The Reds had executed a hundred White prisoners; the Whites executed the members of the Vyborg Soviet and another fifty prisoners. it was rumored that two hundred civilians had been slaughtered.[88] By May 15, 1918, the fighting was over.

The moderate socialists now cooperated with the Germans, issuing a Proclamation to the Workers of Finland (April 16, 1918), denouncing the revolution as a mistake instigated by the Bolsheviks. "So down with the weapons everywhere and let us return to Western, social-democratic methods of struggle, let us return to constructive parliamentary work and unarmed organizational activity." The socialists attempted to participate in Svinhufvud's restored parliamentary regime, but it was only after the government's fall in December 1918 that they were able to return to political life. For their part, those who had supported the failed Bolshevik attempt at revolution in Finland gathered in Moscow, where they formed the kernel of the Finnish Communist Party.[89]

The Finnish Deputation, composed of non-Bolshevik socialists, countenanced the fanaticism of the Red Guards, though they were uneasy with its random, explosive character. They were in any case unable to stop it. The White leadership, by contrast, like the Bolsheviks, adopted terror as a weapon. Between January and mid-May, the Whites executed over eight thousand Red fighters, including over three hundred women, whom they claimed belonged to the Red Guards, as some may well have done. A letter to a respectable newspaper complained: "In spite of the commander in chief's prohibitions, the shootings continue uninterrupted. The Red madness has been followed by the White terror."[90] At the end of May, spontaneous executions were indeed replaced by tribunals, which convicted 67,000 people and executed 265. The remaining eighty thousand prisoners were kept in harsh conditions and treated as criminals; almost twelve thousand of them died of hunger and disease.[91]

In May Svinhufvud invited the German troops to remain. Mannerheim would have preferred to join the aristocratic Russian Whites in toppling the Bolshevik government in Moscow, but the Svinhufvud government had no use for this plan and rejected Mannerheim's authoritarian manner. Mannerheim, for his part, refused to submit to German command, resigned his post, and left for Sweden as a private citizen. On December 12, 1918, a month after the Armistice, Svinhufvud's regime fell and Mannerheim returned to replace him as the head of state of independent Finland.[92] Though Mannerheim was now in charge, Finland was still occupied by von der Goltz's Baltic Division. As a defense against the spread of Bolshevism and the descent into chaos, the Military Inter-Allied Commission of Control, formed in Paris in the wake of the Armistice, had authorized the continued presence of German troops in Finland and the Baltic states. The Armistice required German forces on formerly Russian territory not to leave until "the Allies shall think the moment suitable, having regard to the internal situation of these territories."[93] In Finland, however, Russian-style Bolshevism had decisively failed to spread. Finland had been saved from the threat of Soviet conquest by the German occupation and General Mannerheim's leadership. It was saved from Bolshevism by its own tradition of democratic socialism. As the Finnish Communist Otto Wilhelm Kuusinen complained in October 1918, paying his non-Bolshevik comrades a backhanded compliment, "Finnish Social Democracy did not want to go beyond the representative political system. On the contrary, it wanted to perfect this system, as a genuinely democratic form of government."[94] That ideal had been compromised in the polarized context of the Finns' own civil war, in which the radicalized Red Guards drew the moderates into the bloody combat.[95] After the German defeat, Finland emerged as a conservative republic, avoiding extremes of both right and left. The new country's most important accomplishment was to have escaped imperial Russian borders.

# 4

# Baltic Entanglements

Escaping Imperial Russian borders was also the goal of the lands extending southward from the Gulf of Finland, along the Baltic coast, to the Niemen River—the former imperial provinces that became the independent states of Estonia, Latvia, and Lithuania.[1] Parts of the region had been conquered from Sweden in 1710 by Peter the Great. The traditional social structures of Estonia and Livonia were recognized by the Peace of Nystad in 1721, which allowed the Germanic nobility and the towns to retain their corporate rights. These liminal provinces served both as bridges to Europe and as models for the tsar's project of bringing Russia into the orbit of European civilization.[2] The new capital of St. Petersburg, founded in 1703 as Russia's "window to Europe," in Alexander Pushkin's words, was embraced by the Finnish-Baltic crescent. By 1914, the Baltic periphery, together with the Polish provinces, in particular the area around Warsaw, were the most highly urbanized part of the Empire, after the provinces of Moscow and Petrograd.[3] Their loss would deprive the Russian state of the essential ports of Tallinn (until 1917, Reval), Riga, and Libau (now Liepāja). The region, together with Finland, constituting a direct pathway to the imperial capital of Petrograd, was also a security concern.

Russian patriots considered the subordinate territories and minority populations such as these an integral part of the Empire. This imperial vision was shared by the liberal Kadets no less than the rhetorically anti-imperial Bolsheviks and the militantly pro-Empire anti-Bolshevik Whites, all of whom in different ways tried to keep the pre-1914 territory intact. Although no area of the old Russian Empire was ethnically homogeneous, those that asserted themselves against the center had already begun, before 1914, to think of themselves in ethno-national terms. Otherwise, the struggle for statehood in Finland and the Baltic provinces paralleled the efforts of Russian society itself to enter the political arena and, as in Russia proper, activated tensions endemic to local society. The western periphery also found itself entangled in the conflict between the Central Powers and the emerging Soviet regime.

———

The nation of Latvia was formed out of the Imperial provinces of Courland and lower Livonia.[4] Westernmost Courland, acquired in 1795 in the third Polish partition, was dominated by Baltic barons and inhabited by Latvian-speaking Lutheran peasants; easternmost Latgale (Latgaliia), containing a large Jewish population, along with Polish and Belarussian minorities, had entered Russia in 1772 with the first Polish partition. The Latvian provinces experienced the war with special intensity. The Russian invasion of East Prussia in August 1914 was launched from there. Latvians were among the troops under General Rennenkampf which were defeated at the Masurian Lakes. By summer 1915, the Germans had taken possession of Courland and half of Livonia. As they retreated, the Russians evacuated the industrial infra-structure of Riga and uprooted a good part of the Jewish and Latvian-speaking populations. Riga lost half its half-million population.

The goal of statehood had already been articulated after 1905 by the Latvian delegates to the State Duma, who envisioned an autonomous administration comprising the provinces of Livonia, Courland, and Vitebsk to the east. By February 1917, a good part of this territory was under German occupation. Unwilling to confront the geographical complexities of competing national claims and uncertain of its own authority, the Provisional Government would not grant autonomous status to what remained.[5] The city of Riga, in the unoccupied zone, experienced the same political rivalries as elsewhere after February: in this case, Bolsheviks in the soviets, moderate socialists outside it, and civic leaders in the City Duma. As in the heartland, the Bolsheviks played electoral hardball for as long as elections and ad hoc institutions were still in operation, preparing for the day when they could disable them altogether. As usual, they paid special attention to the soldiers. By May 1917, Bolshevik activists had established a stronghold in the Latvian Riflemen's soviet. By September 3, 1917 (NS), when the Germans captured Riga, the Bolsheviks had gained control of virtually all of the city's governing institutions—by legitimate political methods. In the elections for the Constituent Assembly, they achieved a majority of the vote.

Once the Provisional Government was overthrown, the power struggle continued by other means. In July 1917, the Latvian Social Democrats had formed a Soviet of Soviets (*Iskolat*). After October, the Iskolat declared itself the government of the unoccupied part of Latvia. At the same time, a Latvian National Council invoked the Bolshevik-endorsed principle of national self-determination to demand autonomy, the future form of government to be determined by a Latvian Constituent Assembly. In parallel, a democratic bloc urged the creation of a unified Latvian state. Once the peace was signed at Brest-Litovsk, the Germans took over the remaining Latvian territory and returned power to the Baltic nobility, with the intention of creating a duchy under direct German rule.[6] After the Armistice in November 1918, the Latvian National Council joined with the Riga bloc in declaring independence and establishing a provisional government under Kārlis Ulmanis.[7] The Latvians were not yet masters in their own house, however. As instructed by the Inter-Allied Commission of Control, the German troops under General Rüdiger von der Goltz had not departed. Under those circumstances, the Latvian government appealed to the general for support. The British, despite their "horror of all Bolshevik teachings," as Prime Minister David Lloyd George put it, were unwilling to get involved. They therefore encouraged the Latvians to invite the Germans to create a military force on their behalf.[8]

When the Red Army returned in December 1918, it announced the creation of the Latvian Socialist Soviet Republic, headed by Petr Stuchka (Pēteris Stučka), a native of Livonia, better known for his subsequent role as Soviet Commissar of Justice.[9] On January 3, 1919, the Reds took Riga, and the Provisional Government retreated to Liepāja, on the coast. The Latvian Riflemen had easily assumed control following an insurrection in the factory districts, where the Bolsheviks had genuine support. Stuchka imposed the Red regime with a hard fist, nevertheless. As in the rest of Soviet Russia, food shortages were already extreme, but the problem of supply was aggravated by attempts to impose state control, leading to the expansion of the black market. This in turn provided the excuse, if one were needed, for the hunting of profiteers and anyone designated as class enemies. Since the wealthier citizens of Riga tended to be German, ethnic and class categories overlapped. As hunger intensified, the Riflemen withdrew their allegiance. Occasions for plunder, expropriations, and forced evictions multiplied, alienating the rest of the population.[10] The future U.S. president, Herbert Hoover, then in charge of the American Relief Administration helping war victims in Eastern Europe, described conditions in Bolshevik-controlled

Riga from January to May 1919. Common criminals, as well as political zealots, were running amok, he reported, looting stores and dwellings, shooting "hundreds of innocent people" every day, while many inhabitants were dying of starvation. Hoover's anti-Communist fervor may have colored his terms, but conditions in Riga were truly appalling.[11] In the five months of Soviet occupation, over three thousand executions were carried out in the city and surrounding villages, eight thousand people died of starvation, and another ten thousand were confined to concentration camps.[12]

On February 1, 1919, General von der Goltz arrived in Liepāja, where he organized two forces: the Iron Division, consisting of German volunteers (the Freikorps), and an army technically subordinate to the Latvian government but in fact under the command of aristocratic Baltic officers, who had nothing but disdain for the native Latvians. Major Alfred Fletcher, a German officer of Scottish ancestry, was in charge of the so-called Baltische Landeswehr.[13] In short, the Latvian government was now under the protection of irregular armed forces which it did not control. These forces were at first effective. By March 1, they had cleared the coast, from Ventspils in the north to Liepāja in the south, and then taken Jelgava in the center.[14] On April 16, 1919, the Germans toppled Ulmanis's Provisional Government in Liepāja. The British were not pleased but were still unwilling to intervene, so the Germans remained.

The first step was to recover Riga. Von der Goltz asked Berlin to authorize the move, but the newly installed German president, Social Democrat Friedrich Ebert (whom von der Goltz considered a usurper), did not want to antagonize Britain; von der Goltz was free, however, Ebert informed him, to make use of the formally independent Landeswehr.[15] On May 22, 1919, the Landeswehr, with Freikorps backing, took Riga.[16] In the process, they shot hundreds, if not thousands, of Latvian civilians, horrifying the British and enraging the Latvians, on whose behalf they allegedly fought. As Hoover put it, this time with understatement, the Red horrors had been followed by "another kind of trouble." The Germans established a military field court, which took its revenge on those they held responsible for what had gone before. "There were men on the court whose wives, sons and daughters were among the executed," Hoover observed. "At once a White Terror replaced a Red Terror with its round of executions."[17]

A month later, on June 23, 1919, a joint Latvian-Estonian force defeated Major Fletcher's Iron Division at Cēsis.[18] Five days after that, the peace treaty was signed in Versailles. A British military mission arrived in Latvia, the Latvian government returned to claim power, and the British assumed command of the Landeswehr. Under Allied pressure, on August 5 Ebert removed von der Goltz from his command, but the general, still in pursuit of German power, had one more card up his sleeve. "The whole of southern Livonia could be reconquered," he announced, "and, if supported by a few divisions, St. Petersburg could be taken and thus a place in the East would be won which would considerably change the Versailles Treaty."[19] Unwilling to renounce his plan, he put the Freikorps under the command of a rogue adventurer and poseur, one General Prince Pavel Avalov-Bermondt, a native of Tiflis, who had entered the region early in the year and formed what he called the Russian Army of the West.[20] On August 24, the Iron Division gathered at the Jelgava rail station. Instead of departing, however, it formed a German Legion, led by Avalov-Bermondt, with assistance from von der Goltz, who had returned to join them. On October 8, the Legion attacked Riga, but was defeated, after an artillery battle, by a combination of mobilized citizens, Estonian equipment, and Allied naval backup.[21] The Allies' strategy of containment had misfired.

In January 1920, Latvian and Polish forces gained control of the border area. By early February, a ceasefire between Latvia and Russia had gone into effect. Talks continued into April, when the Latvian Socialist Soviet Republic was dissolved. By the Latvian-Soviet Peace Treaty (Treaty of Riga) of August 11, 1920, the Soviet government recognized Latvian independence. The treaty defined Latvia's borders, accorded reparations from Russia, and stipulated the return of prisoners and property.[22]

———

The situation in what became the country of Estonia had similar features. The first steps toward independence were taken in February 1917 when the Provisional Government granted self-rule to the predominantly Estonian-speaking province of Estland, combined with the northern portion of Livonia. When this territory had been acquired from Sweden in 1721 after the Great Northern War (1700–1721), the tsar became the Duke of Estonia. Local administration was in the hands of the Baltic German nobility.

The Provisional Government first appointed a native Estonian as its representative in the capital city of Tallinn, breaking with the tradition of baronial administration. On March 30, it then acceded to local pressure in recognizing the autonomous role of an elected body, the Maapäev, or Regional Council (Landtag). The pattern of Dual Power was replicated with the establishment of a Soviet of workers, soldiers, and sailors in Tallinn, a naval fortress with large shipyards that employed thousands of workers, most of them Russian. In the September elections to the Maapäev, diverse socialist parties won half the seats, Bolsheviks the fewest.[23] The Bolsheviks naturally concentrated instead on gaining support in the soviets of Tallinn and Narva, the easternmost Estonian city, just over a hundred miles from Petrograd. The Bolshevik-led soviets, invoking proletarian internationalism, opposed independence, thus also serving the geopolitical interests of the new Russia-centered regime. They continued to agitate in the factories and villages, where they promised the peasants access to the Baltic German estates.

Echoing events in the Russian capital, on October 23, the Tallinn Bolsheviks formed a Military Revolutionary Committee. As the Bolsheviks were taking power in Petrograd, the Tallinn committee followed suit. By mid-November it had dissolved the Maapäev, which, in parting, declared itself the supreme power of a future independent Estonia. It cited in justification the Provisional Government's March 30 decree, but left the final determination of the form of government to an anticipated Estonian Constituent Assembly, scheduled for late January, 1918. The Council thus invoked two distinct sources of legitimacy: the constitutional status conferred by the monarchy's successor regime, on the one hand, and the principle of national self-determination, on the other.[24]

Once they had suppressed the Maapäev, the Bolsheviks courted popular support by expropriating the large German-held estates. In characteristic fashion, they also banned the non-Bolshevik press. In the November elections to the All-Russian Constituent Assembly, the party won 40 percent of the Estonian vote; the moderate socialist/democratic bloc did slightly better. When during the vote for the Estonian Constituent Assembly it emerged that the Bolsheviks would not have a majority, they cancelled the election and proceeded to arrest hundreds of local leaders.[25]

By then, of course, the Petrograd Bolsheviks had dispensed with the All-Russian Constituent Assembly. They had also embarked on talks with the Germans at Brest-Litovsk. It was at this point that the moderate Estonian elites embraced the goal of full national independence. At the end of February, 1918, the Germans drove the Red forces out of Tallinn. The surviving leaders of the Maapäev asserted Estonia's status as an independent nation and announced the formation of an Estonian Provisional Government. In this respect, also, they repeated the Petrograd pattern, creating a moderate, democratic inheritor regime reluctant to claim the full rights of power.[26] The German occupation, lasting until the Armistice in November, was welcomed by the Baltic barons, who dreamed of a unified Baltic kingdom under German rule, settled by German farmers. No such Germanic kingdom emerged. The German presence only sharpened the Estonian appetite for independence.[27]

But the path was not yet clear. On the one hand, on November 13, 1918, the Sovnarkom annulled the Brest treaties and claimed the Baltic states as part of Soviet Russia. On the other hand, here too the Allies preferred to keep German troops on hand as an obstacle to Soviet incursion and social breakdown. White leaders also began thinking of the Baltic arena as a staging ground for a military operation aimed at Petrograd.[28] The Estonian Provisional Government announced under the occupation had reestablished itself on November 11, 1918. Its most important act was to initiate land reform as the basis for a socially inclusive national state, thus also winning the support of the peasantry and returning soldiers. The local soviets also returned, however, competing for the same popular constituency. On November 22, 1918, the Red Army launched an attack on Narva and a week later established what it called the Estonian Workers' Commune. On December 7, 1918, the Commune was "recognized" by Moscow as the government of an "independent" Estonia that was nevertheless to remain part of Soviet Russia. The fiction of an Estonian Soviet Republic was intended to obscure the fact that Soviet forces were attempting to impose Russian domination by military means.[29]

The long-anticipated Estonian Constituent Assembly finally convened on April 23, 1919, laying the basis for a left-oriented democratic government dedicated to peace and land reform, stealing the Bolsheviks' thunder.[30] Estonia had thus declared its independence and established a government in Tallinn, but as long as Soviet Russia had not recognized Estonian independence, the Allies refused to do so. They were reluctant at the Paris Peace Conference to affirm the dismemberment of the former Russian Empire.[31] At the end of August, however, Georgii Chicherin, the commissar of foreign affairs, took the first steps toward negotiating independence, and in September the British gave the green light.[32] Estonia's status was resolved finally on February 2, 1920, with the Treaty of Tartu (German Dorpat, Russian Iurev) between the Republic of Estonia and the Russian Soviet Federative Socialist Republic, which confirmed the country's independence. The signatories agreed to a demilitarized zone along their shared border; Estonia pledged to observe diplomatic neutrality. This was the first of the treaties concluded between parts of the former Romanov Empire and the new Soviet state. Estonia had acted without foreign support; the Soviets had established a model for future resolutions of the national question.[33]

---

If by 1920 Estonia and Latvia managed to establish independent governments with internationally recognized borders, the imperial provinces of Kovno and Vilna further south had a more difficult time. Like the lower part of what became Estonia and all of what became Latvia, these provinces, home to speakers of Lithuanian, had belonged to the historic Polish-Lithuanian Commonwealth, destroyed in the late-eighteenth-century partitions.[34] The fate of the future Lithuania was thus entangled with the aspirations of two other emerging nations, all together thwarting the territorial ambitions of the new Soviet Russian regime: the former Russian-ruled Kingdom of Poland, with its capital in Warsaw, which hoped to annex Galicia from the collapsing Hapsburg Empire, and the nine imperial provinces that in 1922 became the Ukrainian Soviet Socialist Republic, with its capital in Kiev. While caught between the Germans and Soviet Russia, the three aspiring nations—Lithuania, Poland, and Ukraine—battled among themselves to define adjoining borders. Internally, each nation's self-appointed political leadership split along ideological and class lines. None of these wars for independence were simple two-way confrontations.

During the war, along with Latvia and lower Estonia, the Germans occupied Kovno and Vilna provinces. They did not object when, on November 28, 1917 (December 11, NS), a Lithuanian national council (Taryba) announced the establishment of an independent state, under German auspices.[35] Repeated on February 16, 1918, the declaration established a democratic republic, recognized by the Germans in March but operating under the continuing occupation.[36] The German surrender at the end of the year, as in the other cases, opened the door to conflict among competing political factions and neighboring states. The German withdrawal exposed the Lithuanians to attack by Bolshevik forces determined to recover the lost territory. Unsuccessful at forming an army of its own, the Lithuanian government retreated from Vilnius to Kaunas, farther to the west, allowing the Reds to take the abandoned city on January 5, 1919. Vilnius then became the capital of a newly created Lithuanian Soviet Socialist Republic, which in February 1919 merged with the freshly minted Belarussian Soviet Socialist

Republic to the southeast, filling the last unclaimed portion of the historic Commonwealth.[37] The right to Vilnius was, however, contested by the Poles, who managed to gain control of it in October 1920 in the course of their war for independence against Soviet Russia.

---

The movement away from the Russian center was not confined to ethnic minorities. In the northwest, as at other points on the periphery, local Russian elites also pushed for greater autonomy. In Arkhangelsk Province, their aspirations derived from the civic ambitions of the local commercial classes, who felt that the needs of the region were not being met. At some point, the northerners went so far as to seek international recognition for the existence of a separate state, but by February 1920 they had been defeated.[38] Their goals were implausible and their efforts failed, but they provided a staging ground in Petrograd's backyard for challenges to the Soviet regime.

Arkhangelsk Province was the largest province in European Russia, a third again the area of France, more than twice the size of today's Germany, extending from the Finnish border to the Ural Mountains, with half a million sparsely distributed inhabitants (Riga's total prewar number), 90 percent rural. Its largest city was the White Sea port of Arkhangelsk, population fifty thousand. Murmansk, on the Barents Sea, built in 1915 by Austro-Hungarian prisoners of war and migrant laborers as a conduit for Allied military shipments, was inaugurated in 1916 as Romanov-on-the-Murman-River (Romanov-na-Murmane) but renamed in 1917, by which time its population had reached fifteen thousand. The north had not experienced serfdom and lacked a landed gentry; the main economic activity was foreign trade, so the local elite consisted mainly of merchants. Importing most of its grain, the area depended for income on the export of timber, flax, hemp, and fish. When the war interrupted the railways, food shortages set in, and grain had to be obtained from the Allies.[39]

The February Revolution opened the door to a proliferation of public organizations. Zemstvos, which had not existed in the region, were established in summer 1917; cooperatives, trade unions, peasant committees flourished. This happy pluralism resulted, however, in administrative disarray. The war had already disrupted the local economy, and the food supply had collapsed; by mid-1917 people were going hungry.[40] In the absence of manorial agriculture, the Arkhangelsk countryside was relatively calm during

1917, but the cities were unstable. Disturbances arose among the garrison soldiers and the workers brought in to help build Murmansk, who now lived in miserable, degraded conditions. Soldiers here as elsewhere assaulted their officers; they plundered local inhabitants and besieged and ransacked the railroad.[41] Food shortages, rising prices, and plant closings created tensions, but here, as in other provincial places, social polarization did not immediately set in. The local soviet did not recognize exclusive Bolshevik rule, but joined with the City Duma, the trade unions, and the moderate socialist parties to form their own revolutionary committee.[42]

Once again, the armed forces played a decisive role. Arctic Fleet sailors and garrison soldiers provided the main Bolshevik support after October. The Bolsheviks also mobilized workers into Red Guards, which descended into the villages and towns to install Bolshevik power, removing zemstvos and local committees and arresting and despoiling the local "bourgeoisie."[43] The situation was complicated by the offshore presence of Allied warships. In February 1918, the Sovnarkom sent a commission to Arkhangelsk to retrieve the Allied military supplies stored on the docks, but the local soviet refused to cooperate for fear of jeopardizing Allied food delivery.[44]

The Sovnarkom, which as late as spring 1918 was itself contemplating possible deals with the Allied forces, could not tolerate resistance from local soviets. By July Moscow had succeeded in getting the region under control, with the help of the garrison and the fleet sailors. Martial law was imposed, elections to the local soviets were rigged, and voters were intimidated, to produce Bolshevik/Left SR majorities. The Arkhangelsk City Duma was abolished, its members arrested as counterrevolutionaries and hauled off to Moscow for trial. Banks, private trading companies, and merchant vessels were seized. The non-Bolshevik press was shuttered.[45] The Red Guards were particularly active in arresting people they considered bourgeois and seizing their possessions. The Cheka set up a local branch, which began arresting socialists and other leading figures.[46] The local economy suffered when the Bolsheviks nationalized the sawmills and requisitioned fishing vessels.[47] By July 1918, many people were eating no more than two ounces of rough bread a day. Many formerly militant soldiers and sailors had gone south in search of food. As Allied intervention loomed, the Bolsheviks instituted a draft, but the peasants in their village assemblies protested, in some cases offering armed resistance.[48]

On August 2, 1918, an Allied Expeditionary Force, consisting largely of British troops, landed in Arkhangelsk. A group associated with the anti-Bolshevik Union for the Regeneration of Russia, established in Moscow in April, with Allied backing and the collaboration of officers still in Petrograd, easily dislodged the Bolsheviks from Arkhangelsk.[49] The group constituted itself the Supreme Administration of the Northern Region (*Verkhovnoe upravlenie Severnoi oblasti*), under the leadership of the Popular Socialist Nikolai Chaikovskii. Their purpose was not to create a local fiefdom but to use the north as a launching pad for the reconstitution of Russia as a whole.[50]

Chaikovskii was a throwback to a bygone era. He had begun his radical career in the 1870s, when he led a circle of young people like himself eager to arouse a peasant revolution. During a few years spent in the United States, he had established a socialist commune in Kansas, worked in a factory near Philadelphia, and lived for a while with the Shakers. In Russia after the 1905 Revolution, he joined the cooperative movement and was briefly arrested. After February 1917, he was elected to the Petrograd Soviet and later to the Constituent Assembly. In the wake of the Bolshevik coup, he joined the Union for the Regeneration of Russia and in 1919 represented the Northern Region at Versailles. He died in England in 1926, at the age of seventy-five.[51] His life had spanned the entire course of the Russian revolutionary movement.

Ousting the Reds from Arkhangelsk was easily accomplished. The change was welcomed by the soviets and trade unions, which still defended the principle of all-socialist government and continued to vest legitimacy in the Constituent Assembly. These grassroots bodies saw the move as a way to fulfill, not abandon, the original promise of the Revolution. The City Dumas, zemstvos, and public organizations also welcomed the change. In the villages, peasants sometimes arrested the local Bolsheviks and helped drive out the Red Guards. The transition initially involved the recognition of the existing non-Bolshevik soviets, but some were then replaced by zemstvos. Village soviets were simply renamed, red flags removed.[52]

The Supreme Administration had difficulty, however, establishing its authority. When it tried to raise a volunteer army, few recruits appeared; when they, like the Bolsheviks before them, instituted a draft, the peasants did not respond. They were willing to take up arms in defense of their homes, but would go no farther afield. The government nevertheless did manage to assemble about ten thousand men, but as their fortunes waned, the troops melted away. The local leaders were no more able than the Soviet commissars to solve the problem of food. Peasants complained they were eating "straw or bread mixed with moss."[53] Nor did the Supreme Administration appeal to the army officers who had assembled in the region. Objecting to their socialist orientation, however mild, in September officers briefly clapped its ministers in jail and in October compelled them to reconstitute themselves as the Provisional Government of the Northern Region (*Vremennoe pravitel'stvo Severnoi oblasti*).[54]

This government then ordered the arrest of all the commissars and soviet and trade union leaders remaining in the area, confining them to prison or labor camps. Quite a number were sentenced to death; in the camps, many succumbed to the terrible conditions. As they retreated, Red partisans plundered villages for food, livestock, and fodder, shot resisters, and executed people at random. They seized hostages and forced their families to help cart away remaining property and grain, leaving the villages destitute. Hostages were subject to particular brutality. Some peasants joined in the plunder, others armed themselves against the partisans in self-defense. Their vengeance was gruesome—Red prisoners were tortured, decapitated, mutilated, dumped in mass graves, or shoved under the ice, as it was now winter.[55]

Popular anger at the departing Reds did not mean the Government of the Northern Region was welcome. Faced with unrest among Arkhangelsk workers and soldiers, in January 1919 it added Evgenii-Ludwig Miller, a lieutenant-general of Baltic German background, to the cabinet. It was then also that Chaikovskii left for Europe to join anti-Bolshevik circles in emigration.[56] Despite his close ties to the late tsar and his reputation as a loyal monarchist, Miller was valued for his record as an honest and competent officer and his imperial patriotism. He had supported the Provisional Government in the early days, but had almost been murdered by his own men when he ordered them to discard their red armbands and red flags. Thrown to the ground, his head bloodied, he nevertheless had not blamed them—"a pitiful unenlightened folk, who can be incited to anything," he pronounced, in patriarchal fashion. He rather blamed Kerensky for having destroyed the army and the country. Had he not been abroad, he might well have supported General Kornilov. Now he found himself close to the Union of Regeneration.[57]

The northwest region was—like Siberia, though to a lesser extent—a staging ground for military mobilization by anti-Bolshevik officers, such as General Miller, who spearheaded the fragmented but Empire-wide White movement. As we have seen, Generals Alekseev and Kornilov had immediately headed south to rally anti-Bolshevik armies. Admiral Aleksandr Kolchak, another supporter of Kornilov's August adventure, found a foothold in Siberia, where by the end of 1918 he had declared himself the Supreme Ruler of Russia. In May 1919, Kolchak designated Miller commander in chief of

White forces in the north. In the absence of competent civilian leaders, the general concentrated both civil and military authority in his own hands.[58]

The principal figure in the northwest, the cause of greatest concern to the Soviet government, and the most closely tied to the fate of the Baltic nations was not, however, General Miller but General Nikolai Iudenich.[59] One of the more successful commanders during the Great War, Iudenich won victories over the Ottomans at Sarıkamış and in Eastern Anatolia. In February 1917, he was commander of the Caucasian Front, but in August he favored Kornilov. After a period of inactivity, in October 1918 Iudenich formed an army in Pskov, just east of the Estonian border. The so-called Russian Northern Corps (*Russkii severnyi korpus*) attracted the support of the German occupiers and also of reactionary figures still remaining in Petrograd. This nexus remains unclear, but it is certain that Iudenich then and later associated himself with the most virulent representatives of the restorationist pre-1917 political right, in particular Nikolai Markov II. A founder of the rabidly anti-Semitic Union of the Russian People and a deputy to the Third and Fourth Dumas, where he was notorious for his intemperate language, Markov was also a member of the Brotherhood of the White Cross of Great Indivisible Russia (*Bratstvo Belogo kresta Velikoi edinoi Rossii*). Markov later ran Iudenich's newspaper, *Belyi krest* (*White Cross*), in the same spirit.[60]

In the wake of the German withdrawal, White leaders began to contemplate opening a Petrograd front, expecting, quite irrationally, to receive support from the aspiring Baltic nations, whose independence they opposed.[61] Iudenich's Northern Corps was powerless, however, to stop the Red Army from taking Narva in November 1918.[62] What remained of the Corps moved west across the Narva River into Estonia, where in December it accepted Estonian command, but the Estonian population proved unwilling to fight for the Russian cause and recruiting failed. The Northern Corps was bested by the Red Army on its way to take Riga on January 3, 1919.[63]

The Reds had taken Pskov on November 25, 1918, and it was not until May 25, 1919, that Estonian troops managed to take it back. As the Reds hastened to leave, recalled Vladimir Gorn, a member of the Pskov City Duma, "the mood of the local citizens revealed certain less than appealing tendencies. Reactionary elements raised their heads and the merchants began to speak of resurrecting the Duma, not the Duma of the Provisional Government, but the 'tsarist' Duma." The Estonians, for their part, now thought of themselves as a democratic country, but their first proclamation

caused the Black Hundreds to rejoice and the Jews to tremble. "The glorious Estonian forces," the commander declared, "have cleared the city of the
Yids and the Communists." When a delegation from the City Duma
objected that his words were calculated to stir up agitation and encourage
pogroms, the commander claimed they had been poorly translated from the
Estonian; he had meant instead to celebrate the liberation of Pskov from the
"Yid-Communists." When the delegates noted that this formulation was
also unlikely to calm the waters, the officer produced a decree warning that
pogroms would be severely punished. Pogrom agitation was indeed nipped
in the bud, to the dismay of the local Black Hundreds.[64] The question of
official responsibility for anti-Jewish pogroms was to be a persistent theme
throughout the Civil War.

The Estonians proved to be civilized, as Gorn put it, and the brief
Estonian interlude was relatively calm. The citizens of Pskov anticipated
their departure with anxiety.[65] The appearance, on May 29, of Lieutenant
Colonel Stanisław Bułak-Bałachowicz, at the head of an unimpressive array
of mounted and foot soldiers, was, however, greeted effusively by the population, who welcomed him as one of their own, a Russian. A native of the
Vilna region, Bułak-Bałachowicz had volunteered for the Imperial Army in
1914. In February 1918, at the head of his own cavalry division, he had
joined the Red Army, but in November had attached himself to General
Iudenich.[66] Addressing the crowd in Pskov's main square, he announced he
was fighting the Bolsheviks "not for tsarist Russia or for the landlords' Russia,
but for the new Constituent Assembly." He pledged "to hang every last
Communist and murderer," and proceeded to fulfill his promise.[67]

Gorn recalled the first time he witnessed the procedure. "High above
the heads of a gaping crowd the corpse of a partly undressed man was
swaying from a lamppost." At first people were frozen in horror, but they
soon grew accustomed to the sight of people hanging from lampposts
along the streets, sometimes grouped together in clusters, "like garlands."
People gathered at appointed hours to watch the executions. Bułak-
Bałachowicz would appear on a white horse, threatening anyone who
dared protest. Later, the hangings were performed at a marketplace outside
the old city wall, in a populous neighborhood, on the spot where earlier
the Reds had executed their victims. The spectacles continued to draw a
public.[68] The victims included petty criminals and Red Army soldiers; later,
peasants were targeted as a method of extortion, because the more prosperous bought themselves off. Jews were a special object both of extortion and

murder. People denounced each other as Bolsheviks. The Bolsheviks, of course, publicized the horrors as propaganda.[69] General Iudenich attempted to curb the outrages, but Bułak-Bałachowicz refused to be corralled. Three months after the events in Pskov, on August 24, 1919, Iudenich declared him a deserter.

Back in May, while Bułak-Bałachowicz was subduing Pskov, the White army which had retreated back beyond the Narva River into Estonia, now emerged in the direction of Petrograd, led at first by the Estonian general Johan Laidoner, former Imperial Army officer, now commander in chief of the Estonian army. Once the troops crossed into Russia, command was transferred to General Aleksandr Rodzianko (nephew of Mikhail Rodzianko, the former president of the State Duma), and only later to Iudenich. Thinking Petrograd was in danger, the Sovnarkom mobilized for the defense of the city. In fact, the objective of the small, ill-equipped army was not to besiege the capital but to establish a foothold in the Russian-inhabited region east of the Estonian border, an area of six thousand square miles.[70]

On July 1, 1919, the Northern Corps was renamed the Northwest Army (*Severno-zapadnaia armiia*), but neither the Finns nor the Estonians wanted anything to do with it. The resurrection of the tsarist anthem did not win friends. By August the Northwest Army was having trouble paying its men; whole units were deserting to the Reds, just as earlier some units had gone the other way. By the end of the month, the Estonians had withdrawn their support and Iudenich lost Pskov, his last foothold in Russia. The Red Army took the city and thousands of refugees headed into Estonia, where they were not welcome.[71]

The British now pressured Iudenich to recognize the independence of the Baltic states. Fearing the Estonians were about to make a deal with Moscow, he reluctantly offered recognition in return for twenty-five thousand men, thus abandoning the core principle of the White movement—integrity of the Empire. The Estonians refused all conditions and observed that Iudenich was in no position to make an offer of any kind, since he was "not backed by any important political organizations, which have received official recognition by the Allied Governments."[72] After further useless complications involving the British, the Estonians and Russians began negotiations in September 1919.[73]

On October 10, 1919, Iudenich embarked on his final military operation. Starting in Narva, he moved toward Petrograd, and a week later his troops were twenty miles from the center of the city. On October 15, the party declared, "Petrograd will not surrender!" and organized the hasty construction of defenses, enlisting the civilian population of both sexes.[74] Focused on the struggle in the south, the Red Army was not in a strong position to push back. The troops available in the northwest were in poor shape, and the chief of staff of the Seventh Red Army was an actual (not imagined) traitor, who communicated its battle plans to Iudenich.[75]

And then, on October 17, Trotsky, the commissar of war, arrived on the special train created for him in August 1918, on which he made the rounds of the active fronts. Heavily armed and guarded (partly by the Latvian Riflemen), equipped with automobiles, a printing press, a generator, telegraph, and radio, the train served as a mobile propaganda platform for rallying the troops.[76] Not only did Trotsky's arrival make an impression, he also doubled the army rations and mobilized the civilian population. The White forces were outmanned and outgunned. They were soon backed up against the Estonian border, where the Estonians disarmed them. Iudenich resigned in November; on January 22, 1920, he disbanded the Northwest Army. Five days later, he was arrested by the same Bułak-Bałachowicz he had dismissed for insubordination and brutality in August. Bułak-Bałachowicz now attempted to deliver the general to the Reds, but Iudenich was rescued by Estonian troops, who handed him to the British instead.[77]

What was left of the Northern Government at the beginning of 1920 tried unsuccessfully to conclude a military agreement with Finland, asserting the existence of the North as an independent nation. Instead, a Red Army offensive forced the government to evacuate Arkhangelsk, ending the illusion of anti-Bolshevik local politics. The Communists then proceeded to execute hundreds of residents of Arkhangelsk; many others were sent to labor camps.[78] General Miller was among the eight hundred officers and civilians who escaped from Arkhangelsk aboard the icebreaker *Kozma Minin* (named after the patriotic Russian merchant celebrated for resisting the Polish invasion of 1612) and finally made his way to Paris. There in 1938 he was seized by Soviet agents, taken to Moscow, and, in 1939, shot.[79]

# 5

# Ukrainian Drama, Act I

Finland, the Baltic states, and Poland were all recognized as discrete parts of the Empire and granted special privileges, to one degree or another. Their special status, which could of course at any time be revoked, encouraged their political classes to develop a sense of nationhood. By contrast, there was no single Ukrainian province in the Empire. There had never been a politically defined Ukrainian state. Situated between Catholic Poland and Orthodox Russia, nine imperial provinces were inhabited by a largely peasant population speaking a Slavic language related to but different from both Polish and Russian.[1]

Even contemporaries disagreed on what to call the region and its inhabitants. As the historian Alexei Miller puts it, "In the nineteenth century the territory of modern Ukraine was made into the object of a real terminological war."[2] The predominantly agricultural area west of the Dnepr River (known as Right Bank Ukraine, with respect to the southward-flowing Dnepr River, or Southwestern Ukraine, from the perspective of the center), had been part of the Polish-Lithuanian Commonwealth until the partitions and continued to be dominated by Polish and German elites. Left Bank, or Eastern, Ukraine, by contrast, extended all the way to the Sea of Azov in the interior. The original Cossack homeland, it had joined the Muscovite lands in the seventeenth century and now included the region's industrial centers.[3] Like the Poles, Ukrainian-speakers were found on both sides of the Russian-Austrian border. Together with the provinces of the Polish Kingdom and Lithuania, the Ukrainian lands were home to the Empire's largest concentration of Jews, most of whom were confined by law to residence in the so-called Pale of Settlement. The Ukrainian provinces were essential to the imperial economy, which depended on them heavily for the production of wheat, rye, and sugar, as well as coal and iron. In 1914 the Ukraine alone had produced over three-quarters of the Empire's grain exports.[4] Odessa, on the

Black Sea, with 670,000 inhabitants in 1914, was the region's largest city; Kiev, on the Dnepr, more or less in the geographic center, with a population of over 600,000, functioned as the capital.[5]

The Cossacks were central figures in the Ukrainian drama and crucial as well to the fate of the White movements based in the Don and Kuban regions. The name "Cossack" first appears in the fifteenth century to designate nomadic warrior bands inhabiting the southern steppe. Of mixed Tatar and Slavic origin, by the sixteenth century they had entered the Orthodox fold and spoke a Slavic language. By then they had formed stable communities centered along the Dnepr and Don rivers and had established service relationships with both the Muscovite princes and the kings of the Polish-Lithuanian Commonwealth. Their settlements (*stanitsa*, sg.) clustered in larger hosts (*voisko*, sg.), centered along the major central waterways—the lower Dnepr, Don, Terek, Kuban, and Ural Rivers.[6]

In the seventeenth and eighteenth centuries, as the Russian rulers consolidated and expanded their power, a handful of charismatic leaders emerged to lead the Cossacks in revolt against the authority of the increasingly powerful state. The last of these revolts was the fierce Pugachev Rebellion of the 1770s under Catherine the Great, who crushed the rebels by force of arms. In its wake, the Cossack hosts were reorganized and their elites bound more closely to the state, which continued to use the cavalrymen to police the frontiers. They became a "military-service estate."[7] Beginning with the wars against Napoleon, the Cossack cavalry became an integral part of the Imperial Army. Indeed, its role in the Napoleonic wars initiated the myth of the bond between tsar and Cossack, which in fact was not very old. Cossacks were used not only on the battlefield but also to pacify domestic unrest, as in the aftermath of the 1905 Revolution. The lawless free men of the periphery had become the enforcers of empire.[8]

The ambivalent position occupied by the Cossacks, as integral to imperial power but also symbols of the frontier that resisted its control, applied to some extent to the Ukraine as a whole. Kiev and the surrounding lands had played a crucial role in the early formation of the Muscovite state, and their subsequent fates were closely intertwined. The idea that Ukraine constituted the core of a separate nation emerged only in the nineteenth century. Until 1905, however, few advocates of this idea understood Ukrainian cultural identity as the basis for political independence. Most continued to see Ukraine as an inextricable part of the greater Russian-Slavic-Orthodox imperial domain.[9] In 1914 Russia occupied Eastern Galicia, thus de facto temporarily uniting the two parts of the future Ukrainian nation imagined by its proponents, but at the same time the authorities prohibited any expression of Ukrainian national identity. In 1915, when Russian forces were forced to abandon Galicia and much of the western region, Ukrainians who remained loyal to the Empire went with them, while those favoring separation stayed behind.[10]

The conflicts that emerged on the territory of today's independent Ukraine (with somewhat different borders) are what in fact created the basis for the later emergence of a politically defined nation. But, as in every other part of the former Romanov Empire, contending native forces fought among themselves for control over territory and resources, attempted to create institutions through which power could be exercised, and struggled to engage popular support and control popular unrest. The battle for the Ukrainian lands, economically and strategically crucial to the survival of any Russian-centered state, was a key element in the unfolding Civil War.

To simplify the picture in relation to the Ukrainian case, one can identify three distinct but interrelated arenas of conflict. The first involved the attempt by the Soviet government in Moscow to assert control over Ukrainian territory. This attempt involved not only the campaign to defeat the Ukrainian nationalist movement but also efforts by the central party leadership to discipline its own operatives in the region. The second conflict unfolded among the various politically and geographically disparate groups aspiring to define and lead an emergent Ukrainian nation. The third arena of conflict involved the vast mass of peasants and the soldiers attached to the numerous armies and armed bands that engaged in chronic insurgency, a continuing rebellion that both animated and threatened the political projects of all contenders for power.

Observers and historians have used the words "kaleidoscopic" or "cinematographic" to describe the succession of claimants that set themselves up, knocked each other down, and tormented, by their instability as well as ruthlessness, the civilian population between 1918 and 1921. Even before the Treaty of Brest-Litovsk, the situation in the Ukrainian lands was extraordinarily confused and complex. Up to a point, the revolution in the south echoed events in the core. In February 1917, officials in Kiev declared their support for the Provisional Government, while hundreds of soviets were formed throughout the region.[11] In greeting the new government in Petrograd, the newly formed Central Rada urged it to reaffirm the principle of national autonomy in the context of a "free federation of free peoples."[12] In mid-March, a hundred thousand demonstrators gathered in Kiev and another twenty-five to thirty thousand in Petrograd, waving blue and yellow flags in support of a Ukrainian nation. Many educated people "suddenly felt themselves to be Ukrainian," as Ukrainian philosopher Miroslav Popovich puts it.[13]

Indeed, over the course of 1917, the Rada functioned as the de facto parliament of a de facto nation-within-a-state (the former Russian Empire, now Russian Republic) calling itself Ukraine. At this point, the Rada did not aspire to national independence but to autonomy within a greater federation. It sponsored a Ukrainian National Congress (*Ukraïn'skyi natsional'nyi kongres*) in Kiev in April, which affirmed these goals but left the final determination to the anticipated All-Russian Constituent Assembly. The mere existence of the Rada and the Congress, however, signaled the emergence of separate institutions claiming to represent national interests and disseminating the national orientation among ever broader segments of the population. Invoking the slogan of national self-determination, the Congress demanded the right of "the Ukrainian people" to send delegates to any future peace conference, while announcing its disagreement with Poland's competing territorial claims.[14]

The Provisional Government in Petrograd hesitated, as we have noted, to address any of the thorny questions of national identity and the relationship of nationally or ethnically identified regions to the former imperial center. It reminded the Rada that it was not an elected body and therefore its claims to popular representation were unconvincing (of course the Provisional Government had not been elected, either). Resolution of the questions of self-government and national borders must await the Constituent Assembly, Petrograd admonished, as everyone seemed to agree.[15] Russian liberals reminded the Ukrainians that they were still part of what was considered Russia and that all citizens of Russia must have a voice in determining their fate.[16] The Kadet Party, for one, continued to reject the Ukrainian claim to independent statehood, refusing to recognize Ukrainian as a separate language, insisting that nationalism was interesting only to a narrow elite, and emphasizing the economic ties binding the region to the center.[17] In terms of the aspiring Ukrainian leadership, however, the national platform provided a focus around which the disparate elements in Ukrainian political life, roused to action by the February Revolution, were able to cohere. The Provisional Government's refusal to recognize their act of self-representation simply magnified the effect. Self-organization, if not formal autonomy, proceeded apace, and attempts were made to propagate the message. An All-Ukrainian Peasant Congress and the Second Ukrainian Military Congress met in early June. An earlier congress in May had created a Ukrainian General Military Commissariat headed by the Social Democrat Symon

Petliura, whom we have encountered among the delegates to the Constituent Assembly.[18]

Petliura went on to play a key role in the Civil War saga. Born in Poltava, about ninety miles west of Kharkov, five months before Trotsky, to an urban family of Cossack origin, he began his education in a seminary, but soon became involved in underground revolutionary activity, for which he was arrested in 1903. In 1909, then in Moscow, he worked as an accountant and soon began writing for Ukrainian-oriented journals. During the war, back in Ukraine he worked for the Zemstvo Union and professed loyalty to the imperial Russian cause, in hopes of Ukraine achieving national rights within the Empire at its conclusion.[19]

Despite such professions, Kerensky condemned the June Military Congress, as did the Petrograd Soviet, in the interests of national unity in wartime. Only Lenin, in the Bolshevik newspaper *Pravda*, defended the rights of what he called "oppressed nationalities."[20] Frustrated by Petrograd's response, on June 10, as noted, the Central Rada therefore issued its First Universal. In the name of all the inhabitants of the Ukrainian lands, the Rada declared itself the elected head of an autonomous nation, within the boundaries of the still emerging post-revolutionary Russian state. "Without separating from all of Russia, without breaking away from the Russian State, let the Ukrainian people on their own territory have the right to manage their own life."[21] The Provisional Government accused the Rada of undermining the war effort, and the Kadets accused it of abetting "the German plan to dismember Russia."[22] The Petrograd Soviet declared its commitment to "the indivisibility of the State."[23]

The Rada, undeterred, on June 15 created a cabinet, called the General Secretariat, to serve as the Rada's executive organ. It was headed by Volodymyr Vynnychenko, a leader of the Ukrainian Social Democrats who had been a delegate, along with Petliura, to the Constituent Assembly.[24] A year younger than Petliura, Vynnychenko was a writer and historian of peasant origin who had begun to study law in Kiev in 1900, but had then become involved in revolutionary activity and in 1905 helped found the Ukrainian Social Democratic Party.[25] Petliura, for his part, became the Rada's secretary of war, though he had no military experience. The Social Democratic leaders of the Rada lacked a working-class base. They have been described by a friendly commentator as belonging to the "nationally oriented intelligentsia, using social slogans to achieve national goals."[26] Their nationalism was not exclusive, however. The Rada recognized four official languages for Ukraine—Ukrainian, Russian, Polish, and Yiddish—and declared Ukraine to be "a common home for all the peoples living on its territory."[27]

In the face of the Rada's persistence, the First All-Russian Congress of Soviets, dominated by Mensheviks and SRs, which met in Petrograd in June, finally voted to support the principle of Ukrainian autonomy.[28] The Provisional Government then bowed to the inevitable and in mid-July recognized the Rada and also permitted the formation of exclusively Ukrainian units in the Russian army.[29] When three hundred thousand Ukrainian-speaking soldiers swore allegiance to the Central Rada, they replicated the situation already created by Order No. 1, which allowed the Petrograd Soviet to dictate conditions of loyalty to the post-imperial military command. Like the Soviet, the Rada became the focus of soldier loyalty.[30] The concession to the Ukraine, as we have seen, precipitated the collapse of the coalition government when three Kadet ministers resigned on July 2.[31] The next day, the Rada's Second Universal confirmed the status of its executive organ, the General Secretariat.[32]

The Rada did not, however, go so far as to declare independence. It adhered to the formula of autonomy, pending final arbitration by the Ukrainian and All-Russian Constituent Assemblies, though its moderation provoked opposition among the more impatient Ukrainian parties.[33] Two weeks after the Second Universal, the Rada presented the Provisional Government with a draft constitution, describing the organs and functions of the ad hoc Ukrainian government.[34] Squaring the circle, the Ukrainians asserted their right to self-rule, while appealing to the higher all-Russian authority for permission.

Both the Rada and the Provisional Government were devoted to the revolution; both defined themselves as temporary expedients pending the Constituent Assembly. The Petrograd cabinet replied to the Rada's claims in the form of Temporary Instructions, objecting to the assertion of autonomy but nevertheless endorsing—and defining—the functions of the General Secretariat as an organ of local self-government.[35] Like the Ukrainians, they were eating their cake and having it, too. Adding to the constitutional confusion, the State Senate, the Empire's supreme court, which was still in operation, rejected the Provisional Government's instructions as exceeding its own legitimate authority.[36] The Rada, for its part, also rejected the Provisional Government's authority to regulate Ukrainian affairs.[37] On Vynnychenko's urging, however, the Rada nevertheless approved the Instructions on August 9, but relations with the Provisional Government were further strained by Kerensky's aggressive remarks at the State Conference in Moscow, three days later.[38]

Despite the friction with Petrograd, the Rada continued to operate as the de facto government, or at least administration, of the Ukrainian provinces, resisting but recognizing the Provisional Government, under the assumption that its final status would be confirmed by the Constituent Assembly. The Rada actually wielded limited authority. It did not create its own institutions, possessing neither an army nor a bureaucracy loyal to itself. The peasants, for their part, were busy helping themselves to land, while the SRs were busy protesting the absence of land reform. If the Provisional Government could not control the Rada, the Rada could not control the various local self-defense squads and soviets that simply ignored its existence. Soon the context would change radically. The Rada's final delegation to the Provisional Government in Petrograd left Kiev on October 22. Given the events in the capital, the emissaries turned around and went home.[39]

The Rada at first supported the Bolshevik coup, which it understood as a deepening of the revolution, but in the same spirit as the Russian-centered socialist parties it continued to put its hopes in the Constituent Assembly. The Ukrainian National Republic inaugurated by the Rada's Third Universal on November 7, 1917, was still conceived as an autonomous part of a future democratic federation, to be defined and authorized by the forthcoming Constituent Assembly. Its platform combined socialist with liberal principles: the abolition of private property in land and state control of industry, on the one hand; rule of law, local self-government, civil liberties, and "national-personal autonomy" for ethnic minorities, on the other. It affirmed its support for the war, but hoped for a peace negotiated by both sides to the conflict and respecting the rights of the Ukrainian nation.[40] Even among the various Ukrainian political parties, some rejected the assertion of national independence—as legally meaningless, as harmful to the revolution.[41]

The Bolsheviks in Petrograd were of course not about to await the verdict of the Constituent Assembly, for which they had no use in any case. Like everyone else, they had proclaimed their adherence to the principle of national self-determination—indeed, this was one of their calling cards. The problem with the Rada was not simply that it wanted to leave the mother ship, but that the Bolsheviks did not control it. On December 4, therefore, the Sovnarkom issued an ultimatum to the Central Rada, accusing it of jeopardizing the revolution. The General Secretariat had recalled Ukrainian units from the front, the commissars complained, blocked the export of food, and informed the Entente of its desire to negotiate an armistice; it had prevented Soviet troops from crossing Ukrainian territory en route to the

Don, where tsarist generals were assembling anti-Bolshevik Cossack forces. The Sovnarkom gave the Rada forty-eight hours to stop "disorganizing the front" and abetting the forces of counterrevolution.[42]

Having endorsed the principle of national self-determination, the Rada expostulated, the Bolsheviks were in no position to instruct the Ukraine on its rights.[43] "Great Russia is more and more becoming the prey of anarchy and economic and political disruption, while the most arbitrary rule and the abuse of all liberties gained by the revolution.... reign supreme in your land," Vynnychenko and Petliura admonished the Russians. "The General Secretariat does not wish to repeat that sad experiment in the Ukraine."[44] Lenin denounced Ukrainian-identified Social Democracy as a "bourgeois" deviation, while Ukrainian Social Democrats accused him of using proletarian internationalism as a cover for Russian neo-imperialism.[45]

In 1917, most Bolsheviks active in the Ukraine were ethnic Russians or Russian-speaking Jews, who focused on the urban proletariat and ignored the Ukrainian issue. An attempted Bolshevik coup in Kiev on November 29, was foiled by Ukrainian troops.[46] The Bolsheviks sought a foothold instead in the local Ukrainian soviets, but even there they were not sure of calling the shots. Anticipating the opening of the All-Ukrainian Congress of Soviets which they themselves had scheduled for December 4, Bolshevik activists from a number of Ukrainian cities gathered in Kiev. They were unable even to agree, however, on what to call themselves. They needed to distinguish themselves from the Petrograd Bolsheviks, but also from the Ukrainian-identified Rada socialists. Some comrades denounced nationalism across the board; others insisted it be appropriated for the benefit of the revolution.[47]

In order to succeed in the Ukrainian situation, local Bolsheviks had to triumph over their competitors on the left, all of whom rejected the domination of Moscow, but in order to counter their appeal, the Kiev Bolsheviks had themselves to resist Lenin's fierce determination to subordinate everything—including his own party—to the center. The Kiev comrades were angry, for example, when they learned of a Sovnarkom threat to send troops against the Rada unless it ceased allowing anti-Bolshevik troops to cross over into the Don. They warned that Lenin was thereby provoking armed conflict between Russia and Ukraine.[48] Lenin, of course, did not think he would be entering a foreign country, but merely bringing a disruptive province into line.

When the First All-Ukrainian Congress of Soviets opened, the Bolshevik and Left SR delegates were in a minority. The industrial centers had not participated, and the Congress ended by endorsing the Central Rada. Unable to control the proceedings, the Bolshevik delegates left for Kharkov, where the regional Congress of Soviets of the Donets–Krivoi Rog (Kryvyi Rih) mining region was then meeting.[49] Once in Kharkov, the Kiev Bolsheviks hijacked the local Congress for their own purposes, renaming it the First All-Ukrainian Congress of Soviets—the name of the Kiev congress they had just walked out on, thus usurping their rivals' claim to represent the region. The replication also makes it harder for historians to follow the already confused sequence of events and the continuous creation of new organizations. On December 14, the rebaptized Kharkov congress announced the formation of a Ukrainian People's (National) Republic, with a People's (National) Secretariat as its executive organ, thus appropriating the terms used by the Rada.[50] Characteristically, the Bolsheviks accompanied their devious move with an outpouring of invective, accusing the Rada of using "the cover of national self-determination [to] promote the interests of the capitalists and bureaucrats, Ukrainian as well as Russian, whose downfall and destruction the workers' and peasants' revolution will accomplish once and for all."[51]

The Kharkov People's Republic and People's Secretariat had no roots in the local population, no army, and no internal coherence. Its own members disagreed on its proper relationship to Moscow. In short, the first putative Soviet government of Ukraine did not really exist.[52] Contradicting Moscow's own rejection of Ukrainian independence, the Kharkov government nevertheless sent delegates to Brest to challenge the Rada's right to represent the Ukrainian nation.[53] When the Central Powers refused to recognize their mandate, they attached themselves to the Soviet Russian delegation, escaping the awkward position of seeming to have endorsed nationalist separatism, but failing to resolve the problem of how to speak for Ukraine.[54] Not all contradictions were resolved, moreover, since the Bolsheviks continued to promote the idea of national self-determination while opposing the steps taken by Ukrainians in that very direction.

The Rada, for its part, continued to claim its right to a seat at the bargaining table. Its Fourth Universal, issued on January 12, 1918 (backdated January 9), asserted the Ukrainian National Republic's complete independence from Soviet Russia. At the same time, the Rada affirmed its commitment to the basic principles of the revolution: an end to private property in land, state control of key elements of the economy, democratic civil liberties, and resistance to the counterrevolution. Despite the claim to independence, however, the Rada still hesitated to define its future relationship to the states emerging from under the umbrella of empire. It postponed the final determination of Ukraine's status to a future Ukrainian Constituent Assembly, which was expected also to legitimate the existence of the Rada's own self-proclaimed regime.[55] The Rada could no longer appeal to the arbitration of the all-Russian Constituent Assembly, to which both Petliura and Vynnychenko had been elected, but which had been shut down by the Bolsheviks in Petrograd a week before.

Meanwhile, the Bolsheviks who remained in Kiev attempted to unseat the Rada by organizing a revolt, principally involving railroad workers, in the course of which they took control of the Arsenal munitions plant. This episode became the subject of Alexander Dovzhenko's 1928 film *Arsenal*. Sailors, students, and officers came to the Rada's defense and successfully resisted the Bolshevik insurgents, who were finally stopped when forces organized by Petliura stormed the city on January 22. Three days later, Lieutenant Colonel Mikhail Murav'ev, at the head of an assemblage of Red Guards imported for the occasion, drove Petliura out.[56] The Rada retreated to Zhitomir (Zhytomyr). A former tsarist officer, though of peasant origin, Murav'ev had been wounded in both the Russo-Japanese War and the Great War. In 1917 he at first supported Kerensky, but after the Kornilov fiasco turned his sympathies to the Left SRs. When the Bolsheviks took over, he helped instigate the murder of General Dukhonin and led the fight against Kerensky and Krasnov.[57]

What became known as "the first Soviet conquest of the Ukraine" was achieved without much resistance. The Ukrainian soldiers who had pledged allegiance to the Rada in summer 1917, while still part of the Imperial Army, were now back in their villages. Petliura had poorly trained men at his disposal, mostly the so-called Free Cossacks (*Vilne kozatstvo*), some of whom found the Bolshevik appeal more attractive and changed sides.[58] In abandoning the city, Petliura's followers not surprisingly had executed as many of the renegades they could get their hands on.[59] Once in possession of Kiev, Colonel Murav'ev introduced his own reign of terror. He gave orders for "all officers and Junkers, Haidamaks, monarchists, and all enemies of the revolution to be ruthlessly destroyed."[60] The Haidamaks (Gaidamaki) were Ukrainian paramilitary bands which had formed on the Austrian side and entered Russian territory together with the Central Powers. They took their name from the eighteenth-century paramilitary units composed of Cossacks and peasants which had staged three revolts against Polish domination and were also known for attacks against the Jews.[61]

Murav'ev was extreme, but his excesses conformed to a recognizable pattern. He began exactly the way the Germans had begun in Kalisz in 1914, by shelling the town from outlying positions. In Kiev, the artillery attack lasted for eleven days and destroyed or damaged a good portion of the city's buildings. The bombardment was followed by a murderous rampage, in the course of which Murav'ev's troops executed as many as five thousand people, at least half of them Russian Imperial Army officers.[62] The soldiers went door to door, dragging men in uniform from their apartments, shooting them point-blank and leaving their naked corpses lying in the snow. Military physicians and "bourgeois" citizens also fell victim to their ferocity.[63] The Rada had required the many officers pouring in from the southwest and Romanian fronts to obtain residence permits. These, ironically red-colored, identity cards became tickets to death when the Bolsheviks made the rounds.[64] It is unlikely that the perpetrators acted from clear political motives, but their targets conformed to the categories Murav'ev supplied— militant Ukrainians, but more important, Russian Imperial Army officers.[65]

A week after signing the peace with the Central Powers, the Rada appealed to the Germans to help them rid Kiev of the Bolshevik occupiers.[66] On February 23, the Rada announced that "the friendly powers, Germany and Austria-Hungary" were "coming to the Ukraine to suppress disorder and anarchy and to establish peace and order."[67] On March 2, Petliura appeared in town with an unimpressive armed cohort, followed immediately by the arrival of German troops, which debarked at the train station.[68] Murav'ev's reign had ended. The treaty finally signed at Brest-Litovsk the following day compelled the Bolsheviks to recognize the independence of the Ukrainian National Republic and accept German occupation of a vast expanse of former imperial land. The local pro-Bolshevik centers fell one by one to German forces. On March 13 the Germans captured Odessa; Soviet Kharkov fell on April 8. Continuing east and south, on May 8 they arrived at Rostov at the mouth of the Don.[69]

The treaty with the Rada, which had been expelled from its own capital by Murav'ev at the moment it was being signed, was intended to provide the Central Powers with access to grain and other resources in exchange for military support. Indeed, the document reads more like a commercial contract than a peace treaty, regulating prices, tariffs, railroads, currency, and customs.[70] The Rada had abolished private property in land, though without endorsing the peasant seizures already transforming the countryside.

The Germans now imposed martial law, assumed control of the railroads, restored private land ownership, and tried more energetically to extract the grain the Rada had failed to wrest from the peasants.[71]

The Rada was doing a poor job of delivering on its promises. General Hoffmann assessed the situation with his usual dry-eyed realism, noting in his diary for March 12, 1918: "The difficulty in the Ukraine is simply that the Central Rada has only our rifles behind it. The moment we withdraw our troops their authority will collapse at once. The cause of this is the land problem. On the land question the more moderate Social Democrats, who compose the Rada, are just as idiotic as the Bolsheviks—*i.e.* they also have confiscated the landed estates and given them to the peasants. Consequently the agricultural industry in the Ukraine is ruined."[72]

The Germans recognized the Rada's impotence, but also their own tenuous position. "Our policy is to walk on eggshells around the Ukrainian government, which has not earned this name and has no roots in the people," wrote Chief of Staff General Wilhelm Gröner to General Ludendorff. "The attitude of the population is generally against us. In favor of us are the large landholders and capitalists, if we help them to recover their property. Otherwise they too will be against us."[73] At the end of March, Gröner received a new commander, General Field Marshal Hermann von Eichhorn. Eichhorn ordered the army to compel the peasants, on pain of death, to sow their fields—a method of obvious futility.[74] In late April, the German ambassador in Kiev, Philipp Freiherr Mumm von Schwarzenstein, expressed his impatience with their supposed partner: "The Ukrainian government must not hinder the military and economic undertakings of the German authorities."[75]

The Rada's failure to play its assigned role reflected the weakness that had driven it into German hands to begin with. On April 29, 1918, the Ukrainian Union of Landowners, with German backing, installed a new government, headed by the Russian-speaking former Imperial Army officer Pavlo Skoropads'kyi, who was anointed hetman of the Ukraine.[76] The Rada, back in Kiev, responded by quickly adopting a constitution and naming the historian Mykhailo Hrushevs'kyi president of the Ukrainian National Republic—a merely symbolic gesture.[77] Born in the spa town of Wiesbaden, Germany, the son of a Russian Imperial Army officer, Skoropads'kyi owned land in Chernigov and Poltava provinces, which is to say, Left Bank Ukraine. He fought as a cavalry commander in both the Russo-Japanese War and the Great War, achieving the rank of lieutenant general in 1916. While aide-de-camp in Nicholas's suite, his political sympathies inclined toward the

Octobrist Party. After October 1917, he transferred to the army of the Ukrainian National Republic.[78] Skoropads'kyi was married to the daughter of Petr Durnovo, minister of the interior during the final phase of the 1905 Revolution.[79] It was Durnovo, in his memorandum of February 1914, who had warned against shifting from a pro-German to a pro-British orientation and correctly predicted the dangerous consequences of embarking on war. Skoropads'kyi's father was a distant collateral relation of the early eighteenth-century Cossack leader Hetman Ivan Skoropads'kyi, who succeeded the notorious Ivan Mazepa after the latter defected to the Poles in 1708. (Mazepa's story is the subject of an opera by Petr Tchaikovsky.) In July 1917, Pavlo received command of the First Ukrainian Corps. In October 1917, he was awarded the resurrected title of hetman (the Polish equivalent, usually used in English, for Ukrainian *otaman* and Russian *ataman*) by the First Congress of Free Cossacks meeting in the old capital of the original Cossack Hetmanate founded by Bohdan Khmel'nyts'kyi in the mid-seventeenth century.[80]

In 1917 the Rada had disliked the Free Cossacks, all the more so when they chose Skoropads'kyi—a former Imperial Army officer—to incarnate the archaic figure of hetman. By January 1918, however, the situation had changed. Now the Free Cossacks were alone in volunteering for the Rada's independent army; about 15,000 of them formed the core of Petliura's entire outfit, the puny contingent which had occupied Kiev after Murav'ev's bloody reign and before the German arrival.[81] The Free Cossacks ended up following Petliura in the name of freedom, but the Rada itself existed only at the sufferance of the occupying power. In contrast to his Russophile ancestor, Pavlo Skoropads'kyi followed Mazepa's example, as well as his father-in-law's strategic advice, in siding with the enemy of Russia. Skoropads'kyi was not, however, the ideal solution to German problems. The hetman was derided by Ukrainian ethnic-cultural nationalists as a Russian in Cossack clothing. He filled his cabinet with men who did not speak Ukrainian and continued to envision the future Ukraine as part of a greater Russian federation. On the left, the members of the deposed Rada who had remained in Kiev complained to the Germans that he was too Russian; monarchists and Russian nationalists saw him as a German tool and plotted against him.[82]

The German tool in fact did not support his sponsors' primary objective, which was to establish an independent Ukrainian state. In the words of German Secretary of State Richard von Kühlmann: "In Russia we have only one interest, namely promotion of the forces of disintegration, the long-term weakening of that country. . . . Our policy must be the establishment of good relations with the newly formed independent states that are in the process of breaking away from Russia."[83] Or, as Ambassador Mumm less delicately put it, "I consider it necessary to support in the Ukraine the fiction of an independent ally state as long as it serves our interests."[84] Skoropads'kyi's regime had a conservative social agenda. Assuming executive and military authority, he reversed the Rada's generally socialist program—reinstating private property and censorship, banning committees and strikes, and restoring the Cossacks to their erstwhile status as a privileged estate, hoping thereby to win the support of the more prosperous peasants.[85] In some respects, however, he managed more than any another temporary officeholder in the months and years of turmoil to create the rudiments of an actual regime—taking steps to organize an army and creating a Ukrainian-language school system, an Academy of Sciences, and a national library. Eleven countries sent ambassadors to Kiev.[86] All this was shielded by the German occupation.

Skoropads'kyi's patrons, however, magnified both popular and political opposition to his rule. Under his aegis, the Germans sent troops to seize reserves that had been withheld from the market. The peasants naturally resisted.[87] Socialist leaders opposed to the hetman's rule began organizing popular opposition. Thousands of delegates to the Second Ukrainian Peasant Congress convened in Kiev in May to express their hostility to Skoropads'kyi and to the reinstatement of the landed classes. A clandestine SD-led Ukrainian workers' congress demanded the return of the Ukrainian National Republic and of land to the peasants. On the nationalist side, a politically broad-based National State Union (*Ukraïns'kyi Natsional'no-Derzhavnyi Soiuz*) opposed the hetman in the name of Ukrainian independence, demanding he remove the non-Ukrainians from his cabinet.[88] In July, the National State Union, renamed the Ukrainian National Union (*Ukraïns'kyi Natsional'nyi Soiuz*), which included Social Democrats and Right SRs, under the leadership of Vynnychenko and Petliura, became the center of nationalist agitation.[89]

In short, Skoropads'kyi, the self-stylized Ukrainian leader, was having trouble with Ukrainians. At the top of the social scale, nationalist intellectuals refused to cooperate. In the villages, peasants refused to cultivate their fields. In the cities, mostly Russian-speaking and SD-inspired factory workers stopped working. On July 12, Petliura was briefly detained. On July 30, the relationship with the Germans reached a crisis when Field Marshal von Eichhorn, the military governor of Ukraine, was assassinated by a Left SR.[90]

The Germans were facing setbacks in the West as well. On August 8, 1918, the first day of the battle of Amiens, German soldiers surrendered in great numbers. Ludendorff called it "the black day of the German army." In late

September, the general admitted the army was on the verge of collapse. On October 3, Prince Max von Baden replaced Georg von Hertling as chancellor and formed a new government with support from the principal Reichstag parties; the request for an armistice was sent to President Woodrow Wilson the following day. When Wilson did not immediately respond, Ludendorff changed his mind, but Wilhelm withdrew his backing and on October 26 accepted Ludendorff's resignation. Two days later, the Reichstag amended the constitution to give Germany a parliamentary government, but this did not calm the waters. On November 4, thousands of mutinous sailors seized the naval base of Kiel, forming a revolutionary council of soldiers and workers on the Soviet model. It looked as though Lenin's predictions might come true. On November 9, as Berlin exploded in revolution, Wilhelm abdicated as emperor; the Social Democrats declared Germany a republic.

Meanwhile, back in the Ukraine, all parties tried to make the best of the rapidly changing situation. On October 10, while approaching Wilson on the subject of an armistice, the German Foreign Office warned Skoropads'kyi that a general peace would not eliminate the German presence. Still in the role of patron and bully, the Germans advised the hetman to institute the long-needed agrarian reform; they urged him to cooperate with Vynnychenko and Petliura's Ukrainian National Union.[91] A coalition cabinet emerged on October 24, but even then Skoropads'kyi could not overcome the contradictions inherent in his position. Some of his ministers wanted to join a reunited Russia, while others resigned. Vynnychenko now took the lead in organizing the National Union for revolt.[92] Many soldiers defected from the hetman's army.[93]

While Ukrainian leaders were attempting to fashion a coherent leadership, the Germans, with the end in sight, looked ahead to the postwar future. On November 5, the day after the start of the Kiel mutiny, Max von Baden dressed the old Ludendorffian wolf in Wilsonian sheep's clothing: "Our fundamental goal remains, within the framework of the Wilson points and the demands of the Entente, to decentralize Russia with the help of the nationality principle and to create for ourselves in the entire eastern territories as much political sympathy and freedom of movement as possible." On November 6, Germany broke diplomatic relations with Soviet Russia, but resolved to maintain a military presence on occupied lands.[94] Three days later, it was a new Germany.

The Armistice declared on November 11, 1918, annulled the conditions imposed by the separate peace at Brest-Litovsk, ending the German occupation of the Ukraine and opening the door to Ukrainian self-government.

The Ukrainians themselves were not, however, united. On November 1, as the fortunes of the Central Powers waned, nationalists on the Austrian side had announced the creation of a Western Ukrainian National Republic (*Zakhidno-Ukraïns'ka Narodna Respublyka*), with its own fighting force, the Ukrainian Galician Army.[95] On November 13, Vynnychenko, on the Russian side, formed a five-man Directory to replace Skoropads'kyi and the next day demanded his resignation. On December 1, the proto-national elites on both sides of the old imperial border joined in announcing the creation of a single identifiably Ukrainian nation. The Germans, however, did not disappear overnight. It was only on December 12 that they agreed to leave the city, allowing Petliura on December 14, to enter Kiev.[96]

When the Germans pulled out, Skoropads'kyi went with them, leaving his supporters in the lurch. As the fictional Colonel Malyshev puts it in Mikhail Bulgakov's *White Guard*, first published in 1925, "the Hetman shamefully abandoned us all to our fate and ran away! Yes, he ran away, like the most miserable scoundrel and coward!" Disguised as a wounded German officer, "swathed in bandages and wrapped in a greatcoat, [he] was carried out on a stretcher," which took him to a departing German train.[97]

The Directory program, as announced on December 26, 1918, reflected Vynnychenko's socialist leanings: expropriation of land, workers' control, government by councils (soviets). Petliura, as secretary of war, took charge of assembling the units of Sich Riflemen (originally Ukrainian soldiers from Galicia in the Austro-Hungarian army), Cossacks, and peasants into a coherent force. On January 22, 1919, with Kiev in Petliura's hands, Ukrainian independence was proclaimed for a second time.[98] The struggle for the Ukrainian future had, however, just begun. German withdrawal removed the last obstacle to unbridled internal conflict—along national, social, and ideological lines. The rest of 1919 unfurled in a welter of competing and conflicting groups, but a general pattern did emerge. The first step in the emancipation of the peripheries from the center and in the articulation of a political alternative to the October coup involved the moderate forces, caught between authoritarians of right and left, leading ultimately to the moderates' defeat. Eventually, in all cases, the contest resulted in military confrontation, in which the ability to create institutions, commandeer resources, and impose discipline proved decisive. The process ending in Soviet victory produced a ruthless, war-based regime, eliciting powerful resistance that only confirmed its determination to eliminate any alternative to itself.

# 6

# Colonial Repercussions

The pattern of civic mobilization followed by the narrowing of political possibilities and ending in military conquest appeared also in the Caucasus and Central Asia, corners of the Empire seemingly "remote from the main centres of action and from the decisive fronts."[1] In its internal fragmentation, social volatility, and entanglement in the Great Powers' fight for supremacy, the southern tier was nevertheless a microcosm of the revolution. Situated at the intersection of Asia and the Near East, bordering Persia on the south and China on the east, the region constituted the Empire's second front—its interface with the Ottoman Empire, its access to the oil riches of the Caucasus and the agricultural riches of the Central Asian steppe, its portal to the Black Sea. Any government aspiring to control the heart of the old Empire must by definition master the circumference, of both strategic and economic importance all the way around.

The southern region was home to the majority of the Empire's approximately fifteen million Muslim subjects. Three million inhabited Transcaucasia, where they constituted a third of the population, and about seven million the Kazakh Steppe and Central Asia, where they constituted 90 percent. Another 3.5 million lived in so-called European Russia, primarily in the Volga-Urals region. Everywhere, adherents of Islam were divided into many distinct ethnic communities, speaking over a dozen different languages, with no sense of collective identity.[2] In general, the autocracy maintained an antagonistic relationship to its own subjects, fearing political challenges from the privileged elites, on which it nevertheless depended, and defiance from the populace. With respect to the Empire's southern rim, St. Petersburg exercised a direct colonial-style rule. The region of Transcaucasia and the vast expanses of Central Asia were annexed by military conquest over the course of two centuries, in both cases against prolonged resistance from the inhabitants.[3]

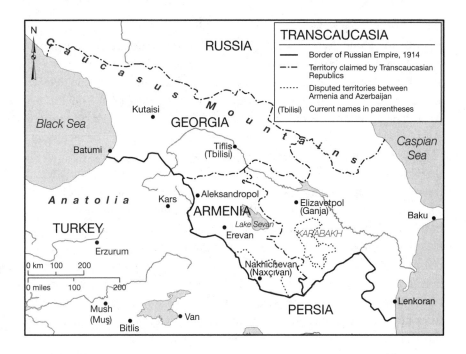

Among the panoply of ethnic groups, distinguished by language, culture, and religion, inhabiting Transcaucasia, the three most important, each claiming a geographic homeland, were the Georgians and Armenians, with their own Christian churches, and the Muslim Azerbaijanis, known at the time as Tatars. Most Georgians lived within imperial Russian borders, but the Armenian population extended into the eastern provinces of Ottoman Anatolia. As a commercial people, Armenians were also present in cities throughout the region. Many Azerbaijanis lived outside Russia as well, in northern Persia. Muslims also inhabited the mountainous North Caucasus, including the regions of Ossetia, Chechnia, and Dagestan. Unlike the predominantly Shiite Azerbaijanis, the mountain peoples (*gortsy*) were largely Sunni.[4]

Russian conquest of the region began, after a war with Persia, with the acquisition of the Caspian port of Baku by Peter the Great in 1824. Georgia, which had earlier been an independent kingdom, was incorporated at the end of the eighteenth century with a promise of autonomy on which the tsars soon reneged. By 1829 the Romanovs had taken Armenia from the Ottomans and dislodged the Azerbaijani khanates. The mountain peoples did not take kindly to Russian rule and remained for decades in a chronic state of insurrection. The most charismatic of the rebel leaders was the Imam Shamil, an ethnic Avar from Dagestan, who led a sustained campaign of guerrilla warfare against Russian forces, ending only with his capture in 1859. The Russian authorities treated Shamil with kid gloves, but demonstrated a ruthless brutality with respect to his followers.[5] The Eastern Anatolian districts of Kars and Ardahan, as well as the Black Sea port of Batumi, were added as a result of the Russo-Turkish War of 1877–1878.

The mountains and their picturesque inhabitants exerted a strong pull on the Russian literary imagination. Pushkin, Lermontov, and Tolstoy were all fascinated by the romance and drama of Russia's exotic south—noble savages, smoky maidens, a place for Russian army officers to prove their manhood. By the twentieth century, the romance had abated and modern life had made itself felt. The Black Sea port of Batumi became a major commercial junction. A Frenchman visiting in the summer of 1920 described its hybrid demeanor: "At the foot of the mountains, where it gently rests, the city of Batum is built on the Russian model. Wide boulevards, colorful one-story houses, onion-shaped church domes...But what is not Russian at all is the tropical vegetation, the palm trees, the aloes along the sidewalks, the cypress, orange trees, bamboo, magnolias." Even in the midst of civil war, when this was written, the port still functioned, "with its great cargoes ready to set out, with its enormous quays piled with goods among which dock hands come and go, with the whistles of the tugboats and the cranes in constant movement."[6] Baku, for its part, was the center of a booming oil industry.

Each of the three principal Transcaucasian peoples, caught between European Russia and Muslim Asia Minor, between deep-seated cultural traditions and the emerging urban world, had its own educated elite and its own political life before 1917. The Armenian Revolutionary Federation (Dashnaktsutiun, known as the Dashnaks), formed in Tiflis in 1890, combined elements of socialism, nationalism, and liberalism. Its goal was to achieve autonomy for the Armenian nation on both sides of the Russo-Ottoman border. Support for the organization spread among respectable Armenian society as a result of increasingly repressive Russian policies toward the century's end.[7] On the Ottoman side, the 1890s were characterized by widespread confrontation between Muslim Kurds and Armenians, with official endorsement or connivance.[8]

The major political tendency in Georgia, by contrast, was not defined in national terms. Although Georgia, like the rest of the region, was predomi-

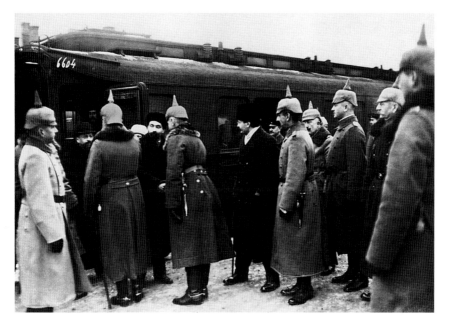

1. Russian delegates arrive in Brest-Litovsk, January 1918. Trotsky center in profile, Lev Kamenev between the German generals, Adolf Ioffe on the left. Getty Images.

2. Leon Trotsky as Commissar of War. Getty Images.

**3.** G. Gasenka, "The Whole World in Ukraine!" Ukrainian poster, Slavonic Library, National Library of the Czech Republic.

**4.** First Red Cavalry, 1920, TASS. Getty Images.

5. Admiral Aleksandr Kolchak. Bain Collection, Prints & Photographs Division, Library of Congress.

6. General Baron Petr Wrangel. Getty Images.

7. Ataman Grigorii Semenov. Ludovic-H. Grondijs, *La guerre en Russie et en Sibérie,* intro Maurice Paléologue, pref. Émile Haumant (Paris: Bossard, 1922). Joseph Regenstein Library, University of Chicago.

8. General Dmitrii Khorvat. Bain Collection, Library of Congress.

**9.** Lenin and Trotsky (center) with delegates to the Tenth Congress of the Russian Communist Party, Moscow, March 8-16, 1921. Getty Images.

**10.** "The Peasant Woman and the Woman Worker. Take the place of brothers and husbands who have left for the Red Front. Your strong alliance guarantees victory over Wrangel and over economic ruin." Ukrainian ROSTA, Nikolaev, 1920. Slavic and East European Collections, The New York Public Library.

nantly rural, a proletariat had begun to form in the railroad yards of Tiflis, serving the line built in the 1880s to link the port of Batumi with the oil fields of Baku. At the turn of the century, when Marxism took hold among the Russian intelligentsia, Georgian intellectuals gravitated toward the Menshevik camp. For them national and social questions merged. The liberation of Georgia from tsarist oppression would be accompanied by the liberation of the working class from the exploitation of the (largely Armenian) bourgeoisie.[9]

Azerbaijan had the smallest Europeanized elite and the weakest sense of nationhood. Its intelligentsia was divided between Turkish-oriented Sunnis and Persian-oriented Shiites, the majority of the population. Inland Elizavetpol (today Ganja) and coastal Baku were its two administrative centers.[10] While Baku contained a large Armenian commercial class and a mixed Russian and Muslim proletariat, Elizavetpol was the heart of nascent Azerbaijani nationalism. The peasants remained largely indifferent to politics, but the intelligentsia formed a range of political parties, including a branch of the Kadets in Baku, the Social Democratic Hummet (Endeavor), the nationalist Musavat (Equality), and the anti-Russian Difai (Defense).[11] After 1908, some Azerbaijanis gravitated to the Young Turks and the ideas of Turkism. The Young Turks were a group of Ottoman intellectuals and army officers belonging to the Committee of Union and Progress, which had ousted the sultan in 1908. Their goal was to build a stronger, modern state, dominated by ethnic Turks.[12] Like them, the leaders of fledgling Azerbaijani nationalism were secular. Until then known as "Tatars" or "Transcaucasian Muslims," they increasingly preferred to call themselves "Turkic."[13]

The Revolution of 1905 in the Caucasus centered, not surprisingly, in the major cities, but it also involved widespread peasant unrest and the emergence of anti-Russian guerrilla bands in Azerbaijan and Dagestan. The breakdown of order unleashed inter-communal violence as well, of which the most dramatic episode was the so-called Armenian-Tatar War of 1905–1906. Which side was the aggressor, or whether the provocation was mutual, is not entirely clear from scholarly accounts, but armed clashes broke out in cities as far-flung as Baku, Elizavetpol, Erevan, Nakhichevan, and Shusha in Western Karabakh, resulting in the destruction of over a hundred villages on each side and many thousands dead. The Armenian Dashnaktsutiun had the advantage of organized armed squads, but damage was well distributed.[14]

The Great War deepened inter-ethnic animosities, while the confrontation between the Ottoman and Romanov Empires raised the political stakes for the leaders of emerging national movements. Having brutalized the Jewish population of occupied Galicia, the Russian High Command was more circumspect in the Caucasus, trying to strike a balance in its treatment of Armenians and Muslims. There was no Russian equivalent on the Caucasian Front of the mass murder of Armenians on the Ottoman side. Like the Ottomans, however, the Russian authorities mobilized ethnic minorities across the border in their own strategic interest and sometimes set hostile or mutually distrustful communities against each other. The Russian military, here as elsewhere, thought of the civilian population as a resource to be exploited, whatever the damage entailed.[15]

On that basis, even lacking an overall plan or a particular ethnic animus as in Galicia, in Transcaucasia the Imperial Army undertook massive relocations. Thus the fifty thousand Armenian refugees who had returned to the Eastern Anatolian cities of Van, Bitlis, and Muş after the slaughter were prevented from resettling there, on the grounds that food was already in short supply. The Imperial Army, here as elsewhere, also drafted civilians into labor battalions, in this case both Armenian and Kurdish.[16] In short, the war endowed the various communities of the Caucasus and neighboring Eastern Anatolia with a heightened sense of incompatible interests and of vulnerability to the machinations of the political powers battling for control of their terrain.

On the international level, the future of the region was laid out in May 1916, when the French and British, with Russia's endorsement, signed the Sykes-Picot accords, delineating postwar zones of influence in the Near East. Russia was promised control of Constantinople and the Straits as well as the eastern end of Anatolia, including Erzurum, Van, and Bitlis, and Trebizond (Trabzon) on the coast, all at the time under Russian occupation.[17] In July 1915, Foreign Minister Sergei Sazonov had said, "the formation of an autonomous Armenia under the sovereignty of the Sultan and under the tripartite protectorate of Russia, France, and England would be the natural result of the longstanding favorable attitude not only of Russia, but of its Allies as well, toward the Turkish Armenians."[18] He was less inclined to welcome an increase in the number of Armenians within imperial Russian borders. "Of all the heterogeneous populations we must rule," the minister commented, "they are the most difficult."[19] The entire region, indeed, continued to present a challenge to his successors.

In February 1917, responsibility changed hands. When news of the revolution in Petrograd reached Transcaucasia a week later, the leaders of civil society moved to fill the vacuum, as they did in most other places. With the departure of Grand Duke Nikolai Nikolaevich, viceroy of the Caucasus since Nicholas had replaced him at Stavka, the regional Duma deputies formed a Special Caucasian Committee (*Osobyi Zakavkazskii Komitet*—Ozakom) to serve as the civilian administration on behalf of the Provisional Government.[20] In Tiflis the Social Democrats immediately established a Soviet on the Petrograd model, but the relationship of Dual Power was not replicated. The Georgian Mensheviks, who dominated the socialist sector, declared their intention of cooperating with the "bourgeoisie" in the pursuit of democracy. Hoping for the defeat of Turkey, Armenian leaders supported the war and welcomed the Provisional Government. Their goal was autonomy within a federated Russian state, to be established by the anticipated Constituent Assembly. The Musavat and other Azerbaijani parties also supported the Provisional Government as a step toward a democratic republic. Bolshevik influence in the region was confined to the ethnically Russian proletariat of Baku. Until Lenin introduced his April Theses, however, the two Social Democratic branches had no trouble working together.[21]

In one of its first official moves, the Sovnarkom had issued a general declaration of the right to national self-determination. Two months later, a separate decree endorsed the right of Armenians to the fulfillment of their national idea, which would include the Russian-occupied territory in Eastern Anatolia, as well as their claims in Transcaucasia.[22] No one in the region seized the opportunity, however, to take them at their word. Mensheviks and SRs denounced the seizure of power, as they did everywhere else, and rejected outright the chance to establish national independence. This is not as odd as it sounds. For the Caucasian intelligentsia, whatever its unhappiness with imperial rule, the sense of vulnerability was overwhelming. "A misfortune has befallen us," declared Noi Zhordaniia, the Georgian Menshevik leader. "The connection with Russia has been broken and Transcaucasia has been left alone. We have to stand on our own feet and either help ourselves or perish through anarchy."[23]

Rejecting the self-proclaimed Petrograd regime and pinning their hopes on the Constituent Assembly, a wide range of organizations uniting all three peoples and involving their primary political parties combined, on November 15, to form a so-called Transcaucasian Commissariat (*Zakavkazskii Komissariat*), to replace the earlier Ozakom.[24] The Commissariat rejected the Bolshevik claim to power, pledging loyalty to Russia and the Constituent Assembly, which it considered "the last thread which could have united Russia and the All-Russian revolutionary democracy."[25] Socialist solidarity and territorial integrity went hand in hand. "Having for over a hundred years joined arms with Russia and linked their fate to hers, the peoples of Transcaucasia in the current historical moment are for the first time left to their own devices, obliged with their own efforts to undertake measures to prevent the approaching economic and social catastrophe." The body declared its opposition to "civil war among the democracy" and called for a Russian Republic "recognized by all."[26]

The reluctant leaders had to deal not only with a new Russian center but with the altered international context. On December 2/15, 1917, the Bolsheviks signed the armistice with the Central Powers; three days later an armistice was concluded between the Ottoman Empire and the remains of the Imperial Caucasian Army.[27] That army, however, was by then falling apart. Its commander endorsed the formation of Georgian and Armenian units, as the only viable remnant of the imperial force.[28] In areas formerly under Russian occupation, these Armenian troops attacked Muslim villages.[29] On February 12 (NS), Turkey broke the armistice and launched an offensive. Turkish leader Enver Pasha aimed to gain control of the lands beyond Anatolia, including Transcaucasia, and sent his brother, Nuri Pasha, to Azerbaijan to create an Army of Islam, composed of Turkish soldiers and Azerbaijani volunteers.[30]

Despite the region's internal tensions, leaders in Transcaucasia nevertheless attempted to transcend ethnic divisions and present a united front against the Bolshevik challenge and the Turkish threat. Musavatists and Dashnaks joined with Georgian Mensheviks to form a Transcaucasian parliament (the Seim), which opened on February 23, 1918, and shortly thereafter voted to conclude peace with Turkey on the basis of the 1914 borders (Russia retaining Kars, Ardahan, and Batumi) and autonomy for Armenians on the Turkish side.[31]

The talks in Trebizond between the Caucasian and Ottoman delegates on conditions for the peace had not yet begun, however, when news arrived from Brest-Litovsk of the impending treaty. Turkey would regain Kars, Ardahan, and Batumi; Armenian forces on both sides of the border would be disarmed and demobilized.[32] In the Seim, Zhordaniia denounced the accord. The Azeri deputies, however, noted the contradiction involved in still claiming to be part of Russia—refusing independence—while rejecting the treaty Russia had signed. The Seim was caught in its own ambivalence. It refused to separate from Russia, but conducted talks with the Ottomans as if it were acting on its own authority and rejected Brest-Litovsk without the authority to do so. Meanwhile, as talks continued in Trebizond, the Turkish Army kept advancing. With the support of Azerbaijani irregulars acting behind the lines, in March and April the Ottomans captured Erzurum, Ardahan, Batumi, and Kars, slaughtering Armenians in their path.[33]

The Georgian Menshevik head of the Transcaucasian peace delegation in Trebizond appealed to the Seim to declare independence and accept Brest-Litovsk. "A country without authority and discipline cannot make war," he said.[34] The Ottomans had an interest in the same outcome, which would have endorsed the return of the contested territory, as stipulated in the Brest accord.[35] The Seim instead recalled the peace delegation and prepared to defend Batumi, which the Turks had ordered them to cede. The Menshevik leader Iraklii Tsereteli would not budge: "Turkish imperialism has issued an ultimatum to the Transcaucasian democracy to recognize the treaty of Brest-Litovsk. We know of no such treaty. We know that in Brest-Litovsk the death sentence was passed upon Revolutionary Russia, and that death sentence to our fatherland we will never sign!"[36] Over the objections of the Azeri deputies, on April 14 the Seim (not having declared independence) declared war on Turkey. The anti-Bolshevik Mensheviks appealed to Moscow to come to their aid and prevent Transcaucasia from leaving Russia. This painfully self-contradictory appeal was ignored.[37]

Fighting dragged on. The Turks took Batumi without resistance on April 15, although four days later Armenians in Kars were still holding out. On April 22, the Seim agreed to the resumption of talks, and voted reluctantly for independence. The Democratic Federative Republic of Transcaucasia (*Zakavkazskaia demokraticheskaia federativnaia respublika*) accepted the treaty of Brest-Litovsk and agreed to evacuate Kars. On April 25, the Turks entered the fortress city and three days later recognized Transcaucasian independence.[38]

It is tempting to puzzle over the Georgian Mensheviks' doctrinaire adherence to the principle of internationalism and their stubborn attachment to a non-Bolshevik Russia that no longer existed. But of all the Caucasian peoples, only the Azerbaijani could contemplate Turkish domination with equanimity; the Armenians, in particular, had reason to fear it. The Georgians and Armenians may have been deluded about the possibilities of democracy in Russia, but they were sober about the dangers of going it alone as small nations caught between antagonistic powers and divided among themselves.

Indeed, the Transcaucasian Federation lasted only until May 26, 1918. During a month of negotiations with Ottoman representatives in Batumi, now under Turkish control, the Ottomans demanded territorial concessions, while at the same time sending troops into Armenia. The Armenians were blocking Ottoman access to northern Persia and to Baku, and the Georgians still controlled the railroads. The Azerbaijanis, for their part, had all along been informing the Turks of what was being said on the Transcaucasian side. The interests of the three partners could no longer be reconciled. The Georgians exited the Federation and with German support declared their national independence. The Germans had an interest in protecting their access to Caucasian oil. The Armenians were still fighting, fearful of what a Turkish victory would mean, a victory the Azerbaijanis eagerly awaited.[39]

The day the Federation folded, Georgia proclaimed itself a democratic republic, with its capital in Tiflis, promising civil rights, respect for ethnic minorities, and neutrality in international affairs. The Tiflis soviet, while clinging to slogans of internationalism, endorsed the move. On May 28, the new country signed an agreement with Germany, recognizing Brest-Litovsk and guaranteeing German use of the railroads, ports, and mines. On the same day, Armenia and Azerbaijan also declared independence, with capitals, respectively, in Erevan and Elizavetpol. Baku was controlled by Bolsheviks, with Dashnak support.[40] On June 4, 1918, by the Treaty of Batumi, the Ottomans recognized the three new republics. Armenian territory was sharply reduced, and the Georgians were subject to German conditions. By contrast, writes historian Firuz Kazemzadeh, "Azerbaijan lost nothing but hoped to gain Baku with Ottoman help."[41]

---

Baku and its oil industry were as important to Bolshevik survival as to the German war effort. The city had been the focus of Bolshevik activity ever since the October coup. In December 1917, Moscow designated Stepan Shaumian, an ethnic Armenian born in Tiflis, as Extraordinary Commissar of the Caucasus, as well as head of the Baku Soviet, the position he had held since March.[42] The same age as Trotsky, Tsereteli, and many other radical leaders, Shaumian had studied philosophy in Berlin and joined the Bolshevik Party at the very beginning.[43] The Soviet faced two competitors for control of the city: the Azerbaijani Musavat and the Armenian Dashnaks, claiming to represent the interests of their respective communities. A quarter of the city's quarter million inhabitants were Armenian, another 40 percent Muslim, and a good third Slavic. Armenians were prominent among factory owners and city officials; they tended to live among themselves and employ their own. The liberal Azeri intelligentsia, for its part, had rallied to the war effort, created a volunteer military detachment, and opened a war hospital in Baku.[44] Of the population in and around the city classified as workers, the majority, particularly in the unskilled ranks, were Muslims, Azerbaijani chief among them.[45]

Given the demography, allegiances based strictly on class could not be counted on, if they could anywhere outside Marxist textbooks. The Musavat earned a proportional 40 percent of the vote in Baku Soviet elections on the eve of the October coup. The party was the dominant political force in the rest of Azerbaijan and therefore the main obstacle to Bolshevik control. After the Bolshevik takeover, Shaumian declared the Soviet to be the sole power in the city. Musavat support for Transcaucasian separatism and its attempts at forming an Azerbaijani armed force were not to his liking.[46]

The Armenians constituted a third force in Baku. By late 1917, Armenian soldiers were deserting from the front, refugees were streaming into Transcaucasia to join those who had fled there after the slaughter in 1915. In Baku each community girded for battle. In February 1918, Armenian commanders in Petrograd sent tanks, cars, and weapons there; three generals appeared in person to mobilize returning Armenian soldiers. The Soviet formed new Red Army detachments and a Red Guard of over ten thousand men, three-quarters ethnic Armenians. The Dashnak had its own armed contingents, financed partly by wealthy members of the community. Shaumian and other ethnic Armenians among the Bolshevik Soviet leaders rejected "national" in favor of "class" politics, but from the Azerbaijani perspective it could easily seem that the (Armenian-led) Soviet was cooperating with the Armenian nationalists to destroy their own national aspirations—and, more directly, to threaten their very existence.

Tensions mounted when the staff of the Caucasian Native Mounted Division, or Savage Division, which had accompanied Kornilov in his unsuccessful August adventure, arrived in Baku from Tiflis on March 9, 1918. Shaumian had them arrested.[47] Despite protests from the Azeri leadership and warnings from Lenin not to stir up trouble, Shaumian did not release them. When a group of Azeri officers on the ship *Evelina* arrived in Baku from Lenkoran, a city on the Persian border, to attend a funeral, rumors spread that the crew was planning a revolt or might be organizing an attack on Russian villagers. The Soviet had them disarmed. The Muslim leadership demanded the weapons be returned, but no action had yet been taken when shooting began. It is unclear who fired first, but a battle soon raged.[48]

The Soviet wanted to think of the confrontation as a political struggle, but it could not avoid the ethnic dimension. The Armenian leadership at first declared its neutrality. Some accounts claim the Armenians offered to back the Musavat but then backed down. In the end the "Russian" parties—including anti-Bolshevik Mensheviks and Kadets—rallied to the Soviet's support. For three days, all accounts agree, Azerbaijanis exchanged fire with Dashnak and Soviet forces, which trained their artillery on the Muslim quarter. All accounts agree that Armenian units went house to house slaughtering the inhabitants and plundering their goods. By April 1, the entire Muslim district had burned to the ground. Corpses were left lying on the streets. The Azerbaijan Democratic Republic later collected testimony from survivors and witnesses for presentation at the Paris Peace Conference, which included descriptions of brutalities and the desecration of corpses. Its report estimated that up to twelve thousand Muslims had been killed, encouraged by Armenian nationalists and what it considered the Armenian-dominated Soviet.[49]

The Muslim inhabitants of Baku were the principal victims of the so-called March Days, but the Armenians were shortly to suffer the consequences. At the end of the month, the Soviet presented an ultimatum to the Musavat, demanding it recognize the Soviet as the sole power in Baku, remove the Savage Division and any other armed units from the city, and open access to the railroads.[50] After the fighting was over, the remaining Muslim population fled the city, as did the leaders of the Musavat. Most Armenian units were incorporated into the Red Army. The "bourgeois" and Menshevik papers were shuttered. The City Duma was closed down. On April 19, the Bolsheviks established a Sovnarkom in Baku, which included only a few Left SRs as partners.[51]

Whatever the exact sequence of events leading up to the crisis, certain facts are clear. In order to achieve a monopoly of power, Shaumian—not as an Armenian, but as a Bolshevik—was determined to undermine the authority and popular base of the Musavat. The appearance of Muslim troops—whether the Savage Division or the officers on the *Evelina*—provided an excuse to mobilize an armed attack. He found his best-equipped ally in the Dashnak formations, which had their own reasons to oppose any sort of

Muslim force. Ethnic and political motives were thus intermingled in this typical atrocity scenario. The leadership on various sides set the stage, and the foot soldiers ran amok, decimating the unarmed civilian population. "We achieved brilliant results," Shaumian boasted to Moscow on April 13. "The enemy was wiped out."[52]

Thus began the period of what became known as the Baku Commune. Shaumian's first order of business was not only to secure Baku's periphery but to extend Soviet power deeper into the region. Once the city had been subdued, Red forces pursued an offensive against Dagestani and Musavat positions to the north and west, and as far south as the Persian border.[53] This was April 1918. Shaumian disapproved not only of the Seim, but of the emergence of independent nations that followed. In early June, he announced the goal of transforming Baku into the nucleus of a new socialist society and ordered the nationalization of the oil industry, but the experiment in building socialism in one city soon ran into trouble. The local peasantry was indifferent to the Soviet appeal; the workers were divided in their allegiances, the politically most experienced gravitating toward the Mensheviks and SRs. Food supply presented the same challenge as it did to every aspiring authority everywhere else, here complicated by competition for control over the railroads, the ongoing war, and ethnic resentments.[54]

While coping with these complications, Shaumian launched a new military campaign to counter the continuing Turkish offensive.[55] Most of the Red troops and their officers were Armenian, many with Dashnak ties, and the Red Army devastated the Muslim population as they headed west toward Elizavetpol. By mid-July, Turkish forces were approaching Baku. Shaumian ordered a full mobilization and put the Cheka in charge, but additional support was needed. Despite Moscow's pact with the Central Powers, the Baku Soviet considered the possibility, urged by the Right SRs, of appealing for British aid. When, after heated debate, on July 15 the question came to a vote, the proposal won by a slim majority, with Menshevik support. The Bolsheviks were defeated.[56] Shaumian continued to beg Moscow for troops, but little help was forthcoming. The Dashnak commanders, for their part, refused to keep fighting, and on July 30 the Armenian leadership decided to surrender to the Turks.[57] The next day, the members of the Baku Sovnarkom boarded ships loaded with their remaining weapons and ammunition and set out for Bolshevik-controlled Astrakhan. They were replaced by something called the Centro-Caspian Dictatorship (*Diktatura Tsentrokaspiia*), consisting mostly of Right SRs, loyal to Russia and the Constituent Assembly.

They sent a gunboat to stop the fleeing commissars, who were returned to Baku and clapped in jail.[58]

Desperate for backup, the Dictatorship invited a British officer stationed in Persia to come to their rescue. When General Lionel Dunsterville and his small force disembarked at Baku on August 17, he was dismayed by the miserable condition of the local army.[59] When a month later the Turks attacked the city, Dunsterville and his men took to their ships, as did a number of Armenian soldiers. On September 15, Azerbaijani troops entered Baku. The truth of what happened next is still hotly contested. The Armenian National Council claimed at the time that Azerbaijani troops spent three days avenging the March events, in the course of which, it contended, almost nine thousand Armenian civilians were massacred.[60] When the Azerbaijani government arrived from Elizavetpol, it admitted that some "excesses" had occurred, but not surprisingly insisted it had done all it could to restrain them, including the execution of "over a hundred Muslims."[61]

Fate was also cruel to the Bolshevik organizers of the March events. Before the Azerbaijani troops entered Baku, the twenty-six members of the Baku Sovnarkom were quickly released and again boarded ship for Astrakhan. The crew, however, had no desire to end up in a Bolshevik-held city and headed instead for Krasnovodsk (now Türkmenbaşy in Turkmenistan), directly across the Caspian Sea. The SRs then in control of Krasnovodsk had the commissars executed, while the British officers present stood by.[62] The overly zealous Shaumian thus met his fate as part of the political war between the Bolsheviks and their SR rivals.

If the British failed to rescue the deposed leaders of Soviet Baku, the Germans took a more energetic interest in the future of nearby Georgia. On June 4, 1918, the Ottomans had recognized Georgian independence, but the Germans were anxious to block Turkish access to Georgian oil and agreed, when invited on June 13 by the Tiflis government, to enter the country as its protectors.[63] The August 27 Supplemental Treaty to Brest-Litovsk opened the way for the conclusion of contracts with major German firms. By August it was clear, however, that Germany was facing defeat in Europe, and the Menshevik government put out feelers to the Allies. When, after the Armistice, Soviet Russia renounced Brest-Litovsk, Armenia and Georgia renewed their claims to Kars and Ardahan, in the one case, and Batumi, in the other.[64]

When Turkey pulled out, the British moved in. The Georgians hoped the British would make common cause against the Bolsheviks and offered

access to ports and railroads as an inducement to accept Georgian indepen-
dence. British troops (actually Indian) remained in Batumi until July 1920.
Armenia also welcomed the Allies. Unwilling to recognize a separate
Azerbaijan, on November 17, 1918, British troops arrived to occupy Baku.
Despite the aspiring nation's uncertain status, the Azerbaijani parliament
convened in December.[65]

Meanwhile conflicts persisted. Georgia and Armenia locked horns over
the definition of their mutual border. Georgia attempted to bring together
the three self-proclaimed republics, plus the Republic of the North Caucasus
Mountain Peoples (*Respublika gortsev Severnogo Kavkaza*), formed in Dagestan
in May 1918, to work out a common platform for the Paris Peace Conference,
but Armenia refused to cooperate. In December 1918 Georgian and
Armenian troops went to war over the disputed region of Borchalo and
desisted only after the Allies intervened.[66]

The Georgian government was still dominated by Mensheviks, who had
won the vast majority of votes in the Constituent Assembly elections. They
proceeded, under the internationalist banner of socialism, to establish
national independence. In decidedly unsocialist fashion, they did away with
the Soviets and renamed the Red Guard the People's Guard; the national
council became the parliament.[67] Having first sought the protection of the
Germans, then of the British, they were denounced by their own Russian
comrades as "allies of the counterrevolutionary bourgeoisie and of Anglo-
American imperialism."[68]

The Tiflis Mensheviks not only violated party principles, but now confronted the challenge of managing an economic crisis and facing the opposition of regions that did not accept them. Determined to maintain its hold
on what it considered national territory, the government sent the People's
Guard to subdue insurgent villages on its own periphery: Ossetia (mountainous northern center), Abkhazia (coastal above Sukhumi), and Mingrelia
(coastal between Sukhumi and Poti). The Caucasus was a bottomless well of
ever more particular national claims. In building the framework of an
umbrella nation, Tiflis created a new flag and imposed the Georgian language in parliament, the courts, and the army to replace Russian, the common language of the professional classes.[69] A British observer called Georgia
"a classic example of an imperialist 'small nation.' Both in territory-snatching
outside and bureaucratic tyranny inside, its chauvinism was beyond all
bounds."[70] In the spring of 1919 Armenia and Georgia were still battling for
contested territory. On July 7, 1920, when the British finally evacuated

Batumi, the Georgians assumed control of the city, against the wishes of the surrounding Adjarian population.[71]

In summer 1920, when American General James G. Harbord, a veteran of the Great War, visited the region at the behest of President Wilson, he noted the mutual mistrust of the three governments, which he characterized as "thoroughly inefficient, without credit and undoubtedly corrupt." In his view, Armenia was the most unfortunate. "Georgia does not hesitate to embargo freight against Armenia," he reported, "and from her position of vantage simply censors the railroad traffic to that unfortunate country. Azerbaijan controls the fuel supply and combines with Georgia against Armenia, which alone of the three has nothing by which to exert leverage."[72]

The Treaty of Batumi had obliged Armenia to renounce the Eastern Anatolian region. Once the Central Powers were defeated, the Armenians took the occasion to renew their claims, announcing their annexation of the area in May 1919.[73] The territory in question was in a state of utter devastation, as difficult for the returning Armenians as for the local Turkish population. The back and forth of Ottoman and Russian armies, the retreat of Russians and Armenian irregulars, "the desperate character of the warfare, with its reprisals of burning and destroying as one side and then the other advanced," General Harbord noted, had left the villages in ruins and the landscape "practically treeless." The "retaliatory cruelties" of the Armenians, he decided, "unquestionably rivaled the Turks in their inhumanity."[74] In the areas where Armenians had returned, he described "roads and lands almost back to the wild... villages and towns in ruins; brigandage rampant in the Transcaucasus; lack of medicines and warm clothing; winter coming on in a treeless land without coal."[75]

Armenia's annexation of Eastern Anatolia was affirmed a year later, on August 10, 1920, when Turkey signed the Treaty of Sèvres with the Allied Powers (Soviet Russia excluded). Turkey did not, however, let the matter rest. In the early fall, Turkish forces seized Sarıkamış, Kars, and Alexandropol (Gyumri, in today's Armenia). The armistice signed on November 18, 1920, allowed Armenia to retain Erevan, but demanded the country's virtual disarmament. Ten days later, a Bolshevik Revolutionary Committee entered Armenia from Azerbaijan, instigated a revolt, and proclaimed the establishment of Soviet power. On December 2, 1920, the Dashnak government signed the Treaty of Alexandropol, by which it renounced the Treaty of Sèvres and with it all territorial claims on Turkey, which obtained the right to use Armenian territory for military purposes. With this final gesture, the

Armenian Council of Ministers ended its existence.[76] On February 18, 1921, however, after two months of Soviet rule and while the Red Army was busy in neighboring Georgia, Armenian troops entered Erevan. Not for long. On April 2, the Red Army retook Erevan and the remaining Dashnaks left for Persia.[77]

Each of the three republics alone was vulnerable, but mutual antagonisms drove them apart. Internally, Azerbaijan was also divided. The interests of the land-hungry peasantry, agitated by news of land reform in Russia and Georgia, collided with those of the big landowners. As often in Russia, a peasant leader arose who inspired his followers to plunder and burn landed estates. Workers also suffered. Oil was of course key to the economy; the civil war had obstructed exports, prices and wages fell, strikes broke out.[78] After the Bolshevik Soviet was replaced by the Centro-Caspian Dictatorship in summer 1918, organized workers had gravitated toward the SRs and the Musavat. When the strikes proved unsuccessful, however, the Baku Bolsheviks stepped up their activity. They first engineered a split in the Social Democratic Hummet Party—the tried-and-true Bolshevik move, from which emerged a separate Communist Party of Azerbaijan, which—another classic moment— was attacked from Moscow for its nationalist orientation. But localism was essential to attract a population that did not see Russians as friendly.[79] The Baku Soviet had been twice damned—as "Armenian" and as "Russian."

The collapse of the Azerbaijani government was ultimately achieved by the Baku Communists, who organized an uprising, followed by the appearance of the Red Army. Parliament formally handed power to the Bolsheviks and announced its own dissolution. On April 28, 1920, Moscow declared victory over the "counterrevolutionary," "criminal" government of Azerbaijan. The only resistance came from peasants in the Elizavetpol region, who staged an uprising in which some Azeri Red Army soldiers also took part.[80] But the deed was done.

After the subjugation of Azerbaijan, the Georgians feared their turn was next. On May 1, they mobilized their forces and blocked the advance of the Red Army. Once again, the local Communists—this time Georgian—staged an uprising. Neither the revolt, planned for May 2, in Tiflis, nor the coup supposed to follow, ended in success. The attempt to destroy the Georgian government having failed, on May 7, Moscow recognized Georgian independence. Georgia pledged not to aid and abet the enemies of Soviet Russia and to tolerate the activities of the Georgian Communist Party, thus in effect renouncing its own sovereignty, since any branch of the party was a tool of Moscow.[81]

Both sides ignored the details. The Georgian government continued to suppress the Communist Party, which continued to pursue its plans to foment insurrection and unseat them. Conflict with Moscow was not the Menshevik regime's only headache. On February 11, 1921, uprisings occurred in the region Georgia had occupied after the war with Armenia in December 1918, while soldiers advancing from the Armenian side engaged Georgian forces. The neighbors were once again at each other's throats. In true Bolshevik fashion, the organizers of the revolts announced the formation of a Soviet regime. They denounced Menshevik aggression and requested Moscow's support. At the same time, Soviet troops entered Georgia from Azerbaijan.[82] Moscow denied any role in the conflict, but the Georgians appealed to fellow socialists. "Comrades, we are sure that you will not sit by while the Government of Moscow, under the mask of Socialism and Communism, annihilates the Georgian Republic."[83] On February 25, 1921, the Red Army announced the conquest of Georgia.[84]

The story was not over yet. Elsewhere the Mensheviks were reviled, but in this case Lenin insisted they be shown a certain consideration. While the fighting was going on, Turkey had used the occasion to demand Batumi and two contested regions, which Georgia had conceded in the vain hope of Turkish support. On March 17, 1921, the Georgian government left Batumi on an Italian ship. The treaty signed in Kutaisi on March 18, 1921, between Soviet Russia and a government which had already been deposed stipulated that Moscow would recover Batumi, which the Georgians preferred to Turkish control and which they helped the Soviets accomplish.[85]

---

Similar conflicts characterized Central Asia during the war and revolution: tensions between indigenous leaders and their own peoples, confrontations between ethnic groups competing for scarce resources, friction between the region and the Russian center. This vast territory extended east from the Caspian Sea to the Irtysh River in western Siberia, southward to the Persian and Chinese borders.[86] Its broad northern rim (the districts of Uralsk, Turgai, Akmolinsk, and Semipalatinsk) constituted the Kazakh Steppe, which had been conquered piecemeal in the early nineteenth century. The conquest of the southern districts of Transcaspia, Samarkand, Semireche,

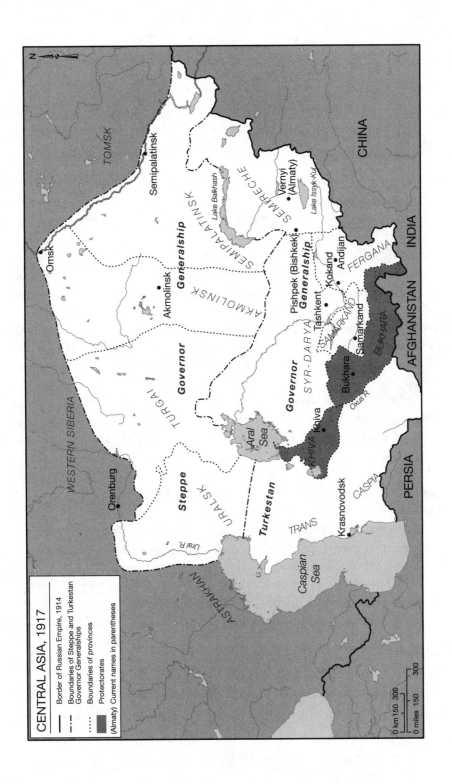

CENTRAL ASIA, 1917

Border of Russian Empire, 1914
Boundaries of Steppe and Turkestan
Governor Generalships
Boundaries of provinces
Protectorates
(Almaty) Current names in parentheses

N

WESTERN SIBERIA

TOMSK

Omsk
Semipalatinsk

Lake Balkhash

SEMIRECHE

Vernyi
(Almaty)

Lake Issyk-Kul

CHINA

INDIA

Akmolinsk

AKMOLINSK

Governor Generalship

SEMIPALATINSK

Pishpek (Bishkek)

Generalship

Kokand
Andijan

FERGANA

AFGHANISTAN

TURGAI

Governor

Tashkent

SAMARKAND

Samarkand

BUKHARA

SYR-DARYA

Governor

Steppe

Aral
Sea

Bukhara

Khiva

KHIVA

Oxus R.

Orenburg

URALSK

Ural R.

Turkestan

ASTRAKHAN

Krasnovodsk

TRANS-

CASPIA

PERSIA

Caspian
Sea

0 km 150 300

0 miles 150 300

Syr-Daria, and Fergana began in 1867 with the establishment of the General-Governorship of Turkestan and continued into the 1880s.[87] The governor-general answered to the Ministry of War, which stationed a large garrison there.[88]

By 1914 Turkestan included a sparsely distributed population of about eleven million.[89] The indigenous peoples were practicing Muslims, but ethnically and linguistically diverse. Most were nomadic herdsmen, though some combined seasonal pasturalism with agricultural labor and some were characterized as peasants. The three principal nomadic peoples were the closely related Kara-Kirgiz and the Kirgiz (known after 1924 as Kyrgyz and Kazakhs, respectively) and the Turkmen of Transcaspia, themselves composed of numerous subgroups or tribes.[90] More confusingly still, the inhabitants of the Kazakh Steppe were mostly known at the time as Kazakh, but the terminology used by Russian sources in some areas is inconsistent. The sedentary Muslims in towns and villages were known at the time as Sarts.[91] The majority of peasants and herdsmen were impoverished, but the villages were dominated by a class of prosperous landowners called *bai* (the Kazakh word for "wealthy"), some of whom made fortunes in the cotton trade.[92]

Russian conquest disturbed the demographic ecology. Toward the end of the nineteenth century, Central Asia became a destination for the settlement of land-hungry Russian peasants and Cossacks.[93] After the completion in 1906 of the railroad between Orenburg and Tashkent, their numbers swelled. The settlers' demand for land put pressure on the nomadic herdsmen who used it for pasture, especially in the agricultural Semireche region.[94] By 1916 settlers constituted a majority in several of the more fertile northern districts of the Kazakh Steppe.[95] In those areas, the contest between newcomers—themselves impoverished—and the nomadic herdsmen was the most acute.[96] Pasture land was formally considered state property, which the tribes had the right to use, but to which they had no legal claim.[97] Settler peasants thus benefited from what amounted to officially sanctioned expropriation, but speculators and corrupt officials profited even more. Their lands appropriated, their herds shrinking, many nomads survived by providing agricultural labor for settlers or for fellow-Muslim landholders.[98] The increasing emphasis on cotton culture in the Fergana Valley also threatened the region's economic equilibrium, reducing the cultivation of cereals and necessitating grain imports from central Russia.[99]

Despite the ruthlessness of conquest and subjugation, the Russians thought of themselves as bringing civilization, not misery, to their new subjects. Administrators cited European colonialism as a positive model.[100] The admiration was returned. A member of the Royal Geographical Society opined in 1882: "The substitution . . . of Russian rule for that of the Kirghiz, Uzbegs and Turkomans throughout a large portion of Central Asia has been an unmixed blessing to humanity."[101] The production of cotton was introduced in the 1880s, and railroads built initially for military purposes became an important stimulus to commercial growth. A line connecting Turkestan and Siberia began construction in 1911. Workers from Russia arrived to build and run the system.[102] By 1914 the cities of Tashkent and Samarkand (both in today's Uzbekistan) had grown into commercial hubs, with the usual attributes of modern urban life. These features were reserved, however, for the European— that is, Russian—inhabitants. Tashkent consisted of two separate cities side by side: the old Muslim city, with its winding streets, bazaars, and traditional architecture, and a newly built modern city, with a planned grid and imperial-style buildings, symbolizing the contrast with native darkness and disorder.[103] Muslim society was not, however, unaffected by change. The region developed a native intelligentsia and sent deputies to the State Duma. A younger generation promoted the values of European culture and modern life, which they had acquired in Russian schools and which they tried to reconcile with local traditions and the needs of their own peoples.[104]

Like Transcaucasia, Central Asia was riven by chronic tensions, both within its various ethnic communities and among them. Sometimes these tensions could work to the Russians' advantage. The conquest of the fertile Fergana Valley, annexed finally in 1876, was facilitated by the struggles between competing tribes and tribal leaders under the Kokand Khanate. Small-scale disturbances continued into the 1890s, but were not directed primarily against the Russian authorities. Rather, the internecine conflicts weakened the authority of the tribal leaders, whose role in the villages was supplanted by that of the Sufi ishans, attracting the loyalty of impoverished peasants and nomads.[105] The first significant revolt against Russian rule, lasting a full decade, from 1837 to 1847, occurred in the Kazakh Steppe.[106] The first important rebellion in Turkestan occurred in 1898 in the Fergana city of Andijan. In the early morning hours of May 17, 1898, over a thousand tribesmen and peasants, armed only with knives and clubs, fell upon the sleeping garrison. In the space of fifteen minutes they managed to kill twenty-two soldiers and wound almost the same number. The rest of the soldiers opened fire, but the attackers fled. Similar attacks planned for other places were foiled by timely betrayals. Eighteen of the Andijan leaders were hanged, more than three hundred exiled or sentenced to hard labor, their villages razed, the inhabitants expelled, and the land transferred to Slavic peasants.[107]

---

The Great War imposed additional hardships and inequities: higher taxes and the requisitioning of food and livestock, both horses and camels in this case. The nomads were hardest hit.[108] The production of cereal crops dropped sharply, and herdsmen began to slaughter and sell their animals. The construction of a planned railroad connecting the city of Vernyi (today Almaty in Kazakhstan) to Tashkent, was suspended, blocking shipments out of the grain-growing Semireche district.[109] Military conscription had an uneven impact. Slavic settlers born in the region were liable to the call-up, but newcomers were exempt.[110] Initially, over 1.5 million draft-age Muslim men in European Russia and the Caucasus and almost 150,000 in Turkestan were deemed unfit or undesirable. At the start of the war and again in 1915, when the need was more pressing, the military and civilian authorities had carefully surveyed the numerous ethnic groups comprising this untapped resource, weighing their political loyalty and capacity to fight in disciplined units. The Savage Division, as noted, was formed immediately, on the basis mostly of Chechen volunteers, including troublemakers who thus earned reprieves from penal sentences, but also including a unit of Azerbaijani troops. By the end of the war, it is estimated that from 800,000 to 1.5 million Muslim men, mostly Tatars, had served in the regular Imperial Army.[111]

In 1916, however, without resolving the question of which groups among the broad Muslim population were best suited to military service, the Ministry of War issued a decree on June 25, abruptly extending conscription to the Muslim populations of Astrakhan Province, Siberia, and Central Asia formerly exempt from the draft. Indigenous men between nineteen and forty-three were to be drafted, not for combat but into labor battalions deployed at the front and behind the lines.[112] The decree arrived during harvest time, when the labor of Kyrgyz men was particularly important, and also during Ramadan.[113] Local officials were given no explanation for the sudden policy change, and no general announcement was provided. Rumors spread that recruits would be made to dig trenches directly under enemy fire.[114] Some Muslim spokesmen expressed support for the draft summons, while demanding the Kyrgyz be used as warriors, not workmen. Others urged the Muslim Duma deputies to press for the order's repeal.[115] General Aleksandr Gippius, the military governor of Fergana, refused to implement the decree, fearing the consequences. He was relieved of his post.[116]

The reaction General Gippius had feared began two weeks later in several Fergana cities, then spread throughout the valley. Village elders and officials charged with drawing up the lists of eligible men were attacked, and over fifty were murdered. In Tashkent on July 11, a crowd of angry Muslim women confronted the authorities. News of the incident spread to the city of Jizzakh in the cattle-grazing area northeast of Samarkand. The local *bais* had managed to keep their sons off the lists. A crowd of resentful workers murdered three officials who tried to appease them. Troops forced the aroused men to retreat to the Muslim quarter, where they gathered swords, knives, and other weapons that came to hand. With no preconceived plan, but following the lead of their *ishan*, the rebels later destroyed miles of railway lines and killed over a dozen railroad workers. By July 16, additional troops had imposed order and restored the trains. The next day martial law was declared in the region. In the course of their rampage, the rebels had seized women and children and killed eighty-three Russians. By the end of the month, however, the revolt had been suppressed. In reprisal, the rebel villages were plundered and burned, their inhabitants shot, and their crops destroyed. Surviving villagers, if they could do so, fled.[117]

General Aleksei Kuropatkin, a former minister of war with a long career behind him in Central Asia, was appointed commander in chief of Turkestan, with orders to pacify the region. When he arrived in Tashkent on August 8, the revolt had spread to the Kazakh Steppe districts.[118] Semireche had the highest concentration of settlers, but also the highest proportion of conscripted working-age men, so that few Slavic men were left in the homesteads. Rifles distributed to the settlers for self-defense had been recalled earlier in the year. By the time revolt broke out, the villages were vulnerable to attack. Bands of tribesmen, several thousand strong, armed with sticks, spears, axes, knives, and the occasional firearm (at one point supplemented by rifles taken from a military convoy), spread through the area surrounding Lake Issyk-Kul, raiding the Russian settlements—killing the men, seizing the women, torching the dwellings, destroying roads and telegraph wires. When heavily armed reinforcements finally joined the available troops, the brutality was returned in kind. Native villages were laid waste, cattle driven away, yurts burned, and hundreds of inhabitants killed, some in cold blood after being arrested. The remaining Cossack and settler population took revenge by pillaging livestock and goods and massacring their owners. Kuropatkin pleaded that "the ruin of the Kirgiz population is not in the interests of the Russian government."[119] But blood was running high. This was a frenzy he himself had brought to the boil. It took until October for the convulsions to be pacified.[120] Military tribunals, meanwhile, sentenced a good fifty rebel leaders to death, and hundreds to hard labor.[121]

The Semireche region was completely devastated. The grain harvested in 1916 was half the yield of 1914.[122] Over two thousand settlers in that area alone were said to have lost their lives, and over a thousand could not be found, while almost three hundred soldiers were dead or unaccounted for.[123] Altogether somewhat over four thousand settlers were killed in the course of the revolt.[124] Figures for losses among the pastoralists are more controversial. They range from "several thousand" dead, to as many as 200,000 dead with another 250,000 fleeing over the border, to a total of 273,000, including both dead and disappeared.[125] One can safely conclude that over a quarter million nomads either were slaughtered outright, perished in flight from starvation or from the rigors of the mountain terrain, or disappeared over the Chinese border. Whatever the exact figures, the loss to the nomadic population was dramatic.[126] In some districts, a third or even two-thirds of the native population was missing by the end of 1916.[127] Those who tried to return were prevented from recovering their land, and those who had remained were expelled en masse, opening a vast expanse around Lake Issyk-Kul to peasant settlement.[128] At a closed session of the Duma, as we know, Alexander Kerensky denounced the government for provoking and brutally repressing the rebellion.

———

The February Revolution, coming eight months after the revolt began, was welcomed with joy in the city of Tashkent. The crowds that filled the central streets and squares of the new city revealed the entire spectrum of local society. Soldiers marched with red rosettes, singing the "Marseillaise." Workers carried red flags and portraits of the new leaders: Rodzianko, Miliukov, Kerensky. A French observer noted the presence of Armenians, Georgians,

Tatars, Persians, Bukharan Jews, and Muslims of the old city, of people in white turbans and flowing robes also bearing red flags. General Kuropatkin was followed by a Cossack entourage—red ribbons affixed to their swords.[129]

The display of solidarity was short-lived, however. The collapse of the monarchy exposed the deep fissures in Turkestani society. The Russian-dominated Tashkent City Duma formed a committee representing civic associations, including only two token Muslims. Railroad workers and soldiers—also Russian—formed their respective soviets. The local Muslim elites, like the educated establishment in most places, supported the Provisional Government, while demanding a role in the administration of regional affairs. Secular activists in the Muslim old city created their own civic committee, paralleled by a Soviet of Muslim Deputies (the Shura).[130] In mid-April, the Provisional Government opened City Duma elections to "citizens of Russia of both sexes, of all nationalities and religious denominations."[131] Local Russians now faced the prospect of a Muslim majority—not only in municipal elections, but also in elections to the forthcoming Constituent Assembly. The Muslim elites did not, however, present a united front. While the clergy (*ulama*) met separately, secular leaders began forming political organizations. In spring and summer, various congresses met in Orenburg and Tashkent, laying the foundations for what would later become a nationally based political party.[132] The modernizers, known as Jadids or enlighteners, differed among themselves on the question of political autonomy; they differed from the *ulama* on the role of religion and the status of women (now suddenly enfranchised). Muslim artisans likewise mobilized, but remained unreceptive to the discourse of Russian Social Democracy. Attempts in the same early months to form trans-regional Muslim organizations also proved ineffective.[133]

Thus, by April 1917, the major divides in Turkestani society—between Slavs and Muslims, between Europeanized and traditional Muslims—had taken political form. At the end of March, the Tashkent Soviet had arrested General Kuropatkin but allowed him to return to Petrograd. In his stead, the Provisional Government appointed a Turkestan Committee divided between Russians and Muslims, all of them outsiders to the region. Arriving in Tashkent, they were welcomed by a large crowd singing the "Marseillaise."[134] The Committee was powerless, however, to deal with the crisis already facing the region, in which ethnic conflicts were exacerbated by deprivation and the collapse of order. In August it reported that "robbery, plunder and violence are perpetrated by [Slavic] peasants against the Kirgiz native population, who are driven to the mountains, are starving, and are suffering from typhus and scurvy."[135] Food shortages increased tension in the cities as well. Russian soldiers in Tashkent pillaged the old town, suspecting its Muslim inhabitants of hoarding provisions.[136] Soldiers attacked native peasants loaded with grain returning by train to their home villages after bringing livestock to market. A massive demonstration summoned by Muslim organizations crossed over into the new city to protest the abuses, but nothing stopped the soldiers, who felt themselves empowered even before the October coup. On September 12, a group from the local garrison established a revolutionary council, claiming to supplant the Provisional Government.[137] The rebels were easily dislodged by loyal troops, but on the heels of the Petrograd coup, after a short but intense armed battle, the Bolsheviks took control of Tashkent. The original soviets were replaced by a Soviet composed of Bolsheviks and their Left SR allies, which announced its claim to power.[138]

This claim was rejected by Muslim leaders across the board, all of whom continued to pin their hopes on the Constituent Assembly, though they could not reconcile the differences among themselves.[139] On November 26, a group of secular Muslims gathered in the Fergana Valley city of Kokand for the Fourth Regional Muslim Congress, which "according to the principles of the great Russian revolution, declared Turkestan to be territorially autonomous in union with the Federated Democratic Russian Republic, deferring the elaboration of the form of autonomy to the Turkestan Constituent Assembly."[140] The Congress created a Provisional Government answerable to a broad-based council, which included non-Muslims. The so-called Kokand Autonomy thus expressed the viewpoint of Russian-educated Muslim intellectuals, with the support of non-Muslim moderates, in opposition both to the *ulama* and the Bolshevik-dominated Soviet.[141]

The attempts of the local elites to establish their authority in the region did not survive the clash of opposing forces, however. The Kokand Autonomy was ousted in February 1918 by Red Guards descending from Bolshevik-controlled Tashkent.[142] Here a configuration emerged that repeated itself in Baku a month later, as we have seen. In opposing the Kokand government, the Bolsheviks enlisted the help of militias formed by the Armenian Dashnak party, composed largely of refugees who had arrived after the 1915 massacres and joined the Armenian community already there. Like the local Russians, the Armenians feared the consequence of Muslim political power.[143] After Kokand was taken, the Armenians joined the Red Guards in pillaging and destroying the Muslim quarter. In the course of the rampage and artillery bombardment, at least ten thousand Muslim inhabitants are said to have been killed.[144]

Soon after the Kokand Autonomy had taken shape, Steppe Kazakh leaders had gathered in Orenburg, at the southern end of the Urals, and formed another Kadet-style government under the name Alash Orda, or Horde of Alash, invoking a mythical ancestor of the Kazakh people. In elections to the Constituent Assembly, the Alash party received a majority among the steppe population.[145] Geographically oriented toward the north, the Orenburg contingent preferred to seek alliances with anti-Bolshevik movements in Siberia.[146] Its fate thus came to depend on the fortunes of the various contending forces in Siberia, all adverse to local autonomy of any kind. Once the Red Army, under the command of Mikhail Frunze, captured Orenburg in spring 1919, the Alash was obliged to come to terms with Soviet rule. In August 1920, the Kazakh Autonomous Soviet Socialist Republic replaced the last vestiges of Kazakh self-government.[147]

The thirty-five-year-old Mikhail Frunze, appearing as the conqueror from the north, was in fact born in Pishpek in Semireche (from 1926 to 1991 named Frunze in his honor; now Bishkek, capital of Kyrgyzstan) and studied in the city of Vernyi. A typical son of the Empire, his mother was Russian, his father a Moldovan peasant who had served as a medical orderly in the Imperial Army. Like many other Bolsheviks of his generation, Frunze joined the party when still in his teens, was arrested a number of times, and was exiled to Siberia. In 1916 he joined the Imperial Army, not in search of a military career but to preach revolution in the trenches. He emerged as a talented commander in 1917, along with the emergence of the Red Army as a fighting force.[148] His victory in Orenburg in 1919 changed the balance of power in Turkestan and the Kazakh Steppe decisively. Between November 1917 and April 1918, the city had gone back and forth four times between the Red Army and the anti-Bolshevik Cossack forces under Ataman Aleksandr Dutov, a native of the Syr-Daria district. From July 1918 to September 1919, Dutov controlled the city and with it the rail connection and telegraph between Russia and Tashkent.[149] The "Orenburg bottleneck"—essentially a blockade—deepened the food crisis in Turkestan and isolated the Bolsheviks in Tashkent from developments in Soviet Russia.[150]

Cut off as they were, on May 1, 1918, the Bolshevik-run Fifth All-Turkestan Congress of Soviets proclaimed the formation of the Turkestan Autonomous Soviet Socialist Republic (*Turkestanskaia avtonomnaia sovetskaia respublika*), as a riposte to the Muslim autonomist intelligentsia, whom the Communists denounced as counterrevolutionary bourgeois nationalists.[151] Yet the party did not have much of a base to count on. Only the workers in the railroad shops of Tashkent and the mass of demobilized soldiers embraced its appeals.[152] As the leading Communist Georgii Safarov admitted, the Tashkent proletariat was "far from understanding revolutionary discipline," and the Red Army men, prone to drunkenness and plunder, were no better.[153] Born in St. Petersburg to Polish and Armenian parents, Safarov joined the Bolshevik Party as a teenager in 1908. Ending up in Zurich, he had returned to Russia in April 1917 on the same sealed train carrying Lenin and his entourage. In summer 1918, then a mere twenty-seven years old, he participated, as a member of the Urals party leadership, in the decision to execute the imperial family in Ekaterinburg.[154] Once in Tashkent, by now a hardened political operator, Safarov realized how tenuous Soviet authority actually was. The principle of "proletarian autonomy," he observed, was nothing more than "a revolutionary phrase," obscuring the fact that the party had no roots in the native population.[155]

Once again, the Bolsheviks faced the issue of how to feed the cities. They began by appropriating the goods of the mostly native merchants to exchange for food from the peasants, but there was soon nothing left to take.[156] As Safarov put it, reflecting on the dilemma of imposing socialism on a colonial society: "The new city fell upon the hungry old cities and the native villages with a hail of requisitions and confiscations, while the Muslim population was dying, not having the power to cope with hunger. Between the Russian new city, in which the Soviet was based, and the broad masses of the native population there opened an unbridgeable gulf." The Communists inherited a situation that was already critical. "In the winter of 1917–1918," Safarov recalled, "the corpses of people who had died of starvation piled up everywhere—on the streets of the new city, in the train stations, on the highways." In February it was reported that "in Semireche hungry Kirgiz have begun to eat the corpses of those who have died of hunger." For the native peasants, Safarov admitted, Communist power unfortunately meant "death from starvation, Red Guard assaults on their centuries-old way of life, indiscriminate reprisals, across-the-board confiscations and requisitions, arbitrary searches."[157]

After July 1918, when Ataman Dutov's Orenburg army blocked rail transport from Russia, the food situation worsened. The Slavic peasants began to feel the brunt as well, as the Red Army seized their grain, plundering and terrorizing the villages.[158] Protective of their supplies, the peasant settlers of Semireche declared they would submit only to the authority of their local soviets. Armed with the weapons they had acquired in the army, the settlers nevertheless retained their advantage over the tribes, ill-equipped to guard their food supplies and land from depredation. Many were already dying.[159]

Soviet-era historians subsequently blamed both the peasants' rejection of Soviet authority and their assaults on the indigenous population on the influence of SR activists, alleged to have been furthering the interests of the wealthiest peasant settlers (kolonizatorskoe kulachestvo) and prosperous tribal landowners (kirgizskie bai) said to exploit the "laboring Kirgiz masses."[160] The party also denounced the armed bands composed of Muslim peasants, known as Basmachi in the local idiom, that sustained a prolonged grassroots insurrection throughout the region. The Bolsheviks dismissed the Basmachi as "bandits," a routine term of abuse for any popular movement that resisted their impositions.[161] These bands were indeed aggressive, but it was their capacity for self-mobilization that presented the greatest threat.

The Basmachi had existed in the region before the revolution, under the leadership of local figures, the kurbashi (qo'rboshi), who now drew their followers from the Muslim peasantry and from the increasingly unemployed and destitute cotton workers. In the Fergana Valley, a third of the population died of starvation in 1918, while the collapse of cotton production caused mass unemployment among field hands and cotton-processing workers.[162] Some kurbashi belonged to Muslim ruling families displaced by the Russian conquest, others were outlaws. All chafed under the increasing dominance of the cities, while defending traditional culture against their own modernizing urban elites.[163] In 1918 the bands spread throughout the Fergana Valley, where their primary role was to protect the villages against the depredations of the Red Army.[164] They also clashed with settler peasants organized by local soviets into a village-based Peasant Army.[165] This army fought alongside Red Army troops in repulsing the Basmachi and taking revenge on the villages they abandoned when fleeing into the mountains.[166]

The two principal kurbashi in Fergana were Irgash-Bek and Madamin-Bek. Both had been serving penal sentences when they were amnestied by the

Provisional Government in early 1917. Madamin-Bek had participated in the 1916 rebellion. Returning to the region, both now saw their mission as the reestablishment of order and the exercise of restraint. After the massacre in Kokand in February 1918, they fled to remote villages, from which they and other *kurbashi* established control over the entire Kokand district. Though attempting to curb the damage inflicted on their own people, they lived off tribute from the local population, in the form of horses, fodder, and food.[167] By 1919 Madamin-Bek had assembled as many as five thousand armed men and created a network of informers, a system of tax collection, and a method of requisition that promised to compensate the peasants for crops and livestock.[168]

The Bolsheviks recognized the need to win support among the indigenous population and in particular to subdue the Basmachi insurgency. At the end of 1917, the Sovnarkom had promised "all toiling Muslims" that their traditions would be respected.[169] Promises were not enough, however. Kazakh Communist Turar Ryskulov became the central figure in a campaign, launched from Moscow, that tried to reconcile Communist class politics with the realities of a pre-capitalist society organized along ethnic and religious lines. A native of the Semireche district, Ryskulov had participated in the 1916 revolt and now, at the ripe old age of twenty-five, represented the face of Central Asian Communism to the Russian party chiefs. His own convictions led him to welcome Moscow's call to bring the nomadic peoples into the apparatus and win acceptance among the Basmachi.[170]

Ryskulov became the head of a newly formed Muslim Office (*Musul'manskoe biuro Kommunisticheskoi partii Turkestana*—Musbiuro).[171] He also obtained positions in the local party organs, allowing him to pursue a policy of ethnic inclusion that gave Muslims, as the demographic majority, a dominant role. He proposed a truce with Madamim-Bek and cracked down on "Russian chauvinists."[172] As the Kazakh historian Kenes Nurpeisov comments, with post-Soviet hindsight, "Ryskulov clearly articulated the idea that the national state of Turkestan must not be merely declarative. This was the state of Kazakhs, Uzbeks, Turkmen, Tajiks, and Kirgiz, who did not want to remain simple spectators of the political process."[173] They were already more than spectators. The problem was not merely to empower them, but also to rein them in. In May 1919, the Tashkent Soviet ordered the Peasant Army to submit to Red Army command. Its leader instead concluded an agreement with Madamin-Bek, by which they pledged jointly to oppose Soviet power.[174]

The Communists had to cope with tensions in their own ranks as well. At regional party conferences in May and June 1919, Musbiuro leaders accused their Russian comrades of arrogance toward the native population, of exacerbating tensions between settler peasants and nomads, of provoking banditism, and of disrespecting Muslim Communists—in essence, of replicating the colonialist posture of the old regime. Ryskulov himself felt he was acting in the spirit of directives from Moscow that called explicitly for proportional representation.[175] Once Frunze had captured Orenburg in spring 1919, opening the rail link to Russia, Moscow's pressure was felt more directly. In early November, the so-called Turkestan Commission (*Turkkomissiia*) arrived in Tashkent from Moscow.[176] Its principal members were Filipp (Isai) Goloshchekin, later to preside over the great Kazakh famine of 1930–1933; Valerian Kuibyshev, a close associate of Stalin's; and Frunze, who at first remained in Orenburg.[177]

In January 1920, the Turkestan Communist Party held a conference at which it outlined policy on the national question. Thinking he was moving in the authorized direction, Ryskulov, as head of the Musbiuro, proposed the formation of a single regional party, with its own Central Committee, subordinate of course to Moscow, in which "the broad laboring masses of the Turkic peoples" would play the dominant role. It was to be called the Communist Party of the Turkic Peoples. The members of the Turkkomissiia indicated their approval and went so far as to recommend the elimination of ethnic denominations—Tatar, Bashkir, Kirgiz—in favor of the omnibus "Turkic" idea.[178] The Muslim Communists—seemingly with official backing—were in effect proposing a form of Soviet-sponsored autonomy, which included the creation of a regional army, enlisting the former Basmachi.[179]

The atmosphere changed abruptly, however, with Frunze's arrival in Tashkent on February 22, 1920.[180] Reversing its initial position, the Turkkomissiia now rejected the notion of a Turkic Party and a Turkic Republic, reaffirmed the various tribal ethnonyms, and christened the region the Turkestan Autonomous Republic of the Russian Soviet Federative Socialist Republic.[181] With the usual Bolshevik invective, Frunze denounced Ryskulov's position as "Kerenskyism," as "narrow nationalism, a concession to the petty-bourgeois classes." Ryskulov was accused of wanting "to organize his own Muslim state," of refusing "to adopt the strictly class point of view on the struggle with colonialism." He was labeled a "national-deviationist."[182] At the end of the year, Moscow appointed less confrontational comrades to the Turkkomissiia, but the attacks on Ryskulov continued.[183]

Frunze's hard line excluded any concessions to the Basmachi, but a number of *kurbashi* had nevertheless begun to recognize Soviet authority. In March 1920, Madamin-Bek accepted what seemed like favorable terms.[184] Frunze was determined, however, to intimidate the natives into subjection. Airplanes flew low over villages to frighten their inhabitants; hostages were taken and threatened with execution if the Basmachi did not give in. Madamin-Bek himself never got to make peace with the new rulers. On his way to Tashkent in mid-May to mark his acceptance of the conditions, he was killed by an angry rival. His own men refused to disarm and melted back into the hinterland of Basmachi resistance.[185] The Basmachi were not entirely subdued until several years later, but at their height they posed a real challenge to Soviet control.[186]

In the end, two forces combined to impose Soviet rule in Central Asia. The first was military—the Red Army moved in to quash any attempt at regional autonomy or popular resistance. The second was economic—the suppression of private trade and the forcible seizure of grain together reduced millions of peasants (and herdsmen) to starvation. Famine hit central Russia in 1921; it began in Turkestan in 1917. Bolshevik policies had unleashed a catastrophe long in the making. The effect of conscription had been to deplete the number of peasants cultivating the fields; productivity dropped, and the grain yield was severely affected. By late 1917, with railroads from Russia blocked, grain shipments no longer reached Central Asia. As the price of grain rose, the nomads sold their animals to be able to afford it. Between 1917 and 1920, the nomads of Russian Turkestan lost almost half their land and two-thirds of their livestock. In the same years, the nomadic population shrank by almost a third—partly as a result of massive flight, partly from starvation.[187]

In the Caucasus and Central Asia, ethnic and cultural differences became organizing principles—and therefore had to be mastered. The failure of Muslim elites to unify across Turkestan and the Kazakh Steppe reflected not only their numerical weakness and their distance from the popular base, but also the many distinctions that separated the indigenous peoples from each other. The Communist constituency in Tashkent was disproportionately Slavic—the workers and urban intelligentsia—but Communism also attracted the support of anti-traditionalist Muslim elites such as Ryskulov, who then found it hard to reconcile the desire for cultural autonomy with the demands of the Russian center. The Soviets claimed to have united the Russian proletariat with the impoverished Muslim peasantry and herdsmen to overthrow imperial Russian colonial power and unseat the privileged classes on which it had been based.[188]

Until the end of 1919, however, the party relied on the same European parts of the population that had anchored imperial power in the region.

Himself a doctrinaire hard-liner in other respects, Safarov strongly criticized the local Russian comrades for having stepped into the old regime's colonial shoes. "The Communist Party," he reflected in 1921, "encounters special conditions in the East. It cannot count on success, since it is the party of the national minority; especially since this national minority belongs to the formerly ruling nation. The example of 'colonial Soviet power' in Turkestan is proof of this." The party must make a special effort, he warned, to root itself in the local culture and strive to represent the interests of the broad native masses against their own class oppressors, at the same time providing them with the cultural and economic tools with which to transform themselves into their own nation.[189] Given his critique of "Communist colonialism," Safarov ought to have embraced Ryskulov and his efforts to nativize the party. Indeed, he sympathized with the difficult position of the "Jadid intelligentsia," such as Ryskulov, faced with the intransigence of "colonialist Russian left communists," by which he meant the original Turkkomissiia.[190] Yet, he too accused Ryskulov of "nationalist opportunism" and called "the nationalist intelligentsia of Ryskulov's type" an obstacle to the participation of the "native masses" in the building of Communism.[191]

Moscow's relationship to Central Asia was thus highly ambivalent, as Safarov's own record makes clear. On the one hand, Lenin insisted the indigenous population be drawn into the party and the local organs; he warned against the application of class politics to a society in which capitalist classes had barely emerged; he denounced Russian chauvinism. On the other hand, Moscow demanded the subordination of regional organizations to its own authority—the power of the Russian center. Safarov seems to have intended his critique of the first Communist activists—imposing the old colonialism in Communist guise—as a warning rather than a final verdict, since it was delivered in 1921 when Communist rule was just getting started. Whatever the specifics of the Central Asian case, the subordination of regions to the center and of local initiative—even within the party—to Moscow's control was a more general pattern. Imposing central control was no easy matter, however, as the rampaging Civil War makes clear. The no-holds-barred struggles in the Cossack heartland of the Don and Kuban and across the Siberian expanse, which impinged on the fight for Central Asia, presented the Moscow leadership with enormous challenges, but also compelled them to forge the institutions on which to build the emerging socialist state.

Isaak Babel, *Konarmiia* (Moscow: Gosudarstvennoe izdatel'stvo, 1926) [*Red Cavalry* (Moscow: State Publishing House, 1926)]. Sterling Memorial Library, Yale University.

# PART V

# War Within

# I

# The Unquiet Don

The Treaty of Brest-Litovsk, as one of its Socialist Revolutionary critics complained, "did not bring peace, but only the start of a new, even more terrible war."[1] In fact, by March 1918, the war against the Bolsheviks was already well under way. As the Mensheviks and Lenin's more cautious comrades had feared, the one-party coup was bound to provoke the domestic enemies of the revolution, some of whom had only reluctantly tolerated the tsar's abdication and the Provisional Government as unfortunate consequences of Nicholas's personal misrule. The Bolsheviks claimed the geographic center. Their opponents gathered along the peripheries—northwest of Petrograd, as we have seen; beyond the Sea of Azov in the Don and Kuban; in Transcaucasia and Central Asia; and across the vast Siberian expanse. Everywhere, leadership was fragmented and the local population divided along class and cultural lines. No single anti-Bolshevik figure or group was able to construct a viable center of authority or an effective fighting force. The Empire, like a porcelain vase, had crashed to the ground, leaving a heap of tiny shards, impossible to reassemble or reshape into a new form.

The chronology of the Civil War is therefore daunting. The period between December 1917 and May 1918 is particularly confusing, as organizations formed, collapsed, merged, diverged, and switched allegiances. The situation with the Germans was still in flux, the Allies were dithering over which horse to back, the Bolsheviks had yet to construct an army worthy of the name, and the diaspora of former tsarist officers was internally riven and unable to inspire a stable following. Demobilization, desertion, the collapse of law enforcement and of laws—the general breakdown of norms and institutions—released criminals and angry masses of hungry men into the social bloodstream. No war is sanitary, and no war stops on a dime. The conflicts that pulverized the remains of the old state structures and the old social order completed the process of dissolution begun in 1914.

The military—functional or in collapse—was central to the entire conflict. The old officer corps, offering professional leadership and expertise, thus constituted the major internal threat to Bolshevik survival—and potentially the key to Bolshevik success. Despite the skills they brought to the task, the anti-Bolshevik officers were hardly assured of success. The challenge was to attract able bodies to do the fighting and to surmount the same logistical and material challenges facing all aspiring regimes amid social and economic crisis: how to feed, equip, arm, and train a fighting force. And how to keep recruits and volunteers from crossing to the other side.

Officers had played a crucial role in 1917 from the start, as we have seen. In February, General Mikhail Alekseev, then chief of staff at Stavka, had endorsed the tsar's abdication. In August, General Lavr Kornilov had attempted to assert the kind of authority Kerensky's government was unable to command. His bid to impose military rule backfired, strengthening the appeal of the Bolshevik message and demonizing the alleged enemies of the revolution. As chief of staff under Kerensky, Alekseev had Kornilov arrested, but soon their fates converged. After the Bolsheviks unseated the Provisional Government, Alekseev departed immediately for Novocherkassk at the base of the Don, upriver from Rostov, where he set about forming the so-called Volunteer Army.[2] By mid-December he had been joined by Kornilov and the other generals released from prison in Bykhov by General Dukhonin. Among them was Anton Denikin, formerly Alekseev's own chief of staff, subsequently Kornilov's co-conspirator, and ultimately his successor at the head of the Volunteer Army.[3]

The Volunteer Army attracted officers with anti-Bolshevik convictions. Others remained at their posts in what was becoming the Red Army. Some felt a patriotic duty to continue fighting the Germans, even under a new flag; some were following their political sympathies. These were joined by newly promoted reserve officers and hastily trained enlisted men who had moved into the upper ranks decimated by the war.[4] By late 1917, recalled the left-leaning writer Viktor Shklovskii, posted with a motorized unit at the time, "Anyone who could be promoted to an officer had been promoted.... A literate man not in an officer's uniform was a rarity; a clerk—a treasure. Sometimes an enormous troop train would arrive and there wouldn't be one literate man in the group—not even anyone to call the roll."[5]

By and large, the commissioned officers had welcomed the February Revolution. "They too were exhausted by the war," Shklovskii remembered. "The best of them stayed and they were the very ones who suffered the most after October."[6] A recent source estimates that 170,000 officers—two-thirds of the surviving Imperial Army officer corps, though most no longer drawn from the privileged classes—ended up fighting against the Bolsheviks. Many were literally pushed into the arms of counterrevolution. In the wake of the October coup and into January 1918, anyone in an officer's uniform was liable to be beaten, stabbed, or shot to death by enraged mobs of often drunken soldiers. Altogether about twenty thousand officers were murdered in this short period, torn from trains and apartments, struck down on the streets.[7]

No matter their personal backgrounds or political views, the officers could not escape their association with the authority of the imperial regime. In Kiev, at first a haven for officers either fleeing the center or unable to return from the front, many were executed in a park which their assailants dubbed "Dukhonin's headquarters."[8] This bit of black humor shows how the wild passions of the mob acquired political coloration. Before his own murder, Dukhonin had been anointed an enemy of the people by the newly fledged People's Commissars, who had not yet managed to decapitate the old army command. The label merely endorsed already inflamed emotions. The gold-braided epaulettes had become a hated symbol of hierarchy from the first days of the revolution. Dukhonin's murderers began by ripping them from his tunic. This act was repeated hundreds of times, sometimes as a prelude to assault, sometimes as a symbolic demonstration. The patriotic Russian officers in Mikhail Bulgakov's *White Guard* hastily remove their own shoulder boards and other insignia as the Reds loom on the horizon.[9]

The officers who organized military opposition to the Bolshevik regime called themselves the Whites. The origin of the label is unclear. It may have referred to the white flag of the royalist Vendée during the French Revolution, since the monarchy still had its supporters among the Russian Whites. It may have been used to evoke the image of General Mikhail Skobelev, known as the White General after the color of his horse. A well-publicized hero of the Russo-Turkish War of 1877–1878, he also participated in the conquest of Central Asia, where he was responsible for one of the more brutal episodes of pacification. St. George, considered a patron of soldiers, who appeared on the Imperial coat-of-arms and lent his name to the Order of St. George, awarded for valor, also rode a white horse. There seems to be no solid explanation.[10]

The Whites were uniformly hostile to Bolshevik rule, but the label implies a coherence they did not possess. Geographically dispersed and internally fragmented, they had difficulty establishing a firm social base in areas that were ethnically and religiously diverse. For the same reason, it was difficult to assemble and retain any kind of army. Nor were the White movement's political goals of a piece. Overall, its leaders represented the interests of the old military and landowning elites, but not all were reactionary. Some represented the civic middle—zemstvos, entrepreneurs, professionals—close in spirit to the Kadet Party. Like the Kadets, they stood for the integrity of the former imperial state, wanting to recover its boundaries and restore its prestige, if not its political tradition.

The color red, by contrast, stood for the generic revolution and was adopted by all the socialist parties. Red flags were brandished in 1905, and red ribbons appeared immediately after February to mark the first victory of the 1917 Revolution. Eventually, as the Bolsheviks bested their rivals on the left, they came to identify the color exclusively with their own Bolshevik enterprise. Between the Bolshevik Reds and the military Whites, however, lay the complex middle ground of revolutionary politics—from the cautious and increasingly right-wing Kadets to the Left and Right SRs, whose allegiances kept shifting. The post-Brest collapse also opened the door to ideologically unclassifiable forces—peasant rebels, self-styled bandits, anarchists, independent socialist-populists—all challenging the Moscow commissars for control over the vast, hard-to-govern expanse whose population had abandoned deep-rooted habits of deference.

If the White-Red dichotomy obscures the complexity of political alignments during the Civil War, the role of the Cossacks illustrates the complexity of popular loyalties. The Cossacks and the Don came to symbolize the anti-Bolshevik counterrevolution, but neither the Cossacks as a community nor the Cossacks as a fighting force were united in opposition to the Soviet regime. What they shared, however, was a reluctance to venture far outside their home territories, which they saw themselves as defending. Overall the Whites had more to offer, since their military leaders joined forces with Cossack spokesmen. But the Cossack cavalrymen had no interest in General Denikin's grand schemes for the restoration of empire. Nor did the Cossacks in the *stanitsa* settlements respond to the socialist call for a society without rank, privilege, or distinctions of wealth, since their identity was inseparable precisely from the privileges they enjoyed and from their relative prosperity.

Despite their continuing military role and their distinctive pageantry, the Cossacks had come more and more to resemble peasants in their everyday lives. Originally nomadic herders, the nineteenth-century Cossacks completed the transition to agriculturalists with settled households. The hosts were run by elected assemblies and controlled the use of land on a collective basis, not unlike the peasant model. There was no single Cossack center, but the various branches shared a distinctive culture, combining highly developed martial skills as saber-wielding horsemen with a style of dress that evoked their Tatar ancestry.[11] They were different from and felt superior to the peasants who lived beside them and envied their status and advantages.[12]

During the Great War, the storied cavalrymen figured as patriotic heroes, the devilish hordes featured in German propaganda—"The Cossacks are coming!" After 1917, by contrast, they came to symbolize the regionalist aspirations of the Ukraine and the Don and Kuban regions, emblems of the counterrevolution, although many also fought for the Reds. The province of the Don stretched north above the Taganrog Inlet at the upper tip of the Sea of Azov. The Kuban lay to its south, east of the Sea of Azov and down to the Black Sea and the northern Caucasus. In both provinces, however, Cossacks constituted just under half the combined seven million inhabitants. Peasants indigenous to the region made up another quarter of the population, recent arrivals the rest.[13] Overall, the Cossacks were more literate and more prosperous than the peasants, though only a minority counted as truly wealthy.[14] Even in the Don and Kuban, moreover, the Cossacks were not a homogeneous lot. Kuban Cossacks were divided between the Black Sea (Zaporozhian) and Caucasian Line (Don) Cossacks, each with a strong sense of identity.[15] Within the Cossack fold, the older generation was more likely to uphold traditional customs, while younger men, affected by the experience of war (the veterans, or *frontoviki*), were less compliant.[16]

As a warrior caste, the Cossacks served in the army in higher proportions than the general peasant population.[17] Their units better resisted the demoralization that affected the peasant-dominated infantry, but the shared experience of the war and the impact of Bolshevik propaganda created a common bond with their peasant neighbors. The high proportion of veterans returning home brought impressions of the revolution with them, but as in the case of every other social group, their views and responses evolved and wavered. The two Don Cossack regiments stationed in Petrograd in February 1917, recently back from the front, had turned the tide by refusing to fire on the gathering crowds, triggering the fall of the monarchy. Yet in July 1917,

Cossacks were employed to suppress the Petrograd street demonstrations.[18] The October coup did not make them any more predictable.

The horsemen with their sabers and fur hats suggested a timeless tradition, but the Cossacks were not isolated from modern life. Cossack officers trained in the military academies; Cossack deputies sat in the State Duma. The region inhabited by Cossacks was itself feeling the impact of modernization. On the Ukrainian side, the cities of Ekaterinoslav (on the Dnepr River, today's Dnipropetrovsk), Donetsk (north of Mariupol), and Rostov (at the mouth of the Don) were centers of heavy industry. The region between the Donets and Don Rivers, known as the Donets Basin (Donbas, for short), produced the coal to smelt the iron ore from Krivoi Rog, southwest of Ekaterinoslav.[19] Heavy industry was also concentrated in the commercial port of Taganrog, on the Sea of Azov, the region's largest city, a site of foreign investment and a funnel for the grain trade. To the east, in the crook of the Volga, Tsaritsyn (now Volgograd) was a major railway junction and a strategic pathway to the Caucasus, possessing munitions factories and a large working class. Railways built in the late nineteenth century linked the principal cities to each other and to the Ukraine and central Russia. The cities and mines were home to a mostly Russian-speaking working class, the target of revolutionary agitation. The regional towns were not mere backwaters, however. The railroad spurred the growth of local urban culture: theaters, universities, health spas, tourism—a world away from the Cossack *stanitsas*.[20]

As in the rest of the Empire, the propertied and urban elites were drawn into political activity during and after 1905. This region sent Kadet delegates to the State Duma. After February 1917, the regionalism that attracted the political classes of the Ukrainian provinces also inspired leaders in the Don to wave the flag of local self-governance. Civic activists in the administrative center of Novocherkassk, just north of Rostov, formed a Don Executive Committee, which was formally recognized by the Provisional Government as the temporary authority in the Don. The Committee was dominated by local civic figures of Cossack origin who identified with the Kadet Party and vowed to defend "the people's interests and the achievements of the Revolution."[21] Later a symbol and stronghold of reaction, the Don thus began as a center of constitutional liberalism. In Cossack clothing, however, this regionalist liberalism was at odds with the Kadet commitment to integrity of empire. The tensions were still to be worked out.

As elsewhere, however, the elites were divided. While the Don Executive Committee was being formed in Novocherkassk, a group of Cossack officers in the same city formed a separate Cossack Union. Meanwhile, in late March and April, congresses organized by the Cossack Duma deputies recognized the authority of the Don Executive Committee, but at the same time called for the convocation of a Cossack Circle (*Krug*), or parliament, based on popular elections.[22] In reviving the historic institutions of Cossack self-rule—the Kuban Rada (Council), the Ural, Don, and Terek Circles—these leaders evoked a partly imagined past in order to operate in a contemporary mode.[23] On May 26, the First Cossack Circle formed a so-called Don Host Government (*Donskoe voiskovoe pravitel'stvo*), electing as leader General Aleksei Kaledin. A conservative cavalry commander, born to a Don Cossack family, who called for the return of traditional army discipline, Kaledin assumed the archaic title of "Ataman of the Don." After the July Days, Kerensky, eager for allies against the troublesome Left, confirmed his support for Kaledin as commander of armed forces in the Don region. In August, however, Kaledin, from his outpost in Novocherkassk, ordered his troops to submit to Kornilov's authority. Kerensky demanded his arrest, but the Don Circle refused to comply, asserting its independent authority.[24]

Though Kaledin spoke in the name of the entire region, in fact the Don Host Government was dedicated not only to independence from the Russian center but also to the maintenance of Cossack estate privileges against the claims of the peasant population. These claims were articulated in May at peasant congresses in the Don, which demanded the equal distribution of land, at the expense of Cossack reserves, and the abolition of the very status distinctions on which Cossack identity depended.[25] Both demands—the redistribution of land and the abolition of the estate hierarchy—were key to the Bolshevik platform. One of the first decrees issued after the October coup announced the "abolition of estates and civil ranks." The Cossacks were not mentioned, but it obviously applied to them, too.[26]

Immediately following the coup, the Novocherkassk Don Host Government welcomed the remnants of the Provisional Government. Numerous Kadet leaders made their way south, seeing Kaledin as a center of anti-Bolshevik authority until the Constituent Assembly should resolve the issue of state power. The Don Host Government dissolved local soviets and imposed martial law in areas where the workers were likely to cause trouble. Indeed, the Constituent Assembly elections in mid-November confirmed the social geography of the region. The Bolsheviks did best in Rostov, Taganrog, and the mining centers, but overall received a mere 15 percent. Kaledin's Don Host Government won 44 percent of the vote and the SRs 34 percent, mostly among peasants, though also some Cossacks. The Kadet vote was negligible.[27] The peasants, for their part, focused their hostility on their Cossack neighbors.[28]

Although in principle Kaledin spoke for Cossack interests, there had always been a disconnect between the urban Cossack elites and the local Cossack population, itself fragmented along communal, geographic, and generational lines. On November 7, Kaledin's Don Circle declared itself sovereign, as the Don Republic, but when the general tried to organize armed opposition to the Bolshevik coup, the Cossack veterans refused to fight.[29] Tension also sharpened between the Cossacks and the local peasants, who were excluded from Cossack organizations. On November 16, in opposition to Kaledin, the miners of Makaevka announced the creation of a Don Soviet Republic and went on strike, crippling coal production. The Don Soviet Republic, however, had little but symbolic importance.[30] As in the Ukraine, here, too, Bolshevik and regionalist institutions—all fragile and in flux—competed for a popular following. Unlike in the Ukraine, where some populist leaders adopted a socialist program, here regionalism suited the purposes of the Cossack elites, appealing to the desire of the Cossack communities to retain their accustomed way of life and economic standing, against the leveling politics of the peasants and their SR and Bolshevik spokesmen.

Although Kaledin promoted local interests that should have attracted Cossack supporters, he was thus faced with competitors on the left with a populist message. He also faced rivals in the anti-Bolshevik camp, who challenged his regionalist aspirations. General Alekseev had arrived in the Don five days before Kaledin made a claim to local sovereignty. Kaledin, for his part, viewed Alekseev as an unwelcome rival. Novocherkassk had become a destination for officers fleeing the dangers and chaos of the center and the collapsing fronts, whom Alekseev tried to recruit for what became the Volunteer Army. Several hundred responded, but many were reluctant to heed his call.[31] Alekseev's enterprise instead attracted a number of leading Kadets, including Pavel Miliukov and Andrei Shingarev (who later returned to Petrograd for the Constituent Assembly, only to be murdered in his hospital bed). It was at this point also that Boris Savinkov, Kornilov's confederate in August, made his appearance.[32]

The anti-Bolshevik officers assembled in the Don thus not only disagreed among themselves but had trouble forming an army. At hand were Cossacks of various descriptions, front veterans tired of the war, officers of every political coloration except Red, and too many competing commanders.

As of February 1918, General Denikin recalled, "all these regiments, battalions, and divisions were but skeleton cadres, and the total 'army' did not exceed *four thousand* fighters, dwindling at times, as during the hard fighting at Rostov, to absolutely insignificant proportions."[33] The troops relied for subsistence on donations from wealthy residents of Moscow and Rostov, on the appropriation of local government funds, and on raiding arms depots. Aside from the donations, which, Denikin complained, were miserly, they depended most heavily on theft. Despite a lack of scruples not peculiar to them, they were nevertheless "short of absolutely everything."[34]

The question of leadership was crucial on both sides after October. While Lenin was imposing his will on the party's inner circle, the opponents of the Bolsheviks were squabbling among themselves. They lacked a single commanding figure. Kornilov and Alekseev were a contrast in style and substance. Kornilov offered panache, Alekseev restraint. "Relations between the two generals were none too cordial, owing to a long-standing mutual antipathy," remarked General Denikin, while insisting that "both knew how to place the national cause above personal disagreements."[35] Neither had much luck, however, attracting officers, much less filling the ranks. Those still loyal to the monarchy were mistrustful. Alekseev had endorsed the tsar's abdication; Kornilov had arrested the imperial family.[36] Alekseev was favored by the Kadet leaders who gathered around him in Novocherkassk. Kornilov hated politicians and moved to Rostov. Some people thought he was planning to unseat Alekseev.

In December, however, the generals settled on a compromise. Alekseev was to handle politics, Kornilov the military, and Kaledin local Cossack affairs. When it came to articulating a political program, the Volunteer Army declared its support for the Constituent Assembly. Its goals were to defeat both the Germans and the Bolsheviks, whom many in this milieu considered direct German agents. In Denikin's words, they were "to fight against anarchy and the Germano-Bolshevist invasion, and to steer the country to the Constituent Assembly, the army pledging itself implicitly to submit to the Government legally elected by the former."[37] This was basically the Kadet program—support for the principles of the February Revolution. When the actual composition of the Constituent Assembly became clear, however, the Volunteer Army withdrew its support, rejecting the SR victory.[38] Each side—Red and White—made a claim to moral superiority, the one in the interests of social justice, the other in those of national honor. Neither side played by the rules. Democracy was an inconvenience.

Savinkov, who in August 1917 had tried to reconcile Kerensky and Kornilov, now tried to smooth relations between Kornilov and Alekseev and was admitted to the Volunteer Army council. Denikin, however, refused to have anything to do with the former terrorist. Too many tensions disturbed this shaky alliance. The putative leaders were at each other's throats, and their base was none too stable. The Don Cossacks did not trust the officers arriving from the interior; Kornilov's right-hand man wanted to have Savinkov assassinated and plotted to depose Kaledin. Left out of the equation, the peasants meanwhile sent delegates to a meeting in Novocherkassk, which, under Bolshevik influence, denounced both Kaledin and the Volunteer Army. More worrisome still, Left SRs had infiltrated Kaledin's Cossack following and turned many of the men against him.[39]

The disarray among the Whites worked to the advantage of the Red forces, which by January 1918 were heading, somewhat unsteadily, for Kaledin's stronghold in Novocherkassk. In command was Vladimir Antonov-Ovseenko, the same figure who in October had flushed the ministers from their refuge in the Winter Palace and in November had joined with local Bolsheviks to capture Rostov. Obliged to work together, Kaledin and Alekseev had retaken the city a week later, although the tension between them did not abate. In mid-January 1918, the Volunteer Army moved its headquarters from Novocherkassk downstream to Rostov, asserting its distance from Kaledin.[40]

Military confrontations always focused on the cities, which gave the Reds an advantage, since the factory districts were hotbeds of Bolshevik agitation. After the Volunteer Army arrived in Taganrog, for example, on January 14, workers plundered the local arsenal and staged an armed rebellion. In the clash with Volunteer Army officers, gruesome brutality was demonstrated on both sides—faces were mutilated, men buried or burned alive.[41] When the Red Army arrived twelve days later, the balance shifted. Unable to marshal his own Cossacks to the defense, on January 29, Kaledin instructed his government to resign in favor of the Novocherkassk City Duma, then took his own life. The Volunteer Army prepared to evacuate the Don, and Kornilov soon followed. In February, the Reds took Rostov and Novocherkassk, where Kaledin's successor as ataman was arrested and executed.[42] At Taganrog, Denikin recalled, "the Volunteer contingents melted away each day, decimated by fighting, disease, frost-bite, and desertion." At Rostov, they were attacked by armed workers, Cossacks, and Red Army troops.[43]

All this was going on as the talks at Brest-Litovsk went back and forth and as the Germans resumed their advance on February 18. Retreating from

Rostov, Kornilov headed for the river-rail junction of Ekaterinodar (from 1920, Krasnodar) in the deep Kuban. Denikin recalled the scene as they set out. Former tsarist officers, with little but knapsacks and a rifle, "leaving behind darkness and moral enslavement to wander into the unknown."[44] "Laying boards and straw on the thawing ice we crossed the River Don. A spectacle never to be forgotten! A dark ribbon winding along the interminable snow-fields; a motley crowd like a gipsy caravan; carts; nondescript civilians plodding along; women in their city clothes and thin shoes stumbling through the snow; and as if lost among them—marching military columns in the midst of the 'caravan'—all that remained of the erstwhile great Russian army."[45]

The stuff of legend. The march, lasting over two months, covered a distance of 155 miles. The procession was not welcomed by the local population. Denikin realized that heroic gestures were not enough. The social issues that galvanized the socialists could not be ignored. "Unwillingly," the general recalled, "we found ourselves drawn into the vicious circle of the general social struggle. One section of the population, the more well-to-do, who stood for law and order, sympathized either openly or secretly with the army; the other which, deservedly or not, built their welfare on the absence of government and chaos, were hostile."[46] A self-serving view, not without merit but less indicative of political insight than of the hostility to popular interests that was to cripple the White cause.

The Whites had other political liabilities. Denikin rejected partisanship; he claimed to defend the Revolution as it stood immediately after the monarchy fell but before the Empire began eroding. He fought for the reestablishment of the old borders under the authority of a future regime constituted by the democratically elected Constituent Assembly. This position, avoiding extremes both of the Left and the Right, coincided with the main tenets of the Kadet Party. It created tensions, however, with anti-Bolshevik monarchists and with proponents of regional autonomy in any form. Association with defenders of the old social order limited Denikin's appeal to the peasant masses; insistence on the restoration of imperial borders and rule from the center troubled his alliance with Ukrainian and Cossack leaders who aspired to self-government.

The Volunteer Army had practical as well as political problems. Many Don Cossacks refused to leave the territory, Kuban Cossacks did not always respond to the call; officers outnumbered men; there was money enough to buy food from the peasants, but little ammunition. In what became known as the First Kuban Campaign, the Volunteer Army skirmished with Red contingents along the way.[47] Denikin recalled their surprise at finding the Bolsheviks already well ensconced in the largely non-Cossack mid-Kuban region. They encountered Circassian settlements decimated by neighboring Cossacks and peasants. Proceeding from village to village, they accumulated wounded as they went along.[48]

Ekaterinodar was the seat of the Kuban regional government, or Rada. On March 14, as Kornilov's troops were approaching, the Reds captured the city. The Cossack troops defending the Rada now joined with Kornilov.[49] As the combined forces departed, the cavalcade, under enemy fire, crossed an icy river, horses up to their shoulders in the current, dragging heavy guns. "The weather changed," Denikin remembered: "it began to freeze hard, the wind increased, and a blizzard set in. Men and horses were covered with an ice crust; everything seemed frozen to the very core, clothes became hard as though wooden, and hampered every movement." Another iconic tableau—what became known to its veterans as the Ice March. Impelled by cold and desperation, Kornilov's men stormed the town of Novodmitrievskaia, in hand-to-hand struggle with the fleeing Reds. Late in the day on March 28, the Volunteer Army arrived at a town called Kaluzhskaia, directly south of Ekaterinodar. It was in Kaluzhskaia, after much wrangling, that the Rada accepted Kornilov's authority. The joint forces now numbered six thousand, mostly Cossacks, under Russian command, a combination that led to considerable tension.[50] Including entourage and refugees, the total rose to nine thousand, accompanied by four thousand horses, six hundred wagons, also guns. All crossed the river by ferry. The goal was to retake Ekaterinodar. Kornilov predicted success.[51]

While the troops took control of the outlying areas, Kornilov, his staff, and the dressing station occupied a farmstead set on an elevation in the midst of an open field. Visible from the town, it was the target of continuous Red shelling. Meanwhile, the Volunteer Army was hemorrhaging, as officers fell in battle and soldiers deserted or collapsed under fire.[52] The commanders estimated the Reds at eighteen thousand, perhaps twice their own number. Afterward they read in the local Soviet *Izvestiia* that five thousand were dead, ten thousand wounded. Altogether the Volunteer Army had no more than three thousand men still able to fight, and these were exhausted, confused, and lacking ammunition.[53] Kornilov insisted on taking the city, seeing no other way out: "Of course we may all be killed," Denikin remembers him saying, but deciding that "retreat now would also be equal to disaster.

Without ammunition it would merely mean a long-drawn-out agony." Postponing the attack for another day, they aimed for April 14.[54]

On April 13, however, the Reds resumed their barrage of the farmstead. "General Kornilov was alone in his room," Denikin remembered, "when an enemy shell burst through the wall by the window and struck the floor beneath his chair. He was apparently blown upwards by the force of the explosion and flung against the stove. When people entered the smoke-filled room, General Kornilov lay on the floor covered with debris of plaster and dust. He was still breathing. Blood oozed from a small wound in the temple and flowed from the fractured thigh." It was uncanny and devastating. "Only a single shell had struck the house, hitting General Kornilov's room while he occupied it, and he alone was killed."[55]

The accidental death, days after Kornilov had threatened to take his own life if the attack did not go forward, had a gruesome aftermath. The general was buried in Gnachbau, a colony of German peasant settlers just north of Ekaterinodar. On April 16 the Reds entered the settlement looking for valuables and found the newly dug grave. Identifying the body by its epaulettes, they stripped it to the shirt and took it to Ekaterinodar, where they dragged it through the streets, hung it on a tree, then burnt it in the slaughterhouse.[56] A ritual cleansing. Epaulettes were deadly, even in death.

General Denikin, who had left Bykhov prison along with Kornilov in December, now replaced him as Volunteer Army commander in chief. Their biographies reflect the complexity of the old empire. Kornilov was of mixed Cossack and Central Asian origin. Denikin, born in Russian Poland, was raised in a bilingual but Orthodox family; his father was a serf who had risen through the ranks in the Imperial Army and married a Polish seamstress.[57] In 1917 and 1918, both men thought of themselves as patriots, defending the integrity of empire. They may have realized in personal terms the danger of trying to pull it apart or letting it disintegrate. Denikin, at least, also realized the extent to which the goal of "a united national front" was impeded by the social conflicts that divided Russian society and permitted the Bolsheviks to harness class antagonism for their own ends.[58]

After the shock of Kornilov's death, Denikin led his troops away from Ekaterinodar northeast towards Tikhoretskaia, a railway junction where they could then head northwest toward Rostov. The railway was controlled by the Reds, who ran armored trains along the line. The Volunteer Army consisted of a core of troops and horses, followed by almost six miles of carts and wagons carrying wounded, supplies, and refugees.[59] This time, the local

Cossacks were more receptive. Denikin believed they were reacting to the experience of Bolshevik control, consisting by his account of "murder, plunder and aggression," sadistic attacks on priests, and the desecration of churches.[60] By Orthodox Easter, the Volunteer Army had crossed the Eia River and turned in the direction of Rostov.[61]

While the Volunteer officers were absorbed by the high drama of desperate guerrilla warfare and heroic marches through brutal weather, rough terrain, and hostile populations, the Red Guards were bent on controlling the major cities and rail lines. Their victims included officers who had chosen not to join Alekseev, among them General von Rennenkampf. Mensheviks and SRs were also targeted. The lesson was clear—there was no middle ground.[62]

The Reds controlled Rostov for two and a half months. Bolshevik propaganda had prepared the soldiers, on entering the city, to encounter gangs of White cadet officers. As in other atrocity scenarios, the nervous men randomly machine-gunned dwellings inhabited by the peaceful population. People were arrested on the streets and in their apartments, some shot on the spot, to the cheers of the assembled populace. Ordinary criminals released from jail mingled with the Red Guards. Officers were assaulted and disfigured before being murdered in cold blood. A professor was shot to death outside his own door. People were denounced for having sheltered White Army soldiers, others were attacked for no reason at all or from mistaken identity. A priest was taken away and shot after completing a marriage ceremony. A witness remembered the "extraordinary calm" with which soldiers lined their victims up against the wall, stripped them naked, fired, tossed the bodies aside, and covered the blood stains on the snow with horse manure. The executioners were happy to take the clothing.[63]

At this point, the Germans were still marching east through Ukraine and might easily enter the Donbas and the Kuban region. To create at least a nominal border, on March 23, 1918, the local Bolshevik Military Revolutionary Committee had announced the formation of (yet another) Don Soviet Republic, as part of the greater Russian Soviet Republic.[64] This Republic lasted only until May 8, when the Germans took Taganrog and Rostov. On June 14, on the nearby Mius River, they perpetrated a massacre of their own. In a conflict with Red soldiers, they killed every last armed man, machine-gunning them to death as they tried to escape into the sea. Later, the Germans rounded up those who had surrendered, together with a large number of civilians who they claimed were armed Bolshevik irregulars, enclosed them in a pen, and slaughtered them en masse. This particular event was carried out on orders of the unit commander, to the discomfort of the German High Command, which, however, found reasons to justify his actions.[65]

Such attacks on the civilian population were entirely counterproductive. As the Whites realized in the Bolshevik case, a taste of Soviet rule was the most effective means of turning the Cossacks against them.[66] Indeed, Red Army abuses and Soviet policies created enemies at many levels. The violence inflicted on Rostov and Taganrog antagonized those officers who had attempted to remain neutral and were now pushed into the White camp.[67] In December the commissars had pursued a mixed approach. On the one hand, they sent Red Guards to the Cossack hosts to suppress any sign of resistance; on the other, they promised not to confiscate the land of "ordinary Cossacks," ending their military service requirement and appealing to the radicalized Cossack veterans.[68] When the *frontoviki* returned home, however, their enthusiasm was often tempered by the influence of their elders. Announcements that Cossacks "as a separate and privileged estate" would be eliminated caused obvious alarm. In Novocherkassk, which the Reds had taken at the end of February, their zealous procurement efforts provoked resistance, which began with the murder of Soviet grain collectors. In early April, the local Cossacks formed a small force, which executed a surprise raid on Novocherkassk, allowing the Cossack officers trapped there to escape and begin organizing an anti-Red Cossack army.[69] The Cossack communities did not respond automatically to the White appeal; they distrusted their own elites and did not care about the greater White mission. Retreating northward from Ekaterinodar and reentering the Don, the Volunteer Army now, however, found Cossacks and peasants united in their anger at the Reds and their strong-arm methods of seizing grain and punishing resistance.[70]

The problems facing the White movement were thus political as well as military. By spring 1918, the Don region sported an array of organizations claiming to represent regional interests, appealing to different segments of the population, and commanding some level of military support. In May General Petr Krasnov, who had attempted in October to squelch the Bolshevik regime and then fled south, was elected ataman of the Don Cossacks. Kaledin's earlier Don Republic, announced in November 1917, had been crushed in January 1918. Now Krasnov, the son of a Don Cossack officer, became the head of a second Don Republic, with its capital in

Novocherkassk, recaptured from the Reds ten days before.[71] By mid-June Krasnov's so-called Don Army, financed by newly printed money, had enlisted forty thousand men. Seeking German support, Krasnov kept his distance from Denikin and the Volunteers. By summertime he had arranged to supply the Germans with food and raw material in exchange for arms and ammunition. Working from headquarters in Rostov, the Germans cooperated in extracting grain from the peasants.[72] Once again, as in the Baltic states and Ukraine, the bid for independence depended on outside backing.[73]

In 1918 the Germans dreamed of uniting the territory extending from the Don to the North Caucasus under Krasnov's leadership. Krasnov, however, was busy quarreling with the other German favorite, Hetman Skoropads'kyi, over the border between the Don and the Ukraine. While Skoropads'kyi wanted to extend his territory eastward, Krasnov insisted that Taganrog, assigned at Brest-Litovsk to the Ukraine, properly belonged in the Don government. On August 11, Skoropads'kyi conceded the point and the Germans ended their three-month occupation of the port. The two native-son leaders of German-sponsored regionalist regimes thus locked horns over their own expansionist ambitions.[74] A well-matched duo.

Denikin, by contrast, disapproved of Krasnov's German game and avoided both Rostov and Novocherkassk. The dislike was mutual. When Krasnov's Don Army had retaken Novocherkassk in early May, he rejected Denikin's offer to join forces. Like Alekseev and Kornilov, this pair was a study in contrasts. Denikin has been described as dull but honest, Krasnov as "vain and devious."[75] Vociferously anti-German, Denikin nevertheless accepted financial support from Krasnov, who took his money from the Germans. While accepting some money from the French and resisting pressure from Volunteer Army officers to compromise with the Germans, Alekseev and Denikin benefited when the Germans tolerated their recruiting efforts in Kiev and acquiesced to their indirect subsidies.[76] Miliukov, for his part, urged Alekseev (Denikin's superior) to ally with Krasnov on the latter's terms (that he maintain command of his own army). At this point in May, Miliukov seriously entertained the idea of collaborating with the Germans, a position that clashed with his own earlier posture and shocked his Kadet colleagues.[77]

The spring and summer months demonstrated how difficult it was in the Don and Kuban to produce a coherent leadership, let alone muster a reliable armed force. Denikin's Volunteer Army lost some followers to Krasnov's

Don Army, but also gained new adherents. The largest contingent was a small army led by Colonel Mikhail Drozdovskii, a veteran commander, which had emerged from the Romanian front to help the Germans crush the Reds at Rostov in early May. Now, in June, Drozdovskii brought Denikin 2,500 disciplined men. By July the Volunteer Army numbered as many as ten thousand.[78] Denikin had problems, however, attracting and holding both staff and men. In his view, the Constituent Assembly still possessed the only authority to determine Russia's future. The posture of neutrality appealed neither to the increasingly reactionary officers now gravitating toward the Volunteer Army nor to disappointed political figures, such as Miliukov, looking to return to the post-February benchmark. Not only were the officers divided by political differences, but they remained as a whole unsympathetic to the Cossacks and their nativist political spokesmen.[79] The Cossacks, for their part, as Krasnov and Denikin realized, would not leave their respective homelands.

Unable to agree, the two generals ended up pursuing their separate goals. Krasnov argued for a coordinated attack on Tsaritsyn, but Denikin preferred to focus on Ekaterinodar.[80] By June, when Denikin launched the Second Kuban Campaign, his 9,000-man-strong Volunteer Army faced a more numerous Red Army, fielding over 75,000. But the Reds, despite their numbers, were not yet strong enough to withstand the more professional White commanders, whose troops were fighting on home ground. On June 25, the Volunteers captured Tikhoretskaia, at the intersection of the region's two major railway lines. In mid-August, Denikin took Ekaterinodar on behalf of the Kuban Rada.[81] A month later, the Volunteer Army took Novorossiisk, on the Black Sea, where they shot the Soviet officials.[82]

The fight for Tsaritsyn was more prolonged and ended, by contrast, in a Red victory. Krasnov's Don Army was at first successful in capturing key railway lines, but in July the Bolsheviks organized a committee to direct military operations in the North Caucasus. The committee included Joseph Stalin and Kliment Voroshilov. Stalin was put in charge of requisitioning and dispatching grain shipments north to Moscow from the rail junction in Tsaritsyn. Upon arriving, he defied the policy introduced by Trotsky as commissar of war, who insisted on retaining trained officers. Stalin, instead, dismissed the general in command and replaced him with Voroshilov. At the same time, he used the local Cheka to conduct sweeping arrests and executions, creating a terror-driven dictatorship in miniature.[83] Though not seriously disciplined, Stalin was reprimanded by Moscow for defying Trotsky's authority, and indeed it was not Voroshilov but the Red commander, Dmitrii Zhloba, who on October 15 led a surprise raid that ousted Krasnov's forces. The so-called Tsaritsyn Affair deepened the growing rivalry between Trotsky and Stalin. In 1925, after Lenin's death, Tsaritsyn was renamed Stalingrad; in 1943 it was the site of an epic Soviet victory. In 1961, after Khrushchev's Secret Speech denouncing Stalin's excesses, it was renamed Volgograd, which it remains. Voroshilov, always close to Stalin, went on to a long career in Soviet military and political life, his major accomplishment being death from natural causes. In 1940 he was among the members of the Politburo who signed the order to execute the Polish officers at Katyń.[84]

Fighting around Tsaritsyn continued sporadically until the end of December 1918, by which time the Red Army outnumbered Krasnov almost three-to-one. In a final attempt to recover his early advantage, Krasnov gathered a group of reactionary officers from the Ukraine and Saratov, at the head of a contingent of Astrakhan Cossacks which he dubbed the Southern Army. A collection of disreputable marginal figures sustained by German money, the Southern Army was a military failure, while its brutal methods and harsh requisitioning only won converts to the Soviet cause.[85]

By the end of 1918, however, Denikin had established his headquarters in Ekaterinodar. By then the Volunteer Army, though it kept its name, was resorting to conscription. Denikin drafted peasants, Cossacks, and officers, even enlisting Red Army prisoners, except for officers, who were shot—an impediment to further recruitment. The men apparently fought just as well for the other side. It was a different matter with the Cossacks, who refused to leave the territory and continued to distrust their Russian commanders.[86] These were not the same officers who had entered the war. Not all were monarchists, but no matter their convictions and personal background, they were unable to avoid representing the old Imperial Army, hence the old social hierarchies as well. Some officers behaved as though Nicholas were still on the throne, disregarding their current superiors and treating the peasant population with high-handed brutality. Living off the riches of the Kuban, the Cossack troops, like all the armies in the Civil War, plundered peasant villages, which repaid them with hostility and mistrust.[87]

Denikin himself continued to profess loyalty to the constitutional principles represented by the February Revolution, relying on the support of Kadet leaders who had fled south in search of a political foothold and who shared his dedication to preserving the geographical integrity of the Empire. Denikin's concept of a politically neutral military to serve as an instrument of state policy depended, however, on the existence of a state capable of exercising authority. Once they had achieved military victory, however local, the Whites needed to establish some kind of civilian administration. On October 8, by the new calendar, General Alekseev succumbed to serious illness. In December Denikin succeeded him as supreme commander of the united Armed Forces of South Russia (*Voennye sily Iuga Rossii*). He was advised by a Special Council (*Osoboe soveshchanie*), conceived as an advisory to the army, but as of February 1919 as a skeleton government, with departments and ministries. Its goal was defined as the "fight to victory over Bolshevism," combined with the re-establishment of "great and indivisible Russia," based on the principles of equal rights, civil liberties, Cossack privileges, the rule of law, and private property—in short, the Kadet agenda.[88]

Aware of the impact of Red propaganda, the Whites had created a propaganda apparatus of their own. An early effort was organized in Ukraine by Vasilii Shul'gin, the editor of the infamous anti-Semitic newspaper, *Kievlianin*. In September 1918, when Alekseev settled in the Kuban, he established an Information Agency (*Osvedomitel'noe agenstvo*—Osvag), at first under the direction of sympathetic Kadets. Among the artists it employed were the talented draftsmen Evgenii Lansere, Ivan Bilibin, and N. Remizov ("Re-mi"), alumni of the left-leaning satirical journals of 1905.[89] Mimicking the techniques used by their opponents, they produced pamphlets, flyers, and posters, even using "agit-trains." Focusing on the worst Bolshevik atrocities while borrowing their techniques, they did not avoid the worst anti-Semitic canards about the Jewish-Communist conspiracy.[90]

Overall, however, Denikin's political profile was unstable. The general thought of himself as an imperial Russian patriot, above partisan politics. "Be Right or Left, but love our harassed fatherland and help us save it."[91] He nevertheless made political choices. In spring 1918, Kadet leaders in Moscow had formed a National Center (*Natsional'nyi tsentr*), which rejected Krasnov in favor of Denikin. By contrast, the independent socialists in the Union for the Regeneration of Russia, formed as an anti-authoritarian alternative to Bolshevik rule, remained hostile to Denikin, who refused to include them in his putative regime.[92] Even within the confines of the Kuban, Denikin failed to mobilize a coherent base. In terms of political allegiances, the Ukraine-oriented Black Sea Cossacks favored the socialist Symon Petliura and contemplated an alliance with the Ukraine, while the Caucasian "line" Cossacks wanted to be part of a Russian federation.[93] Leaders of the surviving Kuban Rada continued to insist on regional autonomy, rejecting

Denikin's authority. The crisis came to a head on November 7, when the Rada dispatched a delegation to the Peace Conference set to open in Paris on January 8, 1919. Denikin denounced them as traitors and had the Rada deputies meeting in Ekaterinodar arrested. One was court-martialed and hanged, the others were deported after agreeing to cooperate.[94]

Denikin himself believed that military rule was the only solution to the fragmentation of authority and to the precariously allied forces confronting the Red threat. By the end of the summer, the Volunteer Army had gained control over the Don and the Kuban, which became its base, but it never articulated a political program with any broad appeal.[95] It had no compelling symbols, no vision except the defense of an empire which had already crumbled. The Cossacks, who themselves became an icon of the counter-revolution, could not be relied upon. At the beginning of 1919, the scene was therefore set for a multi-sided battle for domination over the territories of Ukraine and the Don region. Neither the Whites nor the Reds were internally united; each struggled to impose central control. Between the proletarian dictatorship and the military dictatorship, a host of independent actors vied for appeal, reflecting the fluctuating moods of the local populations. With the Germans gone, the Allies maintained a presence on Russian soil and attempted to influence the outcome.

# 2

# Foreign Bodies

As the Great War slid into Civil War, the foreign powers played a key role, since no internal force was strong enough to win on its own. For Germany and Austria, Brest-Litovsk was a boon; for Britain and France, a betrayal. They, too, now meddled in the internecine conflicts that unfurled across the Eurasian expanse, but it took them a while to decide what form the meddling should take. If Russia could not be drawn back into the war, the alternatives were unclear. The status of the new Soviet state was itself still in doubt. The Allies and the United States had immediately recognized the Provisional Government, on March 22, 1917 (NS), despite its ad hoc character. The Treaty of Brest-Litovsk constituted diplomatic recognition of Soviet Russia by the Central Powers; the treaties of independence of the Baltic states also had the effect of recognizing Soviet Russia, but Allied recognition was delayed and came piecemeal—by France and Britain in 1924; broken off by Britain in 1927, resumed in 1929; by the United States not until 1933.[1]

In 1918 formal relations were suspended, but the Allied ambassadors remained on Russian soil. On February 28, they relocated to the town of Vologda, north of Petrograd, at the intersection of the railways linking Arkhangelsk to Moscow and Petrograd to Siberia, where they received the reports of informal agents who communicated with Soviet leaders on their behalf. For this purpose, the British War Office relied on Bruce R. H. Lockhart, former consul-general in Moscow, the French military mission on the socialist lawyer Jacques Sadoul, the Americans on Raymond Robins, head of the American Red Cross Mission.[2] Their options kept shifting. When talks in Brest-Litovsk broke down and the Germans resumed their advance on February 18, the Allies hoped Russia might still be drawn back into the conflict. The treaty seemed to remove this possibility, but the Germans did not observe its terms. Russia might yet be provoked. Some of the Bolsheviks' opponents still wanted to rekindle the Eastern Front; others were interested simply in dislodging the commissars. Overall, the Allies' decisions were more pragmatic than ideological. They were not primarily concerned to destroy the Bolsheviks as a threat to domestic and world stability, and they were not overly discriminating about the figures and groups they did support.

British anxiety about Russia's fighting capacity had led them in August 1917 to contemplate backing General Kornilov, but they were deterred by his dictatorial ambitions.[3] While the outcome at Brest-Litovsk still hung in the balance, they were prepared to help Trotsky build military strength, but faced with a rapidly evolving situation and uncertain intelligence, they were unsure where to turn. In November 1917, British Ambassador George Buchanan reported that Russian bankers had urged Britain to support General Kaledin. Indeed, in December Foreign Secretary Arthur Balfour briefly considered the possibility of contacting Kaledin, but soon rejected the idea. Realizing the Bolsheviks were not going to continue the fight, he focused on limiting Germany's chance to profit from Russia's weakness.[4]

While the talks at Brest-Litovsk were in abeyance, the possibility of resumed fighting could not be excluded. In view of the renewed German advance, Trotsky was willing to contemplate assistance from the Allies. The French offered officers and experts from the divisions they had pulled from Romania, which had signed an armistice with the Central Powers on December 9, 1917.[5] In a heated Bolshevik Central Committee meeting on February 22, 1918, Nikolai Bukharin had rejected the idea of collaborating with the imperialists, but Lenin insisted that "Comrade Trotsky be authorized to accept the assistance of the brigands of French imperialism against the German brigands."[6] It was for lack of an army that the fledgling regime had found itself vulnerable in the first place. On February 23, as the Petrograd Soviet debated whether to accept the humiliating peace, Krylenko reported the decisive fact that the revolution could not defend itself. "We have no army," he reminded his comrades, "our demoralized soldiers fly panic-stricken before the German bayonets, leaving behind them artillery, transport, and ammunition. The divisions of the Red Guard are swept away like flies. Only the immediate signing of peace can save us from ruin."[7]

Soviet options after March 3, 1918, were limited. German troops controlled the entire territory forfeited by the treaty. In early March, the Allied powers also gained a foothold on Russian soil, when the Murmansk Soviet gave permission for the British to land a group of Royal Marines.[8] They were to protect the Murmansk railway from the threat posed by the nearby

Germans and Finns.[9] It was rumored the Allies had sanctioned a Japanese incursion in the east.[10] Victorious over Russia in 1905, Japan had declared war on Germany on August 23, 1914, with an eye to capturing German colonial possessions in the Pacific. By January 1918, Japan already controlled southern Manchuria and wanted to expand its range. The British and French urged Wilson to endorse a Japanese presence in Vladivostok, Russia's eastern portal, and on the Russian-owned Chinese Eastern Railroad, the section of the Trans-Siberian Railroad crossing northern Manchuria between Irkutsk and Vladivostok. Wilson's stubborn opposition scuttled the idea. In January, nevertheless, one British and four Japanese cruisers had positioned themselves in the bay at Vladivostok.[11]

At the Seventh Party Congress on March 6, 1918, Lenin reminded the comrades of the reality they were facing. No army meant no way to resist invasion from any side. The Bolsheviks put out feelers. Lev Kamenev was dispatched to London, but the self-appointed representative of an unrecognized new regime was not received. Indeed, on the way home, at the Germans' request, he was detained at the Finnish border.[12] Meanwhile, Trotsky lobbied Lockhart to press his superiors for support against both Germany and Japan, but the British saw Japan as a useful counterweight to the German presence in Asia. Both sides were pursuing practical goals. The British were hedging their bets, ready to underwrite both Kornilov and Lenin on the chance that either might revive the Eastern Front—for their very different reasons.[13]

As the ink was drying in Brest-Litovsk, the Bolsheviks pleaded with the Allied representatives to stop Japan and assist them in blocking the German advance, which showed no sign of ending.[14] On both sides it was a gamble. It was not clear that Lenin could bully the Soviet Congress into ratifying the treaty, and it was not clear the Germans would abide by its terms. Lockhart and Robins, for Britain and the United States, respectively, wanted to know whether Lenin would return to war if the Allies offered support. No such assurance was possible. Both men nevertheless urged their governments to intervene on the Soviets' behalf. Balfour refused, recognizing that Lenin had no military force to offer. Japan was the only card the Allies had left to play.[15]

The Western powers at this point saw the political coloration of the Bolshevik government as a problem only insofar as it interfered with their own strategic interests. Wilson indeed took pains to stress his friendly intentions. On February 23, 1918, he rejected the idea of trying to influence the

"form of government" in post-revolutionary Russia, as "in violent contradiction of the principles we have always held, earnestly we should wish to
lend every moral influence to the support of democratic institutions in
Russia and earnestly as we pray that they may survive there and become
permanent." On March 11, the president wired a goodwill message to the
Fourth Soviet Congress, supporting Russia's "complete sovereignty and
independence in her own affairs."[16]

The Germans did not ratify the Brest-Litovsk treaty until March 22,
1918.[17] By then, they had made peace with Finland as well as Ukraine, and
had entered Odessa. Nor did the formalities put an end to the German
threat. And just as the Germans seemed to ignore the terms of the accord,
many Bolsheviks at the local level continued well into the spring to repudiate the consequences of Brest-Litovsk. Soviets in Moscow, Ivanovo-
Voznesensk, Iaroslavl, Perm, Kharkov, Donets, Sevastopol, and Taganrog kept
voting against the treaty in favor of "revolutionary war." Bolshevik activists
in these cities cooperated with pro-war Left SRs and Mensheviks. The
defiant Left SRs organized guerrilla bands to harass the Germans in the
Ukraine.[18]

It might well have seemed from the outside that not much had changed.
To preserve his high-minded principles, Wilson would have preferred the
Soviets to request Allied support in fighting the Germans. This was at first
not such a far-fetched idea. Indeed, in late March Trotsky endorsed the
presence of British and French troops in Murmansk, where they had arrived
to protect military stores and the railroads. On April 4, an American warship
appeared in Murmansk, though ordered not to take action.[19] This activity in
the north was not construed as hostile. Trotsky welcomed technical aid.[20]
But things could change at any minute.

The question of Japanese intervention, which had divided the Allied
powers—France in favor, the United States opposed, Britain on the fence—
was resolved accidentally, or apparently so, when two Japanese civilians were
killed in Vladivostok on April 4. The next day, Japanese troops landed in the
city, accompanied by fifty British Marines to guard the consulate. The
British claimed the move was designed only for the protection of foreign
residents, but the Sovnarkom not unreasonably rejected the excuse. In consort with "the Russian bourgeoisie and its hirelings—the Mensheviks and
SRs," Moscow declared, Japan was pursuing its imperialist ambitions. "The
Japanese authorities were looking for a suitable pretext for their plunderous
raid into Russian territory." In reality, "[t]he imperialists of Japan wish to

strangle the Soviet Revolution, to cut off Russia from the Pacific Ocean, to seize the rich territories of Siberia, and to enslave the Siberian workers and peasants."[21]

Thus, at the same time as the cities in the lower Don were under siege, foreign powers were nibbling away at the outer edges of the old imperial map. Ten days after Japanese and British Marines had landed in Vladivostok, the Turks occupied Batumi and on April 27, took Kars. On April 30, the Germans reached Vyborg in the north, the next day Sevastopol in the south. Soviet Russia was a leaky ship—water coming in from all sides. Occasionally Trotsky managed to plug a hole. Three days before the Germans took Sevastopol, he moved the Black Sea Fleet, slated by treaty for dismantling, from Sevastopol to Novorossiisk on the eastern coast of the Black Sea. He instructed the British naval attaché Captain Francis Cromie, stationed there, to sink the ships rather than let them fall into German hands; on June 8, Cromie carried out the order.[22]

The Germans were still the greatest menace. On April 23, Ambassador von Mirbach arrived in Moscow. On April 26, German troops crossed from the Ukraine into the Don, violating the terms of the accord. The French were the most aggressive in urging a response. "The Germanic states are, in fact, aiming to establish exclusive control over the economic life of all Russia," said French Ambassador Joseph Noulens. "The Allies may be compelled to intervene in order to meet this menace, which is directed against them and, to a much greater extent, against the Russian people. Should the Allies at any time be forced to resort to military operations, they will act solely in the capacity of friends."[23] Indeed, the Allies kept insisting they were only there to help. Until the middle of April, the French and the British went back and forth with Trotsky on the possibility of Allied aid and intervention. The purpose all along was to reopen the Eastern Front, which could only happen with Russian participation, which in turn was possible only with Allied support. The British cabinet went so far as to discuss the conditions of a renewed Russo-British alliance. Trotsky encouraged them, but Noulens remained skeptical of his intentions.[24]

British agent Lockhart arrived in Petrograd at the end of January, having made his way through snowy Finland, where civil war was already raging.[25] In the capital, he met the principal actors in the Bolshevik drama and was impressed. If the storm they unleashed was a whirlwind of destruction, the men at the center were paragons of control. In Lenin's case, the keynote was understatement. "Short of stature, rather plump, with short, thick neck,

broad shoulders, round, red face, high intellectual forehead, nose slightly
turned up, brownish moustache, and short, stubbly beard, he looked at the
first glance more like a provincial grocer than a leader of men. Yet in those
steely eyes there was something that arrested my attention, something in
that quizzing, half-contemptuous, half-smiling look which spoke of bound-
less self-confidence and conscious superiority." Not one to be trifled with:
"In his creed of world-revolution Lenin was an unscrupulous and as uncompromising as a Jesuit, and in his code of political ethics the end to be attained
justified the employment of any weapon."[26] These observations, composed
fifteen years later, of course enjoyed the advantage of hindsight.

Amid the clutter and chaos of Bolshevik headquarters, Trotsky displayed
a similar personal fastidiousness, but mixed with the vanity and volatility
Lenin seemed to lack. He was talented and dynamic, but only second in
command. "Trotsky," Lockhart observed, "was a great organiser and a man
of immense physical courage. But, morally, he was as incapable of standing
against Lenin as a flea would be against an elephant. In the Council of
Commissars there was not a man who did not consider himself the equal of
Trotsky. There was not a Commissar who did not regard Lenin as a demi-
god, whose decision were to be accepted without question. Squabbles
among the Commissars were frequent, but they never touched Lenin." In
this period of tension and uncertainty on the Bolshevik side, in fact the
comrades often challenged the leader. Arguments grew heated in the Central
Committee. Local activists sometimes defied the party line. But Lenin was
the master strategist. His combination of bullying and bravado motivated
and disciplined a core of followers ready to shape a new regime—and a
visionary new social order. Lockhart was "impressed by his tremendous
will-power, his relentless determination, and his lack of emotion."[27]

For all Lenin's steely resolve, however, few at the time—whether outside
observers or his fellow countrymen—believed the Bolsheviks could maintain their tenuous hold on power. It was easier for outsiders to think of
them as puppets than as masters in their own right. Lockhart's advice to his
superiors was pragmatic. "Rather futilely I sought to combat the firmly-
rooted conviction that Lenin and Trotsky were German staff officers in
disguise or at least servile agents of German policy. I was more successful
when I argued that it was madness not to establish some contact with the
men who at that moment were controlling Russia's destinies."[28] Lockhart
made two key points to the War Office. First, that there was no real alternative: "I was convinced that their internal strength was far greater than most

foreign observers realised, and that there was no other power in Russia which was capable of replacing them." Second, that the idea of reopening the Eastern Front was an illusion, since Russians no longer cared about the war: "In so far as Germany was our main enemy . . . , we had nothing to gain by stimulating civil war. If we took sides against the Bolsheviks, we should be backing the weaker horse and would have to employ large forces to ensure even a temporary success."[29]

The Germans were relentless, and their continued advance seemed to cast doubt on the assumption that Lenin was playing their game. On April 27, indeed, Commissar of Foreign Affairs Georgii Chicherin protested German violations of the treaty.[30] Although by this time the two countries had exchanged ambassadors, Ioffe leaving for Berlin and Mirbach arriving in Moscow, the Bolsheviks continued their rhetorical provocations.[31] Mirbach was greeted by an article in *Izvestiia* in which bravado masked the reality of diplomatic defeat: "Not one workman in Berlin will greet the Ambassador of the Russian Socialist Republic with the hate with which every workman in Moscow to-day greets the representative of German capital."[32]

The Allies had reason to be confused. The Bolshevik Party was itself divided over which path to take. Agitated Central Committee meetings in early May debated whether renewed war with Germany could in fact be avoided and whether the Allied option should therefore be retained. Lenin, however, insisted that an alliance with Germany was the only course, although it meant forfeiting Finland and the Ukraine. On May 13, the comrades now voted to reject Allied support. Two days later, Trotsky nevertheless led Lockhart to believe that renewed hostilities with Germany were still on the horizon.[33] Lord Alfred Milner in the British War Office had declared on May 9, "it is desirable to work as well as we can with the Bolshevik government now in power." A week later, he continued to believe the Allies might receive a positive response if they offered to intervene.[34] By now, too, French Ambassador Noulens, who just recently had threatened Allied intervention to stop the German advance, had come around to the idea of working with Trotsky.[35]

The Germans were aware of the Allied efforts to provoke the resumption of war by offering food, arms, and other material incentives. Mirbach knew of the conflicts within the Bolshevik Party and recognized the problem created by the German occupation and the German role in bringing the Hetman Skoropads'kyi to power in the Ukraine. "The more prudent of the

Bolshevik leaders," the ambassador observed, "are still trying to calm those elements which are incensed about the [German] advance in the South and the restoration in the Ukraine."[36] He was doing all he could to support the pro-German side. Keeping the Bolsheviks in power was still in Germany's best interests; their opponents would favor the Entente and reject the Brest peace. He feared that continued German military activity in the south might "drive the Bolsheviks into the arms of the Entente or, in the event of their fall, bring successors favourable to the Entente into power." The Bolsheviks, moreover, now seemed interested in developing economic relations with Germany, conducive to "future economic infiltration."[37] Foreign Minister von Kühlmann agreed. It was time to terminate military operations and consolidate Germany's relationship with the more conservative elements in the Bolshevik fold.[38]

By "conservative" Mirbach and Kühlmann meant Lenin. Addressing a joint session of the Soviet Central Executive Committee, the Moscow Soviet, and the Representatives of Trade Unions and Factory Shop Committees on May 14, Lenin made a convoluted argument for waiting—which is to say, he reiterated, from yet another perspective, his stubborn opposition to any idea of resuming hostilities.[39] "The Russian Socialist Soviet Republic is... an oasis in the midst of a raging ocean of imperialist plundering."[40] The powers were at each other's throats: Germany against Britain in the West, Japan against the United States in the East. The outcome of present hostilities depended on how these conflicts played out. The only hope of salvation was the long-awaited world revolution. "We must remain at our post," he insisted, "until the arrival of our ally, the international proletariat, for this ally is sure to arrive," though, he admitted, it was "moving much slower than we expected and wished."[41] While the Bolsheviks were not in a position to take up arms against the imperialist powers, they must "wag[e] merciless war... against the bourgeoisie in our own country." For this purpose, a strong army and strong political authority—"the dictatorship of the proletariat"— were essential.[42]

Lenin did not wait to translate his pragmatic vision into practical measures. On May 15, the Commissar of Trade, Mikhail Bronskii, presented Mirbach with a plan for economic cooperation and urged him to expedite negotiation of the various issues left to be worked out in the March treaty.[43] In return for substantial loans, Russia would supply raw materials and agree to purchase manufactured goods on the German market. German companies would gain investment opportunities. Germany would pledge not to interfere in Russia's domestic political affairs or in her commercial dealings with the Ukraine, Poland, the Baltics, and the Caucasus, and would not obstruct delivery of ore from eastern Ukraine and the Caucasus. This apparent capitulation to German needs reflected Lenin's desire to enlist the support of German business interests, which in pursuit of private gain would press for an end to German military engagement, thus promoting the cause of Bolshevik survival. In any case, the proposal made no impression in Berlin.[44]

In Moscow, Lenin denounced his critics' reluctance to do business with the Germans as an example of "left-wing childishness and petty-bourgeois mentality." Not only was Germany the model of the type of "state capitalism" that Soviet Russia needed to emulate on its way to developing a modern, industrial socialist economy, but German economic assistance in cash, expertise, and investment was the only realistic path to survival. "Junker-bourgeois" Germany, Lenin declared, was today "'the last word' in modern large-scale capitalist engineering and planned organisation." Under a state "of a different social type, of a different class content—a *Soviet* state, that is, a proletarian state," this same system would offer "the *sum total* of the conditions necessary for socialism," which, he insisted, "is inconceivable without large-scale capitalist engineering based on the latest discoveries of modern science. It is inconceivable without planned state organisation," but only if "the proletariat is the ruler of the state." Lenin saw "the economic, the productive and the socio-economic conditions for socialism" realized in Germany, while the "political conditions" for socialism were embodied in Soviet Russia. While still waiting for the anticipated German revolution, Russia must use "the state capitalism of the Germans" as a model, "and not shrink from adopting *dictatorial* methods" to adopt it.[45]

Germany's short-term needs bolstered Lenin's ambitions. The Bolsheviks had served German purposes by withdrawing from the war. Brest-Litovsk had anticipated economic concessions which the supplementary treaties signed in August later spelled out. The main German goal was still to keep Russia out of the war. In April 1917, they had prized Bolshevik extremism for its potential to "shake the very existence of the Russian empire," thus facilitating Russian military defeat.[46] In May 1918, with the Empire gone, they valued the Bolshevik Party as the most likely means to keep Russia from fighting. Now, with the treaty signed, the party's role, in their eyes, was no longer to undermine state authority but to establish a modicum of authority and administration on its own behalf. Such a foundation would enable the Germans to extract what they needed in economic terms. The Germans were pleased that the Bolsheviks seemed to be "trying gradually to orientate themselves towards the right."[47] By contrast, the anti-German Right SRs were the new firebrands, on whom the Entente were spending "enormous sums" in attempting to bring them to power.[48]

Berlin granted Mirbach as much money as he said he needed precisely to prevent the SRs from succeeding. As Foreign Minister Kühlmann reminded the ambassador, it was "greatly in our interests that Bolsheviks should survive." There was no one else to count on if they fell. "As a party, Kadets are anti-German; Monarchists would also work for revision of Brest peace treaty. We have no interest in supporting Monarchists' ideas, which would reunite Russia. On the contrary, we must try to prevent Russian consolidation as far as possible and, from this point of view, we must therefore support the parties furthest to the left."[49] Furthest to the left, but tilting to the right in pragmatic power-political terms. General Hoffmann commented in late May: "We have information from all sides to the effect that the Bolsheviks will soon collapse from incompetence, but I don't think they will yet awhile. There is no one to take their place, as there is no army to support a new sovereign power."[50] Lenin, for his part, accepted the loss of territory for the sake of economic reconstruction and for the time in which to fashion a plausible military force. Both Lenin and the Germans were being entirely instrumental.

The Bolsheviks were the Germans' best hope, but it was not clear they would last. "The pressure exerted by the Bolsheviks' mailed fist is enormous. People are being shot by the hundreds," reported a German official from Moscow. But terror could not entirely mitigate the effects of hunger, fuel shortages, and the misgivings of the Bolshevik supporters among the poorer classes. The party was banking on the outbreak of revolution in Germany. If the Entente managed to assist in "the resurrection of a reasonably ordered bourgeois Russia," the Ukraine would certainly rejoin the heartland and the specter of a reunited Russia would reemerge. The upshot, however, was hard to predict. Some days the Terror seemed to be working, but popular anger against the Germans, blamed for the shortages of bread and fuel, continued to fester, "and not without some justification," the official had to admit.[51]

The uncertainly caused the Germans to allocate money, not only to keep the Bolsheviks afloat, but in the event they sank and alternatives were needed.[52] By late June, not long before he was to be assassinated by an angry SR, Mirbach was voicing doubts: "After two months' careful observation,

I can now no longer give Bolshevism a favourable diagnosis. We are unquestionably standing by the bedside of a dangerously ill man, who might show apparent improvement from time to time, but who is lost in the long run." He contemplated a maneuver similar to the Skoropads'kyi coup in the Ukraine. The Germans could easily topple the Bolsheviks by force of arms, then throw their support behind the old center—the Octobrists and Kadets—in forming a government that would do Germany's bidding. Such a strategy might entail loss of the Ukraine, but Mirbach considered the occupation no more than a "temporary wartime measure," which Germany should relinquish for long-term political and economic considerations.[53]

During March and April, while the Soviets were courting both Germany and the Entente, trying to buy time, acquire resources, and protect themselves against whichever side they finally renounced, another extraneous factor had entered the equation. The most coherent armed force on Russian soil at this point, beside the German Army, emerged as an inadvertent consequence of the nationality question that continued to haunt the Eastern Front. This was the so-called Czechoslovak Legion. Eager to pursue their own political agenda, which was to extricate their nation from the dying Hapsburg Empire, these foreign soldiers got caught up by happenstance in the fate of the great Empire to the east, also in the throes of death.

In 1914, the Imperial Russian Army had accepted the formation of regiments drawn from the Empire's Czech and Slovak population, which fought alongside Russian troops during the war. In December 1916, Czech national leaders Tomáš Masaryk and Eduard Beneš, then in Paris, proposed the regiments be expanded by the addition of prisoners of war and deserters from the Austro-Hungarian army. The plan was embraced by Kerensky and by British and French representatives in Russia. In September 1917, General Dukhonin authorized the creation of a Czechoslovak Legion, under the authority of the Czechoslovak National Council chaired by Masaryk, with a branch inside Russia.[54] Hesitating to encourage the reverse movement among their own minority populations, the monarchy and then Provisional Government had nevertheless decided to play the same nationality card that in German hands threatened Russia's own borders.

By early 1918, the Legion consisted of about fifty thousand well-organized and equipped soldiers, most located near Kiev.[55] Though some left to join

Kornilov on the Don, Masaryk declined General Alekseev's invitation to join the anti-Bolshevik crusade. He preferred to send the troops east to Vladivostok and from there via the Panama Canal to France, where they would see action under French command. Their transit along the Trans-Siberian Railroad, en route to Europe, was to be financed by subsidies from the British and the French. On February 16, the local Bolsheviks granted permission to begin the Legion's eastward journey. The plan was interrupted, however, by the resumption on February 18, of the German advance. Masaryk, then in Kiev himself, offered to bolster the Red forces against the Germans, but only if the Reds pulled their weight, otherwise, he warned, the Legion would continue on its way eastward. Masaryk and the Allied attachés at this point departed Kiev for Moscow; Masaryk left Russia altogether on March 7, 1918.[56]

Indeed, on their way out of the Ukraine, on March 13, the Legion joined with the local Reds for a minor victory at Bakhmach, after which they climbed back onto their trains.[57] Two days later, the Sovnarkom approved the plan for the Legion to depart via Vladivostok.[58] As the trains proceeded from town to town, they encountered hostility from local Bolsheviks who assumed the armed foreigners were themselves hostile. On March 21, the Omsk soviet halted the trains and asked Moscow to turn them back. Five days later, however, Stalin, as commissar of nationalities, sent an order to let the Legion continue.[59] "The Czechoslovaks," he instructed, "shall proceed not as fighting units but as a group of free citizens taking with them a certain quantity of arms for self-defense against the attacks of counter-revolutionists."[60]

When Japanese troops entered Vladivostok on April 5, and seemed likely to keep going, Lenin ordered the Legion be halted, but the Vladivostok Bolsheviks assured him the Allies were in disarray and intervention was not a sure thing. On April 12, the Sovnarkom again allowed the Legion to proceed, but the Czechoslovaks were suspicious and warned they would not surrender arms. Still pledging to remain neutral, they nevertheless threatened to fight back if attacked.[61] Learning that the Japanese were extending their influence down the Harbin line almost to the fork in the Trans-Siberian Railroad, thus threatening to cut off the east, on April 17 the Sovnarkom imposed martial law in Siberia, and four days later Chicherin again ordered the Legion to stop. Units east of Omsk were allowed to continue, but those to the west were to turn back toward Arkhangelsk-Murmansk. The Legionnaires were surprised at the order, particularly when they discovered it had the Allies' approval. Trotsky promised to facilitate their transit.[62]

This delicate balance was disturbed on May 14, near Cheliabinsk, between Ufa and Omsk, where the Legion got into a scuffle with a group of Hungarian prisoners of war. The Hungarians were among a number who had been recruited into the Red Army, as part of what were called the "international proletarian" brigades.[63] When the local Bolsheviks arrested a few of the Czechoslovaks involved, their comrades forced their way into the prison, disarmed the Red Guards, and seized the arsenal. The affair would apparently have been resolved on site, but the ruckus caused the Sovnarkom to change its mind. On May 20, Trotsky ordered the Legion be disarmed and taken from the trains at Penza, west of the Volga on the Omsk line, and be drafted either into labor battalions or directly into the Red Army. The Czechoslovak National Council endorsed the order, but the leaders of what they called the Czechoslovak Revolutionary Army in Cheliabinsk, while affirming their solidarity with the Russian Revolution, insisted they needed to keep their weapons to assure their safe passage, the Red Army being too weak to provide that guarantee.[64]

On May 25, Trotsky declared war. "All Soviets are hereby ordered to disarm the Czechoslovaks immediately. Every armed Czechoslovak found on the railway is to be shot on the spot; every troop train in which even one armed man is found shall be unloaded, and its soldiers shall be interned in a prisoner of war camp. Local war commissars must proceed at once to carry out this order; every delay will be considered treason and will bring the offender severe punishment."[65] Ambassador Noulens believed Trotsky was acting under pressure from Mirbach.[66]

The results of this order are instructive, and not only for the manner in which the Sovnarkom dealt with its enemies ("shoot on the spot"). They also illuminate the difficulty still experienced by the Sovnarkom in making its authority stick. Upon receiving Trotsky's orders, the Penza soviet, at the western end of the line occupied by the Legion's convoy, met with Legionnaires friendly to the Communist cause and informed Trotsky that they "could not carry out the order in its full sense as you demand."[67] Trotsky replied with the indignation befitting his impotence: "Military orders... should not be discussed but obeyed. Any representative of the War Commissariat who is so cowardly as to evade disarming the Czechoslovaks will be brought by me before the Military Tribunal."[68] In fact, on May 26 the Penza soviet did attempt to disarm the Czechoslovaks, but it did not succeed. Instead, two days later, the Legion took control of Penza and proceeded, over the next two weeks, to capture Cheliabinsk, Omsk, and Samara.

The Reds thus lost control of the Trans-Siberian Railroad, along the almost 1,400 miles beginning west of the Volga all the way to the Irtysh River.[69]

The clash with the Hungarians at Cheliabinsk had transformed the Legion from cautious neutrals to hostile armed agents deep in the heartland. Spread throughout European and Siberian Russia were altogether about two million prisoners of war. Many had been forced to join the Red Army, under threat of punishment. Saturated with pro-Communist propaganda, the former troops of the Central Powers were now used to disarm the Czechoslovak Legion. Both Mirbach and the Allies protested; the Czechoslovaks were convinced, however, that the Central Powers were responsible for the order to disarm them. It was reasonable to assume that Germany would object to an associated Allied force being allowed unmolested to go back into action. On May 26, while the Czechoslovaks were confronting local Bolsheviks in Penza, another contingent arrived by train at Irkutsk, on Lake Baikal, and engaged in serious clashes with nearby German and Austrian prisoners. On June 5, the Czechoslovak National Council informed the French Mission that it was renouncing its neutrality. On June 11, the Sovnarkom ordered that the Council's property be transferred to a group of Czechoslovak Communists controlled by the Commissariat of Nationalities, but the Council refused to comply.[70]

---

In June and July 1918, as the Legion proceeded toward the east, anti-Bolshevik centers established themselves in Samara and Omsk. On July 6, German Ambassador Mirbach was assassinated by SRs in Moscow, as we know, and Boris Savinkov launched his rebellion in Iaroslavl, 165 miles to the northeast. It was a moment of extreme tension. While the fate of Iaroslavl was still in doubt and as the Czechoslovak Legion seemed bent on wresting Siberia from Soviet control, Moscow enacted a drama that dealt a death blow to the remaining symbolic authority of the old regime. The drama was outrageous and highly theatrical—an eloquent message and a point of no return. If violence had been needed to dislodge the Provisional Government, as Lenin had insisted, then violence must also destroy the last vestige of imperial rule. The tsar was, after all, still living, still on Russian soil.

In 1917, in the wake of the July Days, Alexander Kerensky had arranged for the transport of the deposed monarch and the imperial family to the relatively isolated Siberian city of Tobolsk, 1,500 miles east of Moscow, beyond the Ural Mountains, where the family and a small entourage were comfortably established in the governor's mansion. The nearest railroad station was in Tiumen, across three rivers, 155 miles to the west.[71] In early 1918, the Bolsheviks seem to have considered bringing Nicholas to trial, as Louis XVI had been tried in 1793 by the French Convention, but no action had been taken. Well before the Legion had become a threat, the Bolsheviks in Ekaterinburg (from 1924 to 1991, Sverdlovsk), two hundred miles west of Tiumen, warned in March that the coming spring thaw might facilitate the tsar's escape and urged that the imperial family be transferred from Tobolsk. An emissary was sent from Moscow to move the captives from Tobolsk, thinking he was to take the emperor directly to Moscow, but after a confused exchange of messages between the local Communists and the center, Nicholas, Alexandra, and one of the daughters were deposited in Ekaterinburg on April 30, where the other children and the entourage joined them several weeks later.

The imperial family were now in the hands of the Ural Regional Soviet, headed by Aleksandr Beloborodov, a former electrician. The eleven members of the party were installed in the house of a prosperous businessman named Nikolai Ipat'ev, where they occupied the furnished upper floor. The purpose was allegedly to guard them until the emperor's anticipated trial, but they were treated as prisoners from the start—a fence was built, contact with the outside world was restricted. Filipp Goloshchekin, whom we have encountered in his later incarnation as a member of the Turkestan Commission in 1919, was at this point military commissar of the Ural Region. At the end of June, as the Czechoslovak Legion was approaching the city, Goloshchekin urged Moscow to authorize the tsar's execution, warning that a conspiracy was afoot to abduct him. By July 16, Goloshchekin had received the go-ahead and signed the final order.

The murder itself, in all its gruesome detail, has often been described. The members of the imperial party were awakened at 1:30 in the morning and taken to a closed, unfurnished room in the basement of the house, where they were brusquely informed they were about to be shot. The firing squad consisted of six Hungarian prisoners of war and four Russians, instructed to shoot each one through the heart to produce an instant death, with the least possible bloodshed. In fact, the bullets went wild between the four walls, blood spattered profusely, and six of the victims had to be finished off. The bodies were carried away in a truck, first buried in a local mineshaft, then transferred to another spot, disfigured by acid, and buried. The remains were discovered only in 1989.

The execution was an act not merely of political self-defense but of icon-oclasm. In fact, Nicholas had lost his charisma long before. As historian Boris Kolonitskii has amply demonstrated, he had already stopped being loved.[72] But although the tsar was nevertheless executed as a symbol, he himself, his family, his personal physician, and his retainers were murdered in cold blood, as civilians. If the murder was intended to convey a message, the Sovnarkom was cagey about the details of what had transpired, pretend-ing for a long time that Nicholas alone had been executed, while the family was being held in safety, for their own protection. After the Czechoslovak Legion had taken Ekaterinburg on July 25, the Whites investigated the cir-cumstances of the murders. The results of that investigation were published in Paris in 1921. Later, in exile, Trotsky explained: "The execution of the Tsar's family was needed not only to frighten, horrify, and dishearten the enemy, but also in order to shake up our own ranks, to show them that there was no turning back."[73] He claimed that Lenin had endorsed the murders. In any case, Beloborodov and Goloshchekin would not have acted without Moscow's approval.[74]

———

The decision to execute the tsar was taken in the face of the Czechoslovak Legion's transformation into an armed internal threat to Bolshevik power and the decision of the Allied powers to intervene directly in the Russian conflict. On June 1, the Supreme Allied War Council in Versailles authorized the Japanese to proceed inland from Vladivostok (with pious warnings against seizing territory or interfering in internal political affairs). The Allies also decided to increase the number of troops in Murmansk and try to seize Arkhangelsk.[75] On June 4, when the Allied representatives in Vologda pro-tested Trotsky's order to disarm the Legion, Chicherin told them to mind their own business.[76]

On June 20, the French Ministry of War instructed the Legion, still formally under French command, not to surrender arms. On June 29, Legionnaires ousted the Soviet in Vladivostok, while British and Japanese forces took possession of the train station and public buildings. On July 6, a protectorate over Vladivostok was announced by the American, French, Japanese, Chinese, and Czechoslovak military representatives, who promised to take "all necessary measures... for its defense against dangers both external and internal.... This action," they declared, "is taken in a spirit of sympathetic friendship for the Russian people without reference to any political faction or party," in hopes of fruitful cooperation and the defeat of the "Austro-German powers."[77]

Despite the participation of the U.S. Asiatic Fleet in this effort, the United States continued to resist the prospect of military involvement. Such action, it warned the Allies, "would add to the present sad confusion in Russia rather than cure it, injure her rather than help her, and...would be of no advantage in the prosecution of our main design, to win the war against Germany." The United States was therefore unable to "take part in such intervention or sanction it in principle." The Americans nevertheless agreed to participate in guarding military stores and aiding the Czechoslovak Legion.[78]

Earlier, while still fearing German incursion from the north, the Bolsheviks had accepted the British presence in Murmansk. The Czechoslovak revolt changed the situation. On June 7, Lenin instructed the Murmansk Soviet to lodge a protest. Again, as in the Penza case, the local comrades asserted their independence. Instead of protesting, the Murmansk Soviet invited the British to send more men.[79] The Sovnarkom denounced the chairman of the Murmansk Soviet as a traitor and enemy of the people; Trotsky warned of serious sanctions.[80] The chairman replied: "Can you supply the region with the food we are now lacking and send us a force sufficient to carry out your instructions...? If not, there is no need of lecturing us.... We ourselves know that the Germans and the Allies are imperialist, but of two evils we have chosen the lesser."[81]

In May, while relations between the Sovnarkom and the Allies were still in flux, the British had sent General F. C. Poole to Arkhangelsk to assist Trotsky and take command of the Czechoslovaks, originally supposed to leave Russia by the northern route, before it was decided to send them via Vladivostok.[82] Now, on July 6, undeterred by Moscow, the Murmansk Soviet signed an agreement with the British allowing the Allies to enter at Murmansk. As the British began moving south along the Murmansk railroad, Chicherin protested to Lockhart against British aggression. Discovering that the Allies were encouraging the anti-Bolshevik resistance in Iaroslavl, a hundred miles to the south, the Sovnarkom requested that the Allied ambassadors relocate from Vologda to Moscow, but they refused. After General Poole informed them he was preparing to occupy Arkhangelsk in early August, the ambassadors left Vologda for the northern city on July 25.[83]

At the end of July, Lenin announced a state of war with "Anglo-French imperialism." The Soviet Central Executive Committee once again declared

"The Socialist Fatherland in Danger." The Allies were not, however, the main target of invective. A campaign of "mass terror" was launched against the domestic "counterrevolutionary bourgeoisie," accused of abetting the foreign powers.[84] The next day, Chicherin denied that Lenin really meant war. The ambassadors could stay, but the rhetoric of world revolution persisted. On August 1, the Sovnarkom issued an appeal to the "toiling masses of France, England, America, Italy, and Japan," denouncing the perfidious plans of the "hirelings of your exploiters [who] have thrown off their masks and shout openly of a campaign against the workers and peasants of Russia." "The Anglo-French bandits are already shooting Soviet workers on the Murmansk Railway, which they have seized." The Allies were also paying the Czechoslovak Legion to shoot workers in Siberia. "In the interests of capital you are to be the executioners of the Russian workers' revolution."[85] It was the Allies' rejection of Soviet overtures during the talks at Brest-Litovsk, Chicherin reminded the foreign workers, that had forced Russia to sign the humiliating peace. Since then the Allies had been engaged in a campaign of subversion and economic warfare. "German imperialism can be defeated only when the imperialism of all countries is defeated by the united attack of the world proletariat."[86] "Down with the bandits of international imperialism! Long live the International Revolution!"[87]

On August 2, the British landed at Arkhangelsk. The international revolution was still around the corner, but it had not yet arrived.

# 3

# Trotsky Arms, Siberia Mobilizes

Trotsky pursued his flirtation with the Allied powers in the early weeks of 1918 for a number of reasons. It was not clear that negotiations at Brest-Litovsk would actually result in peace. On the Russian side, many Bolsheviks, as well as SRs, wanted to keep fighting, this time in a "revolutionary war." In Germany the "war party" might reject or ignore a peace. The weak Red forces might need the support of Russia's still nominal allies, whose ambivalence invited continued appeals. Finally, the new regime needed urgently to create a functional military force, with assistance from any possible quarter.

The Army's collapse had enabled the October coup. Now the tables were turned, and the victorious rebels needed to reestablish the basis for obedience and authority.[1] They had to master the spirit of defiance which the larger catastrophe had unleashed and on which they had ridden to power. Claims to power, of course, meant nothing without the ability to impose it. To counteract the effects of the Petrograd Soviet's Order No. 1 and stem the army's further dissolution, the Provisional Government had begun sending emissaries to the front. By the end of 1917, as we have seen, authority in the field was divided among the officers, the commissars, and the soldier committees. Insofar as it was divided, it was no authority at all, as subsequent events were to demonstrate.

Even before the October climax, the problem was clear. The writer Viktor Shklovskii recalled his experience on the eve of Kerensky's July 1917 offensive. "For the time being, the regiments were held together by their naive revolutionary ideology, by the 'Marseillaise,' by the red banner and especially by the great momentum of such a huge accumulation of men as an army; they were held together by the residues and habits of everyday army life."

The force of habit was reinforced, paradoxically enough, by the committees, positioned between the ranks and their now disempowered commanders. "The task of the committee members was, above all, the preservation of the army," Shklovskii observed. "How to preserve it they didn't know, and they waited for the storm and feared it and didn't know whether to struggle against it." The worst were the "hastily assembled units" of reserves, "with no traditions, with commanders quarreling among themselves." Men refused to dig trenches, to fight. Commissars who preached the offensive were "nearly beaten...to death."[2]

The Decree on Peace and the Decree on Land, as well as the abolition of capital punishment, all promulgated on October 26, had only made matters worse. Official demobilization of conscripts began two days later, but was soon partially rescinded. The momentum was difficult, however, to stop. The troops were already heading home, from war-weariness and for fear of missing out on the division of land. On the way, they looted storehouses, stole regimental funds, and refused to surrender their weapons. Their numbers overwhelmed the already overburdened railroads. The challenge was to control the potential flood of the millions still in uniform. As officers began defecting to the emerging White opposition and as the Germans continued to move forward, the commissars could not afford to let the process of disintegration run its course. Army Chief of Staff General Mikhail Bonch-Bruevich, brother of a trusted Bolshevik comrade, reported at the start of the new year: "The army is altogether unsuitable for combat and is in no condition to hold back the enemy."[3]

The Soviet Republic needed an army—not the old army, but an army compatible with socialist principles and capable of defending the new regime.[4] The model of a socialist army combining the myth of the "people in arms" with the reality of modern warfare was being worked out in January while the negotiations at Brest-Litovsk were fitfully proceeding and while German troops were advancing toward Petrograd. On January 14/27, the day before the announced formation of what would become the Red Army, Trotsky temporarily left the negotiations. Nikolai Krylenko, still nominally commander in chief, thought Trotsky intended to dissolve the active army and ordered demobilization. Lenin demanded the decree be rescinded, but it did nothing more than increase the tempo of what was already a massive flight.[5]

Part of the problem of reestablishing authority stemmed from the confusion and lack of expertise at the top of the new Red command. In the wake of the coup, leadership of the Commissariat of War was shared by three men, with varying degrees of military experience. Vladimir Antonov-Ovseenko, who had arrested the ministers in 1917, came from an officer's family and had trained as an officer-cadet; Pavel Dybenko had been a sailor in the Black Sea Fleet who had led naval squads against General Krasnov; Krylenko was an ensign.[6] By January 1918, Dybenko had been replaced by Nikolai Podvoiskii, a member of the Military Revolutionary Committee in 1917 who had no military background. They all, of course, deferred to Lenin.[7] After the signing of the peace, a new organ was created to oversee the Commissariat for Military and Naval Affairs. The Supreme Military Council of the Republic (*Vysshii voennyi sovet respubliki*), with Trotsky as chair, undertook the task of creating the Red Army. The Left SRs forfeited the lone position they had occupied on the Council after the Fourth All-Russian Congress of Soviets, in mid-March, where they persisted in championing the model of a socialist militia.[8] But realism was in order. In the crisis of February 1918, the volunteer Red Army, the Red Guards, and the old regiments now in disarray had all failed. It was in this context of weakness and improvisation that the French and British representatives expressed the desire to help Trotsky create a fighting force.[9]

Despite opposition from the Left SRs and from within the Bolshevik Party, Trotsky insisted authority must be restored. He repeated the theme on every possible occasion. "Comrades! Our Soviet Socialist Republic must have a well-organized army." "Exhausted and unarmed Russia will inevitably become the slave of the united forces of international imperialism, unless we are saved in time by the support of the international proletariat and unless we organize our own defense."[10] "The question of creating an army is for us now a question of life or death."[11] Into late April, until German ambassador von Mirbach appeared in Moscow, Trotsky kept the Allies thinking he might turn to them for cooperation and expertise.[12]

From whatever source, the new military needed the skill and discipline of a conventional army. It needed commanders. Trotsky therefore now made an effort to recruit former Imperial Army officers, ending the principle of elected commanders established in Order No. 1. When the soldier committees objected, he ordered them dissolved.[13] They continued in existence nevertheless and kept electing officers into 1919, but a new direction had been set. The democratic ethos could not simply be discarded, however. The urge to break with the past was overwhelming. Already in August 1917, Shklovskii observed the curious case in which "soldiers were wearing

unlaced boots and belts, not around their waists, but over one shoulder like
sword-holders. I understood the reasons for this strange, slovenly costume.
These men wanted everything to be different."[14]

The new regime had to establish its distance from the old culture of
command. A decree in December abolished ranks, along with their privileges and insignia. The term "specialist" replaced "officer"; "Red Army man"
replaced "soldier." The Sovnarkom opened training schools for what were
called Red Commanders, giving priority to workers and peasants over educated men.[15] The career officers were to be monitored by political commissars, a practice already employed in 1917 by the Provisional Government.
This created a structure reminiscent of the post-February Dual Power. The
endorsement of the commander's orders by the commissar was supposed
to ensure that soldiers obeyed them, but the commissars and the officer-
specialists also had to contend with the soldier committees, which were
closest to the men.[16] In the end, over the course of the Civil War, about fifty
thousand former tsarist officers—about 20 percent—of the imperial officer
corps fought with the Reds. Those attached to the old General Staff were
the most likely to remain, as did the core of the old military administration.[17] As far as administration was concerned, Podvoiskii had the good sense
to retain most of the former ministry bureaucrats, under the Commissariat's
supervision.[18]

At the bottom of the hierarchy of command, the Red Army also needed
soldiers. The first step, in April 1918, was to institute "compulsory military
training," though not yet compulsory military service. After the revolt of the
Czechoslovak Legion at the end of May, conscription for men twenty-one
to twenty-five years old was introduced for Siberia, the Urals, and the Volga
region, and the numbers eligible continued to expand.[19] After the Fifth
Congress of Soviets in Moscow in July, which coincided with the SR revolt,
the Red Army was reconstituted on the basis of compulsory military service,
centralized authority, an officer corps assembled from the old Imperial
Army, and application of the death penalty against traitors and deserters. The
goal was still to train a new generation of Red Commanders. Commissars
were still in use as ideological watchdogs, but hierarchy and the threat of
execution were back. Field tribunals were created to impose the death penalty on soldiers, officers, and commissars guilty of treason, sabotage, desertion, or looting.[20]

Authority was the order of the day. "We face enormous tasks," Trotsky
told the Moscow Soviet in March 1918. These were "to reestablish railway

transport, feed the hungry, draw the masses into productive and properly organized labor. There is no doubt that the tasks of the present moment are considerably complicated by the fact that the old discipline instilled in the masses has been eradicated, while the new, revolutionary discipline has not yet taken form."[21] In the case of the volunteers, whether in the Red Army or the Red Guards, a uniform or label put the stamp of approval on behavior that was impossible to control. Some men joined the Red Army or Red Guards as the only way to get a meal; grain-requisitioning detachments were in effect authorized to plunder the peasantry; soldiers could also walk away with their uniforms and weapons, to use or sell as they saw fit.[22]

Nor was conscription a magic solution. The army relied on the villages to identify the eligible men, but the villages were more likely to impede the work of personnel sent to administer the draft; many eligible men simply did not show up. Others who enlisted were later released, because the army needed not only to register but also to feed them. And there the vicious circle kicked in. The same peasants who provided the troops also harvested the grain for the bread they ate; the same workers who entered the Red Guards were those manning the factories producing the products for the peasants to buy with the money they gained from selling their grain. But the factories had largely ceased operation, and the peasants were not getting paid for their grain—instead, the authorities sent men from the cities to steal it. Horses were requisitioned, then died of hunger.[23] Until the industrial and agricultural sectors were back in operation, no mass army could be sustained.

The Red Army emerged nevertheless as the single most effective fighting force in the Civil War and became the cornerstone of the new political regime. Trotsky was its central figure. He was colorful, dramatic, dynamic, a ruthless disciplinarian and gifted propagandist. The special train in which he traversed the country, exhorting and inspiring, communicating, haranguing, impressing the crowds, demonstrating the power of technology—the train itself, the automobiles, the press, a mobile mass media station—combined the genius of propaganda with the devotion to organization and discipline that were Bolshevik hallmarks.[24] A brilliant improviser, Trotsky did better, in the end, at a job for which he had no preparation than many of the professional warriors ranged against him. William Henry Chamberlin describes him as "a Jewish revolutionary who, without any technical military experience, drove the heterogeneous masses of the Red Army to final victory by a combination of ruthless fanaticism, abounding energy and never failing resourcefulness."[25] His Jewishness is relevant in this context only insofar as Jews had been reputed during the Great War to be unfit for military service. Here was the living refutation of the charge that they were good only for book-learning, disputation, and troublemaking. A troublemaker Trotsky certainly was, but also a builder and warrior.

Trotsky's methods combined brutality, organizational skill, and ideological inspiration—the patented Bolshevik formula. The commissar's "passionate, impetuous nature," Chamberlin notes, "sometimes led him to order measures, . . . which would have been not only inhuman, but inexpedient."[26] His hardline response to the Czechoslovak Legion turned them against the Reds, with whom, as socialists, they were in general sympathy. His readiness to execute the wavering or faint-hearted alienated some confederates. In opposition to Stalin and in later exile, Trotsky came to symbolize the left-wing critique of Soviet Communism as a repressive, authoritarian regime, but in his heyday, the commissar of war was himself ruthless and high-handed. Habits of ruthlessness and brutality, however, did not distinguish the Bolsheviks from most of their opponents in the Civil War, and the role of any single personality, however charismatic, cannot explain how the Bolsheviks managed to come out on top in the end.

---

Indeed, the Bolsheviks faced a seemingly overwhelming challenge, as opposition to their rule spread not only up and down the Volga and across the south, but throughout the entire Eurasian continent. Yet in some respects the evolving Civil War favored the Bolshevik project. While highlighting—indeed promoting—the fragmentation of the political opposition, the conflict was welcomed by the Soviet leadership as a means of forging unity within its own ranks and consolidating the kind of central control and uncontested authority that were Lenin's trademarks. In short, the Bolsheviks thrived on civil war, which also had the advantage of combining the battle against the armed enemy with the battle against the unarmed, sometimes invisible enemy lurking within the society they were dismantling in order to rebuild.

The Civil War functioned also to sharpen distinctions within the common vocabulary of the revolution; it clarified the political landscape. Critics of Trotsky's methods, within the party and among its socialist allies, objected to his authoritarian style and to the imposition of conventional discipline and hierarchy in the Red Army as a betrayal of socialist democracy. Socialist opponents of Bolshevik rule also spoke in the name of democracy. Menshevik leader Iulii Martov denounced Lenin's "so-called dictatorship of the proletariat" as a "caricature" created by the "bohemian intelligentsia" propelled by the destructive, "anarchistic" impulses of the "petty bourgeois" classes. True democracy, Martov insisted, must be the work of "organized civic forces" capable of rallying the mass of the people behind the creation of a "democratic republican order, able to regulate the interests of different groups of the population without recourse to civil war." Otherwise, Martov feared, opposition to Bolshevism would result in the victory of "the propertied, monarchist-landowning counterrevolution."[27]

Martov's comments, from 1918, reflect both the wisdom and the weakness of the Menshevik position. Operating with the same Marxist lexicon—intelligentsia, proletariat, petty bourgeoisie—and equally hostile to the counterrevolution, thus unwilling to jeopardize the revolution's success, Martov understood that the Bolshevik concept of dictatorship was fatal to democracy in the political sense. The Bolsheviks preferred war. Wise as to the political consequences of Bolshevism, but hamstrung by the fear of reaction, the moderate socialist opposition thus depended on the same tenuous civic middle ground that had failed to carry the day in 1917. The "struggle for democracy...against Bolshevist Tyranny" became a catchword among the disparate opponents of Soviet rule, but there was little agreement on what this "democracy" meant in practical terms and what means were justified on its behalf.[28]

Indeed, the political and social incoherence of the anti-Bolshevik opposition was nowhere more obvious than in the vast reaches of Siberia, through which in spring and summer 1918 the Czechoslovak Legion was proceeding. The Whites in the Don and Kuban were driven by traditional patriotism, devotion to duty, and defense of the old social order, if not always the old political regime. The anti-Bolshevik forces in Siberia were, by contrast, a political hodgepodge. Liberals, SRs, regionalists, and career officers struggled for predominance, popular support, and the military and financial backing of foreign powers. In spring 1918, French ambassador Noulens recalled, "Siberia presented a spectacle probably unparalleled in history. Representatives of all the belligerent nations and of the hundred nationalities of the tsarist old regime rubbed elbows there in friendly fashion or, on occasion, killed each other." Bolshevik interests, in his view, were promoted by "convicts, outlaws, and political exiles," who had established soviets in all the larger cities.[29]

It is not surprising that Siberia should have hosted such a broad array of groups and interests. It was more a vast territorial expanse than a region

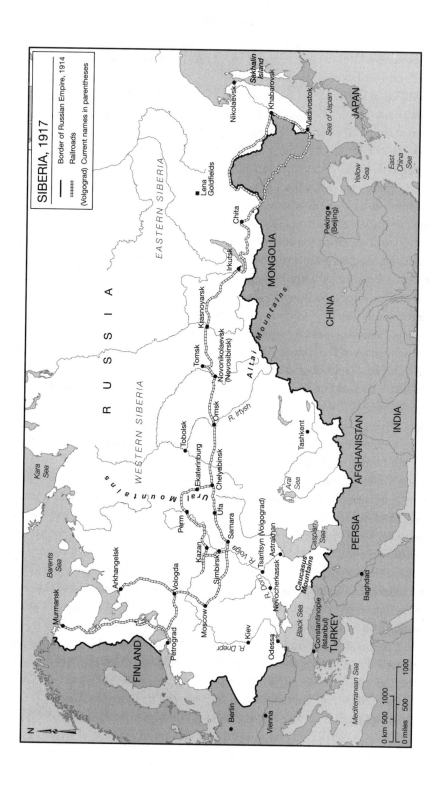

SIBERIA, 1917

Border of Russian Empire, 1914
Railroads
(Volgograd) Current names in parentheses

FINLAND

Murmansk
Arkhangelsk
Barents Sea
Kara Sea

Petrograd
Moscow
Vologda
Kiev
R. Dnepr
Berlin
Vienna

Kazan
Simbirsk
Samara
R. Volga
Tsaritsyn (Volgograd)
Astrakhan
Don
Novocherkassk
Caucasus Mountains
Caspian Sea
Odessa
Constantinople (Istanbul)
TURKEY
Black Sea
Baghdad
Mediterranean Sea

Perm
Ufa
Ekaterinburg
Ural Mountains
Chelyabinsk
Tobolsk
Omsk
R. Irtysh
Aral Sea
Tashkent
PERSIA
AFGHANISTAN
INDIA

RUSSIA

WESTERN SIBERIA
EASTERN SIBERIA

Tomsk
Novonikolaevsk (Novosibirsk)
Krasnoyarsk
Irkutsk
Altai Mountains
Chita
Lena Goldfields
MONGOLIA
CHINA
Peking (Beijing)

Nikolaevsk
Sakhalin Island
Khabarovsk
Vladivostok
Sea of Japan
JAPAN
Yellow Sea
East China Sea

N

0 km 500 1000
0 miles 500 1000

unified either in geographic or ethnic terms.[30] Encompassing almost five million square miles, it covered more than half the territory of the Empire, but contained only about 6 percent of the total population, most of its inhabitants concentrated in the cities along the six thousand miles of the Trans-Siberian Railroad, two-thirds in the western half.[31] Larger than China, Canada, or the United States, Siberia embraced three-quarters the area of today's Russian Federation.

Despite the sparseness of its population, Siberia produced an urban professional and entrepreneurial class. As in the Ukraine, this urban society generated a regionalist movement, which first emerged after the February Revolution. In May 1917, a public meeting in the university city of Tomsk resolved that Siberia should be governed at the local level by an All-Siberian Regional Duma (*Vsesibirskaia oblastnaia duma*—Sibobduma).[32] Regionalists gathered again in August and after the coup, in October, to consider what to do about it. The so-called All-Siberian Regional Congress involved an awkward alliance between the regionalists and an influx of SRs seeking an institutional foothold. By January 1918, the SRs active in Siberia had moved far to the right. They opposed land reform and repudiated their Left SR colleagues. The SR Party had lost control of its brand, which no longer had any political coherence aside from visceral opposition to exclusive Bolshevik rule. SRs played a leading role in the second regionalist gathering at the end of October, which drafted the basic outlines of regional self-government, within the framework of a greater Russia, to be presented for endorsement at the anticipated Empire-wide Constituent Assembly. The executive was to be the Siberian Regional Duma first proposed in May.[33]

Conversation was soon interrupted. In the wake of October, the fledgling Red Army, weak as it was, had no difficulty at first in assuming control of the cities along the Trans-Siberian Railroad. Soviet power was declared in Tomsk, 2,300 miles east of Moscow, on December 8, 1917.[34] The Reds encountered resistance only at Irkutsk, another thousand miles farther east, on Lake Baikal, which they easily overcame. "Soviet rule began the year 1918 in the East in the full flowering of its might," a hostile left-wing observer noted. "On the entire, limitless expanse of the Volga region, the Urals, Turkestan, and Siberia, the Bolsheviks reigned alone. Power fell into their hands painlessly." The same commentator acknowledged Bolshevik success, not only in military terms but in elections to the local soviets and in establishing a network of disciplined agents at all levels of administration. These were indeed the classic Bolshevik methods—relentless propaganda and organized penetration at the grass roots. Only the Ural Cossacks stubbornly resisted the Red advance.[35] In the November 1918 elections to the Constituent Assembly, however, the Bolsheviks won only 10 percent of the Siberian vote.[36]

The patchwork of competing political centers in Siberia illustrates the chaotic nature of political life after October. Among the proliferation of short-lived organizations that filled the political vacuum, a certain pattern nevertheless emerged. The civic organizations that Martov hoped could provide the backbone of a truly democratic political regime, with mass popular support, appeared in the wake of the October coup and resurfaced whenever the Bolsheviks were chased from their temporary strongholds. Imperial Russian civil society on the provincial level—whether in Siberia, the Caucasus, Central Asia, or the Ukraine—was still yearning for the political leadership it had been denied under the tsar. And, as Martov had feared, these efforts were overwhelmed in the end by the collision of extremes on both sides. That is a major theme of the Civil War, which was to engulf the former Empire after the Germans withdrew.

The All-Siberian Regional Duma, slated to open in Tomsk in late January 1918, was dominated by Right SRs who rejected the authority of the regional soviet, in which their erstwhile colleagues, the Left SRs, collaborated with the Bolsheviks. In a repetition of the events in Petrograd earlier in the month, Red Guards appeared on the eve of the Duma meeting and shut it down. Many of the delegates were arrested. A few escaped and met clandestinely to form what they called the Provisional Government of Autonomous Siberia (*Vremennoe pravitel'stvo avtonomnoi Sibiri*).[37] Its flag was green and white, for the forests and snows of Siberia.[38] Its leader was an SR named Petr Derber, a native of Odessa of Jewish background, at this point about thirty years old, who like many of his generation had embarked on a radical career in his teens and been arrested, exiled to Siberia, and escaped to Europe, in Derber's case ending up in Siberia yet again. Soon after his election as head of the Siberian Provisional Government, however, he took off for the Far East, leaving his associates behind.[39] Like other SRs, he fell between two stools—hated by the Whites, persecuted by the Soviet regime.[40] In 1918, as the Bolsheviks charged, the SR Party was indeed an anti-Bolshevik terrorist organization, though not in its own eyes counterrevolutionary. In mid-February, two weeks after Derber headed east, four SR members of his Provisional Government formed an underground organization, the Western Siberian Commissariat (*Zapadno-Sibirskii komissariat*), based just south of Tomsk in Novonikolaevsk (since 1926, Novosibirsk). Their purpose was to create an army that would drive the Reds out of Siberia. The Commissariat remained under-ground until late May, after the Czechoslovak Legion had liberated the city.[41]

Thus, by February, Tomsk, Irkutsk, and Novonikolaevsk had become cen-ters of frenzied political organization. Phantom institutions came and went. For the regionalists, to recapitulate, the First All-Siberian Regional Congress in Tomsk had responded to the Bolshevik coup by creating the Siberian Regional Duma (dispersed by force), whose rump had formed the Provisional Government of Autonomous Siberia (briefly under Derber), which in turn generated the clandestine Western Siberian Commissariat in Novonikolaevsk. The confused terminology was symptomatic. On the Red side, the Second All-Siberian Congress of Soviets, meeting in Irkutsk on February 23, 1918, generated the Central Executive Committee of Siberian Soviets. The Bolsheviks' poor showing for Siberia in the elections to the Constituent Assembly did not stop the Second Congress from again proclaiming Soviet rule in Siberia, a claim first announced in Tomsk in December 1917.[42]

For its part, the Western Siberian Commissariat was unable to muster an armed force, without which no putative government could even pretend to govern. The officers pouring into Siberia from the Russian core at first refused to work with the SRs, however moderate they had become. Anger at Brest-Litovsk, however, moved some to come on board. The Commissariat's platform endorsed the Constituent Assembly, the (no longer existing) Siberian Regional Duma, and cautious army reforms. It spawned similar, clandestine institutions farther east and also delegated its SR members to infiltrate the soviets and Red Guard. The Bolshevik obsession with traitors was not a complete delusion.[43] Support for the Western Siberian Commissariat came from the local SR-led cooperative movement, but without Allied funding all of this was just whistling in the wind. Siberian big business, by contrast, was leery of socialists of any stripe. The entrepreneurs put their money on a monarchist organization formed in Omsk, known as the Group of Thirteen.[44]

As the various groups fragmented and recombined, the Siberian anti-Bolshevik opposition, still flying the democratic flag, moved ever farther to the right. After the Czechoslovak revolt in late May, the Legion easily swept the Reds from the cities they had earlier taken.[45] In the course of June, with the help of SR-oriented officers, the Legion picked off one city after another, from Penza to Vladivostok.[46] Moving from station to station along the Trans-Siberian Railroad, as though clearing a path through the wilds, it became embroiled in the domestic opposition to Bolshevik power. "The cities terrorized by the Bolsheviks," Ambassador Noulens had observed, "received them as liberators and invited them to assume the role of city government, as they had earlier invited the Germans to do. Wherever the Legion stopped it restored order and its presence allowed the moderate governments to replace the Red dictators who had fled."[47] Noulens, not surprisingly, painted the Bolsheviks in the darkest possible colors, but none of the competing armies was kind to the civilian population.

Once the fragile Soviet institutions had been dislodged, the field was open to the many local contenders. In June, the Western Siberian Commissariat moved to liberated Omsk. The officers who now helped the Western Siberian Commissariat form a functioning army had no use for socialism of any kind, and it soon abandoned the remaining elements of the original Siberian Regional Duma program. The Siberian Provisional Government had similarly lost its SR supporters.[48] The trend at the beginning of the year, in which SRs had pushed out the moderate regionalists, now reversed itself. The increasingly right-wing groups were dispensing with their SR partners. The Provisional Government at Omsk announced that "Bolshevik power in Siberia has been abolished and the Siberian Provisional Government, elected by the Siberian Regional Duma,...has assumed the task of governing Siberia." In return, the Sovnarkom denounced the "counter-revolutionary conspirators," whom it described as "trying to play at government." It accused them of plotting to starve the Soviet Republic by strangling the railroad. "Under the guise of the Constituent Assembly there is going on a fight to establish the autocratic rule of rich over poor, of idlers over toilers."[49]

The Provisional Siberian Government in Omsk, endorsed by the Siberian Regional Duma, emerged by the end of June with a council of five men, headed by the liberal lawyer Petr Vologodskii, former president of the Omsk District Court, deputy to the Second Duma from Tomsk.[50] On July 4, 1918, at the very moment that the Fifth All-Russian Congress of Soviets in Moscow was adopting the Constitution of the RSFSR, the Provisional Siberian Government declared itself the head of an independent state.[51]

The contradictions and illusions inherent in these organizational gymnastics emerge from the text of the document in which the Provisional Siberian Government "assumed full authority in the country after the expulsion of the Bolshevik usurpers." Citing the January declaration issued by the Siberian Regional Duma, the new claimants to power now assumed responsibility for deciding what kind of government Siberia should have. "Considering the fact that Russian sovereignty as such no longer exists, since a considerable part of Russian territory is in the de facto possession of the Central Powers, while another part is occupied by the Bolshevik usurpers, the Siberian Provisional Government solemnly declares that henceforth it and the Siberian Regional Duma will be responsible for the future of Siberia." Declaring war against the Soviet contenders, but not against Russia itself, the Vologodskii government asserted that "the severance of Siberia from the territories comprising the former Russian Empire is only temporary and... every effort will be made to reestablish Russian sovereignty." The future of this resurrected state was to be determined by the joint efforts of Siberian and All-Russian Constituent Assemblies.[52] In other words, independent Siberia was a temporary expedient on the road to the restoration of a unified greater Russian political world. The same was true for the Provisional Siberian Government's social program, which included the restoration of private property (the return of confiscated land) and the reintroduction of field courts and the death penalty. These were the very elements which had alienated popular support for the tsarist regime and its post-February successor.[53] The Red Army had by now also introduced harsh disciplinary measures, which in its case conflicted with its professed revolutionary ideals.

Even within the confines of rump Siberia, however, unity was hard to achieve. The vestigial Siberian Regional Duma, whose earlier statements the Provisional Siberian Government had invoked, still existed. Convening at Tomsk University in August, it challenged the authority of Vologodskii and his ministers to represent the region or define its political path.[54] The commander of the Omsk garrison used an excuse to arrest a number of the Duma's SR members, one of whom was killed while under arrest, but the Duma itself refused to disappear.[55] Meanwhile, the Provisional Siberian Government had managed to assemble the elements of what it called the Western Siberian Army. By now called simply the Siberian Army, it included as many as ten thousand officers and thirty thousand men.[56]

By the summer months of 1918, opposition, however dispersed and fragmented, to the Bolshevik regime had thus intensified. One of the first cities cleared by the Czechoslovak Legion was Samara, situated on the Volga River between Simbirsk and Saratov, seven hundred miles east of Moscow. Samara was a major commercial and manufacturing center of over 100,000 inhabitants. There, on June 8, the Legion collaborated with the SRs in establishing an anti-Bolshevik government, calling itself the Committee of Members of the Constituent Assembly (*Komitet chlenov Vserossiiskogo Uchreditel'nogo sobraniia*—Komuch), referred to also as the Samara Government.[57] The Komuch opened its doors to any elected delegates who made their way to the city, with the exception of Bolsheviks and Left SRs, though in the end it consisted exclusively of SRs.[58] It called new elections to the soviets, acknowledged the zemstvos and City Dumas, and announced the restoration of civil liberties. It also formed a so-called People's Army, under the command of sympathetic former imperial officers, composed of volunteers and peasant conscripts, operating without committees or commissars.[59]

The Komuch People's Army flew the three-striped Russian flag, signaling its claim to represent the whole of Russia—though in a nod to the popular revolution, its officers did not wear epaulettes.[60] Acquiring a popular following was more difficult than dispensing with symbols. Peasants had to be compelled to answer to the draft, and those that were taken, "lacking any real military training, unconstrained by any sense of duty or discipline, were as a whole completely useless. Upon encountering Bolsheviks they either surrendered or...abandoned their positions and ran off to the villages."[61] The local peasants were reluctant to fight the Reds, whose policies and strong-arm methods had not yet affected them directly. The workers in the cities preferred to stand aside, and the local elites viewed the socialists with suspicion.[62]

The Provisional Siberian Government, for its part, considered the Komuch almost as objectionable, in its SR leanings, as the Bolsheviks. The two centers refused to cooperate, withholding shipments of grain and manufactured goods and threatening military confrontation.[63] Its critics considered the Komuch a replay of the same SR politics which had doomed that party in 1917. "The same endless meetings with tiresome and empty speeches about 'revolutionary democracy' and the 'bourgeoisie,' and about the 'hydra of counterrevolution insolently raising its head'.... The entire verbal arsenal of the honeymoon of the revolution was taken from mothballs and returned to circulation."[64]

---

If Siberia was the Empire's Wild East, the Volga River was the heartland's vital pulse. Over two thousand miles long, originating in the north between St. Petersburg and Moscow, it formed a great arc east and south to Kazan and Samara, and down through Tsaritsyn to the Caspian Sea. The cities along the Volga, like those along the Trans-Siberian Railroad, were targets of political as

well as military conquest, as the various enemies of Bolshevik rule mobilized
their forces to attack the imperial core. A menacing circle was forming around
the seat of power in Moscow, as the Czechoslovak Legion—the one disciplined
and effective military force in anyone's hands—made its way up the Volga.

The case of Simbirsk, the birthplace of both Kerensky and Lenin, was
particularly painful—a political and military stab in the back. The protagonist
was Lieutenant Colonel Mikhail Murav'ev, who had begun his bloody career
defending Bolshevik power, in January 1918, as we have seen, taking Kiev and
terrorizing the city. By July, his Left SR sympathies had led him into the opposition. Still in command of the Red Eastern Army, he led a unit of a thousand
men down the Volga from Kazan to Simbirsk, which he reached on July 10.
Calling himself the "Garibaldi of the Russian people," he was determined
to link up with the Czechoslovak Legion and renew the fight against the
Germans. His treacherous ambitions were foiled and the Red Eastern Army
saved when he was killed by the Reds in Simbirsk the next day.[65] On July 21,
however, the Czechoslovak Legion, together with the relatively feeble Komuch
People's Army, managed to achieve Murav'ev's goal and chase the Bolsheviks
from Simbirsk.[66]

Murav'ev was replaced at the head of the Red Eastern Army by the ruthless Colonel Ioakim Vatsetis (Jukums Vācietis) of the still-devoted Latvian
Riflemen, who had destroyed the Left SR revolt in Moscow. Now, in the
Volga, the rest of the army collapsed, some of his own officers turned against
him, and Vatsetis suffered a shameful personal defeat.[67] "The soldiers proved
utterly lacking in discipline," he reported. Only the Latvian Riflemen were
still in form. "As regards Russian units, they proved incapable of fighting in
mass because of lack of preparation and discipline."[68] In early August, the
Czechoslovak Legion took Kazan, giving the Samara Government access to
the imperial gold reserves which had been transferred from Petrograd.[69]

As in Siberia, the anti-Bolshevik parties in the Urals also attempted to
form alliances. On August 20, a group of political moderates—including two
Kadets, a Popular Socialist, a Menshevik, and an SR—made yet another claim
to authority—also tentative, also local. They called themselves the Provisional
Regional Government of the Urals (*Vremennoe oblastnoe pravitel'stvo Urala*).
Describing life in the Urals as "completely disorganized," the group resolved
to work for the improvement of local conditions while anticipating the
eventual reunification of Russia on the old scale, with a government determined by the Constituent Assembly. They endorsed civil rights, private
property, the eight-hour day, and food distribution via cooperatives, instead

of requisition. Land for the time being would remain in the hands of the tillers. The self-declared government annulled all Soviet decrees but refrained from undoing recent changes.[70]

Setbacks on the Volga were balanced, however, from the Bolshevik perspective, by news that the Allies were punishing the Germans at Amiens on the Western Front.[71] On August 27, the Supplementary Treaty to Brest-Litovsk pledged the Germans to abandon military action, allowing the Reds to throw their weight into the Volga campaign. The principle of "revolutionary discipline" went into effect. "If any part of the army retreats of its own will, the first to be shot will be the commissar and the second, the commander," Trotsky warned. "Cowards and traitors will not escape the bullets."[72] The problem of loyalty was addressed in an equally draconian manner. "Those peasants and workers who have sold themselves to the White Guards and remain in their armies voluntarily will be shot, along with the officers and the darling sons of the bourgeoisie and capitalists."[73]

For the Bolsheviks, the summer of treachery and defeats ended on August 30, 1918, as we have seen, with the assassination of Uritskii and the attempt on Lenin's life. The Cheka responded the next day by raiding the embassy still maintained by the British in Petrograd. Francis Cromie, the naval officer who in June had executed Trotsky's instructions to scuttle the Russian Baltic Fleet to prevent it falling into German hands, was shot to death during the encounter. British agent Bruce Lockhart was arrested. The Sovnarkom accused the Allies of plotting to overthrow the Soviet government, impose a military dictatorship, and restart the war against Germany.[74] Bolshevik flirtation with the "Anglo-French imperialists" had come to an end, and on September 5, 1918, the Sovnarkom made the Red Terror official.

Meanwhile, the Red Army was making its way down the Volga, seizing Kazan on September 10 and Simbirsk a day later.[75] "The taking of Kazan," Trotsky said, "is the beginning of the death agony for the bourgeois scoundrels on the Volga, in the Urals and Siberia."[76] The scoundrels were certainly up to no good. They were in fact gathering in the east, attempting to establish a unified leadership and acquire foreign support. In the fall of 1918, the Whites also moved farther in the direction of brute repression and force of arms, at the expense of whatever political process had survived until then. The Kadets in the Ukraine had lent their backing to the German puppet-regime of the hetman Skoropads'kyi. Now, in the Far East, the democratic Allied powers of Britain and France gave their endorsement to another native strongman. Enter Admiral Aleksandr Kolchak.

# 4

## Kolchak—the Wild East

Admiral Kolchak was not a dyed-in-the-wool monarchist but a professional soldier who had already experienced the humiliation and dangers of military defeat. As a young officer in the Russo-Japanese War, he had witnessed the destruction of the Imperial Navy. Ill with rheumatism and lightly wounded, he ended up in a Port Arthur hospital as a prisoner of the Japanese, returning eventually to Russia via the United States.[1] In July 1916, he was transferred from the Baltic to the Black Sea Fleet as rear-admiral.[2] In February 1917, recognizing that "the monarchy was unable to carry on this war to its end,"[3] he took the oath to the Provisional Government and instructed his crews to obey the new authorities. Hostile to the Soviet, he recognized Order No. 1 only when Guchkov confirmed it. It was two or three weeks later, by the end of March, he recalled, that the crews first began showing hostility to their commanders.[4] He blamed their growing anger on the relentless barrage of revolutionary propaganda emanating from the soviets and was particularly outraged by the Declaration of Soldiers' Rights. The soviets were destroying the armed forces and the Provisional Government was doing nothing to stop them.[5] A separate peace was not an option, in his view. Even if the Allies were to win without Russian help, Russia would suffer. "We shall lose our political independence, our borderlands, and shall finally be reduced to a 'Muscovy,' an inland state, forced to do whatever they please," he later recalled himself thinking.[6]

The mutinous spirit plaguing the Baltic Fleet, so close to the center of power and the target of intense Bolshevik agitation, did not immediately affect crews in the Black Sea. By May, however, the spirit of Bolshevism was on the ascendant, Kolchak remembered, and had undermined the Sevastopol garrison, as well, "by means of systematic, planned, moral corruption."[7] By then, Kolchak was fed up with Kerensky. What was needed, he believed, was a return to old-fashioned discipline backed by the use of force. As threats to the officers increased and discipline dissolved, Kolchak had resigned his command and returned to Petrograd. When the crews accused their officers of counterrevolution, Kolchak took it as a personal insult and, in a dramatic gesture, threw his sword overboard into the sea. He believed German agents were helping spread the subversive message.[8] And indeed, as General Ludendorff had boasted, the Germans intended their propaganda "to encourage a strong movement for peace in the Russian Army."[9] Once back in Petrograd, Kolchak witnessed the riots in July and what he described as the demoralization of the Baltic sailors: "The Kronstadt crews, which came to Petrograd after this clash, ravaged the town, then got drunk, went back to the ships, and sailed for Kronstadt. It all made the impression of an entirely unorganized move of a perfectly absurd character."[10]

Seeking a way to get back into the war, Kolchak accepted an invitation from the Americans, who had solicited his advice in preparing a naval operation against the Turks.[11] He arrived in the United States to find the plans had been scuttled, but he managed a brief meeting with President Wilson. Taking the eastern route, he left San Francisco on a Japanese ship headed for Vladivostok. Arriving in Yokohama in early November, he learned that rumors of a coup in Petrograd were well founded.[12] He had accepted the authority of the February ministers, but he dismissed the Bolsheviks as usurpers, "a government by a certain party, a group of persons," which "did not express the attitudes and wishes of the whole country." He objected in particular to the break with the Allies and then later to the Treaty of Brest-Litovsk, which, he believed, subordinated Russian to German interests.[13]

Kolchak's global itinerary did not end in Japan. The British had approved his request to join the Indian Army. En route he stopped in Shanghai, but the British now advised him to return to Russia. He also visited Peking, where the Russian ambassador requested he take command of the various groups now active in the eastern territories.[14] In early April 1918, Kolchak reached Harbin, three hundred miles inland from Vladivostok, just as British and Japanese troops were arriving in the port city. There, Kolchak complained, "All the best houses, the best barracks, the best quays were occupied by the Czech, Japanese, and Allied troops who came there, whereas our own position was profoundly humiliating, profoundly sad. I felt that Vladivostok was no longer our Russian city."[15]

From the French point of view, by contrast, Vladivostok was all too Russian. General Maurice Janin, an old Russia hand who had led the French

Military Mission to Russia during the war, returned now at the end of 1918, in charge of Allied forces in the Russian Far East.[16] Arriving in Vladivostok in November, he was treated to a grand banquet for the benefit of the foreign dignitaries. "Dinner was abundant and well lubricated. Many speeches. Then came the songs and the dances, no less 'lubricated,' following the banquet ritual I have witnessed many times in my twenty-five years in Russia. All that continued until three in the morning.... How puzzling that, with their country in shreds, the Russians have the heart to spend their time this way."[17] While the poor suffered, the rich played. In Vladivostok "life was gay. The streets were full and at night the restaurants were packed with people, with no thought of going to fight in the Urals," he observed sanctimoniously, "while the Allies were maintaining law and order on the shores of the Pacific."[18]

By the time Kolchak made his appearance, a number of claimants to leadership of the anti-Bolshevik forces in Siberia had already established headquarters in the Far East. Their activity centered in Vladivostok and Harbin, connected by the Chinese Eastern Railroad. This line, cutting through Manchuria, had been constructed by Russia following an agreement with China in 1896. Since its completion in 1902 and continuing under the Provisional Government, its Russian general manager, based in Harbin, had been a certain Lieutenant General Dmitrii Khorvat. Despite his Hungarian surname, Khorvat came from a Russified gentry family from Poltava in the Ukraine. In 1918, then almost sixty, thus fifteen years Kolchak's senior, he sported a long white beard, which created a hirsute veil over his many medals.[19] He was not a well-known public figure, having spent over a decade as a bureaucrat in a remote eastern outpost.

But Khorvat had ambitions. He began by creating the Far Eastern Committee for Active Defense of the Homeland and the Constituent Assembly (*Dal'ne-vostochnyi komitet aktivnoi zashchity rodiny i Uchreditel'nogo sobraniia*) and organizing what he called an All-Russian Government (*Vserossiiskoe pravitel'stvo*), run by a Business Cabinet (*Delovoi kabinet*) filled with right-wing Kadets, with himself at its head. On July 9, 1918, in a railway station on the Chinese border, General Khorvat declared himself the "Temporary Ruler" of Russia. His term would last, he explained, until "with the participation of the people, order had been restored in the country, and until the convening of a freely elected Constituent Assembly, which will determine the government of the Russian state."[20]

Khorvat's sovereign claims were welcomed not only by conservative Kadets but by businessmen and industrialists from central Russia who had taken refuge in Vladivostok.[21] The self-designated spokesmen of Russia's commercial interests believed Khorvat could lead them back from the abyss and reconstitute both a functioning government and a solid state apparatus. He was, after all, both a bureaucrat and an officer, and far enough from the centers of power and conflict to represent both continuity and a clean slate. "Only in the Far East," his supporters contended, "in the isolated zone of the Chinese Eastern Railroad, was the principle of statehood [gosudarstven-nost'] preserved." Under his leadership it would be possible "to restore order in the country, to resurrect the Army and return Russia to the ranks of the powers fighting our common enemy."[22] The Vladivostok Stock Exchange Committee and the representatives of the city's manufacturing and commercial class reaffirmed a commitment to the Constituent Assembly, the alliance against Germany, and the overthrow of the Bolsheviks. An Orthodox priest hailed Khorvat as a savior: "Russia was in the process of collapse. And would have fallen to pieces if her finest sons had not risen to confront the dark forces.... You, General, are one of those sons."[23]

Khorvat wasn't the only one with ambitions, however. As we recall, in January 1918 the Odessan SR Petr Derber had been elected to head the newly formed Provisional Government of Autonomous Siberia, but had immediately headed east to rally support. Khorvat, who controlled the trains in Harbin, allowed the so-called Derber Government, which he dismissed as meaningless, to operate out of a railway carriage parked on a sideline.[24] After the Czechoslovak Legion had dislodged the Soviet forces remaining in Vladivostok despite the Allied presence, Derber moved to that city, where on July 8, he announced the formation of what he called the Provisional Government of Autonomous Siberia in the Far East.[25]

The competition among would-be rulers of anti–Bolshevik Russia had a comic-opera aspect. Returning Khorvat's animosity, Derber demanded the General "divest yourself immediately of the power you have illegally assumed."[26] He warned the Allies that "any agreement with private individuals or organizations declaring themselves to be the supreme authorities... of Siberia will be condemned by the entire population." The Provisional Government of Autonomous Siberia, he announced, was the only sovereign authority.[27] To be a government, it seemed enough to call yourself one—but it was unclear who would obey you.

---

The Czechoslovak Legion, which by now controlled the Trans-Siberian Railroad, the crucial link between east and west, joined with the Union for the Regeneration of Russia, which had formed in Moscow in April, in urging the various groups and self-proclaimed governments to put aside their differences. The Union itself represented the principle of compromise, as we have seen. Its members included Right SRs, Kadets who rejected Pavel Miliukov's pro-German line, and middle-of-the-road Popular Socialists.[28] With the need for collaboration in mind, in late August 1918 plans were made to hold a broadly based State Conference (*Gosudarstvennoe Soveshchanie*), similar to the Moscow State Conference that Kerensky had convened in August 1917. The similarity did not augur well. The purpose was to form a unified government with authority not only for Siberia but for Russia as a whole. On September 8, 1918, over 150 delegates assembled in Ufa, situated between the Volga River and the Ural Mountains. The group represented the broad middle of the political spectrum. Two-thirds identified themselves as SRs, but the gathering also included pro-war Social Democrats, Popular Socialists, Kadets, Right SRs, and zemstvo activists. The self-appointed governments of the Urals, Siberia, and Estonia sent delegates, as did the Ural Cossacks and the Central Asian regions.[29]

The extent to which the entire "democratic revolution" had moved to the right was demonstrated in the remarks of one of the Kadet delegates. Lev Krol', an electrical engineer from Ekaterinburg, where he ran the municipal power station, had been active in the workers' section of the War Industries Committee and had been elected to the Constituent Assembly on the Kadet ticket from Perm. In 1918 he joined the Union of Regeneration, refusing to collaborate with the SR-dominated Komuch in Samara.[30] His political career thus displayed the typical features of progressive-minded liberalism and civic activism. These liberal postulates were now severely tested. The Kadets had done poorly in the Constituent Assembly elections for Siberia; they hated the SRs, whom they considered little better than Bolsheviks, and ended up supporting the regional industrialists and the army.[31] Now, at the Ufa Conference, Krol' reiterated the party's commitment to "the reestablishment of a great, united, and undivided Russia" and

its conviction that Russia must "reenter the war on the side of the Allies."
Where Krol' departed from the standard Kadet platform was his assertion
that under the present circumstances "the best form of government is a
one-man government."[32]

The Ufa Conference ended, on September 23, by repurposing the
Provisional Siberian Government, formed in Omsk in early July. Now
dubbed the Provisional All-Russian Government, or Directory (*Vremennoe
Vserossiiskoe pravitel'stvo, Direktoriia*), it was to assume leadership until the
convocation of an all-Russian Constituent Assembly—the usual incantation.[33]
It consisted of Petr Vologodskii, the principal figure in the Omsk govern-
ment, along with the same five-man council and thirteen ministers, seven of
them unchanged. General Vasilii Boldyrev, a member of both the Union for
Regeneration and the National Center, was its commander in chief.[34] Its
chair was the SR Nikolai Avksent'ev, one of the leaders of the Petrograd
Soviet in 1917, later minister of internal affairs in the Provisional Government.[35]
It was a composite of what remained of moderate civil society.

When, however, on October 8 the Red Army captured Samara, 260 miles
west of Ufa by rail, the Directory retreated eight hundred miles eastward
from Ufa to Omsk, where it inaugurated its official existence on November 5,
dedicated to demolishing "the German-Magyar hordes and their henchmen, the Bolsheviks."[36] After a seventeen-day journey in the opposite direction, starting in Vladivostok, Kolchak arrived in Omsk after the formation
of the Directory and the death of General Alekseev. General Boldyrev convinced him to remain as minister of army and navy.[37]

The conditions in Omsk dramatized the challenge faced by any pretender
to power. A city of 130,000 in 1917, it had expanded by 1919 to over half a
million, thanks to a flood of refugees, some living in deep misery, others in
ostentatious luxury—horse races, theater, duck shooting.[38] Everyone, however,
was equally subject to lawlessness and fear. Colonel John Ward, in Omsk with
the British Middlesex Regiment, recalled his impressions: "Every night as soon
as darkness set in rifle and revolver shots and shouts could be heard in all directions. The morning sanitary carts picked up from five to twenty dead officers.
There were no police, no courts, no law, no anything. In desperation the officers grouped themselves together and hit back indiscriminately at the people
they thought responsible for the murder of their comrades. So a fair proportion
of civilian bodies became mixed up with those wearing uniforms."[39]

The foundling regime from the start showed the weaknesses of the forced
compromise it entailed. At the State Conference, Krol' had conveyed the

impression that the Kadets supported the venture, but in fact the party's leading figures opposed it. His colleagues in Omsk called him a traitor, while the
regionalists made common cause with the mainstream Kadets. The Samara
SRs denounced the Directory as undemocratic. Neither the Allies nor the
Czechoslovaks (for all their earlier encouragement) were enthusiastic. Hopes
that General Denikin might move east were disappointed.[40]

Colonel Ward attended the Directory's inaugural banquet in Omsk,
together with General Alfred Knox, formerly the British military attaché,
now head of the Allied military mission in Siberia. The Colonel, who
believed the Bolsheviks were German "hirelings" and "Terrorists," was not
impressed by the alternative.[41] He described the new government as "a combination that refused to mix." "Its members were the most unmitigated failures that even poor distracted Russia had so far produced, and the people
waited, hoping and longing, for their speedy removal."[42] These were the
same followers of Kerensky, Ward observed, who in 1917 had betrayed
General Kornilov. Now they "were continuing to play the same double game
which had brought ruin on the first National Assembly and disaster upon the
Russian people. They were members of the same futile crowd of useless char-
latans who by their pusillanimity had made their country a byword and the
Treaty of Brest-Litovsk possible."[43] Ward's dismissive remarks reflected the
British impatience with the quarrelsome moderates and their dubious social-
ist associates. General Knox preferred a strong center of authority.[44]

What with its internal tensions and the skepticism of the foreign powers,
the Directory, which established its office in a railway carriage on a siding,
just as Derber had done in Harbin, lasted all of two weeks. The new cabinet
was supposed to have resolved the tensions between the Provisional Siberian
Government and the Komuch, but the tensions only grew. Representatives
of the Volunteer Army in Omsk distrusted the arrangement. The Siberian
Government, which in theory had renounced its claim to authority but in
fact continued to fulfill its administrative functions, thought the socialists
had too much weight.[45] Of the other competing centers, the Siberian
Regional Duma gave in to pressure from Avksent'ev, the Directory chair,
and accepted its own demise.[46]

The conciliatory work of Avksent'ev and his fellow SR, Vladimir
Zenzinov, was undermined, however, by the SR Party itself. On October 11,
1918, the Central Committee meeting in Ekaterinburg denounced the
Directory for suppressing worker and peasant organizations, violating the
civil rights of their political rivals, and restoring the old hierarchies, discipline,

and insignia to the army, as well as favoring reactionary commanders and the Cossack chieftains. The party resolved "to resist the blow of the counterrevolutionary organizers of civil war in the rear of the anti-Bolshevik front." In Omsk, Avksent'ev and Zenzinov expected to be arrested any moment. "We live, as it were, on a volcano," they reported, "which is ready to begin an eruption at any moment."[47]

At the end of October, the Directory's General Boldyrev noted that "the idea of military dictatorship grows stronger and stronger in political and military circles. I have hints from different sides."[48] On November 15, a Kadet conference in Omsk declared in favor of just such a military dictatorship as the only means of reestablishing Russian statehood and sovereignty.[49] In the absence of any unifying authority, the Kadet Party declared it "not only does not fear a dictatorship, but in the current circumstances considers it a necessity."[50] At the Ufa Conference in September, when Krol' had endorsed the need for a strong authority, he was censured by the party for thinking the Directory would serve the purpose. The Kadets had never embraced that position and now made their opposition clear.

The volcano Avksent'ev and Zenzinov were awaiting erupted soon enough. On the evening of November 17, the two SRs were indeed arrested. Vologodskii then summoned the Directory cabinet, which voted almost unanimously the next day to elevate its minister of war, Admiral Kolchak, to the position of supreme ruler and commander in chief of all Russian land and sea forces, thus combining military and civilian authority.[51] Kolchak was acknowledged in his new role by the other White commanders— Denikin in the south, Evgenii-Ludwig Miller in Arkhangelsk, Iudenich in the northwest.[52] Thus, one year after the Bolsheviks had dislodged the weakened Provisional Government in Petrograd, instituting what they proudly called the "dictatorship of the proletariat," Kolchak displaced the remnants of the self-styled Provisional Government of Siberia, imposing what he trumpeted as old-fashioned military rule.

There was little to stop him. The socialist-oriented Czechoslovak National Council in Cheliabinsk accused Kolchak of having "violated the principle of legality, which must be placed at the foundation of every state," but the Legion took no action. Some Legion commanders, notably Major-General Radola Gajda (Rudolf Geidl), even favored the move. The troops in any case had no stomach for fighting.[53] Gajda, a Montenegrin by birth, was a colorful figure who had spearheaded the Legion's revolt, then demonstrated considerable ability as a commander in capturing the Siberian cities. After the coup, he ended up serving under Kolchak.[54] The Legion itself was now reduced to guarding the railway, along with an assortment of other foreign troops—Japanese, British, American, French, Poles, Romanians, even Italians.[55] The Directory's General Boldyrev had been away at the front. He now resigned in protest and departed for Japan.[56]

Kolchak's assumption of leadership for all of Russia has been called a coup, but it was more like a hostile corporate takeover. The contrasts were telling. In August 1917, Kornilov had tried to topple the flailing provisional regime, and Kerensky may well have colluded in the attempted solution to the problem of authority. That venture failed. In October 1917, Lenin demanded the use of force as a necessary rupture with the existing government, however tenuous its powers actually were. The ministers of the Provisional Government did not, of course, embrace him as their savior. By contrast, Kolchak's move was endorsed by some of the same men he pushed aside. The Directory was not actually displaced but swallowed. With the exception of his own military portfolio, Kolchak retained all the former ministers, including Vologodskii.[57] Within the year, however, most of the holdovers were gone.

In relation to the Allies, Kolchak knew what song to sing. He pledged "as my main objective the creation of an efficient army, victory over Bolshevism and the establishment of law and order, so that the people may choose the form of government which it desires without obstruction and realize the great ideas of liberty which are now proclaimed in the whole world."[58] The French and British were pleased at the turn of events, having indicated their approval beforehand.[59] They were nevertheless unsure what Kolchak's self-proclaimed government actually stood for, since its statements were entirely vague. The conservative Kadet, Vasilii Maklakov, still in Paris, where he had been appointed by the Provisional Government as Russian ambassador, warned him to sound democratic and thus stay in the Allies' good graces, since the admiral still needed arms, still aspired to a place at the Paris Peace Conference, and was seeking a counterweight to Japan. At the same time, Kolchak could not afford to offend his more right-wing backers, so everything he said was qualified as provisional and couched in general terms.[60]

Anxious to be rid of those on the left, Kolchak had the SR members of the Directory escorted across the Chinese border.[61] When the SRs in Ekaterinburg objected, Viktor Chernov and his associates were also arrested.[62] With the Directory's suppression, the final blow was now dealt to the political aspirations of the moderate SRs, who had attempted to unite the progressive elements in the anti-Soviet opposition. When the Komuch in Samara denounced Kolchak's "criminal mutiny," Kolchak ordered its arrest for "endeavoring to arouse an insurrection against the state authority." Within the next two weeks, the remaining SR leaders in Ekaterinburg, Samara, and Ufa were rounded up by troops of the Siberian Army, formerly the Western Siberian Army, now under Kolchak's command. It was hard for the victims to distinguish the lesser evil. As usual, the SR Party was divided. Some wanted to join or tolerate the Reds and concentrate their forces against the Whites; others, including Chernov, wanted to continue the fight "on both fronts."[63]

Complaining of the continued posturing of "the former members of Komuch and the Samara government, refusing to relinquish their claims to power," Kolchak instructed "all Russian military authorities to obstruct the criminal work of the above mentioned persons by the most decisive means, not excluding the use of armed force."[64] Chernov himself made it to Moscow. By mid-1919, he had decided the party should cease its opposition to Soviet rule and focus on defeating the Whites. In 1920 he left for Estonia, moving in 1938 to France and in 1941 to the United States. He died in 1952 in New York, also the final resting place of his SR colleagues Avksent'ev and Zenzinov.[65]

Other members of the SR Party were less fortunate. Kolchak's officers rounded up SR leaders in Ufa and Cheliabinsk, and by early December all were behind bars in Omsk.[66] While their rivals were thus being corralled by their common enemy, Bolshevik activists in Omsk were planning an uprising for December 22. The plot was betrayed by a spy, and the day before, eighty-eight activists, assumed to be Bolshevik ringleaders, were arrested, of whom thirty-three were summarily shot. At the last minute, the party tried to call off the revolt, but the message was not received. When the workers and soldiers took up their posts throughout the city on the designated day, their positions were attacked by two Cossack units under General Pavel Ivanov-Rinov, backed by machine-gunners from the Czechoslovak Legion. Estimates of the number killed range from 1,500 to 2,500.[67] Before Kolchak had time to react, Ivanov-Rinov declared Omsk under martial law, encouraging the Cossacks to rampage through the city, breaking into houses, setting fires, arresting and murdering workers and ordinary citizens. The rebels had had enough time in the early morning to spring two hundred prisoners from jail, including the SRs who had recently been captured. The commander of the Omsk garrison now ordered the fugitives to turn themselves in, on penalty of death, and some were naive enough to return. When their wives approached the prison, they found their husbands' mutilated corpses strewn along the snow-covered banks of the Irtysh River, not far from Kolchak's residence. Shot and slashed, faces smashed, heads severed—the work of Cossack sabers.[68]

A Cossack from Semipalatinsk, Ivanov-Rinov was a veteran of the Russo-Japanese War and the Great War who had participated in the ruthless suppression of the 1916 revolt in Turkestan. An extreme reactionary earlier associated with the Group of Thirteen in Omsk, he used his authority as commander of the Siberian Army to impose old-fashioned discipline on his men, including the use of corporal punishment. His officers paraded in traditional gold-braided epaulettes. In general, Omsk became a center of old-regime ostentation. The tsarist anthem was sung, millionaires congregated, SRs cowered in fear.[69]

At the same time, however, Ivanov-Rinov's campaign against the SRs and alleged Bolshevik supporters represented a challenge to Kolchak, whose democratic posturing the commander found objectionable. Rumors circulated that Ivanov-Rinov aimed to replace the Admiral with Grand Duke Mikhail Aleksandrovich, the tsar's brother, thought to be wandering somewhere in the Siberian vastness, though in fact he had already been murdered in Perm in June.[70] No serious investigation followed the Omsk massacre. Kolchak could not afford to antagonize the officers upon whom he relied. "It remains only for me to pull the trigger," Ivanov-Rinov warned, "and not a trace of you, Admiral, would remain."[71] In the same spirit, Major-General Ivan Krasil'nikov, commander of the Siberian Cossack regiment, was heard to say when in his cups: "I set him up and I can remove him!"[72] The truth of Ivanov-Rinov's rampage was concealed from the Allies, who apparently did not read the indignant reaction in the moderate Siberian press (still in operation). "We feel deeply powerless to express the bottomless depth of horror that has seized our long-suffering homeland," a journalist wrote, "a horror that weighs like a bloody nightmare on every conscious person who retains even an atom of humanity."[73]

Ivanov-Rinov's crimes were overshadowed by the Siberian Army's success immediately thereafter, under the command of General Gajda, who had recently transferred from the Czechoslovak Legion, in repulsing the Red Army and seizing the city of Perm. In the process, the Siberian Army acquired thirty thousand prisoners and a considerable number of weapons, locomotives, and train cars.[74] The victory at Perm, along with Ivanov-Rinov's massacre at Omsk, established the hold exercised by the Siberian Army officers over the Supreme Ruler, whom they only nominally obeyed.

General Ivanov-Rinov was only one of a number of regional commanders, adopting the title of ataman, who operated independently in the Siberian
arena, the most notorious among them being Grigorii Semenov, Ivan
Kalmykov, Ivan Gamov, and Boris Annenkov.[75] In early 1918 the atamans had
begun receiving subsidies from the Japanese, as a way of obstructing the formation of a stable government in Siberia. Like the Germans in the Ukraine,
the Japanese were interested in economic exploitation and counted on the
failure of central authority. Unlike the Germans in the Ukraine, however, the
Japanese were not looking to rule by proxy and therefore did not need a
local administration capable of serving their needs. They had everything to
gain from a policy of disruption.[76] On their own behalf, by contrast, the
Japanese were a stabilizing presence, presiding over the port of Vladivostok as
the Czechoslovak Legion presided over the railways—"two better organized
forces, confident, effective," an observer remarked.[77] By November 1918,
Japan had seventy thousand troops in the Far East and Manchuria, most
deployed on the Chinese Eastern Railroad, and aggressively promoted its
economic interests—fishing, lumber, and merchant shipping.[78]

The atamans were thus free to pursue their own selfish interests. An officer from the Transbaikal Cossack Host, in 1918 Grigorii Semenov was a
young man of twenty-eight. Born in the heart of the Trans-Baikal, between
Chita and Nerchinsk, he was fluent in Mongol and Buriat and knew the
territory well. Decorated on the Polish and Galician fronts during the war,
in 1916 he had fought under General Brusilov. In July 1917, the Provisional
Government sent him back to his native region as a military commissar; his
mentor, General Krymov, committed suicide after the Kornilov fiasco a
month later. After the Bolshevik coup, Semenov headed to Irkutsk, where
he hoped to rally troops in defense of the deposed ministers. By the end of
December 1917, the Reds had gained control of Irkutsk and most of the
Trans-Baikal.[79] When they also tried to seize Harbin, Semenov helped rally
a force that repelled them. Initially, with Japanese encouragement, Semenov
had refused to recognize Kolchak's authority. "Citizens!" his pamphlets
thundered. "Now is a grave political moment and such a mediocre invalid
as Kolchak cannot be permitted to be our leader.... and if he will not go
away of his own accord it will be necessary to remove him."[80] Finally, in
December 1918, under pressure from the French, Semenov acknowledged
Kolchak's authority, but it was a perfunctory move.[81]

By the end of 1918, Semenov was installed in his own fiefdom, in Chita,
six hundred miles by rail east of Irkutsk, which he had captured in September.

Setting up headquarters in an armored railway carriage, he styled himself a new Genghis Khan or Napoleon.[82] From there his brigades terrorized the local population, seizing property, raping women.[83] They roamed the rails, arresting people at will, shooting them at random.[84] Semenov's grandiosity and the harsh impositions of his men stood out even against the general lawlessness and chronic violence that pervaded the Far East. The city of Harbin was described by Kolchak as "a gutter," where the militia consisted of "mostly licentious, drunken men."[85] But if chaos reigned in Harbin, in Chita Semenov exercised a systematic "dictatorship of the whip,"[86] which damaged the Supreme Ruler's reputation. The unchecked depredations of the atamans thus revealed Kolchak's weakness. They represented his "regime," but he could not control them, while his enemies accused him of selling out to the Japanese, their sponsor.[87]

In 1919, when presiding over his stretch of the Trans-Siberian Railway, Semenov's men preyed on private travelers, seizing their belongings, while on a larger scale also seizing locomotives and passenger cars—those rare commodities. The engines were harnessed to Semenov's own armored train or stripped for metal; two hundred carriages went to house his so-called Independent Manchurian Army, another thousand were leased for profit. Dozens of freight trains were also halted at Chita and emptied of their food cargo, which was then sold on the black market. Tolls were exacted on goods passing through Manchuli, the first station within Manchuria on the Chinese Eastern Railroad.[88] Japanese support also allowed Semenov to indulge his more elaborate fantasies of power. In February 1919, Japan approved the convocation of a Pan-Mongol Conference in Chita, at which Semenov announced the formation of a Mongol-Buriat kingdom.[89]

Ivan Kalmykov, by contrast, was not a born Cossack, but he had joined a Cossack Host during the Great War and achieved a new identity. In January 1918, he attached himself nominally to General Khorvat, later refusing to acknowledge Kolchak's authority. No less brazen than Semenov, his brigade patrolled the Trans-Siberian Railroad in the area of Khabarovsk, disrupting traffic, molesting passengers, and indulging in massacres and pillage.[90] He impressed General Janin as even younger than his barely thirty years. "He's a timid young man," the general wrote, "maybe twenty-two or twenty-three. At first ill at ease, he gradually relaxes and recounts his clean-up procedures in an entirely straightforward way." When questioned about a notorious execution, Janin remembered him saying, "I had them arrested, intending to shoot them the next day, but some sort of Jew employed by the Americans raises a fuss, says it can't be done this way, he won't allow it. At that point, of course, I did what you would surely have done in my place. I had them shot that same night."[91]

Kolchak's representatives did their best to conceal the details of the admiral's military associates from his political supporters. Sheltered from the full truth, not wishing to think too hard about whatever they did know, the Kadets and the French and British agents in Siberia seemed unperturbed by Kolchak's methods. The Supreme Ruler even managed to convince at least some foreign observers that he represented the "constitutionalist" alternative for Russia, and he retained the favor of a varied constituency, including local cooperatives, Popular Socialists, commercial and industrial interests, and the Union for Regeneration.[92] The Kadet Party, for its part, pronounced unequivocally in favor of authoritarian rule. In May 1919, Pavel Novgorodtsev, former deputy in the First Duma, signatory of the Vyborg Manifesto, and more recently delegate to the Constituent Assembly, declared: "If nothing remains of our democratism, then that is an excellent thing, since what is needed now is dictatorship, a force for creating authority.... There is now no 'Kadetism' or 'democratism,' there is only the task of national unification."[93]

Not everyone attached to the Allied contingents in Russia accepted either the need for dictatorship or the pseudo-constitutionalist rhetoric in which it was veiled. The French officer Joseph Lasies, though himself an anti-Semitic adherent of the fascist Action française, believed his own government had been "brain-washed." "Admiral Kolchak," Lasies observed, "was surrounded by supporters of tsarism, who did not conceal their counterrevolutionary goals. Personally, the admiral was a generous man, but weak, indecisive, timid, afraid of his entourage, which was the source of his unpopularity." By endorsing his takeover, Lasies complained, the French had betrayed the democratic opponents of Bolshevik power whom he had displaced.[94] In fact, on the subject of the Jews, Kolchak was closer to Lasies's heart than the Frenchman apparently realized. The *Protocols of the Elders of Zion* were the Admiral's favorite reading matter.[95] Such views, however, did not distinguish Kolchak from either the British ambassador George Buchanan or the British general Alfred Knox.[96]

───────────

The demise of moderation and of constitutional illusions and the rise of military power over the course of 1918 repeated the pattern of 1917—only this time toward authoritarianism of the right, not the left. In both cases, the resort to absolute authority seemed a realistic response to an environment in which politics had become a form of war. In both cases, the victors helped create the environment in which politics in any other form had become impossible. A vicious circle.

Admiral Kolchak, the "Supreme Ruler," did not, however, rule supreme. Both of his claims rang hollow—to observe democratic principles and to impose military rule. The shots in his government were called in fact by the vicious and reactionary officers of the Siberian Army. The real character of his regime was reflected in the unbridled violence of Cossack chieftains, both within the army and outside it, who did not even bother with the pretense of subordination. The Allies nevertheless continued to arm and supply Kolchak's forces, insisting still, as late as May 1919, that he pledge to reconvene the Constituent Assembly. They urged him to recognize independent Poland and Finland, but Kolchak, the "champion of empire," could not tolerate Finnish independence.[97]

Officials of the U.S. State Department were among those who looked favorably on Kolchak, as an antidote to "Bolshevism," while turning a blind eye to the depredations of Semenov and other acolytes. A dissenter was General William Graves, commander of the U.S. Expeditionary Force in Siberia, where he arrived with eight thousand troops on September 1, 1918. Graves believed Washington was falling for White propaganda, which tarred all Kolchak's critics with the Bolshevik brush.[98] In repressing such "legal, reliable, and law abiding organizations" as the zemstvos, City Dumas, and cooperative organizations, the admiral's government, in fact, violated the principles America held dear—"the boons of modern civilization"—freedom of speech, press, and other civil liberties.[99] The State Department, in Graves's view, had ended up supporting the proponents of autocracy and the perpetrators of genuine atrocities, the latter enjoying the patronage of America's true rival in the Far East—Japan. "Semenoff and Kalmikoff soldiers, under the protection of Japanese troops, were roaming the country like wild animals, killing and robbing the people, and these murders could have been stopped any day Japan wished. If questions were asked about these brutal murders, the reply was that the people murdered were Bolsheviks and this explanation, apparently, satisfied the world."[100]

Kolchak returned the compliment. "The American troops, consisting of the rejects of the American Army—Jewish immigrants, with a corresponding commanding staff, are a factor only of disintegration and disorders. I consider their removal from Russian territory necessary, because their further presence will lead only to a final discrediting of America and to extremely serious consequences."[101] The Americans in Siberia, he complained, were doing all they could "to spread Bolshevism," which was promoted locally by foreigners, primarily Jews. The American policy, he complained "is basically a Jewish policy, and here in Siberia they are surrounded mainly by Russian Jews."[102] The former Kadet Viktor Pepeliaev, Kolchak's last prime minister, complained: "The behavior of America is disgusting."[103]

In fact, Kolchak should have thanked the Americans for their contribution to the continued functioning of the Trans-Siberian Railroad, on which his existence depended. In May 1917, President Wilson had dispatched John F. Stevens, an engineer who had helped build the Great Northern Railway between Saint Paul and Seattle and later worked on the construction of the Panama Canal, to help the Provisional Government keep the trains running. The United States had granted newly democratic Russia a substantial loan with which to finance the purchase of supplies, which then would have to be transported along the poorly maintained and overburdened rail lines.[104] Stevens was to have been joined by a three-hundred-man Russian Railway Service Corps, but the October coup intervened. Stranded in Japan, the Americans were uncertain of the role they might now play. Tense negotiations among the eight powers with troops in Siberia resulted on January 9, 1919, in the establishment of a commission for the supervision of the Siberian and Chinese Eastern Railroad systems, of which Stevens was the technical head.[105]

Like Kolchak, the Japanese resented the American role, and the commission was hampered by the babble of languages, the general environment of corruption, and the terrible condition of the railways, their vulnerability to attack, and so on. General Graves was unhappy with the idea of supporting the Supreme Ruler, to whom he refused to accord priority on the tracks. He posted notices, in the Wilsonian spirit, asserting that the railroad should serve all Russians "irrespective of a person's nationality, religion or politics."[106] But in fact, despite his efforts, he concluded that "the majority of the people of Siberia enjoyed about the same value from the operation of the railways as did the people of Liberia."[107]

The Allies never did recognize Kolchak, although his military successes in the spring of 1919 impressed them and the flow of arms continued.[108] Their sympathies were aroused by Russian émigrés who barraged the politicians in Paris and London with tales of Bolshevik horrors and assurances of Kolchak's dedication to democracy.[109] Yet Kolchak had reason for suspicion. William C. Bullitt, an unofficial U.S. envoy, was in Moscow feeling out the prospects for peace; the Allies were organizing a relief mission to Soviet

Russia to combat hunger—a plan that threatened to bolster the Soviet regime, by alleviating starvation.[110]

Having crushed whatever seedlings of civilian administration had sprouted in Siberian soil, Kolchak had to prove his mettle as a military dictator. He had three problems. In the first place, he was unable to control the activities of the ataman chiefs funded by the Japanese and operating independently, whose followers showed no restraint in attacking political enemies and the civilian population.[111] In the second place, Kolchak's team made no effort to win the support of the general population. Like the Reds, they needed to draft men into the colors; like the Reds, they requisitioned grain and used force to back their demands. The Omsk administration operated a counterintelligence office that monitored the mood in the villages, factories, and barracks, realizing they could not simply ignore what people felt. They issued newspapers and flyers; they kept track of Bolshevik propaganda.[112] But they had no social policy. Unlike the Reds, who did nothing to stop the peasants from seizing the land, while also abolishing private property (a contradiction with consequences for the future), conducting a murderous assault on the old privileged classes, Kolchak refused to address the land question at all. His army, moreover, embodied the old-style discipline and hierarchy against which the foot soldiers of the monarchy had revolted in the first place.

Finally, Kolchak proved unsuccessful as a military commander and strategist—the very service he was supposed to provide. Initially, in March and April 1919, his forces made progress. They outnumbered the Reds in the East by four to one. Meanwhile, the peasants in the mid-Volga had reacted to intensified Red requisitions by staging a series of revolts, which the Red Army took time to repress. By mid-March 1919, the Whites had taken Ufa and continued on toward Kazan and Samara. But they were hampered by their own weaknesses. Kolchak had bad judgment in his appointments and followed bad advice, and his commanders competed among themselves. The armies lacked the grassroots organization that allowed the Reds to conduct successful drafts in a number of Siberian cities.[113]

The popular mood, moreover, was unstable. In late April, the Ukrainian unit in the White Army murdered its officers and went over to the Reds, who by May had pushed the Whites back eastward from the Volga to the Urals. On June 9, the Red Army took Ufa. A week later, the gun-manufacturing city of Zlatoust, east of the mountains and west of Cheliabinsk, was in Soviet hands and by mid-July, Ekaterinburg had fallen. White soldiers deserted and surrendered. In early August, the Whites were defeated at Cheliabinsk; the Reds took fifteen thousand prisoners, leaving fifty thousand stragglers to retreat back into Siberia. Kolchak had lost the Urals industrial region.[114]

The admiral's military regime got a poor rating, even from his supporters. Major-General Baron Aleksei Budberg, who served as Kolchak's minister of war from late August to late October, 1919, complained to his diary in August: "In the army, collapse; at headquarters, ignorance and stupidity; in the government, moral rot, discord, the reign of careerists and egotists; in the country, uprisings and anarchy; in society at large, panic, self-seeking, bribery, and every abomination."[115] Budberg blamed a failure of leadership all down the line. "Along with a small number of truly capable officers, entire crowds arrive of superficially disciplined but inwardly degenerate youth. They parade their epaulettes and boast of their rights, but are entirely unprepared for hard work or submission to duty." They liked to strike arrogant poses, "but understand nothing about how to lead a platoon or company in battle, on the march, or in daily life. Many have already taken to alcohol and cocaine." Rot started at the head. "Often the instability and even cowardice of the officers," the general observed, "are the reason the soldiers quit the battlefield and flee in panic."[116] Bolshevik propaganda could not have painted a bleaker picture.

Budberg published his diary in Leningrad in 1929, so ideological hindsight may have colored the text, but a staunch anti-Bolshevik, publishing closer to the events, echoes his view. Lev Krol', the Kadet who had prematurely come out in favor of authoritarian rule at the State Conference in September 1918, reported the testimony of a local Siberian official a year later. "The military authorities, from the very lowest rank, interfere in civil matters," the official complained, "bypassing civil authorities. Illegal actions, reprisals without trial, the flogging even of women, the murder of prisoners 'while trying to escape,' arrests by denunciation, the transfer of civil cases to the military authorities ... I do not know of a single case in which military personnel were prosecuted for these actions, while civilians are thrown into prison at the slightest allegation."[117]

The spirit of the atamans—free-lance banditry—infected the armies. Major-General Krasil'nikov, a participant in the infamous Omsk massacre in December 1918, was a typical case. In spring 1919, he was described by Kolchak's own ministry of war as "devot[ing] himself exclusively to drinking and disorderly conduct; his officers act in the same way; the soldiers carry out arbitrary searches with the purpose of robbery and violate women. The whole population is eager for Bolshevism."[118] Krasil'nikov died of typhus in Irkutsk in January 1920 at the age of thirty-two.[119] General Budberg concluded: "The poison of the ataman regime and the lure of lawlessness have penetrated everywhere too deeply and we are unable to put an end to this evil. It will in all likelihood consume us, but it will itself perish in the stench it has produced."[120]

——————

It should have been easy to win support in the villages, which endured the extortions and reprisals of the Reds. By the spring of 1919, the peasants had experienced the rigors of Soviet requisitioning, "the seizure on account of everything down to the last chicken," as Krol' put it, and the shooting of the "family members of any Red Army man who went over to the 'Whites.'"[121] But the peasants who had revolted against the exactions of the Reds now turned against their opponents. The White armies had to contend with the obstruction of traffic on the railroad, with nocturnal attacks along the wooded stretches organized by peasant partisan bands. Revolts were particularly fierce in areas that had been settled by poor peasants arriving from central Russia after the turmoil of 1905. They resented their more prosperous Siberian neighbors. Peasants in general hated the towns.[122]

The towns, however, were no less of a challenge. They were the site of continuing Bolshevik agitation in the factories and railway shops and on the docks. They were also the gathering places for Kolchak's bitterest enemies—the SRs, aided and abetted by discontented elements in the Czechoslovak Legion. Throughout 1919 the Siberian SRs, intent on finding a "third way" between Red and White, plotted the overthrow of the Omsk regime. Some among the officers of the Siberian Army had begun to realize that Kolchak's anti-democratic methods were harming the cause. They lent their voices to the chorus emerging from the remnants of the local civic organizations that had begun to shape a regional Siberian politics in the wake of October 1917—the Siberian zemstvos and City Dumas and the Siberian Regional Council. Perhaps democracy was not yet dead, after all.

Early in 1919, these moderate anti-Bolshevik groups had gathered in Vladivostok to discuss the response to Kolchak's coup. Their leaders were quickly arrested by Ivanov-Rinov and deported to Mongolia and Japan. The Japanese were happy to see the possibility of moderation foiled.[123] By early fall, however, the SRs, once again taking the lead, together with some former Mensheviks and local civic leaders, published a charter and called for the convocation of a "Council of the Land" (*zemskii sobor*). The charter (*gramota*) and the Council of the Land were terms culled from the lexicon of premodern Rus'. They were meant to invoke a deep-seated native democracy, but in fact they signaled the ideological exhaustion of Kolchak's middle-of-the-road foes.[124]

The admiral's response to the political challenge was, once again, the application of force. The aged Khorvat had continued, surprisingly enough, to serve as high plenipotentiary for the Far East, but in July Kolchak replaced him with General Sergei Rozanov. After a brief stint with the Reds, Rozanov had joined the Komuch People's Army, then served the Ufa Directory, finding his place under Kolchak in early 1919. Rozanov was known for the decimation of peasant villages suspected of Bolshevik sympathies and, in Krasnoiarsk, a city of thirty thousand on the Enisei River, for hanging suspected partisans from the telegraph poles.[125] In Vladivostok, the general had brutally suppressed a series of strikes among railroad workers and longshoremen, organized by the SRs in summer 1919 with Bolshevik support.[126] Now, in September, Rozanov summoned Ataman Kalmykov from Khabarovsk, where the latter had established a similar reputation for viciousness, having arrested and tortured two U.S. Marines and demonstratively hanged ten suspected Bolsheviks. Kalmykov arrived with four thousand Cossack troops, who proceeded in the same manner to assault and murder American and Czechoslovak soldiers. "Rozanov's administration," a diplomat remarked, "would have been a disgrace to any government, no matter how desperate."[127]

Yet again, the foreign powers could not be entirely discounted. In late September, the Inter-Allied Committee of Diplomatic Representatives at Vladivostok, which included the Japanese, warned Rozanov to have Kalmykov's troops removed or face serious consequences.[128] When Kolchak denounced the warning as an "infringement of the sovereign rights of the Russian people," the Allies backed off and Kalmykov remained. At the same time, as the Japanese seemed to be weakening in their support for the atamans, a group of SRs were encouraged to think Japan would stand aside.[129] General Gajda, who had helped install Kolchak in November 1918 and led the Siberian Army at Perm in December, by July 1919 had fallen out with the admiral, who had reduced him in rank. By September, Gajda, with eight thousand men in Vladivostok, was ready to help the SRs remove him. On

November 7, Gajda warned the British that he would "seize power on or shortly after the date of the fall of Omsk."[130]

On November 11, as the Red Army was nearing Omsk, Kolchak informed the Allies that he was departing. He traveled with seven trains flying the Allied flags, loaded with the members of his government, their families and possessions, and what remained of the imperial gold reserves. They were guarded by the Czechoslovak Legion under the command of General Janin, who promised to escort him to safety. The Legionnaires, however, had by now had enough. On November 13, the Czechoslovak National Council, residing in Irkutsk, complained that "under the protection of Czechoslovak bayonets, the local Russian military authorities permit themselves activities that horrify the entire civilized world. The burning of villages, the beating of peaceful Russian citizens by the hundreds, the shooting without trial of representatives of democracy on the mere suspicion of political unreliability have become habitual developments."[131] By observing the principle of neutrality with respect to Russia's internal politics, the Legionnaires complained, they had become "accomplices in crime." Now all they wanted was to leave the country and get home. They were no longer willing to occupy this "tragic moral position" on Kolchak's behalf.[132] Kolchak called this protest a form of blackmail.[133]

Meanwhile, on November 12, with the admiral's trains making their way eastward from Omsk to Irkutsk, a distance of fifteen hundred miles, a group of Mensheviks, SRs, and representatives of Siberian zemstvos and City Dumas met secretly in Irkutsk and formed what they called the Political Center, thus replicating the profile of the Directory that Kolchak had displaced.[134] The Center vowed to create an independent Siberian government of some kind—back, in other words, to the drawing board.[135]

On November 14, a year since Kolchak had anointed himself Supreme Ruler, promising to replace spineless moderation with martial resolve, the Red Army seized his now-deserted capital. The remaining democratic forces in the East now launched their comeback. On November 17, the SR plotters in Vladivostok proclaimed the establishment of (yet another) Provisional—this time, People's—Government of Siberia, with General Gajda as commander in chief. Counting on the support of garrison troops and workers, the organizers adopted the green-and-white Siberian flag, now adorned with a thin red (socialist) stripe. The Japanese held the trump card, however. Their troops surrounded the Vladivostok train station where the SR leaders had congregated. The cordon prevented workers from entering and Gajda's handful of still loyal men from getting out. Fish in a barrel. On the morning of November 18, Ataman Kalmykov and General Rozanov trained their guns on the station, massacring three hundred of Gajda's soldiers as they gave themselves up. Gajda himself was spirited away, and General Graves intervened to rescue the heads of the abortive Vladivostok Provisional Government. Rozanov, however, took fifteen hundred prisoners. The leaders were thrown into the harbor and shot as they floundered in the water. As many as five hundred others were taken behind the station and shot.[136] The bloodbath, courtesy of the Japanese occupiers and their ataman clients, ended the SR uprising in Vladivostok.

That same day, November 18, 1919, the anniversary of his coup, Kolchak's cabinet arrived in Irkutsk, where they learned that Omsk had fallen. Warned that the actions of the atamans had destroyed the last shred of his own authority, the admiral made a few feeble attempts to approach the representatives of "society" with an offer to form some kind of "cabinet of solidarity."[137] In reply, the Irkutsk zemstvo activists declared their preference for an alliance on the left, in essence contemplating a truce and even collaboration with the Bolsheviks.[138] The dilemma of the "third path" was not, however, easily resolved. One of Kolchak's ministers, Sergei Tret'iakov, a wealthy Moscow industrialist active in the War Industries Committee during the war and a member of the coalition government in 1917, now warned against the idea that persisted in moderate SR circles that an alliance on the left was an option. "The bloody dictatorship of Lenin and Trotsky," he admonished, "will not get us a step closer to what we understand as truly democratic methods of government." Yet partisan wrangling would doom them. "Our culture is a frail vessel on the raging ocean. We, the representatives of the intelligentsia, ignoring the elements descending upon us, are fighting each other on board the ship. The ocean will swallow the ship and us together with it."[139] The intelligentsia and the officer class might tear each other's eyes out, but none would prevail without confronting the popular anger driving the revolution—and directed also at themselves.

On November 21, his train still a thousand miles from Irkutsk, Kolchak reorganized his cabinet, giving the military even more weight than before. By now his hopes rested on Semenov, moving to challenge the Red Army at Tomsk, and on the Japanese, whom he had earlier resented.[140] The disgruntled Czechoslovak Legion, chaperoning the admiral and his overburdened cortège, deliberately slowed his passage, and it took him two weeks to cover the five hundred miles to Tomsk. Infighting among his supporters further weakened his position. On December 9, his prime minister, Viktor Pepeliaev, in collaboration with his brother, General Anatolii Pepeliaev, had Kolchak's commander in chief, General Konstantin Sakharov, arrested.[141] Georgii Gins (Guins), an erstwhile Kadet and former member of Kolchak's cabinet, described Sakharov's arrest as "a demonstration of the general collapse. It gave the signal for the outbreak of wanton violence and depravity everywhere."[142]

Indeed, the rout was terrible and undignified. Two of Kolchak's armies were stuck behind trains crammed with refugees, of whom the wealthiest had paid for carriages to take them east. The troops defied their commanders. In Novonikolaevsk, just west of Tomsk, drunken soldiers deserted en masse in anticipation of joining the Reds, who arrived on December 14, when they captured two thousand officers and about thirty thousand troops. Kolchak's armies were done for. In the catastrophic conditions, thousands of residents had died of typhus. In Tomsk his remaining soldiers arrested and shot some of their own officers. On December 20, the Red Army conquerors claimed, thirty thousand White soldiers, along with the Tomsk garrison, surrendered. The Political Center managed to hold onto Krasnoiarsk, 350 miles further east of Tomsk, for only two weeks, until January 8, when the Red Army took it.[143]

The so-called Russian Army, comprising Kolchak's remaining forces, including the Siberian Army, meanwhile was covering the nine hundred miles from Omsk to Krasnoiarsk, through the frozen taiga, by horse, by sleigh, on foot—officers, wives, and children, like a gaggle of refugees. Some were more comfortable in railway cars, but they could not advance, given the crowding and confusion on the tracks. Tens of thousands died of typhus en route; frozen corpses were stacked like firewood beside the roads.[144] Kolchak ordered the troops—what remained of them—to retreat without fighting, but orders no longer mattered. Twenty-five thousand men and many officers refused to move. In Krasnoiarsk, an observer reported, "the streets were so thickly littered with epaulettes as to suggest the idea of fallen leaves in autumn."[145]

Finally, the Czechoslovak Legion, which had blocked the eastward march of Red power and had guarded the lifeline across Siberia, now put itself first. With General Janin's endorsement, the Legionnaires refused to let the Russian trains pass until they themselves, followed by the Poles, Romanians, and Serbs, had proceeded. Kolchak protested to the Allies, but in vain.[146] Janin stood firm. A Dutch correspondent reported: "The Russians and

Czechs were positioned like two shipwrecked men, clinging to a plank strong enough to hold only one."[147] Kolchak's collapse brought with it the demise of civil society in Siberia. This was true in a personal, as well as political sense. Officer families and fleeing civilians often perished—of disease, cold, hunger—in the very train carriages supposed to take them east, but immobilized on the track behind the retreating Czechoslovak Legion. Typhus was epidemic.[148]

In mid-December, the now desperate Kolchak, bypassing his own cabinet, summoned Semenov from Chita and installed him as commander in chief of the Far East. Semenov had only eight thousand men to the Legion's thirty thousand, and he agreed to provide very few of them.[149] As Kolchak's trains neared Irkutsk, on December 23 the local military authorities acting on his behalf arrested the leaders of the Political Center.[150] For those who remained, it was time to act. Kolchak's train was approaching from the west, Semenov's men from the east, Red forces were positioned to the north. The Center circulated its program to the garrisons—truce with the Bolsheviks, foreigners out, a separate democratic state in the East. The plotters expected the Legion to support them against the forces backing Kolchak.[151]

Meanwhile, the Allied High Commissioners and General Janin were sitting in railroad cars at the suburban Glaskovo station outside Irkutsk. They observed as troops took over the stations and the arsenals. Inside the city, Kolchak's remaining ministers were waiting in their hotel rooms. The Allies played conflicting roles in the drama. While the Japanese urged Semenov to send reinforcements to back Kolchak, Janin warned General Konstantin Sychev, commander of the Irkutsk garrison still loyal to Kolchak, not to bombard Glaskovo station, as the general had threatened to do.[152] Various futile negotiations went back and forth, the Allied Commissioners refereeing between Kolchak's ministers, who insisted on guaranteed passage for the admiral and the gold, and representatives of the Political Center, who objected. By December 30, General Sychev, together with General Leonid Skipetrov, another of Kolchak's commanders, had driven the Political Center and their armed defenders out of Irkutsk. At this point, however, a miners' militia backed by Red partisans staged a revolt and pushed General Skipetrov out again. On December 31, Sychev's men deserted and the Political Center took control of the city.[153]

On January 1, 1920, the remnants of Kolchak's regime realized that their situation was desperate. The Japanese would not help them, Semenov was miserly with his support, and the Allies favored the Political Center as by now the most likely stabilizing force. A ceasefire was agreed, but General Skipetrov was no longer in control of his men, who ran wild through the city. On January 5, however, the Political Center declared itself the new power, pledging to introduce civil liberties, democratic elections, and— most controversially—truce with the Soviet regime.[154]

Kolchak was meanwhile under virtual house arrest in his train, still west of Irkutsk, which had turned from a refuge into a prison. On January 1, the Allies had insisted Kolchak allow the gold to proceed to Vladivostok under Allied guard and promised to protect him for as long as he requested. Two days later, the admiral announced he was transferring power to General Denikin, but still did not formalize his resignation. His true intentions remained unclear, but his forces were deserting him. When his soldiers pre- ceded him into Irkutsk, singing the "Marseillaise," they joined the rebels. When he relieved his officers of their duties, only a few stayed behind.[155]

The rebellion against Kolchak, led by the predominantly SR Political Center, had succeeded, but the aftermath was bloody. During the brief period when General Sychev had controlled Irkutsk, he had taken thirty-one hostages, including SR-Maximalists, Bolsheviks, and supporters of the Political Center. On leaving the city, the general handed the hostages over to Semenov's men, who on January 6 proceeded to drown them in Lake Baikal. The atrocity caused a stir and fed the animus against Kolchak, though of course the Red partisans had their own brutalities to account for.[156]

In any case, Kolchak's fate was sealed. When his train finally reached Irkutsk in the afternoon of January 15 after two months en route, soldiers loyal to the Political Center were massed on the platform. Japanese troops stood ready to depart with the fallen leader on a special train, but the Czechoslovak Legion refused to release him.[157] Instead, with Allied blessing, General Janin handed him over to the Political Center, which placed him under arrest. Janin had betrayed his promise to convey the Supreme Ruler to safety. The Political Center, for its part, created an Extraordinary Investigating Commission for the purpose of interrogating Kolchak. On January 21, the second day of its proceedings, the Red Army captured Irkutsk and assumed control, but the original investigators were allowed to continue.[158]

Thus began the interrogation of Admiral Kolchak. The questioning was conducted by Konstantin Popov, a Bolshevik now in charge of the Center's political police. A native of Omsk, Popov had begun his revolutionary career in March 1917 as chair of the Omsk Soviet. Arrested by the Czechoslovak Legion in June 1918, he had escaped a prison convoy in August 1919. By then he was urging the local SRs to support Bolshevik power. Among the leaders of the revolt in Irkutsk that ousted the remnants of Kolchak's government in refuge there, Popov now had the satisfaction of presiding over the "Supreme Ruler's" last days.[159]

Over the course of two weeks, Popov listened as Kolchak explained his career and his political views. Meanwhile, however, Kolchak's remaining forces, under General Vladimir Kappel', continued their progress towards Irkutsk. "The starving, half-frozen bands of the remaining Kolchak forces, summoning their last strength," the Irkutsk Military Revolutionary Committee announced, were heading for the city.[160] Describing the troops as a "pitiful handful," the Committee nevertheless warned that Kappel', should he prevail, would institute a compulsory draft and shoot anyone who resisted.[161] When, on Febuary 5, Kappel''s forces won a small victory in nearby Zima, only 150 miles northwest of Irkutsk, Kolchak's captors panicked. The prisoner's account, an autobiography under duress, was therefore interrupted, before reaching the final chapter, by his execution.[162] On the night of February 6–7, 1920, he was taken out and shot, together with his prime minister, Viktor Pepeliaev.[163] Their bodies were thrown under the ice of the Angara River.

To the end, Popov conceded, the admiral maintained the dignity of a "commander of a defeated army."[164] Indeed, he remained more of a soldier than a politician. The Soviet government published the proceedings of his interrogation in 1925.[165] In late May 1920, the other members of Kolchak's government were interrogated as well and brought before a Special Revolutionary Tribunal in Omsk. Thousands of spectators were herded into a specially refurbished building for the ten-day spectacle. Evidence was drawn from Kolchak's own testimony and from material assembled by local branches of the Cheka. Of the twenty-three defendants, four were sentenced to be shot, the others to various terms of hard labor.[166]

The prosecutor was Aleksandr Goichbarg, a prerevolutionary specialist in civil law, at the time close to left-liberal legal circles. Goichbarg had begun as a Menshevik, but in 1918 hitched his wagon to the Bolshevik star and was soon appointed to the Commissariat of Justice under the patronage of Mikhail Reisner, another left-leaning liberal jurist before 1917. Together they helped draft the Soviet Constitution announced in July 1918. In 1919 Goichbarg joined the Communist Party; in 1924 he was expelled. His son was arrested and shot in 1937, but Goichbarg Senior survived untouched, pursuing a slightly impeded career, until 1948. In the heat of Stalin's postwar anti-Semitic campaign, he was not executed but committed instead to a psychiatric institution, from which he was released in 1955. He and his son were rehabilitated in May 1956.[167] Goichbarg had been both an architect and a casualty of the Soviet system of justice.

Indeed, the trial of Kolchak's ministers was the first—and the prototype—of the political show trials that were to reach their apogee in Stalin's purges. The purpose of the exercise was to judge not only the responsible individuals, but the entire counterrevolution. It was political theater intended for the instruction of "the masses," several thousand of whom were compelled to attend. The defendants, knowing they were doomed, addressed a different audience. The erstwhile Menshevik Leonid Shumilovskii, Kolchak's former minister of labor, said he spoke "mainly for history.... Here unseen history and the coming generation are listening.... We are not in a condition to judge each other dispassionately. We are too blinded by battle—those who emerge the victors and those who are struck down."[168]

Kolchak's fall has sometimes been described as a tragedy, that of an honest soldier hampered by his own naiveté, his reputation damaged by the depravity of his cohorts.[169] His fate might have been tragic had it represented the defeat of some noble principle. Kolchak paid lip service to lawfulness, but allowed lawlessness to prevail. As commander, he was implicated in the behavior of his nominal subordinates, however insubordinate they might in fact have been. But not all Kolchak's followers saw Semenov as a liability. In the wake of the Irkutsk disaster, the ataman was hailed by some remaining loyalists as the banner-carrier of "greater Russian statehood" (rossiiskaia gosudarstvennost').[170] Semenov thus provides a dishonorable pendant to the Kolchak saga.

In December 1919, the chieftain had begun to organize a government in Chita, where his advocates hailed him as "a mighty Cossack-warrior...battling the enslavers of our Homeland."[171] Like Kolchak, he posed as a constitutionalist, pledging to call popular elections and affirming his dedication to "law and order on the basis of the people's rule."[172] Preferring the Slavic neologism narodopravstvo to the Latinate demokratiia, 'democracy,' with its revolutionary associations, Semenov became a symbol of authoritarian populism. As Kolchak's star fell, Semenov pursued his own ambitions, still with Japanese support. Pretending to have reformed his ways, he made overtures to the Americans, but General Graves declared he "would have nothing to do with murderers."[173]

Semenov's memoirs, composed in the 1930s in the Chinese port of Dairen (Dalian), present him as a statesman as well as a military leader, the heir to Kolchak's mantle. A well-disciplined army under central, undivided leadership was indispensable to the survival of any state, the memoir declared.[174] The key word was "statehood" (*gosudarstvennost'*), the mantra of the anti-Bolshevik right, beginning with the Kadets. As a local trouble-maker, dependent on foreign support, who undermined the authority of his own superior, Semenov's invocation of these terms was nothing but cynical. He promised now to avoid the mistakes that had lost Kolchak "the rear." He would separate military and civil justice, embrace deserting Red soldiers, limit requisitions to strict military needs, pay for what was taken, and so on—the reverse litany of Kolchak's self-defeating evil deeds.[175] Like Kolchak, the public Semenov talked the talk that was expected of him, but few were listening now. White Russians in emigration scolded the Allies for their accommodation with Soviet power and hailed the Japanese for supporting the ongoing struggle in the Far East.[176] In reality, the Japanese had sup-ported Semenov at the expense of Kolchak and of whatever nuance of moderation separated the commander from his minions. They had deserted him in the end, a move consistent with their overall policy.

Semenov's Trans-Baikal regime, centered in Chita, issued noble decrees and maintained its pattern of brutality, certainly no model of a disciplined central state. After Kolchak's execution, the Reds stopped short of the Trans-Baikal, turning their attention instead back west, to the unfinished Polish campaign. As a placeholder, the Soviets established a Far Eastern Republic, centered in Verkhne-Udinsk (today Ulan-Ude, in the Buriat Republic), which declared its "independence" and was duly recognized by Moscow. When the Japanese withdrew from Chita in October 1920, the Reds cap-tured the city, dislodging what was left of the ataman's vestigial "statehood." Semenov crossed into Mongolia.[177] In 1922 he was allowed to visit the United States, "notwithstanding," as General Graves put it, "that he had bru-tally murdered Americans," among other offenses to civilization.[178]

# 5

# Ukraine, Act II

The foreign powers were involved in the Ukraine as well as Siberia, but whereas Allied intervention amplified the turmoil in Siberia, German occupation in the Ukraine had put an end to armed conflict. When the Germans left, in December 1918, the free-for-all began. The rivals for political domination all faced similar problems, however, in building armies, creating administrations, and controlling their subordinates, deputies, and local agents. As in Siberia, in Ukraine the anti-Red forces faced off against each other. The Bolsheviks had the advantage of ideological unity, if not always strategic agreement. The challenge was to keep the Ukrainian lands within Soviet Russia's political borders. The best way to do this was unclear, and differences emerged within the party. Authority was not easy to achieve even for an authoritarian, whether Lenin or Kolchak.[1]

The Bolsheviks faced opposition in the Ukraine from three sources—Ukrainian nationalists of various stripes, attempting to form an independent state; the White armies; and the foreign powers. The Ukrainians were also fighting on various fronts. Nationalists on the Austrian side faced off against the newly independent and self-assertive Poles, with whom they contested boundaries. Nationalists on the Russian side confronted Communists from Moscow, native Communists, and the Whites, none of whom favored Ukrainian independence.

As the Ukrainian leaders struggled to shape a government, Moscow struggled to attach the region firmly to the center. The Baltic states and Finland had achieved independence with German backing.[2] Lenin had been ready to relinquish the Baltic periphery for the sake of peace, but the German card was no longer in play, and in any case Ukraine was not expendable. The Ukrainian lands belonged to the Slavic core of the Empire, with a closely entwined history, a similar peasant culture, the same predominant Orthodox religion, and a similar Slavic tongue. Ukraine was also the

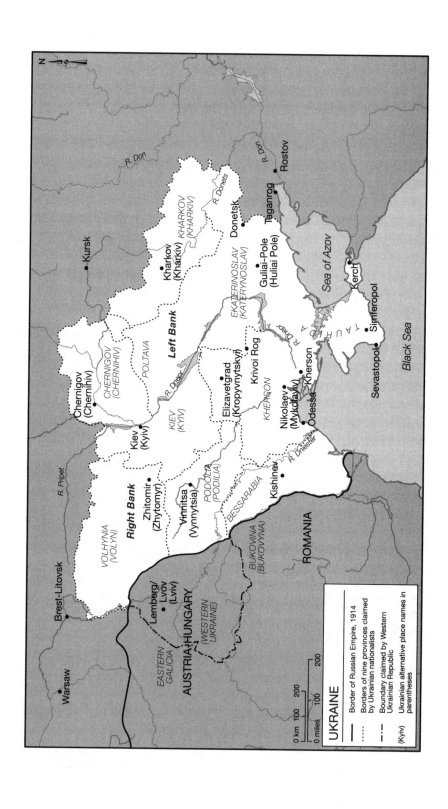

UKRAINE

——— Border of Russian Empire, 1914

··········· Borders of nine provinces claimed
by Ukrainian nationalists

—·—·— Boundary claimed by Western
Ukrainian Republic

(Kyiv)  Ukrainian alternative place names in
parentheses

0 km 100 200
0 miles 100 200

N

R. Don

Kursk

KHARKOV
(KHARKIV)

Kharkov
(Kharkiv)

Donetsk

R. Donets

R. Don

Rostov

Taganrog

Guliai-Pole
(Huliai Pole)

Sea of Azov

Kerch

EKATERINOSLAV
(KATERYNOSLAV)

Left Bank

CHERNIGOV
(CHERNIHIV)

POLTAVA

R. Dnepr

Chernigov
(Chernihiv)

Krivoi Rog

R. Dnepr

T A U R I S

Simferopol

KIEV
(KYIV)

Elizavetgrad
(Kropyvnytskyi)

KHERSON

Kherson

Kiev
(Kyiv)

Nikolaev
(Mykolaiv)

Odessa

Sevastopol

Black Sea

R. Pripet

Right Bank

PODOLIA
(PODILIA)

Zhitomir
(Zhytomyr)

Vinnitsa
(Vynnytsia)

R. Dniester

BESSARABIA

Kishinev

VOLHYNIA
(VOLYN)

Brest-Litovsk

Lemberg/
Lvov
(Lviv)

EASTERN
GALICIA

(WESTERN
UKRAINE)

AUSTRIA-HUNGARY

BUKOVINA
(BUKOVYNA)

ROMANIA

Warsaw

Russian breadbasket. Determined to secure their hold on Ukrainian territory, the Soviets nevertheless had to take Ukrainian nationalism into account. They also had to subordinate their own local operatives to the top party command.

The attempt to establish a Soviet foothold in Ukraine, as we have seen, dated back to December 1917, when the Bolshevik delegates to the First Ukrainian Congress of Soviets in Kiev, dominated by the Rada leadership, had fled to Kharkov to create their own, competing institutions under the same titles used by their rivals—the Ukrainian People's (National) Republic, with a People's (National) Secretariat. These same Bolshevik leaders subsequently relocated to Ekaterinoslav, southeast of Kiev, where a Second Ukrainian Congress of Soviets convened on March 17–19, 1918, under entirely new circumstances. This Second Congress, with a slim Bolshevik majority, reaffirmed Ukrainian independence, though anticipating an eventual union with Soviet Russia. The tactical maneuver was intended to avoid the consequences of the Brest-Litovsk treaty, which obliged Moscow to recognize the Ukrainian nation and prohibited Russia from opposing German occupation.[3]

The Bolsheviks active in Ukraine shared the SRs' discontent with the treaty terms and attempted to establish a certain distance from the Russian-centered leadership. In April 1918, the members of the Bolshevik Secretariat relocated to Taganrog, outside Ukraine, in the lower Don, where they voted to create an independent Bolshevik Communist Party of Ukraine, linked to the Russian (Moscow-centered) party via the Third International. They were not, however, independent, nor were they deeply rooted in Ukraine. Few spoke decent Ukrainian. Indeed, in July the party held its first congress not in Ukraine but in Moscow, where it was formally established under the leadership of Georgii Piatakov, Ukrainian-born but Russian-educated and Russian-identified, and the Podolia native Vladimir Zatonskii (Volodymyr Zatons'kyi). It had its own Central Committee and the right to make decisions in local matters.[4] The Congress reaffirmed the dissolution of the People's (National) Secretariat, supposedly abolished at Taganrog, which had in the meantime continued to operate. In August 1918, yet another Soviet government was formed—the Worker and Peasant Government of Ukraine—which was in turn dissolved by the Second Ukrainian Bolshevik Party Congress, in Moscow, in October.[5] None of these putative governments, with their confusingly similar names, had any power or authority.

The Ukrainian Communist Party was thus not only at odds with Moscow and disconnected from the territory it claimed to represent, but its leaders disagreed among themselves. Bolsheviks based in Ekaterinoslav, known as the "Right," thought the party should concentrate on organizing local workers. They rejected the idea of a separate Ukrainian Communist Party and saw their main enemies as General Krasnov's Don Cossacks and General Denikin's Volunteer Army. Those centered in Kiev, known as the "Left," believed the Ukrainian proletariat was too small to constitute a popular base; the party must focus on the peasantry and must respect the region's desire for administrative autonomy. The creation of a separate Ukrainian Communist Party reflected the triumph of Piatakov's Left position.[6] The Brest treaty had created a neutral zone on the northern border of Ukrainian territory. Under Piatakov's brief leadership, the Ukrainian party used the zone, contrary to its original purpose, as a staging ground for guerrilla attacks on the German occupiers, defying the terms of the treaty. On August 5, the Left faction, on its own initiative, called for a general uprising against Skoropads'kyi and the occupiers.[7] Lenin disapproved of the partisan strategy, which in fact did not succeed.[8]

With the Germans finally out of the way, the center itself decided to launch an attack. On November 12, the day after the armistice, Trotsky ordered Red Army troops into the Ukraine. Soon after, on November 20, a second Ukrainian Soviet government was proclaimed, with Piatakov at its head, Kliment Voroshilov in charge of internal affairs, and Vladimir Antonov-Ovseenko as commander in chief. The commissars operated out of Kursk, north of Kharkov, where they occupied a train carriage next to the station.[9] The government called itself provisional, anticipating the time when Soviet Russia would have conquered Ukraine and a future congress of soviets established its permanent form.[10] In January 1919, Khristian Rakovskii replaced Piatakov as head of the Ukrainian party. Of Bulgarian origin, with Romanian citizenship, the internationalist Rakovskii was hostile to Ukrainian nationalism and rejected the use of Ukrainian as the party's official language.[11] His personal background and political stance exemplified the contradictions of the Bolshevik approach to the Ukrainian question.

The man charged with executing Trotsky's November 12 directive was Antonov-Ovseenko. Like Piatakov, born in the Ukraine but Russian-identified, Antonov-Ovseenko had graduated in military engineering from the St. Petersburg Cadet Academy in 1904, but simultaneously began his career as a full-time revolutionary, having joined the Social Democratic

Party in 1902 at the age of nineteen, a pattern typical of many Bolsheviks of his generation. In 1906 he was arrested for organizing a revolt, escaped from prison, and turned up in Paris, where he helped Trotsky edit a Menshevik newspaper. He joined the Bolsheviks in June 1917. After October, he commanded the Petrograd Military District and, as noted, was part of the troika running the first Commissariat for Military and Naval Affairs.[12]

Antonov-Ovseenko's mission was now to prevent Petliura's Directory from gaining ground, while at the same time creating an army that would stop Denikin from moving west and taking the cities, all before Allied forces could manage to get their hand on what the Germans had left behind and install themselves in their place.[13] Operating out of Kursk, he confronted a panoply of existing groups with varying degrees of self-organization, which could possibly support a pro-Soviet campaign.[14] He faced the same problem on the local level as Trotsky faced in the center: how to fashion existing formations—such as partisan bands, which were undisciplined, used to having their own way, and ready to desert—into a functioning army.[15] Weapons could be had from the Germans, who were eager to get out, but he lacked supplies and he lacked authority.[16]

Ironically, while Antonov-Ovseenko faced the challenge of imposing his will on leaders used to deciding for themselves, he himself resisted subordination.[17] His grandiose schemes did not find favor with Ioakim Vatsetis, now Supreme Commander of the Red Army, who insisted on concentrating strategic decisions in his own hands. Vatsetis had emerged from a peasant family in Courland Province to attend military academy in Vilna, then the General Staff academy, and rise through the ranks during the Great War, in which he commanded a regiment of the Latvian Riflemen. He led them, on behalf of the new Soviet power, in suppressing the revolts of the Left SRs and the Czechoslovak Legion. Though not a party member, he was crucial, along with Trotsky, in building the Red Army.[18]

Where Antonov-Ovseenko stood in relation to his (sometimes merely nominal) subordinates, Vatsetis stood in relation to him. If Antonov-Ovseenko thought of himself as implementing Trotsky's order to descend into Ukraine and perform a miracle of mobilization and penetration, Vatsetis believed he was implementing Trotsky's model of centralized military command and old-style military discipline. Despite the resistance within the nascent Red Army from noncommissioned officers, Old Bolsheviks, and partisan leaders, who for various reasons clung to the Red Guard ethos of decision by committee and dispersed authority,

Trotsky's model prevailed.[19] New organs were created to focus authority at the top, where Trotsky and Vatsetis now had the last word.[20] The tug of war between Antonov-Ovseenko and Vatsetis thus revolved around two cardinal principles: the centralization of authority within the Red Army and the subordination of the regions to the capital. Antonov-Ovseenko remonstrated to Lenin, but was told to obey orders. Trotsky denounced "*partizanshchina*," the partisan spirit, which he equated with amateurism, improvisation, and blindness to the bigger picture.[21] "The Soviet Republic is facing a growing danger of invasion by the united hordes of world imperialism," the Bolshevik Central Committee declared.[22] Soviet Russia must be united in return.

While Antonov-Ovseenko was tussling with Moscow on the issue of military authority, the Kursk Soviet government insisted on the right to make its own decisions with respect to the situation in Ukraine. Piatakov and his associates complained of contradictory messages coming from Moscow, while also rejecting the center's authority to dictate to the region.[23] The quarrel between Kursk and Moscow reflected a clash of realisms— Trotsky's recognition that no army could exist without old-style discipline versus the insistence of Antonov-Ovseenko and Piatakov that local leaders needed the freedom to respond to local conditions. When Vatsetis demanded Antonov-Ovseenko send his troops to fight on the Southern Front, Zatonskii retorted: "Such a degree of discipline as Trotsky dreams about does not exist in a single company, and to hurl units formed with difficulty from partisan sections into the fight against [Krasnov's] Cossacks would mean to destroy them completely."[24] He, too, rejected *partizanshchina*, but at the moment partisans were all they had.

Over Vatsetis's objections, Antonov-Ovseenko proceeded to Kharkov, which his troops managed to wrest from the hands of pro-Petliura forces on January 3, 1919. His success was enabled by a worker revolt in the city and the defection of men from Petliura's side. In recognition, Moscow appointed Antonov-Ovseenko head of the Ukrainian Front, with a staff and Military Revolutionary Council of his own. Bolshevik success motivated many peasants to abandon the Directory; at the same time, the worsening situation of Petliura's forces increased the tendency of his lieutenants to countenance or encourage attacks on Jews and the rough handling of peasants. The peasants responded by welcoming the Reds.[25]

At the beginning of 1918, Soviet forces had swept into the Ukraine with little to impede them, before being driven out again. The second Soviet conquest occurred a year later, at the start of 1919. When the Red Army marched into Ukraine, Chicherin, as commissar for foreign affairs, baldly denied that Ukraine was being invaded. "There are no troops of the Russian Socialist Soviet Republic in the Ukraine at all," he said on January 5, 1919. "Military action on Ukrainian territory is proceeding at this moment between the troops of the Directory and the troops of the Ukrainian Soviet Government, which is completely independent."[26] The independence Moscow was in the process of quashing in its own ranks served it as a rhetorical ploy.

Antonov-Ovseenko was commander in chief of the (second) self-declared Soviet government of Ukraine. Driving out Petliura's forces, on January 12, his troops took Chernigov, eighty miles north of Kiev; on January 20, Poltava (Petliura's birthplace), two hundred miles to the southeast. Meanwhile, Antonov-Ovseenko moved his headquarters to Chernigov, preparing to take Kiev, fearing that Denikin, backed by the French, who had landed in Odessa in December, were heading toward the city. Once again the threat of foreign intervention galvanized the Bolshevik cause.[27]

Confronting the threat, the Directory leadership was divided. Some favored closer relations with Moscow; others saw Moscow as the enemy of Ukrainian independence. Even those sympathetic to the socialist cause, like Vynnychenko himself, deplored what they saw as the Soviet regime's imperialist maneuvers.[28] On January 16, 1919, the Directory declared war on Soviet Russia; four days later, the Ukrainians sent a mission to Odessa to appeal for French support, without which their success was unlikely. The French, however, saw the Bolsheviks and the Directory as equally noxious. Denouncing Vynnychenko as a Bolshevik and Petliura as a bandit, they insisted both resign, while demanding control over railroads, finances, and the army they expected the Directory to raise.[29] Appointing Volunteer Army general Aleksei Grishin-Almazov as military governor of Odessa, they demonstrated their solidarity with Denikin's Great Russia aspirations.[30]

In the absence of outside sponsorship and under pressure from the growing Bolshevik assault, the aspirational Ukrainian government, like the Komuch and the provisional governments of Siberia, moved from the chaos of popular participation and ideological confusion to the relative clarity of military rule. As elsewhere, the authoritarians within the socialist camp won out over the talkers. Under the circumstances, Vynnychenko drew closer to Petliura, who had narrowed his sights to the battle with Bolshevism.[31] Unfortunately, Petliura's competence as a strongman only diminished as the pressure to be one increased. The peasants were deserting, and units were defecting; some joined Denikin, many went over to the Reds.[32] On January 23, 1919, his troops began exiting Kiev. Vynnychenko left the city on February 1, and the Directory departed for Vinnitsa (Vinnytsia) the day after. Meanwhile, Kiev workers were preparing an uprising. When the Red Army arrived on February 5, a year after Colonel Murav'ev had expelled Petliura the first time around, the city was theirs for the taking.[33] On February 10, a week after fleeing Kiev, Vynnychenko resigned his position. Petliura replaced him as head of the Directory, abandoned the Social Democratic party, and appointed a non-socialist cabinet as a sop to the Allies, who were not, however, interested in supporting an independent Ukraine.[34]

The Ukrainians were not alone in struggling to establish military and political institutions. Despite the Red Army's success in capturing the string of cities, it was still a work in progress, and the power struggle between Antonov-Ovseenko and Vatsetis continued, with its paradoxical inner tension. While Antonov-Ovseenko resisted orders from the center, he himself applied principles of hierarchy and top-down authority, which Trotsky had introduced in November 1918 to the Red Army as a whole, in shaping a regular fighting force out of the miscellaneous armed outfits at hand.[35] He did not, of course, succeed. This tension between control and improvisation, center and locality, can be understood as a vulnerability but also an advantage. From the perspective of the emerging system, the Soviet regime needed both the mildly insubordinate Antonov-Ovseenko types and the draconian disciplinarians to cope with a situation of chaos and urgency that needed to be mastered, both by force of arms and by the exercise of recognized authority.

Moving down the chain of command, Antonov-Ovseenko himself faced insubordination and improvisation in the levels below him. Conscripting as many men as possible, capturing abandoned military material, plundering the population, impressing former officers and noncommissioned officers, he brought on board the elders and Cossack atamans who commanded the peasant bands and partisan units of devoted but undisciplined men. Leaders and men were hard to control and hard to integrate into campaigns that transcended their own local issues. The atamans were often the more literate members of their communities, the best equipped to exercise and also defy authority.[36] The technique of implanting commissars to educate or restrain the troops caused problems as well. They were usually city men, often identifiable as Jews or presumed to be Jewish, responsible on behalf of the new regime for requisitioning, confiscating property and weapons, executions, and meddling in the daily life of the units. Sometimes units—nominally of the Red Army—would murder the commissars, Cheka agents, or Soviet officials. At the same time, commanders, in the "partisan spirit," continued to defy Antonov-Ovseenko's orders, make their own decisions, and look the other way at pillaging and anti-Jewish pogroms.[37]

In January 1919, Antonov-Ovseenko faced pressure and criticism from his superiors in the Ukraine, while he blamed them for getting in his way. He appealed to Moscow for resources, but to no avail. Instead of reinforcements, he received orders to send his own troops to the south and east, where Denikin and Kolchak posed threats to the center. The resentful Antonov-Ovseenko could not but comply, but the pressure only intensified the challenge of recruitment.[38] The desperation to fill the ranks and to annex (both use and tame) the charisma of myriad local leaders led the Red Army in Ukraine to make use of characters whose misdeeds blackened their name. One of the most notorious was Matvii Hryhoriïv (Nikifor Grigor'ev).[39]

Hryhoriïv was a peasant with two years of primary education who had served with distinction in the Russo-Japanese War and the Great War, achieving the rank of captain.[40] After October he deserted to his native village in the Ukraine, where he recruited his own peasant following. He at first supported Skoropads'kyi, but in December 1918 joined Petliura's campaign against the hetman. Petliura anointed him the ataman of Zaporozhe, a title that endowed him with the borrowed aura of the legendary Zaporozhian Cossacks, who had run their own community on the lower Dnepr from the sixteenth to the nineteenth century. They served in the war against Turkey under Catherine the Great, but many then joined Pugachev's massive popular uprising, which was suppressed by force of arms in 1775. The Zaporozhian Sech (Sich) was then liquidated, depriving the community of self-rule and its separate identity. The Cossacks had put their military prowess at the sovereign's service, but also defied her authority. Anyone who tried to make use of Hryhoriïv would confront this dangerous ambiguity.

Active in soldier committees during the war, Hryhoriïv allowed his politics to wander. In 1917 he favored the SRs, in 1919 he joined the Borot'bist party, Ukrainian Left SRs who took the name Communist and in August 1919 merged with a splinter group from the Ukrainian Social Democrats.[41] He was an untrained and unskilled commander, but he had outlaw charisma and appealed to the sentiments of his peasant followers, angry at Bolshevik food policies and at the cities the Bolsheviks fed, focused on their own

interests and unwilling to go far from home. By December 1918, Hryhoriïv
had rallied as many as six thousand men, cavalry and infantry, to his side,
bringing together a hundred local outfits.[42] In February 1919, after the Reds
defeated Petliura, he joined the victorious side. He remained commander of
his brigade, which became part of a Red Army division.[43] He did not, however, consider himself subject to their command. "If you continue to organize
authority behind my back," he warned Antonov-Ovseenko and Rakovskii,
"I will refuse to fight."[44] He was dangerous, but effective. "The regiments
formed a mob," one of Petliura's erstwhile followers observed, upon visiting
Hryhoriïv. "But it was an inspired and passionate mob—a beast that would
see the enemy, recognize him and seek to destroy him."[45]

Hryhoriïv's insubordination as well as his ferocity were on display in his
conquest in March 1919 of Nikolaev and Kherson, port cities whose warehouses bulged with goods and equipment. Nikolaev housed fifteen thousand German troops under French command, waiting to return home. In
their usual pragmatic fashion, the Bolsheviks were busy negotiating for the
Germans to hand over their weapons and supplies before departing. They
did not want Hryhoriïv, by an impetuous move, to disturb the deal, but
Hryhoriïv seized Nikolaev on March 12, foiling their plan and taking the
weapons for himself. His success undermined Antonov-Ovseenko's authority but enhanced his own. His numbers swelled, now clothed, armed, and
transported by horses and motor vehicles.[46]

The seizure and conquest of Odessa, which followed, only magnified
Hryhoriïv's self-importance. The Red Army was poised west of the city, but
Vatsetis continued to pick off units to dispatch to the Southern Front. The
French commandant declared a state of siege, but neither the Entente nor
the Volunteer Army took any action, allowing the Red Army to maintain
their assault on the Directory forces. Hryhoriïv in theory was under the
command of Anatolii Skachko, appointed by Antonov-Ovseenko to head
the Odessa Group. They faced at least fifty thousand troops massed in the
city—French, Greeks, Romanians, and a Volunteer Army brigade using
Allied equipment, protected by warships in the harbor.[47] In fact, Hryhoriïv
had no intention of following anyone's orders.

The opposition in Odessa was not as formidable as it seemed. The French
were undermined primarily by the low morale of their own soldiers, who
had no desire to die in Russia after the war had ended. The French command itself was ambivalent. Some officers spoke openly of the futility of any
kind of military operation, and they faced insurmountable obstacles of a

practical sort. Hryhoriïv's capture of Kherson and Nikolaev blocked transport and communication. Odessa already suffered shortages of grain and coal, and factories were closing. The population, swollen with refugees, had expanded by a third; 80 percent of workers were unemployed; typhus raged. Crime was rampant, and wealthy people employed personal bodyguards. The French attempted to suppress news of Hryhoriïv's success, leading to the spread of anxious rumors. The propertied classes panicked; the workers responded to Bolshevik appeals.[48]

Abruptly, on April 2, the French announced they were pulling out, and a hurried evacuation began. Their rapid withdrawal, taking to ship with as many refugees as could wrangle their way on board, seemed like a rout, an impression strengthened by Hryhoriïv's many vainglorious telegrams to all and sundry. Four days later, Hryhoriïv celebrated his own triumph. "After incredible violence, sacrifices, and tactical maneuvers," he declared, "the French, Greeks, Romanians, Turks, Volunteers, and our other enemies have been cut to pieces at Odessa. They have fled in terrible panic."[49] He made much of his own prowess—horse shot out from under him, bullets grazing his flesh. "Odessa was taken exclusively by my units...Not one Red Army soldier of another regiment was in the fight."[50] When he drove through the city, his car was mobbed by cheering crowds; he held his hand out to be kissed. Rumors swirled among the public starved for news.[51]

Antonov-Ovseenko had a different version of local events: "On the sixth of April, Odessa was taken by the Ukrainian Soviet Army. The supports of the allied imperialists in the Black Sea have crumbled. Long live Soviet power! Long live the World Socialist Revolution!" Rakovskii provided additional ideological color. "The strong point of rapacious international imperialism fell in the southern Ukraine on the same day that the telegraph communicated the joyous news about the proclamation of the Soviet Republic in Bavaria and about the invasion of our troops into the Crimean peninsula."[52]

Red Army troops did particulate in the conquest of Odessa. Hryhoriïv was not solely responsible for the rout of the Allied occupiers, but his capture of Kherson and Nikolaev had increased the pressure; moreover, his bravado heartened the workers primed to revolt and his threatening messages spread fear.[53] Antonov-Ovseenko could not control him; indeed, Antonov-Ovseenko's own superiors dealt with Hryhoriïv directly, enhancing the ataman's sense of independence and his self-regard. Antonov-Ovseenko warned against "strengthen[ing] the prestige of the adventurer."[54] His prestige—or fearsome reputation—was one of his weapons. The writer Ivan Bunin, who later received the Nobel Prize for literature, now lent his talents to General Denikin's propaganda agency. In April 1919 he was in Odessa, where he kept a diary in which he noted how "Roughly six hundred of 'Grigoriev's men' blew into town, bowlegged youths led by a pack of convicts and hooligans, who somehow captured an extremely well-to-do city with a million people in it! When they entered, everyone died of fright, they ran and hid."[55]

Hryhoriïv could blow down the walls (though not without assistance), but he could not build a new city and certainly not a new society. This feat the Bolsheviks accomplished with their signature mix of hard and soft power: arrests, executions, confiscations—new icons, new symbols, new alphabet, new calendar, new words in new combinations. Many cultured people, like Bunin, were violently hostile to the upstart rulers, but others were eager to serve the new regime. The Revolution seemed to herald the future—of society, art, human existence. This was an expectation artists and intellectuals had themselves nurtured in the years since 1900—the desire to tear down the old aesthetic, moral, and social constraints. The Bolsheviks enlisted many talents, as they enlisted professional officers in building the army, to design the new world and teach people how to see and think differently. Thus, in Odessa, amid acute shortages and the shock of Bolshevik repression, May Day in 1919 was celebrated with a public spectacle—which some artists were eager to design. Despite the scarcity of fuel and the power outages that kept the city dark at night, Bolshevik newspapers were published and hawked on the street corners.[56] "The newspapers," Bunin commented, "all have one and the same tone—a high-blown yet vulgar jargon—along with the same threats and the same frenzied boasting."[57]

The language grated on literary ears, but it had the power of incantation, formulas easy to repeat, if not always to make sense of. Not all messages, in any case, were vulgar and bombastic. Posters plastered on the city walls often displayed a compelling graphic imagination. The brilliant images and playful verses that had recently celebrated the patriotic war now called for Red victory. Futurist constructions graced the public squares.[58] What workers or average citizens made of these adornments is hard to say, but their presence signaled the allegiance of Russia's cultural elite. Part of it, in any case. The Bolsheviks had craftsmen of the word and image at their disposal. Vladimir Mayakovsky, the provocative poet of the prewar futurist avant-garde, had created colorful cartoons and rhymes for wartime propaganda. Though soon disillusioned, he celebrated the new world for its aesthetic iconoclasm and break with the past. In March 1918, he published *An Order to the Army of Art*. "Comrades! To the barricades!—the barricades of hearts and souls. The only true Communist is the one who has burned the bridges to retreat. Enough, you futurists, of taking it slow, seize the future in one go!"

The new era was not merely an avant-garde concoction. It affected everyday life. Bolshevik *Izvestiia* used the new orthography; the hours conformed to daylight savings time and fell into time zones.[59] A culture snob like Bunin derided the "Red aristocracy" that frequented the newly christened theaters and clubs—"sailors with huge revolvers in their belts, pickpockets, criminal villains, and shaved dandies in service jackets, depraved-looking riding breeches, and dandylike shoes with the inevitable spurs. All have gold teeth and big, dark, cocainelike eyes." Bunin saw "the people" as brutes; he sympathized with the other side—"the Whites, whom the people have profaned, assaulted, and murdered, and from whom they have taken everything away."[60] Yet even Bunin understood that "many everyday citizens" welcomed the Bolsheviks because they "are tired of the change of governments; they want something stable and hope that life will be cheaper, too."[61]

Things, however, did not soon improve. Again to take the case of Odessa, by the end of April electricity was running out. "Thus in one month they have brought chaos to everything," Bunin snarled, "no factories, no railroads, no trams, no water, no bread, no clothes—no nothing!"[62] In fact the Bolsheviks had inherited the chaos and the crisis; they also inherited—and exacerbated—the free-wheeling brutality displayed on all sides and of which (in the person of Hryhoriïv, for example) they were the beneficiaries. To this kind of panache they applied a new moral calculus. As Mayakovsky had put it in 1917, when the excitement was still fresh: "Gorge on pineapple! / Chomp on grouse! / Your days are numbered, / bourgeois louse!"[63] In real terms, class war was less playful. In the name of class justice, clothing and personal possessions were confiscated from propertied inhabitants, even those with little to take, providing new justification for the plunder and pilfering that was going on everywhere and could not be stopped but only relabeled.[64] No longer a personal vice, looting became a public service. Similarly, the arbitrary arrests, executions, and hostage-taking became the official duty of the Cheka.

The rest of the Hryhoriïv saga reflects both the conflict between the Red Army central command and its regional leaders (Antonov-Ovseenko) and the conflict between the regional Red Army command and their partisan accomplices. On March 21, 1919, Béla Kun announced the formation of the Hungarian Republic of Worker, Peasant, and Soldier Soviets and appealed to Moscow for support against troops from Romania and Czechoslovakia, with additional French involvement. Here internationalism and imperialism converged. Bessarabia, the slice of Russian-Ukrainian territory abutting Romania, had opted in November 1918 to become a Romanian province. Hoping simultaneously to support the foreign revolution and recover the lost Ukrainian land, in mid-April 1919 Antonov-Ovseenko planned an offensive via Bessarabia toward Hungary.[65] He did so despite the constant pressure from Vatsetis to release reinforcements for the Southern Front against Denikin, but Antonov-Ovseenko's own powers were limited by resistance from below. His attempt to mobilize Hryhoriïv in support of the Romanian campaign caused the ataman to turn against the Reds in a battle that lasted almost two weeks and diverted the Red Army from its other missions.[66]

Meanwhile, on the Southern Front, the Reds enjoyed the support of another independent operator, the anarchist Nestor Makhno. At first lionized by the Bolsheviks, later denounced, Makhno created his own political domain under its own political banner, centered in his home village of Guliai-Pole (Huliaipole) in Ekaterinoslav Province. Displaying a real talent for partisan-style military leadership, Makhno impressed people with his personal magnetism, but also his quickness to anger, his unstable moods, and his mistrustfulness.[67] At its peak, Makhno's influence extended throughout Ekaterinoslav and upper Tauride provinces, embracing a population of almost 2.5 million.[68] He organized and led a successful peasant force, the Revolutionary Insurgent Army of Ukraine, which sometimes cooperated with the Bolsheviks, sometimes attacked them, while consistently opposing Petliura and the Whites.[69]

Makhno was a peasant with an elementary schooling, who as a young man worked briefly in a factory and by 1906, still in his teens, had participated in anarchist "expropriations," which is to say, robberies. Several arrests landed him in prison, where he was tutored in anarchist principles by inmates better educated than himself. Released from Butyrka Prison in Moscow in the post-February amnesty, he returned home. There he helped organize a peasant union, attracting the participation of some of the officers quartered there, as well as local schoolteachers "eager to take an active part in public life."[70] Still hostile to higher authority, even if it was new, he and his confederates allied with the local soviets and labor unions to resist the power of Provisional Government committees.

Anarchists in general thought of themselves as overturning the old police regime. As Makhno put it, "the February Revolution opened wide the doors of the Russian political prisons."[71] In Guliai-Pole the local anarchist group scoured the police records to discover who had been informing on them. The revolution against power did not abjure violence, however. Concerning the double agents whose identity they had found, Makhno said: "Theirs was the most horrible of crimes, treason. A true Revolution must exterminate them all. A free and united society has no need of traitors. They must all perish by their own hands or be killed by the revolutionary vanguard."[72] A familiar refrain.

As far as Makhno was concerned, the insurgent Bolsheviks seemed to be going in a welcome direction. In Petrograd, anarchist agitators had rallied the sailors and soldiers in support of the October coup; at home Makhno helped install Soviet power and dispossess the landowners.[73] As the new regime took hold, however, anarchists felt deceived. "To seize control of the Revolution," Makhno commented, the Bolsheviks and Left SRs "have made use of anti-governmental slogans that contradict their governmental ideas."[74] Peasants, he insisted, "viewed the new revolutionary socialist government as no different from any other government, which they noticed only when it robbed them through various taxes, drafted them into the army, or intervened in their difficult workers' lives by other acts of violence."[75] Makhno's goal was to organize a movement that would not replicate government institutions but would promote the self-activation of the laboring masses. Its goal was "on the one hand, to abolish, by revolutionary action, private property in land and make it the property of the nation; on the other hand, in concert with the urban proletariat, to abolish the possibility of new privileges and of the domination of one group over another."[76]

Harking back to the early post-February days, he imagined a system of democratic soviets, elected by the local population, not imposed from outside. This would constitute "the authentic soviet system"—without state power.[77] On home territory, Makhno presided in the village manner over a general assembly, in which the peasants were to settle the land question themselves—to determine how to divide the land they had already taken. His followers called him "*bat'ko*"—the traditional designation of an elder or leader. At the same time, he also took a leaf from the socialist handbook, convening his own soviet congresses in Guliai-Pole: one in February, another in April, drawing peasant deputies from a wide area. The congresses rejected "the dictatorship of any one party," demanded socialization of land and industry, substitution of exchange in kind for requisition, organization of cooperatives—in short, a counter-Bolshevik position, clearly influenced in its articulation by SR and anarchist activists.[78]

Despite the enlightened program, endorsed by "the peasants themselves," Makhno's troops behaved in the same rapacious manner as other guerrilla bands—though they had a reputation for being somewhat less ferocious. Makhno discouraged his men from preying on the villages, but of course even his army, which by mid-1919 numbered fifty thousand men—composed of peasants, like all the others—had to live off the land, which is to say off peasants like themselves.[79] Though rejecting the principle of authority or "power," his "insurrectionary army" functioned like a proper state institution. It drew for leadership on the experience of former imperial officers, printed its orders, kept accounts, issued salaries and official papers. At the same time, it was an army on wheels, dragging its machine guns on traditional peasant carts—the perfect hybrid of old and new.[80]

Makhno was indeed remarkably effective. The Skoropads'kyi regime, like all others, had relied on requisitions. The official grain-collecting brigades had been armed.[81] By October 1918, the authorities were complaining that Makhno, based in Guliai-Pole, was organizing armed peasant gangs to overthrow the hetman's regime.[82] Indeed, in concert with Left SRs and anarchists, Makhno had begun in June 1918 to rally the local peasants. Once Skoropads'kyi fell, he refused to cooperate with Petliura but offered his support to the Reds, dispatching ninety train cars to Moscow and Petrograd containing grain and coal confiscated from the Whites as battle trophies.[83]

Makhno was consistent in his opposition to the Whites; the two sides pulled no punches in the brutality they inflicted on each other.[84] Despite his commitment to the social revolution, his relationship with the Reds, by contrast, was unstable. He allied with them three times: at the end of 1918 after Skoropads'kyi's fall; in February 1919, when his brigade was incorporated into the Red Army; and again in October 1920.[85] While in the commissars' good graces, he was described as a folk hero. Thus, *Izvestiia*: "He organizes detachments, leads them into battle, throws his artillery from position to position, overcomes thousands of every possible daily obstacle and complication."[86] When he turned away, he was vilified, but was then taken back again.

---

The intermittent alliance with Makhno reflected the desperate straits in which the Red Army found itself in April 1919. Its forces were stretched to the limit, facing a Cossack rebellion in the Don and Denikin's offensive moving north. Antonov-Ovseenko sent Makhno reinforcements, but Red Army troops in the Ukraine were fighting in Bessarabia, Crimea, and Kiev, while also suppressing pogroms and rebellions in the interior.[87] Vatsetis and Trotsky wanted blood from a stone. "You exaggerate our strength," Antonov-Ovseenko objected. "We have been undermined by incessant fighting, we are badly supplied, the men long for home. Food, uniforms, and cartridge supplies are horrible. There are no cannon." Horses were hard to acquire, because peasants needed them in the fields and were reinforced in their resistance by "the growing influence of the nationalistic parties and the anarchists."[88]

Antonov-Ovseenko complained of too much bureaucracy, not enough equipment or qualified personnel, food collectors antagonizing the peasants, collectivization breeding hatred. He thought it better to work through the local soviets, include the other socialist parties, and stop draining Ukraine of its resources.[89] Lenin, however, focused on the military issue, on which the fate of the entire regime hung. "The Ukraine is obligated to acknowledge the Donets Basin unconditionally as the most important Ukrainian front," he admonished Antonov-Ovseenko. From Lenin's perspective, Rostov was more important than western Ukraine; his own authority must prevail. "I will punish independence," he warned. "Transfer the Ukrainian troops for the taking of Taganrog. The obligation is immediate, no matter what the situation."[90]

Torn in all directions, Antonov-Ovseenko needed Hryhoriïv all the more. The Bolsheviks knew the ataman was unreliable, and that his followers were responsible for attacks on the Jewish population, in particular. Some wanted him taken out ("liquidated"), but he was needed. Needed but insubordinate, ignoring orders, giving his men free rein to plunder, exporting their loot on trains out of Odessa, their carriages blocking the rails. His fifteen-thousand-man division, equipped with artillery and cavalry, fuel, and clothing seized in Odessa, was headquartered in his home village, Aleksandriia, directly north of Krivoi Rog, in the eastern crook of the

Dnepr River.[91] Despite the danger to his own person, Antonov-Ovseenko went there to seek him out. Hryhoriïv complained of Bolshevik policies, the Cheka, the Russian and Jewish commissars, of grain seizures. Antonov-Ovseenko urged him to join up with Makhno in the Donbas against Denikin, but Hryhoriïv equivocated. When Antonov-Ovseenko and a Ukrainian comrade addressed the villagers in person, their listeners seemed to applaud the Red Army, but at the mention of collective farms, they threatened to lynch the speaker.[92] Not only was the peasant mood unstable, but sending Hryhoriïv to join up with Makhno, even if he agreed, was risky. The two chieftains might drop their rivalry and combine against the Reds. Instead, Antonov-Ovseenko suggested Hryhoriïv go to Romania, and Hryhoriïv seemed to agree.[93] Some of his men repaired to the Elizavetgrad region for three weeks to recoup. Most, however, simply returned to their own villages.[94]

Making the rounds of the independent warriors on bended knee, Antonov-Ovseenko next visited Makhno's headquarters in Guliai-Pole. The Soviets had been trying to collect food in his area and had sent political commissars to accompany his troops, but Makhno had stopped the requisitioners and had the commissars arrested. Face to face with Antonov-Ovseenko, he agreed to release the prisoners, but demanded additional military supplies. Blinding himself to the subterfuge and dangers, on his way back Antonov-Ovseenko returned to see Hryhoriïv yet again. The ataman had not yet moved his men, who were running wild, attacking Communists and Jews, incited by Petliura, Left SRs, monarchists, and anti-Semites.[95]

Despite the growing crisis, as May Day was being celebrated on Odessa's public squares, Rakovskii, the Ukrainian party chief, insisted the campaign for Bessarabia proceed and pledged support for the Hungarian comrades.[96] After Denikin's army took the eastern Ukrainian city of Lugansk (Luhansk) on May 5, Lenin warned Antonov-Ovseenko and Rakovskii: "You will be responsible for the catastrophe if you delay serious assistance to the Donets Basin."[97] Lev Kamenev and Adolf Ioffe were sent from Moscow to mobilize workers and soldiers. But Antonov-Ovseenko continued to believe that Hryhoriïv, though delaying, was on their side, and set out once again to see him. He was stopped only by a message from Rakovskii warning him that the chieftain was in fact already in revolt.[98] On May 9, Hryhoriïv disseminated a "Universal to the Ukrainian People," demanding "All power to the soviets of the Ukrainian people without Communists!" and "Ukraine for Ukrainians!" Denouncing the dictatorship of the party, he demanded popularly elected soviets and a real people's government. After several Red Army units had joined him, his force grew to include as many as fifteen thousand men, plus weapons, machine guns, and ten armored trains—a peasant revolt with technology. Ekaterinoslav, Cherkassy, and Kremenchug along the Dnepr River, Nikolaev and Kherson in the south—all fell before them.[99]

Answering Hryhoriïv's challenge, Antonov-Ovseenko declared: "White Guard swine strive to destroy the strength of the Red Army, to incite it against the peaceful population and to throw its regiments against one another. The golden epaulettes [White officers] and the cut-throat Cossack riff-raff still tear at the workers in the Donets mines; they threaten the Ukraine and Russia with weapons obligingly slipped in by the French and English occupation. From the west the Polish pans [gentry] attack, the Romanian boyars plunder Bessarabia to prepare a campaign against the Ukraine. Representatives of the Directory instigate our brothers, the Galicians, against us."[100] Punchy language, classic Bolshevik epithets, but still Antonov-Ovseenko clung to his desperate illusion. On May 10, he contacted Hryhoriïv in his home village, trying to bully him into following orders. To his face, Hryhoriïv denounced "the Cheka and the dictatorship of the Communists" and declared "the government of the adventurist Rakovskii to be deposed." Antonov-Ovseenko was a man of honor, but the Bolsheviks in general were "political speculators, adventurists."[101] The delicate dance was over. A special force under Voroshilov's command recaptured the string of cities Hryhoriïv had taken barely two weeks before, including his base at Aleksandriia.[102]

Hryhoriïv's men had inflicted tremendous damage on the villages they traversed and their inhabitants and particularly on the Jews. The revolt also forced the Red Army to divert resources from the Southern Front in support of Makhno. After the defeat, some of the ataman's followers continued their depredations in the west, others dispersed back to their villages, arms in hand, anger still seething. "Decree and carry out the complete disarming of the population," Lenin ordered Rakovskii. "Mercilessly shoot on the spot anyone hiding a rifle."[103]

"The revolution has taken all it can get from improvised rebel detachments," Trotsky concluded. "Now these detachments have become not only dangerous, but fatal to the revolution." It was time, he said, "to apply the white-hot iron. . . . We must do away with the swashbucklers not just in words, but in action."[104] The challenge was not, however, merely to stop using peasant brigades as adjuncts to the Red Army, but to prevent these mobilized peasants from turning against the regime. Here the "white-hot iron" did not suffice; it was necessary to master the crisis that motivated peasant revolt to begin with. The Ukrainian Communists were incapable of organizing a functioning government. They were unable to extract the amount of grain needed to feed even their own army, let alone satisfy the demands coming from Moscow. Attempts to adjust and implement official policies were impeded by the absence of clear authority. Military and civilian leaders on the local level (Podvoiskii versus Rakovskii) got in each other's way; agents from Moscow (Kamenev, the Cheka) tried to impose their will but only tangled the lines of command. The only way to wrest any resources at all from the towns or villages was by force of arms.

In Odessa the desperate Bolsheviks announced a "Day of Peaceful Uprising," ordering citizens to surrender what the army lacked: underwear, boots, coats—officially sanctioned plunder to satisfy needs usually met by spontaneous looting. In this case, the supplies extracted from unwilling Odessa households tipped the balance, but the men went back and forth continually in both directions, between rebels and Reds. They were the same stock—peasants, weary foot soldiers, ready on both sides to savage a Jewish town, on both sides to denounce capitalists, speculators, and landowners. The Cheka was active everywhere, thus fanning the flames of resentment against the Reds.[105]

In April and May of 1919, Moscow was facing threats from three directions: Kolchak in the east; General Iudenich in the north, heading for Petrograd; and in the south a revolt of the Don Cossacks and Denikin's successful advance.[106] Lenin and Trotsky were determined to impose their will on the Ukrainian Communists, streamlining authority and setting the military agenda. Trotsky insisted on top-down authority in the military, Lenin on authority emanating from Moscow. The Ukrainian Communists dutifully acceded to Moscow's demand for consolidation of the administrative and military organs at the regional level. On the military side, this involved getting the ragtag forces of the Ukraine under control, abolishing the Ukrainian Front, focusing on the Donbas. Trotsky demanded the "radical and merciless liquidation of *partizanshchina*."[107] This meant not only Hryhoriïv, but also

Antonov-Ovseenko's willfulness and his accommodation with partisan confederates. Even Trotsky, however, still could not dispense with Makhno; he could not immediately dissolve the Ukrainian army.[108]

A battle of realisms. "It is necessary," Lenin wrote Antonov-Ovseenko in late May, imposing a three-day deadline, "to throw aside everything but the Donbas." Antonov-Ovseenko replied: "In full consciousness of my responsibility for the defense of Soviet Power in the Ukraine, I declare: 'I cannot execute your command. I will do all that I can do. Spurs are not necessary. Either trust me or dismiss me.'"[109] Voroshilov, sent from Moscow with special powers, established a new military council and demanded Antonov-Ovseenko's dismissal. Trotsky insisted Voroshilov concentrate on strengthening the existing Ukrainian army. Lenin backed Trotsky against Voroshilov, but the Central Committee in Moscow had already decided to remove Antonov-Ovseenko. On June 6, the Ukrainian Front was abolished and the former Ukrainian Army sent to the Southern Front.[110]

This move targeted both Makhno and Antonov-Ovseenko. During the spring, Makhno's Red Army brigade had achieved a number of victories and he was awarded the Order of the Red Banner. In May Antonov-Ovseenko described him as absolutely loyal, devoted to the cause, committed to crushing "the counterrevolutionary Cossack and officer classes." Makhno was no "bandit," Antonov-Ovseenko insisted; he "will not turn against us."[111] Antonov-Ovseenko's view was not shared at the top.[112] Trotsky denounced "the little-known state called Guliai-Pole, ruled by a certain Makhno and his staff. At first he had a partisan detachment, then a brigade, then, it seems, a division, and now all this has been gussied up as something resembling a special insurrectionary 'army.'" As self-proclaimed anarchists, Makhno and his followers were avowed "enemies of Soviet power." It was inconceivable "to permit on the territory of the Soviet republic the existence of armed bands, . . . which do not acknowledge the will of the working class, which seize whatever they want and fight with whomever they please."[113]

On June 8, Trotsky, following Lenin's lead, ended Makhno's connection to the Red Army.[114] The Donbas Extraordinary Military Revolutionary Tribunal accused Makhno of undermining Soviet power and opening the door to White penetration.[115] It was convenient to blame the failures of the Red Army on Makhno. His independence and his appropriation of the core Bolshevik message—soviet-style grassroots power, land to the toilers—made him appealing to the same population the Communists needed to secure for themselves. Makhno resigned his Red Army command but until the end of the year kept up the pressure against Denikin, impressing the Whites with the martial skills of his horsemen.[116]

Makhno was also responsible for removing the threat of insurgency coming from Hryhoriïv. After Makhno's dismissal, the two chiefs had at first joined forces, but their differences proved too great. On July 27, they arranged a meeting near Hryhoriïv's base. A crowd of twenty thousand villagers and armed rebels was present. There, in front of the fearsome throng, Makhno denounced Hryhoriïv's alliance with the White generals and demanded he compensate the victims of the anti-Jewish pogroms perpetrated by his men. "Such blackguards as Grigor'ev degrade all the rebels of the Ukraine, and for them there can be no place in the ranks of the honorable workers of the revolution," Makhno declared. A witness reported that Hryhoriïv then reached for his gun, but Makhno's sidekick "drove him to the ground with several bullets from his Colt, and Makhno, triumphantly proclaiming, 'Death to the Ataman!' shot him dead." It took another "two or three minutes before the eyes of the assembly" for Makhno's men to execute the rest of his rival's entourage.[117] With Hryhoriïv gone, Makhno's Insurgent Army regrouped. Those of his soldiers who had joined the Red Army deserted back to his command, which now numbered fifteen thousand fighters and another fifteen thousand in support. Resisting attempts by the Red Army to bring him back under its wing, Makhno pursued his own campaign against Denikin's rear. His army swelled to 100,000 men, most of them veterans of the Great War and thus experienced fighters, who mobilized behind the classic peasant slogan—"land, liberty, and freedom!"[118]

In the summer of 1919, the military threat to Soviet power seemed very real. Denikin's White forces were proceeding rapidly, west into Ukraine and northward toward Moscow.[119] In Ukraine, the Whites encountered not only Makhno and the Soviet Red Army, but the Ukrainian Galician Army attached to the Western Ukrainian National Republic—not an enemy, but a rival. Occupied since November 1918 fighting against the Poles in Eastern Galicia, in July 1919 the defeated Galicians crossed into Russia. At the end of August, the Ukrainian Galician Army and the Volunteer Army entered Kiev one after the other, ending the Red Army's seven-month tenure. For a single day, both the Imperial Russian flag and the flag of the Ukrainian Republic flew over Kiev, before Denikin forced the Galicians to leave. He then proceeded to restore private property in land, ban the Ukrainian language, and arrest Ukrainian intellectuals.[120]

On the Communist side, the military crisis destroyed whatever vestiges of the Ukrainian administration had remained, and the Ukrainian party was dissolved.[121] At the same time, the incursion of the White forces exposed the divisions within the Ukrainian nationalist leadership. While in November the Galician Army accepted Denikin's command, the Directory rejected the Whites, and in December, under Petliura's leadership, relinquished any claim on Galicia and came to terms with the Poles.[122] By then, however, Denikin's seemingly invincible campaign had ground to a halt and the Red Army had rallied, thanks in part to Makhno's unsolicited support.[123] On December 16, 1919, the Red Army took Kiev for the third time since the beginning of 1918. Having subordinated the Ukrainian party to central command, Moscow now granted formal independence to a Soviet Ukraine within the framework of a Russian federation.[124]

---

In 1920 the game changed yet again. Intensified requisitioning inspired continuous attacks on collection brigades. Red Army intelligence tracked the guerrilla activities of small units of Makhno's Insurgent Army throughout the Ekaterinoslav, Kharkov, and Donets regions in the spring and summer.[125] Makhno had a propaganda office, which described the situation as it appeared in May of that year. "All the dark forces of the former servants of Bloody Nicholas have united and with the help of the Polish Pans, French instructors, and the traitor Petliura are heading for Ukraine, to impose on us autocracy, implant landowners, capitalists, zemstvo officials, policemen, and other executioners of peasants and workers." The "Communist-Bolshevik commissars," with their "punitive squads and Chekas are superb at killing peasants and workers, burning villages and towns. But against the true enemies of the revolution, against Denikin and other bands they flee shamefully, like pitiful cowards."[126]

Indeed, in the first week of May, Polish and Ukrainian forces captured Kiev. At the same time, Dzerzhinskii was sent to Kharkov to wipe out the so-called bandits and propagandize against Makhno. By mid-June, the Reds had retaken Kiev, conquering the city for the fourth and final time in the course of two and a half years. The Communists could at this point afford to do without Makhno, but then in the fall, when they faced their last credible White threat, they took Makhno on board again. Makhno's men followed orders and fought well but were weakened from battle and typhus. The Reds vowed to destroy him. Ordering him to the Polish front, knowing he would refuse, they accused him of insubordination.[127] Almost a year later, still in the process of subduing Makhno's movement, a Ukrainian Communist described the methods used in compelling the peasants to betray the rebels still hidden among them. Selecting at random a handful of substantial or "suspicious" characters, the soldiers would slice them to pieces with their sabers before the eyes of the assembled villagers, who would then hasten to produce the alleged culprits. This method "made an impression."[128]

In August 1921, Makhno and a handful of men were finally driven into Romania. From there he made it to Poland, and after various difficulties and arrests he arrived in Paris in 1925, where he wrote his memoirs and died in poverty of tuberculosis in 1934.[129]

# 6

# War Against the Cossacks

At the start of 1919, the Red Army was in disarray; by the end of the year, the Whites were fleeing. General Denikin reached the high point of his push toward Moscow when the Volunteer Army took Orel, two hundred miles south of the capital, on October 13, 1919, where the campaign stalled. In November, General Iudenich was defeated in the north. In Siberia, as we know, Admiral Kolchak renounced his claim to supreme leadership on January 4, 1920, and was executed a month later. On April 4, 1920, Denikin was succeeded at the head of the Volunteer Army by Baron Petr Wrangel, a scion of the German and Swedish Baltic nobility. The last of the White commanders, Wrangel continued the effort for another six months. On November 2, he retreated to the Crimea; two weeks later, he boarded ship to Constantinople with the remainder of his troops and as many civilian refugees as managed to escape along with him. The challenge to Bolshevik power from the old regime military establishment had been defeated.

In some respects, Red victory reflected certain obvious advantages. The Soviets controlled the geographic center and what was left of the imperial administration; they had a unified mission and a leader of overwhelming authority, equipped with a powerful ideology accessible at every level of the social hierarchy, from sophisticated intellectuals to the last ragged foot soldier. The Whites had a defensive, not an inspirational message; their leadership was fragmented geographically, ideologically, and personally; their forces were scattered around the peripheries. Yet the outcome was far from inevitable, and the Bolsheviks felt themselves vulnerable until the very end.

Although in 1919 the Reds were fighting "on all points of the compass," the focus was on the south.[1] As we have seen, Moscow continuously pressured Vladimir Antonov-Ovseenko in the Ukraine to send troops to the Southern Front. By mid-February, the Red Army had moved a quarter of its men and resources to the Southern Army Group. Ranged against it were three White armies—Denikin's Volunteer Army, Petr Krasnov's Don Army, and Wrangel's Caucasus Volunteer Army—which at the start of the year had combined to form the Armed Forces of South Russia, under Denikin's command, headquartered in Ekaterinodar in the deep Kuban. Krasnov and Denikin had never been able to cooperate. Once the armies joined forces, Krasnov was replaced at the head of a much weakened Don Army by a more accommodating commander.[2]

In January and February 1919, the Armed Forces of South Russia easily swept the Reds out of the North Caucasus, taking fifty thousand prisoners. The commander of the North Caucasus Red Army, Grigorii "Sergo" Ordzhonikidze, wired Lenin that his army had "ceased to exist.... The enemy occupies cities and *stanitsas* almost without resistance.... There are no shells or bullets." Those Red Army men who escaped walked across the desert to the port city of Astrakhan on the Caspian Sea, some dying along the way, from typhus, storms, cold and hunger; after leaving Stavropol, some headed south through the mountains into Georgia.[3]

The Red defeat gave the Whites an important advantage. With the Caucasus Mountains at their back, Denikin could safely head north, on the quest to put the Empire back together again.[4] "A swollen army, really a horde rather than an army," Trotsky remarked, "has clashed with Denikin's properly-organized troops and in a few weeks has been reduced to dust. For the illusion of *partizanstvo* we have once more paid a high price."[5] To counter desertion and insubordination, in late 1918 Red Army Commander in Chief Ioakim Vatsetis had demanded the application of Red Terror in the army, "not only against outright traitors and saboteurs but also against cowards, scoundrels, and their accomplices and concealers." As we have seen, the Bolsheviks had from the start considered the struggle against the class enemy as a form of warfare, authorized and executed by the state, against the domestic population. But in the military itself not all problems could be solved by terror. In the south, the Red Army was far from home base, suffering from a weak supply system and chronic desertion, reliant on relatively young and inexperienced officers and on former tsarist commanders of doubtful loyalty.[6]

By contrast, the Whites were supplied out of the port of Taganrog; they had overall a more professional officer corps and the use of battle-hardened Cossack cavalry. Though troop reinforcements were not forthcoming, the British supplied ammunition and equipment, clothing and boots.[7] Whether the supplies served their purpose is not clear. Of the beds and medical equipment destined for a hospital in Ekaterinodar, British journalist John Ernest Hodgson reported, nothing ever got there. "Beds, blankets, sheets, mattresses, and pillows disappeared as if by magic. They found their way to the houses of staff officers and members of the Kuban Government." Nurses' uniforms were similarly rerouted. "I did not, during the whole of my service with the Army in Russia," Hodgson later recalled, "ever see a nurse in a British uniform; but I have seen girls, who were emphatically not nurses, walking the streets of Novorossisk wearing regulation British hospital skirts and stockings."[8]

Misappropriated or not, British aid continued until the end of the year, bolstering the Whites' military advantage. Red Army troops in the south greatly outnumbered Denikin's forces, yet in the first months of 1919 the Whites conquered one city after another.[9] All attempts by the Red Army between March and May to regain control of the Donbas and the Upper Don ended in failure. By the end of June, they had lost Tsaritsyn, which they had captured in fall 1918, Kharkov, and Ekaterinoslav.[10] Buoyed by success, on July 3, 1919, Denikin issued a secret order, the so-called Moscow Directive, outlining his plan for conquest of the Soviet core. His leading generals were each to follow a railway line and converge on the capital— Wrangel up the Volga, Vladimir Sidorin north along the Don, Vladimir Mai-Maevskii from Kharkov to Moscow. This was an ambitious plan, intended to recruit a peasant army along the way, threaten the regime's geographic hub, and establish a popular base for the counterrevolution.[11] It seemed to be working. Wrangel, after taking Tsaritsyn, moved up along the Volga, chasing the Reds before him. By early August, he was approaching Saratov, 250 miles further up the river.[12]

The Red Army had no choice but to focus on the southern threat. On July 3, Vatsetis had been replaced as commander in chief by Colonel Sergei Kamenev, a former tsarist officer who had welcomed both February and October and soon rose in the Red Army.[13] The appointment of Kamenev and his chief of staff, General Pavel Lebedev, reflected the shift in summer 1919 to greater reliance on old regime holdovers, though accompanied by lingering distrust.[14] But the "military specialists," as they were dubbed, were needed. Trotsky insisted that the use of partisan outfits, with headstrong commanders resistant to central authority, was a recipe for defeat; the army must impose discipline and unitary top-down command.[15]

On July 9, Lenin demanded "All Out for the Fight Against Denikin." The Soviet Republic "must be a single armed camp."[16] Instead of focusing on the

Donbas, with its denser railroad network and a factory work force that would presumably have welcomed the Reds, Kamenev proposed moving into the Kuban, striking at Denikin's heartland, through uncertain Cossack terrain. Trotsky disliked the plan and attempted to resign as commissar of war, but the offer was rejected.[17] Meanwhile, the Whites, under the command of General Mai-Maevskii, gained control of the Donbas.[18] In the Upper Don, the Red Army was hampered behind the lines by Cossack revolts in the very area which had earlier deserted Krasnov and allowed the Reds to enter. The conduct of Soviet officials had since then turned the Cossacks against them. In the course of August, in central Ukraine, the Whites took Poltava, Kherson, Nikolaev, Odessa, and Kiev.[19]

The most spectacular moment in the northward White sweep was the raid executed in August by Lieutenant General Konstantin Mamontov's IV Don Cavalry Corps.[20] His seven to eight thousand fierce Cossacks covered five hundred miles in forty days of pillage and destruction, on a path that included Tambov and reached Voronezh, three hundred miles south of Moscow, in mid-September.[21] Mamontov used the familiar slogan as his rallying cry: "Arm yourself and rise against the common enemy of our Russian land, against the Jewish Bolshevik Communists!"[22] Trotsky denounced his fighters as "mounted bandits," "wild dogs," who "get drunk, rape women, beat up old men." They were not soldiers but degenerates who must be "tracked down like beasts of prey" and annihilated. As usual, though, the enemy also lurked within. Communists must be on guard, Trotsky warned, against anyone giving aid, directly or indirectly, to the bandits. "Cowards, self-seekers, deserters must be punished on the home front as they are in battle—by shooting."[23]

After Voronezh, however, Mamontov's men had taken their loot and gone home.[24] The remnants of the IV Don Corps were destroyed in November. Mamontov died of typhus in Ekaterinodar in February 1920, but he had taught the Red Army a lesson. His men behaved like criminals, but he was a skillful partisan leader and the style of warfare was effective. In Ukraine the Bolshevik leadership had rejected "primitive, inexperienced partisan methods." The regular army had not yet formed, and the independent bands were out of control. At the start of the year, Trotsky had again denounced "the partisan scourge," but now he insisted the Red Army needed a new kind of partisan—disciplined outfits subordinate to the main command but capable of supplementing the regular army with targeted actions behind the lines.[25]

Mamontov raised the issue not only of partisan warfare but of cavalry. And here, too, Trotsky changed course. In mid-September, he issued the incongruous command, "Proletarians, to horse!" "The most conservative type of weapon, almost on the point of extinction," he explained, "has suddenly returned to life and become a most important means of defense and offense in the hands of the conservative and declining classes. We must tear this weapon from their hands and make it our own. The workers' revolution must create a mighty Red Cavalry."[26] By the end of the year the Red Cavalry (*Konarmiia*), under Semen Budennyi's command, counted fifteen thousand horsemen.[27] They were neither proletarians nor even mostly Cossacks, but peasants.

Partisan methods might be needed in extremis, but the Red Army continued to develop in the direction demanded by Lenin and Trotsky, toward greater professionalism and discipline. New men were trained as "Red Commanders," noncommissioned officers were promoted, and party members were recruited into the army, where they helped educate the troops. The Cheka paid special attention to monitoring the conduct and attitudes in the ranks. The army still suffered from lack of equipment, high rates of desertion, illness, and draft dodging, in addition to battle casualties. The campaign against deserters intensified in mid-1919, leading to the return of 1.4 million men in the second half of the year. Technology was still primitive. The Red Army relied mainly on horse-drawn carts to transport machine guns; armored cars were useless on the terrible roads; armored trains fared better, when the tracks were still in place.[28]

Despite these changes, in early fall of 1919, the Soviet regime was still embattled. Denikin resumed his northward offensive in mid-September, following the railroad from Kharkov through Kursk and Orel toward Tula, site of the Red armaments factories, headed for the capital. A week after Kursk fell on September 20, martial law was declared in Moscow.[29] On October 13 Denikin took Orel. General Iudenich's Northwest Army was meanwhile nearing Petrograd. The tide turned quickly, however. By the end of October, as we have seen, Iudenich had been driven back. By then, also, the Latvian Rifle Division had helped the Red Army retake Orel, and Budennyi's Red Cavalry had recaptured Voronezh. It was the turn of the White armies to retreat, this time on a long trek southward. In early January 1920, they crossed the Don.[30]

In August 1919, Trotsky had dismissed Denikin's Moscow Offensive as an audacious gesture born of despair.[31] Wrangel later called the plan "the death sentence of the South Russian armies." "Striving for space," he concluded, "we endlessly stretched ourselves into a spider's web, and wanting to hold on to

RUSSIA IN FLAMES

everything and to be everywhere strong we were everywhere weak." Denikin defended the strategy. "We lengthened the front by hundreds of versts and became from this not weaker, but stronger."[32] At their farthest reach, the White armies had occupied 350,000 square miles with a population of forty-two million, but they were never in any one place for long. The only area they held for more than five months was the North Caucasus and part of the Don, with a population of a mere nine million. The Soviets, by contrast, dominated a population of sixty million on a vastly broader terrain, fielding a vastly bigger army, which, despite its many weaknesses, continued to gain in strength.[33]

Once his fortunes changed, Denikin's forces crumbled. In December 1919 Denikin shifted Wrangel from the Caucasus Army to the Volunteer Army, but Wrangel, then ill with typhus, quarreled with the Volunteer command and was replaced at the start of the new year. The Whites lost Kiev on December 16, Tsaritsyn on January 2, 1920. The Volunteer and Don Armies were tired of fighting. The Red Army took Novocherkassk and Rostov on January 7, and crossed the Don ten days later. Denikin now, belatedly, offered concessions to the Cossacks—the greatest being their own army under the Cossack general Andrei Shkuro—but the White commanders kept quarreling, and the old distrust between former tsarist officers and the Cossack "separatists" endured.[34] The Kuban Cossacks had their own leader and were unwilling to attach themselves to the broader Russian crusade. They were reluctant even to follow their own local but fragmented leadership.[35]

In a last gasp, the Armed Forces of Southern Russia took Rostov yet again on February 20, but it was a futile move. The best of the White cavalry, under General Aleksandr Pavlov, were destroyed by a fierce snowstorm, in which many of the men and horses froze to death.[36] Abandoning Ekaterinodar in mid-March, the White army began a final retreat, this time ignominious, Cossacks and refugees heading toward the sea. At Novorossiisk, on the Black Sea coast directly east of Crimea, the remaining British stores were thrown into the water; Cossacks shot their horses; civilians crammed into the few British ships waiting to take them away. The cavalry that reached Crimea arrived without their mounts. The Kuban Army, which had rejected Denikin, headed for the mountains, but the Georgians would not let them cross over, and some sixty thousand surrendered in April.[37]

The indignity and disorder of the evacuation were echoed in the tensions between the White leaders, who fell out among themselves. In January Wrangel plotted to unseat Denikin, in February Denikin dismissed Wrangel, and in March Denikin's chief of staff was assassinated, probably by another officer. On March 3, now in Crimea, Denikin resigned and Wrangel replaced him. A month later, Denikin left for Constantinople on a British destroyer.[38] The broad southern front had been reduced to the nub of the Crimea, where the final act would play itself out.

After Constantinople, Denikin made his way first to England, then Belgium, spending a few years in Hungary before settling in Paris in 1926. In 1940, after the German occupation, he made his way to the south of France, where he lived undisturbed for the duration of the war. He left for the United States in 1945 and died of a heart attack while visiting Ann Arbor, Michigan, in August 1947. His remains were reburied in Donskoi Monastery in Moscow in 2005, when Patriarch Aleksei II hailed him as a champion of a united Great Russia.[39]

It was one thing for the Reds to assert military superiority over forces organized from outside, which had used the Don and Kuban as staging grounds for their larger imperial ambitions. It was another thing to get a foothold among the population of this turbulent region. As they did everywhere else, the commissars struggled to impose their authority by means both of propaganda and repression: ideological saturation, plus systematically applied reprisals. The point was always to simplify the political landscape, to eliminate rivals on the left, discipline their popular followers, intimidate groups with a vested interest in opposing Bolshevik rule, and dramatize the high costs of noncooperation.

The Cossacks as a people persisted, however, in their complexity. Those who had abandoned General Kaledin in early 1918 later also resisted the Reds. In the region itself, the Bolshevik leaders of the Don Party Bureau and the Southern Front Revolutionary Military Council approached the Cossacks with caution. They had adopted a policy of targeted reprisals against men who had fought with Krasnov and local leaders (priests, atamans) who actively promoted the White cause. They rejected the generalized assault on anyone once connected to Krasnov's army as sure to alienate the broad population. They recognized that many Cossacks had been recruited into the White army, or even joined up for various reasons, without ideological conviction.[40] Of course, it was this very instability, captured in Mikhail Sholokhov's *Quiet Flows the Don* (1928–1932), where Cossacks figure as the collective protagonists, that aroused suspicion.

On January 24, 1919, the Moscow party leadership announced a new, more aggressive approach. Referring to the "Cossack people" (*kazachestvo*) as a whole, the directive informed local officials "that the only correct approach is the merciless fight against all the Cossack elites by means of their complete annihilation. No compromises, no halfway measures can be accepted."[41] The circular called for "mass terror against wealthy Cossacks, exterminating every last one," as well as "merciless mass terror against Cossacks of any kind who have participated directly or indirectly in the fight against Soviet power." A category described as "middle Cossacks" was to be treated preemptively, in such a way as to discourage opposition.[42] The policy was known as "de-Cossackization" (*razkazachivanie*), a concept earlier used in the context of abolishing the estate hierarchy and status privileges. Cossacks stood to forfeit both the burden of military obligation and their favorable access to land. In some areas of the Don, war-weary Cossack veterans preferred to give up their advantages, but most viewed the abolition of estate categories as a threat to their collective existence.[43]

In January 1919, the term acquired a more ominous meaning. The purpose now was literally to decapitate Cossack society and intimidate everyone else. In applying the new decree, the Southern Front Revolutionary Military Council nevertheless continued to favor the execution of ringleaders over the slaughter of ill-defined "Cossack elites." The policy, however construed, was implemented by extraordinary tribunals mounted in the occupied *stanitsas*. Despite the relative moderation of the Don-based commissars and local party leaders, Moscow pressured the tribunals for results. Their energetic decisions, over the course of a mere six weeks, resulted in the deaths of as many as ten thousand Cossacks in the Don territory, where groups of men were systematically rounded up and shot after perfunctory hearings.[44] The military leadership of the Southern Front defined the categories to be executed, on the basis of thoroughgoing sweeps of the Cossack settlements. These included anyone holding any kind of public position; all Krasnov officers, in particular, and anyone associated with Krasnov, in general; figures associated with the old regime; and "all rich Cossacks without exception." Property belonging to the victims was to be confiscated and redistributed.[45] Many Cossack fighters who avoided execution were confined to prisons in conditions that encouraged epidemics.[46]

The application of the January 24 circular has been called a Cossack genocide.[47] The death toll was extreme, the purpose murderous, but the goal of wiping out the entire Cossack population "to the very last one," was never explicitly stated and never achieved. The language of the circular targeted "elites," though it was vague enough to give license to indiscriminate slaughter. If not literally genocidal, the policy was designed to tear apart the fabric of Cossack society and destroy its economic life. The Cossacks were both a fighting force and a community, but they were not now confronted on the battlefield; they were murdered in their homes. The January 24 circular made for excellent White propaganda, and its implementation naturally increased the hostility of the Cossack population as a whole, confirming the presumption that they were endemically hostile to the revolution. A case of terror substantiating its own fears.

Since the party apparatus had barely penetrated the Don, repression was implemented by outsiders with little understanding of the people they were sent to subdue.[48] Their cultural distance no doubt made it easier to accomplish their ruthless task. Indeed, party leaders were explicit about the danger of trying to win over "the counterrevolution" by persuasion rather than crushing it by force. People from the inside were more likely to be soft; what was needed were "experienced, enterprising, energetic, and decisive Communists," the Don Party Bureau advised, if possible from Moscow and Petrograd.[49] The purpose of the campaign was clear both to those in Moscow who defined it and to those who put it into effect. It was not a matter of local comrades going overboard or getting out of hand. The January 24 circular was signed by Iakov Sverdlov, chair of the All-Russian Executive Committee, with the support of Lenin and Trotsky. Inside the Don Party Bureau, some questioned its wisdom, but the enthusiasts, local chair Sergei Syrtsov and Aron Frenkel', were the ones who carried it out.[50]

---

Nevertheless, the Cossacks had to be conquered from within; they could not simply be wiped out. The case of Colonel Filipp Mironov, a talented military commander and charismatic popular leader, illustrates the pathos and contradictions inherent not only in the struggle to secure the loyalty of the Cossack population but also in the wider conflict between the broad peasantry and the emerging institutions of the Soviet state. The story is amply documented in material gathered by the Cheka, which built a case against him in the end.

Mironov was a decorated Cossack officer from the *stanitsa* of Ust-Medveditsa (today the Russian city of Serafimovich), on the Don River northwest of Tsaritsyn. In 1906 he was dismissed from the army after protesting the use of Cossack troops to suppress domestic unrest.[51] In 1917, by then a mature forty-five, he did not immediately welcome the October coup. "I admit," he later reflected, "I was not sympathetic." He set himself to studying the Social Democratic program, he recounted, in order to "take a position that would assure the victory of the popular cause and without too many victims." Returning to his hometown, he took up "civic political activity."[52]

Wary of the Bolsheviks at the start, he was at the same time hostile to their opponents. In December 1917, he addressed a letter to Kaledin's Don Host Government, in which he cited John Stuart Mill on behalf of freedom of speech (citing also the far-from-liberal Slavophile philosopher Konstantin Aksakov) and condemning the imposition of martial law in the Don Republic. He ended with a stirring appeal (which he hoped to publish in local newspapers): "To the Constituent Assembly! To the federative democratic republic! To the truly free liberated Don! ... To free speech, light and truth! ... The Don is not for the adventures of landlords, capitalists, and generals, but for free Cossack citizens! To the laboring Russian people!"[53]

Mironov's understanding of socialism as a liberating creed sometimes jarred with Bolshevik methods. He joined the Ust-Medveditsa Soviet Executive Committee, but then withdrew. Signing himself "Citizen Mironov," he explained his reasons. Arresting the prosecutors and judges of the local courts, he objected, "cannot strengthen the idea of Bolshevism, and I serve only ideas, not persons. The tsarist government perished because it committed atrocities such as no government should permit."[54] Despite these criticisms, Mironov nevertheless affirmed his commitment. "I arrived at the idea of Bolshevism by cautious steps and over many years, but having arrived I will renounce my convictions only at the price of my head."[55] Ideas, not leaders; principles, not policies.

In January 1918, Mironov addressed a passionate appeal to the "Citizen Cossacks of the Ust-Medveditsa district," in which he described socialism as the search for "justice, reason, and freedom." The various socialist parties approached this goal from different angles, he explained; the Bolsheviks were the most resolute, the most determined not to delay or defer.[56] Mironov's understanding of politics obviously derived from the leaflets, proclamations, and newspapers issued by all the parties. He did his own reading as well, but he was no intellectual. His beliefs reflected the extent to which socialism as a culture, as a worldview or value system, had penetrated well beyond the educated elites. His own language has a certain freshness, an engaging naiveté, and indeed naiveté—or excessive cunning—was to be his undoing.

Above all, Mironov was an accomplished military commander. In January 1918, he led a Cossack division from the Romanian front back to the Don, but then refused to fight against the Reds. In the summer, Mironov led a Cossack force on behalf of the recently constituted Don Soviet Republic, preventing Krasnov's Don Army from moving up the Volga. By September his brigade had become a division. In January 1919, Trotsky, as commissar of war, greeted the "heroic warriors" of Mironov's "meritorious division," adding: "All Russia expects great things from you."[57]

Despite his heroism, or perhaps because of it, Mironov was distrusted. Stalin reported to Lenin from Tsaritsyn in early August 1918, complaining of the unreliability of Mironov's forces. The Cossack troops kept moving back and forth, making it impossible to gauge their loyalty. "Entire regiments have gone over to Mironov in order to obtain weapons, to gather information about our forces, and then entice entire regiments back over to Krasnov's side."[58] There is no evidence that such devious strategies were afoot, but Stalin was right about one thing. Mironov toed nobody's line. The local party bosses understood that as well. They considered him unsuited to serve on the Don Executive Committee. "He may be a good military commander," they noted in January 1919, about the same time that Trotsky was praising his battlefield prowess, "but in political terms he is an unknown quantity."[59]

Commenting on Stalin's remark, two distinguished Russian historians, Viktor Danilov and Nonna Tarkhova, writing soon after the fall of the Soviet Union, describe the Bolsheviks as having an "oversimplified understanding of the events of the Civil War, displaying extreme one-sidedness and inflexibility of judgment and evaluation, which deepened social antagonisms, inflamed political passions, and led to ever more victims."[60] Indeed, that was the Bolshevik method—to deepen social divisions, inflame passions, and brandish the sword of terror over everyone's head. Mironov believed these methods were damaging the revolution. He wired Trotsky in early January 1919. "It would be desirable in implementing the decrees of the central authorities in the Don region to pay special attention to the cultural and economic peculiarities of the Don population." Operatives unfamiliar with the region and its customs only antagonized the local population, causing "nothing but harm to the revolution."[61]

Unlike other popular leaders, who encouraged or ignored the spontaneous aggression of their men as a way of retaining their loyalty, Mironov called for austerity and self-control. He warned his troops not to be "inadvertent allies" of the "brigand" Krasnov by abusing the local people and turning them against the revolution, instead of drawing them in. "There is no place for brigands in the Red Army!" he thundered. "In the name of the revolution," he warned against drunkenness, as a breach of discipline, and forbade "the use of violence agains persons, because you are fighting for the rights of individuals, and to be a worthy fighter you must learn to respect the individual person in general."[62] In the same spirit, Mironov resisted the application of the instructions of January 24, 1919, calling for "mass terror" against any Cossack fighters known to have joined the Whites at any time. He preferred to allow those who surrendered to return home with their horses and equipment. "I do not think the ignorance of benighted Cossacks will be considered a crime," he said. "These people deserve to be pitied, not despoiled; indeed, revenge is a two-sided sword and never achieves its goal. The laboring people do not need it."[63]

Mironov thus confronted the party with a natural leader whose message competed with the official line, endorsing discipline, morality, justice, and the bright future. In late February, Trotsky had him transferred to Serpukhov, in central Russia, six hundred miles north of his home base, in order to "look him over."[64] In early March, Mironov was denounced in absentia to the chair of the Don Party Bureau as a demagogue and anti-Semite who agitated against Communist power, having allegedly described the Communists as "robbers, deserters, and cowards" while presenting himself as the champion of the downtrodden.[65] His listeners had apparently taken his message to heart. When later interrogated, peasants who had attended a local meeting reported that "Old Man Mironov told them that for now they were fighting against Krasnov on behalf of the Bolsheviks, but later would fight against the Communists."[66] Indeed, Mironov made no secret of his objection to Soviet methods in the Don. In a message addressed to the Red Army command, Mironov offered his advice. "Time and skillful political workers will destroy the ignorance and fanaticism instilled in the Cossacks by the barracks schooling of the old police regime, which has penetrated the Cossack organism." Communism should be introduced "by means of lectures, conversations, brochures, and so on."[67] Violence would not work.

Mironov here was advocating for wise application of Soviet power, not opposing the Soviet regime, but the Cossacks who took the brunt of its murderous methods drew the obvious conclusions. Rebellion was first reported in Kazanskaia *stanitsa* on March 13, 1919. The rebels seized weapons and ammunition and murdered the local commissar, a certain Kupfervasser, clearly one of the unwelcome outsiders.[68] They issued an announcement, which included the election of a new soviet; the recognition of all kinds of paper money (Kaledin's, Krasnov's, Russian)—in itself a declaration of political instability; and general mobilization, except for certain categories. "Soviet troops that surrender without resistance," the rebels promised, "will be disarmed and allowed to return home. Those that resist will be disarmed by force, arrested, and sent to Veshenskaia *stanitsa*, but without the use of violence or shooting."[69]

The rebels made the by now common distinction between the Soviet regime, standing for the revolution, and the Communist Party, which represented the reality of Soviet rule. "Our rebellion has been launched not against the power of the Soviets and Soviet Russia, but only against the Party of Communists, which has seized power in our homeland." Harsh requisitioning, jeopardizing their very existence, had bred discontent, but finally "the illegal, inappropriate arrests and executions of innocent *peaceful inhabitants*," and other intrusions, had "overfilled the cup of our patience and the population has arisen and overturned Communist power." The rebels had gotten their hands on official documents, including the January decree ordering mass shootings of the Cossack population "by settlers from Russia," as they put it. "We submit to Soviet power, but this power must be elected from among our own population, it must understand our needs and customs, it must be the true expression of the will of the People." Denouncing the collective farms and the mass executions, they concluded, "Long live the Power of the People!"[70]

On March 16, the Military Council of the Southern Front called for "merciless repression," demanding the same energetic measures that had provoked the rebellion to begin with. Instructions to local officials were precise. They were "to torch all rebellious villages; shoot anyone, without exception, taking direct or indirect part in the uprising; in each rebellious village gather five or ten adult males for execution; take mass hostages from neighboring villages; warn that all villages showing support for the rebels will be subject to the merciless annihilation of the entire adult male population and be burned to the ground at the first sign of assistance to the rebels."[71] The list of categories to be repressed was now even longer and more detailed than before.[72]

At the same time, the party began to reconsider. On March 16, the day that Sverdlov, author of the January decree, died in Moscow, probably of influenza, the party's Central Committee heard a report from Grigorii Sokol'nikov, on behalf of the Don Party Bureau, arguing against the anti-Cossack campaign. Lenin, Stalin, Dzerzhinskii, and Trotsky were among

those present. Perhaps because Sverdlov was now dead, the Bolshevik leaders decided to "suspend the application of measures against the Cossack
people." They hoped to win the support of the Upper Don Cossacks, whom
they considered potential allies, against the agitated region of Veshenskaia in
the south.[73]

On March 25, the hard-line Syrtsov instructed the local Bolsheviks to
change course. The Veshenskaia rebels were of course still to be appre-
hended and punished with all possible "ruthlessness," but "indiscriminate
repression must not be applied to *stanitsas* that have not revolted." In other
words, a switch to targeted, not wholesale terror. "Economic measures,
particularly requisitions, should be applied carefully and with discrimination," so as not to provoke further resistance.[74] The message was repeated
in April, to repress the insurrection, but "in relation to peaceful districts do
not resort to mass terror, persecute only active counterrevolutionaries."
Requisitioning and taxation should be applied carefully and in reasonable
proportions.[75]

These decrees obviously acknowledged and described the abuses, which
were clearly still going on a month after the first warning. In what later
became a typical Stalinist move, local officials who had obeyed the January
decree were now punished for implementing its demands. Thus in April, the
head of the revolutionary committee in the village of Morozovskaia was
arrested and tried by a military tribunal for the execution of sixty-four
Cossacks whose corpses had later been found in a barn. The confused commissar had received conflicting instructions—from local officials who considered him too extreme, and from his military superiors who urged him to do
more. He was executed finally for what had since been defined as a crime.[76]
Indeed, the official attitude remained unclear. The Central Committee had
not revoked, but merely halted, the process of de-Cossackization, and pressure on the mutinous southern sector was never intended to stop. On April
22, Moscow reiterated the point. In relation to the "counterrevolutionary
southern Cossacks" terror was to continue; peasants were to be settled among
them, to dilute their presence, and mobilized against them.[77]

In March, just as the trouble was beginning, Mironov had submitted his
report recommending a political, not military, approach to the Cossacks.
Red Army commander in chief Vatsetis had read and approved it. The
southern military authorities, however, did not want Mironov back in the
Don, and he was dispatched to the Belarus-Lithuanian Front. As the Don
and the Volunteer Armies continued their advances, however, Mironov was

ordered to return to the Southern Front and in mid-June was appointed to head a Special Corps of Don Cossacks. In July, he had the chance to present his March report directly to Lenin in Moscow, but his views were opposed by persistent advocates of the former harsh methods. The Special Corps was scuttled.[78]

In July and August, the city of Saransk, three hundred miles southeast of Moscow, between Saratov and Kazan, became the site of meetings at which Cossacks gathered to voice their opposition to the continuing anti-Cossack pressures. Here Mironov learned more about what had been happening in his absence. Writing to Lenin, he condemned "the destruction of everything owned by the laboring peasant, which he has earned through bloody toil, in order on this foundation to begin a new life, full of new dangers and good so far only in theory."[79] He was no friend of Denikin, Kolchak, Petliura, or Hryhoriïv, he said, "but I regard with the same revulsion the violence of the false Communists, which they inflict on the laboring people, and therefore I cannot be on their side."[80]

It is unlikely that Lenin or anyone else ever read Mironov's letter, but it reflected views congenial to Cossacks and peasants suffering under the new order but with no desire to return to the old. In August, Mironov composed the program for a "Worker-Peasant Party," calling for popularly elected soviets and freedom of speech and assembly for all socialist parties. He demanded the abolition of the Sovnarkom and the Cheka, an end to grain requisitions, but also to private property in land. The land must belong on a common basis to the tillers, who were to be gradually schooled in the development of agricultural methods.[81] An "appeal to the long-suffering Russian people," issued in Saransk, announced the formation of a Don Revolutionary Corps under the command of "Citizen Mironov." Deserters were welcome to rally under the red banner for the fight against Denikin and against the Communists. "Land to the peasants, factories to the workers, power to the laboring people as represented by authentic Soviets of worker, peasant, and Cossack deputies elected on the basis of free socialist campaigning. Down with the autocracy of the commissars and the bureaucratism of the Communists, who have doomed the revolution."[82]

In response to this appeal, Trotsky spewed the usual boilerplate invective: "As a turncoat and traitor, Mironov is declared outside the law. Every honest citizen who encounters Mironov has the duty to shoot him like a mad dog. Death to the traitor!"[83] Trotsky admitted that mistakes had been made. "When the Red Army moved into the Don it is clear that in certain places

individual Soviet agents and the worst Red Army units were guilty of injus-
tices and even brutality toward the local Cossack population."These excesses,
he insisted, had been a response to the Cossacks' own support for the White
forces.Yet a true Bolshevik should have put these abuses in perspective, not
used them as an excuse to advance his own personal career.[84]

It is unclear whether Mironov was a power-hungry careerist or the White
Knight of the People's Cause. At the mass meeting of August 22, 1919, in
Saransk that launched his rebellion, he characterized "Citizens Lenin and
Bronshtein-Trotsky" as extremists, ready to spill the blood of the people.
A political commissar reported that his speech was replete with "Black
Hundreds pogrom appeals."[85] Indeed, Mironov had not avoided the question of the Jews, a flashpoint for all anti-Bolshevik propaganda. In June,
while still on the Western Front, Mironov had called for strict discipline and
explicitly denounced pogroms: "Is it possible," he had appealed to his men,
"that the soldiers of the Red Army, bearers and guardians of the ideas of
equality and brotherhood, should commit anti-Jewish pogroms!?" The
answer is "no, no, a thousand times no!!"[86] Now, in August, on home ground,
according to the commissar's report, Mironov had said he regretted his
"proclamations against pogroms.We must destroy the power of the Jews, not
only in the regions, but in the center, where they have implanted the
Bronshteins, Nakhamkises, and other scoundrels." (Iurii Steklov, a member
of the Bolshevik Central Committee, had been born in Odessa as Ovshii
Nakhamkis.) Calling for war against the Communists, he ordered that any
Communists who tried to leave the city be shot on the spot.[87]

Shooting on the spot was, of course, a Bolshevik remedy against which
Mironov had protested, though it was not exclusive to them. On the question of the Jews, it may be that party informants were trying to blacken
Mironov's name, but the identification of the reviled Communists with the
already hated Jews was ubiquitous among resentful peasants and Red Army
men.[88] It was not merely a staple of White propaganda. Mironov indeed
personified the uncertainty of Cossack support for the revolution and the
dangers of heeding the "voice of the people." On September 16, 1919,
Trotsky announced that Mironov had been arrested without resistance,
along with his followers, whom Trotsky characterized as deluded.[89] He was
charged with armed rebellion against Soviet power.[90] The prosecutor was
the Latvian Ivar Smigla, at this point head of the political department of the
Red Army. Mironov, for his part, claimed always to have supported Soviet
power.[91]

The verdict announced on October 7, 1919, listed among Mironov's other offenses the "fomenting of ethnic antagonisms," having denounced the current government as "Yid-Communist." He and nine others were sentenced to be shot.[92] Smigla appealed for clemency. He did not think it was "useful" to kill Mironov or his confederates.[93] Nikolai Rybakov, assigned to be Mironov's defender at the trial, was more explicit. He sent his protest to Mikhail Kalinin, who had succeeded Sverdlov as president of the All-Russian Central Executive Committee. The condemned, said Rybakov, "had for two years fought like lions on the front lines of the Don, had been wounded, had received the highest Red decorations...The names of the convicted are known to everyone on the Don. Their execution will reflect badly on Soviet authorities in the eyes of the Don Cossacks. For political reasons it is desirable to reduce the sentence."[94] Moscow assented.[95] Rybakov was then arrested for publishing his appeal in the local newspaper, but was later released.

The "mad dog" Mironov was in Trotsky's clutches, but instead of being shot he was pardoned and restored to service in the Red Army.[96] In the wake of the rebellion, the Politburo, the party's highest decision-making body, yet again reconsidered its policy toward the Cossacks. "We are giving the Don, the Kuban full autonomy," Trotsky wired Smigla, "our armies are cleaning up the Don. The Cossacks have entirely broken with Denikin. We must establish appropriate guarantees. Mironov and his comrades can serve as intermediaries, whom we can send deep into the Don."[97]

From prison, Mironov called on his followers to make peace with Soviet power. He claimed that the Communists had mended their ways, that Trotsky was "introducing strict control over political workers and purging the Communist Party of unworthy, provocateur, and counterrevolutionary elements."[98] Clearly an astute operator—or else compelled to follow a script—Mironov informed Trotsky that he had been "born again," dedicated to "our common cause—the destruction of the power of capital, the power of the bourgeoisie," and asked for Trotsky's "complete confidence."[99] The party accorded Mironov full amnesty and drafted him into the Don Executive Committee.[100] Trotsky restored his command.[101] Drawing certain lessons from the Mironov case, the Don Committee warned political instructors that "in the fight between the two camps—Red and White, there is no room for a third—yellow or green. Either Lenin, or Denikin.... The Civil War mercilessly destroys everything intermediate, it punishes those who sit between two stools."[102] Mironov took command of the Second Red

Cavalry fighting against Wrangel, but his loyalty remained suspect.[103] He was arrested for a second time on February 13, 1921, on charges of conspiring to organize an insurrection against the Soviet regime.[104] The documents do not tell us if the charges had any foundation. In this period, Moscow was busy liquidating all vestiges of popular opposition, just as it was changing political course and softening the harsh policies of the Civil War. On April 2, 1921, by then almost sixty, Mironov was condemned to death and shot by the Cheka in Moscow.[105] His reputation was formally restored in November 1960.

# 7

# Miracle on the Vistula

Marsz, marsz, Warszawo! "Warszawianka" (1879)
Марш, марш вперед, Рабочий народ! "Varshavianka" (1897)
Forward march, O, Warsaw! O, laboring folk!

Poland was, in one respect, the crucial example in geopolitical terms of the pressure exerted along the borders of the old Empire by rising political elites to break away from Russian domination. The Polish case belongs to the wave of national movements affecting the entire western periphery, from Finland to the Black Sea, which began in the wake of February 1917 and in which the fates of the emerging nations clashed and intertwined. Poland was more, however, than a matter of internal concern to contenders for Russian political leadership. The Polish case also represented, in dramatic terms, the degree to which the Russian Revolution was never merely a domestic affair. The Allies realized that whatever the color of its flag and the details of its borders, Russia as an international presence was not going away and that Germany, despite its defeat, would always be a major player on the European stage. The control of Poland, standing between Germany and Russia, was a key element in maintaining the European balance of power. From the perspective of Soviet Moscow, Poland was the pathway to the spread of world revolution.

Polish leaders, for their part, wanted to close this gate by establishing firm boundaries to a new, sovereign Poland. The same seven years (1914–1921) in which the Russian state wavered, collapsed, and reemerged under new auspices were the years in which the leaders of the divided Poland of the former Polish-Lithuanian Commonwealth struggled to redefine the nation in modern terms as the Second Polish Republic. By 1914 two currents dominated Polish politics: the National Democracy (*Narodowa Demokracja*), which began as the Polish or National League, established by Roman Dmowski; and the Polish Socialist Party (*Polska Partia Socjalistyczna*—PPS), under the leadership of Józef Piłsudski. The Polish-Lithuanian Social Democratic Party, by contrast, was devoted to revolution across borders, not to the Polish national cause. Its members included Rosa Luxemburg and also Feliks Dzerzhinskii, who went on to head the Bolshevik Cheka.

During the war, Dmowski cultivated ties to the Entente, establishing a national committee in London.[1] He conceived of the future Poland as a unified state, whose eastern boundaries would include the westernmost frontier strip of the former Russian Empire with its predominantly Polish-speaking population, but not the ethnically mixed territory further east, which was claimed as part of a future Ukraine by self-designated Ukrainian leaders. To the west, the Polish state would extend, at Germany's expense, to include Poznań and Upper Silesia. Piłsudski, by contrast, envisioned Poland's future as a modern version of the historic Commonwealth, with the lands of the former Grand Duchy of Lithuania incorporated in a federal union with the Polish nation-state. This larger framework would include the diverse eastern borderlands. Piłsudski thus mobilized the concept of self-determination on behalf of a grandiose vision of a Polish sphere of influence covering all of Central Europe between the Adriatic, Baltic, and Black Seas. Though it seemed to offer the friendly hand of federation to the in-between states, Piłsudski's scheme impinged more directly on Russian and Ukrainian territorial claims than Dmowski's more aggressively nationalist but geographically more restricted version.[2]

Differing in their vision of the future, the two Polish leaders also played distinctive roles. At the Paris Peace Conference in late January 1919, Dmowski fashioned himself the diplomat, though his territorial demands and his anti-Semitic remarks were not well received in some quarters. While certain members of the British Foreign Office shared his belief that the Jews exerted a powerful—and harmful—force on world politics, others found his views distasteful.[3] When Britain blocked the extension of Polish borders in the west, Dmowski blamed "the colossal increase of the Jewish influence."[4] He denounced President Wilson as "an instrument of the Jews" and Lloyd George as an "agent of the Jews."[5] The population of Warsaw in 1921, it should be remembered, was one-third Jewish.[6]

Piłsudski in Warsaw left most of the talking to his rival. He was, by contrast, a military man and a man of action. As early as the Russo-Japanese War, he had conceived of organizing extraterritorial Polish Legions and had traveled to Japan to explore the possibility of Japanese support. The first Polish riflemen's associations were eventually formed in 1912 in Austrian Galicia, where they enjoyed official toleration. When war broke out in 1914, Piłsudski created a clandestine military committee (*Polska Organizacja Wojskowa*) and led his sharpshooters across the Russian border. "The decisive hour has come! Poland is no longer a prisoner and wants to decide her own fate, to build her own future."[7] The Legionnaires were not welcomed by the local Poles, however, and the Austrians insisted they submit to Austrian authority.[8]

During the Great War, as we have seen, the Central Powers and Russia competed for the allegiance of the largely Polish-speaking population that lay between them. Grand Duke Nikolai Nikolaevich's lordly gesture of August 1914, promising postwar autonomy did not, of course, contemplate separation.[9] By 1915, however, the Imperial Army had abandoned its share of Polish territory. On November 5, 1916, then in control of the former Polish lands, the Central Powers announced the establishment of "an independent State with a hereditary monarchy and a constitutional government," whose "exact frontiers…will be outlined later."[10] The occupation regime, called the Polish Regency Council, included all but the Prussian sector. In December 1916, the tsar promised support for "a free Poland composed of all three now divided parts," but his words were vague and his days were numbered.[11]

The year 1917 contained a series of landmarks in the evolution of Poland's future. First out of the starting gate was Woodrow Wilson, with his January 22, 1917, "Peace Without Victory" address to the United States Senate, which affirmed the principle of government by consent of the governed. As an example of every people's entitlement "to determine its own polity, its own way of development," Wilson singled out the right of Poland to be "united, independent, and autonomous."[12] It has been suggested that Wilson's attention to Poland reflected the influence of the Polish pianist and future prime minister of the Republic of Poland, Ignacy Jan Paderewski, who in January 1917 was in New York giving concerts and spoke with Wilson's adviser, Colonel Edward M. House. Both Dmowski and Piłsudski, moreover, had established committees in the United States which were lobbying Washington for the Polish cause.[13] Given the timing, however, Wilson was more likely responding to the creation in December 1916 of the German-controlled Regency Council.[14] The case of Poland was in any event a powerful rhetorical choice; it was, indeed, an international issue.

After February 1917, with regard to Poland the Provisional Government continued the monarchy's tradition of vague pronouncements. On the one hand, as republicans, they affirmed the principle of "government by consent of the governed," while on the other they defended the territorial claims of the imperial state they had displaced—a circle it was difficult to square. Kerensky quickly pledged support for Polish independence. Eager to neutralize German influence on the Poles, the British urged him to do more. In late March, a Liquidation Commission for the Kingdom of Poland (*Komisja Likwidacyjna do spraw Królestwa Polskiego*) was created, under the direction of Polish civic activist Aleksander Lednicki. A staunch Kadet, Lednicki had represented Minsk in the First State Duma and signed the Vyborg Manifesto in 1906. During the war he organized relief for Polish prisoners of war in Russia and in 1916 was appointed to head the German-installed Regency Council. He was disappointed when Minister of Foreign Affairs Pavel Miliukov deferred resolution of the Polish question to the ultimate decision of the future all-Russian Constituent Assembly.[15] This was a disappointment Lednicki shared with Dmowski, whose politics he did not otherwise approve. "In this great historical moment," Dmowski complained, "Russia has treated the Polish problem exclusively as her own domestic affair, by which she has proved her total incapacity to meet the requirements of the moment."[16]

In contrast to the Provisional Government, the Petrograd Soviet was unburdened by the conduct of diplomacy and did not hesitate to declare that "Poland has a right to complete independence in national and international affairs." Anticipating a postwar world of fraternal powers, the Soviet expressed the wish that independent Poland establish "a democratic, republican order."[17] Not to be outdone in the duel of pious sentiments, the Provisional Government then recognized "the full right of the fraternal Polish people to decide their own fate . . . by their own free will," still subject, however, to the disposition of the Constituent Assembly. How Polish demands were to be reconciled with those of the Lithuanians and Belarussians was not clear. Despite the urgency of the Polish question, the Russian political establishment (with or without the tsar) was still dedicated to the integrity of Russia's imperial borders.[18]

For the Bolsheviks, by contrast, the international dimension was an advantage. In 1913 Lenin had attacked the Kadets (in his habitual insulting tone) for their reactionary "chauvinism," while he invoked the right of ethnic minorities to form their own separate nations.[19] National movements ("bourgeois," in his terms) were useful not in their own right, but as a stage in the progression from supranational empires to supranational socialism.[20] Affirmed by Wilson in January 1917 (without using the precise term), the right to self-determination was reiterated at the Seventh Bolshevik Party Congress in May 1917.[21] The Decree on Peace, issued immediately after the coup, denounced "annexations" and proclaimed the right of any nation (*natsiia* or *narodnost'*—thus in both the political and ethnic senses) to free itself from domination and determine its own form of government.[22] The Bolsheviks lost nothing by rejecting annexations. Those in question at that moment consisted of German-occupied territories formerly under Russian rule, including Poland. At the Third Congress of Soviets, January 10–18, 1918, Stalin, as commissar of nationalities, said, with reference to the Ukraine (then also under German occupation), that Soviet Russia was ready to recognize the desire for national independence only as an expression of the will of the "working masses," not of "the bourgeoisie."[23] This transparent formulation was a signal that Moscow would acknowledge only the decision of a Soviet-style government loyal to itself.

Poland emerged again as a flashpoint during the negotiations at Brest-Litovsk. In his Fourteen Points of January 8, 1918, Wilson called for the creation of an "independent Polish state" encompassing "the territories inhabited by indisputably Polish populations." As in his "Peace Without Victory" speech the year before, the President's attention to Poland was strategic, not sentimental. Wilson and the American business establishment were eager to prevent Germany from emerging as the dominant economic power in Russia. American engineers had assisted the Provisional Government with management of the Trans-Siberian Railroad, not entirely from selfless motives. They were interested in keeping Russia in the war and positioning America to take advantage of opportunities opened up with Russia's democratic transformation.[24] In January 1918, the Central Powers occupied most of the western half of European Russia, between them controlling the entire expanse of historic Poland. A strong Poland as bulwark against German penetration was surely uppermost in Wilson's mind.

The results of Brest-Litovsk, which consolidated the German presence in the East, only intensified this concern. As we know, the Ukrainians inserted themselves in the negotiations and signed a separate treaty with the Central Powers. By contrast, Germany did not allow the Polish Regency to participate in the talks. Though Lednicki dealt with Georgii Chicherin, commissar of foreign affairs, on refugee matters, neither the Soviets nor the Polish parties recognized the Regency. Two Polish Social Democrats were part of the Russian delegation at Brest; as "internationalists" they insisted that Poland's future lay with Russia, which made a show of endorsing Polish independence.[25]

The rhetoric of self-determination, proletarian style, as in Stalin's formulation, carried them beyond the armistice. On November 13, 1918, Soviet Russia repudiated the Treaty of Brest-Litovsk and declared: "The working masses of Russia, Livonia, Poland, Lithuania, the Ukraine, Finland, the Crimea, and the Caucasus, freed by the German revolution from the yoke of an annexationist treaty, dictated by the German militarists, are now called upon to decide their own fate."[26] In the hands of "the working masses," as Trotsky put it, the border states would "no longer be a wedge but a connecting link between Soviet Russia and the future Soviet Germany and Austria-Hungary. Here is the beginning of a federation, of a European Communist federation."[27] The installation of Soviet-run governments, Lenin explained, would enable the Red Army to arrive as liberators.[28]

That is not, of course, how the local inhabitants saw them. Poland prepared to defend itself against the threat of invasion. Like the Red Army, the Polish Army was constructed of disparate parts, in this case reflecting the trans-border dispersion of the Polish-speaking population. In 1917 there were 600,000 Poles in Russian uniform. In June 1917, General Józef Dowbór-Muśnicki formed the First Polish Army Corps, which was stationed in Belarus; the Second and Third Corps were based in Polish-inhabited areas of Ukraine.[29] After October, Dowbór-Muśnicki refused to cooperate with the Bolsheviks and eventually capitulated to the Germans. Piłsudski's Legions, under the Polish Military Organization, unsuccessfully appealed to the Bolsheviks for permission to form a Polish army inside Russia. The Whites were not an option for Piłsudski, since General Alekseev did not, of course, countenance Polish independence. In addition to the three Polish army corps and Piłsudski's brigades, yet another army formed in France in 1918, under General Józef Haller, formerly a captain in the Austrian army, which fought against the Ukrainians as well as against the Bolsheviks. Poles also fought against the Red Army in Siberia.[30]

In July 1917, the Central Powers had demanded that Piłsudski subordinate his Legions to German command. Many officers refused and were interned; men from the lower ranks were forcibly drafted into the German and Austrian armies or into the Regency's so-called Polish Army (*Polnische Wehrmacht—Polska Siła Zbrojna*). The Legions as such were disbanded.

Piłsudski was confined to house arrest at the Magdeburg Fortress, where he remained until the end of the war. On November 7, 1918, as the outcome became clear, the PPS proclaimed the birth of the People's Republic of Poland (*Ludowa Republika Polska*), based in Lublin, which demanded an end to the Regency Council.[31] On November 8, Piłsudski arrived in Berlin. The following day, Kaiser Wilhelm abdicated, and the new German government under Friedrich Ebert put the Polish leader on a special train to Warsaw, echoing the German-sponsored homecoming of another state-builder, in April 1917.[32]

Piłsudski arrived in Warsaw on November 10; the next day, the Regency Council transferred its powers to him and the Lublin government retired—after a mere four days of existence. On November 14, 1918, Piłsudski became head of state.[33] Like Lenin, Piłsudski was a master of the fait accompli. On November 16, he informed "the belligerent and neutral governments and nations of the existence of the Independent Polish State, embracing all the territories of united Poland."[34]

Meanwhile, Soviet Russia lent its fraternal support to the creation of soviet republics in Lithuania and Belarus, as obstacles in the path of Poland's eastward progress. At the end of February 1919, against the inclination of their own, artificially implanted Bolshevik leaders, the two were amalgamated into the Lithuanian-Belarussian (Litbel) Soviet Socialist Republic (*Litovsko-Belorusskaia SSR*), which itself lasted only until July.[35] Moscow prepared native Communist cadres to run the allegedly independent states, thus using the cover of "self-determination" and "world revolution" to extend and solidify the Soviet regime's political grasp.

In terms of the Versailles Peace Conference, both Poland's borders and the status of Soviet Russia, which was not represented in Paris, remained undecided. Russia, as Herbert Hoover put it, "was the Banquo's ghost sitting at every Council table."[36] The Allies were divided. Lloyd George and Wilson inclined to accept the Bolsheviks as the de facto government. Britain wanted trade, and Wilson thought Russia would mend itself under favorable conditions. The French, by contrast, were aggressively anti-Bolshevik and supported the presence in Paris of a "Conférence Politique Russe" consisting of figures associated with the defunct Provisional Government, hostile not only to the Soviet regime but to the nationalist ambitions of parts of the former Empire.[37] All, however, including Wilson, despite his populist-democratic rhetoric, felt the need to hasten and produce a peace that would avert the spread of revolution, Bolshevism in particular, across Europe.

Concluding a quick peace with Germany would strengthen Ebert's government against the challenge of more radical forces. If they could not defeat Soviet power, they must cordon Russia off and support the states emerging around it. They were nevertheless reluctant to endorse the dismemberment of what had been imperial Russian terrain.[38] The issue of Poland thus presented a dilemma. In February 1919, the Supreme Council created a Commission on Polish Affairs, which in April endorsed as Poland's eastern border the prewar line between the Kingdom of Poland and the Russian provinces, thus favoring Russian over Polish interests, though no formal decision was taken.[39] The Commission also drew up a plan for the so-called Polish Corridor linking Poland by a narrow strip to the Baltic Sea. The port of Danzig (Gdańsk) was designated a free city.[40]

Piłsudski had not waited for the disunited Allies to decide what to do. When the Germans withdrew from core Polish territory, the Polish government feared the Soviets might move into the breach. On December 19, 1918, Warsaw warned Moscow that it would defend "the integrity of the territories inhabited by the Polish nation," including Belarus and Lithuania.[41] On January 1, 1919, the day the Soviet Republic of Belarussia was instituted, Soviet troops and Polish cavalry clashed near Vilnius. On January 5, Polish forces withdrew and the Red Army of the Lithuanian Soviet Republic seized control of the city.[42] The Bolsheviks realized, however, that this army was a shambles and that any further progress into Poland would be perceived by Polish workers not as a brotherly gesture but as a hostile invasion and would arouse patriotic resistance. On February 13, therefore, the Soviet troops instead moved west across the Niemen River toward East Prussia, but were trounced by volunteer German troops on the other side. Plans for an ambitious advance were scuttled.[43]

The Germans, still occupying the border area, permitted Polish forces to move east, where they engaged Red Army troops on February 17, just north of Brest-Litovsk. The Red Army put on a poor show, and several regiments composed of Polish conscripts mutinied. On March 5, the Poles took Pinsk.[44] While these operations were in play, diplomatic exchanges continued between Warsaw and Moscow, concerning the question of recognition for Soviet Russia and the new Soviet republics, which unsurprisingly produced no results. On April 21, the Poles captured Vilnius, which they considered to be Polish Wilno, Piłsudski's hometown.[45] In 1916 the population of Russian Vilna, then under German occupation, had been about 140,000: over half Poles, about two-fifths Jews, 2 percent Lithuanians, and the rest

Russians and Belarussians. By 1923 the city had grown to almost 170,000, about two-thirds Poles, another third Jews.[46] Vilnius, ancient capital of the Grand Duchy of Lithuania, was demographically a Polish (Wilno)—and a Jewish (Vilne)—city.[47]

The Polish conquests made the Allies uneasy. British Prime Minister Lloyd George, criticized Poland's moves against the Lithuanian and Belarussian Soviet Republics as blatant attempts to aggrandize its eastern borders. The French, by contrast, backed the Polish cause.[48] In early February, Joseph Noulens went to Poland as head of an Inter-Allied Mission. Noulens had been French ambassador to Russia in 1917; after October he had championed intervention as a counterweight not only to Bolshevism but also to German influence. Now he insisted the Allies send someone to head the Polish Army, so that it "would not be employed in a way contrary to the intention of the Entente."[49]

It was the Soviet occupation of Vilnius on January 5, 1919, where they remained until late April, when the Poles displaced them, that gave Piłsudski the opportunity to strike back and gain control of territories that for over a century had fallen within Russian state borders. In 1918 the Bolsheviks had annulled the legal basis of the eighteenth-century partitions, thus seeming to renounce any claims.[50] Both sides, however, had self-aggrandizing intentions, which each considered restitution. Poland was indeed asserting its independence, but it was also securing territorial claims. After Vilnius, the Polish armies continued east. In July 1919, they achieved victory in Eastern Galicia, where, as we have seen, they had been fighting the local Ukrainians since November 1918.[51] They then proceeded to gain control of most of Belarus and most of Ukrainian Volhynia. In August, they took Minsk, and in September they approached the city of Daugavpils (Russian Dvinsk) in southern Latvia.[52]

The terrain the Polish forces traversed was not, of course, uniformly Polish in ethnic terms. The invaders received the warmest welcome north of the Niemen, but south of the river the largely Orthodox peasant population was either pro-Russian or pro-Bolshevik, the Poles representing—not merely in Bolshevik propaganda—the return of the Polish landlords (the "pans").[53] "It fills me with despair," Lloyd George commented, with suitable Great Power hauteur, "the way in which I have seen small nations, before they have hardly leaped into the light of freedom, beginning to oppress other races than their own."[54] Poland and Ukraine soon reached an accommodation, however. Piłsudski all along rejected an alliance with the

Whites, resisting Allied pressure to support Denikin. When Denikin took
Kiev at the end of August, Petliura turned to the Poles, with whom he concluded an armistice on September 1, 1919.[55] On December 2, he and
Piłsudski pledged to cooperate and signed a document in which Ukraine
ceded Eastern Galicia to Poland, despite the objections of the Galician representatives present.[56]

   The resolution of these borders was not simply an internal affair, however. Without deciding where they stood on the question of hostilities
between Russia and Poland, on December 8, 1919, the Supreme Council in
Versailles finally proposed an eastern boundary for Poland. It was known as
the Curzon Line, after Lord George Nathaniel Curzon, the British foreign
secretary. The line ran from Grodno in the north through Brest-Litovsk and
down the Bug River to the former Austro-Russian frontier, excluding
Piłsudski's territorial aspirations. The fate of Polish Lwów/Ukrainian Lviv
in Eastern Galicia was left undecided.[57]

———————

As the new year of 1920 dawned, it seemed as though the post-imperial
map of the western borderlands was finally stabilizing. The Sovnarkom
assured the Polish government that it respected "the independence and sovereignty of the Polish Republic," yet again accusing the imperialist Entente
of driving Poland "into a groundless, senseless, and criminal war with Soviet
Russia."[58] In January and February, Russia concluded peace with Estonia
and Latvia; Lithuania was negotiating.[59] Soviet recognition guaranteed the
Baltic states against Polish appeals and White Russian claims.[60] By late
February it seemed, also, that the Allied Supreme Council had managed to
define a position with respect to the border states, offering military support
against Russia only if the Red Army crossed what it called "legitimate frontiers." One of these frontiers could well be the Curzon Line.[61]

   As Warsaw and Moscow went back and forth, ostensibly discussing the
possible terms of a peace accord, Piłsudski pursued the military option.[62] In
early March, Polish troops advanced to a position that interrupted the railway connection between Soviet armies. Chicherin accused Poland of starting an offensive war against Soviet Russia and the "independent Ukrainian
Republic." The Russian and Ukrainian allies were therefore obliged to defend
themselves, he said, while "denying any aggressive intentions toward Poland"
and insisting peace was in the interests of both sides.[63] The Red Army failed,

however, to resist Piłsudski's moves. Talks continued fruitlessly through March and April. Russia proposed peace and prepared for war, concentrating troops on its western front.[64] Poland imposed demands certain to be rejected—the 1772 borders of the Polish-Lithuanian Commonwealth. Moscow, while harping on peace, called Poland an "instrument of the Entente," easily pushed into war.[65] While Chicherin, as commissar of foreign affairs, favored a truce, Lenin and Trotsky pressed for war. Trotsky called for a "focused strike" against Polish forces in Ukraine. The destruction of "White Guard Poland" was necessary, he explained, in order to make "the revolutionary destruction of the Polish bourgeoisie politically and psychologically inevitable."[66]

Confident that Poland could easily get the better of the Red Army, Piłsudski proposed conditions for further discussion that Moscow was sure to reject.[67] In lobbying the Western powers, Polish diplomats accused Russia of provoking war. A Soviet note of April 23, 1920, insisted, to the contrary, that Russia wanted peace. Nevertheless, Chicherin huffed, "Soviet Russia is not a defeated country to which the victor can dictate its will."[68] The Poles believed—correctly—that Russia, despite the righteous palaver, was preparing for war.[69] Yet the Russian terms at this point, had Poland taken them at their word, would have given Poland Belarus and a good swath of Ukraine.[70]

Between Russia and Poland (still undefined in the east) stood not only Belarus and Lithuania but Ukraine, still aspiring to independence. On Ukraine, Polish leaders were divided. Dmowski mistrusted the Ukrainians and did not want to antagonize Russia; the socialists supported Ukrainian independence but not war; Ukrainians in Eastern Galicia opposed Polish domination; Piłsudski wanted to ally with Petliura to secure a privileged position for Poland in Ukraine. In 1919 Kiev had been occupied three times—on February 6 by the Red Army, on August 31 by Denikin, and on December 16 by the Red Army again. Now, on April 21, 1920, Piłsudski and Petliura agreed that Ukraine would get Kiev, while Poland would get Lwów in Eastern Galicia.[71]

Four days later, combined Ukrainian and Polish forces crossed into Ukraine west of Zhytomyr, on a direct course for Kiev. Victory was uncertain—the Poles, no less than the Russians, could be seen as foreign invaders; Ukrainian peasants distrusted them and complained of looting by Polish soldiers.[72] In Warsaw, Dmowski criticized the alliance and rejected Piłsudski's claim that "the reduction of Russia to her historical frontiers" (meaning pre-partition), with the corresponding Polish expansion, was necessary to Poland's existence. After all the diplomatic back-and-forth and rhetorical swordplay, on May 7, Piłsudski and Petliura entered Kiev. Returning to Warsaw in triumph on May 18, Piłsudski was confident Russia would fold.[73]

On the contrary. Polish aggression provided a welcome assist to Soviet mobilization. Lenin and Trotsky objected when the Red Army leadership stressed the assault as an affront to national honor, but *Pravda* allowed the class-war rhetoric to acquire patriotic overtones.[74] Indeed, it was the foreign threat—the (socialist) homeland in danger—that prompted General Aleksei Brusilov, the hero of the 1916 summer offensive, to volunteer to head a special military council and urge fellow officers to join.[75] Brusilov accepted Polish independence as the righting of a historical wrong, but he condemned the Polish offensive as an incursion on "lands that from time immemorial had belonged to the Orthodox Russian people."[76] As Trotsky later observed, "The capture of Kiev by the Poles...did us a great service; it awakened the country."[77] British parliamentary opposition leader Lord Herbert Asquith concurred. "Wantonly undertaken, and connived at by the tacit acquiescence of Europe," the Polish invasion, he noted, had managed "to unite Russia, and to fuse into one body that which has proved a most powerful and effective military force including men of the old as well as the new regime."[78]

Russia was cocky. Soviet leaders considered Poland, like Estonia, a negligible quantity.[79] Cartoonist Boris Efimov prepared a poster captioned, "Red Heroes have taken Warsaw!"[80] Soviet Russia had done everything to keep the peace, Trotsky insisted, "but there is no bourgeoisie in the world greedier, more degenerate, arrogant, thoughtless, and criminal than the gentry-bourgeoisie"—that oxymoron—"of Poland," which now "demands Russian land as far as Smolensk."[81] Soviet victory, by defeating the class enemy, would clear the way for "Polish peasants and workers" to decide their own future.[82]

The Soviet counteroffensive began on April 29, 1920, when Commander in Chief Sergei Kamenev put twenty-seven-year-old Mikhail Tukhachevskii in command of the Western Front.[83] A former lieutenant from an impoverished gentry family of Polish origin on his father's side and a peasant mother, Tukhachevskii was born near Smolensk but raised in Penza. After an elite military education, he had served in the Semenovskii Guards Regiment and was wounded and decorated in the Great War. Captured by the Germans in 1915, he succeeded in his fifth attempt at escape and returned to Russia in the early autumn of 1917. After October, he immediately joined the Red Army and in spring 1918 the party. Ambitious, talented, an ardent patriot, he had embraced the Bolsheviks as fearless exponents of Russian power. As a commander on various fronts, he had been key to victories over Admiral Kolchak and General Denikin.[84] If Kamenev, and by extension Tukhachevskii, enjoyed Trotsky's patronage, the Southwest Front fell under the patronage of Joseph Stalin, whose rivalry with Trotsky was already well advanced. Cheka chief Feliks Dzerzhinskii, ominously, was in charge of the rear.[85] The commander of the Southwest Front was former colonel Aleksandr Egorov. Ten years older than Tukhachevskii, of peasant origin, Egorov had been wounded more than once during the Great War and risen to lead a regiment. In 1917 he initially favored the Left SRs, but then went over to the Bolsheviks.[86]

The Southwest Front included Semen Budennyi's First Cavalry Army, which Stalin had taken under his wing.[87] Budennyi had served as a noncommissioned cavalry officer during both the Russo-Japanese War and the Great War. In 1917 he had joined a regimental committee, in November he fought in the Donbas, and in July 1918 he met Stalin. Whereas Tukhachevskii was his own man—ambitious, arrogant, gifted—Budennyi was Stalin's creature.[88] If Tukhachevskii was the aristocrat, Budennyi was the Russian primitive. General Weygand described him as a reincarnation of "the Tatar chiefs whose hordes once conquered southern Russia."[89] Budennyi was in fact neither Tatar nor even Cossack, but a peasant from the Don. Indeed, barely a fifth of Budennyi's men in 1920 were Cossacks; two-thirds were peasants like him. The First Cavalry Army constituted its own universe, composed of former partisan units, some from single villages, which selected their own commanders, lived off booty, and dragged their families along behind them in a ponderous cortege. Most of the soldiers were barely literate, and some could not read at all; all resented outsiders, in particular their own political commissars, many of whom were Jews.[90] This was the position occupied by Isaac Babel, who described his experience in the stories constituting *The Red Cavalry* (*Konarmiia*, 1926). The army was held together by intense group loyalty and fierce devotion to Budennyi. Budennyi, in turn, was bolstered by the patronage of Stalin and his Tsaritsyn comrades.[91]

The First Cavalry Army had been fighting Denikin in the North Caucasus. Now Sergei Kamenev ordered Budennyi to move west toward Eastern Galicia.[92] Galloping from Rostov across Ukraine, the horsemen reached Elizavetgrad, in Kherson Province, on May 18. On June 9, they headed for Kiev, but circled to the west, reaching Zhytomyr the next day. On June 12, the Poles abandoned Kiev, while Budennyi continued northwest through Rovno and Lutsk (Łuck/Lytsk), then southward into Galicia as far as Lwów.[93] The men had followed a northern arc across a straight distance, Elizavetgrad to Lwów, of seven hundred miles. In the Polish wake, the Red Army took control of Ukraine. Kiev took the brunt from both sides, as each army took its toll.[94]

Tukhachevskii, for his part, had begun moving toward Warsaw a month earlier, pushing the Poles back toward the Vistula. An admirer of Napoleon (as was Piłsudski), at the beginning of July he echoed the call to arms of the French Revolution—"*Formez vos bataillons! Marchons!*" "In the West," he declared, "the fate of world revolution is being decided—over the corpses of White Poland." The men needed more, however, than echoes of Napoleon. Tukhachevskii did his best to stoke their thirst for revenge, invoking Polish atrocities, while also warning against self-seeking or desertion. "There will be no cowards among us."[95]

The opening moves rewarded his expectations. Following the northern arc above the Pripet or Pinsk Marshes (in Polish, Polesie), on July 11 Tukhachevskii took Minsk; over the following week the Persian-born Armenian Gaia Gai (Hayk Bzhishkyan), who had fought on the Caucasian Front in the Great War and was now leading the Third Red Cavalry Corps, took Vilnius and then Grodno.[96] The Lithuanians, eager to regain what they considered their capital, fought on the Russian side. Passing through Białystok, by August 1, Tukhachevskii had taken Brest-Litovsk, 125 miles directly east of Warsaw. Beyond the Bug River, at Brest, began the core of ethnic Poland.[97]

London and Paris became alarmed. On July 11, Lord Curzon had urged Moscow to call a truce at the Bug River, warning that Britain and France might come to Poland's aid if the Red Army continued west. Curzon offered to mediate. Trotsky expressed caution, but Lenin pushed ahead.[98] Commander in Chief Kamenev instructed Tukhachevskii and Egorov to "display the highest intensity in the continuing annihilation of the enemy and the capture of the greatest possible territory in pursuit of the Poles."[99] The Western Front was strong enough to win, Kamenev insisted, but recommended stopping at the Curzon Line, so as not to provoke the Allies.[100] Trotsky, for his part, suspected Curzon of wanting to stall for time while the Entente prepared for another intervention, supporting the Poles, perhaps luring Romania into the fray. Despite his hesitations, on July 17 Trotsky demanded all efforts be directed toward "the rapid and energetic advance on the heels of the retreating Polish White Guard armies." The Western and Southwest Fronts must continue "up to the line indicated by the Entente, as well as beyond this line," but only, he added, "in the event that circumstances force us temporarily to cross beyond it."[101] The last phrase was key. Also on July 17, Chicherin formally rejected Curzon's note and the offer to mediate with Poland, while repeating Russia's desire for peace and offering Poland a more generous eastern border than the Curzon Line.[102]

This was a good moment for posturing. The Second Comintern Congress opened in Moscow on July 19 (it closed August 7, before the military show-down). In the name of the First Cavalry Army, Budennyi dispatched a greet-ing to the foreign comrades: "Our horses' hooves are knocking at the iron gates that the bourgeois order has erected in the shape of gentry Poland between revolutionary Russia and the revolution taking place in Europe." In the coming "brotherhood of nations," Poland would occupy a "distin-guished place," and therefore the fight against Poland—against the mobi-lized world bourgeoisie—would play a "decisive" role.[103]

Momentum seemed to be on the Soviet side. German longshoremen in Danzig went on strike on July 23, refusing to unload arms for Poland, despite the presence of British troops.[104] Locally, the Red Army set up soviets in the towns along their victorious route.[105] On July 30, a newly formed Polish Revolutionary Committee convened in Białystok, south of Grodno, west of the Curzon Line. This was intended as the core of the future Soviet government of soon-to-be-defeated Poland.[106] Once the Red Army had triumphed, the Committee warned, "all representatives of the Polish bourgeoisie and landowners, all who support White Poland, will be arrested and sent to concentration camps."[107] Landowner "para-sites" and their families would be expelled from their estates, their prop-erty confiscated.[108]

Yet for all the martial bluster, talks continued. The diplomatic front left room for maneuver. The Soviets knew that France and Britain differed in their views of the Polish situation and Soviet Russia.[109] While France refused to deal with Soviet Russia, Britain had leverage on both the Polish and Russian sides. After the defeat at Kiev, when the Poles appealed to London for assistance, Lloyd George had insisted they pursue an armistice and accept the Curzon Line. With regard to Russia, the Allied decision in January 1920 to lift economic restrictions kept in place after the peace had been signed in July 1919 and the subsequent opening of economic talks provided London with leverage.[110] Curzon threatened to suspend them if the Soviets pursued their westward advance. London also told Moscow it was ready to mediate.[111]

On July 22, the Poles proposed an armistice. The next day, Chicherin claimed to accept Curzon's offer of an international peace conference—but only after the defeat of the remaining White army, under General Denikin's successor, General Petr Wrangel, had been accomplished. The note also expressed dismay at the threat to stop the negotiations on trade.[112] On July 29, Curzon again urged a truce, to be followed by an international conference to establish the terms of peace, and he opened the door to the Soviet trade delegation.[113] Four days earlier, a joint Anglo-French diplomatic-military mission had arrived in Warsaw to assist the Poles in the event the armistice failed to materialize and Soviet aggression continued. Its leading figures were the British diplomat Edgar Vincent, Viscount D'Abernon, and the French general Maxime Weygand. The Allies realized Moscow was only playing for time. Soviet intentions were transparent, partly because the Poles had deciphered their military signals.[114]

Meanwhile, Tukhachevskii had taken the bit in his teeth and was pursuing the northern course. On August 1, as noted, he took Brest-Litovsk—on a level with Warsaw. Gai quickly made it to Toruń (Thorn), northwest of Warsaw, not far from the German border.[115] While the advance continued, Moscow still pursued the diplomatic path. It weighed the risk of British sanctions, should hostilities escalate, against the desire to wipe out the Polish threat and make good on the boast of spreading revolution. Lenin noted disapprovingly that party leaders were tending toward "support of immediate peace with bourgeois Poland."[116] They believed that defeating General Wrangel should take priority and worried that prospects of encountering revolution in Poland were slim. Doing their best to convince the Allies of their sincerity, the Soviets at the same time did all they could to obstruct any possible agreement until the Red Army had taken Warsaw.[117]

The Soviet reluctance to begin talks with the Poles, as well as the continuing Soviet military offensive, convinced Lloyd George of Russia's bad faith. Leonid Krasin, commissar for foreign commerce, who had earlier been in London for the trade talks, returned to London from Moscow on August 3, together with Politburo member Lev Kamenev, heading a "special peace delegation." Lloyd George warned them that Britain was poised to intervene on Poland's behalf.[118] On August 6, he gave Kamenev twenty-four hours to agree to a truce with Poland. Otherwise, the economic sanctions would resume, trade talks would stop, and the Allies would be free to assist the Poles.[119] Kamenev, for his part, failed to mention that the Red Army had been planning for an extended offensive since Trotsky's directive of July 17, and that on August 5, the party's Central Committee had overcome or silenced its lingering doubts and approved the decision to attack Warsaw. Instead, he assured Lloyd George that the Red Army's continuing advance was "a strictly military operation" and therefore did "not predetermine in the slightest the question of the character of the peace treaty and does not constitute a threat to the independence and integrity of the Polish state in its ethnic borders."[120] Lloyd George and French Prime Minister Alexandre Millerand agreed that if Russia violated Polish independence, they would back Poland with equipment and advisers and resume the Soviet blockade.[121]

On August 9, two days before Russian and Polish delegates were scheduled finally to meet at Minsk, the Soviets informed Britain of their conditions. In exchange for the withdrawal of Soviet troops and recognition of a frontier east of the Curzon Line, Russia demanded a sharp reduction in the size of the Polish army, its immediate demobilization and that of the war industry, and the transfer to Soviet Russia and Ukraine of weapons not needed for the reduced army or for a so-called citizens' militia.[122] The British cabinet deemed these conditions "as reasonable as could be expected." If indeed the Russians at Minsk affirmed their respect for Polish ethnographic borders, then Britain would not take hostile action.[123]

In fact, as Chicherin and Kamenev admitted in telegrams that were intercepted by London, the reference to a militia concealed the intention of using the surrendered weapons to equip the Soviet occupiers of a conquered (now Soviet) Poland. Knowing that Polish Foreign Minister Eustachy Sapieha had rejected the proposed conditions, Kamenev boasted he would "return from Minsk, having shown our moderation and sincerity, won over the British workers completely and kept our hands free." Winston Churchill, then British Secretary of State for War, considered the Soviet wires "an unmistakable avowal of mala fides."[124] Lord D'Abernon, the British diplomat, said of his Soviet counterparts that "they pride themselves in hitting below the belt and in breaking their word."[125] Despite the transparent duplicity of Soviet methods, however, Curzon informed Warsaw that the British would not try to force the Russians to change their terms, a response that infuriated the French. In Warsaw, meanwhile, Piłsudski was attacked for the outcome of the peace maneuvers and reiterated his commitment to "war à outrance against the Bolsheviks."[126]

The wisdom of the Soviet tactics—delaying negotiations while preparing for war; pretending to respect Polish integrity while plotting revolution from abroad; provoking Polish aggression and rallying international support—was not entirely evident to everyone in Moscow. As late as August 11, Trotsky himself still hesitated. Obstruction was a game two could play. He believed the Poles, by impeding the peace talks, were trying to trigger a Russian incursion, so as to get the Western powers involved. "If we pursue the Poles," he cautioned, "we will enter Polish territory and be obliged to take Warsaw. In this case, the Polish government, maliciously dragging out the negotiations, will raise a clamor about our annexationist and imperialist intentions in order to create the possibility of intervention." Behind Poland's transparent but risky ploy, he asserted, stood not England but France. "Russia wants peace on the basis, on the one hand, of the complete inviolability of Poland, on the other hand, of serious and genuine guarantees that Poland will not again become a military weapon in the hands of the French plutocracy directed against Soviet Russia."[127]

While the British were enmeshed in diplomatic maneuvers, the French were assisting Poland in preparing for war. By mid-August, General Weygand had succeeded in remedying some of the defects of the Polish officer corps, composed of alumni of four imperial armies, lacking, in the general's view, in basic discipline and competence. He had helped Piłsudski formulate a plan for the defense of Warsaw and insisted he make better use of the French officers already on hand (including a young Charles de Gaulle).[128]

Though seemingly better positioned and equipped, the Red Army faced its own obstacles in the contest with Poland. These stemmed from conflicts over policy and over authority. Commander in Chief Sergei Kamenev had visited Minsk on July 21, where he was inspired by Tukhachevskii's fervor.[129] That day, in reply to Trotsky's July 17 directive for the Red Army to cross the Curzon line only "temporarily," and only if circumstances demanded, Kamenev reported that the Western Front armies were indeed crossing over. The Southwest Front armies, by contrast, were delaying, he realized, but as long as the discussions with Poland were still in progress, he considered the Western Front armies strong enough on their own.[130] A subsequent directive, sent two days later, on July 23, to the Southwest Front, lacked a sense of urgency. It ordered Budennyi's First Cavalry Army to push the Polish and Ukrainian forces back to the Romanian border and only then, "having accomplished this operation and protected itself from the direction of Lvov," was Budennyi "to concentrate the mass of its horsemen on a narrow front and continue in this fashion in a certain chosen direction." The exact direction was not indicated, but there was clearly no order for Budennyi to move north.[131] That same date—July 23—Kamenev meanwhile ordered the Western Front "to move energetically in the general direction of Warsaw, to strike the decisive blow." The army was to be in position no later than August 12 to then take Warsaw.[132] On July 30, Kamenev repeated the need for speed, to prevent the Poles taking advantage of the armistice talks to catch their breath. The Polish Army, he said, must be "destroyed absolutely."[133]

Poland was not, however, Moscow's only concern in August 1920. Intent on blocking General Wrangel from proceeding northward from Crimea, where his army was based, the Politburo designated the Crimean section of the Southwest Front as an independent Southern Front.[134] To reinforce this sector, on August 2 Kamenev instructed the commanders of the Western and Southwest Fronts to transfer part of their forces to this newly established Southern Front. The following day, in a reverse move, he transferred the First Cavalry Army from the Southwest to the Western command.[135] The first order annoyed Tukhachevskii, who bluntly rejected the transfers.[136] The second displeased Egorov. Tukhachevskii in fact was already fighting the war—his way. He and Kamenev continued to clash not only on troop disposition but on the best path of action. Tukhachevskii insisted on continuing north of the Bug River, partly to block access to Danzig and thus prevent delivery of equipment from France.[137] He demanded assistance from the Twelfth Army and the First Cavalry Army, positioned, respectively, near Kiev and Lwów.[138]

The key move, however, was not in Soviet hands. On August 6, Piłsudski noticed the stretch between Dęblin and Lublin that separated the northern and southern Red Army movements and ordered the Polish armies to advance into this gap, targeting Tukhachevskii from behind. The order fell into Tukhachevskii's hands, but such was his confidence that he did not believe it.[139] Speaking on the phone around midnight of August 9–10, Kamenev told him intelligence indicated the danger would come from the south. Tukhachevskii insisted he was "mistaken." Kamenev, strangely enough, did not persist, and granted Tukhachevskii full "freedom of action," reminding him that "the task remains the quickest possible crushing of Polish forces."[140] On August 10, despite Kamenev's objections, Tukhachevskii proceeded with the attack on Warsaw from the north.

Kamenev seemed to have lost all traction, and the commanders were all at odds. Budennyi and Voroshilov protested the transfer of part of the Red Cavalry to Tukhachevskii's command, while Egorov wanted it for the Crimea campaign. Tukhachevskii insisted on getting additional forces.[141] On August 13, Kamenev again demanded that the Lwów operation be suspended and Budennyi submit to Tukhachevskii's command. This time it was Stalin—Budennyi's patron—who flatly refused. The next day, however, Egorov finally informed the First Cavalry they were to join Tukhachevskii's campaign.[142] On August 15, Tukhachevskii himself ordered Budennyi to get under way, but the order was not countersigned and Budennyi chose not to accept it. When the proper form arrived two days later, the First Cavalry was engaged in heavy fighting around Lwów and did not manage to head north until August 20.[143]

Two problems had emerged: Kamenev was unclear in his directives, and both the political and military command disobeyed him. Stalin, as commissar of the Southwest Front, opposed the northern transfer. Stalin and Egorov were concerned primarily with the south—with Eastern Galicia, the possibility of Romanian intervention, and the Crimea.[144] Stalin made no bones about it. On July 29, while talks with Poland were still in progress, he had ordered Budennyi ("officially," as he put it) to drag his feet. "Until the receipt of a formal order from the Front," he told Budennyi, "you can keep fighting the Poles without worrying about a deadline." The Poles Budennyi was fighting were in Galicia, not Warsaw. "Keep attacking Lwów," Tukhachevskii told him, "we now have time."[145]

In this situation, Stalin acted with what would become his signature style—discrediting his opponents and shielding his favorites. In a message to Lenin, he accused Kamenev of underestimating the importance of the Crimea campaign, delaying the transfer of troops long enough to give Wrangel an advantage. Meanwhile, he excused Budennyi's continuing failure to take Lwów as a minor "hitch," which "did not constitute a turning point in the enemy's favor." He assured Lenin that Budennyi would succeed at Lwów, but "obviously with a certain delay." The priority was Wrangel—and Kamenev must send troops.[146] "It is my impression," Stalin wrote Lenin on August 12, "that the commander in chief and his boys are sabotaging the work of organizing victory over Wrangel. In any case, they do not show a tenth of the desire to win that they certainly show in the fight against Poland."[147]

Whatever Stalin's direct personal role in undermining Kamenev's campaign, his clients Egorov and Budennyi delayed long enough to leave

Tukhachevskii in the lurch. Meanwhile, as Tukhachevskii circled Warsaw from the north, Piłsudski gathered his forces near Dęblin, fifty miles southeast of Warsaw, at the juncture of the Vistula and Wieprz rivers.[148] On August 16, he launched his attack, "if you could even call it an attack," as he put it.[149] To his astonishment, no one stopped him. The Poles drove unimpeded through the opening in the Russian lines, which spanned the north-south distance between Dęblin and Lublin. The Red Cavalry, the "apocalyptic beast" that had terrorized numberless divisions, was nowhere in sight. Piłsudski felt he was dreaming.[150] Lord D'Abernon exclaimed: "The bold stroke has succeeded beyond expectation. A complete Bolshevik rout appears possible."[151]

Tukhachevskii's armies, already weakened, fell back in disarray; obstructed railway lines prevented reinforcements from arriving. By August 21, Piłsudski had destroyed three Soviet armies; another was trapped and forced across the German border into captivity.[152] On the road to Minsk, north of the Pripet Marshes, Piłsudski encountered the remains of the Sixteenth Red Army. "Testifying to its existence were the cannons abandoned in the fields without carts or crew, the numerous corpses of men and horses strewn along the road, and finally the local inhabitants who stopped my car when they recognized me and reported with delight that the 'Bolsheviki' had fled in all directions in disorder and panic."[153] Piłsudski was not exaggerating. Reporting from the area of Siedlice, east of Warsaw, a commissar attached to the same Sixteenth Army described how the troops had fled, under the constant assault not only of Polish forces but of local partisans. The local population, he reported, "were extremely hostile to us....In many cases the retreating units conducted rearguard battles with the local population, during which," he admitted, though perhaps not regretfully, "the Red Army soldiers dealt brutally with the insurgents." Of course, these were not insurgents but inhabitants defending their own lives. In Białystok, the commissar also reported, a Red Army brigade crossing the city, "fought harder against the Białystok population than against the Polish Army. Even the Jewish population," he noted, "took part in the hostile actions." "The Cheka should draw the appropriate conclusions," he advised.[154]

The Red Army was thus doubly defeated—by the Polish Army and by the Polish population. Neither conquest nor socialist revolution had succeeded. "If Poland had become Soviet," Lenin later said, "the Versailles treaty would have been shattered, and the entire international system built up by the victors would have been destroyed."[155] Piłsudski recognized the stakes.

"Soviet Russia waged war against us with the goal of imposing its own, Soviet system upon Poland, and the goal was called revolution from outside."[156] "Revolution from outside" was exactly the phrase used by Tukhachevskii.[157] At the very least, it is clear there was a confused chain of command. Often at cross purposes were the Sovnarkom in Moscow, Commander in Chief Kamenev at army headquarters in Smolensk, Trotsky as commissar of war, Stalin as political commissar of the Southwest Front, and the commanders in the field—Tukhachevskii for the Western Front, Egorov for the Southwest Front, plus cavalry commanders Budennyi and Gai. There was plenty of opportunity for missed and mixed signals. In addition, there was the exuberance of the young, ambitious, ideologically driven warrior— Tukhachevskii, headstrong and hot-headed.

The First Cavalry's failure to appear on time has been blamed for the collapse of the northern strategy.[158] In retrospect the participants all justified their roles. Writing in 1922, Kamenev emphasized the necessary risks taken in Tukhachevskii's northern strategy, based on the need to block the Danzig corridor. At the time, Moscow had believed the Polish proletariat would come to its aid; the earlier Red Army victories led the command to think the Polish Army was seriously damaged and demoralized; Red Army troops had already crossed the Curzon Line, and the threat of English intervention had to be preempted. Yet, Kamenev admitted, he had known that Tukhachevskii's support system was weak.[159] In the event, crucially, the Polish proletariat did not "extend the helping arm" (foiled, alas, by the Polish bourgeoisie) and the southern forces did not move north in time. They were too deeply absorbed in battle to tear themselves away. Wrangel had been an additional distraction.[160]

Whether or not Budennyi's sabers would have saved the day, when they finally moved up from the south they were shelled and battered by Polish airplanes and barely managed to fight their way out.[161] Lenin did not at first want to acknowledge the defeat. On August 18, he was still insisting that "peace can be concluded only on the ruins of White Poland." The battle must go on. Trotsky, however, doubted the army was capable of more.[162] The Politburo designated Wrangel as the primary focus and on August 25 accepted Lenin's belated admission that the time to talk peace had come.[163]

The Poles, meanwhile, built on their success. On September 12, Polish forces recovered Równe and Tarnopol, east and southeast of Lwów, and went on to defeat what was left of Tukhachevskii's Western Army Group on the Niemen River. On October 15, they reached Minsk, which Tukhachevskii had taken three months earlier.[164] While Polish-Soviet talks resumed, talks began between Poland and Lithuania, resulting in a border that left Vilnius on the Lithuanian side. On October 9, however, Polish troops under General Lucjan Żeligowski had seized the city from the Lithuanians, who had received it from the Red Army, which had taken it from Piłsudski in July. In 1923 the Polish occupiers organized a referendum, in which most non-Poles refused to participate; the result, accepted by the Entente, confirmed the city's attachment to Poland.[165]

At Riga, on October 12, 1920, Poland and Soviet Russia signed an armistice and, with the participation of Soviet Ukraine, the final treaty on March 18, 1921. At its greatest extent, the Polish offensive had reached as far as Kiev in the east, including both Vilnius (Lithuania) and Minsk (Belarus) in the north. The Treaty of Riga drew the Polish border east of the Curzon Line, to include Vilnius (Wilno) and Lwów, but excluding Minsk and Kiev. Four to five million Ukrainians and one million Belarussians ended up west of the border, on the Polish side; thirty million Ukrainians and four million Belarussians, on the Soviet side.[166]

----

The Soviet post-mortem was anguished and conflicted. The tangled Soviet wires of command had clearly been responsible for the loss of Warsaw. Subordinates had made decisions on their own, campaigns had not been coordinated, the political leadership in Moscow had kept various options in play—peace, revolution for export, victory at home.[167] There was room for interpretation—and for blame. For years the Soviet military and political establishments argued over who was at fault. At the Ninth Party Conference in Moscow on September 22, 1920, Lenin was on the defensive about the Polish debacle. Both he and Trotsky leveled accusations at Stalin.[168] The men associated with the Southwest group—Budennyi, Voroshilov, and Egorov, among them—clustered around Stalin. Later, Trotsky in exile continued to blame his arch-rival for the disaster.[169] It was Stalin, he claimed, who had delayed sending Budennyi from Lwów to support Tukhachevskii, wanting the glory of Lwów for himself, instead of helping someone else take Warsaw.[170] Whatever Stalin's exact role, the loss of Warsaw demonstrates a broader pattern of authority in the early Soviet years—often a matter of personal allegiances, of freelance revolutionary heroism. Trotsky, too, embodied this troubling combination. A brilliant organizer, ferocious in his demand for military discipline and subordination of authority, he was himself a charismatic figure, who needed to impose his will and call the shots in the name of revolution.

The Battle of Warsaw came to be known in Poland as the Miracle on the Vistula (*Cud nad Wisłą*). For the Russians, it was an ideological as well as military humiliation. In May, when the Poles had the advantage, Trotsky had acknowledged the weakness of the armies on the Western Front. Unable to deny the problem of desertion, he insisted every effort be made to bolster revolutionary morale. "Send movies, phonographs, theaters, musical instruments"—inspiration as well as discipline was needed.[171] Propaganda had also failed to reach the population the Red Army claimed to be liberating. The villages were unreceptive, a commissar reported, also in May, "and those few agitators who arrived were roughed up and murdered by the peasants, who hate the 'Yids' and Communists." In places, the locals "emerged onto the roads, entire villages at a time, armed with rifles, pitchforks, axes, attacking our supply trains, capturing soldiers. Communists, Jews, commissars were shot; Russians were roughed up."[172]

On August 16, as Piłsudski was about to launch his attack, Trotsky had insisted that the Red Army was totally disciplined, on schedule, following orders, and sharply focused on its revolutionary mission—who was the enemy, what was the goal.[173] By September, he was making excuses. After a string of earlier Red Army victories, he wrote, "luck then smiled on the armies of the Polish *szlachta*. Weakened by their glorious march…, exhausted by deprivation, cut off from their base, the Red divisions confronted fresh Polish forces, hitting them from Warsaw—and fell back."[174] Obviously minimizing the disaster ("We are stronger than ever"), and at this point ignoring Stalin's role, he had to concede: "This was a massive failure."[175] From the long-range perspective, however, it was perhaps not a failure at all. Had the Reds taken Warsaw and marched toward the German frontier—hoping to incite an international conflagration—they would have been even more overextended than they already were. The move might well have provoked the Western powers into overcoming their reluctance and mobilizing their armies yet again. Polish victory may have saved Europe from Bolshevism; it also saved Bolshevism from Europe.

# 8

# War Against the Jews

Nothing was more troubling and contradictory, in a troubled and contradictory time, than the question of the Jews in the Russian Revolution and Civil War. Reactionaries blamed the collapse of the Empire on the machinations of a worldwide Jewish cabal. The Whites embraced anti-Semitism, out of conviction and as a mobilizing device, damning the Communists as Jews and inflaming popular passions. As good liberals, the Kadets rejected anti-Semitism and supported Jewish rights, yet they threw in their lot, at the end, with the anti-Semitic General Denikin. Both Petliura and the Bolsheviks condemned anti-Semitism in principle, yet their followers and associates perpetrated anti-Jewish violence on a vast scale. The Communists in Ukraine, for example, partnered with Matvii Hryhoriïv, despite his well-deserved reputation as a thug. Pogroms were the calling card, in particular, of the freelance chieftains, such as Hryhoriïv, who lent their services to the opposing camps. More fundamentally, leaders on all sides fostered the kind of animosities that lent themselves to the anti-Semitic interpretations congenial to followers used to organizing their feelings in stereotyped terms. Both the "bourgeois blood-sucker" and the "blood-soaked Communist" could easily be seen as Jews.

The horror of the pogroms was not only a moral issue but a political one, touching directly on the nature of authority during the crisis of the Revolution and Civil War. The fate of the Jews illustrates the difficulties faced by leaders or would-be leaders on all sides in establishing control over their followers or hangers-on. The ability to impose discipline was a demonstration of power, yet the inability to corral rampaging underlings had its advantages, too. Savagery could be a useful weapon. License to pillage attracted uprooted hungry men; terrorizing the population made it clear who was boss; the brutality of the Cossacks and atamans could always be disavowed once their work was done. Even a professional officer such as

Admiral Kolchak relied on the support of freewheelers, in his case Grigorii Semenov, Ivan Kalmykov, Sergei Rozanov, and Pavel Ivanov-Rinov, who not only defied his orders but violated every norm of disciplined military conduct. He resented their independence, but could neither control nor do without them.

The Civil War, in essence, amounted to a range of free-form armed encounters that pitted the population against itself, as perpetrators and victims. In this context, Petliura's "*atamanshchina*" (use of local chieftains) and Trotsky's reviled "*partizanshchina*" (reliance on free-lance irregulars) were mirror images. Both involved popular mobilization behind captains close to their followers in psychology and social context, who indulged in theatrical brutality, resented formal authority, and were hostile to "outsiders" of various kinds, notably the Jews—the archetypical "intimate alien." In Ukraine, the key element was Symon Petliura's reliance on the delegated authority of chieftains, whom he could not restrain, but on whom his own authority rested. This loose-fitting structure was not accidental, but central to the Directory's power.[1] At the apex of the pyramid, Petliura signed himself "Ataman in Chief" (*Glavnyi ataman*, Ukrainian *Holovnyi otaman*), but his nominal subordinates exercised full command over their units. They were a mixed lot—some loyal to Cossack chiefs, some former Skoropads'kyi supporters, others out simply for excitement and loot. Petliura provided them with money to feed, clothe, and arm their men. His largesse did not guarantee loyalty, but rather allowed them to consolidate their independence, and he did not attempt to curb them.[2]

The chieftains in turn collaborated with numerous local leaders, the *bat'kos*. Though rooted in village life and benefitting from peasant habits of deference, the *bat'kos* were usually not themselves peasants, but men with some schooling and often with experience of the war.[3] Like every soldier or noncommissioned officer, they had absorbed the virulent xenophobic (and anti-Semitic) propaganda emanating from high places and had witnessed or participated in the officially endorsed abuse of civilian populations. They had also experienced the thrill of challenging superior authority. Epaulettes and officers had become fair game. Now the little guys were themselves commanders, and they recruited among a populace which had also abandoned habits of deference.

Revolution and civil war entailed the collapse of social hierarchy, discipline, and moral norms—an overall breakdown of the restraints and inhibitions embedded in communities and in the relationship of subjects or citizens to the state. This collapse was not confined to the lower orders—mobs, bands, armed workers, army deserters, escaped criminals, bandits—who overwhelmed the cities and brought the elites to their knees. The educated and ruling classes also experienced a form of situational depravity. Drunkenness was prevalent among the officers, bribery and pilfering were endemic among former bureaucrats, an atmosphere of every man for himself gripped respectable families on the run, displaced, desperate, vulnerable. The historian Dietrich Beyrau has called the entire period "an unparalleled breakdown of civilization." Yet the civilization that preceded 1917 planted the seeds of what was to come. Indeed, Beyrau cites underlying "cultures of violence" that were freed from constraint by the collapse of state structures during the war.[4]

The disintegration of the old social and moral fabric did not mean, however, that the chaos that followed was nothing but a formless free-for-all. The collective action of peasants and soldiers, often seemingly anarchic, frequently expressed shared values and unfolded in recognizable ways, demonstrating its own, even if sinister, moral economy. The violence often had symbolic as well as practical significance, involving the destruction of cultural objects that signified social status, the humiliation of persons with authority, the desecration of symbols of power. It often had an impudent carnivalesque quality—the inversion of hierarchies, the celebration of demonic impulses. Incidents often began and escalated under the influence of alcohol.

The most notorious of these ritual outbursts of popular violence was the pogrom. The word *pogrom*, from the Russian *gromit'* "to smash" (from a root meaning "thunder"), itself passed into English (as well as German, Polish, and French) to mean mob attacks on Jews, though in Russian it continued to be used in a more general sense as well. Feelings of distrust or hostility toward the Jews were endemic in imperial Russian society at all levels. The lower classes resented them as merchants, tavern-keepers, and middlemen on rural estates, a resentment intensified by the economic crisis accompanying the Great War and Civil War. As an ideology, anti-Semitism was purveyed by intellectuals and public figures and by imperial officials and military commanders. The city of Kiev, in particular, developed a brand of anti-Semitism promoted by the local conservative elite as a form of patriarchal populism, a mass-appeal ideology with a sectionalist twang.[5]

Even while the Empire was still in place, surges of anti-Jewish violence had typically accompanied moments when the highest authorities were

challenged or seemed to have lost their nerve. This was the case in the aftermath of Alexander II's assassination in 1881 and following the October
Manifesto of 1905. The tsars understood the connection between attacks on
the Jews and the more general problem of authority. It was widely believed,
particularly among the Jews themselves, that the tsar authorized the pogroms,
but in fact the tsar and his ministers, personal anti-Semites though they
were, did not encourage or condone mob violence. Local authorities, by
contrast, often aided and abetted the attacks. Pogroms were illegal, culprits
were brought before the courts, but the perpetrators realized they had
another kind of official blessing. The pattern of formal condemnation and
actual complicity was firmly established.

The pogroms of 1881, 1903 (Kishinev), and 1905 were committed by
peasants and workers.[6] By contrast, the attacks on Jews that occurred in the
western provinces during the Great War were the work of soldiers acting in
the context of officially authorized abuses, such as hostage-taking and the
expulsion of civilians, which opened the door to looting, raping, and personal assaults. The Jew was stigmatized as a coward and traitor, a speculator
and spy. Once the lid was off in Ukraine in 1919, the various patterns that
encouraged and orchestrated anti-Jewish attacks converged. No higher
authority commanded allegiance, middle-ranking officers and officials were
themselves vulnerable and corrupt, and anti-Semitism became the rallying
cry of the various anti-Bolshevik forces.

In the interior of Russia there were few pogroms, since Jews were relatively rare. Ukraine was the eye of the storm, because the majority of Jews
had been restricted to the region of the former Pale of Settlement, the territories that emerged as Ukraine, Latvia, Lithuania, and Poland during the
Civil War. Numbering over six and a half million, they constituted about 10
percent of the population in these areas and around 15 percent in the cities
of western Ukraine. Of the core imperial Russian population, including
Siberia, not even 1 percent counted as Jews.[7] Jewish sources at the time did
not consider the Jews in Latvia, Lithuania, or Russia proper to be targets of
special aggression, but the situation in new-born Poland and embryonic
Ukraine was acute.[8]

The fatal brew was thus prepared for the epidemic of anti-Jewish violence
in 1919 and 1920. It was the work of soldiers—and Cossacks—under both
White and Red command, the paramilitaries associated with popular leaders,
as well as peasants and townsmen, workers among them. The breakdown of
authority in the Ukraine was most dramatic after the German departure,

when claimants to power changed almost from day to day, with "cinematographic rapidity."[9] The Jews were a useful target. In mythical terms, the Jew
was all-powerful; in fact, the mass of Jews, those a soldier or peasant would
encounter, were as poor or not much better off than they themselves. Some
might have just enough property to be worth stealing. In the desperate conditions of 1919, every shred counted. "Even a pair of old shoes of a poor Jew
excited the attention of the village population," a witness noted. In the heat
of the pogrom, the victims "were stripped of everything to the last shirt."[10]
The Jews at hand were thus weak enough to prey upon, but the attackers
were motivated by more than poverty or greed. The destruction of the Jews
represented victory over a supposedly powerful force—both the invisible
tentacles of the world Jewish conspiracy invoked by Black Hundred ideologues and the reality of Jews as agents of the new Bolshevik regime, which
like the old one demanded grain, soldiers, and submission. Rape, which combined humiliation and desecration, was endemic to all these attacks.[11]

The Bolsheviks denounced anti-Semitism and discouraged pogroms,
which they blamed on the "enemies of the people."[12] The Bolsheviks and
their followers were nevertheless not themselves free of the anti-Semitic
stain. No more than Petliura or Denikin could Lenin or Trotsky control the
behavior of their lieutenants and popular adherents. Trotsky had adopted a
non-Jewish nom de guerre, partly to downplay the origins that made him a
prime target of anti-Semitic propaganda and of hostility on the part of the
party's own popular base. He himself had little interest in his Jewishness. The
Bronshtein family were, untypically, farmers. The son did not have a religious
education, did not speak Yiddish, and attended a *Realschule* in cosmopolitan
Odessa.[13] Trotsky's indifference did not make him less of a symbol, however.

The Soviet regime had an ambivalent impact on Jewish life and the fate
of the Jews. Accepting Jews in visible positions of authority, it increased
their vulnerability to anti-Semitic hatred, but also provided them with tools
to combat it. In January 1918, the Commissariat of Nationalities established
a special Jewish Commissariat (*Evreiskii komissariat*—Evkom); in July 1918
the party created a special Jewish Section (*Evreiskaia sektsiia*—Evsektsiia), as
part of a broader effort to reach ethnic populations.[14] The Evsektsiia, into
which the Evkom eventually merged, was led by Semen Dimanshtein.
Destined originally to be a rabbi, he had joined the Social Democrats in
1904, at the age of eighteen. As a Bolshevik, he joined in opposing the influence of the Jewish Bund, an anti-Zionist secular labor party founded in Vilna
in 1897, later close to the Mensheviks, that focused on the Yiddish-speaking

working class.[15] The Evsektsiia offered a platform from which Jewish socialists could battle the plague of anti-Semitism and the pogroms. In the interests of consolidating the regime's cultural control, it also repressed autonomous
Jewish organizations, whether socialist or Zionist.[16] In the course of the
anti-religious campaigns that heated up in the 1920s, Jewish religious institutions were targeted as well.

For Russian liberals, who considered the Bolsheviks the greatest evil, the
Jews presented a dilemma. General Denikin's forces conducted a campaign
against the Jews, as virulent as any other.[17] Yet the Kadets, loyal proponents
of Jewish rights, endorsed the White movement and blamed the spread of
anti-Jewish violence on the Bolsheviks, whom they accused of creating an
atmosphere of moral corruption, encouraging naked violence, and raising
the extermination of enemies to a basic principle. At its November 1919
Congress, the Kadet Party even took the argument a step farther. Its pronouncement admonished the "enlightened" leaders of the Jewish community to "declare merciless war" on coreligionists who joined the Bolshevik
cause, thus promoting its success and provoking anti-Jewish violence. In the
end, the Kadets declared, the Jews must recognize that only a "national dictatorship," a strong state power, indeed, the reestablishment of Russian statehood, would be able to protect all citizens, regardless of nationality or
religion, from the "moral barbarization," the "bloody whirlwind" the
Bolsheviks had unleashed.[18] The appeal to the Jews to restrain themselves
was a gesture more commonly adopted by advisors who did not wish them
well, yet the Kadets were not anti-Semites. In May 1918, the Jewish Bund
had similarly blamed the Bolsheviks for "creating particularly favorable conditions for the appearance of anti-Jewish pogroms and the growth of pogromist sentiment."[19] The Kadets were desperate for a realistic option. They
seemed to imagine that if they turned the anti-Semitic illusion on its
head—crediting the Jews with the power to stop what the anti-Semites
thought they had started—they could protect even the Jews from self-
destruction, along with Russia itself.

A more even-handed view of the moral degradation caused by the
Revolution and Civil War was offered by the writer Ivan Bunin. The violently
anti-Bolshevik Bunin had the luxury, unlike the Kadets, of standing on the
political sidelines. In November 1919, he wrote: "It is time for reflection on
the part of the instigators of murder, on both right and left, of revolutionaries
both Russian and Jewish, of everyone who implicitly and explicitly promotes
enmity, malice, conflict of every kind,...relentlessly arousing the beast in the
common people, inciting person against person, class against class."[20] Sergei

Gusev-Orenburgskii, an outspoken Gentile opponent of anti-Semitism during the Great War and a chronicler of pogroms during the Civil War, explained their ubiquity as a product of the endemic warfare to which all sides made a contribution. The pogroms, in his words, reflected "the contempt for human life and other people's property instilled in the masses in the course of many years of external, then civil war, with its Red and White terrors, extorted tributes, requisitions, searches, raids, hostage-taking."[21]

The attacks on the Jews that in 1919–1920 engulfed the area that became the Soviet republics of Belarus and Ukraine and the (overlapping) territory occupied by the Polish Army nevertheless stand out against the general background of plunder and carnage inflicted by all parties to the Civil War. The pogroms of this period amounted to a veritable war against the Jews, in which whole communities were wiped out—despoiled, dismantled, and incinerated. Estimates of the total death toll range widely, from a minimum of 20,000–35,000, perhaps 60,000, to a maximum of 150,000.[22] These pogroms had certain features in common with the prewar model, but in extent and character they represented something new. They formed what has been called a "pogrom movement," whose profile varied in time and place, but overall showed a relentless consistency. The movement drew on the legacy of the Great War and the precedent of the 1905 Revolution, but also reflected the ideologies and social conflicts of the Civil War.

When the headstrong troops of the various armies and loose divisions flooded the small towns of largely Jewish habitation in the western provinces, urged by their leaders to take what they could find, the peasants joined in the plunder. They also joined in the wholesale murder of entire families, young and old, in orgies of rape and humiliation. The pogrom movement was a war within a social war within a political war. Identifying the Jews with the hated Soviet regime, anti-Semitic ideologues fused the class resentments and the pain of economic crisis among the poor and vulnerable populace with their own political ambitions. In 1905 the monarchist Black Hundreds had used rabble-rousing as a political tool, but never before had the demonization of the Jews been propagated with such determination and to such murderous effect. Never had it fueled the actions of whole armies and armed formations.

We know so much about the Civil War pogroms because they attracted foreign attention from the beginning. International Jewish organizations and the Red Cross had agents on the ground, gathering information and providing aid to victims. Beginning in 1919, the efforts of these organizations were supplemented by systematic data-gathering sponsored by the Commissariat of Nationalities. The Soviet authorities were motivated not only by the desire to blacken the reputation of the anti-Soviet camp in the eyes of world opinion, but by the practical desire at the peace negotiations with Poland in Riga in 1919 and the Genoa Conference of 1922 to obtain compensation for damage inflicted.[23] In connection with the 1919 Paris Peace Conference, moreover, the United States and Britain both sent delegations to Poland to investigate the condition and treatment of Jews. Over the course of 1919–1921, while the Civil War was still raging, the results of these investigations were published in English and Russian. In short, an abundance of evidence, including first-person witness and survivor accounts and various forms of statistical data, was available at the time. The question of who was responsible for the pogroms became a matter of international debate in the context of talks for the resolution of the outcome of the war and the establishment of a postwar order. Some of the raw findings ended up in the collections of the YIVO Institute for Jewish Research in New York and in the Moscow archives, where they have attracted the interest of post-Soviet Russian scholars.[24]

The prevalence of anti-Semitism on the terrain of the former Pale of Settlement, encouraged by politically interested elites, nevertheless does not explain the escalation of violence, which had everything to do with the nature of political and military authority under conditions of permanent instability. In Ukraine, as noted, it was not the Directory in Kiev but the atamans and *bat'kos* who led the assault, some operating on their own, others attached to Petliura's Army of the Ukrainian National Republic (*Armiia Ukraïns'koi Narodnoi Respubliky*). In the case of the Reds, Hryhoriïv, while still associated with the Communists, allowed his troops to plunder at will. It was not until he launched his anti-Bolshevik rebellion, however, that he directed their anger against the Jews, whom he now identified with Soviet power. His Universal called for the expulsion of "foreign elements from the ever hungry land of Moscow and the land where Christ was nailed to the cross."[25] Nestor Makhno operated in an area of less dense Jewish habitation and sometimes spoke out against pogroms, but his men also engaged in anti-Jewish violence.[26]

The peak of pogrom activity in the Ukraine occurred in 1919 during the confrontation between Red and White armies and in the midst of widespread peasant rebellion. Each incident resulted in hundreds of deaths; people were not only murdered in their dwellings, but also pulled from trains, drowned on ships, burned alive in synagogues. Women were raped, beards were yanked and snipped, eyes were gouged out with bayonets. After the attacks, people perished from wounds, exposure, hunger, and disease.[27] The vast majority of those counted as dead (excluding the many who eluded calculation) were men of working age, between fifteen and fifty. On the territory of the Ukraine, according to one reliable account, Directory troops tied to Petliura were responsible for 40 percent of incidents (and over half the murders), free-agent partisan bands for 25 percent, the White Army under 20 percent, the Red Army under 10 percent, Hryhoriïv's men under 5 percent, and the Polish Army under 3 percent.[28]

Pogroms on the territory of Belarus occurred in three waves. The first occurred in 1919–1920, during and particularly after the Polish occupation; as the troops withdrew, they plundered Jewish property and torched entire villages, but committed few murders. The second wave took place in 1920, when formations under the leadership of Lieutenant Colonel Stanisław Bułak-Bałachowicz and Boris Savinkov made their way from town to town, stripping the Jews of their property, destroying houses, raping women, and murdering inhabitants en masse. The third wave, in 1921, was not, by contrast, the work of recognizable units, however disorderly, but of independent operators—the remnants of Bułak-Bałachowicz's band, deserters from all sides, criminals, and a significant number of peasants. In the course of these three years of systematic violence, the traditional Jewish settlements were emptied of their occupants, who fled to the cities, and reduced to ashes.[29]

In May 1919, Bułak-Bałachowicz, as we recall, had conducted an anti-Bolshevik reign of terror in Pskov, as part of the unsuccessful White advance on Petrograd, and in January 1920 had had General Iudenich arrested. Between April and August 1920, during the Polish-Soviet War, Bułak-Bałachowicz joined first with Savinkov and later with Petliura to fight the Red Army in Belarus. After peace was concluded in Riga on October 12, 1920, Bułak-Bałachowicz's army was destroyed, and he fled to Poland.[30] Bułak-Bałachowicz was particularly vicious, testing the tolerance even of White generals with a stomach for anti-Semitic violence. But he embodied the recognizable type of the *bat'ko*, the rebellious underling who volunteered for service but resisted authority, the political wild card. Like Semenov and Hryhoriïv, he switched masters and partners. Despite the blood on his hands, despite having turned against Iudenich, he was accepted by Savinkov, whose own hands were not particularly clean, and by Petliura—not surprisingly,

given the profile of his own troops—and by Piłsudski, representing the resurrected Polish nation. Bułak-Bałachowicz was typical also in his cavalier
attitude toward ideology. He fought for the Reds, for Ukraine, for Belarus,
for Estonia, for Poland. He was nationalist only in the sense of defending the
offshoots of the Empire. He was no socialist, in contrast to Petliura and
perhaps also Savinkov. Like the other *bat'kos*, he used anti-Semitism for its
mobilizing power; its justification of plunder, itself a useful tool in the management of irregular forces; and as a stable point of orientation amid the
fluctuating claims of Whites and Reds. The Jew was always the enemy, no
matter where or who you were.

Like many leaders of the anti-Bolshevik crusade, however, Bułak-
Bałachowicz was—incongruously—sensitive to world opinion. He and
Savinkov visited Paris in December 1920, where they spoke with Jewish
journalists. Pressed on the subject of the vicious pogroms committed by
their forces, both denied having "anti-Semitic inclinations." In conversation
with a Russian journalist, also in Paris, Bułak-Bałachowicz said he was not
fighting against the Jews, but against the Communists. "If," however, "it
turned out that among the Jews 80 percent were Communists, I would not
hesitate to exterminate them, not as Jews, but as Communists."[31]

The *bat'kos* may have behaved like independent operators, making up their
own rules, but the Ukrainian national movement was led by men of serious
political convictions. The Jews, for their part, featured not only as helpless
victims. Their interests were represented, in different ways, by political and
community leaders. Not surprisingly, however, given the context, the relationship between the Rada and the Jewish socialists was unstable, with
moments of cooperation and moments of distrust and hostility. Many Jewish
spokesmen supported the Rada in the hope that it would unite the territory
inhabited by the majority of Jews and would guarantee them legal protection and communal self-government.[32] The Bolshevik coup and the
December armistice with Germany had led to a minor outbreak of pogroms
behind the front in late 1917, which Volodymyr Vynnychenko and Petliura
had made a point of condemning. In January 1918, the Rada approved the
formation of Jewish self-defense squads, although Jewish leaders were themselves divided on the wisdom of this tactic.[33] The Jewish parties differed
among themselves on many issues but continued to work with the Rada,
which offered autonomy to Ukraine's Jewish, Polish, and Russian minorities.[34]

Most Jewish leaders were not, however, in favor of separation from Russia and opposed the declaration of Ukrainian independence embodied in the Fourth Universal of January 12.[35]

The opposition of Jewish socialist leaders to Ukrainian separatism is unlikely to have affected the behavior of the troops under Petliura's at least nominal command, but when the Rada, with German backing, returned to Kiev, its troops squeezed the Jewish community for protection money, beat up Jewish passers-by encountered on the streets, and murdered whole families with impunity. Despite Kiev's reputation as a hotbed of ideological anti-Semitism, the city administration was indignant; the Rada itself officially condemned the attacks. After the occupying powers abandoned the Rada and installed Hetman Skoropads'kyi, they accused the Jews of profiteering and of undermining the Ukrainian cause. In July the hetman abolished the law on Jewish autonomy. But the occupiers, by their very presence, also effectively prevented anti-Jewish violence.[36]

The massive violence began once they had departed. In December 1918 and January 1919, the atamans or bat'kos instructed their men to treat the Jews as Bolsheviks, therefore as enemies. Plunder was taken for granted; also rapes, beatings, murders, and ritual humiliations. Abuses were encouraged by slogans, such as "Kill the Jews, also the Jewish children!"[37] Warnings of retribution were not merely rhetorical: "Will you, Jewish rabble, still keep ruling over us?" Occasionally, a "nationalist" note was struck: "Kill the Jews and save the Ukraine!"[38] This was a local variation on the ubiquitous "Smash the Jews, save Russia!" The commander of the Sich Cossacks, Colonel Evgenii (Evhen) Konovalets, had orchestrated the repression of the Arsenal revolt in Kiev in January 1918. He now organized special squads with authorization to plunder.[39] When confronted by Jewish community leaders, the atamans blamed the Jews for starting the pogroms themselves and boasted of having killed them.[40]

The shift from pillage to mass murder occurred early on, in February 1919, as the fortunes of the Directory deteriorated.[41] "The more they were defeated," the Red Cross in Kiev reported, "the more Petliura's troops were forced to retreat, the more violently they revenged themselves on the innocent Jewish population, which they equated with the Communists."[42] The most notorious of the new type of pogrom occurred in the towns of Proskurov (since 1954 Khmelnytskyi) and Felshtin in Podolia.[43] These incidents illustrate the worst behavior of the fanatical ataman commanders, but they also show that local society was not entirely carried away by anti-Semitic zeal. Society was damaged, but not extinguished.

In 1919 Proskurov was a town of fifty thousand inhabitants, half Jewish, located south of Zhytomyr, between Vinnytsia and Lviv, typical of the region of dense Jewish habitation, where the cities were strikingly multicultural. Poles, Jews, and Germans perched on urban islands surrounded by a Ukrainian-speaking peasant sea. As in many such towns, the mayor of Proskurov was a Pole; the city administration was half Jewish and half Gentile. The Directory was represented by the commandant, Colonel Iurii Kiverchuk, the head of a partisan brigade attached to the Army of the Ukrainian National Republic, who was also in charge of the town militia. The city government, however, organized its own self-defense, in the form of a neighborhood guard, under the joint direction of a Pole and a Jew. The town, like every other, harbored representatives of all possible socialist parties, Jewish, Ukrainian, and Russian, including a number of underground Bolshevik activists.[44]

In short, Proskurov was an interethnic provincial town, with an enlightened civic leadership. Trouble here began with the Bolsheviks. In the last week of January 1919, a group of young hotheads gathered in Vinnytsia and decided to launch an uprising across the entire Podolia region, to begin on Saturday morning, February 15. They were convinced that the two divisions quartered in Proskurov, at which they had aimed their appeals, would rise to the call. On February 5, however, Proskurov's profile changed dramatically, with the appearance of a brigade of Zaporozhian Cossacks under the command of a native Zaporozhian, the ataman Ivan Semesenko, along with a division of Gaidamak Cossacks, both attached to the Army of the Ukrainian National Republic. On February 6, Semesenko declared himself head of the town garrison, imposed martial law, and—ironically—threatened to punish anyone who instigated a pogrom.[45] At the same time, he issued an "Order to the Zaporozhian Cossack Brigade of the Ukrainian Republican Army, bearing the name of Ataman in Chief Petliura," in which he warned the Jews, whom he called "a people detested by all the nations," that if they wanted to survive, they must stop troubling "the poor Ukrainian people."[46]

At this point no one in Proskurov knew of the plans being fomented by the Bolsheviks in Vinnytsia. On February 13, when the other socialist leaders learned what was afoot, a representative of the Jewish Bund warned that an uprising would lead to disaster for the Jews.[47] The young Bolsheviks were indifferent to these fears. The leaders of the neighborhood guard, still thinking this was all a bluff, told their men to remain neutral. Alas, at 6:45 the next morning, Saturday, February 15, the Bolsheviks fired some shots to launch the affair, took over the post and telegraph office, and arrested Kiverchuk. The garrison troops, as they had hoped, followed them to the train station. There, unfortunately, they confronted the fierce and more numerous Cossacks emerging from the railway cars in which they were quartered. After firing a few shots, the "rebels" hurried back to their barracks, which the Cossacks treated to a more serious shelling. The outgunned and outnumbered garrison scattered to nearby villages.[48]

Once they realized what was happening, the worried city councilmen paid a visit to Kiverchuk, newly released from his brief detention, who explained that the "Yids" had done it. He now gave his backing to Semesenko, who gathered the Cossacks at the station and provided them with a fine feast and plenty of vodka and cognac. He told them the Jews were the worst enemies of the Ukraine and demanded they take an oath to do their "sacred duty and massacre the Jewish population." They must murder but not rob them. "We need souls, not money."[49] Even among the fierce Cossack warriors, however, there were dissenters. One squad leader proposed exacting a tribute instead, but he was threatened with his life; another, who refused to order his men to shoot unarmed people, was told to leave town. The rest assembled in marching order, musicians at the head, medics in the rear. The Cossacks fanned out in groups of five to fifteen into the streets of the Jewish quarter.[50]

The Jews had grown accustomed to random gunshots and were not troubled on the Saturday morning when they heard the signal supposed to launch the Bolshevik revolt. Returning from synagogue, they consumed the Sabbath meal and retired to nap. They were rudely awakened when the Cossacks broke into their houses, swords drawn, bayonets poised, and proceeded to slash and stab every living person, from the smallest baby to the oldest woman and man. Those who scrambled into attics or cellars were dragged out and slaughtered; hand grenades were lobbed into hiding places.[51]

The event was gruesome, but its conclusion showed that not all vestiges of normal civic life had been expunged by the constant bloodshed and upheaval. The anti-Semitic venom did not penetrate everywhere into Ukrainian society. The slaughter continued for three hours in the afternoon. When the town commissioner, who had been left in the dark, realized what was happening, he telegraphed the Directory in Kamentsy. The front commander, Colonel (later General) German Konovalov, ordered Semesenko to stop. A horn was sounded, and the Cossacks returned in orderly fashion to their quarters at the railway station.[52]

The next morning, the president of the City Duma, the mayor, and other notables visited the commandant and demanded he prevent the violence from resuming. They summoned Semesenko and Kiverchuk to a special session of the Duma. Individual Jews were still being murdered on the street. A local teacher by the name of Trofim Verkhola had served as the Provisional Government district commissar, then been elected to the Constituent Assembly on a Ukrainian joint SD–SR ticket (Spilka). Having been jailed under the hetman, he had just resumed his place in the Proskurov City Duma.[53] At the special Duma sitting, Verkhola accused Semesenko of dressing robbers in Cossack clothing. The pogrom was a disgrace to the Ukraine. "You are fighting against Bolshevists, but were the old men and children whom your Gaidamaks massacred Bolshevists? You insist that only Jews are Bolshevists. Do you not know that there are Bolshevists among the other peoples too, even among Ukrainians?"[54]

Despite the protest, isolated murders and looting continued for the next two days in Proskurov and nearby towns. Verkhola at first tried on his own authority to order the Cossacks out of town, but Semesenko had him arrested and would have had him shot but for the intervention of the mayor and upstanding Ukrainian nationalists.[55] Semesenko explained that "unknown, dishonorable, conscienceless persons," belonging to "the Jewish nation," had been plotting a revolt intending "to take the power into their own hands" for the purpose of reducing Ukraine to "anarchy and disorder." In response, "decisive measures" had been taken. It was unfortunate that some "innocent persons" were among the victims, but "their blood must fall as a curse" on the instigators of rebellion.[56] In the formulation favored by pogrom apologists, the Jews were always responsible for bringing death upon themselves. Verkhola, who was by now the town commissar, demanded the arrest and trial of the perpetrators and the return of stolen goods and announced that "any appeal to national hatred, and particularly to pogroms, is a disgrace to Ukraine and a hindrance to her regeneration."[57] The contrast could not have been sharper.

The Proskurov victims were not anonymous. The Jewish hospital and dressing station that treated the wounded listed them by name and age. They include boys and girls under ten, pierced through the gut, slashed in the head, skewered through the chest, stabbed in the face.[58] A commission established by the Proskurov City Duma to document the facts used an official form with blanks for the names and ages of the victims: "on Aptekar Street, the father Avrum Shuelivich, thirty-six; his wife Khana, twenty-eight, their daughter Leika, seven."[59] The Red Cross relief agency described crazed attacks on entire families, assaulted in their rooms, pulled from under beds. This apparently wild mob attack, the report concluded, was in fact a focused military assault. The violence of February 15 had resulted in 1,500 deaths. Most victims were buried in mass graves. Peasant carts arrived piled with bodies, hired peasants dug a large ditch, while marauders inspected the corpses, cutting off fingers to take the rings, stripping the clothing. Burials continued until four in the morning on Tuesday. For the next two days occasional murders occurred on the roads, as Jews made their way out of town, and also on the streets and in dwellings.[60] On February 16, the Cossacks had proceeded to nearby Felshtin, where in a few hours they murdered another six hundred people, one-third of the town's Jewish inhabitants, raping every woman in sight, and burning the best habitations to the ground.[61] Through all of this, Semesenko was ill with a disease the locals thought was syphilis.[62] If so, he was not alone. Syphilis was widespread in peasant villages. It favored no camp over another. Isaac Babel remarked of the Red Cavalry in Galicia: "All our fighting men—velvet caps, rape, forelocks, battles, revolution and syphilis."[63] Not a figure of speech.

Verkhola was a local hero, but he was not the only one to recoil from the horror of the pogroms. Educated citizens, organized workers, even clergy at times intervened to stop the attacks from unfolding. Peasants could be mobilized to bash the "Yid-Commune," but they would at the same time protect their own Jewish neighbors. One observer concluded that as in Proskurov, "the active interference for defense by the Christian population caused the cessation of the pogroms even in those cases in which the massacres were organized by disciplined military forces."[64] Such intervention was not always successful, however. In March 1919, Zhytomyr went back and forth between Petliura and the Red Army. A rumor circulated that the Jews had massacred 1,700 Christians. A delegation of Jewish and Gentile community leaders approached the troops to refute the rumor, but to no avail. The pogrom in Zhytomyr, which lasted five days, involved murder as well as plunder. The number of victims was limited, however, because many Christians shielded their neighbors and because the Red Army had resumed its advance and the Ukrainian troops were obliged to return to battle.[65] In July 1919, the number of pogroms committed by Directory forces reached a peak, diminishing in August only when Denikin drove the Directory and the Red Army from the Ukraine. From then on, the pogroms became the work of the Volunteer Army.[66]

The question of responsibility—of authority, of power—was key. In fact, the Directory's relationship to the pogroms and to the issue of anti-Semitism was not simple. When it returned to Kiev in December 1918, it had restored Jewish communal autonomy.[67] It included a Ministry of Jewish Affairs and invited the participation of Jewish leaders. Neither Vynnychenko nor Petliura overtly encouraged pogroms or used aggressively anti-Semitic slogans. On January 11, 1919, they issued a proclamation that blamed the violence on "provocateurs from among followers of the hetman, the Volunteer Army, and among those calling themselves Bolsheviks," in order to "disgrace the Ukrainian Republican Army and sow hatred for Ukrainian Cossacks among the population." They called for the arrest and trial of instigators. Unfortunately, the proclamation also echoed a formulation, not exclusive of course to them, that lay at the heart of pogrom logic—that the Jews as a "nation" were somehow responsible for the conduct of individual members of the community. The Directory appealed "to all democratic Jews to fight energetically against the individual anarchist-Bolshevik members of the Jewish nation [*natsiia*], who...provide provocateurs with the basis for the demagogic and harmful agitation they direct against Jews as a whole, who have nothing to do with Bolshevism."[68]

Some Jewish leaders asked Vynnychenko to remove the offending passage, but he claimed it was necessary precisely because collective responsibility was the charge stressed by the anti-Semites.[69] A week later, on January 19, the Army of the Ukrainian National Republic issued a statement that seemed to strengthen the ambiguity. "In whose hands," it asked, "are Ukrainian lands, rivers, factories and so on? In the hands of wealthy Russians, Jews, and Poles. Who always argues against an independent Ukrainian National Republic? Russians, Jews, and Poles."[70] The Directory issued no further statements in February and March, while the violence persisted. By then most Jewish parties had withdrawn their support.[71]

The Directory continued nevertheless to include a Ministry of Jewish Affairs, which focused largely on relief for pogrom victims, and it continued to issue proclamations, insisting it would "not tolerate under any circumstances pogroms against the Jewish population...which dishonor the Ukrainian nation in the eyes of all civilized nations."[72] Additional laws were passed in May, as well, and an investigative commission was established, to try and punish perpetrators.[73] In early July, Petliura sent a telegram to his ministers and army commanders again stressing the need to combat pogroms and the contribution made by Jews to the Ukrainian cause. He blamed the

worst atrocities on the Bolsheviks and claimed to know of cases in which
Ukrainian Cossacks had protected Jewish shops from looting. In August, the
Council of Ministers proposed further penalties for pogromists.[74]

Finally, on August 26, 1919, Petliura issued a decree to the army which
emphasized the degree to which the Jews were also victims of the Bolshevik
regime. He denounced pogroms not only as a crime but as treason against
the Ukrainian state.[75] The Bolsheviks were out for "innocent blood," for
"human meat." Eager to discredit the Ukrainian cause, they had, he admitted, "sometimes incited certain unreliable elements of our army to commit
these terrible deeds." He reminded his "Commanders and Cossacks" that
the world was watching. They must not, by succumbing to Bolshevik provocation, provide the enemy with the means to tarnish the Ukrainian people.[76]
By December 1920, Petliura had taken refuge in the Polish city of Tarnów,
where he learned of charges that Ukrainian troops fighting alongside the
Poles had been guilty of pogroms. Denying that pogroms had occurred,
except perhaps as the work of "robber gangs," he urged his minister of
Jewish affairs to explain to "Jewish circles abroad" that the accusations were
unfounded, implying that Jews were themselves somehow to blame for
damaging the Republic's reputation.[77] Petliura thus repeatedly warned his
armed forces against committing pogroms, sometimes admitting they had
fallen for the temptation, sometimes, against all evidence, denying they had
ever crossed the line. Despite his appeals, as ataman in chief and head of
the Ukrainian National Republic, he nevertheless became a symbol for the
worst excesses of the army of which he was nominally in command. The
historian Henry Abramson notes the irony of a government that was "providing pogrom relief funds to victims of attacks," which its forces were
perpetrating "in the name of that same government."[78] And in Petliura's
name, in particular.

The degree of Petliura's direct responsibility for the pogroms remains a
subject of controversy, revived in its urgency by the desire of post-Soviet
Ukraine to claim him as a national hero.[79] With an eye to world opinion,
the Directory defended its reputation at the time. The Ukrainian delegation
to the Paris Peace Talks in August 1919 blamed the pogroms, which they
could not deny, on "criminal, Black Hundreds elements," attracted by the
possibility of plunder. They repudiated the "rogue actions of individual military units and bands, which directly contradict the basis of our movement
and its leaders."[80] Julian Batchinsky, the Ukrainian Diplomatic Representative
to the United States, explained that the Directory was too weak to stop the

widespread abuses. It was "the strongest possible government under the circumstances," he said, but it was "not powerful enough." Merely eleven months old, it was "expected to assert the principles of right and humanity and to safeguard peace and security in spite of continuous war, and revolution within and without." In the face of armed attacks from all sides, it was expected to establish a viable state, "with a peasant army in rags, with only a strong will to protect their country for their weapon."[81]

The Directory had its Jewish defenders, as well. Arnold Margolin was the son of a wealthy Kiev-based industrialist, educated in Russian schools and trained as a lawyer, who had participated in the defense of Mendel Beilis, then moved to St. Petersburg in 1914 to escape the threats of Black Hundred vigilantes in Kiev. He returned in 1918, believing the future of the Ukrainian Jews lay in their Ukrainian homeland. Having accepted a position in Petliura's cabinet, he resigned over the issue of the pogroms. For all their good intentions, he believed, Petliura and Vynnychenko, as heads of state, were responsible for not being able to stop them. Margolin agreed nevertheless to join the Ukrainian delegation to the Paris Peace talks in 1919.[82] There, he insisted that Petliura had done his best to prevent the assaults, which he described as "instigated by criminals, Black Hundreds, and Bolshevists, who wished to discredit the Ukrainian government."[83] He also contributed to a propaganda pamphlet published in 1919 by the Friends of the Ukraine in the United States defending Petliura's reputation. He explained the plague of pogroms not as the result of Ukrainian nationalism but of the years of Russian domination and what he called "the pogrom habit."[84]

In contrast to Margolin, Elias (Il'ia) Heifetz followed the Soviet line. Appointed by Moscow to chair the All-Ukrainian Relief Committee for the Victims of Pogroms sponsored by the Russian Red Cross, Heifetz concluded, on the basis of testimony gathered by this committee and by Jewish organizations in Kiev, that "the reaction uses the massacre of the Jews as a method for political warfare."[85] The Directory, he maintained, in fact benefited from the depredations it deplored as the work of backward elements. Pretending it was powerless to stop the assaults, could not, he insisted, "exculpate it in any way, not even legally, not to say morally and politically." Understanding the effects of such violence, "it desired them, counted on them and took advantage of them."[86] Insofar as Petliura claimed to be head of state, he bore the responsibility for the deeds that blackened his name and which he had not done enough to prevent. Petliura had issued his August 26, 1919 decree, Heifetz contended, "only after the Denikin reaction had triumphed, when

the Directory rehabilitated itself in the eyes of West European public opinion and had to seek support from the Jewish socialistic parties of the right."[87]

The debate over whether Petliura was or was not personally an anti-
Semite was inflamed in the wake of the exiled leader's assassination in Paris
in 1926 at the hands of a Russian-Jewish refugee and naturalized French
citizen named Solomon Schwarzbard, who claimed to be avenging the
Jewish slaughter. The trial in a Paris courtroom a year later, in which extensive evidence of the pogroms and the policies of the Ukrainian government
were examined and debated, turned not on the issue of the assassin's guilt,
which was never in doubt, but on that of Petliura's reputation.[88] Schwarzbard
was acquitted.

In fact, as its defenders claimed, the Directory's position was one it shared
with other aspiring governments in the Civil War. A power in name only, it
was indeed too weak to impose its will. It is also the case that it needed and
benefited from the authority it delegated to subsidiary chieftains, who did
not have to face the political consequences of their acts. Petliura and
Vynnychenko were not programmatic anti-Semites, but they did not
entirely escape the basic logic of the anti-Semitic world view, which held
the Jews as a collectivity responsible for whatever powerful force seemed
out of their alleged victims' control, whether Bolshevism, capitalism, or the
failure of Ukrainian nationalism. When Jewish socialists complained to
Vynnychenko about the conduct of soldiers under the Ukrainian Army
command, he replied: "Tell your Jews and your young men that they should
not support the Bolshevists. The Jewish workmen organized uprisings in the
towns of Ukrainia to hand over the power to the Bolshevists. We shall soon
be powerless against the anger of our troops against the Jews."[89]

---

As was obvious to all but the blindest anti-Semites, Jewish political allegiances varied widely. Where some individual Jews and Jewish leaders saw
the best hope for their own future in alliance with Ukrainian nationalists,
others viewed Ukrainian nationalism as a danger and banked on the chance
that a greater Russia would better guarantee their rights, just as the Kadet
Party admonished in its November 1919 platform. In both cases, whether
pro-Ukrainian or pro-Kadet, Jewish leaders considered Soviet rule the
greater evil. Some Jews had therefore attached themselves initially to the
White forces. Jews worked in Denikin's propaganda office; some Volunteer

Army officers were Jews. By July 1919, however, all had been dismissed from their positions; an appeal by the officers to be reinstated was repulsed.[90] The Jewish population in the towns at first welcomed the Volunteer Army, distrusting Soviet propaganda, but were soon disillusioned.[91] Margolin, who excused the pogroms committed by Petliura's forces as the work of rogue elements in the turmoil caused by defeat, blamed the pogroms committed by the Volunteer Army on Denikin's official policy. "If in the Ukrainian regular army the rot started at the tail, here the poison of decay began at the head," he said, with officers who "stated baldly that they were not fighting with Bolshevism but with the Jews."[92]

As we have seen, the Volunteer Army spent the summer of 1919 moving progressively deeper into the Ukraine. By the end of August, they had ousted Petliura from Kiev and taken Odessa. By October they had reached Orel, on the way to Moscow, where their progress halted. By December they had been crushed, largely at the hands of the Red Cavalry.[93] Until June the Volunteer Army had operated in areas sparsely populated by Jews. As it advanced westward, the density of Jewish habitation increased and the number of pogroms and their intensity escalated. At first there were individual murders, some looting, some rape. In August, large-scale looting began and Jews were killed in ever greater numbers, but attackers were still sometimes satisfied with money. As the army began its retreat, the ferocity reached its climax.[94]

The White Cossacks and their peasant collaborators were interested mainly in looting, but this motive does not account for the brutality they inflicted—beatings, rapes, murders, obliterating entire communities. When the Volunteer Army entered a town, its publicists plastered the walls with anti-Semitic posters. Hundreds of Jews were murdered at a time, dwellings burned to the ground, women raped, men tortured, people thrown into the Dnepr.[95] The Cossacks did the dirty work (with some personal involvement of officers present), but the commanders set the tone. General Konstantin Mamontov, whom we encountered in the course of Denikin's northward offensive, echoed the signature cry: "Arm yourself and rise against the common enemy of our Russian land, against the Jewish Bolshevik communists."[96] The British journalist John Ernest Hodgson noted with respect to the White Army that it "laid practically all the blame for their country's trouble on the Hebrew. Many held that the whole cataclysm had been engineered by some great and mysterious society of international Jews."[97] Denikin himself did not actively promote the kind of violence that undermined military discipline, but his officers demonstrated what Margolin called a "sadistic hatred for the Jews."[98] And Denikin was reluctant to make the kind of declarations Petliura had offered to placate international public opinion.[99]

Like Petliura, who issued his most emphatic condemnation of pogroms when his fortunes were on the decline, Denikin waited until October 1919, his army then in retreat, to instruct his officers in Kiev to "take energetic measures" to put a stop to "the use of force by the Army against Jews." The Kiev pogroms that followed this announcement, in which at least six hundred Jews were killed, were as violent as any that went before.[100] In the midst of the carnage and mayhem, however, some elements of civic life persisted. Educated society still had something to say. Even in Kiev, there were dissenters. When the main Kiev newspapers claimed, in ritual fashion, that the Jews had started the pogrom by shooting at the troops, the Kiev League to Combat Anti-Semitism, which included the mayor, some magistrates, and an Orthodox priest, came forward to refute the charges.[101]

Not everyone fell for the overheated rhetoric, but the committed anti-Semites spoke loudest. The right-wing ideologue and journalist Vasilii Shul'gin, who in March 1917 had been present at the tsar's abdication, now edited Denikin's official organ, *Velikaia Rossiia*—Great Russia, in both senses of the word, extensive and mighty. On October 8, 1919, he published an article in *Kievlianin*, the leading Kiev newspaper, of which he was the editor, called "Torture by Fear."[102] It became famous. At night in Kiev, it began, "a heart-rending wailing suddenly starts up. It is the Yids. Screaming with fear. Somewhere a handful of 'men with bayonets' will make their way through the darkened streets. At their appearance,...entire streets, seized by mortal horror, cry out in inhuman voices, trembling for their lives." Until the Jews "gather in all the Jewish synagogues and pronounce a public curse" on "the sons of Israel" who support "the Bolshevik frenzy," the terror would continue. "After these terrible nights spent in mortal horror," would they persist instead in denouncing anti-Semitism, "thus inflaming anti-Semitic feelings?" They must either "confess and repent," or continue "to blame everyone except themselves. Which path they choose will determine their fate," Shul'gin warned. The Jews, once again, were responsible, for their own and everyone else's misfortunes.

---

Despite the Bolsheviks' official repudiation of anti-Semitism, some sections of the Red Army were nevertheless responsible for pogroms, as vicious as any other, in which Red officers, Red Army staff, and Soviet commissars themselves participated. In the first months of 1918, the Bolsheviks depended heavily on Red Guard and partisan brigades, which were responsible for pogroms in a series of towns, most egregiously on March 7–9, 1918, in Glukhov (Glukhiv) in the eastern Chernigov region of Left Bank Ukraine.[103] As in the case of Petliura, the top leaders denounced the attacks, which, like him, they blamed on the other side—in this case, on deserters from the White armies and bandit riffraff. Behind the scenes, the Evsektsiia launched an educational campaign against anti-Semitism in the party itself, as well as among the general population.[104] A decree of July 26, 1918 called for "uncompromising measures to tear the anti-Semitic movement out by the roots. Pogromists and pogrom-agitators are to be placed outside the law." Predictably, the decree blamed the "occasional excesses" on the "bourgeois counterrevolution."[105] At the Ukrainian level, party newspapers and leaflets hammered away at the theme. Denunciations of the evil continued, however, to focus on the role of "White Guards" or "kulaks," obscuring the presence of anti-Semitism in the Red Army and in the party's own ranks. In the second half of 1919, partly in reaction to the pogroms staged by anti-Bolshevik troops in the Ukraine, the party began to attract Jewish-identified non-Bolshevik socialists.[106] They complained that not enough had been done to combat the issue on their own side. "Certain Red Army units which are sent to fight the counterrevolution," they reported, "are themselves perpetrating identical criminal pogroms against the Jewish population."[107] *Pravda*, the central party organ, featured a condemnation of anti-Semitism for the first time only in June 1919, on the urging of the Evsetksiia.

Overall, the party's approach was ambivalent—creating and then dismantling special institutions designed to focus on the issue of anti-Semitism, ready to denounce reactionary anti-Semitism but hesitant to acknowledge the sources of anti-Semitism on the Bolshevik side.[108] The Ukraine was a special challenge. On November 21, 1919, Lenin drafted a resolution for the Eighth Party Congress, in which he instructed the party "to keep a tight rein on Jews and city dwellers in Ukraine, transferring them to the front, not letting them into official institutions (except as a negligible percentage, in very exceptional cases, under class supervision)."[109] The resolution, "On Soviet Power in Ukraine," as passed on December 3, altered the original wording, but the meaning was still clear. It instructed that "measures be taken immediately to prevent Soviet institutions from being flooded with the Ukrainian urban petty-bourgeoisie."[110] In general, Soviet propaganda suffered from the problem that its lexicon—bourgeoisie, petty bourgeoisie,

speculators—could easily be interpreted as referring to Jews, and not without reason, as Lenin's first formulation made abundantly clear.

———————

Both the role of Jewish activists as agents of Communist power and the role
of anti-Semitic violence within the regime's own apparatus and popular
base come together in the awful and contradictory case of Budennyi's Red
Cavalry. A commander who was hailed as a Soviet hero led troops that
cursed Soviet power, murdered Soviet officials, plundered, slaughtered, and
terrorized the helpless population, particularly Jews, and were inspired by
the same ferocious slogans preferred by Denikin's anti-Bolshevik army.
Budennyi himself was vicious, defiant, and crude. The Red Army kept him
in harness because he was useful. Born in Rostov of peasant stock, he had
served in the Russo-Japanese War and in the Great War as a noncommissioned officer. Years later, he also served, without distinction, in the Second
World War. For the rest of his life, he appeared as a fixture at ceremonial
occasions. He died of old age in 1973, a Marshal of the Soviet Union.[111]

Budennyi's division was formed in November 1919, when he was a thirty-
six-year-old hellion.[112] A month later, a military commissar denounced the
men as brigands who systematically robbed the towns and villages they
passed through, grabbing everything they could lay their hands on, from the
poor as well as the rich—clothing, boots, chickens, geese, fodder, "breaking
open chests, pulling out women's underwear, money, watches, dishes, etc.
There have been cases of rape and torture.... The peasants ask what's the
difference? the Whites pillaged—now it's the Reds?!"[113] In relation to Soviet
authority, however, Budennyi was his own master. The same commissar
reported an incident in which he and Georgii Piatakov, the Bolshevik leader
in Ukraine, visited Budennyi at his headquarters and threatened to report
him to the highest Soviet military authorities. In reply, the drunken commander uttered a string of obscenities, smashed Piatakov over the head, and
only failed to shoot him when the pistol misfired. "I destroyed Shkuro,
Mamontov, and Ulagai," Budennyi shouted, naming three notorious White
commanders, "and you are going to judge me?!" His men felt a personal
loyalty. "Long live the dictatorship of the proletariat and our chief Budennyi!"
was their cry.[114]

No admonition had any effect. In taking Rostov in January 1920, the cavalry
trashed the wine cellars, went through town plundering houses, committing

"the most degenerate violence and murder." The local Cheka complained that Budennyi took orders from no one. His men controlled the railroads, grabbing fuel, locomotives, and wagons and filling them with stolen goods. They attacked Red patrols and threatened emissaries from the Revolutionary Military Council with their lives when they attempted to restrain them.[115] Another report in February noted that "robbery, violence, banditism, resistance to authority, plunder, and the murder... of political commissars, the taking of trophies all remain unpunished. Prisoners are stripped naked and shot.... The Red Cavalry destroys the counterrevolution as it moves along, but its conduct in the places it captures only revives it." Other reports noted open anti-Semitic agitation, the continuing abuse of prisoners, and attacks on local inhabitants.[116]

The Soviet High Command made excuses. Tukhachevskii deplored the conduct at Rostov but said the Red Cavalry was still an exceptional fighting force. Voroshilov, in March 1920, said all they needed was reeducation.[117] The deputy head of the army political department attached to the Red Cavalry was not so sure. In June 1920, he described the Red Cavalry as composed "mainly of deserters from Denikin and prisoners of war," who behaved like bandits. In the absence of an organized supply system, they robbed the peasants. The Communist personnel were no better, "getting drunk, pillaging along with soldiers, telling their orderlies to get them chickens, geese, clothing, sometimes gold and other valuables." The whistle-blower deputy was dismissed for spreading "lies and defamation."[118] A month later, however, Voroshilov sounded even more severe. "A significant part, probably a majority of our comrades," he noted, "are convinced that a Jew cannot survive in the Red Cavalry, that our soldiers beat and murder Communists and commissars, and in their spare time rape and rob the civilian population."[119] It is clear that among other atrocities rapes were ubiquitous. A report from an incident in October noted that "women were raped in the streets before everyone's eyes and many of the prettiest girls were taken away in the army train."[120]

The Communists responsible for the Red Cavalry denied the charge, which they attributed to "bourgeois-philistine-intelligentsia elements," that it was a "bandit, hooligan, anti-Semitic" outfit, "in which Jews were not permitted, in which commissars were murdered, which plunders, rapes, and tortures." The Red Cavalry, they reported to Moscow, embodied "the peasant masses, rising against Russian landowners and the rich Cossacks of the Don and Kuban." Plunder was needed to feed the men; excesses might occur, but that was true of any army.[121] It was not easy, however, to excuse the role of those Red Army commanders who failed to stop the rampages or even joined in. Some commissars were themselves murdered, to the incongruous chants of "Smash the Yids, Communists, and Commissars, and save Russia."[122] In a contorted fashion the pogromists achieved their goal. The civilian population came to "feel passionate hatred of the Red Army and Soviet power."[123]

Mikhail Frunze, hero of the Turkestan campaign, now commander of the Southern Front, acknowledged the existence of "counterrevolutionary attitudes in Budennyi's army" and urged he be disciplined, but at the same he assured Lenin, "concerning Budennyi's own position and his devotion to Soviet power there are absolutely no doubts."[124] A tribunal was established to investigate the violence and Budennyi's defiance. The evidence repeated the earlier reports. In one town, "twenty-one Jews killed and twelve wounded," in another "drunken Red Army men raped almost every woman," in yet another, "eighteen houses were burned, twenty men killed, women raped in the streets in full view of the townsfolk and the younger women taken away like slaves in transports." Again, the incongruous slogan was usually: "Kill the Jews, Communists, and Commissars."[125] At the end of October, over a hundred perpetrators were sentenced to be shot or jailed. In December nothing had changed. On the Southwest Front, a commissar reported, the men were ready to "finish off Wrangel," while saving Russia from the "Yids and Communists." The pogroms and the plunder had "merged with the military operations and become unnoticeable.... The population where the First Red Cavalry passed through was literally terrorized."[126]

Attached to Budennyi as a political commissar, Isaac Babel noted in his field diary entry for August 18, 1920: "Farther on—the enemy. Two butchered Poles, naked, their small faces slashed to pieces, shining through the rye in the sunlight.... The prisoners are rounded up, made to undress, a strange scene, they undress terribly quickly, shaking their heads, all this out in the sun.... The military commissar and I ride along the line begging the men not to massacre prisoners.... they bayoneted some, shot others, bodies covered by corpses, they strip one man while they're shooting another, groans, screams, death rattles.... It's hell. Our way of bringing freedom—horrible."[127]

Babel, for July 21, 1920: "What sort of person is our Cossack? Many-layered: looting, reckless daring, professionalism, revolutionary spirit, bestial cruelty. We are the vanguard, but of what? The population await their saviors, the Jews look for liberation—and in ride the Kuban Cossacks." August

11, 1920: "This isn't a Marxist revolution, it's a Cossack rebellion. . . . hatred of the rich, of the intelligentsia, an unquenchable hatred."[128] It was on August 20, 1920, that the First Cavalry Army finally set out from Lwów in the direction of Warsaw, to back Tukhachevskii's move from the north, arriving too late to do him any good.

---

The Red Cavalry in 1920 was fighting the Polish Army. Like the Ukrainian Directory, leaders of the newly independent Polish nation struggled to defend themselves against charges of encouraging or failing to stop violence against the Jews. They insisted that the Polish people were not anti-Semitic, they rejected the idea that Jews were special targets in the context of war-time violence and economic collapse, and they blamed the campaign against pogroms for soiling the new government's reputation and harming its prospects in the international area. Some Western statesmen might themselves dislike the Jews, but they did not approve of murdering them. Polish spokesmen returned once again to the notion that the Jews "as a nation" had the responsibility to curb the behavior of those among them who provoked the just wrath of the Gentile population, leading to outbursts of violence that diminished the standing of the former oppressed minorities of the Russian Empire, which is to say, the Poles, in the eyes of the world. The Jews "as a nation"—as an international lobby with deep pockets—had an obligation to stop complaining about what was done to them in response to their own provocations. In short, the Jews were responsible—twice over.

In July 1919, Secretary of State Robert Lansing sent Henry Morgenthau to Poland in charge of an investigative commission. A lawyer and business-man, Morgenthau had served as American ambassador to the Ottoman Empire during the war, where he had publicized the news of the Armenian massacres and helped organize relief aid for the victims. He now spent two months in Poland collecting testimony and data about violence against the Jews. The British government, for its part, dispatched Sir Stuart Montagu Samuel, a banker and former liberal MP, who visited Poland from September to December 1919, together with Captain Peter Wright, a British consular official, who wrote a dissenting report. By the time the reports were published in 1920, the Polish-Soviet war had begun, increasing the urgency of the issue.[129]

Polish Prime Minister Ignacy Jan Paderewski welcomed the investigation. The National Polish Committee of America published the results, hoping to promote a "rapprochement between Poles and Jews in Poland." The Committee was certain the report would "result in complete vindication of the Polish Government." The evidence showed that "in Poland proper" only a handful of Jews had been killed, and in any case it was wrong to "indict a people on the record made by groups of outlaw soldiery on an active front." Even the outlaws were not to blame, it turned out. "If certain elements of the Polish population have at times apparently persecuted the Jews, perhaps there was some real reason for their antagonism."[130] The Jews must have provoked them—and were doing so still. These "apparent persecutions," the Committee complained, did not justify the "inflammatory propaganda" that created "an unjustified hatred of the Polish people." Newspaper stories about "pogrom atrocities" and "all these organized and well financed endeavors to assist Jewry by destroying the dearly won freedom of Poland" only increased the resentment that led to pogroms in the first place and prevented "moderate elements" on both sides from working together.[131] In short, complaining about ill treatment would only result in more of it. This had been the point of Shul'gin's "Torture by Fear."

Morgenthau's findings were intended to be impartial. He even avoided the word "pogrom," because, he complained, it was "applied to everything from petty outrages to premeditated and carefully organized massacres."[132] The events his account detailed, which he referred to as "excesses," seemed, however, to conform to the recognizable pattern. Incidents began immediately after the Central Powers had departed. When the Jews of a town gathered to discuss community issues, local ruffians, released criminals, and Polish Army soldiers, in some combination, would disperse the meeting and beat the participants, sometimes gunning them down. In November, 1918, four Jews had been killed in Kielce and sixty-four in Lwów; in April, 1919, thirty-five men in Pinsk were shot in cold blood, while the women were beaten, and thirty-nine Jews were killed in Lida.[133]

In Vilnius street fighting continued for three days, beginning April 19, 1919, in the course of which thirty-three Polish soldiers were killed and sixty-five Jewish residents, including four women and eight men over fifty. Some were taken outside of town and shot point-blank; others were shot while their homes were being ransacked. Altogether two thousand Jewish dwellings and shops were plundered by Polish soldiers and civilians, who took the shoes and blankets from even the poorest families. Hundreds of Jews were arrested and deported, herded into boxcars, kept without food or water for days. Soldiers broke into the synagogue and mutilated the Torah.

No one was prosecuted.[134] And so on, in Kolbuszowa and Częstochowa in May, in Minsk in August. In Minsk, Morgenthau noted, almost all the shops were owned by Jews, so the looters could not help but damage Jewish property. He did observe, however, that almost all the thirty-one murders "were committed, to all appearances, solely on the ground that the victims were Jews."[135]

Despite this observation, the Morgenthau report categorized most of the violence as political, but not anti-Semitic, insofar as Jews were identified as Bolsheviks and the soldiers were undisciplined and the officers inexperienced. These were the observations most congenial to the Polish Committee of America. The report did, however, note that "the belief that the Jewish inhabitants were politically hostile to the Polish State" was aggravated by "a widespread anti-Semitic prejudice."[136] It could not help but mention "other forms of persecution," such as incidents in which soldiers pulled Jews from trains, beat them, and cut their beards or tore them out. Nor could it ignore the economic boycott promoted by the National Democrats and the attitudes of the non-Jewish press, "which constantly advocates that the economic boycott be used as a means of ridding Poland of its Jewish element."[137]

Morgenthau's collaborators, U.S. Army Brigadier General Edgar Jadwin and Mr. Homer H. Johnson, demurred from his conclusions, striking a posture more favorable to the Polish cause. They stressed the relatively small number of "excesses" and the goodwill of the Polish government in condemning and trying to curb them. They emphasized the reasons why Poles might understandably resent the Jews. "Even in the Middle Ages," they noted, "Jewish separatism, commercial competition and acquisitiveness aroused a certain irritation among the Polish masses, which has persisted as an inherited prejudice to the present day."[138] Wartime conditions had increased this "irritation"—goods were scarce, prices rose, Jews were seen as profiteering. Then, again, irritation turned to violence because the Polish Army and indeed the Polish state were still in the process of formation, but neither had "instigated or approved" the regrettable events.[139] Yet Jadwin and Johnson could not deny that many cases showed "an intelligent and intentional discrimination on the part of the lawless element in the army disclosing a racial antipathy made more patent by the desire to rob and pillage, which was apparently felt not to be wrong or at least not to be severely punished by superiors." The two concluded, however, "that in the highly charged atmosphere there was quite enough fault on both sides."[140] In what sense the Jews had contributed to the violence remained unclear.

The bone of contention was not thus the fact of violence against the Jews, but its extent and the role of the Polish authorities in either encouraging or not sufficiently discouraging the outbreaks, in failing to curb and punish them. It could not be denied that Polish propaganda—like Roman Dmowski's nationalist platform—was overtly anti-Semitic.[141] In 1916 Dmowski had informed the European public that "the Jews in Poland... in their mass do not belong to the Polish nationality: their language is Yiddish, a German dialect, and they are organised as a separate Jewish nationality against the Poles. In these conditions the struggle against the Jews is a national struggle."[142] In 1920, a Polish leaflet appealed—in Russian—to Red Army soldiers "fed up with the power of the Jewish commissars."[143] A poster captioned "Bolshevik Freedom" (*Wolność bolszewicka*) depicted Trotsky with an accentuated Jewish nose.[144] Another poster asked: "Once more those Jewish paws? No, never again!"[145]

Whatever the level of violence in 1919, the war with Russia in 1920 worsened the situation for the Jews, who were now even more emphatically identified with the Soviet enemy. Some conservative Polish Catholics went so far as to demand the expulsion of the Jews from Poland. During the Battle of Warsaw in August 1920, the Polish Army disarmed and interned its three thousand Jewish soldiers, many of them volunteers, allegedly for their own protection. The police arrested the leaders of the Jewish Bund and charged them with treason. As the towns changed hands, the Jews were caught in between. Both armies looted and murdered civilians, among them Jews.[146] Defenders of Polish national honor to this day maintain that the international campaign denouncing the pogroms only sharpened the tension between Poles and Jews in Poland, lending credence to the views of Polish nationalists such as Dmowski, who had always made anti-Semitism central to his appeal.[147] Yet again, the Jews somehow bring misfortune on their own heads by exaggerating their misfortunes.

As an attitude or reflex, anti-Semitism emerges as a constant feature of mass mobilization. The question facing the leadership in each case was what to make of this feature. Programmatically anti-Semitic White officers might worry about loss of discipline when their men went on the rampage, but they themselves fostered the myths that bolstered the popular impulse—indeed they used these myths as a rallying cry. Jews were to blame for Russia's disaster. In the case of the atamans, no conflict of interest was involved—they were in the business of mob violence. Anti-Semitism played an important role in anchoring both Polish and Ukrainian nationalism, drawing on deep-seated feelings of distrust and envy among the general population.

Socialist ideology, by contrast, focused on class conflict and rejected the importance of ethnic or cultural difference. Petliura had a ministry for Jewish affairs to demonstrate his goodwill and also to placate those noisy "Jewish circles." It was only in the Soviet camp, however, that Jews occupied prominent places in the official apparatus. As officials, they interacted directly with the worker and peasant populace, made arrests, and meted out punishments. Yet class categories and ethnic categories often overlapped, and the general virulence of Bolshevik propaganda, which insisted on the utter destruction of the (class) enemy, easily gained traction among followers for whom the social landscape was organized in anti-Semitic terms. The presence of actual Jews in Communist ranks might (and often did) pose a strategic problem. The Jewish question was a question of life or death for the Jews; it was also a symbolic vehicle for the expression of fear, anger, and aggression.

# 9

# The Last Page

In 1920 the Soviet caricaturist Viktor Denisov (Deni) designed a poster with the caption "Reap in Time!" A Russian peasant in a bright red shirt decapitates both the "Polish Landowner" (*Pol'skii Pan*) and "Wrangel"—the Black Baron—with a single sweep of his scythe. Indeed, beginning in spring 1920 the Soviets had faced two simultaneous threats. Once the armistice with Poland was signed in October, the Red Army turned its attention to the south, where the Baltic Baron, General Petr Wrangel, was making a final push against Soviet power. Oddly in parallel, Wrangel and the Bolsheviks were both attempting—under different flags—to reconstruct the map of the former Russian Empire. The Bolsheviks had the greater ambition—not merely to recapture the lost and renegade parts, but to extend the Communist revolution beyond all political borders. Moscow would be the center of a truly global map. The conquest of Poland was to have opened the door to Europe. Instead, over the course of 1920 the Baltic states formalized their independence, as we have seen, and Polish victory turned Soviet Russia inward. It remained to wipe out the remaining threat of military opposition.

---

By the start of 1920, the remnants of the far-flung White movement had taken refuge on the Crimean peninsula. The Crimea constituted the southern part of Tauride Province, which in the north abutted the provinces of Kherson west of the Dnepr and Ekaterinoslav to the northeast. The mountainous peninsula was connected to the broad North Tauride plains, an agricultural steppe region, by the narrow Perekop Isthmus. The Crimea's easternmost point, at the city of Kerch, closed the mouth of the Sea of Azov, across a narrow strait from the Kuban. "How small," General Wrangel reflected, "was this scrap of free Russia compared with the vast Russian territories in the power of the Reds!"[1] The same shard of empire—about a quarter of 1 percent of former imperial lands, not counting Finland—was the site also of the final attempt to construct a moderate alternative to Bolshevik rule.[2] The two challenges—political and military—to Soviet legitimacy lived in uneasy proximity, and both went down to defeat.

Crimea had become part of the Russian Empire in 1783, during the reign of Catherine the Great, after centuries of conquest and reconquest. The great powers did not like Russia's move in the direction of Asia Minor, but did nothing about it at the time. From 1853 to 1856, however, the peninsula was the site of the Crimean War pitting Russia against France, Britain, and the Ottoman Empire.[3] Under Catherine, Russia had triumphed; seventy years later, the humiliation of defeat was among the reasons compelling Tsar Alexander II to abolish serfdom and institute the Great Reforms. As part of the Empire's commercial development, a railroad completed in 1875, through mountainous terrain, linked Sevastopol to central Russia and the European grain market. At the same time, the coastal town of Yalta became a favorite vacation spot for rulers and the Russian upper classes.

The Crimea was not just a playground for Russians elites, however. At the end of the nineteenth century, Tauride Province as a whole had almost 1.5 million inhabitants, a million of them on the mainland, of whom two-thirds were Ukrainian-speaking peasants, another quarter Russian-speaking. The population of the peninsula was more varied. In 1917 its 800,000 inhabitants belonged to thirty-four ethnic groups. About half were Russian and Ukrainian, a quarter Tatars and Turks, and about 8 percent Jews. Among the rest were Crimean Germans (nineteenth-century settlers known as Krimdeutsche), Bulgarians, and Greeks.[4]

The Crimean response to the February Revolution, though reflecting its distinctive profile, followed the general pattern. As soon as the Provisional Government took over in Petrograd, Crimean Tatars began organizing a political movement with the goal of achieving autonomy in cultural and religious affairs. At the end of March, fifteen hundred delegates from all over the Crimea, most with a generally democratic, SR outlook, assembled in the centrally located city of Simferopol, where they formed a Provisional Executive Committee dedicated to the national autonomy of the Crimean Tatars. The leading figure was the thirty-two-year-old writer and political activist Noman Çelebicihan. In July, these secular Tatar democrats issued a program calling for a Constituent Assembly and the reorganization of Russia on a federative basis. They also formed the Milli Firka (National Party), advocating socialist reforms and equal rights for ethnic communities. At the same time, the Tatar moderates faced competition from local representatives of the new Petrograd authorities and from soviets organized in the port cities.[5] The general temper among local leaders, including the socialists, was tolerant and democratic in the broad sense. They faced not only the shock waves from the center, but also tremors closer to home. In July, the Ukrainian Central Rada made a claim to possession of the upper Tauride Province, although by the end of summer they had agreed to acknowledge Crimea's separate status.[6]

The October coup was naturally heralded by the Bolshevik Sevastopol soviet, but the rest of the Crimean political spectrum still put its hopes on the Constituent Assembly. "A handful of anarchist-communists," protested the Yalta soviet, "led by Lenin, Zinov'ev, and others, driven by overweening ambition and the thirst for power, supported by open and concealed agents of the German General Staff and by the Black Hundreds organizations of Petrograd, using deception, lies, and treachery, have lured a part of the Petrograd garrison and workers into armed insurrection against the revolutionary government and the Soviets of soldier, worker, and peasant deputies."[7] The local Mensheviks, separately, also denounced the coup. The Bolsheviks, meanwhile, got down to business, organizing soviets in all the Crimean cities. As in Petrograd, here, too, the socialist Left rejected the single-party takeover. A general congress of soviets that convened in Simferopol in November denounced the coup as a "criminal gamble" and called for the consolidation of democratic forces, from the zemstvos and City Dumas, to the ethno-national organizations. A Soviet of People's Representatives (*Sovet narodnykh predstavitelei*) was formed, with its own embryonic military command. Embracing all parties except the Bolsheviks and the Kadets, the delegates represented a range of workers, factories, municipal organizations, and ethnic groups.[8]

The Tatars, for their part, operated both as a local community and in relation to a broader Muslim context. On November 20, 1917, the Sovnarkom issued an "Appeal to All the Laboring Muslims of Russia and the East" (*Obrashchenie Soveta Narodnykh Komissarov ko vsem trudiashchimsia musul'manam Rossii i Vostoka*), signed by Stalin as commissar of nationalities, promising respect for Muslim beliefs and customs.[9] The Crimean Tatars, however, were determined to decide their own fate. Independent of the (anti-Bolshevik) Soviet of People's Representatives, a Crimean National Constituent Assembly, called the Qurultay, gathered in the Palace of the Khans in Bahçesaray

(Bakhchisarai). Its seventy-eight delegates, representing the cohort of educated young Tatars, formed a Crimean National Democratic Republic (*Krymskaia narodnaia demokraticheskaia respublika*), headed by a Directory. While leaving the last word to the All-Russian Constituent Assembly, they adopted a constitution (*Krymskotatarskie osnovnye zakony*—the Crimean Tatar Fundamental Laws), which promised to respect the rights of all cultural communities. The Directory assumed the task of organizing armed defense against threats from outside and subversion from within, especially from the growing militancy of the Russian fleet. It called on the inhabitants of Crimea to join in forming a "sovereign community." Their motto was "Crimea for the Crimeans!"—but they warned: "If we let the fight for national hegemony tear us apart, as it has in Lithuania, Poland, and Courland, our destiny will be determined by foreigners."[10]

By the end of 1917, the various parties had thus sorted themselves into three centers—the (non-Bolshevik, socialist) Soviet of People's Representatives, the Qurultay, and the Bolshevik Sevastopol soviet.[11] When it came to the elections for the Constituent Assembly in November, an astounding two-thirds of the Crimean population participated. The Russian and Ukrainian SRs together won two-thirds of the votes, the Muslim parties 12 percent, the Kadets 7 percent, the Bolsheviks 6 percent, and the Mensheviks under 3 percent. Among the Baltic Fleet sailors, considered the Bolshevik stronghold, the SRs nevertheless outpolled them two-to-one.[12] By January, however, the Constituent Assembly was nothing but a symbol. Locally, the Sevastopol soviet dissolved the Soviet of People's Representatives and the Qurultay. The Crimean National Republic—admirable on paper—never came into existence.[13]

All the features of revolutionary civic mobilization were thus evident on the small territory of the Crimea. In contrast to Transcaucasia, where intercommunal relations were tense and often bloody, here the leaders of the subnations seemed bent on governing in an inclusive, democratic manner. Yet nationalism was a danger, both inside and out. The Ukrainian Central Rada, which had backed off its claim to Crimea in 1917, would not concede the northern Tauride region. Petliura did, however, allow the Tatar regiment stationed in Ukraine to leave for Crimea.[14] Given the importance of the Baltic Fleet, armed force was clearly going to decide the balance of political power.

The Bolsheviks, for their part, pursued their usual two-pronged strategy, preparing for armed conflict while also mobilizing a popular base. By means of new elections to the local soviets, they secured majorities together with their Left SR allies; in December, a Bolshevik Military Revolutionary Committee took command of Sevastopol. Like their hotheaded northern brothers, for three days the crazed sailors in "the Kronstadt of the South" went on the rampage, terrorizing the city and murdering at least twenty-three officers in the process. "Anarchy is growing," a local journalist wrote. "The furious mob runs wild all over, brigandage, plunder, lynching, shooting, everywhere chaos and destruction, a fratricidal war has broken out, blood flows in the streets—insanity and horror."[15] Another journalist pleaded: "We cannot live on a volcano. Nerves are stretched to the breaking point and life has become pure hell."[16]

More was to come. In January the Sevastopol Military Revolutionary Committee, ignoring the principles of socialist internationalism, issued leaflets inflaming the already overheated sailors against the "Tatar military dictatorship," complaining that Tatar troops were lording it over the population and inciting violence against the crews.[17] Sailors from Sevastopol invaded Yalta, where they conducted a full-scale war against the Tatar squadrons positioned there. During a week of bloody conflict, the city was devastated, two hundred people were killed, and officers were shot and thrown into the sea. The conflict took on an ethnic coloration as the sailors directed their anger against Tatars, while the Tatars forces, on their side, viewed the Greek population as part of the Russian camp. A vicious cycle of attacks and reprisals ensued between the two ethnic communities, ending with the expulsion of almost the entire Greek population from the south.[18]

The Sevastopol sailors were not finished. On January 12, the Red Army defeated the Tatar cavalry near Simferopol and the Tatar parliament disbanded. Among its leaders, Djafer Seïdamet fled to Constantinople. Çelebicihan, who remained in Simferopol, was arrested and taken to Sevastopol, where he was executed and his body thrown into the sea.[19] His murder was part of a three-day wave of bloody terror at the end of February, which left at least six hundred people dead, many having first been subjected to brutal tortures. Lenin's February 21 decree, "The Socialist Fatherland in Danger," calling for the elimination of the recalcitrant bourgeoisie and also targeting a long list of potential enemies, had been widely disseminated. In Sevastopol it provided the impetus for the sailors, mixed in with shiftless men on the docks, to invade the city and take action. The commander of the vessel *Borets za svobodu* (*Freedom Fighter*) instructed the men to "wipe out the bourgeoisie." Another commander ordered this goal to be accomplished "by whatever means necessary." Large sums were extorted from prosperous citizens, who were first held under arrest, then shot. Officers were murdered wherever they were found, often in dramatically gruesome ways. Over the three days of violence, an investigation later concluded, the death toll had reached at least six hundred.[20] Often described as the work of unbridled mobs or fanatical sailors, the terror that seized the port cities in early 1918 reflected the political line coming from Petrograd. The rampages coming from the docks constituted an assault by the periphery on the heart of Crimean society, where the Bolsheviks had little purchase.

Rampaging sailors were nevertheless not enough to establish Soviet power. After the signing of Brest-Litovsk, the Bolsheviks announced the establishment of the Socialist Soviet Republic of the Tauride (*Sotsialisticheskaia sovetskaia respublika Tavridy*), confirmed by the Sovnarkom on March 22, as part of Soviet Russia, its territory limited to the Crimea to avoid conflict with Ukraine or the German occupiers. Not all soviets representing Soviet power were equally militant, but their primary goal seems to have been the seizure of property, often taking the form of barely organized plunder.[21]

It was not long before the reaction began. By mid-April, Mensheviks and SRs had gained control of the Sevastopol and Simferopol soviets.[22] Crucially, between April 17 and 19, German troops, accompanied by Ukrainian soldiers, crossed the Perekop Isthmus heading for Simferopol, in violation of the terms of the treaty. Two thousand Soviet troops were positioned at the base of the Isthmus, but the Bavarian cavalry broke through their defensive lines. In pursuit of the fleeing troops, they massacred everyone they caught.[23] The invasion was a signal for Tatar squadrons to descend from the hills, where they had fled the Bolshevik takeover, and launch an uprising against Soviet power, while also taking revenge on the Christian population for the January events in Yalta. The Tatar forces were in turn soon ousted by Bolshevik sailors. The tide turned yet again on the last day of April, when the Germans took Sevastopol from the sailors and Red Guards who had been defending it.[24] Thus ended the first Socialist Soviet Republic of the Tauride.

As in the Ukraine, the occupiers were interested in stability. The Germans imposed martial law and demanded the population surrender their weapons.[25] The Qurultay leaders returned and welcomed the German occupation as a step toward eventual autonomy and protection against both the Bolsheviks and the Ukrainian nationalists.[26] With German support, the Tatars put together a provisional Crimean government, without the participation of socialists or Kadets, based on the principle of regional autonomy. Many leading Kadets had gravitated toward the south, ending up in Crimea, where some had country houses. Some, following the example of their Kiev colleagues, who had voted to support Hetman Skoropads'kyi, favored an alliance with the occupiers; others remained loyal to the Allies. All agreed there was no future for Crimea outside a greater Russia.[27]

The attempt to form a Tatar government did not succeed, however, and the Germans switched their backing to General Maciej Sulkiewicz (Sul'kevich, Süleyman bey Sulkeviç), who announced the establishment of a so-called Crimean Regional Government (*Krymskoe kraevoe pravitel'stvo*).[28] Sulkiewicz's own background reflected the infinite cultural and demographic complexity of the old Empire. His parents belonged to the Lipka, or Lithuanian Tatars, an originally Turkic-speaking population that settled in what was then the Grand Duchy of Lithuania in the fourteenth century. Lipka Tatar cavalry fought under the banner of the Polish-Lithuanian Commonwealth. Sulkiewicz himself attained the rank of lieutenant general in the Imperial Russian Army in 1915, having served earlier in the war against Japan.

It was clear that Sulkiewicz would not survive without his sponsors. Leading Kadet figures soon began to consider what might happen after they had departed. Some wanted to cooperate with Denikin in a broad Empire-wide movement; others shifted toward a more local orientation, envisioning a regional government with deep social roots and public participation; a few favored military dictatorship as suitable to current turbulent conditions. A zemstvo congress held in Yalta in September 1918, involving SRs and Mensheviks, as well as Kadets, agreed on the choice of Solomon Krym (with an appropriate surname) to head a future post-occupation government. A Crimean Karaite Jew fluent in the Tatar language, Krym was also a landowner, an agronomist, former president of the Tauride zemstvo council, and erstwhile deputy to the First and Fourth State Dumas.[29] Vladimir Nabokov agreed to serve as minister of justice. As minister of foreign affairs Krym chose Maksim Vinaver. A prominent Petersburg lawyer of Polish Jewish origin, known as a vigorous advocate of Jewish rights, who had signed the Vyborg Manifesto and been elected deputy to the Constituent Assembly, Vinaver feared that having two Jews on the masthead would alienate General Denikin and the Volunteer Army, whom they would likely have to rely on for military support. He accepted the position only on the urging of the venerable Ivan Petrunkevich, who denounced anti-Semitism as the bane of the anti-Bolshevik movement. The seventy-five-year-old Petrunkevich was a veteran zemstvo activist, founding member of the pre-1905 Liberation Movement, Kadet deputy to the First State Duma, and Vyborg signatory—in short, the living incarnation of the prolonged liberal effort to create a republican Russia.[30] He died in exile in Prague in 1928, two years after Vinaver had died in Paris, his long quest unrealized.

Just as Skoropads'kyi had fallen when the Germans left the Ukraine, their withdrawal from Crimea ended the tenure of General Sulkiewicz, who headed for Armenia, where he became chief of staff of the armed forces. He was arrested by the Bolsheviks in May 1920 and executed in Baku in July.[31] In his place, on November 16, 1918, the Kadet shadow cabinet, backed by the zemstvo organizations, declared itself the new (provisional) government of Crimea, in anticipation, once again, of the future Constituent Assembly, since it had never been elected or earned any sort of popular acclaim. One of its supporters nevertheless called it "a model laboratory experiment" in democratic government.[32] Gathered in the Simferopol Governor's house, the ministers declared their dedication to a united, indivisible Russia—not the "old, bureaucratic, centralized Russia, based on repression and the suppression of its various peoples," but "a free democratic state, which guarantees the rights of all its peoples to maintain their distinctive cultures."[33]

Indeed, the Crimean Regional Government tried to be all things to all people. It opposed the Bolsheviks, cooperated with the socialists, and maintained the ultimate goal, despite its local orientation, of a future reunified (non-imperial, but all-embracing) Russian state.[34] Tatar demands to postpone the question of independence until the Paris Peace Conference were rejected, although no obstacles were placed in the way of Tatar education and the press, thus allowing Tatar nationalism to flourish.[35] The Crimean Regional Government nevertheless did not include any Tatars in its ranks, and Krym himself was roundly detested by their spokesmen.[36]

The key question of defense was even more difficult to resolve than the conflict between national aspirations and local rights. Without a military force, the government could not enforce its authority or protect itself from attack. As Nabokov put it, sounding not unlike Lenin, the process of establishing a workable government would have to be accompanied by "the process of reestablishing the apparatus of state power. And the first condition of such reestablishment must be the search for an effective coercive force, which constitutes the basis of all state power and without which the existence of power is conceivable only in the theories of anarchism."[37]

One obvious solution was to look to the foreign nations still demonstrating a keen interest in the outcome of the internal Russian struggle. In November the Allies had moved twenty-two vessels—English, French, Greek, and Italian—into Sevastopol harbor, where they were welcomed by Foreign Minister Vinaver. By March 1919, about twenty thousand of their troops had come ashore, but when Vinaver begged for direct military support, the Allies were reluctant. The French did not want to get involved.[38] An alliance with General Denikin therefore seemed the only option, despite his hostility not only to socialist partners of any stripe, but to liberalism itself. The Kadets in Ekaterinodar had endorsed Denikin's cause, but the Kadets in Crimea were wary.[39]

While insisting on civilian control of the government, the Crimean Kadets agreed to recognize the Volunteer Army, "insofar as it is apolitical and insofar as it does not interfere in the internal affairs of the Crimea." The government's socialist supporters were less than enthusiastic about Denikin's followers, among whom they suspected, not unjustly, were many who wished to restore the regime they had helped to destroy.[40] Denikin stoked suspicion by starting off on the wrong foot. In late November, he sent six hundred men into the Crimea, expecting to increase their number with local recruitment. When a military draft was unexpectedly announced, the ministers protested, and Denikin in turn was offended. The mobilization order was withdrawn, but Krym was pressured into issuing one of his own, which Tatar spokesmen energetically rejected. Tensions remained. The ministers, echoed by the trade unions, protested Denikin's increasingly repressive methods. In Ekaterinodar, however, the Kadets continued to support Denikin as the only option and criticized the Crimeans for insisting on their independence. Eventually, the Volunteer Army agreed to step back, and a modus vivendi was established.[41]

---

Meanwhile, on its precarious perch, Krym's Crimean Regional Government did its best to implement liberal principles. It abolished censorship (permitting virulent attacks from Tatar and socialist sources), guaranteed civil rights and minority rights, organized democratic elections, renovated the legal system (Nabokov's work), but hesitated on the question of land, feeling all along that it was provisional.[42] This experiment in moderate utopia did not last and could not have lasted. In addition to the constraints imposed by the geopolitical cul-de-sac in which they were situated, threatened from all sides, they faced a full-scale economic emergency. The peninsula was crammed with refugees, and agriculture and manufacture had collapsed. Unemployment was on the rise, provoking worker unrest. Women began demonstrating for bread in the cities as early as December; rations had been instituted by March.[43] The government was in addition weakened by two (unavoidable) conflicts—with their pro-Denikin colleagues in Ekaterinodar and with Denikin himself, who suspected Krym and his ministers of facilitating Bolshevik penetration by their accommodating attitude toward their socialist allies. In early 1919, as conditions worsened, the Volunteer Army began conducting searches, making arrests, and resorting to executions. Krym himself became less tolerant of the left opposition. The ministers appealed once more for Allied support, yet again without success.[44]

The Volunteer Army seemed to be competing with the Bolsheviks, a local newspaper complained, in its use of arbitrary arrests, searches, threats of reprisals, murders, and confiscations. A compulsory military draft was introduced. The officers seemed to have gone amok. In Yalta they murdered the important Moscow industrialist Jules Goujon, a French national, in cold blood before the eyes of his family.[45] A long-time resident and public figure, in 1915 Goujon had been arrested briefly on suspicion of harboring German sympathies. He did not survive the Russian turmoil in the end—a victim not of the old regime's enemies, but of its defenders. In Sevastopol a group of officers executed the leaders of a trade union. In general, Vinaver complained, the officers "considered it their right," through murders, arrests, and destruction, "to take revenge on anyone they considered a Bolshevik."[46] Even worse, from the political point of view, the Regional Government soon abandoned its democratic pretensions, failing to denounce the repressions and giving Denikin's Special Council carte blanche. Those who had fought against tsarist repression, Nabokov noted sadly, were now using the same methods themselves. The Simferopol City Duma, in the still audible voice of political moderation, declared its absolute repudiation of "these savage acts of class retribution."[47]

By February 1919, the Red Army was driving the Volunteer Army out of the northern Tauride, the Krym government was losing support in municipal and zemstvo circles, and the Tatars were becoming more vocal in their opposition. A trade union conference called for the withdrawal of the Volunteer Army and the transfer of power to a worker and peasant soviet. Sevastopol was hit by a general strike, which the arrest of leaders and the imposition of martial law by the French command did nothing to stop. By now the Regional Government had lost credit with every sector of the population. When the Red Army entered the Perekop Isthmus in early April, Denikin threatened to withdraw his troops if the Krym government did not itself declare martial law and allow him to take over.[48] It was too late. Pushing the White defense aside, the Red Army soon entered Simferopol. With defeat approaching, the ministers decamped to Sevastopol, which was overrun by panicked refugees.[49] On April 15, they boarded an English ship and abandoned their final Russian outpost, just as Soviet forces arrived in the city.[50]

The liberal experiment in good government under impossible conditions had existed for five months, from November 1918 to April 1919. Its principles had not survived. Following the success of the Red Army in chasing it out, the Politburo authorized the establishment of the Provisional Worker and Peasant Government of the Crimean Soviet Socialist Republic (*Vremennoe Raboche-Krest'ianskoe pravitel'stvo Krymskoi SSR*). The nationality question was at the forefront. The commissars included five Crimean Tatars; the Tatar national party, the Milli Firka, was legalized; Tatar military units were authorized. Meanwhile, class politics proceeded with the usual severity, as private property was expropriated, its owners pressed into forced labor. By this time, however, the Armed Forces of South Russia dominated the lower Ukraine. On June 12, White forces entered the peninsula, overwhelming the Red Army, which departed twelve days later, as did the members of the Crimean Soviet Republic, which had lasted all of seventy-five days.[51]

Denikin installed General Nikolai Shilling as military governor of Tauride and Crimea, where he set about revoking all Soviet decrees and repressing the surviving civic organizations. Zemstvos and City Dumas were dissolved, new elections established on a highly undemocratic franchise, and presses shuttered. As commander of forces in the Crimea, Denikin appointed General Iakov Slashchev, a former Guards commander, who had joined the Volunteer Army early in 1918. By now he was a damaged man. General Wrangel later described him as "a slave to drink and drugs," who looked "pale and pasty, with a toothless mouth and mangy hair, a loud unnatural laugh, and chaotic abrupt movements—a man in the throes of mental sickness."[52] His conduct in Crimea did the White cause no favor. Broadly construing its enemies to include socialists of every kind, even ardent anti-Bolsheviks, as well as respectable Russian public figures and Tatar political leaders, Slashchev conducted widespread arrests and used his own system of courts-martial to impose verdicts.[53] The climax came in February in Sevastopol, where fourteen alleged Communists were summarily shot, provoking a massive strike wave in protest, which in turn prompted Slashchev to declare martial law.[54]

Behind the scenes, meanwhile, General Wrangel had begun a campaign to replace General Shilling. Denikin struck back by dismissing Wrangel and several other like-minded commanders. The crisis in White leadership came to a head quickly. In late February, Wrangel left temporarily for Constantinople, where he took refuge in the Russian consulate. Two weeks later, the remains of the White armies, having failed at their northern campaign, began their final trek southward. Twenty-five thousand Volunteer Army troops and another ten thousand Don and Kuban Cossacks, having abandoned their weapons, equipment, and the last shred of discipline, swelled the already overcrowded population of the peninsula, where Denikin established his headquarters on March 17, 1920.

There he encountered unwelcome opinions. The citizens of Sevastopol warned him "that the great cause of the liberation of Russia from Bolshevik oppression is possible only with the triumph of democratic principles, civil liberties, and the absence of administrative repression."[55] To the contrary, the general objected, the time had come for military dictatorship. In December 1919, he had already liquidated his Special Council and created what he called the South Russian Government (*Iuzhnorusskoe Pravitel'stvo*), in which his role as dictator was only slightly mitigated by a council of ministers.[56] A dictator alone is not enough, however, to run a dictatorship, and Denikin's general staff was deserting him. At a meeting of his top commanders in Sevastopol on March 22, which included General Wrangel, Denikin stepped down and Wrangel agreed to replace him.[57]

---

Nothing could be more symbolic—or symmetrical—than the fact that the "last little page" of the Civil War, as Vladimir Mayakovsky called it, was written on the Crimean peninsula, across the Black Sea from Constantinople and the Straits—the object of imperial Russia's ambitions in the Great War.[58] The awkward partners in the opposition to Bolshevik rule—the White military and the exponents of liberal democracy—had shared the desire to maintain Russia's great-power status, but neither had the ability to reestablish the state structures or the political authority to realize their goal.

The strengths and weaknesses of the remaining anti-Bolshevik resistance were both in evidence in these last days. Petr Wrangel, at forty-two the youngest of the leading White commanders, was now the key figure. Tall in stature, aristocratic in origins and bearing, he was often described as the White officer ideal. Trained as a mining engineer and schooled in the General Staff, he had shown his mettle in the Cavalry Guards in the Russo-Japanese War and Great War. After joining Denikin in summer 1918, he gained control of the North Caucasus that winter and took Tsaritsyn on June 30, 1919, though the Whites lost it again six months later. The Soviets called him the Black Baron after his long black Circassian tunic, which he topped by a black or white Circassian fur hat.[59]

By the time Wrangel took command in early April 1920, Crimea had become the final outpost of the displaced remnants of the old regime. The "vast host of refugees," in the words of William Henry Chamberlin, consisted of "bishops and priests who had fled from the persecution of religion, former governors without provinces, former industrialists without factories, former aristocrats without estates, former state officials without appointments."[60] The popular writer known as Teffi recalled how in 1919 she had "rolled [her] way down the map," heading southward from Moscow, to depart Russia for good.[61] Others like her from the artistic intelligentsia, including some who would not depart, such as the poet Osip Mandelstam and the journalist and writer Ilya Ehrenburg, also made the southward journey. High-ranking civil servants, priests, professionals, and prosperous citizens jostled with the penniless and jobless; imperial officers with camp followers, deserters, and the convalescent—like a "large gypsy camp."[62]

Wrangel found an army in complete disarray, officers demoralized, units in no shape to fight.[63] With a shortage of food and fuel, confronting a horde of panicked refugees, menaced by armed peasant bands in the Crimean hills, the general nevertheless managed to assemble an armed force, composed largely of the Don Cossacks and remnants of the Volunteer Army that had accompanied Denikin on his flight, which he named simply the Russian Army.[64] Discipline was restored in Simferopol by the hanging of drunken officers and men.[65] Considering himself a political as well a military leader, Wrangel assumed the title of Commander in Chief of the Russian Army and Ruler of South Russia (*Glavnokomanduiushchii Russkoi armiei i Pravitel' Iuga Rossii*) and announced the establishment of a Government of South Russia (*Pravitel'stvo Iuga Rossii*), the successor to Denikin's South Russian

Government, established in February on the basis of the Special Council to the Armed Forces of South Russia.[66]

Wrangel's was the last of the many self-proclaimed anti-Bolshevik governments—the Komuch, Vologodskii's Provisional All-Russian Government or Directory, Kolchak's All-Russian Provisional Government, and Denikin's Special Council, to name a few. It was led by Aleksandr Krivoshein, tsarist minister of agriculture until 1915 and head of the imperial provisioning committee during the war. The Right Kadet Petr Struve was minister of foreign affairs. Wrangel was a better disciplinarian than Denikin, a devoutly Orthodox monarchist, with an ear cocked to Kadet advisors and attuned to the words that Western statesmen and the respectable world in general wanted to hear.[67] He declared his opposition to Bolshevik "despotism" and announced himself a proponent of democracy. "From the moment when I accepted my present position," he announced, "I repudiated all my own ideas on the question of government and subjected myself absolutely to the will of the Russian people."[68] Presenting himself to foreign powers as the best hope of concerted opposition to Bolshevik rule, Wrangel gestured toward the kind of social policy Denikin had fatally lacked. Proposing the distribution of land parcels to small cultivators, with long-term compensation to former owners, was clearly, however, too little too late and limited even in aspiration to the small patch of land Wrangel could claim to govern.[69] Compared to the politically tone-deaf Denikin, Wrangel's policies were "more progressive and much more flexible,"[70] it has been said, but he was still far from recognizing the enormity of what had occurred and the futility of reversing the course of events.

Nor could he alter the political atmosphere fostered by his predecessors. The general presented himself as a vigorous opponent of pogroms.[71] He rejected the identification of Bolshevism with the Jews and insisted that ethnic hatred was detrimental to the cause, to the army, and to the future of Russia.[72] Alerted by American and French representatives in Crimea to the fact that the head of his press bureau was publishing anti-Semitic articles in a monarchist paper, Wrangel dismissed him.[73] Whether sincere or merely attuned to foreign signals, his efforts had little effect. When Vasilii Maklakov, the staunch defender of Jewish rights, visited the Crimea in September 1920, he was shocked by what he found. The notorious Orthodox archpriest Vladimir Vostokov was giving public sermons that drew large crowds in which he called for a crusade against the Jews, in terms strident enough to draw protests from other priests and some political conservatives.

Maklakov was particularly distressed to find distinguished intellectuals of formerly moderate and politically enlightened views now accepting the equation of Bolshevism with the Jews, as agents of a worldwide conspiracy.[74]

Nor, any more than Denikin or Kolchak, could Wrangel hope to be rescued by foreign angels. On April 6, 1920, the British informed Georgii Chicherin, the commissar of foreign affairs, that they would not permit the destruction of Wrangel's army, but ten days later they told Wrangel to deal with the Soviets on his own—they would not back him. Wrangel refused to negotiate with the Soviets, whom he of course did not recognize.[75] London, however, no longer wished to prolong the conflict with Soviet Russia, with which it was attempting to establish commercial relations.[76] On June 3, the British warned Wrangel not to move north of the Perekop Isthmus. France, by contrast, after extracting certain concessions, formally recognized the Government of South Russia on August 10. By strengthening the White forces in the south with weapons and military supplies, the French hoped in part to divert Soviet resources from the war with Poland, in which it favored the Polish cause. It was Maurice Paléologue, French ambassador to St. Petersburg at the start of the Great War, who communicated the message to Krivoshein. Both were holdovers from the pre-1917 world.[77]

Although he claimed to represent "the whole Russian state" and thus in principle opposed the independence of former imperial territory, Wrangel took the controversial step of extending feelers to the Georgians, Ukrainians, and Poles, all for their own reasons hostile to Soviet power.[78] None responded, but Wrangel was attacked on his own side for contemplating an alliance with the "dismemberers of Russia." The irony was not lost. While the Reds were busy putting Russia back together again, the defenders of empire were proposing deals with those who were breaking it up. All of this, however, was merely academic.[79]

Wrangel in the end was forced to rely on himself. Without the resources of the North Tauride—grain, horses, men—his Russian Army could not survive. "To demand the withdrawal of our troops to the Isthmus," as the British had done, he complained, "is to condemn the Army and the population to death by famine, for the peninsula cannot feed them."[80] Thus, despite the British warning, on June 6 Wrangel launched an offensive, moving from Perekop up the lower Dnepr. In another last-ditch stand, General Slashchev headed for the Sea of Azov, capturing Melitopol along the way.

His forces easily bested the First Red Cavalry commanded by Dmitrii Zhloba, gaining a precious three thousand horses. In the course of a week, Wrangel had managed to secure the North Tauride, taking thousands of prisoners and weapons.[81]

The future Wrangel still hoped for, against all odds, depended most of all on military success, but it also depended on the ability to rally popular support for the anti-Bolshevik crusade outside the tight circumference of the Crimea. In July, Wrangel persisted in trying to access the Don, attempting two landings from the sea, but the Soviets blocked him, and he switched to a land offensive. The Red Army was obliged to reinforce its numbers in the south, straining its resources, but the peasants of southern Ukraine were hostile. An envoy dispatched to court Makhno's favor was hanged.[82] The Kuban Cossacks were in revolt against the Soviet presence, and Wrangel hoped to recruit their leaders. His overtures in early August were nevertheless rebuffed.[83] "The few Cossacks who remained were in a state of absolute terror," he noted, "they had no faith in our success, and expected the Reds to come back at any moment."[84] Pursuing the offensive, the Circassian General Sergei Ulagai, himself a Kuban Cossack, led a Russian Army detachment into the Kuban, reaching the coast of Azov on August 13, soon flushing the Reds from a key railroad junction north of Ekaterinodar. But the massive Red Army reserves in the Kuban stopped his momentum. By September 7, the Reds had pushed Ulagai out of the region. Forces led by White general Fedor Nazarov, which had entered the Don, were decimated. The local Cossacks—emblems of the counterrevolution—did not rally to the White flag.[85]

---

The final campaign against Wrangel was a triumph of Red ingenuity and confirmed the hopelessness of the anti-Bolshevik cause. Trying to sustain French favor, Wrangel minimized the weakness of his position, proposing an alliance with Poland, under French command. By early September 1920, as we have seen, the Red Army had bungled the Battle of Warsaw and was being pursued by the Poles back into the Ukraine. Unlike Kolchak, Wrangel accepted the fact of Polish independence. He emphasized the fight against Bolshevism at all costs. "To the Bolsheviks," he said, "Russia was nothing but a funeral pile, with the help of which they hoped to set alight the whole of Europe."[86]

In September, fighting continued. Wrangel's forces crossed the Dnepr, heading northward to Ekaterinoslav, but the Reds drove them back with heavy losses. A leading commander fell in battle; the troops fell into disarray and retreated. When the talks between Poland and the Soviets seemed finally to be reaching a solution, the general denounced the Poles as "consistent in their duplicity."[87] He and his army, he pronounced in early October, "were now alone in the struggle which will decide the fate not only of our country but of the whole of humanity. Let us strive to free our native land from the yoke of these Red scum who recognize neither God nor country."[88]

In a final move, beginning October 6, 1920, to prove to the Poles and the French that his forces were still in fighting form, Wrangel's army again crossed the Dnepr, but they were vastly outnumbered.[89] Installed at the bridgehead of Kakhovka, above Kherson, the Red Army was poised to attack the North Tauride and Crimea. The Polish-Soviet armistice of October 12 freed the Red Army to focus on the Southern Front.[90] Even earlier, however, the Red command had already begun focusing on Wrangel, creating a new Southern Army group led by Mikhail Frunze, the talented officer who had played a decisive role in the 1919 Turkestan campaign, as we have seen.[91] The heat was on. Now that the peace with Poland had been signed, Trotsky wrote, "We need peace and manpower. Soldiers of the Red Army! Destroy Wrangel! Wipe his gangs from the face of the earth!"[92]

Frunze's goal was to prevent Wrangel from dropping back into the Crimea by keeping him on the vulnerable open terrain above Perekop. By late October, Semen Budennyi's cavalry had arrived from the Polish front (leaving a trail of pogroms as they traveled the intervening three hundred miles). Five Red armies were positioned now in the North Tauride, poised to attack. Wrangel understood the danger of remaining above the Perekop Isthmus, but he needed the harvest. On October 28, the Red Army launched its attack. The results were devastating. Twenty thousand men, half the Russian Army, were captured. The remainder staged a fierce defense at the top of Perekop, along the ancient fortified stone wall that had defended the isthmus since the sixteenth century. West of the Sea of Azov lies an expanse of shallow salt-saturated lagoons, called the Salt Lakes or Putrid Sea (*Gniloe More*), which in the cold weather of early November allowed the Red soldiers to march across and attack Wrangel's remaining men. Frunze, at headquarters in Kharkov, orchestrated the assault, which began on November 7, to coincide with the anniversary of the October Revolution. Wrangel was forced to retreat, but was hit again by the Red Latvians and General Vasilii Bliukher. Despite taking enormous casualties, the Reds prevailed.[93]

It was fitting that the final blow was dealt by Bliukher, a man who had gone from peasant to worker to military commander—the perfect Bolshevik biography. Indeed, he was only a single generation from bondage. The family had acquired its name when his father's master rewarded him for service in the Crimean War with the nickname of Bliukher, after the Prussian field marshal of the Napoleonic wars, Count Gebhard Leberecht von Blücher. The father sent his teenage son to St. Petersburg, where he became a skilled worker at the giant Mytishchinskii railroad car manufacturing plant near Moscow. In 1910 he was arrested after a strike; by 1914 he was employed in a railroad machine shop, another hotbed of worker radicalism. Drafted, decorated, and wounded in the Great War, in 1916 he returned to factory labor. Also in 1916 he joined the Bolshevik Party. Bliukher demonstrated heroic leadership during the Civil War, in 1917 in Samara, in 1918 in the Urals, in 1919 at Kakhovka, in 1920 in Perekop, and later, in 1922, at Volochaevka, near Khabarovsk—the final battle in Zabaikal. Continuing his career in the Soviet army, in 1935 he was elevated to Marshal of the Soviet Union, as was Tukhachevskii. In 1937, during Stalin's Great Purges, Bliukher presided over the tribunal that condemned Tukhachevskii to death. After a failed campaign against the Japanese at Lake Khasan, on October 22, 1938, he himself was arrested and died after a beating in Lefortovo prison.[94]

Frunze offered generous terms for those who surrendered, but Wrangel instead led his remaining forces back into the Crimea. There the situation was desperate—high prices, overcrowding, speculation, food shortages, an enormous civilian "rear" of families and refugees. It was time to cut his losses.[95] The general warned those who wished to leave that the voyage would be difficult and conditions at the other end uncertain.[96] In the course of a relatively well-organized evacuation, the last of the Whites departed Russian soil, in every kind of vessel, from the various Crimean ports. The weather, fortunately, was good. Fittingly, Wrangel himself made the passage on the cruiser *General Kornilov*, which left Sevastopol on November 14, 1920. Almost 150,000 people arrived by ship in Constantinople.[97] Those of Wrangel's supporters who did not make it out of Crimea experienced the full force of Red vengeance. Thousands of officers and bureaucrats, and no doubt many who were nobody and had done nothing at all, were slaughtered.[98] Wiped from the face of the earth, in Trotsky's phrase.

There was irony in the White finale. General Aleksandr Lukomskii had been at General Kornilov's side in August 1917, the very first attempt by imperial officers to put a stop to the leftward course of the revolution. Later he reflected on the final chapter of that crusade. In his memoirs, he recalled "those November days, when the streets of Constantinople were filled with a mass of Russian officers and soldiers, and the Bosporus was covered by ships under Russian flags... and when the cheers of Russian soldiers for their commanders... could be heard... and in the evenings Russian Orthodox evening prayers resounded across the waters..., it seemed that the ancient Russian dream had come true, and Tsargrad had become a Russian city." In fact, as Lukomskii realized, it was the spectacle of defeat and the complete failure of that imperial ambition. He still believed the goal might have been realized had it not been for revolution and Russia's withdrawal from the war. Now the "dream... was replaced by a harsh reality, the remnants of Russian statehood taking refuge on the shores of the Bosporus: not as victors and masters, but unfortunate émigrés."[99]

Not all the refugees in Constantinople were defenders of the old order. To the very end, even some socialists continued to see Wrangel as their only hope. Vladimir Burtsev, an independent socialist and active opponent of anti-Semitism, wrote from Constantinople at the end of 1920, still nursing his faith in the democratic potential of the Russian people. Doubting the Bolsheviks could sustain themselves in power for very long, he described them as "a gang of murderers who have used terror to gather around themselves servile executioners." In the last days in Crimea, the fight against the Bolsheviks had taken priority. Given the alternatives, democratic socialists of like mind had insisted on "struggle to the death against Lenin and limitless support for Wrangel in his fight."[100] Now that fight was over. Another war was yet to be concluded, however. It was the final struggle between the Bolsheviks and the popular masses—the peasants, workers, and soldiers who had lifted them to power, but now fought against their hold.

# 10

# War Against the Peasants

All the protagonists in the Civil War formed armies, but none had the authority to command their allegiance and impose discipline. Achieving this authority was essential to establishing political power—the right and ability to rule. Each side had to secure the loyalty of the men who fought in the ranks, and they had to extract the resources to support them from the same population that supplied the fighting men. In the case of the Cossacks, neither Reds nor Whites were able to attach the warriors firmly to their side. The Bolsheviks addressed the challenge by waging war not only with, but against the Cossacks—the one-sided war of targeted executions, advertised proudly as the Red Terror. For the Red Army to draw resources—men, horses, and grain—from the villages, the allegiance, or at least compliance, of the peasants also had to be secured.

Bread was key to survival—demographic and political. Bread shortages had sparked the February riots that doomed the monarchy. The crisis worsened after the October coup; even Petrograd was short on bread. In meeting the crisis, the Bolsheviks applied their usual methods. First, terror. "Shoot on the spot" hoarders and speculators, Lenin ordered in January 1918, threatening workers who refused to join in the search for hidden stocks with loss of their precious ration cards.[1] And there were already ration cards. The new state was flexing its bureaucratic muscle. Second, the intensification of wartime economic regulation, in particular the state monopoly on grain and control of the market in agricultural and manufactured goods. Third, the application of Communist ideology to the task of economic salvation and reconstruction—the abolition of private property, private trade, and household-based agriculture in the name of social equality and collective ownership. In short, socialism at the point of a gun—a response to immediate catastrophe, but also a first step toward the promised future. The result, which came later to be known as War Communism, defined the regime's relationship to the broad popular masses, in the countryside and in the towns. Its goal was not only to avert collapse but to feed and supply the cities and the troops essential to the defeat of the military opposition, equally in search of food, equipment, manpower, and firepower.

The Bolsheviks directed their invective against the class enemies—the bourgeoisie, the merchants, the officer elite, the landowners—who were in fact, if not in every particular case, their actual opponents. Yet they also faced resistance from the classes on whose behalf they spoke: the workers and peasants. The White generals went down to defeat, but the peasants exerted a more powerful hold on the fate of the Bolshevik regime. They, too, were ultimately defeated, but they managed in the short run to gain the upper hand. The turn from War Communism to market relations, introduced as the New Economic Policy (NEP) in 1921, was dubbed by its critics "the peasant Brest-Litovsk," by analogy with the humiliating peace—a pragmatic concession to external pressure.[2] The retreat came, however, only after millions had starved to death and the methods of state-driven violence and coercion, consistent with Bolshevik practices and justified in ideological terms, had permeated the character of the new regime and its institutions.

———

The broad masses of the population were remote from events in the capital, the squabbles among socialist agitators, and the machinations of imperial generals, but their very lives hung in the balance. After October the villages faced a new form of authority and new policies concerning the vital issues of food and land. The Bolshevik Decree on Land of October 26, 1917, had abolished private property in land, dividing it equitably among those who tilled it.[3] This pronouncement served merely to endorse what was happening already. Peasants across Russia were busy dislodging the owners of landed estates, occasionally murdering them, but always and everywhere claiming their fields, seizing their inventory, and appropriating or destroying their material (including cultural) possessions, down to their clothing and underwear.[4] A report from Saratov Province in the Volga region from December 1917 described manor houses "with only the walls left standing." Windows and doors had disappeared, roads and fields were cluttered with agricultural machines that had been dragged away and abandoned.[5] Plunder, explained Harold H. Fisher, an American involved in famine relief, "brought in many unfamiliar, but prized luxuries:—pianos that could not be played; books that could not be read, but whose pages, happily, made passable cigarette papers; paintings, tapestries, and so forth."[6]

Continuing into the spring of 1918, the peasants continued to seize gentry estates and also acreage belonging to prosperous fellow villagers who had earlier established their own holdings. The movement was not an anarchic outpouring of anger, but an organized campaign, involving intimidation, arson, pillage, and sometimes murder, but orchestrated by the village communes, which administered the seized fields as communal property.[7] If there was an overtly ideological element behind such appropriation, it came from the SR agitators who promoted local soviet rule and endorsed the seizures, which, in any case, no outsider was in a position to stop. The peasants participated widely in elections to the Constituent Assembly, as we have seen, and voted overwhelming for the SRs. The Assembly remained a potent symbol of peasant aspirations, even after it was closed down.[8]

It would have seemed, moreover, that the basic goal of the rural revolution had been achieved. On February 19, 1918, the Sovnarkom issued the Law on the Socialization of Land, repeating the basic provisions of the earlier decree and again promising equitable distribution of land for peasant use, allowing for some forms of household and communal tenure. In a portent of what was to come, however, the decree at the same time projected a future of collective agriculture in which land belonged to the state. The goal of repartition was already being enacted by the peasants in a grassroots collective operation. They were soon to find themselves subjected to new forms of economic and social constraint.[9]

While the villages were in the process of self-generated social revolution, the Bolsheviks were busy negotiating with the Central Powers and creating the basic institutions of state. In regard to the countryside, their first objective was the collection of information. They adopted the method used by armies in the field: daily reports on the position, mood, weapons, resources of the enemy—*svodki*, or digests, as they were called. The Imperial Army had collected data not only about enemy forces but also about the domestic population, particularly in the sensitive border areas; the Soviets extended this practice to the entire country. The military-style intelligence reflected Moscow's view of the countryside as enemy territory in need of conquest. The gathering of information in this form, funneled up to higher bodies by local operatives before reaching key leaders in Moscow, was the task of two bodies: the political police, or Cheka, and the Commissariat of War. In the beginning, reports were irregular, sometimes scribbled on cigarette paper; Trotsky complained they were hard to read. By 1920 the country had been penetrated by a network of informants and the process had become routine.[10]

The food-supply crisis itself was nothing new. In August 1915, the imperial government had set fixed prices for military procurement. In December 1916, grain quotas were introduced, highest in the grain-producing regions. In Tambov Province, later the scene of the most extensive anti-Bolshevik peasant insurrection, zemstvo officials complained: "We do not think we have the right deliberately to drive the population to revolt and famine, therefore the provincial administration finds it impossible to impose the quota in the amount ordered by the Ministry of Agriculture." The Provisional Government continued in the same vein, maintaining the state monopoly on the sale of grain, setting fixed prices, imposing delivery quotas, and sending procurement detachments to the villages to collect them.[11]

In August 1917, the SR minister of agriculture Aleksei Peshekhonov warned that if grain were not delivered before the start of winter, the specter of hunger would justify "extreme measures," that is, the use of armed force, as "dictated by state necessity."[12] The government, however, had neither the means to implement its threats nor the resolve to follow through on them. Its success in meeting its own procurement targets had diminished sharply between May and August, dropping to a miserable 15 percent for the civilian population, 28 percent for the army. The government had vowed not to increase fixed prices again after March, warning the peasants not to hold out for more, but in late August the prices were doubled, pushing the procurement rate up slightly, but still under half of target, and further eroding the government's credibility. Delivery was a problem as well. Rivers were freezing, the railroads were in chaos. Food-supply agents were under attack. Peshekhonov resigned.[13]

The food panic coincided with the political crisis of Kornilov's botched coup in August, implicating Kerensky and bringing down the cabinet. Among Kornilov's supporters was the progressive Moscow textile magnate Pavel Riabushinskii, a constitutionalist opponent of the monarchy active in the War Industries Committee. In the aftermath of the July Days, he had addressed a gathering of industrialists in Moscow, urging them to save Russia from the Soviet menace. Riabushinskii chose his words poorly: "Unfortunately it is necessary for the bony hand of hunger and of the people's poverty to seize by the throat the false friends of the people, the members of various committees and soviets, for them to come to their senses."[14] The Bolsheviks naturally seized this formulation to claim that hunger was a tool being used by the ruling classes to strangle the revolution—sabotage at the highest reaches. Ultimately, the "bony hand of hunger" would come to the Bolsheviks' aid, as a powerful brake on peasant resistance.[15]

The Provisional Government, in fact, realized that its future depended precisely on the conquest of hunger. In the attempt to gain some control over the peasant drive for land, a decree issued in September, in advance of the Constituent Assembly, transferred gentry land and inventory to government land and procurement committees for eventual redistribution.[16] Soon, however, the Food-Supply Ministry was admitting failure: "Famine, genuine famine, has seized a series of towns and provinces—famine vividly expressed by an absolute insufficiency of edibles already leading to death from exhaustion and malnutrition." The crisis of hunger contributed to social breakdown. "Losing the assurance of being able to eat tomorrow, the hungry crowd searches for guilty parties. A primitive and excited psychology is convinced that food products are available [but that] greedy merchants, speculators, and dealers have hidden them." Hunger also caused the localities to turn in on themselves. The Provisional Government's new—and final—minister of food supply, Sergei Prokopovich, said of the Kuban: "They want to remain intact in that sea of anarchy that is flooding the country; they want to save themselves, like an island."[17]

Enter the Bolsheviks, Riabushinskii's "false friends of the people." Before the war, Russia had been a leading exporter of grain, though it fell below Britain, France, or Germany in per capita production. The war and the peasant land seizures had diminished the level of agricultural output; subsistence farming increased, and there was less grain for the market.[18] Before the war, as we recall, Ukraine had produced over three-quarters of the Empire's total grain exports.[19] The German occupation of the Ukraine and the mobilization of counterrevolutionary forces in western Siberia, the Don, Kuban, and the northern Caucasus reduced the grain-growing area accessible to the new regime essentially to the provinces of the central Volga region—Samara, Saratov, Penza, and Simbirsk.[20] Given the shrunken reserves and the disruption of all forms of transport, the problem of extracting and distributing grain had only gotten worse.[21]

In general, tsarist-era officials had at first resisted the new Bolshevik regime, but most continued to exercise their old functions as these functions were newly defined. They remained at their desks out of conviction, or despite their hatred for the new bosses, or for the sake of the food rations provided to state employees.[22] Many among the twice-inherited food-supply officials, who had passed from the monarchy to the Provisional Government without a hitch, in fact yearned for strong state authority to endorse their efforts. The Food-Supply Commissariat served a regime, though in its infancy, that shared its interest in central planning. At the local level, the remaining Provisional Government food-supply committees, many composed of Mensheviks and especially SRs, tried to work with the newly established soviets, but the soviets themselves were under pressure from the peasants to serve local needs. What the Bolsheviks denounced as "localism" reigned everywhere. Producing and consuming regions made direct deals, and factory committees sent their own food expeditions to the villages, ignoring the food-supply officials.[23]

In the case of the military, Moscow condemned the "partisan spirit"—the independent bands, brigades, and detachments under personal leadership—on which, however, the budding Red Army still relied. Analogously, when it came to provisioning, Moscow declared war on "localism"—on private initiative and improvisation, on the market, which it vilified as the "black market." The central organs, in the process of establishing their own authority, aimed to coordinate the requisitioning and distribution of food, to regulate commodity exchange and suppress the role of traders and middlemen, the hundreds of private operators who rode the rails, sacks on their backs, transporting goods from one place to another.[24]

Food was scarce and disease rampant. Typhus, typhoid, and to a lesser extent plague and cholera spread through the Russian heartland. Grain collected for 1917–1918 was a mere fifth of the target.[25] People took matters into their own hands. "Most of the 'bagmen' brought provisions for themselves and their families," the Kadet Ariadna Tyrkova-Williams recalled, "but very soon professional grain smugglers appeared. The railway trains, moving at a snail's pace, were overcrowded with 'bagmen,' and this in spite of the strictest prohibition, under threat of confiscation, to carry foodstuffs in passenger cars."[26] In February 1918, the Sovnarkom nationalized the grain depots and created a Commission for Provisioning and Transportation. Detachments were sent to the countryside to seize grain found in the hands of private persons. Anyone caught on the trains transporting foodstuffs would be arrested; those who resisted would be "shot on the spot." The campaign against the bagmen was indeed a "war with the railway passengers."[27]

In fact, it was part of a greater war. The Food-Supply Commissariat and the army provisioning office worked together.[28] The challenge posed by the detachments, like the one presented by the paramilitary details affiliated with the Red Army, was to mobilize their aggression while keeping them under control. Along with demobilized soldiers and some common criminals, unemployed workers fleeing shortages in the cities joined the grain brigades in hopes of feeding themselves. They arrived in the villages ragged, hungry, and desperate. But many peasants also depended on purchasing grain and were on the brink of starvation. Other workers preferred the black market. Railway hands, for example, took advantage of their position to steal the contents of freight cars and depots; trains often arrived at their destinations empty.[29] Circulars in late March and into May denounced the detachments for their "excesses" and "anarchistic behavior," but with little effect.[30]

The ambiguous role of factory workers in the food crisis, as consumers and enforcers, but also as profiteers, reflects the way class barriers and political identities were breaking down under pressure of economic collapse— all the more reason for the Bolsheviks to insist on clear distinctions. It seemed both practical and ideologically sound to deploy class differences to undermine rural solidarity and produce the desired results. Moscow thus promoted the campaign for grain as an essential component of the class war in the countryside, where the peasantry was supposedly divided between impoverished, landless laborers (a rural proletariat) and the land- and livestock-owning employers of agricultural labor (a rural bourgeoisie), designated with the label "kulak." The term, literally meaning "fist," was already in use before the war to describe the more prosperous peasants, particularly those who after 1905 had formed their own farmsteads outside the communes. A decree of May 13, 1918 attacked the kulaks as "enemies of the people" and called for "merciless struggle" against them.[31]

The Menshevik Fedor Dan, at this point still a member of the Central Soviet Executive Committee, denounced the decree as a declaration of civil war in the countryside, a "crusade against the peasantry," the work of Cain. It was obvious that the wealthier peasants were not alone in concealing grain from official agents, he observed. As everyone knew, peasants everywhere were hiding grain. The regime would have to target the entire countryside.[32] Undeterred, on June 4, 1918, Lenin demanded a "crusade" for bread, mobilizing the village poor against the kulaks.[33] Intent as much on destroying the inner fabric of village communities as on extracting grain, the regime enlisted the most impoverished, landless peasants in "committees of the poor" (*komitety bednoty*, or *kombedy*), which were empowered to despoil their wealthier neighbors, keeping part of the plunder for themselves while delivering the rest to the Food-Supply Commissariat.[34] Successful brigades would be rewarded with discounts on basic food items and farm tools.[35]

Some local soviets had formed their own "poor peasant brigades," but the campaign was officially launched on June 11, 1918. The incentives were obvious. Some *kombedy* were formed from the existing procurement detachments and, like them, attracted workers who had retreated to the countryside after factories closed, as well as peasant-soldiers returning from the front, saturated with Bolshevik slogans and no longer sure of a place in their home villages.[36] The *kombedy* were supposed not only to incite class conflict in the villages; operating directly as arms of the state, they were also intended as counterweights to the local soviets. Moscow did not trust the local examples of Soviet power, because they were still not firmly in Bolshevik hands and because they tended to defend the interests of peasant communities as a whole.[37] With the same goal of strengthening central control, two decrees in May had created a Provisioning Army (*Prodovol'stvennaia armiia*, or Prodarmiia), which was at once a tool of political agitation and a mechanism for the procurement of grain destined for the actual army. The Prodarmiia, like the *kombedy*, consisted of a mix of peasants, former soldiers, and men calling themselves workers, perhaps because they were, perhaps to get better rations or camouflage their actual identities.[38]

In ideological terms, the *kombedy* were supposed to effect the transition from the "bourgeois" phase of the revolution, in which peasants took land for themselves, to the socialist war against the rural "bourgeoisie." The villages were not, however, divided along class lines, as Marxist theory supposed, but defended their interests as collectivities. Usually composed of outsiders, themselves hungry and ill-clothed, the *kombedy* were authorized to extort, intimidate, and threaten. Their various tasks included the confiscation of church property; repression of the ubiquitous practice of home brew, which ate into the peasants' grain reserves; and prevention of the spread of prostitution, another sign of economic desperation.[39] The brigades in fact terrorized the villages, exacting tribute from more prosperous households and bullying anyone who wore a clean shirt.[40]

Far from stimulating hostility between rich and poor, however, the *kombedy* united the villages against them. Ideology provided a road map, here too.

From the official perspective, "the kulaks" were always to blame, not only for hoarding grain but for allegedly infiltrating the *kombedy*, where they were said to provoke the kind of violence against ordinary peasants that turned those peasants against the party. The label "kulak" was not a social descriptor but a political weapon with deadly consequences. Some peasants were of course wealthier than others, but the spontaneous land redistribution in early 1918 had left them alone, since they were not seen by the villagers as hostile to the revolution.[41] There was no "kulak counterrevolution."

It was easy to blame hoarders and speculators, but in fact the crisis was largely the result of damage caused by war and of the normal dynamics of supply and demand. The 1918 harvest was abundant, official prices were higher than those on the private market, and peasants were eager to sell. But much of the yield was never harvested because of the continued fighting, the collapse of estate agriculture, the chaos on the railroads overburdened by troops, the lines damaged, the bridges down, and the unavailability of fuel. The shortage of horses and carts meant that grain often never reached the depots, from which trains often did not depart. The mills stopped working also, for lack of fuel; grain rotted for want of storage space.[42]

The economic collapse coincided, moreover, with a political crisis. The war against the peasants was entangled in the campaign against the Bolsheviks' socialist competitors. In late May 1918, as we know, the Czechoslovak Legion turned against the regime and on June 8 took control of Samara on the Volga River, where the SRs established the headquarters of the Komuch, in a direct challenge to Soviet rule. Given the emergence of organized socialist opposition in the key grain-growing region, it is not surprising that the Mensheviks and SRs should have been expelled from the Central Executive Committee and the local soviets. They, too, became enemies of the people. Undeterred, the Left SRs stood up to rage against the *kombedy* at the Fifth Congress of Soviets, held in Moscow in July 1918, which affirmed the policy of class war in the countryside despite evidence that it wasn't working. Lenin accused them of indifference to the "unspeakable torments of hunger" afflicting the poor peasants, while the fat cats sat on their surpluses. Calling for "pitiless war" against the "friends of the capitalists," the campaign in the countryside was "a war to save socialism," he thundered, "not a war against the peasants! Whoever says that is a great criminal."[43]

It was at this same Fifth Congress, interrupted by news of the assassination of German ambassador Mirbach on July 6, that the Left SRs denounced Lenin as a German tool, ensuring their own political extinction. In August,

Lenin instructed a local party official to "apply the most decisive methods against the kulaks and the Left SR swine who are consorting with them." What was needed was the "merciless suppression of the kulak-bloodsuckers."[44] The Mensheviks and SRs were vilified as "social traitors."[45]

In fact, the peasants—across the board—resisted the forced requisition of grain, livestock, and horses. They refused to dig trenches or be drafted into the Red Army. This was not, however, an ideological protest. When the SR-led Komuch army tried to recruit them, they responded the same way.[46] For the peasants, the issue of horses and livestock was as painful and damaging as the relentless demand for grain. The Imperial Army had drafted a tenth of all civilian horses. At the end of the war, the surviving animals were returned to the peasants, but the Red Army soon demanded them back. Six horse drafts were announced between July 1918 and the end of the year, but as a result of the war and the destruction of estates, horses were in short supply. Offered low prices, which were not always paid, the peasants responded by hiding or even killing their animals. Armored trains were sent to intimidate the reluctant villages; they were equipped with machine guns, which they did not hesitate to use—to no avail. The final horse draft from February to March 1919 in the central regions netted under a third of the target. Though small households were exempt, even one-horse families often lost their animals. Commissars on site warned the central authorities that basic farm work was being endangered; indeed, the removal of work animals contributed to the decline in grain production. In April 1919, the draft was replaced by the offer of market prices. By then, however, the number of livestock and horses in the villages had been drastically reduced.[47]

In the struggle over the procurement of animals, the brutality of Bolshevik methods elicited a brutal response. Reports from local Cheka in August 1918, though filtered through the standard terms of abuse, describe this vicious dynamic. When, for example, officials appeared in Perm Province to draw up grain inventories, they were met by what investigators called "kulak elements," who "made the rounds of neighboring villages, sounded the alarm, and incited people to attack the Red Army soldiers and Soviets. A crowd of seven hundred gathered and murdered eight Red Army soldiers and soviet officials." A detachment sent to arrest the perpetrators dug up the bodies of the murdered comrades. It found mutilated corpses and the wife and child of a peasant who had joined the Red Army. In retaliation, the detachment shot thirty persons, described as "participants in murder and counterrevolutionary actions."[48] In Smolensk Province, also in August, Red

Army detachments sent to take away livestock were assaulted by large crowds of angry peasants. The Cheka accused "kulaks" and "counterrevolutionary former officers" of inciting them to further revolt. Thus aroused, a band of four thousand villagers, equipped with several machine guns, were reported to have murdered nine Red Army men.[49]

Throughout October and November, local Cheka battalions pursued their campaign against what they considered the counterrevolution. At the appearance of procurement brigades, the peasants would rush to the church to sound the alarm. The Cheka would take hostages, whom it threatened to shoot if the quotas were not delivered.[50] In Kazan, a Cheka detachment thwarted a "kulak uprising" and seized ten carts filled with guns, shooting ten men and arresting another thirty. In a case described as an "uprising of deserters and kulaks," forty persons were shot, twenty wounded, three hundred arrested, five hundred weapons taken.[51] And so on.

The Mensheviks and Left SRs, branded "social traitors" and "enemies of the people," were correct. The strategy of sending procurement brigades to the villages to seize their grain and the attempt to mobilize the peasants against each other had failed. As early as August, the Food-Supply Commissariat had blamed the *kombedy* for abusing what it described as the "middle peasants," thus acknowledging not only the failure of the campaign but the fallacy of the categories on which it was based.[52] The notion of the "middle peasant" would provide the rhetorical escape route when the imagined war of poor against rich did not materialize.

By the fall of 1918, the regime had to concede that the strategy of crude requisition was a disaster. "Without the assistance of the peasantry," an official confessed, "it would be impossible to accomplish anything, and the practice of simple raids on the village and of armed requisition was a bad one."[53] By the end of 1918, the *kombedy* had been abolished. Authority in the villages was now vested in the local soviets, supposedly purged of kulaks, which took over the task of grain collection.[54] In January 1919, the *kombedy* were replaced by the *razverstka* (levy, literally "assessment"), which meant higher fixed prices on grain, an alliance with peasant cooperatives, a return to commodity exchange, a tax in kind, and a quota system relying on the collective responsibility of the village, drawing it together rather than tearing it apart.[55] The new approach was supposed to favor the "middle peasant," but the rhetoric of class war was not abandoned. The term "kulak" was now applied to anyone who resisted Soviet authority. And the warlike tone was maintained. At the Sixth Party Congress in November 1918, Lev Zinov'ev warned:"We cannot carry through the proletarian revolution without crushing the village kulaks and without annihilating them psychically and, if necessary, physically."[56]

By early 1919, the food shortage in the cities had driven up prices on the black market. The peasants became even more reluctant to sell to the government, which paid them partly in cash, partly in coupons for a range of basic commodities—kerosene, cloth, tea, soap, agricultural implements. But since manufacturing had also suffered a collapse (witness the unemployed workers fleeing the cities), production had fallen and goods were scarce. Coal production in 1920 had dropped by 75 percent from 1913 levels, production of locomotives by 85 percent, and agricultural machinery by 87 percent. Sugar, textiles, kerosene, soap were all in short supply.[57] The villages therefore relied on local production (cottage industry) and on the black market. The wedge between city and countryside widened.[58]

The *razverstka* was essentially a tax on the peasants. The local soviets were given quotas, which if not met would cost members their jobs or land them in prison.[59] The quotas were established by the central authorities on the basis of crude information, at often arbitrary levels, which set consumption norms too low to feed the peasants themselves and ignored the need to maintain reserves for future planting.[60] The levels were designed to compensate for the portion of the surplus the peasants were presumed to want to hide; the proportion actually taken in fact increased under the new system, doubling the overall imposition. The *razverstka* covered not only grain but also vegetables and dairy products, earlier left to the private traders. The quotas were levied on the villages as a whole, applying the venerable tsarist-era principle of "collective responsibility" (*krugovaia poruka*). This, ironically enough, often burdened the poorest commune members most of all.[61] Detachments of workers still scoured the villages. The Food-Supply Army, consisting mostly of peasants from deficit areas who were unfit for service in the regular army, enforced the quotas. "Blockade detachments" monitored the transport of grain, manhandling peasants carrying sacks, particularly women, which they tore from their unwilling hands.[62] In theory less hostile to the average peasant, the *razverstka* represented a physical assault on the countryside, carried out by a variety of agencies at Moscow's command.

The challenge for Moscow was not only to force the peasantry into compliance; it was to control its own agents in the field, to discipline its own apparatus. The local soviets had been originally little more than rechristened communal assemblies, operating in the name of Soviet power though in fact independent of the central authorities.[63] They existed on the village and district level and were genuinely popular with the peasants in the early months. After the transition to *razverstka*, they performed a balancing act between the amount required to feed the village and the amount needed to satisfy the quota, between the demands of the more prosperous peasants oriented to the market and the poor, who still relied on the commune to guarantee their bare existence. In general they tended to favor trade over requisition as the more effective way of moving grain.[64] On the village level, the peasants responded to the market and devised strategies for meeting their own needs. In short, the countryside, so denigrated by Marxist theory, produced forms of allegiance and integration into functioning social systems that effectively (or as much as possible) responded to change. It was not so much anarchy as coherence that threatened the Bolshevik plan.

Indeed, the peasant response to state impositions displayed both extreme violence and communal solidarity. Under the pressure of relentless requisitions, whether by *kombedy* or the perhaps more insidious, because self-administered, *razverstka*, the peasants reacted initially in spurts of resistance, village riots, and attacks on local officials, but eventually their anger took a more organized and widespread form.[65] Hundreds of personalities emerged to lead armed insurrections, some of considerable size and coherence, almost everywhere. Once the threat of White victory receded and with it the danger of a return to the hated pre-1917 social order, the peasants turned their wrath against the Bolsheviks, who had betrayed them. "In the fight between Bolshevism and the peasant movement," historians Alexis Berelowitch and Viktor Danilov observe, "the armies confronting each other were of the same composition—peasants, fighting under the same red banner, for the same slogan: 'Victory to the real revolution!' But they understood the meaning of this revolution in different ways."[66]

In this sense, the peasant movements of 1918–1921 resembled the ferocious popular uprising led by the Cossack Emelian Pugachev in the reign of Catherine the Great. That charismatic figure offered his followers freedom from state control, though he presented himself as a better form of the same authority—the "true tsar," whose court mirrored the operations of the real one. Now, too, the rebel leaders rejected the power of the state, though once again in shared terms—not the "true tsar" this time, but "true socialism." In

Tambov, the most spectacular case, the rebels created a network of institutions and adopted measures, such as their own grain quotas, very like the ones they opposed. They used the term "comrade" and even flew the red flag.[67]

Perhaps for this very reason it was important for the party to discredit the peasant rebels as criminals, class enemies, or both. It was useful to think of the entire phenomenon as a product of the unstable transition from one social system to another. Crime, "hooliganism," "banditism," and revolt were the response to economic hardship, hunger in particular. The charge of "banditism" was not entirely off the mark. Armed bands attracted a broad range of peasants, especially among the younger men, who in fact appropriated food and animals from the villages; some of their members were indeed no better than thugs. The same could be said, however, about grassroots Bolshevik supporters. The authorities sometimes also denounced the rebels not just as bandits, but as "partisans," a term that remained pejorative, if more respectful. Respect was not unwarranted. The more coherent movements showed a remarkable ability to create operational networks and mobilize local support.

The Cheka, as a good bureaucratic organization, busily gathered information about the participants and the extent of the rebellions. Though all were denounced as "banditism," the authorities nevertheless made distinctions. At the end of 1920, the Cheka drew up a list of incidents and a map of unrest. The invective is instructive, both as a reflection of the social vocabulary disseminated by the new regime and as a key (behind the abuse) to actual social categories. The leadership was said to emerge from the former elites. White officers and tsarist bureaucrats, sometimes "camouflaged" as Soviet officials, allegedly offered ideological direction and organizational skills. In the frontier regions—Bashkiria, Kirgizia, Turkestan, the Caucasus—it was said to be the "feudal, patriarchal clan plutocracy" at work. These class enemies were said to attract a range of followers: common criminals, soldiers fleeing the Red Army, kulaks, and Cossacks, "the most dangerous reserve for banditism," who often fought against each other while also joining forces against Soviet power. None of these groups could be trusted, since they continually switched sides.[68]

In terms of geographic extent, at the end of 1920 the Cheka admitted that only the areas around Moscow and Petrograd and in the north were relatively calm. The Ukraine and the core provinces were the most troubled. In Ukraine the movement coalesced around the figures of Makhno and Petliura, but the Cheka acknowledged that even when the armed "kulak gangs" had been repressed, the spirit of revolt associated with their names (the "*Makhnovshchina*" or "*Petliurovshchina*") persisted. The other volatile region included the central provinces of Tambov, Saratov, Penza, and Voronezh, southeast of Moscow, above the Don, particularly Tambov Province. In Siberia, the Cheka complained, the vast expanses and deep forests provided cover for extensive "bandit gangs." In all cases, the reports attributed a key role to "kulaks" and army deserters, sometimes also described as kulaks. At the same time, the Cheka could not but acknowledge that revolt was stimulated by the policies of requisition and *razverstka*, a pressure clearly felt by peasants everywhere.[69]

The regime liked to think that only the prosperous peasants had turned against it, aided and abetted by their political rivals, the SRs. There was some truth to the charge. The SRs did not, however, represent a unified position. The fate of the SR Party indeed illustrates the dangers of ideo-logical and organizational incoherence that Lenin had always taken pains to avoid in the Social Democratic camp. At this point, some Right SRs continued to work in local soviets; others followed Viktor Chernov in proposing to fight on as a "third force" against both Red and White; the most violently anti-Communist among them chose to support Admiral Kolchak. The Left SRs, by contrast, went underground, pursuing a strategy of terror against the Cheka and Soviet institutions, at the same time dis-tributing anti-Communist literature aimed at the peasants. By summer 1919, the Cheka had wiped out both Left and Right SR organizations.[70] At various moments in 1919, and even into 1920, individual SR activists nevertheless managed to form organizations and participate in the rebel-lions embracing the countryside. Whatever they achieved in practical terms, their message had an impact all on its own. Many of the rebel lead-ers adopted SR slogans and organizing strategies. Their positions resonated with the mood in the villages.[71]

----

Beginning in fall 1917 and continuing into summer 1918, peasant resistance to the procurement brigades and *kombedy* was widespread but disorganized. By 1919 the rebellions had increased in size and coherence. Their ranks were enhanced by the massive influx of former Red Army soldiers, who flooded the countryside in 1919. The Cheka branded them "deserters" and "bandits," but the category of desertion (*dezertirstvo*) covered a range of evasive moves.

Compulsory military service had been introduced in the second half of 1918, as we have seen, but in the countryside almost half the eligible men failed to present themselves. A decree issued in April 1919, demanded that each village produce ten to twenty "volunteers," preferably from Red Army veterans. If no one volunteered, the village was supposed to designate substitutes. Despite an energetic educational campaign, few men responded.[72] Among those considered deserters, most thus simply refused to sign up; others disappeared at the recruitment points or on the way to the front. The returning or escaping men found refuge in the villages or hid in the woods, where they were known as "Greens."[73] Living off the peasants' food and livestock, they encouraged other men to avoid the army and murdered or otherwise attacked the soldiers sent to find them. They also murdered Communists and local soviet officials.[74]

The peasant revolts endemic to the year 1919 almost all involved the participation of these disaffected, still armed former soldiers. Between July and December 1919, the number of deserters at large in European Russia swelled to well over a million. An anti-desertion commission had been formed in December 1918, but six months later it was still trying to get results. Military commissars threatened to confiscate the land and property of the deserters' families and to shoot troublemakers. The rate of desertion only abated when Denikin's forces advanced on Moscow, threatening the return of the old manorial regime. Then the village assemblies themselves began to demand the fugitives turn themselves in. Penalties were perfunctory.[75]

Against the turmoil that enveloped European Russia in 1919, a few cases stand out. The revolt of peasants in the Volga region began in the first week of March 1919 as a reaction to the requisitioning of grain and livestock, the imposition of demands above the norm and beyond what the peasants could come up with, and the Red Army search for deserters. The rebels called themselves "*chapany*," from the robes worn by the local peasants, to symbolize their difference from the city. Organizing their own army, they attacked the food brigades, seized post and telegraph offices, and murdered Communist officials. The movement, which had no outside leaders, spread like wildfire through Simbirsk and Samara provinces, involving as many as 150,000 men and an armed force of 20,000. Leadership came from within the village communities, and decisions were taken by the collective; individual SR activists and the occasional local priest sometimes played a part but did not control the groundswell. The well-organized army, which included many

Red Army deserters, favored guerrilla tactics. Its campaigns were accompanied by bursts of sometimes grisly violence, including the particularly brutal murders of party operatives.[76]

From March 9 to 13, 1919, the rebels managed to occupy Stavropol, in the Kuban, where they created an anti-Communist soviet that included workers as well. Their slogans were: "Down with the Communists! Long live the soviets!" "Down with the Communists! Long live the Bolsheviks!" "Long live Lenin! Down with Trotsky!"—or the reverse! In short, an imagined re-creation of the unsullied revolution. On a less idealistic note, the occupiers also looted bakeries and shops of all kinds.[77] Their slogans included the inevitable "Down with the Yids!"[78] By the end of the month, the Red Army had regained control of the region, though small rebel bands continued to haunt the nearby forests.[79]

A year later, between February and March 1920, the provinces of Kazan, Ufa, and Samara were seized by the "Uprising of the Black Eagle and the Agriculturalist" (*Vosstanie Chernogo orla i zemledel'tsa*), taking its name from an organization created by Right SRs and former Kolchak officers. Also known as the "pitchfork uprising" (*vilochnoe vosstanie*), the rebellion was provoked by the conduct of procurement agents, making arrests and shooting the recalcitrant, in the face of a bad harvest and shrunken reserves. Again, Red Army deserters provided manpower, experience, weapons— and resentment. The rebels operated in the woods, supported by the local villagers, destroying railroad lines, murdering party and soviet officials. Overall, forty thousand peasants were involved; they were stopped finally by a force of ten thousand Red Army men, armed with bayonets, artillery, and armored trains.[80]

The rank-and-file deserters were not ideologically motivated, and they easily changed sides. More worrying perhaps was defection by Red Army officers. Such was the case of Aleksandr Sapozhkov. Originally a peasant from Samara Province, a veteran of the Great War, with the rank of second lieutenant, Sapozhkov joined the Left SRs in 1917. After October, he helped organize support for the Bolshevik coup in the Saratov region. In 1918 he participated in the campaigns against the Cossacks and the Komuch. By early 1919, he was commanding a Red Army cavalry division, but in summer 1919 he began having doubts and resigned from the local soviet. In February 1920, he lost his command, but surprisingly was given another, this time of the Second Turkestan Cavalry Division newly formed in May 1920.[81]

Sapozhkov used this division to help the peasants avoid requisition; he also refused to use his troops to suppress peasant resistance. In July he was ordered to resign, but instead he and his men declared their opposition to Bolshevik rule. His political program called for freeing the soviets from Communist control, ending requisitions, abolishing the Cheka, and restoring free trade. "Down with the commissars, the specialists, and the regional provisions committees! Long live free trade!" With the support of local peasants, his forces captured the town of Buzuluk, directly east of Samara, arresting its Communist officials. The revolt spread to six provinces in the Volga-Urals region. Additional deserters swelled his ranks, but the three thousand or so men in Sapozhkov's Red Army of Justice (*Krasnaia Armiia Pravdy*) were unable to resist the mobilized Red Army assault. On September 6, 1920, Sapozhkov himself was killed in battle. Of the 150 men tried, fifty-two, including eighteen former Red Army officers, were sentenced to be shot. What remained of the Red Army of Justice finally scattered into small guerrilla bands operating from the forests.[82]

The most formidable of the insurrections, however, occurred in Tambov Province. The case provides a good example of the dynamics of peasant revolt and the regime's style of response. The province, with a population of four million, was a key grain-producing area. Its peasants had suffered for decades from an ever-increasing shortage of land and in 1905 engaged in the widespread destruction of manors. In the fall of 1917, even before the Bolshevik coup, they were already destroying gentry property and redistributing the acreage among themselves. Despite the Bolshevik Decree on Land, which favored their cause, when it came to elections for the Constituent Assembly the vast majority of Tambov voters opted for the SRs, whose long-standing position on land the Bolsheviks had now adopted.[83]

It was not until April 1918 that the last Provisional Government officials left Tambov. The transition was followed rapidly by the Sovnarkom decrees in May instituting the state monopoly on grain. With their high quotas and ruthless methods, the procurement brigades and *kombedy* soon aroused massive protests.[84] After military conscription began in June, the combined impact of requisitions and the draft intensified resistance. The grain brigades continued their work into the fall of 1918, when a second draft was instituted, producing another wave of protests and riots, which were subdued by Red Army troops.[85]

Soldiers played a crucial role in the escalating confrontation between peasants and the state. Half the male population of Tambov Province had served in the Imperial and Red Armies. Demobilized soldiers, as well as actual deserters, returned to their villages with weapons in hand and a spirit of defiance. They were joined in the forests by the men who had refused to show up for the draft in the first place. Military patrols combed the villages, looking for shirkers and strafing the fields when necessary to flush out anyone hiding in the grain.[86]

Though the switch from requisition of everything above the consumption norm, implemented by procurement brigades composed of village outsiders, to the system of *razverstka*, or quotas imposed on the villages as collective units, occurred at the beginning of 1919, the *razverstka* was not necessarily less burdensome, as we have seen, and the brigades did not immediately cease their operations. The government had not fulfilled its promise to provide the manufactured goods needed in the villages, and the imposition of grain quotas and horse and labor drafts, in addition to the military call-ups, continued to inflame the peasants against the towns and the regime they represented.[87]

The Bolsheviks blamed the SRs for instigating the "bandit" movement. SR organizers did not in fact mobilize the rebels, but their slogans resonated widely and they had established a network of organizations in Tambov Province that provided the movement with coherence.[88] Years before, in the wake of 1905, SR-identified activists had created a Union of the Laboring Peasantry (*Soiuz trudovogo krest'ianstva*) as a way to draw peasants into the political process. In 1919 this Peasant Union became the basis of a powerful insurrection.[89] Its leader was a thirty-one-year-old Moscow native called Aleksandr Antonov. Antonov himself was not a peasant; his father, a former noncommissioned officer, ran a metalworking shop, his mother was a seamstress. The son received a basic education and worked at times as a district clerk, a factory hand, and a schoolteacher. In 1905, merely sixteen, he began calling himself an SR, later took part in SR-organized robberies, and spent time in prison after 1909, where he was tutored in revolutionary ideology by activist cellmates. In 1917 he joined a militia.[90] In short, Antonov was exactly the kind of rabble-rouser from the literate upper reaches of the popular classes that the Bolsheviks themselves tried to attract. Though raised in a city, his loyalties seem to have been attached more to the region and its peasant life than to any kind of proletariat. His father was a Tambov native, and the local peasants considered the son "one of their own."

In June 1918, the military draft had provoked riots in Tambov, which momentarily undermined Bolshevik control of the city. Aleksandr's younger brother Dmitrii had taken part in the riot, then gone into hiding. By the end of the year, a group of former militiamen had begun to attack local soviets and murder local Communists, living off the proceeds of armed robberies. By summer 1919, the group had attracted over a hundred men.[91] A year later, in August 1920, the villages of Khitrovo and Kamenka rose in open revolt against the procurement brigades, and by September Aleksandr Antonov had become the leader of four thousand armed men and another ten thousand equipped only with pitchforks and scythes. The rebels formed a regular army, supplemented by irregular units drawn from the local population as the need arose. They used partisan tactics and employed a network of propagandists who issued leaflets and proclamations with slogans, such as "Death to the Communists!" and "Long Live the Laboring Peasantry!" At its peak consisting of forty thousand men, the army operated in the forests, supported by nearby villagers. It destroyed railway lines, attacked collective farms, and murdered Soviet officials, but it operated well only in its own locale and never linked up with rebellions outside the region.[92]

The peasant response to Bolshevik procurement policy was destructive and destabilizing, not only because the countryside was out of control, but because the regime's survival depended on extracting enough grain to feed the cities and the army. Although the various revolts remained localized, the regime was having trouble stopping the momentum. Not only had grain collection been interrupted by the revolt, but towns were increasingly cut off by sabotage of the railways. Red Army soldiers garrisoned in the region were deserting; authority was crumbling. In November 1920 a local official reported: "Bands now cover practically the entire district. Soviet authority has ceased to exist."[93] Recruiting from among former Red Army soldiers in the villages, in December 1920 the rebel forces began calling themselves the Partisan Army of the Tambov Region (*Partizanskaia armiia Tambovskogo kraia*). Divided into regiments, it now established a hierarchy of command.[94]

The rebellion was more than an army. Competing with the Soviet authorities at all levels, the movement provided a mirror-image alternative. The rebels, like the socialist parties, recognized the importance of having some kind of program. In late 1920, as they were insisting on their identity as partisans, not bandits, the Union of the Laboring Peasantry announced the goal of overthrowing "Communist-Bolshevik power" in the name of principles derived from the general SR platform: restoration of civil liberties, equality of all citizens, distribution of land, workers' control, privatization of small industry, self-determination for national minorities, and—what had become the core symbol of the anti-Soviet opposition—reconvocation of the Constituent Assembly.[95]

It is unlikely that almost three years after its demise, the peasants cared much about the Constituent Assembly for its own sake, but they clung to what it stood for. Having a program was in itself, moreover, a symbol of authority. When the Partisan Army entered a village, the leader would distribute pamphlets and read the program aloud. A committee of the Union of the Laboring Peasantry would be created in the village, charged with food supply, draft mobilization, and propaganda. Villages were asked to join the movement and given a chance to refuse. The partisans would show up in leather jackets (mimicking the signature Cheka attire), pistols in hand. They sang the "Internationale" and held public funerals for fallen comrades.[96] In short, the rebels displayed the attributes of power as popularly understood—weapons, toughness, a program (itself a weapon), a network of organizations, and a hierarchy of command. The villages would draw up their own statements, obviously drafted by some schoolteacher or clerk. "We declare to our cursed bolshevik enemies"—lower case—"on Russian land there will not remain one single Communist. We send a brotherly welcome to all partisan units and to all those comrade peasants who have risen up or are now rebelling."[97] The villages were asked to vote, required to create a militia, and pressed to engage in some act of sabotage (wrecking rail lines, for example) as a form of initiation. Their adherence was voluntary, but coerced.[98]

The Partisan Army recruited among demobilized Red Army soldiers and deserters, and, like the Red Army, among former tsarist officers. Special privileges were granted to soldier families, lists were kept of loyal households (mirroring the Cheka-compiled lists). The Union of the Laboring Peasantry regulated food supply, fed the army, and applied a tax on grain. At the same time, like the Reds, they denounced looting. Looters were threatened with trial in army courts. The rebels were intent on showing that unlike the "robber-Communists," they were not bandits.[99]

The appeals to "comrades" in the Red Army, the appropriation of the socialist message, the widespread popular response—all presented a real challenge, which demanded action. Top Bolsheviks Nikolai Bukharin and Anatolii Lunacharskii visited the region in February 1921. A plenipotentiary commission was created with Vladimir Antonov-Ovseenko in charge. The Ukraine had taught him something about pacification. As in that case, two issues were again at stake: mounting an effective enough campaign to wipe out the rebellion in military terms; and installing a local party and Soviet administration that was both effective and beholden to the center.[100] The rhetorical high ground had to be seized, improvised violence had to be met with organized force, and the underlying grievances had to be confronted. The face-off with the mass of the laboring population in the countryside was not yet over.

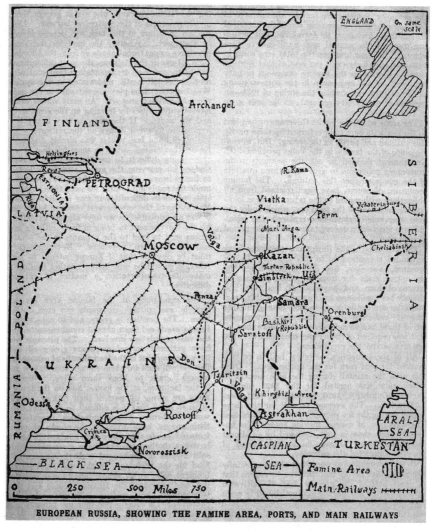

EUROPEAN RUSSIA, SHOWING THE FAMINE AREA, PORTS, AND MAIN RAILWAYS

"Famine in the Volga Provinces," *Russian Information and Review*, vol. 1, no. 1 (October 1, 1921), 3. Information Department of the Russian Trade Delegation, London. Joseph Regenstein Library, University of Chicago.

# PART VI

## Victory and Retreat

# I

# The Proletariat in the
# Proletarian Dictatorship

Astounding as it may seem, given the chaos and violence of the Civil War, the shaky Bolshevik regime was managing to lay the foundations for a noncapitalist economy. The Bolsheviks had inherited some of the problems, strategies, and institutions of their predecessors, primarily the requisitioning of grain and the mobilization of war-related industry, but the state apparatus they inherited was in collapse, and their policies contributed to its further disintegration. Their goal was nevertheless to put that apparatus back on a solid footing.

War under any political system requires enhanced state control and planning. Yet the socialist model contained elements at odds with each other, and socialists came in a variety of hues. Even within the Bolshevik Party, there were differences. Clearly, Bolshevik leaders were guided by the basic postulates of Marxist ideology: that socialism would replace private property with state ownership, the self-regulating market with central planning, disparity of wealth with economic equality. Debates raged, however, in the party's inner circles about how to apply these principles in practice. The specific measures enacted in the course of the Civil War did not reflect a well-crafted plan, but responded to problems created by the pressures of war and economic collapse. They were not introduced all at once, but piecemeal over the course of three years, between 1917 and 1920.[1] While state control implied central authority, the Bolshevik state—not yet fully a state—at this point consisted of competing, ill-coordinated organs. As in every other sphere, there were tensions between central authority and local party bosses; between ideology and necessity; between grand visions and crisis management.

Ideology, the historian Silvana Malle observes, "acted as a filter for acceptable alternatives," but did not dictate specific measures.[2] The term War

Communism was first applied retroactively by Lenin in April 1920, when he insisted that "a peculiar war communism...was forced on us by extreme want, ruin and war...it was not, and could not be, a policy that corresponded to the economic tasks of the proletariat."[3] Yet the basic components were exactly those of the imagined communist future.[4] They were also weapons in the class war. As Anatolii Lunacharskii, the commissar of education, put it: "We had to decimate the bourgeoisie, to destroy all the property in its hands, since it was using that property as a weapon against us." "Expropriate the expropriators!"—"Loot what was looted!"—were slogans, moreover, that give the stamp of approval to the massive wave of plunder that followed immediately upon the October coup.[5] To accuse the Bolsheviks of robbery is not a reproach; they knew what they were doing.

The Soviet government during the Civil War was thus run by a party dedicated to the primacy of economic relations, which aimed to achieve modernization (industry, urbanization, literacy, productivity) through state planning and control, but which also improvised as it went along. Lenin, as always, was both an ideologue and a pragmatist. Trotsky, shaped by the experience of forming and maintaining the Red Army, had no truck with socialist sentimentalism. Both turned to the enemy for models of how to proceed in beating them at their own game. For Trotsky this was an army of ranks and central command, for Lenin a capitalism of giant enterprises and technical expertise, in which the role of the state had been magnified by wartime exigency. German "state capitalism" was Lenin's prototype, to be imposed, he said, by any means, "however dictatorial," on "barbaric medieval Russia"— not hesitating to use "barbaric methods in the fight against barbarism."[6] This was no heresy. Marxists recognized the structural similarity between monopoly capitalism and communism—the massification of the means of production and of labor at the highest level of industrial development, in the first case in private hands, in the second under state control.

While pursuing their power-political goals (survival of the Soviet regime, reconstruction of the country it claimed to rule), the commissars nevertheless had to rely on the compliance of the popular masses, who, as socialist theory rightly stressed, constituted society's productive forces. Without the masses, no economy; without an economy, no willing masses. We have seen how the urgent need to extract grain from the countryside came up against peasant resistance, how approaches had to be modified, and how different strategies were tried, failed, were amended. Ultimately, coercion and famine forced the producers into line. The "bony hand of hunger."

In relation to the manufacturing sector, the state needed to sustain productivity while also exercising political control. Two key issues were involved, ownership and regulation. The Decree on Workers' Control of November 14, 1917, endorsed the demands of the grassroots factory committees to take over management themselves. The concept embodied in the decree did not, however, give workers authority over production; "control" meant the right to monitor the activity of qualified technicians and administrators, which is to say, those already in place. The key policy decisions governing the economy were not, moreover, to be taken at the level of individual plants or localities, but at the center of power, hence the establishment at the beginning of December of the Supreme Council of the National Economy (VSNKh).[7]

At first it seemed as though state ownership and worker input went hand in hand. The complement to the democratization of authority on the shop floor was the seizure of private assets. The factory committees, eager for an even greater role, pressed for a swift transition; often individual factories, mines, or local soviets took the initiative, ousting former owners. By contrast, the Sovnarkom and the VSNKh, anxious to maintain production, tried to halt or retard the process but nevertheless endorsed many of the expropriations, affixing an official label to what they were unable to prevent. In early 1918, moreover, the VSNKh continued to negotiate with proprietors of the largest metallurgical plants concerning the terms of expropriation and elements of continuity. In April 1918, however, the regime decreed full nationalization of the crucial metallurgical industry.[8]

Brest-Litovsk provided a strong incentive to proceed in this direction. The treaty required the return of German-owned property, with the exception of enterprises seized by the state before July 1, 1918, for which it merely exacted compensation. Thus, on June 28, 1918, joint-stock companies, many German-owned, were suddenly taken over. Overall nationalization was not imposed until November 1920, at that point including all large-scale and most medium-scale enterprises, together employing almost 90 percent of the factory workforce.[9] Ownership of the means of production by the workers' state did not, however, mean that the workers became the masters. Trade unions and committees often resisted existing management, pressing for higher wages and a greater role in setting production agendas, but Lenin was concerned with the fate of the economy as a whole. Socialism, he declared, could be achieved only by passing first through the stage of "state capitalism," regulated from the center of political authority.[10]

The transition was not, of course, instantaneous. Throughout 1918, private ownership still prevailed and negotiations persisted among the various involved partners—entrepreneurs, trade unions, the state. Factory committees continued to function in privately held concerns, where they acted as political watchdogs. It was not until the Ninth Party Congress in April 1920 that the committees were finally subordinated to the trade unions, themselves now arms of the state.[11] It was on this occasion that Trotsky pressed for the use of technical experts, the imposition of discipline in the workplace, and the use of coercion—the model behind Red Army victory. Decisions taken at this congress and at the trade union congress that followed subordinated the worker committees to the authority of qualified managers.[12] As Lenin observed, workers were not equipped to run factories. The state, in its own interests, needed the cooperation of "the class enemy." Or, in Marxist terms, the class (the proletariat) which had (in theory) acquired political power was not capable of wielding economic power. Its position contrasted with that of the French bourgeoisie in 1789, which had first dominated the economy before seizing the political reins.[13]

The inherent tension in the communist model between top-down control and grassroots (proletarian) democracy was supposed to be resolved in the operation of a state genuinely representing the real interests of the proletariat. The tension was resolved ultimately in the Soviet case by the suppression of popular initiative and the fiction of proletarian rule. In the meantime, however, "the state" was itself riven by tensions. Achieving central control even at the center was not an easy task. Like the monarchy, which also repressed civic initiative and also faced the challenge of running a war, the Bolshevik proto-state experienced not only the tension between center and locality, top and bottom, but also between the administration of the overall economy and the needs specific to the military. As before 1917, the conflict was expressed in institutional terms. Now, the central economic administration (VSNKh) competed with the Red Army for the mobilization of production and material resources. Indeed, the army created its own economic command center, which shared oversight of military production with VSNKh. Various bodies at the center and in the provinces competed for scarce raw materials and fuel. It was not until the recapture of the Urals in July 1919 that the supply of metal resumed.[14]

Another deficit that emerged under the pressure of economic collapse was a shortage of labor. The cities were shrinking as people fled to the countryside in search of food. Rationing had been introduced immediately after October, but delivery was uncertain and the amounts were meager. Between 1917 and 1920, Petrograd lost two-thirds of its population, Moscow half.[15] Overall, the industrial labor force dropped by 60 percent, from 3.6 to 1.5 million. The suffering of workers, who were favored with the most generous rations, is an index of the seriousness of the food shortage and the degradation of living conditions in the cities. About a quarter of those who left the factories entered the Red Army.[16] The volunteers tended to come from the least qualified workers, who benefited the most from the various material incentives the Red Army had to offer—especially meals and wages. In general, many workers simply did not want to fight in any war.[17] The more qualified workers who remained were those most likely to have shared the political vision of educated ideologues. They were therefore better able to grasp the political betrayal involved in the turn away from grassroots power and more likely to resist Bolshevik rule.

Disciplining the workers became a high priority. Not only was the proletariat, even at its most skilled, unequipped to run the factories, let alone the economy, but it had now to be forced to work. The Commissariat of Labor drafted manpower for construction, transport, and other emergency tasks. Labor cards were introduced in Moscow and Petrograd in June 1919; proof of employment was needed to obtain ration cards. General labor conscription began in April 1920.[18] Yet absenteeism (flight) and low productivity persisted. Food became a weapon. Rations were allocated by type of work, skill level, and production rates. So-called specialists were rewarded, absenteeism and lateness penalized. The trade unions protested against the system of wage incentives and bonuses, as violations of socialist principles; by 1920, given inflation, workers demanded to be paid in kind. They took matters into their own hands by stealing factory property, an act now considered a crime against the state.[19] In addition to conscription, the authorities also turned to another form of coercion. Beginning in early 1920, demobilized soldiers, mostly unskilled peasant laborers, were formed into labor armies and used to gather timber for fuel, in mining, transport, industry, and on the railroads. At the Ninth Party Congress, Trotsky called for the militarization of factory labor as well. Registration with the Commissariat of Labor became compulsory, and avoidance was punished as desertion.[20]

As in every other domain, but surprising in relation to their own purported constituency, the Bolsheviks were neither squeamish nor apologetic about the use of force. "Under proletarian dictatorship," Nikolai Bukharin boasted in 1920, "compulsion is for the first time really the tool of the majority in the interest of this majority." As Lenin put it: "The dictatorship of the proletariat does not fear any resort to compulsion and to the most severe, decisive and ruthless forms of coercion by the state. The advanced class, the class most oppressed by capitalism, is entitled to use compulsion."[21] In this case, it would seem, the proletariat (if it was indeed the proletariat) was therefore using compulsion against itself.

These were thus the basic and paradoxical elements of what became known as War Communism—nationalization of industry, labor conscription, militarization of labor, grain requisitioning. It was a coercive system that extracted from the laboring population what it was unwilling or reluctant to give—labor and the fruits of labor without adequate compensation. It was a system also that mobilized one element of the population (hungry workers) against the other (stubborn, but themselves also hungry, peasants). Workers to some extent, in the Red Guard and food brigades, became instruments of the state power that claimed to represent them but more and more constrained them; peasants, insofar as they were soldiers, entered the apparatus themselves. Both peasants and workers also reacted against that apparatus with violent forms of resistance.

Worker organization (committees, unions, soviets, leaders from the ranks)—the structured opposition to the nascent capitalist order, an opposition shaped by revolutionary activists of every stripe—was the platform from which the Bolsheviks had outmaneuvered the competition. But worker organizations also provided a platform for socialist resistance to Bolshevik rule. These critics on the left gave structure to the workers' own desperation and anger in the face of economic and social crisis. Sometimes, as before, workers at the base reacted against their own leaders. In short, the same anger and energy that helped undermine the tsarist regime, and was nurtured and appropriated by the Bolsheviks on their way to power, posed a challenge once they tried to wield power themselves.

The basic postulates of socialism, boiled down to essentials, resonated with workers and peasants—the dichotomy of exploiters and exploited, "the democracy" versus "the bourgeoisie," those at the bench versus those in the offices, wage-earners versus bosses. The fine points of ideology made little difference in the abstract; the varying appeal of Mensheviks, SRs (both parties internally divided), or Bolsheviks reflected specific situations. Factory workers were indeed capable of creating their own institutions, of generating their own leaders; socialist intellectuals were not merely deluded. But the mass of workers was also capable of wild, undisciplined violence, of switching camps, of opposing the self-appointed spokesmen of their own alleged interests.

After October 1917, collective action continued—this time directed against the regime, which had positioned itself as the supreme master of economic life. This supreme master had not, however, achieved mastery over its own apparatus. The application and impact of policies varied by location and the style of local rule. In Petrograd, the site of the most advanced enterprises and sophisticated trade unions, the local Bolsheviks imposed strict controls on worker organizations. In Moscow, Lenin's pragmatic approach made compromise easier. In the Urals, Left Bolsheviks, Left SRs, and Mensheviks battled for influence—the atmosphere was volatile. Indeed, it was in the Urals that the most serious worker revolts against Soviet authority occurred.[22]

The aftermath of October in the Urals was catastrophic. Civic organizations, such as the City Dumas and zemstvos, collapsed. The Bolsheviks applied emergency measures—brutal requisitions, arrests, plundering the villages for food, banning private trade (confiscations), all of which "reduced the population to exhaustion," as the historian Igor Narskii puts it, setting off a wave of peasant protests. Each city, each large industrial plant closed in on itself, becoming a separate universe of deprivation.[23]

The agenda represented by the soviets and by the various socialist parties, in addition to promising social and economic equality, pledged to address the workers' basic material needs. Marx had said the workers had nothing to lose but their chains; having no property and no stake in the system, they were in a position to overthrow it. But in fact, as the historian Sergei Pavliuchenkov puts it, the "chains" that subjected them to the power of the factory owners were not simply constraints but also links that connected them to the wider economy and provided their means of survival. With the collapse of trade networks, the disruption of production, the loss of jobs, the breakdown of ties between city and countryside, the shortage of fuel and raw materials, the chains were shattered and the workers were left to fend for themselves.[24] Freed of their fetters, they reached a new level of destitution; they went hungry.

Worker attitudes toward Bolshevik rule indeed varied directly with the food supply. Dissatisfaction was strongest in the two capitals, with their grain-poor hinterlands, and in places to which the workers had fled in search of food. Slogans abounded. Left SRs and Mensheviks denounced the dictatorship of the Communist Party, its betrayal of the principles of the revolution, the repression of opposition parties, the decrees binding workers to the factories, but the more widespread and fundamental demands were for food and an end to armed conflict. "If you have taken power, then give us bread," was the refrain. "If you can't, then go to the devil and let someone else take your place."[25]

Slogans were not enough; work stoppages were endemic, meetings and street demonstrations proliferated. In some local soviet elections in 1919 and 1920, Mensheviks won majorities. Workers also engaged in direct action, walking off with products and equipment from the factories and exchanging them for food in the villages.[26] Some workers took up arms and formed detachments which forcibly extracted grain. Relabeled as "food brigades" (*prodotriady*), they were incorporated into the official requisitioning campaign. Yet again, the Bolsheviks coopted what they could not stop. Instead of deserters from the labor front, they got militants on the grain front.[27]

Not all subversive behavior could be easily camouflaged, however. Charges of wrecking were not unfounded. The Cheka, always on its toes, monitored the spread of unrest. It reported cases in which workers damaged equipment, set fire to the premises, burned down warehouses, undermined production. The authorities responded by shutting the agitated plants, dismissing the payroll, prosecuting as deserters those who did not return to reregister. Cavalry were called in on occasion to disperse demonstrations. After 1920 troublesome workers could be drafted into the army or sent to concentration camps.[28]

------

Overall, workers reacted to the new Soviet regime in three ways. First, they protested against measures and conditions resulting from policies that threatened their survival. Protests took both organized and unorganized form. The fact that workers resisted the regime acting in their name did not, however, mean that most or all of them wished to overthrow it, that the Bolsheviks had "lost their base." It was a sign above all that laboring people needed to survive no matter who was in power. It was a sign that this regime was not yet in control of the social forces which had undermined its predecessors and lifted it to the top. The workers were still capable of formulating goals and mobilizing their own forces. The proletarian civic sphere was not yet dead, and it was still socialist.

Second, workers—the same kind at different times, or different kinds at different times—became part of the machinery administering these same policies. Sometimes the motive was also simple survival—joining the army, or the Red Guard, or a food brigade was a way of getting fed. Sometimes joining up was an extension of the leadership already shown from within the factory masses by the most skilled and literate among them. A third way was to go on the rampage, steal, murder, loot, get drunk—a reflection of the general disintegration of social norms and moral constraints and a consequence of the failure of regular mechanisms of repression, all of which February and October had set in train.

The search for alternatives to Bolshevik victory raises the question of why the other socialist parties, which also appealed to worker interests and used the same class-oriented language, were unable to create a movement that successfully challenged Bolshevik rule. Immediately after the dispersal of the Constituent Assembly, the Mensheviks, as we have seen, rejected the possibility of collaborating with the commissars, while the Left SRs went on to join the government. The Mensheviks stuck to their position as the loyal opposition, fierce in their anti-Bolshevik rhetoric but unwilling to jeopardize the triumph of October, which had displaced the "bourgeois" parties in the name of the Socialist Revolution. The SRs, by contrast, soon turned against their partners over Brest-Litovsk and the treatment of the peasantry. The socialist opposition challenged the Communists in their own terms. Throughout 1918, SRs and Mensheviks of varying description continued to propagate the anti-Bolshevik, pro-soviet (lower case) message in the factories, where worker dissatisfaction and spontaneous unrest percolated. Fellow socialists were a menace, but only because their words fell on eager ears. The shared vocabulary made them particularly dangerous.

The year 1918 presents a varied picture. In the beginning, worker protests were widespread but local, mostly focused on material conditions. The early months were also marked by attempts on the part of moderate socialists, mostly Mensheviks, to establish the basis for a politically coherent socialist opposition to Bolshevik rule.[29] The seeds were planted in January 1918 with the creation of a Committee for the Defense of Freedom of the Press (*Komitet bor'by za svobodu pechati*) and a worker-based Union for the Defense of the Constituent Assembly (*Soiuz zashchity Uchreditel'nogo sobraniia*). On the eve of the Fourth Congress of Soviets scheduled to meet in Moscow in mid-March, Menshevik and SR activists hosted the first meeting in Petrograd of what they called the Extraordinary Assembly of Deputies from Factories and Plants (*Chrezvychainoe sobranie upolnomochennykh ot fabrik i zavodov*), based on the model of the worker groups in the War Industries Committees. Of the more than a hundred deputies from the major Petrograd factories, a third were Menshevik, a third were SR, one was a Popular Socialist, and the rest were nonparty.[30]

The meeting reflected the agitated mood in the capital after the Brest treaty had been signed and while the Germans were still advancing. The workers were particularly worried about the effects of the demobilization of industry, the plans for possible evacuation of the factories, the loss of jobs, irregular pay, and the docking of wages as punishment for expressing unwelcome political opinions. The organizers proposed three resolutions, which, despite a few objections from the floor, were in the end adopted: rejection of the Brest peace, resignation of the Sovnarkom, and a new summoning of the Constituent Assembly. This was, of course, the SR agenda in 1918. For all the appeal of its slogans, however, the Assembly of Deputies did little to address concrete problems. "In general," one worker delegate objected, "the Constituent Assembly can be compared during peaceful times to good white bread; at the present time it's duck paté, but you're making it the central task for a moment when the Russian people are eating chaff, horsemeat, and even oats."[31]

Overall, it seems the Assembly of Deputies may have represented as many as fifty thousand Petrograd workers, perhaps a third—impressive, but not a majority—of the total city work force. Branches formed in a number of other cities, and delegates from Petrograd propagandized the workers in Moscow. The Muscovites responded, but not until June, when economic conditions had deteriorated even further. The Moscow city authorities banned their meetings and arrested the delegates. The printers, with a history of Menshevik affiliation, protested the arrests, denouncing the regime of "violence and abuse of authority." Leaders of the railroad union were also arrested. The Petrograd Soviet voted to dissolve the Petrograd Assembly. Its leaders answered by calling for a general strike, but they were not heeded.[32]

Despite the widespread discontent, the Assembly of Deputies would have had difficulty unseating the Bolshevik regime from within the stronghold of the proletariat, though it was not the only alternative organization to emerge in 1918. All in general espoused the SR-Menshevik line, calling for an all-socialist government, defending the Constituent Assembly, and denouncing the Bolsheviks for inflicting "monstrous terror," "arousing the bloody fires of anarchy," destroying the economy, and so on.[33] But if the Bolsheviks were riding the tiger, their rivals were trying to domesticate the beast. Paradoxically, the role of the various worker organizations in 1918 was less to foment insurrection than to stabilize the volatile situation. As one Menshevik leader put it in June 1918: "At the moment there is a great danger in the appearance among the masses of naked revolt, pure hungry movements, blind and fatal for the entire cause. And the Assembly is obliged to use all its influence and powers to counteract these forms, to lead the movement in an organized 'course,' in order not to allow the movement to turn into anarchy."[34]

Discouraged as they may have been, Menshevik organizers persisted in trying to establish a platform for independent worker action. The Assembly of Deputies took the initiative in calling an all-Russia workers' congress to be held in Moscow. It issued a statement, addressed to "the proletariat of all Russia," denouncing not only the Brest peace but the regime itself. "We are governed without constraint by people whom we have long ceased to trust, whom we did not elect, who hold us in contempt, who do not recognize the law, justice, honor, who love only power and for its sake have betrayed us....Our name has been used to camouflage a regime, hostile to us, an anti-popular regime, a regime that has brought us nothing but torment and dishonor. It must go."[35] The gauntlet was thrown down.

---

The moderate socialists had reason to believe the workers would respond to their anti-Bolshevik appeal. Grassroots worker protests, both anarchic and coherent, had begun in the immediate wake of the coup. Food supply in Petrograd was already a problem in November 1917. That and the sense of impunity in the wake of the takeover led to widespread looting, trashing of wine depots, drunkenness, turmoil in the factories as well as on the streets. In one of the major plants, formerly a Bolshevik stronghold, where activists had earlier urged unskilled workers to demand equal pay, the same workers now demanded equal pay of their new masters. They directed their anger at fellow workers, the skilled hands, who had a vested interest in the continuing welfare of the factory. Order was restored only by the appearance of Red Army soldiers.[36]

In January 1918, protests emerged as well among railroad workers in the south, also on the subject of wages. The SR-led railroad union, which had spearheaded the first organized protest against the Bolshevik takeover immediately after the event under the direction of its leadership (Vikzhel), now declared a strike. Its statements denounced the Bolsheviks for "shooting not just bourgeois, not capitalists, but us, workers and peasants.... This is not class war. This is mass murder." Unrest occurred in April in the big metallurgical plants of Moscow and the armaments plants in Tula.[37]

An incident in the town on Kolpino, fifteen miles southeast of Petrograd, in May 1918, was a flashpoint in the evolution of worker protest. Once again, it began with food, this time a delay in bread delivery. Women in line for bread began to grumble, a crowd gathered in the central square, and the Red Guards this time, not Cossacks as in February 1917, tried to disperse them. A boy who ran to the firehouse to sound the alarm was shot dead. Workers at the giant Izhorsk metallurgical plant assembled in a mass meeting, demanding a new soviet. As they left the plant, the Guards took aim, killing one and wounding several others. In the evening, there were searches and arrests; the next day, martial law was declared and meetings were forbidden. Cavalry arrived from Petrograd, while the Red Guards encircled the factory with machine guns. The workers nevertheless managed to send delegates to the Putilov works in Petrograd and other large plants, which organized protest meetings. A delegation from Petrograd took the train to Kolpino for the funeral of the Izhorsk worker who had been shot. A procession a thousand strong, singing revolutionary songs and carrying banners with SR slogans, followed its own orchestra to the cemetery. Confrontations between workers and Red Guards or Red Army troops occurred also at other factories in May.[38]

Work stoppages remained episodic, however, in the summer of 1918, appearing most often in the Central Industrial Region around Moscow. Moscow printers struck in June to protest the arrest of union leaders and also the closing of nonofficial publications, a blow not only to freedom of the press but to employment. Unrest affected a number of key cities—Tula, Klin, Tver, Nizhnii Novgorod—and the railroads, but the call for a general strike in early July failed.[39] The pattern suggests that workers with a history of protest were more likely to do the same thing now, perhaps adopting SR or Menshevik slogans, but in fact demanding that Soviet authorities do a better job and deliver on their promises. The trigger was hunger, and purposeful actions were paralleled by (sometimes mixed with) outbursts of rage and criminality.

As the historian Dmitrii Churakov puts it, 1918 was characterized by conflict "on the same side of the barricades."[40] Sometimes instead of imposing order the Red Guards created trouble themselves. Influenced by the so-called SR-Maximalists, the anarchist wing of the SR Party, they occasionally aimed their violence at Soviet officials and worker leaders, mainline SRs or Mensheviks, who they felt had betrayed the revolution. The Guards themselves might indulge in looting, public executions, arrests, beatings—an arsenal of grassroots terror, which the authorities condemned because they did not direct it. The Petrograd Red Guards were disarmed in March, after the signing of the Brest treaty.[41] These "small wars," or minor insurgencies, which unfolded in the context of the great Civil War were not easily harnessed to the larger anti-Bolshevik cause.[42] The workers, however unhappy, endorsed the basic socialist vision of an egalitarian society in which they themselves would play a key role. Thus, during the Iaroslavl uprising in July, as we have seen, some hundred railroad workers joined the anti-Bolshevik forces, but the rest stood aside, unwilling to accept the unquestioned authority of army commanders. They did not wish to submit to the old harness.[43]

The congress of worker delegates which the Extraordinary Assembly of Deputies from Factories and Plants had announced a month earlier opened in Moscow on July 22, 1918, two weeks after the start of the Iaroslavl revolt and Ambassador Mirbach's murder. The timing was unpropitious. Only thirty-six delegates were present, most from Petrograd, mostly Mensheviks, plus a few SRs and Bundists, no Bolsheviks or Left SRs. A number of large plants were represented, but the size of their constituency is hard to judge.[44] On the second day, everyone was arrested. Latvian riflemen broke in, guns cocked, led by a commissar from the Cheka. The case was taken up by the highest tribunal.[45] *Izvestiia* denounced "the anti-worker congress, which its sponsors call 'worker,' reminding us again of the paradoxical role of 'socialists' taking action in time of socialist revolution against the workers and peasants who are fighting for socialism." These "social-traitors," it charged, in fact constituted a "counterrevolutionary conspiracy."[46] Many workers, some in the showcase radical plants, thought otherwise. Protests against the arrests came from labor organizations and factories. But the leadership had lost its spirit. The last delegates from the workers' congress still in prison were amnestied in November 1918, on the anniversary of the revolution.[47]

The congress of worker delegates was speedily repressed, but grassroots unrest was not immediately quieted. The large state-owned plants of the Urals, an essential source of weapons for both Reds and Whites, were particularly volatile in the first half of 1918. Thirty-seven anti-Bolshevik revolts had to be repressed by force of arms.[48] In August two serious insurrections broke out in the Kama Valley cities of Izhevsk and Votkinsk, which lasted until November. They did not ignite a larger movement, but they reflected widespread problems and anger, which enhanced their symbolic importance. Situated 240 miles northeast of Kazan, Izhevsk had a population of fifty thousand, of whom twenty thousand were employed by the state arms factory dating back to the eighteenth century, which remained a key producer of rifles and steel. Votkinsk, forty miles to the northeast, was the birthplace of composer Petr Tchaikovsky. In 1918 a third of its population of thirty thousand worked in the state metallurgical factory that produced engines and other machinery. Both towns had their own rail junctions and were better supplied with fuel and raw materials than most enterprises at this point. In 1917 both factories had been active Bolshevik supporters.[49]

The official version of these events, compiled as they were still unfolding, could not deny that workers had challenged Bolshevik power, but it depicted the protesters as dupes of the White counterrevolution. The Right SR and Menshevik activists who provided the mobilizing slogans thought of themselves, of course, as restoring the revolution to its original purpose, not jeopardizing its existence. Some leaders of the revolt were indeed returning army officers, as we shall see, but, as post-Soviet scholarship has shown, they were themselves former workers. Organized White forces were not involved. The revolt was a genuine response to Bolshevik policies that in a short time had managed to alienate the majority of formerly radical workers. There was good reason for Soviet-era myths to obscure the facts of the case.

The workers in the state armament plants of the Urals were a special breed—and they represent an anomaly in terms of the usual criteria for "proletarian identity." Though employed in modern enterprises, the archetypal site of capitalist exploitation, they constituted an almost hereditary caste—generation after generation at the same job, enjoying the privileged status of skilled masters. They were often also property owners, many possessing their own plots of land. A good third lived in substantial brick houses, with gardens and baths. Another half also owned their own dwellings, though on a more modest scale. The classic "proletarian" was supposed to have broken his ties to the land, to have nothing to lose but his chains. There was a lot to lose here.

This privileged group was distinct both from the workers employed in the private factories of the region and from the unskilled minority of workers, who were by and large not native to the area. In the elections to the Constituent Assembly, the Bolsheviks did best in the private factories, among the least skilled, least well integrated laborers. The original soviets established after October 1917 consisted mostly of these relative newcomers. Eager to deprive the worker-elites of their property, they resorted to massive confiscations, down to the smallest articles of clothing. These original soviets in the Urals prohibited the use of meadowland, forbade fishing in the ponds, tried to repress private trade, and destroyed the district

administration. The better-qualified workers saw their way of life threatened. Indeed, state factories throughout central Russia became centers of
worker protest against the new regime.[50]

Later elections to the local soviets in the Izhevsk area returned anti-
Bolshevik majorities. A resolution of May 27, 1918, in the SR-Menshevik
spirit, declared:"The regime whose slogans promised peace, bread, the guarantee of freedom, the timely summons of the Constituent Assembly, and the
regulation of industry, in practice has given us the worst form of war, hunger, the violation of freedom, the dispersal of the Constituent Assembly, and
massive unemployment. This regime must go."[51] At this very moment, the
Czechoslovak Legion had embarked on its rebellion in Cheliabinsk, and
two weeks later the SRs established the Komuch in Samara. The moderate
socialists in Izhevsk continued to do well in local elections, which continued to be held, and by June had acquired a working majority. Bolsheviks
sent from Moscow therefore dispersed the soviet and arrested the leading
deputies. The Mirbach murder on July 6 provided another reason to crack
down on socialist opponents.[52] In the Urals, local soviet elections nevertheless continued to return SR and Menshevik deputies, but they were expelled
and arrested.[53]

A month later, the local mood was still unstable. When urged by Bolshevik
emissaries from Moscow to join the Red Army against the counterrevolution, the Izhevsk workers refused. The Red Army nevertheless persisted in
trying to recruit them. A draft was announced on August 5, while the Reds
were struggling to defend Kazan from the Czechoslovaks. Two days later,
the Legion drove them out. The Bolshevik military command in Izhevsk
imposed martial law. The rumor circulated that the Bolsheviks were preparing to slaughter the factory administration and the propertied classes. The
streets emptied. In the early hours of August 7, the factory siren sounded.
People rushed into the streets. Militia and Red Army troops instructed
everyone to gather in the main square, where the Bolshevik commander
announced the fall of Kazan and the general mobilization.[54]

The ground was prepared for revolt. Among the numerous organizations
that had emerged after February in Izhevsk was the Union of Front Soldiers
(*Izhevskii soiuz frontovikov*). Most of its over three thousand members had
been employed by the Izhevsk works before the war. The Union's main
function had been to help returning soldiers find a footing in civilian life.
About a third of the core three to four hundred were officers, who now,
with their professional leadership skills and close ties to the factory rank and

file, provided the backbone of the emerging revolt. Similar unions had appeared in the spring in the Volga region, where they played a leading role in stimulating unrest.[55]

On August 8, the day after the Bolshevik summons, the Izhevsk factory siren sounded again. The Front Soldiers' Union called a general meeting at which officers and socialists joined in demanding "Soviet power, not Party power."[56] The balance was tipped in the direction of violence by a small incident. People were still gathered in the square when three militiamen appeared on horseback. Their commander, unwisely, gave the order to disperse the crowd, which began shouting and threatening the three riders. One of them discharged his gun into the air, another escaped, but the third was pulled from his mount and murdered. His dismembered corpse was thrown into a pond.[57]

The Front Soldiers' Union and the socialist leaders now constituted themselves the head of an armed insurrection, of which they were not of course in control. The first twelve hours consisted of revenge. Bolsheviks were torn from their dwellings, murdered on the streets, in soviet offices, in hospitals. The rebels managed to capture a store of cartridges, and the officers tried to organize regular formations. Rebels and Red Army troops traded fire. After more confusion and more shooting, by the morning of August 9 the rebels had secured control of the city and rounded up the remaining Bolshevik leaders. This was the start of a "small" civil war, inside the greater Civil War, that spread through the Kama Valley.[58]

In nearby Votkinsk, a similar pattern emerged. The town had its own Front Soldiers' Union, which faced the same issues of the draft and the question of arms and was in contact with the Izhevsk union. When the revolt started in Izhevsk, the two groups agreed to coordinate. On August 17, armed men arrived from Izhevsk and joined with local men to chase the Red Army troops into the forests. Bolshevik workers fled; three hundred Bolshevik activists were arrested. The rebels here, too, took their revenge. Dozens of corpses lay on the streets, and almost the entire leadership was captured. By noon it was over. Church bells rang throughout the city as on Easter.[59]

The Red troops were now centered in Sarapul, down the Kama River from Votkinsk. On August 18, under the command of the ubiquitous Vladimir Antonov-Ovseenko, they began shelling Izhevsk. Once again the siren sounded, and the Reds retreated. Indeed, Sarapul itself soon escaped their control. A confusing situation emerged in which SR-Maximalists and Left Bolsheviks resisted the local Bolshevik military council—in the name of Bolshevik power. Antonov-Ovseenko had them arrested. The chaos made it easier for the Izhevsk rebels, when they appeared in Sarapul on August 31, to take over the city. An orchestra played, and reprisals began.[60]

At their fullest extent, the rebels controlled a territory of about five thousand square miles with a population of about 800,000.[61] The most interesting part of the story, however, is what happened after they established control, during the three months when they had to run the city themselves. As in other grassroots revolts that called for "soviets without Communists," leaders here at first returned to the pre-October soviet model, with Mensheviks and Right SRs setting the agenda. But soon the soviet declared itself to be a local branch of the Komuch, which had formed in Samara in early June, thus adopting the ideal of a democratic republican government. Newspapers published in both towns (on scarce and shoddy paper) disseminated the Komuch message, excoriating "those who sold out Russian democracy to German imperialism, drowned the country in blood, suffocated the free word, shot down workers, and reduced the country to hunger, collapse, and despair." Their purpose, they said, was "to overthrow the reign of the commissars [komissaroderzhavie], to restore the democratic state organization destroyed by the Bolsheviks."[62]

The rebels made an effort to reestablish the basic elements of daily life. Stores reopened, work in the factories resumed, and some version of a police force was formed, but crime and spontaneous revenge against Communists continued, sometimes at bayonet point. The rebels also created an army—the Kama People's Army (Prikamskaia narodnaia armiia), led by a decorated former imperial colonel. At its peak, the army numbered at least twenty thousand men from Izhevsk, almost all workers, and another forty thousand from Votkinsk and Sarapul.[63] The army relied for support on the local peasants, with whom the workers maintained close ties and whom they supplied with weapons to use against the Red Army.

As autumn set in, however, divisions within the leadership became more apparent. Tensions increased between the soldiers and the socialists. The officers in the People's Army resented the committees that restricted their authority, and they opposed the abolition of the death penalty—the two patented moves of revolutionary "soldiers' power." Serious conflicts deepened also within the Menshevik fold, between those who endorsed the revolt and those, led by Iulii Martov, who had decided to make their peace with the Bolshevik regime. On August 7, the Menshevik Central Committee had published a resolution denouncing the revolt as harmful to the interests of the working class. The Bolsheviks naturally distributed this proclamation widely. Local Menshevik leaders condemned their party's position, for their own reasons, as "a stab in the back of the democratic proletariat fighting against the butcher-Bolsheviks for the political rights of the working class and the freedom of the entire Russian people."[64]

The skilled workers spearheading the revolt rejected the extremes of Bolshevik labor policies, but they, like the Martovite Mensheviks, wished to preserve the advances of the revolution—notably, the banner issues of the eight-hour day and workers' control. The local peasants who had supported the revolt were disappointed that goods proved as scarce as ever and grain requisitioning failed to disappear. In short, the rebel leaders faced the same problems as all other claimants to "power." Their vulnerability was most apparent when it came to the army. Unable to fill the ranks with volunteers, the insurgents resorted to the draft, which they tried to enforce by executing shirkers and deserters. Anticipating the approach of the Red Army, the People's Army also mobilized civilians for the work of digging trenches. Adults were summoned to the central square and informed that "the spade will save Izhevsk. The deeper we dig, the stronger our defense." Failure to appear "will be considered a crime against the people."[65] Everyone used the same words.

Taking another leaf from the Bolshevik handbook, the Izhevsk insurrection introduced its own local terror. Penalties were exacted for failure to surrender arms; curfews were imposed, unauthorized meetings forbidden; arrests were made, prisons improvised—three thousand prisoners were confined to barges on the river. An investigative commission was established to root out hidden Bolshevik sympathizers, and people were shot on suspicion of disloyalty. With the predictable pendulum effect, brutality ended by enhancing the Bolshevik appeal. Whole units of the People's Army went over to the Reds, though it was clear that the Bolsheviks were no less brutal.

Despite the wavering and disenchantment, the People's Army nevertheless put up a good fight when the Reds attacked in late October. The decisive battle occurred on November 7, involving artillery on both sides. By early evening, Izhevsk had succumbed. "Greetings to the glorious Red Army troops who have taken Izhevsk," Lenin applauded. "Congratulations on the anniversary of the revolution. Long live the socialist Red Army." Three days later, Izhevsk celebrated the Red victory and the first anniversary of October. A crowd of ten thousand workers assembled in the main square, red banners held high, songs resounding, welcoming Soviet power. On November 12, the last of the Kama People's Army in Votkinsk crossed the Kama River, heading east.[66]

For most of 1919 and 1920, worker protests were motivated by economic hardship, not abstract principles. The basic grievances were concrete—inequality of rations, inadequate wages, prohibition on foraging for food and engaging in barter with the villages.[67] Workers also protested the forced imposition of labor discipline—harsh penalties for absenteeism or attempting to change jobs. They objected to the nature of the punishments—exile to hard labor, withholding of rations, arrests.

Railroad shops and munitions production were the two industrial sectors most crucial to economic recovery and to the military fortunes of the regime, and for that reason were subject to the strictest application of War Communist principles. They were also the sectors most prone to organized protest. Railroad workers had been militant since 1905; the umbrella railroad union (Vikzhel) had played an active though unsuccessful role, as we have seen, in organizing a non-Bolshevik alternative after October; the SRs had long had a foothold in the repair shops and, despite the party's misfortunes, continued to provide leadership for grassroots unrest. Both the railroad shops and the armaments plants relied heavily on skilled workers, precisely the type most likely to be involved in union activity, and indeed, given the labor shortage, some Vikzhel activists had been rehired as skilled hands.

The intensification of disciplinary measures in this population not surprisingly provoked an angry response. In spring 1920, unrest was endemic on the railroads. All the main Petrograd railroad shops engaged in periodic work stoppages. Practical issues were at the core, but workers also targeted the policies of War Communism and the methods the party used to enforce them.[68] In response, the party cracked down on the trade unions, which lost whatever autonomy they had so far enjoyed. The arrest of worker leaders, as well as Menshevik and SR activists, succeeded in limiting the extent of worker protests.[69]

Despite the economic collapse and the shrinking size of the factory workforce, even in the most advanced sector, elements of the former labor culture survived, including patterns of self-mobilization, but the question of power affected the less skilled, less politicized workers as well. "Sometimes," the historian Sergei Iarov comments, "the impression of anarchy and disorder 'at the top,' even without any deterioration in the workers' material situation, promoted an oppositional mood. And, conversely, the strengthening of Bolshevik power, even without any material improvement, quickly changed the vector of worker support."[70]

This pattern echoes the dynamic that emerged in 1905 among soldiers and sailors and among peasants at all times. When the authorities showed weakness, they were easily defied; once they asserted their competence, resistance abated. Many protests were directed against the regime's punitive and coercive methods, which were intended to demonstrate its power and authority, when in fact both were still insecure. It can be argued that War Communism, for all its ruthlessness, was experienced not as a sign of authority but as a symptom of weakness, a desperate attempt to exact compliance at the population's expense. In any case, it is clear that repression did not prevent the demonstrative work stoppages in the Russian core, which persisted throughout 1920. Food remained a central concern.[71]

It is also clear that the mood in the factories during the Civil War was above all unstable. Workers responded to hunger and to the drastically degraded conditions of existence. In areas of the Urals controlled by the Reds, by summer 1918 the cities already lacked basic foodstuffs, peasants no longer dared come to town for fear of arrest, prices skyrocketed. Refugees crammed into the Urals city of Perm, where a shortage of housing and lack of sanitation led to epidemics of cholera and typhus. Rations calculated according to revolutionary class status were miserable at best—a half pound of bread a day in the top category.[72] In 1919 bread consumption in the Urals was under half what it had been in 1913, the prewar benchmark. Here, as elsewhere, workers protested the inadequacy and unfairness of rations. They denounced abuses by Soviet officials, whom they derided as "so-called Communists" or "pretend Communists." They denounced the Red Army for exploiting the working poor. A popular ditty chastised the Red Army, which "lets the bourgeois get away, but from the worker takes his pay." The smallest protest for whatever cause was mercilessly repressed.[73]

The Motovilikha weapons and military equipment factory in Perm provides an example of the political disillusionment that affected the region. Founded in 1736 and run by the state until 1917, the plant continues in operation to this day under the same name. In December 1918, the Motovilikha workers issued a number of proclamations. In a language that departs from the formulas of professional revolutionaries, they expressed their accumulated anger. They demanded an end to the use of torture and the death penalty—and the return of free trade in bread. They called for an investigation into "what the commissars were eating" and demanded that "their leather jackets be taken away and used to make shoes for the population." Somewhat incoherently, but eloquently, they appealed to those in power: "We do not recognize your existing Bolshevik regime, we do not recognize where it's headed, we're forced to go against our brothers. We workers won't go for it, you mobilize us against ourselves."[74]

In response, the Red Army shut down the Motovilikha works and declared a state of siege. Arrests were made. The Perm Cheka declared that "anyone agitating against Soviet authorities and spreading false, ridiculous rumors, will be subject by the Cheka to the harshest penalties and when caught in the act will be shot without pity." The Military Revolutionary Committee made it clear that workers were not exempt from revolutionary justice. "Our revolutionary conscience and duty demand we finish off anyone out to destroy the Russian and international revolution, whether purposeful— the bourgeoisie, the capitalists and their henchmen, or unthinking— benighted workers and peasants."[75] The Red Army man would storm the bastions of the bourgeoisie, warned a Communist newspaper, even if it meant stepping over "the dead bodies of the hungry and poor" who mistook their own interests.[76]

Repressing worker activism was one part of the overall project of beating the population into submission, while also mobilizing its forces on behalf of the very same power that held it in check. A difficult balance. Overall, the combination of continuous armed conflict; the policies of War Communism; the pressure exerted by all competing armies on the domestic population in terms of labor power, military service, livestock, food, and fuel; the displacement of masses of the homeless and destitute into the already overcrowded cities; the collapse of any sanitary or medical services; the destruction of urban infrastructure—all this resulted in chronic hunger, starvation, and the spread of disease. Reference to the "dead bodies of the hungry and poor" was not a figure of speech.

# 2

# The Revolution Turns
# Against Itself

The Red Terror was based on the premise that treachery was always lurking, that any collective action which escaped the regime's control was a potential threat to its existence, that no social identity was what it seemed, no group or person incapable of turning colors, and therefore that repression must be not only preemptive but arbitrary. The events of February to March 1921, which closed out the period of the Civil War, replicated the dynamics of popular mobilization that set off the revolution to begin with. They proved that no front was safe in a war without fronts.

The Petrograd proletariat and the Baltic Fleet were icons of Bolshevik grassroots militancy. In February 1917, strikes and street demonstrations in Petrograd had unleashed the cascade of events, including the mutiny of sailors and soldiers, that caused the monarchy to crumble. Four years later, in February 1921, strikes and protests once again rocked Petrograd. The capital had moved to Moscow; Lenin had replaced Nicholas. The workers in the large industrial plants who had welcomed the end of the old regime and expected to benefit from Soviet power now turned against leaders who claimed to govern in their name, but whose policies contributed to the social and economic crisis that threatened their very existence. Unrest in the factory districts inspired sailors in the nearby Kronstadt fortress to mount protests of their own. Fervent Bolsheviks in October 1917, the crews now directed their fury at the "Communist autocracy."

Kronstadt is an island in the Finnish Gulf, about twenty miles from Petrograd. The fortress was erected by Peter the Great at the beginning of the eighteenth century, in defense of his new capital. A city occupied the eastern end of the island, its central square large enough for twenty-five thousand soldiers on parade. In summer, steamers arrived from Petrograd; from late

November to early March, the Gulf was frozen. Altogether a population of some fifty thousand inhabited the island, half military, half civilian.[1]

The Baltic Fleet sailors had all along represented the radical edge of the revolution. We encountered them in February 1917, when they lynched over fifty of their own officers, including two admirals. During the July Days, they arrived in the city to support the mobilized Petrograd workers and were barely prevented from murdering the SR leader Viktor Chernov. As the Menshevik Fedor Dan recalled, "in those memorable days they went on an unprovoked shooting spree and wounded quite a few people."[2] In August the sailors rallied against General Kornilov, demanding his arrest and execution. Most of the officers on Kronstadt also opposed Kornilov, but four refused to join the call for his execution. The sailors arrested and shot them.[3] The Kadets Andrei Shingarev and Fedor Kokoshkin were murdered in their hospital beds in February 1918 by Red Guards and Kronstadt sailors.[4] These were dangerous men when aroused.

By February 1921, some of the original sailors had been replaced by new recruits; the recent additions were perhaps less disciplined, less professional, but the propensity for violence and the hostility to authority were the same as before, though perhaps for somewhat different reasons.[5] What was once a resource for the Bolsheviks was now a threat, but the myth of the loyal vanguard could not be abandoned. The party denounced the Kronstadt rebels as dupes of a counterrevolutionary White conspiracy—and this remained the official interpretation throughout the Soviet years.[6] As in the case of other post-October revolts, the insurgents in fact had no intention of restoring the old regime. This time, in the name of the revolution, they protested the policies associated with War Communism—compulsory labor, requisitioning, repression of the small-scale trade on which many depended for food, the despoiling of the villages. They were angered by the return of inequality—rations pegged to status, privileges enjoyed by officials of the new regime. If they denounced the "Communists," it was not because they had fallen under the spell of reactionary Whites. They rejected the Bolsheviks at this moment for the same reasons they had welcomed them before, not because they had become any less revolutionary.[7]

To some it seemed as though February 1917 was again "in the air."[8] As in 1917, hunger and deprivation, not abstract principles, pushed the demonstrators over the edge. By early 1921, popular resistance to the regime was endemic throughout the Russian core. In the cities, the heart of Bolshevik support, food was scarce, factories closed their doors for lack of fuel and raw material, and workers were out on the streets—facing starvation. In late January, the authorities imposed a cut in rations.[9] Even the Petrograd garrison was short of food; soldiers were said to be fainting from hunger. Some went begging. Soldiers and workers were restless in Moscow, as well. They gathered in continuous meetings.[10]

On February 11, the regime announced the imminent closing of almost a hundred Petrograd factories, including hotbeds of radical mobilization, such as the Putilov works, the Sestroretsk weapons factory, and the vast brick Treugolnik compound; altogether twenty-seven thousand workers were losing their jobs. Protest began with a meeting ten days later, at the Trubochnyi plant, which declared its support for genuine popular rule (*narodovlastie*), the catchword of the non-Bolshevik left opposition. The Petrograd Soviet shut it down. The lockout deprived the workers not only of wages but of rations. On February 24, the streets began filling with workers from Trubochnyi and other factories, swelling to twenty-five hundred in the industrial Vasilevskii Island district.[11]

The authorities in Petrograd created an emergency Defense Committee and imposed a state of martial law.[12] On February 27, the commissar of the Baltic Fleet reported disturbances among the twenty-six thousand Kronstadt sailors.[13] The next day, the movement spread to the militant Putilov works, a mere shadow of its former size, but still six thousand strong. The protesters demanded the removal of Communist armed squads from the factories, abolition of the labor armies, and the restoration of political rights.[14]

The political demands may have reflected the influence of Menshevik and SR agitators, who had been distributing leaflets in the factories. The SRs were calling for revolt; the Mensheviks remained the loyal opposition. They called for policy changes but did not see this moment of unrest as a replay of 1917; now the workers were exhausted and disorganized, their numbers depleted. They were concerned with physical survival, not political ideals. Work stoppages were no threat when the factories were in any case shutting down for lack of fuel and raw material. The authorities made some concessions (extra rations, permission to forage, an end to the confiscation of foodstuffs) and arrested the Menshevik Central Committee.[15] By March 3, the protests had died down.

Fedor Dan remembered the circumstances of his own arrest. On February 26, as the action was just starting, he went to the Mariinskii Theater to hear the famed bass Feodor Chaliapin in Nikolai Rimsky-Korsakov's opera *The Maid of Pskov*. The details are telling: that Dan was interested in the theater at such a moment; that tickets were no longer for sale, but could only be obtained through connections; that performances ended early. Upon returning home at ten in the evening, he was greeted by an agent of the Cheka. Having "thanked the fates to have been able one last time to enjoy Chaliapin's singing," Dan was driven away through the dark and deserted streets.[16]

In the building that once had housed the tsarist secret police, the Okhrana, where he himself had been imprisoned twenty-five years before in the earliest days of the Social Democratic movement, Dan was now searched, stripped, and subjected to interrogation. His captors were not hardened professionals but poorly educated young men, proud of their new power and mindlessly spouting party slogans. They denounced the strikers as traitors to the socialist cause. The real workers had volunteered for the front or joined the food brigades, they said. These were "scum, self-seekers, shopkeepers, who had taken refuge in the factories during the war to escape the draft." The sailors would make mincemeat of them. The Mensheviks were traitors, too. Dan despaired of this "Communism" which "called the proletariat scum, and counted on sailors to impose socialism."[17]

After a year's detention, Dan was expelled from the country and eventually settled in New York.[18] Chaliapin, who ever since 1905 had considered himself a friend of the revolution, left Russia on his own account in 1922 and died finally in Paris.

---

Meanwhile, on Kronstadt, the armored artillery warships *Sevastopol* and *Petropavlovsk* (the major fighting vessels, the "ships of the line") were restless. In 1918 the crews had already demonstrated their unhappiness with Bolshevik policies, adopting the SR critique of Brest-Litovsk and resenting the replacement of their own elected committee by political commissars. They had called for free soviet elections. In December 1920, the mood was angry, and desertions increased. The sailors sent a delegation to Moscow to complain about poor conditions. The delegates were arrested.[19] In January 1921, grievances still festered. The crews of the *Sevastopol* and the *Petropavlovsk* resented a recent transfer from Petrograd to Kronstadt, followed by stricter discipline, including suspension of shore leaves. More basically, the men resented the new hierarchy of privilege—including unequal rations. News from the countryside added to their discontent. The last horse, the last cow were being taken from families and neighbors.[20]

Hearing of the work stoppages in Petrograd, the crews of the *Petropavlovsk* and *Sevastopol* sent delegates to investigate. On March 1, the sailors formulated a platform. It began with a series of political demands. It called for new elections to the soviets, by secret ballot and with the right to pre-election campaigning, since the existing soviets "do not express the will of the workers and peasants." The platform demanded freedom of speech, press, and assembly—but only "for workers and peasants, anarchists, and left socialist parties." It insisted that no single party should have a monopoly on propaganda. It demanded the release of "all political prisoners of the socialist parties, also all workers and peasants, Red Army men and sailors arrested in connection with the worker and peasant movements" and a review of cases in prisons and concentration camps. It demanded the removal of Communist political controls and armed guards. It demanded that peasants have the right to land and livestock, so long as they did not employ hired labor themselves.[21]

Summoned by the Kronstadt soviet, a crowd of sixteen thousand sailors, Red Army men, and city residents gathered on the island's central square to celebrate the anniversary of the February Revolution. A transitional moment. Making a special appearance, Mikhail Kalinin, head of the All-Russian Central Executive Committee, was greeted by music, flags, and military honors. Proceedings were opened by the chair of the Kronstadt soviet, Pavel Vasil'ev. Rising to the podium, Kalinin and Nikolai Kuz'min, commissar of the Baltic Fleet, urged the sailors to abandon their political demands. They were shouted down. A clerk on the *Petropavlovsk* by the name of Stepan Petrichenko called for a vote on the sailor's platform. It was approved "unanimously" by the sailors in the square.[22]

Like many of the other popular leaders on the revolutionary side, Petrichenko perfectly fit the profile of the grassroots activist the Bolsheviks cultivated. Born into a peasant family in Kaluga Province, he moved to the Ukrainian city of Zaporozhe, where he acquired two years of schooling and experience as a metal worker. In 1914, at the age of twenty-two, he was drafted into the navy. In 1919 he joined the Communist Party.[23] He was typical of the seasoned hands, particularly in the technical service, who provided leadership in naval revolts, a pattern already evident in 1905.[24]

Not only the leadership but the process of mobilization adhered to the standard revolutionary script. In the grassroots soviet tradition, the sailors elected delegates, organized elections, demanded a return to the original participatory model. On March 2, Petrichenko summoned a meeting of sailor delegates, who in turn elected a presidium and planned for new elections to the Kronstadt soviet, inviting all socialist parties to participate. A group of thirty delegates was sent to Petrograd to explain their demands in the factories; they were arrested and disappeared.[25]

Instead of responding to the sailors' complaints, commissar Kuz'min issued a warning. All was calm in Petrograd, he announced, no support forthcoming from that quarter, but the fate of the revolution itself was at stake. Piłsudski was lurking across the border, the West was waiting to pounce. The delegates "could shoot him if they cared to," he was reported to have said, "but if they wanted an armed battle, then they would get one—the Communists would not renounce power willingly and would fight to the last breath."[26] For their part, the sailors insisted they sought a compromise with authority; Bolsheviks on Kronstadt were not excluded from the proceedings. Nerves were stretched, however. It was rumored that armed contingents were headed to the island. In anticipation of conflict, the meeting created a Provisional Revolutionary Committee (*Vremennyi revoliutsionnyi komitet*), under Petrichenko's direction.[27]

The sailors distrusted Kuz'min's claim that unrest in Petrograd had abated; they expected widespread worker support for what they called their own "third revolution." Some of the large plants did respond, but most Petrograd workers held back. They were tired of war and conflict, and they feared a new upsurge of terror. They resented what they thought of as the sailors' already privileged position, compared to their own. They may well have accepted the relentless official propaganda, blaming the Kronstadt "mutiny" on the influence of the "White" general Aleksandr Kozlovskii. Posters plastered all over the factory districts denounced Kozlovskii and the alleged counterrevolutionary conspiracy.[28] Workers hesitated to challenge the official view for fear of being arrested.[29] There was indeed a General Kozlovskii on the island. A former major-general in the tsarist army, he had joined the Red Army in 1918 as a "military specialist." As the commander of the Kronstadt artillery, he lent his support to the uprising, but he was hardly its inspiration—and he never showed any sympathy for the White cause. "The Communists," he announced, "have used my name in order to depict the Kronstadt uprising as a White Guard conspiracy, simply because I was the only 'general' on the fortress."[30] Back in Petrograd, his family were seized as hostages.[31]

The rebels rejected the charges. Addressing "Our Comrade Workers and Peasants," they warned, "Our enemies are deceiving you. They say the

Kronstadt uprising is organized by Mensheviks, SRs, spies of the Entente, and tsarist generals.... Bald-faced lies.... We do not want to return to the past. We are not the servants of the bourgeoisie or hirelings of the Entente. We are defenders of the power of the laboring masses, not the unbridled, tyrannical power of a single party." The Bolsheviks were "worse than Nicholas." They "cling to power and are ready to drown all Russia in blood if only to preserve their autocratic rule."[32] There was no White plot behind the rumblings in Kronstadt, but the rebels did echo SR language. Petrichenko was no SR, however, and most of the rebels would have refused a party affiliation. They did, nevertheless, accept the shared language of socialism and popular liberation.

This was a battle of "comrades" against the "Communist dictatorship." Actual enemies of the revolution might welcome this battle, the leaders explained to the men, but from "opposite motives." "You, comrades...are inspired by the fervent intention of restoring true soviet power," the desire to give the workers and peasants what they need. The enemies of the revolution, by contrast, are inspired "by the hope of restoring the tsarist whip and the privilege of generals.... You seek freedom, they want to entrap you once again in the bonds of slavery."[33]

The spokesmen explained what they were fighting for: "Having accomplished the October revolution, the working class hoped to achieve its own emancipation. The result was an even greater enslavement of the individual person. The power of the police-gendarme monarchy fell into the hands of its assailants—the Communists, who instead of bringing the laboring masses freedom brought the constant fear of the Cheka torture chamber, more horrible by far than the tsarist gendarme regime." The sailors' own "third revolution" would "throw off the remaining chains from the laboring masses and open a wide new path for the creation of socialism."[34] Socialism was still the goal.

---

Believing they were under attack, the Kronstadt Provisional Revolutionary Committee organized the takeover of the island. Sailors occupied the arsenals, the telephone exchange, the administrative buildings. The Committee published a newspaper—called *Izvestiia*, like the official Soviet organ—which appealed for order and warned against bloodshed.[35] On March 3, two days after the sailors' mass demonstration and even as worker unrest was abating in Petrograd, the authorities imposed a state of siege in the city and surrounding region. A decree signed by Lenin and Trotsky the following day condemned the "mutiny" and declared the rebels "outside the law." Hostages were taken among the ringleaders' families. The possibility of negotiation was rejected. The choice was capitulate or fight. On March 5, the Kronstadt officers ("military specialists" like Kozlovskii) agreed to assist the rebels in organizing an armed defense.[36]

That same day, Moscow made the decision to attack. Trotsky issued a "final warning"—all who have challenged "the socialist fatherland" must "immediately lay down arms." "Only those who surrender unconditionally can count on clemency from the Soviet Republic." Orders have been issued "to crush the mutiny and the mutineers by force of arms. Responsibility for the damage thereby done to the civilian population falls entirely on the White Guard mutineers."[37] The warning was transmitted by radio to Kronstadt. Leaflets were dropped from airplanes, blaming the Whites, blaming General Kozlovskii.[38] The rebels insisted they were defending "the freedoms won by the Revolution." A meeting of the Kronstadt garrison resolved: "We will die but will not retreat. Long live the Free Russia of the Laboring People."[39]

The ultimatum was extended for twenty-four hours. On March 7, the Provisional Revolutionary Committee announced that the "Revolution of the Laboring Masses" was ready "to sweep away the vile slanderers and butchers who have defiled the face of Soviet Russia. We don't need your clemency, Mr. Trotsky!"[40] The Seventh Army, under the command of Mikhail Tukhachevskii, was to initiate the attack on March 8, the day the Tenth Party Congress was scheduled to open in Moscow, so that success could be announced.[41] It was time, a Cheka agent warned, "to eradicate the spreading illness by surgical means, since it was already too late for an organic cure."[42]

Among their other demands, the Kronstadters insisted on the end of forced requisitions. A year earlier, in February 1920, Trotsky had been led to reconsider the wisdom even of the grain levy, the *razverstka*, which had replaced the disastrous *kombedy*. Experience in the Urals had shown that the *razverstka* did not increase procurement and indeed only caused peasants to restrict their planting to the consumption norm. He had proposed instead a tax in kind (*prodnalog*), a percentage of what was harvested, encouraging the peasants to plant more.[43] In March 1920, however, Lenin reaffirmed that the party's attitude to "petty-bourgeois property owners, to small-scale speculators, who number in the millions...is an attitude of war." Most Bolsheviks agreed that intensified coercion was called for.[44] A year later, by February 1921, Lenin and the top figures in the party and Cheka had now also begun to reconsider the *razverstka*.[45] The question of introducing the *prodnalog* was in fact on the agenda for the Tenth Congress, but the new policy was not announced until the assault on Kronstadt was already under way. The rebels' demand had been preempted. The issue was power. In Lenin's words: "Now is precisely the moment for us to teach this public a lesson, so that for decades to come they will not dare even to contemplate resistance."[46]

If the Tenth Congress had begun two days earlier, on March 6, the rebels might have learned of the change in policy and perhaps, feeling vindicated, might have backed off, but that is not what Lenin wanted.[47] Massive peasant insurgency had compelled the party to modify its approach to grain requisition. Worker protests had caused a group within the party, known as the Workers' Opposition, to urge that trade unions be given a greater role in economic affairs. Lenin insisted, however, on the need to tighten political controls, even within the party. Resolutions endorsing Party unity and condemning "anarchist and syndicalist deviations" signaled the end of the era in which serious differences could be expressed within the party, even among the higher-ups. A renewed ideological rigor thus accompanied the economic concessions exacted by the force of popular unrest.

It was easy to blame the grassroots challenge to party rule on the enemy— the Black Hundreds, the White officers, the Mensheviks, or the SRs—but it was no secret that the revolutionary sailors of the Baltic Fleet acted on their own. It was not so easy, however, to "teach this public a lesson." The revolt was not repressed with surgical precision on March 8. At that point, there were about thirteen thousand sailors and soldiers and another two thousand armed civilians ready to repel an attack. They were shielded somewhat by the eleven miles of ice-covered water that separated them from the mainland, which the assailants would have to cross under fire. They could not, however, withstand a long siege, since supplies of ammunition, fuel, and food were limited.[48] Indeed, hunger was a weapon that could be used against them. "Inevitable hunger will force Kronstadt to submit to the power of the Bolsheviks," an official report predicted.[49]

The first phase of the assault began on the evening of March 7 to 8; the sound of the guns could be heard in Petrograd, but snow and fog soon put an end to the action. The next morning, Red Army troops dressed in white winter gear struggled through a predawn snowstorm. Machine gun fire broke the ice; some soldiers fell in, others refused to continue. When daylight broke around nine o'clock, corpses were revealed lying on the snow.[50] That evening, now March 8, a group of Red Army soldiers approached the island bearing a white flag. Two unarmed leaders went out on horseback to meet them. One of them, Sergei Vershinin, a twenty-six-year-old *Sevastopol* electrician, apparently appealed to the emissaries to join the struggle against the Communists. A later Soviet source claims Vershinin invited them to "get together and beat the Yids." It would not have been surprising if he had actually used the common phrase, but it is also possible that the account wished to depict him as a "backward" or corrupt element, not a disillusioned but loyal revolutionary son. In any case, Vershinin was immediately arrested, although his companion managed to get away.[51]

On March 10, Trotsky insisted they act fast, before the Gulf thawed and the rebels gained access to Finland. "Emergency measures are needed. I fear that neither the party nor the Central Committee is sufficiently aware of the extraordinary seriousness of the Kronstadt question," he fumed.[52] Part of the problem had to do with the condition of the forces needed to repress them. Morale was an issue on both sides—indeed, as everyone realized, there weren't two sides. These were the same men, the same fighting forces of the revolution arrayed against each other.

The trouble was, wrote Tukhachevskii to Lenin that same day, that the challenge was arising on their side of the barricades. "Petrograd workers are not reliable," the commander complained. "In Kronstadt workers supported the sailors.... A large number of Mensheviks were elected to the Smolensk city soviet." So long as economic conditions were difficult, the workers might at any time "turn against Soviet power." The regime needed a real, well-trained army, because it would always be confronted with the challenge of war, war on the inside. "There will be no such thing as peacetime," Tukhachevskii warned.[53]

Tukhachevskii's task at this moment was to complete the military suppression of the challenge from within. Air and artillery bombardment began on March 10 and continued intermittently, fog permitting, for another four days, when Tukhachevskii paused to regroup.[54] The situation, as he had realized, was unstable: some railway workers refused to move troops; some units refused to be deployed. The men balked. "We will not go to the front," "Enough war—give us bread," and the chronic, "Beat the Jews." They would not fight their brothers.[55]

It was rumored the soldiers were being led onto the ice in order on purpose to drown them. Two regiments spilled out of their barracks, weapons in hand, crying "we won't go onto the ice," "let's spread out to the villages," "let's rally the other outfits."[56] The command now applied surgical measures to their own forces. Two hundred men were arrested; seventy-four ringleaders were shot; the regiments returned to order. Just in case, special squads were put in place along the line, "in the event of cowardice and attempts to retreat."[57] Indeed, harsh discipline was in order—field tribunals; informers; the disarming of unreliable units; the death penalty for disobeying, for deserting; public executions. Recalcitrant units were placed under arrest and executed on the spot; men were shot, thirty and forty at a time.[58] Discipline was restored; Petrograd workers were quiescent.[59]

On the night of March 15 to 16, the artillery shelling of Kronstadt resumed. The defenders were running low on fuel, ammunition, medical supplies—and food, as their assailants had foreseen. Vastly outnumbered, they faced troops supplied with special rations, equipped with wire cutters, and led by the same former tsarist officers accused of being counterrevolutionary on their own side. On the evening of March 16, the *Sevastopol* was hit by a shell.[60] A day later, the entire Revolutionary Committee, including Petrichenko, took off across the ice to take refuge in Finland. Altogether eight thousand Kronstadters made it to safety.[61]

By the morning of March 18, the Red Army had gained control. The date coincided with the fiftieth anniversary of the beginning of the Paris Commune, on March 18, 1871. Petrograd newspapers rejoiced. The two renegade battleships were renamed *Marat* and *Paris Commune*. The remaining sailors and the Red Army troops involved were reassigned and dispersed. Estimates of the number of dead vary. Corpses were left on the streets and on the ice. At the end of the month, Russian and Finnish representatives discussed what to do with the bodies that had surfaced with the thaw.[62]

The crews of the *Petropavlovsk* and *Sevastopol* were treated with particular severity. Most of those arrested had played no role in the events, but all were charged in public trials with mutiny and armed insurrection. By summer 1921, the Cheka and various field tribunals had sentenced over two thousand to death and over six thousand to prison. A year later, thousands of family members were expelled from the fortress, emptying it of its former population.[63] Many of the men executed were peasants in their twenties.[64] Vershinin, the Kronstadt emissary seized on the first day of the assault in connection with the ruse of the white flag, was among those interrogated and shot.[65]

Trotsky made no bones about the purpose of the formal proceedings. The trial could have "an important agitational significance. In any case, reports, speeches for the prosecution, and so on, would have a much more powerful impact than brochures and leaflets."[66] The goal was to eradicate SR influence, which Trotsky identified with the Kronstadt events, and the remains of anarchism, primarily associated with Makhno, but also implicated in the sailors' revolt. The consequences of opposing—or questioning—Communist authority from within the revolutionary fold needed to be demonstrated in no uncertain terms.

The Kronstadt sailors were all-purpose icons. The Bolsheviks lionized the Baltic Fleet sailors for the role they had played in the early phase of the revolution. Partisans of the 1921 revolt hailed the insurgents for opposing new forms of oppression, depicting them as freedom-loving "anarchists," champions of popular liberation. The American anarchist Alexander Berkman, a native of Vilna, had been in Russia at the time. "Kronstadt fell," he wrote a year after the events, "but it fell victorious in its idealism and moral purity, its generosity and higher humanity. Kronstadt was superb....The untutored, unpolished sailors, rough in manner and speech, were too noble to follow the Bolshevik example of vengeance: they would not shoot even the hated Commissars." The Bolshevik "triumph," Berkman continued, "held within itself the defeat of Bolshevism. It exposed the true character of the Communist dictatorship....Kronstadt sounded the death knell of Bolshevism with its Party dictatorship, mad centralisation, Tcheka terrorism and bureaucratic castes. It struck into the very heart of Communist autocracy."[67]

Contra Berkman, Bolshevism was not defeated. Threats to the revolution could be used to strengthen the party's hand, but real opposition had by now abated. The SRs and Mensheviks were accused of collaborating with the "White general" Kozlovskii to defeat the revolution. The revolt was said to have been inspired and funded by foreign powers. In fact, among the party's critics on the left, many were loath to strike out against it. The leading Mensheviks, as we have seen, discouraged the workers from escalating their protests. The anarchist Victor Serge considered Kronstadt to be "the beginning of a fresh, liberating revolution for popular democracy," but he nevertheless defended the Bolshevik dictatorship as the last bulwark against "chaos, and through chaos to a peasant rising, the massacre of the Communists, the return of the émigrés, and in the end, through the sheer force of events, another dictatorship, this time anti-proletarian."[68]

Many émigrés did still hope for a return to the old regime; some still dreamed of reestablishing authority on a constitutional basis. In 1918 a group of Kadets in Moscow had founded what they called a National Center, now based in various European cities, which lent its support to General Iudenich in 1919. It welcomed the unrest in Kronstadt and attempted to mobilize support, in the form of food and weapons. Efforts were made to involve the Red Cross and the French; some funds were collected, but no aid of any kind ever reached the rebels. The British, engaged at the time in trade negotiations with the Russians, were unresponsive.[69]

In short, the charges of a counterrevolutionary conspiracy were wrong on all counts. General Kozlovskii had no connection with officers on the other side; the anti-Bolshevik liberal opposition, once allied with Iudenich, was by now stranded abroad and helpless to intervene. The Mensheviks, both at home and in emigration, continued to oppose any fundamental challenge to the Soviet regime, which they persisted in seeing as the best hope for a socialist future.

In early 1921, the Sovnarkom was thus confronted with the militant opposition of what it claimed as the revolution's core base—the industrial proletariat and the radical Kronstadt sailors. The peasants, by contrast, had always been considered suspiciously "bourgeois." Once the Kronstadters had been repressed and demonstrative reprisals inflicted, it was time finally to get control of the countryside. Though the peasants fit awkwardly into the Marxist scheme, they, too, aspired to a better life and imagined the revolution as a new kind of freedom, as the nineteenth-century Populists and their SR successors understood. Hunger was not the only source of their anger; peasants resented the demands imposed by the new power and the violence directed against them. In relation to the lingering insurgency in the Tambov region, the brutal end game showed just how far the regime was prepared to go in showing who got to define that goal and who was master. The Tambov operation was a counterinsurgency campaign and ultimately an act of conquest.

In spring 1921, even after the Kronstadters had been repressed and the Tenth Party Congress had inaugurated the New Economic Policy, the countryside was still unquiet. Vladimir Antonov-Ovseenko, heading a special plenipotentiary commission empowered by Moscow to liquidate what remained of Aleksandr Antonov's revolt, demanded military reinforcements. "The bandit elements," he complained, "have returned and have begun to punish the peasants loyal to us." Whenever the Red Army withdrew, "the bandits once more find themselves masters of the situation."[70] The party put Tambov in the hands of its star commander, Mikhail Tukhachevskii, who arrived in Tambov on May 6 with a large contingent of the most reliable Red Army troops, motorized units, reconnaissance airplanes, and a thousand political commissars to keep the troops in line.[71] In this war, Tukhachevskii insisted, the constraints governing proper armies—even nominally—did not obtain.[72] At best the rebel Antonov was to be treated as a partisan—an irregular; at worst a "bandit," an outlaw, a criminal. At some point in the campaign, Tukhachevskii even authorized the use of poison gas against rebels lurking in the forests. It is not clear whether the gas was actually employed, but the threat was publicized as a means of intimidation.[73]

It was not enough, however, to defeat Antonov in the field. "Skillful methods," warned Tukhachevskii, "must also be applied to cure the local population of this epidemic of banditism."[74] A series of edicts in May defined what methods these were.[75] A month later, Order No. 171 launched a war deep into the peasant households, expanding the sinister practices of hostage-taking and collective responsibility, aiming to destroy social—even familial—solidarity at the root, dispensing with any kind of formal procedures. "1) Citizens refusing to provide their own names will be shot on the spot without trial. 2) In villages where weapons are hidden, the political commissar will take hostages and shoot them if the weapons are not surrendered. 3) When hidden weapons are found, the oldest worker in the family will be shot on the spot without trial. 4) In families harboring a bandit, the entire family will be arrested, expelled from the province, its property confiscated, the eldest worker shot without trial. 5) Households hiding family members or concealing the property of bandits will be treated as bandits, the eldest worker in the family shot on the spot without trial. 6) In cases in which the bandit's family has left, its property will be divided among peasants loyal to Soviet power and the house burned down or dismantled. 7) The order will be applied harshly and ruthlessly."[76] As indeed it was.[77] A commander reported in late June on his technique of "separating the masses into bandits and nonbandits." He would give the village thirty minutes to reveal the culprits, after which the hostages—women as well as men—would be shot in front of the others. "This method produced positive results," he reported.[78]

The systematic campaign was intended not only to squelch resistance, but also to strengthen Soviet institutions. The local Cheka had shrunk in numbers in the course of the rebellion, but Antonov-Ovseenko called for purges and arrests. Aleksandr Antonov had earlier compiled lists of the peasant households he could rely on. Cheka agents now compiled lists of loyal and suspect villagers, as guides to hostage-taking. The Partisan Army had begun by destroying the local soviets; Antonov-Ovseenko now replaced existing soviets with "revolutionary committees," composed of loyal party members, though many were reluctant to leave the relative safety of the towns for fear of being murdered.[79]

For the peasants, of course, cooperation was not always an easy option. The Union of the Laboring Peasantry took revenge on families of Communist Party members or those who succumbed to Red Army threats. Meanwhile, the Cheka was at work, tracking outposts of the union, capturing their leaders, and keeping records of their supporters in the villages. While local commanders justified the effectiveness of shooting hostages, by July party leaders in Moscow had begun to question the psychological impact of the rural terror campaign.[80] Some wanted to rescind Order No. 171, but in the end Antonov-Ovseenko and Tukhachevskii were lauded for having decimated the remnants of Antonov's forces.[81] Tukhachevskii himself boasted of having succeeded in the difficult task not only of rooting out the sources of support for the "bandits," but of achieving the "sovietization" (*sovetizatsiia*) of the villages.[82]

For a while, pacification in fact continued. Although in July, Order No. 171 was officially cancelled, its effectiveness was praised and it continued to be applied, "in all its severity," in certain areas.[83] The number of concentration camps (the term already in circulation during the war, as we have seen) used to lodge the hostages kept expanding, as did the number of their occupants, including women and children. By August, ten camps in Tambov Province were housing over thirteen thousand inmates, among them those convicted of "banditry" or "speculation" by the Cheka or revolutionary tribunals, as well as Polish prisoners of war, former Volunteer Army soldiers, actual criminals, and peasants deemed to be kulaks. Conditions were, not surprisingly, dreadful.[84]

By July, the organizations of the Union of the Laboring Peasantry had been destroyed, its leaders killed or arrested. The Cheka had also wiped out the remaining SR centers in the area and made a clean sweep of the neighboring provinces as well. A few captured rebels were pressured to return home and infiltrate remaining groups. By October, the occupation-eradication campaign was winding down. It was not until June 1922, however, that Antonov and his brother Dmitrii were finally captured and killed. They had been hiding in a village, cared for by a pair of women, one of whom inadvertently revealed their location when she went to a pharmacy for drugs. Surrounded by a group of Cheka marksmen, the brothers were flushed from the house by a grenade, then struck down by bullets. They were buried in a former monastery in Tambov, now housing the local Cheka. A photo of their corpses was published in the newspapers as proof of their demise.[85]

In liquidating the Tambov rebellion, the Communist rulers showed their willingness to destroy the population they needed to enlist on their own behalf. Murderous methods were on one level successful. The army and the terror put an end to organized resistance. On another level, their methods defeated their own cause. The destruction of the grain-producing regions and their manpower by coercive requisitioning and military subjugation had a catastrophic effect on the economy as a whole. The Sovnarkom was caught in a vicious cycle. First it drained the agricultural provinces of the men, horses, and grain needed to build the army that defended the state's very existence. These exactions provoked a violent response among the population whose loyalty and cooperation were no less crucial than the army to the regime's survival. The army built upon the extracted resources was then deployed to extinguish the unrest, but the mere presence of a massive number of troops, which themselves indulged in continuous depredations, did enormous physical and economic damage to the area, resulting in continuing discontent and further deficits.[86]

In 1921, the Russian countryside was pacified by a combination of military force and a change in policy, not only the turn away from forced requisitions but the relaxation of controls on trade and commerce, sanctioning what had been a fragile and risky lifeline until then, the black market. But the damage had been done, and the crisis of spring 1921 was profound. Famine was the deciding factor. The harvests in 1918 and 1919 in Soviet Russia had netted three-quarters the yield of the last imperial prewar harvest, in 1913; the 1920 harvest was little over half, the 1921 harvest not quite half.[87] At the first signs of drought in 1920, the peasants had pleaded for release from their delivery obligations. "The spring was hot and almost rainless," wrote Harold H. Fisher of the American Relief

Administration, "and the land at the time of the spring planting was caked and dry." The summer and autumn were also parched, but the pressure applied in 1920 was less forgiving than ever.[88] The colony of formerly prosperous German settlers, inhabitants of the Tambov region since the reign of Catherine the Great and now numbering half a million, were among those who felt the brunt. Armed workers descended upon them from Tula, their ruthlessness earning them the moniker "Iron Broom." "Like roaring lions they came to the settlements," a German pastor recalled, "all houses, barns, stables, cellars, lofts were searched and literally swept of everything they contained down to the last dried apple and the last egg." Anyone who resisted was beaten or whipped. In response to a futile attempt at organized resistance, hundreds were summarily shot. By the end, 10 percent of the settlers were dead and many had fled, reducing the community to a quarter of its former size.[89]

The drought that reached its zenith in summer 1921, covering the Volga basin, the southern Ukraine, the Crimea, and into the Urals, completed the disaster. "Early in the summer great numbers of peasants were already without food," Fisher reported, "and all up and down the Volga and as far east as the Urals they were beginning to mix grain with ground straw, weeds, and bark. Those who were without food and those who were in sight of the end of their resources, in panic joined the swelling multitudes of refugees in flight from the scorched lands."[90] Famine conditions gripped 190 districts in thirty-six provinces with a total population of 57.1 million.[91] The predominantly Turkic-speaking Muslim communities of the Crimea and Kazan region were particularly hard hit, some areas losing half their population. Kazan itself was inundated with desperate refugees; with water and sewerage systems in collapse, human waste and human bodies piled up in the streets. Abandoned children wandered the city, and disease spread, as did crime and prostitution.[92]

Thanks to the work of American and other foreign relief organizations, the famine's overall toll was less severe than it would otherwise have been. The number of famine-related deaths from starvation and disease was calculated variously by Soviet and visiting relief workers. Estimates range from 1.5 million to ten million. The official Soviet figure provided in 1922 was five million.[93] The famine can also be described in terms of mortality rates. Compared to the normal year of 1913, the 1919 morality rates in Petrograd, Moscow, and the Volga city of Saratov were twice to three times as high. The overall mortality rate for 1919 in European Russia was 39/1,000, in Petrograd and Saratov around 70/1,000. The rate for the famine region overall in 1920 was 50–60/1,000, for 1921 70–80/1,000.[94]

The famine was not only exacerbated by the policy decisions of the Soviet regime, but the response was also highly political. The American Relief Administration was formed in 1919, under the direction of future president Herbert Hoover, to provide food for hungry children in postwar Europe. In the Soviet case, the ARA insisted that food be apportioned according to need, irrespective of socialist class categories. In 1921 a compromise was reached, by which foreign aid workers, including those sent by European-based organizations, were allowed to travel to the sites, while Soviet authorities retained control over geographical distribution. Shortly before the agreements were concluded, the Soviets created their own Committee for Aid to the Starving (*Komitet pomoshchi golodaiushchim*), consisting of seventy-three prominent personalities, including Maxim Gorky. Once the papers were signed, its members were promptly arrested, Gorky excepted.[95]

Foreign relief did not alter the overall picture. The peasants, in the end, were vanquished not only by force of arms but also by the desperation of famine.[96] Industrialist Pavel Riabushinskii's "bony hand of hunger," invoked in August 1917, was the ultimate counterinsurgency weapon. The 1921 famine was an early example of the Soviet regime's cannibalistic relationship to its own population, at a cost that would only escalate in the Stalinist years. It is remarkable how much damage in demographic terms and in terms of human suffering Soviet society could manage to sustain, much of it self-inflicted, while also generating a powerful ethos of ideological devotion. The kind of blanket counterinsurgency practiced during the Civil War grew into the delusional counterinsurgency of the Stalin era, when indeed "the population became the class enemy."

And yet, many in the professional and creative intelligentsia cast their lot with the new regime, despite the horrors unfolding around them. Some were not permitted to remain. Over two hundred intellectuals critical of the Soviet project were preemptively expedited out of the country in 1922, the majority on German vessels departing from Petrograd, in what became known as the "philosophical steamship."[97] Not the steamship of modernity, which the futurists scrambled to board, but the ocean liner of lost values. Many professionals and intellectuals—as well as ordinary people—emigrated of their own accord. Others did not want to leave, or could not afford to. Among those who remained, some were hostile or ambivalent. Evgenii

Zamiatin kept his principles and his irony, until Stalin allowed him out in 1931. Mayakovsky screamed loudly on behalf of the great leap into the future, then fell into despair and exited his own way. Innumerable artists and writers nevertheless found a chance to use their talents, and some found the Soviet experiment an inspiration. Ideological wars were fought for cultural principles by artists and writers impelled by their own convictions. For others the experiment was an aesthetic and spiritual death sentence. Many perished or were murdered, usually in the bacchanal that began fifteen years after the end of the Civil War. Some of the victims in the 1930s had themselves orchestrated the early repressions with exemplary zeal.

Despite the outcome of what had begun in 1917 in the euphoria of expectation, the vision of something new, of a political system in which citizens were citizens—with rights and the responsibility of power—exercised a continuing hold on the imagination of many of the old Empire's former subjects. This vision seemed to return in the 1980s and then after 1991, when the product of Lenin's statist ambition came to the end of its exhausted ideological road. Since then, in new circumstances, more than a few societies in Eurasia and the Middle East have experienced similar hopes. But the world more recently seems to be evolving in ways that remind us how fragile democratic aspirations and democratic institutions always are.

# Conclusion

Power was supposed to be a means by which to realize their ideas, to bring about the triumph of "socialism," and in this they miserably failed. *Their* victory has dealt socialism the most devastating possible blow.

—Vasilii Maklakov, 1924[1]

The greatest paradox in Russian life and the Russian Revolution lies in this, that liberal ideas, ideas of right as well as ideas of social reform appeared, in Russia, to be utopian. Bolshevism on the other hand shewed itself to be much less utopian and much more realist, much more in accord with the whole complex situation in Russia in 1917.

— Nicholas Berdyaev, 1937[2]

The Revolutions of 1917 and the Civil War that ensued created a new form of state power. This new state, which became the Soviet Union, substituted the forced mobilization of popular participation for the formal institutions of political democracy, a negation of the original spirit of the Revolution that began in February 1917 as a response to the hardships engendered by the war, but also as a demand for "freedom" that permeated all levels of imperial Russian society.[3] The combination of popular revolt and elite disaffection had led to the downfall of the monarchy. The notables and moderate socialists who assumed the leadership of an improvised interim regime failed over the next eight months to solve the problems that had undermined the old institutions. They failed either to stop the war or to invigorate its prosecution. They failed to feed the cities. They failed to reestablish the political authority lost when Nicholas stepped aside. And they failed to summon the promised Constituent Assembly in time.

The Bolsheviks advertised their takeover in October 1917 as the culmination of the revolution, its radical high point, claiming to have channeled the people's anger at existing leaders who had failed to satisfy their demands.

The events of October 1917 were not the culmination of the revolution, however, but a coup d'état, a blow directed against its fundamental impulse, which was the desire for democratic political participation. It was a coup that not only toppled the Provisional Government but, perhaps more important, destroyed the Constituent Assembly just as it finally convened in January 1918.

The elections to the Constituent Assembly, which was supposed to establish a new, revolutionary legitimacy by democratic means, attracted the participation of almost fifty million people, almost a third of the imperial population. Parties campaigned, lists were distributed, and people of every social station came to the polls, as though the pent-up desire for modern political life long stifled under the autocracy had finally burst forth. The dispersal of the delegates when they arrived in Petrograd thus constituted a decisive blow against this fundamental aspiration, the underlying spirit of the revolution.

The desire for democracy was not, of course, easily adapted to the tensions within Russian imperial society which had set the revolution in motion to begin with. The desire for liberation in 1917 took different forms, not all of them easily reconciled. Workers and peasants imagined release from subordination, the power to act as communities and collectivities in governing their own lives. The ubiquitous assault on hierarchy, focused on the tsar and the army officers representing his authority, reflected not only the demand for dignity and equal standing but a leveling impulse that was economic as well as social. The generic discourse of socialism, though propagated by educated outsiders, conformed to this vision of an equitable social order. By contrast, urban and provincial property-owners and professionals, who had resented the limits on civic life and political power under the old regime, imagined freedom on the Western liberal model—a system of rights, laws, and political representation. The collectivist model of social and economic equality was thus at odds with the "bourgeois," constitutionalist model of a society and state based on private property, economic and cultural hierarchy, and the primacy of the individual person.

"Democracy" (demokratiia) was another term with wide resonance, which also meant different things to different people. It was often used to designate the laboring masses and their allies, as opposed to those with economic and cultural privilege. In this sense, the Petrograd Soviet formed simultaneously with the Provisional Government was said to represent "the Democracy" against the "bourgeois" ministers. But "democracy" in a looser sense is a good term with which to describe the political aspirations of many classes of the population, whatever their other differences. "Democracy" also meant representation—participation in a political process capable of expressing and adjudicating conflicting social interests. If industrialists and professors wanted a parliament and a constitution, workers wanted soviets—that is, councils of elected representatives. Even peasants—not all, but a considerable number—joined unions and sent delegates to meetings.

The Constituent Assembly, for which so many had voted, remained a potent symbol, even after its dispersal and despite the fact that no popular protest followed. The moderate socialists have been rebuked by historians for their refusal to bite the bullet and block the slide to extremism that swept the Bolsheviks to their goal, but their failure to take power in mid-1917 reflected their belief in democracy, a reluctance to preempt the will of the people, however that will was divined. Socialist ideology has been blamed for its hostility to the formal attributes of political democracy, yet much of the appeal of socialism inhered in its vision of a deeper, higher democracy—Social Democracy.

Had the Constituent Assembly been allowed to function, it might have established a political system capable of expressing and managing the conflicting interests and aspirations that emanate from any complex society. It might have failed, but the attempt was nipped in the bud by radicals whose concept of the revolution was fundamentally anti-democratic. Yet the Bolsheviks belonged to the broad socialist brotherhood. They shared the discourse of social and economic justice. They called themselves Social Democrats, at least at the start. Lenin was astute in waving the banner of Soviet power—the shared socialist endeavor—to camouflage the party's monopolistic advance. This was the banner to which the people rallied.

But the Bolsheviks diverged from the socialist ethos in crucial ways. When they knocked out the "bourgeois" ministers, as the Soviet leaders had not dared or wanted to do, their socialist colleagues protested loudly. Protests arose even within the party, from some who saw the move as unwise and unprincipled. Unprincipled it was—on purpose. Lenin rejected the kind of democracy represented by the soviets, though he used them as cover; he rejected democracy altogether. It took until the end of the Civil War for uniformity and compliance to be imposed inside the party itself, but conformity was the goal. Leninism, in short, was an authoritarian version of socialism, as critics such as the Menshevik Iulii Martov realized all along. This was the version that triumphed in the end, defeating the democratic promise of the revolution, as a great social groundswell, embracing masses of the population whose clashing interests were not easily reconciled but whose desire to escape the constraints of the old regime propelled them to collective action.

The Bolsheviks were triumphant because they focused on power. Lenin designed the party as an instrument of war, the headquarters of insurrection, the "vanguard of the Revolution." There was no model of deliberative process, of respect for different opinions or rival socialist parties which had to be abandoned in the fight for power that ensued after February 1917. Everything from then on was operational—how best to destroy the competition and establish a monopoly of control, how to fashion a new kind of power, a new state capable of destroying the underpinnings of the old social order and on its ruins erecting something new. The Bolsheviks realized that the vanguard needed troops, the popular discontent that challenged the old authorities needed to be harnessed, and they began by building a movement—factory by factory, garrison by garrison, neighborhood by neighborhood, newspaper by newspaper, slogan by slogan, election by election, using the institutions generated by the revolution as a base from which to rebuild the failed imperial state. They were indeed state-builders—on ruins partly of their own making.

In the process, they improvised; there was no manual for seizing and reanimating a state. Lenin and his brain trust had to evaluate each twist and turn, each moment of opportunity, in order to emerge in October in a position from which to dominate the field. Victory was not predestined. The old Empire was an immense territory, in a condition of profound disorganization and distress. Russia was still at war. The bourgeois ministers and the soviet leaders had all, in their respective ways, supported the war effort. The Bolsheviks used the peace platform as their calling card. Lenin's boldest move after October was to act on that promise. Instead of mobilizing the revolution on behalf of the war, he insisted capitulation was necessary to save the revolution. In this he was opposed even by his own comrades. Revolutionaries did not simply lay down arms. World revolution was expected to pull Russia's irons out of the fire, ending the war on an international scale. Sharing this expection, Lenin was nevertheless prepared for Russia to go it alone, at least for now. The illusion of coming world revolution was maintained, the Comintern Congress gathered in Moscow in August 1920, but defeat by Poland soon after put paid to any ambition to extend Communist rule beyond Russian borders. Indeed, the circumstances of Polish victory in 1920, in which the coterie around Stalin frustrated Tukhachevskii's effort to break through Poland into Europe, nicely anticipated Stalin's eventual consolidation of "socialism in one country," which was the consequence of defeat, though one already anticipated by the concession of Brest-Litovsk two years earlier.

Indeed, Brest-Litovsk had turned Russia's attention away from the international arena, toward its own internal conflicts. Energizing opposition from the left, the treaty also intensified the antagonism of the leading tsarist officers, only conditionally supportive of the revolution, who had already begun to mobilize in the aftermath of the coup. The onset of armed civil war was an opportunity for the Bolsheviks as well as a challenge, a welcome process of clarification—us against them—and a laboratory of political and institutional mobilization. Brest-Litovsk demobilized the old Imperial Army. The Civil War created the Red Army, not only as a weapon but as the new society in embryo.

Despite their ingenuity, it took over three years of struggle for the Bolsheviks to gain the upper hand. In the course of those years, just about every sector of the old society rose in protest against their policies, rejecting their claims to authority and their demands on resources. The Red Terror and the Cheka did not emerge, however, in reaction to the outbreak of civil war. Civil war was inherent from the start, and indeed, as we have seen, the Cheka was one of the first institutions created after October. The Red Terror was anticipatory. It took aim not only at actual armed and declared enemies of Bolshevik rule, but also at the implicit and latent enemies of the new society that was emerging from the carnage. The Civil War did not distort the original nature of Bolshevism. As Lenin made perfectly clear, violence was key to October—a preemptive conquest of "the Democracy," before it had the chance to convene one last time. Violence was key to establishing the authority of the emerging Communist state. Needless to say, the Bolsheviks were not alone on the bloody fields of the Civil War. Terror came in White as well as Red, and also Green, alienating the populace in all directions. In the absence of firm authority, in the face of threats from all sides, the dispossessed of the old regime, who had destabilized the ship of state in February 1917, enacted bloody vengeance of their own in the course of the prolonged upheaval. They were perpetrators as well as victims.

In helping make the revolution, these same peasants, workers, and enlisted men embraced the basic socialist message, a broad socialist culture that focused on class oppression and the promise of a brighter life—land to the tillers, the eight-hour day, the management of communal affairs—in the regiment, the factory, and the village—by collective means. The Bolshevik commissars sent to extract grain and force peasants into the army were, however, only the latest in a line of emissaries, bureaucrats, bosses, and land-lords demanding labor, the products of labor, and life itself. They were rejected for their generic function—yet another oppressive state. They were rejected for their particular methods. These methods exacted an enormous human toll, not the least in mass starvation, and set the precedent for the even more brutal and uncompromising application of the same principles that followed down the line. The sacrifice of lives was both pragmatic and punitive, a necessity and a technique of rule.

It was the Russian Civil War that prompted German sociologist Max Weber to reflect on the role of violence in anchoring political authority. In 1919, while Germany was itself in the midst of revolutionary upheaval, Weber invoked a statement attributed to Leon Trotsky at Brest-Litovsk in 1918. "Every state is founded on force," Weber agreed. Its power depended, in good part, on being recognized as "the sole source of the 'right' to use violence."[4] In 1919, as commissar of war, Trotsky was trying to establish this right—to achieve a monopoly on the use of force—while using the power of violence to establish a new authority. Soviet Russia was not supposed to be yet another modern state in the bourgeois mold, but a new kind of state, resting on a different kind of authority. Weber saw the exceptional moment, however, as key to a general principle. Some historians similarly view the Soviet state not as a "totalitarian" aberration, and certainly not a throwback to archaic Russian traditions of autocracy, but as a variation on the broader theme of modern governance. This modern state power is characterized by its direct intrusion into the management of society and into the physical life of the population. It is not merely repressive, but an active organizing and shaping force.[5]

Systematic, state-organized use of extreme violence, as in the Red Terror—as systematic as possible, even in the unsettled conditions of civil war—is not the only type of violence to challenge interpretation. The Great War entailed, in addition to armed combat, a more diffuse violence, affect-ing whole populations at and behind the front. This was a pervasive menace that persisted even after 1918 in areas destabilized by the war. Historians thus see the war itself as one point in a "continuum of violence," which did not abruptly end with the peace.[6] With the collapse of institutions and the mobilization for internecine conflict, the vast Russian Empire emerges as a

playing field saturated by ubiquitous, uncontrolled aggression, which various leaders aspired to capture and direct for their own purposes.

Rejecting the orthodox Soviet interpretation of the October Revolution
as the expression of the will of the organized, class-conscious proletariat,
some historians in post-Soviet Russia, in a similar spirit, now emphasize the
anarchic nature of popular unrest. They acknowledge the blurry line
between Red and White when it comes to pillage, mass slaughter, and in
particular anti-Jewish pogroms. Other scholars, while also rejecting sche-
matic notions of class consciousness on the Marxist model, have looked for
the cultural and sociological patterns structuring the popular response.
Indeed, up and down the social scale, Russian society, for all the obstacles the
autocracy put in its way, demonstrated a remarkable degree of coherence,
even in the heart of the storm.

In the 1920s, Antonio Gramsci famously said that in tsarist Russia "civil
society was primordial and gelatinous," and thus, when the state foundered,
there was no "powerful system of fortresses and earthworks" to prevent a
new tyrant from taking the autocrat's place.[7] The realm was indeed large,
and the popular classes, animated by fierce resentments and anger, were
capable of brutality and mayhem. Nevertheless, as this narrative has shown,
under the carapace of the old imperial state civil society and community
existed. These embedded structures proved surprisingly durable under the
strain of collapse. The popular movements we have examined—among
them, the Antonov saga, Makhno's domain, the Basmachi—benefited from
internal organization and pursued defined goals. The "Russian riot" was
"pitiless," as Pushkin said, but not "senseless." Indeed, the Bolsheviks had to
work hard at destroying the robust remnants of the old order—at all levels.

The Bolsheviks had to work hard to restore the armature of state, as well.
Their only rivals at state-building were the leaders of some of the breakaway nations. Under the nationalist banner, Józef Piłsudski and General
Mannerheim, not without foreign backing, managed to extract their ethnically bounded territories (despite the ambiguity of frontiers and mixed
populations) out from under Russian domination. The Ukrainians did not
succeed. The White generals failed utterly at recovering what had existed
before. They had no sense that political power had to be constructed, that
power is not something that floats unattached over a social organism but
must sink roots. The Bolsheviks understood that the apparatus must go deep
and, while disrupting existing loyalties and connections, they also created
new ones.

Soviet rule was brutal and uncompromising from the start—unapologet-
ically so, since it conceived the struggle as an all-or-nothing fight against an
entire social order. This no-holds-barred assault on the old society was in
fact what led many people, both unschooled and highly literate, to accept or
even welcome the new power, despite the challenge it sometimes posed to
their own existence. For many, confronting extreme deprivation and the
brutality not only of the commissars but of their opponents as well, the central concern was physical survival. Few were in a position to make real
choices. But the new regime neverthless aroused devotion. At the top of the
cultural pyramid, writers and artists rallied to the Soviet cause and found
new inspiration. The new apparatus and the new army opened their doors
to those formerly excluded from power of any kind. The process of modernization that had begun under the monarchy proceeded at an even hand-
ier pace. Literacy spread, the professions expanded, and many people
benefited, as they would have from economic progress under any regime.

At home and abroad, some people forgot, or chose to forget, that the
dream of democracy had been abandoned. In 1989 and in 1991, that dream
resurfaced in a series of revolutions that rejected the original revolution in
the name of the promise it had betrayed. In 2017, a hundred years since the
momentous events of 1917, the future of democracy is once again in doubt,
as demagogues and hate-mongers in many countries seize the podiums and
the highest offices. Soviet socialism was not socialism; capitalism has still not
collapsed, but it has not solved its fundamental inequities, either. The early
phases of the 1917 Revolution were tentative and experimental. Even Lenin,
with the full force of his personality and with the desperation of deepening
crisis, had difficulty extricating Russia from the war. How much harder even
to contemplate this possibility earlier on, how much harder to achieve a
unified center of authority, when the process of dissolution was still in full
swing. In the end, authoritarian contenders from left and right faced off
against each other—Lenin against Denikin and Wrangel—while the Crimean
Kadets took to their ships and the remaining Mensheviks ended in prison.
Many over the years have considered the Revolution of 1917 a "landmark in
the emancipation of mankind from past oppression," again to cite British
historian E. H. Carr.[8] If the same can still be said today, it is only with regard
to the revolution Lenin defeated, not the one he saved.

# Notes

## FRONT MATTER

1. Quoted in Teffi, *Memories: From Moscow to the Black Sea*, intro. Edythe Haber, trans. Robert Chandler et al. (Paris, 1928–1930; New York: New York Review of Books, 2016), 156.

2. Max Weber, "Politics as a Vocation," in *From Max Weber: Essays in Sociology*, ed. and trans. H. H. Gerth and C. Wright Mills (New York: Oxford University Press, 1946), 77–78.

3. Vadim Erlikhman, *Poteri narodonaseleniia v XX veke: Spravochnik* (Moscow: Russkaia panorama, 2004), 18–19. The population of the area within 1923 Soviet borders was 92 percent of its population in 1913. The number of "excess" deaths (beyond normal mortality) on the reduced territory remaining in 1923 has been estimated at 1,626,000 military deaths for 1914–1917 and 11,411,000 military and civilian deaths for 1918–1923, or about 8 percent of the 1913 base. See Andrei Markevich and Mark Harrison, "Great War, Civil War, and Recovery: Russia's National Income, 1913 to 1928," *Journal of Economic History* 71.3 (2011): 676, 679, 695.

4. "Ves' vopros—kto kogo operedit?...Nuzhno smotret' na eti veshshi trezvo: kto kogo?" ["The whole question is—who will come out ahead?...One has to view these things soberly: who bests whom?"], "Novaia ekonomicheskaia politika i zadachi politprosvetov, Doklad 17 okt. 1921 g., II Vserossiiskii s"ezd politprosvetov," in Lenin, *Polnoe sobranie sochinenii* 44:161. Available at http://leninvi.com/t44/p161 (accessed September 30, 2016).

5. Robert Service, "Introduction," in V. I. Lenin, *The State and Revolution* (London: Penguin, 1992).

6. Edward Hallett Carr, *The Russian Revolution: From Lenin to Stalin (1917–1929)*, intro. R. W. Davies (1979; New York: Palgrave-Macmillan, 2004), 1. Quoted (in Russian) in *Oktiabr' 1917: Velichaishee sobytie veka ili sotsial'naia katastrofa?*, ed. P. V. Volobuev (Moscow: Politicheskaia literatura, 1991), 3.

7. B. I. Kolonitskii, "Predskazuemoe proshloe v nepredskazuemom budushchem? Iubilei revoliutsii, politika pamiati i kul'turnaia pamiat' sovremennoi Rossii" [Predictable Past in an Unpredictable Future? The Anniversary of the Revolution, the Politics of Memory and Cultural Memory in Contemporary Russia] (2016, unpublished ms., courtesy of the author), 15 and 16.

8. *Alash-Orda: Sbornik dokumentov*, ed. N. Martynenko (Alma-Ata: Aikap, 1992), 3.

## PART I

1. "Witte," in D. N. Shilov, *Gosudarstvennye deiateli Rossiiskoi imperii: Biobibliograf-icheskii spravochnik* (St. Petersburg: Bulanin, 2001), 122–130; S. Iu. Witte, *The Memoirs of Count Witte*, ed. Sidney Harcave (Armonk: M. E. Sharpe, 1990); B.V. Anan'ich and R. Sh. Ganelin, *Sergei Iul'evich Vitte i ego vremia* (St. Petersburg: Bulanin, 1999); Francis W. Wcislo, *Tales of Imperial Russia: The Life and Times of Sergei Witte, 1849–1915* (Oxford: Oxford University Press, 2011).

2. Robert Service, "Lenin," in *Critical Companion to the Russian Revolution, 1914–1921*, ed. Edward Action, Vladimir Iu. Cherniaev, and William G. Rosenberg (Bloomington: Indiana University Press, 1997), 150–160.

3. G. I. Il'iashchuk and V. I. Miller, "Martov," in *Politicheskie deiateli Rossii 1917: Biograficheskii slovar'*, ed. P. V. Volobuev (Moscow: Bol'shaia rossiiskaia entsik-lopediia, 1993), 204–208.

4. Theodore Dan, *The Origins of Bolshevism*, ed. and trans. Joel Carmichael (1945; New York: Harper & Row, 1964); Leopold H. Haimson, *The Russian Marxists and the Origins of Bolshevism* (1955; Boston: Beacon Press, 1966); J. L. H. Keep, *The Rise of Social Democracy in Russia* (Oxford: Clarendon, 1963).

5. *Partiia sotsialistov-revoliutsionerov: Dokumenty i materialy*, ed.V.V. Shelokhaev et al., 3 vols. (Moscow: ROSSPEN, 1996–2000).

6. Abraham Ascher, *The Revolution of 1905: A Short History* (Stanford: Stanford University Press, 2004), 16. Ascher (2004) provides the framework for my account. See at greater length Abraham Ascher, *The Revolution of 1905*, 2 vols. (Stanford: Stanford University Press, 1988–1992). The literature on 1905 is exhaustive; I cite only a few sources in this chapter.

7. G. D. Alekseeva, K. V. Gusev, and A. V. Manykin, "Chernov," in *Politicheskie deiateli*, 347–351.

8. V. L. Boechin, "Struve," in *Politicheskie deiateli*, 307–310; Richard Pipes, *Struve: Liberal on the Left, 1870–1944* (Cambridge, MA: Harvard University Press, 1970).

9. Ascher, *Revolution* (2004), 20–21.

10. Gerald D. Surh, *1905 in St. Petersburg: Labor, Society, and Revolution* (Stanford: Stanford University Press, 1989), 73; Steve A. Smith, "Petrograd in 1917: The View from Below," in *Revolutionary Russia: New Approaches*, ed. Rex A. Wade (New York: Routledge, 2004), 18 (30,000 by 1917).

11. Ascher, *Revolution* (2004), 26–27.

12. Richard S. Wortman, *Scenarios of Power: Myth and Ceremony in Russian Monarchy*, 2 vols. (Princeton: Princeton University Press, 1995–2000), 2:463 (Trubetskoi family).

13. Laura Engelstein, *Moscow, 1905: Working-Class Organization and Political Conflict* (Stanford: Stanford University Press, 1982), 93–94.

14. Ascher, *Revolution* (2004), 53.

15. Ibid., 55–56. See also: Robert Edelman, *Proletarian Peasants: The Revolution of 1905 in Russia's Southwest* (Ithaca: Cornell University Press, 1987); Scott Seregny,

*Russian Teachers and Peasant Revolution: The Politics of Education in 1905* (Bloomington: Indiana University Press, 1989); Dietrich Beyrau, "Janus in Bastschuhen: Die Bauern in der russischen Revolution 1905–1917," *Geschichte und Gesellschaft* 21.4 (1995): 585–603.

16. John Bushnell, *Mutiny amid Repression: Russian Soldiers in the Revolution of 1905– 1906* (Bloomington: Indiana University Press, 1985).

17. Count Lamsdorf, "Proposed Anti-Semitic Triple Alliance: Secret Russian Memorandum, January 3, 1906," in Lucien Wolf, *Notes on the Diplomatic History of the Jewish Question* (London: Jewish Historical Society of England, 1919), 57.

18. Robert Blobaum, *Rewolucja: Russian Poland, 1904–1907* (Ithaca: Cornell University Press, 1995). On the geography and nomenclature of the incorporation, see Norman Davies, *God's Playground: A History of Poland*, 2 vols. (New York: Columbia University Press, 1982), 2:81–82.

19. Ascher, *Revolution* (2004), 49–50; James D. White, "The 1905 Revolution in Russia's Baltic Provinces," in *The Russian Revolution of 1905: Centenary Perspectives*, ed. Jonathan D. Smele and Anthony Heywood (London: Routledge, 2005), 55–78; Antti Kujala, "Finland in 1905: The Political and Social History of the Revolution," ibid., 79–93; Ralph Tuchtenhagen, "Autonomy, Sovereignty, Class Struggle? Motifs of Rioting in Finland 1905–06," in *The Russian Revolution of 1905 in Transcultural Perspective: Identities, Peripheries, and the Flow of Ideas*, ed. Felicitas Fischer von Weikersthal et al. (Bloomington: Slavica, 2013), 197–211; Malte Rolf, "A Continuum of Crisis? The Kingdom of Poland in the Shadow of Revolution (1905–15)," ibid., 159–174.

20. V. I. Startsev, *Russkaia burzhuaziia i samoderzhavie v 1905–1907 gg.* (Leningrad: Nauka, 1977), 14–16; Howard D. Mehlinger and John M. Thompson, *Count Witte and the Tsarist Government in the 1905 Revolution* (Bloomington: Indiana University Press, 1972).

21. Vladimir Nabokov, *Speak, Memory: An Autobiography Revisited* (New York: Putnam's, 1966), 155; ch. 8 (wonderful portrait of the writer's father). Also: *Vladimir Dmitrievich Nabokov: Svoboda slova po-russki* (St. Petersburg: Severnaia zvezda, 2015); A. L. Fedorenko, "Nabokov," in *Politicheskie deiateli*, 226–227.

22. V. A. Maklakov, *Pervaia Gosudarstvennaia Duma: Vospominaniia sovremennika* (1939; rpt. Moscow: ZAO Tsentr-poligraf, 2006), 308; M. E. Golostenov, "Maklakov," in *Politicheskie deiateli*, 201–202.

23. A. S. Senin, "Guchkov," in *Politicheskie deiateli*, 92–94.

24. Numerous other groupings and fractions emerged after October, but these were the main tendencies. See "Predislovie," in *Partiia "Soiuz 17 oktiabria": Protokoly s"ezdov, konferentsii, zasedanii TsK, 1905–1915 gg.*, ed. D. B. Pavlov, V. V. Shelokhaev et al., 2 vols. (Moscow: ROSSPEN, 1996–2000), 1:5.

25. "Proposed Anti-Semitic Triple Alliance: Secret Russian Memorandum, January 3, 1906," quoted in Wolf, *Notes on the Diplomatic History*, 57 and 59.

26. Ascher, *Revolution* (2004), 82–84, 149 (figures); Victoria Khiterer, "The October 1905 Pogroms and the Russian Authorities," *Nationalities Papers: The Journal of*

*Nationalism and Ethnicity* 43.5 (2015): 788–803. For a famous literary rendition of the post-October pogrom in the southern city of Nikolaev, see Isaac Babel, "The Story of My Dovecote" (1926), in Isaac Babel, *Odessa Stories*, trans. Boris Dralyuk (London: Pushkin Press, 2016), 127–143.

27. Franziska Schedewie, "Peasant Protest and Peasant Violence in 1905: Voronezh Province, Ostrogozhskii uezd," in *Russian Revolution of 1905*, ed. Smele, 137–155; Burton Richard Miller, *Rural Unrest during the First Russian Revolution: Kursk Province, 1905–1906* (Budapest and New York: Central European University, 2013).

28. Leon Trotsky, *My Life: An Attempt at an Autobiography*, intro. Joseph Hansen (1929; New York: Pathfinder Press, 1970), 184, 186–187, 190–191; Ian D. Thatcher, "Leon Trotsky and 1905," in *Russian Revolution of 1905*, ed. Smele, 241–259. Isaac Deutscher, *The Prophet Armed: Trotsky, 1879–1921* (New York: Oxford University Press, 1954) is the (partisan) classic.

29. Ascher, *Revolution* (2004), 115 (hundreds in 1906); Anna Geifman, *Thou Shalt Kill: Revolutionary Terrorism in Russia, 1894–1917* (Princeton: Princeton University Press, 1993), 20–21 (3,000 in 1906, another 1,000 in 1907).

30. Ascher, *Revolution* (2004), 122–123.

31. Ibid., 124.

32. Quoted, ibid., 130.

33. Ibid., 128–129.

34. Ibid., 146.

35. On June 8 and 26, 1906: *Gosudarstvennaia Duma. Stenograficheskie otchety 1906 god. Sessiia pervaia. Tom II. Zasedaniia 19–38 (s 1 iiunia po 4 iiulia)* (St. Petersburg: Gosudarstvennaia tipografiia, 1906): Sessiia I, zasedanie 23 (8 VI 1906 g.), pp. 1125–1141; Sessiia I, zasedanie 33 (26 VI 1906 g.), pp. 1723–1746. The trial of the perpetrators was held two years later: *Delo o pogrome v Belostoke 1–3 iiunia 1906 g.: Obvinitel'nyi akt, sudebnoe sledstvie, rechi poverennykh* (St. Petersburg: tip-lit Busselia, 1909). See Aleksandr Mindlin, *Gosudarstvennaia Duma Rossiiskoi imperii i evreiskii vopros* (St. Petersburg: Aleteiia, 2014), 91–116.

36. Edward H. Judge, *Easter in Kishinev: Anatomy of a Pogrom* (New York: New York University Press, 1992), 72 (about 50 killed, 400 wounded); *Kishinevskii pogrom 1903 goda: Sbornik dokumentov i materialov*, ed. Ia. M. Konanskii et al. (Kishinev: Ruxanda, 2000).

37. *Gosudarstvennaia Duma. Stenograficheskie otchety 1906 god. Sessiia pervaia. Tom II. Zasedaniia 19–38 (s 1 iiunia po 4 iiulia)* (St. Petersburg: Gosudarstvennaia tipografiia, 1906): Sessiia I, zasedanie 23 (8 VI 1906 g.), 1129–1132. Prince Sergei Urusov, *Zapiski gubernatora: Kishinev, 1903–1904* (Berlin: Ladyschnikow, 1907); Prince Serge Dmitriyevich Urussov, *Memoirs of a Russian Governor*, trans. and ed. Herman Rosenthal (London and New York: Harper & Brothers, 1908). The publication of the translation was sponsored by Jacob Schiff, the Jewish-American banker, as part of a campaign against Russian policy on Jews: Brian Horowitz, *Empire Jews: Jewish Nationalism and Acculturation in 19th- and Early 20th-Century Russia* (Bloomington: Slavica, 2009), 265–266.

38. Abraham Ascher, *P. A. Stolypin: The Search for Stability in Late Imperial Russia* (Stanford: Stanford University Press, 2001).

39. Ascher, *Revolution* (2004), 172–174; Hans Rogger, "Russian Ministers and the Jewish Question 1881–1917," in Hans Rogger, *Jewish Policies and Right-Wing Politics in Imperial Russia* (Berkeley: University of California Press, 1986), 93.

40. Ascher, *Revolution* (2004), 168; Geifman, *Thou Shalt Kill*, 74; "Predislovie," in *Taina ubiistva Stolypina*, ed. I. I. Demidov, S. V. Mironenko, and V. V. Shelokhaev (Moscow: ROSSPEN, 2003), 3–5.

41. *Soiuz eserov-maksimalistov: Dokumenty, publitsistika, 1906–1924 gg.*, ed. D. B. Pavlov (Moscow: ROSSPEN, 2002); Manfred Hildermeier, *The Russian Socialist Revolutionary Party Before the First World War* (New York: St. Martin's, 2000), 123–128.

42. N. L. Barsukova, "Tsereteli," in *Politicheskie deiateli*, 339–341; A. L. Raikhtsaum, "Purishkevich," ibid., 265–266.

43. Ascher, *Revolution* (2004), 201–203.

44. Ibid., 208–209.

45. Peter Waldron, *Between Two Revolutions: Stolypin and the Politics of Renewal in Russia* (DeKalb: Northern Illinois University Press, 1998), ch. 5.

46. "Predislovie," in *Taina ubiistva Stolypina*, 4–15.

47. Geifman, *Thou Shalt Kill*, 238–239.

48. Michael S. Melancon, *The Lena Goldfields Massacre and the Crisis of the Late Tsarist State* (College Station: Texas A&M University Press, 2006), 102–104 (casualty figures).

49. Victoria E. Bonnell, *Roots of Rebellion: Workers' Politics and Organizations in St. Petersburg and Moscow, 1900–1914* (Berkeley: University of California Press, 1983), 390–393; Geoffrey A. Hosking, *The Russian Constitutional Experiment: Government and Duma, 1907–1914* (Cambridge: Cambridge University Press, 1973), 206; Wortman, *Scenarios*, 2:430.

50. Boris I. Kolonitskii, "Kerensky," in *Critical Companion to the Russian Revolution*, 138–149.

51. The Fourth Duma had five sittings (OS): 1) November 15, 1912 to June 25, 1913; 2) October 15, 1913 to June 14, 1914, plus a special one-day meeting, July 26, 1914 for war credits; 3) January 27–29, 1915, dissolved; 4) July 19 to September 3, 1915, dissolved; reconvenes February 9 to June 20, 1916; 5) November 1 to December 16, 1916, dissolved; February 14–25, 1917, dissolved. See: "Raspisanie zasedanii Dumy," in Mindlin, *Gosudarstvennaia Duma*, 446 (error for July 19, 1915).

52. Hosking, *Experiment*, 191–194. A more positive assessment, emphasizing predominance of moderates: Raymond Pearson, *The Russian Moderates and the Crisis of Tsarism 1914–1917* (London: Macmillan, 1977), 14.

53. Quoted, Hosking, *Experiment*, 197.

54. Ibid., 199–202; Pearson, *Russian Moderates*, 11–12; K. A. Solov'ev, "Gosudarstvennye instituty," in *Rossiia v gody Pervoi mirovoi voiny: Ekonomicheskoe polozhenie, sotsial'nye protsessy, politicheskii krizis*, ed. Iu. A. Petrov (Moscow: ROSSPEN, 2014), 648–649.

55. Rogger, "The Question of Jewish Emancipation: Russia in the Mirror of Europe," in Rogger, *Jewish Policies*, 234 (notes).

56. Rogger, "Russian Ministers," 97.

57. *Gosudarstvennaia Duma. Stenograficheskie otchety.* Tretii sozyv. 1911 g. Sessiia chetvertaia. Chast' II. Zasedaniia 39–73 (s 17 ianvaria po 5 marta 1911 g.) (St. Petersburg: Gosudarstvennaia tipografiia, 1911): Zasedanie 54, February 9, 1911: cols. 1549–1550.

58. O. V. Budnitskii, "V. A. Maklakov i evreiskii vopros: Iz istorii russkogo liberalizma," *Vestnik Evreiskogo universiteta* 1 (19) (1999): 50, 53–54; V. A. Maklakov, "Spasitel'noe predosterezhenie: Smysl dela Beilisa," *Russkaia mysl'* 11 (1913): 135–143 (second pagination). Also V. A. Maklakov, *Ubiistvo A. Iushchinskogo: Rech' v Kievskom okruzhnom sude 25 oktiabria 1913 g. (po stenograficheskomu otchetu)* (St. Petersburg: Zubkov, 1914).

59. Hans Rogger, "The Beilis Case: Anti-Semitism and Politics in the Reign of Nicholas II," in Rogger, *Jewish Policies*, 40–55; *Delo Mendelia Beilisa: Materialy Chrezvychainoi sledstvennoi komissii Vremennogo pravitel'stva o sudebnom protsesse 1913 g. po obvineniiu v ritual'nom ubiistve*, ed. G. M. Reznik et al.; comp. R. Sh. Ganelin, V. E. Kel'ner, and I. V. Lukoianov (St. Petersburg: Bulanin, 1999); Robert Weinberg, *Blood Libel in Late Imperial Russia: The Ritual Murder Trial of Mendel Beilis* (Bloomington: Indiana University Press, 2014); Mindlin, *Gosudarstvennaia Duma*, 277–292.

60. Wortman, *Scenarios*, 2:410. See the relatively sober Joseph T. Fuhrmann, *Rasputin: The Untold Story* (Hoboken, NJ: John Wiley, 2013); most authoritative is Douglas Smith, *Rasputin: Faith, Power, and the Twilight of the Romanovs* (New York: Farrar, Straus and Giroux, 2016).

61. Sergei Trufanov (Ier. Iliodor), *Sviatoi chort: Zapiski o Rasputine*, intro S. P. Mel'gunov (Moscow: tip. Riabushinskikh, 1917).

62. Quoted, Hosking, *Experiment*, 211; Wortman, *Scenarios*, 2: 429.

63. Quoted, Hosking, *Experiment*, 212 (March 9, 1913, from Duma records).

64. Wortman, *Scenarios*, 2: 439–440.

65. Ibid., 459–460, 460–461 (quote, 461), 462, 465, 471–472, 475, 477.

66. Quoted, Hosking, *Experiment*, 185.

67. Quoted, ibid., 186.

68. Quoted, ibid., 213.

69. Hans Rogger, "Russia in 1914," *Journal of Contemporary History* 1.4 (1966): 95–119.

## PART II: CHAPTER 1

1. John W. Wheeler-Bennett, *Brest-Litovsk, The Forgotten Peace, March 1918* (London: Macmillan; New York: St. Martin's, 1938), 93 (armistice). For an overview of recent scholarship on the war, see Peter Gatrell, "Tsarist Russia at War: The View from Above, 1914–February 1917," *Journal of Modern History* 87.3 (2015): 668–700. The centenary has generated even more; among them: *Russia's Great War*

*and Revolution*, 3 vols. in 5, ed. Anthony Heywood, David M. McDonald, and John W. Steinberg (Bloomington: Slavica, 2014–2016); *Rossiia v gody Pervoi mirovoi voiny: Ekonomicheskoe polozhenie, sotsial'nye protsessy, politicheskii krizis*, ed. Iu. A. Petrov (Moscow: ROSSPEN, 2014); *Rossiia v gody Pervoi mirovoi voiny 1914–1918*, ed. A. N. Artizov et al. (Moscow: Institut rossiiskoi istorii RAN, 2014); A. B. Astashov, *Russkii front v 1914–nachale 1917 goda: Voennyi opyt i sovremennost'* (Moscow: Novyi khronograf, 2014); V. P. Buldakov and T. G. Leont'eva, *Voina, porodivshaia revoliutsiiu, Rossiia, 1914–1917 gg.* (Moscow: Novyi khronograf, 2015); *Die vergessene Front—der Osten 1914/15: Ereignis, Wirkung, Nachwirkung*, ed. Gerhard P. Gross (Paderborn: Ferdinand Schöningh, 2006).

2. For example: Alfred Knox, *With the Russian Army 1914–1917: Being Chiefly Extracts from the Diary of a Military Attaché* (London: Hutchinson, 1921), xix; Peter Gatrell, *Russia's First World War: A Social and Economic History* (Harlow, UK: Pearson-Longman, 2005), 13; Norman Stone, *The Eastern Front, 1914–1917* (1975; London: Penguin, 1998), 42.

3. Michael Freiherr von Taube, *Der Großen Katastrophe entgegen: Die russische Politik der Vorkriegszeit und das Ende des Zarenreiches (1904–1917): Erinnerungen*, 2nd ed. rev. (Leipzig: Koehlers Antiquarium, 1937), 368; Richard S. Wortman, *Scenarios of Power: Myth and Ceremony in Russian Monarchy*, 2 vols. (Princeton: Princeton University Press, 1995–2000), 2:509.

4. On prewar anxiety and unawareness of its approach: Fedor Stepun, *Byvshee i nesbyvsheesia* (New York: Chekhov, 1956; St. Petersburg: Aleteiia; Moscow: Progress-Litera, 1994), 236–238, 257.

5. Dominic Lieven, *The End of Tsarist Russia: The March to World War I and Revolution* (New York: Viking, 2015), 72–76, 284, 288–290.

6. Ibid., 303–307; text of Durnovo memo (February 1914) in *Documents of Russian History, 1914–1917*, ed. Frank Alfred Golder, trans. Emanuel Aronsberg (New York and London: The Century, 1927), 3–23; David M. McDonald, "The Durnovo Memorandum in Context: Official Conservatism and the Crisis of Autocracy," *Jahrbücher für Geschichte Osteuropas* 44 (1996): 481–502; I. I. Tolstoi, *Dnevnik, 1906–1916*, ed. L. I. Tolstaia (St. Petersburg: Evropeiskii dom, 1997), 674 (September 12, 1915, on Durnovo's anti-Semitism).

7. Wortman, *Scenarios*, 2:509.

8. Analysis from Dominic Lieven, "Pro-Germans and Russian Foreign Policy, 1890–1914," *International History Review* 2.1 (1980): 34–54; 47 (Rozen quote); Lieven, *The End*, 128. On the views of political leaders across the board on the eve of the war, see F. A. Gaida, "Politicheskaia obstanovka v Rossii nakanune Pervoi mirovoi voiny v otsenke gosudarstvennykh deiatelei i liderov partii," *Rossiiskaia istoriia* 6 (2011): 123–135.

9. On Sazonov's anti-German, Slavophile position, see Lieven, *The End*, 127.

10. Maurice Paléologue, *La Russie des tsars pendant la Grande Guerre*, vol. 1: *20 juillet 1914–2 juin 1915* (Paris: Plon, 1921), 4. The incongruity plagued the Franco-Russian

alliance from its inception: see Faith Hillis, "The 'Franco-Russian Marseillaise': International Exchange and the Making of Anti-Liberal Politics in *Fin-de-Siècle* France," *Journal of Modern History* 89 (March 2017): 39–78.

11. Paléologue, *La Russie*, 1:8.

12. J. F. Hutchinson, "The Octobrists and the Future of Russia as a Great Power," *Slavonic and East European Review* 50.119 (1972): 220–237.

13. Lieven, *The End*, 334–335.

14. Christopher Clark, *Sleepwalkers: How Europe Went to War in 1914* (London: Allen Lane, 2012), 513.

15. Lieven, *The End*, 336–337; on Nicholas's reluctance to declare full mobilization and the generals' dismay, see Paléologue, *La Russie* 1:37–40.

16. Orlando Figes, *A People's Tragedy: The Russian Revolution, 1891–1924* (New York: Penguin, 1998), 150–151; W. Bruce Lincoln, *Passage through Armageddon: The Russians in War and Revolution, 1914–1918* (New York: Simon and Schuster, 1986), 37–40.

17. Paléologue, *La Russie*, 1:37–38 (July 30, 1914).

18. Ibid., 1:30, 32 (quotes).

19. Ibid., 1:44 (August 1, 1914); Clark, *Sleepwalkers*, 552.

20. Lieven, *The End*, 295–296; "Krivoshein Aleksandr Vasil'evich," in D. N. Shilov, *Gosudarstvennye deiateli Rossiiskoi imperii, 1802–1917: Biobibliograficheskii spravochnik* (St. Petersburg: Bulanin, 2001), 330–333.

21. Lieven, *The End*, 147.

22. Bruce W. Menning, *Bayonets before Bullets: The Imperial Russian Army, 1861–1914* (Bloomington: Indiana University Press, 1992), 218–222; Lieven, *The End*, 149 (promotion of incompetents); David R. Stone, *The Russian Army in the Great War: The Eastern Front, 1914–1917* (Lawrence: University Press of Kansas, 2015), 43–44 (positive contribution).

23. Menning, *Bayonets before Bullets*, 227, 230–235; Stone, *Russian Army*, 48–51.

24. Stone, *Eastern Front*, 39, 19–20.

25. Stone, *Russian Army*, 47, 57. Thanks to Bill Rosenberg for this point.

26. D. A. Iusov, "*Polozhenie o polevom upravlenii voisk v voennoe vremia,*" in *Rossiia v Pervoi mirovoi voine 1914–1918: Entsiklopediia v trekh tomakh*, ed. A. K. Sorokin et al. (Moscow: ROSSPEN, 2014), 2:790–791 (*teatr voennykh deistvii*); Peter Holquist, "Les violences de l'armée russe à l'encontre des Juifs en 1915: Causes et limites," in *Vers la guerre totale: Le tournant de 1914–1915*, ed. John Horne (Paris: Tallandier, 2010), 204; Daniel Graf, "Military Rule Behind the Russian Front, 1914–1917: The Political Ramifications," *Jahrbücher für Geschichte Osteuropas* 22.3 (1974): 390–392.

27. General Fedor Palitsyn, quoted in K. A. Solov'ev, "Gosudarstvennye instituty," in *Rossiia v gody Pervoi mirovoi voiny*, ed. Petrov, 649.

28. Tolstoi, *Dnevnik*, 521 (July 9, 1914; figure of 150,000); Paléologue, *La Russie*, 1:6, 11 (July 20–21, 1914).

29. Paléologue, *La Russie*, 1:40 (July 31, 1914), 49 (August 3, 1914).

30. Ibid., 45–46 (August 2, 1914); Wortman, *Scenarios*, 2:510.

31. Paléologue, *La Russie*, 1:41 (August 4, 1914).

32. *Novoe vremia*, no. 13779 (July 23, 1914), 2; *Novoe vremia*, no. 13780 (July 24, 1914), 2 (100 arrested).

33. Paléologue, *La Russie*, 1:51 (August 4, 1914).

34. Personal reports: "Nadia," Groznyi, Tver' oblast', July 28, 1914, to Evgenii Robertovich Etter, Petersburg: GARF [Gosudarstvennyi arkhiv Rossiiskoi federatsii], f. 102, op. 265, d. 991, l. 1069; "Aleksandr," Mariinsk, Tomsk Prov., July 28, 1914, to polkovnik General'nogo Shtaba N. S. Elizarov, Moscow: GARF, f. 102, op. 265, d. 991, l. 1071.

35. V.V. Rozanov, *Voina 1914 goda i russkoe vozrozhdenie* (Petrograd: Suvorin, 1915), 9; Tolstoi, *Dnevnik*, 526 (condemnation); *Memorandum Concerning the Treatment of German Consuls in Russia and the Destruction of the German Embassy in St. Petersburg* (Berlin: Carl Heymanns, 1915).

36. Rozanov, *Voina 1914 goda*, 16.

37. *Birzhevye vedomosti*, no. 14266 (July 23, 1914), 1.

38. Tolstoi, *Dnevnik*, 526 (July 23, 1914), 524 (July 20, 1914).

39. Ibid., 530 (July 30, 1914).

40. Ibid., 531 (July 31, 1914).

41. V. P. Ponomarev, "Rennenkampf," in *Rossiia v Pervoi mirovoi voine*, 3:48; F. A. Gaida, "Sabler," ibid, 119.

42. Otkrytoe zakaznoe pis'mo, no sig., Moscow, May 19, 1915, to General Aleksandr Germanovich Preis, stantsiia Khlebnikovo, Savelovskaia zhel. dor.: GARF, f. 102, op. 265, d. 1006, l. 8. On distrusting officers with German names: Gruzinov, active army, December 31, 1914, to Ego P. Mikhailov, Moscow: GARF, f. 102, op. 265, d. 1002, l. 2189.

43. Governor-General Anton Ottovich Essen, Governor Semen Nikolaevich Korf, head of the state bank Tuzengauzen: "Pokazaniia A. R. Lednitskogo, 27 sentiabria 1917 g.," in *Padenie tsarskogo rezhima: Stenograficheskie otchety doprosov i pokazanii, dannykh v 1917 g. v Chrezvychainoi sledstvennoi komissii Vremennogo pravitel'stva*, ed. P. E. Shchegolev, 7 vols. (Moscow and Leningrad: Gosizdatel'stvo, 1924–1927), 7:239. Commenting on the same fact: illeg. signature Piatigorsk, December 4, 1914, to S. D. Protopopov Petrograd: GARF, f. 102, op. 265, d. 1000, l. 1991.

44. *Ober-gofmarshal, shtats-sekretar', kamerger, shtalmeister, egermeister, fligel'-ad"jutant, freilina*, etc.: Paléologue, *La Russie*, 3:119 (December 24, 1916).

45. *Rossiia nakanune Pervoi mirovoi voiny: Statistiko-dokumental'nyi spravochnik* (Moscow: Samoteka, 2008), 11, 22; Menning, *Bayonets before Bullets*, 227; Joshua A. Sanborn, *Imperial Apocalypse: The Great War and the Destruction of the Russian Empire* (Oxford: Oxford University Press, 2014), 23 (4 million); Stone, *Russian Army*, 11 (3 million, with caution); William G. Rosenberg, "Reading Soldiers' Moods: Russian Military Censorship and the Configuration of Feeling in World War I," *American Historical Review* 119.3 (2014): 718 (5 million by December

1914); G. F. Krivosheev et al., *Rossiia i SSSR v voinakh XX veka: Kniga poter'* (Moscow: Veche, 2010), 83 (5,130 million), which I take to be most reliable. Also: Astashov, *Russkii front*, 19.

46. Lieutenant-General Nicholas N. Golovine, *The Russian Army in the World War* (New Haven: Yale University Press, for the Carnegie Endowment for International Peace, 1931), 18–19.

47. Krivosheev, *Rossiia i SSSR*, 83–84. Totals vary: Golovine, *Russian Army*, 50 (15,500,000); N. A. Ivanov, "Demograficheskie i sotsial'nye protsessy," in *Rossiia v gody Pervoi mirovoi voiny*, ed. Petrov, 192 (15,793,000), 193 (40 percent); *Rossiia nakanune Pervoi mirovoi voiny*, 19 (15,694,000); Gatrell, *Russia's First World War*, 1 (15,694,000), but also 22 (18,600,000), the latter repeated in Peter Gatrell, "Poor Russia, Poor Show: Mobilising a Backward Economy," in *The Economics of World War I*, ed. Stephen Broadberry and Mark Harrison (Cambridge: Cambridge University Press, 2005), 251; Rosenberg, "Reading Soldiers' Moods," 719 (about 16,000,000); A. V. Oleinikov, "Poteri russkoi armii 1914–17," in *Rossiia v Pervoi mirovoi voine*, 2:834 (15,500,000).

48. Gatrell, "Poor Russia," 251; Stanislas Kohn, "The Vital Statistics of European Russia During the World War 1914–1917," in Stanislas Kohn and Alexander F. Meyendorff, *The Cost of the War to Russia* (New Haven: Yale University Press; London: Oxford University Press for the Carnegie Endowment for International Peace, Division of Economics and History, 1932), 23–24.

49. A. B. Astashov, "Russkii krest'ianin na frontakh Pervoi mirovoi voiny," *Otechestvennaia istoriia* 2 (2003): 73; Astashov, *Russkii front*, 29–30.

50. Stone, *Russian Army*, 36.

51. Stepun, *Byvshee*, 260.

52. T. V. Osipova, *Rossiiskoe krest'ianstvo v revoliutsii i grazhdanskoi voine* (Moscow: Strelets, 2001), 198–199.

53. "Osobyi zhurnal Soveta ministrov, 17 iuliia 1914 goda, no. 58: O vvedenii voen-no-avtomobil'noi povinnosti vo vsekh mestnostiakh Imperii, za iskliucheniem Velikogo Kniazhestva Finliandskogo," in *Osobye zhurnaly Soveta ministrov Rossiiskoi imperii, 1914 god*, ed. B. D. Gal'perina et al. (Moscow: ROSSPEN, 2006), 205–208.

54. N. Chikhachev, Peresna, Smolensk Prov., July 23, 1914 to V. A. Blium, Kiev: GARF, f. 102, op. 265, d. 990, l. 999.

55. Participants writing not long after the revolution differed in their assessment of the extent and meaning of draft protests; see Joshua A. Sanborn, *Drafting the Russian Nation: Military Conscription, Total War, and Mass Politics, 1905–1925* (DeKalb: Northern Illinois University Press, 2003), 202–204.

56. On prohibition, its motives and impact: Petr L'vovich Bark, Minister of Finance, 1914–1917, unpublished memoirs (n.d.): Bakhmeteff Archive, Columbia University, typescript, 11–24. On officers drinking: V. V. Shulgin, *The Years: Memoirs of a Member of the Russian Duma, 1906–1917*, trans. Tanya Davis, intro. Jonathan Sanders (New York: Hippocrene, 1991), 171; V. B. Aksenov, "'Sukhoi

zakon' 1914 goda: Ot pridvornoi intrigi do revoliutsii," *Rossiiskaia istoriia* 4 (2011): 126–139.

57. Igor V. Narskii, *Zhizn' v katastrofe: Budni naseleniia Urala v 1917–1922 gg.* (Moscow: ROSSPEN, 2001), 176.

58. V.V. Kanishchev, *Russkii bunt, bessmyslennyi i besposhchadnyi: Pogromnoe dvizhenie v gorodakh Rossii v 1917–1918 gg.* (Tambov: Tambovskii gos. un-t im. G. R. Derzhavina, 1995), 36–43; Sanborn, *Drafting*, 30–31.

59. A. V. Posadskii, *Krest'ianstvo vo vseobshchei mobilizatsii armii i flota 1914 goda (Po materialam Saratovskoi gubernii)* (Saratov: Saratovskii universitet, 2002), 88, 92, 94.

60. Iu. I. Kir'ianov, *Sotsial'no-politicheskii protest rabochikh Rossii v gody Pervoi mirovoi voiny (iul' 1914 – fevral' 1917 gg.)* (Moscow: Institut Rossiiskoi istorii RAN, 2005), 40 and 44; Sanborn, *Imperial Apocalypse*, 23.

61. von Taube, *Der Großen Katastrophe entgegen*, 366–367; Sanborn, *Imperial Apocalypse*, 23.

62. Oleinikov, "Poteri," 834 (his totals); 820 (on divergent figures). On divergence in available figures, see Astashov, *Russkii front*, 20–22.

63. Vadim Erlikhman, *Poteri narodonaseleniia v XX veke: Spravochnik* (Moscow: Russkaia panorama, 2004), 18; Krivosheev, *Rossiia i SSSR*, 90; Jonathan D. Smele, *The "Russian" Civil Wars 1916–1926: Ten Years That Shook the World* (Oxford: Oxford University Press, 2015), 256 (citing Erlikhman); "The Economics of World War I: An Overview," in *The Economics of World War I*, ed. Stephen Broadberry and Mark Harrison (Cambridge: Cambridge University Press, 2005), 27; Golovine, *Russian Army*, 93–94 (soldiers from all causes, 1,650,000, plus 3,850,000 surviving wounded). In addition to other problems of accounting, desertion was a chronic problem throughout the war; some were caught, but many disappeared: A. B. Astashov, "Dezertirstvo i bor'ba s nim v tsarskoi armii v gody Pervoi mirovoi voiny," *Rossiiskaia istoriia* 4 (2011): 44–52.

64. S.V. Volkov, *Tragediia russkogo ofitserstva* (Moscow: Fokus, 1999), 7–8.

65. Ibid., 6 (these figures). See also, A.V. Maryniak, "K voprosu o komplektovanii ofitserskogo korpusa russkoi armii v gody Pervoi mirovoi voiny," in *Rossiia v gody Pervoi mirovoi voiny 1914–1918*, ed. Artizov, 290 (44,000 in 1914), 295 (September 1917: 132,500, plus 17,300 reserve); Peter Kenez, "Changes to the Social Composition of the Officer Corps during World War I," *Russian Review* 31.4 (1972): 369 (40,590 in 1914 to 145,916, January 1917); Matthew Rendle, *Defenders of the Motherland: The Tsarist Elite in Revolutionary Russia* (Oxford: Oxford University Press, 2010), 116 (45,000 in 1914; 145,000 by 1917, 250,000 by October 1917); Krivosheev, *Rossiia i SSSR*, 88 (38,156 October 1914, 58,011 September 1915, 115,201 November 1916, 136,600 May 1917).

66. Figures for noncommissioned ranks: Krivosheev, *Rossiia i SSSR*, 88 (fall 1914, 17,500; May 1917, 53,000).

67. Kenez, "Changes," 373–374; Gatrell, *Russia's First World War*, 23–24; Lincoln, *Passage*, 53; Viktor Shklovsky, *A Sentimental Journey: Memoirs, 1917–1922*, trans. Richard Sheldon (1923; Ithaca: Cornell University Press, 1984), 65–66; Rosenberg, "Reading

Soldiers' Moods," 216–217 (over a quarter of foot soldiers were illiterate; the rest had some degree of literacy); Stone, *Russian Army*, 33 (one-third illiterate in 1913, but 60 percent wartime draft); Astashov, *Russkii front*, 32 (48 percent literate before the war, by 1916 40–45 percent literate).

68. Golovine, *Russian Army*, 205–206 ("*Za Veru, Tsaria i Otechestvo*").

69. Stepun, *Byvshee*, 269–271. Recent study of peasant-soldier mentality: Astashov, *Russkii front*.

70. Boris Kolonitskii, "Russian Leaders of the Great War and Revolutionary Era in Representations and Rumors," in *Russian Culture in War and Revolution, 1914–22: Political Culture, Identities, Mentalities, and Memories*, ed. Murray Frame, Boris Kolonitskii, Steven G. Marks, and Melissa K. Stockdale (Bloomington: Slavica, 2014), 29–36.

71. Golovine, *Russian Army*, 185.

72. These were *Grenzsicherungstruppen* from Silesia: see Imanuel Geiss, "Die Kosaken kommen! Ostpreussen im August 1914," in Imanuel Geiss, *Das Deutsche Reich und der Erste Weltkrieg* (Munich: Hanser, 1978), 60–61.

73. Alfred Knox, *With the Russian Army 1914–1917: Being Chiefly Extracts from the Diary of a Military Attaché* (London: Hutchinson, 1921), 41.

74. See Laura Engelstein, "'A Belgium of Our Own': The Sack of Russian Kalisz, August 1914," *Kritika* 10.3 (2009):1–33; Ryszard Bieniecki and Bogumiła Celer, *Katastrofa Kaliska 1914: Materiały źródłowe* (Lakisz: Kaliskie Towarzystwo Przyjaciół Nauk, 2014).

75. "Introduction," *State, Society, and Mobilization in Europe during the First World War*, ed. John Horne (Cambridge: Cambridge University Press, 1997), 29–21; Jürgen von Ungern-Sternberg and Wolfgang von Ungern-Sternberg, *Der Aufruf 'An die Kulturwelt!': Das Manifest der 93 und die Anfänge der Kriegspropaganda im Ersten Weltkrieg* (Stuttgart: Franz Steiner, 1996).

76. For example: A. S. Rezanov, *Nemetskie zverstva: Kniga sostavlena po rasskazam poterpevshikh i ochevidtsev, a takzhe po ofitsial'nym dokumentam* (Petrograd: M. A. Suvorin, 1915).

77. P. L. Bark, "Iiul'skie dni 1914 goda: Nachalo velikoi voiny," *Vozrozhdenie: Literaturno-politicheskie tetradi*, no. 91 (Paris, 1959), 43–44.

78. "Privetstvennoe slovo Ego Imperatorskogo Velichestva Gosudaria Imperatora Gosudarstvennomu Sovetu i Gosudarstvennoi Dume, skazannoe v Imperatorskom Zimnem Dvortse 26 Iiulia 1914 g."; "Slovo vremenno ispolniaiushchego obiazannosti Predsedatelia Gosudarstvennogo Soveta Golubeva, skazannoe v Imperatorskom Zimnem Dvortse 26 Iiulia 1914 g."; "Slovo Predsedatelia Gosudarstvennoi Dumy Rodzianko, skazannoe v Imperatorskom Zimnem Dvortse 26 Iiulia 1914 g.," in *Gosudarstvennaia Duma. Stenograficheskie otchety*, Chetvertyi sozyv, Sessiia II, Chast' V (Petrograd: Gosudarstvennaia tipografiia, 1914), unpaginated. For excerpts in English of this and the Duma speeches, see Golder, *Documents*, 29–37.

79. *Velikaia voina: Chto dolzhen znat' o nei kazhdyi russkii?* (Petrograd:Tekhnicheskoe izdatel'stvo inzhenera N. G. Kuznetsova, [1914]), 39.

80. Zasedanie Gosudarstvennoi Dumy, sozvannoi na osnovanii Vysochaishego Ukaza Pravitel'stvuiushchemu Senatu ot 20 iiulia 1914 g. Subbota, 26 Iiulia 1914 g., in *Gosudarstvennaia Duma. Stenograficheskie otchety*, Chetvertyi sozyv, Sessiia II, Chast'V (Petrograd: Gosudarstvennaia tipografiia, 1914), col. 1–32; here, 2. Speeches covered in the press; e.g., *Novoe vremia*, no. 13783 (July 27, 1914), 5.

81. Zasedanie Gosudarstvennoi Dumy (July 26, 1914), 4–5.

82. Ibid., 9 (Sazonov), 10–11.

83. Ibid., 24–25 (*rossiiskie grazhdane*). On Miliukov's previously pacifist stand and the party pressure to strike a patriotic note in July 1914, see Raymond Pearson, *The Russian Moderates and the Crisis of Tsarism 1914–1917* (London: Macmillan, 1977), 19.

84. Zasedanie Gosudarstvennoi Dumy (July 26, 1914), 18–19 (*nerusskie narodnosti*).

85. Pearson, *Moderates*, 22–25.

86. Zasedanie Gosudarstvennoi Dumy (July 26, 1914), 20, 22–23 (*natsional'nost'*; *russkii narod*).

87. Ibid., 21.

88. Ibid., 23–24. N. M. Fridman's August 9, 1914 speech widely circulated: see Mark Levene, *War, Jews, and the New Europe: The Diplomacy of Lucien Wolf, 1914–1919* (Oxford: Oxford University Press, 1992), 48; text in Golder, *Documents*, 36.

89. Zasedanie Gosudarstvennoi Dumy (July 26, 1914), 28.

90. Golovine, *Russian Army*, 212–213; Stone, *Eastern Front*, 35, 42, 49.

91. Stone, *Eastern Front*, 25, 28–32.

92. Lincoln, *Passage*, 54; "Perepiska V. A. Sukhomlinova s N. N. Ianushkevichem (cont.)," *Krasnyi arkhiv* 2 (1922), various.

93. "Perepiska V. A. Sukhomlinova," 143–144 (December 6, 1914); on boot shortage: *Sovet ministrov Rossiiskoi imperii v gody Pervoi mirovoi voiny: Bumagi A. N. Iakhontova*, ed. B. D. Gal'perina (St. Petersburg: Bulanin, 1999), 108 (December 12, 1914); Golovine, *Russian Army*, 177–178.

94. Because of unfamiliarity with the technology or lack of equipment, sending messages *en clair* was not confined to the Russians: Stone, *Russian Army*, 71–72.

95. Lincoln, *Passage*, 57–58.

96. Ibid., 71 (quote), 72–73.

97. Peter Kenez, *Civil War in South Russia, 1918: The First Year of the Volunteer Army* (Berkeley: University of California Press, 1971), 19–20.

98. Lincoln, *Passage*, 75–76; Stone, *Eastern Front*, 66–67 (100,000 POWs/400 guns). These figures and those presented by Golovine are challenged by Oleinikov, "Poteri," 826–827. I accept his lower figures.

99. General Basil Gourko, *Memories and Impressions of War and Revolution in Russia 1914–1917* (London: John Murray, 1918), 70. Sukhomlinov called him "an

arrogant Prussian" and considered him a coward and liar. "Perepiska V. A. Sukhomlinova," 139, 145, 148.

100. Stone, *Russian Army*, 79. In October 1915, he was released from service for personal reasons: Ponomarev, "Rennenkampf," 48–50. On March 16, 1918 he was shot by the Bolsheviks.

101. Stone, *Eastern Front*, 66.

102. Lincoln, *Passage*, 78.

103. Golovine, *Russian Army*, 217; Oleinikov, "Poteri," 830, 834.

104. All preceding from Lincoln, *Passage*, 84–91.

105. Rosenberg, "Reading Soldiers' Moods."

106. Astashov, "Dezertirstvo."

107. Golovine, *Russian Army*, 216–217.

108. von Taube, *Der Großen Katastrophe entgegen*, 369–370. Baron von Taube was Russian-born, of Swedish-German Baltic heritage, a convert to Catholicism; after 1917 in emigration.


### PART II: CHAPTER 2

1. David R. Stone, *The Russian Army in the Great War: The Eastern Front, 1914–1917* (Lawrence: University Press of Kansas, 2015), 132–134.

2. Lieutenant-General Nicholas N. Golovine, *The Russian Army in the World War* (New Haven: Yale University Press, for the Carnegie Endowment for International Peace, 1931), 221.

3. V. V. Shulgin, *The Years: Memoirs of a Member of the Russian Duma, 1906–1917*, trans. Tanya Davis, intro. Jonathan Sanders (New York: Hippocrene, 1991), 165; William Henry Chamberlin, *The Russian Revolution, 1917–1921*, 2 vols. (1935; New York: Grosset & Dunlap, 1965), 2:144 (Dmitriev refused to join the Red Army, was executed by the Cheka on October 31, 1918); S. V. Potrashkov, "Dmitriev (Radko-Dmitriev)," in *Rossiia v Pervoi mirovoi voine 1914–1918: Entsiklopediia v trekh tomakh*, ed. A. K. Sorokin et al. (Moscow: ROSSPEN, 2014), 622.

4. Maurice Paléologue, *La Russie des tsars pendant la Grande Guerre*, vol. 2: *3 juin 1915–18 août 1916*, 23rd ed. (Paris: Plon, 1922), 28 (July 20, 1915), quote; 35 (August 4, 1915).

5. Peter Gatrell, *A Whole Empire Walking: Refugees in Russia during World War I* (Bloomington: Indiana University Press, 1999), 20.

6. Ibid.

7. Eric Lohr, *Nationalizing the Russian Empire: The Campaign Against Enemy Aliens During World War I* (Cambridge, MA: Harvard University Press, 2003), 122–123.

8. I. I. Tolstoi, *Dnevnik, 1906–1916*, ed. L. I. Tolstaia (St. Petersburg: Evropeiskii dom, 1997), 561 (*Novoe vremia*, in particular), 562–563. Another decree at the end of December 1914 ordered the expulsion of all remaining German civilians: ibid., 584.

9. Lohr, *Nationalizing*, 122.

10. Reinhard Nachtigal, "Germans in Russia during World War I," in *Russia's Home Front in War and Revolution 1914–22*, Book 2: *The Experience of War and Revolution*, ed. Adele Lindenmeyr, Christopher Read, and Peter Waldron (Bloomington: Slavica, 2016), 327–342.

11. S. G. Nelipovich, "Naselenie okkupirovannykh territorii rassmatrivalos' kak rezerv protivnika: Internirovanie chasti zhitelei Vostochnoi Prussii, Galitsii, i Bukoviny v 1914–1915," *Voenno-istoricheskii zhurnal* 2 (2000): 60–69 (electronic unpaginated); Mark von Hagen, "The Great War and the Mobilization of Ethnicity in the Russian Empire," in *Post-Soviet Political Order: Conflict and State Building*, ed. Barnett Rubin and Jack Snyder (London and New York: Routledge, 1998), 46.

12. Daniel Graf, "Military Rule Behind the Russian Front, 1914–1917: The Political Ramifications," *Jahrbücher für Geschichte Osteuropas* 22.3 (1974): 390–411; also "General ot infanterii N. N. Ianushkevich: 'Nemetskuiu pakost' uvolit', i bez nezhnostei...': Deportatsii v Rossii 1914–1918 gg.," ed. S. G. Nelipovich, *Voenno-istoricheskii zhurnal* 1 (1997): 42–53; Graf, "Military Rule," 394.

13. Gatrell, *Empire Walking*, 23–24.

14. "General ot infanterii N. N. Ianushkevich," 50.

15. Gatrell, *Empire Walking*, 17–18 (citing *Iz chernoi knigi*); Alexander V. Prusin, "The Russian Military and the Jews in Galicia, 1914–1915," in *The Military and Society in Russia: 1450–1917*, ed. Eric Lohr and Marshall Poe (Leiden and Boston: Brill, 2002), 529, 534–536.

16. Gatrell, *Empire Walking*, 18.

17. Krivoshein quoting an earlier remark by Ianushkevich: *Sovet ministrov Rossiiskoi imperii v gody Pervoi mirovoi voiny: Bumagi A. N. Iakhontova*, ed. B. D. Gal'perina (St. Petersburg: Bulanin, 1999), 260 (September 2, 1915).

18. Prusin, "Russian Military," 537–538.

19. On the Germans: "General ot infanterii N. N. Ianushkevich," 45–47; on the Jews: Prusin, "Russian Military," 539.

20. Nelipovich, "Naselenie okkupirovannykh territorii" (electronic unpaginated).

21. Gatrell, *Empire Walking*, 28–29.

22. S. A. An-sky [S. A. Rappoport], *The Enemy at his Pleasure: A Journey Through the Jewish Pale of Settlement During World War I*, ed. and trans. Joachim Neugroschel (New York: Metropolitan, 2002), 226–227.

23. "Rech' N. M. Fridmana v zasedanii 20 iiulia 1915 goda," *Chertvertaia Gosudarstvennaia Duma. Fraktsiia narodnoi svobody, "voennye" sessii, 26 iiulia 1914 goda–3 sentiabria 1915 goda. Chast' 1: Otchet Fraktsii. Chast' 2: Rechi deputatov* (Petrograd: Ekateringofskoe Pechatnoe Delo, 1916), 24–34 (quote, 27); see also Mark Levene, *War, Jews, and the New Europe: The Diplomacy of Lucien Wolf, 1914–1919* (Oxford: Oxford University Press, 1992), 48–49.

24. S. Elachich, Samara, January 26, 1915, to Ego Prev. N. A. Elachich, Petrograd: GARF, f. 102, op. 265, d. 1012, l. 216-ob. The addressee was possibly Nikolai Aleksandrovich Elachich (1872–1938), the writer possibly his mother Sofia

Kirillovna. See E. E. Shergalin, "Evgenii Aleksandrovich Elachich (1880–1944) – naturalist, prosvetitel' i pedagog," *Russkii ornitologicheskii zhurnal* 20 (2011): 1539–1549. Available online at http://www.russiangrave.ru/assets/files/88613717 _Elacic.pdf (accessed August 18, 2016).

25. Maurice Paléologue, *La Russie des tsars pendant la Grande Guerre*, vol. 1: *20 juillet 1914–2 juin 1915* (Paris: Plon, 1921), 335–336 (March 30, 1915).

26. Paléologue, *La Russie*, 2:16 (June 19, 1915).

27. Ibid., 36 (August 8, 1915).

28. Peter Holquist, "Les violences de l'armée russe à l'encontre des Juifs en 1915: Causes et limites," in *Vers la guerre totale: Le tournant de 1914–15*, ed. John Horne (Paris: Tallandier, 2010), 211.

29. Ibid., 201. See Peter Jahn, "'Zarendreck, Barbarendreck': Die russische Besetzung Ostpreußens 1914 in der deutschen Öffentlichkeit," *Verführungen der Gewalt: Russen und Deutsche im Ersten und Zweiten Weltkrieg*, ed. Karl Eimermacher and Astrid Volpert (Munich: Fink, 2005); Alexander Watson, "'Unheard-of Brutality': Russian Atrocities against Civilians in East Prussia, 1914–1915," *Journal of Modern History* 86.4 (2014): 780–825.

30. Nelipovich, "Naselenie okkupirovannykh territorii" (electronic unpaginated).

31. Konrad Zieliński, *Stosunki polsko-żydowskie na ziemiach Królestwa Polskiego w czasie pierwszej wojny światowej* (Lublin: Uniwersytet Marii Curie-Skłodowskiej, 2005), 101–104, 112–113.

32. Michael Freiherr von Taube, *Der Großen Katastrophe entgegen: Die russische Politik der Vorkriegszeit und das Ende des Zarenreiches (1904–1917): Erinnerungen*, 2nd ed. rev. (Leipzig: Koehlers Antiquarium, 1937), 372–373.

33. General Basil Gourko, *Memories and Impressions of War and Revolution in Russia 1914–1917* (London: John Murray, 1918), 23–32. Also preceding paragraph.

34. Imanuel Geiss, "Die Kosaken kommen! Ostpreussen im August 1914," in Imanuel Geiss, *Das Deutsche Reich und der Erste Weltkrieg* (Munich: Hanser, 1978), 58–66.

35. Gourko, *Memories*, 38–39.

36. Order to First Army August 23, 1914 from Verkhovnyi Glavnokomanduiushchii, cited in M. K. Lemke, *250 dnei v tsarskoi Stavke (25 sent. 1915–2 iiulia 1916)* (Petersburg: Gosudarstvennoe Izdatel'stvo, 1920), 82.

37. Gourko, *Memories*, 83.

38. Official German testimony and remonstrance concerning Russian atrocities in East Prussia: Auswärtiges Amt, *Greueltaten russischer Truppen gegen deutsche Zivilpersonen und deutsche Kriesgefangene* (Berlin, 1915). Pamphlets on same theme: Robert Heymann, *Der Weltkrieg 1914: Kosakengreuel* (Dresden: Max Fischer, [1915]); Germanicus (pseud. Valerian Hugo Tornius), *Das russische Gespenst: Kriegs-Zeitschriften: Eine Sammlung aufklärender Schriften für die Allgemeinheit* (Leipzig: Schulze, [1915]); Robert Franke, *Russische Verwüstungen und Greuel: Meine Fahrt durch Ostpreussens Ruinen*, 2nd ed. rev. (Danzig: Kafemann, 1917).

39. Peter Holquist, "The Role of Personality in the First (1914–1915) Russian Occupation of Galicia and Bukovina," in *Anti-Jewish Violence: Rethinking the Pogrom in European History*, ed. Jonathan Dekel-Chen (Bloomington: Indiana University Press, 2010); Mark von Hagen, *War in a European Borderland: Occupations and Occupation Plans in Galicia and Ukraine, 1914–1918* (Seattle: University of Washington Press, 2007), 30–31.

40. Prusin, "Russian Military," 526–527; Peter Holquist, "'In the Russo-Turkish War of 1877–78 Russian Forces Conducted Themselves Differently—But That Was a Different Era': Forms of Violence in the First (1914–15) and Second (1916–17) Occupations of Galicia" (unpublished paper, 2005); and Holquist, "Les violences." Propaganda on theme of historic Galicia: L. Kusnishchskii, *Chervonnaia rus' (Galitsiia)*, Vyp. 1, *Mir i voina*, Biblioteka obshchedostupnykh ocherkov, posviashchennykh voine 1914 g. (Moscow: Obshchee delo, 1914).

41. Gabriella Safran, *Wandering Soul: The Dybbuk's Creator, S. An-sky* (Cambridge, MA: Harvard University Press, 2010), 226.

42. An-sky, *Enemy at his Pleasure*, 64–65, 143; Safran, *Wandering Soul*, 227–228.

43. Wlad. W. Kaplun-Kogan, *Der Krieg: Eine Schicksalsstunde des jüdischen Volkes* (Bonn: Marcus and Weber, 1915), 10–11.

44. Yohanan Petrovsky-Shtern, "The 'Jewish Policy' of the Late Imperial War Ministry: The Impact of the Russian Right," *Kritika* 3.2 (2002): 217–254; Holquist, "Role of Personality," 65. See also Dietrich Beyrau, *Militär und Gesellschaft im vorrevolutionären Russland* (Cologne: Böhlaw, 1984), ch. 8.

45. N. Kozlovskii, "Ob otnoshenii narodnostei Rossii k ispolneniiu voinskoi povinnosti (Po dannym o prizyvakh 1909–11 gg.)," *Voennyi sbornik* 1 (January 1915): 141, 147.

46. Leonid Efremovich Gorizontov, "Pol'sko-evreiskie otnosheniia vo vnutrennei politike i obshchestvennoi mysli Rossiiskoi imperii (1831–1917)," in *Istoriia i kul'tura rossiiskogo i vostochnoevropeiskogo evreistva: Novye istochniki, novye podkhody*, ed. O. V. Budnitskii et al. (Moscow: Dom evreiskoi knigi, 2004).

47. Tolstoi, *Dnevnik*, 543 (*beshennyi antisemitizm*).

48. Reported in ibid., 550 (September 17, 1914).

49. Ibid., 573 (November 30, 1914); John Klier, "Gintsburg Family," *YIVO Encyclopedia of Jews in Eastern Europe* (2010), available online at http://www.yivoencyclopedia.org/article.aspx/Gintsburg_Family (accessed June 17, 2015).

50. Emile Verhaeren, *La Belgique sanglante* (Paris: Nouvelle revue française, [1915]), 129–139.

51. Quoted, Levene, *War, Jews, and the New Europe*, 51, 54 (Bernard Pares agreed; so did *Times* correspondent Stanley Washburn and General Alfred Knox, British military attaché at Russian Army Headquarters).

52. L. Andreev, "Pervaia stupen'," *Shchit: Literaturnyi sbornik*, ed. Leonid Andreev, Maksim Gor'kii, and Fedor Sologub, 3rd ed. rev. (Moscow: Mamontov, 1916), 5.

53. For graphic descriptions of such abuses, see Carnegie Endowment for International Peace, *Report of the International Commission to Inquire into the*

*Causes and Conduct of the Balkan Wars* (Washington, DC: The Endowment, 1914). The Russian Kadet leader Pavel Miliukov was a member of the committee.

54. See: Peter Holquist, "Russo-Turkish War"; Peter Holquist, "Role of Personality."

55. Holquist, "Les violences," 197.

56. *Gosudarstvennaia Duma. Stenograficheskie otchety.* Chetvertyi sozyv. Sessiia tret'ia. Zasedaniia 1–3 (27–29 ianvaria 1915 g.) (Petrograd: Gosudarstvennaia tipografiia, 1915), Zasedanie pervoe (27 ianvaria 1915 g.), col. 15.

57. Peter Holquist, "Russo-Turkish War"; Holquist, "Role of Personality"; official remonstrance concerning Galicia in fall 1914: Austro-Hungarian Monarchy, Ministerium des K. und K. Hauses und des Äussern, *Sammlung von Nachweisen für die Verletzungen des Völkerrechtes durch die mit Österreich-Ungarn Krieg-führenden Staaten*. I. Nachtrag (Vienna: K. K. Hof- und Staatsdruckerei, 1915). See also: An-sky, *Enemy at his Pleasure*; Prusin, "Russian Military"; Alexander Victor Prusin, *Nationalizing a Borderland: War, Ethnicity, and Anti-Jewish Violence in East Galicia, 1914–1920* (Tuscaloosa: University of Alabama Press, 2005).

58. Nicholas read three radical-right newspapers, *Novoe vremia, Russkii invalid*, and *Zemshchina*: A. A. Polivanov, *Memuary: Iz dnevnikov i vospominanii po dolzhnosti Voennogo ministra i ego pomoshchnika 1907–1916 g.*, ed. A. M. Zaionchkovskii (Moscow: Vysshii voennyi redaktsionnyi sovet, 1924), 189.

59. Quoted, Nelipovich, "Naselenie okkupirovannykh territorii" (electronic unpaginated).

60. Quoted (March 4/17, 1915), ibid.

61. Holquist, "Role of Personality," 61; Lohr, *Nationalizing*, 138–139.

62. Lohr, *Nationalizing*, 150–152.

63. Gatrell, *Empire Walking*, 18; von Hagen, "Great War," 45.

64. An-sky, *Enemy at his Pleasure*, 68; Holquist, "Role of Personality," 55.

65. Prusin, *Nationalizing*, 30–32, as cited by Holquist, "Role of Personality," 70.

66. Alekseev quoted, Nelipovich, "Naselenie okkupirovannykh territorii" (electronic unpaginated).

67. David M. Goldfrank, "Berlin, Congress of," *Encyclopedia of Russian History*, ed. James R. Millar, 4 vols. (New York: Macmillan, 2004), 1:144.

68. Michael A. Reynolds, *Shattering Empires: The Clash and Collapse of the Ottoman and Russian Empires 1908–1918* (Cambridge: Cambridge University Press, 2011), 109–115; Ronald Grigor Suny, *"They Can Live in the Desert but Nowhere Else": A History of the Armenian Genocide* (Princeton: Princeton University Press, 2015), 218.

69. Suny, *They Can Live*, 108–129, 166–172.

70. von Hagen, "Great War," 40–41.

71. Quoted, Suny, *They Can Live*, 230.

72. Reynolds, *Shattering*, 116–117.

73. Suny, *They Can Live*, 221–223, 230.

74. Ibid., 213; von Hagen, "Great War," 44.

75. Donald Bloxham, *The Great Game of Genocide: Imperialism, Nationalism, and the Destruction of the Ottoman Armenians* (Oxford: Oxford University Press, 2005), 72–74; Peter Holquist, "The Politics and Practice of the Russian Occupation of Armenia, 1915–February 1917," in *A Question of Genocide: Armenians and Turks at the End of the Ottoman Empire*, ed. Ronald Grigor Suny, Fatma Müge Goçek, and Norman M. Naimark (New York: Oxford University Press, 2011), 158.

76. Suny, *They Can Live*, 235–236.

77. Ibid., 236.

78. Bloxham, *The Great Game*, 75–76; Suny, *They Can Live*, 235.

79. Holquist, "Politics and Practice," 158–159.

80. Reynolds, *Shattering*, 144.

81. Bloxham, *The Great Game*, 78; Suny, *They Can Live*, 240–242.

82. Suny, *They Can Live*, 243–253.

83. Ibid., 255–258.

84. Ibid., 278–279.

85. Ibid., 259; Reynolds, *Shattering*, 146. See, also: Ronald Grigor Suny, "Truth in Telling: Reconciling Realities in the Genocide of the Ottoman Armenians," *American Historical Review* 114.4 (2009): 930–994.

86. Suny, *They Can Live*, 261.

87. Ibid., 283–284, 288–289.

88. Ibid., 309.

89. Ibid., 347; Bloxham, *The Great Game*, 1 and 10.

90. Suny, *They Can Live*, 262–263.

91. See: Henry Morgenthau, *Ambassador Morgenthau's Story* (New York: Doubleday, 1919); Johannes Lepsius, *Le rapport secret du Dr. Johannès Lepsius, président de la Deutsche orient-mission et de la Société germano-arménienne. Sur les massacres d'Arménie*, ed. and pref. René Pinon (Paris: Payot, 1918); *Archives du génocide des arméniens: Recueil de documents diplomatiques allemands: Extraits de Deutschland und Armenien (1914–1918)*, ed. Johannes Lepsius, trans. Marie-France Letenoux, pref. Alfred Grosser (Paris: Fayard, 1986); Johannes Lepsius, *Deutschland und Armenien, 1914–1918: Sammlung diplomatishcher Aktenstücke* (Potsdam: Tempelverlag, 1919); Johannes Lepsius, *Der Todesgang des armenischen Volkes: Bericht über das Schicksal des armenischen Volkes in der Türkei während des Weltkrieges*, 2nd ed. (Potsdam: Missionshandlung und Verlag, 1919). Comparison made by observers at the time, who also noted the difference in degree: Holquist, "Les violences," 211.

### PART II: CHAPTER 3

1. Lieutenant-General Nicholas N. Golovine, *The Russian Army in the World War* (New Haven: Yale University Press, for the Carnegie Endowment for International Peace, 1931), 222, 224–225; A. V. Oleinikov, "Poteri russkoi armii 1914–17," in *Rossiia v Pervoi mirovoi voine 1914–1918: Entsiklopediia v trekh tomakh*,

ed. A. K. Sorokin et al. (Moscow: ROSSPEN, 2014), 2:832–833; David R. Stone, *The Russian Army in the Great War: The Eastern Front, 1914–1917* (Lawrence: University Press of Kansas, 2015), 146–147.

2. Biblioteka Narodowa, Warsaw, Czytelnia dokumentów życia społecznego: *Aux peuples civilisés: Protestation* (Grodzisk, 7 août 1915): IA5 1915 Grodzisk.

3. "At Novo Georgievsk Just Before Fall," *New York Times* (August 25, 1915), 1.

4. Golovine, *Russian Army*, 222.

5. Krivoshein, quoted in *Sovet ministrov Rossiiskoi imperii v gody Pervoi mirovoi voiny: Bumagi A. N. Iakhontova*, ed. B. D. Gal'perina (St. Petersburg: Bulanin, 1999), 221 (August 16, 1915). Krivoshein was one of a group of technocratic bureaucrats serving in the Ministry of Agriculture, which during the war had responsibility for grain procurement. See Peter Holquist, "'In Accord with State Interests and the People's Wishes':The Technocratic Ideology of Imperial Russia's Resettlement Administration," *Slavic Review* 69.1 (2010): 151–179.

6. Peter Holquist, "Les violences de l'armée russe à l'encontre des Juifs en 1915: Causes et limites," in *Vers la guerre totale: Le tournant de 1914–15*, ed. John Horne (Paris: Tallandier, 2010), 212–213.

7. "Bark Petr L'vovich," in D. N. Shilov, *Gosudarstvennye deiateli Rossiiskoi imperii, 1802–1917: Biobibliograficheskii spravochnik* (St. Petersburg: Bulanin, 2001), 60–62.

8. *Sovet ministrov*, 163 (May 8, 1915). On Bark's interest in Jewish money and his well-founded anxieties, see Mark Levene, *War, Jews, and the New Europe: The Diplomacy of Lucien Wolf, 1914–1919* (Oxford: Oxford University Press, 1992), 59–60, 68–69.

9. Objections by Maklakov: *Sovet ministrov*, 169 (May 29, 1915). On Goujon: John P. McKay, *Pioneers for Profit: Foreign Entrepreneurship and Russian Industrialization, 1885–1913* (Chicago: University of Chicago Press, 1970), 53.

10. Academic A. Sobolevskii, personal letter June 16, 1915, quoted from GARF perlustration file, in Iu. I. Kir'ianov, *Sotsial'no-politicheskii protest rabochikh Rossii v gody Pervoi mirovoi voiny (iul' 1914–fevral' 1917 gg.)* (Moscow: Institut Rossiiskoi istorii RAN, 2005), 57.

11. Kir'ianov, *Sotsial'no-politicheskii protest*, 54–56.

12. *Sovet ministrov*, 178 (June 9, 1915).

13. Eric Lohr, *Nationalizing the Russian Empire: The Campaign Against Enemy Aliens During World War I* (Cambridge, MA: Harvard University Press, 2003), ch. 2; Iu. I. Kir'ianov, "'Maiskie besporiadki' 1915 g. v Moskve," *Voprosy istorii* 12 (1994):137–150; "Nemetskoe vliianie i nemetskoe zasil'e: Rech' F. I. Rodicheva po voprosu o komissii po vyrabotke mer dlia bor'by s nemetskim zasil'em v zasedanii 3 avg. 1915 goda," *Chertvertaia Gosudarstvennaia Duma. Fraktsiia narodnoi svobody, "voennye" sessii, 26 iiulia 1914 goda–3 sentiabria 1915 goda. Chast' 1: Otchet Fraktsii. Chast' 2: Rechi deputatov* (Petrograd: Ekateringofskoe Pechatnoe Delo, 1916), 85–91.

14. Maurice Paléologue, *La Russie des tsars pendant la Grande Guerre*, vol. 2: *3 juin 1915–18 août 1916*, 23rd ed. (Paris: Plon, 1922), 2 (June 11, 1915). On the collapse

of the tsar's charisma: Boris Kolonitskii, *"Tragicheskaia erotika": Obrazy imperator-skoi sem'i v gody Pervoi mirovoi voiny* (Moscow: NLO, 2010).

15. Paléologue, *La Russie*, 2:3 (June 13, 1915).
16. Ibid., 5 (June 16, 1915).
17. Ibid., 26–27 (July 18 and 19, 1915); William C. Fuller, Jr., *The Foe Within: Fantasies of Treason and the End of Imperial Russia* (Ithaca: Cornell University Press, 2006); *Sovet ministrov*, 176–177 (June 5, 1915).
18. Paléologue, *La Russie*, 2:5 (June 16 and 18, 1915); Raymond Pearson, *The Russian Moderates and the Crisis of Tsarism 1914–1917* (London: Macmillan, 1977), 41–42.
19. *Sovet ministrov*, 191–192 (June 26, 1915).
20. Ibid., 211 (August 6, 1915).
21. Shcherbatov on locusts; Krivoshein on ruin: ibid., 239 (August 24, 1915).
22. Ibid., 211–212 (August 6, 1915).
23. *The Jews in the Eastern War Zone* (New York: American Jewish Committee, 1916); Holquist, "Les violences," 215; R. Ganelin, "Evreiskii vopros vo vnutren-nei politike Rossii v 1915 godu," *Vestnik Evreiskogo universiteta v Moskve* 1(14) (1997): 43; Peter Gatrell, *A Whole Empire Walking: Refugees in Russia during World War I* (Bloomington: Indiana University Press, 1999), 147; Levene, *War, Jews, and the New Europe*, 49–69.
24. M. M. Vinaver, "Doklad po evreiskomu voprosu Tsentral'nogo Komiteta partii" (June 7, 1915), in *S"ezdy i konferentsii konstitutsionno-demokraticheskoi partii 1905–1920 gg.*, 3 vols. Vol. 3, bk. 1: 1915–1917 gg., ed. P. V. Volobuev et al. (Moscow: ROSSPEN, 2000), 52–80; Maklakov, response to Vinaver, "Doklad po evreis-komu voprosu," ibid., 89–91.
25. Cited, Ganelin, "Evreiskii vopros," 54.
26. Ibid., 56; Michael F. Hamm, "Liberalism and the Jewish Question: The Progressive Bloc," *Russian Review* 31.2 (1972): 163–172; R. Sh. Ganelin, "Gosudarstvennaia duma i antisemitskie tsirkuliary 1915–1916 gg.," *Vestnik Evreiskogo universiteta v Moskve* 3(10) (1995), 4–37; Aleksandr Mindlin, *Gosudarstvennaia Duma Rossiiskoi imperii i evreiskii vopros* (St. Petersburg: Aleteiia, 2014), 391–440.
27. *Sovet ministrov*, 189 (June 18, 1915).
28. Ibid., 199–200 (July 8, 1915).
29. Ibid., 202 (July 16, 1915).
30. Iakhontov, quoted in Golovine, *Russian Army*, 229–230.
31. Paléologue, *La Russie*, 2:5 (June 16 and 18, 1915), 17 (July 3, 1915), 32–33 (July 30, 1915).
32. Ibid., 35 (August 5, 1915). The charge was failing to provide adequate arms and ammunition: A. A. Polivanov, *Memuary: Iz dnevnikov i vospominanii po dolzhnosti Voennogo ministra i ego pomoshchnika 1907–1916 g.*, ed. A. M. Zaionchkovskii (Moscow: Vysshii voennyi redaktsionnyi sovet, 1924), 192; Norman Stone, *The Eastern Front, 1914–1917* (1975; London: Penguin, 1998), 25 ("Sukhomlinov, as a sort of uniformed Rasputin, belongs to the demonology of 1917"). Transferred

to house arrest three months later, he was rearrested in March 1917, sentenced to hard labor in September, commuted to a prison term, from which he was released in May 1918 when he turned seventy. Left for Finland, settled in Wannsee in Berlin, where he died in 1926: O. V. Chistiakov, "Sukhomlinov," in *Rossiia v Pervoi mirovoi voine*, 3:288–289. For the proceedings, see General V. A. Sukhomlinov: *Dnevnik, Pis'ma, Dokumenty: Sbornik dokumentov*, ed. E. G. Machikin (Moscow: ROSSPEN, 2014).

33. Paléologue, *La Russie*, 2:43–44 (August 14, 1915).

34. On the fall of Kovno, see *Source Records of the Great War*, ed. Charles F. Horne, 7 vols. (New York: National Alumni, 1923), 3:239.

35. Paléologue, *La Russie*, 2:50 (August 18, 1915); O. V. Chistiakov, "Grigor'ev," *Rossiia v Pervoi mirovoi voine*, 1:556–557.

36. *Monarkhiia pered krusheniem, 1914–1917: Bumagi Nikolaia II i drugie dokumenty: Stat'i V. P. Semennikova* (Moscow: Gosudarstvennoe izdatel'stvo, 1927), 270–275 ("Gosudarstvennaia duma i voennye porazheniia 1915 g."). On Shingarev's approach to Polivanov: Polivanov, *Memuary*, 231.

37. Paléologue, *La Russie*, 2:54–55 (August 25, 1915). On her role: K. A. Solov'ev, "Gosudarstvennye instituty," in *Rossiia v gody Pervoi mirovoi voiny: Ekonomicheskoe polozhenie, sotsial'nye protsessy, politicheskii krizis*, ed. Iu. A. Petrov (Moscow: ROSSPEN, 2014), 650.

38. Polivanov, *Memuary*, 203.

39. Kolonitskii, *Tragicheskaia erotika*.

40. Solov'ev, "Gosudarstvennye instituty," 651–655.

41. Paléologue, *La Russie*, 2:67–68 (September 6, 1915). Letter to Nikolai Nikolaevich also described in Polivanov, *Memuary*, 203–204.

42. Paléologue, *La Russie*, 2:53–54 (August 25, 1915).

43. Samarin, in *Sovet ministrov*, 216 (August 10, 1915).

44. Samarin, in ibid., 222 (August 16, 1915).

45. Ibid., 218 (August 11, 1915).

46. Polivanov, *Memuary*, 232–233.

47. *Sovet ministrov*, 232–237 (August 21, 1915), 233 (Sazonov: "*Tsar' verolomnyi*").

48. On Moscow city council resolution: Polivanov, *Memuary*, 221–222.

49. *Sovet ministrov*, 232–237 (August 21, 1915), 236 ("*Armii net, a vooruzhennyi narod*").

50. Ibid., 232–237 (August 21, 1915).

51. Polivanov, *Memuary*, 235–236.

52. M. V. Rodzianko, *The Reign of Rasputin: An Empire's Collapse*, trans. Catherine Zvegintzoff, intro. Sir Bernard Pares (London: A. M. Philpot, 1927), 173.

53. Pearson, *Moderates*, 30–31.

54. Ibid., 27; A. S. Tumanova, "Obshchestvennye organizatsii," in *Rossiia v gody Pervoi mirovoi voiny*, ed. Petrov, 424–445.

55. Pearson, *Moderates*, 32–33. Shut down April 1, 1915.

56. Ibid., 32–35; Peter Gatrell, *Russia's First World War: A Social and Economic History* (Harlow, UK: Pearson-Longman, 2005), 43–44; O. R. Airapetov, "Voenno-promyshlennye komitety," in *Rossiia v Pervoi mirovoi voine*, 1:390–393; Lewis H. Siegelbaum, *The Politics of Industrial Mobilization in Russia, 1914–17: A Study of the War-Industries Committees* (London: Macmillan, 1983).

57. Pearson, *Moderates*, 38.

58. Polivanov, *Memuary*, 206; Gatrell, *Russia's First World War*, 40–42.

59. A. P. Korelin, "Sozdanie sistemy voenno-reguliruiushchikh organov i samoor-ganizatsiia predprinimatel'skoi sredy," in *Rossiia v gody Pervoi mirovoi voiny*, ed. Petrov, 117–166; *Zhurnaly osobogo soveshchaniia: Dlia obsuzhdeniia i ob"edineniia meropriiatii po oborone gosudarstva (osoboe soveshchanie po oborone gosudarstva), 1915–1918*, 3 vols., ed. Iu. A. Petrov et al. (Moscow: ROSSPEN, 2013).

60. Polivanov, *Memuary*, 237.

61. Gatrell, *Russia's First World War*, 90–95.

62. K. A. Solov'ev, "Progressivnyi blok: Popytka konsolidatsii konservativnykh i liberal'nykh sil," in *Rossiia v gody Pervoi mirovoi voiny*, ed. Petrov, 689–697.

63. Polivanov, *Memuary*, 222–223.

64. Ibid., 219–221; Pearson, *Moderates*, 49–54.

65. *Sovet ministrov*, 244–249 (August 26, 1915); F. A. Gaida, "Progressivnyi blok," in *Rossiia v Pervoi mirovoi voine*, 2:868.

66. *Sovet ministrov*, 249.

67. Ibid., 253–255.

68. Paléologue, *La Russie*, 2:72 (September 15, 1915).

69. *Sovet Ministrov*, 248–249 (August 26, 1915): Samarin's opinion of Miliukov; Sazonov, by contrast, called Miliukov a "great bourgeois," concerned only to protect the interests of capital.

70. Pearson, *Moderates*, 58.

71. *Sovet ministrov*, 260 (September 2, 1915); 264 (September 5, 1915); also, Kir'ianov, *Sotsial'no-politicheskii protest*, 119–120.

72. Paléologue, *La Russie*, 2:76 (September 20, 1915); Pearson, *Moderates*, 60–61.

73. *Sovet ministrov*, 280–281 (September 25, 1915).

74. Ibid., 273 (September 18, 1915), 297 (November 17, 1915).

75. Ibid., 267–269 (September 11, 1915).

76. Ibid., 271–284 (September 13, 18, 22, 23, 25, 1915, October 2, 1915).

77. Ibid., 273, 291 (September 13 and October 13, 1915).

### PART II: CHAPTER 4

1. Mark von Hagen, "The Great War and the Mobilization of Ethnicity in the Russian Empire," in *Post-Soviet Political Order: Conflict and State Building*, ed. Barnett Rubin and Jack Snyder (London and New York: Routledge, 1998), 38–44.

2. William W. Hagen, *Germans, Poles, and Jews: The Nationality Conflict in the Prussian East, 1772–1914* (Chicago: University of Chicago Press, 1980), 168.

3. Prof. A. L. Pogodin, "Russko-pol'skie otnosheniia," *Birzhevye vedomosti*, no. 14257 (July 18, 1914), 1.

4. General-Ad"iutant Nikolai, "Vozzvanie Verkhovnogo Glavnokomanduiu-shchego—Poliaki!" (dated August 1, 1914), *Voennyi sbornik* 12 (December 1914): 205–206. For texts of both German and Russian appeals and summaries of press coverage, see *Novoe zveno*, no. 32 (August 2, 1914), 15–17. On the popular level: "Poliaki!," *Niva*, no. 33 (August 16, 1914), 641. On authorship: A. Iu. Bakhturina, "Vozzvanie k poliakam 1 avgusta 1914 g. i ego avtory," *Voprosy istorii* 8 (1998): 134. On the reaction of Polish political leaders to the Appeal, see Baron B. E. Nol'de, "Politika Romana Dmovskogo," in *Dalekoe i blizkoe: Istoricheskie ocherki* (Paris: Sovremennye zapiski, 1930), 108–114.

5. Imanuel Geiss, *Der polnische Grenzstreifen 1914–1918: Ein Beitrag zur deutschen Kriegszielpolitik im Ersten Weltkrieg* (Lübeck and Hamburg: Matthiesen, 1960), 23; *Nashi vragi: Obzor deistvii Chrezvychainoi sledstvennoi kommissii s 29 aprelia 1915 g. po 1 ianvaria 1916 g.*, 2 vols. (Petrograd: Senatskaia tip., 1916), 1: 320. On November 5, 1916, the Germans occupying Poland issued a decree promising to create "an independent state with a hereditary monarchy and a constitution": "Manifest über die Errichtung des Königreichs Polen," in *Amtliche Kriegs-Depeschen: Nach Berichten des Wolff'schen Telegr.-Bureaus*, vol. 5 (Berlin: Nationaler Verlag, 1917), available at http://www.stahlgewitter.com/16_11_05.htm (accessed Sept. 13, 2016). Maurice Paléologue, *La Russie des tsars pendant la Grande Guerre*, vol. 3: *19 août 1916–17 mai 1917* (Paris: Plon, 1922), 77 (November 8, 1916).

6. *New York Times* (August 18, 1914), 2. Prusin says the proclamation, though "meaningless" in practical terms, was intended by the Russians to deflect Polish nationalism away from its Russian target and onto the Jews, a strategy he claims was successful: Alexander Victor Prusin, *Nationalizing a Borderland: War, Ethnicity, and Anti-Jewish Violence in East Galicia, 1914–1920* (Tuscaloosa: University of Alabama Press, 2005), 6.

7. Prof. Iu. Kulakovskii, Kiev, August 8, 1914, to Ee Prev-vu E. P. Kulakovskaia, Pushkino: GARF, f. 102, op. 265, d. 992, l. 1191.

8. "Vash S. Koval…", Vil'na, August 10, 1914, to Ego Prev-vu P. G. Byval'kevich, Petersburg: GARF, f. 102, op. 265, d. 993, ll. 1217–12170b.

9. D. Khomiakov, Moscow, November 30, 1914, to Count I. L. Morinoki, Riga: GARF, f. 102, op. 265, d. 1000, l. 1972.

10. V, n. p., (n.d.), to Ee Prev E. A. Sokolova, Moscow: GARF, f. 102, op. 265, d. 1002, l. 2190.

11. Princess Shakhovskaia, Piukhtitsa, Estliand Gub., August 18, 1914, to Ego Prev. V. A. Evreinov, Petrograd: GARF, f. 102, op. 265, d. 993, l. 1299.

12. General-Ad"iutant Nikolai, "Vozzvanie," 207–208 (the terms are *narodnost'* and *inozemtsy*). On motive for second appeal: M. K. Lemke, *250 dnei v tsarskoi Stavke (25 sent. 1915–2 iiulia 1916)* (Petersburg: Gosudarstvennoe Izdatel'stvo, 1920), 15.

13. Allan K. Wildman, *The End of the Russian Imperial Army*, 2 vols. (Princeton: Princeton University Press, 1980, 1987), 1:103.

14. Eugeniusz de Henning-Michaelis, *Burza dziejowa: Pamiętnik z wojny światowej 1914–1917*, 2 vols. (Warsaw: Gebethner and Wolff, 1928), 1:25, 27.

15. Władysław Goździkowski, *Co każdy Polak o obecnej wojnie wiedzieć ma i czynić powinien*, 4th ed. (Piotrków: Druk. Państwowa, 1915), 28, 11–12.

16. Bakhturina, "Vozzvanie k poliakam," 133. On the suspiciously high percentage of German surnames among Russian officials in Poland: "Pokazaniia A. R. Lednitskogo, 27 sentiabria 1917 g.," in *Padenie tsarskogo rezhima: Stenograficheskie otchety doprosov i pokazanii, dannykh v 1917 g. v Chrezvychainoi sledstvennoi komissii Vremennogo pravitel'stva*, ed. P. E. Shchegolev, 7 vols. (Moscow and Leningrad: Gosizdatel'stvo, 1924–1927), 7:239.

17. Aleksander Lednicki, *Pamiętnik 1914–1918*, ed. Zbigniew Koziński (Cracow: Nakladem Biblioteki Jagiellońskiej, 1994). On Lednicki (1866–1934), see the obituary: Paul Milyukov and W. B., "Alexander Lednicki," *Slavonic and East European Review* 13.39 (1935): 677–680.

18. "Pokazaniia A. R. Lednitskogo," 239–241.

19. Zasedanie pervoe. 27 ianvaria 1915 g. *Gosudarstvennaia Duma. Stenograficheskie otchety*. Chetvertyi sozyv. Sessiia tret'ia. Zasedaniia 1–3 (27–29 ianvaria 1915 g.) (Petrograd: Gosudarstvennaia tipografiia, 1915), col. 5.

20. Maurice Paléologue, *La Russie des tsars pendant la Grande Guerre*, vol. 2: *3 juin 1915–18 août 1916*, 23rd ed. (Paris: Plon, 1922), 92 (October 15, 1915); 95 (October 28, 1915).

21. Zasedanie pervoe. 27 ianvaria 1915 g., col. 7 (*narodnosti*), 10, 14.

22. Ibid., col. 28 (*narody*), 31, 33, 34.

23. Ibid., col. 63.

24. Ibid., col. 50–52.

25. Ibid., col. 45–46 (*natsional'nye idealy*).

26. G. I. Il'iashchuk and V. I. Miller, "Chkheidze," in *Politicheskie deiateli Rossii 1917: Biograficheskii slovar'*, ed. P. V. Volobuev (Moscow: Bol'shaia rossiiskaia entsiklopediia, 1993), 353–355.

27. Zasedanie pervoe. 27 ianvaria 1915 g., col. 42–44. Socialists from the neutral countries of Sweden, Norway, Denmark, and Holland met in Copenhagen (January 17–18, 1915) in order to restore the Second International. They resolved to appeal to their governments to intervene between the belligerent powers, to hasten the end of the war.

28. See Laura Engelstein, "The Old Slavophile Steed: Failed Nationalism and the Philosophers' Jewish Problem," in *Slavophile Empire: Imperial Russia's Illiberal Path* (Ithaca: Cornell University Press, 2009).

29. Laura Engelstein, "Against the Grain: Russians in Defense of the Jews," in *On Not Being an Anti-Semite: Exemplary Cases from Russia, Ukraine, and Poland* (Waltham, MA: Brandeis University Press, forthcoming).

30. Paléologue, *La Russie*, 2:155 (January 21, 1916); on munitions supply and losses, also 154–155 (January 19, 1916).

31. Lieutenant-General Nicholas N. Golovine, *The Russian Army in the World War* (New Haven: Yale University Press, for the Carnegie Endowment for

International Peace, 1931), 240–241; Norman Stone, *The Eastern Front, 1914–1917* (1975; London: Penguin, 1998), 227–232. On Kuropatkin's military career: V. P. Ponomarev, "Kuropatkin," in *Rossiia v Pervoi mirovoi voine 1914–1918: Entsiklopediia v trekh tomakh*, ed. A. K. Sorokin et al. (Moscow: ROSSPEN, 2014), 2:191–194.

32. Golovine, *Russian Army*, 241–242; Stone, *Eastern Front*, 245–254.

33. Stone, *Eastern Front*, 265–266.

34. Ibid., 279–280.

35. Golovine, *Russian Army*, 242, 244 (quote).

36. "Khronologiia sobytii, sviazannykh s vosstaniem Kirgizov v 1916 godu," in *Vosstanie 1916 goda: Dokumenty i materialy*, ed. K. I. Mambetaliev (Bishkek: Abykeev, 2015), 243–247. On the uprising, see Part 4, ch. 6.

37. D. A. Amanzholova, ed., "'Takoe upravlenie gosudarstvom—nedopustimo': Doklad A. F. Kerenskogo na zakrytom zasedanii Gosudarstvennoi dumy. Dekabr' 1916 g.," *Istoricheskii arkhiv* 2 (1997): 4–22, 7 ("*takoe upravlenie gosudarstvom—nedopustimo*").

38. Figures vary: Golovine, *Russian Army*, 244 (over a million killed and wounded, over 200,000 taken captive); G. F. Krivosheev et al., *Rossiia i SSSR v voinakh XX veka: Kniga poter'* (Moscow: Veche, 2010), 71 (500,000 casualties).

39. Guchkov to Alekseev (August 15, 1916), from *Monarkhiia pered krusheniem, 1914–1917: Bumagi Nikolaia II i drugie dokumenty: Stat'i V. P. Semennikova* (Moscow: Gosudarstvennoe izdatel'stvo, 1927), 282; quoted, Golovine, *Russian Army*, 246; Paléologue, *La Russie*, 3:44–45 (October 9, 1916).

40. Peter Gatrell, *Russia's First World War: A Social and Economic History* (Harlow, UK: Pearson-Longman, 2005), 71; A. B. Astashov and V. P. Buldakov, "Massovye dvizheniia v 1914–1916 gg.," in *Rossiia v gody Pervoi mirovoi voiny: Ekonomicheskoe polozhenie, sotsial'nye protsessy, politicheskii krizis*, ed. Iu. A. Petrov (Moscow: ROSSPEN, 2014), 725. Figures differ, but relative proportions agree.

41. Astashov and Buldakov, "Massovye dvizheniia," 724–725, 732.

42. Iu. I. Kir'ianov, *Sotsial'no-politicheskii protest rabochikh Rossii v gody Pervoi mirovoi voiny (iul' 1914–fevral' 1917 gg.)* (Moscow: Institut Rossiiskoi istorii RAN, 2005), 45, 49.

43. Ibid., 61.

44. Ibid., 57–60.

45. *Sovet ministrov Rossiiskoi imperii v gody Pervoi mirovoi voiny: Bumagi A. N. Iakhontova*, ed. B. D. Gal'perina (St. Petersburg: Bulanin, 1999), 217–218 (August 11, 1915).

46. Kir'ianov, *Sotsial'no-politicheskii protest*, 61–62, 64–65; Astashov and Buldakov, "Massovye dvizheniia," 729.

47. Kir'ianov, *Sotsial'no-politicheskii protest*, 65–67.

48. *Sovet ministrov*, 244–245 (August 26, 1915), 260 (September 2, 1915), 264 (September 5, 1915), 280–281 (September 25, 1915), 318 (February 7, 1916, on Putilov).

49. Gatrell, *Russia's First World War*, 71.

50. Paléologue, *La Russie*, 3:66–67 (October 31, 1916); 78 (November 9, 1916).

51. Astashov and Buldakov, "Massovye dvizheniia," 735–741.

52. Barbara Alpern Engel, "Not by Bread Alone: Subsistence Riots in Russia during World War I," *Journal of Modern History* 69.4 (1997): 696–721.

53. Astashov and Buldakov, "Massovye dvizheniia," 735–741; Gatrell, *Russia's First World War*, 164–170.

54. Boris Kolonitskii, *"Tragicheskaia erotika": Obrazy imperatorskoi sem'i v gody Pervoi mirovoi voiny* (Moscow: NLO, 2010).

55. S. P. Mel'gunov, *Na putiakh k dvortsovomu perevorotu: Zagovory pered revoliutsiei 1917 goda* (Paris: Rodnik, 1931). On actual plots, see Semion Lyandres, *The Fall of Tsarism: Untold Stories of the February Revolution* (Oxford: Oxford University Press, 2013), ch. 13.

56. People mentioned this example explicitly: Paléologue, *La Russie*, 3:118 (December 23, 1916).

57. Paléologue, *La Russie*, 2:170–171 (February 5, 1916).

58. Ibid., 232 (March 30, 1916).

59. Ibid., 236 (April 2, 1916).

60. Ibid., 194–196 (February 22, 1916).

61. Quoted, ibid., 328 (August 3, 1916).

62. Ibid., 179–180 (February 13, 1916).

63. Ibid., 281–282 (May 31, 1916). More on the alleged Jewish-German influence: Paléologue, *La Russie*, 3:58 (October 21, 1916).

64. The Jewish Manus, originally from Odessa, converted to Orthodoxy, was active in the stock market, invested in railroads, and was investigated in March 1916 by the intelligence service for suspicious ties to Germany, with which he had business connections; he was shot by the Bolsheviks in 1918. Rubinshtein, founder of the Russo-French Bank and a stockholder in *Novoe vremia*, fell out with Rasputin in March 1916; in July he was arrested on suspicion of treason, but freed from exile on Alexandra's intervention. V. Iu. Gessen, "Ignatii Porfir'evich Manus: Promyshlennik, bankovskii i birzhevoi deiatel'," online at: http://www .hist.msu.ru/Banks/sources/gessen/gessen.htm (accessed February 2, 2017). For Krivoshein's remark, see previous chapter.

65. Paléologue, *La Russie*, 3:2 (August 19, 1916).

66. Ibid., 41–42 (October 5, 1916).

67. Ibid., 60–61 (October 24, 1916).

68. Ibid., 75 (November 5, 1916).

69. Ibid., 84–86 (November 13, 1916).

70. Kolonitskii, *Tragicheskaia erotika*, 289.

71. Paléologue, *La Russie*, 3:87–88 (November 14, 1916).

72. "Miliukov's Speech in the Duma" (November 1/14, 1916), in *Documents of Russian History 1914–1917*, ed. Frank Alfred Golder, trans. Emanuel Aronsberg (New York: Century, 1927), 154–166. Russian original: A. S. Rezanov, *Shturmovoi*

*signal P. N. Miliukova: S prilozheniem polnogo teksta rechi, proiznesennoi Miliukovym v zasedanii Gosud. Dumy 1 noiabria 1916 g.* (Paris: Izdanie avtora, 1924), online at http://www.pravoslavie.ru/jurnal/625.htm (accessed September 13, 2010). Quotes here are in my translation. The ministers he had in mind were Shcherbatov, Samarin, Krivoshein, Kharitonov, Polivanov, and Sazonov: "Miliukov's Speech in the Duma," 157 (note). See Kolonitskii, *Tragicheskaia erotika*, 289–293.

73. Kolonitskii, *Tragicheskaia erotika*, 289.
74. Ibid., 290.
75. Ibid., 292; Paléologue, *La Russie*, 3:89–90 (November 16, 1916).
76. Paléologue, *La Russie*, 3:90–91 (November 17, 1916); 97–98 (November 23, 1916); 100 (November 25, 1916).
77. Ibid., 105 (December 1, 1916).
78. Andrei Belyi (Boris Bugaev), *Peterburg: Roman v vos'mi glavakh s prologom i epilogom* (Petrograd: Stasiulevich, 1916).
79. Kolonitskii, *Tragicheskaia erotika*, 9–10.
80. Teffi (Nadezhda Buchinskaia, née Lokhvitskaia), "Rasputin" (1932), in Teffi, *Subtly Worded and Other Stories*, trans. Anne Marie Jackson et al. (London: Pushkin Press, 2014), 100, 136. On Rozanov, see Laura Engelstein, *The Keys to Happiness: Sex and the Search for Modernity in Fin-de-Siècle Russia* (Ithaca: Cornell University Press, 1992), ch. 8.
81. Paléologue, *La Russie*, 3:6 (August 29, 1916); Kolonitskii, *Tragicheskaia erotika*, ch. 5.
82. Paléologue, *La Russie*, 3:126 (December 29, 1916).
83. "Purishkevich's Speech in the Duma," in Golder, *Documents*, 166–175, 174 (quote). Source given as *Revue de Paris*, vol. 5 (Paris, 1923), 721–746.
84. Paléologue, *La Russie*, 3:106 (December 2, 1916), 109 (December 9, 1916).
85. Joseph T. Fuhrmann, *Rasputin: The Untold Story* (Hoboken, NJ: John Wiley, 2013), 228–231; Douglas Smith, *Rasputin: Faith, Power, and the Twilight of the Romanovs* (New York: Farrar, Straus and Giroux, 2016), 590.
86. Based on Fuhrmann, *Rasputin*; see also Smith, *Rasputin*.
87. Paléologue, *La Russie*, 3:129 (December 31, 1916); "Plot to Kill Rasputin," in Golder, *Documents*, 175–177.
88. "V. A. Maklakov, Ia. E. Povolotskii i Ko." (Paris, 1923), in V. M. Purishkevich, *Iz dnevnika V. M. Purishkevicha: Ubiistvo Rasputina* (1918; Paris: Povolotskii, 1923), 3–10. On Purishkevich's earlier scurrilous persona: Engelstein, *The Keys to Happiness*, 313. Also: V. Pourichkevitch, *Comment j'ai tué Raspoutine: Pages du journal, traduit du russe* (Paris: Povolozky, 1924). This edition does not mention that it is a reprint. The Paris publisher of the "diary" (actually memoir) of this rabid anti-Semite was Jacques Povolozky (Povolotskii), born Iakov Benderskii in Odessa, who took French citizenship in 1909 and published Russian authors in the original and in French. See https://fantlab.ru/publisher6511.

### PART III: CHAPTER I

1. A. A. Bublikov, *Russkaia revoliutsiia: Ee nachalo, arest Tsaria, perspektivy, vpechatle-niia i mysli ochevidtsa i uchastnika* (New York: s.n., 1918), 8, 9.

2. Baron B. E. Nol'de, *Dalekoe i blizkoe: Istoricheskie ocherki* (Paris: Sovremennye zapiski, 1930), 118.

3. Basil [Vasilii] Maklakov, "On the Fall of Tsardom [review of Bernard Pares]," *Slavonic and East European Review* 18.52 (1939): 76 (blames Alexandra).

4. William Henry Chamberlin, *The Russian Revolution, 1917–1921*, 2 vols. (1935; New York: Grosset & Dunlap, 1965), 1:66–67 (Miliukov quote). Line from Pushkin's *The Captain's Daughter* (*Kapitanskaia dochka*, 1836): "*bunt bessmyslennyi i besposhchadnyi.*"

5. Iu. I. Kir'ianov, *Sotsial'no-politicheskii protest rabochikh Rossii v gody Pervoi mirovoi voiny (iul' 1914 – fevral' 1917 gg.)* (Moscow: Institut Rossiiskoi istorii RAN, 2005), 78–82, 100–101; Ziva Galili, *The Menshevik Leaders in the Russian Revolution: Social Realities and Political Strategies* (Princeton: Princeton University Press, 1989), 15.

6. Tsuyoshi Hasegawa, *The February Revolution: Petrograd, 1917* (Seattle: University of Washington Press, 1981), 215–216. This chapter relies heavily on Hasegawa's account.

7. Maurice Paléologue, *La Russie des tsars pendant la Grande Guerre*, vol. 3: *19 août 1916–17 mai 1917* (Paris: Plon, 1922), 213 (March 6, 1917).

8. Igor V. Narskii, *Zhizn' v katastrofe: Budni naseleniia Urala v 1917–1922 gg.* (Moscow: ROSSPEN, 2001), 170–171.

9. Hasegawa, *February Revolution*, 215–221.

10. Ibid., 221–224. In November 1918, it was renamed Insurrection Square (*Ploshchad' Vosstaniia*), in honor of its role in the February days. In 1937 the monument was removed; the church was dismantled in 1941.

11. A. P. Balk, "Gibel' tsarskogo Petrograda: Fevral'skaia revoliutsiia glazami gra-donachal'nika A. P. Balka," *Russkoe proshloe* 1 (1991): 26. Balk mentions middle-class women and "few workers" on Nevskii; Wildman mentions "housewives," but says the crowds on February 23 did not contain middle-class people: Allan K. Wildman, *The End of the Russian Imperial Army*, 2 vols. (Princeton: Princeton University Press, 1980, 1987), 1:131.

12. Hasegawa, *February Revolution*, 224–225.

13. Ibid., 226–229.

14. Ibid., 232–234; on Cossack reluctance, see Wildman, *Army*, 1:132.

15. Hasegawa, *February Revolution*, 235–236.

16. N. N. Sukhanov, *The Russian Revolution 1917*, ed. and trans. Joel Carmichael (Princeton: Princeton University Press, 1984), 16, 19 (quote); A. A. Kornikov, "Sukhanov (Gimmer)," in *Politicheskie deiateli Rossii 1917: Biograficheskii slovar'*, ed. P. V. Volobuev (Moscow: Bol'shaia rossiiskaia entsiklopediia, 1993), 311–312.

17. Hasegawa, *February Revolution*, 236–239; Wildman, *Army*, 1:142–143 (the Volynskii); Steve A. Smith, "Petrograd in 1917: The View from Below," in

*Revolutionary Russia: New Approaches*, ed. Rex A. Wade (New York: Routledge, 2004), 17 (200,000 for February 24).

18. Hasegawa, *February Revolution*, 243–245.

19. Original words by Wacław Święcicki (1848–1900) to commemorate the 1863–1864 Polish Uprising against tsarist rule; Russian text by Bolshevik Gleb Krzhizhanovskii (1872–1959) while in prison in 1897. Became the anthem of the 1905 Polish insurrection, hence known as the *Warszawianka 1905*. Available at http://a-pesni.org/starrev/varsavianka.htm (accessed June 19, 2015).

20. Tsuyoshi Hasegawa, "*Gosudarstvennost', obshchestvennost'* and *klassovost'*: Crime, the Police, and the State in the Russian Revolution in Petrograd," *Canadian-American Slavic Studies* 35.2–3 (2001): 157–188.

21. Sukhanov, *Russian Revolution*, 19 (Cossack chopped off policeman's hand); Wildman, *Army*, 1:133 (account of the incident vary, but all agree it made a dramatic impression).

22. Chamberlin, *Russian Revolution*, 1:76–77; Hasegawa, *February Revolution*, 432.

23. For February 25, Hasegawa, *February Revolution*, ch. 14.

24. Point made by Wildman, *Army*, 1:136.

25. Edward T. Heald, *Witness to Revolution: Letters from Russia, 1916–1919*, ed. James B. Gidney (Kent, OH: Kent State University Press, [1972]), 52.

26. Wildman, *Army*, 1:124; 140 (map of locations).

27. Ibid., 139, 129 (companies comprised of soldiers brought back from the front to be trained as noncoms; they were considered the most reliable units to be used against civilian disturbances); Hasegawa, *February Revolution*, 269. Kirpichnikov turned against the Bolsheviks after October, but when he tried to join Kornilov's Volunteer Army, he was executed.

28. Sukhanov, *Russian Revolution*, 25.

29. Ibid., 26-27.

30. Ibid., 29; Hasegawa, *February Revolution*, 272 (different version: no crowd, but the soldiers fire directly at the police); Wildman, *Army*, 1:142.

31. Hasegawa, *February Revolution*, 273–274.

32. Ibid., 274.

33. Dokument 43: "'Protokol sobytii' Fevral'skoi revoliutsii" (February 27–March 4, 1917), in *Fevral'skaia revoliutsiia, 1917: Sbornik dokumentov i materialov*, ed. O. A. Shashkova (Moscow: RGGU, 1996), 110.

34. Hasegawa, *February Revolution*, 433 (quote).

35. Dokument 16: "Soobshchenie gazety *Utro Rossii* o sobytiiakh v Gosudarstvennoi dume" (February 26, 1917, published February 27), in *Fevral'skaia revoliutsiia*, 71–72.

36. Quoted, Dokument 43: "Protokol sobytii," in *Fevral'skaia revoliutsiia*, 111 (*poslednii oplot poriadka*).

37. Hasegawa, *February Revolution*, 279–280.

38. Ibid., 281; Wildman, *Army*, 1:143–144.

39. V. B. Stankevich, *Vospominaniia, 1914–1919 g.* (Berlin: Ladyschnikow, 1920), 66.

40. Hasegawa, *February Revolution*, 281.

41. Ibid., 283–285.

42. Ibid., 287–288; Wildman, *Army*, 1:146.

43. Sukhanov, *Russian Revolution*, 44.

44. Viktor Shklovsky, *A Sentimental Journey: Memoirs, 1917–1922*, trans. Richard Sheldon (1923; Ithaca: Cornell University Press, 1984), 16.

45. Hasegawa, *February Revolution*, 294–295; Wildman, *Army*, 1:148–149.

46. Wildman, *Army*, 1:127–128; Shklovsky, *Sentimental Journey*, 15.

47. Hasegawa, *February Revolution*, 298–299.

48. Ibid., 298–302.

49. Dokument 43: "Protokol sobytii," in *Fevral'skaia revoliutsiia*, 112.

50. Until recently, historians have described the deputies as responding to the decree by then assembling in the Tauride Palace and proposing the special session: Hasegawa, *February Revolution*, 276. Hasegawa has now revised his own narrative to reflect information presented in A. B. Nikolaev, *Gosudarstvennaia Duma v Fevral'skoi revoliutsii: Ocherki istorii* (Riazan: Tribunskii, 2002); and A. B. Nikolaev, *Revoliutsiia i vlast': IV Gosudarstvennaia Duma 27 fevralia–3 marta 1917 goda* (St. Petersburg: RGPU, 2005). See Tsuyoshi Hasegawa, "Review of A. B. Nikolaev, *Revoliutsiia i vlast'*: How Has Nikolaev Changed the Interpretation of the February Revolution?" *Journal of Modern Russian History and Historiography* 6.1 (2013): 1–16; Tsuyoshi Hasegawa, "Could the February Revolution Have Been a Liberal Revolution?" (unpublished paper, 2016, courtesy of author). I follow the revisions he proposes. Further revisions of the narrative include a new emphasis on plans to unseat the monarchy on the part of Duma moderates before February 1917: Semion Lyandres, *The Fall of Tsarism: Untold Stories of the February 1917 Revolution* (Oxford: Oxford University Press, 2013), citing among other sources S. P. Mel'gunov, *Na putiakh k dvortsovomu perevorotu: Zagovory pered revoliutsiei 1917 goda* (Paris: Rodnik, 1931).

51. Quoted, Dokument 43: "Protokol sobytii," in *Fevral'skaia revoliutsiia*, 112.

52. Lyandres, *Fall of Tsarism*, 285.

53. Hasegawa, *February Revolution*, 353. On role of Progressive Bloc and public organizations, see Galili, *Menshevik Leaders*, 22–23; Dokument 43: "Protokol sobytii," in *Fevral'skaia revoliutsiia*, 113–115; Dokument 45: "Soobshchenie Vremennogo komiteta Gos. dumy o ego sostave" (February 27, 1917), in ibid., 148–49.

54. Hasegawa, "Review," 8–9; Hasegawa, "Could," 6–7; Dokument 43: "Protokol sobytii," in *Fevral'skaia revoliutsiia*, 117.

55. Dokument 43: "Protokol sobytii," in *Fevral'skaia revoliutsiia*, 119.

56. B. Maklakoff, "Vers la Révolution: La Russie de 1900 à 1917: Le Dénouement," *La Revue de Paris* 31.19 (October 1, 1924): 519.

57. On Protopopov: Raymond Pearson, *The Russian Moderates and the Crisis of Tsarism 1914–1917* (London: Macmillan, 1977), 128, 143.

58. Hasegawa, *February Revolution*, 303–304.

59. Ibid., 436; E. E. Petrova and K. O. Bitiukov, *Velikokniazheskaia oppozitsiia v Rossii 1915–1917 gg.* (St. Petersburg: Asterion, 2009), 157–158.
60. Dokument 43: "Protokol sobytii," in *Fevral'skaia revoliutsiia*, 115–117.
61. Hasegawa, *February Revolution*, 306, 308–309.
62. Dokument 43: "Protokol sobytii," in *Fevral'skaia revoliutsiia*, 119 (my translation); cf. "First Steps of the Temporary Committee of the State Duma," *Izvestiia Revoliutsionnoi Nedeli*, no. 2 (February 28, 1917), 1, in *The Russian Provisional Government 1917: Documents*, ed. Robert Paul Browder and Alexander F. Kerensky, 3 vols. (Stanford: Stanford University Press, 1961), 1:50. Cited in Galili, *Menshevik Leaders*, 22; Wildman, *Army*, 1:171.
63. Maklakoff, "Vers la Révolution," 517–518.
64. Dokument 43: "Protokol sobytii," in *Fevral'skaia revoliutsiia*, 120.
65. Bublikov, *Russkaia revoliutsiia*, 21, 22–23.
66. Hasegawa, "Could," 7–8.
67. Hasegawa, *February Revolution*, 367.
68. Death dates in D. N. Shilov, *Gosudarstvennye deiateli Rossiiskoi imperii 1802–1917: Biobibliograficheskii spravochnik* (St. Petersburg: Bulanin, 2001), 391 (Maklakov), 550 (Protopopov), 757 (Shtiurmer), 765 (Shcheglovitov).
69. Paul Avrich, *Kronstadt, 1921* (New York: Norton, 1974), 59; Wildman, *Army*, 1:234; Anthony F. Upton, *The Finnish Revolution, 1917–1918* (Minneapolis: University of Minnesota Press, 1980), 26–27.
70. Hasegawa, *February Revolution*, 363–364; V. D. Nabokov, "The Provisional Government," in *V. D. Nabokov and the Russian Provisional Government, 1917*, ed. Virgil D. Medlin and Steven L. Parsons (New Haven: Yale University Press, 1976), 41.
71. Quoted, Hasegawa, *February Revolution*, 354.
72. Sukhanov, *Russian Revolution*, 48.
73. Ibid., 40.
74. Hasegawa, *February Revolution*, 323–325.
75. Ibid., 327.
76. Dokument 43: "Protokol sobytii," in *Fevral'skaia revoliutsiia*, 112, 115.
77. *Fevral'skaia revoliutsiia*, 314 (notes).
78. On worker perceptions of the Duma, see Galili, *Menshevik Leaders*, 20. The Fourth Duma had contained twenty-two socialist deputies: five Bolshevik, seven Menshevik, and ten Laborite (*Trudovik*): Pearson, *Moderates*, 15.
79. This characterization from Galili, *Menshevik Leaders*, 27.
80. Hasegawa, *February Revolution*, 380–381.
81. Ibid., 340.
82. Boris I. Kolonitskii, "Kerensky," in *Critical Companion to the Russian Revolution, 1914–1921*, ed. Edward Acton, Vladimir Iu. Cherniaev, and William G. Rosenberg (Bloomington: Indiana University Press, 1997), 139–140.
83. Sukhanov, *Russian Revolution*, 50, 65.
84. Nabokov, "Provisional Government," 43–44 (scene from March 2).

85. Fedor Stepun, *Byvshee i nesbyvsheesia* (New York: Chekhov, 1956; St. Petersburg: Aleteiia; Moscow: Progress-Litera, 1994), 328.

86. On the Commission, see Wildman, *Army*, 1:168–169; Dokument 43: "Protokol sobytii," in *Fevral'skaia revoliutsiia*, 117.

87. Hasegawa, *February Revolution*, 336.

88. Quoted, ibid., 336.

89. Ibid., 342.

90. Dokument 23: "K naseleniiu Petrograda i Rossii ot Soveta rabochikh deputatov" (February 28, 1917), in *Fevral'skaia revoliutsiia*, 81–82.

91. Sukhanov, *Russian Revolution*, 74.

92. B. I. Kolonitskii, *Pogony i bor'ba za vlast' v 1917 godu* (St. Petersburg: Ostrov, 2001).

93. Hasegawa, *February Revolution*, 373.

94. Galili, *Menshevik Leaders*, 51 (officers' support for Duma).

95. Hasegawa, *February Revolution*, 374–375.

96. Ibid., 390.

97. Ibid., 376; Wildman, *Army*, 1:190.

98. Wildman, *Army*, 1:183. This was the night of February 28 to March 1.

99. Hasegawa, *February Revolution*, 437–438.

100. Ibid., 469–471.

101. Ibid., 445–446; Lyandres, *Fall of Tsarism*, 277–278.

102. Hasegawa, *February Revolution*, 440; Chamberlin, *Russian Revolution*, 1:90.

103. Hasegawa, *February Revolution*, 477; Wildman, *Army*, 1:207–208.

104. Wildman, *Army*, 1:212; *Fevral'skaia revoliutsiia*, 318–319 (note).

105. Wildman, *Army*, 1:211.

106. Ibid.; Hasegawa, *February Revolution*, 479–480, 482, 484.

107. Wildman, *Army*, 1:193 (including an SR from the motor vehicle division of the Red Cross and a Menshevik from the Finland Regiment); Hasegawa, *February Revolution*, 396; Dokument 30: "Iz protokola zasedaniia Petrogradskogo Soveta rabochikh i soldatskikh deputatov" (March 1, 1917), in *Fevral'skaia revoliutsiia*, 88–89.

108. Quoted in Hasegawa, *February Revolution*, 396.

109. Sukhanov, *Russian Revolution*, 80–82.

110. Hasegawa, *February Revolution*, 396.

111. Ibid., 400.

112. Shliapnikov, quoted, Hasegawa, *February Revolution*, 401. For an account of its genesis, see Wildman, *Army*, 1:182–189, same passage cited, 186, slightly different translation.

113. "Order No. 1" (March 1, 1917), in *Russian Provisional Government*, 2:848–849; "Prikaz No. 1 Petrogradskogo Soveta rabochikh i soldatskikh deputatov po garnizonu Petrogradskogo voennogo okruga" (March 1, 1917), in *Fevral'skaia revoliutsiia*, 89–90, 316 (note).

114. Dokument 43: "Protokol sobytii," in *Fevral'skaia revoliutsiia*, 127–128.

115. Hasegawa, *February Revolution*, 534–537; Chamberlin, *Russian Revolution*, 1:84.

116. Hasegawa, *February Revolution*, 413–414.

117. Dokument 43: "Protokol sobytii," in *Fevral'skaia revoliutsiia*, 130–131.

118. Hasegawa, *February Revolution*, 415–419; Dokument 43, "Protokol sobytii," in *Fevral'skaia revoliutsiia*, 131–132.

119. Hasegawa, *February Revolution*, 421.

120. "Order No. 1" (March 6, 1917), in *Russian Provisional Government*, 2:851–852.

121. *Fevral'skaia revoliutsiia*, 316 (note).

122. Hasegawa, "Could," 20.

123. Hasegawa, *February Revolution*, 383–384.

124. Ibid., 452–454.

125. "Speech of Miliukov in the Ekaterininskii Hall of the Tauride Palace," *Izvestiia Revoliutsionnoi Nedeli*, no. 6 (March 2, 1917), 1, in *Russian Provisional Government*, 1:129–133; quote, 130. These sentences cited in Hasegawa, *February Revolution*, 530, in slightly different translation. See, Dokument 53: "Rech' chlena Vremennogo Komiteta Gosudarstvennoi dumy P. N. Miliukova na mitinge v Tavricheskom dvortse ob obrazovanii Vremennogo pravitel'stva" (March 2, 1917), in *Fevral'skaia revoliutsiia*, 154–159; Paul Miliukov, *Political Memoirs, 1905–1917*, ed. Arthur P. Mendel, trans. Carl Goldberg (Ann Arbor: University of Michigan Press, 1967), 406.

126. "Statement of Miliukov Concerning His Reference to the Dynasty in His Ekaterininskii Hall Speech," *Izvestiia Revoliutsionnoi Nedeli*, no. 4 (March 23, 1917), 3, in *Russian Provisional Government*, 1:133.

127. Hasegawa, *February Revolution*, 508.

128. Chamberlin, *Russian Revolution*, 1:90–91; Wildman, *Army*, 1:208–209.

129. Hasegawa, *February Revolution*, 514–515.

130. Wildman, *Army*, 1:212 (tsar's designation of L'vov).

131. Both quotes, Chamberlin, *Russian Revolution*, 1:95.

132. "The Refusal of the Grand Duke Mikhail Aleksandrovich to Assume the Supreme Power Pending the Determination in the Constituent Assembly of the Form of Government and the New Fundamental Laws of the Russian State," in *Russian Provisional Government*, 1:116. Cited in Wildman, *Army*, 1:215; Lyandres, *Fall of Tsarism*, 284–285 (claims Rodzianko had contemplated the removal of Nicholas even before 1917).

133. On absence of legal grounds: Nabokov, "The Provisional Government," 71. On Nicholas perceived as traitor to country: Paléologue, *La Russie*, 3:272 (March 24, 1917).

134. Nabokov, "Provisional Government," 109.

135. Chamberlin, *Russian Revolution*, 1:96–97.

136. Nabokov, "Provisional Government," 43 (quote), 49–53; Baron B. E. Nol'de, "V. D. Nabokov in 1917," in *V. D. Nabokov and the Russian Provisional Government*, 18–20 (trans. of B. E. Nol'de, "V. D. Nabokov v 1917 g.," *Arkhiv russkoi revoliutsii*, ed. I. V. Gessen [Berlin, 1922]), 7:7–8).

137. Nabokov, "Provisional Government," 35.

## PART III: CHAPTER 2

1. "A. F. Kerensky's Statement in the Soviet of Workers' Deputies," *Izvestiia Revoliutsionnoi Nedeli*, no. 7 (March 3, 1917), 1, in *The Russian Provisional Government, 1917: Documents*, ed. Robert Paul Browder and Alexander F. Kerensky, 3 vols. (Stanford: Stanford University Press, 1961), 1:128–129; Tsuyoshi Hasegawa, *The February Revolution: Petrograd, 1917* (Seattle: University of Washington Press, 1981), 540–541.

2. Boris I. Kolonitskii, "Kerensky," in *Critical Companion to the Russian Revolution, 1914–1921*, ed. Edward Acton, Vladimir Iu. Cherniaev, and William G. Rosenberg (Bloomington: Indiana University Press, 1997), 141.

3. Tsuyoshi Hasegawa, "Could the February Revolution Have Been a Liberal Revolution?" (unpublished paper, 2016, courtesy of author), 24–29.

4. Hasegawa, "Could," 29–32; Dokument 55: "Zhurnal zasedaniia Vremennogo pravitel'stva No. 2" (March 2, 1917), in *Fevral'skaia revoliutsiia, 1917: Sbornik dokumentov i materialov*, ed. O. A. Shashkova (Moscow: RGGU, 1996), 161–163 (Hasegawa, "Could," 29, citing Nikolaev, notes that the correct date is March 3).

5. "From the Provisional Government," *Izvestiia Revoliutsionnoi Nedeli*, no. 7 (March 3, 1917), 1, in *Russian Provisional Government*, 1:135–136.

6. William Henry Chamberlin, *The Russian Revolution, 1917–1921*, 2 vols. (1935; New York: Grosset & Dunlap, 1965), 1:88.

7. "Order of the Temporary Committee of the State Duma, March 2, 1917," *Izvestiia Revoliutsionnoi Nedeli*, no. 7 (March 3, 1917), 1, in *Russian Provisional Government*, 1:134.

8. B. I. Kolonitskii, "Fevral'skaia? Burzhuaznaia? Demokraticheskaia? Revoliutsiia...," *Neprikosnovennyi zapas: Debaty o politike i kul'ture* 2 (22) (Moscow: NLO, 2002): 82–88.

9. Kolonitskii, "Kerensky," 138–139.

10. V. D. Nabokov, "The Provisional Government," in *V. D. Nabokov and the Russian Provisional Government, 1917*, ed. Virgil D. Medlin and Steven L. Parsons (New Haven: Yale University Press, 1976), 77, 76, respectively; Kolonitskii, "Kerensky," 138–149.

11. Kolonitskii, "Kerensky," 139–140; see also Chamberlin, *Russian Revolution*, 1:149–150.

12. Chamberlin, *Russian Revolution*, 1:103; Maurice Paléologue, *La Russie des tsars pendant la Grande Guerre*, vol. 3: *19 août 1916–17 mai 1917* (Paris: Plon, 1922), 269–270 (March 24, 1917).

13. Paléologue, *La Russie*, 3:273 (March 25, 1917).

14. Officially endorsed by the State Senate, which no longer had the legal right to do so: see B. Maklakoff, "Vers la Révolution: La Russie de 1900 à 1917: Le Dénouement," *La Revue de Paris* 31.19 (October 1, 1924): 513.

15. Nabokov, "Provisional Government," 62–63.

16. "The Proclamation of the Provisional Government to the Poles" (March 16, 1917), in *Russian Provisional Government*, 1:321–323; also 334–335.

17. Entire paragraph based on Chamberlin, *Russian Revolution*, 1:103–105.

18. I.A.Tropov, *Revoliutsiia i provintsiia: Mestnaia vlast' v Rossii (fevral'–oktiabr' 1917 g.)* (St. Petersburg: Evropeiskii dom, 2011), 119–156; N. N. Kabytova, *Vlast' i obshchestvo v rossiiskoi provintsii v revoliutsii 1917 goda* (Samara: Samarskii universitet, 2002); Liudmila Novikova, "The Russian Revolution from a Provincial Perspective," *Kritika* 16.4 (2015): 769–785.

19. Matthew Rendle, "The Problem of the 'Local' in Revolutionary Russia: Moscow Province, 1914–22," in *Russia's Home Front in War and Revolution, 1914–22: Russia's Revolution in Regional Perspective*, ed. Sarah Badcock, Liudmila G. Novikova, and Aaron B. Retish (Bloomington: Slavica, 2015), 23.

20. Novikova, "The Russian Revolution from a Provincial Perspective," 771–773.

21. Igor V. Narskii, *Zhizn' v katastrofe: Budni naseleniia Urala v 1917–1922 gg.* (Moscow: ROSSPEN, 2001), 36.

22. Sarah Badcock, "Structures and Practices of Power: 1917 in Nizhegorod and Kazan' Provinces," in *Russia's Home Front in War and Revolution*, ed. Sarah Badcock et al., 355.

23. Narskii, *Zhizn'*, 179, quoting *Orenburgskaia zhizn'* (March 3, 1917).

24. Narskii, *Zhizn'*, 184–185.

25. Ibid., 34–35.

26. Ibid., 180–181.

27. Quoted, Allan K. Wildman, *The End of the Russian Imperial Army*, 2 vols. (Princeton: Princeton University Press, 1980, 1987), 1:218.

28. Wildman, *Army*, 1:234.

29. Quoted, ibid., 245.

30. Quoted, ibid., 260.

31. Lenin, "Peace Without Annexations and the Independence of Poland as Slogans of the Day in Russia," *Sotsial-demokrat*, no. 51 (February 29, 1916), available at https://www.marxists.org/archive/lenin/works/1916/feb/29.htm.

32. Adam Tooze, *The Deluge: The Great War and the Remaking of Global Order, 1916–1931* (London: Allen Lane, 2014), 53–54; "Address of President Woodrow Wilson to the U.S. Senate 22 January 1917," available at http://www.firstworldwar.com/source/peacewithoutvictory.htm.

33. "The Government's Initial Statement on Foreign Policy" (March 4, 1917), in *Russian Provisional Government*, 2:1042.

34. Rex A. Wade, *The Russian Search for Peace, February–October 1917* (Stanford: Stanford University Press, 1969), 20–21; "The Debate in the Soviet on the Appeal" (*Izvestiia*, no. 16, March 16, 1917), in *Russian Provisional Government*, 2:1076–1077; "Soviet Appeal to the Peoples of All the World" (*Izvestiia*, no. 15, March 15, 1917), ibid., 2:1077–1078. See Wildman, *Army*, 1:293.

35. "Press Interview with Miliukov" (*Rech'*, no. 70, March 23, 1917), in *Russian Provisional Government*, 2:1044–1045.

36. "The Provisional Government's Declaration of March 27 on War Aims" (*Rech'*, no. 73, March 28, 1917), in *Russian Provisional Government*, 2:1045–1046.

37. Chamberlin, *Russian Revolution*, 1:112. Known as the All-Russian Soviet Conference: see N. N. Sukhanov, *The Russian Revolution 1917*, ed. and trans. Joel Carmichael (Princeton: Princeton University Press, 1984), 304.

38. The contrasting slogans were "war to victory" (*voina do pobednogo kontsa*) vs. "war without annexations or indemnities" (*voina bez anneksii i kontributsii*): André Mazon, *Lexique de la guerre et de la révolution en Russie (1914–1918)* (Paris: Champion, 1920), 51.

39. Nabokov, "Provisional Government," 137–138.

40. Ibid., 139–140.

41. Quoted in Wildman, *Army*, 1:335.

42. "Miliukov's Denial that the Government Has Renounced the Agreement on Constantinople and the Straits" (April 1, 1917)," in *Russian Provisional Government*, 2:1058.

43. "The Note of April 18" (*Rech'*, no. 91, April 20, 1917), in *Russian Provisional Government*, 2:1089.

44. "*Rech'* on the Note" (*Rech'*, no. 91, April 20, 1917), in *Russian Provisional Government*, 2:1099.

45. Wildman, *Army*, 2:11–12.

46. Sukhanov, *Russian Revolution*, 317.

47. Ibid., 318–320.

48. Wildman, *Army*, 2:13.

49. Nabokov, "Provisional Government," 113.

50. Ibid., 87.

51. On the strategy of supporting the Bolsheviks and the decision to ship them back, see role of Helphand in: *Germany and the Revolution in Russia 1915–1918: Documents from the Archives of the German Foreign Ministry*, ed. Z. A. B. Zeman (London: Oxford University Press, 1958); Herfried Münkler, "Spiel mit dem Feure: Die 'Politik der revolutionären Infektion,'" *Osteuropa* 64.2 (2014):109–125; Catherine Merridale, *Lenin on the Train* (London: Metropolitan, 2017).

52. Basil [Vasilii] Maklakov, "On the Fall of Tsardom [review of Bernard Pares]," *Slavonic and East European Review* 18.52 (1939): 78.

53. Karl Freiherr von Bothmer, *Moskauer Tagebuch 1918*, ed. Gernot Böhme, annotated Winfried Baumgart (Paderborn: Ferdinand Schöningh, 2010), 90.

54. Fedor Stepun, *Byvshee i nesbyvsheesia* (New York: Chekhov, 1956; St. Petersburg: Aleteiia; Moscow: Progress-Litera, 1994), 340.

55. On mobilization: Sukhanov, *Russian Revolution*, 275.

56. Ibid., 269.

57. Ibid., 270, 272.

58. Chamberlin, *Russian Revolution*, 1:115–117.

59. Quoted, Sukhanov, *Russian Revolution*, 273.

60. Ibid., 273–274.

61. Ibid., 280.

62. Chamberlin, *Russian Revolution*, 1:441–442.

63. Ibid., 1:118–119, 441–443 (text).

64. Sukhanov, *Russian Revolution*, 286.

65. Ibid., 289, 324.

66. Chamberlin, *Russian Revolution*, 1:119.

67. Sukhanov, *Russian Revolution*, 298–299.

68. Quoted, Wildman, *Army*, 2:15; Ziva Galili and Albert P. Nenarokov, "Tsereteli," in *Companion*, 201; Ziva Galili, *The Menshevik Leaders in the Russian Revolution: Social Realities and Political Strategies* (Princeton: Princeton University Press, 1989), 158.

69. This sequence from Wildman, *Army*, 2:13–14.

70. Melissa Kirschke Stockdale, *Paul Miliukov and the Quest for a Liberal Russia, 1880–1918* (Ithaca: Cornell University Press, 1996), 256; Paul Miliukov, *Political Memoirs, 1905–1917*, ed. Arthur P. Mendel, trans. Carl Goldberg (Ann Arbor: University of Michigan Press, 1967), 454.

71. On negotiations between the Provisional Government and Soviet leaders to form the coalition, see Sukhanov, *Russian Revolution*, 329–339.

72. M. E. Golostenov, "Tereshchenko," in *Politicheskie deiateli Rossii 1917: Biograficheskii slovar'*, ed. P. V. Volobuev (Moscow: Bol'shaia rossiiskaia entsiklopediia, 1993), 313–314.

73. A. L. Raikhtsaum, "Skobelev," in *Politicheskie deiateli*, 291–292.

74. Sukhanov, *Russian Revolution*, 348–352.

75. Ibid., 346.

76. "The Provisional Government's Declaration of March 27 on War Aims" (*Rech'*, no. 73, March 28, 1917), in *Russian Provisional Government*, 2:1045–1046; Wade, *Russian Search for Peace*, 48.

77. Sukhanov, *Russian Revolution*, 360 (quotes); "Interview with Prince L'vov" (*Rech'*, no. 106, May 7, 1917), in *Russian Provisional Government*, 2:1102; "Communiqué to the Press from Foreign Minister Tereshchenko" (May 6, 1917), in *Russian Provisional Government*, 2:1103–1105. See Wildman, *Army*, 2:21.

78. Sukhanov, *Russian Revolution*, 348–352; T. O. Maksimova, "Aksel'rod," in *Politicheskie deiateli*, 13–14.

79. Quoted, Wildman, *Army*, 2:17–18, 21.

80. Ibid., 5–6.

81. S. G. Nelipovich, "Iiun'skoe (letnee) nastuplenie 1917," in *Rossiia v Pervoi mirovoi voine 1914–1918: Entsiklopediia v trekh tomakh*, ed. A. K. Sorokin et al. (Moscow: ROSSPEN, 2014), 1:813–818.

82. Thanks to Bill Rosenberg for this point.

83. Wildman's point, *Army*, 2:22.

84. "Order No. 8 on the Rights of Servicemen (Declaration of Soldiers' Rights)" (May 11, 1917), in *Russian Provisional Government*, 2:880–883; Wildman, *Army*, 2:22–24.

85. "The Reply of *Izvestiia* to *Pravda*'s Attacks on the Declaration" (no. 65, May 26, 1917), in *Russian Provisional Government*, 2:883–885.

86. Chamberlin, *Russian Revolution*, 1:151.
87. Quoted, Sukhanov, *Russian Revolution*, 361.
88. Wildman, *Army*, 2:24–26.
89. Ibid., 27.
90. Quoted, ibid., 30.
91. Ibid., 31.
92. Quoted, ibid., 32.
93. Sukhanov, *Russian Revolution*, 368.
94. Ibid., 368–369.
95. Ibid., 370.
96. Ibid., 386.
97. Ibid., 378–380; Chamberlin, *Russian Revolution*, 1:159.
98. Sukhanov, *Russian Revolution*, 384.
99. Chamberlin, *Russian Revolution*, 1:155.
100. Ibid., 161; Sukhanov, *Russian Revolution*, 390–391.
101. Quoted, Sukhanov, *Russian Revolution*, 398–399.
102. Rex A. Wade, "The Red Guards: Spontaneity and the October Revolution," in *Revolution in Russia: Reassessments of 1917*, ed. Edith Rogovin Frankel, Jonathan Frankel, and Baruch Knei-Paz (Cambridge: Cambridge University Press, 1992), 54–59; S. A. Smith, *Red Petrograd: Revolution in the Factories, 1917–1918* (Cambridge: Cambridge University Press, 1983), 101.
103. Sukhanov, *Russian Revolution*, 403 (his italics).
104. Ibid., 405–406.
105. Ibid., 414–417; Chamberlin, *Russian Revolution*, 1:162–163.
106. Sukhanov, *Russian Revolution*, 418.
107. Chamberlin, *Russian Revolution*, 1:163.
108. Wildman, *Army*, 2:75, 77.
109. Ibid., 39, 37–43.
110. Ibid., 77, 83–84.
111. Ibid., 74.
112. Quoted, ibid., 78; O. R. Airapetov, "Alekseev," in *Rossiia v Pervoi mirovoi voine*, 1:57.
113. Wildman, *Army*, 2:83–84, quoting incident from Shklovsky.
114. Quoted, ibid., 89.
115. Ibid., 105–106.
116. Report of June 30, quoted, ibid., 93.
117. Ibid., 97.
118. Ibid., 99.
119. Ibid., 116–117.
120. Quoted, Chamberlin, *Russian Revolution*, 1:164.
121. Wildman, *Army*, 2:117–123.
122. Doc. 349. "The First Universal of the Central Rada" (June 10, 1917), in *Russian Provisional Government*, 1:383–385.

123. Doc. 350. "Appeal of the Provisional Government to the Ukrainian People" (June 17, 1917), in *Russian Provisional Government*, 1:385–386; Doc. 353. "*Izvestiia* on the First Universal" (June 16, 1917), ibid., 1:388–389 (endorsing this plea); Doc. 354. "The Agreement Reached Between the Central Rada and the Provisional Government" (*Rech'*, July 4, 1917), ibid., 1:389–390; Serhy Yekelchyk, *Ukraine: Birth of a Modern Nation* (New York: Oxford University Press, 2007), 70–71.

124. Doc. 355. "The Resignation of the Kadet Ministers in Protest Against the Ukrainian Agreement" (*Rech'*, July 4, 1917), in *Russian Provisional Government*, 1:390–392; Doc. 1182. "The Kadets Explain the Resignation of Their Members in the Government" (*Rech'*, July 5, 1917), ibid., 3:1383–1384.

125. The Provisional Government conducted an investigation into the July events: *Sledstvennoe delo bol'shevikov: Materialy Predvaritel'nogo sledstviia o vooruzhennom vystuplenii 3–5 iuliia 1917 g. v g. Petrograde protiv gosudarstvennoi vlasti, iiul'–oktiabr' 1917 g.: Sbornik dokumentov*, 2 vols. in 4, ed. O. K. Ivantsova (Moscow: ROSSPEN, 2012).

126. Sukhanov, *Russian Revolution*, 426–427.

127. Ibid., 428.

128. Ibid., 430–431.

129. Chamberlin, *Russian Revolution*, 1:172–173.

130. Sukhanov, *Russian Revolution*, 432.

131. Ibid., 453.

132. Ibid., 433–436.

133. Ibid., 439–441; Chamberlin, *Russian Revolution*, 171–172.

134. Sukhanov, *Russian Revolution*, 442.

135. Quoted, Chamberlin, *Russian Revolution*, 1:174.

136. Sukhanov, *Russian Revolution*, 443; Chamberlin, *Russian Revolution*, 1:173.

137. Sukhanov, *Russian Revolution*, 442.

138. Ibid., 443.

139. Chamberlin, *Russian Revolution*, 1:174–175 (quotes, 175).

140. Sukhanov, *Russian Revolution*, 444.

141. Ibid., 452 (Martov).

142. Ibid., 445 (quote), 446–447.

143. Chamberlin, *Russian Revolution*, 1:176; Sukhanov, *Russian Revolution*, 449.

144. Sukhanov, *Russian Revolution*, 450.

145. Ibid., 456.

146. Chamberlin, *Russian Revolution*, 1:167.

147. Ibid., 176–181.

148. Sukhanov, *Russian Revolution*, 454, 455, 457–459.

149. Ibid., 459–464.

150. Ibid., 470–472.

151. Chamberlin, *Russian Revolution*, 1:183.

152. Sukhanov, *Russian Revolution*, 473, 478.

153. Quoted, William G. Rosenberg, *Liberals in the Russian Revolution: The Constitutional Democratic Party, 1917–1921* (Princeton: Princeton University Press, 1974), 179; Doc. 1186. "Statement by Prince L'vov Concerning His Resignation" (July 9, 1917), in *Russian Provisional Government*, 3:1388–1389; Doc. 1190. "*Rech'* on the Withdrawal of the Kadet Ministers and Prince L'vov" (July 8, 1917), ibid., 3:1395–1396.

154. Doc. 1191. "*Delo naroda* on the Resignation of Prince L'vov" (July 9, 1917), in *Russian Provisional Government*, 3:1396–1397; quote, 1397.

155. Sukhanov, *Russian Revolution*, 473.

156. Ibid., 476–477.


PART III: CHAPTER 3

1. Allan K. Wildman, *The End of the Russian Imperial Army*, 2 vols. (Princeton: Princeton University Press, 1980, 1987), 2:119–221. On the Kornilov affair, see Geoffrey Swain, *The Origins of the Russian Civil War* (London: Longmans, 1996), ch. 1.

2. Wildman, *Army*, 2:123, 142.

3. W. Bruce Lincoln, *Passage through Armageddon: The Russians in War and Revolution, 1914–1918* (New York: Simon and Schuster, 1986), 412; Alexander Rabinowitch, *The Bolsheviks Come to Power: The Revolution of 1917 in Petrograd* (New York: Norton, 1976), 96–97; Peter Kenez, *Civil War in South Russia, 1918: The First Year of the Volunteer Army* (Berkeley: University of California Press, 1971), 21–22, 31; S. M. Iskhakov, "Pervaia mirovaia voina glazami rossiiskikh musul'man," in *Rossiia i Pervaia mirovaia voina*, ed. N. N. Smirnov (St. Petersburg: Bulanin, 1999), 423. Rabinowitch and Wildman are the essential sources for this chapter.

4. Denikin quoted, William Henry Chamberlin, *The Russian Revolution, 1917–1921*, 2 vols. (1935; New York: Grosset & Dunlap, 1965), 1:197; 192–195 (on Kornilov).

5. Ia. V. Mel'nichuk, "Vvedenie," in B. V. Savinkov, *Vo Frantsii vo vremia voiny: Sentiabr' 1914–iiun' 1915*, ed. Ia. V. Mel'nichuk (Moscow: Gos. publichnaia istoricheskaia biblioteka Rossii, 2008), 9–13, 16–19.

6. Richard B. Spence, *Boris Savinkov: Renegade on the Left* (New York: Columbia University Press, 1991), 106, 109–111; K. V. Gusev, "Savinkov," in *Politicheskie deiateli Rossii 1917: Biograficheskii slovar'*, ed. P. V. Volobuev (Moscow: Bol'shaia rossiiskaia entsiklopediia, 1993), 283–286.

7. Wildman, *Army*, 2:124–127, 129–133.

8. Ibid., 153.

9. Kenez, *Civil War 1918*, 29.

10. Wildman, *Army*, 2:158–160.

11. Ibid., 181.

12. S. G. Nelipovich, "Iiun'skoe nastuplenie 1917," in *Rossiia v Pervoi mirovoi voine 1914–1918: Entsiklopediia v trekh tomakh*, ed. A. K. Sorokin et al. (Moscow: ROSSPEN, 2014), 1:817–818.

13. "Gosudarstvennoe soveshchanie" (Moscow, August 12–15, 1917), in *Politicheskie deiateli*, 381.

14. Rabinowitch, *Bolsheviks Come to Power*, 110–114; Chamberlin, *Russian Revolution*, 1:202.

15. Rabinowitch, *Bolsheviks Come to Power*, 110–114.

16. Wildman, *Army*, 2:189; "Kornilov's Speech," in *The Russian Provisional Government 1917: Documents*, ed. Robert Paul Browder and Alexander F. Kerensky, 3 vols. (Stanford: Stanford University Press, 1961), 3:1476, 1478.

17. Quoted, Wildman, *Army*, 2:186.

18. Rabinowitch, *Bolsheviks Come to Power*, 116–118.

19. Wildman, *Army*, 2:187–190. See Wladimir S. Woytinsky, *Gody pobed i porazhenii*, 2 vols. (Berlin, St. Petersburg, Moscow: Grzhebin, 1923–1924).

20. Rabinowitch, *Bolsheviks Come to Power*, 118–119; Chamberlin, *Russian Revolution*, 1:208.

21. Rabinowitch, *Bolsheviks Come to Power*, 120, 122–125, 127, 126 (quote).

22. Chamberlin, *Russian Revolution*, 1:215–216.

23. Rabinowitch, *Bolsheviks Come to Power*, 133–134.

24. Ibid., 316, 136–137 (quote).

25. Wildman, *Army*, 2:205.

26. Rabinowitch, *Bolsheviks Come to Power*, 142.

27. Chamberlin, *Russian Revolution*, 1:217.

28. Rabinowitch, *Bolsheviks Come to Power*, 277–278; Chamberlin, *Russian Revolution*, 1:218–219. On arrests among the officers implicated in Kornilov's plan: Matthew Rendle, *Defenders of the Motherland: The Tsarist Elite in Revolutionary Russia* (Oxford: Oxford University Press, 2010), 186–187.

29. Rabinowitch, *Bolsheviks Come to Power*, 149–150.

30. V. B. Stankevich, *Vospominaniia, 1914–1919 g.* (Berlin: Ladyschnikow, 1920), 243, quoted in Chamberlin, *Russian Revolution*, 1:236–237.

31. Wildman, *Army*, 2:219–221.

32. Quoted, ibid., 223; 197–223 (preceding account).

33. Ibid., 226, 227 (quotes).

34. Ibid., 225.

35. Ibid., 233.

36. Quoted, ibid., 260.

37. Isaac Deutscher, *The Prophet Armed: Trotsky, 1879–1921* (New York: Oxford University Press, 1954), 282.

38. Rabinowitch, *Bolsheviks Come to Power*, 152–154.

39. Ibid., 159–160.

40. Ibid., 162–164.

41. Iu. V. Aksiutin, "Kamenev (Rozenfel'd)," in *Politicheskie deiateli*, 131–136; Iu. V. Aksiutin, "Zinov'ev (Radomysl'skii)," ibid., 117–121.

42. Quoted, Rabinowitch, *Bolsheviks Come to Power*, 171.

43. Quoted, V. I. Miller, "'Shestoi s"ezd RSDRP(b)" (July 26–August 3, 1917), in *Politicheskie deiateli*, 380.

44. Rabinowitch, *Bolsheviks Come to Power*, 173–174.

45. Chamberlin, *Russian Revolution*, 1:280; on cooperatives see Swain, *Origins*, 45; A. L. Raikhtsaum, "Vserossiiskoe Demokraticheskoe soveshchanie" (September 14–22, 1917), in *Politicheskie deiateli*, 383–384.

46. Figures from Raikhtsaum, "Vserossiiskoe Demokraticheskoe soveshchanie," 383.

47. Rabinowitch, *Bolsheviks Come to Power*, 187.

48. Quotes, ibid., 179–180.

49. John Reed, *Ten Days that Shook the World* (1919; New York: Penguin, 1977), 40.

50. A. L. Raikhtsaum, "Spisok chlenov i kandidatov v chleny Vremennogo Soveta rossiiskoi respubliki (Predparlamenta)," in *Politicheskie deiateli*, 386–390.

51. See Swain, *Origins*, 44–45.

52. V. I. Miller, "Vtoroi Vserossiiskii s"ezd Sovetov rabochikh i soldatskikh deputatov" (October 25–27, 1917), in *Politicheskie deiateli*, 390–391.

53. Rabinowitch, *Bolsheviks Come to Power*, 187.

54. Quotes, ibid., 193, 194.

55. Quoted, Chamberlin, *Russian Revolution*, 1:289.

56. Quoted, Rabinowitch, *Bolsheviks Come to Power*, 201–202.

57. Chamberlin, *Russian Revolution*, 1:284–285; Deutscher, *Prophet Armed*, 225–226 (Zimmerwald).

58. Chamberlin, *Russian Revolution*, 1:285–286.

59. Rabinowitch, *Bolsheviks Come to Power*, 202–208.

## PART III: CHAPTER 4

1. Allan K. Wildman, *The End of the Russian Imperial Army*. 2 vols. (Princeton: Princeton University Press, 1980, 1987), 2:267.

2. Ibid., 265 (his phrase).

3. This interpretation from ibid., 279–288.

4. Quotes, Alexander Rabinowitch, *The Bolsheviks Come to Power: The Revolution of 1917 in Petrograd* (New York: Norton, 1976), 220. Rabinowitch is a key source for this chapter.

5. Quotes, ibid., 220.

6. I. I. Vainberg, "Gor'kii," in *Politicheskie deiateli Rossii 1917: Biograficheskii slovar'*, ed. P. V. Volobuev (Moscow: Bol'shaia rossiiskaia entsiklopediia, 1993), 82–85. *Novaia zhizn'*, edited by Gorky, appeared in Petrograd from April 1917 to June 1918.

7. Rabinowitch, *Bolsheviks Come to Power*, 226.

8. See Michael B. Barrett, *Operation Albion: The German Conquest of the Baltic Islands* (Bloomington: Indiana University Press, 2008).

9. Rabinowitch, *Bolsheviks Come to Power*, 226–229.

10. Ibid., 232–236, 239.

11. Ibid., 236–237; 241 (quote).
12. N. N. Sukhanov, *The Russian Revolution 1917*, trans. and ed. Joel Carmichael (Princeton: Princeton University Press, 1984), 584; quoted, Rabinowitch, *Bolsheviks Come to Power*, 243.
13. Sukhanov, *Russian Revolution*, 584.
14. Ibid., 585.
15. Rabinowitch, *Bolsheviks Come to Power*, 242.
16. Sukhanov, *Russian Revolution*, 550–551.
17. Rabinowitch, *Bolsheviks Come to Power*, 243–248.
18. "Directive Number One," quoted, ibid., 249.
19. Quoted, ibid., 256.
20. Ibid., 258–260.
21. Ibid., 261–263.
22. Quoted, ibid., 265–266.
23. Ibid., 263–266.
24. Ibid., 269–272.
25. B. Maklakoff, "Vers la Révolution: La Russie de 1900 à 1917: Le Dénouement," *La Revue de Paris* 31.23 (December 1, 1924): 609.
26. Quoted, Rabinowitch, *Bolsheviks Come to Power*, 274–275.
27. Ibid., 276–278.
28. Quoted, ibid., 278.
29. Quoted, ibid., 279.
30. Quoted, ibid.
31. Ibid., 281.
32. Ibid., 288–289.
33. Quoted, ibid., 291.
34. Ibid., 291–292; Ziva Galili, *The Menshevik Leaders in the Russian Revolution: Social Realities and Political Strategies* (Princeton: Princeton University Press, 1989), 416; V. I. Miller, "Vtoroi Vserossiiskii s"ezd Sovetov rabochikh i soldatskikh deputatov" (October 25–27, 1917), in *Politicheskie deiateli*, 390–391.
35. Quoted, Rabinowitch, *Bolsheviks Come to Power*, 293; Sukhanov, *Russian Revolution*, 294 (quote).
36. "Resolution of Martov," in *The Russian Provisional Government 1917: Documents*, ed. Robert Paul Browder and Alexander F. Kerensky, 3 vols. (Stanford: Stanford University Press, 1961), 3:1797.
37. Rabinowitch, *Bolsheviks Come to Power*, 295; Galili, *Menshevik Leaders*, 392–394.
38. Quoted from minutes of the meeting, Rabinowitch, *Bolsheviks Come to Power*, 296.
39. Quoted, ibid.
40. Quoted, ibid.
41. Sukhanov, Russian Revolution, 646; quoted, Rabinowitch, *Bolsheviks Come to Power*, 294.
42. Quoted, Rabinowitch, *Bolsheviks Come to Power*, 303 (minor modification), from *Russian Provisional Government*, 3:1797–1798.

43. Rabinowitch, *Bolsheviks Come to Power*, 304.

44. "Lenin's Speech on the Peace Declaration" (November 8/October 26, 1917), in James Bunyan and H. H. Fisher, *The Bolshevik Revolution 1917–1918: Documents and Materials* (Stanford: Stanford University Press, 1934), 124–128; "Lenin's Speech on the Land Decree" (November 8/October 26, 1917), in ibid., 128–132. "Dekret II Vserossiiskogo s"ezda Sovetov o mire (26 oktiabria/8 noiabria, 1917 g.)," in *Dekrety Sovetskoi vlasti*, vol. 1 (Moscow: Politicheskaia literatura, 1957), 12–16 ("peace without annexations, i.e., without the seizure of foreign lands, without the violent incorporation of foreign nations or peoples, and without indemnities"); "Dekret II Vserossiiskogo s"ezda Sovetov o zemle (26 oktiabria/8 noiabria, 1917 g.)," ibid., 17–20. "Dekret o mire" available at http://www.hist.msu.ru/ER/Etext/DEKRET/o_mire.htm, "Dekret o zemle" at http://www.hist.msu.ru/ER/Etext/DEKRET/o_zemle.htm (both accessed January 24, 2017).

45. I. N. Steinberg, *In the Workshop of the Revolution* (New York: Rinehart, 1953), 46. Of the original sixteen incumbents, one (Trotsky) was assassinated, ten were executed or died in the 1930s purges, and five died of natural causes—all, except Stalin, before the purges began.

46. Quoted, Alexander Rabinowitch, *The Bolsheviks in Power: The First Year of Soviet Rule in Petrograd* (Bloomington: Indiana University Press, 2007), 21.

47. This and preceding paragraph from Dmitrii Churakov, *Revoliutsiia, gosudarstvo, rabochii protest: Formy, dinamika i priroda massovykh vystuplenii rabochikh v Sovetskoi Rossii, 1917–1918 gody* (Moscow: ROSSPEN, 2004), 13–17.

48. Wildman, *Army*, 2:264.

49. Peter Kenez, *Civil War in South Russia, 1918: The First Year of the Volunteer Army* (Berkeley: University of California Press, 1971), 46.

50. Rabinowitch, *Bolsheviks Come to Power*, 306.

51. Ibid., 23–24.

52. Ibid., 25.

53. V. N. Zabotin, "Nogin," in *Politicheskie deiateli*, 237–238.

54. Diane Koenker, *Moscow Workers and the 1917 Revolution* (Princeton: Princeton University Press, 1981), 332–346.

55. Churakov, *Revoliutsiia*, 13 (*odnorodnoe sotsialisticheskoe pravitel'stvo*).

56. Quoted, ibid., 19.

57. Ibid., 21.

58. Quoted, ibid., 24.

59. Ibid., 23.

60. Ibid., 25. "Popular Socialists," in Jonathan D. Smele, *Historical Dictionary of the Russian Civil Wars, 1916–1926*, 2 vols. (Lanham, MD: Rowman & Littlefield, 2015), 2:886 (1906–1918, non-Marxist democratic socialists).

61. Quoted, Churakov, *Revoliutsiia*, 26, from An-skii, "Posle perevorota 25-go oktiabria 1917," *Arkhiv russkoi revoliutsii* 8 (Moscow, 1991), 49.

62. On Vikzhel episode, overall: Churakov, *Revoliutsiia*, 19–28; also Wildman, *Army*, 2:303–307.

63. Rabinowitch, *Bolsheviks Come to Power*, 305, 308.

64. Quoted, Igor V. Narskii, *Zhizn' v katastrofe: Budni naseleniia Urala v 1917–1922 gg.* (Moscow: ROSSPEN, 2001), 198.

65. Ibid., 199.

66. Ibid., 205.

67. Wildman, *Army*, 2: 310.

68. Geoffrey Swain, *The Origins of the Russian Civil War* (London: Longmans, 1996), 83–84.

69. "Lenin's Speech on the Peace Declaration" (November 8/October 26, 1917), in Bunyan and Fisher, *Bolshevik Revolution*, 125; text in *Izvestiia*, October 27/November 9, 1917.

70. "Order to Dukhonin to Open Armistice Negotiations" (Radiogram from the Sovnarkom, November 8/21, 1917), in Bunyan and Fisher, *Bolshevik Revolution*, 233. See Wildman, *Army*, 2:380.

71. John W. Wheeler-Bennett, *Brest-Litovsk: The Forgotten Peace, March 1918* (London: Macmillan; New York: St. Martin's, 1938), 72–73.

72. "Dukhonin's Appeal to the People and the Army" (November 12/25, 1917), in Bunyan and Fisher, *Bolshevik Revolution*, 253–254; Kenez, *Civil War 1918*, 50–53.

73. George F. Kennan, *Soviet-American Relations, 1917–1920*. Vol. 1: *Russia Leaves the War* (London: Faber and Faber, 1956), 89–91; "Dukhonin Declines to Open Armistice Negotiations (Conversation by Direct Wire with Lenin, Stalin, and Krylenko, 2:00 A.M., November 9/22, 1917)," in Bunyan and Fisher, *Bolshevik Revolution*, 233–235.

74. "Lenin Urges the Soldiers to Negotiate with the Enemy" (Proclamation to Soldiers and Sailors, November 9/22, 1917), published *Izvestiia*, November 23, 1917, in Bunyan and Fisher, *Bolshevik Revolution*, 236–237; quoted, Wildman, *Army*, 2:381; Kennan, *Russia Leaves the War*, 95.

75. "Krylenko's Order No. 2" (November 13/26, 1917, published *Izvestiia*, November 15/28, 1917), in Bunyan and Fisher, *Bolshevik Revolution*, 256–257.

76. "The Soviet Delegation Leaves for Brest-Litovsk (Telegram from Dvinsk, November 20/December 3, 1917)," signed by Skliansky, President of the Congress of the 5th Army and the Army Committee, in Bunyan and Fisher, *Bolshevik Revolution*, 269.

77. "Krylenko Arrives at Dvinsk" (General Boldyrev, Commander of Russian 5th Army, to Dukhonin, November 11/24, 1917), in Bunyan and Fisher, *Bolshevik Revolution*, 251; "The Army and the Negotiations" (General A.V. Cheremisov to Dukhonin, November 13/26, 1917), ibid., 254–255.

78. "Order of the Mogilev Military Revolutionary Committee" (November 19/December 2, 1917), in Bunyan and Fisher, *Bolshevik Revolution*, 266.

79. General A. Denikine, *The White Army*, trans. Catherine Zvegintzov (London: Jonathan Cape, 1930), 23–25.

80. Geoffrey Swain, "Russia's Garibaldi: The Revolutionary Life of Mikhail Artemevich Muraviev," *Revolutionary Russia* 11:2 (1998): 58.

81. Described in Wheeler-Bennett, *Brest-Litovsk*, 74; also Wildman, *Army*, 2:400–401. "The Bolsheviks Take Control of the Stavka (Krylenko's Proclamation to the Soldiers, November 20/December 3, 1917)," in Bunyan and Fisher, *Bolshevik Revolution*, 267; "The Murder of General Dukhonin" (Extracts from Krylenko's Report to the Sovnarkom, *Novaia zhizn'*, November 30/December 13, 1917), ibid., 267–268 (note); Kenez, *Civil War 1918*, 52–53.

82. "The Bolsheviks Take Control of the Stavka," in Bunyan and Fisher, *Bolshevik Revolution*, 267; "The Murder of General Dukhonin," ibid., 267–268.

83. Note to Krylenko's account, Bunyan and Fisher, *Bolshevik Revolution*, 268.

84. The Russian language has two distinct adjectives—*russkii* and *rossiiskii*—both translated in English as "Russian." *Russkii* refers to the language, the culture, the ethnic category. *Rossiiskii*, derived from *Rossiia*, is a political term, designating the Russian (*russkii*)-centered state, but including the non-Russian populations.

### PART III: CHAPTER 5

1. Alexander Rabinowitch, *The Bolsheviks in Power: The First Year of Soviet Rule in Petrograd* (Bloomington: Indiana University Press, 2007), 34.

2. Quoted, ibid., 36.

3. Quoted, ibid., 37.

4. Quoted, ibid., 47.

5. Ibid.

6. V. N. Zabotin, "Nogin," in *Politicheskie deiateli Rossii 1917: Biograficheskii slovar'*, ed. P. V. Volobuev (Moscow: Bol'shaia rossiiskaia entsiklopediia, 1993), 238.

7. Rabinowitch, *Bolsheviks in Power*, 55, 57.

8. Both paragraphs: ibid., 68–69 (Petrograd); the rest: L. G. Protasov, *Liudi Uchreditel'nogo sobraniia: Portret v inter'ere epokhi* (Moscow: ROSSPEN, 2008), 55, 84, 108, 125, 136, 149; George Leggett, *The Cheka: Lenin's Political Police* (Oxford: Clarendon 1981), 42 (similar figures).

9. From Protasov, *Liudi*. Krylenko was shot in 1938; Rozmirovich died in 1953; Chernov emigrated in 1920 and died in New York in 1952; Sletova-Chernova died in prison in 1938; Bosh committed suicide in 1925 after an illness; Piatakov was shot. Iakovleva worked in the Cheka/NKVD and died in prison in 1944. Leggett, *Cheka*, 450.

10. Rabinowitch, *Bolsheviks in Power*, 69–70.

11. Ibid., 70–71.

12. Bukharin at November 29 (December 12) Bolshevik Central Committee meeting, quoted, ibid., 72.

13. Rabinowitch, *Bolsheviks in Power*, 75–76.

14. Ibid., 76.

15. "Arrest of the Cadet Leaders" (Decree of Sovnarkom, December 11/November 28, 1917), in James Bunyan and H. H. Fisher, *The Bolshevik Revolution 1917–1918: Documents and Materials* (Stanford: Stanford University Press, 1934), 359.

16. "Cadet Party Declared an Enemy of the People" (Proclamation of Sovnarkom, December 11/November 28, 1917), in Bunyan and Fisher, *Bolshevik Revolution*, 357–359.

17. Quoted, Rabinowitch, *Bolsheviks in Power*, 78.

18. Ibid., 83–84.

19. Ibid., 82; Leggett, *Cheka*, 10; "Cheka," in Jonathan D. Smele, *Historical Dictionary of the Russian Civil Wars, 1916–1926*, 2 vols. (Lanham, MD: Rowman & Littlefield, 2015), 1:264–268.

20. Leggett, *Cheka*, 6–15.

21. A. S. Velidov, "Dzerzhinskii," in *Politicheskie deiateli*, 100–101; Leggett, *Cheka*, 22–26.

22. Rabinowitch, *Bolsheviks in Power*, 83–87; Leggett, *Cheka*, 44; I. N. Steinberg, *In the Workshop of the Revolution* (New York: Rinehart, 1953), 64.

23. Quoted, S. P. Mel'gunov, *"Krasnyi terror" v Rossii 1918–1923* (Berlin: Vataga, 1924), 12–20.

24. Quoted, ibid., 20 (*obezvrezhen*).

25. A. L. Litvin, *Krasnyi i belyi terror, 1918–1922* (Moscow: Eksmo, 2004), 30; Leggett, *Cheka*, 17 (same passage).

26. Rabinowitch, *Bolsheviks in Power*, 88–91 (Kamenev, David Riazanov, Aleksei Rykov, Iurii Larin, and Vladimir Miliutin).

27. "Declaration of the Rights of the Toiling and Exploited Peoples," in Bunyan and Fisher, *Bolshevik Revolution*, 372–374 (my trans. differs); "Deklaratsiia prav trudiashchegosia i eksplotiruemogo naroda" (January 3/16, 1918), in *Dekrety Sovetskoi vlasti*, vol. 1 (Moscow: Politicheskaia literatura, 1957), 321–322.

28. *The Debate on Soviet Power: Minutes of the All-Russian Central Executive Committee of Soviets, Second Convocation, October 1917–January 1918*, trans. and ed. John L. H. Keep (Oxford: Clarendon, 1979); *Uchreditel'noe sobranie: Stenograficheskii otchet* (Petrograd: Tip. Arend. akts. o-va "Dom pechati," 1918).

29. Rabinowitch, *Bolsheviks in Power*, 99–101.

30. Ibid., 100.

31. Victor Serge, "During the Civil War: Petrograd: May–June 1919" (January 1920), in Victor Serge, *Revolution in Danger: Writings from Russia 1919–1921*, trans. Ian Birchall (Chicago: Haymarket Books, 2011), 37.

32. Rabinowitch, *Bolsheviks in Power*, 104–106.

33. Ibid., 108–109; N. P. Okunev, *Dnevnik Moskvicha (1917–1924)* (Paris: YMCA, 1990), 129–130.

34. "Rezoliutsiia TsK RSDRP(o) po povodu rasstrela mirnoi demonstratsii v podderzhku uchreditel'nogo sobraniia" (January 5, 1918); "Vozzvanie TsK RSDRP (o) 'K grazhdanam vsei Rossii!'" (after January 5, 1918); "Vozzvanie TsK RSDRP (o) 'Rabochie i rabotnitsy!'" (after January 5, 1918); "Vozzvanie TsK RSDRP (o) 'K soldatam i krasnogvardeitsam!'" (January 6, 1918), in *Men'sheviki v 1918 godu*, ed. Ziva Galili and A. P. Nenarokov (Moscow: ROSSPEN, 1999), 92–97.

35. Sergei A. Pavliuchenkov, *Voennyi kommunizm v Rossii: Vlast' i massy* (Moscow: RKT-Istoriia, 1997), 144–145.

36. M. V. Vishniak, *Vserossiiskoe uchreditel'noe sobranie* (Paris: Sovremennye zapiski, 1932), 100.

37. Richard Pipes, *The Russian Revolution* (New York: Knopf, 1990), 552.

38. "Sverdlov (Movshevich)," in Smele, *Historical Dictionary*, 2:1133–1134.

39. "The Opening of the Constituent Assembly" (from Stenographic Report, January 18, 1918), in Bunyan and Fisher, *Bolshevik Revolution*, 371–372.

40. Quoted, Rabinowitch, *Bolsheviks in Power*, 118.

41. Ibid., 120–122.

42. Ibid., 122–123.

43. Steinberg, *Workshop*, 54–55; quote, 55.

44. Okunev, *Dnevnik Moskvicha*, 131.

45. Rabinowitch, *Bolsheviks in Power*, 122–124; Bunyan and Fisher, *Bolshevik Revolution*, 375–379.

46. Rabinowitch, *Bolsheviks in Power*, 124.

47. Quote from *Pravda*: Leggett, *Cheka*, 43.

48. I am mixing English, as quoted, Rabinowitch, *Bolsheviks in Power*, 125–126; and Bunyan and Fisher, *Bolshevik Revolution*, 382.

49. Quoted from Trotsky's account, Leggett, *Cheka*, 45.

50. Rabinowitch, *Bolsheviks in Power*, 126–127.

51. Leggett, *Cheka*, 44 (arrest of delegates); William G. Rosenberg, *Liberals in the Russian Revolution: The Constitutional Democratic Party, 1917–1921* (Princeton: Princeton University Press, 1974), 277–278.

52. Steinberg, *Workshop*, 75–78; "The Assassination of Shingarev and Kokoshkin," in Bunyan and Fisher, *Bolshevik Revolution*, 386–387. See A. I. Shingarev, *Kak eto bylo: Dnevnik A. I. Shingareva* (Royal Oak, MI: Strathcona, 1978); *The Shingarev Diary: How It Was*, trans. Felicity Ashbee and Irina Tidmarsh (Royal Oak, MI: Strathcona, 1978).

53. Bruce R. H. Lockhart, *British Agent* (New York and London: Putnam, 1933), 216.

54. V. B. Stankevich, *Vospominaniia, 1914–1919 g.* (Berlin: Ladyschnikow, 1920), 302.

55. Stankevich, *Vospominaniia*, 302–303.

56. Leggett, *Cheka*, 30–32; *Arkhiv VChK: Sbornik dokumentov*, ed. V. Vinogradov, A. Litvin, and V. Khristoforov (Moscow: Kuchkovo pole, 2007), covering the years 1917–1921.

57. Leggett, *Cheka*, 49–51.

58. Quoted, ibid., 55.

59. Steinberg, *Workshop*, 65.

60. Ibid., 61. For June 1918 contacts with Germans, contemplating overthrow of Bolshevik regime: John W. Wheeler-Bennett, *Brest-Litovsk, The Forgotten Peace, March 1918* (London: Macmillan; New York: St. Martin's, 1938), 335–336.

61. Geoffrey Swain, *The Origins of the Russian Civil War* (London: Longmans, 1996), 87.

62. Quoted, ibid., 85, from Keep, *Debate on Soviet Power*, 177.

63. Quoted, Steinberg, *Workshop*, 60.

64. Quoted, Leggett, *Cheka*, 56.

65. Rosenberg, *Liberals*, 282–285.

## PART III: CHAPTER 6

1. Orlando Figes, *Peasant Russia, Civil War: The Volga Countryside in Revolution (1917–1921)* (Oxford: Clarendon, 1989), 17–18.
2. *Rossiia 1913: Statistiko-dokumental'nyi spravochnik*, ed. A. M. Anfimov and A. P. Korelin (St. Petersburg: BLITs, 1995), 63, citing *Dinamika zemlevladeniia v Rossii: 1906–1914 gg.*, ed. A. M. Anfimov and I. F. Makarov (Moscow: Inst. istorii SSSR AN SSSR, 1989), 54–55.
3. Figes, *Peasant Russia*, 34.
4. James W. Heinzen, *Inventing a Soviet Countryside: State Power and the Transformation of Rural Russia, 1917–1929* (Pittsburgh: University of Pittsburgh Press, 2004), 20; Figes, *Peasant Russia*, 33–46.
5. Figes, *Peasant Russia*, 33–46.
6. Ibid., 47–61.
7. Ibid., 62.
8. Ibid., 62–68.
9. R. Scotland Liddell, *Actions and Reactions in Russia* (London: Chapman and Hall, 1917), 146. Liddell was a British journalist who also commanded a Russian company at the front.
10. Ibid., 148.
11. Quoted, V. V. Kanishchev, *Russkii bunt, bessmyslennyi i besposhchadnyi: Pogromnoe dvizhenie v gorodakh Rossii v 1917–1918 gg.* (Tambov: Tambovskii gos. un-t im. G. R. Derzhavina, 1995), 48.
12. This analysis in Naum Jasny, *Soviet Economists of the Twenties: Names to Be Remembered* (Cambridge: Cambridge University Press, 1972), 94; Liddell, *Actions*, 151–152.
13. Lars T. Lih, *Bread and Authority in Russia, 1914–1921* (Berkeley: University of California Press, 1990), 7–21.
14. Jasny, *Soviet Economists of the Twenties*, 91–93.
15. Lih, *Bread*, 26.
16. Quoted, ibid. Iakov Bukshpan worked at the St. Petersburg Polytechnic Institute and published in liberal newspapers; arrested 1930, released 1932, ran the economics department of the Soviet food production academy; rearrested 1938, shot 1939.
17. Lih, *Bread*, 29–31, 33–34.
18. Ibid., 36–39.
19. Ibid., 41–43, 45–47.
20. Quoted, ibid., 53, 48–53 (discussion).
21. Ibid., 53–56.
22. Ibid., 59–65.
23. Diane Koenker, *Moscow Workers and the 1917 Revolution* (Princeton: Princeton University Press, 1981), 75.
24. Diane P. Koenker and William G. Rosenberg, "Strikes and Revolution in Russia, 1917," in *Revolutionary Russia: New Approaches*, ed. Rex A. Wade (New York: Routledge, 2004), 37.

25. Koenker, *Moscow Workers*, 88–89.
26. S. A. Smith, *Red Petrograd: Revolution in the Factories 1917–18* (Cambridge: Cambridge University Press, 1983), ch. 3.
27. Ibid., 82–102.
28. Koenker, *Moscow Workers*, chs. 4–7.
29. Silvana Malle, *The Economic Organization of War Communism, 1918–1921* (Cambridge: Cambridge University Press, 1985), 90.
30. Smith, *Red Petrograd*, ch. 5.
31. Ibid., 139–152.
32. "Polozhenie o rabochem kontrole (14/27 noiabria 1917 g.)," in *Dekrety Sovetskoi vlasti*, vol. 1 (Moscow: Politicheskaia literatura, 1957), 78–85, available at http://www.hist.msu.ru/ER/Etext/DEKRET/rab_ctrl.htm (accessed January 25, 2017).
33. Malle, *Economic Organization*, 89–95. "Dekret ob uchrezhdenii Vysshego soveta narodnogo khoziaistva (2/15 dekabria 1917 g.)," in *Dekrety Sovetskoi vlasti*, 1:172–174, available at http://www.hist.msu.ru/ER/Etext/DEKRET/vsnh.htm (accessed January 25, 2017).
34. Koenker, *Moscow Workers*, 337–338.
35. Sergei A. Pavliuchenkov, *Voennyi kommunizm v Rossii: Vlast' i massy* (Moscow: RKT-Istoriia, 1997), 61.
36. Rex A. Wade, "The Red Guards: Spontaneity and the October Revolution," in *Revolution in Russia: Reassessments of 1917*, ed. Edith Rogovin Frankel, Jonathan Frankel, and Baruch Knei-Paz (Cambridge: Cambridge University Press, 1992), 54–75.
37. S. V. Iarov, *Proletarii kak politik: Politicheskaia psikhologiia rabochikh Petrograda v 1917–1923 gg.* (St. Petersburg: Bulanin, 1999), 7.
38. S. P. Postnikov and M. A. Fel'dman, *Sotsiokul'turnyi oblik promyshlennykh rabochikh Rossii v 1900–1941 gg.* (Moscow: ROSSPEN, 2009), 304–305.
39. Dmitrii Churakov, *Revoliutsiia, gosudarstvo, rabochii protest: Formy, dinamika i priroda massovykh vystuplenii rabochikh v Sovetskoi Rossii, 1917–1918 gody* (Moscow: ROSSPEN, 2004), 12–13.
40. V. B. Stankevich, *Vospominaniia, 1914–1919 g.* (Berlin: Ladyschnikow, 1920), 76–78.
41. P. V. Volobuev, "Istoricheskie korni oktiabr'skoi revoliutsii," in *Anatomiia revoliutsii: 1917 god v Rossii: Massy, partii, vlast'*, ed. V. Iu. Cherniaev et al. (St. Petersburg: Glagol, 1994), 41.
42. Malle, *Economic Organization*, 35, quoting Lenin, "Can the Bolsheviks Retain State Power" (end September 1917).
43. John L. H. Keep, *The Russian Revolution: A Study in Mass Mobilization* (New York: Norton, 1976), comments that during the revolution, in contrast to the politically oriented "educated minority,...the popular masses, especially in the towns,...became increasingly preoccupied with the struggle to protect or advance their material interests" (67); workers were indifferent to the abstraction of the "proletariat" (88). Commenting on the lack of popular response to

the dispersal of the Constituent Assembly, Richard Pipes writes: "The 'popular masses' demonstrated that they understood only private and regional interests." *The Russian Revolution* (New York: Knopf, 1990), 556. Neither index contains the word "proletariat," though obviously it appears in both texts.

44. Social history examples: Smith, *Red Petrograd*; Koenker, *Moscow Workers*; Mark Steinberg, *Moral Communities: The Culture of Class Relations in the Russian Printing Industry, 1867–1907* (Berkeley: University of California Press, 1992).

45. B. I. Kolonitskii, "Antiburzhuaznaia propaganda i 'antiburzhuiskoe' soznanie," in *Anatomiia revoliutsii*, 190–192, 193, citing A. Kizevetter, "Moda na sotsializm," *Russkie vedomosti* (June 25, 1917).

46. Kolonitskii, "Antiburzhuaznaia," 195–197.

47. Aleksandr Kizevetter, "Itogi moskovskikh vyborov," *Russkie vedomosti* (June 28, 1917), cited Kolonitskii, "Antiburzhuaznaia," 196.

48. André Mazon, *Lexique de la guerre et de la révolution en Russie (1914–1918)* (Paris: É. Champion, 1920), 51–53.

49. Iarov, *Proletarii kak politik*, 10–15; echoed in Postnikov and Fel'dman, *Sotsiokul'turnyi oblik*, 315.

50. Mazon, *Lexique*, 48.

51. Kolonitskii, "Antiburzhuaznaia," 196.

52. Above passages overall based on Orlando Figes and Boris Kolonitskii, *Interpreting the Russian Revolution: The Language and Symbols of 1917* (New Haven: Yale University Press, 1999), ch. 4.

53. "Ves' vopros kto kogo operedit? …Nuzhno smotret' na eti veshshi trezvo: kto kogo?" Doklad 17 okt. 1921 g. II Vserossiiskii s"ezd politprosvetov. Lenin, 44:161, available at http://leninvi.com/t44/p161 (accessed February 12, 2017).

54. Quoted, Kolonitskii, "Antiburzhuaznaia," 201, from N. Berdiaev, "Torzhestvo i krushenie narodnichestva," *Russkaia svoboda*, no. 14/15 (1917), 5.

55. Kolonitskii, "Antiburzhuaznaia," 202.

56. Quoted, Churakov, *Revoliutsiia*, 177, from "Pis'mo K. M. Ermolaeva P. B. Aksel'rodu v Stokgol'm" (Petrograd, June 17, 1918), in *Mensheviki v 1918 godu*, ed. Z. Galili and A. Nenarokov (Moscow: ROSSPEN, 1999), 558.

## PART IV: CHAPTER 1

1. George F. Kennan, *Soviet-American Relations, 1917–1920,* Vol. 1: *Russia Leaves the War* (London: Faber and Faber, 1956), 87.

2. Adam Tooze, *The Deluge: The Great War and the Remaking of Global Order, 1916–1931* (London: Allen Lane, 2014), ch. 2.

3. Ibid., 57; Erez Manela, *The Wilsonian Moment: Self-Determination and the International Origins of Anticolonial Nationalism* (New York: Oxford University Press, 2007), 16.

4. Tooze, *Deluge*, 218–219.

5. John W. Wheeler-Bennett, *Brest-Litovsk, The Forgotten Peace, March 1918* (London: Macmillan; New York: St. Martin's, 1938), 103.

6. Wheeler-Bennett, *Brest-Litovsk,* 100–101.

7. "Lenin's Speech on the Peace Declaration" (November 8/October 26, 1917), in James Bunyan and H. H. Fisher, *The Bolshevik Revolution 1917–1918: Documents and Materials* (Stanford: Stanford University Press, 1934), 125. Delivered at Second All-Russian Congress of Soviets of Worker and Soldier Deputies; published *Izvestiia,* October 27/November 9, 1917.

8. Bunyan and Fisher, *Bolshevik Revolution,* 128.

9. Richard Pipes, *Russian Revolution* (New York: Knopf, 1990), 571; Kennan, *Russia Leaves the War,* 74–76.

10. Pipes, *Russian Revolution,* 576.

11. Kennan, *Russia Leaves the War,* 86.

12. Ibid., 91, 95. "Lenin Urges the Soldiers to Negotiate with the Enemy" (Proclamation to Soldiers and Sailors, November 9/22, 1917, published *Izvestiia,* November 10/23, 1917), in Bunyan and Fisher, *Bolshevik Revolution,* 236–237.

13. "Publication of the 'Secret Treaties'" (Trotsky on Secret Diplomacy, November 9/22, 1917, published *Izvestiia,* November 10/23, 1917), in Bunyan and Fisher, *Bolshevik Revolution,* 243–244; quoted, Kennan, *Russia Leaves the War,* 92.

14. Kennan, *Russia Leaves the War,* 92–93. "Protest of the Allied Military Missions Against Separate Negotiations (Letter to Dukhonin, November 10/23, 1917)," in Bunyan and Fisher, *Bolshevik Revolution,* 245; "The Allies Urge Dukhonin to Ask the Parties to Cease Demoralizing Agitation on the Front (Allied Military Missions to Dukhonin, November 11/24, 1917)," ibid., 247.

15. Wheeler-Bennett, *Brest-Litovsk,* 72–74; "Trotsky's Reply [to Allied Protest]" (November 11/24, 1917), in Bunyan and Fisher, *Bolshevik Revolution,* 245–246.

16. "Krylenko's Order No. 3" (November 14/27, 1917, published *Izvestiia,* November 15/28, 1917), in Bunyan and Fisher, *Bolshevik Revolution,* 258; Wheeler-Bennett, *Brest-Litovsk,* 75.

17. Wheeler-Bennett, *Brest-Litovsk,* 84; "The Sovnarkom to the People of the Belligerent Countries" (Radiogram, November 1/27, 1917), signed Trotsky and Lenin, in Bunyan and Fisher, *Bolshevik Revolution,* 258–259; "Trotsky Invites the Allies to Join the Armistice Negotiations" (November 16/29, 1917), ibid., 264.

18. See discussion of responses: Bunyan and Fisher, *Bolshevik Revolution,* 259–263.

19. From Peace Decree, quoted, Wheeler-Bennett, *Brest-Litovsk,* 69.

20. "First Negotiations at Brest" (Joffe Proposes a General Armistice, December 3, 1917), in Bunyan and Fisher, *Bolshevik Revolution,* 269–270; "Hoffmann Proposes a Separate Armistice" (December 3, 1917), ibid., 270; on duration, 271.

21. Alexander Rabinowitch, *The Bolsheviks in Power: The First Year of Soviet Rule in Petrograd* (Bloomington: Indiana University Press, 2007), 71–72 (November 26/December 9).

22. Wheeler-Bennett, *Brest-Litovsk,* 89–92.

23. "Armistice Agreement of Brest-Litovsk" (December 2/15), in ibid., 379–384; also, Bunyan and Fisher, *Bolshevik Revolution,* 273.

24. Quoted, Bunyan and Fisher, *Bolshevik Revolution,* 274 (dated December 6/19).

25. Wheeler-Bennett, *Brest-Litovsk,* 113, 116.

26. On their role: Winfried Baumgart, *Deutsche Ostpolitik 1918: Von Brest-Litowsk bis zum Ende des Ersten Weltkrieges* (Vienna and Munich: Oldenbourg, 1966), 15.

27. Wheeler-Bennett, *Brest-Litovsk*, 84–85.

28. Remark of February 13, 1918, cited in Pipes, *Russian Revolution*, 586.

29. Wheeler-Bennett, *Brest-Litovsk*, 84. Anti-Semitism aside, it is true that the leading Bolshevik delegates were Jews: Trotsky, Grigorii Sokol'nikov (Brilliant), Karl Radek, Ioffe, Lev Kamenev (Rozenfel'd).

30. In 1927, seriously ill, he committed suicide after Stalin had expelled Trotsky from the Party. See B. Ia. Khazanov, "Ioffe," in *Politicheskie deiateli Rossii 1917: Biograficheskii slovar'*, ed. P. V. Volobuev (Moscow: Bol'shaia rossiiskaia entsiklopediia, 1993), 126.

31. "The Russian Conditions of Peace (Joffe's Statement of the 'Six Points')" (December 9/22, 1917), in Bunyan and Fisher, *Bolshevik Revolution*, 477–478.

32. Wheeler-Bennett, *Brest-Litovsk*, 99, 103.

33. Ibid., 117, 120.

34. Ibid., 75, 84, 92.

35. Ibid., 76, quote, 76–77.

36. Baumgart, *Deutsche Ostpolitik 1918*, 15. See also Fritz Fischer, *Germany's Aims in the First World War*, intro. Hajo Holborn and James Joll (German, 1961; New York: Norton, 1967).

37. "Czernin's Reply for the Quadruple Alliance" (December 25, 1917), in Bunyan and Fisher, *Bolshevik Revolution*, 479–481; Wheeler-Bennett, *Brest-Litovsk*, 120.

38. Bunyan and Fisher, *Bolshevik Revolution*, 484 (December 14/27).

39. Wheeler-Bennett, *Brest-Litovsk*, 121–122.

40. Kennan, *Russia Leaves the War*, 247–248; Bunyan and Fisher, *Bolshevik Revolution*, 485–486 (December 16/29); Wheeler-Bennett, *Brest-Litovsk*, 136.

41. Quoted, Kennan, *Russia Leaves the War*, 254. See Bunyan and Fisher, *Bolshevik Revolution*, 486, citing *The Soviet Union and Peace: The Most Important of the Documents Issued by the Government of the U.S.S.R. Concerning Peace and Disarmament from 1917 to 1929*, intro Henri Barbusse (New York: International Publishers, [1929?]), 35–39.

42. Wheeler-Bennett, *Brest-Litovsk*, 117–118, 120–125.

43. Hoffmann, quoted, ibid., 126–127.

44. Quoted, Rabinowitch, *Bolsheviks in Power*, 135.

45. Mark von Hagen, *War in a European Borderland: Occupations and Occupation Plans in Galicia and Ukraine, 1914–1918* (Seattle: University of Washington Press, 2007), ch. 3.

46. Quoted, ibid., 60, from Fischer, *War Aims*.

47. Wheeler-Bennett, *Brest-Litovsk*, 103–105.

48. Bunyan and Fisher, *Bolshevik Revolution*, 487; Wheeler-Bennett, *Brest-Litovsk*, 140.

49. Wheeler-Bennett, *Brest-Litovsk*, 166.

50. "Declaration of the Ukrainian Delegation" (January 10, 1918), in Bunyan and Fisher, *Bolshevik Revolution*, 491–492.

51. Full text available at http://avalon.law.yale.edu/20th_century/wilson14.asp (accessed January 26, 2017).

52. On these motives, Kennan, *Russia Leaves the War*, 249–251. Gaddis and Hobsbawm agree that Wilson was intent on stopping Bolshevism: E. J. Hobsbawm, *Age of Extremes: A History of the World, 1914–1991* (New York: Pantheon, 1994), 67; John Lewis Gaddis, *The Cold War: A New History* (New York: Penguin, 2005), 121; cf. David W. McFadden, *Alternative Paths: Soviets and Americans, 1917–1920* (New York: Oxford University Press, 1993), 191.

53. Wheeler-Bennett, *Brest-Litovsk*, 144–145.

54. Quoted, Kennan, *Russia Leaves the War*, 254; "Address by the President of the United States, Woodrow Wilson, at a joint session of the two Houses of Congress, January 8, 1918," in *American Foreign Relations Since 1898: A Documentary Reader*, ed. Jeremy Suri (Chichester, UK: Wiley-Blackwell, 2010), 27.

55. Quoted, Kennan, *Russia Leaves the War* 255; "Address by the President of the United States," 28.

56. "Address by the President of the United States," 29.

57. Ibid., 30.

58. Kennan, *Russia Leaves the War*, 258, makes the point.

59. Charges that the Bolsheviks were acting with German support go back to 1917, when Lenin and his associates returned to Russia on the sealed train. Charges that the Germans were paying Lenin to make a separate peace were leveled in 1918 by Edgar Sisson, an employee of the U.S. propaganda agency in Petrograd, who was at the same time bankrolling the Soviet propaganda office: Kennan, *Russia Leaves the War*, 251. See George F. Kennan, "The Sisson Documents," *Journal of Modern History* 28 (1956): 130–154. Also, Kennan, *Russia Leaves the War*, ch. 22 (The Sisson Papers). German SPD leader Eduard Bernstein accused the Bolsheviks of essentially having sold themselves: Wheeler-Bennett, *Brest-Litovsk*, 184. The charge came from various quarters in 1918, as the treaty negotiations unfolded and the results were revealed; e.g., Wheeler-Bennett, *Brest-Litovsk*, 261.

60. Kennan, *Russia Leaves the War*, 260–261.

61. On German policy: Udo Gehrmann, "Turbulenzen am Stillen Don: Zur deutschen Kriegsziel- und Ostpolitik in der Zeit des Brest-Litovsker Friedens," *Jahrbücher für Geschichte Osteuropas*, n.s., 41.3 (1993): 394–421.

62. Wheeler-Bennett, *Brest-Litovsk*, 153–154.

63. Quoted, Wheeler-Bennett, *Brest-Litovsk*, 156, from Czernin's memoirs, Ottokar Theobald Otto Maria Czernin von und zu Chudenitz, *Im Weltkriege* (Berlin and Vienna: Ullstein, 1919); *In the World War* (New York: Harper & Bros, 1919). "Their only choice is what sauce they want to be served in." "Just like us."

64. Remarks of December 28/January 10, in Wheeler-Bennett, *Brest-Litovsk*, 156–157; quote, 157.

65. Quoted, Bunyan and Fisher, *Bolshevik Revolution*, 493.

66. Rabinowitch, *Bolsheviks in Power*, 136–142. For similar illusions about the possibility of mass mobilization after the war, see Michael Geyer, "Insurrectionary

Warfare: The German Debate about a *Levée en Masse* in October 1918," *Journal of Modern History* 73 (2001): 459–527.

67. "The Russian Proposal Regarding Self-Determination of Occupied Territories (From Kamenev's Statement in the Special Commission on Political Questions, January 12, 1918)," in Bunyan and Fisher, *Bolshevik Revolution*, 494–495.

68. "Hoffmann's Reply" (January 12, 1918), in Bunyan and Fisher, *Bolshevik Revolution*, 495–496.

69. Hoffmann summarized in ibid., 497.

70. Wheeler-Bennett, *Brest-Litovsk*, 169–170.

71. Ibid., 173–175; "Extract from Trotsky's Statement" (January 5/18, 1918), in Bunyan and Fisher, *Bolshevik Revolution*, 498.

72. Wheeler-Bennett, *Brest-Litovsk*, 183–184; Bunyan and Fisher, *Bolshevik Revolution*, 507.

73. Wheeler-Bennett, *Brest-Litovsk*, 184–186; quote, 196.

74. Ibid., 188.

75. "Revolutionary War or German Peace (Lenin's Argument for Peace, January 7/20, 1918)," in Bunyan and Fisher, *Bolshevik Revolution*, 500–505 (Lenin's text); also quoted, Wheeler-Bennett, *Brest-Litovsk*, 188–190; quote, 189.

76. Wheeler-Bennett, *Brest-Litovsk*, 193; Bunyan and Fisher, *Bolshevik Revolution*, 499; "*Pravda* Hails the International Revolution (January 22–February 1, 1918)," ibid., 505.

77. Wheeler-Bennett, *Brest-Litovsk*, 194.

78. Ibid., 195; "Trotsky on the Peace Terms (Extracts from His Report to the Third Congress, January 13/26, 1918)," in Bunyan and Fisher, *Bolshevik Revolution*, 506.

79. A. J. Ryder, *The German Revolution of 1918: A Study of German Socialism in War and Revolt* (Cambridge: Cambridge University Press, 1967), 117; Wheeler-Bennett, *Brest-Litovsk*, 196–197.

80. Rabinowitch, *Bolsheviks in Power*, 143–148.

81. Wheeler-Bennett, *Brest-Litovsk*, 203.

82. Ibid., 207–209.

83. Ibid., 210.

84. Ibid.

85. Quoted, ibid., 211.

86. Ibid., 231.

87. Rabinowitch, *Bolsheviks in Power*, 151; Wheeler-Bennett, *Brest-Litovsk*, 219–221; "The Treaty of Peace Between Ukraine and the Central Powers (Signed at Brest-Litovsk, February 9, 1918)," in Wheeler-Bennett, *Brest-Litovsk*, 392–402. Text available online at http://www.firstworldwar.com/source/ukrainianpeacetreaty.htm (accessed March 19, 2013).

88. Photos: http://humus.livejournal.com/2896160.html (accessed December 22, 2016). Wheeler-Bennett, *Brest-Litovsk*, 220 (filming).

89. Wheeler-Bennett, *Brest-Litovsk*, 221–224.

90. Ibid., 225–228; "No Peace and No War (From the Declaration of the Russian Delegation, February 10, 1918)," in Bunyan and Fisher, *Bolshevik Revolution*, 510. Text available online at http://www.firstworldwar.com/source/brestlitovsk_trotskywithdrawal.htm (accessed January 26, 2017).

91. Bruce R. H. Lockhart, *British Agent* (New York and London: Putnam, 1933), 226–227.

92. Rabinowitch, *Bolsheviks in Power*, 152; Wheeler-Bennett, *Brest-Litovsk*, 229–232; also on German differences: Bunyan and Fisher, *Bolshevik Revolution*, 511.


PART IV: CHAPTER 2

1. Alexander Rabinowitch, *The Bolsheviks in Power: The First Year of Soviet Rule in Petrograd* (Bloomington: Indiana University Press, 2007), 155–160. Rabinowitch is a key source for this chapter.

2. Major-General Max Hoffmann, *War Diaries and Other Papers*, trans. Eric Sutton, 2 vols. (London: Martin Secker, 1929), 1:205.

3. Ibid., 207.

4. Evan Mawdsley, *The Russian Civil War* (Boston: Allen and Unwin, 1987), 35.

5. Quoted, John W. Wheeler-Bennett, *Brest-Litovsk, The Forgotten Peace, March 1918* (London: Macmillan; New York: St. Martin's, 1938), 249.

6. *The Bolshevik Revolution, 1917–1918: Documents and Materials*, ed. James Bunyan and H. H. Fisher (Stanford: Stanford University Press, 1934), 511–513.

7. Rabinowitch, *Bolsheviks in Power*, 164.

8. "The Sovnarkom Accepts the Peace Terms" (Radiogram, February 18–19, 1918, *Pravda*, no. 30, February 20, 1918), in Bunyan and Fisher, *Bolshevik Revolution*, 513–514.

9. Iurii Fel'shtinskii, *Krushenie mirovoi revoliutsii: Brestskii mir: Oktiabr' 1917–noiabr' 1918* (Moscow: Terra, 1992), 259–260.

10. Rabinowitch, *Bolsheviks in Power*, 168–170.

11. "The Socialist Fatherland Is in Danger" (Proclamation of the Sovnarkom, February 21, 1918), in Bunyan and Fisher, *Bolshevik Revolution*, 517; V. A. Antonov-Ovseenko, *Zapiski o grazhdanskoi voine*, 3 vols. (Moscow: Vysshii voennyi redaktsionnyi sovet, 1924), 1:274–275; Wheeler-Bennett, *Brest-Litovsk*, 253; Rabinowitch, *Bolsheviks in Power*, 182 (quote).

12. Wheeler-Bennett, *Brest-Litovsk*, 250–252.

13. Ibid., 254–255; Iu. I. Korablev, "Trotskii," in *Politicheskie deiateli Rossii 1917: Biograficheskii slovar'*, ed. P. V. Volobuev (Moscow: Bol'shaia rossiiskaia entsiklopediia, 1993), 324.

14. "Chicherin," in Jonathan D. Smele, *Historical Dictionary of the Russian Civil Wars, 1916–1926*, 2 vols. (Lanham, MD: Rowman & Littlefield, 2015), 1:275–277.

15. Wheeler-Bennett, *Brest-Litovsk*, 245; Rabinowitch, *Bolsheviks in Power*, 173.

16. Wheeler-Bennett, *Brest-Litovsk*, 255–257 (Lenin quote, 257); "The Germans Refuse to Stop the Advance" (Hoffmann to Krylenko, February 24, 1918);

"Signing the Treaty: Arrival of Soviet Delegation at Brest" (Karakhan to the Sovnarkom, March 1, 1918), in Bunyan and Fisher, *Bolshevik Revolution*, 521.

17. Rabinowitch, *Bolsheviks in Power*, 173–178; Wheeler-Bennett, *Brest-Litovsk*, 258.

18. Kollontai quoted, Wheeler-Bennett, *Brest-Litovsk*, 259.

19. Quoted, ibid., 260.

20. V. B. Stankevich, *Vospominaniia, 1914–1919 g.* (Berlin: Ladyschnikow, 1920), 308.

21. Wheeler-Bennett, *Brest-Litovsk*, 245–246; Mawdsley, *Russian Civil War*, 33.

22. Rabinowitch, *Bolsheviks in Power*, 173–178; "The Sovnarkom Accepts the Ultimatum" (Telegram of February 24, 1918), in Bunyan and Fisher, *Bolshevik Revolution*, 520.

23. Rabinowitch, *Bolsheviks in Power*, 182–183.

24. Ibid., 183–186.

25. Karsten Brüggemann, "National and Social Revolution in the Empire's West: Estonian Independence and the Russian Civil War, 1917–20," trans. Martin Pearce, in *Russia's Home Front in War and Revolution, 1914–22*, Book 1: *Russia's Revolution in Regional Perspective*, ed. Sarah Badcock, Liudmila G. Novikova, and Aaron B. Retish (Bloomington: Slavica, 2015), 146–147; Geoffrey Swain, "The Disillusioning of the Revolution's Praetorian Guard: The Latvian Riflemen, Summer–Autumn 1918," *Europe-Asia Studies* 51.4 (1999): 667–686.

26. Rabinowitch, *Bolsheviks in Power*, 199–200.

27. "The Germans Make New Demands" (Karakhan to the Sovnarkom, March 2, 1918)," in Bunyan and Fisher, *Bolshevik Revolution*, 522.

28. Wheeler-Bennett, *Brest-Litovsk*, 266–269.

29. "Statement of the Russian Delegation" (March 3, 1918), in Bunyan and Fisher, *Bolshevik Revolution*, 522–523; quote, 522.

30. Wheeler-Bennett, *Brest-Litovsk*, 269, 275; 403–408 (text).

31. Stankevich, *Vospominaniia*, 307–308, 310.

32. Rabinowitch, *Bolsheviks in Power*, 186–188.

33. Ibid., 197; Lenin quoted, Bunyan and Fisher, *Bolshevik Revolution*, 526.

34. Quoted, Wheeler-Bennett, *Brest-Litovsk*, 280; also "The Seventh Bolshevik Party Congress and Peace (March 8, 1918): Majority Resolution for Peace," in Bunyan and Fisher, *Bolshevik Revolution*, 527.

35. Wheeler-Bennett, *Brest-Litovsk*, 281.

36. "Minority Resolution for Revolutionary War," in Bunyan and Fisher, *Bolshevik Revolution*, 528–529.

37. Rabinowitch, *Bolsheviks in Power*, 200–203.

38. Wheeler-Bennett, *Brest-Litovsk*, 283.

39. Ibid., 299.

40. I. S. Rat'kovskii, *Krasnyi terror i deiatel'nost' VChK v 1918 godu* (St. Petersburg: S.-Peterburgskii universitet, 2006), 46–47.

41. On these feelers: Bunyan and Fisher, *Bolshevik Revolution*, 535–537; Wheeler-Bennett, *Brest-Litovsk*, 288–295.

42. "Wilson's Message to the Congress of Soviets," in Bunyan and Fisher, *Bolshevik Revolution*, 538.

43. Wheeler-Bennett, *Brest-Litovsk*, 299.

44. "The Fourth Congress of Soviets Ratifies the Treaty: Summary of Lenin's Argument for Ratification" (March 1918), in Bunyan and Fisher, *Bolshevik Revolution*, 530–531; quote, 531.

45. Quoted, Bunyan and Fisher, *Bolshevik Revolution*, 531; A. I. Razgon, "Kamkov," *Politicheskie deiateli*, 136–139.

46. Quoted, Bunyan and Fisher, *Bolshevik Revolution*, 533.

47. "The Socialist-Revolutionaries of the Left Repudiate the Ratification" (March 16, 1918), in Bunyan and Fisher, *Bolshevik Revolution*, 533.

48. *Pravda*, March 19, 1918, in Bunyan and Fisher, *Bolshevik Revolution*, 534.

49. William G. Rosenberg, *Liberals in the Russian Revolution: The Constitutional Democratic Party, 1917–1921* (Princeton: Princeton University Press, 1974), 291–292.

50. Ibid., 292 (quote); "The Union for the Regeneration of Russia," in James Bunyan, *Intervention, Civil War, and Communism in Russia, April–December 1918: Documents and Materials* (Baltimore: Johns Hopkins Press, 1936), 182–185; *Krasnaia kniga V.Ch.K.*, vol. 2, ed. M. I. Latsis (Moscow: Gosizdat, 1922); rpt., ed. A. S. Velidov (Moscow: Politicheskaia literatura, 1989), 32–35 ("Soiuz vozrozhdeniia"); 79–87 ("Spravka S. P. Mel'gunova").

51. Rabinowitch, *Bolsheviks in Power*, 237–238.

52. Ibid., 239–243. A fierce proponent of the Red Terror from its inception, Krylenko went on to become commissar of justice and prosecutor general of the RSFSR; see V. N. Zabotin, "Krylenko," in *Politicheskie deiateli*, 171.

53. Rabinowitch, *Bolsheviks in Power*, 314.

54. Ibid., 244–246.

55. Ibid., 247.

56. Ibid., 252–256.

57. Ibid., 213–222, 224.

58. Ibid., 257–258.

59. Ibid., 283–284.

60. Lutz Häfner, "The Assassination of Count Mirbach and the 'July Uprising' of the Left SRs in Moscow, 1918," *Russian Review* 50 (1991): 324; Rabinowitch, *Bolsheviks in Power*, 285–286.

61. Quoted, George Leggett, *The Cheka: Lenin's Political Police* (Oxford: Clarendon, 1981), 58. For more such language: S. P. Mel'gunov, *"Krasnyi terror" v Rossii 1918–1923* (Berlin: Vataga, 1924), 30, 34. Mel'gunov is acidic on the subject of Left SR Commissar of Justice Shteinberg, who in retrospect condemned the Bolshevik terror, but at the time participated in the Bolshevik government.

62. Leggett, *Cheka*, 53.

63. I. N. Steinberg, *In the Workshop of the Revolution* (New York: Rinehart, 1953), 97–99.

64. Häfner, "Assassination," 324.

65. Of a total 1,164 deputies: 773 Bolsheviks, 353 Left SRs, 17 SR-Maximalists, 4 anarchists, 4 Menshevik-Internationalists, 1 Dashnak (Armenian), 1 Poalei-Tsion (Zionist), 1 Right SR, 10 nonparty; the Presidium: 14 Bolsheviks, 6 Left SRs: "Piatyi Vserossiiskii s"ezd Sovetov...," in *Politicheskie deiateli*, 412; Häfner, "Assassination," 326.

66. Bruce R. H. Lockhart, *British Agent* (New York and London: Putnam, 1933), 295.

67. Ibid., 296.

68. Wheeler-Bennett, *Brest-Litovsk*, 338–339.

69. "Piatyi Vserossiiskii s"ezd Sovetov...," in *Politicheskie deiateli*, 412 (Kamkov, udochka).

70. Quoted, Lockhart, *British Agent*, 299, repeated from this source in Wheeler-Bennett, *Brest-Litovsk*, 339.

71. Rabinowitch, *Bolsheviks in Power*, 287–289.

72. Ibid., 290–291; Lockhart, *British Agent*, 300–301; Häfner, "Assassination," 326–328; Karl Freiherr von Bothmer, *Moskauer Tagebuch 1918*, ed. Gernot Böhme, annotated Winfried Baumgart (Paderborn: Ferdinand Schöningh, 2010), 75–78. Also: Boris Chavkin, "Die Ermordung des Grafen Mirbach," *Forum für osteuropäische Ideen- und Zeitgeschichte* 10 (2006), 91–114.

73. Rabinowitch, *Bolsheviks in Power*, 292–295; Mawdsley, *Russian Civil War*, 41 (Latvian rifles).

74. Rabinowitch, *Bolsheviks in Power*, 289–304.

75. Mikhail Samoilovich Frenkin, *Tragediia krest'ianskikh vosstanii v Rossii, 1918–1921 gg.* (Jerusalem: "Leksikon," 1987), 90–91.

76. *Krasnaia kniga VChK*, vol. 1, ed. P. Makintsian (Moscow: Gosizdat, 1920); rpt., ed. A. S.Velidov (Moscow: Politicheskaia literatura, 1989), 49–178; V. Vinogradov and V. Safonov, "Boris Savinkov—protivnik bol'shevikov," in *Boris Savinkov na Lubianke: Dokumenty*, ed. A. L. Litvin (Moscow: ROSSPEN, 2001), 4–7.

77. Dmitrii Churakov, *Revoliutsiia, gosudarstvo, rabochii protest: Formy, dinamika i priroda massovykh vystuplenii rabochikh v Sovetskoi Rossii, 1917–1918 gody* (Moscow: ROSSPEN, 2004), 107–108; Rat'kovskii, *Krasnyi terror*, 125 (2,000).

78. "Vozzvanie k zhiteliam goroda Iaroslavlia o sverzhenii vlasti Bol'shevikov i svoei programme" (no later than July 6, 1918), in *Iaroslavskoe vosstanie 1918*, ed. E. A. Ermolin and V. N. Kozliakov (Moscow: Mezhdunarodnyi fond "Demokratiia," 2007), 28; "The Yaroslav Revolt (Proclamation of the Insurrectionists, July 6, 1918)," in Bunyan, *Intervention*, 193–194.

79. Telegram of July 16, 1918, quoted, *Iaroslavskoe vosstanie*, 13.

80. Quoted, ibid., 15.

81. Ibid., 15; Rat'kovskii, *Krasnyi terror*, 126–127.

82. Quoted, *Iaroslavskoe vosstanie*, 15.

83. Rabinowitch, *Bolsheviks in Power*, 295–296.

84. Leggett, *Cheka*, 61–63 (quote, 63).

85. Rabinowitch, *Bolsheviks in Power*, 321–324.

86. See Lockhart, *British Agent*, 263–265.

87. Quoted, Rabinowitch, *Bolsheviks in Power*, 324.

88. Ibid., 325.

89. Quoted, ibid., 326.

90. Ibid., 328–329.

91. Elektronnaia evreiskaia entsiklopediia, available at http://www.eleven.co.il/article/14228 (accessed April 1, 2013).

92. Elektronnaia evreiskaia entsiklopediia, available at http://www.eleven.co.il/article/11951 (accessed April 1, 2013).

93. On personal motives, see John E. Malmstad and Nikolay Bogomolov, *Mikhail Kuzmin: A Life in Art* (Cambridge, MA: Harvard University Press, 1999), 266. Thanks to Stephen Dodson for suggesting the source.

94. Quoted, V.V. Voroshilov, "Zasulich," in *Politicheskie deiateli*, 117.

95. *VChK upolnomochena soobshchit'—: 1918 g.*, ed. V. K. Vinogradov (Moscow: Kuchkovo pole, 2004), 35.

96. Quoted, Rabinowitch, *Bolsheviks in Power*, 332; *Arkhiv VChK: Sbornik dokumentov*, ed. V. Vinogradov, A. Litvin, and V. Khristoforov (Moscow: Kuchkovo pole, 2007), 77 (September 5, 1918).

97. Rabinowitch, *Bolsheviks in Power*, 331–334; quote, 333.

98. "Protokol zasedaniia Kollegii otdela po bor'be s kontrrevoliutsiei, 5 sentiabria 1918 g.," in *Arkhiv VChK*, 267.

99. "Protokol zasedaniia Prezidiuma kollektiva Otdela K.P. ot 24 sentiabria 1918 g.," in *Arkhiv VChK*, 275.

100. Mel'gunov, *"Krasnyi terror,"* 7–8.

101. Quotes, ibid., 10–11.

102. Quoted, ibid., 11 (*protivozaraznaia privivka*).

103. Quoted, ibid., 34 (September 23, 1918).

104. Rabinowitch, *Bolsheviks in Power*, 334–339.

105. Ibid., 340–341.

106. Ibid., 342, 346–347. See *Moskovskii Politicheskii Krasnyi Krest (Moskovskii Komitet Obshchestva Krasnogo Kresta dlia pomoshchi politicheskim zakliuchennym v Rossii), 1918–1922: Sbornik dokumentov*, ed. L. A. Dolzhanskaia et al. (Moscow: Formika-S, 2015).

107. Quoted, Mel'gunov, *"Krasnyi terror,"* 15.

108. Ibid., 13–14.

109. Quoted, ibid., 16.

110. Ibid., 30.

111. Ibid., 16–17.

## PART IV: CHAPTER 3

1. Andreas Kappeler, *The Russian Empire: A Multiethnic History*, trans. Alfred Clayton (Harlow: Longman-Pearson Education, 2001), 331 (1905).

2. Anthony F. Upton, *The Finnish Revolution, 1917–1918* (Minneapolis: University of Minnesota Press, 1980), 3–4. Upton is the key source for this chapter.

3. Kappeler, *Russian Empire*, 260–261.

4. Upton, *Finnish Revolution*, 3–8.

5. Ibid., 10–12; Irina N. Novikova, *"Finskaia karta" v nemetskom pas'ianse: Germaniia i problema nezavisimosti Finliandii v gody Pervoi mirovoi voiny* (St. Petersburg: Peterburgskii universitet, 2002).

6. Upton, *Finnish Revolution*, 19–24.

7. The 1878 conscription law was suspended 1900–1917: Upton, *Finnish Revolution*, 322; Joshua A. Sanborn, *Imperial Apocalypse: The Great War and the Destruction of the Russian Empire* (Oxford: Oxford University Press, 2014), 176.

8. Upton, *Finnish Revolution*, 26–27; Semion Lyandres, *The Fall of Tsarism: Untold Stories of the February 1917 Revolution* (Oxford: Oxford University Press, 2013), 211; A. D. Bazhanov, "Ubiistvo komanduiushchego Baltiiskim flotom vitse-admirala A. I. Nepenina 4 marta 1918 g.," in *Revoliutsiia 1917 goda v Rossii: Novye podkhody i vzgliady* (St. Petersburg: RGPU, 2010), 30–39.

9. Upton, *Finnish Revolution*, 27.

10. Henning Söderhjelm, *The Red Insurrection in Finland in 1918: A Study Based on Documentary Evidence*, trans. Anne I. Fausbøll (London: Harrison and sons, [1919]), 16.

11. Söderhjelm, *Red Insurrection*, 20–21.

12. Upton, *Finnish Revolution*, 27–28.

13. Ibid., 28.

14. Malbone W. Graham, *New Governments of Eastern Europe* (New York: Henry Holt, 1927), 180–184.

15. Upton, *Finnish Revolution*, 86–90.

16. Ibid., 92–93.

17. Graham, *New Governments*, 185–186; Upton, *Finnish Revolution*, 96–97 (quote, 96).

18. Upton, *Finnish Revolution*, 120.

19. Ibid., 127; B. M. Shaposhnikov, *Vospominaniia: Voenno-nauchnye trudy*, intro. A. M. Vasilevskii and M. V. Zakharov (Moscow: Voenizdat, 1974), 228, cited in http://ruskline.ru/monitoring_smi/2005/05/16/general_vladimir_oranovskij/ (accessed February 13, 2017).

20. Upton, *Finnish Revolution*, 128–129; Elena Dubrovskaia, "The Russian Military in Finland and the Russian Revolution," in *Russia's Home Front in War and Revolution, 1914–22*, book 1: *Russia's Revolution in Regional Perspective*, ed. Sarah Badcock, Liudmila G. Novikova, and Aaron B. Retish (Bloomington: Slavica, 2015), 247–266.

21. Upton, *Finnish Revolution*, 127–132.

22. Quoted, ibid., 137.

23. Ibid., 134–137.

24. Ibid., 138–141.

25. Ibid., 144–147.

26. Ibid., 150–153.

27. Ibid., 170–174.
28. Ibid., 178.
29. "Svinhufvud," in Jonathan D. Smele, *Historical Dictionary of the Russian Civil Wars, 1916–1926*, 2 vols. (Lanham, MD: Rowman & Littlefield, 2015), 2:1134–1135.
30. Upton, *Finnish Revolution*, 180–181.
31. Quotes, ibid., 182.
32. Ibid., 183; Graham, *New Governments*, 190–191 (date given incorrectly as November 24/December 7, 1917).
33. Upton, *Finnish Revolution*, 184–185.
34. Ibid., 185.
35. November 16/29 statement; November 27/December 10 and December 15/28 statements, quoted, ibid., 186.
36. Ibid., 186–187 (quote, 186).
37. Ibid., 187–190.
38. Quoted, ibid., 192.
39. Ibid., 192–193.
40. Ibid., 195.
41. Ibid., 196–197; quote, 197.
42. Ibid., 198–200.
43. Quoted, ibid., 201.
44. Ibid., 206–210.
45. Quoted, ibid., 227.
46. Ibid., 224–225.
47. Quoted, ibid., 230.
48. Ibid., 210–212.
49. Ibid., 212–216, 236–237.
50. Ibid., 237–238.
51. Ibid., 239–241.
52. Ibid., 247.
53. Ibid., 254–255.
54. Ibid., 256–257.
55. Quoted, ibid., 266.
56. Quoted, ibid., 262.
57. Ibid., 269–271.
58. Quoted, ibid., 276.
59. Ibid., 285–287.
60. Ibid., 288–290, 293, 295.
61. Ibid., 294 (all quotes).
62. Ibid., 415–416.
63. Quoted, ibid., 303.
64. Ibid., 304–305.
65. Quoted, ibid., 311.

66. Quoted from March 13, 1918, order for Tampere offensive, ibid., 313.

67. Quoted, ibid., 323.

68. Ibid., 405–407.

69. Quoted, ibid., 413–414.

70. Ibid., 419, 421–422.

71. Ibid., 352.

72. Ibid., 379–381.

73. Ibid., 385–388.

74. Quotes, ibid., 316.

75. Ibid., 322–328, 348–349.

76. Ibid., 310, 328.

77. Ibid., 336–337.

78. Quoted, ibid., 339.

79. Ibid., 340, 342.

80. Ibid., 350–351, 474. See Rüdiger von der Goltz, *Meine Sendung in Finnland und im Baltikum* (Leipzig: Koehler, 1920). This was not the late Colmar Freiherr von der Goltz, responsible for the atrocities in Belgium.

81. Quoted, Upton, *Finnish Revolution*, 474, 475.

82. Ibid., 477–481.

83. Ibid., 468–469.

84. Ibid., 468–470; quote, 469.

85. Ibid., 483.

86. Ibid., 492–498.

87. Quoted, ibid., 512.

88. Ibid., 510–513.

89. Ibid., 516–519 (quote, 516).

90. Ibid., 519–520 (quote, 520, from letter dated May 25, 1918).

91. Ibid., 521–522. Pertti Haapala and Marko Tikka, "Revolution, Civil War, and Terror in Finland in 1918," in *War in Peace: Paramilitary Violence after the Great War*, ed. Robert Gerwarth and John Horne (Oxford: Oxford University Press, 2012), 83 (overall estimate, the Red Terror in Finland took the lives of 1,600 people, the White Terror of over 8,000).

92. Upton, *Finnish Revolution*, 532–534.

93. Text in John M. Thompson, *Russia, Bolshevism, and the Versailles Peace* (Princeton: Princeton University Press, 1966), 24; Herbert Hoover, *The Memoirs of Herbert Hoover*, 3 vols., Vol. 1: *Years of Adventure, 1874–1920* (New York: Macmillan, 1951), 369.

94. Otto Wille Kuusinen, *Révolution en Finlande: Essai d'autocritique sur les luttes de 1918* (Petrograd: Éditions de l'Internationale Communiste, 1920), 21; "Kuusinen," in Smele, *Historical Dictionary*, 1:646–647.

95. Söderhjelm, *Red Insurrection*, 157.

PART IV: CHAPTER 4

1. See, recently, Andrejs Plakans, *A Concise History of the Baltic States* (Cambridge: Cambridge University Press, 2011).
2. Andreas Kappeler, *The Russian Empire: A Multiethnic History*, trans. Alfred Clayton (Harlow: Longman-Pearson Education, 2001), 71–75 (bridge and model).
3. Courland, 27 percent; Livonia, 39 percent; Poland, 25 percent (Warsaw province, 40 percent); Petrograd, 74 percent; Moscow Province, 53 percent, against the Empire average of 15 percent: *Rossiia 1913 god: Statistiko-dokumental'nyi spravochnik*, ed. A. M. Anfinov and A. P. Korelin (St. Petersburg: BLITs, 1995), 18–22.
4. Olavi Arens and Andrew Ezergailis, "The Revolution in the Baltics: Estonia and Latvia," in *Critical Companion to the Russian Revolution 1914–1921*, ed. Edward Acton, Vladimir Iu. Cherniaev, and William G. Rosenberg (Bloomington: Indiana University Press, 1997), 667–678. See also: Andrew Ezergailis, *The 1917 Revolution in Latvia* (New York: Columbia University Press, 1973); Andrew Ezergailis, *The Latvian Impact on the Bolshevik Revolution: The First Phase, September 1917 to April 1918* (New York: Columbia University Press, 1983); Malbone W. Graham, *New Governments of Eastern Europe* (New York: Henry Holt, 1927), ch. 10.
5. Graham, *New Governments*, 324–325.
6. Ibid., 326–329; Karsten Brüggemann, "National and Social Revolution in the Empire's West: Estonian Independence and the Russian Civil War, 1917–20," trans. Martin Pearce, in *Russia's Home Front in War and Revolution, 1914–22: Russia's Revolution in Regional Perspective*, ed. Sarah Badcock, Liudmila G. Novikova, and Aaron B. Retish (Bloomington: Slavica, 2015), 151. The work of Brüggemann and Novikova is key to this chapter.
7. Graham, *New Governments*, 330; *The Bolshevik Revolution, 1917–1918: Documents and Materials*, ed. James Bunyan and H. H. Fisher (Stanford: Stanford University Press, 1934), 460–461.
8. Robert G. L. Waite, *Vanguard of Nazism: The Free Corps Movement in Post-War Germany, 1918–1923* (Cambridge, MA: Harvard University Press, 1952), 103–104 (quote, 103).
9. Andres Kasekamp, *A History of the Baltic States* (New York: Palgrave Macmillan, 2010), 101; "Stuchka," in Jonathan D. Smele, *Historical Dictionary of the Russian Civil Wars, 1916–1926*, 2 vols. (Lanham, MD: Rowman & Littlefield, 2015), 2:1122. He died a natural death in 1932.
10. Karsten Brüggemann, "Cities of Imperial and National Utopias: A Transnational Approach to Riga and Tallinn, 1914–1924" (unpublished ms., courtesy of the author, 2016), 18–19.
11. Herbert Hoover, *The Memoirs of Herbert Hoover*, 3 vols., vol. 1: *Years of Adventure, 1874–1920* (New York: Macmillan, 1951), 375; Brüggemann, "Cities," 18–20; Mark T. Hatlie, "Voices from Riga: Ethnic Perspectives on a Wartime City, 1914–1919," *Zeitschrift für Ostmitteleuropa-Forschung* 56.3 (2007): 318–346; Mark T.

Hatlie, *Riga at War: War and Wartime Experience in a Multi-Ethnic Metropolis* (Marburg: Herder-Institut, 2014).

12. George Stewart, *The White Armies of Russia: A Chronicle of Counter-Revolution and Allied Intervention* (New York: Macmillan, 1933), 215.

13. Waite, *Vanguard*, 109.

14. Ibid., 111.

15. Ibid., 116–117.

16. Brüggemann, "National and Social Revolution," 160, confirms that the Landeswehr under von der Goltz was the force that took Riga on May 22, 1919.

17. Hoover, *Memoirs*, 1:375.

18. Waite, *Vanguard*, 116–119; Brüggemann, "National and Social Revolution," 160.

19. Quoted, Waite, *Vanguard*, 116.

20. Ibid., 120–124.

21. Ibid., 125–131; Brüggemann, "Cities," 20–21.

22. Graham, *New Governments*, 333–335.

23. Brüggemann, "National and Social Revolution," 147–148; Arens and Ezergailis, "The Revolution in the Baltics: Estonia and Latvia," 667–678; Graham, *New Governments*, chs. 8–9.

24. Brüggemann, "National and Social Revolution," 148–149; Graham, *New Governments*, 256.

25. Brüggemann, "National and Social Revolution," 149–150.

26. Account in Bunyan and Fisher, *Bolshevik Revolution*, 460; Karsten Brüggemann, *Die Gründung der Republik Estland und das Ende des "Einen und unteilbaren Russland": Die Petrograder Front des russischen Bürgerkriegs 1918–1920* (Wiesbaden: Harrassowitz, 2002), 451; Brüggemann, "National and Social Revolution," 151.

27. Brüggemann, "National and Social Revolution," 151.

28. Ibid., 152–153.

29. Ibid., 155.

30. Graham, *New Governments*, 265; Brüggemann, "National and Social Revolution," 158.

31. Graham, *New Governments*, 281–284.

32. Brüggemann, "National and Social Revolution," 167, 170.

33. Graham, *New Governments*, 286–287.

34. Tomas Balkelis, *The Making of Modern Lithuania* (London: Routledge, 2009).

35. Timothy Snyder, *The Reconstruction of Nations: Poland, Ukraine, Lithuania, Belarus, 1569–1999* (New Haven: Yale University Press, 2003), ch. 3; here 61–62; Kasekamp, *History*, 97–98.

36. Kasekamp, *History*, 98.

37. Jerzy Borzęcki, *The Soviet-Polish Peace of 1921 and the Creation of Interwar Europe* (New Haven: Yale University Press, 2008), 14–16; Kasekamp, *History*, 101.

38. Liudmila G. Novikova, "A Province of a Non-Existent State: The White Government in the Russian North and Political Power in the Russian Civil War, 1918–20," *Revolutionary Russia* 18.2 (2005): 121.

39. Yanni Kotsonis, "Arkhangel'sk, 1918: Regionalism and Populism in the Russian Civil War," *Russian Review* 51.4 (1992): 528–530.

40. Novikova, "A Province," 126.

41. Liudmila G. Novikova, "Russia's Red Revolutionary and White Terror, 1917–1921: A Provincial Perspective," *Europe-Asia Studies* 65.9 (2013): 1757–1758.

42. Kotsonis, "Arkhangel'sk," 530–531.

43. Novikova, "Russia's Red Revolutionary and White Terror," 1759.

44. Kotsonis, "Arkhangel'sk," 532; Liudmila G. Novikova, "Northerners into Whites: Popular Participation in the Counter-Revolution in Arkhangel'sk Province, Summer–Autumn 1918," *Europe-Asia Studies* 60.2 (2008): 282.

45. Kotsonis, "Arkhangel'sk," 532.

46. Novikova, "Russia's Red Revolutionary and White Terror," 1759.

47. Novikova, "A Province," 126.

48. Novikova, "Northerners into Whites," 280, 282–283.

49. Kotsonis, "Arkhangel'sk," 535; *Krasnaia kniga V.Ch.K.*, vol. 1, ed. M. I. Latsis (Moscow: Gosizdat, 1922); rpt., ed. A. S. Velidov (Moscow: Politicheskaia literatura, 1989), 32–35 ("Soiuz vozrozhdeniia"), 79–87 ("Spravka S. P. Mel'gunova").

50. Novikova, "A Province," 127–128; Kotsonis, "Arkhangel'sk," 535–536.

51. V. I. Goldin, "Chaikovskii," in *Politicheskie deiateli Rossii 1917: Biograficheskii slovar'*, ed. P. V. Volobuev (Moscow: Bol'shaia rossiiskaia entsiklopediia, 1993), 342–343. See: S. P. Mel'gunov, *N. V. Chaikovskii v gody grazhdanskoi voiny: Materialy dlia istorii russkoi obshchestvennosti* (Paris: Rodnik, 1929); *Nikolai Vasil'evich Chaikovskii: Religioznye i obshchestvennye iskaniia*, ed. A. A. Titov (Paris: Rodnik, 1929).

52. Novikova, "Northerners into Whites," 283–284, 286.

53. Quoted, ibid., 288–289.

54. Ibid., 280; Novikova, "A Province," 128–129.

55. Novikova, "Russia's Red Revolutionary and White Terror," 1760–1762, 1765.

56. Novikova, "A Province," 132; Novikova, *Provintsial'naia*, 112.

57. Novikova, *Provintsial'naia*, 108–111.

58. Ibid., 114, 116; Novikova, "A Province," 133–134 (*diktatura po soglasheniiu*); Sergei Volkov, "Miller," in *Grazhdanskaia voina v Rossii: Entsiklopediia katastrofy*, ed. Dmitrii Volodikhin and Sergei Volkov (Moscow: Sibirskii tsiriul'nik, 2010), 147.

59. Sergei V. Volkov, *Belaia Bor'ba na Severo-Zapadne Rossii* (Moscow: Tsentrpoligraf, 2003).

60. Brüggemann, *Die Gründung*, 88–91; Brüggemann, "National and Social Revolution," 153, 163; "Iudenich," in Smele, *Historical Dictionary*, 1:510–512; G. Kirdetsov, *U vorot Petrograda (1919–1920)* (Berlin: "Moskva," 1921). In emigration in Germany, Markov published works with titles such as *The Wars of the Dark Forces…the Jews as Enemies of Mankind* (1935) and *The Jew is a Parasite on the Peasantry* (1944). He died a natural death in Wiesbaden in 1945, at the ripe old age of eighty. See "Markov," in Aleksandr Mindlin, *Gosudarstvennye, politicheskie i obshchestvennye deiateli Rossiiskoi imperii v sud'bakh evreev, 1762–1917* (St. Petersburg: Aleteiia, 2007), 210–216.

61. Brüggemann, "National and Social Revolution," 152–153.

62. Brüggemann, *Die Gründung*, 92; Brüggemann, "National and Social Revolution," 154.

63. Brüggemann, "National and Social Revolution," 156.

64. Vasilii Gorn, *Grazhdanskaia voina na severno-zapade Rossii* (Berlin: Gamaiun, 1923), 5–8.

65. Ibid., 8–9.

66. Valerii Klaving, *Grazhdanskaia voina v Rossii: Belye armii* (Moscow: AST, 2003), 402–404; Sergei Volkov, "Bulak-Balakhovich," in *Grazhdanskaia voina v Rossii*, ed. Volodikhin and Volkov, 301; "Bułak-Bałachowicz," in Smele, *Historical Dictionary*, 1:241–243. Bułak-Bałachowicz will be discussed at greater length in connection with the anti-Jewish pogroms that engulfed the western provinces in 1919–1920.

67. Quoted, Gorn, *Grazhdanskaia voina*, 11–12.

68. Ibid., 12–13.

69. Brüggemann, "National and Social Revolution," 164; Brüggemann, *Die Gründung*, 234–236; Gorn, *Grazhdanskaia voina*, 14.

70. Evan Mawdsley, *The Russian Civil War* (Boston: Allen and Unwin, 1987), 196–199; Brüggemann, "National and Social Revolution," 157, 159.

71. Brüggemann, "National and Social Revolution," 161–163, 168; Konstantin Zalesskii, "Pervoe nastuplenie Iudenicha na Petrograd," in *Grazhdanskaia voina v Rossii*, ed. Volodikhin and Volkov, 232–234.

72. August 8, 1919 quoted, Brüggemann, "National and Social Revolution," 165.

73. Brüggemann, "National and Social Revolution," 167.

74. Konstantin Zalesskii, "Vtoroe nastuplenie Iudenicha na Petrograd," in *Grazhdanskaia voina v Rossii*, 235–237; Sergei Volkov, "Iudenich," ibid., 235 and 237; Brüggemann, "National and Social Revolution," 169.

75. Mawdsley, *Russian Civil War*, 199–200.

76. William Henry Chamberlin, *The Russian Revolution, 1917–1921*, 2 vols. (1935; New York: Grosset & Dunlap, 1965), 2:38; N. S. Tarkhova, "Trotsky's Train: An Unknown Page in the History of the Civil War," in *The Trotsky Reappraisal*, ed. Brian Pearce, Jenny Brine, and Andrew Drummond (Edinburgh: Edinburgh University Press, 1992), 163–173.

77. Mawdsley, *Russian Civil War*, 199–201; Klaving, *Grazhdanskaia voina*, 403–404, 601. Iudenich died in 1933 in Nice.

78. Novikova, "Russia's Red Revolutionary and White Terror," 1768.

79. Sergei Volkov, "Miller," in *Grazhdanskaia voina v Rossii*, ed. Volodikhin and Volkov, 147.

## PART IV: CHAPTER 5

1. Imperial Provinces constituting "Ukraine" in 1917: Chernigov, Ekaterinoslav, Kharkov, Kherson, Kiev, Podolia, Poltava, Taurida, Volhynia (Chernihiv, Katerynoslav, Kharkiv, Kherson, Kyiv, Podillia, Poltava, Tavriia, Volyn). Five had Ukrainian ethnic majorities: Chernigov, Kiev, Podolia, Poltava, Volhynia. See

Serhy Yekelchyk, *Ukraine: Birth of a Modern Nation* (New York: Oxford University Press, 2007), 70–71. Basic works are: Stephen Velychenko, *State Building in Revolutionary Ukraine: A Comparative Study of Government and Bureaucrats, 1917–22* (Toronto: University of Toronto Press, 2010); Serhii Plokhy, *The Gates of Europe: A History of Ukraine* (New York: Basic Books, 2015).

2. Alexei Miller, *The Ukrainian Question: The Russian Empire and Nationalism in the Nineteenth Century* (Budapest: Central European University Press, 2003), 25 (quote), 30–36.

3. Serhiy Bilenky, "Children of Rus': From the Little Russian Idea to the Russian World," *Russian History* 42 (2015): 426–427; Paul Robert Magocsi, *A History of Ukraine* (Toronto: University of Toronto Press, 1996), 324.

4. Magocsi, *History of Ukraine*, 6, 326.

5. Bilenky, "Children of Rus'," 426–427; Magocsi, *History of Ukraine*, 324.

6. Shane O'Rourke, *The Cossacks* (Manchester: Manchester University Press, 2007), 27–53, 146–150.

7. Term from V. P. Danilov and N. S. Tarkhova, "Vvedenie," in *Filipp Mironov: Tikhii Don v 1917–1921 gg.*, ed. V. P. Danilov and Teodor Shanin (Moscow: Mezhdunarodnyi fond "Demokratiia," 1997), 6.

8. See Shane O'Rourke, "The Cossacks," in *Critical Companion to the Russian Revolution, 1914–1921*, ed. Edward Acton, Vladimir Iu. Cherniaev, and William G. Rosenberg (Bloomington: Indiana University Press, 1997), 499–506; O'Rourke, *Cossacks*, 136–145.

9. Faith Hillis, *Children of Rus': Right-Bank Ukraine and the Invention of a Russian Nation* (Ithaca: Cornell University Press, 2013).

10. Alexei I. Miller, "The Role of the First World War in the Competition between Ukrainian and All-Russian Nationalism," in *The Empire and Nationalism at War*, ed. Eric Lohr, Vera Tolz, Alexander Semyonov, and Mark von Hagen (Bloomington: Slavica, 2014), 73–89.

11. V. F. Soldatenko, *Grazhdanskaia voina v Ukraine, 1917–1920 gg.* (Moscow: Novyi khronograf, 2012), 24.

12. "Telegrams from the Ukrainian Central Rada to Prince L'vov and Kerensky, March 6, 1917," in *The Russian Provisional Government 1917: Documents*, ed. Robert Paul Browder and Alexander F. Kerensky, 3 vols. (Stanford: Stanford University Press, 1961), 1:370.

13. Miroslav Popovich, "Petliura: Vstupitel'naia stat'ia," in Simon Petliura, *Glavnyi ataman: B plenu nesbytochnykh nadezhd*, ed. Miroslav Popovich and Viktor Mironenko, trans. from Ukrainian G. Lesnaia (Moscow and St. Petersburg: Letnii sad, 2008), 7–8.

14. Wolodymyr Stojko, "Ukrainian National Aspirations and the Russian Provisional Government," in *The Ukraine 1917–1921: A Study in Revolution*, ed. Taras Hunczak (Cambridge, MA: Harvard Ukrainian Research Institute, 1977), 7; "From the Resolutions of the Ukrainian National Congress" (April 5–8, 1917), in *Russian Provisional Government*, 1:372–373.

15. "Official *Communiqué* on the Rejection of the Ukrainian Demands" (June 3, 1917), in *Russian Provisional Government*, 1:376–377.

16. "*Russkiia Vedomosti* on the Ukrainian Memorandum" (June 1, 1917), in *Russian Provisional Government*, 1:377–378.

17. I. V. Shklovsky (Dioneo), "The Ukrainian Question," in *The Reconstruction of Russia*, ed. Paul Vinogradoff (Oxford: Oxford University Press, 1919), 52–68.

18. Popovich, "Petliura," 12–13.

19. Ibid., 6–7, 10.

20. Sources for this and preceding paragraph: "From the Resolutions on Ukrainian Autonomy of the All-Ukrainian Peasant Congress" (May 29–June 2, 1917), in *Russian Provisional Government*, 1:379; "Kerensky's Prohibition of the Ukrainian Military Congress" (June 2, 1917), ibid., 379–380; "Resolution of the Second Ukrainian Military Congress (June 5–10) Concerning the Action of Kerensky," ibid., 380; "Against the Unity of Forces of the Revolution" (Editorial in [Petrograd Soviet] *Izvestiia*, June 2, 1917), ibid., 381–382; "Lenin on the Ban Against the Ukrainian Military Congress" ("It is not Democratic, Citizen Kerensky," *Pravda*, June 2, 1917), ibid., 382–383. On military congress, Serhy Yekelchyk, "Bands of Nation Builders? Insurgency and Ideology in the Ukrainian Civil War," in *War in Peace: Paramilitary Violence after the Great War*, ed. Robert Gerwarth and John Horne (Oxford: Oxford University Press, 2012), 110.

21. "The First Universal of the Central Rada" (June 10, 1917), in *Russian Provisional Government*, 1:383–385.

22. "Appeal of the Provisional Government to the Ukrainian People" (June 17, 1917), signed Prince L'vov, in *Russian Provisional Government*, 1:385–386; "*Rech'* on the First Universal" (June 14, 1917), ibid., 386–387.

23. "*Izvestiia* on the First Universal" (June 16, 1917), in *Russian Provisional Government*, 1:388–389.

24. Note to Document 354: *Russian Provisional Government*, 1:389; Arthur E. Adams, *The Bolsheviks in the Ukraine: The Second Campaign, 1918–1919* (New Haven: Yale University Press, 1963). 4.

25. "Vynnychenko," in Jonathan D. Smele, *Historical Dictionary of the Russian Civil Wars, 1916–1926*, 2 vols. (Lanham, MD: Rowman & Littlefield, 2015), 2:1296–1297. After going into exile in 1920, he remained a critic of the Soviet regime, but refused to cooperate with the Nazis in helping to undermine it. He was interned in a concentration camp, which damaged his health but did not kill him.

26. Popovich, "Petliura," 10.

27. Quoted, ibid., 11.

28. On All-Russian Soviet Congress: Stojko, "Ukrainian National Aspirations," 17–19.

29. "The Agreement Reached Between the Central Rada and the Provisional Government" (*Rech'*, July 4, 1917), in *Russian Provisional Government*, 1:389–390; Stojko, "Ukrainian National Aspirations," 18–19.

30. Miller, "Role of the First World War," 85.
31. "The Resignation of the Kadet Ministers in Protest Against the Ukrainian Agreement" (*Rech'*, July 4, 1917), in *Russian Provisional Government*, 1:390–392.
32. "The Second Universal of the Central Rada" (*Rech'*, July 6, 1917), in *Russian Provisional Government*, 1:392–393.
33. Stojko, "Ukrainian National Aspirations," 20–22.
34. "Draft Proposal of the Small Rada on the Administration of the Ukraine" (July 16, 1917), in *Russian Provisional Government*, 1:394–396.
35. "The Temporary Instructions of the Provisional Government to the General Secretariat" (August 4, 1917), in *Russian Provisional Government*, 1:396–397.
36. "The Refusal of the Senate to Publish the Temporary Instructions" (published October 5, 1917), in *Russian Provisional Government*, 1:397–398.
37. "Resolution of the Rada on the Instruction of August 4," in *Russian Provisional Government*, 1:398–399.
38. Stojko, "Ukrainian National Aspirations," 26–27.
39. Ibid., 28–31; Yekelchyk, *Ukraine*, 70–71.
40. "Proclamation of the Ukrainian People's Republic" (The Third Universal of [the] Ukrainian Rada, Kiev, November 7/20, 1917), in James Bunyan and H. H. Fisher, *The Bolshevik Revolution 1917–1918: Documents and Materials* (Stanford: Stanford University Press, 1934), 435–437, from "Universal Ukrainskoi Tsentral'noi Rady," in S. Piontkovskii, *Grazhdanskaia voina v Rossii (1918–1921 gg.): Khrestomatiia* (Moscow: Kom. Universitet im. Sverdlova, 1925), 344–346.
41. "Resolution of the Kiev City Duma" (Session of November 14/27, 1917), in Bunyan and Fisher, *Bolshevik Revolution*, 438–439.
42. "Soviet Ultimatum to the Ukrainian Rada" (Decree of the Sovnarkom, December 4/17, 1917), in Bunyan and Fisher, *Bolshevik Revolution*, 439–440; Jurij Borys, *The Sovietization of Ukraine, 1917–1923: The Communist Doctrine and Practice of National Self-Determination* (Edmonton: Canadian Institute of Ukrainian Studies, 1980), 175–184.
43. "Reply of the Rada" (December 6/19, 1917), in Bunyan and Fisher, *Bolshevik Revolution*, 440–441, cf. "Pozitsiia Tsentral'noi Rady: Telegramma Sovetu Narodnykh Komissarov ot 5-go dekabria," in Piontkovskii, *Grazhdanskaia voina*, 347–349.
44. Quoted, Bunyan and Fisher, *Bolshevik Revolution*, 441; Piontkovskii, *Grazhdanskaia voina*, 347 (quote).
45. John S. Reshetar, "The Communist Party of the Ukraine and Its Role in the Ukrainian Revolution," in Hunczak, ed., *Ukraine*, 160–163.
46. Ibid., 164–166; Yaroslav Bilinsky, "The Communist Take-over of the Ukraine," in Hunczak, ed., *Ukraine*, 108.
47. Reshetar, "Communist Party," 167–169.
48. Ibid., 170.
49. Ibid., 170–171; Bilinsky, "Communist Take-over," 108; Borys, *Sovietization*, 182–183.

50. Reshetar, "Communist Party," 171–172; Borys, *Sovietization*, 188. English translation adds to the confusion, since the Ukrainian adjective *narodna* can be rendered either as "the people's" or "national." In the case of the Sovnarkom, the Russian adjective *narodnykh* clearly means "people's," but in *Ukraïns'ka Narodna Respublyka* the emphasis was on "national." For the same reason, the Polish *Narodowa Demokracja* translates as "National Democracy," not "People's Democracy." From the Bolshevik point of view, in this case the ambiguity would have been useful.

51. "Formation of a Soviet Government of the Ukraine" (Declaration of the Ukrainian Central Executive Committee, December 14/27, 1917), in Bunyan and Fisher, *Bolshevik Revolution*, 442–444, from Soviet Executive Committee, "Manifest ko vsem rabochim, krest'ianam i soldatam Ukrainy ot 14 dek. 1917 g.," in Piontkovskii, *Grazhdanskaia voina*, 349–352, 350 (quote); Bilinsky, "Communist Take-over," 108.

52. Borys, *Sovietization*, 189–191.

53. Reshetar, "Communist Party," 171.

54. Ibid., 174.

55. "Fourth Universal of the Ukrainian Central Rada" (Proclamation of January 9/22, 1918), in Bunyan and Fisher, *Bolshevik Revolution*, 444–448.

56. Reshetar, "Communist Party," 173; Soldatenko, *Grazhdanskaia voina*, 164–165, 165 (1,500 workers shot), 166; Yekelchyk, "Bands," 115 (300 workers shot); Borys, *Sovietization*, 187 (Red Guard).

57. Geoffrey Swain, "Russia's Garibaldi: The Revolutionary Life of Mikhail Artemevich Muraviev," *Revolutionary Russia* 11.2 (1998): 54–81; also, "Murav'ev," in Smele, *Historical Dictionary*, 2:772–773; and "Murav'ev Uprising," ibid., 773–774.

58. Yekelchyk, *Ukraine*, 71–72; Reshetar, "Communist Party," 173.

59. "Bolshevik Occupation of Kiev" (Extract from Report of the United States Consul at Kiev, March 1, 1918), signed Douglas Jenkins, in Bunyan and Fisher, *Bolshevik Revolution*, 449–451; on departing executions, 449.

60. V. A. Antonov-Ovseenko, *Zapiski o grazhdanskoi voine*, 3 vols. (Moscow: Vysshii Voennyi Redaktsionnyi Sovet, 1924), 1:154; Soldatenko, *Grazhdanskaia voina*, 165 (quote).

61. Mark von Hagen, *War in a European Borderland: Occupations and Occupation Plans in Galicia and Ukraine, 1914–1918* (Seattle: University of Washington Press, 2007), 64, 93.

62. Yekelchyk, *Ukraine*, 73; Bunyan and Fisher, *Bolshevik Revolution*, 448–451; A. Gol'denveizer, "Iz kievskikh vospominanii," in *1918 god na Ukraine*, ed. S. V. Volkov (Moscow: Tsentrpoligraf, 2001), 77–78; Soldatenko, *Grazhdanskaia voina*, 166 (2,500 executed officers).

63. S. V. Volkov, *Tragediia russkogo ofitserstva* (Moscow: Fokus, 1999), 49.

64. Ibid., 48; Gol'denveizer, "Iz kievskikh vospominanii," 80.

65. Yekelchyk, "Bands," 115 ("not ideological fanatics but rag-tag irregulars loyal only to their own commanders").

66. "The Rada Appeals to the Germans" (Notes of February 17, 1918), in Bunyan and Fisher, *Bolshevik Revolution*, 451.

67. Quoted, Taras Hunczak, "The Ukraine Under Hetman Pavlo Skoropadsky," in Hunczak, ed., *Ukraine*, 61.

68. Gol'denveizer, "Iz kievskikh vospominanii," 83–84.

69. Evan Mawdsley, *The Russian Civil War* (Boston: Allen and Unwin, 1987), 36.

70. "The Treaty of Peace Between Ukraine and the Central Powers" (signed at Brest-Litovsk, February 9, 1917), in John W. Wheeler-Bennett, *Brest-Litovsk, The Forgotten Peace, March 1918* (London: Macmillan; New York: St. Martin's, 1938), 392–402.

71. Yekelchyk, *Ukraine*, 72–73.

72. Major-General Max Hoffmann, *War Diaries and Other Papers*, trans. Eric Sutton, 2 vols. (London: Martin Secker, 1929), 1:209.

73. Quoted, von Hagen, *European Borderland*, 109.

74. Ibid., 90.

75. Quoted, Hunczak, "Ukraine Under Hetman Pavlo Skoropadskyi," 64.

76. von Hagen, *European Borderland*, 93–94.

77. Yekelchyk, *Ukraine*, 74.

78. *Getman P. P. Skoropadskii: Ukraina na perelome, 1918 goda*, ed. O. K. Ivantsova (Moscow: ROSSPEN, 2014), 1045–1046.

79. Ibid., 668.

80. Ibid., 1045–1046. See: Iaroslav Lebedynsky, *Skoropadsky et l'édification de l'Etat ukrainien (1918)* (Paris: Harmattan, 2010); Pavlo Petrovych Skoropads'kyi, *Erinnerungen: 1917 bis 1918* (Stuttgart: Steiner, 1999).

81. Yekelchyk, "Bands," 113–114. The self-described Free Cossacks who followed the lead of nationalist intellectuals in reviving the myth of ancient freedoms were Ukrainian men either too young or too old to serve in the regular army.

82. von Hagen, *European Borderland*, 96–97.

83. Quoted, Peter Borowsky, "Germany's Ukrainian Policy during World War I and the Revolution of 1918–19," in *German-Ukrainian Relations in Historical Perspective*, ed. Hans-Joachim Torke and John-Paul Himka (Edmonton: Canadian Institute of Ukrainian Studies Press, 1994), 87.

84. Comment of May 19, 1918, quoted, Hunczak, "Ukraine Under Hetman Pavlo Skoropadskyi," 71.

85. Yekelchyk, *Ukraine*, 74; Hunczak, "Ukraine Under Hetman Pavlo Skoropadskyi," 68–69.

86. Yekelchyk, *Ukraine*, 75.

87. Ibid., 74–75.

88. Hunczak, "Ukraine Under Hetman Pavlo Skoropadskyi," 71–73.

89. Ibid., 76; Yekelchyk, *Ukraine*, 75.

90. Hunczak, "Ukraine Under Hetman Pavlo Skoropadskyi," 76.

91. Borowsky, "Germany's Ukrainian Policy," 90.

92. Martha Bohachevsky-Chomiak, "The Directory of the Ukrainian National Republic," in Hunczak, ed., *Ukraine*, 82–83; Soldatenko, *Grazhdanskaia voina*, 17.

93. Yekelchyk, *Ukraine*, 75.

94. Borowsky, "Germany's Ukrainian Policy," 91 (quote).

95. Yekelchyk, *Ukraine*, 77; Bohachevsky-Chomiak, "Directory," 90; Soldatenko, *Grazhdanskaia voina*, 19 (Galician Army was 90 percent of UNR's armed forces); Bilinsky, "Communist Take-over," 119 (by April 1919 had mobilized over 200,000 men).

96. Yekelchyk, *Ukraine*, 75–76; Yekelchyk, "Bands," 116, 118; Adams, *Bolsheviks in Ukraine*, 13; Mikhail Bulgakov, *The White Guard*, trans. Michael Glenny (1923; Chicago: Academy, 1987), 248, mentions well-organized troops marching into the city, wearing "German cloth" and German helmets.

97. Bulgakov, *White Guard*, 114 and 110; Hunczak, "Ukraine Under Hetman Pavlo Skoropadskyi," 79–81; disguise also in Yekelchyk, *Ukraine*, 75–76; Skoropads'kyi settled in Germany, where he was killed in an Allied bombing raid in Bavaria in 1945: *Getman P. P. Skoropadskii*, 1046.

98. Bohachevsky-Chomiak, "Directory," 84–87, 91–92.

### PART IV: CHAPTER 6

1. William Henry Chamberlin, *The Russian Revolution*, 2 vols. (1935; New York: Grosset and Dunlap, 1965), 2:398.

2. Robert D. Crews, *For Prophet and Tsar: Islam and Empire in Russia and Central Asia* (Cambridge, MA: Harvard University Press, 2006), 13–14; see also Eileen Kane, *Russian Hajj: Empire and the Pilgrimage to Mecca* (Ithaca: Cornell University Press, 2015).

3. Austin Jersild, *Orientalism and Empire: North Caucasus Mountain Peoples and the Georgian Frontier, 1845–1917* (Montreal: McGill-Queen's University Press, 2002).

4. In 1917 the North Caucasian peoples created their own political organization: Timur Muzaev, *Soiuz gortsev: Russkaia revoliutsiia i narody Severnogo Kavkaza, 1917–mart 1918 goda*, 2nd ed. (Nalchik: Arkhivnoe upravlenie Pravitel'stva Chechenskoi Respubliki, 2012).

5. Firuz Kazemzadeh, *The Struggle for Transcaucasia (1917–1921)* (New York: Philosophical Library, 1951), 7. Kazemzadeh is a basic source for this chapter.

6. Paul Gentizon, *La résurrection géorgienne* (Paris: Leroux, 1921), 27, 26.

7. Kazemzadeh, *Struggle*, 9–10; Ronald Grigor Suny, *"They Can Live in the Desert but Nowhere Else": A History of the Armenian Genocide* (Princeton: Princeton University Press, 2015), 87–89.

8. Suny, *They Can Live*, 115–122.

9. Kazemzadeh, *Struggle*, 12–13.

10. Tadeusz Swietochowski, "National Consciousness and Political Orientations in Azerbaijan, 1905–1920," in *Transcaucasia, Nationalism, and Social Change: Essays in the History of Armenia, Azerbaijan, and Georgia*, ed. Ronald Grigor Suny (Ann Arbor: University of Michigan Press, 1996), 211–212.

11. Kazemzadeh, *Struggle*, 8–17, 19–22.

12. Michael A. Reynolds, *Shattering Empires: The Clash and Collapse of the Ottoman and Russian Empires 1908–1918* (Cambridge: Cambridge University Press, 2011), 1–2, 22–23; Taner Akçam, *A Shameful Act: The Armenian Genocide and the Question of Turkish Responsibility*, trans. Paul Bessemer (New York: Metropolitan Books, 2006), 48–49.

13. Swietochowski, "National Consciousness," 218–220; A. Iu. Khabutdinov, *Obshchestvennoe dvizhenie molodezhi u tatar-musul'man v nachale XX veka* (Nizhnii Novgorod: NII im. Kh. Faizkhanova, 2005).

14. Kazemzadeh, *Struggle*, 19 (mutual); Swietochowski, "National Consciousness," 214–216 (figures); Svante E. Cornell, *Small Nations and Great Powers: A Study of Ethnopolitical Conflict in the Caucasus* (Richmond, UK: Curzon, 2001), 55–56 (range of interpretation), citing Charles van der Leeuw, *Storm over the Caucasus: In the Wake of Independence* (New York: St. Martin's, 1998), 70–71; Haidar Bammate, "The Caucasus and the Russian Revolution (From a Political Viewpoint)," *Central Asian Survey*, no. 1–2 (1991)—reprinting 1929 Paris article. On the development of Dashnak organization: Anahide Ter Minassia, "Nationalism and Socialism in the Armenian Revolutionary Movement (1887–1912)," in *Transcaucasia, Nationalism, and Social Change*, 176–177.

15. Argument of Peter Holquist, "The Politics and Practice of the Russian Occupation of Armenia, 1915–February 1917," in *A Question of Genocide, 1915: Armenians and Turks at the End of the Ottoman Empire*, ed. Ronald Grigor Suny, Fatma Müge Göçek, and Norman M. Naimark (New York: Oxford University Press, 2011).

16. Ibid., 169, 171–172.

17. Kazemzadeh, *Struggle*, 30–31; Reynolds, *Shattering*, 135.

18. Quoted, Suny, *They Can Live*, 296.

19. Quoted, Holquist, "Politics and Practice," 156.

20. Reynolds, *Shattering*, 191–192.

21. Kazemzadeh, *Struggle*, 34–52.

22. "Dekret o 'Turetskoi Armenii'" (December 29, 1917/January 11, 1918), in *Dekrety Sovetskoi vlasti*, vol. 1 (Moscow: Politicheskaia literatura, 1957), 298–299, cited in Solmaz Rustamova-Togidi, *Mart 1918 g. Baku: Azerbaidzhanskie pogromy v dokumentakh* (Baku: Nauchno-issledovatel'skii tsentr Min. Natsional'noi Bezopasnosti Azerbaidzhanskoi Respubliki, 2009), 21.

23. Quoted, Kazemzadeh, *Struggle*, 55, from N. N. Zhordaniia, *Za dva goda: Doklady i rechi* (Tiflis: Istoricheskaia komissiia I. K. Soveta rabochikh deput. g. Tiflisa, 1919), 51–52.

24. Kazemzadeh, *Struggle*, 54–58; "Prikaz ob obrazovanii Zakavkazskogo Komissariata" (November 15/28, 1917), in *Dokumenty i materialy po vneshnei politike Zakavkaz'ia i Gruzii*, ed. G. S. Mamulia (1919; Tbilisi: Naimon, 1990), 7–8.

25. Quoted, Kazemzadeh, *Struggle*, 85.

26. "Pervaia deklaratsiia Zakavkazskogo Komissariata k narodam Zakavkaz'ia" (Tiflis, November 18/December 1, 1917), in *Dokumenty i materialy po vneshnei politike*, 8.

27. Reynolds, *Shattering*, 171, 173; "Tekst peremiriia (Telegramma po korpusam Kavkazskoi armii)" (December 5/18, 1917), in *Dokumenty i materialy po vneshnei politike*, 18–23.

28. Reynolds, *Shattering*, 194; Kazemzadeh, *Struggle*, 81–83.

29. Kazemzadeh, *Struggle*, 85–86 (Erzinjan/Erzincan, on January 2–3/15–16, 1918); Reynolds, *Shattering*, 194 (Kars). See complaints from the Turkish army to the Russian command, in *Dokumenty i materialy po vneshnei politike*, 41–46, and reply of Russian commander, who declares respect for the Muslim population and pledges to punish perpetrators: ibid., 46–47.

30. Kazemzadeh, *Struggle*, 86–87; Ronald Grigor Suny, *The Baku Commune, 1917–1918: Class and Nationality in the Russian Revolution* (Princeton: Princeton University Press, 1972), 262.

31. Kazemzadeh, *Struggle*, 87–90.

32. Ibid., 91–92.

33. Ibid., 86–87, 95–97; Suny, *Baku Commune*, 262.

34. Quoted, Kazemzadeh, *Struggle*, 98.

35. Reynolds, *Shattering*, 202–203.

36. Kazemzadeh, *Struggle*, 99–100; quote, 100.

37. Ibid., 101–102.

38. Ibid., 102–103, 105–108; Reynolds, *Shattering*, 206.

39. Kazemzadeh, *Struggle*, 109–117.

40. Reynolds, *Shattering*, 213, 216; Kazemzadeh, *Struggle*, 119–124.

41. Kazemzadeh, *Struggle*, 127.

42. Ibid., 64–66.

43. V. N. Zabotin, "Shaumian," in *Politicheskie deiateli Rossii 1917: Biograficheskii slovar'*, ed. P. V. Volobuev (Moscow: Bol'shaia rossiiskaia entsiklopediia, 1993), 357–358.

44. Suny, *Baku Commune*, 19–20.

45. Ibid., 13–14.

46. This and following from Rustamova-Togidi, "Martovskie sobytiia," in *Mart 1918 g. Baku*, 9–24.

47. All of above, ibid.

48. Kazemzadeh, *Struggle*, 70.

49. Its findings are published from the archival records in Rustamova-Togidi, "Martovskie sobytiia," and cited in Dzhamil' Gasanly, *Russkaia revoliutsiia i Azerbaidzhan: Trudnyi put' k nezavisimosti 1917–1920*, ed. S. M. Iskhakov (Moscow: Fainta, 2011); *Claims of the Peace Delegation of the Republic of Caucasian Azerbaijan presented to the Peace Conference in Paris* ([Paris, 1919]), the published text, cited in Kazemzadeh, *Struggle*, 72. See *Azerbaidzhanskaia Demokraticheskaia Respublika, 1918–1920* (Baku: Izd-vo Azerbaidzhan, 1998).

50. Suny, *Baku Commune*, 223; Gasanly, *Russkaia revoliutsiia*, 123; Kazemzadeh, *Struggle*, 72.
51. Suny, *Baku Commune*, 227–231; Kazemzadeh, *Struggle*, 76–77.
52. Quoted, Kazemzadeh, *Struggle*, 75 ("For us the results of the battle were brilliant. The destruction of the enemy was complete.") and Gasanly, *Russkaia revoliutsiia*, 124 (my translation).
53. Suny, *Baku Commune*, 263.
54. Ibid., 295–296, 299–301.
55. Ibid., 268–270.
56. Kazemzadeh, *Struggle*, 128–131, 135–137; Suny, *Baku Commune*, 272, 306–308, 312–315.
57. Suny, *Baku Commune*, 317.
58. Kazemzadeh, *Struggle*, 138–139; Suny, *Baku Commune*, 321.
59. L. C. [Lionel Charles] Dunsterville, *The Adventures of Dunsterforce* (London: Arnold, 1920), 215, quoted in Kazemzadeh, *Struggle*, 140.
60. Kazemzadeh, *Struggle*, 140–144 (claim reproduced with some skepticism); Suny, *They Can Live*, 331 (20,000 Armenian victims).
61. Kazemzadeh, *Struggle*, 146; Gasanly, *Russkaia revoliutsiia*, 249–252; 249 (quote). Gasanly endorses the claim that the invaders acted with relative restraint and that victims were nowhere as numerous as the Armenian nationalists—and Soviet-era historians—have asserted. He does not provide an exact count, but suggests the total might have been as low as 700. By contrast, he accepts the figure of 12,000 for the Muslim victims of the March massacres.
62. Kazemzadeh, *Struggle*, 144–145; Suny, *Baku Commune*, 340–342; Gasanly, *Russkaia revoliutsiia*, 243–246.
63. Kazemzadeh, *Struggle*, 147–148; Suny, *Baku Commune*, 286.
64. Kazemzadeh, *Struggle*, 150–151, 160–162.
65. Ibid., 169–170, 202, 172–173, 164–165, 167.
66. Ibid., 174–181; see Muzaev, *Soiuz gortsev*.
67. Kazemzadeh, *Struggle*, 187, 184, 330, 186.
68. Quoted, Ibid., 185.
69. Ibid., 189–192, 198–199.
70. C. E. Bechhofer, *In Denikin's Russia and the Caucasus, 1919–1920* (London: W. Collins, 1921), 14, cited in Kazemzadeh, *Struggle*, 199.
71. Kazemzadeh, *Struggle*, 199–203.
72. J. G. Harbord, "American Military Mission to Armenia," *International Conciliation*, no. 151 (June 1920, New York), 32/290, cited in part, Kazemzadeh, *Struggle*, 215.
73. Kazemzadeh, *Struggle*, 211–213, 286.
74. Harbord, "American Military Mission," 25/283 (all quotes).
75. Ibid., 28/286.
76. Kazemzadeh, *Struggle*, 288–290.
77. Ibid., 323, 328.
78. Ibid., 222–226.

79. Ibid., 230–231, 314.

80. Ibid., 283–284 (quotes), 297.

81. Ibid., 209–210, 296–299.

82. Ibid., 316, 318–319.

83. Quoted, ibid., 320, from Gentizon, *La résurrection géorgienne*, 310–311.

84. Kazemzadeh, *Struggle*, 323.

85. Ibid., 325–328.

86. Richard A. Pierce, *Russian Central Asia 1867–1917: A Study in Colonial Rule* (Berkeley: University of California Press, 1960); Daniel R. Brower, *Turkestan and the Fate of the Russian Empire* (London: Routledge, 2003), 1.

87. On brutality of conquest: Hans Rogger, "The Skobelev Phenomenon: The Hero and His Worship," *Oxford Slavonic Papers*, ed. Robert Auty, J. L. I. Fennell, and I. P. Foote, n.s., vol. IX (Oxford: Clarendon, 1976), 51, 56–57.

88. Edward Dennis Sokol, *The Revolt of 1916 in Russian Central Asia* (Baltimore: Johns Hopkins University Press, 1954; rpt. 2016), 37–38; Robert D. Crews, "An Empire for the Faithful, A Colony for the Dispossessed," *Cahiers d'Asie centrale* 17/18: *Turkestan russe: Une colonie comme les autres?*, ed. Svetland Gorshenina and Sergei Abashin (Tashkent and Paris: Collection de l'IFEAC, 2009): 79–106.

89. *Rossiia 1913 god: Statistiko-dokumental'nyi spravochnik*, ed. A. M. Anfimov and A. P. Korelin (St. Petersburg: BLITs, 1995), 22; Brower, *Turkestan*, 2 (7 million).

90. Arne Haugen, *The Establishment of National Republics in Soviet Central Asia* (Basingstoke and New York: Palgrave Macmillan, 2003), 167–168. Thanks to Sarah Cameron for this reference and for her clarifications on this and other points. On Turkmen identity and conquest: Adrienne Lynn Edgar, *Tribal Nation: The Making of Soviet Turkmenistan* (Princeton: Princeton University Press, 2004), 21–30. I cannot be sure of using the correct term in any particular case, since I rely on sources that may not themselves be making the right distinctions.

91. Sokol, *Revolt*, 3–4.

92. Ibid., 22, 29 (definition).

93. Sarah Cameron, *The Hungry Steppe: Famine, Violence and the Making of Soviet Kazakhstan* (Cornell University Press, forthcoming; ms. courtesy of the author), ch. 1.

94. Marco Buttino, "Central Asia (1916–20): A Kaleidoscope of Local Revolutions and the Building of the Bolshevik Order," in *The Empire and Nationalism at War*, ed. Eric Lohr, Vera Tolz, Alexander Semyonov, and Mark von Hagen (Bloomington: Slavica, 2014), 112–113.

95. Glenda Fraser, "Basmachi—I," *Central Asian Survey* 6:1 (1987): 1 and 65; Alexander Morrison, "Peasant Settlers and the Civilizing Mission in Russian Turkestan 1865–1917," *The Journal of Imperial and Commonwealth History* 43.3 (2015): 394, 396 (similar proportions: 16–17 percent); Robert P. Geraci, "Going Abroad or Going to Russia? Orthodox Missionaries in the Kazakh Steppe,

1881–1917," in *Of Religion and Empire: Missions, Conversion, and Tolerance in Tsarist Russia*, ed. Robert P. Geraci and Michael Khodarkovsky (Ithaca: Cornell University Press, 2001), 284 (40 percent, higher in the Kazakh Steppe); but see Gulnar Kendirbai, *Land and People: The Russian Colonization of the Kazak Steppe* (Berlin: ANOR, 2002), 18 (23 percent). In general, the numbers vary with the source; see also: A. P. Fomenko, *Russkie poseleniia v Turkestanskom krae v kontse XIX–nachale XX v.: Sotsial'no-ekonomicheskii aspekt* (Tashkent: "Fan" Uzbekskoi SSR, 1983), 71–72; George J. Demko, *The Russian Colonization of Kazakhstan 1896–1916* (Bloomington: Indiana University, 1969), 134, 136 (tables), 137–139. The statistics are inconsistent and the territories defined in different ways, but a general picture emerges.

96. Demko, *Russian Colonization*, 112, 114; Morrison, "Peasant Settlers," 402, 404.

97. Brower, *Turkestan*, 129; Sokol, *Revolt*, 27–28, 166.

98. Sokol, *Revolt*, 34, 32.

99. Marco Buttino, "Study of the Economic Crisis and Depopulation in Turkestan, 1917–1920," *Central Asian Survey* 9.4 (1990): 59.

100. Crews, "An Empire," 80.

101. Quoted, Sokol, *Revolt*, 8.

102. Ibid., 17–19, 23.

103. Robert D. Crews, "Civilization and the City: Architecture, Urbanism, and the Colonization of Tashkent," in *Architectures of Identity in Russia, 1500–2000*, ed. James Cracraft and Daniel Rowland (Ithaca: Cornell University Press, 2003), 117–132; Pierce, *Russian Central Asia*, 102–106.

104. Sokol, *Revolt*, 64–65; Adeeb Khalid, *The Politics of Muslim Cultural Reform: Jadidism in Central Asia* (Berkeley: University of California Press, 1998); D. A. Amanzholova, *Kazakhskii avtonomizm i Rossiia: Istoriia dvizheniia Alash* (Moscow: Rossiia molodaia, 1994), 19. On Muslim political activity during the Civil War, see *Grazhdanskaia voina v Rossii i musul'mane: Sbornik dokumentov i materialov*, ed. S. M. Iskhakov (Moscow: Tsentr stratigicheskoi kon"iunktury, 2014).

105. Beatrice Forbes Manz, "Central Asian Uprisings in the Nineteenth Century: Ferghana under the Russians," *Russian Review* 46.3 (1987): 269–275.

106. Yuriy Malikov, "The Kenesary Kasymov Rebellion (1837–1947): A National-Liberation Movement or 'a Protest of Restoration,'" *Nationalities Papers* 33.4 (2005): 569–597.

107. Sokol, *Revolt*, 50–51, 57; Brower, *Turkestan*, 95–96; Manz, "Central Asian Uprisings," 276–278; Pierce, *Russian Central Asia*, 226–233.

108. Brower, *Turkestan*, 154; Jörn Happel, *Nomadische Lebenswelten und zaristische Politik: Der Aufstand in Zentralasien 1916* (Stuttgart: Franz Steiner, 2010), 97.

109. Buttino, "Study," 61; Buttino, "Central Asia," 113.

110. Brower, *Turkestan*, 155.

111. S. M. Iskhakov, "Pervaia mirovaia voina glazami rossiiskikh musul'man," in *Rossiia i Pervaia mirovaia voina*, ed. N. N. Smirnov (St. Petersburg: Bulanin,

1999), 421–424; A. B. Astashov, *Russkii front v 1914–nachale 1917 goda: Voennyi opyt i sovremennost'* (Moscow: Novyi khronograf, 2014), 18 (exempt groups).

112. Brower, *Turkestan*, 156–157; Buttino, "Central Asia," 114; Sokol, *Revolt*, 74. "Tsarskii ukaz o mobilizatsii 'inorodcheskogo' naseleniia Astrakhanskoi gubernii, Sibiri i Srednei Azii dlia rabot po ustroistvu oboronitel'nykh sooruzhenii v raione deistvuiushchei armii" (June 25, 1916), in *Vosstanie 1916 goda v Srednei Azii i Kazakhstane: Sbornik dokumentov*, ed. A. V. Piaskovskii and S. G. Agadzhanov (Moscow: Akad. nauk SSSR, 1960), 25–26; Iskhakov, "Pervaia mirovaia voina," 422.

113. D. A. Amanzholova, ed., "'Takoe upravlenie gosudarstvom—nedopustimo': Doklad A. F. Kerenskogo na zakrytom zasedanii Gosudarstvennoi dumy. Dekabr' 1916 g.," *Istoricheskii arkhiv* 2 (1997): 10; *Alash-Orda: Sbornik dokumentov*, ed. N. Martynenko (Alma-Ata: Aikap, 1992), 8.

114. Sokol, *Revolt*, 80; Amanzholova, ed., "Takoe upravlenie gosudarstvom," 11.

115. Sokol, *Revolt*, 101–102; Amanzholova, *Kazakhskii avtonomizm*, 23.

116. Amanzholova, ed., "Takoe upravlenie gosudarstvom," 11.

117. Sokol, *Revolt*, 82–92.

118. Sokol, *Revolt*, 94, 98–99.

119. Ibid., 111–126; Brower, *Turkestan*, 158–160, 162, 163 (quote); Buttino, "Central Asia," 114–115. Some Turkmen were also involved in the revolt and were affected by the repression: Edgar, *Tribal Nation*, 34.

120. "Khronologiia sobytii, sviazannykh s vosstaniem Kirgizov v 1916 godu," in *Vosstanie 1916 goda: Dokumenty i materialy*, ed. K. I. Mambetaliev (Bishkek: Abykeev, 2015), 243–247.

121. Brower, *Turkestan*, 163; Sokol, *Revolt*, 153.

122. Brower, *Turkestan*, 162, 164.

123. Sokol, *Revolt*, 155–156. Same figures in A. V. Ganin, "Vosstanie v Turkestane i stepnom krae 1916–17," in *Rossiia v Pervoi mirovoi voine 1914–1918: Entsiklopediia v trekh tomakh*, ed. A. K. Sorokin et al. (Moscow: ROSSPEN, 2014), 1:422.

124. Ganin, "Vosstanie v Turkestane," 422 (Russian bias, therefore 4,145 dead and missing can be taken as maximum); cf. Happel, *Nomadische Lebenswelten*, 15 (10,000 Russians and Ukrainians).

125. Ganin, "Vosstanie v Turkestane," 424 ("*neskol'ko tysiach miatezhnikov*"); Happel, *Nomadische Lebenswelten*, 15 (100,000–200,000—no apparent bias); K. Mambetaliev, "Posleslovie," in *Vosstanie 1916 goda*, ed. Mambetaliev, 248 (273,222 total dead and missing—current Kyrgyz version can be taken as maximum); Vadim Erlikhman, *Poteri narodonaseleniia v XX veke: Spravochnik* (Moscow: Russkaia panorama, 2004), 18 (75,000 pastoralists dead, the rest of the 250,000 fleeing); Cloé Drieu, "L'impact de la Première Guerre mondiale en Asie centrale: Des révoltes de 1916 aux enjeux politiques et scientifiques de leur historiographie," *Histoire@politique* 22 (2014): 4/178 (53,000 dead, 220,000 fled for Semireche alone).

126. Buttino, "Study," 65.

127. T. R. Ryskulov, *Vosstanie tuzemtsev Srednei Azii v 1916 godu* (Kzyl-Orda, 1927), in T. R. Ryskulov, *Sobranie sochinenii v trekh tomakh* (Almaty: Izd. "Kazakhstan," 1997), 2:113 (29 percent)—this figure cited in Drieu, "L'impact," 4/178. Cf. T. R. Ryskulov, "Predislovie," in L. V. Lesnaia, *Vosstanie 1916 g. v Kirgizstane: Dokumenty i materialy*, ed. T. R. Ryskulov (Moscow: Gos. sotsial'no-ekon. izd., 1937), 11 (66 percent—not the same districts).

128. Brower, *Turkestan*, 167; "Plan Kuropatkina o vyselenii Kirgiz iz raionov vos-staniia: Protokol soveshchaniia 16 oktiabria 1916 g.," in Lesnaia, *Vosstanie 1916 g.*, 85–88.

129. Joseph Castagné, "Le Turkestan depuis la Révolution russe (1917–1921)," *Revue du monde musulman* 50 (1922): 32–34.

130. Khalid, *Politics*, 246–248.

131. "Temporary Rules for Holding Elections of Municipal Duma Members" (April 15, 1917), in *The Russian Provisional Government 1917*, ed. Robert Paul Browder and Alexander F. Kerensky, 3 vols. (Stanford: Stanford University Press, 1961), 1:262.

132. Martynenko, *Alash-Orda*, 21–61; Amanzholova, *Kazakhskii avtonomizm*, 26.

133. Khalid, *Politics*, 254–264, 267–269.

134. Ibid., 265; Adeeb Khalid, *Making Uzbekistan: Nation, Empire, and Revolution in the Early USSR* (Ithaca: Cornell University Press, 2015), 90.

135. Quoted, Brower, *Turkestan*, 172.

136. Khalid, *Politics*, 270–271.

137. Ibid., 271–272.

138. Buttino, "Central Asia," 117–118; Castagné, "Le Turkestan," 42–43.

139. Khalid, *Politics*, 273–274.

140. Text of resolution in G. I. Safarov, *Kolonial'naia revoliutsiia (Opyt Turkestana)* (Moscow: Gos. izd-vo, 1921), 71; also quoted, Khalid, *Politics*, 275. Turkmen from Transcaspia sent delegates to the Kokand meeting: Edgar, *Tribal Nation*, 35.

141. Khalid, *Politics*, 275–276; Buttino, "Central Asia," 118–119; Castagné, "Le Turkestan," 46–47.

142. Buttino, "Central Asia," 120.

143. Marco Buttino, "Ethnicité et politique dans la guerre civile: À propos du *bas-mačestvo* au Fergana," *Cahiers du monde russe* 38.1–2 (1997): 207–208.

144. Buttino, "Ethnicité," 200, 204 ("thousands of Muslims"), 207; Sh. A. Shamagdiev, *Ocherki istorii grazhdanskoi voiny v Ferganskoi doline* (Tashkent: Akademiia nauk Uzbekskoi SSR, 1961), 54 (10,000). Dashnak-sponsored Armenian militias played a similar role in Andijan in the summer of 1918, where they came to the support of Soviet forces pursuing rebel bands and joined in devastating the city's Muslim section: Buttino, "Ethnicité," 208–209.

145. Amanzholova, *Kazakhskii avtonomizm*, 27.

146. Buttino, "Central Asia," 119; Tomohiko Uyama, "The Alash Orda's Relations with Siberia, the Urals, and Turkestan: The Kazakh National Movement and

the Russian Imperial Legacy," in *Asiatic Russia: Imperial Power in Regional and International Contexts*, ed. Tomohiko Uyama (London: Routledge, 2012), 275–281; "Iz polevogo shtaba predsedatelia kirgizskogo s"ezda o zakliuchenii dogovora s ural'skimi kazakami" and "Zapiska pravitel'stva Uil'skogo oliaiata voinskomu pravitel'stvu i glavshtabu orenburgskogo kazach'ego voiska—o snabzhenii oruzhiem i ofitserami," in Martynenko, *Alash-Orda*, 114–117.

147. Buttino, "Central Asia," 131; Amanzholova, *Kazakhskii avtonomizm*, 125–157 ("1919 god: perelom"); "Alash Orda," in Jonathan D. Smele, *Historical Dictionary of the Russian Civil Wars, 1916–1926*, 2 vols. (Lanham, MD: Rowman & Littlefield, 2015), 1:100–101.

148. "Frunze," in Smele, *Historical Dictionary*, 1:429–430.

149. "Dutov," in Valerii Klaving, *Grazhdanskaia voina v Rossii: Belye armii* (Moscow: AST, 2003), 441–442. Dutov fled to China in May 1920, where ten months later he was assassinated by an agent of the NKVD.

150. Safarov, *Kolonial'naia*, 75–76.

151. K. N. Nurpeisov and V. K. Grigor'ev, "Turar Ryskulov i ego vremia," in Ryskulov, *Sobranie sochinenii*, 1:18.

152. Safarov, *Kolonial'naia*, 76.

153. Ibid., 84 (quote), 94.

154. Mikhail Konstantinovich Diterikhs, *Ubiistvo tsarskoi sem'i i chlenov Doma Romanovykh na Urale*, 2 vols. (Vladivostok: Voennaia Akademiia, 1922), 1:288; mentioned in *Gibel' tsarskoi sem'i: Materialy sledstviia po delu ob ubiistve Tsarskoi sem'i (avgust 1918–fevral' 1920)*, ed. Nikolai Ross (Frankfurt: Posev, 1987).

155. Safarov, *Kolonial'naia*, 77–80, 86.

156. Buttino, "Ethnicité," 202.

157. Safarov, *Kolonial'naia*, 80–82; quote, 80–81.

158. Buttino, "Ethnicité," 202, 197.

159. Buttino, "Central Asia," 123.

160. T. R. Ryskulov, "Predislovie," *Revoliutsiia i korennoe naselenie Turkestana* (Tashkent: Uzbekskoe gos. izd., 1925), in Ryskulov, *Sobranie sochinenii*, 1:53.

161. S. A. Shumov and A. R. Andreev, "Kratkaia istoriia basmachestva," in *Basmachestvo*, ed. S. A. Shumov and A. R. Andreev (Moscow: Eksmo, 2005), 5 (from the Turkish, "to attack"); Sokol, *Revolt*, 124 ("oppress," "violate"); Edgar, *Tribal Nation*, 38–39 ("bandit"). See Baymirza Hayit, *"Basmatchi": Nationaler Kampf Turkestans in den Jahren 1917 bis 1934* (Cologne: Dreisam, 1992).

162. Safarov, *Kolonial'naia*, 90.

163. Khalid, *Making*, 86–88.

164. Buttino, "Ethnicité," 198; Buttino, "Central Asia," 124.

165. Buttino, "Central Asia," 127.

166. Buttino, "Ethnicité," 203.

167. Ibid., 204; Glenda Fraser, "Basmachi—I," 4.

168. Buttino, "Central Asia," 126.

169. Khalid, *Making*, 91 (decree of December 3, 1917 [November 20, OS]).

170. Nurpeisov and Grigor'ev, "Turar Ryskulov," 21–22.
171. Nurpeisov and Grigor'ev, "Turar Ryskulov," 22; Buttino, "Ethnicité," 215; Buttino, "Central Asia," 128. Ryskulov was shot in 1938; his accounts of the events in Central Asia, published in the 1920s, when he was part of the Soviet apparatus, are still cited: K. Mambetaliev, "Posleslovie," 248; see also: Khalid, *Making*, 110–112. Ryskulov's approach and role are criticized in Safarov, *Kolonial'naia*, 114–115.
172. Nurpeisov and Grigor'ev, "Turar Ryskulov," 22–23.
173. Ibid., 26.
174. Buttino, "Central Asia," 127–128.
175. Safarov, *Kolonial'naia*, 99–100.
176. Buttino, "Ethnicité," 216.
177. Nurpeisov and Grigor'ev, "Turar Ryskulov," 26–27. Kuibyshev was shot in 1935, Goloshchekin in 1941.
178. Ibid., 28–30.
179. Buttino, "Central Asia," 130–131; Buttino, "Ethnicité," 216.
180. Buttino, "Ethnicité," 217.
181. Nurpeisov and Grigor'ev, "Turar Ryskulov," 30–31.
182. Ibid., 31, 32, 33, 27 (quotes).
183. Ibid., 35–37.
184. Buttino, "Ethnicité," 217; Buttino, "Central Asia," 129–130.
185. Fraser, "Basmachi—I," 34; Buttino, "Ethnicité," 217–218.
186. Glenda Fraser, "Basmachi—II," *Central Asian Survey* 6.2 (1987): 8, 24.
187. Buttino, "Study," 61–65; Buttino, "Central Asia," 114.
188. P. G. Galuzo, *Turkestan-koloniia: Ocherk istorii Turkestana ot zavoevaniia russkimi do revoliutsii 1917 goda* (Moscow: Kommunisticheskii universitet trudiash-chikhsia Vostoka, 1929), 217–220.
189. Safarov, *Kolonial'naia*, 124; Buttino, "Central Asia," 109, says "the principal objective of the Bolshevik Revolution in Turkestan was to maintain the dominant position of the Russian colonial minority and prevent decolonization." He thus applies Safarov's critique of the early phase to the entire character of Soviet rule in the region.
190. Safarov, *Kolonial'naia*, 96.
191. Ibid., 114–115.

## PART V: CHAPTER 1

1. V. B. Stankevich, *Vospominaniia, 1914–1919 g.* (Berlin: Ladyschnikow, 1920), 306.
2. Geoffrey Swain, *The Origins of the Russian Civil War* (London: Longmans, 1996), 87.
3. Peter Kenez, *Civil War in South Russia, 1918: The First Year of the Volunteer Army* (Berkeley: University of California Press, 1971), 54–55, 24–25 (Denikin).
4. Ibid., 19.
5. Viktor Shklovsky, *A Sentimental Journey: Memoirs, 1917–1922*, trans. Richard Sheldon (1923; Ithaca: Cornell University Press, 1984), 65.

6. Ibid., 66.

7. S.V.Volkov, *Tragediia russkogo ofitserstva* (Moscow: Fokus, 1999), 306–307.

8. Ibid., 49.

9. B. I. Kolonitskii, *Pogony i bor'ba za vlast' v 1917 godu* (St. Petersburg: Ostrov, 2001); B. I. Kolonitskii, *Simvoly vlasti i bor'ba za vlast': K izucheniiu politicheskoi kul'tury rossiiskoi revoliutsii 1917 goda* (St. Petersburg: Bulanin, 2001), 140–228.

10. "Whites," in Jonathan D. Smele, *Historical Dictionary of the Russian Civil Wars, 1916–1926*, 2 vols. (Lanham, MD: Rowman & Littlefield, 2015), 2:1313–1314; Hans Rogger, "The Skobelev Phenomenon: The Hero and his Worship," *Oxford Slavonic Papers*, ed. Robert Auty, J. L. I. Fennell, and I. P. Foote, n.s., vol. IX (Oxford: Clarendon, 1976), 46–78.

11. Shane O'Rourke, *The Cossacks* (Manchester: Manchester University Press, 2007), 27–53, 146–150.

12. Stephen M. Brown, "Communists and the Red Cavalry: The Political Education of the *Konarmiia* in the Russian Civil War, 1918–20," *Slavonic and East European Review* 73.1 (1995): 89.

13. For Don: Peter Holquist, *Making War, Forging Revolution: Russia's Continuum of Crisis, 1914–1921* (Cambridge, MA: Harvard University Press, 2002), 8 (39 percent); Kenez, *Civil War 1918*, 38 (49 percent).

14. Shane O'Rourke, "The Cossacks," in *Critical Companion to the Russian Revolution, 1914–1921*, ed. Edward Acton, Vladimir Iu. Cherniaev, and William G. Rosenberg (Bloomington: Indiana University Press, 1997), 500; V. P. Danilov and N. S. Tarkhova, "Vvedenie," in *Filipp Mironov: Tikhii Don v 1917–1921 gg.*, ed. V. P. Danilov and Teodor Shanin (Moscow: Mezhdunarodnyi fond "Demokratiia," 1997), 7.

15. Kenez, *Civil War 1918*, 43; O'Rourke, *Cossacks*, 152.

16. Kenez, *Civil War 1918*, 38–41.

17. O'Rourke, *Cossacks*, 209.

18. Ibid., 212 (garrisons); O'Rourke, "The Cossacks," 501.

19. Kenez, *Civil War 1918*, 142.

20. Willard Sunderland, *Taming the Wild Field: Colonization and Empire on the Russian Steppe* (Ithaca: Cornell University Press, 2004), 159, 197.

21. Holquist, *Making War*, 52–55; quote, 55.

22. Ibid., 66–72.

23. O'Rourke, *Cossacks*, 217–219.

24. Kenez, *Civil War 1918*, 41–42; Swain, *Origins*, 85; Holquist, *Making War*, 73, 90–93; "Kaledin," in Smele, *Historical Dictionary*, 1:536–537.

25. Danilov and Tarkhova, "Vvedenie," 8–9.

26. Ibid., 12 (dated November 11/24, 1917).

27. Holquist, *Making War*, 115–117.

28. Kenez, *Civil War 1918*, 61.

29. Ibid., 59–61.

30. Ibid., 63–64.

31. General A. Denikine, *The White Army*, trans. Catherine Zvegintzov (London: Jonathan Cape, 1930), 27–28; Kenez, *Civil War 1918*, 62.

32. Swain, *Origins*, 87–88; Kenez, *Civil War 1918*, 73–74.

33. Denikin, *White Army*, 31.

34. Ibid., 31–32 (his italics).

35. Ibid., 30.

36. Kenez, *Civil War 1918*, 73–79; V. Iu. Cherniaev, "The White Generals," in *Critical Companion*, 208.

37. Denikin, *White Army*, 34–35.

38. Kenez, *Civil War 1918*, 75–82; on triumvirate, see also Swain, *Origins*, 88.

39. Kenez, *Civil War 1918*, 86–90.

40. Swain, *Origins*, 87–88.

41. Kenez, *Civil War 1918*, 92.

42. Kenez, *Civil War 1918*, 91–95; William G. Rosenberg, *Liberals in the Russian Revolution: The Constitutional Democratic Party, 1917–1921* (Princeton: Princeton University Press, 1974), 313 (Kaledin suicide); Denikin, *White Army*, 43–44 (Kaledin suicide). On Red occupation of Rostov, see the account by Menshevik A. S. Lokerman, *Les Bolcheviks à l'oeuvre: Soixante-quatorze jours de dictature bolcheviste à Rostov-sur-le-Don*, pref. Vladimir Zenzinoff (Paris: Rivière, 1920).

43. Denikin, *White Army*, 44–45.

44. Ibid., 46.

45. Ibid., 47–48 (slightly modified quote).

46. Ibid., 53.

47. Kenez, *Civil War 1918*, 96–103; Rosenberg, *Liberals*, 313 ("Icy March," which he numbers at 3,000, mostly officers).

48. Denikin, *White Army*, 62–73.

49. Ibid., 76–78.

50. Ibid., 80–82; Kenez, *Civil War 1918*, 110–111.

51. Denikin, *White Army*, 84.

52. Ibid., 88–90.

53. Ibid., 92.

54. Ibid., 93–95.

55. Ibid., 94–96.

56. Ibid., 97–98.

57. Kenez, *Civil War 1918*, 24–25; "Denikin," in Smele, *Historical Dictionary*, 1:321–324.

58. Denikin, *White Army*, 129.

59. Ibid., 101–107.

60. Ibid., 108–109; Kenez, *Civil War 1918*, 121 (not exaggerating).

61. Denikin, *White Army*, 110–113.

62. Kenez, *Civil War 1918*, 120–122.

63. Lokerman, *Les Bolcheviks à l'oeuvre*, 8, 11–17, 21–22.

64. Holquist, *Making War*, 131, 137.

65. Michael Geyer, "Ein Exerzierfeld extremer Gewalt: Zur Mikro-Geschichte des 'Gefechts am Mius-See'" (unpublished ms., November 2013); Reinhard Nachtigal, "Das Gefecht an der Mius-Bucht: Ein unbeachtetes Kapitel der deutschen Besetzung Südrußlands 1918," *Jahrbücher für Geschichte Osteuropas*, n.s., 53.2 (2005): 221–246.

66. Kenez, *Civil War 1918*, 118; Danilov and Tarkhova, "Vvedenie," 10 (dates).

67. Kenez, *Civil War 1918*, 120–122; Holquist, *Making War*, 136.

68. O'Rourke, *Cossacks*, 229–230.

69. Kenez, *Civil War 1918*, 121–123 (April 14, 1918 raid).

70. Denikin, *White Army*, 116.

71. "Don Republic," in Smele, *Historical Dictionary*, 1:336; "Krasnov," ibid., 621–622; Evan Mawdsley, *The Russian Civil War* (Boston: Allen and Unwin, 1987), 85–86, 87.

72. Kenez, *Civil War 1918*, 138–148; Mawdsley, *Russian Civil War*, 86–88.

73. Mawdsley, *Russian Civil War*, 88, 166. Krasnov was consistent in his reactionary politics. He left for Germany in February 1919, where he later became a Nazi sympathizer. Repatriated by the British in 1945, he was hanged by the Soviets in 1947 at the age of seventy-seven.

74. Kenez, *Civil War 1918*, 144–148.

75. Ibid., 154.

76. Ibid., 156–158, 159–164.

77. Rosenberg, *Liberals*, 314–315.

78. Kenez, *Civil War 1918*, 126–131, 149–151; "Drozdovskii," in Smele, *Historical Dictionary*, 1:342–344; Denikin, *White Army*, 116–118, 120–122.

79. Kenez, *Civil War 1918*, 151–155.

80. Mawdsley, *Russian Civil War*, 91–92.

81. Kenez, *Civil War 1918*, 166–172; Mawdsley, *Russian Civil War*, 93.

82. William Henry Chamberlin, *The Russian Revolution, 1917–1921*, 2 vols. (1935; New York: Grosset & Dunlap, 1965), 2:141.

83. Stephen Kotkin, *Stalin*, vol. 1: *Paradoxes of Power, 1878–1928* (New York: Penguin, 2014), 300–307; Mawdsley, *Russian Civil War*, 88–91.

84. Kenez, *Civil War 1918*, 173–175; Konstantin Zalesskii, "Voroshilov," in *Grazhdanskaia voina v Rossii: Entsiklopediia katastrofy*, ed. Dmitrii Volodikhin and Sergei Volkov (Moscow: Sibirskii tsiriul'nik, 2010), 233–234; "Voroshilov," in Smele, *Historical Dictionary*, 2:1288–1290.

85. Kenez, *Civil War 1918*, 174 (figures), 175–177.

86. Ibid., 177–178.

87. Ibid., 191–208.

88. A. G. Zarubin and V. G. Zarubin, *Bez pobeditelei: Iz istorii grazhdanskoi voiny v Krymu* (Simferopol: Tavriia, 1997), 146–148, 150.

89. "Osvag," in Smele, *Historical Dictionary*, 2: 831–832; Andrei Kruchinin, "Osvag," in *Grazhdanskaia voina v Rossii*, ed. Volodikhin and Volkov, 207–208. On Osvag in relation to anti-Semitism, see O.V. Budnitskii, *Rossiiskie evrei mezhdu krasnymi i belymi, 1917–1920* (Moscow: ROSSPEN, 2005), 222–229.

90. Christopher Lazarski, "White Propaganda Efforts in the South during the Russian Civil War, 1918–19 (The Alekseev-Denikin Period)," *Slavonic and East European Review* 70 (1992): 688–707.

91. Quoted, Kenez, *Civil War 1918*, 210.

92. Rosenberg, *Liberals*, 297–298; "Natsional'nyi tsentr," in *Krasnaia kniga V.Ch.K.*, vol. 2, ed. M. I. Latsis (Moscow: Gosizdat, 1922); rpt., ed. A. S. Velidov (Moscow: Politicheskaia literatura, 1989), 38–52; "Soiuz vozrozhdeniia," ibid., 32–38.

93. Kenez, *Civil War 1918*, 220–223.

94. Chamberlin, *Russian Revolution*, 2:260–261; Kenez, *Civil War 1918*, 230.

95. Mawdsley, *Russian Civil War*, 96–97.

### PART V: CHAPTER 2

1. "Editorial Comment: Recognition of Russia," *American Journal of International Law* 28.1 (1934): 94, 97.

2. W. P. Coates and Zelda K. Coates, *Armed Intervention in Russia, 1918–1922* (London: Victor Gollancz, 1935), 62; Bruce R. H. Lockhart, *British Agent* (New York and London: Putnam, 1933); Jacques Sadoul, *Notes sur la révolution bolchevique (octobre 1917–janvier 1919)*, pref. Henri Barbusse (Paris: Éditions de la Sirène, 1919); William Hard, *Raymond Robins' Own Story* (New York and London: Harper & Brothers, 1920). U.S. engineers had been in Russia maintaining the railway system since February 1917: Kendall Bailes, "The American Connection: Ideology and the Transfer of American Technology to the Soviet Union, 1917–1941," *Comparative Studies in Society and History* 23.3 (1981): 425–426; Clifford M. Foust, *John Frank Stevens: Civil Engineer* (Bloomington: Indiana University Press, 2013).

3. Geoffrey Swain, *The Origins of the Russian Civil War* (London: Longmans, 1996), 102.

4. Ibid., 111–112, 121–122.

5. Ibid., 133–134.

6. John W. Wheeler-Bennett, *Brest-Litovsk, The Forgotten Peace, March 1918* (London: Macmillan; New York: St. Martin's, 1938), 253–254 (quote 254).

7. Quoted, ibid., 258–259.

8. Evan Mawdsley, *The Russian Civil War* (Boston: Allen and Unwin, 1987), 50.

9. James Bunyan, *Intervention, Civil War, and Communism in Russia, April–December 1918: Documents and Materials* (Baltimore: Johns Hopkins Press, 1936), 62.

10. Wheeler-Bennett, *Brest-Litovsk*, 278; Swain, *Origins*, 106 (rumors of Japanese intervention).

11. Betty Miller Unterberger, "Woodrow Wilson and the Russian Revolution," in *Woodrow Wilson and a Revolutionary World*, ed. Arthur S. Link (Chapel Hill: University of North Carolina Press, 1982), 57–58; Bunyan, *Intervention*, 64–67.

12. Wheeler-Bennett, *Brest-Litovsk*, 280, 284–285.

13. Ibid., 286–287.

14. Ibid., 288–290.

15. Ibid., 291–295.

16. Quoted, Unterberger, "Woodrow Wilson," 62; Wheeler-Bennett, *Brest-Litovsk*, 297.

17. Wheeler-Bennett, *Brest-Litovsk*, 307.

18. Swain, *Origins*, 128–130.

19. Unterberger, "Woodrow Wilson," 62–63.

20. Bunyan, *Intervention*, 62–63.

21. Ibid., 64–69.

22. Wheeler-Bennett, *Brest-Litovsk*, 331–332.

23. Bunyan, *Intervention*, 71.

24. Swain, *Origins*, 138–141.

25. Lockhart, *British Agent*, 217.

26. Ibid., 237–239.

27. Ibid., 238.

28. Ibid., 197.

29. Ibid., 236.

30. Wheeler-Bennett, *Brest-Litovsk*, 330; "Protest against Germany's Violation of the Brest treaty" (Chicherin to German Government, April 27, 1918), in Bunyan, *Intervention*, 114–115.

31. Wheeler-Bennett, *Brest-Litovsk*, 328–329.

32. Radek in *Izvestiia*, April 28, 1918, quoted, ibid., 330.

33. Swain, *Origins*, 150.

34. Quotes, ibid., 141.

35. Bunyan, *Intervention*, 71.

36. "The Minister in Moscow to the Foreign Ministry, May 10, 1918," in *Germany and the Revolution in Russia 1915–1918: Documents from the Archives of the German Foreign Ministry*, ed. Z. A. B. Zeman (London: Oxford University Press, 1958), 123–124.

37. "The Minister in Moscow to the Foreign Ministry, May 13, 1918," in ibid., 124–125.

38. Protocol of a Meeting at Spa, May 13, 1918, in ibid., 125.

39. "Soviet Russia's Foreign Relations" (Lenin's speech at Plenary Session of CEC, Moscow Soviet, and Representatives of Trade Unions and Factory-Shop Committees, May 14, 1918), in Bunyan, *Intervention*, 116–121.

40. Ibid., 116.

41. Ibid., 120.

42. Ibid., 121.

43. Reporting Bronskii's visit: "The Minister in Moscow to the Foreign Ministry, May 15, 1918," in Zeman, *Germany*, 126.

44. This and above paragraph: Winfried Baumgart, *Deutsche Ostpolitik 1918: Von Brest-Litowsk bis zum Ende des Ersten Weltkrieges* (Vienna and Munich: Oldenbourg, 1966), 167–168 (on the May 15 proposal, favors the latter view); Swain, *Origins*, 151.

45. On the polemic: Baumgart, *Deutsche Ostpolitik*, 268–269. "'Left-Wing' Childishness and the Petty-Bourgeois Mentality," written April 1918, published May 9, 10, 11, 1918, in *Pravda*; available at http://www.marxists.org/archive/lenin/works/1918/may/09.htm (accessed January 31, 2017).

46. "The Minister in Copenhagen (Brockdorff-Rantzau) to the Foreign Ministry (April 2, 1917)," in Zeman, *Germany*, 31.

47. Kühlmann, "Protocol of a Meeting at Spa" (May 13, 1918), in ibid., 125.

48. "The Minister in Moscow to the Foreign Ministry" (May 16, 1918), in ibid., 128.

49. "The State Secretary to the Minister in Moscow" (May 18, 1918), in ibid., 128–129.

50. Major-General Max Hoffmann, *War Diaries and Other Papers*, trans. Eric Sutton, 2 vols. (London: Martin Secker, 1929), 1:218–219.

51. "The Counsellor of Legation in Moscow (Riezler) to Minister Bergen" (June 4, 1918), in Zeman, *Germany*, 130–132.

52. "The State Secretary of the Foreign Ministry to the State Secretary of the Treasury" (June 8, 1918), in Zeman, *Germany*, 132–133.

53. "The Minister in Moscow (Mirbach) to the State Secretary" (June 25, 1918), in Zeman, *Germany*, 137–139.

54. "Czechoslovak Legion," in Jonathan D. Smele, *Historical Dictionary of the Russian Civil Wars, 1916–1926*, 2 vols. (Lanham, MD: Rowman & Littlefield, 2015), 1:305–306; Joseph Noulens, *Mon ambassade en Russie soviétique 1917–1919*, 2 vols. (Paris: Plon, 1933), 2:80–81; William Henry Chamberlin, *The Russian Revolution, 1917–1921*, 2 vols. (1935; New York: Grosset & Dunlap, 1965), 2:2.

55. Peter Kenez, *Civil War in South Russia, 1918: The First Year of the Volunteer Army* (Berkeley: University of California Press, 1971), 136 (50,000); Bunyan, *Intervention*, 75 (45,000); Noulens, *Mon ambassade*, 2:81 (48,000); Mawdsley, *Russian Civil War*, 47 (40,000).

56. Swain, *Origins*, 113–115, 118.

57. Bunyan, *Intervention*, 76; Swain, *Origins*, 118; Wheeler-Bennett, *Brest-Litovsk*, 311–312.

58. "Soviet Commander in Chief Authorizes the Czechoslovaks to Leave the Ukraine" (Antonov's announcement, March 16, 1918), in Bunyan, *Intervention*, 80; on ice blocking Arkhangelsk: Noulens, *Mon ambassade*, 2:86–87.

59. Bunyan, *Intervention*, 77–78; "Omsk Soviet Orders the Stopping of the Czechoslovak Legion" (minutes of Tsentrosibir, March 22, 1918), in Bunyan, *Intervention*, 80–81.

60. "Soviet Government Grants the Czechoslovaks Passage to Vladivostok" (Stalin to Czechoslovak National Council, March 26, 1918), in Bunyan, *Intervention*, 81–82, quote, 81; Chamberlin, *Russian Revolution*, 2:3.

61. Bunyan, *Intervention*, 82–85; "The Czechoslovaks Threaten Resistance to the Soviets (Kirsanov Resolution, April 14, 1918), ibid., 83–85.

62. Bunyan, *Intervention*, 85–86.

63. Noulens, *Mon embassade*, 2:82.

64. Bunyan, *Intervention*, 86–87, 88–90.

65. "Orders to Disarm the Czechoslovaks" (Trotsky's Telegram, May 25, 1918), in Bunyan, *Intervention*, 91.

66. Noulens, *Mon ambassade*, 2:85.

67. "Penza Soviet to Trotsky" (May 26, 1918), in Bunyan, *Intervention*, 92.

68. "Trotsky's Reply" (May 26, 1918), in Bunyan, *Intervention*, 92.

69. Bunyan, *Intervention*, 87.

70. Ibid., 92–101.

71. Richard Pipes, *The Russian Revolution* (New York: Knopf, 1990), 438.

72. Boris Kolonitskii, *"Tragicheskaia erotika": Obrazy imperatorskoi sem'i v gody Pervoi mirovoi voiny* (Moscow: NLO, 2010).

73. Quoted, L. Bruce Lincoln, *Red Victory: A History of the Russian Civil War, 1918–1921* (New York: Simon and Schuster, 1989; rpt. Da Capo Press, 1999), 155.

74. This account relies primarily on Pipes, *Russian Revolution*, ch. 17, with attention to sources he also uses. *Gibel' tsarskoi sem'i: Materialy sledstviia po delu ob ubiistve Tsarskoi sem'i (avgust 1918–fevral' 1920)*, ed. Nikolai Ross (Frankfurt: Posev, 1987)—results of the White commission headed by Nikolai Sokolov, who emigrated to France and took the evidence with him; Nikolai Sokolov, *Ubiistvo tsarskoi sem'i* (Berlin: Slovo, 1925); *Ubiistvo tsarskoi sem'i i ee svity: Ofitsial'nye dokumenty* (Constantinople: Pressa, 1920); P. M. Bykov, *Les derniers jours des Romanov* (Paris: Payot, 1931)—the official, but frank version; M. K. Diterikhs, *Ubiistvo tsarskoi sem'i i chlenov Doma Romanovykh na Urale*, 2 vols. (Vladivostok: Voennaia Akademiia, 1922)—blaming the murder on the Jews; *Ispoved' tsareubiits: Ubiistvo tsarskoi sem'i v materialakh predvaritel'nogo sledstviia i v vospominaniiakh lits, prichastnykh k soversheniii*, ed. Iu. A. Zhuk (Moscow: Veche, 2008). See also "The Execution of the Imperial Family (Pierre Billiard)," and "Announcement of the Presidium of the Ural Regional Soviet," in Bunyan, *Intervention*, 230–231; Lincoln, *Red Victory*, 150–155; Orlando Figes, *A People's Tragedy: A History of the Russian Revolution* (New York: Viking, 1996), 638–639.

75. Bunyan, *Intervention*, 104.

76. Ibid., 101–102.

77. Ibid., 104–108 (commentary); "Overthrow of the Vladivostok Soviet" (June 29, 1918), ibid., 316; "Establishment of an Allied Protectorate Over Vladivostok" (Proclamation by the Commanders of the Allied and Associated Powers at Vladivostok, July 6, 1918), ibid., 317–318.

78. "American Plan for intervention in Russia" (from Communication of Secretary of State to Allied Ambassadors, July 17, 1918), in ibid., 109–110; quote, 109.

79. "Murmansk Soviet Approves Cooperation with Allies" (June 30, 1918), in ibid., 132–133.

80. "Chairman of Murmansk Soviet Declared an Enemy of the People" (Sovnarkom announcement July 1, 1918), in ibid., 134–135; A. A. Kiselev, "Iur'ev," in

*Politicheskie deiateli Rossii 1917: Biograficheskii slovar'*, ed. P.V.Volobuev (Moscow: Bol'shaia rossiiskaia entsiklopediia, 1993), 367.

81. "Statement of July 1, 1918," in Bunyan, *Intervention*, 134; Yanni Kotsonis, "Arkhangel'sk, 1918: Regionalism and Populism in the Russian Civil War," *Russian Review* 51.4 (1992): 534.

82. Swain, *Origins*, 144. Collection of Major General Sir Frederick Cuthbert Poole, General Officer Commanding, North Russia Expeditionary Force, 1918–1919. King's College London, available at http://www.kingscollections.org/serving-soldier/collection/revolutionary-russia-a-british-view (accessed January 31, 2017).

83. Bunyan, *Intervention*, 132–137.

84. "Socialist Fatherland in Danger" (July 29, 1918), in ibid., 138–139.

85. Quoted, ibid., 139–141.

86. Quoted, ibid., 141–142.

87. "To the Toiling Masses of France, England, America, Italy, and Japan" (Appeal of Sovnarkom, August 1, 1918), in ibid., 139–143, 143 (final quote).


PART V: CHAPTER 3

1. M. A. Molodtsygin, *Krasnaia armiia: Rozhdenie i stanovlenie 1917–1920 gg.* (Moscow: Institute Rossiiskoi istorii RAN, 1997).

2. Viktor Shklovsky, *A Sentimental Journey: Memoirs, 1917–1922*, trans. Richard Sheldon (1923; Ithaca: Cornell University Press, 1984), 27, 34, 35, 39.

3. Quoted, Mark von Hagen, *Soldiers in the Proletarian Dictatorship: The Red Army and the Soviet Socialist State, 1917–1930* (Ithaca: Cornell University Press, 1990), 19.

4. Preceding two paragraphs: ibid., 17–20.

5. S. S. Voitikov, "Razvitie vzgliadov vysshego rukovodstva Sovetskoi Rossii na voennoe stroitel'stvo v noiabre 1917–marte 1918 g.," *Voprosy istorii* 10 (2007): 4, citing "Telegramma V. A. Antonova-Ovseenko V. I. Leninu, N. I. Povoiskomu," protesting the decree, in *Bol'shevistskoe rukovodstvo: Perepiska, 1912–1927* (Moscow: ROSSPEN, 1996), 35–36; 36 (note).

6. Voitikov, "Razvitie vzgliadov," 3–4; John Erickson, *The Soviet High Command: A Military-Political History, 1918–1941*, 3rd ed. (London: Frank Cass, 2001), 835 (Antonov-Ovseenko), 837 (Dybenko).

7. Voitikov, "Razvitie vzgliadov," 4.

8. Ibid., 9–10.

9. Geoffrey Swain, *The Origins of the Russian Civil War* (London: Longmans, 1996), 132–134.

10. "Nam nuzhna armiia" (Rech' na zasedanii Moskovskogo Soveta Rab., Sold., i Kr. Deput., 19 marta 1918 g., *Pravda*, March 21, 1918), in L. Trotskii, *Kak vooruzhalas' revoliutsiia (na voennoi rabote)*, vol. 1: *Tysiacha deviat'sot vosemnadtsatyi god* (Moscow: Vysshii voennyi redaktsionnyi sovet, 1923), 26.

11. "Trud, distsiplina, poriadok" (Doklad na Moskovskoi Gorodskoi Konferentsii RKP, March 28, 1918), in ibid., 1:45.

12. Swain, *Origins*, 136–138.

13. The order was repeated in June 1918: von Hagen, *Soldiers*, 28.

14. Shklovsky, *Journey*, 63.

15. A. G. Kavtaradze, *Voennye spetsialisty na sluzhbe Respubliki Sovetov 1917–1920 gg.* (Moscow: Nauka, 1988), 39–40; von Hagen, *Soldiers*, 24.

16. von Hagen, *Soldiers*, 26–28.

17. S. V. Volkov, *Tragediia russkogo ofitserstva* (Moscow: Fokus, 1999), 306 (55,000–58,000 out of 276,000); Evan Mawdsley, *The Russian Civil War* (Boston: Allen and Unwin, 1987), 60.

18. Voitikov, "Razvitie vzgliadov," 5–6.

19. von Hagen, *Soldiers*, 28–30; Francesco Benvenuti, *The Bolsheviks and the Red Army, 1918–1922*, trans. Christopher Woodall (Cambridge: Cambridge University Press, 1988), 24; T. V. Osipova, *Rossiiskoe krest'ianstvo v revoliutsii i grazhdanskoi voine* (Moscow: Strelets, 2001), 301.

20. von Hagen, *Soldiers*, 34–37.

21. Trotsky, "Nam nuzhna armiia," 27.

22. Orlando Figes, "The Red Army and Mass Mobilization during the Russian Civil War, 1918–1920," *Past and Present* 129 (1990): 175; V. B. Stankevich, *Vospominaniia, 1914–1919 g.* (Berlin: Ladyschnikow, 1920), 313.

23. Figes, "Red Army," 175–180.

24. William Henry Chamberlin, *The Russian Revolution, 1917–1921*, 2 vols. (1935; New York: Grosset & Dunlap, 1965), 2:38.

25. Ibid., 37.

26. Ibid., 39.

27. Quoted, G. I. Il'iashchuk and V. I. Miller, "Martov," in *Politicheskie deiateli Rossii 1917: Biograficheskii slovar'*, ed. P. V. Volobuev (Moscow: Bol'shaia rossiiskaia entsiklopediia, 1993), 207.

28. Paul Dotsenko, *The Struggle for a Democracy in Siberia, 1917–1920: Eyewitness Account of a Contemporary* (Stanford: Hoover Institution Press, 1983); Col. Vladimir I. Lebedeff, *The Russian Democracy in its Struggle Against the Bolshevist Tyranny* (New York: Russian Information Bureau in the U. S., 1919).

29. Joseph Noulens, *Mon ambassade en Russie soviétique 1917–1919*, 2 vols. (Paris: Plon, 1933), 2:88.

30. Jonathan D. Smele, *Civil War in Siberia: The Anti-Bolshevik Government of Admiral Kolchak, 1918–1920* (Cambridge: Cambridge University Press, 1996), 16. Smele is a principal source for this chapter.

31. Ibid., 450; *Rossiia 1913 god: Statistiko-dokumental'nyi spravochnik* (St. Petersburg: BLITs, 1995), 14, 20, 22; *The Statesman's Year-Book: Statistical and Historical Annual of the States of the World for the Year 1916*, ed. J. Scott Keltie and M. Epstein (London: Macmillan, 1916), 1282.

32. V. I. Shishkin, "Pervaia sessiia Sibirskoi oblastnoi dumy (ianvar' 1918 goda)," in *Istoriia beloi Sibiri: Sbornik nauchnykh statei* (Kemerovo: KGU, 2011), 54–61.

Available online at http://zaimka.ru/shishkin-duma/ (accessed November 30, 2013; no pagination).

33. Smele, *Civil War in Siberia*, 17–19.

34. Ibid., 20.

35. Anton S. Soloveichik, *Bor'ba za vozrozhdenie Rossii na Vostoke: Povolzh'e, Ural i Sibir' v 1918 godu* (Rostov na Donu, [July] 1919), 5–6.

36. Smele, *Civil War in Siberia*, 14.

37. Ibid., 18–20; *S Kolchakom—protiv Kolchaka*, ed. A. V. Kvakin (Moscow: Agraf, 2007), 180; William G. Rosenberg, *Liberals in the Russian Revolution: The Constitutional Democratic Party, 1917–1921* (Princeton: Princeton University Press, 1974), 386.

38. Chamberlin, *Russian Revolution*, 2:12; *The Testimony of Kolchak and Other Siberian Materials*, ed. Elena Varneck and H. H. Fisher (Stanford: Stanford University Press, 1935), 160.

39. Smele, *Civil War in Siberia*, 20.

40. Derber bio from Memorial website: http://socialist.memo.ru/lists/bio/l6.htm (accessed August 9, 2014); also "Derber," in Jonathan D. Smele, *Historical Dictionary of the Russian Civil Wars, 1916–1926*, 2 vols. (Lanham, MD: Rowman & Littlefield, 2015), 1:325–327.

41. Smele, *Civil War in Siberia*, 21; "Western Siberian Commissariat," in Smele, *Historical Dictionary*, 2:1307–1308; "Zapadno-Sibirskii komissariat," in Kvakin, *S Kolchakom*, 198; *Zapadno-Sibirskii komissariat vremennogo Sibirskogo pravitel'stva (26 maia–30 iiunia 1918 g.): Sbornik dokumentov i materialov*, ed. V. I. Shishkin (Novosibirsk: Novosibirskii gos. un-t, 2005).

42. Smele, *Civil War in Siberia*, 13.

43. Ibid., 21–22.

44. Ibid., 25, 23.

45. Ibid., 13–14.

46. Ibid., 26–27.

47. Noulens, *Mon ambassade*, 2:87–88.

48. Smele, *Civil War in Siberia*, 28–30.

49. "The Sovnarkom Declares War on the Siberian Provisional Government" (June, 10, 1918), in James Bunyan, *Intervention, Civil War, and Communism in Russia, April-December 1918: Documents and Materials* (Baltimore: Johns Hopkins Press, 1936), 325–328.

50. Smele, *Civil War in Siberia*, 30; "Establishment of the Provisional Government of Western Siberia" (Announcement of the Chairman of the Siberian Regional Duma, June 30, 1918), including the members of what it called "the Siberian Provisional Government," in Bunyan, *Intervention*, 329. On Vologodskii: *Testimony*, notes, 234. See *Vremennoe Sibirskoe Pravitel'stvo: 26 maia–3 noiabria 1916 g.: Sbornik dokumentov i materialov*, ed. V. I. Shishkin (Novosibirsk: Sova, 2007).

51. "Declaration of Siberian Independence" (July 4, 1918), in Bunyan, *Intervention*, 329–330; "Deklaratsiia Vremennogo Sibirskogo pravitel'stva o gosudarstvennoi samostoiatel'nosti Sibiri" (July 4/17, 1918), in Omsk. Available online at http://

www.oldchita.org/documents/7-xxc-documents/446-1918declaration.html (accessed February 1, 2017).

52. Bunyan, *Intervention*, 330 (both quotes).

53. Smele, *Civil War in Siberia*, 31; Chamberlin, *Russian Revolution*, 2:14; "Policies of the Siberian Provisional Government," in Bunyan, *Intervention*, 331.

54. Smele, *Civil War in Siberia*, 32–33.

55. "Prorogation of the Siberian Regional Duma" (decree of September 21, 1918), in Bunyan, *Intervention*, 338; "The Siberian Regional Duma Dismisses the Administrative Council" (September 22, 1918), ibid., 339.

56. Smele, *Civil War in Siberia*, 31.

57. Mawdsley, *Russian Civil War*, 56; Smele, *Civil War in Siberia*, 33. See Stephen M. Berk, "The Democratic Counter-revolution: Komuch and the Civil War on the Volga," *Canadian-American Slavic Studies* 7.4 (1973):443–459.

58. Smele, *Civil War in Siberia*, 33; Bunyan, *Intervention*, 283–290 (Komuch decrees); Soloveichik, *Bor'ba*, 13–14.

59. Lebedeff, *The Russian Democracy*, 14; Chamberlin, *Russian Revolution*, 2:14–15.

60. *Testimony*, 161.

61. Soloveichik, *Bor'ba*, 16.

62. Mawdsley, *Russian Civil War*, 64–65.

63. Smele, *Civil War in Siberia*, 33–34.

64. Soloveichik, *Bor'ba*, 14.

65. *1918 god na Ukraine*, ed. S. V. Volkov (Moscow: Tsentrpoligraf, 2001), 382 (killed after arrest); *Krasnaia kniga V.Ch.K.*, vol. 1, ed. P. Makintsian (Moscow: Gosizdat, 1920); rpt., ed. A. S. Velidov (Moscow: Politicheskaia literatura, 1989), 259; Geoffrey Swain, "Russia's Garibaldi: The Revolutionary Life of Mikhail Artemevich Muraviev," *Revolutionary Russia* 11.2 (1998): 54–81, 75 (accounts of death vary, some sources say he resisted arrest, some that he committed suicide); Bruce R. H. Lockhart, *British Agent* (New York and London: Putnam, 1933), 302 (his own men arrest him, he shoots himself); A. Gol'denveizer, "Iz kievskikh vospominanii," in *1918 god na Ukraine*, ed. Volkov, 80; Swain, *Origins*, 177 (invited to soviet meeting in Simbirsk and "gunned down"); Mawdsley, *Russian Civil War*, 57 (ambushed and killed by head of Simbirsk Soviet while repressing anti-Bolshevik revolt); also, "Murav'ev," in Smele, *Historical Dictionary*, 2:772–73; and "Murav'ev Uprising," ibid., 773–774 (773 for his death).

66. Mawdsley, *Russian Civil War*, 56–57.

67. Ibid., 58–59; "Vācietis," in Smele, *Historical Dictionary*, 2:1255–1256.

68. Quoted, Bunyan, *Intervention*, 292.

69. Chamberlin, *Russian Revolution*, 2:16, 530; Smele, *Civil War in Siberia*, 33; Bunyan, *Intervention*, 292.

70. Bunyan, *Intervention*, 296–299.

71. Mawdsley, *Russian Civil War*, 66.

72. Trotsky, "What the Taking of Kazan Means" (August 24, 1918), in Bunyan, *Intervention*, 301.

73. Trotsky, "Do Not Join the Enemy!" (August 27, 1918), in ibid., 303.

74. "Accusations Against Allied Diplomatic Representatives" (Announcement of the Sovnarkom, September 2, 1918, *Izvestiia*, September 3, 1918), in ibid., 145–146; "Raid on the British Embassy at Petrograd" (Bolshevik Statement, September 5, 1918, *Izvestiia*, September 5, 1918, as "Appeal to the Civilized World"), ibid., 147–148.

75. Bunyan, *Intervention*, 300.

76. Trotsky, "What the Taking of Kazan Means," 301.

## PART V: CHAPTER 4

1. *The Testimony of Kolchak and Other Siberian Materials*, ed. Elena Varneck and H. H. Fisher (Stanford: Stanford University Press, 1935), 17–18. Rpt. and trans., with annotation, of *Dopros Kolchaka: Protokoly zasedanii Chrezvychainoi sledstvennoi komissii v Irkutske, stenograficheskii otchet*, ed. K. A. Popov (Leningrad: Gos. Izd-vo, 1925).

2. *Testimony*, 33.

3. Ibid., 48.

4. Ibid., 54–60.

5. Ibid., 66–69.

6. Ibid., 71.

7. Ibid., 74–75, 84.

8. Ibid., 76–77, 79–84.

9. General Ludendorff, *My War Memories, 1914–1918*, 2 vols. (London: Hutchinson, 1919), 1:414.

10. *Testimony*, 91.

11. Ibid., 85–87.

12. Ibid., 98–102.

13. Ibid., 104.

14. Ibid., 107–110.

15. Ibid., 146.

16. "Janin," in Jonathan D. Smele, *Historical Dictionary of the Russian Civil Wars, 1916–1926*, 2 vols. (Lanham, MD: Rowman & Littlefield, 2015), 1:520.

17. Général Janin, *Ma mission en Sibérie 1918–1920* (Paris: Payot, 1933), 14–15.

18. Ibid., 23–24.

19. *Protsess nad kolchakovskimi ministrami: Mai 1920*, ed. V. I. Shishkin (Moscow: Mezhdunarodnyi fond "Demokratiia," 2003), 473; Valerii Klaving, *Grazhdanskaia voina v Rossii: Belye armii* (Moscow: AST, 2003), 571; "Khorvat," in *S Kolchakom—protiv Kolchaka: Kratkii biograficheskii slovar': Ukazatel' uchrezhdenii i organizatsii: Kratkii ukazatel' literatury po istorii Grazhdanskoi voiny*, ed. A.V. Kvakin (Moscow: Agraf, 2007), 150–151.

20. *Testimony*, 235 (note); Kvakin, *S Kolchakom*, 247, 150–151; "Proclamation of a Government by Khorvat" (July 9, 1918), in James Bunyan, *Intervention, Civil War,*

*and Communism in Russia, April–December 1918: Documents and Materials* (Baltimore: Johns Hopkins Press, 1936), 320–332; *Protsess nad kolchakovskimi ministrami*, 473.

21. William G. Rosenberg, *Liberals in the Russian Revolution: The Constitutional Democratic Party, 1917–1921* (Princeton: Princeton University Press, 1974), 386–387.

22. V. D. Vatrantsev, A. I. Romanenko, M. V. Kolodov, and A. Kh. Temiukov, "K chitateliu," *Dmitrii Leonidovich Khorvat* (Vladivostok, [November] 1918), i.

23. *Dmitrii Leonidovich Khorvat*, 46, 55 (quote).

24. *Testimony*, 118.

25. "Declaration of the Provisional Government of Autonomous Siberia" (Vladivostok, July 8, 1918), in Bunyan, *Intervention*, 319–320; Kvakin, *S Kolchakom*, 54, 172.

26. "A Warning to Khorvat" (Derber's Note of July 28, 1918), in Bunyan, *Intervention*, 323.

27. "Note of the Siberian Government to the Allied Powers" (July 25, 1918), in Bunyan, *Intervention*, 323.

28. "The Czechoslovaks Urge the Formation of a Central Government" (Memorandum Presented to the Second Cheliabinsk Conference, August 20, 1918), in Bunyan, *Intervention*, 336–337; "Soiuz vozrozhdeniia Rossii," in Kvakin, *S Kolchakom*, 301; "Soiuz vozrozhdeniia," *Krasnaia kniga V.Ch.K.*, vol. 2, ed. M. I. Latsis (Moscow: Gosizdat, 1922); rpt., ed. A. S. Velidov (Moscow: Politicheskaia literatura, 1989), 32–36.

29. "The Ufa State Conference" (Opening session, September 8, 1918, including statements by individual delegations), in Bunyan, *Intervention*, 340–351, 339 (number of delegates), 352 (identity of delegates); Rosenberg, *Liberals*, 292, 390–391; Jonathan D. Smele, *Civil War in Siberia: The Anti-Bolshevik Government of Admiral Kolchak, 1918–1920* (Cambridge: Cambridge University Press, 1996), 36, 45–48; Susan Z. Rupp, "Conflict and Crippled Compromise: Civil-War Politics in the East and the Ufa State Conference," *Russian Review* 56.2 (1997): 249–264. Smele is the principal source for this chapter.

30. "Krol'," in L. G. Protasov, *Liudi Uchreditel'nogo sobraniia: Portret v inter'ere epokhi* (Moscow: ROSSPEN, 2008), 321.

31. Smele, *Civil War in Siberia*, 51–56.

32. "Declaration of the Party of the People's Freedom," in Bunyan, *Intervention*, 349; Rosenberg, *Liberals*, 389–390; L. A. Krol', *Za tri goda: Vospominaniia, vpechatleniia i vstrechi* (Vladivostok: "Svobodnaia Rossiia," 1921).

33. "Constitution of the Ufa Directorate" (Resolution of the State Conference, September 23, 1918), in Bunyan, *Intervention*, 352–356; "Ufimskoe Gosudarstvennoe Soveshchanie," in Kvakin, *S Kolchakom*, 305.

34. Smele, *Civil War in Siberia*, 680 (table); "Direktoriia," in Kvakin, *S Kolchakom*, 190; *Protsess nad kolchakovskimi ministrami*, 473 (Avksent'ev); 73 (Zenzinov); 473–474 (Boldyrev); 474–475 (Vologodskii).

35. "Avksent'ev," in Kvakin, *S Kolchakom*, 3.

36. "Proclamation of the All-Russian Provisional Government" (November 4, 1918), in Bunyan, *Intervention*, 368–370; quote, 370.

37. *Testimony*, 154–155, 157.

38. Smele, *Civil War in Siberia*, 369 (figures).

39. Col. John Ward, *With the "Die-Hards" in Siberia* (London: Cassell, 1920), 126–127.

40. Rosenberg, *Liberals*, 391–393.

41. Ward, *With the "Die-Hards,"* x, 9.

42. Ibid., 112, 127.

43. Ibid., 126.

44. Janin, *Ma mission*, 19; William Henry Chamberlin, *The Russian Revolution, 1917–1921*, 2 vols. (1935; New York: Grosset & Dunlap, 1965), 2:180; William Sidney Graves, *America's Siberian Adventure, 1918–1920* (New York: J. Cape and Smith, 1931), 99.

45. *Testimony*, 157, 160; Chamberlin, *Russian Revolution*, 2:175.

46. Chamberlin, *Russian Revolution*, 2:175.

47. Quotes, ibid., 175–177.

48. Quoted from Boldyrev's diary, ibid., 174.

49. Rosenberg, *Liberals*, 394–395 (*gosudarstvennost'*).

50. "V. N. Pepeliaev, "Konspekt doklada Vostochnogo otdela Tsentral'nogo Komiteta Partii narodnoi svobody v Omske" (15/XI [1918]), in *S"ezdy i konferentsii konstitutsionno-demokraticheskoi partii*, vol. 3, bk. 2: *1918–1920 gg.* (Moscow: ROSSPEN, 2000), 58.

51. Smele, *Civil War in Siberia*, 681; Chamberlin, *Russian Revolution*, 2:177–178.

52. Chamberlin, *Russian Revolution*, 2:180. "Miller," in Smele, *Historical Dictionary*, 2:756–758.

53. Quoted, Chamberlin, *Russian Revolution*, 2:182; Smele, *Civil War in Siberia*, 195.

54. "Gajda (Geidl)," in Smele, *Historical Dictionary*, 1:437–439.

55. Chamberlin, *Russian Revolution*, 2:162; Smele, *Civil War in Siberia*, 195 (Czechoslovak National Council at Cheliabinsk open letter to Kolchak: "The Czechoslovak Army, fighting for the ideals of freedom and democracy, cannot and will not either unite or cooperate with the makers of *coups d'état* which run contrary to these principles.").

56. Chamberlin, *Russian Revolution*, 2:183; Kvakin, *S Kolchakom*, 23–25. For the next two years, Boldyrev collaborated with the Japanese occupation forces, which did not leave Vladivostok until October 1922. Arrested by the victorious Soviet authorities, he was released from prison in 1926 upon pledging to serve the new regime. He was arrested again in 1933 and shot. His extensive memoirs were published in 1925, while he was in prison. See Klaving, *Grazhdanskaia voina*, 397–398; General Vasilii G. Boldyrev, *Direktoriia, Kolchak, interventy:*

*Vospominaniia iz tsikla "Shest' let" 1917–1922 gg.*, ed.V. D.Vegman (Novonikolaevsk: Sibkraiizdat, 1925).

57. Smele, *Civil War in Siberia*, 681.
58. Quoted, Chamberlin, *Russian Revolution*, 2:178.
59. Ibid., 180.
60. Smele, *Civil War in Siberia*, 184–186.
61. Ibid., 113.
62. Ibid., 163–165.
63. Chamberlin, *Russian Revolution*, 2:183–184.
64. Quoted, Smele, *Civil War in Siberia*, 166, citing "Prikaz no. 56: Verkhovnogo Pravitelia i Verkhovnogo Glavnokomanduiushchego vsemi sukhoputnymi i morskimi vooruzhennymi silami Rossii" (Omsk, November 30, 1918), in S. Piontkovskii, *Grazhdanskaia voina v Rossii, 1918–1921 gg.: Khrestomatiia* (Moscow: Kom. Universitet im. Ia. M. Sverdlova, 1925), 300–301; quote (my translation), 301.
65. "Chernov," in Kvakin, *S Kolchakom*, 154; G. D. Alekseeva, K. V. Gusev, and A. V. Manykin, "Chernov," in *Politicheskie deiateli Rossii 1917: Biograficheskii slovar'*, ed. P. V. Volobuev (Moscow: Bol'shaia rossiiskaia entsiklopediia, 1993), 351.
66. Smele, *Civil War in Siberia*, 167.
67. Ibid., 169.
68. Ibid., 170–173.
69. Ibid., 80–84; "Ivanov-Rinov," in Smele, *Historical Dictionary*, 1:515–517.
70. Smele, *Civil War in Siberia*, 172–174. On murders of other Romanovs, Richard Pipes, *The Russian Revolution* (New York: Knopf, 1990), 763–765.
71. Quoted, Smele, *Civil War in Siberia*, 175, from Budberg.
72. Quoted, ibid., 175, from G. K. Gins (George K. Guins), *Sibir', soiuzniki i Kolchak: Povorotnyi moment russkoi istorii, 1918–1920 gg.: Vpechatleniia i mysli chlena Omskogo pravitel'stva* (Peking: Russkaia dukhovnaia missiia, 1921), 398.
73. Quoted, S. P. Mel'gunov, *Tragediia Admirala Kolchaka: Iz istorii grazhdanskoi voiny na Volge, Urale i v Sibiri*, 3 vols. in 4 pts. (Belgrade: Russkaia tipografiia, 1930–1931), 3:1, 57.
74. Smele, *Civil War in Siberia*, 181; "Gajda," in Smele, *Historical Dictionary*, 1:437–439.
75. *Testimony*, 114, 120–121.
76. This point made by Graves, *American's Siberian Adventure*, 107 and elsewhere.
77. Joseph Kessel, *Les temps sauvages* (Paris: Gallimard, 1975), 68.
78. Smele, *Civil War in Siberia*, 458.
79. Jamie Bisher, *White Terror: Cossack Warlords of the Trans-Siberian* (London and New York: Frank Cass, 2005), 23–39; Willard Sunderland, *The Baron's Cloak: A History of the Russian Empire in War and Revolution* (Ithaca: Cornell University Press, 2014); Ataman Semenov, *O sebe: Vospominaniia, mysli i vyvody*, ed. O. Prudkov (1936–1938; Moscow: AST, 1999).
80. Smele, *Civil War in Siberia*, 189–191; 190 (quote).

81.  Janin, *Ma mission*, 36.

82.  Smele, *Civil War in Siberia*, 188–189.

83.  Ibid., 386.

84.  *Testimony*, 132; Janin, *Ma mission*, 27–28.

85.  *Testimony*, 136, 143.

86.  Smele, *Civil War in Siberia*, 385.

87.  Ibid., 195; Mel'gunov, *Tragediia*, 3:1, 342.

88.  Smele, *Civil War in Siberia*, 456.

89.  Ibid., 193–194.

90.  "Kalmykov," in Smele, *Historical Dictionary*, 538–539.

91.  Quoted, Janin, *Ma mission*, 17.

92.  Ward, *With the "Die-Hards,"* x; Anton S. Soloveichik, *Bor'ba za vozrozhdenie Rossii na Vostoke: Povolzh'e, Ural i Sibir' v 1918 godu* (Rostov na Donu, [July] 1919), 59–60.

93.  Pavel Novgorodtsev, May 1919, quoted, Rosenberg, *Liberals*, 410; "Novgorodtsev," in Protasov, *Liudi*, 354.

94.  Joseph Lasies, *La tragédie Sibérienne: Le drame d'Ékaterinbourg, la fin de l'amiral Koltchak* (Paris: Édition française illustrée, 1920), 40 (quote), 41.

95.  Gins, *Sibir'*, 2:368.

96.  Mark Levene, *War, Jews, and the New Europe: The Diplomacy of Lucien Wolf, 1914–1919* (Oxford: Oxford University Press, 1992), 51, 54, 115. On Knox's views during Civil War, see Richard H. Ullman, *Britain and the Russian Civil War, November 1918–February 1920* (Princeton: Princeton University Press, 1968), 30, 113–114.

97.  Chamberlin, *Russian Revolution*, 2:160–161, 186.

98.  "Graves," in Smele, *Historical Dictionary*, 1:473–474.

99.  Graves, *America's Siberian Adventure*, 103.

100. Chamberlin, *Russian Revolution*, 2:163; Graves, *America's Siberian Adventure*, 108.

101. Quoted, Chamberlin, *Russian Revolution*, 2:163, from I. Subbotovskii, *Soiuzniki, russkie reaktsionery i interventsiia: Kratkii obzor* (Leningrad: Leningradskii Gublit, 1926), 102 (quote with my minor corrections from the original text); also Graves, *America's Siberian Adventure*, 111.

102. L. H. Grondijs [Lodewijk Hermen], *La guerre en Russie et in Sibérie*, intro. Maurice Paléologue (Paris: Éditions Bossard, 1922), 524 (Bolshevik Jews), 525 (U.S. and Jews).

103. Quoted, Chamberlin, *Russian Revolution*, 2:163, from Mel'gunov, *Tragediia*.

104. On background and loan: Adam Tooze, *The Deluge: The Great War and the Remaking of Global Order, 1916–1931* (London: Allen Lane, 2014), 80.

105. Smele, *Civil War in Siberia*, 465–467. On Stevens and the American project of economic intervention in Siberia, see Leo J. Bacino, *Reconstructing Russia: U.S. Policy in Revolutionary Russia, 1917–1922* (Kent, OH: Kent State University Press, 1999), esp. ch. 2.

106. Quoted, Smele, *Civil War in Siberia*, 471, from Graves, *America's Siberian Adventure*, 186.

107. Ibid., 470, from Graves, *America's Siberian Adventure*, 179–180.

108. Smele, *Civil War in Siberia*, 211–215.

109. Ibid., 109–111.

110. Ibid., 209; Chamberlin, *Russian Revolution*, 2:159.

111. Chamberlin, *Russian Revolution*, 2:187–188.

112. For example: "Svodka svedenii nachal'nika kontr-razvedki o nastroeniiakh naseleniia po irkutskomu voennomu okrugu" (December 8, 1919), "Telegrammy shifrovannye ot nachal'nikov kontr-razvedyvatel'nykh punktov o nastroenii voennych chastei i naseleniia" (December 1919), in *Poslednie dni Kolchakovshchiny*, ed. M. M. Konstantinov (Moscow and Leningrad: Gos. izdat., 1926), 71–74; "Politicheskaia svodka za 23 oktiabria 1919 goda," ibid., 106.

113. Chamberlin, *Russian Revolution*, 2:189–190.

114. Ibid., 190–194.

115. Baron A. P. Budburg, "Dnevnik," *Akhiv russkoi revoliutsii*, xi (1924), 269, quoted, Rosenberg, *Liberals*, 413; same quote, Chamberlin, *Russian Revolution*, 2:195. Translation from text in Baron Aleksei Budberg, *Dnevnik belogvardeitsa (Kolchakovskaia epopeia)* (Leningrad: Priboi, 1929), 211, modified by me.

116. Entry of August 14, 1919, in Budberg, *Dnevnik*, 211.

117. L. A. Krol', *Za tri goda: Vospominaniia, vpechatleniia i vstrechi* (Vladivostok: "Svobodnaia Rossiia," 1921), 169. Partially quoted from Miliukov, Chamberlin, *Russian Revolution*, 2:194. Passage also cited, Igor V. Narskii, *Zhizn' v katastrofe: Budni naseleniia Urala v 1917–1922 gg.* (Moscow: ROSSPEN, 2001), 237 (my translation from Narskii).

118. Quoted, Chamberlin, *Russian Revolution*, 2:197.

119. "Krasil'nikov," in Kvakin, *S Kolchakom*, 83–84; "Krasil'nikov," in Smele, *Historical Dictionary*, 1:617.

120. Budberg, *Dnevnik*, 218 (August 18, 1919).

121. Krol', *Za tri gody*, 168.

122. Chamberlin, *Russian Revolution*, 2:195–197.

123. Smele, *Civil War in Siberia*, 271–272.

124. Ibid., 552–556.

125. Ibid., 560; "Rozanov," in Kvakin, *S Kolchakom*, 123–124; "Rozanov," in Smele, *Historical Dictionary*, 2:955–956.

126. Smele, *Civil War in Siberia*, 557.

127. Quoted, ibid., 561; Graves, *America's Siberian Adventure*, 325 (Rozanov's reputation for murder).

128. Smele, *Civil War in Siberia*, 561.

129. Ibid., 562.

130. Ibid., 553, 564–566, 567 (quote).

131. Quoted, Chamberlin, *Russian Revolution*, 2:200; also in Smele, *Civil War in Siberia*, 572, citing "Memorandum predstavitelei chekho-slovatskoi armii po

povodu kolchakovskoi politiki" (November 13, 1919), in Konstantinov, *Poslednie dni*, 112–113 (translation modified).

132. Additional quotes, from Konstantinov, *Poslednie dni*, 113.

133. "Telegrammy admirala Kolchaka v otvet na cheshskii memorandum" (November 25, 1919), in Konstantinov, *Poslednie dni*, 113.

134. "Politicheskii tsentr," in Kvakin, *S Kolchakom*, 245–246; Smele, *Civil War in Siberia*, 653.

135. Smele, *Civil War in Siberia*, 573.

136. Ibid., 567–570.

137. Ibid., 570, 574–576.

138. Ibid., 579, citing Gins, *Sibir'*, 2:460–461.

139. Tret'iakov, quoted, Gins, *Sibir'*, 2:461, 464.

140. Smele, *Civil War in Siberia*, 581–583.

141. Ibid., 585–586.

142. Gins, *Sibir'*, 2:465 (*proizvol* and *raspushchennost'*).

143. Smele, *Civil War in Siberia*, 587, 589–592.

144. Ibid., 592–594.

145. Quoted, ibid., 597, from Francis McCullagh, *A Prisoner of the Reds: The Story of a British Officer Captured in Siberia* (New York: Dutton, 1922), 22.

146. Smele, *Civil War in Siberia*, 600–602.

147. Quoted, ibid., 602, from Grondijs, *La guerre*, 532 (Smele citation, my translation from original).

148. Chamberlin, *Russian Revolution*, 2:203.

149. Smele, *Civil War in Siberia*, 602–606.

150. Ibid., 612–613.

151. Ibid., 608–609.

152. Ibid., 614–615.

153. Ibid., 618–619.

154. Ibid., 620–624.

155. Ibid., 629–634.

156. Grondijs, *La guerre*, 543–547; Mel'gunov, *Tragediia*, 3:2, 121–123.

157. Smele, *Civil War in Siberia*, 636–637.

158. Ibid., 653; K. A. Popov, "Introduction," in *Testimony*, 3.

159. "Popov," in Kvakin, *S Kolchakom*, 117; "Sledstvennaia komissiia," ibid., 297–298.

160. "Ob"iavlenie Voennogo Komissariata Irkutskogo Soveta Rab. i Sold. Deputatov"—"Krasnyi Irkutsk v opasnosti" (February 2, 1920), in Konstantinov, *Poslednie dni*, 203 (quote).

161. "Operativnaia svodka shtaba vostochno-sibirskoi sovetskoi armii" (January 29, 1920), in Konstantinov, *Poslednie dni*, 198–199; "Ob"iavlenie Irkutskogo Voenno-Revoliutsionnogo Komiteta" (February 1, 1920), ibid., 201; "Vozzvanie Voenno-Revoliutsionnogo Komiteta: K naseleniiu" (February 5, 1920), ibid., 204; "Telegramma tov. Nesterova shtabu vost.-sibirskoi sovetskoi armii"

(February 4, 1920), ibid., 205; "Operativnaia svodka shtaba vostochno-sibirskoi sovetskoi armii za 3 fevralia" (February 5, 1920), ibid., 205.

162. "Postanovlenie Irkutskogo Voenno-Revoliutsionnogo Komiteta" (February 6, 1920), in Konstantinov, *Poslednie dni*, 208–209.

163. Graves, *America's Siberian Adventure,* 301.

164. These two paragraphs from *Testimony*, 3–4, 7, 215.

165. *Dopros Kolchaka*, ed. Popov.

166. Vladimir Shishkin, "Vvedenie," in *Protsess nad kolchakovskimi ministrami*, 6–7; "Zasedanie odinnadtsatoe" (May 30, 1920), ibid., 432.

167. On Goichbarg, *Protsess nad kolchakovskimi ministrami*, 451 (biography). Also T. A. Moriashkina, in Istoricheskii portal "Moskoviia"—Zhurnal Russkaia istoriia/RUS-ISTORIA.RU, available at http://ist-konkurs.ru/raboty/2014/ 1525-aleksandr-grigorevich-gojkhbarg-v-avangarde-sovetskogo-gosudarstvenno-pravovogo-stroitelstva (accessed December 6, 2015).

168. Quoted, *Protsess nad ministrami*, 5; Shumilovskii biography, ibid., 454.

169. For example, Mel'gunov, *Tragediia Admirala Kolchaka*.

170. B. Borisov, *Dal'nii vostok* (Vienna: "Novaia Rossiia," 1921), 13.

171. Quoted, ibid., 45.

172. Ibid., 16.

173. Graves, *America's Siberian Adventure*, 290.

174. Semenov, *O sebe*.

175. Borisov, *Dal'nii vostok*, 31.

176. Ibid., 3–4, 50–53.

177. Sunderland, *Baron's Cloak*, 162–163.

178. Graves, *America's Siberian Adventure*, 314–315.


PART V: CHAPTER 5

1. Recently: Stephen Velychenko, *State Building in Revolutionary Ukraine: A Comparative Study of Government and Bureaucrats, 1917–22* (Toronto: University of Toronto Press, 2010); Mikhail Akulov, "War Without Fronts: Atamans and Commissars in Ukraine, 1917–1919" (Ph.D. dissertation, Harvard University, 2013); *Die Besatzung der Ukraine 1918: Historischer Kontext, Forschungsstand, wirschaftliche und soziale Folgen*, ed. Wolfram Dornik (Graz: Verein zur Förderung von Folgen nach Konflikten und Kriegen, 2008); *Die Ukraine: Zwischen Selbstbestimmung und Fremdherrschaft 1917–1922*, ed. Wolfram Dornik et al. (Graz: Leykam, 2011).

2. Anthony F. Upton, *The Finnish Revolution, 1917–1918* (Minneapolis: University of Minnesota Press, 1980), 189–190.

3. John S. Reshetar, "The Communist Party of the Ukraine and Its Role in the Ukrainian Revolution," in *The Ukraine 1917–1921: A Study in Revolution*, ed. Taras Hunczak (Cambridge, MA: Harvard Ukrainian Research Institute, 1977), 174–176; Jurij Borys, *The Sovietization of Ukraine, 1917–1923: The Communist*

*Doctrine and Practice of National Self-Determination* (Edmonton: Canadian Institute of Ukrainian Studies, 1980), 193.

4. Reshetar, "Communist Party," 175–176; Yaroslav Bilinsky, "The Communist Take-over of the Ukraine," in Hunczak, ed., *Ukraine*, 109; Arthur E. Adams, *The Bolsheviks in the Ukraine: The Second Campaign, 1918–1919* (New Haven: Yale University Press, 1963), 14–19; "Piatakov," in Jonathan D. Smele, *Historical Dictionary of the Russian Civil Wars, 1916–1926*, 2 vols. (Lanham, MD: Rowman & Littlefield, 2015), 2:867–869. Adams is the principal source for this chapter.

5. Borys, *Sovietization*, 146, 194.

6. Adams, *Bolsheviks*, 14–19.

7. The leader was Andrei Bubnov, a Russian from Ivanovo-Voznesensk, who sympathized with the Left Communists and opposed the Brest treaty. "Bubnov," in Smele, *Historical Dictionary*, 1:323–333.

8. Reshetar, "Communist Party," 177.

9. Ibid., 177–179; Adams, *Bolsheviks*, 55–60.

10. Borys, *Sovietization*, 214–215.

11. "Rakovski," in Smele, *Historical Dictionary*, 2:911–913; Borys, *Sovietization*, 215.

12. Adams, *Bolsheviks*, 26–28; "Antonov-Ovseenko," in Smele, *Historical Dictionary*, 1:125–126.

13. Adams, *Bolsheviks*, 25.

14. Ibid., 30–32, 37.

15. Ibid., 67.

16. Ibid., 71.

17. Ibid., 73–74.

18. Ibid., 40–41; "Vācietis," in Smele, *Historical Dictionary*, 2:1255–1256.

19. Adams, *Bolsheviks*, 45–46.

20. "A Revolutionary War Council and a Council of Defense: Decree of the Central Executive Committee, October 30, 1918," in James Bunyan, *Intervention, Civil War, and Communism in Russia, April–December 1918: Documents and Materials* (Baltimore: Johns Hopkins Press, 1936), 275; "Decree of the Central Executive Committee, November 30, 1918," ibid., 275–276.

21. Adams, *Bolsheviks*, 50–52 (quote, 52).

22. "Decree of the Central Executive Committee, November 30, 1918," in Bunyan, *Intervention*, 275.

23. Adams, *Bolsheviks*, 54–64.

24. Quoted, ibid., 62.

25. Ibid., 88–89, 90, 92.

26. Quoted, ibid., 100.

27. Ibid., 93, 94–95, 99.

28. Ibid., 100–101.

29. Ibid., 104–106.

30. Ibid., 102–103.

31. Ibid., 108–109.

32. V. F. Soldatenko, *Grazhdanskaia voina v Ukraine, 1917–1920 gg.* (Moscow: Novyi khronograf, 2012), 280.

33. Adams, *Bolsheviks*, 113–114.

34. Martha Bohachevsky-Chomiak, "The Directory of the Ukrainian National Republic," in Hunczak, ed., *Ukraine*, 89, 93; Adams, *Bolsheviks*, 80; Yekelchyk, *Ukraine*, 80.

35. Adams, *Bolsheviks*, 137–140.

36. This from excellent discussion in ibid., 139–141.

37. Ibid., 142–144.

38. Ibid., 145–148.

39. Ibid., 158, 161; "Hryhoriiv" and "Hryhoriiv Uprising," in Smele, *Historical Dictionary*, 1:491–492.

40. Petr Aleshkin and Iurii Vasil'ev, "Grigor'evshchina," in *Grazhdanskaia voina v Rossii: Entsiklopediia katastrofy*, ed. Dmitrii Volodikhin and Sergei Volkov (Moscow: Sibirskii tsiriul'nik, 2010), 245.

41. Adams, *Bolsheviks*, 149–150.

42. Ibid., 150–151; Soldatenko, *Grazhdanskaia voina*, 282 (figure of 5,000–6,000).

43. Adams, *Bolsheviks*, 155–157; Aleshkin and Vasil'ev, "Grigor'evshchina," 245.

44. Quoted, Adams, *Bolsheviks*, 161.

45. Quoted, ibid., 167.

46. Adams, *Bolsheviks*, 178–180, 182–184; Soldatenko, *Grazhdanskaia voina*, 282.

47. Adams, *Bolsheviks*, 191–192 (35,000 troops); Soldatenko, *Grazhdanskaia voina*, 282 (60,000 Entente troops).

48. Adams, *Bolsheviks*, 196–197, 210, 205–208.

49. Quoted, ibid., 197–199.

50. Quoted, ibid., 203.

51. Ibid., 201–203; Ivan Bunin, *Cursed Days: A Diary of Revolution*, trans. and ed. Thomas Gaiton Marullo (London: Phoenix Press, 2000), 79, 81 (April 12/25, 1919); see Ivan Bunin, *Okaiannye dni: Dnevniki, stat'i, vospominaniia* (Moscow: Eksmo, 2011). Fragments first published in 1926 in an emigré monarchist newspaper.

52. Adams, *Bolsheviks*, 200 (both quotes).

53. Ibid., 201.

54. Quoted, ibid., 214.

55. Bunin, *Cursed Days*, 84 (April 15/28, 1919).

56. Ibid., 82 (April 13/26, 1919); ibid., 87–89 (April 17/30, 1919).

57. Ibid., 93 (April 20/May 3, 1919).

58. Ibid., 122–123 (April 24/May 7, 1919), 131 (April 25/May 8, 1919).

59. Note to Bunin, *Cursed Days*, 103.

60. Bunin, *Cursed Days*, 107, 108 (April 22/May 5, 1919).

61. Ibid., 121 (April 24/May 7, 1919).

62. Ibid., 127 (April 24/May 7, 1919).

63. Quoted in Teffi, *Memories: From Moscow to the Black Sea*, intro. Edythe Haber, trans. Robert Chandler et al. (Paris, 1928–1930; New York: New York Review of Books, 2016), 156.

64. Bunin, *Cursed Days*, 102 (April 21/May 4, 1919).

65. Adams, *Bolsheviks*, 239–242.

66. Soldatenko, *Grazhdanskaia voina*, 320.

67. Ibid., 327; T. Shanin, V. Kondrashin, and N. Tarkhova, "Vvedenie," in *Nestor Makhno:Krest'ianskoe dvizhenie na Ukraine, 1918–1921: Dokumenty i materialy*, ed. V. Danilov et al. (Moscow: ROSSPEN, 2006), 26 ("genius").

68. Soldatenko, *Grazhdanskaia voina*, 322.

69. "Makhno" and "Makhnovshchina," in Smele, *Historical Dictionary*, 2:700–704.

70. Nestor Makhno, *La Révolution russe en Ukraine (mars 1917–avril 1918)* (Paris: La Brochure mensuelle, 1927), 25.

71. Ibid., 13.

72. Ibid., 40–41.

73. "Vvedenie," in *Nestor Makhno*, ed. Danilov, 8.

74. Makhno, *La Révolution russe*, 163.

75. Ibid., 166.

76. Ibid., 108.

77. "Vvedenie," in *Nestor Makhno*, ed. Danilov, 12–13 (*podlinnyi sovetskii stroi—bez vlasti*).

78. Soldatenko, *Grazhdanskaia voina*, 315–316.

79. "Vvedenie," in *Nestor Makhno*, ed. Danilov, 13–15; Soldatenko, *Grazhdanskaia voina*, 323 (size).

80. "Vvedenie," in *Nestor Makhno*, ed. Danilov, 17.

81. "Rasporiazhenie Chernigovskomu, Poltavskomu i Kievskomu gubernial'nym starostam" (August 13, 1918), in *Nestor Makhno*, ed. Danilov, 49.

82. "Dokladnaia zapiska…" (October 20, 1918), in *Nestor Makhno*, ed. Danilov, 50–51.

83. "'Bat'ko Makhno' – soobshchenie…" (February 9, 1919), in *Nestor Makhno*, ed. Danilov, 66–67.

84. "Nikolai Borisovich Karamanov, 25 let, pravoslavnyi, krest'ianin s. Guliai-Pole" (testimony), "Iz materialov denikinskoi 'Osoboi komissii po rassledovaniiu zlodeianii bol'shevikov'—protokol doprosa zhitelei sel Guliai-Pole i Pologi o deiatel'nosti Makhno i ego povstancheskikh otriadov" (August 7–8, 1919), in *Nestor Makhno*, ed. Danilov, 195.

85. "Vvedenie," in *Nestor Makhno*, ed. Danilov, 19.

86. "'Makhno'—stat'ia iz gazety Izvestiia—organa VTsIK RSFSR" (April 6, 1919), in *Nestor Makhno*, ed. Danilov, 104.

87. Adams, *Bolsheviks*, 249–250.

88. Quoted, ibid., 252.

89. Adams, *Bolsheviks*, 264–266.

90. Quotes, ibid., 256, 257.

91. Ibid., 259–263.

92. Ibid., 270–273.

93. Ibid., 275–277.

94. Aleshkin and Vasil'ev, "Grigor'evshchina," 246.

95. Adams, *Bolsheviks*, 278–283.

96. Ibid., 284.

97. Quoted, ibid., 352.

98. Ibid., 185–188.

99. Soldatenko, *Grazhdanskaia voina*, 320; Aleshkin and Vasil'ev, "Grigor'evshchina," 246.

100. Quoted, Adams, *Bolsheviks*, 296.

101. Quotes, ibid., 305, 298.

102. Ibid., 307–312; Soldatenko, *Grazhdanskaia voina*, 320.

103. Adams, *Bolsheviks*, 355–357, 358 (quote).

104. Soldatenko, *Grazhdanskaia voina*, 320, 321.

105. Adams, *Bolsheviks*, 328–348.

106. Ibid., 350.

107. Ibid., 359, 360 (quote).

108. Ibid., 360–361.

109. Quotes, ibid., 363.

110. Ibid., 364–367.

111. "Zapiska o Makhno komanduiushchego Ukrainskim frontom V. A. Antonova-Ovseenko predsedateliu SNK U[k]SSR Kh. G. Rakovskomu i narkomvoenu N. I. Podvoiskomu" (May 2, 1919), in *Nestor Makhno*, ed. Danilov, 129–130.

112. Soldatenko, *Grazhdanskaia voina*, 323.

113. "Stat'ia L. D. Trotskogo 'Makhnovshchina'" (June 2, 1919), reprinted from L. Trotskii, *Kak vooruzhalas' revoliutsiia (na voennoi rabote)*, vol. 2: *Tysiacha deviat'sot deviatnadtsatyi god*, bk. 1 (Moscow: Vysshii voennyi redaktsionnyi sovet, 1924), 189–191, in *Nestor Makhno*, ed. Danilov, 162.

114. Adams, *Bolsheviks*, 367; "Vvedenie," in *Nestor Makhno*, ed. Danilov, 23–24.

115. Soldatenko, *Grazhdanskaia voina*, 324 (dated June 18, 1919).

116. "Vvedenie," in *Nestor Makhno*, ed. Danilov, 22–24; "Iz zapisi razgovora po priamomu provodu nachal'nika shtaba 3-go armeiskogo korpusa Dobrovol. armii V.V. Chernavina so shtabom komaduiushchego voiskami Novorossiiskoi oblasti" (September 13, 1919), ibid., 200.

117. Adams, *Bolsheviks*, 402–404; quote within quoted testimony by Arshinov, ibid. 404.

118. Soldatenko, *Grazhdanskaia voina*, 326 ("*zemlia, volia, svoboda*").

119. Adams, *Bolsheviks*, 372–373.

120. Yekelchyk, *Ukraine*, 78, 81–82.

121. Adams, *Bolsheviks*, 382–384.

122. Yekelchyk, *Ukraine*, 81–82; Bilinsky, "Communist Take-over," 119–120.

123. Adams, *Bolsheviks*, 373–374.

124. Ibid., 382–385; Yekelchyk, *Ukraine*, 82.

125. Documents no. 221–226, "Iz informatsionnykh svodok osobogo otdela Iugo-Zapadnogo fronta o deistviiakh makhnovskikh otriadov" (April 30–August 13, 1920), in *Nestor Makhno*, ed. Danilov, 359–367; "Iz biulleteniia No. 7: Ob usloviiakh bor'by s makhnovshchinoi" (June 3, 1920), ibid., 357.

126. "Obrashchenie kul'turno-prosvetitel'skogo otdela Povstancheskoi armii 'Ko vsem rabotnikam sokhi i molota' s prizyvom ob"ediniat'sia protiv vsekh vragov Ukrainy" (May 1920), in *Nestor Makhno*, ed. Danilov, 375.

127. "Vvedenie," *Nestor Makhno*, ed. Danilov, 25–26; "Iz prikaza armiiam Iuzhnogo fronta o nachale nastupleniia" (October 24, 1920, signed Southern Front Commander M.V. Frunze), in *Nestor Makhno*, ed. Danilov, 511.

128. Quoted, "Vvedenie," *Nestor Makhno*, ed. Danilov, 26, from: "Iz biulletenei sekretno-informatsionnogo otdela SNK U[k]SSR o makhnovskom dvizhenii na Ukraine" (July 2–August 13, 1921): "Iz biulletenia No. 116" (July 2, 1921), in *Nestor Makhno*, ed. Danilov, 647.

129. "Makhno," in Smele, *Historical Dictionary*, 2:700–702.

## PART V: CHAPTER 6

1. Vatsetis quoted, Evan Mawdsley, *The Russian Civil War* (Boston: Allen and Unwin, 1987), 181. Mawdsley is a principal source for this chapter.

2. William Henry Chamberlin, *The Russian Revolution, 1917–1921*, 2 vols. (1935; New York: Grosset & Dunlap, 1965), 2:209–210; Mawdsley, *Russian Civil War*, 163–166. See R. G. Gagkuev, *Beloe dvizhenie na Iuge Rossii: Voennoe stroitel'stvo, istochniki komplektovaniia, sotsial'nyi sostav, 1917–1920 gg.* (Moscow: Posev, 2012).

3. Chamberlin, *Russian Revolution*, 2:146.

4. Ibid., 148.

5. Quoted, Mawdsley, *Russian Civil War*, 162; Chamberlin, *Russian Revolution*, 2:138.

6. Mawdsley, *Russian Civil War*, 162–163, 170; quote, 163.

7. Ibid., 167.

8. Chamberlin, *Russian Revolution*, 2:263–264, citing John Ernest Hodgson, *With Denikin's Armies, Being a Description of the Cossack Counter-Revolution in South Russia, 1918–1920* (London: Williams, 1932), 180; Charlotte Alston, "British Journalism and the Campaign for Intervention in the Russian Civil War, 1918–20," *Revolutionary Russia* 20.1 (2007): 42.

9. Mawdsley, *Russian Civil War*, 161–162, 169 (Red Army: February 1919, 152,000; May, 228,000; June, 259,000; Denikin: March, 45,000 Volunteers and Cossacks; May, 50,000, plus 14,000 in North Caucasus); cf. 163 (117,000 Red Army total in south in early 1919).

10. Ibid., 171–172, 174.

11. Peter Kenez, *Civil War in South Russia, 1919–1920: The Defeat of the Whites* (Berkeley: University of California Press, 1977), 42; Chamberlin, *Russian Revolution*, 2:245.

12. Mawdsley, *Russian Civil War*, 173; Chamberlin, *Russian Revolution*, 2:244.

13. Mawdsley, *Russian Civil War*, 175; "Kamenev, Sergei," in Jonathan D. Smele, *Historical Dictionary of the Russian Civil Wars, 1916–1926*, 2 vols. (Lanham, MD: Rowman & Littlefield, 2015), 1:543–545.

14. Mawdsley, *Russian Civil War*, 179–180.

15. "Prichiny neudach na Iuzhnom fronte" (July 8, 1919), in L. Trotskii, *Kak vooruzhalas' revoliutsiia (na voennoi rabote)*, vol. 2: *Tysiacha deviat'sot deviatnadtsatyi god*, bk. 1 (Moscow: Vysshii voennyi redaktsionnyi sovet, 1924), 221–223.

16. Quoted, Mawdsley, *Russian Civil War*, 175.

17. Kenez, *Civil War, 1919*, 42–43; Chamberlin, *Russian Revolution*, 2:210–211.

18. Chamberlin, *Russian Revolution*, 2:210–211; "Mai-Maevskii," in Valerii Klaving, *Grazhdanskaia voina v Rossii: Belye armii* (Moscow: AST, 2003), 486–487.

19. Chamberlin, *Russian Revolution*, 2:211, 246; Mawdsley, *Russian Civil War*, 172–173.

20. "Mamontov," in Klaving, *Grazhdanskaia voina*, 487–88; "Mamontov" and "Mamontov Raid," in Smele, *Historical Dictionary*, 2:707–708.

21. Chamberlin, *Russian Revolution*, 2:247–248.

22. Quoted, Kenez, *Civil War 1919*, 175.

23. Prikaz no. 146: "Predsedatelia Revvoensoveta Respubliki i Narkomvoenmora ot 4 sentiabria 1919 g.: Na bor'bu s razboinikami mamontovskoi shaiki"; Prikaz no. 147: "Predsedatelia Revvoensoveta Respubliki i Narkomvoenmora ot 4 sentiabria 1919 g."; "Rabochie i krest'iane, vykhodite na oblavu!" (September 4, 1919), in Trotskii, *Kak*, 2:1, 278–282; Kenez, *Civil War 1919*, 43–44.

24. Mawdsley, *Russian Civil War*, 174.

25. "Nuzhny li nam partizany?" (September 6, 1919), in Trotskii, *Kak*, 2:1, 283–284.

26. "Proletarii, na konia!" (September 11, 1919), in ibid., 287–288. See Stephen M. Brown, "Communists and the Red Cavalry: The Political Education of the *Konarmiia* in the Russian Civil War, 1918–20," *Slavonic and East European Review* 73.1 (1995): 82–99.

27. Mawdsley, *Russian Civil War*, 220.

28. Ibid., 180–184.

29. Ibid., 195–196.

30. Ibid., 202–203.

31. "Khrabrost' ot otchaianiia" (August 19, 1919), Trotskii, *Kak*, 2:1, 273.

32. Quotes, Mawdsley *Russian Civil War*, 206.

33. Ibid., 211–215.

34. Ibid., 221–222.

35. Chamberlin, *Russian Revolution*, 2:286.

36. Ibid.

37. Mawdsley, *Russian Civil War*, 223–224. A. S. Lukomskii, *Vospominaniia generala A. S. Lukomskogo: Period Evropeiskoi voiny, nachalo razrukhi v Rossii, bor'ba s bol'shevikami*, 2 vols. (Berlin: Otto Kirchner, 1922), 2:213; Chamberlin, *Russian Revolution*, 2:288.

38. Mawdsley, *Russian Civil War*, 224–225.

39. "Denikin," in Smele, *Historical Dictionary*, 1:324.

40. Peter Holquist, *Making War, Forging Revolution: Russia's Continuum of Crisis, 1914–1921* (Cambridge, MA: Harvard University Press, 2002), 178–179. Holquist is an important source for this chapter.

41. Quoted, ibid., 180; Doc. 88: "Tsirkuliarnoe pis'mo Orgbiuro TsK RKP(b) ob otnoshenii k kazakam (24 ianvaria 1919 g.)," in *Filipp Mironov: Tikhii Don v 1917–1921 gg.*, ed. V. P. Danilov and Teodor Shanin (Moscow: Mezhdunarodnyi fond "Demokratiia," 1997), 137–138 (my translation).

42. Doc. 88: "Tsirkuliarnoe pis'mo Orgbiuro TsK RKP(b) ob otnoshenii k kazakam (24 ianvaria 1919 g.)," in Danilov-Shanin, eds., *Mironov*, 137–138 (my translation).

43. Danilov and Tarkhova, "Vvedenie," in Danilov-Shanin, eds., *Mironov*, 12.

44. Holquist, *Making*, 182–184. See also: Peter Holquist, "'Conduct Merciless Mass Terror': Decossackization on the Don, 1919," *Cahiers du monde russe* 38 (1997): 127–162.

45. Doc. 96: "Instruktsiia Revvoensoveta Iuzhfronta k provedeniiu direktivy TsK RKP(b) s kontrrevoliutsiei na Donu" (February 7, 1919), in Danilov-Shanin, *Mironov*, 145.

46. Doc. 99–100: "Zapiski po priamomu provodu Revvoensoveta Iuzhnogo fronta v Tsentr o sud'be plennykh kazakov" (February 9 and 24, 1919), in Danilov-Shanin, *Mironov*, 147–148.

47. Shane O'Rourke, *The Cossacks* (Manchester: Manchester University Press, 2007), 244 ("The Genocide of the Cossacks").

48. Danilov and Tarkhova, "Vvedenie," 13; Doc. 86: "Telegramma chlena Donbiuro RKP(b) A. A. Frenkelia sekeretariu TsK RKP(b) Ia. M. Sverdlovu" (January 23, 1919), in Danilov-Shanin, *Mironov*, 137 (lack of agitators).

49. Doc. 89: "Zakliuchenie Donskogo biuro RKP (b) o doklade t. Kovaleva o Donskom pravitel'stve" (January 25, 1919), in Danilov-Shanin, *Mironov*, 139.

50. Danilov and Tarkhova, "Vvedenie," 12, 13, 14; Danilov-Shanin, *Mironov*, 740, 741.

51. Danilov and Tarkhova, "Vvedenie," 5.

52. Doc. 7: "Zaiavlenie F. K. Mironova v Ust'-Medveditskii ispolnitel'nyi komitet o vykhode iz sostava komiteta" (March 9, 1918), in Danilov-Shanin, *Mironov*, 42 (*obshchestvennaia politicheskaia deiatel'nost'*).

53. Doc. 1: "Otkrytoe pis'mo F. K. Mironova chlenu Donskogo Voiskovogo pravitel'stva P. M. Ageevu" (December 15, 1917), in Danilov-Shanin, *Mironov*, 25–31.

54. Doc. 7: "Zaiavlenie F. K. Mironova v Ust'-Medveditskii ispolnitel'nyi komitet o vykhode iz sostava komiteta" (March 9, 1918), in Danilov-Shanin, *Mironov*, 43 (*bezobraziia*).

55. Quoted, Danilov and Tarkhova, "Vvedenie," 10; Doc 7: "Zaiavlenie F. K. Mironova v Ust'-Medveditskii ispolnitel'nyi komitet o vykhode iz sostava komiteta" (March 9, 1918), in Danilov-Shanin, *Mironov*, 42.

56. Excerpt quoted in Danilov and Tarkhova, "Vvedenie," 10, from Doc. 4: "Obrashchenie polkovogo komiteta 32-go Donskogo kazach'ego polka" (January 25, 1918), in Danilov-Shanin, *Mironov*, 34–37.

57. Quoted, Danilov and Tarkhova, "Vvedenie," 10, 11; Doc. 75: "Telegramma L. D. Trotskogo F. K. Mironovu s privetstviem boitsam 23-i divizii" (January 12, 1919), in Danilov-Shanin, *Mironov*, 109.

58. Doc. 46: "Iz pis'ma I. V. Stalina V. I. Leninu o polozhenii na Tsaritsynskom fronte" (August 4, 1918), in Danilov-Shanin, *Mironov*, 77.

59. Doc. 89: "Zakliuchenie Donskogo biuro RKP(b) o doklade t. Kovaleva o Donskom pravitel'stve" (January 25, 1919), in Danilov-Shanin, *Mironov*, 139.

60. Danilov-Tarkhova, "Vvedenie," 11.

61. Doc. 83: "Telegramma F. K. Mironova predsedateliu Revvoensoveta Respubliki L. D. Trotskomu ob otnoshenii k kazachestvu" (no later than January 18, 1919), in Danilov-Shanin, *Mironov*, 134.

62. Doc. 84: "Vozzvanie F. K. Mironova k krasnoarmeitsam" (January 21, 1919), in Danilov-Shanin, *Mironov*, 134–135.

63. Doc. 103: "Pis'mo-proshenie ot gruppy kazakov, pereshedshikh na storonu Krasnoi Armii i reshenie F. K. Mironova" (February 15, 1919), in Danilov-Shanin, *Mironov*, 150.

64. Doc. 104: "Rasporiazhenie Revvoensoveta 9-i armii ob otkomandirovanii F. K. Mironova v Serpukhov" (February 23, 1919), in Danilov-Shanin, *Mironov*, 150.

65. Doc. 106: "Peregovory po priamonu provodu predsedatelia Ust'-Medveditskogo okruzhnogo biuro RKP(b) K. F. Grodnera i predsedatelia Donbiuro RKP(b) S. I. Syrtsova" (March 6, 1919), in Danilov-Shanin, *Mironov*, 151–152; also Doc. 111: "Iz doklada v Donbiuro o deiatel'nosti Mikhailovskogo raionnogo biuro RKP(b)" (March 14, 1919), ibid., 155.

66. Doc. 110: "Iz protokola No. 1 obshchego sobraniia chlenov RKP(b) sl. Mikhailovki Ust'-Medveditskogo raiona" (March 9, 1919), in Danilov-Shanin, *Mironov*, 154.

67. Doc. 125: "Doklad F. K. Mironova o putiakh privlecheniia kazachestva na storonu Sovetskoi vlasti" (no later than March 16, 1919), in Danilov-Shanin, *Mironov*, 168–169.

68. Doc. 113: "Telegramma zavpolitotdelom Iuzhnogo fronta Krzhizhanovskogo v Sovnarkom V. I. Leninu, VTsIK Ia. M. Sverdlovu i TsK RKP(b) o volneniiakh kazakov v st. Kazanskoi" (March 15, 1919), in Danilov-Shanin, *Mironov*, 157.

69. Doc. 114: "Prikaz po Verkhne-Donskomu okrugu No. 1 " (Veshenskaia, mid-March 1919), in Danilov-Shanin, *Mironov*, 158–159.

70. Doc. 115: "Vozzvanie 'Ko vsemu trudovomu narodu Dona!'" (mid-March 1919), in Danilov-Shanin, *Mironov*, 159–160.

71. Doc. 118: "Direktiva Revvoensoveta Iuzhnogo fronta o merakh po podavleniiu vosstaniia" (March 16, 1919), in Danilov-Shanin, *Mironov*, 163.

72. Doc. 122: "Instruktsiia komissarov-kommunistov dlia podavleniia vosstaniia na Donu" (n. d.), in Danilov-Shanin, *Mironov*, 165–166.

73. Doc. 119: "Reshenie plenuma TsK RKP(b) o priostanovke primeneniia mer protiv kazachestva" (March 16, 1919), in Danilov-Shanin, *Mironov*, 164.

74. Doc. 132: "Telegramma S. I. Syrtsova rairevkomam o peresmotre Direktivy IsK ot 24 ianvaria 1919 g." (March 25, 1919), in Danilov-Shanin, *Mironov*, 175–176.

75. Doc. 134: "Direktiva Revvoensoveta Iuzhnogo fronta revvoensovetam armii i revkomam po voprosam obshchei politiki v Donskoi oblasti" (April 5, 1919), in Danilov-Shanin, *Mironov*, 177–178.
76. Holquist, *Making*, 190–191.
77. Cited, Danilov and Tarkhova, "Vvedenie," 14, from Doc. 139: "Iz protokola zasedaniia Orgbiuro TsK RKP(b) o polozhenii del na Donu" (April 22, 1919), in Danilov-Shanin, *Mironov*, 187–188.
78. Danilov and Tarkhova, "Vvedenie," 16–17, citing Doc 149: "Prikaz komanduiushchego Zapadnym frontom D. N. Nadezhnogo F. K. Mironovu o srochnom vyezde na Iuzhnyi front" (June 13, 1919), in Danilov-Shanin, *Mironov*, 208–209.
79. Danilov and Tarkhova, "Vvedenie," 18; Doc. 176: "'Trebuiu imenem revoliutsii i ot litsa izmuchennogo kazachestva prekratit' politiku ego istrebleniia" (Letter from Mironov to Lenin, July 31, 1919), in Danilov-Shanin, *Mironov*, 255–271.
80. Danilov and Tarkhova, "Vvedenie," 18; Doc. 176.
81. Danilov and Tarkhova, "Vvedenie," 19, citing Doc. 284: "Tiuremnyi dnevnik F. Mironova" (September 16–October 9, 1919), in Danilov-Shanin, *Mironov*, 433–435.
82. Danilov and Tarkhova, "Vvedenie," 20; Doc. 211: "Vozzvanie F. K. Mironova" (August 24, 1919), in Danilov-Shanin, *Mironov*, 325.
83. "Prikaz Predsedatelia Revvoensoveta Respubliki i Narkomvoenmora po N-skoi armii ot 12 sentiabria 1919 g.," in Trotskii, *Kak*, 2:1, 292 (To be read to all military formations).
84. "Polkovnik Mironov" (September 13, 1919), in Trotskii, *Kak*, 2:1, 293–295.
85. Doc. 244: "Doklad politkoma komendantskoi komandy shtaba Donskogo korpusa A. Ia. Kutyreva v Kazachii otdel VTsIK o vystupleniiakh F. K. Mironova na mitinge 22 avgusta" (September 8, 1919), in Danilov-Shanin, *Mironov*, 371–372.
86. Doc. 150: "Pis'mo-obrashchenie F. K. Mironova k krasnoarmeitsam o distsipline" (June 13, 1919), in Danilov-Shanin, *Mironov*, 209–211.
87. Doc. 244: "Doklad politkoma komendantskoi komandy shtaba Donskogo korpusa," in Danilov-Shanin, *Mironov*, 371–372.
88. Brown, "Communists and the Red Cavalry," 86, 94 (examples from Budennyi's First Cavalry Army).
89. Doc. 256: "Stat'ia L. D. Trotskogo 'Uroki mironovshchiny'" (September 16, 1919), in Danilov-Shanin, *Mironov*, 389–391 (in *Pravda*, September 21, 1919).
90. Doc. 276: "Obvinitel'naia rech' I. T. Smigli na sude" (October 5, 1919), in Danilov-Shanin, *Mironov*, 415–423.
91. Doc. 277: "Rech' F. K. Mironova na sude" (October 6, 1919), in Danilov-Shanin, *Mironov*, 423–427.
92. Doc. 278: "Prigovor Chrezvychainogo tribunala po delu Mironova" (October 7, 1919), in Danilov-Shanin, *Mironov*, 427–430.
93. Doc. 279: "Zapis' razgovora po priamomu provodu V. A. Trifonova i I. T. Smigli o sud'be podsudimykh" (October 7, 1919), in Danilov-Shanin, *Mironov*, 430–431.

94. Doc. 281: "Telegramma zashchitnika N.V. Rybakova M. I. Kalininu o smiag-chenii prigovora po delu Mironova" (October 7, 1919), in Danilov-Shanin, *Mironov*, 432.

95. Doc. 283: "Iz protokola zasedaniia Politbiuro TsK RKP(b) ob izmenenii prigovora po delu Mironova" (October 7, 1919), in Danilov-Shanin, *Mironov*, 433.

96. Holquist, *Making*, 200, 274 (arrest and pardon as policy change).

97. Doc. 288: "Telegramma L. D. Trotskogo I. T. Smigle" (October 10, 1919), in Danilov-Shanin, *Mironov*, 447.

98. Doc. 289: "Obrashchenie F. K. Mironova 'Donskim kazakam i vsem, kto na fronte Denikina'" (October 11, 1919), in Danilov-Shanin, *Mironov*, 445.

99. Doc. 295: "Zaiavlenie F. K. Mironova v Revvoensovet Respubliki s predlozhe-niem ispol'zovat' ego v budushchem" (October 18, 1919), in Danilov-Shanin, *Mironov*, 456–457 (*ia vnov' rozhdennyi*).

100. Doc. 298: "Iz protokola zasedaniia Politbiuro TsK RKP(b) o polnoi amnistii Mironova i vvedenii ego v sostav Donispolkoma" (October 23, 1919), in Danilov-Shanin, *Mironov*, 459.

101. Doc. 299: "Iz protokola zasedaniia Politbiuro TsK RKP(b) o dal'neishei sud'by Mironova" (October 26, 1919), in Danilov-Shanin, *Mironov*, 460.

102. Doc. 304: "Iz tezisov Donkoma RKP(b) dlia dokladov na partiinykh sobrani-iakh i agitatsionnykh vystupleniiakh" (October 22, 1919), in Danilov-Shanin, *Mironov*, 478–484 (quote, 483).

103. Danilov and Tarkhova, "Vvedenie," 21.

104. Doc. 376: "Soobshchenie nachal'nika operativnogo otdeleniia OO VChK ob areste i obyske F. K. Mironova i soprovozhdavshikh ego lits" (February 21, 1921), in Danilov-Shanin, *Mironov*, 616; Doc. 395: "Zakliuchitel'nyi akt po delu F. K. Mironova i ego spodvizhnikov, sostavlennyi v Donskoi ChK" (March 28, 1921), ibid., 637–640.

105. Danilov and Tarkhova, "Vvedenie," 22; Doc. 424: "Opredelenie Voennoi kol-legii Verkhovnogo suda SSSR o prekrashchenii dela F. K. Mironova" (November 15, 1960), in Danilov-Shanin, *Mironov*, 681.

### PART V: CHAPTER 7

1. Paul Latawski, "Roman Dmowski, the Polish Question, and Western Opinion, 1915–18: The Case of Britain," in *The Reconstruction of Poland, 1914–1923*, ed. Paul Latawski (New York: St. Martin's, 1992), 2.

2. Piotr Wandycz, *Soviet-Polish Relations, 1917–1921* (Cambridge, MA: Harvard University Press, 1969), 104, 120, 121. Wandycz is a principal source for this chapter.

3. Latawski, "Roman Dmowski," 4, 5, 6, 8. For the context of English anti-Sem-itism: Anthony Julius, *Trials of the Diaspora: A History of Anti-Semitism in England* (Oxford: Oxford University Press, 2010); also Lucien Wolf, *The Myth of the Jewish Menace in World Affairs* (New York: Macmillan, 1921). On positive views

held by Lloyd George and Balfour: Hillel Halkin, *Jabotinsky: A Life* (New Haven: Yale University Press, 2014), 104; Mark Levene, *War, Jews, and the New Europe: The Diplomacy of Lucien Wolf, 1914–1919* (Oxford: Oxford University Press, 1992), 189–190. On Dmowski's visit to Britain: Sam Johnson, *Pogroms, Peasants, Jews: Britain and Eastern Europe's "Jewish Question," 1867–1925* (Houndmills, UK: Palgrave Macmillan, 2011), 159–166.

4. Roman Dmowski, *Separatyzm Żydów i jego źródła* (Warsaw: Gazeta Warszawska, 1909), 27; Piotr Wandycz, "Dmowski's Policy at the Paris Peace Conference: Success or Failure?" in *Reconstruction of Poland*, ed. Latawski, 122.

5. Wandycz, "Dmowski's Policy," 122–123; Kay Lundgreen-Nielsen, *The Polish Problem at the Paris Peace Conference: A Study of the Policies of the Great Powers and the Poles, 1918–1919* (Odense: Odense University Press, 1979), 343–344.

6. Antony Polonsky, "Warsaw," in *The YIVO Encyclopedia of Jews in Eastern Europe*, ed. Gershon David Hundert, 2 vols. (New Haven: Yale University Press, 2008), 2:2001.

7. "Odezwa na wkroczenie wojsk polskich do Królestwa Kongresowego," signed Józef Piłsudski, Komendant Główny Wojka Polskiego (Cracow, August 12, 1914), in Józef Piłsudski, *Odezwy, dekrety, mowy* (Skultuna, Sweden: Ligatur, 2008), 9.

8. Wacław Jędrzejewicz, *Piłsudski: A Life for Poland* (New York: Hippocrene, 1982), 35, 49–57.

9. Text, in *Reconstruction of Poland*, ed. Latawski, 196; Ronald Bobroff, "Devolution in Wartime: Sergei D. Sazonov and the Future of Poland, 1910–1916," *International History Review* 22.3 (2000): 505–528.

10. Text, in *Reconstruction of Poland*, ed. Latawski, 196.

11. Wandycz, *Soviet-Polish Relations*, 34.

12. "Address of President Woodrow Wilson to the U.S. Senate 22 January 1917," available at http://www.firstworldwar.com/source/peacewithoutvictory.htm (accessed February 4, 2017).

13. Eugene Kusielewicz, "Woodrow Wilson and the Rebirth of Poland," *Polish American Studies* 12.1–2 (1955): 1–10.

14. Jędrzejewicz, *Piłsudski*, 64.

15. Wandycz, *Soviet-Polish Relations*, 36; Levene, *War, Jews, and the New Europe*, 188.

16. Dmowski, "Memorandum on the Territory of the Polish State" (March 26, 1917), in *Reconstruction of Poland*, ed. Latawski, 197.

17. Quotes, Wandycz, *Soviet-Polish Relations*, 37.

18. Ibid., 38 (quote), 39–40.

19. Ibid., 26. "Natsional-liberalizm i pravo natsii na samoopredelenie" (*Proletarskaia Pravda*, December 12/20, 1913), in V. I. Lenin, *Polnoe sobranie sochinenii*, 58 vols. (Moscow: Politicheskaia literatura, 1958–1970), 24:247–249; 248 ("right to the formation of independent national states"), available at http://leninism.su/works/62-tom-24/2257-nacional-liberalizm-i-pravo-naczij-na-samoopre-delenie.html/ (accessed February 4, 2017).

20. Adam Tooze, *The Deluge: The Great War and the Remaking of Global Order, 1916–1931* (London: Allen Lane, 2014), 79–80.

21. Wandycz, *Soviet-Polish Relations*, 40.

22. "Lenin's Speech on the Peace Declaration" (November 8 [October 26], 1917), in *The Bolshevik Revolution, 1917–1918: Documents and Materials*, ed. James Bunyan and H. H. Fisher (Stanford: Stanford University Press, 1934), 125. Delivered at Second All-Russian Congress of Soviets of Worker and Soldier Deputies. Text in *Izvestiia*, October 27/November 9, 1917.

23. Wandycz, *Soviet-Polish Relations*, 42–45.

24. Leo J. Bacino, *Reconstructing Russia: U.S. Policy in Revolutionary Russia, 1917–1922* (Kent, OH: Kent State University Press, 1999).

25. Wandycz, *Soviet-Polish Relations*, 43, 60, 47–48.

26. Ibid., 65–66; quote, 66; Jerzy Borzęcki, *The Soviet-Polish Peace of 1921 and the Creation of Interwar Europe* (New Haven: Yale University Press, 2008), 8.

27. Quoted, Wandycz, *Soviet-Polish Relations*, 66.

28. Lenin quoted, ibid., 67; Stephen Blank, "Soviet Nationality Policy and Soviet Foreign Policy: The Polish Case, 1917–1921," *International History Review* 7.1 (1985): 119.

29. Wandycz, *Soviet-Polish Relations*, 54–55.

30. Ibid., 58; Maxime Weygand, *Mémoires: Mirages et realité*, 3 vols. (Paris: Flammarion, 1957), 2:109–110.

31. Wandycz, *Soviet-Polish Relations*, 72.

32. Adam Zamoyski, *Warsaw 1920: Lenin's Failed Conquest of Europe* (London: Harper Press, 2008), 4–5; Klaus Zernack, *Polen und Rußland: Zwei Wege in der europäischen Geschichte* (Berlin: Propyläen, 1994), 408; Jędrzejewicz, *Piłsudski*, 71.

33. Wandycz, *Soviet-Polish Relations*, 73; Zernack, *Polen*, 409.

34. Borzęcki, *Soviet-Polish Peace*, 28; text in *Reconstruction of Poland*, ed. Latawski, 199–200 (incorrect date). "Depesza do szefów mocarstw notyfikująca powstanie Państwa Polskiego" (Warsaw, November 16, 1918), in Piłsudski, *Odezwy, dekrety, mowy*, 12.

35. Borzęcki, *Soviet-Polish Peace*, 14–16. On the political calculations behind the joint republic, see Blank, "Soviet Nationality Policy," 121–124; Wandycz, *Soviet-Polish Relations*, 69–71, 84.

36. Herbert Hoover, *The Memoirs of Herbert Hoover*, 3 vols. (New York: Macmillan, 1951–1952), 1:411.

37. Wandycz, *Soviet-Polish Relations*, 101, 103.

38. Ibid., 104; John M. Thompson, *Russia, Bolshevism, and the Versailles Peace* (Princeton: Princeton University Press, 1966), 384–390; Dan Diner, *Cataclysms: A History of the Twentieth Century from Europe's Edge* (Madison: University of Wisconsin Press, 2008), 66.

39. Wandycz, *Soviet-Polish Relations*, 106.

40. Margaret MacMillan, *Paris 1919: Six Months that Changed the World* (New York: Random House, 2002), 215–218.

41. Quoted, Borzęcki, *Soviet-Polish Peace*, 13.

42. Ibid., 11–12; Zamoyski, *Warsaw 1920*, 8.

43. Borzęcki, *Soviet-Polish Peace*, 12–13.

44. Ibid., 13–14.

45. Ibid., 19–21.

46. *Der Grosse Brockhaus*, 15th ed., vol. 20 (1935), 348 (for 1923). On Jewish population (50 percent in 1905), see *YIVO Encyclopedia of Jews in Eastern Europe*, 2:1974.

47. Joanna Januszewski-Jurkiewicz, "Together or Apart? Nations Living in the Vilnius Region Towards a Perspective of Self-Determination after the First World War," *Wieki stare i nowe* 2.7 (2013): 39–55.

48. Evan Mawdsley, *The Russian Civil War* (Boston: Allen and Unwin, 1987), 254; Titus Komarnicki, *Rebirth of the Polish Republic: A Study in the Diplomatic History of Europe, 1914–1920* (London: Heinemann, 1957), 198, 400; Wandycz, *Soviet-Polish Relations*, 103.

49. Quoted, Komarnicki, *Rebirth of the Polish Republic*, 401.

50. Borzęcki, *Soviet-Polish Peace*, 27.

51. Ibid., 34.

52. Ibid., 26–27.

53. Ibid., 24–25.

54. Quoted, MacMillan, *Paris 1919*, 226.

55. Wandycz, *Soviet-Polish Relations*, 127; John Erickson, *The Soviet High Command: A Military-Political History, 1918–1941*, 3rd ed. (London: Frank Cass, 2001), 85.

56. Wandycz, *Soviet-Polish Relations*, 155–157..

57. Ibid., 149–150.

58. Ibid., 152–154; "Zaiavlenie Soveta Narodnykh Komissarov R.S.F.S.R. Pravitel'stvu Pol'shi i pol'skomu narodu" (January 28, 1920), signed Lenin, Chicherin, Trotskii, in *"Krasnaia kniga": Sbornik diplomaticheskikh dokumentov o russko-pol'skikh otnosheniiakh 1918–1920 g.* (Moscow: Gos. izd., 1920), 84–85; Kalinin, "Obrashchenie V.Ts.I.K. k pol'skomu narodu" (February 2, 1920), ibid., 88.

59. Wandycz, *Soviet-Polish Relations*, 167.

60. Ibid., 136.

61. Ibid., 166.

62. Ibid., 163.

63. Chicherin, "Ministru Inostrannykh Del Pateku" (March 6, 1920), in *Krasnaia kniga*, 93.

64. Wandycz, *Soviet-Polish Relations*, 168–171, 173–174.

65. Ibid., 176–178; Trotskii, "Pol'skii front: Beseda s predstavitelem Sovetskoi pechati" (May 2, 1920), in L. Trotskii, *Kak vooruzhalas' revoliutsiia (na voennoi rabote)*, vol. 2.2: *Tysiacha deviat'sot dvadtsatyi god* (Moscow: Vysshii voennyi redaktsionnyi sovet, 1924), 102 (quote).

66. Wandycz, *Soviet-Polish Relations*, 179–180; Erickson, *Soviet High Command*, 86; Trotskii, "Pol'skii front: Beseda," 105, 104 (quotes).

67. Wandycz, *Soviet-Polish Relations*, 182.

68. "Zaiavlenie Narodnogo Komissariata Inostrannykh Del RSFSR o mirnykh peregovorakh s Pol'shei" (April 3, 1920), in *Dokumenty vneshnei politiki SSSR*, 21 vols. (Moscow: Politicheskaia literatura, 1958), 2:480–482; quote, 480.

69. Wandycz, *Soviet-Polish Relations*, 187–188.

70. Stephen Kotkin, *Stalin*, vol. 1: *Paradoxes of Power, 1878–1928* (New York: Penguin, 2014), 354.

71. Wandycz, *Soviet-Polish Relations*, 190–193; Mawdsley, *Russian Civil War*, 251.

72. Wandycz, *Soviet-Polish Relations*, 193–196.

73. Ibid., 198 (quote), 197.

74. Ibid., 200–201.

75. William Henry Chamberlin, *The Russian Revolution, 1917–1921*, 2 vols. (1935; New York: Grosset & Dunlap, 1965), 2:302; "Po povodu sozdaniia osobogo soveshchaniia pri Glavkomanduiushchem" (May 7, 1920), in Trotskii, *Kak*, 2:2, 119–120.

76. "Pis'mo A. A. Brusilova N. I. Ratteliu v sviazi s nastupleniem pol'skikh voisk" (Moscow, May 1, 1920), in *Pol'sko-sovetskaia voina 1919–1920: Ranee ne opubliko-vannye dokumenty i materialy*, ed. I. I. Kostiushchko, 2 vols. (Moscow: RAN Institut slavianovedeniia i balkanistiki, 1994), 1:75.

77. Leon Trotsky, *My Life* (1929; New York: Pathfinder Press, 1970), 456.

78. Quoted, Richard H. Ullman, *Anglo-Soviet Relations, 1917–1921*, 3 vols. (Princeton: Princeton University Press, 1961–1972), 3:231.

79. Wandycz, *Soviet-Polish Relations*, 178.

80. A. S. Puchenkov, "'Daesh' Varshavu!': Iz istorii sovetsko-pol'skoi voiny 1920 g.," *Noveishaia istoriia Rossii* 2 (2012): 28, citing Boris Efimov, *Desiat' desiatiletii: O tom, chto videl, perezhil, zapomnil* (Moscow: Vagrius, 2000), 74. "Warsaw Taken by Red Heroes." Efimov (b. Fridliand) was a leading Soviet caricaturist; his brother was the writer Mikhail Kol'tsov. Alice Nakhimovsky, "Efimov, Boris Efimovich" (2010), YIVO Encyclopedia of Jews in Eastern Europe, available at http://www.yivoencyclopedia.org/article.aspx/Efimov_Boris_Efimovich (accessed June 14, 2015). For images of the Red Army and its evolution from Imperial Army deserters in 1917 to the Red Army in 1924, see Boris Efimov, *Karikatury*, pref. L. D. Trotskii (Moscow: Izvestiia TsIK SSSR i VTsIK, 1924), 57–63.

81. Trotskii, "Smert' pol'skoi burzhuazii" (April 29, 1920), in *Kak*, 2:2, 91; also Trotskii, "Pol'skii front i nashi zadachi: Tezisy" (April 30, 1920), ibid., 93–96; quotes, 94.

82. "Obrashchenie Vserossiiskogo Tsentral'nogo Ispolnitel'nogo Komiteta k rabo-chim, krest'ianam i soldatam Pol'shi" (May 7, 1920), in *Dokumenty vneshnei poli-tiki*, 2:507–509 (quote 509), cited, Wandycz, *Soviet-Polish Relations*, 203.

83. Kotkin, *Stalin*, 356–357; Erickson, *Soviet High Command*, 57–58; Konstantin Zalesskii, "Kamenev," in *Grazhdanskaia voina v Rossii: Entsiklopediia katastrofy*, ed. Dmitrii Volodikhin and Sergei Volkov (Moscow: Sibirskii tsiriul'nik, 2010), 85–87.

84. Dmitrii Mikhailovich, "Tukhachevskii," in *Grazhdanskaia voina v Rossii*, ed. Volodikhin and Volkov, 341; "Tukhachevskii," in Jonathan D. Smele, *Historical*

*Dictionary of the Russian Civil Wars, 1916–1926*, 2 vols. (Lanham, MD: Rowman & Littlefield, 2015), 2:1187–1190; Erickson, *Soviet High Command*, 57–58.

85. Erickson, *Soviet High Command*, 89.

86. Ibid., 73; "Egorov," in Smele, *Historical Dictionary*, 1:361–362.

87. Stephen M. Brown, "Communists and the Red Cavalry: The Political Education of the *Konarmiia* in the Russian Civil War, 1918–20," *Slavonic and East European Review* 73.1 (1995): 85.

88. Erickson, *Soviet High Command*, 70, 401.

89. Weygand, *Mémoires*, 2:114.

90. Brown, "Communists and the Red Cavalry," 88–89, 94.

91. Ibid., 91–92; Isaak Babel, *Red Cavalry*, ed. Nathalie Babel, trans. Peter Constantine (New York: Norton, 2003); Isaak Babel', *Konarmiia* (Moscow: Gos. izd-vo, 1926).

92. Erickson, *Soviet High Command*, 86–87.

93. Ibid., 90–91; Chamberlin, *Russian Revolution*, 2:304.

94. Erickson, *Soviet High Command*, 90–91; Trotskii, "Pochto-telegramma," to Chicherin, Lenin, Radek, L. Kamenev et al. (June 29, 1920), in Trotskii, *Kak*, 2:2, 145–146; "Prikaz Predsedatelia Revoliutsionnogo Voennogo Soveta Respubliki po voiskam Zapadnogo i iugo-zapadnogo frontov" (June 17, 1920), in ibid., 155.

95. Cited in part, Wandycz, *Soviet-Polish Relations*, 213. Here from text: "Komandarmam 4, 15, 3, 16 i komanduiushchemu Mozyrskoi gruppoi" (July 2, 1920), signed Tukhachevskii; members R.V.S. Smigla and Unshlikht, in N. E. Kakurin, *Grazhdanskaia voina v Rossii: Voina s belopoliakami* (1925; rpt. Moscow: AST, 2002), 669–670.

96. Chamberlin, *Russian Revolution*, 2:304; Kotkin, *Stalin*, 359; Mawdsley, *Russian Civil War*, 253; Sergei Shokarev, "Gai," in *Grazhdanskaia voina v Rossii*, ed. Volodikhin and Volkov, 183; "Gai," in Smele, *Historical Dictionary*, 1:435–436.

97. Chamberlin, *Russian Revolution*, 2:305–306.

98. Wandycz, *Soviet-Polish Relations*, 212–214; Trotskii, "Zakliuchitel'noe slovo na 2-i konferentsii komiacheek vysshikh voenno-uchebnykh zavedenii 10 dekabria 1921 goda," in L. Trotskii, *Kak vooruzhalas' revoliutsiia (na voennoi rabote)*, vol. 3.2: *Tysiacha deviat'sot dvadtsat' pervyi–tretii god* (Moscow: Vysshii voennyi redaktsionnyi sovet, 1925), 91 ("I favored peace, because I greatly doubted we had the strength to attack Warsaw, or even to get there").

99. "Direktiva Glavnogo komandovaniia komandovaniiu zapadnogo i iugo-za-padnogo frontov o reshitel'nom prodvizhenii vpered" (July 13, 1920), signed S. Kamenev, in *Direktivy Glavnogo komandovaniia Krasnoi armii (1917–1920): Sbornik dokumentov*, ed. G. A. Belov et al. (Moscow: Voenizdat, 1969), 640.

100. Wandycz, *Soviet-Polish Relations*, 213–215; *Grazhdanskaia voina na Ukraine, 1918–1920: Sbornik dokumentov i materialov*, ed. S. M. Korolivskii et al., 3 vols. (Kiev: Nauk. dumka, 1967), 3:395 (July 16 Glavkom note).

101. "Glavnokomanduiushchemu vsemi vooruzhennymi silami Respubliki" (signed Trotsky, July 17, 1920), in Kakurin, *Grazhdanskaia voina*, 677–678.

102. Wandycz, *Soviet-Polish Relations*, 220–221.

103. "Privetstvennaia telegramma komandovaniia 1-i Konnoi Armii vtoromu kongressy III Kommunisticheskogo internatsionala" (July 14, 1920), in *Grazhdanskaia voina na Ukraine, 1918–1920*, 3:275 (dated five days before Comintern Congress opened, signed also by Voroshilov and Sergei Minin).

104. The blocked shipments did finally make it to Warsaw on August 3, then were blocked again until August 27. See F. Russel Bryant, "Lord D'Abernon, the Anglo-French Mission, and the Battle of Warsaw, 1920," *Jahrbücher für Geschichte Osteuropas* 38 (1990): 533–534, 536, 544; Wandycz, *Soviet-Polish Relations*, 235; Ullman, *Anglo-Soviet Relations*, 3:220 (dock workers).

105. Chamberlin, *Russian Revolution*, 2:306, 309; Mawdsley, *Russian Civil War*, 254.

106. Kotkin, *Stalin*, 361.

107. "Direktiva Pol'revkoma ob areste protivnikov sotsialisticheskoi revoliutsii v Pol'she" (Moscow, to distribute to the Western Front armies, August 4, 1920), in *Pol'sko-sovetskaia voina*, ed. Kostiushchko, 1:165.

108. "Prikaz No. 22 Vremennogo Revoliutsionnogo Komiteta Pol'shi ot 15 avgusta 1920 g." (signed Julian Marchlewski and Edward Próchniak), in *Pol'sko-sovetskaia voina*, ed. Kostiushchko, 1:190–191.

109. Wandycz, *Soviet-Polish Relations*, 219–220.

110. Norbert H. Gaworek, "From Blockade to Trade: Allied Economic Warfare against Soviet Russia, June 1919 to January 1920," *Jahrbücher für Geschichte Osteuropas* 23.1 (1975): 43, 59–60, 63–64, 67; Bryant, "Lord D'Abernon," 530 (propaganda); Ullman, *Anglo-Soviet Relations*, 3:220–221 (pro-Soviet feeling in British trade unions); 224 (Soviet support for Labor, including funds). On the blockade: V. A. Shishkin, *Antisovetskaia blokada i ee krushenie* (Leningrad: Nauka, 1989).

111. Bryant, "Lord D'Abernon," 527–528.

112. Ibid., 530; "Nota Narodnogo Komissara Inostrannykh Del RSFSR Ministru Inostrannykh Del Velikobritanii Kerzonu" (July 23, 1920), signed Chicherin, in *Dokumenty vneshnei politiki*, 3:61–62.

113. Wandycz, *Soviet-Polish Relations*, 222–225; Bryant, "Lord D'Abernon," 536. A trade agreement between Britain and Soviet Russia was finally concluded in March 1921.

114. Bryant, "Lord D'Abernon," 529–530.

115. Kotkin, *Stalin*, 361.

116. Quoted, I. V. Mikhutina, *Pol'sko-sovetskaia voina 1919–1920 gg.* (Moscow: In-t slavianovedeniia i balkanistiki RAN, 1994), 187. See also Wandycz, *Soviet-Polish Relations*, 233.

117. Wandycz, *Soviet-Polish Relations*, 233; Ullman, *Anglo-Soviet Relations*, 3:186.

118. Ullman, *Anglo-Soviet Relations*, 3:193, 196–197; Wandycz, *Soviet-Polish Relations*, 232–233, 235; Bryant, "Lord D'Abernon," 537.

119. Ullman, *Anglo-Soviet Relations*, 3:206.

120. Ibid., 196; Wandycz, *Soviet-Polish Relations*, 233, citing N. F. Kuz'min, *Krushenie poslednego pokhoda Antanty* (Moscow: Gosizdat, 1958), 256–257. "Nota Predsedatelia Delegatsii Sovetskogo Pravitel'stva v Londone Prem'er-Ministru Velikobritanii

Lloid-Dzhordzhu" (August 6, 1920), in *Dokumenty vneshnei politiki*, 3:85 (my translation); cited, Wandycz, *Soviet-Polish Relations*, 236. See also Trotskii, "Pol'skii front i nashi zadachi: Tezisy" (April 30, 1920), in Trotskii, *Kak*, 2:2, 93–96. On disagreements between Kamenev, Chicherin, and Litvinov in Copenhagen about the details of tactics, see Ullman, *Anglo-Soviet Relations*, 3:208.

121. Wandycz, *Soviet-Polish Relations*, 237; Ullman, *Anglo-Soviet Relations*, 3:209–210, 218; Bryant, "Lord D'Abernon," 540. August 8–9 meeting in the English coastal town of Lympne.

122. Ullman, *Anglo-Soviet Relations*, 3:213; "Nota Predsedatelia Delegatsii Sovetskogo Pravitel'stva v Londone Prem'er-Ministru Velikobritanii Lloid-Dzhordzhu" (August 9, 1920), in *Dokumenty vneshnei politiki*, 3:100–101.

123. Ullman, *Anglo-Soviet Relations*, 3:230 (quote), 231.

124. Quotes, ibid., 255, 259, 258.

125. Quoted, Bryant, "Lord D'Abernon," 545.

126. Wandycz, *Soviet-Polish Relations*, 238, 239 (quote); Bryant, "Lord D'Abernon," 540–541.

127. Trotskii, "Tezisy voenno-politicheskoi kampanii po povodu zakliucheniia mira s Pol'shei" (August 11, 1920; presented to Moscow Party Committee), in Trotskii, *Kak*, 2:2, 164–165. When it was over, he repeated the claim that Poland had forced Russia into war, while pretending to talk peace: Trotskii, "Nuzhen vtoroi urok?" (September 8, 1920), ibid., 170–171.

128. Bryant, "Lord D'Abernon," 541–542; Erickson, *Soviet High Command*, 688, downplays Weygand's contribution, as do Wandycz and Norman Davies, as a way of emphasizing the importance of Piłsudski's role, which was denigrated by his opponents and by the French Right. Piłsudski himself slighted Weygand in his memoirs: Bryant, "Lord D'Abernon," 546–547.

129. Erickson, *Soviet High Command*, 93.

130. Also for preceding paragraph: "Glavkom doklad na imia predrevvoensoveta za No. 481" (July 21, 1920), text in Kakurin, *Grazhdanskaia voina*, 302–303; quote here, 302.

131. Quoted, Kakurin, *Grazhdanskaia voina*, 304 (*v opredelennom vybrannom napravlenii*), and Kakurin comment.

132. "Direktiva Glavnogo komandovaniia o nanesenii okonchatel'nogo porazheniia protivniku i ovladenii Varshavoi" (no. 4344), Document 635, in *Direktivy*, 643–644 (dated July 22, but actually midnight into July 23); quote, 643. Also in Kakurin, *Grazhdanskaia voina*, 304–305; quote, 305. Later the same day, Kamenev again urged speed: "Ukazanie..." (no. 2160, July 23, 1920), in *Direktivy*, 644–645.

133. "Direktiva..." (no. 4502, July 30, 1920), in *Direktivy*, 645.

134. *Direktivy*, 806 (n. 114).

135. "Direktiva Glavnogo komandovaniia komandovaniiu zapadnogo i iugo-zapadnogo frontov o peredache zapadnomu frontu 12 i 1 konnoi armii" (no. 4587), Document 639, in *Direktivy*, 646.

136. *Direktivy*, 806 (n. 115).

137. Erickson, *Soviet High Command*, 688 (n. 46), 96–97. On Danzig maneuver: General L. Sikorski, *La Campagne polono-russe de 1920*, trans. M. Larcher, pref. Maréchal Foch (Paris: Payot, 1928), 122; S. S. Kamenev, *Zapiski o grazhdanskoi voine i voennom stroitel'stve: Izbrannye stat'i*, ed. N. S. Kameneva, L. M. Spirin, and P. P. Chernyshkov (Moscow: Voennoe izdatel'stvo Min. Oborony SSSR, 1963), 167. Also: "Ukazanie polevogo shtaba o zakhvate v Dantsigskom koridore imushchestva, postavliaemogo Pol'she Antantoi" (no. 4796), signed Lebedev (August 14, 1920), Document 647, in *Direktivy*, 655.

138. Erickson, *Soviet High Command*, 95.

139. Ibid., 95–96.

140. "Iz zapisi razgovora po priamomu provodu Glavkoma s M. N. Tukhachevskim po povodu plana general'nogo srazheniia na Visle" (August 10, 1920), Document 644, in *Direktivy*, 650–652; quote, 652.

141. Erickson, *Soviet High Command*, 97; "Glavkomu, Trotskomu, Khar'kov R.V.S. Iugo-Zap. fronta" (Berdichev, August 10, 1920), signed Budennyi, Voroshilov, Minin, in Kakurin, *Grazhdanskaia voina*, 710; "Razgovor Glavkoma s komandzapom po priamomu provodu" (August 13, 1920), ibid., 710–712; also as "Iz zapisi razgovora po priamomu provodu Glavkoma s M. N. Tukhachevskim o peredache frontu armii iugo-zapadnogo fronta" (August 13, 1920), Document 645, in *Direktivy*, 652–654.

142. "Telegramma I. V. Stalina V. I. Leninu" (August 12, 1920), *Bol'shevistskoe rukovodstvo: Perepiska, 1912–1927*, ed. A. V. Kvashonkin (Moscow: ROSSPEN, 1996), 155 (note); Kuz'min, *Krushenie*, 261.

143. Erickson, *Soviet High Command*, 97.

144. Mikhutina, *Pol'sko-sovetskaia voina*, 182.

145. "Telegramma I. V. Stalina S. M. Budennomu, K. E. Voroshilovu" (July 29, 1920), in *Bol'shevistskoe rukovodstvo*, 150.

146. "Telegramma I. V. Stalina V. I. Leninu" (August 4, 1920), in *Bol'shevistskoe rukovodstvo*, 153–154.

147. "Telegramma I. V. Stalina V. I. Leninu" (August 12, 1920), in *Bol'shevistskoe rukovodstvo*, 155 ("Moe vpechatlenie takovo, chto Glavkom i brat'ia sabotiruiut rabotu...").

148. Erickson, *Soviet High Command*, 98; Chamberlin, *Russian Revolution*, 2:311.

149. Józef Piłsudski, *Rok 1920* (Warsaw: Ignis, 1924), 181 ("Dnia 16-go rozpocząłem atak, o ile w ogóle atakiem nazwać to można."). The book is a refutation of Tukhachevskii's published account of the war, which it opens by reproducing in Polish translation.

150. Piłsudski, *Rok 1920*, 181 ("Przecież była to jakaś apokaliptyczna bestja, przed którą cofały się przez miesiąc liczne dywizje. Wydawało mi się, że śnię."), 182–183.

151. Quoted, Bryant, "Lord D'Abernon," 542.

152. Erickson, *Soviet High Command*, 98.

153. Piłsudski, *Rok 1920*, 183.

154. "Telegramma chlena RVS 16-i armii G. L. Piatakova o panicheskom otstuplenii chastei armii" (to Lenin and Trotsky, August 28, 1920), in *Pol'sko-sovetskaia voina*, ed. Kostiushchko, 2:5–6; for harsh and counterproductive policies in occupied Białystok, see Wandycz, *Soviet-Polish Relations*, 227.

155. Statement October 2, 1920, cited Wandycz, *Soviet-Polish Relations*, 214.

156. Piłsudski, *Rok 1920*, 203.

157. M. N. Tukhachevskii, "Revoliutsiia izvne," *Voina Klassov: Stat'i 1919–1920 g.* (Moscow: Gosizdat, 1921).

158. Mikhutina, *Pol'sko-sovetskaia voina*, 189 (problem was the Red Army was just not up to it).

159. Kamenev, *Zapiski*, 164–165; Erickson, *Soviet High Command*, 100 ("an ill-assorted jumble of peasant-carts, ammunition trains, artillery parks and straining locomotives").

160. Kamenev, *Zapiski*, 167–168.

161. Erickson, *Soviet High Command*, 98–99.

162. Wandycz, *Soviet-Polish Relations*, 241, citing Trotskii, "Zakliuchitel'noe slovo na 2-i konferentsii komiacheek vysshikh voenno-uchebnykh zavedenii 10 dekabria 1921 goda," in Trotskii, *Kak*, 3:1, 91 (on debate after defeat).

163. Wandycz, *Soviet-Polish Relations*, 241.

164. Erickson, *Soviet High Command*, 98; Mawdsley, *Russian Civil War*, 256.

165. Timothy Snyder, *The Reconstruction of Nations: Poland, Ukraine, Lithuania, Belarus, 1569–1999* (New Haven: Yale University Press, 2003), 63–64, 68–69.

166. Mawdsley, *Russian Civil War*, 256–257.

167. Trotsky, *My Life*, 459, describes the hesitations, even Lenin's own, about what to do with Poland—continue the war or make peace.

168. Kotkin, *Stalin*, 376–377. Most historians accept Stalin's responsibility for the defeat. Most recently, Kotkin, *Stalin*, 362, calls Stalin insubordinate, but also says he was "scapegoated" (378). By contrast, Thomas Fiddick, "The 'Miracle on the Vistula': Soviet Policy versus Red Army Strategy," *Journal of Modern History* 45.4 (1973): 642–643, in a convoluted argument, asserts that Lenin did not want victory, and therefore Stalin was not insubordinate but fulfilling his master's wishes.

169. Erickson, *Soviet High Command*, 101–102; 108 (Budennyi and Voroshilov insubordinate, abetted by Stalin).

170. Trotsky, *My Life*, 458.

171. Trotskii, "Prikaz," to commanders of Western Front (May 9, 1920), in Trotskii, *Kak*, 2:2, 125; "Sovetskaia i shliakhetskaia" (May 15, 1920), ibid., 140–141; "Telegramma L. D. Trotskogo TsK RKP o nedostatke sil i sredstv na Zapadnom fronte i neobkhodimosti napravleniia na etot front luchshikh rabotnikov" (May 9, 1920), direct wire to Sklianskii in Moscow for the Cheka, in *Pol'sko-sovetskaia voina*, ed. Kostiushchko, 1:91.

172. "Dokladnaia zapiska N. I. Muralova o sostoianii 12-i armii, polozhenii v ee tylu i ego soobrazheniiakh o postanovke voennogo dela" (May 17, 1920), to Lenin, in *Pol'sko-sovetskaia voina*, ed. Kostiushchko, 1:102, 95, 96. The case cited concerned Berdichev (Berdychiv).

173. Trotskii, "Oproverzhenie" (August 16, 1920), in Trotskii, *Kak*, 2:2, 167.

174. Trotskii, "Nuzhen vtoroi urok?" (September 8, 1920), in Trotskii, *Kak*, 2:2, 170–171.

175. Trotskii, "My sil'nee, chem byli" (September 10, 1920), in Trotskii, *Kak*, 2:2, 173 (*Razumeetsia, eto krupnaia neudacha*).

PART V: CHAPTER 8

1. V. F. Soldatenko, *Grazhdanskaia voina v Ukraine, 1917–1920 gg.* (Moscow: Novyi khronograf, 2012), 289.

2. Martha Bohachevsky-Chomiak, "The Directory of the Ukrainian National Republic," in *The Ukraine 1917–1921: A Study in Revolution*, ed. Taras Hunczak (Cambridge, MA: Harvard Ukrainian Research Institute, 1977), 87–88; Arthur E. Adams, *The Bolsheviks in the Ukraine: The Second Campaign, 1918–1919* (New Haven: Yale University Press, 1963), 79, 81–82; Soldatenko, *Grazhdanskaia voina*, 286.

3. Elias Heifetz, *The Slaughter of the Jews in the Ukraine in 1919* (New York: Seltzer, 1921), 61–62. Report published for the Jewish People's Relief Committee of America.

4. Dietrich Beyrau, "Brutalization Revisited: The Case of Russia," *Journal of Contemporary History* 50.1 (2015): 17; also Stefan Plaggenborg, "Weltkrieg, Bürgerkrieg, Klassenkrieg. Mentalitätsgeschichtliche Versuche über Gewalt in Sowjetrussland," *Historische Anthropologie* 3 (1995): 493–505.

5. Faith Hillis, *Children of Rus': Right-Bank Ukraine and the Invention of a Russian Nation* (Ithaca: Cornell University Press, 2013).

6. *Kishinevskii pogrom 1903 goda: Sbornik dokumentov i materialov*, ed. Ia. M. Kopanskii (Kishinev: Ruxanda, 2000).

7. *American Jewish Year Book 5862 (October 3, 1921 to September 22, 1922)*, vol. 23, ed. Harry Schneiderman (Philadelphia: Jewish Publication Society of America, 1921), 280; Stephen Velychenko, *State Building in Revolutionary Ukraine: A Comparative Study of Government and Bureaucrats, 1917–22* (Toronto: University of Toronto Press, 2010), 277–278.

8. *American Jewish Year Book 5862*, 330–347.

9. Heifetz, *Slaughter*, 59.

10. Ibid., 63.

11. On prevalence of rape, see Henry Abramson, *A Prayer for the Government: Ukrainians and Jews in Revolutionary Times, 1917–1920* (Cambridge, MA: Ukrainian Research Institute and Center for Jewish Studies, Harvard University, 1999), 122; *Les pogromes en Ukraine sous les gouvernements ukrainiens (1917–1920): Aperçu historique et documents* (Paris: Comité des Délégations Juives, 1927), 75–76 (Les viols). Rape figures centrally in the poem by Hayim Nahman Bialik about the Kishinev pogrom, "In the City of Slaughter" (1903), which he wrote and published after seeing the results with his own eyes: "... on each daughter of

your people…Seven uncircumcised savages piled, / Despoiling child in front of mother, mother in front of child." Excerpt from Hillel Halkin, *Jabotinsky: A Life* (New Haven: Yale University Press, 2014), 52.

12. Oleg Budnitskii, *Russian Jews Between the Reds and the Whites, 1917–1920*, trans. Timothy J. Portice (Philadelphia: University of Pennsylvania Press, 2012), 97–99. See also Oleg Budnitskii, *Rossiiskie evrei mezhdu krasnymi i belymi (1917–1920)* (Moscow: ROSSPEN, 2005).

13. Isaac Deutscher, *The Prophet Armed: Trotsky, 1879–1921* (New York: Vintage, 1954), 8–13; Leon Trotsky, *My Life*, intro. Joseph Hansen (New York: Pathfinder, 1970), in which the first two chapters barely mention the Jewish religion.

14. Budnitskii, *Russian Jews*, 81; Arkadi Zeltser, "Commissariat for Jewish National Affairs," in *The YIVO Encyclopedia of Jews in Eastern Europe* (2010), available at http://www.yivoencyclopedia.org/article.aspx/Commissariat_for_Jewish_National_Affairs (accessed December 1, 2016); Zvi Gitelman, "Evsektsiia," in ibid., available at http://www.yivoencyclopedia.org/article.aspx/Evsektsiia (accessed November 30, 2016).

15. Arkadi Zeltser, "Dimanshtein, Semen Markovich," in ibid., available at http://www.yivoencyclopedia.org/article.aspx/Dimanshtein_Semen_Markovich (accessed December 1, 2016).

16. Budnitskii, *Russian Jews*, 76–90.

17. William Henry Chamberlin, *The Russian Revolution, 1917–1921*, 2 vols. (1935; New York: Grosset & Dunlap, 1965), 2:231.

18. "Postanovleniia Khar'kovskogo soveshchaniia chlenov partii narodnoi svobody (3–6 noiabria 1919 g.): Po evreiskomu voprosu," in *S"ezdy i konferentsii konstitutsionno-demokraticheskoi partii*, vol. 3, bk. 2: *1918–1920 gg.* (Moscow: ROSSPEN, 2000), 147.

19. Quoted, Brendan Francis McGeever, "The Bolshevik Confrontation with Antisemitism in the Russian Revolution, 1917–1919" (Ph.D. dissertation, University of Glasgow, 2015), 118 (translation modified).

20. Ivan Bunin, *Okaiannye dni: Dnevniki, stat'i, vospominaniia* (Moscow: Eksmo, 2011), 485 (my translation).

21. S. I. Gusev-Orenburgskii, *"Bagrovaia kniga": Pogromy 1919–20 g.g. na Ukraine* (Harbin: Lemberg, 1922), 16. Published by the Far East Jewish Social Committee for Aid to Orphan Victims of the Pogroms.

22. Figures proposed as most reasonable, citing not only data collected at the time by various Jewish and Soviet agencies, but also the data presented at Genoa by the Soviet delegation, hoping to extract compensation from the Entente for having bankrolled the anti-Soviet forces most active in the destruction of the Jews (the figures thus represent a high end, but tally overall with other methods of calculation): L. B. Miliakova, "Vvedenie," *Kniga pogromov: Pogromy na Ukraine, v Belorussii i evropeiskoi chasti Rossii v period Grazhdanskoi voiny 1918–1922 gg.: Sbornik dokumentov*, ed. L. B. Miliakova (Moscow: ROSSPEN, 2007), xii, xiii.

Also, Lidia Miliakova and Irina Ziuzina, "Le travail d'enquête des organisations juives sur les pogroms d'Ukraine, de Biélorussie et de Russie soviétique pendant la guerre civile (1918–1922)," *Le Mouvement social* 222 (2008): 61. Miliakova provides a detailed description of the sources on which these data are based. See also Abramson, *Prayer*, 110.

23. On the organizations involved, the relationship to the Soviet government, and the archiving of the data, see Miliakova and Ziuzina, "Le travail."

24. Miliakova, "Vvedenie," iv, xiii, xviii–xxvii.

25. Quoted, Heifetz, *Slaughter*, 67, 68 (quote).

26. Miliakova, "Vvedenie," ix; Heifetz says Makhno occasionally did call for pogroms: Heifetz, *Slaughter*, 72–75, 85, 89.

27. Miliakova, "Vvedenie," xii.

28. Ibid., xiv. Figure for murders from Lars Fischer, "Whither *pogromshchina*—Historiographical Synthesis or Deconstruction?" *East European Jewish Affairs* 38.3 (2008): 305, citing Nahum Gergel, *Di lage fun di Yidn in Rusland* (Warsaw: Bzshazo, 1929).

29. Miliakova, "Vvedenie," viii.

30. In May 1926, he supported Piłsudski's coup; in 1937 he fought on Franco's side in Spain; in 1939 he participated in the defense of Warsaw, then joined the anti-Nazi underground. He was murdered on a street in Warsaw on May 10, 1940, by a German patrol. See Valerii Klaving, *Grazhdanskaia voina v Rossii: Belye armii* (Moscow: AST, 2003), 402–404; Sergei Volkov, "Bulak-Balakhovich," in *Grazhdanskaia voina v Rossii: Entsiklopediia katastrofy*, ed. Dmitrii Volodikhin and Sergei Volkov (Moscow: Sibirskii tsiriul'nik, 2010), 301; "Bułak-Bałachowicz," in Jonathan D. Smele, *Historical Dictionary of the Russian Civil Wars, 1916–1926*, 2 vols. (Lanham, MD: Rowman & Littlefield, 2015), 1:241–243.

31. Interview reported in *L'Univers israélite: Journal des Principes Conservateurs du Judaïsme*, no. 15 (December 17, 1920), 352.

32. Henry Abramson, "Jewish Representation in the Independent Ukrainian Governments of 1917–1920," *Slavic Review* 50.3 (1991): 543.

33. Abramson, *Prayer*, 80–81, 83–84; Abramson, "Jewish Representation," 544.

34. Abramson, *Prayer*, 90–98; Abramson, "Jewish Representation," 544.

35. Heifetz, *Slaughter*, 12–16; Abramson, *Prayer*, 88.

36. Abramson, *Prayer*, 89–90, 100–101; Abramson, "Jewish Representation," 546.

37. Heifetz, *Slaughter*, 28–30, 33 (quote).

38. Quotes, ibid., 78, 79.

39. Ibid., 23. After a complicated life in emigration, Konovalets was assassinated by an NKVD agent in Rotterdam in 1938. "Konovalets," in Smele, *Historical Dictionary*, 1:602–603.

40. Heifetz, *Slaughter*, 37–38.

41. Ibid., 39.

42. Quoted, Arnol'd Davidovich Margolin, *Ukraina i politika antanty: Zapiski evreia i grazhdanina* (Berlin: Efron, 1921), 310.

43. Bohdan Khmelnyts'kyi was a seventeenth-century Zaporozhian Cossack hetman who led an uprising against the Polish-Lithuanian Commonwealth, in the course of which thousands of Jews were slaughtered. He ended by concluding a treaty with the Russian tsar, bringing the lands of what later became Ukraine into the Russian orbit. In the nineteenth century, Khmelnyts'kyi became a symbol of the Ukrainian intelligentsia's nationalist aspirations, imbued with a xenophobic ideology directed against Poles and Jews. In the Soviet period, Khmelnyts'kyi represented the unification of Ukraine and Russia—the Friendship of Nations. On his place in emerging Ukrainian nationalism, see Hillis, *Children of Rus'*.

44. Document No. 15. "Doklad upolnomochennogo Otdela pomoshchi pogromlennym pri ROKK na Ukraine A. I. Gillersona o pogromakh, ustroennykh voinskimi chastiami armii UNR v g. Proskurove i m. Fil'shtin Podol'skoi gub. 15 i 16 fevralia 1919 g." (not before June 1919), *Kniga pogromov*, 47 (*kvartal'naia okhrana*).

45. Ibid., 48; 845 (biography); Hillerson, in Heifetz, *Slaughter*, 204.

46. "Ordre à la Brigade des Cosaques de Zaporojie de L'Armee Républicaine d'Ukraine, portant le nom de l'Ataman en Chef Petlioura," Proskourov, 6 février 1919, signed Semessenko, YIVO, Tcherikower Archive, File 453, #38195. My translation from Annexe no. 25, in *Les pogromes en Ukraine*, 52. Cf. Abramson, *Prayer*, 122, quoting English text, 187; also Heifetz, *Slaughter*, 42–43.

47. On this point, also Heifetz, *Slaughter*, 39–40.

48. Document 15, *Kniga pogromov*, 49–50.

49. This phrase from: "Kratkii konspekt moikh pokazanii," by name illegible, chair of the Direction of the Jewish Community in Proskurov, chair of the Committee to Aid Pogrom Victims, YIVO, Tcherikower Archive, File 406, #35317.

50. Document 15, *Kniga pogromov*, 51.

51. Ibid.

52. Heifetz, *Slaughter*, 211; "Konovalov, German," in Smele, *Historical Dictionary*, 1:603–604.

53. Heifetz, *Slaughter*, 213, 214; "Verkhola," in L. G. Protasov, *Liudi Uchreditel'nogo sobraniia: Portret v inter'ere epokhi* (Moscow: ROSSPEN, 2008), 271.

54. Quoted, Heifetz, *Slaughter*, 139; also 214.

55. Ibid., 217, 215.

56. Quoted, ibid., 216 (cf. Annexe no. 26, 52–53).

57. Quoted, ibid., 217.

58. Document No. 16, "Vypiska iz registratsionnogo zhurnala evreiskoi gorodskoi bol'nitsy o ranenykh, nakhodivshikhsia na izlechenii posle pogroma v g. Proskurove Podol'skoi gub. v fevrale 1919 g." (August 1, 1921), in *Kniga pogromov*, 70–79; Document No. 17, "Vypiska iz registratsionnogo zhurnala pereviazochnogo punkta No. 3 o ranenykh, nakhodivshikhsia na izlechenii posle pogroma v g. Proskurove Podol'skoi gub. v fevrale 1919 g." (August 1, 1921), ibid., 80–84.

59. Example with information entered on April 20, 1919, YIVO, Tcherikower Archive, File 391, #34792.

60. Heifetz, *Slaughter*, 218; Abramson, *Prayer*, 129.

61. Heifetz, *Slaughter*, 43.

62. Abramson, *Prayer*, 122.

63. Isaac Babel, *1920 Diary*, trans. H. T. Willetts, ed. Carol J. Avins (New Haven: Yale University Press, 1995), 41 (July 28, 1920).

64. Heifetz, *Slaughter*, 134–137, 138.

65. Ibid., 45–47.

66. Ibid., 51–52.

67. Abramson, "Jewish Representation," 546.

68. Quotes, Margolin, *Ukraina*, 270–271. Full text in French translation in "Appel du Directoire sur les pogromes" (Annexe no. 20), *Les pogromes en Ukraine*, 36–37.

69. Abramson, *Prayer*, 144–146; Margolin, *Ukraina*, 271.

70. Quoted, Abramson, *Prayer*, 132, from archives.

71. Abramson, "Jewish Participation," 549.

72. Quoted, Margolin, *Ukraina*, 272.

73. "Zakon Direktorii UNR o sozdanii Osoboi Sledstvennoi Komissii dlia rassledovaniia evreiskikh pogromov" (May 27, 1919), in Symon Petliura, *Glavnyi ataman: V plenu nesbytochnykh nadezhd*, ed. Miroslav Popovich and Viktor Mironenko, trans. from Ukrainian G. Lesnaia (Moscow and St. Petersburg: Letnii sad, 2008), 240–243.

74. Margolin, *Ukraina*, 273–275; "Biulleten' Ministerstva informatsii UNR o telegramme S. Petliury o reshitel'noi bor'be s bol'shevistskimi provokatorami evreiskikh pogromov" (July 1919), in Petliura, *Glavnyi ataman*, 244–245.

75. "Soldiers of the Ukrainian People's Republic Ordered to Respect and Protect the Jews: Daily Order by the Supreme Commander [Petliura] to the Troops of the Ukrainian People's Republic" (August 26, 1919), in *The Jewish Pogroms in Ukraine: Authoritative Statements on the Question of Responsibility for Recent Outbreaks Against the Jews in Ukraine* (Washington, DC: Friends of Ukraine, 1919), 15–16; Heifetz, *Slaughter*, 54–55; Margolin, *Ukraina*, 274; "La première proclamation de Petlioura contre les pogromes: Ordre du jour du Commandant suprême des troupes de la République populaire ukrainienne, no. 131 (26 août 1919)," in *Les pogromes en Ukraine*, 75–76.

76. "Prikaz glavnogo komandovaniia voisk UNR" (August 26, 1919), in Petliura, *Glavnyi ataman*, 245–247 (signed Petliura).

77. "Pis'mo Predsedatelia Direktorii UNR S. Petliury Ministru po evreiskim delam P. Krasnomu s pros'boi dat' ras"iasneniia zarubezhnym evreiskim krugam otnositel'no situatsii s pogromami na Ukraine" (December 29, 1920), in Petliura, *Glavnyi ataman*, 304–305.

78. Abramson, *Prayer*, 131.

79. Fischer, "Whither *pogromshchina?*": 303-305; Volodymyr Serhiychuk, *Symon Petliura and the Jewry*, trans. from Ukrainian Olexandr Terekh (Kiev: Universe,

2000); Taras Hunczak, *Symon Petliura and the Jews: A Reappraisal* (Toronto: Ukrainian Historical Association, 1985); Miroslav Popovich, "Petliura: Vstupitel'naia stat'ia," in Petliura, *Glavnyi ataman*, 5–6.

80. Margolin, *Ukraina*, 277, 279.

81. Julian Batchinsky (Ukrainian Diplomatic Representative to the United States), "The Jewish Pogroms in Ukraine and the Ukrainian People's Republic" (November 1919, letter to newspapers, mostly Jewish), in *Jewish Pogroms in Ukraine* (Washington, 1919), 10.

82. Victoria Khiterer, "Arnold Davidovich Margolin: Ukrainian-Jewish Jurist, Statesman and Diplomat," *Revolutionary Russia* 18.2 (2005):145–167; On resignation: Margolin, *Ukraina*, 125–132.

83. Quoted from *Jewish Chronicle* (May 15, 1919), in Heifetz, *Slaughter*, 53; also "The Jews in the Ukraine: Interview appearing in the 'Jewish Chronicle' of London, England, granted by Dr. Arnold Margolin, Representative of the Ukraine at the Paris Peace Conference," in *Jewish Pogroms in Ukraine* (Washington, 1919), 17–20; also Margolin, *Ukraina*.

84. "The Jews in the Ukraine: Interview," 17–20, quote, 20.

85. Heifetz, *Slaughter*, i–iii. Miliakova, "Vvedenie," xxii.

86. Heifetz, *Slaughter*, 81.

87. Ibid., 56.

88. Laura Engelstein, "That Scoundrel Petliura," in *On Not Being an Anti-Semite: Exemplary Cases from Russia, Ukraine, and Poland* (Waltham, MA: Brandeis University Press, forthcoming).

89. Quoted, Heifetz, *Slaughter*, 47.

90. Peter Kenez, *Civil War in South Russia, 1919–1920: The Defeat of the Whites* (Berkeley: University of California Press, 1977), 174–175.

91. Heifetz, *Slaughter*, 100.

92. Margolin, *Ukraina*, 312.

93. Adams, *Bolsheviks*, 373–374.

94. Kenez, *Civil War 1919*, 167–168.

95. Heifetz, *Slaughter*, 111–112.

96. Quoted, Kenez, *Civil War 1919*, 175.

97. Quote from John Ernest Hodgson, *With Denikin's Armies, Being a Description of the Cossack Counter-Revolution in South Russia, 1918–1920* (London: Williams, 1932), 54–55, in Kenez, *Civil War 1919*, 176.

98. Margolin, *Ukraina*, 312.

99. "Belye i evrei (Po materialam rossiiskogo posol'stva v Parizhe i lichnogo arkhiva V. A. Maklakova)," in *Evrei i russkaia revoliutsiia: Materialy i issledovaniia*, ed. O.V. Budnitskii (Moscow and Jerusalem:"Gesharim," 1999), 274.

100. Kenez, *Civil War 1919*, 175 (and quote).

101. Heifetz, *Slaughter*, 112.

102. Quoted in English in Heifetz, *Slaughter*, 113–114 (my translation from the original Russian text). Article mentioned, citing Heifetz, in William Henry

Chamberlin, *The Russian Revolution, 1917–1921*, 2 vols. (1935; New York: Grosset & Dunlap, 1965), 2:230–231.

103. McGeever, "Bolshevik Confrontation," 103–110.

104. Ibid., 116–117; "Obrashchenie Komissariata po evreiskim delam g. Moskvy i Moskovskoi oblasti v SNK o merakh po bor'be s pogromami" (April 19, 1918), signed Tsvi Fridliand, in Miliakova, *Kniga pogromov*, 754–55; "Pis'mo zamestitelia komissara po evreiskim delam NKN RSFSR I. G. Dobkovskogo predsedateliu SNK V. I. Leninu ob obsuzhdenii voprosa bor'by s pogromami" (April 19, 1918), ibid., 755–756.

105. Quotes, McGeever, "Bolshevik Confrontation," 141–142.

106. Ibid., 194–199, 210–213.

107. Quoted, ibid., 223.

108. Ibid., 239–245.

109. Quoted, ibid., 262–263; here my translation.

110. Quoted, ibid., 264 (*gorodskoe meshchanstvo*).

111. "Budenny," in Smele, *Historical Dictionary*, 1:234–237; Evan Mawdsley, *The Russian Civil War* (Boston: Allen and Unwin, 1987), 220.

112. Mawdsley, *Russian Civil War*, 220.

113. Quoted, V. L. Genis, "Pervaia Konnaia armiia: Za kulisami slavy," *Voprosy istorii* 12 (1994): 65, citing report by military commissar of 42nd Rifle Division of the 13th Army, December 1919.

114. Quoted, Genis, "Pervaia Konnaia armiia," 66.

115. Ibid., 66–67.

116. Quoted, ibid., 68.

117. Ibid., 68.

118. Quoted, ibid., 69.

119. Stephen M. Brown, "Communists and the Red Cavalry: The Political Education of the *Konarmiia* in the Russian Civil War, 1918–20," *Slavonic and East European Review* 73.1 (1995): 88, from archival source.

120. Genis, "Pervaia Konnaia armiia," 71–72; quote, 71.

121. Ibid., 69–70.

122. Ibid., 71.

123. Quoted, ibid., 72 (telegram of October 14, 1920, from Rakovskii, chair of Ukrainian Sovnarkom).

124. Quoted, ibid., 73.

125. Archival report, cited in Brown, "Communists and the Red Cavalry," 86.

126. Quoted, Genis, "Pervaia Konnaia armiia," 73, 74 (quote).

127. Babel, *1920 Diary*, 71, 73, 74.

128. Ibid., 28, 64, 77.

129. Norman Davies, "Great Britain and the Polish Jews, 1918–20," *Journal of Contemporary History* 8.2 (1973): 129–130.

130. Preface, *The Jews in Poland: Official Reports of the American and British Investigating Missions* (Chicago: National Polish Committee of America, 1920), 3.

131. Ibid., 2.
132. "Morgenthau Report: American Commission to Negotiate Peace, Mission to Poland," dated Paris, October 3, 1919, in *The Jews in Poland* (1920), 5.
133. Ibid., 5–6.
134. Ibid., 6.
135. Ibid., 7.
136. Ibid.
137. Ibid., 8.
138. Jadwin and Johnson Report, in *The Jews in Poland* (1920), 11.
139. Ibid., 12, 14, 16.
140. Ibid., 15.
141. Brian Porter, *When Nationalism Began to Hate: Imagining Modern Politics in Nineteenth-Century Poland* (Oxford: Oxford University Press, 2000), 227–232.
142. Cited, Sam Johnson, *Pogroms, Peasants, Jews: Britain and Eastern Europe's "Jewish Question," 1867–1925* (Houndmills, UK: Palgrave Macmillan, 2011), 159, from Roman Dmowski, "Poland, Old and New," in *Russian Realities and Problems*, ed. J. D. Duff (Cambridge: Cambridge University Press, 1916), 115.
143. *The Year 1920: The War between Poland and Bolshevik Russia* (Warsaw: KARTA Centre; City of Warsaw History Museum, 2005), 30.
144. Ibid., 64.
145. Ibid., 127 (Znowu łapy żydowskie? Nie, przenigdy!). See also Irena Kamińska-Szmaj, *Judzi, zohydza, ze czci odziera: Język propagandy politycznej w prasie 1919–1923* (Wroclaw: Tow. Przyjaciół Polonistyki Wrocławskiej, 1994).
146. Davies, "Great Britain and the Polish Jews," 132–135.
147. Ibid., 142; Porter, *When Nationalism Began to Hate*, 213.

### PART V: CHAPTER 9

1. General Baron Peter N. Wrangel, *Always With Honour*, foreword Herbert Hoover (New York: Robert Speller, 1957), 247.
2. *Rossiia 1913 god: Statistiko-dokumental'nyi spravochnik*, ed. A. M. Afimov and A. P. Korelin (St. Petersburg: BLITs, 1995), 12, 14.
3. M. S. Anderson, "The Great Powers and the Russian Annexation of the Crimea, 1783–4," *Slavonic and East European Review* 37.88 (1958): 39, 41; Orlando Figes, *The Crimean War: A History* (New York: Metropolitan Books, 2010).
4. A. G. Zarubin and V. G. Zarubin, *Bez pobeditelei: Iz istorii grazhdanskoi voiny v Krymu* (Simferopol: Tavriia, 1997), 6–7.
5. Djafer Seïdamet, *La Crimée* (Lausanne: Vaney-Burnier, 1921), 67; Zarubin and Zarubin, *Bez pobeditelei*, 24–25; William G. Rosenberg, *Liberals in the Russian Revolution: The Constitutional Democratic Party, 1917–1921* (Princeton: Princeton University Press, 1974), 358; Alan W. Fisher, *The Crimean Tatars* (Stanford: Hoover, 1978), 112–113. Zarubin and Zarubin and Rosenberg are the principal sources for this chapter.

6. Zarubin and Zarubin, *Bez pobeditelei*, 28–30.

7. Quoted, ibid., 42–43.

8. Ibid., 44–45.

9. Text at http://constitution.garant.ru/history/act1600-1918/5310/ (accessed December 17, 2016).

10. Seïdamet, *La Crimée*, 73 (quote), 74–76; Zarubin and Zarubin, *Bez pobeditelei*, 31, 50 (quote).

11. Zarubin and Zarubin, *Bez pobeditelei*, 53.

12. Ibid., 46–47.

13. Ibid., 52, 64.

14. Ibid., 48–49.

15. Ibid., 52–53, 54 (quote).

16. Quoted, ibid., 57.

17. Ibid., 58.

18. Ibid., 62.

19. Ibid., 65; Fisher, *Crimean Tatars*, 19–20.

20. Zarubin and Zarubin, *Bez pobeditelei*, 66–72. On February 21 decree, see Part 4, Chapter 2.

21. Ibid., 83, 88.

22. Ibid., 89–90.

23. Wolfram Dornik and Peter Lieb, "Die militärischen Operationen," in Wolfram Dornik et al., *Die Ukraine zwischen Selbstbestimmung und Fremdherrschaft, 1917–1922* (Graz: Leykam, 2011), 216 (thanks to Michael Geyer for the reference); Zarubin and Zarubin, *Bez pobeditelei*, 91 (mentions incursion but not massacre).

24. Zarubin and Zarubin, *Bez pobeditelei*, 90–94.

25. Ibid., 101–102.

26. Fisher, *Crimean Tatars*, 122–124.

27. Rosenberg, *Liberals*, 360–361; Zarubin and Zarubin, *Bez pobeditelei*, 103–104.

28. Fisher, *Crimean Tatars*, 122–124.

29. Rosenberg, *Liberals*, 361–363; "Krym," in Jonathan D. Smele, *Historical Dictionary of the Russian Civil Wars, 1916–1926*, 2 vols. (Lanham, MD: Rowman & Littlefield, 2015), 1:633.

30. Rosenberg, *Liberals*, 363; M. E. Golostenov, "Petrunkevich," in *Politicheskie deiateli Rossii 1917: Biograficheskii slovar'*, ed. P. V. Volobuev (Moscow: Bol'shaia rossiiskaia entsiklopediia, 1993), 249–250. See also M. Vinaver, *Nashe pravitel'stvo Krymskie vospominaniia, 1918–1919 gg.* (Paris: Voltaire, 1928).

31. "Sul'kevich," in Smele, *Historical Dictionary*, 2:1126–1127.

32. Rosenberg, *Liberals*, 357, citing Daniil Pasmanik, *Revoliutsionnye gody v Krymu: Prilozhenie: Pis'mo I. I. Petrunkevicha o russkoi intelligentsii* (Paris: Société anonyme imprimerie de Navarre, 1926), 113.

33. Quoted, Zarubin and Zarubin, *Bez pobeditelei*, 158.

34. Rosenberg, *Liberals*, 364–366.

35. Fisher, *Crimean Tatars*, 127; Rosenberg, *Liberals*, 373–374; Seïdamet, *La Crimée*, 80.
36. Zarubin and Zarubin, *Bez pobeditelei*, 158, 168.
37. Quoted, ibid., 160–161.
38. Ibid., 141–142, 145; Rosenberg, *Liberals*, 371.
39. Rosenberg, *Liberals*, 330–331.
40. Zarubin and Zarubin, *Bez pobeditelei*, 160 (quote).
41. Ibid., 169; Rosenberg, *Liberals*, 368–370.
42. Zarubin and Zarubin, *Bez pobeditelei*, 166.
43. Ibid., 162–164.
44. Rosenberg, *Liberals*, 375–376.
45. Zarubin and Zarubin, *Bez pobeditelei*, 176.
46. Quoted, ibid., 177.
47. Ibid., 180–181, 185 (quote).
48. Ibid., 183; Rosenberg, *Liberals*, 376–377.
49. Zarubin and Zarubin, *Bez pobeditelei*, 189.
50. Rosenberg, *Liberals*, 377–378.
51. Zarubin and Zarubin, *Bez pobeditelei*, 206–210.
52. Wrangel, *Always With Honour*, 257; Wrangel quoted in Zarubin and Zarubin, *Bez pobeditelei*, 240.
53. Zarubin and Zarubin, *Bez pobeditelei*, 241–242.
54. Ibid., 253–254. Pushed into exile by White defeat, in 1921 Slashchev accepted the Soviet offer of amnesty and returned to Russia, where he held teaching posts in Red Army academies. On January 11, 1929, one of his students, a young man by the name of Kolenberg, shot the former White officer to death in his own apartment. Kolenberg was declared mentally unfit to stand trial and was released. He explained his act as revenge for the death of his brother, who had been murdered during a pogrom committed by Slashchev's men in Nikolaev. "Slashchev," in Valerii Klaving, *Grazhdanskaia voina v Rossii: Belye armii* (Moscow: AST, 2003), 547; "Slashchov," in Smele, *Historical Dictionary*, 2:1061–1062; Ia. A. Slashchov-Krymskii, *Trebuiu suda obshchestva i glasnosti: Oborona i sdacha Kryma: Memuary i dokumenty* (Constantinople: Shulman, 1921); O. S. Smyslov, *General Slashchev-Krymskii: Pobedy, emigratsiia, vozrashchenie* (Moscow: Veche, 2013).
55. Quoted, Zarubin and Zarubin, *Bez pobeditelei*, 216.
56. Ibid., 212–226.
57. Ibid., 254–262.
58. Vladimir Maiakovskii, "The Last Little Page of the Civil War" ("Posledniaia stranichka grazhdanskoi voiny," 1920–1921), in V. V. Maiakovskii, *Polnoe sobranie sochinenii*, 13 vols. (Moscow: Goslitizdat, 1956), vol. 2. Available at http://www .ilibrary.ru/text/2381/index.html (accessed March 2, 2017).
59. "Uniforms (White Armies)," in Smele, *Historical Dictionary*, 2:1241.
60. William Henry Chamberlin, *The Russian Revolution, 1917–1921*, 2 vols. (1935; New York: Grosset & Dunlap, 1965), 2:318.

61. Teffi [Nadezhda Buchinskaia, née Lokhvitskaia], *Memories: From Moscow to the Black Sea*, intro. Edythe Haber, trans. Robert Chandler et al. (Paris, 1928–1930; New York: New York Review of Books, 2016), 130.

62. Zarubin and Zarubin, *Bez pobeditelei*, 236.

63. Following paragraphs: Evan Mawdsley, *The Russian Civil War* (Boston: Allen and Unwin, 1987), 262–267.

64. A. S. Lukomskii, *Vospominaniia generala A. S. Lukomskogo: Period Evropeiskoi voiny, nachalo razrukhi v Rossii, bor'ba s bol'shevikami*, 2 vols. (Berlin: Otto Kirchner, 1922), 2:215–216.

65. Chamberlin, *Russian Revolution*, 2:320.

66. Zarubin and Zarubin, *Bez pobeditelei*, 263.

67. Chamberlin, *Russian Revolution*, 2:282–283.

68. Wrangel, *Always With Honour*, 238.

69. Lukomskii, *Vospominaniia*, 2:214–219; Chamberlin, *Russian Revolution*, 2:323.

70. Chamberlin, *Russian Revolution*, 2:328.

71. Wrangel, *Always With Honour*, 28–29.

72. Ibid., 239; Oleg Budnitskii, *Russian Jews Between the Reds and the Whites, 1917–1920*, trans. Timothy J. Portice (Philadelphia: University of Pennsylvania Press, 2012), 210.

73. O. V. Budnitskii, *Rossiiskie evrei mezhdu krasnymi i belymi (1917–1920)* (Moscow: ROSSPEN, 2005), 266–267; statement, 267; Budnitskii, *Russian Jews*, 210.

74. Budnitskii, *Rossiiskie evrei*, 213–219; 216 (Maklakov); Budnitskii, *Russian Jews*, 211–215.

75. Anthony Kröner, *The White Knight of the Black Sea: The Life of General Peter Wrangel* (The Hague: Leuxenhoff, 2010), 237–238.

76. Lukomskii, *Vospominaniia*, 2:216; Chamberlin, *Russian Revolution*, 2:321.

77. Chamberlin, *Russian Revolution*, 2:321; Wrangel, *Always With Honour*, 241–242, 254 (Millerand's message to M. Basily, Russian Chargé d'Affaires in Paris, August 10, 1920).

78. Wrangel, *Always With Honour*, 242 (quote); Lukomskii, *Vospominaniia*, 2:234.

79. Lukomskii, *Vospominaniia*, 2:240.

80. Wrangel, *Always With Honour*, 241.

81. Mawdsley, *Russian Civil War*, 268; Lukomskii, *Vospominaniia*, 2:233–234.

82. Chamberlin, *Russian Revolution*, 2:232–234; John Erickson, *The Soviet High Command: A Military-Political History, 1918–1941*, 3rd ed. (London: Frank Cass, 2001), 102–103.

83. Chamberlin, *Russian Revolution*, 2:325.

84. Wrangel, *Always with Honour*, 259.

85. Chamberlin, *Russian Revolution*, 2:327.

86. Wrangel, *Always with Honour*, 261–262, 265, 277, 285 ("pile" as in text).

87. Ibid., 281, 291–292, 294–295; quote, 295.

88. Ibid., 296 (October 6, 1920 statement).

89. Mawdsley, *Russian Civil War*, 269; Erickson, *Soviet High Command*, 106.

90. Chamberlin, *Russian Revolution*, 2:328–329; Lukomskii, *Vospominaniia*, 2:236.

91. Mawdsley, *Russian Civil War*, 269; Konstantin Zalesskii, "Frunze," in *Grazhdanskaia voina v Rossii: Entsiklopediia katastrofy*, ed. Dmitrii Volodikhin and Sergei Volkov (Moscow: Sibirskii tsiriul'nik, 2010), 173 and 175.

92. "Prikaz Predsedatelia Revoliutsionnogo Voennogo Soveta Respubliki po armiiam Iuzhnogo fronta" (October 13, 1920), in L. Trotskii, *Kak vooruzhalas' revoliutsiia (na voennoi rabote)*, vol. 2.2: *Tysiacha deviat'sot dvadtsatyi god* (Moscow: Vysshii voennyi redaktsionnyi sovet, 1924), 213.

93. Mawdsley, *Russian Civil War*, 269–270.

94. Gleb Eliseev, "Bliukher," in *Grazhdanskaia voina v Rossii*, ed. Volodikhin and Volkov, 329.

95. Lukomskii, *Vospominaniia*, 2:236–237.

96. Wrangel, *Always with Honour*, 319.

97. Mawdsley, *Russian Civil War*, 270; Lukomskii, *Vospominaniia*, 2:238–239; Chamberlin, *Russian Revolution*, 2:330–232; Wrangel, *Always with Honour*, 320–327 (evacuation).

98. Stephen Kotkin, *Stalin*, vol. 1: *Paradoxes of Power, 1878–1928* (New York: Penguin, 2014), 332 (no accurate figures).

99. Lukomskii, *Vospominaniia*, 2: 237–238; Mawdsley, *Russian Civil War*, 271 (quote).

100. *Poslednie dni Kryma: Vpechatleniia, fakty i dokumenty*, ed. V. L. Burtsev (Constantinople: Pressa, 1920), 46–47.

## PART V: CHAPTER 10

1. Sergei A. Pavliuchenkov, *Krest'ianskii Brest, ili predystoriia bol'shevistkogo NEPa* (Moscow: Russkoe knigoizd., 1996), 25; Mauricio Borrero, *Hungry Moscow: Scarcity and Urban Society in the Russian Civil War, 1917–1921* (New York: Peter Lang, 2003), ch. 5.

2. Pavliuchenkov, *Krest'ianskii Brest*, 3.

3. Text in *Documents of Russian History, 1914–1917*, ed. Frank Alfred Golder (New York and London: The Century, 1927), 623–625.

4. December 31, 1917, testimony, cited in G. K. Gins (George K. Guins), *Sibir', soiuzniki i Kolchak: Povorotnyi moment russkoi istorii, 1918–1920 gg.: Vpechatleniia i mysli chlena Omskogo pravitel'stva* (Peking: Russkaia dukhovnaia missiia, 1921), 31; Orlando Figes, *Peasant Russia, Civil War: The Volga Countryside in Revolution (1917–1921)* (Oxford: Clarendon, 1989), 52–53. Figes is a principal source for this chapter.

5. Cited, Figes, *Peasant Russia*, 53.

6. Harold H. Fisher, *The Famine in Soviet Russia, 1919–1923: The Operations of the American Relief Administration* (New York: Macmillan, 1927), 486.

7. Figes, *Peasant Russia*, 47–49, 56–57, 70–71.

8. Aaron B. Retish, *Russia's Peasants in Revolution and Civil War: Citizenship, Identity, and the Creation of the Soviet State, 1914–1922* (Cambridge: Cambridge University Press, 2008), 120, 128, 133.

9. Figes, *Peasant Russia*, 102, 105.

10. A. Berelovich and V. Danilov, "Dokumenty VChK-OGPU-NKVD o sovetskoi derevne (1918–1939 gg.)," in *Sovetskaia derevnia glazami VChK-OGPU-NKVD: Dokumenty i materialy*, ed. A. Berelovich and V. Danilov, 4 vols. (Moscow: ROSSPEN, 1998–2000), vol. 1, *1918–1922* (2000), 8–12.

11. V. Danilov et al., "Nauchno-issledovatel'skii proekt 'Krest'ianskaia revoliutsiia v Rossii, 1902–1922 gg.' (Vmesto predisloviia)," in *Krest'ianskoe vosstanie v Tambovskoi gubernii v 1919–1921 gg., "Antonovshchina": Dokumenty i materialy*, ed. V. Danilov, T. Shanin et al. (Tambov: Intertsentr, 1994), 9 (quote).

12. Quoted, Lars T. Lih, *Bread and Authority in Russia, 1914–1921* (Berkeley: University of California Press, 1990), 106; also Danilov et al., "Nauchno-issledovatel'skii proekt," 9. Lih is a principal source for this chapter.

13. Lih, *Bread*, 107–109.

14. Quoted, ibid., 101.

15. Figes, *Peasant Russia*, 353.

16. Danilov et al., "Nauchno-issledovatel'skii proekt," 8 (September 13/26, 1917).

17. Lih, *Bread*, 111, 117 (quotes).

18. James W. Heinzen, *Inventing a Soviet Countryside: State Power and the Transformation of Rural Russia, 1917–1929* (Pittsburgh: University of Pittsburgh Press, 2004), 13–14, 24–25.

19. Paul Robert Magocsi, *A History of Ukraine* (Seattle: University of Washington Press, 1996), 326.

20. Figes, *Peasant Russia*, 249.

21. Lih, *Bread*, 134.

22. Heinzen, *Inventing*, 37; Danilov et al., "Nauchno-issledovatel'skii proekt," 9.

23. Lih, *Bread*, 119–121, 123–127; Figes, *Peasant Russia*, 258.

24. Lih, *Bread*, 128–130; see A. Iu. Davidov, *Meshochniki: Nelegal'noe snabzhenie rossi-iskogo naseleniia i vlast' 1917–1921 gg.* (St. Petersburg: Nauka, 2002).

25. Alessandro Stanziani, "La gestion des approvisionnements et la restauration de la *gosudarstvennost'*: Le *Narkomprod*, l'armée et les paysans (1918–1921)," *Cahiers du Monde russe* 38.1/2 (1997): 85–86.

26. A. Tyrkova-Williams, *Why Soviet Russia is Starving* (London: Russian Liberation Committee, 1919), 5.

27. Ibid., 6.

28. Stanziani, "La gestion," 85.

29. Danilov et al., "Nauchno-issledovatel'skii proekt," 9; Figes, *Peasant Russia*, 256, 258, 264.

30. Stanziani, "La gestion," 85.

31. May 9, 1918, at Soviet Executive Committee, quoted A. V. Shestakov, *Kombedy RSFSR: Sbornik dekretov i dokumentov o komitetakh bednoty* (Moscow: Sovetskoe zakonodatel'stvo, 1933), 11.

32. Shestakov, *Kombedy*, 13 (including quote).

33. Ibid., 11–12.

34. Stanziani, "La gestion," 86.

35. Shestakov, *Kombedy*, 12–13, 20.

36. Ibid., 19.

37. Erik C. Landis, *Bandits and Partisans: The Antonov Movement in the Russian Civil War* (Pittsburgh: University of Pittsburgh Press, 2008), 10–11. Landis is a principal source for this chapter.

38. Stanziani, "La gestion," 86–87, 100.

39. Figes, *Peasant Russia*, 190–192, 194–198.

40. Landis, *Bandits*, 13.

41. Shestakov, *Kombedy*, 19; Figes, *Peasant Russia*, 155–156.

42. Figes, *Peasant Russia*, 253–255.

43. Shestakov, *Kombedy*, 15, 16 (quote).

44. Ibid., 15, 16 (August 17, 1918, quote).

45. No. 46, "Neskol'ko slov o predotvrashchenii belogvardeiskikh i kulatskikh vystuplenii v derevne" (iz *Ezhenedel'nika chrezvychainykh komissii po bor'be s kontrrevoliutsiei i spekuliatsiei*) (September 29, 1918), in *Sovetskaia derevnia*, ed. Berelovich and Danilov, 86; Figes, *Peasant Russia*, 188–189 (class war, merciless struggle).

46. L. Borisova, V. Vinogradov, A. Ivnitskii, and V. Kondrashin, "Informatsionnye materialy VChK-OGPU za 1918–1922 gg. kak istoricheskii istochnik," in *Sovetskaia derevnia*, ed. Berelovich and Danilov, 23–24.

47. T. V. Osipova, *Rossiiskoe krest'ianstvo v revoliutsii i grazhdanskoi voine* (Moscow: Strelets, 2001), 299–301.

48. No. 33, "Iz biulletenia VChK (August 6, 1918) – Okhanskaia chrezvychainaia komissiia (Permskaia gub.)," in *Sovetskaia derevnia*, ed. Berelovich and Danilov, 80.

49. No. 34, "Iz biulletenia VChK (August 8, 1918) – Smolenskaia gub.," in *Sovetskaia derevnia*, ed. Berelovich and Danilov, 81.

50. No. 46, "Neskol'ko slov," 87.

51. No. 60, "Iz svodki operativnogo otdela shtaba korpusa voisk VChK ob uchastii chastei korpusa v podavlenii kontrrevoliutsionnykh vosstanii za period s 1 oktiabria po 25 noiabria 1918 g.," in *Sovetskaia derevnia*, ed. Berelovich and Danilov, 105.

52. Stanziani, "La gestion," 87.

53. Quoted, Lih, *Bread*, 169.

54. Figes, *Peasant Russia*, 198–220; Stanziani, "La gestion," 89 (abolished December 2, 1918); Lih, *Bread*, 178–179.

55. Lih, *Bread*, 168–172; Figes, *Peasant Russia*, 260 (translates *prodrazverstka* as "food levy"); Silvana Malle, *The Economic Organization of War Communism, 1918–1921* (Cambridge: Cambridge University Press, 1985), 401 ("the law on *prodrazverstka* represented an enormous effort in organizing a state market in cereals, as compared with the rough policy of requisition carried out in 1918.").

56. Quoted, Lih, *Bread*, 175.

57. Fisher, *Famine*, 495–496. Import of agricultural machinery ceased in 1914; the value of domestic production shrank by 95 percent between 1914 and 1921: Serguei Adamets, *Guerre civile et famine en Russie: Le pouvoir bolchevique et la population face à la catastrophe démographique, 1917–1923* (Paris: Institut d'études slaves, 2003), 48.

58. Figes, *Peasant Russia*, 258–260.

59. Lih, *Bread*, 179–180, 184.

60. Figes, *Peasant Russia*, 249–251; Osipova, *Rossiiskoe krest'ianstvo*, 298.

61. Figes, *Peasant Russia*, 260–261, 268–271.

62. Lih, *Bread*, 193–194.

63. Figes, *Peasant Russia*, 66–67.

64. Ibid., 73–89.

65. Figes, *Peasant Russia*, 323–324.

66. Berelovich and Danilov, "Dokumenty VChK-OGPU-NKVD," 10–11, 11 (quote).

67. Danilov et al., "Nauchno-issledovatel'skii proekt," 12.

68. No. 189, "Doklad sekretnogo otdela VChK o povstancheskom dvizhenii po sostoianiiu na noiabr' 1920 g." (December 11, 1920), in *Sovetskaia derevnia*, ed. Berelovich and Danilov, 363–365.

69. Ibid., 365–379.

70. Osipova, *Rossiiskoe krest'ianstvo*, 296–297.

71. Mikhail Frenkin, *Tragediia krest'ianskikh vosstanii v Rossii, 1918–1921 gg.* (Jerusalem: "Leksikon," 1987), 78–79.

72. Osipova, *Rossiiskoe krest'ianstvo*, 301–302.

73. Erik C. Landis, "Who Were the 'Greens'? Rumor and Collective Identity in the Russian Civil War," *Russian Review* 69 (2010): 30–46.

74. Osipova, *Rossiiskoe krest'ianstvo*, 304.

75. Ibid., 302–305, 316–317, 320.

76. Figes, *Peasant Russia*, 324–328.

77. Ibid., 330 (quotes), 329.

78. Osipova, *Rossiiskoe krest'ianstvo*, 307.

79. Figes, *Peasant Russia*, 332–333.

80. Ibid., 333–335; Osipova, *Rossiiskoe krest'ianstvo*, 324.

81. Figes, *Peasant Russia*, 336–337; Osipova, *Rossiiskoe krest'ianstvo*, 326–327; *Sovetskaia derevnia*, ed. Berelovich and Danilov, 803.

82. Figes, *Peasant Russia*, 336–340, 339 (quote); Osipova, *Rossiiskoe krest'ianstvo*, 328.

83. Danilov et al., "Nauchno-issledovatel'skii proekt," 8, 10–11.

84. Ibid., 10.

85. Landis, *Bandits*, 5–8, 15–17.

86. Ibid., 15, 24; Danilov et al, "Nauchno-issledovatel'skii proekt," 10.

87. Danilov et al, "Nauchno-issledovatel'skii proekt," 10.

88. *Sovetskaia derevnia*, ed. Berelovich and Danilov, 762; Landis, *Bandits*, 72; Osipova, *Rossiiskoe krest'ianstvo*, 328.

89. Landis, *Bandits*, 2, 72; *Sovetskaia derevnia*, ed. Berelovich and Danilov, 762 (origins of Union).

90. Danilov et al., "Nauchno-issledovatel'skii proekt," 17; Landis, *Bandits*, 43–45, 47.

91. Landis, *Bandits*, 52–58.

92. Danilov et al., "Nauchno-issledovatel'skii proekt," 13–14.

93. Quoted, Landis, *Bandits*, 105.

94. "Prikazy po 1-i partizanskoi armii Tambovskogo kraia," in *Antonovshchina*, ed. Danilov and Shanin, 86–89; Landis, *Bandits*, 106, 110–111, 118.

95. Quoted, Landis, *Bandits*, 124–125, from *Antonovshchina*, ed. Danilov and Shanin, 79–80.

96. Landis, *Bandits*, 144–145. On the self-representation of peasant movements and the importance of programs, see Viktor Kondrashin, "Lozungi i programa krest'ianskogo povstancheskogo dvizheniia v gody grazhdanskoi voiny," in *Krest'ianskii front, 1918-1922 gg.: Sbornik statei i materialov*, ed. A. V. Posadskii (Moscow: AIRO-XXI, 2013), 80–98.

97. Quoted, Landis, *Bandits*, 131.

98. Ibid., 127–135.

99. Ibid., 142–143, quote, 142.

100. Ibid., 158–163.

## PART VI: CHAPTER 1

1. Sergei A. Pavliuchenkov, *Voennyi kommunizm v Rossii: Vlast' i massy* (Moscow: RKT-Istoriia, 1997), 46.

2. Silvana Malle, *The Economic Organization of War Communism, 1918–1921* (Cambridge: Cambridge University Press, 1985), 24–25.

3. Quoted, ibid., 11.

4. Pavliuchenkov, *Voennyi kommunizm*, 8–9, 11.

5. Ibid., 57, 144.

6. Quoted ibid., 52, from spring 1918.

7. Malle, *Economic Organization*, 47.

8. Ibid., 50–56.

9. Ibid., 59–62, 64, 55–67.

10. Ibid., 101.

11. Ibid., 102–104.

12. Ibid., 129, 132–137.

13. Ibid., 89.

14. Ibid., 469–476.
15. Mauricio Borrero, *Hungry Moscow: Scarcity and Urban Society in the Russian Civil War, 1917–1921* (New York: Peter Lang, 2003), 65–66. Same percentages in Diane Koenker, "Urbanization and Deurbanization in the Russian Revolution and Civil War," *Journal of Modern History* 57.3 (1985): 424; cf. Stephen Wheatcroft, "Soviet Statistics and Nutrition and Mortality During Times of Famine, 1917–22 and 1931–33," *Cahiers du monde russe* 30.4 (1997): 527 (same figure for Petrograd, only one-third for Moscow).
16. S. P. Postnikov and M. A. Fel'dman, *Sotsiokul'turnyi oblik promyshlennykh rabochikh Rossii v 1900–1941 gg.* (Moscow: ROSSPEN, 2009), 311–312; A. A. Il'iukhov, *Zhizn' v epokhu peremen: Material'noe polozhenie gorodskikh zhitelei v gody revoliutsii i grazhdanskoi voiny* (Moscow: ROSSPEN, 2007), 3 and overall.
17. Postnikov and Fel'dman, *Sotsiokul'turnyi oblik*, 312–313; Ol'ga Porshneva, "Vlast' i rabochie Urala: Evoliutsiia vzaimootnoshenii v usloviiakh Grazhdanskoi voiny," *Rossiiskaia istoriia* 1 (2013): 50–51.
18. Malle, *Economic Organization*, 478–479.
19. Ibid., 483–485. Thanks to Bill Rosenberg for this point and other comments on this chapter.
20. Ibid., 485–486.
21. Ibid., 487, 488 (quotes).
22. Dmitrii Churakov, *Revoliutsiia, gosudarstvo, rabochii protest: Formy, dinamika i priroda massovykh vystuplenii rabochikh v Sovetskoi Rossii, 1917–1918 gody* (Moscow: ROSSPEN, 2004), 352–353. Churakov is the principal reference for this chapter.
23. Igor V. Narskii, *Zhizn' v katastrofe: Budni naseleniia Urala v 1917–1922 gg.* (Moscow: ROSSPEN, 2001), 38–39.
24. Pavliuchenkov, *Voennyi kommunizm*, 146–147.
25. Ibid., 147–149, 152 (quote).
26. Ibid., 151–153.
27. Churakov, *Revoliutsiia*, 354–355.
28. Pavliuchenkov, *Voennyi kommunizm*, 155, 157.
29. For an early treatment of this subject, see Vladimir N. Brovkin, *The Mensheviks after October: Socialist Opposition and the Rise of the Bolshevik Dictatorship* (Ithaca: Cornell University Press, 1987), and other of his works. More recently: *Men'sheviki v 1918 godu*, ed. A. P. Nenarokov and Ziva Galili (Moscow: ROSSPEN, 1999); *Men'sheviki v 1919–1920 gg.*, ed. A. P. Nenarokov and Ziva Galili (Moscow: ROSSPEN, 2000); A. P. Nenarokov, *Pravyi men'shevizm: Prozreniia rossiiskoi sotsial-demokratii* (Moscow: Novyi khronograf, 2011).
30. Churakov, *Revoliutsiia*, 118–120, 125–128; *Rabochee oppozitsionnoe dvizhenie v bol'shevistskoi Rossii 1918 g.: Sobraniia upolnomochennykh fabrik i zavodov: Dokumenty i materialy*, ed. D. B. Pavlov (Moscow: ROSSPEN, 2006); *Sobranie upolnomochennykh i piterskie rabochie v 1918 godu: Dokumenty i materialy*, ed. E. Tsudzi (St. Petersburg: Sankt-Peterburgskii universitet, 2006).

31. Churakov, *Revoliutsiia*, 129–130, 131–132 (quote).
32. Ibid., 136–159.
33. Ibid., 170.
34. Quoted, ibid., 177, from "Pis'mo K. M. Ermolaeva P. B. Aksel'rodu v Stokgol'm" (Petrograd, June 17, 1918), in *Mensheviki v 1918 godu*, ed. Galili and Nenarokov, 558.
35. Quoted, Churakov, *Revoliutsiia*, 200.
36. Ibid., 66–67.
37. Ibid., 68–69; quote, 68.
38. Ibid., 70–73.
39. Ibid., 74–76.
40. Ibid., 89.
41. Ibid., 89–93.
42. Ibid., 104, citing M. A. Drobov, *Malaia voina: Partizanstvo i diversii* (Moscow: Al'manakh "Vympel," 1998), first published 1931, then suppressed, discovered, and reissued.
43. Churakov, *Revoliutsiia*, 107–108.
44. Ibid., 213–215.
45. Ibid., 223, 225–226.
46. Quoted, ibid., 230.
47. Ibid., 232–236.
48. Porshneva, "Vlast' i rabochie Urala," 48–49.
49. Churakov, *Revoliutsiia*, 258–260; Aaron B. Retish, "The Izhevsk Revolt of 1918: The Fateful Clash of Revolutionary Coalitions, Paramilitarism, and Bolshevik Power," in *Russia's Home Front in War and Revolution, 1914–22*, book 1: *Russia's Revolution in Regional Perspective*, ed. Sarah Badcock, Liudmila G. Novikova, and Aaron B. Retish (Bloomington: Slavica, 2015), 299–322; A. V. Korobeinikov, *Votkinskaia Narodnaia armiia v 1918 g.*, pt. 1 (Izhevsk: Idnakar, 2013).
50. Sociology from M. A. Fel'dman, "Izhevsko-Votkinskoe rabochee vosstanie skvoz' prizmu sotsial'noi istorii Rossii," *Rossiiskaia istoriia* 3 (2012): 13–14; Postnikov and Fel'dman, *Sotsiokul'turnyi oblik*, 311 (state factories).
51. Quoted, Fel'dman, "Izhevsko-Votkinskoe rabochee vosstanie," 16.
52. Churakov, *Revoliutsiia*, 258–263.
53. Porshneva, "Vlast' i rabochie Urala," 49–50.
54. Churakov, *Revoliutsiia*, 272–277.
55. A. V. Posadskii, *Ot Tsaritsyna do Syzrani: Ocherki grazhdanskoi voiny na Volge* (Moscow: AIRO-XXI, 2010), 44–46 (on *frontovik* unions).
56. Quoted, Churakov, *Revoliutsiia*, 274.
57. Ibid., 271–274.
58. Ibid., 274–277.
59. Ibid., 281–283.
60. Ibid., 284–288.
61. Ibid., 290.

62. Ibid., 299, quoting *Izhevskii zashchitnik* (August 30, September 3, 1918).
63. Ibid., 306–307; Fel'dman, "Izhevsko-Votkinskoe rabochee vosstanie," 16–17 (figures and percentage of workers).
64. Quoted, Churakov, *Revoliutsiia*, 313 (*nasil'niki-bol'sheviki*).
65. Quoted, ibid., 319.
66. Ibid., 291–325; quote, 324.
67. S. V. Iarov, *Proletarii kak politik: Politicheskaia psikhologiia rabochikh Petrograda v 1917–1923 gg.* (St. Petersburg: Bulanin, 1999), 144–145.
68. Above paragraphs from Jonathan Aves, *Workers Against Lenin: Labour Protest and the Bolshevik Dictatorship* (London: Tauris, 1996), 39–47 (railroads); 47–56 (munitions).
69. Iarov, *Proletarii kak politik*, 136–138; Aves, *Workers*, 55.
70. Iarov, *Proletarii kak politik*, 19.
71. Aves, *Workers*, 69–71.
72. Narskii, *Zhizn'*, 242–243.
73. Porshneva, "Vlast' i rabochie Urala," 60, 52 (quote), 53–54, citing Iarov.
74. Quotes, Porshneva, "Vlast' i rabochie Urala," 51.
75. Quotes, ibid., 51, 52, citing Narskii, *Zhizn'*, 392. The contrasting terms are *soznatel'nye* and *bessoznatel'nye*.
76. Quoted, Porshneva, "Vlast' i rabochie Urala," 52.

## PART VI: CHAPTER 2

1. Paul Avrich, *Kronstadt 1921* (Princeton: Princeton University Press, 1970; rpt. New York: Norton, 1974), 51–54.
2. Fedor Gurvich [Dan], *Dva goda skitanii (1919–1921)* (Berlin: Russische Bücherzentrale "Obrasowanije," 1922), 199; G. I. Il'iashchuk, "Dan," in *Politicheskie deiateli Rossii 1917: Biograficheskii slovar'*, ed. P. V. Volobuev (Moscow: Bol'shaia rossiiskaia entsiklopediia, 1993), 94–96.
3. This incident from the diary of Captain I. I. Rengarten, in *Posledniia novosti*, no. 5813 (February 22, 1937), excerpted in *The Russian Provisional Government, 1917: Documents*, ed. Robert Paul Browder and Alexander F. Kerensky, 3 vols. (Stanford: Stanford University Press, 1961), 3:1582.
4. Avrich, *Kronstadt 1921*, 61.
5. Ibid., 89–90.
6. A. S. Pukhov, *Kronshtadtskii miatezh v 1921* (Leningrad: Molodaia gvardiia, 1931); *Kronshtadtskii miatezh: Sbornik statei, vospominanii i dokumentov*, ed. N. A. Kornatovskii (Leningrad: Leningradskii institut istorii VKP/b/, 1931).
7. "Vvedenie," in *Kronshtadt 1921: Dokumenty o sobytiiakh v Kronshtadte vesnoi 1921 g.*, ed. V. P. Naumov and A. A. Kosakovskii (Moscow: Mezhdunarodnyi fond "Demokratiia," 1997), 7; Avrich, *Kronstadt 1921*, 36.
8. Dan, *Dva goda*, 106.
9. Avrich, *Kronstadt 1921*, 35.

10. "Shifrogramma sekretaria Petrogradskogo Gubkoma Partii Zorina zamestiteliu predsedatelia Revvoensoveta Sklianskomu" (February 11, 1921), in *Kronshtadt 1921*, 24; "Zapiska Podvoiskogo, Mekhonoshina, Muralova, Kedrova, Menzhinskogo, Iagody v TsK RKP/b/" (February 31, 1921), ibid., 24–25; "Iz svodki Petrogradskoi gubcheka v VChK o polozhenii v Petrograde" (reports from February 1–15, 1921), ibid., 25–27; "Telegramma…Dzerzhinskomu o polozhenii v Moskve na 23 fevralia 1921 g. i meropriiatiiakh MChK v sviazi s zabastovkami i volneniiami na moskovskikh predpriiatiiakh" (February 23, 1921), ibid., 27–29; "Telegramma…Dzerzhinskomu o polozhenii v Moskve na 24 fevralia 1921 g." (February 24, 1921), ibid., 29. On begging soldiers: Dan, *Dva goda*, 105.

11. "Vvedenie," in *Kronshtadt 1921*, 8.

12. "Telegramma…Dzerzhinskomu o polozhenii v Moskve na 24 fevralia 1921 g.," in *Kronshtadt 1921*, 29; "Iz protokola zasedaniia biuro petrogradskogo komiteta RKP/b/" (February 24, 1921), ibid., 32–33.

13. "Vvedenie," in *Kronshtadt 1921*, 8; "Prikaz VChK 'Ob usilenii bor'by s kontr-revoliutsiei'" (February 28, 1921), ibid., 36–37.

14. Avrich, *Kronstadt 1921*, 42.

15. Ibid., 48–49; Dan, *Dva goda*, 108, 110–113, 120–121.

16. Dan, *Dva goda*, 114–116.

17. Dan, *Dva goda*, 115–118, 120–122.

18. *Kronshtadt 1921*, 385 (note); "Protokol doprosa Dana" (April 19, 1921), ibid., 266–269.

19. Avrich, *Kronstadt 1921*, 63–68.

20. "Doklad nachal'nika 1-go Spetsial'nogo otdela VChK Fel'dmana v osobyi otdel VChK" (December 10, 1920), in *Kronshtadt 1921*, 19–23; Trotskii, "O sobytiiakh v Kronshtadte: Interv'iu, dannoe predstaviteliam inostrannoi pechati" (March 16, 1921), in L. Trotskii, *Kak vooruzhalas' revoliutsiia (na voennoi rabote)*, vol. 3, pt. 1: *Tysiacha deviat'sot dvadtsat' pervyi–tretii gody* (Moscow: Vysshii voennyi redaktsionnyi sovet, 1924), 204; "Nachalo dvizheniia v Kronshtadte," in *Pravda o Kronshtadte: Ocherk geroicheskoi bor'by kronshtadttsev protiv diktatury Kommunisticheskoi partii* (Prague: Volia Rossii, 1921), 7.

21. Avrich, *Kronstadt 1921*, 71–73; *Pravda o Kronshtadte*, 46–47; "Vvedenie," in *Kronshtadt 1921*, 9; "Obrashchenie Kronshtadtskogo revkoma k zhelezno-dorozhnikam" (n.d.), in ibid., 136.

22. "Nachalo dvizheniia," in *Pravda o Kronshtadte*, 8; "Vvedenie," in *Kronshtadt 1921*, 9; Alexander Berkman, *The Kronstadt Rebellion* (Berlin: Der Syndikalist, 1922), 9.

23. Biographical note, *Kronshtadt 1921*, 402.

24. On naval sociology: Avrich, *Kronstadt*, 90.

25. "Vvedenie," in *Kronshtadt 1921*, 9 ; "Nachalo dvizheniia," in *Pravda o Kronshtadte*, 10; on leaflets with the platform distributed among the workers: Victor Serge, *Memoirs of a Revolutionary*, trans. Peter Sedgwick with George Paizis (1951; New York: New York Review of Books, 2012), 147, 149 (arrest).

26. *Kronshtadt 1921*, 83, quoting from *Pravda o Kronshtadte*, 116; Kuz'min's words reproduced in Berkman, *Kronstadt Rebellion*, 13.

27. "Vvedenie," in *Kronshtadt 1921*, 9; "Kak sozdalsia vremennyi revoliutsionnyi komitet," in *Pravda o Kronshtadte*, 115–116; Avrich, *Kronstadt 1921*, 84–85.

28. "Vvedenie," in *Kronshtadt 1921*, 10–11; on worker response: S. V. Iarov, *Proletarii kak politik: Politicheskaia psikhologiia rabochikh Petrograda v 1917–1923 gg.* (St. Petersburg: Bulanin, 1999), 8–9, 115–119; Serge, *Memoirs*, 147.

29. Iarov, *Proletarii kak politik*, 115.

30. "Kronshtadt prinimaet mery samooborony," in *Pravda o Kronshtadte*, 13–15; quote 14; Avrich, *Kronstadt 1921*, 99.

31. "Soobshchenie iz Petrograda o vziatii zalozhnikov" (March 4, 1921), in *Kronshtadt 1921*, 95; "Spisok sledstvennykh materialov po delu 'Kronshtadtskii miatezh' na zalozhnikov za generala Kozlovskogo," ibid., 96.

32. "K tovarishcham rabochim i krest'ianam!" (no date), in *Pravda o Kronshtadte*, 119–120.

33. "'Gospoda' ili 'tovarishchi'" (March 6, 1921), in *Pravda o Kronshtadte*, 61; quoted, Avrich, *Kronstadt 1921*, 114.

34. "Za chto my boremsia," in *Pravda o Kronshtadte*, 82–84 (*lichnost' cheloveka*).

35. Avrich, *Kronstadt 1921*, 86–87.

36. "Vvedenie," in *Kronshtadt 1921*, 11.

37. "Poslednee preduprezhdenie: K garnizonu i naseleniiu Kronshtadta i miatezhnykh fortov" (March 5, 1921), in Trotskii, *Kak*, 3:1, 202; reprinted, "Trotskii ugrozhaet rasgromom," in *Pravda o Kronshtadte*, 73; cited, Avrich, *Kronstadt 1921*, 144.

38. Avrich, *Kronstadt 1921*, 145.

39. "Vozzvanie 'Krasnoarmeitsev' k 'Krasnoflottsam,'" in *Pravda o Kronshtadte*, 74; "Rezoliutsii II," ibid., 75.

40. "Patronov ne zhalet'," *Izvestiia VRK* (March 7, 1921), in *Pravda o Kronshtadte*, 68; cited Avrich, *Kronstadt 1921*, 145.

41. "Vvedenie," in *Kronshtadt 1921*, 12.

42. "Raport upolnomochennogo Osobogo otdela VChK predsedateliu Revvoensoveta Respubliki" (March 7, 1921), in V. P. Naumov and A. A. Kosakovskii, eds., "Kronshtadtskaia tragediia 1921 goda" [Pt. 2], *Voprosy istorii* 5 (1994): 10.

43. V. Danilov et al., "Nauchno-issledovatel'skii proekt 'Krest'ianskaia revoliutsiia v Rossii, 1902–1922 gg.' (Vmesto predisloviia)," in *Krest'ianskoe vosstanie v Tambovskoi gubernii v 1919–1921 gg., "Antonovshchina": Dokumenty i materialy*, ed. V. Danilov, T. Shanin et al. (Tambov: Intertsentr, 1994), 13; T. V. Osipova, *Rossiiskoe krest'ianstvo v revoliutsii i grazhdanskoi voine* (Moscow: Strelets, 2001), 322–323.

44. Osipova, *Rossiiskoe krest'ianstvo*, 323 (including quote).

45. Erik C. Landis, *Bandits and Partisans: The Antonov Movement in the Russian Civil War* (Pittsburgh: University of Pittsburgh Press, 2008), 165–166. Landis is a principal reference for this chapter.

46. "Vvedenie," in *Kronshtadt 1921*, 12 (quote).

47. Ibid.

48. Avrich, *Kronstadt 1921*, 150–151.

49. "Iz dokladnoi zapiski po voprosu ob organizatsii vosstaniia v Kronshtadte" (n.d. [1921]), no signature, in *Kronshtadt 1921*, 42.

50. "Vvedenie," in *Kronshtadt 1921*, 13; Avrich, *Kronstadt 1921*, 152–154.

51. Avrich, *Kronstadt 1921*, 155 (on Jews, citing *Kronshtadtskii miatezh*, ed. Kornatovskii, 95), 179–180; *Pravda o Kronshtadte*, 94–98, 129 (no mention of Jews).

52. "Pis'mo Trotskogo v Politbiuro TsK RKP/b/" (March 10, 1921), in V. P. Naumov and A. A. Kosakovskii, eds., "Kronshtadtskaia tragediia 1921 goda" [Pt. 3], *Voprosy istorii* 6 (1994): 26.

53. "Pis'mo komanduiushchego 7-oi armii M. Tukhachevskogo V. I. Leninu" (March 10, 1921), in ibid., 27–28.

54. Avrich, *Kronstadt 1921*, 197.

55. "Raport o nastroenniiakh polkov 27-i strelkovoi divizii Nachal'niku ODTChK, Ptrgrd, Balt." (March 12, 1921), in Naumov and Kosakovskii, eds., "Kronshtadtskaia tragediia 1921 goda," [Pt. 3], 28. Also "Raport upolnomochennogo informatsionnoi chasti V. Nasonova v informchast' 1-go Osobogo otdeleniia" (n.d.), ibid., 31.

56. "Postanovlenie chrezvychainoi revoliutsionnoi troiki 1-go Osobootdeleniia Osobogo Otdela okhrany finliandskoi granitsy respubliki" (March 15, 1921), in Naumov and Kosakovskii, eds., "Kronshtadtskaia tragediia 1921 goda" [Pt. 3], 37.

57. "Prikaz voiskam 7-i armii no. 11/015 (Petrograd, March 15, 1921), signed Tukhachevskii, in ibid., 38; "Telegramma nachal'nika Osobogo otriada A. Nikolaeva" (March 17, 1921), ibid., 39; "Raport Predsedatelia Troek pri 1-m i 2-m Osobotdelenii Osobotdela Okhrfingran" (April 20, 1921), in V. P. Naumov and A. A. Kosakovskii, eds., "Kronshtadtskaia tragediia 1921 goda" [Pt. 4], *Voprosy istorii* 7 (1994): 24 (seventy-four executed).

58. "Vvedenie," in *Kronshtadt 1921*, 13–14.

59. Avrich, *Kronstadt 1921*, 200.

60. Ibid., 201–203.

61. "Vvedenie," in *Kronshtadt 1921*, 14.

62. Ibid.; Avrich, *Kronstadt 1921*, 213–214.

63. "Vvedenie," in *Kronshtadt 1921*, 14–15; "Raport Predsedatelia Troek pri 1-m i 2-m Osobotdelenii Osobotdela Okhrfingran" (April 20, 1921), in Naumov and Kosakovskii, eds., "Kronshtadtskaia tragediia 1921 goda" [Pt. 4], 25–26.

64. "Iz protokola zasedaniia prezidiuma Petrogradskoi chrezvychainoi komissii po bor'be s kontrrevoliutsiei, spekuliatsiei i prestupleniiami po dolzhnosti 20 aprelia 1921 g.," in *Kronshtadt 1921*, 307–330.

65. "Protokol doprosa Vershinina, chlena Kronshtadtskogo revkoma" (March 21, 1921), in ibid., 305–306.

66. "Zapiska Trotskogo Molotovu, Leninu i Dzerzhinskomu" (March 24, 1921), in Naumov and Kosakovskii, eds., "Kronshtadtskaia tragediia 1921 goda" [Pt. 4], 3.

67. Berkman, *Kronstadt Rebellion*, 42, 41.

68. Serge, *Memoirs*, 150–151.

69. Avrich, *Kronstadt 1921*, 103–125.

70. Quoted, Landis, *Bandits*, 209.

71. Ibid., 210–212; V. Danilov et al., "Nauchno-issledovatel'skii proekt," 14, 16.

72. Osipova, *Rossiiskoe krest'ianstvo*, 337 (Tukhachevskii's view of the campaign as a war against the population).

73. No. 199, Order No. 116: "Prikaz komandovaniia voiskami Tambovskoi gubernii o primenenii udushlivykh gazov protiv povstantsev" (June 12, 1921), signed Commander Tukhachevskii, in *Antonovshchina*, ed. Danilov and Shanin, 179; Landis, *Bandits*, 266–268.

74. No. 176, "Instruktsiia po iskoreneniu banditizma v Tambovskoi gubernii" (May 12, 1921—secret), signed Tukhachevskii, in *Antonovshchina*, ed. Danilov and Shanin, 163 (*epidemiia banditizma*).

75. No. 174, Order No. 130. "Prikaz komanduiushchego voiskami Tambovskoi gubernii M. N. Tukhachevskogo o merakh bor'by s povstantsami" (May 12, 1921); No. 175, "Prikaz Polnomochnoi komissii VTsIK s ob"iavleniem pravil poriadka vziatiia zalozhnikov i konfiskatsii imushchestva" (May 12, 1921); No. 176, "Instruktsiia po iskoreneniu banditizma v Tambovskoi gubernii" (May 12, 1921—secret), signed Tukhachevskii, in *Antonovshchina*, ed. Danilov and Shanin, 162–164.

76. No. 198, Order No. 171: "Prikaz Polnomochnoi komissii VTsIK o nachale provedeniia repressivnykh mer protiv otdel'nykh banditov i ukryvaiushchikh ikh semei" (June 11, 1921), signed Antonov-Ovseenko and Tukhachevskii, in *Antonovshchina*, ed. Danilov and Shanin, 179.

77. S. P. Mel'gunov, *"Krasnyi terror" v Rossii 1918–1923* (Berlin: Vataga, 1924), 17.

78. No. 232, "Iz doklada predsedatelia Tambovskoi uezdnoi politkomissii 4-go boeuchastka o rezul'tatakh okkupatsii naselennykh punktov Tambovskogo uezda" (not before June 23, 1921), in *Antonovshchina*, ed. Danilov and Shanin, 188; cited in different translation in Landis, *Bandits*, 236–237.

79. Landis, *Bandits*, 205–209.

80. Ibid., 237–239.

81. No. 267, "Doklad Glavkoma S. S. Kameneva predsedateliu Soveta truda i oborony o khode bor'by s povstanchestvom v Tambovskoi gubernii" (July 16, 1921), in *Antonovshchina*, ed. Danilov and Shanin, 224; Landis, *Bandits*, 239.

82. No. 266, "Zapiska komanduiushchego voiskami Tambovskoi gubernii M. N. Tukhachevskogo V. I. Leninu o polozhenii del v gubernii" (July 16, 1921—secret), in *Antonovshchina*, ed. Danilov and Shanin, 222; term cited in Landis, *Bandits*, esp. ch. 8.

83. Quoted, Landis, *Bandits*, 241, from No. 276, "Sekretnye tsirkuliary Polnomochnoi komissii VTsIK uezdnym politkomissiam o poriadke provedeniia prikazov No. 171 i 234" (July 20, 1921—secret), in *Antonovshchina*, ed. Danilov and Shanin, 228 (*so vsiu surovost'iu*).

84. Landis, *Bandits*, 242–244, 246–247, 250–252.

85. Ibid., 273–279.

86. Ibid., 280–281.

87. Harold H. Fisher, *The Famine in Soviet Russia, 1919–1923: The Operations of the American Relief Administration* (New York: Macmillan, 1927), 483; Serguei Adamets, "À l'origine de la diversité des mesures de la famine soviétique: La statistique des prix, des récoltes et de la consommation," *Cahiers du monde russe* 30.4 (1997): 575–577 (1921 harvest in Russian provinces half prewar level, in Ukrainian provinces only a quarter); Serguei Adamets, *Guerre civile et famine en Russie: Le pouvoir bolchevique et la population face à la catastrophe démographique, 1917–1923* (Paris: Institut d'études slaves, 2003), 47 (slightly different figures).

88. Fisher, *Famine*, 497 (quote), 499.

89. Ibid., 500–501 (quote, 500); James W. Long, "The Volga Germans and the Famine of 1921," *Russian Review* 51.4 (1992): 510–525.

90. Fisher, *Famine*, 504–505 (quote, 504).

91. Adamets, "À l'origine," 561.

92. Hakan Kirimli, "The Famine of 1921–22 in the Crimea and the Volga Basin and the Relief from Turkey," *Middle Eastern Studies* 39.1 (2003): 37–88.

93. Bertrand M. Patenaude, *The Big Show in Bololand: The American Relief Expedition to Soviet Russia in the Famine of 1921* (Stanford: Stanford University Press, 2002), 197–198.

94. Adamets, *Guerre civile*, 250–251, 260–261.

95. Ibid., 168–169.

96. D. A. Safonov, *Velikaia krest'ianskaia voina 1920–1921 gg. i Iuzhnyi Ural* (Orenburg: n.p., 1998), 90 ("krest'ianskii protest v itoge byl zadushen golodom"), quoted, Igor V. Narskii, *Zhizn' v katastrofe: Budni naseleniia Urala v 1917–1922 gg.* (Moscow: ROSSPEN, 2001), 44.

97. *"Ochistim Rossiiu nadolgo . . ." Repressii protiv inakomysliashchikh, konets 1921–nachalo 1923 g.*, ed. A. N. Artizov and V. S. Khristoforov (Moscow: Mezhdunarodnyi fond "Demokratiia," 2008).

## CONCLUSION

1. B. Maklakoff, "Vers la Révolution: La Russie de 1900 à 1917: Le Dénouement," *La Revue de Paris* 31.23 (December 1, 1924): 609.

2. Nicholas Berdyaev, *The Origin of Russian Communism*, trans. R. M. French (1937; Ann Arbor: University of Michigan Press, 1960), 112–113. First published in English in 1937; in Russian as *Istoki i smysl russkogo kommunizma* (Paris: YMCA, 1955).

3. S. A. Smith, *Russia in Revolution: An Empire in Crisis, 1890–1928* (Oxford: Oxford University Press, 2017), 377.

4. Max Weber, "Politics as a Vocation," in *From Max Weber: Essays in Sociology*, ed. and trans. H. H. Gerth and C. Wright Mills (New York: Oxford University Press, 1946), 77–78.

5. Peter Holquist, "'Information is the Alpha and Omega of Our Work': Bolshevik Surveillance in its Pan-European Perspective," *Journal of Modern History* 69.3 (1997): 415–450.

6. See Peter Holquist, *Making War, Forging Revolution: Russia's Continuum of Crisis, 1914–1921* (Cambridge, MA: Harvard University Press, 2002); Felix Schnell, *Räume des Schreckens: Gewalt und Gruppenmilitanz in der Ukraine, 1905–1933* (Hamburg: Hamburger Edition, 2012); Robert Gerwarth, *The Vanquished: Why the First World War Failed to End* (New York: Farrar, Straus and Giroux, 2016).

7. Quoted, Laura Engelstein, "The Dream of Civil Society in Tsarist Russia: Law, State, and Religion," in *Civil Society Before Democracy: Lessons from Nineteenth-Century Europe*, ed. Nancy Bermeo and Philip Nord (Lanham, MD: Rowman & Littlefield, 2000), 23.

8. Edward Hallett Carr, *The Russian Revolution: From Lenin to Stalin (1917–1929)*, intro. R. W. Davies (1979; New York: Palgrave Macmillan, 2004), 1.

# Acknowledgments

This book relies primarily on the work of other scholars, without whose research and narratives a synthesis of this kind would be impossible. Those to whom I am especially indebted are noted in the references and the Bibliographic Essay. I would also like to express my gratitude to colleagues in Russia who have labored over the past twenty-five years to edit and publish new archival sources, to the benefit of the international scholarly community. Most of my research has been done in the United States, in the outstanding collections of Yale University's Sterling Memorial Library and the Joseph Regenstein Library at the University of Chicago. In addition to the many published volumes on its shelves, including the latest titles from Russia and Europe, Regenstein offers a wide array of digitized material, which it shares with the patrons of other university libraries. Thanks, especially, to the Hathi Trust for transforming the way research is conducted. Thanks as well to the American Academy in Berlin, where I began work on the First World War. I am particularly grateful to the Slavonic Library of the National Library of Finland, in Helsinki, which has been a scholarly home away from home, and to its presiding spirit, Irina Lukka, who has been a true friend over the years. Thanks to her and to Lukáš Babka, at the Slavonic Library of the National Library of the Czech Republic, in Prague, for the use of images in their collections.

The book owes its existence to my editor at Oxford University Press in New York, Timothy Bent, who invited me to write a book that nonspecialist readers would find challenging and engaging—on a big topic, a "pivotal moment in history." Tim has served as coach, interlocutor, and first reader—a true editor in the best sense of the word. The entire team at Oxford University Press, New York, has been a model of professionalism and good spirit in the face of an implacable deadline. My thanks, in particular, to Amy Whitmer, and to outgoing Alyssa O'Connell and incoming Mariah White; thanks also to Russian-ready copy editor Stephen Dodson for "*chapany*."

I am fortunate also to have had the moral and intellectual support of a close group of friends and colleagues, on whose expertise and opinions I was able to draw. Conversations with Francine Hirsch, Boris Kolonitskii, William G. Rosenberg, and S. A. Smith enabled me to sharpen my ideas. Fran Hirsch, with her pitiless editorial eye, constructively demolished early versions of the introduction. Steve Smith's recent book on the revolution initiated a fruitful dialogue which has helped me formulate my point of view. Having a companion in the centenary run-up has been a great boon. Bill Rosenberg offered not only encouragement but a detailed reading of the manuscript, catching slips and misunderstandings and sharing wisdom derived from years of immersion in the subject. Boris Kolonitskii has inspired me with the originality of his own work and his scholarly civic-mindedness. Ziva Galili provided cogent observations and a reminder of the Menshevik point of view—to which I have not done justice, I know. For the errors and misconceptions that remain, the responsibility is all mine.

In personal terms, three ghosts have hovered over the proceedings: my maternal grandfather, Morris Greenfield (1886–1961), who lived through the events I am describing but escaped in time; my father, Stanley Engelstein (1920–2010), who obsessed over them all his life; and my forever missed colleague, friend, and mentor, Reggie Zelnik (1936–2004), who would have set me straight on many points.

Most crucially, this book has been written in constant conversation with Michael Geyer, who pressed me to decide what I really wanted to say—and come out with it. His wisdom as a historian, his intellectual courage and generosity, and his deep moral commitments have all contributed in fundamental ways to this project. He has broadened my outlook, as well as my life. In his company I am "mehr als ich bin."

Finally, I have always had in mind, as I wrote, my two ideal readers—and two ideal brothers—Daniel Engelstein and Larry Engelstein, who took the time to read the manuscript from beginning to end and asked very good questions. Both have spent their working lives in the cause of fairness and justice, which is what many of the revolution's participants thought it was about.

# Bibliographic Essay

Innumerable books have been published over the last century about the Russian Revolution, in all its many dimensions. Despite the constraints imposed by Soviet orthodoxy, historians in the Soviet Union managed to produce serious scholarly work on the highly political subject of the Russian Revolution and Civil War, just as some of us in the West managed to conduct serious research despite even more limited access to sources and our own political biases. The situation for everyone changed for the better, however, in the 1990s. As soon as the archives relaxed their restrictions, the Russians began actively publishing previously inaccessible documents and new kinds of books, and a new dialogue opened between native and foreign scholars. The recent publications of Russian colleagues and their search for fresh interpretations have strongly influenced my own thinking. I have also relied heavily on the work of Western colleagues, before and after 1991. This essay points to the sources to which I am most indebted and which might be of interest to general readers.

To begin with the home team. In the 1990s, the senior academic, Pavel V. Volobuev, began posing new questions focused on the role of individuals in the political process and on the ultimate political and ethical value of the revolution itself. His seminar published a series of volumes on these themes, whose titles tell the story: *Oktiabr' 1917: Velichaishee sobytie veka ili sotsial'naia katastrofa?* [*October 1917: The Greatest Event of the Century or a Social Catastrophe?*], ed. P.V. Volobuev (Moscow: Politicheskaia literatura, 1991); *Oktiabr'skaia revoliutsiia: Narod—ee tvorets ili zalozhnik?* [*The October Revolution: The People—Its Creator or Its Hostage?*], ed. P.V. Volobuev (Moscow: Nauka, 1992); *Revoliutsiia i chelovek: Sotsial'no-psikhologicheskii aspekt* [*Revolution and the Person: The Social-Psychological Dimension*] (Moscow: Institut rossiiskoi istorii RAN, 1996); and *Revoliutsiia i chelovek: Byt, nravy, povedenie, moral'* [*Revolution and the Person: Everyday Life, Customs, and Morality*], ed. P. V. Volobuev (Moscow: Institut rossiiskoi istorii RAN, 1997). Two biographical dictionaries (indispensable to this book) reflect the same post-Soviet concern with the role of personalities in the revolution, not just at the summit of power but as members of politically activated society: *Politicheskie deiateli Rossii 1917: Biograficheskii slovar'*, ed. P. V. Volobuev [*Political Figures, Russia 1917: A Biographical Dictionary*] (Moscow: Bol'shaia rossiiskaia entsiklopediia, 1993) and L. G. Protasov, *Liudi Uchreditel'nogo sobraniia: Portret v inter'ere epokhi* [*The People of the Constituent Assembly: An Inside Portrait of the Era*] (Moscow: ROSSPEN, 2008).

This critical tendency has inspired continuing innovations. In a challenge to the Soviet-era insistence on the central role of a disciplined, politically aware proletariat,Vladimir P. Buldakov has focused on the impact of diffuse violence. For example, *Krasnaia smuta: Priroda i posledstviia revoliutsionnogo nasiliia* [*The Red Turmoil: The Nature and Consequences of Revolutionary Violence*] (Moscow: ROSSPEN, 1997), in expanded form, ROSSPEN, 2010. The theme of violence and disorder emerges again in his *Khaos i etnos: Etnicheskie konflikty v Rossii, 1917–1918 gg.* [*Chaos and Ethnos: Ethnic Conflicts in Russia, 1917–1918 gg.*] (Moscow: Novyi khronograf, 2010). Interest in the role of personality and psychology can be discerned also in Sergei V. Iarov's *Proletarii kak politik: Politicheskaia psikhologiia rabochikh Petrograda v 1917–1923 gg.* [*The Proletarian as Politician: The Political Psychology of Petrograd Workers in 1917–1923*] (St. Petersburg: Bulanin, 1999). The focus on diffuse violence, on everyday life circumstances, and on local conditions characterizes the original treatment of the Civil War from a ground-level regional perspective in Igor V. Narskii, *Zhizn' v katastrofe: Budni naseleniia Urala v 1917–1922 gg.* [*Life during the Catastrophe: Everyday Existence in the Urals in 1917–1922*] (Moscow: ROSSPEN, 2001), which spends more time on drunkenness than on class consciousness.

The Western literature has long been divided between partisans of the revolution as an emancipatory promise, if not its realization, and opponents of the revolution in principle. Heightened during the Cold War, the intensity of this opposition diminished once it ended. This is not the place to count the milestones in this debate, but merely to signal some works from the 1990s that reflect the continuing contrast. In *The Russian Revolution* (New York: Knopf, 1990), Richard Pipes is critical not only of the outcome of 1917 but of the revolutionary project itself. Orlando Figes, in *A People's Tragedy: The Russian Revolution, 1891–1924* (London: Cape, 1996), is critical but sympathetic, as is Sheila Fitzpatrick, *The Russian Revolution*, 3rd ed. (Oxford: Oxford University Press, 2008). For radiantly partisan, dramatic accounts, see, of course, John Reed, *Ten Days that Shook the World* (1919) and Leon Trotsky, *History of the Russian Revolution* (1932). For a lucid, even-handed overall narrative, still worth consulting, see William Henry Chamberlin, *The Russian Revolution, 1917–1921*, 2 vols. (1935; New York: Grosset & Dunlap, 1965). For serious scholarship in the form of a reference manual, involving collaboration between Western and Russian scholars, see *Critical Companion to the Russian Revolution, 1914–1921*, ed. Edward Acton, Vladimir Iu. Cherniaev, and William G. Rosenberg (Bloomington: Indiana University Press, 1997). For a masterful treatment of the revolutionary process as a whole, integrating the latest sources, see S. A. Smith, *Russia in Revolution: An Empire in Crisis, 1890–1928* (Oxford: Oxford University Press, 2017); more briefly and from a different perspective, see his *The Russian Revolution: A Very Short Introduction* (Oxford: Oxford University Press, 2002). The longer work is now probably the best introduction to the issues raised by the revolution as a long-term process and its interpretation over the years.

The literature on the last decade of the Empire is also vast. On the 1905 Revolution, this book owes a particular debt to Abraham Ascher: *The Revolution of*

*1905*, 2 vols. (Stanford: Stanford University Press, 1988–1992) and the shorter version, *The Revolution of 1905: A Short History* (Stanford: Stanford University Press, 2004). A flood of new scholarship has appeared on the centenary of the First World War. A sensible treatment of the lead-up to the war on the Russian side, building on his earlier work, is Dominic Lieven, *The End of Tsarist Russia: The March to World War I and Revolution* (New York: Viking, 2015). For the military aspect, the classic is still Norman Stone, *The Eastern Front, 1914–1917* (1975; London: Penguin, 1998); more recently, David R. Stone, *The Russian Army in the Great War: The Eastern Front, 1914–1917* (Lawrence: University Press of Kansas, 2015). For the social-political history of the army, the classic remains Allan K. Wildman, *The End of the Russian Imperial Army*, 2 vols. (Princeton: Princeton University Press, 1980, 1987). The question of borderlands and wartime politics is taken up in Mark von Hagen, *War in a European Borderland: Occupations and Occupation Plans in Galicia and Ukraine, 1914–1918* (Seattle: University of Washington Press, 2007) and Michael A. Reynolds, *Shattering Empires: The Clash and Collapse of the Ottoman and Russian Empires 1908–1918* (Cambridge: Cambridge University Press, 2011). Reflecting the recent scholarly interest in the dynamics of empire, Joshua A. Sanborn, *Imperial Apocalypse: The Great War and the Destruction of the Russian Empire* (Oxford: Oxford University Press, 2014) interprets the war as a process of decolonization.

For the question of how the war affected Russian society, see Joshua A. Sanborn, *Drafting the Russian Nation: Military Conscription, Total War, and Mass Politics, 1905–1925* (DeKalb: Northern Illinois University Press, 2003) and Eric Lohr, *Nationalizing the Russian Empire: The Campaign Against Enemy Aliens During World War I* (Cambridge, MA: Harvard University Press, 2003). Peter Gatrell has made two key contributions to the study of the war's domestic impact: *Russia's First World War: A Social and Economic History* (Harlow, UK: Pearson-Longman, 2005) and his original and stunning *A Whole Empire Walking: Refugees in Russia during World War I* (Bloomington: Indiana University Press, 1999). On Rasputin, the least sensationalist recent study is Douglas Smith, *Rasputin: Faith, Power, and the Twilight of the Romanovs* (New York: Farrar, Straus and Giroux, 2016).

Two cases involving mass violence against civilian populations in the course of the war in which Russia played a role concern the Armenian massacres and the anti-Jewish pogroms. For the Armenian case, the latest, most judicious treatment is Ronald Grigor Suny, *"They Can Live in the Desert but Nowhere Else": A History of the Armenian Genocide* (Princeton: Princeton University Press, 2015); notable also is Donald Bloxham, *The Great Game of Genocide: Imperialism, Nationalism, and the Destruction of the Ottoman Armenians* (Oxford: Oxford University Press, 2005), as well as the essays in *A Question of Genocide, 1915: Armenians and Turks at the End of the Ottoman Empire*, eds. Ronald Grigor Suny, Fatma Müge Göçek, and Norman M. Naimark (New York: Oxford University Press, 2011). On anti-Jewish violence, see Alexander Victor Prusin, *Nationalizing a Borderland: War, Ethnicity, and Anti-Jewish Violence in East Galicia, 1914–1920* (Tuscaloosa: University of Alabama Press, 2005), and the first-person account of S. A. An-sky [S. A. Rappoport], *The Enemy at his*

*Pleasure: A Journey Through the Jewish Pale of Settlement During World War I*, ed. and trans. Joachim Neugroschel (New York: Metropolitan Books, 2002).

On the Central Asian insurrection of 1916, also part of the war, the centenary has prompted the reissue of Edward Dennis Sokol, *The Revolt of 1916 in Russian Central Asia* (Baltimore: Johns Hopkins University Press, 1954; rpt. 2016). See the more recent Jörn Happel, *Nomadische Lebenswelten und zaristische Politik: Der Aufstand in Zentralasien 1916* (Stuttgart: Franz Steiner, 2010). A documentary collection published in Kyrgyzstan, *Vosstanie 1916 goda: Dokumenty i materialy* [*The 1916 Uprising: Documents and Materials*], ed. K. I. Mambetaliev (Bishkek: Abykeev, 2015), is an example of the recent historical research published in Russian, but emanating from the regions involved.

In Russian-language scholarship, two essay collections provide samples of new work on the war. See *Rossiia v gody Pervoi mirovoi voiny: Ekonomicheskoe polozhenie, sotsial'nye protsessy, politicheskii krizis* [*Russia in the First World War: Economic Conditions, Social Processes, Political Crisis*], ed. Iu. A. Petrov (Moscow: ROSSPEN, 2014) and *Rossiia v gody Pervoi mirovoi voiny 1914–1918* [*Russia in the First World War, 1914–1918*], ed. A. N. Artizov et al. (Moscow: Institut rossiiskoi istorii RAN, 2014). Another excellent resource is the scholarly compendium *Rossiia v Pervoi mirovoi voine 1914–1918: Entsiklopediia v trekh tomakh* [*Russia in the First World War, 1914–1918: An Encyclopedia in Three Volumes*], ed. A. K. Sorokin et al. (Moscow: ROSSPEN, 2014). For focus on the culture and psychology of peasant recruits, see A. B. Astashov, *Russkii front v 1914–nachale 1917 goda: Voennyi opyt i sovremennost'* [*The Russian Front from 1914 to Early 1917: Military Experience and Modernity*] (Moscow: Novyi khronograf, 2014); on the war's contribution to the revolution, V. P. Buldakov and T. G. Leont'eva, *Voina, porodivshaia revoliutsiiu: Rossiia, 1914–1917 gg.* [*The War that Gave Rise to the Revolution: Russia, 1914–1917*] (Moscow: Novyi khronograf, 2015). For a thought-provoking and novel approach to the broad question of political culture and in particular the declining fortunes of the monarchy's popularity during the war, see Boris Kolonitskii, *"Tragicheskaia erotika": Obrazy imperatorskoi sem'i v gody Pervoi mirovoi voiny* [*"Tragic Eros": Images of the Imperial Family during the First World War*] (Moscow: NLO, 2010).

On the Revolutions of 1917, the enduring account of the social dynamics of the February events, on which I have heavily relied, is Tsuyoshi Hasegawa, *The February Revolution: Petrograd, 1917* (Seattle: University of Washington Press, 1981). Hasegawa has revised some of his earlier views in response to the recent work of A. B. Nikolaev, *Revoliutsiia i vlast': IV Gosudarstvennaia Duma 27 fevralia – 3 marta 1917 goda* [*Revolution and Power: The Fourth State Duma, February 27 to March 3, 1917*] (St. Petersburg: RGPU, 2005) and Semion Lyandres, *The Fall of Tsarism: Untold Stories of the February 1917 Revolution* (Oxford: Oxford University Press, 2013), who emphasize the revolutionary significance of the early actions of Duma leaders in bringing about the monarchy's fall. Important documents bearing on this political turn are assembled in *Fevral'skaia revoliutsiia, 1917: Sbornik dokumentov i materialov* [*The February Revolution, 1917: A Collection of Documents and Materials*], ed. O. A. Shashkova

(Moscow: RGGU, 1996). For innovative studies of revolutionary political culture, see Orlando Figes and Boris Kolonitskii, *Interpreting the Russian Revolution: The Language and Symbols of 1917* (New Haven: Yale University Press, 1999) and B. I. Kolonitskii, *Simvoly vlasti i bor'ba za vlast': K izucheniiu politicheskoi kul'tury rossiiskoi revoliutsii 1917 goda* [*Symbols of Power and the Struggle for Power: Toward the Study of Political Culture in the Russian Revolution of 1917*] (St. Petersburg: Bulanin, 2001).

On the Provisional Government, see *The Russian Provisional Government 1917: Documents*, ed. Robert Paul Browder and Alexander F. Kerensky, 3 vols. (Stanford: Stanford University Press, 1961). For the role of mainstream center and left parties, see William G. Rosenberg, *Liberals in the Russian Revolution: The Constitutional Democratic Party, 1917–1921* (Princeton: Princeton University Press, 1974) and Ziva Galili, *The Menshevik Leaders in the Russian Revolution: Social Realities and Political Strategies* (Princeton: Princeton University Press, 1989).

For October, see the memoirs of N. N. Sukhanov, *The Russian Revolution 1917*, trans. and ed. Joel Carmichael (Princeton: Princeton University Press, 1984), a key primary source. On popular mobilization, see S. A. Smith, *Red Petrograd: Revolution in the Factories, 1917–1918* (Cambridge: Cambridge University Press, 1983) and Diane Koenker, *Moscow Workers and the 1917 Revolution* (Princeton: Princeton University Press, 1981), both emphasizing the active political role of organized workers. On Bolshevik strategy, see Alexander Rabinowitch, *The Bolsheviks Come to Power: The Revolution of 1917 in Petrograd* (New York: Norton, 1976). For a refreshingly original post-Soviet reflection on the workers' movement, see Dmitrii Churakov, *Revoliutsiia, gosudarstvo, rabochii protest: Formy, dinamika i priroda massovykh vystuplenii rabochikh v Sovetskoi Rossii, 1917–1918 gody* [*Revolution, the State, and Worker Protest: The Forms, Dynamics, and Nature of Mass Labor Action in Soviet Russia, 1917–1918*] (Moscow: ROSSPEN, 2004), from which I have drawn ideas and interpretations.

On the Civil War, or Civil Wars, the basic, comprehensive English-language narrative remains Evan Mawdsley, *The Russian Civil War* (Boston: Allen and Unwin, 1987). More recently, Jonathan D. Smele, *The "Russian" Civil Wars, 1916–1926: Ten Years that Shook the World* (Oxford: Oxford University Press, 2015) draws on newer material and offers extensive references (including a list of websites). See also his invaluable *Historical Dictionary of the Russian Civil Wars, 1916–1926*, 2 vols. (Lanham, MD: Rowman & Littlefield, 2015). For a political narrative of 1918 focused on the capital, see Alexander Rabinowitch, *The Bolsheviks in Power: The First Year of Soviet Rule in Petrograd* (Bloomington: Indiana University Press, 2007).

On Brest-Litovsk and the international environment, the masterly account remains John W. Wheeler-Bennett, *Brest-Litovsk: The Forgotten Peace, March 1918* (London: Macmillan; New York: St. Martin's, 1938). From the same period, but still useful: James Bunyan, *Intervention, Civil War, and Communism in Russia, April–December 1918: Documents and Materials* (Baltimore: Johns Hopkins Press, 1936). See also: George F. Kennan, *Soviet-American Relations, 1917–1920*, vol. 1: *Russia Leaves the War* (London: Faber and Faber, 1956); Richard H. Ullman, *Anglo-Soviet Relations, 1917–1921*, 3 vols. (Princeton: Princeton University Press, 1961–1972); and Leo J.

Bacino, *Reconstructing Russia: U.S. Policy in Revolutionary Russia, 1917–1922* (Kent, OH: Kent State University Press, 1999).

On nationalism and the imperial dimension, for the Baltic states, critical sources are Karsten Brüggemann, "National and Social Revolution in the Empire's West: Estonian Independence and the Russian Civil War, 1917–20," trans. Martin Pearce, in *Russia's Home Front in War and Revolution, 1914–22*, book 1: *Russia's Revolution in Regional Perspective*, ed. Sarah Badcock, Liudmila G. Novikova, and Aaron B. Retish (Bloomington: Slavica, 2015) and his *Die Gründung der Republik Estland und das Ende des "Einen und unteilbaren Russland": Die Petrograder Front des russischen Bürgerkriegs 1918–1920* (Wiesbaden: Harrassowitz, 2002). Also Anthony F. Upton, *The Finnish Revolution, 1917–1918* (Minneapolis: University of Minnesota Press, 1980). For an overview, Timothy Snyder, *The Reconstruction of Nations: Poland, Ukraine, Lithuania, Belarus, 1569–1999* (New Haven: Yale University Press, 2003).

Ukraine is a separate topic in itself. My primary references have been Arthur E. Adams, *The Bolsheviks in the Ukraine: The Second Campaign, 1918–1919* (New Haven: Yale University Press, 1963); the essays in *The Ukraine 1917–1921: A Study in Revolution*, ed. Taras Hunczak (Cambridge, MA: Harvard Ukrainian Research Institute, 1977); and Jurij Borys, *The Sovietization of Ukraine, 1917–1923: The Communist Doctrine and Practice of National Self-Determination* (Edmonton: Canadian Institute of Ukrainian Studies, 1980). Recent work, on which I have also drawn, includes Alexei Miller, *The Ukrainian Question: The Russian Empire and Nationalism in the Nineteenth Century* (Budapest: Central European University Press, 2003); Serhy Yekelchyk, *Ukraine: Birth of a Modern Nation* (New York: Oxford University Press, 2007); Stephen Velychenko, *State Building in Revolutionary Ukraine: A Comparative Study of Government and Bureaucrats, 1917–22* (Toronto: University of Toronto Press, 2010); and Serhii Plokhy, *The Gates of Europe: A History of Ukraine* (New York: Basic Books, 2015). Recent works by Ukrainian scholars, publishing in Russian, have moved away from both Communist-era and nationalist approaches. The introduction to a volume of documents on Petliura's record is particularly useful: Simon Petliura, *Glavnyi ataman: B plenu nesbytochnykh nadezhd* [*Ataman in Chief: Prisoner of Impossible Hopes*], ed. Miroslav Popovich and Viktor Mironenko, trans. from Ukrainian G. Lesnaia (Moscow and St. Petersburg: Letnii sad, 2008). I have also drawn on sections of V. F. Soldatenko, *Grazhdanskaia voina v Ukraine, 1917–1920 gg.* [*The Civil War in Ukraine, 1917–1920*] (Moscow: Novyi khronograf, 2012). For examples of recently published documentary collections, see *Nestor Makhno: Krest'ianskoe dvizhenie na Ukraine, 1918–1921: Dokumenty i materialy* [*Nestor Makhno: The Peasant Movement in Ukraine, 1918–1921: Documents and Materials*], ed. V. Danilov et al. (Moscow: ROSSPEN, 2006), and *Getman P. P. Skoropadskii: Ukraina na perelome, 1918 goda* [*Hetman P. P. Skoropadskii: Ukraine at the Turning Point, 1918*], ed. O. K. Ivantsova (Moscow: ROSSPEN, 2014).

For Poland, the classic source is still Piotr Wandycz, *Soviet-Polish Relations, 1917–1921* (Cambridge, MA: Harvard University Press, 1969), supplemented by *The Reconstruction of Poland, 1914–1923*, ed. Paul Latawski (New York: St. Martin's, 1992), and Adam Zamoyski, *Warsaw 1920: Lenin's Failed Conquest of Europe* (London:

Harper Press, 2008). In addition to sources published before 1991, see *Pol'sko-sovetskaia voina 1919–1920: Ranee ne opublikovannye dokumenty i materialy* [*The Polish-Soviet War, 1919–1920: Previously Unpublished Documents and Materials*], ed. I. I. Kostiushchko, 2 vols. (Moscow: RAN Institut slavianovedeniia i balkanistiki, 1994).

For Central Asia, the basic reference remains Firuz Kazemzadeh, *The Struggle for Transcaucasia (1917–1921)* (New York: Philosophical Library, 1951). A useful overview is provided by Marco Buttino, "Central Asia (1916–20): A Kaleidoscope of Local Revolutions and the Building of the Bolshevik Order," in *The Empire and Nationalism at War*, ed. Eric Lohr, Vera Tolz, Alexander Semyonov, and Mark von Hagen (Bloomington: Slavica, 2014). For a perspective emanating from Kazakhstan, see *Alash-Orda: Sbornik dokumentov* [*Alash-Orda: A Document Collection*], ed. N. Martynenko (Alma-Ata: Aikap, 1992). See also D. A. Amanzholova (Kiseleva), *Kazakhskii avtono-mizm i Rossiia: Istoriia dvizheniia Alash* [*Kazakh Autonomy and Russia: The History of the Alash Movement*] (Moscow: Rossiia molodaia, 1994).

For the Caucasus, Ronald Grigor Suny is a major authority. See his *The Baku Commune, 1917–1918: Class and Nationality in the Russian Revolution* (Princeton: Princeton University Press, 1972) and *Transcaucasia, Nationalism, and Social Change: Essays in the History of Armenia, Azerbaijan, and Georgia*, ed. Ronald Grigor Suny (Ann Arbor: University of Michigan Press, 1996). The Azerbaijan government has sponsored the publication of *Mart 1918 g. Baku: Azerbaidzhanskie pogromy v dokumen-takh* [*March 1918 in Baku: The Azerbaijan Pogroms in Documents*], ed. Solmaz Rustamova-Togidi (Baku: Nauchno-issledovatel'skii tsentr Min. Natsional'noi Bezopasnosti Azerbaidzhanskoi Respubliki, 2009); also *Azerbaidzhanskaia Demokraticheskaia Respublika, 1918–1920* [*The Azerbaijan Democratic Republic, 1918–1920*] (Baku: Izd-vo Azerbaidzhan, 1998). The Moscow-based historian Salavat M. Iskhakov provides an overview of Muslim political activity during the Civil War: *Grazhdanskaia voina v Rossii i musul'mane: Sbornik dokumentov i materialov* [*Muslims and the Civil War in Russia: A Collection of Documents and Materials*], ed. S. M. Iskhakov (Moscow: Tsentr stratigicheskoi kon"iunktury, 2014), and has edited Dzhamil' Gasanly, *Russkaia revoliut-siia i Azerbaidzhan: Trudnyi put' k nezavisimosti 1917–1920* [*The Russian Revolution and Azerbaijan: The Difficult Path to Independence, 1917–1920*], ed. S. M. Iskhakov (Moscow: Fainta, 2011).

On the White movement, the work of Peter Kenez is still essential: *Civil War in South Russia, 1918: The First Year of the Volunteer Army* (Berkeley: University of California Press, 1971) and *Civil War in South Russia, 1919–1920: The Defeat of the Whites* (Berkeley: University of California Press, 1977). More recent are S. V. Volkov, *Tragediia russkogo ofitserstva* [*The Tragedy of the Russian Officer Corps*] (Moscow: Fokus, 1999), and R. G. Gagkuev, *Beloe dvizhenie na Iuge Rossii: Voennoe stroitel'stvo, istochniki komplektovaniia, sotsial'nyi sostav, 1917–20 gg.* [*The White Movement in the South of Russia: Military Formation, Manpower Sources, Social Profile, 1917–20*] (Moscow: Posev, 2012). For the situation in Crimea, there is the somewhat dated Alan W. Fisher, *The Crimean Tatars* (Stanford: Hoover, 1978), and the refreshing work of the brothers A. G. and V. G. Zarubin *Bez pobeditelei: Iz istorii grazhdanskoi voiny v Krymu* [*No

*Victors: From the History of the Civil War in Crimea*] (Simferopol: Tavriia, 1997). On the Cossacks and their fate, as a window into the basic dynamics of the civil war and revolution, see the pathbreaking study by Peter Holquist, *Making War, Forging Revolution: Russia's Continuum of Crisis, 1914–1921* (Cambridge, MA: Harvard University Press, 2002).

The basic English-language work on the anti-Bolshevik movement in Siberia, on which I principally rely, is Jonathan D. Smele, *Civil War in Siberia: The Anti-Bolshevik Government of Admiral Kolchak, 1918–1920* (Cambridge: Cambridge University Press, 1996). Records of Kolchak's interrogation can be found in *The Testimony of Kolchak and Other Siberian Materials*, ed. Elena Varneck and H. H. Fisher (Stanford: Stanford University Press, 1935), based on the 1925 Russian publication. The testimony of his ministers is now also available: *Protsess nad kolchakovskimi ministrami: Mai 1920* [*The Trial of Kolchak's Ministers, May 1920*], ed. V. I. Shishkin (Moscow: Mezhdunarodnyi fond "Demokratiia," 2003). Kolchak's context is illuminated in *S Kolchakom—protiv Kolchaka: Kratkii biograficheskii slovar': Ukazatel' uchrezhdenii i organizatsii: Kratkii ukazatel' literatury po istorii Grazhdanskoi voiny* [*With Kolchak, Against Kolchak: A Short Biographical Dictionary, Guide to Institutions and Organizations, A Short Guide to the Literature on the History of the Civil War*], ed. A. V. Kvakin (Moscow: Agraf, 2007). Most of the important scholarship on the history of Siberia in this period is associated with Vladimir I. Shishkin, at the Russian Academy of Sciences in Novosibirsk.

On the Civil War pogroms, see the balanced treatment by Henry Abramson, *A Prayer for the Government: Ukrainians and Jews in Revolutionary Times, 1917–1920* (Cambridge, MA: Ukrainian Research Institute and Center for Jewish Studies, Harvard University, 1999). Oleg Budnitskii's 2005 account has been translated into English as *Russian Jews Between the Reds and the Whites, 1917–1920*, trans. Timothy J. Portice (Philadelphia: University of Pennsylvania Press, 2012). The most important source for primary documents and the history of their accumulation is *Kniga pogromov: Pogromy na Ukraine, v Belorussii i evropeiskoi chasti Rossii v period Grazhdanskoi voiny 1918–1922 gg.: Sbornik dokumentov* [*The Book of Pogroms: Pogroms in Ukraine, Belorussia, and European Russia during the Civil War, 1918–1922: A Documentary Collection*], ed. L. B. Miliakova (Moscow: ROSSPEN, 2007). Two important articles on the Red pogroms are V. L. Genis, "Pervaia Konnaia armiia: Za kulisami slavy" [The First Cavalry Army: Behind the Glory], *Voprosy istorii* 12 (1994): 64–77, and Stephen M. Brown, "Communists and the Red Cavalry: The Political Education of the *Konarmiia* in the Russian Civil War, 1918–20," *Slavonic and East European Review* 73.1 (1995): 82–99. Easily accessible primary sources are Elias Heifetz, *The Slaughter of the Jews in the Ukraine in 1919* (New York: Seltzer, 1921), and Isaac Babel, *1920 Diary*, trans. H. T. Willetts, ed. Carol J. Avins (New Haven: Yale University Press, 1995).

Recent years have provided a series of key publications on peasant mobilization. An early reference remains Orlando Figes, *Peasant Russia, Civil War: The Volga Countryside in Revolution (1917–1921)* (Oxford: Clarendon, 1989).

For an example of moving beyond Soviet categories, see V. V. Kanishchev, *Russkii bunt, bessmyslennyi i besposhchadnyi: Pogromnoe dvizhenie v gorodakh Rossii v 1917–1918 gg.* [*The Russian Riot, Senseless and Pitiless: The Pogrom Movement in the Cities of Russia, 1917–1918*] (Tambov: Tambovskii gos. un-t im. G. R. Derzhavina, 1995). The distinguished Russian historian, the late Viktor P. Danilov, organized a series of documentary volumes with interpretive introductions and commentary: *Krest'ianskoe vosstanie v Tambovskoi gubernii v 1919–1921 gg., "Antonovshchina": Dokumenty i materialy* [*Peasant Insurrection in Tambov Province in 1919–1921: The "Antonov Saga": Documents and Materials*], ed. V. Danilov, T. Shanin et al. (Tambov: Intertsentr, 1994); *Filipp Mironov: Tikhii Don v 1917–1921 gg.* [*Filipp Mironov: The Quiet Don, 1917–1921*], ed. V. P. Danilov and Teodor Shanin (Moscow: Mezhdunarodnyi fond "Demokratiia," 1997); *Sovetskaia derevnia glazami VChk-OGPU-NKVD: Dokumenty i materialy* [*The Soviet Countryside Through the Eyes of the All-Russian Cheka-OGPU-NKVD: Documents and Materials*], ed. A. Berelovich [Berelowitch] and V. Danilov, 4 vols. (Moscow: ROSSPEN, 1998–2000). Additional sources are provided by *Iaroslavskoe vosstanie 1918* [*The Iaroslav Insurrection, 1918*], ed. E. A. Ermolin and V. N. Kozliakov (Moscow: Mezhdunarodnyi fond "Demokratiia," 2007). Two recent studies, on which I have also drawn, are T. V. Osipova, *Rossiiskoe krest'ianstvo v revoliutsii i grazhdanskoi voine* [*The Russian Peasantry in the Revolution and Civil War*] (Moscow: Strelets, 2001); and the astute Erik C. Landis, *Bandits and Partisans: The Antonov Movement in the Russian Civil War* (Pittsburgh: University of Pittsburgh Press, 2008).

The study of worker activism after 1917 has also flourished in recent years. Jonathan Aves, *Workers Against Lenin: Labour Protest and the Bolshevik Dictatorship* (London: Tauris, 1996) can still be consulted, but recent Russian work is now indispensable. Again, the original study by Dmitrii Churakov, noted above; also A. V. Korobeinikov, *Votkinskaia Narodnaia armiia v 1918 g.* [*The Votkinsk People's Army, 1918*] (Izhevsk: Idnakar, 2013). For worker organizations, see *Rabochee oppozitsionnoe dvizhenie v bol'shevistskoi Rossii 1918 g.: Sobraniia upolnomochennykh fabrik i zavodov: Dokumenty i materialy* [*The Workers' Opposition Movement in Bolshevik Russia, 1918: The Assemblies of Deputies from Factories and Plants: Documents and Materials*], ed. D. B. Pavlov (Moscow: ROSSPEN, 2006); *Sobranie upolnomochennykh i piterskie rabochie v 1918 godu: Dokumenty i materialy* [*The Assembly of Deputies and Petersburg Workers in 1918: Documents and Materials*], ed. E. Tsudzi (St. Petersburg: Sankt-Peterburgskii universitet, 2006). On the Kronstadt revolt, the English-language classic remains Paul Avrich, *Kronstadt 1921* (Princeton: Princeton University Press, 1970; rpt. New York: Norton, 1974); more recently, *Kronshtadt 1921: Dokumenty o sobytiiakh v Kronshtadte vesnoi 1921 g.* [*Kronstadt, 1921: Documents on the Events of Spring 1921 in Kronstadt*], ed. V. P. Naumov and A. A. Kosakovskii (Moscow: Mezhdunarodnyi fond "Demokratiia," 1997).

On political opposition to Bolshevik rule, see Vladimir N. Brovkin, *The Mensheviks after October: Socialist Opposition and the Rise of the Bolshevik Dictatorship* (Ithaca: Cornell University Press, 1987) and others of his works, and Scott B. Smith, *Captives of Revolution: The Socialist Revolutionaries and the Bolshevik Dictatorship, 1918–1923*

(Pittsburgh: University of Pittsburgh Press, 2011). The records of the major political parties from 1905 through the Revolution and Civil War have been published over the last two decades by the Moscow publishing house ROSSPEN—The Russian Political Encyclopedia, also responsible for many of the documentary collections cited here.

On economic policy and the famine, still basic are Silvana Malle, *The Economic Organization of War Communism, 1918–1921* (Cambridge: Cambridge University Press, 1985), and Lars T. Lih, *Bread and Authority in Russia, 1914–1921* (Berkeley: University of California Press, 1990). Also, Sergei A. Pavliuchenkov, *Voennyi kommunizm v Rossii: Vlast' i massy* [*War Communism in Russia: Government and the Masses*] (Moscow: RKT-Istoriia, 1997). For the famine, see the participant account of Harold H. Fisher, *The Famine in Soviet Russia, 1919–1923: The Operations of the American Relief Administration* (New York: Macmillan, 1927). For the demography, see Serguei Adamets, *Guerre civile et famine en Russie: Le pouvoir bolchevique et la population face à la catastrophe démographique, 1917–1923* (Paris: Institut d'études slaves, 2003). On famine relief, see Bertrand M. Patenaude, *The Big Show in Bololand: The American Relief Expedition to Soviet Russia in the Famine of 1921* (Stanford: Stanford University Press, 2002).

On the Red Terror, I have relied on primary accounts, as well as the basic work by George Leggett, *The Cheka: Lenin's Political Police* (Oxford: Clarendon, 1981); A. L. Litvin, *Krasnyi i belyi terror v Rossii, 1918–1922 gg.* [*Red and White Terror in Russia, 1918–1922*] (Moscow: Eksmo, 2004); I. S. Rat'kovskii, *Krasnyi terror i deiatel'nost' VChK v 1918 godu* [*The Red Terror and the Activity of the All-Russian Cheka in 1918*] (St. Petersburg: S.-Peterburgskii universitet, 2006); and *Arkhiv VChK: Sbornik dokumentov* [*The Archive of the All-Russian Cheka: A Documentary Collection*], ed. V. Vinogradov, A. Litvin, and V. Khristoforov (Moscow: Kuchkovo pole, 2007).

I have also been influenced by work on the general nature of violence in this period and region. Examples include Peter Holquist, "Violent Russia, Deadly Marxism? Russia in the Epoch of Violence, 1905–21," *Kritika* 4.3 (2003): 627–652 (and other essays by him); Dietrich Beyrau, "Der Erste Weltkrieg als Bewährungsprobe: Bolschewistische Lernprozesse aus dem 'imperialistischen' Krieg," *Journal of Modern European History* 1 (2003): 96–124; Felix Schnell, *Räume des Schreckens: Gewalt und Gruppenmilitanz in der Ukraine 1905–1933* (Hamburg: Hamburger Edition, 2012); Dietrich Beyrau, "The Long Shadow of the Revolution: Violence in War and Peace in the Soviet Union," in *Legacies of Violence: Eastern Europe's First World War*, ed. Jochen Böhler, Włodzimierz Borodziej, and Joachim von Puttkamer (Munich: Oldenbourg, 2014), 285–316 (and other essays in this volume).

For further reading, see Jonathan D. Smele, *The Russian Revolution and the Civil War, 1917–1921: An Annotated Bibliography* (London: Continuum, 2003), and the bibliography to his 2015 study of the Civil War, cited above. This essay, of course, reflects my own linguistic limitations.

# Index

Page numbers in *italics* denote illustrations.